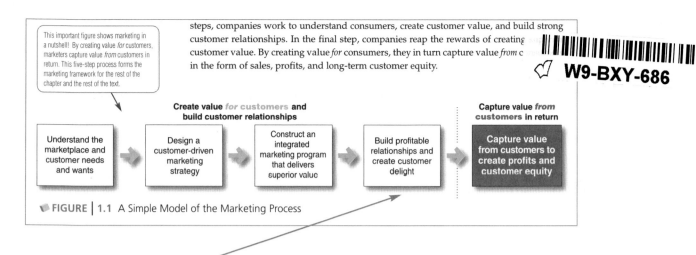

steps, companies work to understand consumers, create customer value, and build strong customer relationships. In the final step, companies reap the rewards of creating customer value. By creating value *for* consumers, they in turn capture value *from* c in the form of sales, profits, and long-term customer equity.

This important figure shows marketing in a nutshell! By creating value *for* customers, marketers capture value *from* customers in return. This five-step process forms the marketing framework for the rest of the chapter and the rest of the text.

Create value *for* customers and build customer relationships

| Understand the marketplace and customer needs and wants | Design a customer-driven marketing strategy | Construct an integrated marketing program that delivers superior value | Build profitable relationships and create customer delight |

Capture value *from* customers in return

Capture value from customers to create profits and customer equity

FIGURE | 1.1 A Simple Model of the Marketing Process

4 Redesigned figures integrate closely with the text, using annotations to connect you to the key points.

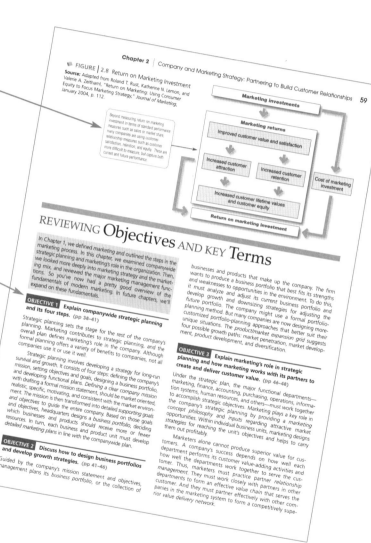

FIGURE | 2.8 Return on Marketing Investment
Source: Adapted from Roland T. Rust, Katherine N. Lemon, and Valerie A. Zeithaml, "Return on Marketing: Using Consumer Equity to Focus Marketing Strategy," *Journal of Marketing,* January 2004, p. 112.

Beyond measuring return on marketing investment in terms of standard performance measures such as sales or market share, many companies are using customer relationship measures such as customer satisfaction, retention, and equity. These are more difficult to measure, but capture both current and future performance.

Marketing investments

Marketing returns

Improved customer value and satisfaction

Increased customer attraction

Increased customer retention

Cost of marketing investment

Increased customer lifetime values and customer equity

Return on marketing investment

5 Summary and Key Terms are tied back to chapter objectives and page numbers – guiding you to exactly where they are covered.

REVIEWING Objectives AND KEY Terms

In Chapter 1, we defined *marketing* and outlined the steps in the marketing process. In this chapter, we examined companywide strategic planning and marketing's role in the organization. Then, we looked more deeply into marketing strategy and the marketing mix, and reviewed the major marketing management functions. So you've now had a pretty good overview of the fundamentals of modern marketing. In future chapters, we'll expand on these fundamentals.

OBJECTIVE 1 Explain companywide strategic planning and its four steps. (pp 38–41)

Strategic planning sets the stage for the rest of the company's planning. Marketing contributes to strategic planning, and the overall plan defines marketing's role in the company. Although formal planning offers a variety of benefits to companies, not all companies use it or use it well.

Strategic planning involves developing a strategy for long-run survival and growth. It consists of four steps: defining the company's mission, setting objectives and goals, designing the company's business portfolio, and developing functional plans. Defining a clear *company mission* starts with drafting a formal mission statement, which should be market oriented, realistic, specific, motivating, and consistent with the market environment. The mission is then transformed into detailed *supporting goals and objectives* to guide the entire company. Based on those goals and objectives, headquarters designs a *business portfolio,* deciding which businesses and products should receive more or fewer resources. In turn, each business and product unit must develop detailed *marketing plans* in line with the companywide plan.

OBJECTIVE 2 Discuss how to design business portfolios and develop growth strategies. (pp 41–46)

Guided by the company's mission statement and objectives, management plans its *business portfolio,* or the collection of businesses and products that make up the company. The firm wants to produce a business portfolio that best fits its strengths and weaknesses to opportunities in the environment. To do this, it must analyze and adjust its *current business portfolio* and develop growth and downsizing strategies for adjusting the *future portfolio.* The company might use a formal portfolio-planning method. But many companies are now designing more-customized portfolio-planning approaches that better suit their unique situations. The *product/market expansion grid* suggests four possible growth paths: market penetration, market development, product development, and diversification.

OBJECTIVE 3 Explain marketing's role in strategic planning and how marketing works with its partners to create and deliver customer value. (pp 46–48)

Under the strategic plan, the major functional departments—marketing, finance, accounting, purchasing, operations, information systems, human resources, and others—must work together to accomplish strategic objectives. Marketing plays a key role in the company's strategic planning by providing a *marketing concept philosophy* and *inputs* regarding attractive market opportunities. Within individual business units, marketing designs strategies for reaching the unit's objectives and helps to carry them out profitably.

Marketers alone cannot produce superior value for customers. A company's success depends on how well each department performs its customer value-adding activities and how well the departments work together to serve the customer. Thus, marketers must practice partner *relationship management.* They must work closely with partners in other departments to form an effective *value chain* that serves the customer. And they must partner effectively with other companies in the marketing system to form a competitively superior *value delivery network.*

Kotler | Armstrong

PRINCIPLES OF
Marketing

Marketing Enriched Beverage
with pomegranate

20FL OZ

Marketing enriched content

KA

PRINCIPLES OF
Marketing

PHILIP KOTLER
Northwestern University

GARY ARMSTRONG
University of North Carolina

Prentice Hall
Upper Saddle River, New Jersey 07458

Library of Congress Cataloging-in-Publication Data

Kotler, Philip.
    Principles of marketing / Philip Kotler, Gary Armstrong.—13th ed.
        p. cm.
    Includes bibliographical references and index.
    ISBN-13: 978-0-13-607941-5 (casebound : alk. paper)
    ISBN-10: 0-13-607941-5
    1. Marketing. I. Armstrong, Gary (Gary M.) II. Title.
    HF5415.K636 2010
    658.8--dc22

                        2008048626

AVP/Executive Editor: Melissa Sabella
Editorial Director: Sally Yagan
Product Development Manager: Ashley Santora
Editorial Project Manager: Melissa Pellerano
Editorial Assistant: Karin Williams
Media Project Manager: Denise Vaughn
Director of Marketing: Patrice Lumumba Jones
Marketing Manager: Anne K. Fahlgren
Marketing Assistant: Susan Osterlitz
Permissions Coordinator: Charles Morris
Associate Director, Production Editorial: Judy Leale
Production Project Manager: Kerri Tomasso
Senior Operations Specialist: Arnold Vila
Creative Director: John Christiana
Interior and Cover Design: Blair Brown
Art Director: Blair Brown
Cover Photo: Photographer: Jupiter Images/Jack Anderson/Blair Brown
Image Manager: Keri Jean Miksza
Director, Image Resource Center: Melinda Patelli
Manager, Rights and Permissions: Zina Arabia
Manager, Visual Research: Beth Brenzel
Image Permission Coordinator: Fran Toepfer
Composition/Full-Service Project Management: GEX Publishing Services
Printer/Binder: Courier/Kendallville
Cover Printer: Lehigh-Phoenix Color/Hagerstown
Typeface: 8.5/11.5 Palatino

Credits and acknowledgments borrowed from other sources and reproduced, with permission, in this textbook appear on the appropriate page within text or on page C1.

Pearson Education Ltd., London
Pearson Education Singapore, Pte. Ltd
Pearson Education, Canada, Inc.
Pearson Education–Japan
Pearson Education Australia PTY, Limited

Pearson Education North Asia Ltd., Hong Kong
Pearson Educación de Mexico, S.A. de C.V.
Pearson Education Malaysia, Pte. Ltd.
Pearson Education, Upper Saddle River, New Jersey

Prentice Hall
is an imprint of

www.pearsonhighered.com

10 9 8 7 6 5 4 3 2 1
ISBN-13: 978-0-13-607941-5
ISBN-10: 0-13-607941-5

Dedication

To Kathy, Betty, Mandy, Matt, KC, Keri, Delaney, Molly, Macy, and Ben; and Nancy, Amy, Melissa, and Jessica

About the Authors

As a team, Philip Kotler and Gary Armstrong provide a blend of skills uniquely suited to writing an introductory marketing text. Professor Kotler is one of the world's leading authorities on marketing. Professor Armstrong is an award-winning teacher of undergraduate business students. Together they make the complex world of marketing practical, approachable, and enjoyable.

Philip
Kotler is the S. C. Johnson & Son Distinguished Professor of International Marketing at the Kellogg School of Management, Northwestern University. He received his master's degree at the University of Chicago and his PhD at MIT, both in economics. Dr. Kotler is the author of *Marketing Management* (Pearson Prentice Hall), now in its thirteenth edition and the most widely used marketing text book in graduate business schools worldwide. He has authored dozens of other successful books and has written more than 100 articles in leading journals. He is the only three-time winner of the coveted Alpha Kappa Psi award for the best annual article in the *Journal of Marketing*.

Professor Kotler was named the first recipient of two major awards: the *Distinguished Marketing Educator of the Year Award*, given by the American Marketing Association and the *Philip Kotler Award for Excellence in Health Care Marketing*, presented by the Academy for Health Care Services Marketing. His numerous other major honors include the Sales and Marketing Executives International *Marketing Educator of the Year Award*; the European Association of Marketing Consultants and Trainers *Marketing Excellence Award*; the *Charles Coolidge Parlin Marketing Research Award*; and the *Paul D. Converse Award*, given by the American Marketing Association to honor "outstanding contributions to science in marketing." In a recent *Financial Times* poll of 1,000 senior executives across the world, Professor Kotler was ranked as the fourth "most influential business writer/guru" of the twenty-first century.

Dr. Kotler has served as chairman of the College on Marketing of the Institute of Management Sciences, a director of the American Marketing Association, and a trustee of the Marketing Science Institute. He has consulted with many major U.S. and international companies in the areas of marketing strategy and planning, marketing organization, and international marketing. He has traveled extensively throughout Europe, Asia, and South America, advising companies and governments about global marketing practices and opportunities.

Gary
Armstrong is the Crist W. Blackwell Distinguished Professor of Undergraduate Education in the Kenan-Flagler Business School at the University of North Carolina at Chapel Hill. He holds undergraduate and master's degrees in business from Wayne State University in Detroit, and he received his PhD in marketing from Northwestern University. Dr. Armstrong has contributed numerous articles to leading business journals. As a consultant and researcher, he has worked with many companies on marketing research, sales management, and marketing strategy.

But Professor Armstrong's first love has always been teaching. His Blackwell Distinguished Professorship is the only permanent endowed professorship for distinguished undergraduate teaching at the University of North Carolina at Chapel Hill. He has been very active in the teaching and administration of Kenan-Flagler's undergraduate program. His administrative posts have included Chair of Marketing, Associate Director of the Undergraduate Business Program, Director of the Business Honors Program, and many others. He has worked closely with business student groups and has received several campuswide and Business School teaching awards. He is the only repeat recipient of the school's highly regarded Award for Excellence in Undergraduate Teaching, which he has received three times. Most recently, Professor Armstrong received the UNC Board of Governors Award for Excellence in Teaching, the highest teaching honor bestowed by the 16-campus University of North Carolina system.

Brief Contents

Contents

Preface

The Thirteenth Edition of Principles of Marketing! Creating More Value for You!

The goal of every marketer is to create more value for customers. So it makes sense that our goal for the thirteenth edition is to continue creating more value for you—*our* customer. Our goal is to introduce you to the fascinating world of modern marketing in an innovative yet practical and enjoyable way. We've redesigned the book to make it easier to learn and study from, and we've added mymarketinglab, our online personalized study and assessment tool.

Marketing: Creating Customer Value and Relationships

A recent survey of top marketers showed that they all share a common goal: putting the consumer at the heart of marketing. Today's marketing is all about creating customer value and building profitable customer relationships. It starts with understanding consumer needs and wants, deciding which target markets the organization can serve best, and developing a compelling value proposition by which the organization can attract, keep, and grow targeted consumers. If the organization does these things well, it will reap the rewards in terms of market share, profits, and customer equity.

Five Major Value Themes

From beginning to end, the thirteenth edition of *Principles of Marketing* develops an innovative customer-value and customer-relationships framework that captures the essence of today's marketing. It builds on five major value themes:

1. *Creating value for customers in order to capture value from customers in return*. Today's marketers must be good at *creating customer value* and *managing customer relationships*. Outstanding marketing companies understand the marketplace and customer needs, design value-creating marketing strategies, develop integrated marketing programs that deliver customer value and delight, and build strong customer relationships. In return, they capture value from customers in the form of sales, profits, and customer loyalty.

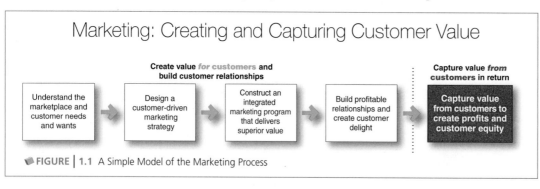

FIGURE | 1.1 A Simple Model of the Marketing Process

This innovative *customer-value framework* is introduced at the start of Chapter 1 in a five-step marketing process model, which details how marketing *creates* customer value and *captures* value in return. The framework is carefully explained in the first two chapters and then fully integrated throughout the remainder of the text.

2. *Building and managing strong, value-creating brands.* Well-positioned brands with strong brand equity provide the basis upon which to build customer value and profitable customer relationships. Today's marketers must position their brands powerfully and manage them well. They must build close brand relationships and experiences with customers.

3. *Measuring and managing return on marketing.* Marketing managers must ensure that their marketing dollars are being well spent. In the past, many marketers spent freely on big, expensive marketing programs, often without thinking carefully about the financial returns on their spending. But all that has changed rapidly. "Marketing accountability"—measuring and managing return on marketing investments—has now become an important part of strategic marketing decision making. This emphasis on marketing accountability is addressed throughout the thirteenth edition.

4. *Harnessing new marketing technologies.* New digital and other high-tech marketing developments are dramatically changing how consumers and marketers relate to one another. The thirteenth edition thoroughly explores the new technologies impacting marketing, from "Web 2.0" in Chapter 1 to new-age digital marketing and online technologies in Chapters 15 and 17 to the exploding use of online social networks and customer-generated marketing in Chapters 1, 5, 14, 17, and elsewhere.

5. *Sustainable marketing around the globe.* As technological developments make the world an increasingly smaller and more fragile place, marketers must be good at marketing their brands globally and in responsible and ethical ways. New material throughout the thirteenth edition emphasizes the concept of sustainable marketing—meeting the present needs of consumers and businesses while also preserving or enhancing the ability of future generations to meet their needs.

New in the Thirteenth Edition

We've thoroughly revised the thirteenth edition of *Principles of Marketing* to reflect the major trends and forces impacting marketing in this era of customer value and relationships. Here are just some of the major changes you'll find in this edition.

- The thirteenth edition has a **completely new learning design**! The text's more active and integrative presentation includes new in-chapter learning enhancements such as annotated chapter-opening stories, an opening objectives outline, and explanatory author comments on major chapter sections and figures. The newly designed chapter-opening layout helps to preview and position the chapter and its key concepts. Redesigned figures, annotated with author comments, help students to simplify and organize chapter material. End-of-chapter features help to summarize important chapter concepts and highlight important themes, such as marketing technology, ethics, and financial marketing analysis. In all, the new design facilitates student understanding and eases learning.

- Throughout the thirteenth edition, you will find important new coverage of the rapidly **changing nature of customer relationships** with companies and brands. Today's marketers aim to create deeper consumer involvement and a sense of community surrounding a brand—to make the brand a meaningful part of consumers' conversations and their lives. New relationship-building tools include everything from blogs, Web sites, in-person events, and video sharing, to online communities and social networks, such as MySpace, Facebook, YouTube, or a company's own social networking sites.

- A revised Chapter 20 pulls marketing together under an important new **sustainable marketing** framework. It shows how sustainable marketing calls for socially and environmentally responsible actions that meet both the immediate and the future needs of customers, the company, and society as a whole.

- Increasingly, marketing is taking the form of two-way conversations between consumers and brands. The thirteenth edition contains new material on the exciting trend toward **consumer-generated marketing**, by which marketers invite consumers to play a more active role in providing customer insights (Chapter 4), shaping new products (Chapter 9), developing or passing along brand messages (Chapter 15), interacting in customer communities (Chapters 5, 15, and 17), and other developments.

- This edition provides new and expanded discussions of new **marketing technologies**, from "Web 2.0" in Chapter 1 to neuromarketing in Chapter 5 to RFID in Chapter 12 to the new-age digital marketing and online technologies in Chapters 1, 14, 15, and 17.

- In line with the text's emphasis on **measuring and managing return on marketing**, we've added end-of-chapter financial and quantitative marketing exercises that let students apply analytical thinking to relevant concepts in each chapter and link chapter concepts to the text's innovative Appendix 2: Marketing by the Numbers.

- The thirteenth edition provides refreshed and expanded coverage of the explosive developments in integrated **marketing communications** and **direct and online marketing**. It tells how marketers are incorporating a host of new digital and direct approaches to build and create more targeted, personal, and interactive customer relationships. No other text provides more current or encompassing coverage of these exciting developments.

Real Value Through Real Marketing

Principles of Marketing features in-depth, real-world examples and stories that show concepts in action and reveal the drama of modern marketing. In the thirteenth edition, every chapter opening vignette and "Real Marketing" highlight has been updated or replaced to provide fresh and relevant insights into real marketing practices.

- Trader Joe's unique "cheap gourmet" price-value strategy has earned it an almost cult-like following of devoted customers who love what they get for the prices they pay.
- Patagonia sets the standard for sustainable marketing—its reason for being is to make the best product and cause no unnecessary environmental harm.
- Apple founder Steve Jobs used dazzling customer-driven innovation to first start the company and then to remake it again 20 years later.
- Nike gives consumers more than just good athletic gear. It markets a way of life, a sports culture, and a just-do-it attitude.
- McDonald's, the quintessential all-American company, now sells more burgers and fries outside the United States than within.
- Design consultancy ZIBA's new-product designs don't start in the research lab—its first design step is to research consumers and get to know them—*really* get to know them.
- Starbucks has brewed up an ambitious—perhaps overly ambitious—growth strategy to maintain its lead in an increasingly overcaffeinated marketplace.
- Big-box retailer Costco bullies even giant Wal-Mart by creating a merchandising magic that other big retailers just can't match.
- Dunkin' Donuts targets the "Dunkin' Tribe"—not the Starbucks snob but the average Joe.
- Once little-known GEICO used an industry-changing advertising campaign featuring a likable spokes-lizard, an indignant clan of cavemen, and an enduring tagline, to become an industry leader.

Each chapter is packed with countless real, relevant, and timely examples that reinforce key concepts and bring marketing to life.

Valuable Learning Aids

A wealth of chapter-opening, within-chapter, and end-of-chapter learning devices help students to learn, link, and apply major concepts:

- *Chapter Preview.* As part of a new, more active and integrative chapter-opening design, a brief section at the beginning of each chapter previews chapter concepts, links them with previous chapter concepts, and introduces the chapter-opening story.
- *Chapter-opening marketing stories.* Each chapter begins with an engaging, deeply developed, illustrated, and annotated marketing story that introduces the chapter material and sparks student interest.
- *Objective outline.* This chapter-opening feature provides a helpful preview outline of chapter contents and learning objectives.
- *Author comments and figure annotations.* Throughout the chapter, author comments ease and enhance student learning by introducing and explaining major chapter sections and organizing figures.

- *Real Marketing highlights.* Each chapter contains two highlight features that provide an in-depth look at real marketing practices of large and small companies.
- *Reviewing the Objectives and Key Terms.* A summary at the end of each chapter reviews major chapter concepts, chapter objectives, and key terms.
- *Discussing and Applying the Concepts.* Each chapter contains a set of discussion questions and application exercises covering major chapter concepts.
- *Focus on Technology.* Application exercises at the end of each chapter provide discussion of important and emerging marketing technologies in this digital age.
- *Focus on Ethics.* Situation descriptions and questions highlight important issues in marketing ethics at the end of each chapter.
- *Marketing by the Numbers.* An exercise at the end of each chapter lets students apply analytical and financial thinking to relevant chapter concepts and links the chapter to Appendix 2: Marketing by the Numbers.
- *Company Cases.* All new or revised company cases for class or written discussion are provided at the end of each chapter. These cases challenge students to apply marketing principles to real companies in real situations.
- *Video Cases.* Short cases and discussion questions appear at the end of every chapter, to be used with the set of 4- to 6-minute videos that accompany this edition.
- *Marketing Plan appendix.* Appendix 1 contains a sample marketing plan that helps students to apply important marketing planning concepts.
- *Marketing by the Numbers appendix.* An innovative Appendix 2 provides students with a comprehensive introduction to the marketing financial analysis that helps to guide, assess, and support marketing decisions.

More than ever before, the thirteenth edition of *Principles of Marketing* creates value for you—it gives you all you need to know about marketing in an effective and enjoyable total learning package!

A Valuable Learning Package

A successful marketing course requires more than a well-written book. A total package of resources extends this edition's emphasis on creating value for you. The following aids support *Principles of Marketing*.

Videos

The video library features 20 exciting segments for this edition. All segments are on DVD (ISBN: 0-13-608017-0) and in mymarketinglab. Here are just a few of the videos offered:

Live Nation's Customer Relationships

TOMS Shoes' Marketing Environment

E*TRADE's Advertising and PR Strategies

Principle Financial Group's Personal Selling

Umpqua Bank's Competitive Advantage

Study Guide (ISBN: 0-13-608075-8)

The thirteenth edition study guide provides students on the go with a valuable resource. It consists of detailed chapter outlines, student exercises, plus exercises correlated to award-winning print advertisements. There is also a section providing suggested answers for all exercises, offering the students feedback on their responses. The study guide can be packaged at a low cost with new copies of this text. The study guide can also be purchased separately at www.pearsonhighered.com/marketing.

PEARSON mymarketinglab™

mymarketinglab (www.mymarketinglab.com) gives you the opportunity to test yourself on key concepts and skills, track your own progress through the course, and use the personalized study plan activities—all to help you achieve success in the classroom.
Features include:

- **Personalized study plans**—Pre- and posttests with remediation activities directed to help you understand and apply the concepts where you need the most help.

- **Self-assessments**—Prebuilt self-assessments allow you to test yourself.

- **Interactive elements**—A wealth of hands-on activities and exercises let you experience and learn firsthand. Whether it is with the online e-book where you can search for specific keywords or page numbers, highlight specific sections, enter notes right on the e-book page, and print reading assignments with notes for later review or with other materials including "Real People Real Choices Video Cases," online end-of-chapter activities, "Active Flashcards," and much more.

- **iQuizzes**—Study anytime, anywhere—iQuizzes work on any color-screen iPod and are comprised of a sequence of quiz questions, specifically created for the iPod screen.

Find out more at **www.mypearsonmarketinglab.com**.

More Valuable Resources

CourseSmart is an exciting new *choice* for students looking to save money. As an alternative to purchasing the print textbook, students can purchase an electronic version of the same content and save up to 50 percent off the suggested list price of the print text. With a CourseSmart eTextbook, students can search the text, make notes online, print out reading assignments that incorporate lecture notes, and bookmark important passages for later review. For more information, or to purchase access to the CourseSmart eTextbook, visit **www.coursesmart.com**.

VangoNotes

Study on the go with VangoNotes—chapter reviews from your text in downloadable mp3 format. Now wherever you are—whatever you're doing—you can study by listening to the following for each chapter of your textbook:

- *Big Ideas:* Your "need to know" for each chapter
- *Practice Test:* A gut check for the Big Ideas—tells you if you need to keep studying
- *Key Terms:* Audio "flashcards" to help you review key concepts and terms
- *Rapid Review:* A quick drill session—use it right before your test

VangoNotes are **flexible**; download all the material directly to your player, or only the chapters you need. And they're **efficient**. Use them in your car, at the gym, walking to class, or wherever. So get yours today at VangoNotes.com and get studying.

Acknowledgments

No book is the work only of its authors. We greatly appreciate the valuable contributions of several people who helped make this new edition possible. We owe very special thanks to Keri Jean Miksza for her deep and valuable involvement and advice throughout *every* phase of the project, and to her new daughter Lucy for sharing Keri with us during this project. We thank Andy Norman of Drake University for his skillful development of company cases and video cases, and Lew Brown of the University of North Carolina at Greensboro for his able assistance in helping to prepare selected marketing stories. Thanks also go to Laurie Babin of the University of Louisiana at Monroe for her dedicated efforts in preparing end-of-chapter materials and keeping our Marketing by the Numbers appendix fresh; Marian Burk Wood for her help in revising the Marketing Plan appendix; Tony L. Henthorne at the University of Nevada, Las Vegas, for his work on the Instructor's Manual; Deborah Utter at Boston University for developing the PowerPoints; Bonnie Flaherty for creating the Test Item File, Study Plan, and iQuizzes; and Tracy Tuten for her quality work on the Study Guide.

Many reviewers at other colleges and universities provided valuable comments and suggestions for this and previous editions. We are indebted to the following colleagues for their thoughtful input:

Thirteenth Edition Reviewers

Praveen Aggarwal, University of Minnesota, Duluth

Mary Albrecht, Maryville University

Lydia E. Anderson, Fresno City College

Roger Berry, California State University, Dominguez Hills

Amit Bhatnagar, University of Wisconsin, Milwaukee

Donald L. Brady, Millersville University

Kirsten Cardenas, University of Miami

Rod Carveth, Naugatuck Valley Community College

Hongsik John Cheon, Frostburg State University

Mary Conran, Temple University

Michael Coolsen, Shippensburg University

Douglas A. Cords, California State University, Fresno

James L. Giordano, La Guardia Community College

Karen Gore, Ivy Tech Community College, Evansville Campus

David Houghton, Charleston Southern University

Debra Laverie, Texas Tech University

Charles Lee, Chestnut Hill College

Marilyn Liebrenz-Himes, George Washington University

Samuel McNeely, Murray State University

Chip Miller, Drake University

Ted Mitchell, University of Nevada, Reno

David Murphy, Madisonville Community College

Susan Peterson, Scottsdale Community College

Gregory A. Rich, Bowling Green State University

William Ryan, University of Connecticut

Randy Stewart, Kennesaw State University

Donna Waldron, Manchester Community College

Former Reviewers

Ron Adams, University of North Florida

Sana Akili, Iowa State University

Mark Alpert, University of Texas at Austin

Mark Anderson, Eastern Kentucky University

Allan L. Appell, San Francisco State University

Laurie Babin, University of Southern Mississippi

Michael Ballif, University of Utah

Pat Bernson, County College of Morris

Roger Berry, California State University, Dominguez Hills

Amit Bhatnagar, University of Wisconsin

Thomas Brashear, University of Massachusetts, Amherst

Fred Brunel, Boston University

Jeff Bryden, Bowling Green University

David J. Burns, Youngstown State University

Glenn Chappell, Coker College

Sang T. Choe, University of Southern Indiana

Glenn L. Christensen, Brigham Young University

Kathleen Conklin, St. John Fisher College

Mary Conran, Temple University

Alicia Cooper, Morgan State University

Preyas Desai, Purdue University

Philip Gelman, College of DuPage

Hugh Guffey, Auburn University

Kenny Herbst, Saint Joseph's University

Terry Holmes, Murray State University

Pat Jacoby, Purdue University

Carol Johanek, Washington University

Eileen Kearney, Montgomery County Community College

Thomas R. Keen, Caldwell College

Tina Kiesler, California State University at North Ridge

Dmitri Kuksov, Washington University in St. Louis

Bruce Lammers, California State University at North Ridge

J. Ford Laumer, Auburn University

Kenneth Lawrence, New Jersey Institute of Technology

Richard Leventhal, Metropolitan State College, Denver

Dolly D. Loyd, University of Southern Mississippi

Kerri Lum, Kapiolani Community College

Larry Maes, Davenport University

Tamara Mangleburg, Florida Atlantic University

Patricia M. Manninen, North Shore Community College

Wendy Martin, Judson College, Illinois

Patrick H. McCaskey, Millersville University

June McDowell-Davis, Catawba College/High Point University

H. Lee Meadow, Indiana University East

H. Lee Meadow, Northern Illinois University

John Mellon, College Misericordia

Mohan K. Menon, University of Southern Alabama

Martin Meyers, University of Wisconsin, Stevens Point

William Mindak, Tulane University

David M. Nemi, Niagra County Community College

Carl Obermiller, Seattle University

Howard Olsen, University of Nevada at Reno

Betty Parker, Western Michigan University

Vanessa Perry, George Washington University

Abe Qastin, Lakeland College

Paul Redig, Milwaukee Area Technical College

William Renforth, Angelo State University

Melinda Schmitz, Pamlico Community College

Roberta Schultz, Western Michigan University

Alan T. Shao, University of North Carolina, Charlotte

Lynne Smith, Carroll Community College

Martin St. John, Westmoreland County Community College

Karen Stone, Southern New Hampshire University

John Stovall, University of Illinois, Chicago

Jeff Streiter, SUNY Brockport

Ruth Taylor, Texas State University

Donna Tillman, California State Polytechnic University

Donna Tillman, California Polytechnic University, Pomona

Janice Trafflet, Bucknell University

Rafael Valiente, University of Miami

Simon Walls, University of Tennessee

Mark Wasserman, University of Texas

Alvin Williams, University of Southern
Mississippi

Douglas E Witt, Brigham Young University

Andrew Yap, Florida International
University

Irvin A. Zaenglein, Northern Michigan
University

Larry Zigler, Highland Community
College

We also owe a great deal to the people at Pearson Prentice Hall who helped develop this book. Executive Editor Melissa Sabella provided fresh ideas and support throughout the revision. Project Manager Melissa Pellerano provided invaluable assistance and ably managed many facets of this complex revision project. Blair Brown developed the thirteenth edition's exciting new learning design and worked tirelessly in helping to make the design a reality. We'd also like to thank Kerri Tomasso, Anne Fahlgren, and Judy Leale. We are proud to be associated with the fine professionals at Pearson Prentice Hall. We also owe a deep debt of gratitude to Kelly Morrison and the wonderful team at GEX Publishing Services.

Finally, we owe many thanks to our families for all of their support and encouragement—Kathy, Betty, Mandy, Matt, KC, Keri, Delaney, Molly, Macy, and Ben from the Armstrong family and Nancy, Amy, Melissa, and Jessica from the Kotler family. To them, we dedicate this book.

Philip Kotler
Gary Armstrong

PRINCIPLES OF
Marketing

Marketing enriched content

KA

Marketing Enriched Beverage
with pomegranate

Marketing Enriched Beverage

20FL.OZ

Chapter 1

Part 1   Defining Marketing and the Marketing Process (Chapters 1, 2)
Part 2   Understanding the Marketplace and Consumers (Chapters 3, 4, 5, 6)
Part 3   Designing a Customer-Driven Strategy and Mix (Chapters 7, 8, 9, 10, 11, 12, 13, 14, 15, 16, 17)
Part 4   Extending Marketing (Chapters 18, 19, 20)

Marketing Creating and Capturing **Customer Value**

Chapter **PREVIEW**

In this chapter, we introduce you to the basic concepts of marketing. We start with the question, "What *is* marketing?" Simply put, marketing is managing profitable customer relationships. The aim of marketing is to create value *for* customers and to capture value *from* customers in return. Next, we discuss the five steps in the marketing process—from understanding customer needs, to designing customer-driven marketing strategies and programs, to building customer relationships and capturing value for the firm. Finally, we discuss the major trends and forces affecting marketing in this age of customer relationships. Understanding these basic concepts and forming your own ideas about what they really mean to you will give you a solid foundation for all that follows.

Let's start with a good story about marketing in action at Procter & Gamble, one of the world's largest and most respected marketing companies. P&G makes and markets a who's who list of consumer megabrands, including the likes of Tide, Crest, Bounty, Charmin, Puffs, Pampers, Pringles, Gillette, Dawn, Ivory, Febreze, Swiffer, Olay, CoverGirl, Pantene, Scope, NyQuil, Duracell, and a hundred more. It's also the world's largest advertiser, spending an eye-popping $8.2 billion each year on advertising worldwide, "telling and selling" consumers on the benefits of using its products. But look deeper and you'll see that this premier marketer does far more than just "tell and sell." The company's stated purpose is to provide products that "improve the lives of the world's consumers." P&G's products really do create value for consumers by solving their problems. In return, customers reward P&G with their brand loyalty and buying dollars. You'll see this theme of creating customer value to capture value in return repeated throughout the first chapter and throughout the text.

Creating customer value and building meaningful customer relationships sounds pretty lofty, especially for a company like P&G, which sells seemingly mundane, low-involvement consumer products such as detergents and shampoos, toothpastes and fabric softeners, and toilet paper and disposable diapers. Can you really develop a meaningful relationship with a laundry detergent? For P&G, the resounding answer is *yes*.

For example, take P&G's product Tide. More than 60 years ago, Tide revolutionized the industry as the first detergent to use synthetic compounds rather than soap chemicals for cleaning clothes. Tide really does get clothes clean. For decades, Tide's marketers have positioned the brand on superior functional performance, with hard-hitting ads showing before-and-after cleaning comparisons. But as it turns out Tide means a lot more to consumers than just getting grass stains out of that old pair of jeans.

For several years, P&G has been on a mission to unearth and cultivate the deep connections that customers have with its products. Two years ago, P&G global marketing chief James Stengel mandated that the company's brands must "speak to consumers eye-to-eye" rather than relentlessly driving product benefits. "We need to think beyond consuming . . . and to really directly understand the role and the meaning the brand has in [consumers'] lives," says Stengel. Behind this strategy lies the realization that competitors can quickly copy product benefits, such as cleaning power.

However, they can't easily copy how consumers *feel* about a brand. Consequently, P&G's true strength lies in the relationships that it builds between its brands and customers.

Under this mandate, the Tide marketing team decided that it needed a new message for the brand. Tide's brand share, although large, had been stagnant for several years. Also, as a result of its hard-hitting functional advertising, consumers saw the Tide brand as arrogant, self-absorbed, and very male. The brand needed to recapture the hearts and minds of its core female consumers.

So the team set out to gain a deeper understanding of the emotional connections that women have with their laundry. Rather than conducting the usual focus groups and research surveys, however, marketing executives and strategists from P&G and its longtime ad agency, Saatchi & Saatchi, went into a two-week consumer immersion. They tagged along with shadowed women in Kansas City, Missouri, and Charlotte, North Carolina, as they worked, shopped, and ran errands, and they sat in on discussions to hear women talk about

> **P&G's true strength lies in the relationships that it builds between brands and customers: "Tide knows fabrics best."**

knows fabrics best

what's important to them. "We got to an incredibly deep and personal level," says a Tide marketing executive. "We wanted to understand the role of laundry in their life." But "one of the great things," adds a Saatchi strategist, "is we didn't talk [to consumers] about their laundry habits [and practices]. We talked about their lives, what their needs were, how they felt as women. And we got a lot of rich stuff that we hadn't tapped into before."

For members of the Tide team who couldn't join the two-week consumer odyssey, including Saatchi's creative people, the agency videotaped the immersions, prepared scripts, and hired actresses to portray consumers in an hour-long play titled "Pieces of Her." "They were actually very good actresses who brought to life many dimensions of women," says the Saatchi executive. "It's difficult to inspire creatives sometimes. And [their reaction to the play] was incredible. There was crying and laughing. And you can see it in the [later] work. It's just very connected to women."

From the customer immersions, the marketers learned that, although Tide and laundry aren't the most important things in customers' lives, women are very emotional about their clothing. For example, "there was the joy a plus-size, divorced woman described when she got a whistle from her boyfriend while wearing her "foolproof (sexiest) outfit." According to one P&G account, "Day-to-day fabrics in women's lives hold meaning and touch them in many ways. Women like taking care of their clothes and fabrics because they are filled with emotions, stories, feelings, and memories. The fabrics in their lives (anything from jeans to sheets) allow them to express their personalities, their multidimensions as women, their attitudes." Such insights impacted everything the brand did moving forward. Tide, the marketers decided, can do more than solve women's laundry problems. It can make a difference in something they truly care about—the fabrics that touch their lives.

Based on these insights, P&G and Saatchi developed an award-winning advertising campaign, built around the theme "Tide knows fabrics best." Rather than the mostly heartless demonstrations and side-by-side comparisons of past Tide advertising, the new campaign employs rich visual imagery and meaningful emotional connections. The "Tide knows fabrics best" slogan says little about cleaning. Instead, the message is that Tide lets women focus on life's important things. "One of our rallying cries was to get out of the laundry basket and into [your] life," says a Tide marketer.

The "Tide knows fabrics best" ads have just the right mix of emotional connections and soft sell. In one TV commercial, a pregnant woman dribbles ice cream on the one last shirt that still fits. It's Tide with Bleach to the rescue, so that "your clothes can outlast your cravings." Another ad shows touching scenes of a woman first holding a baby and then cuddling romantically with her husband, all to the tune of "Be My Baby." Tide with Febreze, says the ad, can mean "the difference between smelling like a mom and smelling like a woman." In a third ad, a woman plays with her daughter at a park, still in her white slacks from the office, thanks to her confidence in Tide with Bleach: "Your work clothes. Your play clothes. Yup, they're the same clothes," the ad concludes. "Tide with bleach: For looking great, it's child's play." In all, the "Tide knows fabrics best" campaign shows women that Tide really does make a difference in fabrics that touch their lives.

So . . . back to that original question: Can you develop a relationship with a laundry detergent brand? Some critics wonder if P&G is taking this relationship thing too seriously. "Everybody wants to elevate their brand to this kind of more rarefied level," says one brand consultant, "but at the end of the day detergent is detergent." But it's hard to argue with success, and no brand is more successful than Tide. P&G's flagship brand captures an incredible 43 percent share of the cluttered and competitive laundry detergent market. That's right, 43 percent and growing—including a 7 percent increase in the year following the start of the "Tide knows fabrics best" campaign.

If you ask P&G global marketing chief Stengel, he'd say that this kind of success comes from deeply understanding consumers and connecting the company's brands to their lives. Stengel wants P&G to be more than a one-way communicator with customers. He wants it to be "a starter of conversations and a solver of consumers' problems." "It's not about telling and selling," he says. "It's about bringing a [customer] relationship mind-set to everything we do."[1]

> If you had wanted a pair of **yellow pants**, you wouldn't have paid **$46 for these.**
>
> TIDE WITH BLEACH ALTERNATIVE KEEPS WHITES WHITER, LONGER, SO THE LOOK YOU LOVE WILL LAST.
>
> *Tide*
> knows fabrics best

P&G is on a mission to unearth and cultivate the deep connections that customers have with its products. Can you really develop a meaningful relationship with a laundry detergent? For P&G, the resounding answer is yes.

Procter & Gamble, one of the world's largest and most respected marketing companies, really does create value for consumers by solving their problems. In return, customers reward P&G with their brand loyalty and buying dollars.

Objective Outline

Today's successful companies have one thing in common: Like Procter & Gamble, they are strongly customer-focused and heavily committed to marketing. These companies share a passion for understanding and satisfying customer needs in well-defined target markets. They motivate everyone in the organization to help build lasting customer relationships based on creating value. P&G's chief global marketer, Jim Stengel, puts it this way: "If we're going to make one big bet on our future—right here, right now—I'd say that the smart money is on building [customer] relationships."[2]

Author Comment | Stop here for a second and think about how you'd answer this question before studying marketing. Then, see how your answer changes as you go through the chapter.

What Is Marketing? (pp 4–6)

Marketing, more than any other business function, deals with customers. Although we will soon explore more-detailed definitions of marketing, perhaps the simplest definition is this one: *Marketing is managing profitable customer relationships.* The twofold goal of marketing is to attract new customers by promising superior value and to keep and grow current customers by delivering satisfaction.

Wal-Mart has become the world's largest retailer—and the world's largest *company*—by delivering on its promise, "Save money. Live Better." At Disney theme parks, "imagineers" work wonders in their quest to "make a dream come true today." Apple fulfills its motto to "Think Different" with dazzling, customer-driven innovation that captures customer imaginations and loyalty. Its wildly successful iPod grabs more than 70 percent of the music player market; its iTunes music store captures nearly 90 percent of the song download business.[3]

Sound marketing is critical to the success of every organization. Large for-profit firms such as Procter & Gamble, Google, Target, Toyota, Apple, and Marriott use marketing. But so do not-for-profit organizations such as colleges, hospitals, museums, symphony orchestras, and even churches.

You already know a lot about marketing—it's all around you. Marketing comes to you in the good old traditional forms: You see it in the abundance of products at your nearby shopping mall and in the advertisements that fill your TV screen, spice up your magazines, or stuff your mailbox. But in recent years, marketers have assembled a host of new marketing approaches, everything from imaginative Web sites, Internet chat rooms, and social networks to interactive TV and your cell phone. These new approaches aim to do more than just blast out messages to the masses. They aim to reach you directly and personally. Today's marketers want to become a part of your life and to enrich your experiences with their brands—to help you *live* their brands.

At home, at school, where you work, and where you play, you see marketing in almost everything you do. Yet, there is much more to marketing than meets the consumer's casual eye. Behind it all is a massive network of people and activities competing for your attention and purchases. This book will give you a complete introduction to the basic concepts and practices of today's marketing. In this chapter, we begin by defining marketing and the marketing process.

Marketing Defined

What *is* marketing? Many people think of marketing only as selling and advertising. And no wonder—every day we are bombarded with TV commercials, direct-mail offers, sales calls, and e-mail pitches. However, selling and advertising are only the tip of the marketing iceberg.

Today, marketing must be understood not in the old sense of making a sale—"telling and selling"—but in the new sense of *satisfying customer needs*. If the marketer understands consumer needs; develops products that provide superior customer value; and prices, distributes, and promotes them effectively, these products will sell easily. In fact, according to management guru Peter Drucker, "The aim of marketing is to make selling unnecessary."[4] Selling and advertising are only part of a larger "marketing mix"—a set of marketing tools that work together to satisfy customer needs and build customer relationships.

Broadly defined, marketing is a social and managerial process by which individuals and organizations obtain what they need and want through creating and exchanging value with others. In a narrower business context, marketing involves building profitable, value-laden exchange relationships with customers. Hence, we define **marketing** as the process by which companies create value for customers and build strong customer relationships in order to capture value from customers in return.[5]

Marketing
The process by which companies create value for customers and build strong customer relationships in order to capture value from customers in return.

The Marketing Process

 **Figure 1.1** presents a simple five-step model of the marketing process. In the first four steps, companies work to understand consumers, create customer value, and build strong customer relationships. In the final step, companies reap the rewards of creating superior customer value. By creating value *for* consumers, they in turn capture value *from* consumers in the form of sales, profits, and long-term customer equity.

This important figure shows marketing in a nutshell! By creating value *for* customers, marketers capture value *from* customers in return. This five-step process forms the marketing framework for the rest of the chapter and the rest of the text.

Create value *for customers* and build customer relationships

| Understand the marketplace and customer needs and wants | → | Design a customer-driven marketing strategy | → | Construct an integrated marketing program that delivers superior value | → | Build profitable relationships and create customer delight | → | **Capture value *from* customers in return** Capture value from customers to create profits and customer equity |

FIGURE | 1.1 A Simple Model of the Marketing Process

In this chapter and the next, we will examine the steps of this simple model of marketing. In this chapter, we will review each step but focus more on the customer relationship steps—understanding customers, building customer relationships, and capturing value from customers. In Chapter 2, we'll look more deeply into the second and third steps—designing marketing strategies and constructing marketing programs.

> **Author Comment** | Marketing is all about creating value for customers. So, as the first step in the marketing process, the company must fully understand consumers and the marketplace in which it operates.

Understanding the Marketplace and Customer Needs (pp 6–8)

As a first step, marketers need to understand customer needs and wants and the marketplace within which they operate. We now examine five core customer and marketplace concepts: (1) *needs, wants, and demands*; (2) *market offerings (products, services, and experiences)*; (3) *value and satisfaction*; (4) *exchanges and relationships*; and (5) *markets*.

Customer Needs, Wants, and Demands

Needs
States of felt deprivation.

The most basic concept underlying marketing is that of human needs. Human **needs** are states of felt deprivation. They include basic *physical* needs for food, clothing, warmth, and safety; *social* needs for belonging and affection; and *individual* needs for knowledge and self-expression. These needs were not created by marketers; they are a basic part of the human makeup.

Wants
The form human needs take as shaped by culture and individual personality.

Wants are the form human needs take as they are shaped by culture and individual personality. An American *needs* food but *wants* a Big Mac, french fries, and a soft drink. A person in Papua New Guinea *needs* food but *wants* taro, rice, yams, and pork. Wants are shaped by one's society and are described in terms of objects that will satisfy needs. When backed by buying power, wants become **demands.** Given their wants and resources, people demand products with benefits that add up to the most value and satisfaction.

Demands
Human wants that are backed by buying power.

Outstanding marketing companies go to great lengths to learn about and understand their customers' needs, wants, and demands. They conduct consumer research and analyze mountains of customer data. Their people at all levels—including top management—stay close to customers. For example, at Southwest Airlines, all senior executives handle bags, check in passengers, and serve as flight attendants once every quarter. At P&G, executives from the CEO down routinely spend time with consumers in their homes and other settings. "We all go out and really spend time with consumers," notes P&G's global marketing officer, Jim Stengel, "just to look at the differences in how they [think] about brands [and what's] important in their lives."[6]

Market Offerings—Products, Services, and Experiences

Market offering
Some combination of products, services, information, or experiences offered to a market to satisfy a need or want.

Consumers' needs and wants are fulfilled through **market offerings**—some combination of products, services, information, or experiences offered to a market to satisfy a need or want. Market offerings are not limited to physical *products*. They also include *services*—activities or benefits offered for sale that are essentially intangible and do not result in the ownership of anything. Examples include banking, airline, hotel, tax preparation, and home repair services.

More broadly, market offerings also include other entities, such as *persons*, *places*, *organizations*, *information*, and *ideas*. ▲For example, UNCF powerfully markets the idea that "A Mind Is a Terrible Thing to Waste." The nation's oldest and most successful African American education assistance organization, UNCF has helped more than 350,000 minority students graduate from college.[7]

Marketing myopia
The mistake of paying more attention to the specific products a company offers than to the benefits and experiences produced by these products.

Many sellers make the mistake of paying more attention to the specific products they offer than to the benefits and experiences produced by these products. These sellers suffer from **marketing myopia**. They are so taken with their products that they focus only on existing wants and lose sight of underlying customer needs.[8] They forget that a product is only a tool to solve a consumer problem. A manufacturer of quarter-inch drill bits may think that the customer needs a drill bit. But what the customer *really* needs is a quarter-inch hole. These sellers will have trouble if a new product comes along that serves the customer's need better or less expensively. The customer will have the same *need* but will *want* the new product.

Smart marketers look beyond the attributes of the products and services they sell. By orchestrating several services and products, they create *brand experiences* for consumers. For example, you don't just watch a NASCAR race, you immerse yourself in the exhilarating NASCAR experience. Similarly, Hewlett-Packard recognizes that a personal computer is much more than just a collection of wires and electrical components. It's an intensely personal user experience. As noted in a recent HP ad, "There is hardly anything that you own that is *more* personal. Your personal computer is your backup brain. It's your life. . . . It's your astonishing strategy, staggering proposal, dazzling calculation. It's your autobiography, written in a thousand daily words."[9]

Customer Value and Satisfaction

Consumers usually face a broad array of products and services that might satisfy a given need. How do they choose among these many market offerings? Customers form expectations about the value and satisfaction that various market offerings will deliver and buy accordingly. Satisfied customers buy again and tell others about their good experiences. Dissatisfied customers often switch to competitors and disparage the product to others.

Marketers must be careful to set the right level of expectations. If they set expectations too low, they may satisfy those who buy but fail to attract enough buyers. If they raise expectations too high, buyers will be disappointed. Customer value and customer satisfaction are key building blocks for developing and managing customer relationships. We will revisit these core concepts later in the chapter.

UNCF helps thousands of deserving students. But we have to turn away thousands more. So please give to the United Negro College Fund. Your donation will make a difference. Visit uncf.org or call 1-800-332-8623.

UNITED NEGRO COLLEGE FUND
A mind is a terrible thing to waste.®

▲ Market offerings are not limited to physical products. UNCF powerfully markets the idea that "A mind is a terrible thing to waste."

Exchanges and Relationships

Marketing occurs when people decide to satisfy needs and wants through exchange relationships. **Exchange** is the act of obtaining a desired object from someone by offering something in return. In the broadest sense, the marketer tries to bring about a response to some market offering. The response may be more than simply buying or trading products and services. A political candidate, for instance, wants votes, a church wants membership, an orchestra wants an audience, and a social action group wants idea acceptance.

Marketing consists of actions taken to build and maintain desirable exchange *relationships* with target audiences involving a product, service, idea, or other object. Beyond simply attracting new customers and creating transactions, the goal is to retain customers and grow their business with the company. Marketers want to build strong relationships by consistently delivering superior customer value. We will expand on the important concept of managing customer relationships later in the chapter.

Exchange
The act of obtaining a desired object from someone by offering something in return.

Markets

The concepts of exchange and relationships lead to the concept of a market. A **market** is the set of actual and potential buyers of a product. These buyers share a particular need or want that can be satisfied through exchange relationships.

Marketing means managing markets to bring about profitable customer relationships. However, creating these relationships takes work. Sellers must search for buyers, identify their needs, design good market offerings, set prices for them, promote them, and store and deliver them. Activities such as consumer research, product development, communication, distribution, pricing, and service are core marketing activities.

Market
The set of all actual and potential buyers of a product or service.

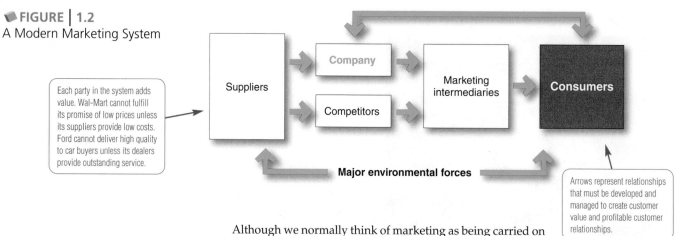

Each party in the system adds value. Wal-Mart cannot fulfill its promise of low prices unless its suppliers provide low costs. Ford cannot deliver high quality to car buyers unless its dealers provide outstanding service.

Arrows represent relationships that must be developed and managed to create customer value and profitable customer relationships.

Although we normally think of marketing as being carried on by sellers, buyers also carry on marketing. Consumers do marketing when they search for products and interact with companies and obtain information and make their purchases. In fact, today's digital technologies, from Web sites and blogs to cell phones and other wireless devices, have empowered consumers and made marketing a truly interactive affair. Marketers are no longer asking only "How can we reach our customers?" but also "How should our customers reach us?" and even "How can our customers reach each other?"

◆ **Figure 1.2** shows the main elements in a marketing system. Marketing involves serving a market of final consumers in the face of competitors. The company and competitors research the market and interact with consumers to understand their needs. Then they create and send their market offerings and messages to consumers, either directly or through marketing intermediaries. All of the parties in the system are affected by major environmental forces (demographic, economic, physical, technological, political/legal, and social/cultural).

Each party in the system adds value for the next level. All of the arrows represent relationships that must be developed and managed. Thus, a company's success at building profitable relationships depends not only on its own actions but also on how well the entire system serves the needs of final consumers. Wal-Mart cannot fulfill its promise of low prices unless its suppliers provide merchandise at low costs. And Ford cannot deliver high quality to car buyers unless its dealers provide outstanding sales and service.

Author Comment | Now that the company fully understands consumers and the marketplace, it must decide which customers it will serve and how it will bring them value.

Marketing management
The art and science of choosing target markets and building profitable relationships with them.

Designing a Customer-Driven Marketing Strategy (pp 8–12)

Once it fully understands consumers and the marketplace, marketing management can design a customer-driven marketing strategy. We define **marketing management** as the art and science of choosing target markets and building profitable relationships with them. The marketing manager's aim is to find, attract, keep, and grow target customers by creating, delivering, and communicating superior customer value.

To design a winning marketing strategy, the marketing manager must answer two important questions: *What customers will we serve (what's our target market)?* and *How can we serve these customers best (what's our value proposition)?* We will discuss these marketing strategy concepts briefly here, and then look at them in more detail in the next chapter.

Selecting Customers to Serve

The company must first decide *who* it will serve. It does this by dividing the market into segments of customers (*market segmentation*) and selecting which segments it will go after (*target marketing*). Some people think of marketing management as finding as many customers as possible and increasing demand. But marketing managers know that they cannot serve all customers in every way. By trying to serve all customers, they may not serve any customers well. Instead, the company wants to select only customers that it can serve well and profitably. For example, Nordstrom stores profitably target affluent professionals; Family Dollar stores profitably target families with more modest means.

Some marketers may even seek *fewer* customers and reduced demand. For example, Yosemite National Park is overcrowded in the summer and many power companies have trouble meeting demand during peak usage periods. In these and other cases of excess demand, companies may practice *demarketing* to reduce the number of customers or to shift their demand temporarily or permanently. For instance, many power companies now sponsor programs that help customers reduce their power usage through peak-load control devices, better energy use monitoring, and heating system tune-up incentives. Progress Energy even offers an Energy Manager on Loan program that provides school systems and other public customers with a cost-free on-site energy expert to help them find energy-savings opportunities.

Ultimately, marketing managers must decide which customers they want to target and on the level, timing, and nature of their demand. Simply put, marketing management is *customer management* and *demand management*.

Choosing a Value Proposition

The company must also decide how it will serve targeted customers—how it will *differentiate and position* itself in the marketplace. A company's *value proposition* is the set of benefits or values it promises to deliver to consumers to satisfy their needs. BMW promises "the ultimate driving machine," whereas ▲ Land Rover lets you "Go Beyond"—to "get a taste of adventure, whatever your tastes." And with cell phones, Nokia is "Connecting People—anyone, anywhere," whereas with Apple's iPhone, "Touching is believing."

Such value propositions differentiate one brand from another. They answer the customer's question "Why should I buy your brand rather than a competitor's?" Companies must design strong value propositions that give them the greatest advantage in their target markets.

Marketing Management Orientations

Marketing management wants to design strategies that will build profitable relationships with target consumers. But what *philosophy* should guide these marketing strategies? What weight should be given to the interests of customers, the organization, and society? Very often, these interests conflict.

There are five alternative concepts under which organizations design and carry out their marketing strategies: the *production, product, selling, marketing,* and *societal marketing concepts.*

Production concept
The idea that consumers will favor products that are available and highly affordable and that the organization should therefore focus on improving production and distribution efficiency.

DEFENDER

LAND ROVER
GO BEYOND

▲ Value propositions: Land Rover lets you "Go Beyond"—to "get a taste of adventure, whatever your tastes."

The Production Concept

The **production concept** holds that consumers will favor products that are available and highly affordable. Therefore, management should focus on improving production and distribution efficiency. This concept is one of the oldest orientations that guides sellers.

The production concept is still a useful philosophy in some situations. For example, computer maker Lenovo dominates the highly competitive, price-sensitive Chinese PC market through low labor costs, high production efficiency, and mass distribution. However, although useful in some situations, the production concept can lead to marketing myopia. Companies adopting this orientation run a major risk of focusing too narrowly on their own operations and losing sight of the real objective—satisfying customer needs and building customer relationships.

The Product Concept

The **product concept** holds that consumers will favor products that offer the most in quality, performance, and innovative features. Under this concept, marketing strategy focuses on making continuous product improvements.

Product quality and improvement are important parts of most marketing strategies. However, focusing *only* on the company's products can also lead to marketing myopia. For example, some manufacturers believe that if they can "build a better mousetrap, the world will beat a path to their door." But they are often rudely shocked. Buyers may be looking for a better solution to a mouse problem, but not necessarily for a better mousetrap. The better solution might be a chemical spray, an exterminating service, or something else that works even better than a mousetrap. Furthermore, a better mousetrap will not sell unless the manufacturer designs, packages, and prices it attractively; places it in convenient distribution channels; brings it to the attention of people who need it; and convinces buyers that it is a better product.

The Selling Concept

Many companies follow the **selling concept,** which holds that consumers will not buy enough of the firm's products unless it undertakes a large-scale selling and promotion effort. The selling concept is typically practiced with unsought goods—those that buyers do not normally think of buying, such as insurance or blood donations. These industries must be good at tracking down prospects and selling them on product benefits.

Such aggressive selling, however, carries high risks. It focuses on creating sales transactions rather than on building long-term, profitable customer relationships. The aim often is to sell what the company makes rather than making what the market wants. It assumes that customers who are coaxed into buying the product will like it. Or, if they don't like it, they will possibly forget their disappointment and buy it again later. These are usually poor assumptions.

The Marketing Concept

The **marketing concept** holds that achieving organizational goals depends on knowing the needs and wants of target markets and delivering the desired satisfactions better than competitors do. Under the marketing concept, customer focus and value are the *paths* to sales and profits. Instead of a product-centered "make and sell" philosophy, the marketing concept is a customer-centered "sense and respond" philosophy. The job is not to find the right customers for your product but to find the right products for your customers.

Figure 1.3 contrasts the selling concept and the marketing concept. The selling concept takes an *inside-out* perspective. It starts with the factory, focuses on the company's existing products, and calls for heavy selling and promotion to obtain profitable sales. It focuses primarily on customer conquest—getting short-term sales with little concern about who buys or why.

In contrast, the marketing concept takes an *outside-in* perspective. As Herb Kelleher, Southwest Airlines' colorful CEO, puts it, "We don't have a marketing department; we have a customer department." The marketing concept starts with a well-defined market, focuses on customer needs, and integrates all the marketing activities that affect customers. In turn, it yields profits by creating lasting relationships with the right customers based on customer value and satisfaction.

Product concept
The idea that consumers will favor products that offer the most quality, performance, and features and that the organization should therefore devote its energy to making continuous product improvements.

Selling concept
The idea that that consumers will not buy enough of the firm's products unless it undertakes a large-scale selling and promotion effort.

Marketing concept
The marketing management philosophy that holds that achieving organizational goals depends on knowing the needs and wants of target markets and delivering the desired satisfactions better than competitors do.

FIGURE | 1.3
The Selling and Marketing Concepts Contrasted

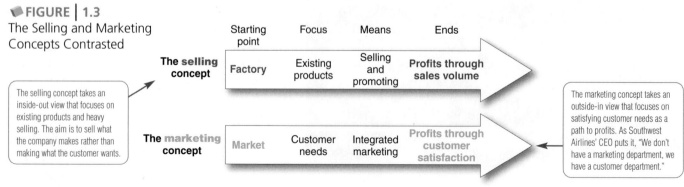

The selling concept takes an inside-out view that focuses on existing products and heavy selling. The aim is to sell what the company makes rather than making what the customer wants.

	Starting point	Focus	Means	Ends
The selling concept	Factory	Existing products	Selling and promoting	Profits through sales volume
The marketing concept	Market	Customer needs	Integrated marketing	Profits through customer satisfaction

The marketing concept takes an outside-in view that focuses on satisfying customer needs as a path to profits. As Southwest Airlines' CEO puts it, "We don't have a marketing department, we have a customer department."

▲ Customer-driving marketing: Even 20 years ago, how many consumers would have thought to ask for now-commonplace products such as cell phones, personal digital assistants, notebook computers, iPods, and digital cameras. Marketers must often understand customer needs even better than the customers themselves do.

Implementing the marketing concept often means more than simply responding to customers' stated desires and obvious needs. *Customer-driven* companies research current customers deeply to learn about their desires, gather new product and service ideas, and test proposed product improvements. Such customer-driven marketing usually works well when a clear need exists and when customers know what they want.

In many cases, however, customers *don't* know what they want or even what is possible. For example, even 20 years ago, how many consumers would have thought to ask for now-commonplace products such as cell phones, notebook computers, iPods, digital cameras, 24-hour online buying, and satellite navigation systems in their cars? Such situations call for ▲ *customer-driving* marketing— understanding customer needs even better than customers themselves do and creating products and services that meet existing and latent needs, now and in the future. As an executive at 3M puts it, "Our goal is to lead customers where they want to go before *they* know where they want to go."

The Societal Marketing Concept

Societal marketing concept

The idea that a company's marketing decisions should consider consumers' wants, the company's requirements, consumers' long-run interests, and society's long-run interests.

The **societal marketing concept** questions whether the pure marketing concept overlooks possible conflicts between consumer *short-run wants* and consumer *long-run welfare.* Is a firm that satisfies the immediate needs and wants of target markets always doing what's best for consumers in the long run? The societal marketing concept holds that marketing strategy should deliver value to customers in a way that maintains or improves both the consumer's *and society's* well-being.

Consider today's flourishing bottled water industry. You may view bottled water companies as offering a convenient, tasty, and healthy product. Its packaging suggests "green" images of pristine lakes and snow-capped mountains. Yet making, filling, and shipping billions of plastic bottles generates huge amounts of carbon dioxide emissions that contribute substantially to global warming. Further, the plastic bottles pose a substantial recycling and solid waste disposal problem. Thus, in satisfying short-term consumer wants, the highly successful bottled water industry may be causing environmental problems that run against society's long-run interests.[10]

As ◗ **Figure 1.4** shows, companies should balance three considerations in setting their marketing strategies: company profits, consumer wants, *and* society's interests.

◗ FIGURE | 1.4
The Considerations Underlying the Societal Marketing Concept

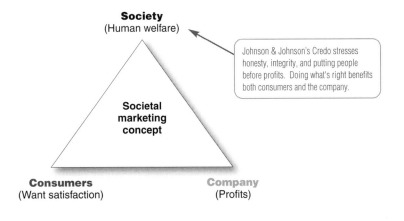

Society
(Human welfare)

Societal marketing concept

Johnson & Johnson's Credo stresses honesty, integrity, and putting people before profits. Doing what's right benefits both consumers and the company.

Consumers
(Want satisfaction)

Company
(Profits)

Our Credo

We believe our first responsibility is to the doctors, nurses and patients,
to mothers and fathers and all others who use our products and services.
In meeting their needs everything we do must be of high quality.
We must constantly strive to reduce our costs
in order to maintain reasonable prices.
Customers' orders must be serviced promptly and accurately.
Our suppliers and distributors must have an opportunity
to make a fair profit.

We are responsible to our employees,
the men and women who work with us throughout the world.
Everyone must be considered as an individual.
We must respect their dignity and recognize their merit.
They must have a sense of security in their jobs.
Compensation must be fair and adequate,
and working conditions clean, orderly and safe.
We must be mindful of ways to help our employees fulfill
their family responsibilities.
Employees must feel free to make suggestions and complaints.
There must be equal opportunity for employment, development
and advancement for those qualified.
We must provide competent management,
and their actions must be just and ethical.

We are responsible to the communities in which we live and work
and to the world community as well.
We must be good citizens — support good works and charities
and bear our fair share of taxes.
We must encourage civic improvements and better health and education.
We must maintain in good order
the property we are privileged to use,
protecting the environment and natural resources.

Our final responsibility is to our stockholders.
Business must make a sound profit.
We must experiment with new ideas.
Research must be carried on, innovative programs developed
and mistakes paid for.
New equipment must be purchased, new facilities provided
and new products launched.
Reserves must be created to provide for adverse times.
When we operate according to these principles,
the stockholders should realize a fair return.

Johnson & Johnson

The societal marketing concept: Johnson & Johnson's Credo stresses putting people before profits.

▲ Johnson & Johnson does this well. Its concern for societal interests is summarized in a company document called "Our Credo," which stresses honesty, integrity, and putting people before profits. Under this credo, Johnson & Johnson would rather take a big loss than ship a bad batch of one of its products.

Consider the tragic tampering case in which eight people died in 1982 from swallowing cyanide-laced capsules of Tylenol, a Johnson & Johnson brand. Although Johnson & Johnson believed that the pills had been altered in only a few stores, not in the factory, it quickly recalled all of its product and launched an information campaign to instruct and reassure consumers. The recall cost the company $100 million in earnings. In the long run, however, the company's swift recall of Tylenol strengthened consumer confidence and loyalty, and today Tylenol remains one of the nation's leading brands of pain reliever.

Johnson & Johnson management has learned that doing what's right benefits both consumers and the company. Says former CEO Ralph Larsen, "The Credo should not be viewed as some kind of social welfare program . . . it's just plain good business. If we keep trying to do what's right, at the end of the day we believe the marketplace will reward us." Thus, over the years, Johnson & Johnson's dedication to consumers and community service has made it one of America's most admired companies *and* one of the most profitable.[11]

Author Comment | The customer-driven marketing strategy discussed in the last section outlines which customers the company will serve (the target market) and how it will serve them (the value proposition). Now, the company develops marketing plans and programs—a marketing mix—that will actually deliver the intended customer value.

Preparing an Integrated Marketing Plan and Program (p 12)

The company's marketing strategy outlines which customers the company will serve and how it will create value for these customers. Next, the marketer develops an integrated marketing program that will actually deliver the intended value to target customers. The marketing program builds customer relationships by transforming the marketing strategy into action. It consists of the firm's *marketing mix,* the set of marketing tools the firm uses to implement its marketing strategy.

The major marketing mix tools are classified into four broad groups, called the *four Ps* of marketing: product, price, place, and promotion. To deliver on its value proposition, the firm must first create a need-satisfying market offering (product). It must decide how much it will charge for the offering (price) and how it will make the offering available to target consumers (place). Finally, it must communicate with target customers about the offering and persuade them of its merits (promotion). The firm must blend all of these marketing mix tools into a comprehensive *integrated marketing program* that communicates and delivers the intended value to chosen customers. We will explore marketing programs and the marketing mix in much more detail in later chapters.

Author Comment | Doing a good job with the first three steps in the marketing process sets the stage for step four, building and managing lasting customer relationships.

Building Customer Relationships (pp 12-21)

The first three steps in the marketing process—understanding the marketplace and customer needs, designing a customer-driven marketing strategy, and constructing marketing programs—all lead up to the fourth and most important step: building profitable customer relationships.

Customer Relationship Management

Customer relationship management is perhaps the most important concept of modern marketing. Some marketers define customer relationship management narrowly as a customer data management activity (a practice called *CRM*). By this definition, it involves managing detailed information about individual customers and carefully managing customer "touchpoints" in order to maximize customer loyalty. We will discuss this narrower CRM activity in Chapter 4 when dealing with marketing information.

Most marketers, however, give the concept of customer relationship management a broader meaning. In this broader sense, **customer relationship management** is the overall process of building and maintaining profitable customer relationships by delivering superior customer value and satisfaction. It deals with all aspects of acquiring, keeping, and growing customers.

Relationship Building Blocks: Customer Value and Satisfaction

The key to building lasting customer relationships is to create superior customer value and satisfaction. Satisfied customers are more likely to be loyal customers and to give the company a larger share of their business.

Customer Value.   Attracting and retaining customers can be a difficult task. Customers often face a bewildering array of products and services from which to choose. A customer buys from the firm that offers the highest **customer-perceived value**—the customer's evaluation of the difference between all the benefits and all the costs of a market offering relative to those of competing offers.

For example, consider the "premium denim" trend that has recently sent the price of jeans skyrocketing. A pair of Paige Premium Denim jeans, for instance, starts at $169. A woman who buys a pair of Paige jeans gains a number of benefits. Owner and designer Paige Adams-Geller uses the knowledge she learned as a jeans model to design jeans from the female perspective. Says Paige, "Most of us weren't blessed with perfect genes but we're bringing you the next best thing: perfect jeans." Her denim "will lift the derriere, lengthen your legs, and slenderize your hips and thighs—all with an uncompromising commitment to feminine detail and quality." In all, says Paige, her jeans are a real value—they will fit you better and last longer. When deciding whether to purchase a pair, customers will weigh these and other perceived values of owning Paige jeans against the money and psychic costs of acquiring them.

Customers often do not judge values and costs "accurately" or "objectively." They act on *perceived* value. For example, as compared to a pair of less expensive jeans that you'd pull off the shelf at Gap, do Paige jeans really provide superior quality and that perfect fit and look? If so, are they worth the much higher price? It's all a matter of personal value perceptions but for many women the answer is yes. One woman notes that, for her, premium jeans always seem to fit just right, making the price irrelevant. "I work, so I have the money to buy them," she says. "I think they're worth it."[12]

Customer Satisfaction.   **Customer satisfaction** depends on the product's perceived performance relative to a buyer's expectations. If the product's performance falls short of expectations, the customer is dissatisfied. If performance matches expectations, the customer is satisfied. If performance exceeds expectations, the customer is highly satisfied or delighted.

Outstanding marketing companies go out of their way to keep important customers satisfied. Most studies show that higher levels of customer satisfaction lead to greater customer loyalty, which in turn results in better company performance. Smart companies aim to delight customers by promising only what they can deliver, then delivering more than they promise. Delighted customers not only make repeat purchases, they become willing marketing partners and "customer evangelists" who spread the word about their good experiences to others (see **Real Marketing 1.1**).[13]

For companies interested in delighting customers, exceptional value and service are more than a set of policies or actions—they are a companywide attitude, an important part of the overall company culture. For example, year after year, Ritz-Carlton ranks at or near

Customer relationship management
The overall process of building and maintaining profitable customer relationships by delivering superior customer value and satisfaction.

Customer-perceived value
The customer's evaluation of the difference between all the benefits and all the costs of a marketing offer relative to those of competing offers.

Customer satisfaction
The extent to which a product's perceived performance matches a buyer's expectations.

Real Marketing 1.1

iRobot's Roomba:

The Power of Customer Delight

When you were a child, you probably didn't like it much when your mother made you vacuum around the house. You probably still don't much like vacuuming—it's a thankless, seemingly never-ending task. But there's one group of people who don't mind vacuuming at all. In fact, they're absolutely delighted about it. They are the folks who own an iRobot Roomba, the cute little robotic vacuum that zips around rooms, avoiding furniture and other obstacles, tirelessly sniffing up dirt, dust, and dog hair.

People love their little Roombas. They name them, talk to them, and even buy a second Roomba so that the first one won't be lonely. Many Roomba owners spend more time watching their little petlike robots than they would spend vacuuming a room themselves. Recognizing the strong attachments that many Roomba owners have to these personable little machines, iRobot does all it can to involve its customers in everything from product development to technical support, turning them into an army of Roomba consumer evangelists and marketing partners.

iRobot began in the 1990s, building devices for the U.S. military—small robots called PackBots now used to diffuse improvised explosive devices (IEDs) in Iraq or explore caves in Afghanistan. Based on this advanced technology, the company introduced its first Roomba in 2002. Made up of more than 100 plastic parts, motors, controllers, sensors, brushes, and a dustbin, the 10-pound Roomba uses a sophisticated algorithm to scoot around a room, even going under tables, chairs, sofas, and beds. When it runs into obstacles, it figures out how to clean around them. And when its rechargeable battery begins to lose its charge, the Roomba finds its way to its home base unit, plugs itself in, and recharges automatically. Owners can even program more expensive models to clean at certain times of the day or days of the week, even when no one is home.

In the summer of 2002, iRobot negotiated distribution deals with Brookstone and Sharper Image, and Roomba sales took off. Soon, the company began getting calls from major chains

Costumes for your iRobot Roomba and now your Scooba!!!

Delighting customers: People love their pet-like little Roombas. They name them, talk to them, and even buy a second Roomba so that the first one won't be lonely. Recognizing this, iRobot has turned customers into an army of Roomba consumer evangelists.

such as Target, Kohl's, and Linens 'n Things. iRobot's factory churned out 50,000 units just to meet that year's holiday demand.

Then the real fun began. As iRobot received Roombas back for servicing, customer-service reps noted that many owners were customizing and humanizing their little robotic assistants. Rather than selling just a high-tech household appliance, it seems that iRobot had invented a new kind of family pet. Reps reported that owners were often painting their Roombas and referring to them by name and gender. The most popular name was Rosie, after the robotic maid on the classic animated TV series, *The Jetsons.*

Before long, delighted Roomba owners became iRobot's best marketing partners. An independent Web site sprang up, myRoomBud. com, offering RoomBud costumes that transform a Roomba from "just a naked vacuum" into a lovable character such as "Roobit the Frog," "Mooba the Cow," or "RoomBette La French Maid." The site even lets Roomba enthusiasts print out official-looking birth certificates for their newly adopted robotic pets.

Smitten Roomba owners by the hundreds began posting video clips of their Roombas in action on YouTube. One mounted a camera on his Roomba to create a RoombaCam. Other

Roomba customers created the Roomba Review Web site (www.RoombaReview.com), which features news, chats, product reviews, and hacker information. Billed as the official Roomba lover's forum, Roomba Review is loaded with posts and comments on everything from shared Roomba experiences and adventures to information on differences between models, tips on finding a Roomba at a good price, and tech support questions and answers—all supplied by customers. A disclaimer at the bottom notes that the Web site "is not affiliated with iRobot Corporation (We're just really big fans of the Roomba vacuum!)"

Noting all of this customer enthusiasm and delight, iRobot developed programs to strengthen and organize the growing sense of community among Roomba owners. For example, it opened its programmatic interface, encouraging owners, amateur robotics enthusiasts, and others to develop their own programs and uses for the Roomba. It also set up an iRobot Create Web site (www.irobot. com/create/), where customers could show off their latest inventions. These actions turned Roomba owners into a community of amateur tinkerers and hobbyists. Customers

Continued on next page

Real Marketing 1.1 Continued ▼

themselves began to develop improved features that iRobot would later adopt.

By monitoring interactions with and among enthusiastic Roomba customers, iRobot was able to discover product problems and additional customer needs. Complaints that animal hair often clogged the machines led the company to introduce the Roomba for Pets model, featuring easy-to-clean brushes that make removing pet hair easier. For customers who wanted a robotic "floor mopper," iRobot introduced the Scooba floor washer, another personable little gizmo that preps, washes, scrubs, and squeegees tile, linoleum, and hardwood floors "so that you don't have to!" For customers who complained about cleaning gutters, iRobot developed the Looj Gutter Cleaning Robot. The Verro Pool Cleaning Robot "gets pools deep-down clean from floor to waterline—just

drop it in and let it go!" Customers are now clamoring for a Roomba lawn mower!

Based on interactions with its customer community, iRobot has also continued to improve the original Roomba. Last year, it introduced the 500 series, even smarter Roombas that can free themselves from almost any jam, including rug tassels and power cords, reducing the need to prep a room before unleashing the little sniffer. The new model also features a built-in voice tutorial for new users that explains the Roomba's features right out of the box.

Thus, iRobot has discovered the power of customer delight. More than that, it's working to harness that power by partnering with its satisfied-customer community to improve current products, develop new ones, and help spread the word to new customers. So far, iRobot has sold more than two million Roombas. Last year, the company's sales reached nearly $250 million, up 75 percent in only the last two years. Profits surged 175 percent. With the help of its delighted customers, iRobot is filling the vacuum and really cleaning up.

Sources: Based on information found in Paul Gillin, "Cleaning Up with Customer Evangelists," *BtoB*, August 13, 2007, p. 10; Ben McConnell, "Roomba Robot Love," December 30, 2006, accessed at www.churchofthecustomer.com; Faith Arner, "How the Roomba Was Realized," *BusinessWeek*, October 6, 2003, p. 10; Joel Garreau, "Robots That Fill an Emotional Vacuum," *Washington Post*, December 29, 2006, p. C1; "iRobot Corporation," *Hoover's Company Records*, August 1, 2008, p. 132607; and www.myroombud.com and www.roombareview.com, accessed November 2008.

the top of the hospitality industry in terms of customer satisfaction. ▲ Its passion for satisfying customers is summed up in the company's Credo, which promises that its luxury hotels will deliver a truly memorable experience—one that "enlivens the senses, instills well-being, and fulfills even the unexpressed wishes and needs of our guests."

THE RITZ-CARLTON®

CREDO

The Ritz-Carlton is a place where the genuine care and comfort of our guests is our highest mission.

We pledge to provide the finest personal service and facilities for our guests who will always enjoy a warm, relaxed, yet refined ambience.

The Ritz-Carlton experience enlivens the senses, instills well-being, and fulfills even the unexpressed wishes and needs of our guests.

▲ Customer satisfaction: Ritz-Carlton's passion for satisfying customers is summed up in its Credo, which promises a truly memorable experience—one that "enlivens the senses, instills well-being, and fulfills even the unexpressed wishes and needs of our guests."

Check into any Ritz-Carlton hotel around the world, and you'll be amazed by the company's fervent dedication to anticipating and meeting even your slightest need. Without ever asking, they seem to know that you want a king-size bed, a nonallergenic pillow, and breakfast with decaffeinated coffee in your room. Each day, hotel staffers—from those at the front desk to those in maintenance and housekeeping—discreetly observe and record even the smallest guest preferences. Then, every morning, each hotel reviews the files of all new arrivals who have stayed previously at a Ritz-Carlton and prepares a list of suggested extra touches that might delight each guest. And once they identify a special customer need, The Ritz-Carlton employees go to legendary extremes to meet it. For example, to serve the needs of a guest with food allergies, a Ritz-Carlton chef in Bali located special eggs and milk in a small grocery store in another country and had them delivered to the hotel. In another case, when the hotel's laundry service failed to remove a stain on a guest's suit before the guest departed, the hotel manager traveled to the guest's house and personally delivered a reimbursement check for the cost of the suit. As a result of such customer-service heroics, an amazing 95 percent of departing guests report that their stay has been a truly memorable experience. More than 90 percent of Ritz-Carlton's delighted customers return.[14]

However, although the customer-centered firm seeks to deliver high customer satisfaction relative to competitors, it does not attempt to *maximize* customer satisfaction. A company can always increase customer satisfaction by lowering its price or increasing its services. But this may result in lower profits. Thus, the purpose of marketing is to generate customer value profitably. This requires a very delicate balance: The marketer must continue to generate more customer value and satisfaction but not "give away the house."

Customer Relationship Levels and Tools

Companies can build customer relationships at many levels, depending on the nature of the target market. At one extreme, a company with many low-margin customers may seek to develop *basic relationships* with them. For example, Procter & Gamble does not phone or call on all of its Tide consumers to get to know them personally. Instead, P&G creates relationships through brand-building advertising, sales promotions, and its Tide Fabric Care Network Web site (www.Tide.com). At the other extreme, in markets with few customers and high margins, sellers want to create *full partnerships* with key customers. For example, P&G customer teams work closely with Wal-Mart, Safeway, and other large retailers. In between these two extreme situations, other levels of customer relationships are appropriate.

Today, most leading companies are developing customer loyalty and retention programs. Beyond offering consistently high value and satisfaction, marketers can use specific marketing tools to develop stronger bonds with consumers. For example, many companies now offer *frequency marketing programs* that reward customers who buy frequently or in large amounts. Airlines offer frequent-flyer programs, hotels give room upgrades to their frequent guests, and supermarkets give patronage discounts to "very important customers."

Other companies sponsor *club marketing program*s that offer members special benefits and create member communities. ▲For example, Harley-Davidson sponsors the Harley Owners Group (H.O.G.), which gives Harley riders a way to share their common passion of "making the Harley-Davidson dream a way of life." H.O.G. membership benefits include two magazines (*Hog Tales* and *Enthusiast*), a *H.O.G. Touring Handbook*, a roadside assistance program, a specially designed insurance program, theft reward service, a travel center, and a "Fly & Ride" program enabling members to rent Harleys while on vacation. The worldwide club now numbers more than 1,500 local chapters and more than one million members.[15]

To build customer relationships, companies can add structural ties as well as financial and social benefits. A business marketer might supply customers with special equipment or online linkages that help them manage their orders, payroll, or inventory. For example, McKesson Corporation, a leading pharmaceutical wholesaler, has set up a Supply Management Online system that helps retail pharmacy customers manage their inventories, order entry, and shelf space. The system also helps McKesson's medical-surgical supply and equipment customers optimize their supply purchasing and materials management operations.

▲ Building customer relationships: Harley-Davidson sponsors the Harley Owners Group (H.O.G.), which gives Harley owners "an organized way to share their passion and show their pride." The worldwide club now numbers more than 1,500 local chapters and 1 million members.

The Changing Nature of Customer Relationships

Significant changes are occurring in the ways in which companies are relating to their customers. Yesterday's big companies focused on mass marketing to all customers at arm's length. Today's companies are building deeper, more direct, and more lasting relationships with more carefully selected customers. Here are some important trends in the way companies and customers are relating to one another.

Relating with More Carefully Selected Customers

Few firms today still practice true mass marketing—selling in a standardized way to any customer who comes along. Today, most marketers realize that they don't want relationships with every customer. Instead, they now are targeting fewer, more profitable customers. Called *selective relationship management,* many companies now use customer profitability analysis to weed out losing customers and to target winning ones for pampering. Once they identify profitable customers, firms can create attractive offers and special handling to capture these customers and earn their loyalty.

But what should the company do with unprofitable customers? If it can't turn them into profitable ones, it may even want to "fire" customers that are too unreasonable or that cost more to serve than they are worth. ▲For example, consumer electronics retailer Best Buy recently rolled out a new "Customer-Centricity" strategy that distinguishes between its best customers (called *angels*) and less profitable ones (called *demons*). The aim is to embrace the angels while ditching the demons.[16]

▲ Best Buy's "Customer-Centricity" strategy serves its best customers (angels) and exorcizes less profitable ones (demons). Clerks steer high-income "Barrys" into the store's Magnolia Home Theater Center, a comfy store within a store that mimics the media rooms popular with home-theater fans.

The *angels* include the 20 percent of Best Buy customers who produce the bulk of its profits. They snap up high-definition televisions, portable electronics, and newly released DVDs without waiting for markdowns or rebates. In contrast, the demons form an "underground of bargain-hungry shoppers intent on wringing every nickel of savings out of the big retailer. They load up on loss leaders . . . then flip the goods at a profit on eBay. They slap down rock-bottom price quotes from Web sites and demand that Best Buy make good on its lowest-price pledge."

To attract the angels, Best Buy's Customer-Centricity stores now stock more merchandise and offer better service to these good customers. For example, the stores set up digital photo centers and a "Geek Squad," which offers one-on-one in-store or at-home computer assistance to high-value buyers. Best Buy also set up a Reward Zone loyalty program, in which regular customers can earn points toward discounts on future purchases. To discourage the demons, Best Buy removed them from its marketing lists, reduced the promotions and other sales tactics that tended to attract them, and installed a 15 percent restocking fee.

However, Best Buy didn't stop there. Customer analysis revealed that its best customers fell into five groups: "Barrys," high-income men; "Jills," suburban moms; "Buzzes," male technology enthusiasts; "Rays," young family men on a budget; and small business owners. Each Customer-Centricity store now aligns its product and service mix to reflect the make-up of these customers in its market area. Best Buy then trains store clerks in the art of serving the angels and exorcising the demons. At stores targeting Barrys, for example, blue-shirted sales clerks steer promising candidates to the store's Magnolia Home Theater Center, a comfy store within a store that mimics the media rooms popular with home-theater fans. With sales up more than $10 billion in just the past three years, the customer-centric strategy appears to be a winner for Best Buy and its customers. As one store manager puts it, "The biggest thing now is to build better relationships with [our best] customers."

Relating More Deeply and Interactively

Beyond choosing customers more selectively, companies are now relating with chosen customers in deeper, more meaningful ways. Rather than relying only on one-way, mass-media messages, today's marketers are incorporating new, more interactive approaches that help build targeted, two-way customer relationships.

The deeper nature of today's customer relationships results in part from the rapidly changing communications environment. New technologies have profoundly changed the ways in which people relate to one another. For example, thanks to explosive advances in Internet and computer technology, people can now interact in direct and surprisingly personal ways with large groups of others, whether nearby or scattered around the world. New tools for relating include everything from e-mail, blogs, Web sites, and video sharing to online communities and social networks such as MySpace, Facebook, YouTube, and Second Life.

This changing communications environment also affects how consumers relate to companies and products. Increasingly, marketers are using the new communications approaches in building closer customer relationships. The aim is to create deeper consumer involvement and a sense of community surrounding a brand—to make the brand a meaningful part of consumers' conversations and lives. "Becoming part of the conversation between consumers is infinitely more powerful than handing down information via traditional advertising," says one marketing expert. "It [makes] consumers . . . a part of the process, rather than being dumb recipients of the message from on high—and that is of huge potential value to brands."[17]

However, at the same time that the new communications tools create relationship-building opportunities for marketers, they also create challenges. They give consumers greater power and control. Today's consumers have more information about brands than ever before, and they have a wealth of platforms for airing and sharing their brand views with other consumers. And more than ever before, consumers can choose the brand conversations and exchanges in which they will participate. According to Mark Parker, chief executive of Nike, the new power of the consumer is "the most compelling change we've seen over the past four or five years. They are dictating what the dialogue is, how we're conducting it, and it's definitely a two-way conversation."[18]

Greater consumer control means that, in building customer relationships, companies can no longer rely on marketing by *intrusion*. They must practice marketing by *attraction*—creating market offerings and messages that involve consumers rather than interrupt them. Hence, most marketers now augment their mass-media marketing efforts with a rich mix of direct marketing approaches that promote brand–consumer interaction.

For example, many are participating in the exploding world of *online social networks* or creating online communities of their own. Toyota, the world's fifth-largest advertiser, spends $3.1 billion a year on media advertising. But it also sells Scions at Second Life and maintains a Scion presence on MySpace, Gaia Online, and other cyber hangouts. And the company's Toyota.com/hybrids site creates a community in which more than 17,500 Prius, Camry, and Highlander hybrid "believers" meet to share their reasons for buying hybrid vehicles and videos and messages on their experiences, both good and bad. "There's value in being totally authentic and transparent [with your customers]," says a manager of consumer-generated media at Toyota, "as much as it hurts sometimes."[19]

Similarly, Nike has recently shifted a bigger chunk of its media budget toward new, more direct interactions with consumers. It now spends just 33 percent of its almost $700 million annual ad budget on television and other traditional media, down 55 percent from 10 years ago. Nike's new media include not only the Internet, but also in-person events and other activities designed to build brand community and deeper customer relationships.[20]

▲ Twice a week, 30 or more people gather at the Nike store in Portland, Oregon, and go for an evening run. Afterward the members of the Niketown running club chat in the store over refreshments. Nike's staff keeps track of

▲ Creating community with customers: Nike's new, more interactive media include in-person events and other activities designed to build brand community and deeper customer relationships.

their performances and hails members who have logged more than 100 miles. The event is a classic example of up-close-and-personal relationship building with core customers. Nike augments such events with an online social network aimed at striking up meaningful long-term interactions with even more runners. Its Nike Plus running Web site lets customers with iPod-linked Nike shoes upload, track, and compare their performances. More than 200,000 runners are now using the Nike Plus site and more than half visit the site at least four times a week. The goal is to have 15 percent of the world's 100 million runners using the system.

As a part of the new customer control and dialogue, consumers themselves are now creating brand conversations and messages on their own. And increasingly, companies are even *inviting* consumers to play a more active role in shaping brand messages and ads. For example, Frito-Lay, Southwest, and Heinz have run contests for consumer-generated commercials that have been aired on national television. Other companies, including marketing heavyweights such as Coca-Cola, McDonald's, and Apple, have snagged brand-related consumer videos from YouTube and other popular video-sharing sites and turned them into commercial messages.

Consumer-generated marketing

Marketing messages, ads, and other brand exchanges created by consumers themselves—both invited and uninvited.

Consumer-generated marketing, whether invited by marketers or not, has become a significant marketing force. In fact, last year, *Advertising Age* magazine awarded its coveted Ad Agency of the Year designation to—you guessed it—the consumer. "The explosion of video, blogs, Web sites, [and consumer-generate ads] confirmed what we knew all along," says the magazine. When it comes to creative messages, "the consumer is king."[21] (See **Real Marketing 1.2**.)

Partner Relationship Management

> **Author Comment** | Marketers can't create customer value and build customer relationships by themselves. They need to work closely with other company departments and with partners outside the firm.

When it comes to creating customer value and building strong customer relationships, today's marketers know that they can't go it alone. They must work closely with a variety of marketing partners. In addition to being good at *customer relationship management*, marketers must also be good at **partner relationship management.** Major changes are occurring in how marketers partner with others inside and outside the company to jointly bring more value to customers.

Partners Inside the Company

Partner relationship management

Working closely with partners in other company departments and outside the company to jointly bring greater value to customers.

Traditionally, marketers have been charged with understanding customers and representing customer needs to different company departments. The old thinking was that marketing is done only by marketing, sales, and customer-support people. However, in today's more connected world, every functional area can interact with customers, especially electronically. The new thinking is that every employee must be customer-focused. David Packard, late cofounder of Hewlett-Packard, wisely said, "Marketing is far too important to be left only to the marketing department."[22]

Today, rather than letting each department go its own way, firms are linking all departments in the cause of creating customer value. Rather than assigning only sales and marketing people to customers, they are forming cross-functional customer teams. For example, Procter & Gamble assigns "customer development teams" to each of its major retailer accounts. These teams—consisting of sales and marketing people, operations specialists, market and financial analysts, and others—coordinate the efforts of many P&G departments toward helping the retailer be more successful.

Marketing Partners Outside the Firm

Changes are also occurring in how marketers connect with their suppliers, channel partners, and even competitors. Most companies today are networked companies, relying heavily on partnerships with other firms.

Marketing channels consist of distributors, retailers, and others who connect the company to its buyers. The *supply chain* describes a longer channel, stretching from raw materials to components to final products that are carried to final buyers. For example, the supply chain for personal computers consists of suppliers of computer chips and other

Real Marketing 1.2

Consumer-Generated Marketing:

Ad Agency of the Year? YOU!

Advertising Age, a must-read magazine for advertising professionals, recently awarded its prestigious Ad Agency of the Year award not to the usual big Madison Avenue agency, but to you, the consumer. Here's its explanation of why it picked consumer-generated advertising content over that prepared by seasoned advertising professionals.

Stop me if you've heard this one before. A pair of Maine theater geeks decide to film an experiment in which a certain mint is dropped into a bottle of a certain no-calorie soft drink, unleashing a foamy geyser. Flavoring this bit of schoolyard chemistry lore with Vegas show-manship, they produce a cola version of the Bellagio fountain and put the clip on the Web, where it goes viral. Really viral. So viral, in fact, that millions watch it, hundreds of media out-lets cover it, and the mint in question enjoys a 15 percent spike in sales.

It's a sign of our times: The most impor-tant piece of commercial content last year was created by a juggler named Fritz Grobe and a lawyer Stephen Voltz. "The Diet Coke & Mentos Experiment" sensation raises a key question that gnaws at just about every com-pany that wants to sell a product to con-sumers in the twenty-first century: Should I try to get my consumers to do something like this? Even if they haven't worked out exactly how to make that happen, many leading marketers have already answered with a resounding yes. Company after company, including the makers of blue-chip brands such as Pepsi, Jeep, Heinz, Sprint, and Converse have given up at least some control and turned their brands over to consumers.

In truth, consumers have always had some measure of control, and a brand has only ever been as good as consumers' experi-ences with it. The difference today is that con-sumers have lots of ways of communicating those experiences, and they trust each other's views above marketers' overt sales pitches. Consequently, consumers are influencing marketing strategy as never before. And that's why last year's *Advertising Age* Ad Agency of the Year was (drum roll, please) . . . the con-sumer. A portfolio of consumer-generated

Harnessing consumer-generated marketing: When H.J. Heinz recently invited consumers to submit homemade ads for its ketchup brand on YouTube, it received more than 8,000 entries—some very good but most only so-so or even downright dreadful.

commercial content over the past few years would easily beat out any single advertising agency's offering.

Today, as in our cola fountain story, not only do everyday people make the videos that earn that oh-so-coveted water-cooler buzz, they also reign supreme as distributors of content of all kinds. YouTube's explosion glopped a big new pile of distractions into an already cluttered communications world, which means that if you want anybody to see your ad, you'd better hope people are frenet-ically e-mailing links to it.

Here are just a few examples of consumer-generated marketing content. Two moon-lighting comedians threw together video of themselves amateurishly rapping about Chicken McNuggets and slapped it on the Internet— McDonald's used the video in a popular New York-area commercial. Apple discovered an amateur video produced by a British teenager on YouTube. With the teen's permission, Apple recreated the ad for TV. MasterCard invited cus-tomers to help create a new "Priceless" com-mercial, received 100,000 submissions, and showed the winning ad on regular TV. The credit card giant's priceless.com site is now loaded with good consumer video.

And then there's the Super Bowl. Long a showcase for ad agencies' finest productions, the 2007 ad spectacular was invaded success-fully by the unwashed masses. Frito-Lay's Doritos solicited 30-second ads from con-sumers and ran the best two during the game. One of the ads, which showed a supermarket checkout girl getting frisky with a shopper, was judged in one poll as 67 percent more effective than the average Super Bowl ad in

improving viewer opinion of the advertised product. The other Doritos ad, showing a young driver flirting with a pretty girl, cost only $12.79 to produce (the cost of four bags of chips) but was judged 45 percent more effec-tive. The ads were extremely popular with viewers, both during and after the big game. "What this means is: You've got some kid with a video camera and he's playing on the same field as everyone else," says one ad agency veteran. Frito-Lay followed up in 2008 by invit-ing consumers to submit original songs at snackstrongproductions.com—its Second Life-inspired Doritos Web environment. Frito-Lay then gave winner Kina Grannis the stage of a lifetime by airing a 60-second music video fea-turing her winning song on the Super Bowl.

Does the new wave of consumer-generated marketing mean the end of the big ad agency as we know it? Not likely. But the fact that an amateur could turn out a winning Doritos ad for $12.79, versus the $1 million or more that many large agencies spent crafting more spectacular but less effective ads, sug-gests that there are some lessons to be learned. As one ad agency creative executive suggests, "It's gonna keep professional idea makers on their toes." Marketers now "perk up when you talk about this stuff," he says.

The big question is how to harness consumer-generated creativity—so unpol-ished and unaccountable—and deploy it in the service of a brand. There's a big poten-tial downside to putting your brand in the hands of consumers. For every Diet Coke & Mentos clip that's grown into a viral craze,

Continued on next page ▼

Real Marketing 1.2 Continued ▼

there are several marketer-led disasters. For example, General Motors' Chevy Tahoe off-roaded into the consumer-content arena and, to its shock, found that some people aren't so crazy about the gas-guzzling SUV. At Chevy's invitation, consumers created some very creative ads, but many of the ads centered on the big vehicle's poor gas mileage and negative environmental impact.

Harnessing consumer-generated content can be time consuming and costly, and companies may find it difficult to glean even a little gold from all the garbage. H.J. Heinz recently invited consumers to submit home-made ads for its ketchup brand on its YouTube page, offering a $57,000 top prize and the promise of airing the winning ad on primetime TV. Heinz sifted through more than 8,000 entries, of which nearly 4,000 are posted on YouTube. Some of the amateur ads are very good—entertaining and potentially effective. Most, however, are so-so at best, and others are downright dreadful. In one ad, a contestant chugs ketchup straight from the bottle. In another, a teen contestant rubs ketchup over his face like acne cream, then puts pickles on his eyes. In still another, the

would-be filmmaker brushes his teeth, washes his hair, and shaves his face with Heinz's product.

Heinz had to reject many of the submitted ads because they include copyrighted songs, displayed other brands, or "wouldn't be appropriate to show mom." But rejected submissions continue showing up on YouTube anyway. One of the most viewed Heinz videos, seen more than 12,800 times, ends with a close-up of a mouth with crooked, yellowed teeth—oops. Despite such problems, however, Heinz continues to invite consumers to submit their masterpieces. In all, the campaign has been very successful. Within only a few months, consumers had logged more than 2.3 million views of the spots on YouTube,

and spent more than 80,000 hours watching them. The YouTube exposure gives the venerable old brand lots of contemporary attention.

Today, more and more big marketers are loosening up and turning at least a piece of their brand marketing over to consumers. At a recent Association of National Advertisers meeting, P&G's CEO, A. G. Lafley, urged companies to invite more customer interaction and to "let go" of their brands. Coming from the normally tightly controlling P&G, such a provocative statement deeply impacted the advertiser audience. The same could be said of Lafley showing an animated Pringles commercial made by a U.K. teen to the audience full of advertisers. And you know what? The clip was pretty good.

Sources: Portions adapted from Matthew Creamer, "John Doe Edges Out Jeff Goodby," *Advertising Age*, January 8, 2007, pp. S4–S5; with information from Frank Ahrens, "$2 Million Airtime, $13 Ad: In the YouTube Era, Even Super Bowl Advertisers Are Turning to Amateurs," *Washington Post*, January 31, 2007, accessed at www.washingtonpost.com; Elinor Mills, "Frito-Lay Turns to Netizens for Ad Creation," *CNET News*, March 21, 2007, accessed at www.cnetnews.com; Laura Petrecca, "Amateurs' Ad Ideas Come Up with Winners," *USA Today*, February 13, 2007, p. 2B; Gavin O'Malley, "Entries Pour in for Heinz Catsup Commercial Contest," August 13, 2007, accessed at http://publications.mediapost.com; and "Fans Vote 22-Year-Old Singer/Songwriter Kina Grannis Winner in Doritos Crash the Super Bowl Challenge," PR Newswire, February 3, 2008.

components, the computer manufacturer, and the distributors, retailers, and others who sell the computers.

Through *supply chain management*, many companies today are strengthening their connections with partners all along the supply chain. They know that their fortunes rest not just on how well they perform. Success at building customer relationships also rests on how well their entire supply chain performs against competitors' supply chains. These companies don't just treat suppliers as vendors and distributors as customers. They treat both as partners in delivering customer value. On the one hand, for example, Lexus works closely with carefully selected suppliers to improve quality and operations efficiency. On the other hand, it works with its franchise dealers to provide top-grade sales and service support that will bring customers in the door and keep them coming back.

> **Author Comment** | Check back to Figure 1.1. In the first four steps of the marketing process, the company creates value *for* target customers and builds strong relationships with them. If it does that well, it can capture value *from* customers in return in the form of loyal customers who buy and continue to buy the company's brands.

Capturing Value from Customers (pp 21-24)

The first four steps in the marketing process outlined in Figure 1.1 involve building customer relationships by creating and delivering superior customer value. The final step involves capturing value in return in the form of current and future sales, market share, and profits. By creating superior customer value, the firm creates highly satisfied customers who stay loyal and buy more. This, in turn, means greater long-run returns for the firm. Here, we discuss the outcomes of creating customer value: customer loyalty and retention, share of market and share of customer, and customer equity.

Creating Customer Loyalty and Retention

Good customer relationship management creates customer delight. In turn, delighted customers remain loyal and talk favorably to others about the company and its products. Studies show big differences in the loyalty of customers who are less satisfied, somewhat

Customer lifetime value
The value of the entire stream of purchases that the customer would make over a lifetime of patronage.

satisfied, and completely satisfied. Even a slight drop from complete satisfaction can create an enormous drop in loyalty. Thus, the aim of customer relationship management is to create not just customer satisfaction, but customer delight.[23]

Companies are realizing that losing a customer means losing more than a single sale. It means losing the entire stream of purchases that the customer would make over a lifetime of patronage. For example, here is a dramatic illustration of **customer lifetime value:**

▲ Customer lifetime value: To keep customers coming back, Stew Leonard's has created the "Disneyland of dairy stores." Rule #1: The customer is always right. Rule #2: If the customer is ever wrong, reread Rule #1.

▲Stew Leonard, who operates a highly profitable four-store supermarket in Connecticut and New York, says that he sees $50,000 flying out of his store every time he sees a sulking customer. Why? Because his average customer spends about $100 a week, shops 50 weeks a year, and remains in the area for about 10 years. If this customer has an unhappy experience and switches to another supermarket, Stew Leonard's has lost $50,000 in revenue. The loss can be much greater if the disappointed customer shares the bad experience with other customers and causes them to defect. To keep customers coming back, Stew Leonard's has created what the *New York Times* has dubbed the "Disneyland of Dairy Stores," complete with costumed characters, scheduled entertainment, a petting zoo, and animatronics throughout the store. From its humble beginnings as a small dairy store in 1969, Stew Leonard's has grown at an amazing pace. It's built 29 additions onto the original store, which now serves more than 300,000 customers each week. This legion of loyal shoppers is largely a result of the store's passionate approach to customer service. Rule #1: at Stew Leonard's—The customer is always right. Rule #2: If the customer is ever wrong, reread rule #1![24]

Stew Leonard is not alone in assessing customer lifetime value. Lexus, for example, estimates that a single satisfied and loyal customer is worth more than $600,000 in lifetime sales.[25] Thus, working to retain and grow customers makes good economic sense. In fact, a company can lose money on a specific transaction but still benefit greatly from a long-term relationship. This means that companies must aim high in building customer relationships. Customer delight creates an emotional relationship with a brand, not just a rational preference. And that relationship keeps customers coming back.

L.L.Bean, which regularly rates among the nation's top five brands in the Brand Keys Customer Loyalty Engagement Index, was founded on a philosophy of customer satisfaction and long-term customer relationships. Founder L.L.Bean posted the following notice on the wall of his first store: "NOTICE: I do not consider a sale complete until goods are worn out and customer still satisfied." The company still preaches the following "golden rule": "Sell good merchandise, treat your customers like a human beings, and they'll always come back for more."[26]

Growing Share of Customer

Share of customer
The portion of the customer's purchasing that a company gets in its product categories.

Beyond simply retaining good customers to capture customer lifetime value, good customer relationship management can help marketers to increase their **share of customer**—the share they get of the customer's purchasing in their product categories. Thus, banks want to increase "share of wallet." Supermarkets and restaurants want to get more "share of stomach." Car companies want to increase "share of garage," and airlines want greater "share of travel."

To increase share of customer, firms can offer greater variety to current customers. Or they can create programs to cross-sell and up-sell in order to market more products and services to existing customers. For example, Amazon.com is highly skilled at leveraging relationships with its 66 million customers to increase its share of each customer's purchases. Originally an online bookseller, Amazon.com now offers customers music, videos, gifts, toys, consumer electronics, office products, home improvement items, lawn and garden products, apparel and accessories, jewelry, tools, and even groceries. In addition, based on each customer's purchase history, the company recommends related products that might be of interest. This recommendation system may influence up to 30 percent of all sales.[27] In these ways, Amazon.com captures a greater share of each customer's spending budget.

Building Customer Equity

We can now see the importance of not just acquiring customers, but of keeping and growing them as well. One marketing consultant puts it this way: "The only value your company will ever create is the value that comes from customers—the ones you have now and the ones you will have in the future. Without customers, you don't have a business."[28] Customer relationship management takes a long-term view. Companies want not only to create profitable customers, but to "own" them for life, earn a greater share of their purchases, and capture their customer lifetime value.

What Is Customer Equity?

Customer equity

The total combined customer lifetime values of all of the company's customers.

The ultimate aim of customer relationship management is to produce high *customer equity.*[29] **Customer equity** is the total combined customer lifetime values of all of the company's current and potential customers. Clearly, the more loyal the firm's profitable customers, the higher the firm's customer equity. Customer equity may be a better measure of a firm's performance than current sales or market share. Whereas sales and market share reflect the past, customer equity suggests the future. Consider Cadillac:

In the 1970s and 1980s, Cadillac had some of the most loyal customers in the industry. To an entire generation of car buyers, the name "Cadillac" defined American luxury. Cadillac's share of the luxury car market reached a whopping 51 percent in 1976. Based on market share and sales, the brand's future looked rosy. However, measures of customer equity would have painted a bleaker picture. Cadillac customers were getting older (average age 60) and average customer lifetime value was falling. Many Cadillac buyers were on their last car. Thus, although Cadillac's market share was good, its customer equity was not. Compare this with BMW. Its more youthful and vigorous image didn't win BMW the early market share war. However, it did win BMW younger customers with higher customer lifetime values. The result: In the years that followed, BMW's market share and profits soared while Cadillac's fortunes eroded badly. Thus, market share is not the answer. We should care not just about current sales but also about future sales. Customer lifetime value and customer equity are the name of the game. ▲Recognizing this, in recent years, Cadillac has attempted to make the Caddy cool again by targeting a younger generation of consumers with new high-performance models and more vibrant advertising. The average consumer aspiring to own a Cadillac is now about 36 years old.[30]

▲ To increase customer lifetime value and customer equity, Cadillac is cool again. It's highly successful ad campaigns target a younger generation of consumer.

Building the Right Relationships with the Right Customers

Companies should manage customer equity carefully. They should view customers as assets that need to be managed and maximized. But not all customers, not even all loyal customers, are good investments. Surprisingly, some loyal customers can be unprofitable, and some disloyal customers can be profitable. Which customers should the company acquire and retain?

The company can classify customers according to their potential profitability and manage its relationships with them accordingly. **Figure 1.5** classifies customers into one of four relationship groups, according to their profitability and projected loyalty.[31] Each group requires a different relationship management strategy. "Strangers" show low potential profitability and little projected loyalty. There is little fit between the company's offerings and their needs. The relationship management strategy for these customers is simple: Don't invest anything in them.

"Butterflies" are potentially profitable but not loyal. There is a good fit between the company's offerings and their needs. However, like real butterflies, we can enjoy them for only a short while and then they're gone. An example is stock market investors who trade shares often and in large amounts but who enjoy hunting out the best deals without building a regular relationship with any single brokerage company. Efforts to convert butterflies into loyal customers are rarely successful. Instead, the company should enjoy the butterflies for the moment. It should use promotional blitzes to attract them, create satisfying and profitable transactions with them, and then cease investing in them until the next time around.

"True friends" are both profitable and loyal. There is a strong fit between their needs and the company's offerings. The firm wants to make continuous relationship investments to delight these customers and nurture, retain, and grow them. It wants to turn true friends into "true believers," who come back regularly and tell others about their good experiences with the company.

"Barnacles" are highly loyal but not very profitable. There is a limited fit between their needs and the company's offerings. An example is smaller bank customers who bank regularly but do not generate enough returns to cover the costs of maintaining their accounts. Like barnacles on the hull of a ship, they create drag. Barnacles are perhaps the most problematic customers. The company might be able to improve their profitability by selling them more, raising their fees, or reducing service to them. However, if they cannot be made profitable, they should be "fired."

The point here is an important one: Different types of customers require different relationship management strategies. The goal is to build the *right relationships* with the *right customers*.

FIGURE | 1.5 Customer Relationship Groups

Source: Reprinted by permission of *Harvard Business Review*. Adapted from "Mismanagement of Customer Loyalty" by Werner Relnartz and V. Kumar, July 2002, p. 93. Copyright © by the president and fellows of Harvard College; all rights reserved.

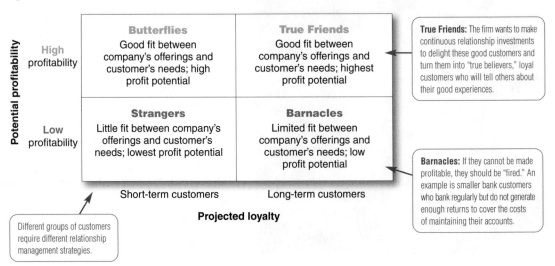

Author Comment | Marketing doesn't take place in a vacuum. Now that we've discussed the five steps in the marketing process, let's examine how the ever-changing marketplace affects both consumers and the marketers who serve them. We'll look more deeply into these and other marketing environment factors in Chapter 3.

The Changing Marketing Landscape (pp 25–30)

Every day, dramatic changes are occurring in the marketplace. Richard Love of Hewlett-Packard observes, "The pace of change is so rapid that the ability to change has now become a competitive advantage." Yogi Berra, the legendary New York Yankees catcher and manager, summed it up more simply when he said, "The future ain't what it used to be." As the marketplace changes, so must those who serve it.

In this section, we examine the major trends and forces that are changing the marketing landscape and challenging marketing strategy. We look at four major developments: the digital age, rapid globalization, the call for more ethics and social responsibility, and the growth of not-for-profit marketing.

The Digital Age

The recent technology boom has created a digital age. The explosive growth in computer, communications, information, and other digital technologies has had a major impact on the ways companies bring value to their customers. Now, more than ever before, we are all connected to each other and to information anywhere in the world. Where it once took days or weeks to receive news about important world events, we now learn about them as they are occurring through live satellite broadcasts and news Web sites. Where it once took weeks to correspond with others in distant places, they are now only moments away by cell phone, e-mail, or Web cam.

The digital age has provided marketers with exciting new ways to learn about and track customers and to create products and services tailored to individual customer needs. It's helping marketers to communicate with customers in large groups or one-to-one. Through Web videoconferencing, marketing researchers at a company's headquarters in New York can look in on focus groups in Chicago or Paris without ever stepping onto a plane. With only a few clicks of a mouse button, a direct marketer can tap into online data services to learn anything from what car you drive to what you read to what flavor of ice cream you prefer. Or, using today's powerful computers, marketers can create their own detailed customer databases and use them to target individual customers with offers designed to meet their specific needs.

Digital technology has also brought a new wave of communication, advertising, and relationship building tools—ranging from online advertising, video sharing tools, cell phones, and video games to Web widgets and online social networks. The digital shift means that marketers can no longer expect consumers to always seek them out. Nor can they always control conversations about their brands. The new digital world makes it easy for consumers to take marketing content that once lived only in advertising or on a brand Web site with them wherever they go and to share it with friends. More than just add-ons to traditional marketing channels, the new digital media must be fully integrated into the marketer's customer-relationship-building efforts. Says one marketer, "We're [now] building a network of experiences."[32]

Perhaps the most dramatic new digital technology is the **Internet.** The number of Internet users worldwide now stands at more than 1.2 billion and will reach an estimated 3.4 billion by 2015. Today's typical Internet users spend 47 percent of their time online looking at online content—watching video, reading the news, or getting the lowdown on friends and celebrities on MySpace or Facebook. They spend another 33 percent of their online time communicating with each other, 15 percent shopping, and 5 percent googling or using other search engines. Computers and the Internet have become an indispensable part of our lives.[33]

Internet
A vast public web of computer networks that connects users of all types all around the world to each other and to an amazingly large information repository.

What do we value most? Judging by how we spend our time, our computers. Most people spend more time with their computers than with their spouse or significant other. More than 80 percent report that they grow more dependent on their computer every year. Computers are also a growing source of stress. The average consumer experiences frustrating computer problems twice a month and wastes 12 hours a month due to computer problems. Eleven percent say they'd be willing to implant a device in their brains that would allow them to access the Internet. Twenty-four percent say the Internet can serve as a substitute for a significant other. Ten percent say the Web brings them close to God.

Internet usage surged in the 1990s with the development of the user-friendly World Wide Web. During the overheated Web frenzy of the late 1990s, dot-coms popped up everywhere. The frenzy cooled during the "dot-com meltdown" of 2000, when many poorly conceived e-tailers and other Web start-ups went out of business. ▲Today, a new version of the Internet has emerged—a "second coming" of the Web often referred to as *Web 2.0*. Web 2.0 involves a more reasoned and balanced approach to marketing online. It also offers a fast-growing set of new Web technologies for connecting with customers, such as Weblogs (blogs) and vlogs (video-based blogs), social-networking sites, and video-sharing sites. The interactive, community-building nature of these new technologies makes them ideal for relating with consumers.[34]

Online marketing is now the fastest-growing form of marketing. These days, it's hard to find a company that doesn't use the Web in a significant way. In addition to the "click-only" dot-coms, most traditional "brick-and-mortar" companies have now become "click-and-mortar" companies. They have ventured online to attract new customers and build stronger relationships with existing ones. Today, more than 65 percent of American online users use the Internet to shop.[35] Business-to-business online commerce is also booming. It seems that almost every business has set up shop on the Web.

Thus, the technology boom is providing exciting new opportunities for marketers. We will explore the impact of the new digital marketing technologies in future chapters, especially Chapter 17.

▲ Web 2.0—a "second coming" of the Internet—offers a fast-growing set of new Web technologies for connecting with customers. Here, Dunkin' Donuts offers a popular YouTube space where people can share their "that's why America runs on Dunkin'" stories and videos.

Rapid Globalization

As they are redefining their relationships with customers and partners, marketers are also taking a fresh look at the ways in which they relate with the broader world around them. In an increasingly smaller world, many marketers are now connected *globally* with their customers and marketing partners.

Today, almost every company, large or small, is touched in some way by global competition. A neighborhood florist buys its flowers from Mexican nurseries, and a large U.S. electronics manufacturer competes in its home markets with giant Korean rivals. A fledgling Internet retailer finds itself receiving orders from all over the world at the same time that an American consumer-goods producer introduces new products into emerging markets abroad.

American firms have been challenged at home by the skillful marketing of European and Asian multinationals. Companies such as Toyota, Nokia, Nestlé, Sony, and Samsung have often outperformed their U.S. competitors in American markets. Similarly, U.S. companies in a wide range of industries have developed truly global operations, making and selling their products worldwide. ▲Quintessentially American McDonald's now serves 52 million customers daily in 31,600 restaurants worldwide—some 65 percent of its revenues come from outside the United States. Similarly, Nike markets in more than 160 countries, with non-U.S. sales accounting for 53 percent of its worldwide sales. Even MTV

Networks has joined the elite of global brands—its 150 channels worldwide deliver localized versions of its pulse-thumping fare to 419 million homes in 164 countries around the globe. And it reaches millions more daily via the more than 5,000 mobile, console, and online games and virtual worlds that it shares on its more than 300 Web sites worldwide.[36]

Today, companies are not only trying to sell more of their locally produced goods in international markets, they also are buying more supplies and components abroad. For example, Isaac Mizrahi, one of America's top fashion designers, may choose cloth woven from Australian wool with designs printed in Italy. He will design a dress and e-mail the drawing to a Hong Kong agent, who will place the order with a Chinese factory. Finished dresses will be airfreighted to New York, where they will be redistributed to department and specialty stores around the country.

Thus, managers in countries around the world are increasingly taking a global, not just local, view of the company's industry, competitors, and opportunities. They are asking: What is global marketing? How does it differ from domestic marketing? How do global competitors and forces affect our business? To what extent should we "go global"? We will discuss the global marketplace in more detail in Chapter 19.

The Call for More Ethics and Social Responsibility

Marketers are reexamining their relationships with social values and responsibilities and with the very Earth that sustains us. As the worldwide consumerism and environmentalism movements mature, today's marketers are being called upon to take greater responsibility for the social and environmental impact of their actions. Corporate ethics and social responsibility have become hot topics for almost every business. And few companies can ignore the renewed and very demanding environmental movement. Every company action can affect customer relationships:[37]

▲ U.S. companies in a wide range of industries have developed truly global operations. Quintessentially American McDonald's captures 65 percent of its revenues from outside of the United States.

There is an unwritten contract today between customers and the brands they buy. First, they expect companies to consistently deliver what they advertise. Second, they expect the companies they do business with to treat them with respect and to be honorable and forthright. . . . Everything a company does affects the brand in the eyes of the customer. For example, Celestial Seasonings incurred customers' wrath by ignoring its advertised corporate image of environmental stewardship when it poisoned prairie dogs on its property. By contrast, Google's decision to use solar energy for its server farms reinforces what Google stands for and strengthens the Google brand.

The social-responsibility and environmental movements will place even stricter demands on companies in the future. Some companies resist these movements, budging only when forced by legislation or organized consumer outcries. More forward-looking companies, however, readily accept their responsibilities to the world around them. They view socially responsible actions as an opportunity to do well by doing good. They seek ways to profit by serving the best long-run interests of their customers and communities.

Some companies—such as Patagonia, Ben & Jerry's, Honest Tea, Ethos Water, and others—are practicing "caring capitalism," setting themselves apart by being civic-minded and responsible. They are building social responsibility and action into their company value and mission statements. For example, when it comes to environmental responsibility, outdoor gear marketer Patagonia is "committed to the core." "Those of us who work here share a strong commitment to protecting undomesticated lands and waters," says the company's Web site. "We believe in using business to inspire solutions to the environmental crisis." Patagonia backs these words with actions. Each year it pledges at least 1 percent of its sales or 10 percent of its profits, whichever is greater, to the protection of the natural environment.[38] We will revisit the topic of marketing and social responsibility in greater detail in Chapter 20.

The Growth of Not-for-Profit Marketing

In the past, marketing has been most widely applied in the for-profit business sector. In recent years, however, marketing also has become a major part of the strategies of many not-for-profit organizations, such as colleges, hospitals, museums, zoos, symphony orchestras, and even churches. The nation's not-for-profits face stiff competition for support and membership. Sound marketing can help them to attract membership and support.[39] Consider the marketing efforts of St. Jude Children's Research Hospital of Memphis:

> St. Jude is like no other pediatric research facility in the world. Its discoveries have profoundly changed how the world treats children with cancer and other catastrophic diseases. St. Jude houses some of the world's most gifted researchers, and doctors from across the world send their toughest cases there. At St. Jude, no one pays for treatment beyond what is covered by insurance, and those without insurance are never asked to pay. All of this comes at a very high cost, a voracious $1.2 million per day. So, to help fund its medical miracles, St. Jude aggressively markets its powerful mission—"Finding Cures. Saving Children."

> St. Jude's marketing efforts include everything from cutting-edge public relations and television commercials to online auctions, contests, and even merchandise licensing. St. Jude also co-sponsors innovative cause-related marketing programs with corporate partners such as Target, Williams-Sonoma, Domino's Pizza, CVS Pharmacy, Gymboree, and Stanford Financial Group. ▲For example, Stanford Financial sponsors The Eagles for St. Jude program, in which Stanford donates $1,000 for every eagle made on the PGA tour. St. Jude invites the golfing public to follow suit with its own donations. Last year alone, Stanford Financial donated more than $1.7 million. Golfer Vijay Singh, PGA TOUR Ambassador for the program, was himself deeply touched by St. Jude's good works, donating $50,000 of his own money: "All the research, all the cures, all the misery that people face—but you get there and see the kids with their smiles," he says. "It's just overwhelming."

> When St. Jude applies its sophisticated public relations efforts on behalf of its life-saving programs, the results can be spectacular. For example, during last year's annual *Thanks and Giving* campaign, some 50–75 million viewers watched weeklong St. Jude's segments on NBC's *Today* show featuring St. Jude National Outreach Director Marlo Thomas and patient families. The Monday segment of *Today* showing host Meredith Vieira's tour of the hospital coincided with the highest single day rating ever in the history of the *Today* show. Thomas also appeared on *Larry King Live, This Week with George Stephanopoulos, Rachael Ray, FOX and Friends,* and *The View.* As a result, St. Jude enlisted a record 50 corporate sponsors and millions of individual donors heeded the call. Through such strong marketing, St Jude earns tens of millions of dollars each year in donations, of which 85 percent go directly to research and treating children.[40]

▲ Not-for-profit marketing: St. Jude aggressively markets its powerful mission—"Finding Cures. Saving Children." For example, it works with Stanford Financial and PGA TOUR Ambassador Vijay Singh to sponsor The Eagles for St. Jude program.

Government agencies have also shown an increased interest in marketing. For example, the U.S. military has a marketing plan to attract recruits to its different services, and various government agencies are now designing *social marketing campaigns* to encourage energy conservation and concern for the environment or to discourage smoking, excessive drinking, and drug use. Even the once-stodgy U.S. Postal Service has developed innovative marketing to sell commemorative stamps, promote its priority mail services, and lift its image as a contemporary and competitive organization. In all, the U.S. government is the nation's 29th largest advertiser, with an annual advertising budget of more than $1.2 billion.[41]

> **Author Comment** | Remember Figure 1.1 outlining the marketing process? Now, based on everything we've discussed in this chapter, we'll expand that figure to provide a road map for learning marketing throughout the rest of the text.

So, What is Marketing? Pulling It All Together (pp 29–30)

At the start of this chapter, Figure 1.1 presented a simple model of the marketing process. Now that we've discussed all of the steps in the process, **Figure 1.6** presents an expanded model that will help you pull it all together. What is marketing? Simply put, marketing is the process of building profitable customer relationships by creating value for customers and capturing value in return.

The first four steps of the marketing process focus on creating value for customers. The company first gains a full understanding of the marketplace by researching customer needs and managing marketing information. It then designs a customer-driven marketing strategy based on the answers to two simple questions. The first question is "What consumers will we serve?" (market segmentation and targeting). Good marketing companies know that they cannot serve all customers in every way. Instead, they need to focus their resources on the customers they can serve best and most profitably. The second marketing strategy question is "How can we best serve targeted customers?" (differentiation and

> This expanded version of Figure 1.1 at the beginning of the chapter provides a good road map for the rest of the text. The underlying concept of the entire text is that marketing creates value *for* customers in order to capture value *from* customers in return.

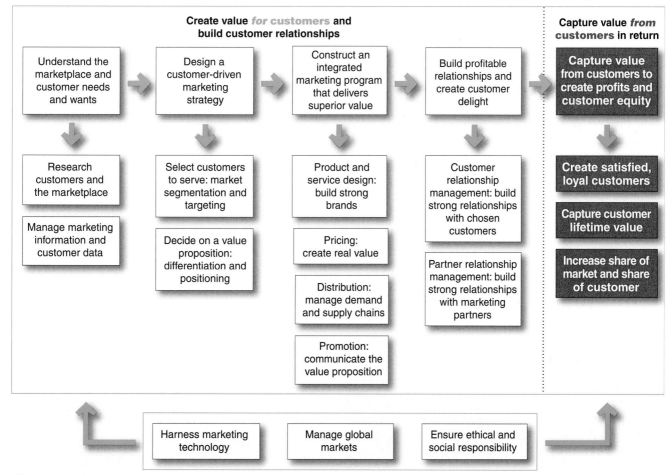

FIGURE | 1.6 An Expanded Model of the Marketing Process

positioning). Here, the marketer outlines a value proposition that spells out what values the company will deliver in order to win target customers.

With its marketing strategy decided, the company now constructs an integrated marketing program—consisting of a blend of the four marketing mix elements, or the four Ps—that transforms the marketing strategy into real value for customers. The company develops product offers and creates strong brand identities for them. It prices these offers to create real customer value and distributes the offers to make them available to target consumers. Finally, the company designs promotion programs that communicate the value proposition to target consumers and persuade them to act on the market offering.

Perhaps the most important step in the marketing process involves building value-laden, profitable relationships with target customers. Throughout the process, marketers practice customer relationship management to create customer satisfaction and delight. In creating customer value and relationships, however, the company cannot go it alone. It must work closely with marketing partners both inside the company and throughout the marketing system. Thus, beyond practicing good customer relationship management, firms must also practice good partner relationship management.

The first four steps in the marketing process create value *for* customers. In the final step, the company reaps the rewards of its strong customer relationships by capturing value *from* customers. Delivering superior customer value creates highly satisfied customers who will buy more and will buy again. This helps the company to capture customer lifetime value and greater share of customer. The result is increased long-term customer equity for the firm.

Finally, in the face of today's changing marketing landscape, companies must take into account three additional factors. In building customer and partner relationships, they must harness marketing technology, take advantage of global opportunities, and ensure that they act in an ethical and socially responsible way.

Figure 1.6 provides a good road map to future chapters of the text. Chapters 1 and 2 introduce the marketing process, with a focus on building customer relationships and capturing value from customers. Chapters 3, 4, 5, and 6 address the first step of the marketing process—understanding the marketing environment, managing marketing information, and understanding consumer and business buyer behavior. In Chapter 7, we look more deeply into the two major marketing strategy decisions: selecting which customers to serve (segmentation and targeting) and deciding on a value proposition (differentiation and positioning). Chapters 8 through 17 discuss the marketing mix variables, one by one. Chapter 18 sums up customer-driven marketing strategy and creating a competitive advantage in the marketplace. Then, the final two chapters examine special marketing considerations: global marketing and marketing ethics and social responsibility.

REVIEWING Objectives AND KEY Terms

Today's successful companies—whether large or small, for-profit or not-for-profit, domestic or global—share a strong customer focus and a heavy commitment to marketing. The goal of marketing is to build and manage customer relationships. Marketing seeks to attract new customers by promising superior value and to keep and grow current customers by delivering satisfaction. To be successful, companies will have to be strongly market focused.

OBJECTIVE 1 **Define marketing and outline the steps in the marketing process.** (pp 4–6)

Marketing is the process by which companies create value for customers and build strong customer relationships in order to capture value from customers in return.

The marketing process involves five steps. The first four steps create value *for* customers. First, marketers need to understand the marketplace and customer needs and wants. Next, marketers design a customer-driven marketing strategy with the goal of getting, keeping, and growing target customers. In the third step, marketers construct a marketing program that actually delivers superior value. All of these steps form the basis for the fourth step, building profitable customer relationships and creating customer delight. In the final step, the company reaps the rewards of strong customer relationships by capturing value *from* customers.

OBJECTIVE 2 **Explain the importance of understanding customers and the marketplace, and identify the five core marketplace concepts. (pp 6–8)**

Outstanding marketing companies go to great lengths to learn about and understand their customers' needs, wants, and demands. This understanding helps them to design want-satisfying market offerings and build value-laden customer relationships by which they can capture customer lifetime value and greater share of customer. The result is increased long-term customer equity for the firm.

The core marketplace concepts are needs, wants, and demands; market offerings (products, services, and experiences); value and satisfaction; exchange and relationships; and markets. Wants are the form taken by human needs when shaped by culture and individual personality. When backed by buying power, wants become demands. Companies address needs by putting forth a value proposition, a set of benefits that they promise to consumers to satisfy their needs. The value proposition is fulfilled through a market offering, which delivers customer value and satisfaction, resulting in long-term exchange relationships with customers.

OBJECTIVE 3 **Identify the key elements of a customer-driven marketing strategy and discuss the marketing management orientations that guide marketing strategy. (pp 8–12)**

To design a winning marketing strategy, the company must first decide *who* it will serve. It does this by dividing the market into segments of customers (*market segmentation*) and selecting which segments it will cultivate (*target marketing*). Next, the company must decide *how* it will serve targeted customers (how it will *differentiate and position* itself in the marketplace).

Marketing management can adopt one of five competing market orientations. The *production concept* holds that management's task is to improve production efficiency and bring down prices. The *product concept* holds that consumers favor products that offer the most in quality, performance, and innovative features; thus, little promotional effort is required. The *selling concept* holds that consumers will not buy enough of the organization's products unless it undertakes a large-scale selling and promotion effort. The *marketing concept* holds that achieving organizational goals depends on determining the needs and wants of target markets and delivering the desired satisfactions more effectively and efficiently than competitors do. The *societal marketing concept* holds that generating customer satisfaction *and* long-run societal well-being are the keys to both achieving the company's goals and fulfilling its responsibilities.

OBJECTIVE 4 **Discuss customer relationship management and identify strategies for creating value *for* customers and capturing value *from* customers in return. (pp 12–24)**

Broadly defined, *customer relationship management* is the process of building and maintaining profitable customer relationships by delivering superior customer value and satisfaction. The aim of customer relationship management is to produce high *customer equity,* the total combined customer lifetime values of all of the company's customers. The key to building lasting relationships is the creation of superior *customer value* and *satisfaction.*

Companies want not only to acquire profitable customers but also to build relationships that will keep them and grow "share of customer." Different types of customers require different customer relationship management strategies. The marketer's aim is to build the *right relationships* with the *right customers.* In return for creating value *for* targeted customers, the company captures value *from* customers in the form of profits and customer equity.

In building customer relationships, good marketers realize that they cannot go it alone. They must work closely with marketing partners inside and outside the company. In addition to being good at customer relationship management, they must also be good at *partner relationship management.*

OBJECTIVE 5 **Describe the major trends and forces that are changing the marketing landscape in this age of relationships. (pp 25–30)**

Dramatic changes are occurring in the marketing arena. The boom in computer, telecommunications, information, transportation, and other technologies has created exciting new ways to learn about and track customers, and to create products and services tailored to individual customer needs. It has also allowed new approaches by which marketers can target consumers more selectively and build closer, two-way customer relationships.

In an increasingly smaller world, many marketers are now connected *globally* with their customers and marketing partners. Today, almost every company, large or small, is touched in some way by global competition. Today's marketers are also reexamining their ethical and societal responsibilities. Marketers are being called upon to take greater responsibility for the social and environmental impact of their actions. Finally, in the past, marketing has been most widely applied in the for-profit business sector. In recent years, however, marketing also has become a major part of the strategies of many not-for-profit organizations, such as colleges, hospitals, museums, zoos, symphony orchestras, and even churches.

Pulling it all together, as discussed throughout the chapter, the major new developments in marketing can be summed up in a single word: *relationships.* Today, marketers of all kinds are taking advantage of new opportunities for building relationships with their customers, their marketing partners, and the world around them.

KEY Terms

OBJECTIVE 1

Marketing (p 5)

OBJECTIVE 2

Needs (p 6)
Wants (p 6)
Demands (p 6)
Market offering (p 6)
Marketing myopia (p 6)
Exchange (p 7)
Market (p 7)

OBJECTIVE 3

Marketing management (p 8)
Production concept (p 9)
Product concept (p 10)
Selling concept (p 10)
Marketing concept (p 10)
Societal marketing concept (p 11)

OBJECTIVE 4

Customer relationship
management (p 13)

Customer-perceived value (p 13)
Customer satisfaction (p 13)
Consumer-generated marketing (p 19)
Partner relationship
management (p 19)
Customer lifetime value (p 22)
Share of customer (p 22)
Customer equity (p 23)

OBJECTIVE 5

Internet (p 25)

DISCUSSING & APPLYING THE Concepts

Discussing the Concepts

1. What is marketing and what is its primary goal? (AASCB: Communication)

2. Compare and contrast customer needs, wants, and demands. Describe the need versus the want for the following products: Gatorade, Nike shoes, and iPod. (AACSB: Communication; Reflective Thinking)

3. Explain how a company designs a customer-driven marketing strategy. (AACSB: Communication)

4. What are the five different marketing management orientations? Which orientation do you believe your school follows when marketing itself? (AACSB: Communication; Reflective Thinking)

5. Explain the difference between *share of customer* and *customer equity.* Why are these concepts important to marketers? (AACSB: Communication; Reflective Thinking)

6. How has the Internet changed consumers? Marketers? (AACSB: Communication)

Applying the Concepts

1. Ask five businesspeople from different industries (for example, food service, retailing, consumer-product manufacturing, industrial-product manufacturing, education, and so on) what they think marketing is. Evaluate their definitions and discuss whether or not they are consistent with the goal of creating customer value and managing profitable customer relationships. (AACSB: Communication; Reflective Thinking)

2. In a small group, develop a marketing plan for a pet boarding service. Who is your target market? How will you enable customers to get the best value? Define what you mean by value and develop the value proposition of your offering for this target market. (AACSB: Communication; Reflective Thinking)

3. Define the different relationship levels companies can build with customers. Pick a company and describe the types of relationships you have with it. (AACAB: Communication; Reflective Thinking)

FOCUS ON Technology

Embracing the marketing concept is one thing; implementing it is another. How do marketers know what consumers' needs and wants are so that they can develop a marketing strategy and mix to satisfy those needs and wants? Research, of course. But that takes time and resources, so many companies are turning to the Internet to get continuous, timely, and innovative information from customers. For example, software maker SAP developed its Business Process Expert (BPX) community by which customers share feedback in forums, blogs, and articles. Procter & Gamble wants you to "Share Your Thoughts" at www.pg.com/getintouch/. But if you have a really good idea, perhaps you should look into

licensing with P&G (see https://secure3.verticali.net/pg-connection-portal/ctx/noauth/PortalHome.do).

1. Explore the Web sites of other companies to learn how they get feedback from customers. Start by clicking on "Contact Us," then dig deeply to see if you can find a place where each company seeks or accepts feedback and ideas. Write a brief report of what you find. (AACSB: Communication; Use of IT)

2. Discuss other ways in which businesses can use the Internet to create greater customer value. (AACSB: Communication; Reflective Thinking)

FOCUS ON Ethics

Did you drive a car today? Use a laptop computer? Buy a product in a store? If so, you emitted carbon dioxide (CO2) and created a carbon footprint. All of us do that every day. Individuals and companies emit carbon dioxide in everyday activities. Many consumers feel bad about doing this; others expect companies to take action. What's the answer? Reducing carbon emissions is one solution, but another one is to offset your carbon emissions by purchasing carbon offsets and renewable energy certificates (RECs). Individual consumers do this, and companies are flocking to purchase carbon offsets for themselves or to offer to their customers, resulting in an estimated $100 million market. And experts predict exponential growth over the next few years. Airlines routinely offer flyers the option of paying a few extra dollars to offset their carbon emissions. For example, JetBlue Airways introduced its

Jetting to Green program that allows flyers to make their flight "carbon-neutral" for as little as $2.00. Flyers' donations will then support reforestation, wind, and waste management projects.

1. Learn more about carbon offsets and discuss four examples of how businesses are using them. In your opinion, are these companies embracing the societal marketing concept? (AACSB Communication; Reflective Thinking)

2. One criticism of carbon offsetting is that companies are not really helping the environmental by changing their own behavior; instead they're merely buying "environmental pardons." Do you think carbon offsets are a responsible solution to environmental concerns? Write a brief essay debating this issue. (AACSB: Communication; Ethical Reasoning)

MARKETING BY THE Numbers

How much are you worth to a given company if you continue to purchase its brand for the rest of your life? Many marketers are grappling with that question, but it's not easy to determine how much a customer is worth to a company over his or her lifetime. Calculating customer lifetime value can be very complicated. Intuitively, however, it can be a fairly simple net present value calculation. To determine a basic customer lifetime value, each stream of profit is discounted back to its present value (PV) and then summed. The basic equation for calculating net present value (NPV) is as follows:

$$NPV = \sum_{t=0}^{N} \frac{C_t}{(1+r)^t}$$

Where,

t = time of the cash flow
N = total customer lifetime
r = discount rate

C_t = net cash flow (the profit) at time t (The initial cost of acquiring a customer would be a negative profit at time 0.)

NPV can be calculated easily on most financial calculators or by using one of the calculators available on the Internet, such as the one found at www.investopedia.com/calculator/NetPresentValue.aspx. For more discussion of the financial and quantitative implications of marketing decisions, see Appendix 2, Marketing by the Numbers.

1. Assume that a customer shops at a local grocery store spending an average of $150 a week and that the retailer earns a five percent margin. Calculate the customer lifetime value if this shopper remains loyal over a 10-year lifespan, assuming a five percent annual interest rate and no initial cost to acquire the customer. (AACSB Communication; Analytic Reasoning)

2. Discuss how a business can increase a customer's lifetime value. (AACSB: Communication; Reflective Thinking)

VIDEO Case

Harley-Davidson

Few brands engender such intense loyalty as that found in the hearts of Harley-Davidson owners. Long ago, the folks at Harley-Davidson realized that the best way to create lasting relationships with its customers was to understand them on their own terms. The company spends a great deal of time and money in pursuit of that goal. It wants to know who its customers are, how they think and feel, and why they buy a Harley. That customer-centric strategy has helped build Harley-Davidson into a multibillion-dollar company with the largest company-sponsored owner's group in the world.

Harley-Davidson has learned that it sells much more than motorcycles. The company sells a feeling of independence, individualism, and freedom. These strong emotional connections have made Harley-Davidson ownership much more of a lifestyle than merely a product consumption experience. To support that lifestyle, Harley-Davidson recognizes that its most important marketing tool is the network of individuals who ride Harleys. For this reason, Harley-Davidson engages its customer base through company-sponsored travel adventures, events, and other things, such as clothes and accessories both for riders and for those who simply like to associate with the brand.

After viewing the video featuring Harley-Davidson, answer the following questions about managing profitable customer relationships:

1. How does Harley-Davidson build long-term customer relationships?

2. What is Harley-Davidson's value proposition?

3. Relate the concept of customer equity to Harley-Davidson. How does Harley-Davidson's strategy focus on the right relationships with the right customers?

COMPANY Case

Build-A-Bear: Build-A-Memory

In the late 1990s, it was all about the dot-com. While venture capital poured into the high-tech sector and the stock prices of dot-com start-ups rose rapidly, the performance of traditional companies paled in comparison. That era seemed like a bad time to start a chain of brick-and-mortar mall stores selling stuffed animals. Indeed, when Maxine Clark founded Build-A-Bear Workshop in 1996, many critics thought that she was making a poor business decision.

But with its first decade of doing business behind it, Build-A-Bear Workshop now has more cheerleaders than naysayers. In the last few years, it has won numerous awards, including being named one of the five hottest retailers by one retail consultancy. The company hit number 25 on *BusinessWeek's* Hot Growth list of fast-expanding small companies. And founder and CEO Maxine Clark won Fast Company's Customer-Centered Leader Award. How does a small start-up company achieve such accolades?

THE PRODUCT

On paper, it all looks simple. Maxine Clark opened the first company store in 1996. Since then, the company has opened more than 370 stores and has custom-made tens of millions of teddy bears and other stuffed animals. Annual revenues reached $474 million for 2007 and are growing at a steady and predictable 15 percent annually. After going public in November of 2004, the company's stock price soared 56 percent in just two years. Annual sales per square foot are $600, roughly double the average for U.S. mall stores. In fact, Build-A-Bear Workshops typically earns back almost all of its investment in a new store within the first year, a feat unheard of in retailing. On top of all this, the company's Internet sales are exploding.

But what all these numbers don't illustrate is *how* the company is achieving such success. That success comes not from the tangible object that children clutch as they leave a store. It comes from what Build-A-Bear is really selling: the experience of participating in the creation of personalized entertainment.

When children enter a Build-A-Bear store, they step into a cartoon land, a genuine fantasy world organized around a child-friendly assembly line comprised of clearly labeled work stations. The process begins at the "Choose Me" station where customers select an unstuffed animal from a bin. At the "Stuff Me" station, the animal literally comes to life as the child operates a foot pedal that blows in the amount of "fluff" that she or he (25 percent of Build-A-Bear customers are boys) chooses. Other stations include "Hear Me" (where customers decide whether or not to include a "voice box"), "Stitch Me" (where the child stitches the animal shut), "Fluff Me" (where the child can give the animal a blow-dry spa treatment), "Dress Me" (filled with accessories galore), and

"Name Me" (where a birth certificate is created with the child-selected name).

Unlike most retail stores, waiting in line behind other customers is not an unpleasant activity. In fact, because the process is much of the fun, waiting actually enhances the experience. By the time children leave the store, they have a product unlike any they've ever bought or received. They have a product that they have created. More than just a stuffed animal that they can have and hold, it's imbued with the memory created on their visit to the store. And because of the high price-to-delight ratio (bears start as low as $10 and average $25), parents love Build-A-Bear as much as the kids.

WHY THE CONCEPT WORKS

The outside observer might assume that Build-A-Bear is competing with other toy companies or with other makers of stuffed animals, such as the Vermont Teddy Bear Company. Touting its product as the only bear made in America and guaranteed for life, Vermont Teddy Bear hand-makes all of its bears at a central factory in Vermont. Customers choose their bears through a catalogue or Web site, receiving their bear in the mail without the experience of having taken part in the creation of the bear. Quality is the key selling point (reinforced by its price of $50–$100).

Although Vermont Teddy Bear has achieved great success since it sold its first bear in 1981, Maxine Clark does not consider it to be a serious Build-A-Bear competitor. "Our concept is based on customization," says Clark. "Most things today are high-tech and hard-touch. We are soft-touch. We don't think of ourselves as a toy store—we think of ourselves as an experience." It is widely recognized in many industries that the personalization feature builds fiercely loyal customers. As evidence, Clark points out that unlike the rest of the toy industry, Build-A-Bear sales do not peak during the holiday season, but are evenly distributed throughout the year.

Although not very common in the toy industry, Maxine Clark asserts that personalization is emerging because it lets customers be creative and express themselves. It provides far more value for the customer than they receive from mass-produced products. "It's empowerment—it lets the customer do something in their control," she adds. Build-A-Bear has capitalized on this concept by not just allowing for customization, but by making it a key driver of customer value. The extensive customer involvement in the personalization process is more of the "product" than the resulting item.

Although Build-A-Bear has performed impressively, some analysts question whether or not it is just another toy industry fad, comparing the brand to Beanie Babies and Cabbage Patch Kids. Although Maxine Clark has considered this, she is confident that the Build-A-Bear product and experience will evolve as quickly as the fickle tastes of children. Whereas some outfits and accessories might be trendy (the company added Spiderman costumes to the bear-size clothing line at the peak of the movie's popularity), accessories assortments are changed 11 times each year.

KNOWING THE CUSTOMER

Maxine Clark has been viewed as the strategic visionary—and even the genius—who has made the Build-A-Bear concept work. But her success as CEO derives from more than just business skills relating to strategy development and implementation. Clark attributes her success to "never forgetting what it's like to be a customer." Given that Clark has no children of her own, this is an amazing feat indeed. Although understanding customers is certainly not a new concept, Clark has employed both low-tech and high-tech methods for making Build-A-Bear a truly customer-centric organization.

To put herself in the customer's shoes, Clark walks where they walk. Every week, she visits two or three of the more than 370 Build-A-Bear stores. She doesn't do this just to see how the stores are running operationally. She takes the opportunity to interact with her customer base by chatting with preteens and parents. She actually puts herself on the front line, assisting employees in serving customers. She even hands out business cards.

As a result, Clark receives thousands of e-mails each week, and she's added to the buddy lists of preteens all over the world. Clark doesn't take this honor lightly, and tries to respond to as many of those messages as possible via her BlackBerry. Also, to capitalize on these customer communications, she has created what she calls the "Virtual Cub Advisory Council," a panel of children on her e-mail list. And what does Clark get in return from all this high-tech communication? "Ideas," she says. "I used to feel like I had to come up with all the ideas myself but it's so much easier relying on my customers for help."

From the location of stores to accessories that could be added to the Build-A-Bear line, Build-A-Bear actually puts customer ideas into practice. As the ideas come in, Clark polls the Cub Council to get real-time feedback from customers throughout the areas where the company does business. Mini-scooters, Hello Kitty bears, mascot bears at professional sports venues, and sequined purses are all ideas generated by customers that have become very successful additions.

Clark sees accessories as a tool for building the child/bear relationship. Build-A-Bear Workshops house in-store galleries of bear-sized furniture designed by kids for kids. An exclusive partnership with Skechers shoes makes Build-A-Bear Workshop the seller of more bear shoes, sandals, boots, and slippers than any other company worldwide. And with the sports licensing agreements that it has with the NBA, WNBA, MLB, NHL, NFL, and NASCAR, Build-A-Bear's offspring can become part of a child's affinity for a sports team. Clark's research efforts have also lead to a media campaign focusing on the tween segment by playing up ideas of fashion and imagination.

As a means of further expanding the Build-A-Bear experience beyond the retail store, the company has created a Web site that connects real-world toys with the online world. Dubbed "BuildABearVille.com," the interactive site contains games and activities that feature the same themes as the brick-and-mortar stores. "The new virtual world was carefully created so that it reflects the core values of Build-A-Bear Workshop," Clark said. "It allows children to have fun as they grow their friendships and learn about being an active participant in the community." Although any child can register, the premium content is only accessible via a code that comes with the purchase of a bear from one of the chain's retail stores.

But growth for Build-A-Bear will come from more than just these improvements to same-store sales. Clark's expansion efforts include building a base of at least 350 stores in the United States, 120 stores in Europe, and franchising an additional 300 stores in other parts of the world. And Clark is taking action on the flood of "build-your-own" concepts that have come across her desk since the first Build-A-Bear Workshop opened. She will give much more attention to a new line of stores called "Friends 2B Made," a concept built around the personalization of dolls rather than stuffed animals. She's opened up the first "Build-A-Dino" stores. And Build-A-Bear has a 25 percent ownership stake in the start-up "Ridemakerz," a make-and-outfit your own toy car shop.

Although Maxine Clark may communicate with only a fraction of her customers, she sees her efforts as the basis for a personal connection with all customers. "With each child that enters our store, we have an opportunity to build a lasting memory," she says. "Any business can think that way, whether you're selling a screw, a bar of soap, or a bear."

Questions for Discussion

1. Give examples of needs, wants, and demands that Build-A-Bear customers demonstrate, differentiating each of these three concepts. What are the implications of each on Build-A-Bear's actions?

2. In detail, describe all facets of Build-A-Bear's product. What is being exchanged in a Build-A-Bear transaction?

3. Which of the five marketing management concepts best describes Build-A-Bear Workshop?

4. Discuss in detail the value that Build-A-Bear creates for its customers.

5. Is Build-A-Bear likely to be successful in continuing to build customer relationships? Why or why not?

Sources: James Bickers, "Virtual Friends," *Retail Customer Experience*, April 2008, p. 20; Joanne Kaufman, "After Build-A-Bear, Build-A-Toy-Car," *New York Times*, May 29, 2007, p. C3; "Build-A-Bear Brings Out the Bulls," *BusinessWeek*, June 28, 2007, accessed at www.businessweek.com; Lucas Conley, "Customer-Centered Leader: Maxine Clark," *Fast Company*, October 2005, p. 54; Staff writer, "This Bear Doesn't Hibernate," *BusinessWeek*, June 6, 2005, accessed at www.businessweek.com; and Roger Crockett, "Build-A-Bear Workshop: Retailing Gets Interactive with Toys Designed by Tots," *BusinessWeek*, June 6, 2005, p. 77.

Chapter 2

Part 1 Defining Marketing and the Marketing Process (Chapters 1, 2)
Part 2 Understanding the Marketplace and Consumers (Chapters 3, 4, 5, 6)
Part 3 Designing a Customer-Driven Strategy and Mix (Chapters 7, 8, 9, 10, 11, 12, 13, 14, 15, 16, 17)
Part 4 Extending Marketing (Chapters 18, 19, 20)

Company and Marketing

Strategy Partnering to Build Customer Relationships

Chapter PREVIEW

In the first chapter, we explored the marketing process by which companies create value for consumers in order to capture value from them in return. We will now dig deeper into steps two and three of the marketing process—designing customer-driven marketing strategies and constructing marketing programs. First, we look at the organization's overall strategic planning, which guides marketing strategy and planning. Next, we discuss how, guided by the strategic plan, marketers partner closely with others inside and outside the firm to create value for customers. We then examine marketing strategy and planning—how marketers choose target markets, position their market offerings, develop a marketing mix, and manage their marketing programs. Finally, we look at the important step of measuring and managing return on marketing investment.

But first, let's look under NASCAR's hood. In only a few years, NASCAR (the National Association for Stock Car Auto Racing) has grown swiftly from a pastime for beer-guzzling bubbas into a national marketing phenomenon. How? Through customer-driven companywide and marketing strategies. NASCAR creates high-octane experiences that result in strong relationships with its tens of millions of fans. In return, NASCAR captures value from these fans, both for itself and for its many sponsors. Read on and see how NASCAR does it.

When you think of NASCAR, do you think of tobacco-spitting rednecks in pickup trucks at run-down race tracks? Think again! These days, NASCAR is much, much more. In fact, it's one great marketing organization. And for fans, NASCAR is a lot more than stock car races. It's a high-octane, totally involving experience.

As for the stereotypes, throw them away. NASCAR is now the second-highest rated regular season sport on TV—only the NFL draws more viewers—and races are seen in 150 countries in 23 languages. NASCAR fans are young, affluent, and decidedly family oriented—40 percent are women. What's more, they are 75 million strong and passionate about NASCAR. A hardcore NASCAR fan spends nearly $700 a year on NASCAR-related clothing, collectibles, and other items.

What's NASCAR's secret? Perhaps no organization is more customer-driven—NASCAR focuses single-mindedly on creating customer relationships. For fans, the NASCAR relationship develops through a careful blend of live racing events and abundant media and Web coverage.

Each year, fans experience the adrenalin-charged, heart-stopping excitement of NASCAR racing firsthand by attending national tours to some two dozen tracks around the country. NASCAR is America's number-one live spectator sport, holding 17 of the 20 top-attended sporting events last year. More than 200,000 people attended the recent Daytona 500, compared to the 70,000 who attended the latest Super Bowl.

At these events, fans hold tailgate parties, camp and cook out, watch the cars roar around the track, meet the drivers, and swap stories with other NASCAR enthusiasts. Track facilities even include RV parks next to and right inside the racing oval. What other sport lets you drive your RV or camper into the stadium and sit on it to watch the event? Rather than fleecing fans with over-priced food and beer, NASCAR tracks encourage fans to bring their own. Such actions mean that NASCAR might lose a sale today, but it will keep the customer tomorrow.

To further the customer relationship, NASCAR makes the sport a wholesome family affair. The environment is safe for kids—uniformed security guards patrol the track to keep things in line. The family atmosphere extends to the drivers, too. Unlike the aloof and often distant athletes in other sports, NASCAR drivers seem like regular people. They are friendly and readily available to mingle with fans and sign autographs.

Can't make it to the track? No problem. Campaigns featuring NASCAR drivers and cars have proliferated across a broad range of media, from TV and multiple Web sites to cell phones, satellite radio, video game consoles, and mobile devices. "It's incredibly important to reach the fans in different ways as they engage with our sport in different ways," says NASCAR's chief marketing officer.

> More than 200,000 avid NASCAR fans attended the recent Daytona 500, compared to the 70,000 who attended the latest Super Bowl.

An average televised NASCAR event reaches 18 million TV viewers. Last year alone, through network partners like ABC, ESPN2, Fox Broadcasting, and Speed, NASCAR events captured more than 300 million viewers. NASCAR's most avid fans, roughly 30 million of them, consume eight hours a week of NASCAR media. Well-orchestrated coverage and in-car cameras put fans in the middle of the action, giving them vicarious thrills that keep them glued to the screen. "When the network gets it right, my surround-sound bothers my neighbors but makes my ears happy," says Angela Kotula, a 35-year-old human resources professional.

NASCAR also delivers the NASCAR experience through engaging Web sites. NASCAR fans can often be found surfing NASCAR sites while watching a race on TV. Many NASCAR sponsors, such as Office Depot and Best Western, also offer popular microsites devoted to their NASCAR sponsorships.

NASCAR.com, which attracts almost four million unique visitors each month, serves up a glut of information and entertainment—in-depth news, stats, standings, driver bios, background information, online games, community discussions, and merchandise. More than 300,000 die-hard fans subscribe to TrackPass to get up-to-the-minute standings, race video, streaming audio from the cars, and access to a host of archived audio and video highlights. TrackPass with PitCommand even delivers a real-time data feed, complete with the GPS locations of cars and data from drivers' dashboards.

But a big part of the NASCAR experience is the feeling that the sport, itself, is personally accessible. Anyone who knows how to drive feels that he or she, too, could be a champion NASCAR driver. As 48-year-old police officer Ed Sweat puts it, "Genetics did not bless me with the height of a basketball player, nor was I born to have the bulk of a lineman in the NFL. But . . . on any given Sunday, with a rich sponsor, the right car, and some practice, I could be draftin' and passin', zooming to the finish line, trading paint with Tony Stewart. . . . Yup, despite my advancing age and waistline, taking Zocor, and driving by a gym, I could be Dale Jarrett!"

Ultimately, such fan enthusiasm translates into financial success for NASCAR—and for its sponsors. Television networks pay on average $560 million per year for the rights to broadcast NASCAR events, and in turn charge advertisers nearly $600,000 per thirty-second advertising slot. With everything from NASCAR-branded bacon to its own series of Harlequin romance novels, the sport is third in licensed merchandise sales, behind only the NFL and the NCAA. NASCAR itself sells more than $2 billion in merchandise a year.

Marketing studies show that NASCAR's fans are three times more loyal to the sport's sponsors than fans of any other sport. Seventy-two percent of NASCAR fans consciously purchase sponsors' products because of the NASCAR connection. Just ask dental hygienist Jenny German, an ardent fan of driver Jeff Gordon. According to one account, "She actively seeks out any product he endorses. She drinks Pepsi instead of Coke, eats Edy's ice cream for desert, and owns a pair of Ray-Ban sunglasses. 'If they sold underwear with the number 24 on it, I'd have it on,' German says."

Because of such loyal fan relationships, NASCAR has attracted more than 250 big-name sponsors, from Wal-Mart, Home Depot, and Target to Procter & Gamble, UPS, Coca-Cola, and the U.S. Army. In all, corporations spend more than $1 billion a year for NASCAR sponsorships and promotions. Sprint Nextel is shelling out $750 million over a span of 10 years to be a NASCAR sponsor and to put its name on the NASCAR Sprint Cup Series. "I could pay you $1 million to try and not run into our name at a NASCAR race and you would lose," says a Sprint Nextel spokesperson.

Other sponsors eagerly pay on average $18 million to $20 million per year to sponsor a top car and to get their corporate colors and logos emblazoned on team uniforms and on the hoods or side panels of team cars. Or they spend big bucks to become the "official" (fill-in-the-blank) of NASCAR racing. For example, Molson Coors recently signed a $25 million contract to have Coors Light be the official beer of NASCAR for five years. Is it worth the price? Office Depot certainly thinks so. It began sponsoring a car when its surveys showed that 44 percent of rival Staples' customers would switch office supply retailers if Office Depot hooked up with NASCAR.

So if you're still thinking of NASCAR as rednecks, pickup trucks, and moonshine, you'd better think again. NASCAR is a premier customer-driven marketing organization that knows how to create customer value that translates into deep and lasting customer relationships. "Better than any other sport," says a leading sports marketing executive, "NASCAR listens to its fans and gives them what they want." In turn, fans reward NASCAR and its sponsors with deep loyalty and the promise of lasting profits.[1]

> Because of its loyal fan relationships, NASCAR has attracted more than 250 big-name sponsors, who spend more than $1 billion a year for NASCAR sponsorships and promotions.

> NASCAR is a premier customer-driven marketing organization that knows how to create customer value that translates into deep and lasting customer relationships. "Better than any other sport," says a leading sports marketing executive, "NASCAR listens to its fans and gives them what they want." In turn, fans reward NASCAR and its sponsors with deep loyalty and the promise of lasting profits.

Objective Outline

Like NASCAR, outstanding marketing organizations employ strongly customer-driven marketing strategies and programs that create customer value and relationships. These marketing strategies and programs, however, are guided by broader companywide strategic plans, which must also be customer focused. Thus, to understand the role of marketing, we must first understand the organization's overall strategic planning process.

Author Comment | Companywide strategic planning guides marketing strategy and planning. Like marketing strategy, the company's broad strategy must also be customer focused.

Strategic planning
The process of developing and maintaining a strategic fit between the organization's goals and capabilities and its changing marketing opportunities.

Companywide Strategic Planning: Defining Marketing's Role (pp 38–46)

Each company must find the game plan for long-run survival and growth that makes the most sense given its specific situation, opportunities, objectives, and resources. This is the focus of **strategic planning**—the process of developing and maintaining a strategic fit between the organization's goals and capabilities and its changing marketing opportunities.

Strategic planning sets the stage for the rest of the planning in the firm. Companies usually prepare annual plans, long-range plans, and strategic plans. The annual and long-range plans deal with the company's current businesses and how to keep them going. In contrast, the strategic plan involves adapting the firm to take advantage of opportunities in its constantly changing environment.

At the corporate level, the company starts the strategic planning process by defining its overall purpose and mission (see **Figure 2.1**). This mission is then turned into detailed supporting objectives that guide the whole company. Next, headquarters decides what portfolio of businesses and products is best for the company and how much support to give each one. In turn, each business and product develops detailed marketing and other departmental plans that support the companywide plan. Thus, marketing planning occurs at the business-unit, product, and market levels. It supports company strategic planning with more detailed plans for specific marketing opportunities.

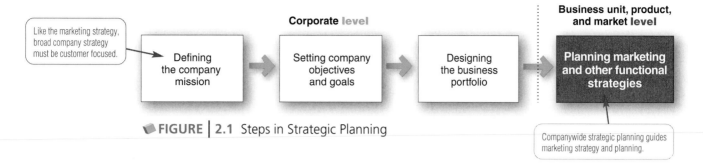

Like the marketing strategy, broad company strategy must be customer focused.

Corporate level

Defining the company mission → Setting company objectives and goals → Designing the business portfolio

Business unit, product, and market level

Planning marketing and other functional strategies

Companywide strategic planning guides marketing strategy and planning.

FIGURE | 2.1 Steps in Strategic Planning

Defining a Market-Oriented Mission

An organization exists to accomplish something, and this purpose should be clearly stated. Forging a sound mission begins with the following questions: What is our business? Who is the customer? What do consumers value? What *should* our business be? These simple-sounding questions are among the most difficult the company will ever have to answer. Successful companies continuously raise these questions and answer them carefully and completely.

Many organizations develop formal mission statements that answer these questions. A **mission statement** is a statement of the organization's purpose—what it wants to accomplish in the larger environment. A clear mission statement acts as an "invisible hand" that guides people in the organization. Studies have shown that firms with well-crafted mission statements have better organizational and financial performance.[2]

Mission statement

A statement of the organization's purpose—what it wants to accomplish in the larger environment.

Some companies define their missions myopically in product or technology terms ("We make and sell furniture" or "We are a chemical-processing firm"). But mission statements should be *market oriented* and defined in terms of satisfying basic customer needs. Products and technologies eventually become outdated, but basic market needs may last forever. ▲Cold Stone Creamery's mission isn't simply to sell ice cream. Its mission is to "make people happy around the world by selling the highest quality, most creative ice cream experience with passion, excellence, and innovation." Likewise, eBay's mission isn't simply to hold online auctions and trading. It aims "to provide a global trading platform where practically anyone can trade practically anything"—with eBay, "Shop victoriously!" It wants to be a unique Web community in which people can safely shop around, have fun, and get to know each other, for example, by chatting at the eBay Café. ● **Table 2.1** provides several other examples of product-oriented versus market-oriented business definitions.[3]

Mission statements should be meaningful and specific yet motivating. They should emphasize the company's strengths in the marketplace. Too often, mission statements are written for public relations purposes and lack specific, workable guidelines. Says former GE super-CEO, Jack Welch:[4]

Few leaders actually get the point of forging a mission with real grit and meaning. [Mission statements] have largely devolved into fat-headed jargon. Almost no one can figure out what they mean. [So companies] sort of ignore them or gussy up a vague package deal along the lines of: "our mission is to be the best fill-in-the-blank company in our industry." [Instead, Welch advises, CEOs should] make a choice about how your company will win. Don't mince words! Remember Nike's old mission, "Crush Reebok"? That's directionally correct. And Google's mission statement isn't something namby-pamby like "To be the world's best search engine." It's "To organize the world's information and make it universally accessible and useful." That's simultaneously inspirational, achievable, and completely graspable.

Cold Stone Creamery's mission is "to make people happy around the world by selling the highest quality, most creative experience with passion, excellence, and innovation."

● TABLE | 2.1   Market-Oriented Business Definitions

Company	Product-Oriented Definition	Market-Oriented Definition
Amazon.com	We sell books, videos, CDs, toys, consumer electronics, hardware, housewares, and other products online.	We make the Internet buying experience fast, easy, and enjoyable—we're the place where you can find and discover anything you want to buy online.
Disney	We run theme parks.	We create fantasies—a place where dreams come true and America still works the way it's supposed to.
Google	We provide the world's best online search engine.	We help you organize the world's information and make it universally accessible and useful.
Home Depot	We sell tools and home repair and improvement items.	We empower consumers to achieve the homes of their dreams.
Nike	We sell athletic shoes and apparel.	We bring inspiration and innovation to every athlete* in the world. (*If you have a body, you are an athlete.)
Charles Schwab	We are a brokerage firm.	We are the guardian of our customers' financial dreams.
Revlon	We make cosmetics.	We sell lifestyle and self-expression; success and status; memories, hopes, and dreams.
Ritz-Carlton Hotels	We rent rooms.	We create the Ritz-Carlton experience—one that enlivens the senses, instills well-being, and fulfills even the unexpressed wishes and needs of our guests.
Wal-Mart	We run discount stores.	We deliver low prices every day and give ordinary folks the chance to buy the same things as rich people. "Save Money. Live Better."

> Companies should define themselves not in terms of what they do or make ("We sell athletic shoes") but in terms of how they create value for customers ("We bring inspiration and innovation to every athlete in the world").

Finally, a company's mission should not be stated as making more sales or profits—profits are only a reward for creating value for customers. A company's employees need to feel that their work is significant and that it contributes to people's lives. For example, Microsoft's aim is to help people to "realize their potential." "Your potential, our passion," says the company. Target tells customers to "Expect more. Pay less."

Setting Company Objectives and Goals

The company needs to turn its mission into detailed supporting objectives for each level of management. Each manager should have objectives and be responsible for reaching them. For example, giant chemical company BASF makes and markets a diverse product mix that includes everything from chemicals, plastics, and agricultural products to crude oil and natural gas. But BASF does more than just make chemicals. Its mission is to work with commercial customers in numerous industries to help them employ these chemicals to find innovative solutions and better products for their consumers.

This broad mission leads to a hierarchy of objectives, including business objectives and marketing objectives. ▲BASF's overall objective is to build profitable customer relationships by developing better products. It does this by investing in research—nearly 10 percent of BASF's employees work in research and development. R&D is expensive and requires improved profits to plow back into research programs. So improving profits becomes another major BASF objective. Profits can be improved by increasing sales or reducing costs. Sales can be increased by improving the company's share of domestic and international markets. These goals then become the company's current marketing objectives.[5]

BASF's overall marketing objective is to work with commercial customers/partners to "help make products better." For example, it works with packaging firms to create biodegradable plastic bags and packaging that are "shelf stable for one full year, then completely decompose in compost within a few weeks."

Business portfolio
The collection of businesses and products that make up the company.

Portfolio analysis
The process by which management evaluates the products and businesses that make up the company.

Growth-share matrix
A portfolio-planning method that evaluates a company's strategic business units in terms of its market growth rate and relative market share. SBUs are classified as stars, cash cows, question marks, or dogs.

Marketing strategies and programs must be developed to support these marketing objectives. To increase its market share, BASF might increase its products' availability and promotion in existing markets. To enter new global markets, the company can create new local partnerships within targeted countries. For example, BASF's Agricultural Products division has begun targeting China's farmers with a line of insecticides. To bring the right crop protection solutions to these farmers, BASF has formed working relationships with several Chinese agricultural research organizations, such as Nanjing Agricultural University.[6]

These are BASF's broad marketing strategies. Each broad marketing strategy must then be defined in greater detail. For example, increasing the product's promotion may require more salespeople, advertising, and public relations efforts; if so, both requirements will need to be spelled out. In this way, the firm's mission is translated into a set of objectives for the current period.

Designing the Business Portfolio

Guided by the company's mission statement and objectives, management now must plan its **business portfolio**—the collection of businesses and products that make up the company. The best business portfolio is the one that best fits the company's strengths and weaknesses to opportunities in the environment. Business portfolio planning involves two steps. First, the company must analyze its *current* business portfolio and decide which businesses should receive more, less, or no investment. Second, it must shape the *future* portfolio by developing strategies for growth and downsizing.

Analyzing the Current Business Portfolio

The major activity in strategic planning is business **portfolio analysis**, whereby management evaluates the products and businesses that make up the company. The company will want to put strong resources into its more profitable businesses and phase down or drop its weaker ones.

Management's first step is to identify the key businesses that make up the company, called *strategic business unit* (SBUs). An SBU can be a company division, a product line within a division, or sometimes a single product or brand. The company next assesses the attractiveness of its various SBUs and decides how much support each deserves. When designing a business portfolio, it's a good idea to add and support products and businesses that fit closely with the firm's core philosophy and competencies.

The purpose of strategic planning is to find ways in which the company can best use its strengths to take advantage of attractive opportunities in the environment. So most standard portfolio analysis methods evaluate SBUs on two important dimensions—the attractiveness of the SBU's market or industry and the strength of the SBU's position in that market or industry. The best-known portfolio-planning method was developed by the Boston Consulting Group, a leading management consulting firm.[7]

The Boston Consulting Group Approach. Using the now-classic Boston Consulting Group (BCG) approach, a company classifies all its SBUs according to the **growth-share matrix** as shown in **Figure 2.2**. On the vertical axis, *market growth rate* provides a measure of market attractiveness. On the horizontal axis, *relative market share* serves as a measure of company strength in the market. The growth-share matrix defines four types of SBUs:

Stars. Stars are high-growth, high-share businesses or products. They often need heavy investments to finance their rapid growth. Eventually their growth will slow down, and they will turn into cash cows.

◗FIGURE | 2.2
The BCG Growth-Share Matrix

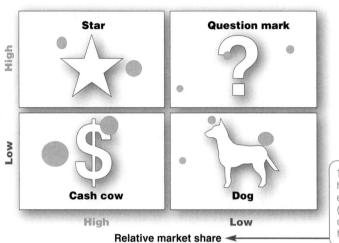

Under this classic Boston Consulting Group portfolio planning approach, the company invests funds from mature, successful products and businesses (cash cows) to support promising products and businesses in faster-growing markets (stars and question marks), hoping to turn them into future cash cows.

The company must decide how much it will invest in each product or business (SBU). For each SBU, it must decide whether to build, hold, harvest, or divest.

Cash cows. Cash cows are low-growth, high-share businesses or products. These established and successful SBUs need less investment to hold their market share. Thus, they produce a lot of cash that the company uses to pay its bills and to support other SBUs that need investment.

Question marks. Question marks are low-share business units in high-growth markets. They require a lot of cash to hold their share, let alone increase it. Management has to think hard about which question marks it should try to build into stars and which should be phased out.

Dogs. Dogs are low-growth, low-share businesses and products. They may generate enough cash to maintain themselves but do not promise to be large sources of cash.

The 10 circles in the growth-share matrix represent a company's 10 current SBUs. The company has two stars, two cash cows, three question marks, and three dogs. The areas of the circles are proportional to the SBU's dollar sales. This company is in fair shape, although not in good shape. It wants to invest in the more promising question marks to make them stars and to maintain the stars so that they will become cash cows as their markets mature. Fortunately, it has two good-sized cash cows. Income from these cash cows will help finance the company's question marks, stars, and dogs. The company should take some decisive action concerning its dogs and its question marks.

Once it has classified its SBUs, the company must determine what role each will play in the future. One of four strategies can be pursued for each SBU. The company can invest more in the business unit in order to *build* its share. Or it can invest just enough to *hold* the SBU's share at the current level. It can *harvest* the SBU, milking its short-term cash flow regardless of the long-term effect. Finally, the company can *divest* the SBU by selling it or phasing it out and using the resources elsewhere.

As time passes, SBUs change their positions in the growth-share matrix. Many SBUs start out as question marks and move into the star category if they succeed. They later become cash cows as market growth falls, then finally die off or turn into dogs toward the end of their life cycle. The company needs to add new products and units continuously so that some of them will become stars and, eventually, cash cows that will help finance other SBUs.

Problems with Matrix Approaches. The BCG and other formal methods revolutionized strategic planning. However, such centralized approaches have limitations: They can be difficult, time consuming, and costly to implement. Management may find it difficult to define SBUs and measure market share and growth. In addition, these approaches focus on classifying *current* businesses, but provide little advice for *future* planning.

Because of such problems, many companies have dropped formal matrix methods in favor of more customized approaches that better suit their specific situations. Moreover, unlike former strategic-planning efforts that rested mostly in the hands of senior managers

▲ Managing the business portfolio: Most people think of Disney as theme parks and wholesome family entertainment, but over the past two decades it's become a sprawling collection of media and entertainment businesses that requires big doses of the famed "Disney Magic" to manage.

at company headquarters, today's strategic planning has been decentralized. Increasingly, companies are placing responsibility for strategic planning in the hands of cross-functional teams of divisional managers who are close to their markets.

For example, consider ▲The Walt Disney Company. Most people think of Disney as theme parks and wholesome family entertainment. But in the mid-1980s Disney set up a powerful, centralized strategic planning group to guide the company's direction and growth. Over the next two decades, the strategic planning group turned The Walt Disney Company into a huge and diverse collection of media and entertainment businesses. The sprawling Disney grew to include everything from theme resorts and film studios (Walt Disney Pictures, Touchstone Pictures, Hollywood Pictures, and others) to media networks (ABC plus Disney Channel, ESPN, A&E, History Channel, and a half dozen others) to consumers products and a cruise line. The newly transformed company proved hard to manage and performed unevenly. Recently, Disney disbanded the centralized strategic planning unit, decentralizing its functions to Disney division managers.

Developing Strategies for Growth and Downsizing

Beyond evaluating current businesses, designing the business portfolio involves finding businesses and products the company should consider in the future. Companies need growth if they are to compete more effectively, satisfy their stakeholders, and attract top talent. "Growth is pure oxygen," states one executive. "It creates a vital, enthusiastic corporation where people see genuine opportunity." At the same time, a firm must be careful not to make growth itself an objective. The company's objective must be to manage "profitable growth."[8] (See **Real Marketing 2.1**.)

Marketing has the main responsibility for achieving profitable growth for the company. Marketing needs to identify, evaluate, and select market opportunities and lay down strategies for capturing them. One useful device for identifying growth opportunities is the **product/market expansion grid**, shown in ◖**Figure 2.3**.[9] We apply it here to Crocs, Inc., the five-year-old company that markets those neon rubbery clogs with Swiss-cheese holes that people either love or hate. With their slip-resistant non-marking soles, Crocs shoes were originally marketed as a boating and outdoor shoe. However, consumers quickly adopted them as a shoe worn for comfort.[10]

First, Crocs might consider whether the company can achieve deeper **market penetration**—making more sales without changing its original product. It can spur growth through marketing mix improvements—adjustments to its product design, advertising, pricing, and distribution efforts. For example, Crocs now offers a rainbow of colors and styles to match any personality or outfit. The company keeps prices of many of its

Product/market expansion grid
A portfolio-planning tool for identifying company growth opportunities through market penetration, market development, product development, or diversification.

Market penetration
A strategy for company growth by increasing sales of current products to current market segments without changing the product.

◖FIGURE | 2.3
The Product/Market
Expansion Grid

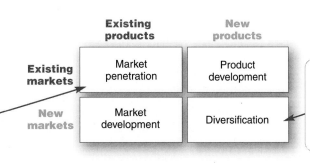

Through market penetration, companies can grow by doing a better job of penetrating current markets with current products. For example, Crocs now offers a rainbow of colors and styles, keeps prices low, and is broadening distribution channels to include everything from sporting good stores and gift shops to a colorful, upbeat Web site.

	Existing products	**New products**
Existing markets	Market penetration	Product development
New markets	Market development	Diversification

Through diversification, companies can grow by starting up or buying businesses outside their current product/markets. For example, Crocs recently acquired the Fury brand, under which it launched an Aeorflex Series of hockey gloves made from Crocs's Croslite material.

Real Marketing 2.1

Starbucks Coffee:
Where Growth Is Hot—But Boiling Over?

More than 25 years ago, Howard Schultz hit on the idea of bringing a European-style coffeehouse to America. He believed that people needed to slow down, to "smell the coffee," and enjoy life a little more. The result is Starbucks. This coffeehouse doesn't sell just coffee, it sells *The Starbucks Experience*—one that "provides an uplifting experience that enriches people's lives one moment, one human being, one extraordinary cup of coffee at a time." Starbucks gives customers what it calls a "third place"—a place away from home and away from work.

Starbucks is now a powerhouse premium brand in a category in which only cheaper commodity products once existed. Some 40 million customers a week flock to its more than 15,000 shops in over 40 countries. Growth has been the engine that has kept Starbucks perking, and over the past two decades, the company's sales and profits have risen like steam off a mug of hot java. Starbucks targets (and regularly achieves) amazing revenue growth exceeding 20 percent each year. During the past decade, Starbucks has delivered a nearly 26 percent average annual return to investors.

Starbucks's success, however, has drawn a host of competitors. These days it seems that everyone is peddling their own brand of premium coffee. To maintain its phenomenal growth in an increasingly overcaffeinated marketplace, Starbucks brewed up an ambitious, multipronged growth strategy. Let's examine the key elements of this strategy:

More store growth: Starbucks has opened new stores at a breakneck pace. A dozen years ago, Starbucks had just 1,015 stores, total—that's about 1,550 fewer than opened last year alone. Starbucks's strategy has been to put stores *everywhere*. One three-block stretch in Chicago contains six of the trendy coffee bars. In New York City, there are two Starbucks in one Macy's store. In fact, cramming so many stores close together caused one satirical publication to run this headline: "A New Starbucks Opens in the Restroom of Existing Starbucks."

To maintain its phenomenal growth, Starbucks brewed up an ambitious growth strategy. But it must be careful to manage growth in a way that enhances the warm and rich *Starbucks Experience*: "Life happens over coffee."

Enhanced Starbucks Experience: Beyond opening new shops, Starbucks has added in-store products and features that get customers to stop in more often, stay longer, and buy more. Over the years, the retailer has beefed up its menu to include hot breakfast sandwiches plus lunch and dinner items, increasing the average customer purchase. To get customers to hang around longer, Starbucks offers wireless Internet access in most of its stores. The chain also offers in-store music downloads, letting customers burn their own CDs while sipping their lattes. Out of cash? No problem—just swipe your prepaid Starbucks Card, "a Starbucks store in your wallet," which now accounts for 15 percent of Starbucks's transactions.

New retail channels: The vast majority of coffee in America is bought in retail stores and brewed at home. To capture this demand, Starbucks has also pushed into America's supermarket aisles. It has a co-branding deal with Kraft, under which Starbucks roasts and packages its coffee and Kraft markets and distributes it. Beyond supermarkets, Starbucks kiosks have popped up everywhere, and service businesses from airlines to car dealerships, now proudly announce "We serve Starbucks coffee." Starbucks has installed coffee shops in Borders Books and Target stores as well as coffee stands in many supermarkets. It also sells gourmet coffee, tea, gifts, and related goods through business and consumer catalogs. And its Web site, www.StarbucksStore.com, has become a kind of "lifestyle portal" on which it sells coffee, tea, coffee-making equipment, compact discs, gifts, and collectibles.

New products and store concepts: Starbucks has partnered over the years with several firms to extend its brand into new categories. For example, it joined with PepsiCo to stamp the Starbucks brand on bottled Frappuccino and its DoubleShot espresso drink. Starbucks ice cream, marketed in a joint venture with Dreyer's, is now the leading brand of coffee ice cream; and Starbucks recently teamed with Hershey to develop a line of coffee-flavored chocolates. Starbucks has also diversified into the entertainment business. Starbucks Entertainment offers customers "the best in music, books, and film" as a part of their daily coffee experience. The entertainment initiative includes Hear Music, which produces and sells music CDs under its own label and also runs its own XM Satellite Radio station.

International growth: Finally, Starbucks has taken its American-brewed concept global. In 1996, the company had only 11 coffeehouses outside North America. By last year, the number had grown to more than 5,000 stores in 42 international markets, from Paris to Osaka, to Oman and Beijing.

Although Starbucks's growth strategy so far has met with amazing success, many analysts have long worried that the company's almost obsessive focus on growth for growth's sake might take a toll on the Starbucks experience. According to one critic, far from its roots

Continued on next page

Real Marketing 2.1 Continued ▼

as a warm and intimate coffeehouse, the Starbucks chain "has evolved into more of a filling station. It is now battling fast-food outlets for some of the same customers in real dollars. Today, about 80 percent of the orders purchased at U.S. Starbucks are consumed outside the store. The average income and education levels of Starbucks customers have gone down."

Additions such as drive-through windows and breakfast sandwiches similar to the Egg McMuffin may spur growth, critics contend, but they have commoditized the brand and diluted the customer experience. More and more, Starbucks now finds itself competing with the likes of—gasp!—McDonald's, which recently began installing coffee bars of its own with baristas serving cappuccinos, lattes, mochas, and the Frappe, similar to the Starbucks ice-blended Frappuccino. In the words of one Chicago barista, "the more and more business they get in the store, the more it seems like another fast-food job."

Even Schultz, who stepped down as CEO in 2000, grew worried. In a 2007 memo to Starbucks management, Schultz lamented that "in order to achieve the growth, development, and scale necessary to go from less than 1,000 stores to 15,000 stores and beyond, [Starbucks had made decisions that may] have led to the watering down of the Starbucks experience"—that Starbucks may be "losing its soul." Something needed to be done, he noted, to shift Starbucks's focus away from its big-business "bureaucracy" and back to customers—to "reignite the emotional attachment with customers."

Sure enough, Starbucks may already be showing signs of overheating. For the first time ever, in the fourth quarter of 2007, the average number of transactions per U.S. store fell off and same-store sales growth slowed. As a result, the company's high-flying share price tumbled. Although suggesting that concerns of overexpansion are exaggerated, Starbucks reacted quickly. In early 2008, Schultz reassumed his role as Starbucks president and CEO. "As we grew rapidly and had phenomenal success," Shultz confirmed, "we started to lose sight of our focus on the customer and

our commitment to continually and creatively enhance the Starbucks Experience."

Schultz quickly promised to cool down the pace of U.S. store growth, close underperforming locations, and initiate store enhancements in all areas that "touch the customer" and advance the customer experience. In spring 2008, Starbucks dramatically closed all of its U.S. locations for three hours to conduct nationwide employee training in the interests of producing more satisfied consumers.

Thus, growth is still perking at Starbucks, but the company must be careful that it doesn't boil over. Growth is important, but Starbucks must manage growth in a way that enhances its core competitive strengths. "At the core, we are a coffee company," says Shultz. "At our core, we celebrate the interaction between us and our customers through the coffee experience. Life happens over coffee."

Sources: Quotes and other information from Janet Adamy, "McDonald's Takes on a Weakened Starbucks," *Wall Street Journal*, January 7, 2008, p. A1; Janet Adamy, "Schultz Takes over to Try to Perk Up Starbucks," *Wall Street Journal*, January 8, 2008, p. B1; "It's Not You, It's Us: Communicating to Employees during Transitions," *PRNews*, March 10, 2008, www.PRnewsonline.com; Emily Bryson York, "Starbucks Plots New Course, Charges Full Steam Ahead," *Advertising Age*, March 19, 2008, http://adage.com/article?article_id=125829; and Starbucks annual reports and other information accessed at www.starbucks.com, November 2008.

Market development
A strategy for company growth by identifying and developing new market segments for current company products.

models low ($29.99), and it is broadening distribution channels to include everything from shoe and department stores to sporting goods stores and gift shops to mail-order catalogs and a colorful, upbeat Web site.

Second, Crocs management might consider possibilities for **market development**— identifying and developing new markets for its current products. For instance, managers could review new *demographic markets*. Perhaps new groups—such as senior consumers—could be encouraged to try Crocs shoes, based on their comfort, slip-resistant sole, and youthful appeal. Managers also could review new *geographical markets*. Crocs is expanding swiftly into international markets. It sells its products in more than 80 countries, generating a third of its revenues outside of the United States.

Third, management could consider **product development**— offering modified or new products to current markets. Many analysts see the original Crocs shoes as a fad. To avoid the swift slide that often accompanies fad products, Crocs has a variety of new designs. ▲For example, over the past five years, the Crocs footwear line has grown to more than 30 rubbery styles, including boots, faux fur lined shoes, flip-flops, and all-terrain shoes. The company has also forged licensing agreements with organizations such as the NFL, MLB, Nickelodeon, and various universities to create sports and entertainment Crocs shoes, allowing fans to sport Red Sox Crocs, Dora Crocs, or Clemson Crocs shoes. The company also has has a new line of high-end designer shoes called YOU by Crocs.

▲ Product development: The Crocs line has grown to more than 30 rubbery styles, including boots, faux fur lined shoes, flip-flops, and all-terrain shoes. The company has also added sports and entertainment Crocs shoes.

Product development
A strategy for company growth by offering modified or new products to current market segments.

Diversification
A strategy for company growth through starting up or acquiring businesses outside the company's current products and markets.

Downsizing
Reducing the business portfolio by eliminating products of business units that are not profitable or that no longer fit the company's overall strategy.

Fourth, Crocs might consider **diversification**—starting up or buying businesses outside of its current products and markets. For example, Crocs recently purchased Jibbitz, LLC, which makes accessories that can be snapped into existing air holes in Crocs shoes. It also purchased Ocean Minded, Inc., which makes sandals for the beach, adventure, and action sport markets, taking Crocs into the surf and skate footwear category. Through still another acquisition, Fury, Crocs is entering the market for hockey and lacrosse equipment, such as sticks, shin pads, and elbow pads. Under the Fury name, Crocs recently launched an Aeroflex Series line of hockey gloves that feature Crocs's Croslite material.

Companies must not only develop strategies for *growing* their business portfolios, but also strategies for **downsizing** them. There are many reasons that a firm might want to abandon products or markets. The market environment might change, making some of the company's products or markets less profitable. The firm may have grown too fast or entered areas where it lacks experience. This can occur when a firm enters too many international markets without the proper research, or when a company introduces new products that do not offer superior customer value. Finally, some products or business units simply age and die.

When a firm finds brands or businesses that are unprofitable or that no longer fit its overall strategy, it must carefully prune, harvest, or divest them. Weak businesses usually require a disproportionate amount of management attention. Managers should focus on promising growth opportunities, not fritter away energy trying to salvage fading ones.

Author Comment | Marketing, alone, can't create superior customer value. Under the companywide strategic plan, marketers must work closely with other departments to form an effective company value chain and then must work with other companies in the marketing system to create an overall value delivery network that jointly serves customers.

Planning Marketing: Partnering to Build Customer Relationships (pp 46–48)

The company's strategic plan establishes what kinds of businesses the company will operate and its objectives for each. Then, within each business unit, more detailed planning takes place. The major functional departments in each unit—marketing, finance, accounting, purchasing, operations, information systems, human resources, and others—must work together to accomplish strategic objectives.

Marketing plays a key role in the company's strategic planning in several ways. First, marketing provides a guiding *philosophy*—the marketing concept—that suggests that company strategy should revolve around building profitable relationships with important consumer groups. Second, marketing provides *inputs* to strategic planners by helping to identify attractive market opportunities and by assessing the firm's potential to take advantage of them. Finally, within individual business units, marketing designs *strategies* for reaching the unit's objectives. Once the unit's objectives are set, marketing's task is to help carry them out profitably.

Customer value is the key ingredient in the marketer's formula for success. However, as we noted in Chapter 1, marketers alone cannot produce superior value for customers. Although marketing plays a leading role, it can be only a partner in attracting, keeping, and growing customers. In addition to *customer relationship management*, marketers must also practice *partner relationship management*. They must work closely with partners in other company departments to form an effective *value chain* that serves the customer. Moreover, they must partner effectively with other companies in the marketing system to form a competitively superior *value delivery network*. We now take a closer look at the concepts of a company value chain and a value delivery network.

Partnering with Other Company Departments

Value chain
The series of departments that carry out value-creating activities to design, produce, market, deliver, and support a firm's products.

Each company department can be thought of as a link in the company's **value chain**.[11] That is, each department carries out value-creating activities to design, produce, market, deliver, and support the firm's products. The firm's success depends not only on how well each department performs its work, but also on how well the various departments coordinate their activities.

For example, Wal-Mart's goal is to create customer value and satisfaction by providing shoppers with the products they want at the lowest possible prices. Marketers at Wal-Mart play an important role. They learn what customers need and stock the stores' shelves with the

▲ The value chain: Wal-Mart's ability to help you "Save money. Live Better." by offering the right products at lower prices depends on the contributions of people in all of the company's departments.

desired products at unbeatable low prices. They prepare advertising and merchandising programs and assist shoppers with customer service. Through these and other activities, Wal-Mart's marketers help deliver value to customers.

However, the marketing department needs help from the company's other departments. ▲Wal-Mart's ability to offer the right products at low prices depends on the purchasing department's skill in developing the needed suppliers and buying from them at low cost. Wal-Mart's information technology department must provide fast and accurate information about which products are selling in each store. And its operations people must provide effective, low-cost merchandise handling.

A company's value chain is only as strong as its weakest link. Success depends on how well each department performs its work of adding customer value and on how well the activities of various departments are coordinated. At Wal-Mart, if purchasing can't obtain the lowest prices from suppliers, or if operations can't distribute merchandise at the lowest costs, then marketing can't deliver on its promise of lowest prices.

Ideally then, a company's different functions should work in harmony to produce value for consumers. But, in practice, departmental relations are full of conflicts and misunderstandings. The marketing department takes the consumer's point of view. But when marketing tries to develop customer satisfaction, it can cause other departments to do a poorer job *in their terms*. Marketing department actions can increase purchasing costs, disrupt production schedules, increase inventories, and create budget headaches. Thus, the other departments may resist the marketing department's efforts.

Yet marketers must find ways to get all departments to "think consumer" and to develop a smoothly functioning value chain. The idea is to "maximize the customer experience across the organization and its various customer touch points," says a marketing consultant. ▲Jack Welch, the highly regarded former GE CEO, told his employees, "Companies can't give job security. Only customers can!" He emphasized that all GE people, regardless of their department, have an impact on customer satisfaction and retention. His message: "If you are not thinking customer, you are not thinking."[12]

▲ "If you are not thinking customer, you are not thinking." *Jack Welch, former GE CEO*

Partnering with Others in the Marketing System

In its quest to create customer value, the firm needs to look beyond its own value chain and into the value chains of its suppliers, distributors, and, ultimately, its customers. Consider McDonald's. McDonald's nearly 30,000 restaurants in more than 100 countries serve more than 52 million customers daily, capturing over 40 percent of the burger market.[13] People do not swarm to McDonald's only because they love the chain's hamburgers. In fact, consumers typically rank McDonald's behind Burger King and Wendy's in taste. Consumers flock to the McDonald's *system*, not just to its food products. Throughout the world, McDonald's finely tuned system delivers a high standard of what the company calls QSCV—quality, service, cleanliness, and value. McDonald's is effective only to the extent that it successfully partners with its franchisees, suppliers, and others to jointly deliver exceptionally high customer value.

Value delivery network
The network made up of the company, suppliers, distributors, and, ultimately, customers who "partner" with each other to improve the performance of the entire system.

More companies today are partnering with the other members of the supply chain to improve the performance of the customer **value delivery network**. For example, Toyota knows the importance of building close relationships with its suppliers. In fact, it even includes the phrase "achieve supplier satisfaction" in its mission statement:

Achieving satisfying supplier relationships has been a cornerstone of Toyota's stunning success. In one recent survey of parts makers—which measured items such as degree of trust, open and honest communication, amount of help given to reduce costs, and the opportunity to make a profit—Toyota scored far higher than competitors. On a scale of 1 to 500, with an industry mean of 270, Toyota rated 415, whereas GM rated 174 and Ford rated just 162. U.S. competitors often alienate their suppliers through self-serving,

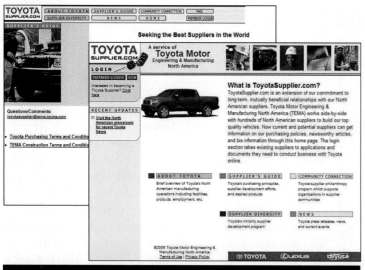

▲ Toyota partners with its suppliers and helps them meet its very high expectations. Creating satisfied suppliers helps Toyota produce lower-cost, higher-quality cars, which in turn result in more satisfied customers.

heavy-handed dealings. "The [U.S. automakers] set annual cost-reduction targets [for the parts they buy]," says one supplier. "To realize those targets, they'll do anything. [They've unleashed] a reign of terror, and it gets worse every year." Says another, "[Ford] seems to send its people to 'hate school' so that they learn how to hate suppliers."

By contrast, rather than bullying suppliers, ▲ Toyota partners with them and helps them to meet its very high expectations. Toyota learns about their businesses, conducts joint improvement activities, helps train supplier employees, gives daily performance feedback, and actively seeks out supplier concerns. It even recognizes top performers with annual performance awards. The high supplier satisfaction means that Toyota can rely on suppliers to help it improve its own quality, reduce costs, and develop new products quickly. For example, when Toyota recently launched a program to reduce prices by 30 percent on 170 parts that it would buy for its next generation of cars, suppliers didn't complain. Instead, they pitched in, trusting that Toyota would help them achieve the targeted reductions, in turn making them more competitive and profitable in the future. In all, creating satisfied suppliers helps Toyota to produce lower-cost, higher-quality cars, which in turn results in more satisfied customers.[14]

Increasingly in today's marketplace, competition no longer takes place between individual competitors. Rather, it takes place between the entire value delivery networks created by these competitors. Thus, Toyota's performance against Ford depends on the quality of Toyota's overall value delivery network versus Ford's. Even if Toyota makes the best cars, it might lose in the marketplace if Ford's dealer network provides more customer-satisfying sales and service.

Author Comment | Now that we've set the context in terms of companywide strategy, it's time to talk about customer-driven marketing strategy and programs!

Marketing Strategy and the Marketing Mix (pp 48–53)

The strategic plan defines the company's overall mission and objectives. Marketing's role and activities are shown in ⬥ **Figure 2.4**, which summarizes the major activities involved in managing a customer-driven marketing strategy and the marketing mix.

Consumers stand in the center. The goal is to create value for customers and build profitable customer relationships. Next comes **marketing strategy**—the marketing logic by which the company hopes to create this customer value and achieve these profitable relationships. The company decides which customers it will serve (segmentation and targeting) and how (differentiation and positioning). It identifies the total market, then divides it into smaller segments, selects the most promising segments, and focuses on serving and satisfying the customers in these segments.

Guided by marketing strategy, the company designs an integrated *marketing mix* made up of factors under its control—product, price, place, and promotion (the four Ps). To find the best marketing strategy and mix, the company engages in marketing analysis, planning, implementation, and control. Through these activities, the company watches and adapts to the actors and forces in the marketing environment. We will now look briefly at each activity. Then, in later chapters, we will discuss each one in more depth.

Marketing strategy
The marketing logic by which the business unit hopes to create customer value and achieve profitable customer relationships.

Customer-Driven Marketing Strategy

As we emphasized throughout Chapter 1, to succeed in today's competitive marketplace, companies need to be customer centered. They must win customers from competitors, then keep and grow them by delivering greater value. But before it can satisfy consumers, a

FIGURE | 2.4
Managing Marketing Strategies
and the Marketing Mix

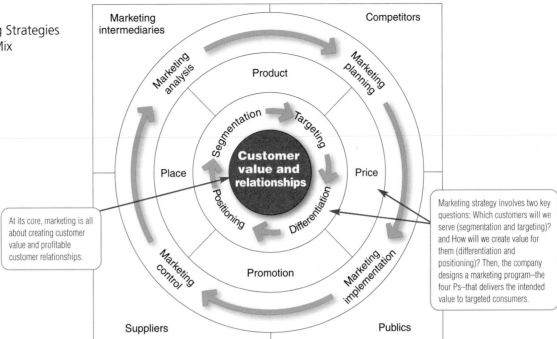

FIGURE | 2.4
Managing Marketing Strategies
and the Marketing Mix

At its core, marketing is all about creating customer value and profitable customer relationships.

Marketing strategy involves two key questions: Which customers will we serve (segmentation and targeting)? and How will we create value for them (differentiation and positioning)? Then, the company designs a marketing program—the four Ps—that delivers the intended value to targeted consumers.

company must first understand their needs and wants. Thus, sound marketing requires a careful customer analysis.

Companies know that they cannot profitably serve all consumers in a given market—at least not all consumers in the same way. There are too many different kinds of consumers with too many different kinds of needs. And most companies are in a position to serve some segments better than others. Thus, each company must divide up the total market, choose the best segments, and design strategies for profitably serving chosen segments. This process involves *market segmentation*, *market targeting*, *differentiation*, and *positioning*.

Market Segmentation

The market consists of many types of customers, products, and needs. The marketer has to determine which segments offer the best opportunities. Consumers can be grouped and served in various ways based on geographic, demographic, psychographic, and behavioral factors. The process of dividing a market into distinct groups of buyers who have different needs, characteristics, or behaviors, and who might require separate products or marketing programs is called **market segmentation**.

Every market has segments, but not all ways of segmenting a market are equally useful. For example, Tylenol would gain little by distinguishing between low-income and high-income pain reliever users if both respond the same way to marketing efforts. A **market segment** consists of consumers who respond in a similar way to a given set of marketing efforts. In the car market, for example, consumers who want the biggest, most comfortable car regardless of price make up one market segment. Consumers who care mainly about price and operating economy make up another segment. It would be difficult to make one car model that was the first choice of consumers in both segments. Companies are wise to focus their efforts on meeting the distinct needs of individual market segments.

Market Targeting

After a company has defined market segments, it can enter one or many of these segments. **Market targeting** involves evaluating each market segment's attractiveness and selecting one or more segments to enter. A company should target segments in which it can profitably generate the greatest customer value and sustain it over time.

A company with limited resources might decide to serve only one or a few special segments or "market niches." Such "nichers" specialize in serving customer segments that major competitors overlook or ignore. For example, Ferrari sells only 1,500 of its very high-performance cars in the United States each year, but at very high prices—from an

Market segmentation
Dividing a market into distinct groups of buyers who have different needs, characteristics, or behaviors, and who might require separate products or marketing programs.

Market segment
A group of consumers who respond in a similar way to a given set of marketing efforts.

Market targeting
The process of evaluating each market segment's attractiveness and selecting one or more segments to enter.

eye-opening $190,000 for its Ferrari F430 model to an astonishing $2 million for its FXX super sports car, which can be driven only on race tracks (it sold 10 in the United States last year). Most nichers aren't quite so exotic. White Wave, maker of Silk Soymilk, has found its niche as the nation's largest soymilk producer. And Veterinary Pet Insurance is tiny compared with the insurance industry giants, but it captures a profitable 60 percent share of all health insurance policies for our furry—or feathery—friends (see **Real Marketing 2.2**).

Alternatively, a company might choose to serve several related segments—perhaps those with different kinds of customers but with the same basic wants. Abercrombie & Fitch, for example, targets college students, teens, and kids with the same upscale, casual clothes and accessories in three different outlets: the original Abercrombie & Fitch, Hollister, and Abercrombie. Or a large company might decide to offer a complete range of products to serve all market segments.

Most companies enter a new market by serving a single segment, and if this proves successful, they add more segments. Large companies eventually seek full market coverage. They want to be the General Motors of their industry. GM says that it makes a car for every "person, purse, and personality." The leading company normally has different products designed to meet the special needs of each segment.

Market Differentiation and Positioning

Positioning
Arranging for a product to occupy a clear, distinctive, and desirable place relative to competing products in the minds of target consumers.

Differentiation
Actually differentiating the market offering to create superior customer value.

After a company has decided which market segments to enter, it must decide how it will differentiate its market offering for each targeted segment and what positions it wants to occupy in those segments. A product's *position* is the place the product occupies relative to competitors' products in consumers' minds. Marketers want to develop unique market positions for their products. If a product is perceived to be exactly like others on the market, consumers would have no reason to buy it.

Positioning is arranging for a product to occupy a clear, distinctive, and desirable place relative to competing products in the minds of target consumers. As one positioning expert puts it, positioning is "why a shopper will pay a little more for your brand."[15] Thus, marketers plan positions that distinguish their products from competing brands and give them the greatest advantage in their target markets.

Thus, Wal-Mart promises "Save Money. Live Better."; Target says "Expect More. Pay Less."; MasterCard gives you "priceless" experiences; and whether it's an everyday moment or the moment of a lifetime, "Life Takes VISA." Similarly, Epicurious.com is a site "for people who love to eat." Its ads tell you to "get closer to your food." Such deceptively simple statements form the backbone of a product's marketing strategy. For example, ▲ VISA has designed its entire integrated marketing campaign around the "Life Takes VISA" slogan.

In positioning its product, the company first identifies possible customer value differences that provide competitive advantages upon which to build the position. The company can offer greater customer value either by charging lower prices than competitors, or by offering more benefits to justify higher prices. But if the company *promises* greater value, it must then *deliver* that greater value. Thus, effective positioning begins with **differentiation**—actually *differentiating* the company's market offering so that it gives consumers more value. Once the company has chosen a desired position, it must take strong steps to deliver and communicate that position to target consumers. The company's entire marketing program should support the chosen positioning strategy.

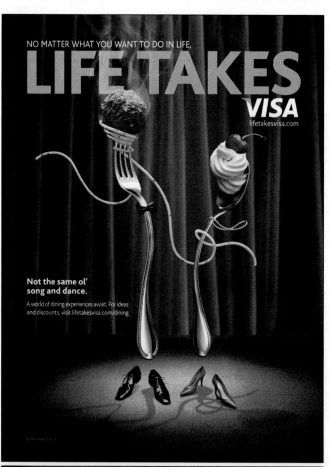

NO MATTER WHAT YOU WANT TO DO IN LIFE,
LIFE TAKES
VISA
lifetakesvisa.com

Not the same ol' song and dance.
A world of dining experiences await. For ideas and discounts, visit lifetakesvisa.com/dining

▲ Positioning: VISA has designed its entire integrated marketing campaign around the deceptively simple "Life Takes VISA" slogan. Ads like this one take you to lifetakesvisa.com microsites with articles, tips, and special offers tailored to specific interests and lifestyles—here the world of food and restaurants.

Real Marketing 2.2

Niching:

Health Insurance for Our Furry— or Feathery— Friends

Health insurance for pets? MetLife, Prudential, Northwestern Mutual, and most other large insurance companies haven't paid much attention to it. But that leaves plenty of room for more-focused nichers, for whom pet health insurance has become a lucrative business. The largest of the small competitors is Veterinary Pet Insurance (VPI). VPI's mission is to "make the miracles of veterinary medicine affordable to all pet owners."

Pet insurance is a still-small but fast-growing segment of the insurance business. Insiders think the industry offers huge potential. Currently, 63 percent of all U.S. households own at least one pet. Collectively, Americans own some 75 million dogs, 88 million cats, 142 million freshwater fish, 10 million saltwater fish, 16 million birds, 24 million small animals, 13 million reptiles, and 14 million horses. More than two-thirds have included their pets in holiday celebrations and one-third characterize their pet as a child. Some 42 percent of dogs now sleep in the same bed as their owners. Americans spend a whopping $41 billion a year on their pets, more than the gross domestic product of all but 64 countries in the world. They spend $9.8 billion of that on pet health care.

Unlike in Britain and Sweden, where almost half of all pets owners carry pet health insurance, relatively few pet owners in the United States now carry such coverage. However, a recent study of pet owners found that nearly 75 percent are willing to go into debt to pay for veterinary care for their furry— or feathery—companions. And for many pet medical procedures, they'd have to! If not diagnosed quickly, even a mundane ear infection in a dog can result in $1,000 worth of medical treatment. Ten days of dialysis treatment can reach $12,000 and cancer treatment as much as $40,000. All of this adds up to a lot of potential growth for pet health insurers.

VPI plans cover a multitude of pet medical problems and conditions. The insurance helps pay for office calls, prescriptions, treatments,

FAMILY *Redefined.*

Enroll Today at **PETINSURANCE.COM** *or* **800-944-1649**

He's not just a dog. He's your baby and deserves the best medical care. VPI Pet Insurance helps pay for your pet's lab fees, medications, surgeries, X-rays, and more. We even offer coverage for routine care, including vaccinations and prescription flea control. Plus, you're free to use any veterinarian. That's the kind of protection you need for all your family members. Call today for a free quote.

All applications are subject to underwriting approval. / Read your policy for complete coverage details / Underwritten by Veterinary Pet Insurance Company (CA). Brea, CA / National Casualty Company (NAIC). Madison, WI, an A+15 rated company / ©2008 Veterinary Pet Insurance Company

VPI PET Insurance

Nichers: Market nicher VPI is growing faster than a new-born puppy. Its mission is to "be the trusted choice of America's pet lovers."

lab fees, x-rays, surgery, and hospitalization. Like its handful of competitors, VPI issues health insurance policies for dogs and cats. Unlike its competitors, VPI covers a menagerie of exotic pets as well. Among other critters, the Avian and Exotic Pet Plan covers birds, rabbits, ferrets, rats, guinea pigs, snakes and other reptiles, iguanas, turtles, hedgehogs, and potbellied pigs. "There's such a vast array of pets," says a VPI executive, "and people love them. We have to respect that."

How's VPI doing in its niche? It's growing like a newborn puppy. VPI is by far the largest of the handful of companies that offer pet insurance, providing more than 60 percent of all U.S. pet insurance policies. Since its inception, VPI has issued more than one million policies, and it now serves more than 460,000 policyholders. Sales have grown rapidly, exceeding $148 million in policy premiums last year. That might not amount to

much for the likes of MetLife, Prudential, or Northwestern Mutual, which rack up tens of billions of dollars in yearly revenues. But it's profitable business for nichers like VPI. And there's room to grow. Only about 3 percent of pet owners currently buy pet insurance.

"Pet health insurance is no longer deemed so outlandish in a world where acupuncture for cats, hospice of dogs, and Prozac for ferrets are part of a veterinarian's routine," says one analyst. Such insurance is a real godsend for VPI's policyholders. Just ask Joe and Paula Sena, whose cocker spaniel, Elvis, is receiving radiation treatments for cancer. "He is not like our kids—he is our kid," says Ms. Sena. "He is a kid in a dog's body." VPI is making Elvis's treatment possible by picking up a lion's share of the costs. As more people adopt the Sena's view towards their pets, it's hard to think the pet industry isn't just beginning to stretch its paws.

Sources: See Diane Brady and Christopher Palmeri, "The Pet Economy," *BusinessWeek*, August 6, 2007, pp. 45–54; Yilu Zhao, "Break a Leg, Fluffy, If You Have Insurance," *New York Times*, June 30, 2002, p. 9.11; Damon Darlin, "Vet Bills and the Priceless Pet: What's a Practical Owner to Do?" *New York Times*, May 13, 2006, p. C1; "New National Pet Owners Survey Details Two Decades of Evolving American Pet Ownership," American Pet Products Manufacturers Association, June 18, 2007, www.appma.com; "Multiple Pet Owners with VPI Pet Insurance Represent 17% of All Policyholders," *PR Newswire*, July 30, 2007, p. 1; "All in the Family," *Marketing Management*, January/February 2008, p. 7; and information accessed at www.petinsurance.com, September 2008.

Developing an Integrated Marketing Mix

After deciding on its overall marketing strategy, the company is ready to begin planning the details of the marketing mix, one of the major concepts in modern marketing. The **marketing mix** is the set of controllable, tactical marketing tools that the firm blends to produce the response it wants in the target market. The marketing mix consists of everything the firm can do to influence the demand for its product. The many possibilities can be collected into four groups of variables known as "the four Ps": *product, price, place,* and *promotion.* ◗ **Figure 2.5** shows the marketing tools under each *P.*

Product means the goods-and-services combination the company offers to the target market. Thus, a Ford Escape consists of nuts and bolts, spark plugs, pistons, headlights, and thousands of other parts. Ford offers several Escape models and dozens of optional features. The car comes fully serviced and with a comprehensive warranty that is as much a part of the product as the tailpipe.

Price is the amount of money customers must pay to obtain the product. Ford calculates suggested retail prices that its dealers might charge for each Escape. But Ford dealers rarely charge the full sticker price. Instead, they negotiate the price with each customer, offering discounts, trade-in allowances, and credit terms. These actions adjust prices for the current competitive situation and bring them into line with the buyer's perception of the car's value.

Place includes company activities that make the product available to target consumers. Ford partners with a large body of independently owned dealerships that sell the company's many different models. Ford selects its dealers carefully and supports them strongly. The dealers keep an inventory of Ford automobiles, demonstrate them to potential buyers, negotiate prices, close sales, and service the cars after the sale.

Promotion means activities that communicate the merits of the product and persuade target customers to buy it. Ford Motor Company spends more than $2.5 billion each year on U.S. advertising to tell consumers about the company and its many products.[16] Dealership salespeople assist potential buyers and persuade them that Ford is the best car for them. Ford and its dealers offer special promotions—sales, cash rebates, low-financing rates—as added purchase incentives.

An effective marketing program blends all of the marketing mix elements into an integrated marketing program designed to achieve the company's marketing objectives by

Marketing mix
The set of controllable tactical marketing tools—product, price, place, and promotion—that the firm blends to produce the response it wants in the target market.

◗ FIGURE | 2.5
The Four Ps of the Marketing Mix

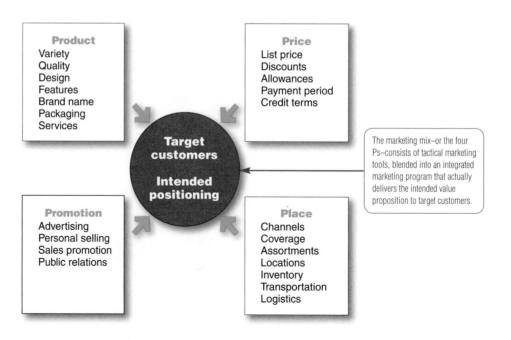

Product
Variety
Quality
Design
Features
Brand name
Packaging
Services

Price
List price
Discounts
Allowances
Payment period
Credit terms

Target customers

Intended positioning

Promotion
Advertising
Personal selling
Sales promotion
Public relations

Place
Channels
Coverage
Assortments
Locations
Inventory
Transportation
Logistics

The marketing mix—or the four Ps—consists of tactical marketing tools, blended into an integrated marketing program that actually delivers the intended value proposition to target customers.

delivering value to consumers. The marketing mix constitutes the company's tactical tool kit for establishing strong positioning in target markets.

Some critics think that the four Ps may omit or underemphasize certain important activities. For example, they ask, "Where are services?" Just because they don't start with a *P* doesn't justify omitting them. The answer is that services, such as banking, airline, and retailing services, are products too. We might call them *service products*. "Where is packaging?" the critics might ask. Marketers would answer that they include packaging as just one of many product decisions. All said, as Figure 2.5 suggests, many marketing activities that might appear to be left out of the marketing mix are subsumed under one of the four Ps. The issue is not whether there should be four, six, or ten Ps so much as what framework is most helpful in designing integrated marketing programs.

There is another concern, however, that is valid. It holds that the four Ps concept takes the seller's view of the market, not the buyer's view. From the buyer's viewpoint, in this age of customer value and relationships, the four Ps might be better described as the four Cs:[17]

4Ps	4Cs
Product	Customer solution
Price	Customer cost
Place	Convenience
Promotion	Communication

Thus, whereas marketers see themselves as selling products, customers see themselves as buying value or solutions to their problems. And customers are interested in more than just the price; they are interested in the total costs of obtaining, using, and disposing of a product. Customers want the product and service to be as conveniently available as possible. Finally, they want two-way communication. Marketers would do well to think through the four Cs first and then build the four Ps on that platform.

Author Comment | So far we've focused on the *marketing* in marketing management. Now, let's turn to the *management*.

Managing the Marketing Effort (pp 53–57)

In addition to being good at the *marketing* in marketing management, companies also need to pay attention to the *management*. Managing the marketing process requires the four marketing management functions shown in Figure 2.6—*analysis*, *planning*, *implementation*, and *control*. The company first develops companywide strategic plans and then translates them into marketing and other plans for each division, product, and brand. Through implementation, the company turns the plans into actions. Control consists of measuring and evaluating the results of marketing activities and taking corrective action where needed. Finally, marketing analysis provides information and evaluations needed for all of the other marketing activities.

Marketing Analysis

Managing the marketing function begins with a complete analysis of the company's situation. The marketer should conduct a **SWOT analysis**, by which it evaluates the company's overall strengths (S), weaknesses (W), opportunities (O), and threats (T) (see Figure 2.7). Strengths include internal capabilities, resources, and positive situational factors that may help the company to serve its customers and achieve its objectives. Weaknesses include internal limitations and negative situational factors that may interfere with the company's performance. Opportunities are favorable factors or trends in the external environment that the company may be able to exploit to its advantage. And threats are unfavorable external factors or trends that may present challenges to performance.

The company should analyze its markets and marketing environment to find attractive opportunities and identify environmental threats. It should analyze company strengths and weaknesses as well as current and possible marketing actions to determine which opportunities it can best pursue. The goal is to match the company's strengths to attractive

SWOT analysis
An overall evaluation of the company's strengths (S), weaknesses (W), opportunities (O), and threats (T).

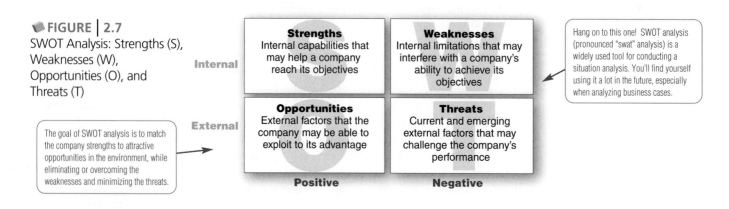

FIGURE | 2.6
Managing Marketing: Analysis, Planning, Implementation, and Control

Analysis

Planning
Develop strategic plans

Develop marketing plans

Implementation
Carry out the plans

Control
Measure results

Evaluate results

Take corrective action

> The first part of the chapter dealt with this—developing companywide and marketing strategies and plans.

> We'll close the chapter by looking at how marketers manage those strategies and plans—how they implement marketing strategies and programs and evaluate the results.

opportunities in the environment, while eliminating or overcoming the weaknesses and minimizing the threats. Marketing analysis provides inputs to each of the other marketing management functions. We discuss marketing analysis more fully in Chapter 3.

Marketing Planning

Through strategic planning, the company decides what it wants to do with each business unit. Marketing planning involves deciding on marketing strategies that will help the company attain its overall strategic objectives. A detailed marketing plan is needed for each business, product, or brand. What does a marketing plan look like? Our discussion focuses on product or brand marketing plans.

● **Table 2.2** outlines the major sections of a typical product or brand marketing plan. (See Appendix 1 for a sample marketing plan.) The plan begins with an executive summary that quickly reviews major assessments, goals, and recommendations. The main section of the plan presents a detailed SWOT analysis of the current marketing situation as well as potential threats and opportunities. The plan next states major objectives for the brand and outlines the specifics of a marketing strategy for achieving them.

A *marketing strategy* consists of specific strategies for target markets, positioning, the marketing mix, and marketing expenditure levels. It outlines how the company intends to create value for target customers in order to capture value in return. In this section, the planner explains how each strategy responds to the threats, opportunities, and critical issues spelled out earlier in the plan. Additional sections of the marketing plan lay out an action program for implementing the marketing strategy along with the details of a supporting *marketing budget*. The last section outlines the controls that will be used to monitor progress, measure return on marketing investment, and take corrective action.

FIGURE | 2.7
SWOT Analysis: Strengths (S), Weaknesses (W), Opportunities (O), and Threats (T)

Internal

Strengths
Internal capabilities that may help a company reach its objectives

Weaknesses
Internal limitations that may interfere with a company's ability to achieve its objectives

External

Opportunities
External factors that the company may be able to exploit to its advantage

Threats
Current and emerging external factors that may challenge the company's performance

Positive   **Negative**

> Hang on to this one! SWOT analysis (pronounced "swat" analysis) is a widely used tool for conducting a situation analysis. You'll find yourself using it a lot in the future, especially when analyzing business cases.

> The goal of SWOT analysis is to match the company strengths to attractive opportunities in the environment, while eliminating or overcoming the weaknesses and minimizing the threats.

Marketing Implementation

Marketing implementation
The process that turns marketing strategies and plans into marketing actions in order to accomplish strategic marketing objectives.

Planning good strategies is only a start toward successful marketing. A brilliant marketing strategy counts for little if the company fails to implement it properly. **Marketing implementation** is the process that turns marketing *plans* into marketing *actions* in order to accomplish strategic marketing objectives. Whereas marketing planning addresses the *what* and *why* of marketing activities, implementation addresses the *who*, *where*, *when*, and *how*.

Many managers think that "doing things right" (implementation) is as important as, or even more important than, "doing the right things" (strategy). The fact is that both are critical to success, and companies can gain competitive advantages through effective implementation. One firm can have essentially the same strategy as another, yet win in the marketplace through faster or better execution. Still, implementation is difficult—it is often easier to think up good marketing strategies than it is to carry them out.

In an increasingly connected world, people at all levels of the marketing system must work together to implement marketing strategies and plans. At Black & Decker, for example,

● TABLE | 2.2   Contents of a Marketing Plan ◄— To see this in action, check out the sample marketing plan in Appendix 1.

Section	Purpose
Executive summary	Presents a brief summary of the main goals and recommendations of the plan for management review, helping top management to find the plan's major points quickly. A table of contents should follow the executive summary.
Current marketing situation	Describes the target market and company's position in it, including information about the market, product performance, competition, and distribution. This section includes, • a *market description*, that defines the market and major segments, then reviews customer needs and factors in the marketing environment that may affect customer purchasing. • a *product review* that shows sales, prices, and gross margins of the major products in the product line. • a review of *competition* that identifies major competitors and assesses their market positions and strategies for product quality, pricing, distribution, and promotion. • a review of *distribution* that evaluates recent sales trends and other developments in major distribution channels.
Threats and opportunities analysis	Assesses major threats and opportunities that the product might face, helping management to anticipate important positive or negative developments that might have an impact on the firm and its strategies.
Objectives and issues	States the marketing objectives that the company would like to attain during the plan's term and discusses key issues that will affect their attainment. For example, if the goal is to achieve a 15 percent market share, this section looks at how this goal might be achieved.
Marketing strategy	Outlines the broad marketing logic by which the business unit hopes to create customer value and relationships and the specifics of target markets, positioning, and marketing expenditure levels. How will the company create value for customers in order to capture value from customers in return? This section also outlines specific strategies for each marketing mix element and explains how each responds to the threats, opportunities, and critical issues spelled out earlier in the plan.
Action programs	Spells out how marketing strategies will be turned into specific action programs that answer the following questions: *What* will be done? *When* will it be done? *Who* will do it? *How* much will it cost?
Budgets	Details a supporting marketing budget that is essentially a projected profit-and-loss statement. It shows expected revenues (forecasted number of units sold and the average net price) and expected costs of production, distribution, and marketing. The difference is the projected profit. Once approved by higher management, the budget becomes the basis for materials buying, production scheduling, personnel planning, and marketing operations.
Controls	Outlines the control that will be used to monitor progress and allow higher management to review implementation results and spot products that are not meeting their goals. It includes measures of return on marketing investment.

marketing implementation for the company's power tools, outdoor equipment, and other products requires day-to-day decisions and actions by thousands of people both inside and outside the organization. Marketing managers make decisions about target segments, branding, packaging, pricing, promoting, and distributing. They talk with engineering about product design, with manufacturing about production and inventory levels, and with finance about funding and cash flows. They also connect with outside people, such as advertising agencies to plan ad campaigns and the news media to obtain publicity support. The sales force urges Home Depot, Lowe's, and other retailers to advertise Black & Decker products, provide ample shelf space, and use company displays.

Marketing Department Organization

The company must design a marketing organization that can carry out marketing strategies and plans. If the company is very small, one person might do all of the research, selling, advertising, customer service, and other marketing work. As the company expands, a marketing department emerges to plan and carry out marketing activities. In large companies, this department contains many specialists. They have product and market managers, sales managers and salespeople, market researchers, advertising experts, and many other specialists.

To head up such large marketing organizations, many companies have now created a *chief marketing officer* (or CMO) position. The CMO heads up the company's entire marketing operation and represents marketing on the company's top management team. The CMO position puts marketing on equal footing with other C-level executives, such as the chief executive officer (CEO) and the chief financial officer (CFO).[18]

Modern marketing departments can be arranged in several ways. The most common form of marketing organization is the *functional organization*. Under this organization, different marketing activities are headed by a functional specialist—a sales manager, advertising manager, marketing research manager, customer-service manager, or new-product manager. A company that sells across the country or internationally often uses a *geographic organization*. Its sales and marketing people are assigned to specific countries, regions, and districts. Geographic organization allows salespeople to settle into a territory, get to know their customers, and work with a minimum of travel time and cost.

Companies with many very different products or brands often create a *product management organization*. Using this approach, a product manager develops and implements a complete strategy and marketing program for a specific product or brand. Product management first appeared at Procter & Gamble in 1929. A new company soap, Camay, was not doing well and a young P&G executive was assigned to give his exclusive attention to developing and promoting this product. He was successful, and the company soon added other product managers.[19] Since then, many firms, especially consumer-products companies, have set up product management organizations.

For companies that sell one product line to many different types of markets and customers that have different needs and preferences, a *market* or *customer management organization* might be best. A market management organization is similar to the product management organization. Market managers are responsible for developing marketing strategies and plans for their specific markets or customers. This system's main advantage is that the company is organized around the needs of specific customer segments. Many companies develop special organizations to manage their relationships with large customers. For example, companies such as Procter & Gamble and Black & Decker have large teams, or even whole divisions, set up to serve large customers such as Wal-Mart, Target, Safeway, or Home Depot.

Large companies that produce many different products flowing into many different geographic and customer markets usually employ some *combination* of the functional, geographic, product, and market organization forms. This ensures that each function, product, and market receives its share of management attention. However, it can also add costly layers of management and reduce organizational flexibility. Still, the benefits of organizational specialization usually outweigh the drawbacks.

Marketing organization has become an increasingly important issue in recent years. As we discussed in Chapter 1, today's marketing environment calls for less focus on

▲ Marketers must continually plan their analysis, implementation, and control activities.

Marketing control
The process of measuring and evaluating the results of marketing strategies and plans and taking corrective action to ensure that objectives are achieved.

products, brands, and territories and more focus on customer relationships. More and more, companies are shifting their brand management focus toward *customer management*—moving away from managing just product or brand profitability and toward managing profitability and customer equity. They think of themselves not as managing portfolios of brands, but as managing portfolios of customers.

Marketing Control

Because many surprises occur during the implementation of marketing plans, marketers must practice constant **marketing control**—evaluating the results of marketing strategies and plans and taking corrective action to ensure that objectives are attained. Marketing control involves four steps. Management first sets specific marketing goals. It then measures its performance in the marketplace and evaluates the causes of any differences between expected and actual performance. Finally, management takes corrective action to close the gaps between its goals and its performance. This may require changing the action programs or even changing the goals.

Operating control involves checking ongoing performance against the annual plan and taking corrective action when necessary. Its purpose is to ensure that the company achieves the sales, profits, and other goals set out in its annual plan. It also involves determining the profitability of different products, territories, markets, and channels. *Strategic control* involves looking at whether the company's basic strategies are well matched to its opportunities. Marketing strategies and programs can quickly become outdated, and each company should periodically reassess its overall approach to the marketplace.

The marketing audit covers *all* major marketing areas of a business, not just a few trouble spots. It assesses the marketing environment, marketing strategy, marketing organization, marketing systems, marketing mix, and marketing productivity and profitability. The audit is normally conducted by an objective and experienced outside party. The findings may come as a surprise—and sometimes as a shock—to management. Management then decides which actions make sense and how and when to implement them.

Author | Measuring ROI has
Comment | become a major
marketing emphasis recently. But it can be difficult. For example, a Super Bowl ad reaches nearly 100 million consumers but may cost as much as $3 million for 30 seconds of airtime alone. How do you measure the specific return on such an investment in terms of sales, profits, and building customer relationships? We'll look into that question again in Chapter 15.

➤ Measuring and Managing Return on Marketing Investment (pp 57–59)

Marketing managers must ensure that their marketing dollars are being well spent. In the past, many marketers spent freely on big, expensive marketing programs, often without thinking carefully about the financial returns on their spending. They believed that marketing produces intangible outcomes, which do not lend themselves readily to measures of productivity or return. But all that is changing:

For years, corporate marketers have walked into budget meetings like neighborhood junkies. They couldn't always justify how well they spent past handouts or what difference it all made. They just wanted more money—for flashy TV ads, for big-ticket events, for, you know, getting out the message and building up the brand. But those heady days of blind budget increases are fast being replaced with a new mantra: measurement and accountability. Armed with reams of data, increasingly sophisticated tools, and growing evidence that the old tricks simply don't work, there's hardly a marketing executive today who isn't demanding a more scientific approach to help defend marketing strategies in front of the chief financial officer. Marketers want to know the actual return on investment (ROI) of each dollar. They want to know it often, not just annually.... Companies in every segment of American business have become obsessed with honing the science of measuring marketing performance. "Marketers have been pretty unaccountable for many years," notes one expert. "Now they are under big pressure to estimate their impact."[20]

In response, marketers are developing better measures of *return on marketing investment*. **Return on marketing investment** (or *marketing ROI*) is the net return from a marketing investment divided by the costs of the marketing investment. It measures the profits generated by investments in marketing activities.

It's true that marketing returns can be difficult to measure. In measuring financial ROI, both the *R* and the *I* are uniformly measured in dollars. But there is as of yet no consistent definition of marketing ROI. "It's tough to measure, more so than for other business expenses," says one analyst. "You can imagine buying a piece of equipment . . . and then measuring the productivity gains that result from the purchase," he says. "But in marketing, benefits like advertising impact aren't easily put into dollar returns. It takes a leap of faith to come up with a number."[21]

One recent survey of CMOs from top marketing companies found that "make marketing accountable" emerged as a top strategic theme, second only to "put the consumer at the heart of marketing." However, another recent survey of top marketing executives found that although 58 percent of the companies surveyed have formal accountability programs, only 28 percent are satisfied with their ability to use marketing ROI measures to take action.[22]

A company can assess return on marketing in terms of standard marketing performance measures, such as brand awareness, sales, or market share. Many companies are assembling such measures into ▲*marketing dashboards*—meaningful sets of marketing performance measures in a single display used to monitor strategic marketing performance. Just as automobile dashboards present drivers with details on how their cars are performing, the marketing dashboard gives marketers the detailed measures they need to assess and adjust their marketing strategies.[23]

Increasingly, however, beyond standard performance measures, marketers are using customer-centered measures of marketing impact, such as customer acquisition, customer retention, customer lifetime value, and customer equity. These measures capture not just current marketing performance but also future performance resulting from stronger customer relationships. ▼**Figure 2.8** views marketing expenditures as investments that produce returns in the form of more profitable customer relationships.[24] Marketing investments result in improved customer value and satisfaction, which in turn increases customer attraction and retention. This increases individual customer lifetime values and the firm's overall customer equity. Increased customer equity, in relation to the cost of the marketing investments, determines return on marketing investment.

Regardless of how it's defined or measured, the return on marketing investment concept is here to stay. "Marketing ROI is at the heart of every business," says an AT&T marketing executive. "[We've added another P to the marketing mix]—for *profit and loss* or *performance*. We absolutely have to . . . quantify the impact of marketing on the business. You can't improve what you can't measure."[25]

Return on marketing investment (or *marketing ROI*)
The net return from a marketing investment divided by the costs of the marketing investment.

▲ Many companies are assembling marketing dashboards—meaningful sets of marketing performance measures in a single display used to set and adjust their marketing strategies.

◆ FIGURE | 2.8
Return on Marketing Investment

Source: Adapted from Roland T. Rust, Katherine N. Lemon, and Valerie A. Zeithaml, "Return on Marketing: Using Consumer Equity to Focus Marketing Strategy," *Journal of Marketing*, January 2004, p. 112.

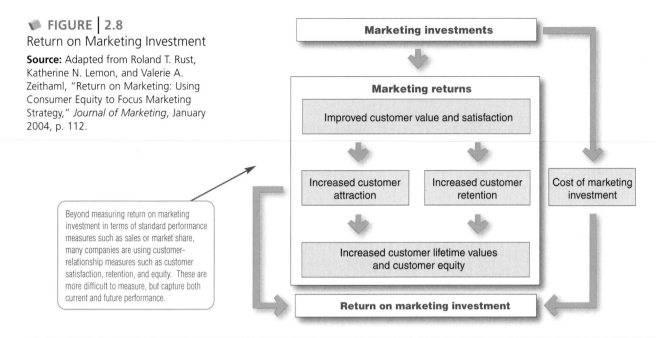

Beyond measuring return on marketing investment in terms of standard performance measures such as sales or market share, many companies are using customer-relationship measures such as customer satisfaction, retention, and equity. These are more difficult to measure, but capture both current and future performance.

REVIEWING Objectives AND KEY Terms

In Chapter 1, we defined *marketing* and outlined the steps in the marketing process. In this chapter, we examined companywide strategic planning and marketing's role in the organization. Then, we looked more deeply into marketing strategy and the marketing mix, and reviewed the major marketing management functions. So you've now had a pretty good overview of the fundamentals of modern marketing. In future chapters, we'll expand on these fundamentals.

OBJECTIVE 1 Explain companywide strategic planning and its four steps. (pp 38–41)

Strategic planning sets the stage for the rest of the company's planning. Marketing contributes to strategic planning, and the overall plan defines marketing's role in the company. Although formal planning offers a variety of benefits to companies, not all companies use it or use it well.

Strategic planning involves developing a strategy for long-run survival and growth. It consists of four steps: defining the company's mission, setting objectives and goals, designing a business portfolio, and developing functional plans. *Defining a clear company mission* with drafting a formal mission statement, should be market oriented, realistic, specific, motivating, and consistent with the market environment. The mission is then transformed into detailed *supporting goals and objectives* to guide the entire company. Based on those goals and objectives, headquarters designs a *business portfolio*, deciding which businesses and products should receive more or fewer resources. In turn, each business and product unit must develop *detailed marketing plans* in line with the companywide plan.

OBJECTIVE 2 Discuss how to design business portfolios and develop growth strategies. (pp 41–46)

Guided by the company's mission statement and objectives, management plans its *business portfolio*, or the collection of businesses and products that make up the company. The firm wants to produce a business portfolio that best fits its strengths and weaknesses to opportunities in the environment. To do this, it must analyze and adjust its *current* business portfolio and develop growth and downsizing strategies for adjusting the *future* portfolio. The company might use a formal portfolio-planning method. But many companies are now designing more-customized portfolio-planning approaches that better suit their unique situations. The *product/market expansion grid* suggests four possible growth paths: market penetration, market development, product development, and diversification.

OBJECTIVE 3 Explain marketing's role in strategic planning and how marketing works with its partners to create and deliver customer value. (pp 46–48)

Under the strategic plan, the major functional departments—marketing, finance, accounting, purchasing, operations, information systems, human resources, and others—must work together to accomplish strategic objectives. Marketing plays a key role in the company's strategic planning by providing a *marketing concept philosophy* and *inputs* regarding attractive market opportunities. Within individual business units, marketing designs *strategies* for reaching the unit's objectives and helps to carry them out profitably.

Marketers alone cannot produce superior value for customers. A company's success depends on how well each department performs its customer value-adding activities and how well the departments work together to serve the customer. Thus, marketers must practice partner *relationship management*. They must work closely with partners in other departments to form an effective *value chain* that serves the customer. And they must partner effectively with other companies in the marketing system to form a competitively superior *value delivery network*.

OBJECTIVE 4   **Describe the elements of a customer-driven marketing strategy and mix, and the forces that influence it.** (pp 48–53)

Consumer value and relationships are at the center of marketing strategy and programs. Through market segmentation, targeting, differentiation, and positioning, the company divides the total market into smaller segments, selects segments it can best serve, and decides how it wants to bring value to target consumers. It then designs an *integrated marketing mix* to produce the response it wants in the target market. The marketing mix consists of product, price, place, and promotion decisions.

OBJECTIVE 5   **List the marketing management functions, including the elements of a marketing plan, and discuss the importance of measuring and managing return on marketing investment.** (pp 53–59)

To find the best strategy and mix and to put them into action, the company engages in marketing analysis, planning, implementation, and control. The main components of a *marketing plan* are the executive summary, current marketing situation, threats and opportunities, objectives and issues, marketing strategies, action

programs, budgets, and controls. To plan good strategies is often easier than to carry them out. To be successful, companies must also be effective at *implementation*—turning marketing strategies into marketing actions.

Much of the responsibility for implementation goes to the company's marketing department. Marketing departments can be organized in one or a combination of ways: *functional marketing organization*, *geographic organization*, *product management organization*, or *market management organization*. In this age of customer relationships, more and more companies are now changing their organizational focus from product or territory management to customer relationship management. Marketing organizations carry out *marketing control*, both operating control and strategic control. They use *marketing audits* to determine marketing opportunities and problems and to recommend short-run and long-run actions to improve overall marketing performance.

Marketing managers must ensure that their marketing dollars are being well spent. Today's marketers face growing pressures to show that they are adding value in line with their costs. In response, marketers are developing better measures of *return on marketing investment*. Increasingly, they are using customer-centered measures of marketing impact as a key input into their strategic decision making.

KEY Terms

OBJECTIVE 1

Strategic planning (p 38)
Mission statement (p 39)

OBJECTIVE 2

Business portfolio (p 41)
Portfolio analysis (p 41)
Growth-share matrix (p 41)
Product/market expansion grid (p 43)
Market penetration (p 43)
Market development (p 45)

Product development (p 45)
Diversification (p 46)
Downsizing (p 46)

OBJECTIVE 3

Value chain (p 46)
Value delivery network (p 47)

OBJECTIVE 4

Marketing strategy (p 48)
Market segmentation (p 49)

Market segment (p 49)
Market targeting (p 49)
Positioning (p 50)
Differentiation (p 50)
Marketing mix (p 52)

OBJECTIVE 5

SWOT analysis (p 53)
Marketing implementation (p 55)
Marketing control (p 57)
Return on marketing investment (p 58)

DISCUSSING & APPLYING THE Concepts

Discussing the Concepts

1. Define strategic planning and briefly describe the four steps that lead managers and the firm through the strategic planning process. Discuss the role marketing plays in this process. (AASCB: Communication)

2. Describe the Boston Consulting Group's approach to portfolio analysis. Briefly discuss why management may find it difficult to dispose of a "question mark." (AACSB: Communications; Reflective Thinking)

3. Name and describe the four product/market expansion grid strategies. KFC is now rolling out a new Kentucky Grilled Chicken line to add to its traditional fried chicken lineup. Which growth strategy does this represent? (AACSB: Communications; Reflective Thinking)

4. Discuss the differences between market segmentation, targeting, differentiation, and positioning. What two simple questions do they address? (AACSB: Communication)

5. Define each of the four Ps. Does the four Ps framework do an adequate job of describing marketer responsibilities in preparing and managing marketing programs? Why? Do you see any issues with this framework in relation to service products? (AACSB: Communication; Reflective Thinking)

6. What is return on marketing investment? Why is it difficult to measure? (AACSB: Communication; Reflective Thinking)

Applying the Concepts

1. Explain what a SWOT analysis involves. Develop a SWOT analysis for a travel agency in your community. (AACSB: Communication; Reflective Thinking)

2. In a small group, discuss whether the following statement from Burton Snowboards North America, manufacturers and marketers of a leading snowboard brand, meets the five criteria of a good mission statement: "Burton Snowboards is a rider-driven company solely dedicated to creating the best snowboarding equipment on the planet." (AACSB: Communication; Reflective Thinking)

3. Explain the role of a chief marketing officer (CMO). Learn more about this C-level executive position and find an article that describes the importance of this position, the characteristics of an effective CMO, or any issues surrounding this position. (AACSB: Communication; Reflective Thinking)

FOCUS ON Technology

Mobile marketing is touted as the next "big thing," offering the promise of connecting with consumers on the most personal medium—their cell phones. Technological advances are letting marketers send not only text messages to cell phones but also video messages. In Japan, QR Codes (quick response codes) originally developed for manufacturing purposes are now placed on outdoor, print, and other media advertisements so that consumers can snap pictures of them and be taken directly to mobile Web sites. Although not widely practiced yet, some U.S. marketers are now dabbling in mobile marketing. For example, Jaguar used a mobile campaign and sold over 1,100 XFs in one month. Visa used mobile marketing in China to encourage consumers to pass video commercials on to their friends via mobile phones. Even textbook publishers are using mobile marketing to send updated information to students and teachers. Although

there are still technical roadblocks stifling rapid expansion of this marketing method, some experts claim that marketers had better jump on this bandwagon or risk being left behind.

1. Visit the Mobile Marketing Association's Web site at www.mmaglobal.com and click on "Resources" and then "MMA Member Case Studies" on the left. Discuss one case study and describe the factors you think made that application of mobile marketing a success. (AACSB: Communication; Use of IT; Reflective Thinking)

2. Analysis is an important first step in the marketing management process. The rapid advance in mobile technology poses opportunities as well as threats for marketers. Discuss both the opportunities and threats for marketers. (AACSB: Communication; Reflective Thinking)

FOCUS ON Ethics

Four dollars a gallon? Five dollars a gallon? Six dollars or more a gallon? Perhaps gas prices will be even higher by the time you read this. Consumers stuck with gas-guzzling SUVs are flocking to fuel-saving gadgets to increase their fuel economy. Enterprising marketers are answering the call with do-it-yourself products that supposedly increase mileage. For $150, Water4Gas uses hydrogen to convert a car into a water-fueled hybrid. For $170, Fuel Saver 7000 will treat your fuel with a vaporization process. For only $35 to $65, you can outfit your engine with a Turbonator, CycloneFuelSaver, or Spiral Max, fans that swirl incoming air. Many other devices are available that supposedly enable an automobile to burn fuel more efficiently. However, the Environmental Protection Agency and the Federal Trade Commission are not convinced these product really do

enhance fuel economy. Many consumers are also unaware that installing such products may void their automobile's factory warranty. The makers of these products counter that, although some products don't measure up, others do, and that the EPA and FTC reports are too broad.

1. Many of these products are offered by manufacturers of other auto-part products. What product-market growth strategy does this represent for these companies? (AACSB: Communication; Reflective Thinking)

2. If these products do not deliver the benefits claimed, should marketers be allowed to continue selling them? (AACSB: Communication; Ethical Reasoning)

MARKETING BY THE Numbers

Appendix 2, Marketing by the Numbers, discusses other marketing profitability metrics beyond the return on marketing investment (marketing ROI) measure described in this chapter. The following is a profit-and-loss statement for a business. Review Appendix 2 and answer the following questions.

1. Calculate the net marketing contribution (NMC) for this company. (AACSB: Communication; Analytic Thinking)

2. Calculate both marketing return on sales (or marketing ROS) and marketing return on investment (or marketing ROI) as described in Appendix 2. Is this company doing well? (AACSB: Communication; Analytic Reasoning; Reflective Thinking)

Net sales		$800,000,000
Cost of goods sold		(375,000,000)
Gross margin		$425,000,000
Marketing Expenses		
Sales expenses	$70,000,000	
Promotion expenses	30,000,000	
		(100,000,000)
General and Administrative Expenses		
Marketing salaries and expenses	$10,000,000	
Indirect overhead	60,000,000	(70,000,000)
Net profit before income tax		$255,000,000

VIDEO Case

Live Nation

Live Nation may not be a household name. But if you've been to a concert in the past few years, chances are you've purchased a Live Nation product. In fact, Live Nation has been the country's largest concert promoter for many years, promoting as many as 29,000 events annually. But through very savvy strategic planning, Live Nation is shaking up the structure of the music industry.

A recent $120 million deal with Madonna illustrates how this concert promoter is diving into other businesses as well. Under this deal, Live Nation will become Madonna's record label, concert promoter, ticket vendor, and merchandise agent. Similar deals have been reached with other performers such as Jay-Z and U2.

But contracting with artists is only part of the picture. Live Nation is partnering with other corporations as well. A venture with Citi will expand its reach to potential customers through a leveraging of database technologies. Joining forces with ticket reseller powerhouses such as StubHub will give Live Nation a position in the thriving business of secondary ticket sales.

After viewing the video featuring Live Nation, answer the following questions about the role of strategic planning:

1. What is Live Nation's mission?

2. Based on the product/market expansion grid, provide support for the strategy that Live Nation is pursuing.

3. How does Live Nation's strategy provide better value for customers?

COMPANY Case

Trap-Ease America: The Big Cheese of Mousetraps

CONVENTIONAL WISDOM

One April morning, Martha House, president of Trap-Ease America, entered her office in Costa Mesa, California. She paused for a moment to contemplate the Ralph Waldo Emerson quote that she had framed and hung near her desk:

> If a man [can] . . . make a better mousetrap than his neighbor . . . the world will make a beaten path to his door.

Perhaps, she mused, Emerson knew something that she didn't. She *had* the better mousetrap—Trap-Ease—but the world didn't seem all that excited about it.

The National Hardware Show

Martha had just returned from the National Hardware Show in Chicago. Standing in the trade show display booth for long hours and answering the same questions hundreds of times had been tiring. Yet, all the hard work had paid off. Each year,

National Hardware Show officials held a contest to select the best new product introduced at that year's show. The Trap-Ease had won the contest this year, beating out over 300 new products.

Such notoriety was not new for the Trap-Ease mousetrap, however. *People* magazine had run a feature article on the trap, and the trap had been the subject of numerous talk shows and articles in various popular press and trade publications.

Despite all of this attention, however, the expected demand for the trap had not materialized. Martha hoped that this award might stimulate increased interest and sales.

BACKGROUND

A group of investors had formed Trap-Ease America in January after it had obtained worldwide rights to market the innovative mousetrap. In return for marketing rights, the group agreed to pay the inventor and patent holder, a retired rancher, a royalty fee for each trap sold. The group then hired Martha to serve as president and to develop and manage the Trap-Ease America organization.

Trap-Ease America contracted with a plastics-manufacturing firm to produce the traps. The trap consisted of a square, plastic tube measuring about 6 inches long and 1-1/2 inches in diameter. The tube bent in the middle at a 30-degree angle, so that when the front part of the tube rested on a flat surface, the other end was elevated. The elevated end held a removable cap into which the user placed bait (cheese, dog food, or some other aromatic tidbit). The front end of the tube had a hinged door. When the trap was "open," this door rested on two narrow "stilts" attached to the two bottom corners of the door. (See Exhibit 1.)

The simple trap worked very efficiently. A mouse, smelling the bait, entered the tube through the open end. As it walked up the angled bottom toward the bait, its weight made the elevated end of the trap drop downward. This action elevated the open end, allowing the hinged door to swing closed, trapping the mouse. Small teeth on the ends of the stilts caught in a groove on the bottom of the trap, locking the door closed. The user could then dispose of the mouse while it was still alive, or the user could leave it alone for a few hours to suffocate in the trap.

Martha believed the trap had many advantages for the consumer when compared with traditional spring-loaded traps or poisons. Consumers could use it safely and easily with no risk of catching their fingers while loading it. It posed no injury or poisoning threat to children or pets. Furthermore, with Trap-Ease, consumers avoided the unpleasant "mess" they often encountered with the violent spring-loaded traps. The Trap-Ease created no "clean-up" problem. Finally, the user could reuse the trap or simply throw it away.

Martha's early research suggested that women were the best target market for the Trap-Ease. Men, it seemed, were more willing to buy and use the traditional, spring-loaded trap. The targeted women, however, did not like the traditional trap. These women often stayed at home and took care of their children. Thus, they wanted a means of dealing with the mouse problem that avoided the unpleasantness and risks that the standard trap created in the home.

To reach this target market, Martha decided to distribute Trap-Ease through national grocery, hardware, and drug chains such as Safeway, Kmart, Hechingers, and CB Drug. She sold the trap directly to these large retailers, avoiding any wholesalers or other middlemen.

The traps sold in packages of two, with a suggested retail price of $2.49. Although this price made the Trap-Ease about five to ten times more expensive than smaller, standard traps, consumers appeared to offer little initial price resistance. The manufacturing cost for the Trap-Ease, including freight and packaging costs, was about 31 cents per unit. The company paid an additional 8.2 cents per unit in royalty fees. Martha priced the traps to retailers at 99 cents per unit (two units to a package) and estimated that, after sales and volume discounts, Trap-Ease would produce net revenue from retailers of 75 cents per unit.

To promote the product, Martha had budgeted approximately $60,000 for the first year. She planned to use $50,000 of this amount for travel costs to visit trade shows and to make sales calls on retailers. She planned to use the remaining $10,000 for advertising. So far, however, because the mousetrap had generated so much publicity, she had not felt that she needed to do much advertising. Still, she had placed advertising in *Good Housekeeping* (after all, the trap had earned the *Good Housekeeping* Seal of Approval) and in other "home and shelter" magazines. Martha was the company's only salesperson, but she intended to hire more salespeople soon.

Martha had initially forecasted Trap-Ease's first-year sales at five million units. Through April, however, the company had only sold several hundred thousand units. Martha wondered if

most new products got off to such a slow start, or if she was doing something wrong. She had detected some problems, although none seemed overly serious. For one, there had not been enough repeat buying. For another, she had noted that many of the retailers upon whom she called kept their sample mousetraps on their desks as conversation pieces— she wanted the traps to be used and demonstrated. Martha wondered if consumers were also buying the traps as novelties rather than as solutions to their mouse problems.

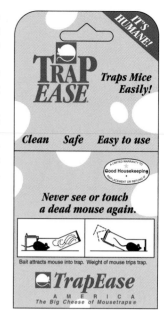

Martha knew that the investor group believed that Trap-Ease America had a "once-in-a-lifetime chance" with its innovative mousetrap, and she sensed the group's impatience with the company's progress so far. She had budgeted approximately $250,000 in administrative and fixed costs for the first year (not including marketing costs). To keep the investors happy, the company needed to sell enough traps to cover those costs and make a reasonable profit.

BACK TO THE DRAWING BOARD

In these first few months, Martha had learned that marketing a new product was not an easy task. Some customers were very demanding. For example, one national retailer had placed a large order with instructions that Trap-Ease America was to deliver the order to the loading dock at one of the retailer's warehouses between 1:00 and 3:00 p.m. on a specified day. When the truck delivering the order arrived after 3:00 p.m., the retailer had refused to accept the shipment. The retailer had told Martha it would be a year before she got another chance.

As Martha sat down at her desk, she realized she needed to rethink her marketing strategy. Perhaps she had missed something or made some mistake that was causing sales to be so slow. Glancing at the quotation again, she thought that perhaps she should send the picky retailer and other customers a copy of Emerson's famous quote.

Questions for Discussion

1. Martha and the Trap-Ease America investors believe they face a once-in-a-lifetime opportunity. What information do they need to evaluate this opportunity? How do you think the group would write its mission statement? How would *you* write it?

2. Has Martha identified the best target market for Trap-Ease? What other market segments might the firm target?

3. How has the company positioned the Trap-Ease for the chosen target market? Could it position the product in other ways?

4. Describe the current marketing mix for Trap-Ease. Do you see any problems with this mix?

5. Who is Trap-Ease America's competition?

6. How would you change Trap-Ease's marketing strategy? What kinds of control procedures would you establish for this strategy?

Chapter 3

Part 1	Defining Marketing and the Marketing Process (Chapters 1, 2)
Part 2	Understanding the Marketplace and Consumers (Chapters 3, 4, 5, 6)
Part 3	Designing a Customer-Driven Strategy and Mix (Chapters 7, 8, 9, 10, 11, 12, 13, 14, 15, 16, 17)
Part 4	Extending Marketing (Chapters 18, 19, 20)

Analyzing the Marketing
Environment

Chapter PREVIEW

In Part 1 (Chapters 1 and 2), you learned about the basic concepts of marketing and the steps in the marketing process for building profitable relationships with targeted consumers. In Part 2, we'll look deeper into the first step of the marketing process—understanding the marketplace and customer needs and wants. In this chapter, you'll discover that marketing operates in a complex and changing environment. Other *actors* in this environment—suppliers, intermediaries, customers, competitors, publics, and others—may work with or against the company. Major environmental *forces*—demographic, economic, natural, technological, political, and cultural—shape marketing opportunities, pose threats, and affect the company's ability to build customer relationships. To develop effective marketing strategies, you must first understand the environment in which marketing operates.

Let's start with a look at an American icon, Xerox. A half-century ago, this venerable old company harnessed changing technology to create a whole new industry—photocopying—and dominated that industry for decades. But did you know that, barely a decade ago, Xerox was on the verge of bankruptcy? Don't worry, the company is once again growing and profitable. But Xerox's harrowing experience provides a cautionary tale of what can happen when a company—even a dominant market leader—fails to adapt to its changing marketing environment.

Xerox introduced the first plain-paper office copier nearly 50 years ago. In the decades that followed, the company that invented photocopying flat-out dominated the industry it had created. The name Xerox became almost generic for copying (as in "I'll Xerox this for you"). Through the years, Xerox fought off round after round of rivals to stay atop the fiercely competitive copier industry. In 1998, Xerox's profits were growing at 20 percent a year and its stock price was soaring.

Then, things went terribly wrong for Xerox. The legendary company's stock and fortunes took a stomach-churning dive. In only 18 months, Xerox lost some $38 billion in market value. By mid-2001, its stock price had plunged from almost $70 in 1999 to under $5. The once-dominant market leader found itself on the brink of bankruptcy. What happened? Blame it on change, or—rather—on Xerox's failure to adapt to its rapidly changing marketing environment. The world was quickly going digital but Xerox hadn't kept up.

In the new digital environment, Xerox customers no longer relied on the company's flagship products—stand-alone copiers—to share information and documents. Rather than pumping out and distributing stacks of black-and-white copies, they created digital documents and shared them electronically. Or they popped out copies on their nearby networked printer. On a broader level, while Xerox was busy perfecting copy machines, customers were looking for more sophisticated "document management solutions." They wanted systems that would let them scan documents in Frankfurt, weave them into colorful, customized showpieces in San Francisco, and print them on demand in London—altering for American spelling.

As digital technology changed, so did Xerox's customers and competitors. Instead of selling copiers to equipment purchasing managers, Xerox found itself trying to develop and sell document management systems to high-level information technology managers. And instead of competing head-on with copy machine competitors such as Sharp, Canon, and Ricoh, Xerox was now squaring off against information technology companies such as HP and IBM.

Xerox's large and long-respected sales force—made up of those guys in the toner-stained shirts trained to sell and repair copy machines—simply wasn't equipped to deal effectively in the brave new world of digital document solutions. Xerox, the iconic "copier company," just wasn't cutting it in the new digital environment. Increasingly, Xerox found itself occupying the dusty and dying "copy machine" corner of the analog office.

Since those dark days on the brink, however, Xerox has rethought, redefined, and reinvented itself. The company has undergone a remarkable transformation. Xerox no longer defines itself as a "copier company." In fact, it doesn't even make stand-alone copiers anymore. Instead, Xerox bills itself as "the world's leading document-management technology and services enterprise." Xerox's newly minted mission is to help companies and people "be smarter about their documents." Says the company in a recent annual report

Documenting any communication used to mean committing it to paper, getting it down in

Xerox's new brand logo better fits the changing digital environment, helping to complete the transformation of the company's image.

black and white. Now communication is generally scanned, sent, searched, archived, merged, and personalized—often in color. It can move back and forth, many times, from physical to digital. So when we say our mission is to help people be smarter about their documents, it really means giving them a range of tools and techniques to capture, organize, facilitate, and enhance how they communicate. In any form. To an audience of one or many millions.

The Xerox transformation started with a new focus on the customer. Before developing new products, Xerox researchers held seemingly endless customer focus groups. Xerox's Chief Technology Officer, Sophie Vandebroek, calls this "dreaming with the customer." The goal, she argues, is "involving experts who know the technology with customers who know the pain points. . . . Ultimately innovation is about delighting the customer." Xerox even employed anthropologists, ethnographers, sociologists, and psychologists—what it calls "work-practice specialists"—to spend time with customers, understand their problems, and help develop customer-focused solutions. The new Xerox believes that understanding customers is just as important as understanding technology.

As a result, the Xerox now offers a broad portfolio of customer-focused products, software, and services that help its customers manage documents and information. Xerox has introduced 100 innovative new products in the last three years. It now offers digital products and systems ranging from network printers and multifunction devices to color printing and publishing systems, digital presses, and "book factories." It also offers an impressive array of consulting and outsourcing services that help businesses develop online document archives, operate in-house print shops or mailrooms, analyze how employees can most efficiently share documents and knowledge, and build Web-based processes for personalizing direct mail, invoices, and brochures.

Now that Xerox has transformed its business, it's setting out to transform its image as well. Befitting its new identity, Xerox recently unveiled a new brand logo.

Xerox recently retired the staid red capital X and block-lettered XEROX that has dominated its logo for 40 years. In its place is "a brand identity that reflects the Xerox of today." The new brand logo consists of a bright red lowercase "xerox" that sits alongside a red sphere sketched with lines that link to form a stylized X. Xerox chose a ball to suggest forward movement and a holistic company, and to reflect the company's connection to customers, partners, industry, and innovation. The logo retains the good things that Xerox stands for (dependability and stability), jettisons the not-so-nice (formal, somewhat stodgy), and, most importantly, adds in such attributes as modern, innovative, and flexible.

Like the new Xerox, the new brand logo better fits the changing digital environment. For example, the ball is designed to be animated easily for use in multimedia formats, particularly in messages that can be beamed to handheld devices. Xerox settled on lowercase letters

because they seemed friendlier, and on a deeper red and a thicker font to stand out better on the Web and on high-definition television. Xerox thinks that the new logo and supporting marketing campaign will help to complete the transformation of the company's image.

Xerox has rethought, redefined, and reinvented itself. The company now "connects closely with customers in a content-rich digital marketplace."

Xerox CEO Anne Mulcahy sums things up this way: "We have transformed Xerox into a business that connects closely with customers in a content-rich digital marketplace. Our new brand reflects who we are, the markets we serve, and the innovation that differentiates us in our industry. We have expanded into new markets, created new businesses, acquired new capabilities, developed technologies that launched new industries—to ensure we make it easier, faster, and less costly for our customers to share information." A major Xerox customer agrees: "From the outside looking in, I've watched Xerox transition its business from a copier and printer company to a true partner in helping companies better manage information—whether it's digital, paper, or both. Changing the brand is the next logical step. Now the face of Xerox matches the tech savvy, innovative company Xerox is today."

Thus, Xerox isn't an old, fusty copier company anymore. And thanks to a truly remarkable turnaround, Xerox is once again growing and profitable. But the message remains clear. Even the most dominant companies can be vulnerable to the often turbulent and changing marketing environment. Companies that understand and adapt well to their environments can thrive. Those that don't risk their very survival.[1]

Xerox invented photocopying and for decades flat-out dominated the industry it had created. But Xerox's harrowing experience provides a cautionary tale of what can happen when a company—even a dominant market leader—fails to adapt to its changing marketing environment.

Objective Outline

Marketing environment
The actors and forces outside marketing that affect marketing management's ability to build and maintain successful relationships with target customers.

Microenvironment
The actors close to the company that affect its ability to serve its customers—the company, suppliers, marketing intermediaries, customer markets, competitors, and publics.

Macroenvironment
The larger societal forces that affect the microenvironment—demographic, economic, natural, technological, political, and cultural forces.

Author Comment | The microenvironment includes all of the actors close to the company that affect, positively or negatively, its ability to create value for and relationships with its customers.

A company's **marketing environment** consists of the actors and forces outside marketing that affect marketing management's ability to build and maintain successful relationships with target customers. Like Xerox, companies constantly watch and adapt to the changing environment.

More than any other group in company, marketers must be the environmental trend trackers and opportunity seekers. Although every manager in an organization needs to observe the outside environment, marketers have two special aptitudes. They have disciplined methods—marketing research and marketing intelligence—for collecting information about the marketing environment. They also spend more time in customer and competitor environments. By carefully studying the environment, marketers can adapt their strategies to meet new marketplace challenges and opportunities.

The marketing environment is made up of a *microenvironment* and a *macroenvironment*. The **microenvironment** consists of the actors close to the company that affect its ability to serve its customers—the company, suppliers, marketing intermediaries, customer markets, competitors, and publics. The **macroenvironment** consists of the larger societal forces that affect the microenvironment—demographic, economic, natural, technological, political, and cultural forces. We look first at the company's microenvironment.

The Company's Microenvironment (pp 66–69)

Marketing management's job is to build relationships with customers by creating customer value and satisfaction. However, marketing managers cannot do this alone. ⬛ Figure 3.1 shows the major actors in the marketer's microenvironment. Marketing success will require building relationships with other company departments, suppliers, marketing

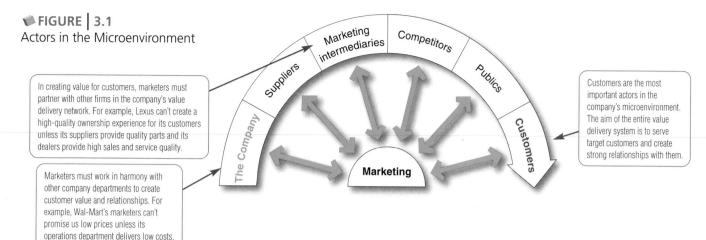

FIGURE | 3.1
Actors in the Microenvironment

In creating value for customers, marketers must partner with other firms in the company's value delivery network. For example, Lexus can't create a high-quality ownership experience for its customers unless its suppliers provide quality parts and its dealers provide high sales and service quality.

Marketers must work in harmony with other company departments to create customer value and relationships. For example, Wal-Mart's marketers can't promise us low prices unless its operations department delivers low costs.

Customers are the most important actors in the company's microenvironment. The aim of the entire value delivery system is to serve target customers and create strong relationships with them.

intermediaries, customers, competitors, and various publics, which combine to make up the company's value delivery network.

The Company

In designing marketing plans, marketing management takes other company groups into account—groups such as top management, finance, research and development (R&D), purchasing, operations, and accounting. All of these interrelated groups form the internal environment. Top management sets the company's mission, objectives, broad strategies, and policies. Marketing managers make decisions within the strategies and plans made by top management. As we discussed in Chapter 2, marketing managers must work closely with other company departments. Other departments have an impact on the marketing department's plans and actions. And under the marketing concept, all of these functions must "think consumer." They should work in harmony to provide superior customer value and relationships.

Suppliers

Suppliers form an important link in the company's overall customer value delivery system. They provide the resources needed by the company to produce its goods and services. Supplier problems can seriously affect marketing. Marketing managers must watch supply availability and costs. Supply shortages or delays, labor strikes, and other events can cost sales in the short run and damage customer satisfaction in the long run. Rising supply costs may force price increases that can harm the company's sales volume.

Most marketers today treat their suppliers as partners in creating and delivering customer value. For example, Home Depot works closely with its army of almost 12,000 suppliers. Its Supplier Center Web site (https://suppliercenter.homedepot.com) provides valuable supplier information and assistance. Supplier scorecards give important feedback that helps suppliers improve their performance. The giant retailer also hosts regular international supplier workshops, held in the local language so that factory leaders can attend. In return, Home Depot's Supplier Council, consisting of its 15 most strategic suppliers, meets four times a year to provide supplier feedback. In these and other ways, Home Depot actively solicits the "voice of the supplier." It knows that good partner relationship management results in success for all—Home Depot, its suppliers, and, ultimately, its customers.[2]

Marketing Intermediaries

Marketing intermediaries
Firms that help the company to promote, sell, and distribute its goods to final buyers.

Marketing intermediaries help the company to promote, sell, and distribute its products to final buyers. They include resellers, physical distribution firms, marketing services agencies, and financial intermediaries. *Resellers* are distribution channel firms that help the company find customers or make sales to them. These include wholesalers and retailers who buy and resell merchandise. Selecting and partnering with resellers is not easy. No longer do manufacturers have many small, independent resellers from which to choose. They now face large and growing reseller organizations such as Wal-Mart, Target, Home Depot, Costco, and Best Buy. These organizations frequently have enough power to dictate terms or even shut smaller manufacturers out of large markets.

Physical distribution firms help the company to stock and move goods from their points of origin to their destinations. *Marketing services agencies* are the marketing research firms, advertising agencies, media firms, and marketing consulting firms that help the company target and promote its products to the right markets. *Financial intermediaries* include banks, credit companies, insurance companies, and other businesses that help finance transactions or insure against the risks associated with the buying and selling of goods.

Like suppliers, marketing intermediaries form an important component of the company's overall value delivery system. In its quest to create satisfying customer relationships, the company must do more than just optimize its own performance. It must partner effectively with marketing intermediaries to optimize the performance of the entire system.

Thus, today's marketers recognize the importance of working with their intermediaries as partners rather than simply as channels through which they sell their products. ▲For example, when Coca-Cola signs on as the exclusive beverage provider for a fast-food chain, such as McDonald's, Wendy's, or Subway, it provides much more than just soft drinks. It also pledges powerful marketing support.

Coke assigns cross-functional teams dedicated to understanding the finer points of each retail partner's business. It conducts a staggering amount of research on beverage consumers and shares these insights with its partners. It analyzes the demographics of U.S. zip code areas and helps partners to determine which Coke brands are preferred in their areas. Coca-Cola has even studied the design of drive-through menu boards to better understand which layouts, fonts, letter sizes, colors, and visuals induce consumers to order more food and drink. Based on such insights, the Coca-Cola FoodService group develops marketing programs and merchandising tools that help its retail partners to improve their beverage sales and profits. For example, it recently created its Ponle Mas Sabor Con Coca-Cola program designed to help retail partners take full advantage of opportunities in the fast-growing Hispanic market. Coca-Cola FoodService's Web site, www.CokeSolutions.com, provides retailers with a wealth of information, business solutions, and merchandising tips. Such intense partnering efforts have made Coca-Cola a runaway leader in the U.S. fountain soft-drink market.[3]

▲ Partnering with marketing intermediaries: Coca-Cola provides its retail partners with much more than just soft drinks. It also pledges powerful marketing support.

Competitors

The marketing concept states that to be successful, a company must provide greater customer value and satisfaction than its competitors do. Thus, marketers must do more than simply adapt to the needs of target consumers. They also must gain strategic advantage by positioning their offerings strongly against competitors' offerings in the minds of consumers.

No single competitive marketing strategy is best for all companies. Each firm should consider its own size and industry position compared to those of its competitors. Large firms with dominant positions in an industry can use certain strategies that smaller firms cannot afford. But being large is not enough. There are winning strategies for large firms, but there are also losing ones. And small firms can develop strategies that give them better rates of return than large firms enjoy.

Publics

Public
Any group that has an actual or potential interest in or impact on an organization's ability to achieve its objectives.

The company's marketing environment also includes various publics. A **public** is any group that has an actual or potential interest in or impact on an organization's ability to achieve its objectives. We can identify seven types of publics:

- *Financial publics.* This group influences the company's ability to obtain funds. Banks, investment houses, and stockholders are the major financial publics.

- *Media publics.* This group carries news, features, and editorial opinion. It includes newspapers, magazines, and radio and television stations.

- *Government publics.* Management must take government developments into account. Marketers must often consult the company's lawyers on issues of product safety, truth in advertising, and other matters.

- *Citizen-action publics.* A company's marketing decisions may be questioned by consumer organizations, environmental groups, minority groups, and others. Its public relations department can help it stay in touch with consumer and citizen groups.

- *Local publics.* This group includes neighborhood residents and community organizations. Large companies usually appoint a community relations officer to deal with the community, attend meetings, answer questions, and contribute to worthwhile causes. ▲For example, the Avon Foundation's long-running Walk for Breast Cancer efforts recognize the importance of community publics.

- *General public.* A company needs to be concerned about the general public's attitude toward its products and activities. The public's image of the company affects its buying.

- *Internal publics.* This group includes workers, managers, volunteers, and the board of directors. Large companies use newsletters and other means to inform and motivate their internal publics. When employees feel good about their company, this positive attitude spills over to external publics.

A company can prepare marketing plans for these major publics as well as for its customer markets. Suppose the company wants a specific response from a particular public, such as goodwill, favorable word of mouth, or donations of time or money. The company would have to design an offer to this public that is attractive enough to produce the desired response.

Customers

As we've emphasized throughout, customers are the most important actors in the company's microenvironment. The aim of the entire value delivery system is to serve target customers and create strong relationships with them. The company might target any or all of five types of customer markets. *Consumer markets* consist of individuals and households that buy goods and services for personal consumption. *Business markets* buy goods and services for further processing or for use in their production process, whereas *reseller markets* buy goods and services to resell at a profit. *Government markets* are made up of government agencies that buy goods and services to produce public services or transfer the goods and services to others who need them. Finally, *international markets* consist of these buyers in other countries, including consumers, producers, resellers, and governments. Each market type has special characteristics that call for careful study by the seller.

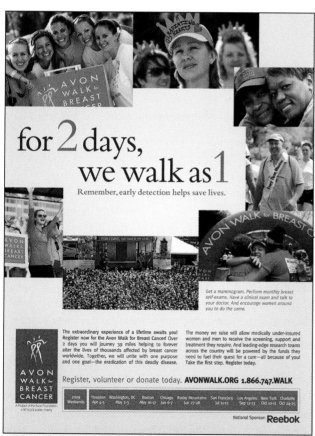

▲ Publics: The Avon Foundation's long-running Walk for Breast Cancer efforts recognize the importance of community publics. The campaign dramatically impacts the lives of millions affected by breast cancer.

Author Comment | The macroenvironment consists of broader forces that affect the actors in the microenvironment.

The Company's Macroenvironment
(pp 70–91)

The company and all of the other actors operate in a larger macroenvironment of forces that shape opportunities and pose threats to the company. ❥**Figure 3.2** shows the six major forces in the company's macroenvironment. In the remaining sections of this chapter, we examine these forces and show how they affect marketing plans.

Demographic Environment

Author Comment | Changes in demographics—in the nature of human populations—mean changes in markets. So they are very important to marketers. We'll start by looking at perhaps the biggest demographic trend in the United States and the world—the changing age structure of the population.

Demography is the study of human populations in terms of size, density, location, age, gender, race, occupation, and other statistics. The demographic environment is of major interest to marketers because it involves people, and people make up markets. The world population is growing at an explosive rate. It now exceeds 6.6 billion people and will grow to 8.1 billion by the year 2030.[4] The world's large and highly diverse population poses both opportunities and challenges.

Changes in the world demographic environment have major implications for business. For example, consider China. More than a quarter century ago, to curb its skyrocketing population, the Chinese government passed regulations limiting families to one child each. ▲As a result, Chinese children—known as "little emperors and empresses"—have been showered with attention and luxuries under what's known as the "six-pocket syndrome." As many as six adults—two parents and four doting grandparents—may be indulging the whims of each only child.

Demography
The study of human populations in terms of size, density, location, age, gender, race, occupation, and other statistics.

Baby boomers
The 78 million people born during the baby boom following World War II and lasting until 1964

The little emperors, now ranging in age from newborns to mid-20s, are affecting markets for everything from children's products to financial services, restaurants, and luxury goods. Parents with only one child at home now spend about 40 percent of their income on their cherished child, creating huge market opportunities for children's educational products. For example, Time Warner targeted the lucrative Chinese coddled-kiddies market with an interactive language course called English Time, a 200-lesson, 40-CD set that takes as long as four years for a child to complete. The course sells for $3,300, more than a year's salary for many Chinese parents.[5]

At the other end of the spectrum, Starbucks is targeting China's older little emperors, positioning itself as a new kind of informal but indulgent meeting place.[6]

China's one-child rule created a generation who have been pampered by parents and grandparents and have the means to make indulgent purchases. Instead of believing in traditional Chinese collective goals, these young people embrace individuality. "Their view of this world is very different," says the president of Starbucks Greater China. "They have never gone through the hardships of our generation." Starbucks is in sync with that, he says, given its customized drinks, personalized service, and original music compilations.

Thus, marketers keep close track of demographic trends and developments in their markets, both at home and abroad. They track changing age and family structures, geographic population shifts, educational characteristics, and population diversity. Here, we discuss the most important demographic trends in the United States.

Changing Age Structure of the Population

The U.S. population stood at over 302 million in 2007 and may reach almost 364 million by the year 2030.[7] The single most important demographic trend in the United States is the changing age structure of the population. The U.S. population contains several generational groups. Here, we discuss the three largest groups—the baby boomers, Generation X, and the Millennials—and their impact on today's marketing strategies.

The Baby Boomers. The post–World War II baby boom produced 78 million **baby boomers**, born between 1946 and 1964. Over the years, the baby boomers have been one of the most powerful forces shaping the marketing environment.

▲ Demographics and business: Chinese regulations limiting families to one child have resulted in what's known as the "six-pocket syndrome." Chinese children and teens are being showered with attention and luxuries, creating opportunities for marketers.

FIGURE | 3.2
Major Forces in the Company's Macroenvironment

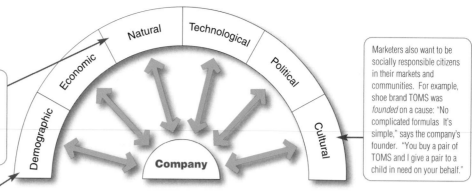

Concern for the natural environment has spawned a so-called green movement in industries ranging from PCs to diesel locomotives. For example, last year HP recovered and recycled 250 million pounds of electronics globally, equivalent to some 800 jumbo jets. The goal of many companies today is **environmental sustainability**—strategies and practices that the planet can support indefinitely.

Changing demographics mean changes in markets, which in turn require changes in marketing strategies. For example, Amerprise Financial now targets aging baby boomers with the promise that it will help them "envision what exactly you want to do in the next phase of your life."

Marketers also want to be socially responsible citizens in their markets and communities. For example, shoe brand TOMS was *founded* on a cause: "No complicated formulas It's simple," says the company's founder. "You buy a pair of TOMS and I give a pair to a child in need on your behalf."

Today's baby boomers account for nearly 30 percent of the population, spend about $2.3 trillion annually, and hold three-quarters of the nation's financial assets.[8]

The youngest boomers are now in their mid forties; the oldest are entering their sixties. The maturing boomers are rethinking the purpose and value of their work, responsibilities, and relationships. As they reach their peak earning and spending years, the boomers constitute a lucrative market for financial services, new housing and home remodeling, travel and entertainment, eating out, health and fitness products, and just about everything else.

It would be a mistake to think of the aging boomers as phasing out or slowing down. Today's boomers think young no matter how old they are. In fact, the boomers are spending $30 billion a year on *anti*aging products and services. And unlike previous generations, boomers are retiring later and working more after retirement. Rather than viewing themselves as phasing out, they see themselves as entering new life phases. According to one observer:[9]

> The boomers thrive on change and reinvention. They did not grow up with the Internet, but they readily go online to plot out vacations and seek bargains. They grew up with television, but they have embraced TiVo and VCR's and other technologies that let them scoot past commercials. They may not like rap music, but they'll listen to their own music on the same types of iPods that their children use. For example, take Frank Zacherl and his wife Dixie. Frank is a Windows Vista guru. He loves to rip music, post videos on YouTube, and Skype his grandchildren. Frank is 65. His wife, Dixie is an iPod fanatic and fellow Skype user. The older boomers get, it seems, the younger they seem to feel. . . . They see retirement not as an end but as just another stage in life.

Toyota recognizes these changing boomer life phases. Ads for its Toyota Highlander show empty-nest boomers and declare "For your newfound freedom." Similarly, Curves fitness centers targets older women, but not grandmas in rocking chairs. Curves' older regulars "want to be strong and fit," says the expert. "They just don't want to go into Gold's Gym and be surrounded by spandex-clad Barbie dolls."[10]

Similarly, cosmetics brands such as Dove, L'Oréal, CoverGirl, and Olay use 50- or 60-something spokesmodels such as Christie Brinkley and Diane Keaton to appeal to boomer women. And they use sensible, aspirational appeals aimed at confident older consumers who aren't trying to fight the aging process. "Boomers are saying 'I'm aging, but I'm going to do it in a way that's graceful and still about who I am'" says a marketer for Unilever's Dove Pro.Age brand. Says another marketer, "I don't think boomers want to be young again—I don't think they feel old in the first place."[11]

Perhaps no one is targeting the baby boomers more fervently than the financial services industry. In coming years, the aging boomers will transfer some $30 trillion in retirement nest eggs and other savings into new investments. They'll also be inheriting $8 trillion as their parents pass away. Thus, the boomers will be needing lots of money management help. An Ameriprise Financial marketer explains, "It's not just about the rational numbers. It's about how you are going to reinvent yourself for what could be 30 or 40 years of retirement." An Ameriprise ad promises retiring boomers that the company will "help you envision what exactly you want to do in the next phase of your life."[12] (See **Real Marketing 3.1**.)

Real Marketing 3.1

Ameriprise Financial:

Still a Boomer Market

As the largest demographic bulge in America's history, the baby boomers have always been a hot market to companies across a wide range of industries. These days, as the boomers reach their peak earning years and look ahead toward retirement, they've become downright irresistible to the financial services industry. In fact, Ameriprise Financial, a long-standing company (formerly American Express Financial Advisors) with a new brand name and a fresh new start, is pretty much staking its future on cultivating the baby boomers. Its entire positioning rests on a bedrock of helping the aging baby boomers realize their pre-retirement and retirement experiences through its Dream > Plan > Track approach to financial planning.

The baby boomers make up a huge and growing financial services market. Ameriprise Financial estimates that America's 41 million affluent and mass-affluent households hold more that $19 trillion in investable assets. More than half of these affluent households are headed by baby boomers. What's more, the first boomers, now in their 60s, will initiate a retirement gold rush that will continue for more that two decades. By the time that the last boomer turns 65 in 2029, the boomers will control more than 40 percent of the nation's disposable income. During that time and beyond, the boomers will need a heap of financial planning help.

Consequently, whereas the eyes of marketers in some industries are now wandering toward the younger and fresher Millennials generation, the aging boomers comprise the

Targeting the baby boomers: The positioning of Ameriprise Financial rests on a bedrock of helping the boomers to discover and realize their retirement dreams. And "Dreams don't retire."

bulk of revenues for Ameriprise Financial and other financial services firms. According to one expert, "If you are in the financial services industry, *this* is the baby-boomer decade."

But Ameriprise Financial knows that the boomers are very different from previous generations of preretirees and that connecting with them will require a deep understanding of what makes them tick. The image of the doddering old fool in mismatched flannel, pouring lemonade for the grandkids

simply doesn't resonate with today's boomer consumer. The boomers don't think of themselves as getting old. And they don't think of themselves as retiring—it's more like shifting gears and striking out in new directions. The boomers won't need help just managing their money, they'll need help planning for and realizing life's next phases. For Ameriprise Financial, says the company's CEO, "it all begins with understanding our client's dreams." And "Dreams don't retire."

Generation X

The 45 million people born between 1965 and 1976 in the "birth dearth" following the baby boom.

Generation X. The baby boom was followed by a "birth dearth," creating another generation of 49 million people born between 1965 and 1976. Author Douglas Coupland calls them **Generation X** because they lie in the shadow of the boomers and lack obvious distinguishing characteristics.

The Generation Xers are defined as much by their shared experiences as by their age. Increasing parental divorce rates and higher employment for their mothers made them the first generation of latchkey kids. Having grown up during times of recession and corporate downsizing, they developed a more cautious economic outlook. Although they seek success, they are less materialistic; they prize experience, not acquisition. For many of the 30 million Gen Xers that are parents, family comes first, career second.[13] From a marketing viewpoint, the Gen Xers are a more skeptical bunch. They tend to research products before they consider a purchase, and they tend to be less receptive to overt marketing pitches.

To better understand just what those retirement dreams entail, Ameriprise Financial linked up with baby-boomer experts to conduct a large-scale "New Retirement Mindscape" study. It learned that retirement is characterized by five distinct stages, such as imagination (the 6 to 15 years preceding retirement when people envision the retirement they want) and liberation (the year following retirement when people begin reconnecting with their families, pursuing hobbies, traveling, and starting new businesses). Another key finding was that people want a financial advisor who understands them—this was rated just as important as return on their investments.

Based on these findings, Ameriprise Financial developed a *Dream Book* guide—a planning guide that helps boomers to explore their retirement dreams and create a life strategy for retirement. It's "the best book on retirement—the one you'll write—that will help you get to a retirement defined by your dreams." The *Dream Book* guide becomes one of the first steps in the Dream > Plan > Track approach to financial planning through which more than 11,800 personal advisors from Ameriprise Financial form long-term relationships with clients. So far, the company has distributed more than three million of the popular planning guides.

Ameriprise Financial also used the New Retirement Mindscape study results to shape an innovative "Dreams don't retire" advertising campaign. The new campaign shuns the typical industry "Are *you* ready for retirement?" message of fear. Instead, it focuses on the positive, aspirational aspects of retirement—on what's next. The first phase of the ad campaign features 1960s icon Dennis Hopper, star of boomer-era counterculture classics such as *Easy Rider*. At 71 years old, Hopper himself is not a boomer. But boomers see him as an older brother type, one who has lived true to himself and done things his own way.

In the ads, Hopper talks plainly about what retirement means before the action shifts to boomers tackling ambitious retirement tasks, such as building a boat or designing an eco-friendly new home. One commercial, set in a field of yellow daisies, hits the old flower-power boomers right where they live. Speaking and looking directly into the lens, an impassioned Hopper says, "Some people say that dreams are like delicate little flowers. Wrong! Dreams are powerful. Dreams are what make you say 'When I'm 64, I'm going to start a new business. I want to make my own movie.' Flower power was then—your dreams are now."

In another commercial, Hopper stands on an expansive white, sandy beach reading from a dictionary. "To withdraw, to go away, to disappear—that's how the dictionary defines retirement," he intones. Tossing the dictionary aside, he continues, "Time to redefine! Your generation is definitely not headed for bingo night. In fact, you can write a book about how you're going to turn retirement upside down. I just don't see you playing shuffleboard—'ya know what I mean? The thing about dreams is—they don't retire." All of the ads employ a 1960s-style red chair as a visual icon. The chair symbolizes the launching pad for boomers' retirement dreams—it is an "anti-rocking chair."

The boomer-focused campaign has hit the right target with the right message. Although they scored low with the general audience, the ads hit it big with boomers.

Half of the target group liked the ads a lot or somewhat, and 79 percent rated the ads as very effective or somewhat effective (both very good numbers, given that they're, well, ads). Perhaps more important, thanks to the campaign, the newly minted Ameriprise Financial brand achieved 56 percent awareness, up from just 24 percent two years ago. And the company experienced double-digit sales and profits growth in the year following the start of the campaign. Says the Ameriprise Financial chief marketing officer, "In just two years [of running the campaign], we've established a powerful and respected brand that has transformed financial services advertising and the way people look at financial planning."

According to an industry analyst, "Ameriprise Financial looks well on the way to securing a perch among the largest financial service providers serving baby boomers headed for retirement—it's a sleeping giant." But when it comes to catering to baby boomers, this giant isn't napping. It's working face to face with more than two million clients, "Putting millions of dreams on track. One dream at a time." As one ad promises: "What do you dream of doing in retirement? Maybe you want to go back to school. Start a second career. Visit the Spanish Steps. Work on that short game. Or maybe you're not even sure. . . . Ameriprise Financial [will help you] envision what exactly you want to do in the next phase of your life . . . and develop a plan to help get you there."

Sources: Quotes and other information from Laura Petrecca, "More Marketers Target Boomers' Eyes, Wallets," *USA Today*, February 26, 2007, p. 6B; "New Evolution of Ameriprise Financial Advertising Emphasizes That 'Dreams Don't Retire,'" September 7, 2006, accessed at www.ameriprise.com; Jack Willoughby, "Ameriprise Comes Alive," *Wall Street Journal*, August 27, 2006; Claudia H. Deutsch, "Not Getting Older, Just More Scrutinized," *New York Times*, October 11, 2006, accessed at www.nyt.com; Lisa Shidler, "Baby Boomers Are Tough Customers," *Investment News*, March 12, 2007, p. 28; "Online Strategy Plays a Primary Role in New Evolution of Ameriprise Financial Advertising," *Business Wire*, September 10, 2007; and annual reports and various pages at www.ameriprise.com, accessed December 2008.

Once labeled as "the MTV generation" and viewed as body-piercing slackers who whined about "McJobs," the Gen Xers have grown up and are now taking over. The Gen Xers are displacing the lifestyles, culture, and materialistic values of the baby boomers. They represent close to $1.4 trillion in annual purchasing power. With so much potential, many companies are focusing on Gen Xers as an important target segment. For example, unlike Ameriprise Financial, which targets baby boomers, Charles Schwab recently launched a campaign targeting Gen Xers.[14]

Most Gen Xers are woefully behind in saving for retirement—and they worry about it. Still, nearly half of Gen Xers say they are so saddled with debt or live on such tight budgets that they can't even think about saving. Recognizing these pressures, Schwab has started offering solutions linked with this generation's approach to savings. For

How can we start a
nest egg when we're still
saving for the nest?

You'll be surprised what we can help you with.
Too many things to save for to think about investing? Even
if you're saving for something short term, like a down
payment, Schwab can give you real investment help, plus
the research and online resources to help you get ahead.
We can also help you roll over your 401(k) and invest in
an IRA to help better prepare for your future. It's all about
getting your eggs in the right baskets, so to speak.
Talk to a Schwab Investment Professional today.
1-800-4SCHWAB / SCHWAB.COM

TALK TO
CHUCK

charles SCHWAB

▲ Targeting Gen Xers: Schwab's "Talk to Chuck"
campaign speaks directly to Gen Xers and promotes
solutions linked with their approach to savings.

Millennials (or Generation Y)
The 83 million children of the baby
boomers, born between 1977 and 2000.

example, it has lowered account minimums to $1000 and offers a high-yield checking account linked to a brokerage account. "If they can start with a checking account, they can invest easily over time," says a Schwab marketing executive.

To engage Gen Xers, instead of talking about "portfolio diversification" or "free trades," ▲Schwab's "Talk to Chuck" advertising campaign focuses on everyday issues, such as saving for a home or paying down college debt. By speaking to Gen Xers in their language, Schwab makes investing a viable option for these "savers." The campaign avoids the business and finance publications traditionally used by financial services advertisers, instead concentrating on lifestyle publications in the area of parenting, home, fitness, and style. Digital media also concentrate on lifestyle platforms. Schwab places ads on baby shower and children's party invitations on Evite.com, mortgage calculators on BankRate.com, and Gen X–oriented entertainment and travel areas of Yahoo! and AOL, along with Wi-Fi sponsorships in airports and sponsorship of MSN's instant messaging platforms. National television ads support the overall communications effort. The result: Six months into the campaign, younger investors new to Schwab increased 118 percent over the previous year.

Millennials.   Both the baby boomers and Gen Xers will one day be passing the reins to the **Millennials** (also called Generation Y or the echo boomers). Born between 1977 and 2000, these children of the baby boomers number 83 million, dwarfing the Gen Xers and larger even than the baby boomer segment. This group includes several age cohorts: *tweens* (aged 8–12), *teens* (13–18), and *young adults* (the 20-somethings). The younger Millennials are just beginning to wield their buying power. The older ones have now graduated from college and are moving up in their careers, significantly expanding both their earning and their spending. The Millennials are a diverse bunch. Whereas the baby boomers were 80 percent white, 45 percent of Millennials describe their race as something other than white.[15]

One thing that all of the Millennials have in common is their utter fluency and comfort with computer, digital, and Internet technology. "Whereas Gen X spent a lot of time in front of the TV," says one expert, the Millennials "are always 'on.' They're consumers of every imaginable means of communication: TV, radio, cell phone, Internet, video games—often simultaneously."[16] Here's a typical Millennial profile:[17]

A.J. Hunter can't start the day without first pulling out his laptop. Each morning, the 21-year-old Ball State University junior downloads his schedule onto his Mac Powerbook, which—along with his iPod and cell phone—is always close at hand. Hunter is a typical tech-savvy college student. He can access the social networking site Facebook from his cell phone. He uses e-mail and instant messaging anywhere on the wireless campus. He downloads music to his laptop and his iPod, and he uses a 4-gigabyte flash drive provided by the university to transfer files and songs and to access his digital portfolio. Technology is so second nature, "I can't even think of when I use it and when I don't. It's such a part of life," he says. Hunter isn't a techno-geek. He's just a "digital native"—a term that has been used to describe Millennials, the first generation who grew up in a world filled with computers, cell phones, cable TV, and online social networks.

Each Millennials segment constitutes a huge and attractive market. However, reaching these message-saturated segments effectively requires creative marketing approaches. For example, P&G's Tide, normally known for targeting women who are responsible for their

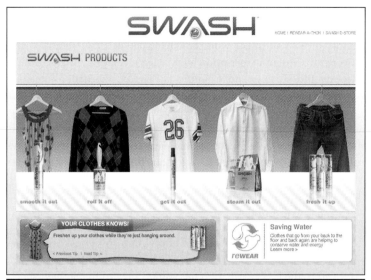

▲ Targeting the Millennials: Tide's new Swash line targets the great unwashed—college students—telling them that it's not just okay to rewear their clothes between washes, but even environmentally heroic.

household's laundry, has now set its marketing sights on the great, unwashed Millennial masses—college students:[18]

Tide is experimenting with a new line of products, called Swash. ▲ Not only is Tide telling college students that it's okay to rewear their clothes between washes, it's *encouraging* them to do so. Swash offers students dewrinkling sprays, stain-removing pens, odor-removing sprays, clothes dryer sheets, and lint rollers that can help give their clothes the look and smell of having been washed without the trouble or expense of actual washing. In the process, the brand's helping eliminate the one domestic chore most college students do. The Swash products aren't actually new—they are old offerings cleverly repositioned to fit the lifestyle of multislackers—students who are juggling the demands of not doing their laundry, not finishing their home-work, and not cleaning their rooms. Swash is here to tell them that it's okay, even environmentally heroic, to pick their wardrobes off the floor in the morning. A seg-ment on SwashItOut.com, labeled "The Rewear Movement," touts reuse of unwashed clothes as "the effortless way to save water." Says the site, "Swash brings the experience and trust of Tide into a revolutionary way to care for clothes, helping you rewear with confidence and conserve water between washes."

Generational Marketing.   Do marketers need to create separate products and market-ing programs for each generation? Some experts warn that marketers need to be careful about turning off one generation each time they craft a product or message that appeals effectively to another. Others caution that each generation spans decades of time and many socioeconomic levels. For example, marketers often split the baby boomers into three smaller groups—leading-edge boomers, core boomers, and trailing-edge boomers—each with its own beliefs and behaviors. Similarly, they split the Millennials into tweens, teens, and young adults.

Thus, marketers need to form more precise age-specific segments within each group. More important, defining people by their birth date may be less effective than segmenting them by their lifestyle, life stage, or the common values they seek in the products they buy. We will discuss many other ways to segment markets in Chapter 7.

The Changing American Family

The "traditional household" consists of a husband, wife, and children (and sometimes grandparents). Yet, the once American ideal of the two-child, two-car suburban family has lately been losing some of its luster.

In the United States today, married couples with children make up only 23 percent of the nation's 114 million households; married couples without children make up 29 percent; and single parents comprise another 16 percent. A full 32 percent are nonfamily house-holds—single live-alones or adult live-togethers of one or both sexes.[19]

More people are divorcing or separating, choosing not to marry, marrying later, or marrying without intending to have children. Marketers must increasingly consider the special needs of nontraditional households, because they are now growing more rapidly than traditional households. Each group has distinctive needs and buying habits.

The number of working women has also increased greatly, growing from under 40 per-cent of the U.S. workforce in the late 1950s to 59 percent today. Both husband and wife work in 57 percent of all married-couple families. Meanwhile, more men are staying home with their children, managing the household while their wives go to work. According to the census, the number of stay-at-home dads has risen 18 percent since 1994—some 159,000 fathers now stay at home.[20]

The significant number of women in the workforce has spawned the child day care business and increased consumption of career-oriented women's clothing, financial services, and convenience foods and services. An example is Peapod, the nation's leading Internet grocer. Using Peapod, instead of trekking to the grocery store, battling traffic, and waiting in line, busy working moms and dads can simply buy their groceries online. Peapod offers a virtual selection of more than 10,000 grocery store products and delivers customers' orders to their doorsteps. We "bring a world of food to your door," says Peapod—it's "the solution to today's busy lifestyles." Peapod fulfilled its 10 millionth order this year. More important, it figures that it has saved its busy customers about 10 million hours in trips to the grocery store.[21]

Geographic Shifts in Population

This is a period of great migratory movements between and within countries. Americans, for example, are a mobile people, with about 14 percent of all U.S. residents moving each year. Over the past two decades, the U.S. population has shifted toward the Sunbelt states. The West and South have grown, whereas the Midwest and Northeast states have lost population.[22] Such population shifts interest marketers because people in different regions buy differently. For example, research shows that people in Seattle buy more toothbrushes per capita than people in any other U.S. city; people in Salt Lake City eat more candy bars; and people in Miami drink more prune juice.

Also, for more than a century, Americans have been moving from rural to metropolitan areas. In the 1950s, they made a massive exit from the cities to the suburbs. Today, the migration to the suburbs continues. And more and more Americans are moving to "micropolitan areas," small cities located beyond congested metropolitan areas, such as Bozeman, Montana; Natchez, Mississippi; and Torrington, Connecticut. Drawing refugees from rural and suburban America, these smaller micros offer many of the advantages of metro areas—jobs, restaurants, diversions, community organizations—but without the population crush, traffic jams, high crime rates, and high property taxes often associated with heavily urbanized areas.[23]

The shift in where people live has also caused a shift in where they work. For example, the migration toward micropolitan and suburban areas has resulted in a rapid increase in the number of people who "telecommute"—work at home or in a remote office and conduct their business by phone, fax, modem, or the Internet. This trend, in turn, has created a booming SOHO (small office/home office) market. An estimated 10 percent of today's workforce works from home with the help of electronic conveniences such as PCs, cell phones, fax machines, PDA devices, and fast Internet access. And a recent study estimates that two million American businesses support some kind of telecommuting program.[24]

Many marketers are actively courting the lucrative telecommuting market. ▲For example, WebEx, the Web-conferencing division of Cisco, helps overcome the isolation that often accompanies telecommuting. With WebEx, people can meet and collaborate online, no matter what their work location. "All you need to run effective online meetings is a browser and a phone," says the company. With WebEx, people working anywhere can interact with other individuals or small groups to make presentations, exchange documents, and share desktops, complete with audio and full-motion video. WebEx's

▲ Cisco targets the growing telecommuter market with WebEx, which lets people meet and collaborate online, no matter what their work location.

MeetMeNow service can be launched from desktops, Microsoft Outlook and Office, and instant messaging clients such as Yahoo! Messenger and MSN Messenger. MeetMeNow automatically finds and configures users' Webcams and lets meeting hosts switch among participants' video streams to form a virtual roundtable. More than 2.2 million people participate in WebEx sessions every day.[25]

A Better-Educated, More White-Collar, More Professional Population

The U.S. population is becoming better educated. For example, in 2004, 86 percent of the U.S. population over age 25 had completed high school and 29 percent had completed college, compared with 69 percent and 17 percent in 1980. Moreover, nearly two-thirds of high school graduates now enroll in college within 12 months of graduating.[26] The rising number of educated people will increase the demand for quality products, books, magazines, travel, personal computers, and Internet services.

The workforce also is becoming more white-collar. Between 1983 and 1999, the proportion of managers and professionals in the workforce increased from 23 percent to more than 30 percent. Job growth is now strongest for professional workers and weakest for manufacturing workers. Between 2006 and 2016, the number of professional workers is expected to increase 23 percent, while manufacturing workers are expected to decline more than 10 percent.[27]

Increasing Diversity

Countries vary in their ethnic and racial makeup. At one extreme is Japan, where almost everyone is Japanese. At the other extreme is the United States, with people from virtually all nations. The United States has often been called a melting pot—diverse groups from many nations and cultures have melted into a single, more homogenous whole. Instead, the United States seems to have become more of a "salad bowl" in which various groups have mixed together but have maintained their diversity by retaining and valuing important ethnic and cultural differences.

Marketers now face increasingly diverse markets, both at home and abroad as their operations become more international in scope. The U.S. population is about 66 percent white, with Hispanics at 15 percent and African Americans at a little more than 13 percent. The U.S. Asian American population now totals about 5 percent of the population, with the remaining 1 percent made up of American Indian, Eskimo, and Aleut. Moreover, more than 34 million people living in the United States—more than 12 percent of the population—were born in another country. The nation's ethnic populations are expected to explode in coming decades. By 2050, whites will comprise an estimated 47 percent of the population, while Hispanics will grow to just under one-third, African Americans will hold steady at about 13 percent, and Asians will almost double to 9 percent.[28]

Most large companies, from Procter & Gamble, Sears, Wal-Mart, Allstate, and Bank of America to Levi Strauss and General Mills, now target specially designed products, ads, and promotions to one or more of these groups. ▲For example, Energizer recently launched an award-winning campaign to introduce Spanish-speaking consumers to its Energizer Bunny. For many Americans, the pink bunny is an advertising icon synonymous with long-lasting batteries. The challenge was to make the Energizer Bunny just as recognizable to Hispanic immigrants who didn't grow up in the United States:[29]

▲ Multicultural marketing: Energizer recently launched an award-winning campaign to introduce Spanish-speaking consumers to its Energizer Bunny.

Energizer teamed up with Latin Grammy-nominated musician Elvis Crespo and the band Camila to craft a Latin music campaign dubbed

"Musica Que Sigue y Sigue" ("Music That Goes On and On"). The musicians wrote and recorded the longest songs of their careers, tipping their hats to the bunny's reputation for "going and going and going." Energizer then used clips of the songs in television commercials that premiered during the Latin Grammy ceremonies. In the ads, Crespo sings in front of a huge mound of sheet music and Camila's lead singer fights a sore throat from singing so long. The goal of the ads, which aired on the Univision and Telemundo Spanish-language networks, was to drive people to Energizer's new Hispanic Web site, www.SigueYSigue.com. The site offers free downloads of Camila's 5-minute, 19-second, written-for-Energizer ballad, called "Amor Eterno" ("Eternal Love"), ring tones, and behind-the-scenes footage that has since popped up on YouTube. The site also allows visitors to upload their own original videos to contribute to the longest song. This site now draws tens of thousands of visitors each week.

Diversity goes beyond ethnic heritage. For example, many major companies have recently begun to explicitly target gay and lesbian consumers. According to PlanetOut Inc., a leading global media and entertainment company that exclusively serves the lesbian, gay, bisexual, and transgender (LGBT) community, the U.S. gay and lesbian segment has buying power of $610 billion. PlanetOut's audience is twice as likely as the general population to have a household income over $250,000. A Simmons Research study of readers of the National Gay Newspaper Guild's 12 publications found that, compared to the average American, respondents are 12 times more likely to be in professional jobs, almost twice as likely to own a vacation home, 8 times more likely to own a notebook computer, and twice as likely to own individual stocks. More than two-thirds have graduated from college and 21 percent hold a master's degree.[30]

With hit TV shows such as Carson Kressley's (of *Queer Eye For the Straight Guy*) *How to Look Good Naked*, *The Graham Norton Show*, and *The Ellen DeGeneres Show*, and Oscar-winning movies such as *Brokeback Mountain* and *Capote*, the LGBT community has increasingly emerged into the public eye. A number of media now provide companies with access to this market. For example, PlanetOut Inc. offers several successful magazines (*Out*, the *Advocate, Out Traveler*) and Web sites (Gay.com and PlanetOut.com). In 2005, media giant Viacom's MTV Networks introduced LOGO, a cable television network aimed at gays and lesbians and their friends and family. LOGO is now available in 27 million U.S. households. More than 60 mainstream marketers have advertised on LOGO, including Ameriprise Financial, Anheuser-Busch, Continental Airlines, Dell, Levi Strauss, eBay, Johnson & Johnson, Orbitz, Sears, Sony, and Subaru.

Companies in a wide range of industries are now targeting the LGBT community with gay-specific marketing efforts. For example, IBM fields a paid, full-time sales force dedicated to bringing LGBT decision makers in contact with the company. IBM also targets the gay small-business community with ads in the *Advocate*, *Out*, and 30 other gay-themed publications. American Airlines has a dedicated LGBT sales team, sponsors gay community events, and offers a special gay-oriented Web site (www.aa.com/rainbow) that features travel deals, an e-newsletter, podcasts, and a gay events calendar. The airline's focus on gay consumers has earned it double-digit revenue growth from the LGBT community each year for more than a decade. And Levi's recently ran the same ad with different endings for gay and straight audiences:[31]

A spot from the jeans maker features a young, attractive male in his second-floor apartment slipping on his Levi's. The motion of yanking up his pants inexplicably causes the street below his apartment to get pulled up as well, crashing through his floor and bringing with it an equally attractive female in a telephone booth. In the end, the guy gets the girl. But if you watch the ad on gay cable network LOGO, the same guy with the magic jeans is greeted by a fetching blond gentleman, and the two of them run off together in the same manner as their heterosexual counterparts.

Another attractive diversity segment is the nearly 54 million adults with disabilities in the United States—a market larger than African Americans or Hispanics—representing

more than $200 billion in annual spending power. Many individuals with disabilities are active consumers. For example, a recent study found that more than two-thirds of adults with disabilities had traveled at least once for business or pleasure during the preceding two years. Thirty-one percent had booked at least one flight, more than half had stayed in hotels, and 20 percent had rented a car. Over 75 percent of people with disabilities dine out at least once a week.[32]

How are companies trying to reach consumers with disabilities? Many marketers now recognize that the worlds of people with disabilities and those without disabilities are one in the same. Says one marketer, "The 'us and them' paradigm is obsolete." Marketers such as McDonald's, Verizon Wireless, Sears, and Honda have featured people with disabilities in their mainstream advertising. For instance, Target features disabled models in sales circulars.

Other companies use specially targeted media to reach this attractive segment. ▲The new Web site Disaboom.com reaches people with disabilities though social networking features akin to Facebook combined with relevant information, everything from medical news to career advice, dating resources, and travel tips. Several large marketers, including Johnson & Johnson, Netflix, Avis, GM, and Ford have already signed on as Disaboom.com marketing partners. Ford uses the site to highlight its Mobility Motoring Program. Among other things, the program provides $1,000 allowances for new car buyers to defray costs of adding adaptive equipment such as wheelchair or scooter lifts, pedal extensions, and steering wheel knobs. Marketing on Disaboom.com has "been a new concept for us and we are pleased with the performance so far," says Ford's mobility motoring manager.[33]

As the population in the United States grows more diverse, successful marketers will continue to diversify their marketing programs to take advantage of opportunities in fast-growing segments.

Economic Environment

Markets require buying power as well as people. The **economic environment** consists of factors that affect consumer purchasing power and spending patterns. Marketers must pay close attention to major trends and consumer spending patterns both across and within their world markets.

Nations vary greatly in their levels and distribution of income. Some countries have *industrial economies*, which constitute rich markets for many different kinds of goods. At the other extreme are *subsistence economies*—they consume most of their own agricultural and industrial output and offer few market opportunities. In between are *developing economies*—which can offer outstanding marketing opportunities for the right kinds of products.

Consider India with its population of 1.1 billion people. In the past, only India's elite could afford to buy a car. In fact, only one in seven Indians now owns one. But recent dramatic changes in India's economy have produced a growing middle class and rapidly rising incomes. Now, to meet the new demand, European, North American, and Asian automakers are introducing smaller, more-affordable vehicles into India. But they'll have to find a way to compete with India's Tata Motors, which has unveiled the least expensive car

> **Author Comment** | The economic environment can offer both opportunities and threats. For example, a recent economic downturn took a big bite out of Apple's sales growth and stock performance. Premium products such as iPhones and iPods are often hardest hit in troubled economic times. Said CEO Steve Jobs, "Our stock is being buffeted by factors much larger than ourselves."

Economic environment
Factors that affect consumer buying power and spending patterns.

▲ Economic environment: To capture India's growing middle class, Tata Motors introduced the small, affordable Tata Nano, designed to be India's Model T—the car that puts the developing nation on wheels.

ever in this market, ▲ the Tata Nano. Dubbed "the people's car," the Nano sells for only 100,000 rupees (about US $2,500). It can seat four passengers, gets 50 miles per gallon, and travels at a top speed of 60 miles per hour. The car is designed to be India's Model T—the car that puts the developing nation on wheels. For starters, Tata hopes to sell one million of these vehicles a year.[34]

Following are some of the major economic trends in the United States.

Changes in Income

In recent years, American consumers fell into a consumption frenzy, fueled by income growth, a boom in the stock market, rapid increases in housing values, and other economic good fortune. They bought and bought, seemingly without caution, amassing record levels of debt. However, the free spending and high expectations of those days were dashed by the recent economic downturn. Today's "tapped-out" consumers are now repaying debts acquired during earlier spending splurges, sweating out increased mortgage and household expenses, and saving ahead for children's college tuition payments and retirement.

These financially squeezed consumers are spending more carefully. *Value marketing* has become the watchword for many marketers. Rather than offering high quality at a high price, or lesser quality at very low prices, marketers are looking for ways to offer today's more financially cautious buyers greater value—just the right combination of product quality and good service at a fair price.

Changing economic conditions can have a big impact on even the most successful companies. For example, the recent economic downturn took a big bite out of Apple's sales growth and stock performance. Premium digital devices, such as the iPhone and iPod, account for more than 40 percent of Apple's sales. In a troubled economy, such products are often the hardest hit. When Apple issued lower-than-expected sales forecasts, its stock price hit an air pocket. "Apple sells premium products, and every [sign] we get on the economy is a negative one," said an analyst at the time. "[Not even] Apple's products are immune to that." Said Apple CEO Steve Jobs, "Our stock is being buffeted by factors a lot larger than ourselves."[35]

Marketers should pay attention to *income distribution* as well as income levels. Over the past several decades, the rich have grown richer, the middle class has shrunk, and the poor have remained poor. The top 1 percent of American earners get 21.2 percent of the country's adjusted gross income, and the top 10 percent of earners capture 46.4 percent of all income. In contrast, the bottom 50 percent of American earners receive just 12.8 percent of total income.[36]

This distribution of income has created a tiered market. Many companies—such as Nordstrom and Neiman-Marcus department stores—aggressively target the affluent. Others—such as Dollar General and Family Dollar stores—target those with more modest means. In fact, such dollar stores are now the fastest-growing retailers in the nation. Still other companies tailor their marketing offers across a range of markets, from the affluent to the less affluent. For example, many high-end fashion designers whose designs sell at sky-high prices to those who can afford it now also sell merchandise at prices that the masses can manage.[37]

Isaac Mizrahi, a high-end fashion designer, pioneered the "fashion for the masses" trend by offering a line of clothing and accessories at Target. Now, other designers such as Nicole Miller and Stella McCartney are offering less expensive lines at JCPenney and H&M, respectively. And Vera Wang, known for her $10,000 wedding gowns found in boutiques and high-end retailers such as Bergdorf Goodman, offers a line called "Simply Vera—Vera Wang" at Kohl's. In one fall collection, a Vera Wang gold brocade skirt that is nearly identical to a skirt that fetches $890 at a high-end department store will sell for $68 at Kohl's.

Changing Consumer Spending Patterns

Food, housing, and transportation use up the most household income. However, consumers at different income levels have different spending patterns. Some of these differences were noted over a century ago by Ernst Engel, who studied how people shifted their spending as their income rose. He found that as family income rises, the percentage spent on food declines, the percentage spent on housing remains about constant (except for such utilities as gas, electricity, and public services, which decrease), and both the percentage spent on most other categories and that devoted to savings increase. **Engel's laws** generally have been supported by later studies.

Changes in major economic variables such as income, cost of living, interest rates, and savings and borrowing patterns have a large impact on the marketplace. Companies watch these variables by using economic forecasting. Businesses do not have to be wiped out by an economic downturn or caught short in a boom. With adequate warning, they can take advantage of changes in the economic environment.

Natural Environment

The **natural environment** involves the natural resources that are needed as inputs by marketers or that are affected by marketing activities. Environmental concerns have grown steadily during the past three decades. In many cities around the world, air and water pollution have reached dangerous levels. World concern continues to mount about the possibilities of global warming, and many environmentalists fear that we soon will be buried in our own trash.

Marketers should be aware of several trends in the natural environment. The first involves growing *shortages of raw materials*. Air and water may seem to be infinite resources, but some groups see long-run dangers. Air pollution chokes many of the world's large cities, and water shortages are already a big problem in some parts of the United States and the world. By 2030, more than one in three of the world's human beings will not have enough water to drink.[38] Renewable resources, such as forests and food, also have to be used wisely. Nonrenewable resources, such as oil, coal, and various minerals, pose a serious problem. Firms making products that require these scarce resources face large cost increases, even if the materials remain available.

A second environmental trend is *increased pollution*. Industry will almost always damage the quality of the natural environment. Consider the disposal of chemical and nuclear wastes; the dangerous mercury levels in the ocean; the quantity of chemical pollutants in the soil and food supply; and the littering of the environment with nonbiodegradable bottles, plastics, and other packaging materials.

A third trend is *increased government intervention* in natural resource management. The governments of different countries vary in their concern and efforts to promote a clean environment. Some, such as the German government, vigorously pursue environmental quality. Others, especially many poorer nations, do little about pollution, largely because they lack the needed funds or political will. Even the richer nations lack the vast funds and political accord needed to mount a worldwide environmental effort. The general hope is that companies around the world will accept more social responsibility, and that less expensive devices can be found to control and reduce pollution.

In the United States, the Environmental Protection Agency (EPA) was created in 1970 to set and enforce pollution standards and to conduct pollution research. In the future, companies doing business in the United States can expect continued strong controls from government and pressure groups. Instead of opposing regulation, marketers should help develop solutions to the material and energy problems facing the world.

Concern for the natural environment has spawned the so-called green movement. Today, enlightened companies go beyond what government regulations dictate. They are developing strategies and practices that support **environmental sustainability**—an effort to create a world economy that the planet can support indefinitely. They are responding to consumer demands with more environmentally responsible products.

For example, ▲General Electric is using its "ecomagination" to create products for a better world—cleaner aircraft engines, cleaner locomotives, cleaner fuel technologies.

Engel's laws
Differences noted over a century ago by Ernst Engel in how people shift their spending across food, housing, transportation, health care, and other goods and services categories as family income rises.

Author Comment | Today's enlightened companies are developing *environmentally sustainable* strategies in an effort to create a world economy that the planet can support indefinitely.

Natural environment
Natural resources that are needed as inputs by marketers or that are affected by marketing activities.

Environmental sustainability
Developing strategies and practices that create a world economy that the planet can support indefinitely.

▲ Responding to the consumer demands for more environmentally responsible products, GE is using "ecomagination" to create products for a better world.

Taken together, for instance, all the GE Energy wind turbines in the world could produce enough power for 2.4 million U.S. homes. And in 2005, GE launched its Evolution series locomotives, diesel engines that cut fuel consumption by 5 percent and emissions by 40 percent compared to locomotives built just a year earlier. Up next is a triumph of sheer coolness: a GE hybrid diesel-electric locomotive that, just like a Prius, captures energy from braking and will improve mileage another 10 percent.[39]

Other companies are developing recyclable or biodegradable packaging, recycled materials and components, better pollution controls, and more energy-efficient operations. For example, HP is pushing legislation to force recycling of old TVs, computers, and other electronic gear:[40]

HP wants your old PCs back. For decades the computer maker has invested in recycling systems, giving it a head start against competitors. Last year, HP recovered 250 million pounds of electronics globally—equivalent to more than 800 jumbo jets. HP also reused 65 million pounds of hardware to be refurbished for resale or donation. And it's goal is to reduce PC energy usage 25 percent by 2010. No other electronics maker has a recycling, reuse, and resale program on this scale. HP's efforts have made it the darling of environmentalists, but its agenda isn't entirely altruistic. "We see legislation coming," says HP's vice president for corporate, social, and environmental responsibility. "A lot of companies haven't stepped up to the plate. . . . If we do this right, it becomes an advantage to us."

Thus, companies today are looking to do more than just good deeds. More and more, they are recognizing the link between a healthy ecology and a healthy economy. They are learning that environmentally responsible actions can also be good business.

Technological Environment

Author Comment | Technological advances are perhaps the most dramatic forces affecting today's marketing strategies. Just think about the tremendous impact of the Web, which emerged only in the mid-1990s, on marketing. You'll see examples of the surging world of online marketing many times in every chapter and we'll discuss it in detail in Chapter 17.

Technological environment
Forces that create new technologies, creating new product and market opportunities.

The **technological environment** is perhaps the most dramatic force now shaping our destiny. ▲Technology has released such wonders as antibiotics, robotic surgery, miniaturized electronics, laptop computers, and the Internet. It also has released such horrors as nuclear missiles, chemical weapons, and assault rifles. It has released such mixed blessings as the automobile, television, and credit cards.

Our attitude toward technology depends on whether we are more impressed with its wonders or its blunders. For example, what would you think about having tiny little transmitters implanted in all of the products you buy that would allow tracking products from their point of production though use and disposal? On the one hand, it would provide many advantages to both buyers and sellers. On the other hand, it could be a bit scary. Either way, it's already happening:[41]

Envision a world in which every product contains a tiny transmitter, loaded with information. As you stroll through the supermarket aisles, shelf sensors detect your selections and beam ads to your shopping cart screen, offering special deals on related products. As your cart fills, scanners detect that you might be buying for a dinner party; the screen suggests a wine to go with the meal you've planned. When you leave the store, exit scanners total up your purchases and automatically charge them to your credit card. At home,

▲ Technological environment: Technology is perhaps the most dramatic force shaping the marketing environment.

readers track what goes into and out of your pantry, updating your shopping list when stocks run low. For Sunday dinner, you pop a Butterball turkey into your "smart oven," which follows instructions from an embedded chip and cooks the bird to perfection.

Seem far-fetched? Not really. In fact, it might soon become a reality, thanks to tiny radio-frequency identification (RFID) transmitters—or "smart chips"—that can be embedded in the products you buy. Beyond benefits to consumers, the RFID chips also give producers and retailers an amazing new way to track their products electronically—anywhere in the world, anytime, automatically—from factories, to warehouses, to retail shelves, to recycling centers. Many large firms are adding fuel to the RFID fire. For example, Wal-Mart requires all suppliers shipping products to its Sam's Club's distribution centers to apply RFID tags to their pallets. If they don't, it charges $2 a pallet to do it for them. Sam's Club plans to use RFID tags on every pallet, case, and item by the fall of 2010. One study found that by using RFID, Wal-Mart can improve its inventory accuracy by 13 percent, saving millions and millions of dollars a year.

The technological environment changes rapidly. Think of all of today's common products that were not available 100 years ago, or even 30 years ago. Abraham Lincoln did not know about automobiles, airplanes, radios, or the electric light. Woodrow Wilson did not know about television, aerosol cans, automatic dishwashers, air conditioners, antibiotics, or computers. Franklin Delano Roosevelt did not know about xerography, synthetic detergents, tape recorders, birth control pills, jet engines, or earth satellites. John F. Kennedy did not know about personal computers, cell phones, the Internet, or googling.

New technologies create new markets and opportunities. However, every new technology replaces an older technology. Transistors hurt the vacuum-tube industry, xerography hurt the carbon-paper business, CDs hurt phonograph records; and digital photography hurt the film business. When old industries fought or ignored new technologies, their businesses declined. Thus, marketers should watch the technological environment closely. Companies that do not keep up will soon find their products outdated. And they will miss new product and market opportunities.

The United States leads the world in research and development spending. Total U.S. R&D spending reached an estimated $367 billion last year. The federal government was the largest R&D spender at about $102 billion.[42] Scientists today are researching a wide range of promising new products and services, ranging from practical solar energy, electric cars, paint-on computer and entertainment video displays, and powerful computers that you can wear or fold into your pocket to go-anywhere concentrators that produce drinkable water from the air.

Today's research usually is carried out by research teams rather than by lone inventors such as Thomas Edison, Samuel Morse, or Alexander Graham Bell. Many companies are adding marketing people to R&D teams to try to obtain a stronger marketing orientation. Scientists also speculate on fantasy products, such as flying cars, three-dimensional televisions, and space colonies. The challenge in each case is not only technical but also commercial—to make *practical*, *affordable* versions of these products.

As products and technology become more complex, the public needs to know that these are safe. Thus, government agencies investigate and ban potentially unsafe products. In the United States, the Food and Drug Administration (FDA) has set up complex regulations for testing new drugs. The Consumer Product Safety Commission sets safety standards for consumer products and penalizes companies that fail to meet them. Such regulations have resulted in much higher research costs and in longer times between new-product ideas and their introduction. Marketers should be aware of these regulations when applying new technologies and developing new products.

Author Comment | Even the most liberal advocates of the free-market system agree that the system works best with at least some regulation. But beyond regulation, most companies *want* to be socially responsible. Check the Web site of almost any company and you'll find long lists of good deeds and environmentally responsible actions. For example, try the Nike Responsibility page (www.nikebiz.com/responsibility/) or Johnson & Johnson's Community page (www.jnj.com/community/index.htm). We'll focus directly on marketing and social responsibility in Chapter 20.

Political environment

Laws, government agencies, and pressure groups that influence and limit various organizations and individuals in a given society.

Political and Social Environment

Marketing decisions are strongly affected by developments in the political environment. The **political environment** consists of laws, government agencies, and pressure groups that influence or limit various organizations and individuals in a given society.

Legislation Regulating Business

Even the most liberal advocates of free-market economies agree that the system works best with at least some regulation. Well-conceived regulation can encourage competition and ensure fair markets for goods and services. Thus, governments develop *public policy* to guide commerce—sets of laws and regulations that limit business for the good of society as a whole. Almost every marketing activity is subject to a wide range of laws and regulations.

Increasing Legislation. Legislation affecting business around the world has increased steadily over the years. The United States has many laws covering issues such as competition, fair trade practices, environmental protection, product safety, truth in advertising, consumer privacy, packaging and labeling, pricing, and other important areas (see ●**Table 3.1**). The European Commission has been active in establishing a new framework of laws covering competitive behavior, product standards, product liability, and commercial transactions for the nations of the European Union.

Understanding the public policy implications of a particular marketing activity is not a simple matter. For example, in the United States, there are many laws created at the national, state, and local levels, and these regulations often overlap. Aspirins sold in Dallas are governed both by federal labeling laws and by Texas state advertising laws. Moreover, regulations are constantly changing—what was allowed last year may now be prohibited, and what was prohibited may now be allowed. Marketers must work hard to keep up with changes in regulations and their interpretations.

Business legislation has been enacted for a number of reasons. The first is to *protect companies* from each other. Although business executives may praise competition, they sometimes try to neutralize it when it threatens them. So laws are passed to define and prevent unfair competition. In the United States, such laws are enforced by the Federal Trade Commission and the Antitrust Division of the Attorney General's office.

The second purpose of government regulation is to *protect consumers* from unfair business practices. Some firms, if left alone, would make shoddy products, invade consumer privacy, tell lies in their advertising, and deceive consumers through their packaging and pricing. Unfair business practices have been defined and are enforced by various agencies.

The third purpose of government regulation is to *protect the interests of society* against unrestrained business behavior. Profitable business activity does not always create a better quality of life. Regulation arises to ensure that firms take responsibility for the social costs of their production or products.

Changing Government Agency Enforcement. International marketers will encounter dozens, or even hundreds, of agencies set up to enforce trade policies and regulations. In the United States, Congress has established federal regulatory agencies, such as the Federal Trade Commission, the Food and Drug Administration, the Federal Communications Commission, the Federal Energy Regulatory Commission, the Federal Aviation Administration, the Consumer Product Safety Commission, and the Environmental Protection Agency. Because such government agencies have some discretion in enforcing the laws, they can have a major impact on a company's marketing performance.

New laws and their enforcement will continue to increase. Business executives must watch these developments when planning their products and marketing programs. Marketers need to know about the major laws protecting competition, consumers, and society. They need to understand these laws at the local, state, national, and international levels.

● TABLE | 3.1   Major U.S. Legislation Affecting Marketing

Legislation	Purpose
Sherman Antitrust Act (1890)	Prohibits monopolies and activities (price fixing, predatory pricing) that restrain trade or competition in interstate commerce.
Federal Food and Drug Act (1906)	Forbids the manufacture or sale of adulterated or fraudulently labeled foods and drugs. Created the Food and Drug Administration.
Clayton Act (1914)	Supplements the Sherman Act by prohibiting certain types of price discrimination, exclusive dealing, and tying clauses (which require a dealer to take additional products in a seller's line).
Federal Trade Commission Act (1914)	Establishes a commission to monitor and remedy unfair trade methods.
Robinson-Patman Act (1936)	Amends Clayton Act to define price discrimination as unlawful. Empowers FTC to establish limits on quantity discounts, forbid some brokerage allowances, and prohibit promotional allowances except when made available on proportionately equal terms.
Wheeler-Lea Act (1938)	Makes deceptive, misleading, and unfair practices illegal regardless of injury to competition. Places advertising of food and drugs under FTC jurisdiction.
Lanham Trademark Act (1946)	Protects and regulates distinctive brand names and trademarks.
National Traffic and Safety Act (1958)	Provides for the creation of compulsory safety standards for automobiles and tires.
Fair Packaging and Labeling Act (1966)	Provides for the regulation of packaging and labeling of consumer goods. Requires that manufacturers state what the package contains, who made it, and how much it contains.
Child Protection Act (1966)	Bans sale of hazardous toys and articles. Sets standards for child resistant packaging.
Federal Cigarette Labeling and Advertising Act (1967)	Requires that cigarette packages contain the following statement: "Warning: The Surgeon General Has Determined That Cigarette Smoking Is Dangerous to Your Health."
National Environmental Policy Act (1969)	Establishes a national policy on the environment. The 1970 Reorganization Plan established the Environmental Protection Agency.
Consumer Product Safety Act (1972)	Establishes the Consumer Product Safety Commission and authorizes it to set safety standards for consumer products as well as exact penalties for failure to uphold those standards.
Magnuson-Moss Warranty Act (1975)	Authorizes the FTC to determine rules and regulations for consumer warranties and provides consumer access to redress, such as the class action suit.
Children's Television Act (1990)	Limits number of commercials aired during children's programs.
Nutrition Labeling and Education Act (1990)	Requires that food product labels provide detailed nutritional information.
Telephone Consumer Protection Act (1991)	Establishes procedures to avoid unwanted telephone solicitations. Limits marketers' use of automatic telephone dialing systems and artificial or prerecorded voices.
Americans with Disabilities Act (1991)	Makes discrimination against people with disabilities illegal in public accommodations, transportation, and telecommunications.
Children's Online Privacy Protection Act (2000)	Prohibits Web sites or online services operators from collecting personal information from children without obtaining consent from a parent and allowing parents to review information collected from their children.
Do-Not-Call Implementation Act (2003)	Authorized the FTC to collect fees from sellers and telemarketers for the implementation and enforcement of a National Do-Not-Call Registry.

Increased Emphasis on Ethics and Socially Responsible Actions

Written regulations cannot possibly cover all potential marketing abuses, and existing laws are often difficult to enforce. However, beyond written laws and regulations, business is also governed by social codes and rules of professional ethics.

Socially Responsible Behavior. Enlightened companies encourage their managers to look beyond what the regulatory system allows and simply "do the right thing." These socially responsible firms actively seek out ways to protect the long-run interests of their consumers and the environment.

The recent rash of business scandals and increased concerns about the environment have created fresh interest in the issues of ethics and social responsibility. Almost every aspect of marketing involves such issues. Unfortunately, because these issues usually involve conflicting interests, well-meaning people can honestly disagree about the right course of action in a given situation. Thus, many industrial and professional trade associations have suggested codes of ethics. And more companies are now developing policies, guidelines, and other responses to complex social responsibility issues.

The boom in Internet marketing has created a new set of social and ethical issues. Critics worry most about online privacy issues. There has been an explosion in the amount of personal digital data available. Users, themselves, supply some of it. They voluntarily place highly private information on social networking sites such as MySpace or on genealogy sites, which are easily searched by anyone with a PC.

However, much of the information is systematically developed by businesses seeking to learn more about their customers, often without consumers realizing that they are under the microscope. Legitimate businesses plant cookies on consumers' PCs and collect, analyze, and share digital data from every mouse click consumers make at their Web sites. Critics are concerned that companies may now know *too* much, and that some companies might use digital data to take unfair advantage of consumers. Although most companies fully disclose their Internet privacy policies, and most work to use data to benefit their customers, abuses do occur. As a result, consumer advocates and policymakers are taking action to protect consumer privacy.

Throughout the text, we present "Real Marketing" exhibits that summarize the main public policy and social responsibility issues surrounding major marketing decisions. These exhibits discuss the legal issues that marketers should understand and the common ethical and societal concerns that marketers face. In Chapter 20, we discuss a broad range of societal marketing issues in greater depth.

Cause-Related Marketing.   To exercise their social responsibility and build more positive images, many companies are now linking themselves to worthwhile causes. These days, every product seems to be tied to some cause. Buy a pink mixer from KitchenAid and support breast cancer research. Purchase Ethos water from Starbucks and help bring clean water to children around the world. For every Staples Easy Button you buy, the office supplies retailer will donate about $5 to Boys and Girls Clubs of America. ▲ Buy a pair of TOMS shoes and the company will give another pair to a child in need on your behalf. Pay for these purchases with the right charge card and you can support a local cultural arts group or help fight heart disease.

Cause-related marketing has become a primary form of corporate giving. It lets companies "do well by doing good" by linking purchases of the company's products or services with fundraising for worthwhile causes or charitable organizations. Companies now sponsor dozens of cause-related marketing campaigns each year. Many are backed by large budgets and a full complement of marketing activities. For example, consider P&G's "Pantene Beautiful Lengths" campaign, which last year received Cause Marketing Forum's Golden Halo Award for the best cause-related health campaign.[43]

The Pantene Beautiful Lengths campaign has involved a broad-based marketing effort, including a campaign Web site, public service TV and prints ads, and promotional items

▲ Cause-related marketing: TOMS pledges, "No complicated formulas, it's simple . . . you buy a pair of TOMS and we give a pair to a child on your behalf."

and events. P&G kicked off the Pantene Beautiful Lengths with celebrity spokes-woman Diane Lane having her hair cut for donation on the *Today Show*. Since then the campaign has generated more than 700 million media impressions in major publications, TV shows, and Web sites. To date, the campaign has received more than 24,000 donated ponytails and more than 3,000 free wigs have been distributed through the American Cancer Society's nationwide network of wig banks. Compare that to the 2,000 wigs created over the past 10 years by charity Locks of Love. Pantene Beautiful Lengths has also contributed more than $1 million to the EIF Women's Cancer Research Fund, which raises funds and awareness for millions of women and their families affected by cancer. This year, two-time Oscar winner Hilary Swank cut her hair for Pantene and is partnering with the Beautiful Lengths campaign to raise an incredible one million additional inches of hair to make more free wigs.

Cause-related marketing has stirred some controversy. Critics worry that cause-related marketing is more a strategy for selling than a strategy for giving—that "cause-related" marketing is really "cause-exploitative" marketing. Thus, companies using cause-related marketing might find themselves walking a fine line between increased sales and an improved image, and facing charges of exploitation.

However, if handled well, cause-related marketing can greatly benefit both the company and the cause. The company gains an effective marketing tool while building a more positive public image. The charitable organization or cause gains greater visibility and important new sources of funding and support. Spending on cause-related marketing in the United States skyrocketed from only $120 million in 1990 to more than 1.5 billion by 2008.[44]

Cultural Environment

Author Comment | Cultural factors strongly affect how people think and how they consume. So marketers are keenly interested in the cultural environment.

Cultural environment
Institutions and other forces that affect society's basic values, perceptions, preferences, and behaviors.

The **cultural environment** is made up of institutions and other forces that affect a society's basic values, perceptions, preferences, and behaviors. People grow up in a particular society that shapes their basic beliefs and values. They absorb a world view that defines their relationships with others. The following cultural characteristics can affect marketing decision making.

Persistence of Cultural Values

People in a given society hold many beliefs and values. Their core beliefs and values have a high degree of persistence. For example, most Americans believe in working, getting married, giving to charity, and being honest. These beliefs shape more specific attitudes and behaviors found in everyday life. *Core* beliefs and values are passed on from parents to children and are reinforced by schools, churches, business, and government.

Secondary beliefs and values are more open to change. Believing in marriage is a core belief; believing that people should get married early in life is a secondary belief. Marketers have some chance of changing secondary values but little chance of changing core values. For example, family-planning marketers could argue more effectively that people should get married later than not getting married at all.

Shifts in Secondary Cultural Values

Although core values are fairly persistent, cultural swings do take place. Consider the impact of popular music groups, movie personalities, and other celebrities on young people's hairstyling and clothing norms. Marketers want to predict cultural shifts in order to spot new opportunities or threats. Several firms offer "futures" forecasts in this connection. For example, the Yankelovich Monitor has tracked consumer value trends for years. Its annual State of the Consumer report analyzes and interprets the forces that shape consumers' lifestyles and their marketplace interactions. The major cultural values of a society are expressed in people's views of themselves and others, as well as in their views of organizations, society, nature, and the universe.

People's Views of Themselves.   People vary in their emphasis on serving themselves versus serving others. Some people seek personal pleasure, wanting fun, change, and escape. Others seek self-realization through religion, recreation, or the avid pursuit of careers or other life goals. People use products, brands, and services as a means of self-expression, and they buy products and services that match their views of themselves.

The Yankelovich Monitor identifies several consumer segments whose purchases are motivated by self-views. Here are two examples:[45]

Do-It-Yourselfers—Recent Movers. Embodying the whole do-it-yourself attitude, these active consumers not only tackle home improvement projects on their own, but they also view the experience as a form of self-expression. They view their homes as their havens, especially when it's time to kick back and relax. Undertaking decorating, remodeling, and auto maintenance projects to save money and have fun, Do-It-Yourselfers view their projects as personal victories over the high-priced marketplace. Mostly GenX families with children at home, these consumers also enjoy playing board and card games and renting movies. As recent movers, they're actively spending to turn their new home into a castle.

Adventurers. These adventuresome individuals rarely follow a single path or do the same thing twice. These folks view the experience as far more exciting than the entertainment value. Although they may be appreciative of the arts (including movies, museums, photography and music), they are more likely to engage in activities most think are too dangerous, and they like to view themselves as doing things others wouldn't dare to do.

Marketers can target their products and services based on such self-views. ▲For example, MasterCard targets Adventurers who might want to use their credits cards to quickly set up the experience of a lifetime. It tells these consumers, "There are some things in life that money can't buy. For everything else, there's MasterCard."

People's Views of Others.   In past decades, observers have noted several shifts in people's attitudes toward others. Recently, for example, many trend trackers have seen a new wave of "cocooning," in which people are going out less with others and are staying home more to enjoy the creature comforts of home and hearth—from the networked home office, to home entertainment centers, to just finding a quiet spot to plug into their iPods while they check into their favorite Web hangouts. "Call it Cocooning in the Digital Age," says one observer. "With DVD players in most homes, broadband connections proliferating, scores of new video game titles being released each year, and nearly 400 cable channels, consumers can be endlessly entertained right in their own living room or home theater."[46]

This trend suggests less demand for theater-going and greater demand for home improvement, home office, and home entertainment products. And "as the . . . 'nesting' or 'cocooning' trend continues, with people choosing to stay home and entertain more often, the trend of upgrading outdoor living spaces has [grown

2 week vacation to Chile: $4,500

(deciding to miss your return flight: priceless)

There are 192 countries in the world and MasterCard® can help you see every single one. From Kathmandu to the Great Wall of China, no other card is more accepted worldwide. Go to priceless.com for fresh travel ideas and great escapes. there are some things money can't buy. for your next adventure, there's MasterCard.™

MasterCard

▲ People's self-views: With its "priceless" campaign, MasterCard targets "Adventurers" who imagine themselves doing things others wouldn't dare do. MasterCard can help them quickly set up the experience of a lifetime—"deciding to miss your return flight: priceless."

rapidly]," says a home industry analyst. People are adding bigger decks with fancy gas-ready barbeques, outdoor Jacuzzis, and other amenities that make the old house "home, sweet home" for family and friends.[47]

People's Views of Organizations.   People vary in their attitudes toward corporations, government agencies, trade unions, universities, and other organizations. By and large, people are willing to work for major organizations and expect them, in turn, to carry out society's work.

The past two decades have seen a sharp decrease in confidence in and loyalty toward America's business and political organizations and institutions. In the workplace, there has been an overall decline in organizational loyalty. Waves of company downsizings bred cynicism and distrust. In just the last decade, corporate scandals at Enron, WorldCom, and Tyco; record-breaking profits for big oil companies during a time of all-time high prices at the pump; and other questionable activities have resulted in a further loss of confidence in big business. Many people today see work not as a source of satisfaction but as a required chore to earn money to enjoy their nonwork hours. This trend suggests that organizations need to find new ways to win consumer and employee confidence.

People's Views of Society.   People vary in their attitudes toward their society—patriots defend it, reformers want to change it, malcontents want to leave it. People's orientation to their society influences their consumption patterns and attitudes toward the marketplace. American patriotism has been increasing gradually for the past two decades. It surged, however, following the September 11 terrorist attacks and the Iraq war. For example, the summer following the start of the Iraq war saw a surge of pumped-up Americans visiting U.S. historic sites, ranging from the Washington, D.C., monuments, Mount Rushmore, the Gettysburg battlefield, and the *USS Constitution* ("Old Ironsides") to Pearl Harbor and the Alamo. Following these peak periods, patriotism in the United States still remains high. A recent global survey on "national pride" found that Americans ranked number one among the 34 democracies polled.[48]

Marketers respond with patriotic products and promotions, offering everything from floral bouquets to clothing with patriotic themes. Although most of these marketing efforts are tasteful and well received, waving the red, white, and blue can prove tricky. Except in cases where companies tie product sales to charitable contributions, such flag-waving promotions can be viewed as attempts to cash in on triumph or tragedy. Marketers must take care when responding to such strong national emotions.

People's Views of Nature.   People vary in their attitudes toward the natural world—some feel ruled by it, others feel in harmony with it, and still others seek to master it. A long-term trend has been people's growing mastery over nature through technology and the belief that nature is bountiful. More recently, however, people have recognized that nature is finite and fragile, that it can be destroyed or spoiled by human activities.

This renewed love of things natural has created a 41-million-person "lifestyles of health and sustainability" (LOHAS) market, consumers who seek out everything from natural, organic, and nutritional products to fuel-efficient cars and alternative medicine. This segment spends nearly $215 billion annually on such products. In the words of one such consumer,[49]

> I am not an early adopter, a fast follower, or a mass-market stampeder. But I am a gas-conscious driver. So that's why I was standing in a Toyota dealership . . . this week, the latest person to check out a hybrid car. Who needs $40 fill-ups? After tooling around in three different hybrid car brands—Toyota, Honda and a Ford—I thought, How cool could this be? Saving gas money and doing well by the environment. Turns out there's a whole trend-watchers' classification for people who think like that: LOHAS. Lifestyles of Health and Sustainability. Buy a hybrid. Shop at

places like Whole Foods. Pick up the Seventh Generation paper towels at Albertsons. No skin off our noses. Conscientious shopping with no sacrifice or hippie stigma.

Many marketers are now tracking and responding to such cultural trends. For example, Wal-Mart recently developed a Live Better Index by which it tracks the attitudes of its 180 million annual shoppers. The first Live Better Index tracked consumers' decisions regarding eco-friendly products such as compact florescent lightbulbs, organic milk, and concentrated liquid laundry detergents in reduced packaging. The index shows that 11 percent of Americans now consider themselves to be converts to more sustainable living and that 43 percent say they will be "extremely green" within the next five years.[50]

Food producers have also found fast-growing markets for natural and organic products. ▲Consider Earthbound Farm, a company that grows and sells organic produce. It started in 1984 as a 2.5-acre raspberry farm in California's Carmel Valley. Founders Drew and Myra Goodman wanted to do the right thing by farming the land organically and producing food they'd feel good about serving to their family, friends, and neighbors. Today, Earthbound Farm has grown to become the world's largest producer of organic vegetables, with 40,000 acres under plow, annual sales of $480 million, and products available in 75 percent of America's supermarkets.[51]

In total, the U.S. organic-food market generated $17.8 billion in sales last year, a more than 20 percent increase over the year before. Niche marketers, such as Whole Foods Markets, have sprung up to serve this market, and traditional food chains such as Kroger and Safeway have added separate natural and organic food sections. Even pet owners are joining the movement as they become more aware of what goes into Fido's food. Almost every major pet food brand now offers several types of natural foods.[52]

Our organic greens show their true colors long before they begin to peek through the soil. We raise our crops without harmful chemicals, in healthy soil that supports strong, nutrient-rich plants. Sure, organic farming can be more challenging in the short term, but the reward is delicious organic produce and a healthy planet. That's something we can all feel good about.

Get our new Pocket Guide to Choosing Organic at www.ebfarm.com.

Earthbound Farm. ORGANIC

Food to live by.

▲ Riding the trend of all things natural, Earthbound Farm has grown to become the world's largest producer of organic salads, fruits, and vegetables, with products in 75 percent of America's supermarkets.

People's Views of the Universe. Finally, people vary in their beliefs about the origin of the universe and their place in it. Although most Americans practice religion, religious conviction and practice have been dropping off gradually through the years. Some futurists, however, have noted a renewed interest in spirituality, perhaps as a part of a broader search for a new inner purpose. People have been moving away from materialism and dog-eat-dog ambition to seek more permanent values—family, community, earth, faith—and a more certain grasp of right and wrong.

"Americans are on a spiritual journey, increasingly concerned with the meaning of life and issues of the soul and spirit," observes one expert. People "say they are increasingly looking to religion—Christianity, Judaism, Hinduism, Islam, and others—as a source of comfort in a chaotic world." This new spiritualism affects consumers in everything from the television shows they watch and the books they read to the products and services they buy. "Since consumers don't park their beliefs and values on the bench outside the marketplace," adds the expert, "they are bringing this awareness to the brands they buy.

Tapping into this heightened sensitivity presents a unique marketing opportunity for brands."[53]

Author | Rather than simply
Comment | watching and reacting,
companies should take proactive steps
with respect to the marketing
environment.

Responding to the Marketing Environment (pp 91–93)

Someone once observed, "There are three kinds of companies: those who make things happen, those who watch things happen, and those who wonder what's happened."[54] Many companies view the marketing environment as an uncontrollable element to which they must react and adapt. They passively accept the marketing environment and do not try to change it. They analyze the environmental forces and design strategies that will help the company avoid the threats and take advantage of the opportunities the environment provides.

Other companies take a *proactive* stance toward the marketing environment. Rather than simply watching and reacting, these firms take aggressive actions to affect the publics and forces in their marketing environment. Such companies hire lobbyists to influence legislation affecting their industries and stage media events to gain favorable press coverage. They run advertorials (ads expressing editorial points of view) to shape public opinion. They press lawsuits and file complaints with regulators to keep competitors in line, and they form contractual agreements to better control their distribution channels.

By taking action, companies can often overcome seemingly uncontrollable environmental events. For example, whereas some companies view the seemingly ceaseless online rumor mill as something over which they have no control, others work proactively to prevent or counter negative word of mouth. Kraft foods did this last year when its Oscar Mayer brand fell victim to a potentially damaging e-mail hoax:[55]

> The bogus e-mail, allegedly penned by a Sgt. Howard C. Wright, claimed that Marines in Iraq had written Oscar Mayer saying how much they liked its hot dogs and requesting that the company send some to the troops there. According to the e-mail, Oscar Mayer refused, saying that it supported neither the war nor anyone in it. The soldier called on all patriotic Americans to forward the e-mail to friends and to boycott Oscar Mayer and its products. As the e-mail circulated widely, rather than waiting and hoping that consumers would see through the hoax, Kraft responded vigorously with its own e-mails, blog entries, and a "Rumor and Hoaxes" Web page. It explained that Kraft and Oscar Mayer does, in fact, strongly support American troops, both in Iraq and at home. It works with the military to ensure that Kraft products are available wherever in the world troops are stationed. On the home front, Kraft explained, Oscar Mayer Weinermobiles visit about half of all major U.S. military bases each year, about 70 total. The offending e-mail turned out to be a nearly verbatim copy of a 2004 chain e-mail circulated against Starbucks, signed by the same fictitious soldier but with "Oscar Mayer" and "hot dog" substituted for "Starbucks" and "coffee." Kraft's proactive counter campaign quickly squelched the rumor, and Oscar Mayer remains America's favorite hot dog.

Marketing management cannot always control environmental forces. In many cases, it must settle for simply watching and reacting to the environment. For example, a company would have little success trying to influence geographic population shifts, the economic environment, or major cultural values. But whenever possible, smart marketing managers will take a *proactive* rather than *reactive* approach to the marketing environment (see **Real Marketing 3.2**).

Real Marketing 3.2

YourCompany Sucks.com

The Internet has been hailed by marketers as the great new relational medium. Companies use the Web to engage customers, gain insights into their needs, and create customer community. In turn, Web-empowered consumers share their brand experiences with companies and with each other. All of this back-and-forth helps both the company and its customers. But sometimes, the dialog can get nasty. Consider the following examples:

MSN Money columnist Scott Burns accuses Home Depot of being a "consistent abuser" of customers' time. Within hours, MSN's servers are caving under the weight of 14,000 blistering e-mails and posts from angry Home Depot customers who storm the MSN comment room, taking the company to task for pretty much everything. It is the biggest response in MSN Money's history.

Blogger Jeff Jarvis posts a series of irate messages to his BuzzMachine blog about the many failings of his Dell computer and his struggles with Dell's customer support. The post quickly draws national attention, and an open letter posted by Jarvis to Dell founder Michael Dell becomes the third most linked-to post on the blogosphere the day after it appears. Jarvis's headline—Dell Hell—becomes shorthand for the ability of a lone blogger to deliver a body blow to an unsuspecting business.

Systems engineer Michael Whitford wakes up one morning to find that his favorite-ever laptop, an Apple Macbook, still under warranty, has "decided not to work." Whitford takes the machine to his local Apple store, where the counter person obligingly sends it off for repairs. However, Whitford later gets a call from an Apple Care representative, who claims that the laptop has "spill damage" not covered by the warranty and says that repairs will cost him $774. "I did not spill anything on my laptop," declares Whitford. "Too bad," says the Apple rep, and the Macbook is returned unrepaired. But that's not the end of the story—far from it. A short time later, Whitford posts a video on YouTube (www.youtube.com/watch?v=hHbrQqrgVgg). In the video, a seemingly rational Whitford calmly selects among a golf club, an ax, and a sword before finally deciding on a sledgehammer as his weapon of choice for bashing his nonfunctioning Macbook to smithereens. More than 428,000 people have viewed the smash-up on YouTube and the video has been passed along on countless blogs and other Web sites.

Extreme events? Not anymore. "Web 2.0" has turned the traditional power relationship between businesses and consumers upside-down. In the good old days, disgruntled consumers could do little more than bellow at a company service rep or shout out their complaints from a street corner. Now, armed with only a PC and a broadband connection, they can take it public, airing their gripes to millions on blogs, chats, online communities, or even hate sites devoted exclusively to their least favorite corporations.

"I hate" and "sucks" sites are becoming almost commonplace. These sites target some highly respected companies with some highly *dis*respectful labels: PayPalSucks.com (aka NoPayPal); WalMart-blows.com; Microsucks.com; NorthWorstAir.org (Northwest Airlines); AmexSux.com (American Express); IHateStarbucks.com; DeltaREALLYsucks.com; and UnitedPackageSmashers.com (UPS), to name only a few.

Some of these sites and other Web attacks air legitimate complaints that should be addressed. Others, however, are little more than anonymous, vindictive slurs that unfairly ransack brands and corporate reputations. Some of the attacks are only a passing nuisance; others can draw serious attention and create real headaches.

How should companies react to Web attacks? The real quandary for targeted companies is figuring out how far they can go to protect their images without fueling the already raging fire. One point upon which all experts seem to agree: Don't try to retaliate in kind. "It's rarely a good idea to lob bombs at the fire starters," says one analyst. "Preemption, engagement, and diplomacy are saner tools."

Some companies have tried to silence the critics through lawsuits but few have succeeded. The courts have tended to regard such criticism as opinion and therefore as protected speech. As it turns out, a company has legal recourse only when the unauthorized use of its trademarks, brand names, or other intellectual property is apt to be confusing to the public. And no reasonable person is likely to be confused that Wal-Mart maintains and supports a site tagged Walmart-blows.com. Beyond the finer legal points, companies also fear that a lawsuit will only draw more attention to the consumer hate site.

Given the difficulties of trying to sue consumer online criticisms out of existence, some companies have tried other strategies. For example, most big companies now routinely

Today, armed only with a PC and a broadband connection, the little guy can take it public against corporate America. By listening and proactively responding to such seemingly uncontrollable environmental events, companies can prevent the negatives from spiraling out of control or even turn them into positives.

Continued on next page ▼

Real Marketing 3.2 Continued ▼

buy up Web addresses for their firm names preceded by the words "Ihate" or followed by "sucks.com." For example, Procter & Gamble has registered ihateprocterandgamble.com and, interestingly, febrezekillspets.com. But this approach is easily thwarted, as Wal-Mart learned when it registered ihatewalmart.com, only to find that someone else then registered ireallyhatewalmart.com.

In general, attempts to block, counterattack, or shut down consumer attacks may be shortsighted. Such criticisms are often based on real consumer concerns and unresolved anger. Hence, the best strategy might be to proactively monitor these sites and respond to the concerns they express. "The most obvious thing to do is talk to the customer and try to deal with the problem, instead of putting your fingers in your ears," advises one consultant. For example, Home Depot CEO Francis Blake drew praise when he heeded the criticisms expressed in the MSN Money onslaught and responded positively. Blake posted a heartfelt letter in which he thanked critic Scott Burns, apologized to angry customers, and promised

to make things better. He also created a new company site and a "dedicated taskforce" to deal specifically with Home Depot service problems. And within a month of the YouTube video, Apple fessed up to its misdeeds and replaced Michael Whitford's laptop. "I'm very happy now," says Whitford. "Apple has regained my loyalty. I guess I finally got their attention."

Many companies have now set up teams of specialists that monitor Web conversations and engage disgruntled consumers. Others hire firms such as BuzzLogic, which creates "conversation maps" tracking not just who's talking about a company's product but also which opinions matter most. BuzzLogic recently helped computer maker Lenovo head off its own Dell Hell moment. When

tech-oriented blogger Rick Klau posted his frustrations over his Lenovo ThinkPad's faulty hard drive, BuzzLogic quickly picked up the post and alerted Lenovo. Within only a few hours, Klau received a phone call from David Churbuck, Lenovo's VP of global Web marketing. Churbuck offered to fix the problem, turning Klau's rants into raves. The *good* news was picked up by other bloggers before the *bad* news could catch fire.

Thus, by listening and proactively responding to seemingly uncontrollable events in the environment, companies can prevent the negatives from spiraling out of control or even turn them into positives. Who knows? With the right responses, WalMart-blows.com might even become WalMart-rules.com. Then again, probably not.

Sources: Quotes, excerpts, and other information from Michelle Conlin, "Web Attack," *BusinessWeek,* April 16, 2007, pp. 54–56; Oliver Ryan, "The Buzz Around Buzz," *Fortune,* March 19, 2007, p. 46; Gemma Charles, "Complaints Are There to Be Heard," *Marketing,* January 10, 2007, p. 15; "Top 10 Service Complaint Sites," *Time Out New York,* March 8, 2007, accessed at www.timeout.com; "Corporate Hate Sites," New Media Institute, accessed at www.newmedia.org/categories/Hot-Topics-&-Issues/Corporate-Hate-Sites/, February 2008; "Consumer Vigilantes," *BusinessWeek,* March 3, 2008, p. 38; and Christopher L. Marting and Nathan Bennett, "Corporate Reputation; What to Do About Online Attacks," *Wall Street Journal,* March 10, 2008, p. R6.

REVIEWING Objectives AND KEY Terms

In this chapter and the next two chapters, you'll examine the environments of marketing and how companies analyze these environments to better understand the marketplace and consumers. Companies must constantly watch and manage the *marketing environment* in order to seek opportunities and ward off threats. The marketing environment consists of all the actors and forces influencing the company's ability to transact business effectively with its target market.

OBJECTIVE 1   Describe the environmental forces that affect the company's ability to serve its customers.
(pp 66–70)

The company's *microenvironment* consists of other actors close to the company that combine to form the company's value delivery network or that affect its ability to serve its customers. It includes the company's *internal environment*—its several departments and management levels—as it influences marketing decision making. *Marketing channel firms*—suppliers and marketing intermediaries, including resellers, physical distribution firms, marketing services agencies, and financial intermediaries—cooperate to create customer value. Five types of customer *markets* include consumer, business, reseller, government, and international markets. *Competitors* vie with the company in an effort to serve customers better. Finally, various *publics* have an actual or potential interest in or impact on the company's ability to meet its objectives.

The *macroenvironment* consists of larger societal forces that affect the entire microenvironment. The six forces making up the company's macroenvironment include demographic, economic, natural, technological, political, and cultural forces. These forces shape opportunities and pose threats to the company.

OBJECTIVE 2   Explain how changes in the demographic and economic environments affect marketing decisions.
(pp 70–81)

Demography is the study of the characteristics of human populations. Today's *demographic environment* shows a changing age structure, shifting family profiles, geographic population shifts, a better-educated and more white-collar population, and increasing diversity. The *economic environment* consists of factors that affect buying power and patterns. The economic environment is characterized by more consumer concern for value and shifting consumer spending patterns. Today's squeezed consumers are seeking greater value—just the right combination of good quality and service at a fair price. The distribution of income also is shifting. The rich have grown richer, the middle class has shrunk, and the poor have remained poor, leading to a two-tiered market. Many companies now tailor their marketing offers to two different markets—the affluent and the less affluent.

OBJECTIVE 3 **Identify the major trends in the firm's natural and technological environments. (pp 81–83)**

The *natural environment* shows three major trends: shortages of certain raw materials, higher pollution levels, and more government intervention in natural resource management. Environmental concerns create marketing opportunities for alert companies. The *technological environment* creates both opportunities and challenges. Companies that fail to keep up with technological change will miss out on new product and marketing opportunities.

OBJECTIVE 4 **Explain the key changes in the political and cultural environments. (pp 84–91)**

The *political environment* consists of laws, agencies, and groups that influence or limit marketing actions. The political environment has undergone three changes that affect marketing worldwide: increasing legislation regulating business, strong government agency enforcement, and greater emphasis on ethics and socially responsible actions. The *cultural environment* is made up of institutions and forces that affect a society's values, perceptions, preferences, and behaviors. The environment shows trends toward digital "cocooning," a lessening trust of institutions, increasing patriotism, greater appreciation for nature, a new spiritualism, and the search for more meaningful and enduring values.

OBJECTIVE 5 **Discuss how companies can react to the marketing environment. (pp 91–93)**

Companies can passively accept the marketing environment as an uncontrollable element to which they must adapt, avoiding threats and taking advantage of opportunities as they arise. Or they can take a *proactive* stance, working to change the environment rather than simply reacting to it. Whenever possible, companies should try to be proactive rather than reactive.

KEY Terms

OBJECTIVE 1

Marketing environment (p 66)
Microenvironment (p 66)
Macroenvironment (p 66)
Marketing intermediaries (p 67)
Public (p 69)

OBJECTIVE 2

Demography (p 70)
Baby boomers (p 70)
Generation X (p 72)
Millennials (Generation Y) (p 74)
Economic environment (p 79)
Engel's laws (p 81)

OBJECTIVE 3

Natural environment (p 81)
Environmental sustainability (p 81)
Technological environment (p 82)

OBJECTIVE 4

Political environment (p 84)
Cultural environment (p 87)

DISCUSSING & APPLYING THE Concepts

Discussing the Concepts

1. Name and describe the elements of a company's microenvironment and give an example illustrating why each is important. (AASCB: Communication; Reflective Thinking)

2. List some of the demographic trends of interest to marketers in the United States and discuss whether these trends pose opportunities or threats for marketers. (AACSB: Communication; Reflective Thinking)

3. Discuss current trends in the economic environment of which marketers must be aware and provide examples of companies' responses to each trend. (AACSB: Communication; Reflective Thinking)

4. Discuss the primary reasons why a company would hire a lobbyist in Washington, D.C. Would it make sense for the same company to also hire lobbyists at the state level? Why? (AACSB: Communication; Reflective Thinking)

5. Compare and contrast core beliefs/values and secondary beliefs/values. Provide an example of each and discuss the potential impact marketers have on each. (AACSB: Communication; Reflective Thinking)

6. How should marketers respond to the changing environment? (AACSB: Communication)

Applying the Concepts

1. Much of U.S. culture is influenced by products from Hollywood, including movies and television programs. In a small group, select a current television program and explain how it might affect the cultural environment. (AACSB: Communication; Reflective Thinking)

2. The Federal Trade Commission (FTC) has regulatory authority over marketing practices. Visit www.ftc.gov to learn about this agency and how it regulates business activities in general and marketing activities in particular. Describe the process the FTC uses if a complaint is made and discuss one FTC case related to marketing. (AACSB: Communication; Use of IT)

3. Cause-related marketing has grown considerably over the past 10 years. Visit www.causemarketingforum.com and learn about companies winning Halo Awards for outstanding cause-related marketing programs. Present two award-winning case studies to your class. (AACSB: Communication; Use of IT)

FOCUS ON Technology

Have you ever gone phishing? Probably not, but the Internet enables unscrupulous individuals to "phish" for your personal information. This and other types of attacks aimed at stealing your identity or your money are called "social engineering." Social engineering is a remake of an old-fashioned con game that tricks people into giving information and then uses it to rob them. You might receive an e-mail, supposedly from PayPal, Amazon.com, or your bank, asking you to update your personal information. To make it easier for you, says the message, just click on the link in the e-mail to input your information. Don't do it! The click will take you to a site that looks legitimate but is really a skillfully designed fake, often located in another country. Even if you don't enter any personal information, just clicking on the link might put software on your computer that can track your keystrokes, revealing login and password information to the crooks.

1. Discuss two recommendations for how consumers might protect themselves from such Internet scams. (AACSB: Communication; Reflective Thinking)

2. Phishing scams also victimize businesses. Visit the Federal Trade Commission's Web site (www.ftc.gov) to learn how businesses can deal with this problem and discuss recommendations for marketers who face this threat. (AACSB: Communication; Reflective Thinking; Use of IT)

FOCUS ON Ethics

Since the mid-1990s, companies such as Northfield Laboratories and Biopure have been testing blood substitutes in hopes of attaining approval by the U.S. Food and Drug Administration (FDA). Blood substitutes are oxygen-carrying products designed to replace donated human blood. Unlike human donor blood, these products can be stored without refrigeration for long periods and don't have to be crossed-matched with a patient's blood. These characteristics offer significant advantages in battlefield and trauma applications. However, clinical trials indicate that using blood substitutes results in a 30 percent death risk increase and nearly as high of a risk of having a heart attack, leading some to criticize the FDA for allowing continued clinical trials. A recent study published in the *Journal of the American Medical Association* faulted the FDA for not conducting prompt analysis of previous studies and claimed that the risks of using blood substitutes were evident as early as 2000. The FDA claimed it was aware of these risks but deemed some products worthy of further research. Some critics are pushing for more stringent legislation governing product testing, particularly if there are potentially significant health risks.

1. Discuss the environmental forces acting on these companies. What are Northfield's and Biopure's responsibilities and possible reactions to these environmental forces? (AACSB: Communication; Reflective Thinking)

2. Is it ethical for these companies to continue clinical trials in this case? (AACSB: Communication; Ethical Reasoning)

MARKETING BY THE Numbers

China and India are emerging markets that will have a significant impact on the world in coming years. With China's population at over 1.3 billion and India's at 1 billion, they are the two most populous countries, comprising almost 40 percent of the world's population. The economies of both countries are growing at phenomenal rates as well. The term "Chindia" is used to describe the growing power of these two countries, and predictions are that these two will overtake the United States as the largest economies in the world within just a few decades.

1. Discuss a demographic and an economic trend related to Chindia's power and its impact on marketers in the United States. Support your discussion of these trends with statistics. (AACSB: Communication; Reflective Thinking)

2. Using the chain ratio method described in Appendix 2: Marketing by the Numbers, discuss factors to consider when estimating total market demand for automobiles in China or India. (AACSB: Communication, Analytical Reasoning)

VIDEO Case

TOMS Shoes

"Get involved: Changing a life begins with a single step." This sounds like a mandate from a nonprofit volunteer organization. But in fact, this is the motto of a for-profit shoe company located in Santa Monica, California. In 2006, Tom Mycoskie founded TOMS Shoes because he wanted to do something different. He wanted to run a company that would make a profit while at the same time helping the needy of the world.

Specifically, for every pair of shoes that TOMS sells, it gives a pair of shoes to a needy child somewhere in the world. So far, the company has given away tens of thousands of pairs of shoes and is on track to give away hundreds of thousands. Can TOMS succeed and thrive based on this idealistic concept? That all depends on how TOMS executes its strategy within the constantly changing marketing environment.

After viewing the video featuring TOMS Shoes, answer the following questions about the marketing environment:

1. What trends in the marketing environment have contributed to the success of TOMS Shoes?

2. Did TOMS Shoes first scan the marketing environment in creating its strategy, or did it create its strategy and fit the strategy to the environment? Does this matter?

3. Is TOMS's strategy more about serving needy children or about creating value for customers? Explain.

COMPANY Case

Prius: Leading a Wave of Hybrids

Americans love their cars. In a country where SUVs have dominated the roads for more than a decade and the biggest sport is stockcar racing, it seems unlikely that a small, sluggish, hybrid vehicle would become such a hit. But against all odds, the Toyota Prius has become one of the top 10 selling vehicles in America. Introducing a fuel sipper in a market where vehicle size and horsepower have reigned led one Toyota executive to profess, "Frankly, it was one of the biggest crapshoots I've ever been involved in." Considering these issues, it is nothing short of amazing that only five years later, the president of Toyota Motor Sales U.S.A., Jim Press, dubbed the Prius "the hottest car we've ever had."

THE NUTS AND BOLTS OF THE PRIUS

Like other hybrids currently available or in development, the Prius combines a gas engine with an electric motor. Different hybrid vehicles employ this combination of power sources in different ways to boost both fuel efficiency and power. The Prius runs on only the electric motor when starting up and under initial acceleration. At roughly 15 mph, the gas engine kicks in. This means that the auto gets power from only the battery at low speeds, and from both the gas engine and electric motor during heavy acceleration.

Once up to speed, the gas engine sends power directly to the wheels and, through the generator, to the electric motor or battery. When braking, energy from the slowing wheels—energy that is wasted in a conventional car—is sent back through the electric motor to charge the battery. At a stop, the gas engine shuts off, saving fuel. When starting up and operating at low speeds, the auto makes no noise, which seems eerie to some drivers and to pedestrians who don't hear it coming!

The Prius first sold in the United States in the 2001 model year. It was a small, cramped, slow compact car with a dull design. Three years later, the second-generation Prius benefited from a modest power increase. But it was still anything but a muscle car. However, there were countless other improvements. The sleek, Asian-inspired design was much better looking than the first generation Prius and came in seven colors. The interior was roomy and practical, with plenty of rear leg room and gobs of storage space.

The Gen II Prius also provided expensive touches typically found only in luxury vehicles. A single push button brought the car to life. A seven-inch energy monitor touch screen displayed fuel consumption, outside temperature, and battery charge level. It also indicated when the car was running on gas, electricity, regenerated energy, or a combination of these. Multiple screens within the monitor also provided controls for air conditioning, audio, and a satellite navigation system. And whereas the first Prius averaged an astounding 42 miles per gallon, its successor did even better at 48.

A RUNAWAY SUCCESS

Apparently, consumers liked the improvements. In its inaugural year, the Prius saw moderate sales of just over 15,000 units—not bad considering that Toyota put minimal promotional effort behind the new vehicle. But sales for the carbon fuel miser have increased exponentially ever since. In 2007, Toyota sold 181,000 Priuses in the United States alone, a 70 percent increase over 2006 sales. That makes the Prius Toyota's third-best-selling passenger car following the Camry and Corolla. Perhaps more significantly, in May of 2008, Toyota announced that it had sold a total of 1,028,000 Prius cars worldwide since the vehicle first went on sale in Japan in 1997.

The rapid increase in demand for the Prius created a rare automotive phenomenon. During a period when most automotive companies had to offer substantial incentives to move vehicles, many Toyota dealers had no problem getting price premiums of up to $5,000 over sticker price for the Prius. Waiting lists for the Prius stretched up to six months. At one point, spots on dealers' waiting lists were being auctioned on eBay for $500. By 2006, the Prius had become the "hottest" car in the United States, based on industry metrics of time spent on dealer lots, sales incentives, and average sale price relative to sticker price. In fact, according to Kelley Blue Book, demand for new Priuses became so strong that, even after one year and more than 20,000 miles, a Prius could fetch thousands more than its original sticker price.

There are many reasons for the success of the Prius. For starters, Toyota's targeting strategy has been spot-on from the beginning. It focused first on early adopters, techies who were attracted by the car's advanced technology. Such buyers not only bought the car but found ways to modify it by hacking into the Prius's computer system. Soon, owners were sharing their hacking secrets through chat rooms such as Priusenvy.com, boasting such modifications as using the dashboard display screen to play video games, show files from a laptop, watch TV, and look at images taken by a rear-view camera. One savvy owner found a way to plug the Prius into a wall socket and boost fuel efficiency to as much as 100 miles per gallon.

In addition to Toyota's effective targeting tactics, various external incentives helped to spur Prius sales. For example, some states issued permits for hybrids to drive in HOV (High Occupancy Vehicle) lanes, even if they only had one occupant. Some cities, including Albuquerque, Los Angeles, San Jose, and New Haven, provide free parking. But the biggest incentives were monetary.

The federal government gave huge tax breaks amounting to thousands of dollars. Some state governments gave additional tax breaks, in some cases matching the federal tax break. On top of all that, some eco-friendly companies such as Timberland, Google, and Hyperion Solutions also joined in the incentive game, giving employees as much as $5,000 toward the purchase of hybrids.

But after some time, the early adopter market had been skimmed and the government incentives were slowly phased out. Just as these changes were taking place, Toyota was already well into a $40 million campaign targeting a different set of consumers, the environmentally conscious and those desiring greater fuel efficiency. With the accuracy of a fortune teller, Toyota hit the nail right on the head. Gas prices skyrocketed, first to $3 a gallon, then past $4. By the spring of 2008, Prius hysteria had reached an all-time high. Just as demand for full-sized SUVs began to tank, waiting lists and dealer mark-ups over sticker for the Prius once again became the norm.

"I'm selling every one I can get my hands on," said Kenny Burns, a general sales manager at a California Toyota dealer. With a 30-day waiting list for a new Prius, "The day the car comes in is the day the car goes out."

FUELING THE HYBRID CRAZE

The overall category of gas-electric vehicles in the United States is hotter than ever. Although hybrids accounted for only about 3 percent of total U.S. car sales in 2007, their share is growing rapidly. For the first quarter of 2008, hybrid sales were up 25 percent over the previous year. In April of that year, sales jumped a whopping 58 percent. The Prius alone commands more than 50 percent of the market and is largely responsible for category growth.

While various hybrid models have hit the market in recent years, it appears that consumers like their green cars very green. Sales of the ultra-high-mileage Prius and Civic have grown significantly each year since their introductions. But less efficient (and more expensive) hybrid models such as the Honda Accord (now discontinued), the Ford Escape, and the Mercury Mariner have not fared nearly as well. Some analysts believe it is because consumers are doing the math and realizing that even with better fuel efficiency, they may not save money with a hybrid. In fact, a widely publicized 2006 report by *Consumer Reports* revealed that of six hybrid models studied, the Prius and the Civic were the only two to recover the price premium and save consumers money after five years and 75,000 miles. But as the price of gas rises, the break-even period for the price of a hybrid gets shorter and shorter. That may just mean greater demand for all hybrid models as consumers perceive that even the less efficient hybrids make financial sense.

Almost every automotive nameplate now wants a piece of the growing pie. In 2008, there were 15 hybrid models available in the United States from 9 different brand nameplates. General Motors offers both the only full-sized SUV hybrid in the Tahoe and the lowest priced hybrid option at $2,000 for the Saturn Vue and Aura. GM plans to extend the Saturn hybrid line to almost every vehicle in the lineup while continuing to introduce hybrids in other divisions. Ford plans to produce 250,000 hybrids a year by 2012. And while Subaru, Hyundai, and Honda are all promoting upcoming hybrid models, Audi, BMW, and numerous others are busy developing hybrid vehicles of their own.

Even with all the activity from these automotive brands, Toyota is currently the clear leader in hybrid sales and likely will be for some time to come. It makes 6 of the current 15 U.S. hybrid models (including 3 Lexus models). And with market conditions changing, Toyota is also showing its ability to adapt. In addition to the increased level of competition, the Prius faces more internal competition from new Toyota models like the Camry. Toyota faces a greater challenge in ramping up production to meet demand than from external competition.

All indications show that Toyota plans to maintain its hybrid momentum, doubling its line to 12 models and increasing its worldwide hybrid sales to 1 million vehicles per year by the early 2010s. At that time, it plans to unleash an entirely new lineup of hybrids based on next-generation lithium-ion batteries, which pack more power than the current nickel-metal-hydride batteries. If the past is any indication, Toyota's future looks very green.

Questions for Discussion

1. What microenvironmental factors affected both the first generation and second generation models of the Toyota Prius? How well has Toyota dealt with these factors?

2. Outline the major macroenvironmental factors—demographic, economic, natural, technological, political and cultural—that have affected Prius sales. How well has Toyota dealt with each of these factors?

3. Evaluate Toyota's marketing strategy so far. What has Toyota done well? How might it improve its strategy?

4. GM's marketing director for new ventures, Ken Stewart, says "If you want to get a lot of hybrids on the road, you put them in vehicles that people are buying now." This seems to summarize the U.S. auto makers' approach to hybrids. Would you agree with Mr. Stewart? Why or why not?

Sources: Martin Zimmerman, "Hybrid Car Sales Are Zoomin," *Los Angeles Times*, May 23, 2008, p. A1; David Welch, "Prius: Over 1 Million Sold," *BusinessWeek*, May 15, 2008, accessed at www.businessweek.com; Peter Valdes-Dapena, "Prius Still King as Hybrid Auto Sales Rise," *CNNMoney.com*, August 2, 2007; Peter Valdes-Dapena, "Mad Market for Used Fuel-Sippers," *CNNMoney.com*, May 18, 2006; David Kiley and David Welch, "Invasion of the Hybrids," *BusinessWeek*, January 10, 2006; and Brian Twomey, "The Prius Is the World's Best Selling Hybrid," *Mirror*, May 23, 2008, p. 44.

Chapter 4

Part 1   Defining Marketing and the Marketing Process (Chapters 1, 2)
Part 2   Understanding the Marketplace and Consumers (Chapters 3, 4, 5, 6)
Part 3   Designing a Customer-Driven Strategy and Mix (Chapters 7, 8, 9, 10, 11, 12, 13, 14, 15, 16, 17)
Part 4   Extending Marketing (Chapters 18, 19, 20)

Managing Marketing Information to Gain Customer Insights

Chapter PREVIEW

In the previous chapter, you learned about the complex and changing marketing environment. In this chapter, we continue our exploration of how marketers gain insights into consumers and the marketplace. We look at how companies develop and manage information about important marketplace elements—customers, competitors, products, and marketing programs. To succeed in today's marketplace, companies must know how to turn mountains of marketing information into fresh customer insights that will help them deliver greater value to customers.

We'll start this chapter with a story about ZIBA, a brand and product design consultancy that helps its clients to create new products that connect strongly with customers. ZIBA's designs don't start in a research lab. ZIBA's first step is to research consumers and get to know them—*really* get to know them. Then, based on the deep insights garnered from consumer research, ZIBA designs products that turn consumers' heads and open their wallets.

ZIBA is a brand and new-product design consultancy. In its own words, it "helps companies to create meaningful ideas, designs, and experiences that consumers crave." ZIBA knows that good product design begins with good marketing research. But it does much, much more than just gather facts about market demographics and consumer buying patterns. It digs in and *really* gets to know consumers. More than just gathering facts and figures, it develops deep customer and market insights. Driven by a self-described "almost unnatural obsession for understanding consumers," ZIBA innovates with soul. "ZIBA's process is about more than design," says a design analyst. "It's about creating something that will evoke emotion—even love."

The company's long odyssey into the hearts and hungers of consumers began in 1989 with—of all things—a squeegee. An entrepreneur hired the consultancy to craft a hip-looking tool for cleaning gunky shower stalls. Rather than pouring through market data or conducting the usual consumer surveys, ZIBA dispatched a small team of designers to plumb the mysteries of the American bathroom. It spent 10 days shadowing people as they bent to their noxious task, photographing the ballet-like movements of window washers, and even studying silk screeners to glean the ergonomics of handling a squeegee-like device.

Such surveillance eventually led to a sculptured, cylindrical handle, about the size of a shampoo bottle, which held two removable, wave-shaped plastic blades. Dubbed the Clerét, the freestanding cleaning tool looked like no other squeegee that had come before. Elegantly simple in its design and effective in its performance, it landed in the Smithsonian's permanent design collection. It also claimed the Industrial Designers Society of America's best-designed new consumer product award (check it out at www.cleret.com/aboutus.html). Best of all, since the Clerét's launch, the start-up has sold $40 million

worth of the thing. From that point on, every ZIBA design would grow out of its unique research approach of first decoding the consumer's mind in order to forge key customer insights.

At the heart of ZIBA's success is its Consumer Insights and Trends Group, an interesting mix of social anthropologists, cultural ethnographers, user-experience wizards, trend trackers, brand translators, and cool hunters, headed by creative director Steve McCallion. McCallion argues that it's not enough to study the average user and ask them what they want. "We're going for something deeper—to understand *why* people want what they want," he says. "Our ability to invent is solely dependent on our ability to capture that dynamic relationship between the brand and the culture that finds it relevant."

So when Sirius Satellite Radio enlisted ZIBA to fashion a handheld receiver (what would later become the Sirius S50 and the new Stiletto), McCallion and his consumer insights squad went in for a deep dive, spreading out across Portland, Boston, and Nashville to spend some quality time with 44 Sirius subscribers. They toured people's CD collections, hung out with them at Saturday afternoon tailgating parties, studied how they accessorized their cars, and got them to rift on why music matters to them.

> Before designing the Sirius satellite radio, ZIBA's consumer insight squad went in for a "deep dive" with customers, resulting in a "discovery, portability, personalization" positioning statement that drove the entire design process.

Then, back at ZIBA's studios, the team spent weeks harvesting raw data, photographs, and field notes, seeking deeper customer insights. McCallion edited the material down to a design target—the "iPod fatigued"—and assembled more-focused profiles of Sirius users, such as the "intelligent fan" (dials into a wide range of sports and listens to the radio while attending Red Sox games) and the "business charismatic" (drives a BMW 5 Series and holds a platinum frequent-flier card).

Working from the profiles, McCallion and the insights team crafted a perceptive positioning statement—"discovery, portability, personalization"—that drove the entire design process as ZIBA tested and refined scores of prototypes. They knew the business charismatic was looking for a device that wouldn't detract from a car's interior, so they urged designers to give the S50 and the Stiletto a simple, accessible interface. The intelligent fan was keen on portability, and by storyboarding scenarios for the S50, the team discovered that many people wanted to use it to record programming and play it back later. They also pushed for a prominent media dial and a lustrous black finish, based on the conviction that both were powerfully reminiscent of "radio."

"We all have memories of listening to the radio when we were kids," says McCallion. "We wanted to tap into those memories; they help you emotionally connect with the product." Apparently, McCallion and ZIBA scored a hit—the S50 became one of the holiday season's top sellers and took yet another Gold Idea Award, presented by the Industrial Designers Society of America.

ZIBA has come a long way from contemplating shower stalls. Thanks to its innovative research approach, ZIBA is now one of the nation's hottest brand and design consultancies. It has fashioned everything from waffle makers for KitchenAid to winches for Oregon's Warn Industries to a new community development for Portland's South Waterfront. Today, ZIBA's clients include a who's who list of *Fortune* 100 heavyweights such as P&G, Microsoft, FedEx, and Whirlpool as well as an assortment of small technology start-ups and service organizations. ZIBA's doing something right: Over the past several years, it's walked off with a shelf full of Industrial Design Excellence Awards.

ZIBA teaches its clients that successful new products don't begin in their R&D labs. They begin with a deep understanding of customers and their emotional connections to the products they buy and use. "They're terrific designers but it's their ability to capture what your customers are about and then connect with them that's truly fascinating," says one client. Whether it's a squeegee or a high-tech consumer communications device, at ZIBA, innovative new products start with innovative consumer research that provides fresh customer and market insights.[1]

> Based on deep customer insights, ZIBA designs products that turn consumers' heads and open their wallets.

> ZIBA's product designs don't start in the research lab. The design consultancy's first step is to research consumers and get to know them—*really* get to know them.

As the ZIBA story highlights, good products and marketing programs begin with good customer information. Companies also need an abundance of information on competitors, resellers, and other actors and marketplace forces. But more than just gathering information, marketers must *use* the information to gain powerful *customer and market insights*.

Author Comment | Marketing information by itself has little value. The value is in the *customer insights* gained from the information and how these insights are used to make better marketing decisions.

Marketing Information and Customer Insights (pp 99–102)

To create value for customers and to build meaningful relationships with them, marketers must first gain fresh, deep insights into what customers need and want. Companies use such customer insights to develop competitive advantage. "In today's hypercompetitive

Objective Outline

world," states a marketing expert, "the race for competitive advantage is really a race for customer and market insights." Such insights come from the good marketing information.[2]

Consider Apple's phenomenally successful iPod. ▲The iPod wasn't the first digital music player but Apple was the first to get it right. Apple's research uncovered a key insight about how people want to consume digital music—they want to take all their music with them but they want personal music players to be unobtrusive. This insight led to two key design goals—make it as small as a deck of cards and build it to hold 1,000 songs. Add a dash of Apple's design and usability magic to this insight, and you have a recipe for a blockbuster. Apple's expanded iPod line now captures more than 75 percent market share.

However, although customer and market insights are important for building customer value and relationships, these insights can be very difficult to obtain. Customer needs and buying motives are often anything but obvious—consumers themselves usually can't tell you exactly what they need and why they buy. To gain good customer insights, marketers must effectively manage marketing information from a wide range of sources.

Today's marketers have ready access to plenty of marketing information. With the recent explosion of information technologies, companies can now generate information in great quantities. In fact, most marketing managers are overloaded with data and often overwhelmed by it. For example, Wal-Mart refreshes sales data from checkout scanners hourly, adding a billion rows of data a day, equivalent to about 96,000 DVD movies. That's a *lot* of data to analyze.[3] Still, despite this data glut, marketers frequently complain that they lack enough information of the right kind. They don't need *more* information, they need *better* information.

▲ Key customer insights, plus a dash of Apple's design and usability magic, have made the iPod a blockbuster. It now captures more than 75 percent market share.

And they need to make better *use* of the information they already have. Says another marketing information expert, "transforming today's vast, ever-increasing volume of consumer information into actionable marketing insights . . . is the number-one challenge for digital-age marketers."[4]

Thus, a company's marketing research and information system must do more than simply generate lots of information. The real value of marketing research and marketing information lies in how it is used—in the **customer insights** that it provides. "The value of the market research department is not determined by the number of studies that it does," says a marketing expert, "but by the business value of the *insights* that it produces and the decisions that it influences." Says another expert, "Companies that gather, disseminate, and apply deep customer insights obtain powerful, profitable, sustainable competitive advantages for their brands."[5]

Based on such thinking, many companies are now restructuring and renaming their marketing research and information functions. They are creating "customer insights teams," headed by a vice president of customer insights and made up of representatives from all of the firm's functional areas. For example, the head of marketing research at Kraft Foods is called the director of consumer insights and strategy.

Customer insights groups collect customer and market information from a wide variety of sources—ranging from traditional marketing research studies to mingling with and observing consumers to monitoring consumer online conversations about the company and its products. Then, they *use* the marketing information to develop important customer insights from which the company can create more value for its customers. For example, Unilever's customer insights group states its mission simply as "getting better at understanding our consumers and meeting their needs."

In gathering and using customer insights, however, companies must be careful not to go too far and become *customer controlled*. The idea is not to give customers everything they request. Rather, it's to understand customers to the core and give them what they need— to create value for customers as a means of capturing value for the firm in return.[6]

Thus, companies must design effective marketing information systems that give managers the right information, in the right form, at the right time and help them to use this information to create customer value and stronger customer relationships. A **marketing information system (MIS)** consists of people and procedures for assessing informational needs, developing the needed information, and helping decision makers to use the information to generate and validate actionable customer and market insights.

Figure 4.1 shows that the MIS begins and ends with information users—marketing managers, internal and external partners, and others who need marketing information. First, it interacts with these information users to *assess information needs*. Next, it interacts with the

Customer insights
Fresh understandings of customers and the marketplace derived from marketing information that become the basis for creating customer value and relationships.

Marketing information system (MIS)
People and procedures for assessing information needs, developing the needed information, and helping decision makers to use the information to generate and validate actionable customer and market insights.

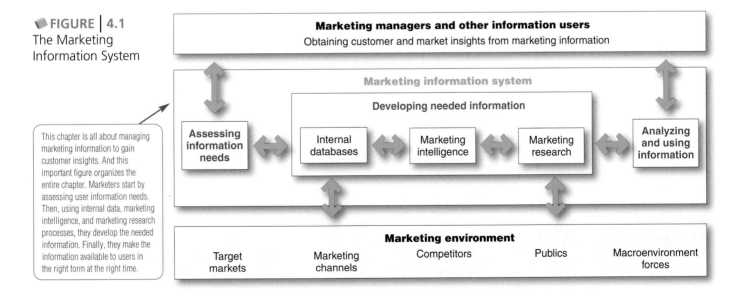

FIGURE | 4.1
The Marketing Information System

This chapter is all about managing marketing information to gain customer insights. And this important figure organizes the entire chapter. Marketers start by assessing user information needs. Then, using internal data, marketing intelligence, and marketing research processes, they develop the needed information. Finally, they make the information available to users in the right form at the right time.

marketing environment to *develop needed information* through internal company databases, marketing intelligence activities, and marketing research. Finally, the MIS helps users to analyze and use the information to develop customer insights, make marketing decisions, and manage customer relationships.

Author Comment | The marketing information system begins and ends with users—with assessing their information needs and then delivering information that meets those needs.

Assessing Marketing Information Needs (p 102)

The marketing information system primarily serves the company's marketing and other managers. However, it may also provide information to external partners, such as suppliers, resellers, or marketing services agencies. For example, Wal-Mart's RetailLink system gives key suppliers access to information on customer buying patterns and inventory levels. And Dell creates tailored Premium Pages for large customers, giving them access to product design, order status, and product support and service information. In designing an information system, the company must consider the needs of all of these users.

A good marketing information system balances the information users would *like* to have against what they really *need* and what is *feasible* to offer. The company begins by interviewing managers to find out what information they would like. Some managers will ask for whatever information they can get without thinking carefully about what they really need. Too much information can be as harmful as too little.

Other managers may omit things they ought to know, or they may not know to ask for some types of information they should have. For example, managers might need to know about surges in favorable or unfavorable consumer "word-of-Web" discussions about their brands on blogs or online social networks. Because they do not know about these discussions, they do not think to ask about them. The MIS must monitor the marketing environment in order to provide decision makers with information they should have in order to better understand customers and make key marketing decisions.

Sometimes the company cannot provide the needed information, either because it is not available or because of MIS limitations. For example, a brand manager might want to know how competitors will change their advertising budgets next year and how these changes will affect industry market shares. The information on planned budgets probably is not available. Even if it is, the company's MIS may not be advanced enough to forecast resulting changes in market shares.

Finally, the costs of obtaining, analyzing, storing, and delivering information can mount quickly. The company must decide whether the value of insights gained from additional information is worth the costs of providing it, and both value and cost are often hard to assess. By itself, information has no worth; its value comes from its *use*. In many cases, additional information will do little to change or improve a manager's decision, or the costs of the information may exceed the returns from improved customer insights and decision making. Marketers should not assume that additional information will always be worth obtaining. Rather, they should weigh carefully the costs of getting more information against the benefits resulting from it.[7]

Author Comment | The problem isn't *finding* information—the world is bursting with information from a glut of sources. The real challenge is to find the *right* information—from inside and outside sources—and to turn it into customer insights.

Developing Marketing Information (pp 102–105)

Marketers can obtain the needed information from *internal data, marketing intelligence,* and *marketing research.*

Internal Data

Internal databases
Electronic collections of consumer and market information obtained from data sources within the company network.

Many companies build extensive **internal databases**, electronic collections of consumer and market information obtained from data sources within the company network. Marketing managers can readily access and work with information in the database to identify marketing opportunities and problems, plan programs, and evaluate performance.

Information in the database can come from many sources. The marketing department furnishes information on customer transactions, demographics, psychographics, and buying behavior. The customer service department keeps records of customer satisfaction or service problems. The accounting department prepares financial statements and keeps detailed records of sales, costs, and cash flows. Operations reports on production schedules, shipments, and inventories. The sales force reports on reseller reactions and competitor activities, and marketing channel partners provide data on point-of-sale transactions. Harnessing such information can provide powerful customer insights and competitive advantage.

Here is an example of how one company uses its internal database to make better marketing decisions:

Internal databases: Pizza Hut can slice and dice its extensive customer database by favorite toppings, what you ordered last, and whether you buy a salad with your cheese and pepperoni pizza, targeting coupon offers to specific households based on past buying behaviors and preferences.

▲ Pizza Hut's database contains detailed customer data on 40 million U.S. households, gleaned from phone orders, online orders, and point-of-sale transactions at its more than 7,500 restaurants around the nation. The company can slice and dice the data by favorite toppings, what you ordered last, and whether you buy a salad with your cheese and pepperoni pizza. It then uses all this data to enhance customer relationships. For example, based on extensive analysis of several years of purchase transactions, Pizza Hut designed a VIP (Very Into Pizza) program to retain its best customers. It invites these customers to join the VIP program for $14.95 and receive a free large pizza. Then, for every two pizzas ordered each month, VIP customers automatically earn a coupon for another free large pizza. Pizza Hut tracks VIP purchases and targets members with additional e-mail offers. In all, the campaign not only retained Pizza Hut's top customers but attracted new customers as well. The program also generated a lot of online buzz. Says one blogger, "So who is always on my mind when I feel like pizza? Who is sending me coupons and free things that make me want to get pizza rather than make dinner? You got it, Pizza Hut. They had me buy in and now they'll have my loyalty. They make it so easy that I wouldn't want to bother getting it anywhere else."[8]

Internal databases usually can be accessed more quickly and cheaply than other information sources, but they also present some problems. Because internal information was often collected for other purposes, it may be incomplete or in the wrong form for making marketing decisions. For example, sales and cost data used by the accounting department for preparing financial statements must be adapted for use in evaluating the value of a specific customer segment, sales force, or channel performance. Data also ages quickly; keeping the database current requires a major effort. In addition, a large company produces mountains of information, which must be well integrated and readily accessible so that managers can find it easily and use it effectively. Managing that much data requires highly sophisticated equipment and techniques.

Marketing Intelligence

Marketing intelligence

The systematic collection and analysis of publicly available information about consumers, competitors, and developments in the marketing environment.

Marketing intelligence is the systematic collection and analysis of publicly available information about consumers, competitors, and developments in the marketplace. The goal of marketing intelligence is to improve strategic decision making by understanding the consumer environment, assessing and tracking competitors' actions, and providing early warnings of opportunities and threats.

Marketing intelligence gathering has grown dramatically as more and more companies are now busily eavesdropping on the marketplace and snooping on their competitors. Techniques range from monitoring Internet buzz or observing consumers firsthand to quizzing the company's own employees, benchmarking competitors' products, researching the Internet, lurking around industry trade shows, and even rooting through rivals' trash bins.

Many companies routinely monitor consumers' online chatter with the help of monitoring services such as Nielsen Online.

Good marketing intelligence can help marketers to gain insights into how consumers talk about and connect with their brands. Many companies send out teams of trained observers to mix and mingle with customers as they use and talk about the company's products. ▲Other companies routinely monitor consumers' online chatter with the help of online monitoring services such as Nielsen Online or BrandIntel. For example, Ford employs marketing intelligence firm BrandIntel to monitor blogs and other Internet sites. Ford wants to know what people are saying about its products, their performance, and their looks. It also wants to know about any important issues—positive or negative—that might have consumers buzzing online about specific Ford models. For example, if BrandIntel discovers unanswered product questions or service complaints, it forwards them to Ford's customer-service staff. When appropriate, the service staff can respond online, identifying themselves and asking if they can join the online discussions.[9]

Companies also need to actively monitor competitors' activities. Firms use competitive intelligence to gain early warnings of competitor moves and strategies, new-product launches, new or changing markets, and potential competitive strengths and weaknesses. A recent analysis by consulting firm PricewaterhouseCoopers found that companies employing competitive intelligence as a critical element in their strategic thinking grow 20 percent faster than those that do not.[10]

Much competitor intelligence can be collected from people inside the company—executives, engineers and scientists, purchasing agents, and the sales force. The company can also obtain important intelligence information from suppliers, resellers, and key customers. Or it can get good information by observing competitors and monitoring their published information. It can buy and analyze competitors' products, monitor their sales, check for new patents, and examine various types of physical evidence. For example, one company regularly checks out competitors' parking lots—full lots might indicate plenty of work and prosperity; half-full lots might suggest hard times.

Some companies have even rifled their competitors' garbage, which is legally considered abandoned property once it leaves the premises. ▲In one classic garbage-snatching incident, Procter & Gamble admitted to "dumpster diving" at rival Unilever's headquarters. Unilever's dumpsters yielded a wealth of information about strategies for Unilever's hair care brands. However, when news of the questionable tactics reached top P&G managers, they were shocked and immediately stopped the project. Although P&G claims it broke no laws, it noted that dumpster raids violated its business policies.

Competitors often reveal intelligence information through their annual reports, business publications, trade show exhibits, press releases, advertisements, and Web pages. The Web has become an invaluable source of competitive intelligence. Using Internet search engines, marketers can search specific competitor names, events, or trends and see what turns up. Moreover, most companies now place volumes of information on their Web sites, providing details to attract customers, partners, suppliers, investors, or franchisees. This can provide a wealth of useful information about competitors' strategies, markets, new products, facilities, and other happenings.

Intelligence seekers can also pore through any of thousands of online databases. Some are free. For example, the U.S. Security and

Marketing Intelligence: Procter & Gamble admitted to "dumpster diving" at rival Unilever's Helene Curtis headquarters. When P&G's top management learned of the questionable practice, it stopped the project, voluntarily informed Unilever, and set up talks to right whatever competitive wrongs had been done.

Exchange Commission's database provides a huge stockpile of financial information on public competitors, and the U.S. Patent Office and Trademark database reveals patents competitors have filed. And for a fee, companies can subscribe to any of the more than 3,000 online databases and information search services such as Hoover's, LexisNexis, and Dun & Bradstreet's Online Access. Notes a marketing intelligence consultant, companies "are often surprised that there's so much out there to know. They're busy with their day-to-day operations and they don't realize how much information can be obtained with a few strategic keystrokes."[11]

The intelligence game goes both ways. Facing determined marketing intelligence efforts by competitors, most companies are now taking steps to protect their own information. For example, Unilever conducts widespread competitive intelligence training. Employees are taught not just how to collect intelligence information but also how to protect company information from competitors. According to a former Unilever staffer, "We were even warned that spies from competitors could be posing as drivers at the minicab company we used." Unilever even performs random checks on internal security. Says the former staffer, "At one [internal marketing] conference, we were set up when an actor was employed to infiltrate the group. The idea was to see who spoke to him, how much they told him, and how long it took to realize that no one knew him. He ended up being there for a long time."[12]

The growing use of marketing intelligence raises a number of ethical issues. Although most of the preceding techniques are legal, and some are considered to be shrewdly competitive, some may involve questionable ethics. Clearly, companies should take advantage of publicly available information. However, they should not stoop to snoop. With all the legitimate intelligence sources now available, a company does not need to break the law or accepted codes of ethics to get good intelligence.

Author Comment | Whereas marketing intelligence involves actively scanning the general marketing environment, marketing research involves more focused studies to gain customer insights relating to specific marketing decisions.

Marketing Research (pp 105–120)

In addition to marketing intelligence information about general consumer, competitor, and marketplace happenings, marketers often need formal studies that provide customer and market insights for specific marketing situations and decisions. For example, Budweiser wants to know what appeals will be most effective in its Super Bowl advertising. Google wants to know how Web searchers will react to a proposed redesign of its site. Or Samsung wants to know how many and what kinds of people will buy its next-generation LCD televisions. In such situations, marketing intelligence will not provide the detailed information needed. Managers will need marketing research.

Marketing research
The systematic design, collection, analysis, and reporting of data relevant to a specific marketing situation facing an organization.

Marketing research is the systematic design, collection, analysis, and reporting of data relevant to a specific marketing situation facing an organization. Companies use marketing research in a wide variety of situations. For example, marketing research gives marketers insights into customer motivations, purchase behavior, and satisfaction. It can help them to assess market potential and market share or to measure the effectiveness of pricing, product, distribution, and promotion activities.

Some large companies have their own research departments that work with marketing managers on marketing research projects. This is how Procter & Gamble, GE, and many other corporate giants handle marketing research. In addition, these companies—like their smaller counterparts—frequently hire outside research specialists to consult with management on specific marketing problems and conduct marketing research studies. Sometimes firms simply purchase data collected by outside firms to aid in their decision making.

The marketing research process has four steps (see 🐭 **Figure 4.2**): defining the problem and research objectives, developing the research plan, implementing the research plan, and interpreting and reporting the findings.

Defining the Problem and Research Objectives

Marketing managers and researchers must work closely together to define the problem and agree on research objectives. The manager best understands the decision for which information is needed; the researcher best understands marketing research and how to obtain

⬤ **FIGURE** | 4.2
The Marketing Research
Process

| Defining the problem and research objectives | → | Developing the research plan for collecting information | → | Implementing the research plan— collecting and analyzing the data | → | Interpreting and reporting the findings |

This first step in the marketing research process is probably the most difficult, but is also the most important one. It guides the entire research process. It's pretty frustrating to reach the end of a large and expensive research project only to learn that you were addressing the wrong problem!

Exploratory research
Marketing research to gather preliminary information that will help define problems and suggest hypotheses.

Descriptive research
Marketing research to better describe marketing problems, situations, or markets, such as the market potential for a product or the demographics and attitudes of consumers.

Causal research
Marketing research to test hypotheses about cause-and-effect relationships.

the information. Defining the problem and research objectives is often the hardest step in the research process. The manager may know that something is wrong, without knowing the specific causes.

After the problem has been defined carefully, the manager and researcher must set the research objectives. A marketing research project might have one of three types of objectives. The objective of **exploratory research** is to gather preliminary information that will help define the problem and suggest hypotheses. The objective of **descriptive research** is to describe things, such as the market potential for a product or the demographics and attitudes of consumers who buy the product. The objective of **causal research** is to test hypotheses about cause-and-effect relationships. For example, would a 10 percent decrease in tuition at a private college result in an enrollment increase sufficient to offset the reduced tuition? Managers often start with exploratory research and later follow with descriptive or causal research.

The statement of the problem and research objectives guides the entire research process. The manager and researcher should put the statement in writing to be certain that they agree on the purpose and expected results of the research.

Developing the Research Plan

Once the research problems and objectives have been defined, researchers must determine the exact information needed, develop a plan for gathering it efficiently, and present the plan to management. The research plan outlines sources of existing data and spells out the specific research approaches, contact methods, sampling plans, and instruments that researchers will use to gather new data.

Research objectives must be translated into specific information needs. ▲For example, suppose Unilever decides to conduct research on how consumers would react to a proposed new premium cologne line sold under its Axe brand. The Axe line of body sprays, shower gels, and deodorants has grown rapidly in recent years to become the world's top male grooming brand. Axe targets 18- to 24-year-old males with a coolly seductive, adventurous, and unconventional positioning that promises to give them "an edge in the dating game." However, as younger consumers of Axe age, research suggests that many see themselves as outgrowing "inexpensive" body scents and switching to cologne.[13] Creating a line of cologne fragrances for the Axe brand would be expensive but it might help to keep current customers as they mature. The proposed research might call for the following specific information:

▲ The decision by the Axe brand to offer a new cologne line that would give maturing customers a new "edge in the dating game" might call for marketing research that provides lots of specific information.

- The demographic, economic, and lifestyle characteristics of current Axe users. (Maturing teen and young adult users might move readily to Axe cologne if it's priced right, carries a more mature scent, and is positioned to meet their changing lifestyles.)

- Characteristics and usage patterns of young male cologne users: What do they need and expect from their fragrances, where do they buy them, when and how do they use them, and what existing cologne brands and price points are most popular? (The new Axe cologne will need strong, relevant positioning in the crowed men's fragrance market.)

- Retailer reactions to the proposed new product line: Would they stock it? Where would they display it? (Failure to get retailer support would hurt sales of the premium cologne.)

- Forecasts of sales of both the new and current Axe products. (Will the new cologne line create new sales or simply take sales from the current Axe products? Will the cologne increase Unilever's overall profits?)

Axe brand managers will need these and many other types of information to decide whether and how to introduce the new cologne product.

The research plan should be presented in a *written proposal*. A written proposal is especially important when the research project is large and complex or when an outside firm carries it out. The proposal should cover the management problems addressed and the research objectives, the information to be obtained, and the way the results will help management decision making. The proposal also should include research costs.

To meet the manager's information needs, the research plan can call for gathering secondary data, primary data, or both. **Secondary data** consist of information that already exists somewhere, having been collected for another purpose. **Primary data** consist of information collected for the specific purpose at hand.

Secondary data
Information that already exists somewhere, having been collected for another purpose.

Primary data
Information collected for the specific purpose at hand.

Commercial online databases
Computerized collections of information available from online commercial sources or via the Internet.

Gathering Secondary Data

Researchers usually start by gathering secondary data. The company's internal database provides a good starting point. However, the company can also tap into a wide assortment of external information sources, including commercial data services and government sources (see ● **Table 4.1**).

Companies can buy secondary data reports from outside suppliers. For example, ACNielsen sells buyer data from a consumer panel of more than 260,000 households in 27 countries worldwide, with measures of trial and repeat purchasing, brand loyalty, and buyer demographics. ▲Experian Consumer Research (Simmons) sells information on more than 8,000 brands in 450 product categories, including detailed consumer profiles that assess everything from the products consumers buy and the brands they prefer to their lifestyles, attitudes, and media preferences. The MONITOR service by Yankelovich sells information on important social and lifestyle trends. These and other firms supply high-quality data to suit a wide variety of marketing information needs.[14]

Using **commercial online databases**, marketing researchers can conduct their own searches of secondary data sources. General database services such as Dialog, ProQuest, and LexisNexis put an incredible wealth of information at the keyboards of marketing decision makers. Beyond commercial Web sites offering information for a fee, almost every industry association, government agency, business publication, and news medium offers free information to those tenacious enough to find their Web sites. There are so many Web sites offering data that finding the right ones can become an almost overwhelming task.

Web search engines can also be a big help in locating relevant secondary information sources. However, they can also be very frustrating and inefficient. For example, an Axe marketer googling "mens cologne" would come up with some 1,470,000 hits! Still, well-structured, well-designed Web searches can be a good starting point to any marketing research project. For example, the fourth hit in the "mens cologne" Google search list would take the Axe marketing to a shopping.yahoo.com page containing consumer reviews and price comparisons of hundreds of men's cologne brands.

▲ Consumer database services such as Experian Consumer Research sell an incredible wealth of information on everything from the products consumers buy and the brands they prefer to their lifestyles, attitudes, and media preferences. Experian Consumer Research is "The Voice of the American Consumer."

● **TABLE** | **4.1**   Selected External Information Sources

For business data:

ACNielsen Corporation (http://acnielsen.com) provides point-of-sale scanner data on sales, market share, and retail prices; data on household purchasing; and data on television audiences (a unit of VNU NV).

Experian Consumer Research (Simmons) (http://smrb.com) provides detailed analysis of consumer patterns in 400 product categories in selected markets.

Information Resources, Inc., (www.infores.com) provides supermarket scanner data for tracking grocery product movement and new product purchasing data.

IMS Health (http://imshealth.com) tracks drug sales, monitors performance of pharmaceutical sales representatives, and offers pharmaceutical market forecasts.

Arbitron (http://arbitron.com) provides local-market and Internet radio audience and advertising expenditure information, among other media and ad spending data.

J.D. Power and Associates (http://jdpower.com) provides information from independent consumer surveys of product and service quality, customer satisfaction, and buyer behavior.

Dun & Bradstreet (http://dnb.com) maintains a database containing information on more than 50 million individual companies around the globe.

comScore Networks (http://comscore.com) provides consumer behavior information and geodemographic analysis of Internet and digital media users around the world.

Thomson Dialog (www.dialog.com) offers access to more than 900 databases containing publications, reports, newsletters, and directories covering dozens of industries.

LexisNexis (http://lexisnexis.com) features articles from business, consumer, and marketing publications plus tracking of firms, industries, trends, and promotion techniques.

Factiva (http://factiva.com) specializes in in-depth financial, historical, and operational information on public and private companies.

Hoover's, Inc., (http://hoovers.com) provides business descriptions, financial overviews, and news about major companies around the world.

CNN (http://cnn.com) reports U.S. and global news and covers the markets and news-making companies in detail.

American Demographics (http://adage.com/americandemographics/) reports on demographic trends and their significance for businesses.

For government data:

Securities and Exchange Commission Edgar database (http://sec.gov/edgar.shtml) provides financial data on U.S. public corporations.

Small Business Administration (http://sba.gov) features information and links for small business owners.

Federal Trade Commission (http://ftc.gov) shows regulations and decisions related to consumer protection and antitrust laws.

Stat-USA (http://stat-usa.gov), a Department of Commerce site, highlights statistics on U.S. business and international trade.

U.S. Census (www.census.gov) provides detailed statistics and trends about the U.S. population.

U.S. Patent and Trademark Office (http://uspto.gov) allows searches to determine who has filed for trademarks and patents.

For Internet data:

ClickZ (http://clickz.com) brings together a wealth of information about the Internet and its users, from consumers to e-commerce.

Interactive Advertising Bureau (http://iab.net) covers statistics about advertising on the Internet.

Jupiter Research (http://jupiterresearch.com) monitors Web traffic and ranks the most popular sites.

Secondary data can usually be obtained more quickly and at a lower cost than primary data. Also, secondary sources can sometimes provide data an individual company cannot collect on its own—information that either is not directly available or would be too expensive to collect. For example, it would be too expensive for Axe marketers to conduct a continuing retail store audit to find out about the market shares, prices, and displays of competitors' brands. But it can buy the InfoScan service from Information Resources, Inc., which provides this information based on scanner and other data from 34,000 retail stores in markets around the nation.[15]

Secondary data can also present problems. The needed information may not exist—researchers can rarely obtain all the data they need from secondary sources. For example, Unilever will not find existing information about consumer reactions to a new cologne line that it has not yet placed on the market. Even when data can be found, the information might not be very usable. The researcher must evaluate secondary information carefully to make certain it is *relevant* (fits research project needs), *accurate* (reliably collected and reported), *current* (up-to-date enough for current decisions), and *impartial* (objectively collected and reported).

Primary Data Collection

Secondary data provide a good starting point for research and often help to define research problems and objectives. In most cases, however, the company must also collect primary data. Just as researchers must carefully evaluate the quality of secondary information, they also must take great care when collecting primary data. They need to make sure that it will be relevant, accurate, current, and unbiased. ● **Table 4.2** shows that designing a plan for primary data collection calls for a number of decisions on *research approaches*, *contact methods*, *sampling plan*, and *research instruments*.

Research Approaches

Research approaches for gathering primary data include observation, surveys, and experiments. Here, we discuss each one in turn.

Observational research

Gathering primary data by observing relevant people, actions, and situations.

Observational Research. **Observational research** involves gathering primary data by observing relevant people, actions, and situations. For example, a bank might evaluate possible new branch locations by checking traffic patterns, neighborhood conditions, and the location of competing branches.

Researchers often observe consumer behavior to glean customer insights they can't obtain by simply asking customers questions. For instance, Fisher-Price has set up an observation lab in which it can observe the reactions of little tots to new toys. The Fisher-Price Play Lab is a sunny, toy-strewn space where lucky kids get to test Fisher-Price prototypes, under the watchful eyes of designers who hope to learn what will get kids worked up into a new-toy frenzy. Others employ "Mindcams," which allow a company to observe through the consumer's eye in their natural environments. For example, Kimberly-Clark used camera-equipped "glasses" to observe behavior of consumers of their Huggies brand:[16]

A few years back, Kimberly-Clark saw sales of its Huggies baby wipes slip just as the company was preparing to launch a line of Huggies baby lotions and bath products. When traditional research didn't yield any compelling customer insights, K-C's marketers decided they could get more useful feedback just from watching customers' daily lives. They came up with camera-equipped "glasses" to be worn by consumers at home, so that researchers could see what they saw. It didn't take long to spot the problems—and the opportunities. Although women in focus groups talked about changing babies at a diaper table, the truth was they changed them on beds, floors, and on top of washing machines in awkward

● **TABLE** | 4.2 Planning Primary Data Collection

Research Approaches	Contact Methods	Sampling Plan	Research Instruments
Observation	Mail	Sampling unit	Questionnaire
Survey	Telephone	Sample size	Mechanical instruments
Experiment	Personal	Sampling procedure	
	Online		

positions. The researchers could see they were struggling with wipe containers and lotions requiring two hands. So the company redesigned the wipe package with a push-button one-handed dispenser and designed lotion and shampoo bottles that can be grabbed and dispensed easily with one hand.

Observational research can obtain information that people are unwilling or unable to provide. In some cases, observation may be the only way to obtain the needed information. In contrast, some things simply cannot be observed, such as feelings, attitudes and motives, or private behavior. Long-term or infrequent behavior is also difficult to observe. Finally, observations can be very difficult to interpret. Because of these limitations, researchers often use observation along with other data collection methods.

Ethnographic research
A form of observational research that involves sending trained observers to watch and interact with consumers in their "natural habitat."

A wide range of companies now use **ethnographic research**. Ethnographic research involves sending trained observers to watch and interact with consumers in their "natural habitat." Consider this example:[17]

Mobile phone maker Nokia wants to add two billion new customers by the end of the decade. To do so, it has invested heavily in ethnographic research, focusing especially on emerging economies. ▲Nokia deploys teams of anthropologists to study deeply the behavior of mobile-phone owners in vast markets such as China, Brazil, and Indian. By "living with the locals," from the shanty towns of Soweto to the bedrooms of Seoul's painfully tech-savvy teens, Nokia gleens subtle insights into nuances of each local culture. For example, it knows first-hand that 50 percent of the world's women keep their phones in their handbags (and miss 20 percent of their calls) and that most Asian early adopters who watch mobile TV ignore the mobile part and tune in from home.

Survey research
Gathering primary data by asking people questions about their knowledge, attitudes, preferences, and buying behavior.

One of the biggest discoveries came from researchers studying how people in poor rural areas overcome some of the barriers to communication they face in their daily lives. Surprisingly, although usually considered a one-owner item, mobile phones in these areas are often used by entire families or even villages because of the cost. Based on this finding, Nokia designed its 1200 and 1208 phones, which make shared use the top priority. The affordable phones offer many useful and durable features and are robust enough to accommodate many different people using them. For example, they contain a long-life battery and multiple phone books so each member of a family or village can keep his or her own contacts and numbers separately from others.

▲ Ethnographic research: Teams of Nokia anthropologists "live with the locals" in emerging economies to glean subtle insights into each local culture. Such insights resulted in the robust Nokia 1200 phone, which makes shared use a top priority.

Observational and ethnographic research often yield the kinds of details that just don't emerge from traditional research questionnaires or focus groups. Whereas traditional quantitative research approaches seek to test known hypotheses and obtain answers to well-defined product or strategy questions, observational research can generate fresh customer and market insights. "The beauty of ethnography," says a research expert, is that it "allows companies to zero in on their customers' unarticulated desires." Agrees another researcher, "Classic market research doesn't go far enough. It can't grasp what people can't imagine or articulate. Think of the Henry Ford quote: 'If I had asked people what they wanted, they would have said faster horses.'"[18]

Survey Research.   **Survey research**, the most widely used method for primary data collection, is the approach best suited for gathering *descriptive* information. A company that wants to know about people's knowledge, attitudes, preferences, or buying behavior can often find out by asking them directly.

The major advantage of survey research is its flexibility—it can be used to obtain many different kinds of information in many different situations. Surveys addressing almost any marketing question or decision can be conducted by phone or mail, in person, or on the Web. However, survey research also presents some problems. Sometimes people are unable to answer survey questions because they cannot remember or have never thought about what they do and why. People may be unwilling to respond to unknown interviewers or about things they consider private. Respondents may answer survey questions even when they do not know the answer in order to appear smarter or more informed. Or they may try to help the interviewer by giving pleasing answers. Finally, busy people may not take the time, or they might resent the intrusion into their privacy.

Experimental research. Whereas observation is best suited for exploratory research and surveys for descriptive research, **experimental research** is best suited for gathering *causal* information. Experiments involve selecting matched groups of subjects, giving them different treatments, controlling unrelated factors, and checking for differences in group responses. Thus, experimental research tries to explain cause-and-effect relationships.

For example, before adding a new sandwich to its menu, McDonald's might use experiments to test the effects on sales of two different prices it might charge. It could introduce the new sandwich at one price in one city and at another price in another city. If the cities are similar, and if all other marketing efforts for the sandwich are the same, then differences in sales in the two cities could be related to the price charged.

Contact Methods

Information can be collected by mail, telephone, personal interview, or online. ● **Table 4.3** shows the strengths and weaknesses of each of these contact methods.

Mail, Telephone, and Personal Interviewing. *Mail questionnaires* can be used to collect large amounts of information at a low cost per respondent. Respondents may give more honest answers to more personal questions on a mail questionnaire than to an unknown interviewer in person or over the phone. Also, no interviewer is involved to bias the respondent's answers.

However, mail questionnaires are not very flexible—all respondents answer the same questions in a fixed order. Mail surveys usually take longer to complete, and the response rate—the number of people returning completed questionnaires—is often very low. Finally, the researcher often has little control over the mail questionnaire sample. Even with a good mailing list, it is hard to control *whom* at the mailing address fills out the questionnaire.

Telephone interviewing is one of the best methods for gathering information quickly, and it provides greater flexibility than mail questionnaires. Interviewers can explain difficult questions and, depending on the answers they receive, skip some questions or probe on

---

Experimental research

Gathering primary data by selecting matched groups of subjects, giving them different treatments, controlling related factors, and checking for differences in group responses.

● TABLE | 4.3   Strengths and Weaknesses of Contact Methods

	Mail	**Telephone**	**Personal**	**Online**
Flexibility	Poor	Good	Excellent	Good
Quantity of data that can be collected	Good	Fair	Excellent	Good
Control of interviewer effects	Excellent	Fair	Poor	Fair
Control of sample	Fair	Excellent	Good	Excellent
Speed of data collection	Poor	Excellent	Good	Excellent
Response rate	Poor	Poor	Good	Good
Cost	Good	Fair	Poor	Excellent

Source: Adapted with permission of the authors from *Marketing Research: Measurement and Method*, 7th ed., by Donald S. Tull and Del I. Hawkins. Copyright 1993 by Macmillan Publishing Company.

others. Response rates tend to be higher than with mail questionnaires, and interviewers can ask to speak to respondents with the desired characteristics or even by name.

However, with telephone interviewing, the cost per respondent is higher than with mail questionnaires. Also, people may not want to discuss personal questions with an interviewer. The method introduces interviewer bias—the way interviewers talk, how they ask questions, and other differences may affect respondents' answers. Different interviewers may interpret and record responses differently, and under time pressures some interviewers might even cheat by recording answers without asking questions. Finally, in this age of do-not-call lists and promotion-harassed consumers, potential survey respondents are increasingly hanging up on telephone interviewers rather than talking with them.

Personal interviewing takes two forms—individual and group interviewing. *Individual interviewing* involves talking with people in their homes or offices, on the street, or in shopping malls. Such interviewing is flexible. Trained interviewers can guide interviews, explain difficult questions, and explore issues as the situation requires. They can show subjects actual products, advertisements, or packages and observe reactions and behavior. However, individual personal interviews may cost three to four times as much as telephone interviews.

Group interviewing consists of inviting six to ten people to meet with a trained moderator to talk about a product, service, or organization. Participants normally are paid a small sum for attending. The moderator encourages free and easy discussion, hoping that group interactions will bring out actual feelings and thoughts. At the same time, the moderator "focuses" the discussion—hence the name **focus group interviewing**.

Researchers and marketers watch the focus group discussions from behind one-way glass and comments are recorded in writing or on video for later study. Today, focus group researchers can even use videoconferencing and Internet technology to connect marketers in distant locations with live focus group action. Using cameras and two-way sound systems, marketing executives in a far-off boardroom can look in and listen, using remote controls to zoom in on faces and pan the focus group at will.

Along with observational research, focus group interviewing has become one of the major qualitative marketing research tools for gaining fresh insights into consumer thoughts and feelings. However, focus group studies present some challenges. They usually employ small samples to keep time and costs down, and it may be hard to generalize from the results. Moreover, consumers in focus groups are not always open and honest about their real feelings, behavior, and intentions in front of other people.

Thus, although focus groups are still widely used, many researchers are tinkering with focus group design. For example, Cammie Dunaway, chief marketing officer at Yahoo!, prefers "immersion groups"—four or five people with whom Yahoo!'s product designers talk informally, without a focus group moderator present. That way, rather than just seeing videos of consumers reacting to a moderator, Yahoo! staffers can work directly with select customers to design new products and programs. "The outcome is richer if [consumers] feel included in our process, not just observed," says Dunaway.[19]

Other researchers are combining focus groups with hypnosis in an effort to get deeper, more vivid insights. Consider this example:[20]

> Volvo equals safety. In focus group after focus group, participants said the same thing. But to check these findings, Volvo called in a hypnotist. Members of Volvo focus groups were asked to test-drive a car. Immediately afterwards, they were hypnotized and asked their true feelings about the brand. It wasn't pretty: Many revealed that Volvo also equals being middle-aged. That idea "for some people was suffocating," says a Volvo researcher. "Hypnosis helped get past the clichés. We needed the conversation taken to a deeper, more emotional place."

Still other researchers are changing the environments in which they conduct focus groups. To help consumers relax and to elicit more authentic responses, they use settings that are more comfortable and more relevant to the products being researched. ▲For example, to get a better understanding of how women shave their legs, Schick Canada

Focus group interviewing
Personal interviewing that involves inviting six to ten people to gather for a few hours with a trained interviewer to talk about a product, service, or organization. The interviewer "focuses" the group discussion on important issues.

created the "Slow Sip" sessions designed to be like a simple get-together with girlfriends.

In these Slow Sip sessions, participants gathered round at a local café to sip coffee or tea and munch on snacks together. The structure was loose, and the congenial setting helped the women to open up and share personal shaving and moisturizing stories on a subject that might have been sensitive in a more formal setting. The Slow Sip sessions produced a number of new customer insights. For example, researchers discovered that the message for their Schick Quattro for Women razor—that Quattro has four-blade technology—was too technical. Women don't care about the engineering behind a razor, they care about shaving results. As a result, Schick Canada repositioned the Quattro as offering a smooth, long-lasting shave. As a side benefit, participants enjoyed the sessions so much that they wanted to stick around for more. They became a kind of ongoing advisory board for Schick's marketers and "brand ambassadors" for Schick's products.[21]

▲ New focus group environments: To create a more congenial setting in which women could open up and share personal shaving and moisturizing stories, Schick Canada sponsored "Slow Sip" sessions in local cafés.

Online marketing research
Collecting primary data online through Internet surveys, online focus groups, Web-based experiments, or tracking consumers' online behavior.

Online Marketing Research.   The growth of the Internet has had a dramatic impact on the conduct of marketing research. Increasingly, researchers are collecting primary data through **online marketing research**—*Internet surveys, online panels, experiments,* and *online focus groups.* By one estimate, global online research spending reached an estimated $4.4 billion in 2008, triple the amount spent in 2005. An estimated one-quarter to one-third of all research will be conducted online by 2010.[22]

Online research can take many forms. A company can use the Web as a survey medium. It can include a questionnaire on its Web site and offer incentives for completing it. It can use e-mail, Web links, or Web pop-ups to invite people to answer questions and possibly win a prize. It can create online panels that provide regular feedback or conduct live discussions or online focus groups. Beyond surveys, researchers can conduct experiments on the Web. They can experiment with different prices, use different headlines, or offer different product features on different Web sites or at different times to learn the relative effectiveness of their offers. Or they can set up virtual shopping environments and use them to test new products and marketing programs. Finally, a company can learn about the behavior of online customers by following their click streams as they visit the Web site and move to other sites.

The Internet is especially well suited to *quantitative* research—conducting marketing surveys and collecting data. Two-thirds of all Americans now have access to the Web, making it a fertile channel for reaching a broad cross section of consumers. As response rates for traditional survey approaches decline and costs increase, the Web is quickly replacing mail and the telephone as the dominant data collection methodology. One industry analyst estimates that consumer packaged-goods firms may now invest as much as two-thirds of their total quantitative survey budgets online. And Internet surveys now command nearly 80 percent of all online research spending.[23]

Web-based survey research offers some real advantages over traditional phone and mail approaches. The most obvious advantages are speed and low costs. "Faster. Cheaper. It boils down to that," concludes a marketing research executive.[24] By going online, researchers can quickly and easily distribute Internet surveys to thousands of respondents simultaneously via e-mail or by posting them on selected Web sites. Responses can be almost instantaneous, and because respondents themselves enter the information, researchers can tabulate, review, and share research data as they arrive.

Online research usually costs much less than research conducted through mail, phone, or personal interviews. Using the Internet eliminates most of the postage, phone, interviewer, and data-handling costs associated with the other approaches. As a result, Internet surveys typically cost 15 to 20 percent less than mail surveys and 30 percent less than phone surveys. Moreover, sample size has little impact on costs. Once the questionnaire is set up, there's little difference in cost between 10 and 10,000 respondents on the Web.

Beyond their speed and cost advantages, Web-based surveys also tend to be more interactive and engaging, easier to complete, and less intrusive than traditional phone or mail surveys. As a result, they usually garner higher response rates. The Internet is an excellent medium for reaching the hard-to-reach—the often-elusive teen, single, affluent, and well-educated audiences. It's also good for reaching working mothers and other people who lead busy lives. Such people are well represented online, and they can respond in their own space and at their own convenience.

Whereas marketing researchers have rushed to use the Internet for quantitative surveys and data collection, they are now also adopting *qualitative* Web-based research approaches—such as online focus groups or depth interviews. Many marketers have learned that the Internet can provide a fast, low-cost way to gain qualitative customer insights. For example, Anheuser-Busch uses the Web—both formally and informally—as a research "test-lab" for advertising ideas.[25]

Anheuser-Busch is increasingly using the Web to spread and fine-tune its advertising. The Web allows it to test-drive edgy material that, in years past, would never have seen the light of day for fear of causing offense on TV. Witness the strange life of "Swear Jar," a commercial that portrays an effort to clean up office language by fining staffers 25 cent per profanity. The twist: the cash goes toward buying Bud Light—and the wholesome plan backfires spectacularly. Although the language was too raw for TV, A-B tested it out on the Internet. Someone sent it to YouTube, where it got more than 2.5 million hits, despite never appearing on television. "The digital space . . . can be an incubator for ideas," says an Anheuser-Busch media executive. Using the Web to gauge fervor for offbeat ads promises broader and quicker insight than the traditional way—peeking through a one-way window as a test group watches new TV commercials. "The Web gives instant credibility or thumbs-down," says the executive.

Online focus groups
Gathering a small group of people online with a trained moderator to chat about a product, service, or organization and gain qualitative insights about consumer attitudes and behavior.

The primary qualitative Web-based research approach is **online focus groups**. Such focus groups offer many advantages over traditional focus groups. Participants can log in from anywhere—all they need is a laptop and a Web connection. Thus, the Internet works well for bringing together people from different parts of the country or world, especially those in higher-income groups who can't spare the time to travel to a central site. Also, researchers can conduct and monitor online focus groups from just about anywhere, eliminating travel, lodging, and facility costs. Finally, although online focus groups require some advance scheduling, results are almost immediate.

Online focus groups can take any of several formats. Most occur in real time, in the form of online chat room discussions in which participants and a moderator sit around a virtual table exchanging comments. Alternatively, researchers might set up an online message board on which respondents interact over the course of several days or a few weeks. Participants log in daily and comment on focus group topics. The focus group moderator monitors the online interactions and redirects the discussion as required to keep the group on track. This ongoing message board format gives participants a chance to reflect on their responses, talk to others, and check out products in the real world as the group progresses. It also gives researchers the opportunity to make ongoing adjustments as the discussion unfolds. As a result, this online approach can produce much more data and deeper insights than single-session, in-person focus groups.

Although low in cost and easy to administer, online focus groups can lack the real-world dynamics of more personal approaches. The online world is devoid of the eye contact, body language, and direct personal interactions found in traditional focus group research. And the Internet format—running, typed commentary and online "emoticons" (punctuation marks that express emotion, such as :-) to signify happiness)—greatly restricts respondent expressiveness. The impersonal nature of the Internet can prevent people from interacting with each other in a normal way and getting excited about a concept.

Some researchers have now added real-time audio and video to their online focus groups. For example, Channel M2 "puts the human touch back into online research" by assembling focus group participants in people-friendly "virtual interview rooms."

To overcome these shortcomings, some researchers are now adding real-time audio and video to their online focus groups. ▲For example, online research firm Channel M2 "puts the human touch back into online research" by assembling focus group participants in people-friendly "virtual interview rooms."[26]

Participants are recruited using traditional methods and then sent a Web camera so that both their verbal and nonverbal reactions can be recorded. Participants are then provided instructions via e-mail, including a link to the Channel M2 online interviewing room and a toll-free teleconference number to call. At the appointed time, when they click on the link and phone in, participants sign on and see the Channel M2 interview room, complete with live video of the other participants, text chat, screen or slide sharing, and a whiteboard. Once the focus group is underway, questions and answers occur in "real time" in a remarkably lively setting. Participants comment spontaneously—verbally, via text messaging, or both. Researchers can "sit in" on the focus group from anywhere, seeing and hearing every respondent. Or they can review a recorded version at a later date.

Although the use of online marketing research is growing rapidly, both quantitative and qualitative Web-based research does have drawbacks. For one, restricted Internet access can make it difficult to get a broad cross section of respondents—about 30 percent of all U.S. adults still lack Web access.[27] However, with Internet penetration growing, this is less of a problem. Another major problem is controlling who's in the online sample. Without seeing respondents, it's difficult to know who they really are. Finally, online surveys can be dry and lacking in dynamics compared with other, more-personal approaches.

To overcome such sample and context problems, many online research firms use opt-in communities and respondent panels. For example, online research firm Greenfield Online provides access to 12 million opt-in panel members in more than 40 countries. Advances in technology—such as the integration of animation, streaming audio and video, and virtual environments—also help to overcome online research dynamics limitations. In another recent development, many companies are developing their own custom social networks and using them to gain customer inputs and insights (see **Real Marketing 4.1**).

Perhaps the most explosive issue facing online researchers concerns consumer privacy. Some fear that unethical researchers will use the e-mail addresses and confidential responses gathered through surveys to sell products after the research is completed. They are concerned about the use of technologies that collect personal information online without the respondents' consent. Failure to address such privacy issues could result in angry, less-cooperative consumers and increased government intervention. Despite these concerns, most industry insiders predict healthy growth for online marketing research.[28]

Sampling Plan

Marketing researchers usually draw conclusions about large groups of consumers by studying a small sample of the total consumer population. A **sample** is a segment of the population selected for marketing research to represent the population as a whole. Ideally, the sample should be representative so that the researcher can make accurate estimates of the thoughts and behaviors of the larger population.

Sample
A segment of the population selected for marketing research to represent the population as a whole.

Real MARKETING 4.1

Custom Social Networks:
Del Monte Unleashes Dog-Lover Insights

When Del Monte Foods—maker of such well-known dog food brands as Kibbles 'n Bits, Gravy Train, and Milk-Bone—was considering a new breakfast treat for dogs, it sent out a note to an online community of dog owners, called "I Love My Dog," asking them what they most wanted to feed their pets in the morning. The consensus answer was something with a bacon-and-egg taste. The result: Del Monte introduced Snausages Breakfast Bites, born out of insights that a dedicated segment of dog owners love to share holiday events and mealtimes with their pets. The Snausages Breakfast Bites are flavored like bacon and eggs and contain an extra dose of vitamins and minerals, which the dog owners said was also important to them.

The "I Love My Dog" online community isn't some random chat room or yet another Web site for dog enthusiasts—it's a custom social network created by Del Monte working with research firm MarketTools. Its 400 members were handpicked to join the

Del Monte's "I Love My Dog" custom social network lets the company continuously observe and interact with important customers to obtain authentic, in-depth insights.

private social network, which the company uses to help create products, test marketing campaigns, and stir up buzz. "The idea is to develop a relationship . . . create ad hoc surveys and get feedback," says Del Monte Senior Customer Insights Manager Gala Amoroso. "If one of the brand managers has a new product idea or a different positioning, instead of

Designing the sample requires three decisions. First, *who* is to be surveyed (what *sampling unit*)? The answer to this question is not always obvious. For example, to study the decision-making process for a family automobile purchase, should the researcher interview the husband, wife, other family members, dealership salespeople, or all of these? The researcher must determine what information is needed and who is most likely to have it.

Second, *how many* people should be surveyed (what *sample size*)? Large samples give more reliable results than small samples. However, larger samples usually cost more, and it is not necessary to sample the entire target market or even a large portion to get reliable results. If well chosen, samples of less than 1 percent of a population can often give good reliability.

Third, *how* should the people in the sample be *chosen* (what *sampling procedure*)? ● **Table 4.4** describes different kinds of samples. Using *probability samples*, each population member has a known chance of being included in the sample, and researchers can calculate confidence limits for sampling error. But when probability sampling costs too much or takes too much time, marketing researchers often take *nonprobability samples*, even though their sampling error cannot be measured. These varied ways of drawing samples have different costs and time limitations as well as different accuracy and statistical properties. Which method is best depends on the needs of the research project.

just internal brainstorming within the company and before putting real research dollars behind it, we'll float it with the [online] community."

Such online networks are now rapidly spreading to companies ranging from Coca-Cola and P&G to Walt Disney's ABC Television Studios. They are often cheaper and more effective than phone surveys or traditional focus groups because companies can draw on the participants in a much broader and deeper way than they could in an offline setting.

Del Monte found that traditional market research techniques simply weren't providing enough depth of customer understanding. Traditional qualitative methods (such as ethnographies and focus groups) were either too time-consuming or too shallow. Surveys and other quantitative methods, although helpful in answering specific questions, did not allow for interactive exploration. In contrast, the custom dog-lover network lets Del Monte continuously observe and interact with important customers to obtain authentic, in-depth insights.

The "I Love My Dog" site and other custom networks bear a resemblance to other online social networking sites, where members create profile pages and post to discussion boards. Companies use them to administer polls, chat in real time with consumers, and even ask members to go to the store to try out specific products. The rapid back-and-forth between the company and the online community can help to substantially shorten the product-development cycle, a process that typically takes a year or more

from the time a company comes up with a product idea until the item arrives in stores.

For Snausages Breakfast Bites, that process took only six months. During that time, Del Monte contacted "I Love My Dog" members dozens of times, both as a group and individually. The company has also tapped network members for prelaunch insights into other products, including its Pup-Peroni treat that recently landed on store shelves. "It is not just a focus group that you see for three hours; you are developing a relationship with these pet parents," says Amoroso.

As with any social-networking site, these private networks face the constant risk of member boredom and, ultimately, member dropout. There can be a fair amount of turnover on the private networks, and to keep members around, the companies that set them up have to constantly add games and other features, along with incentives such as coupons, giveaways, and sneak peeks at new products. Properly tended, however, networks such as "I Love My Dog" help remove some of the guesswork for marketers by letting brands know exactly to whom they are talking and giving them more control over the discussions.

Based on the success of the "I Love My Dog" network, Del Monte has now worked with MarketTools to create another custom network, this one consisting of 10,200 moms. It plans to tap this Moms Insight Network for advice and collaboration on current brands as well as new product launches. One key insight already gleaned from the moms network is that moms trust experts less than ever and are more interested in hearing from other moms in similar situations. This finding lends even greater importance to the Moms Insight Network, which not only seeks in-depth inputs from mothers but connects them with each other in the context of Del Monte brands.

Amoroso has high hopes for Del Monte's custom social networks. "The online community Web sites give us a wealth of information about our target consumers' pains and needs and provides a platform for us to explore and understand their attitudes and behaviors," she says. "It helps us anticipate and identify opportunities, and it enables us to collaborate with our target market to develop new solutions that truly meet their needs. It's different than receiving a report from a study. It's about taking the time to go to the community and listen."

Sources: Portions adapted from Emily Steel, "The New Focus Groups: Online Networks," *Wall Street Journal*, January 14, 2008, p. B6; with quotes and other information from Abbey Klaassen, "Del Monte to Take Its Cues from Moms," *Advertising Age*, July 2, 2007, accessed at http://adage.com/print?article_id=118908; and "Del Monte Foods Turns to Dog Owners to Unleash Innovation," MarketTools Case Study, May 2008, accessed at http://www.markettools.com/resources/files/CS_DelMonte.pdf.

● TABLE | 4.4   Types of Samples

Probability Sample	
Simple random sample	Every member of the population has a known and equal chance of selection.
Stratified random sample	The population is divided into mutually exclusive groups (such as age groups), and random samples are drawn from each group.
Cluster (area) sample	The population is divided into mutually exclusive groups (such as blocks), and the researcher draws a sample of the groups to interview.
Nonprobability Sample	
Convenience sample	The researcher selects the easiest population members from which to obtain information.
Judgment sample	The researcher uses his or her judgment to select population members who are good prospects for accurate information.
Quota sample	The researcher finds and interviews a prescribed number of people in each of several categories.

Research Instruments

In collecting primary data, marketing researchers have a choice of two main research instruments—the *questionnaire* and *mechanical devices*.

Questionnaires. The *questionnaire* is by far the most common instrument, whether administered in person, by phone, or online. Questionnaires are very flexible—there are many ways to ask questions. *Closed-end questions* include all the possible answers, and subjects make choices among them. Examples include multiple-choice questions and scale questions. *Open-end questions* allow respondents to answer in their own words. In a survey of airline users, Southwest might simply ask, "What is your opinion of Southwest Airlines?" Or it might ask people to complete a sentence: "When I choose an airline, the most important consideration is. . . ." These and other kinds of open-end questions often reveal more than closed-end questions because they do not limit respondents' answers.

Open-end questions are especially useful in exploratory research, when the researcher is trying to find out *what* people think but not measuring *how many* people think in a certain way. Closed-end questions, on the other hand, provide answers that are easier to interpret and tabulate.

Researchers should also use care in the *wording* and *ordering* of questions. They should use simple, direct, unbiased wording. Questions should be arranged in a logical order. The first question should create interest if possible, and difficult or personal questions should be asked last so that respondents do not become defensive. A carelessly prepared questionnaire usually contains many errors (see ● **Table 4.5**).

Mechanical Instruments. Although questionnaires are the most common research instrument, researchers also use *mechanical instruments* to monitor consumer behavior. Nielsen Media Research attaches *people meters* to television sets in selected homes to record who watches which programs. Retailers use *checkout scanners* to record shoppers' purchases.

Other mechanical devices measure subjects' physical responses. For example, advertisers use eye cameras to study viewers' eye movements while watching ads—at what points their eyes focus first and how long they linger on any given ad component. IBM's BlueEyes technology interprets human facial reactions by tracking pupil, eyebrow, and mouth movements. BlueEyes offers a host of potential marketing uses, such as marketing machines that "know how you feel" and react accordingly. An elderly man squints at a bank's ATM screen and the font size doubles almost instantly. A woman at a shopping center kiosk smiles at a travel ad, prompting the device to print out a travel discount coupon.[29]

Still other researchers are applying "neuromarketing," measuring brain activity to learn how consumers feel and respond. Marketing scientists using MRI scans have learned that

● TABLE | 4.5   A "Questionable Questionnaire"

Suppose that a summer camp director has prepared the following questionnaire to use in interviewing the parents of prospective campers. How would you assess each question?

1. What is your income to the nearest hundred dollars? *People don't usually know their income to the nearest hundred dollars, nor do they want to reveal their income that closely. Moreover, a researcher should never open a questionnaire with such a personal question.*

2. Are you a strong or weak supporter of overnight summer camping for your children? *What do "strong" and "weak" mean?*

3. Do your children behave themselves well at a summer camp? Yes ( ) No ( ) *"Behave" is a relative term. Furthermore, are yes and no the best response options for this question? Besides, will people answer this honestly and objectively? Why ask the question in the first place?*

4. How many camps mailed or e-mailed information to you last year? This year? *Who can remember this?*

5. What are the most salient and determinant attributes in your evaluation of summer camps? *What are salient and determinant attributes? Don't use big words on me!*

6. Do you think it is right to deprive your child of the opportunity to grow into a mature person through the experience of summer camping? *A loaded question. Given the bias, how can any parent answer yes?*

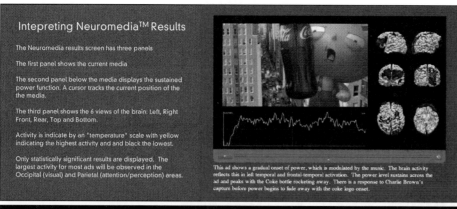

Interpreting Neuromedia™ Results

The Neuromedia results screen has three panels

The first panel shows the current media

The second panel below the media displays the sustained power function. A cursor tracks the current position of the media.

The third panel shows the 6 views of the brain: Left, Right Front, Rear, Top and Bottom.

Activity is indicate by an "temperature" scale with yellow indicating the highest activity and and black the lowest.

Only statistically significant results are displayed. The largest activity for most ads will be observed in the Occipital (visual) and Parietal (attention/perception) areas.

This ad shows a gradual onset of power, which is modulated by the music. The brain activity reflects this in left temporal and frontal-temporal activation. The power level sustains across the ad and peaks with the Coke bottle rocketing away. There is a response to Charlie Brown's capture before power begins to fade away with the coke logo onset.

▲ Neuromarketing: When researchers strapped electrode-loaded caps on the noggins of test subjects during last year's Super Bowl, they learned that brain activity soared for some ads but lagged for others.

"strong brands trigger activity in parts of the brain associated with self-identification, positive emotions, and rewards." According to one observer, it "turns out the Nike's swoosh is more than just a feel-good brand logo. It actually lights up your brain." ▲Similarly, when researchers strapped electrode-loaded caps on the noggins of test subjects during last year's Super Bowl to measure advertising engagement, they learned that brain activity soared for some ads but lagged for others.[30] Here's an example of neuromarketing at work:[31]

Thirty-four bathroom-cleanser users recently went to a research lab to watch "Prison Visitor," the much-awarded TV spot for Unilever's Vim line of home cleaners, positioned as a product that "deals with the toughest dirt." The ad shows a young girl visiting her distraught mother, who appears to be behind a prison glass but is revealed to be scrubbing a grimy shower. Researchers wanted a "clean read" on the ad, so they tested consumers in places where the ad never aired and where the product wasn't yet available. Participants reacted strongly to a "hands on glass" sequence, particularly during a dramatic "I love you, Momma!" "I love you too, baby!" exchange. However, the scenes showing the product demonstration and brand message evoked a much weaker response. In all, the ad stirred up very strong, mostly negative emotions. Follow-up interviews showed that consumers actually hated the ad. How did researchers measure viewers' response to such emotionally charged advertising? Easy. Each participant in the study was asked how they felt about the ad. Oh, and even more telling, there were six electrodes attached to each person's head. Welcome to the world of neuromarketing, which peers into consumers' minds by measuring brain activity to discover how consumers respond to brands and marketing.

Although neuromarketing techniques can measure consumer involvement and emotional responses minute by minute, such brain responses can be difficult to interpret. Thus, neuromarketing is usually used in combination with other research approaches to gain a more complete picture of what goes on inside consumers' heads.[32]

Implementing the Research Plan

The researcher next puts the marketing research plan into action. This involves collecting, processing, and analyzing the information. Data collection can be carried out by the company's marketing research staff or by outside firms. The data collection phase of the marketing research process is generally the most expensive and the most subject to error. Researchers should watch closely to make sure that the plan is implemented correctly. They must guard against problems with contacting respondents, with respondents who refuse to cooperate or who give biased answers, and with interviewers who make mistakes or take shortcuts.

Researchers must also process and analyze the collected data to isolate important information and findings. They need to check data for accuracy and completeness and code it for analysis. The researchers then tabulate the results and compute statistical measures.

Interpreting and Reporting the Findings

The market researcher must now interpret the findings, draw conclusions, and report them to management. The researcher should not try to overwhelm managers with numbers and fancy statistical techniques. Rather, the researcher should present important findings and insights that are useful in the major decisions faced by management.

However, interpretation should not be left only to the researchers. They are often experts in research design and statistics, but the marketing manager knows more about the problem and the decisions that must be made. The best research means little if the manager blindly accepts faulty interpretations from the researcher. Similarly, managers may be biased—they might tend to accept research results that show what they expected and to reject those that they did not expect or hope for. In many cases, findings can be interpreted in different ways, and discussions between researchers and managers will help point to the best interpretations. Thus, managers and researchers must work together closely when interpreting research results, and both must share responsibility for the research process and resulting decisions.

Analyzing and Using Marketing Information (pp 120–122)

Information gathered in internal databases and through marketing intelligence and marketing research usually requires additional analysis. And managers may need help applying the information to gain customer and market insights that will improve their marketing decisions. This help may include advanced statistical analysis to learn more about the relationships within a set of data. Information analysis might also involve the application of analytical models that will help marketers make better decisions.

Once the information has been processed and analyzed, it must be made available to the right decision makers at the right time. In the following sections, we look deeper into analyzing and using marketing information.

Customer Relationship Management (CRM)

Author Comment We've talked generally about managing customer relationships throughout the book. But here, "Customer Relationship Management" (CRM) has a much narrower data-management meaning. It refers to capturing and using customer data from all sources to manage customer interactions and build customer relationships.

The question of how best to analyze and use individual customer data presents special problems. Most companies are awash in information about their customers. In fact, smart companies capture information at every possible customer *touch point*. These touch points include customer purchases, sales force contacts, service and support calls, Web site visits, satisfaction surveys, credit and payment interactions, market research studies—every contact between the customer and the company.

The trouble is that this information is usually scattered widely across the organization. It is buried deep in the separate databases and records of different company departments. To overcome such problems, many companies are now turning to **customer relationship management (CRM)** to manage detailed information about individual customers and carefully manage customer touch points in order to maximize customer loyalty.

Customer relationship management (CRM)
Managing detailed information about individual customers and carefully managing customer "touch points" in order to maximize customer loyalty.

CRM first burst onto the scene in the early 2000s. Many companies rushed in, implementing overly ambitious CRM programs that produced disappointing results and many failures. More recently, however, companies are moving ahead more cautiously and implementing CRM systems that really work. By 2012, U.S. companies will spend an estimated $6.6 billion on CRM systems from companies such as Oracle, Microsoft, Salesforce.com, and SAS.[33]

CRM consists of sophisticated software and analytical tools that integrate customer information from all sources, analyze it in depth, and apply the results to build stronger customer relationships. CRM integrates everything that a company's sales, service, and marketing teams know about individual customers to provide a 360-degree view of the customer relationship.

CRM analysts develop *data warehouses* and use sophisticated *data mining* techniques to unearth the riches hidden in customer data. A data warehouse is a companywide electronic database of finely detailed customer information that needs to be sifted through for gems. The purpose of a data warehouse is not just to gather information, but to pull it together into a central, accessible location. Then, once the data warehouse brings the data together, the company uses high-powered data mining techniques to sift through the mounds of data and dig out interesting findings about customers.

These findings often lead to marketing opportunities. For example, Wal-Mart's huge database provides deep insights for marketing decisions. A few years ago, as Hurricane Ivan roared toward the Florida coast, reports one observer, the giant retailer "knew exactly what to rush onto the shelves of stores in the hurricane's path—strawberry Pop Tarts. By mining years of sales data from just prior to other hurricanes, [Wal-Mart] figured out that shoppers would stock up on Pop Tarts—which don't require refrigeration or cooking."[34]

By using CRM to understand customers better, companies can provide higher levels of customer service and develop deeper customer relationships. They can use CRM to pinpoint high-value customers, target them more effectively, cross-sell the company's products, and create offers tailored to specific customer requirements.

For example, ▲Harrah's Entertainment, the world's largest casino operator, uses CRM to manage day-to-day relationships with important customers at its Harrah's, Caesars, Horseshoe, Bally's, Flamingo, and Showboat casinos around the world. During the past decade, Harrah's Total Rewards Program has become *the* model for good CRM and customer-loyalty management.[35]

More than 80 percent of Harrah's customers worldwide—40 million in all—use a Harrah's Total Rewards card. Information from every swipe of every card at each of Harrah's 40 casinos zips off to a central computer in Memphis, Tennessee, creating a vast customer database. Harrah's carefully mines this mother lode of information to gain insights into customer characteristics and behavior. It then uses these insights to manage day-to-day customer relationships. In fact, Harrah's now processes customer information in real time, from the moment customers swipe their rewards cards, creating the ideal link between data and the customer experience.

Based on up-to-the-minute customer information, casino personnel know which customers should be rewarded with free show tickets, dinner vouchers, or room upgrades. Says Harrah's chief information officer, "A person might walk up to you while you're playing and offer you $5 to play more slots, or a free meal, or maybe just wish you a happy birthday." Compared with nonmembers, Total Rewards customers visit the company's casinos more frequently, stay longer, and spend a lot more of their dollars in Harrah's rather than in rival casinos. Through smart CRM, Harrah's has hit the customer-loyalty jackpot. In just the past five years, the entertainment giant's sales have nearly tripled while profits have more than doubled.

▲ Customer relationship management: Harrah's CRM system helps the company to focus its branding, marketing, and service development strategies on the needs of its most important customers. "We're trying to figure out which products sell, and we're trying to increase our customer loyalty."

CRM benefits don't come without cost or risk, either in collecting the original customer data or in maintaining and mining it. The most common CRM mistake is to view CRM only as a technology and software solution. But technology alone cannot build profitable customer relationships. "CRM is not a technology solution—you can't achieve . . . improved customer relationships by simply slapping in some software," says a CRM expert. Instead, CRM is just one part of an effective overall *customer relationship management strategy*. "Focus on the *R*," advises the expert. "Remember, a relationship is what CRM is all about."[36]

When it works, the benefits of CRM can far outweigh the costs and risks. Based on a study by SAP, customers using its mySAP CRM software reported an average 10 percent increase in customer retention and a 30 percent increase in sales leads. Overall, 90 percent of the companies surveyed increased in value from use of the software and reported an attractive return on investment. The study's conclusion: "CRM pays off."[37]

Distributing and Using Marketing Information

Marketing information has no value until it is used to gain customer insights and make better marketing decisions. Thus, the marketing information system must make the information readily available to the managers and others who make marketing decisions or deal with customers. In some cases, this means providing managers with regular performance reports, intelligence updates, and reports on the results of research studies.

But marketing managers may also need nonroutine information for special situations and on-the-spot decisions. For example, a sales manager having trouble with a large customer may want a summary of the account's sales and profitability over the past year. Or a retail store manager who has run out of a best-selling product may want to know the current inventory levels in the chain's other stores. Increasingly, therefore, information distribution involves entering information into databases and making it available in a timely, user-friendly way.

Many firms use a company *intranet* to facilitate this process. The intranet provides ready access to research information, reports, shared work documents, contact information for employees and other stakeholders, and more. For example, iGo, a catalog and Web retailer, integrates incoming customer service calls with up-to-date database information about customers' Web purchases and e-mail inquiries. By accessing this information on the intranet while speaking with the customer, iGo's service representatives can get a well-rounded picture of each customer's purchasing history and previous contacts with the company.

In addition, companies are increasingly allowing key customers and value-network members to access account, product, and other data on demand through *extranets*. Suppliers, customers, resellers, and select other network members may access a company's extranet to update their accounts, arrange purchases, and check orders against inventories to improve customer service. For example, Wal-Mart's RetailLink extranet system provides suppliers with a two-year history of every product's daily sales in every Wal-Mart store worldwide, letting them track when and where their products are selling and current inventory levels. And Target's PartnersOnline extranet lets its supplier/partners review current sales, inventory, delivery, and forecasting data. Such information sharing helps Target, its suppliers, and its customer by elevating the performance of the supply chain.[38]

Thanks to modern technology, today's marketing managers can gain direct access to the information system at any time and from virtually any location. They can tap into the system while working at a home office, from a hotel room, or from the local Starbucks through a wireless network—anyplace where they can turn on a laptop and link up. Such systems allow managers to get the information they need directly and quickly and to tailor it to their own needs. From just about anywhere, they can obtain information from company or outside databases, analyze it using statistical software, prepare reports and presentations, and communicate directly with others in the network.

Other Marketing Information Considerations (pp 122–128)

This section discusses marketing information in two special contexts: marketing research in small businesses and nonprofit organizations and international marketing research. Finally, we look at public policy and ethics issues in marketing research.

Marketing Research in Small Businesses and Nonprofit Organizations

Just like larger firms, small organizations need market information and the customer and market insights that it can provide. Start-up businesses need information about their potential customers, industries, competitors, unfilled needs, and reactions to new market offers.

Existing small businesses must track changes in customer needs and wants, reactions to new products, and changes in the competitive environment.

Managers of small businesses and nonprofit organizations often think that marketing research can be done only by experts in large companies with big research budgets. True, large-scale research studies are beyond the budgets of most small businesses. However, many of the marketing research techniques discussed in this chapter also can be used by smaller organizations in a less formal manner and at little or no expense. ▲Consider how one small-business owner conducted market research on a shoestring before even opening his doors:[39]

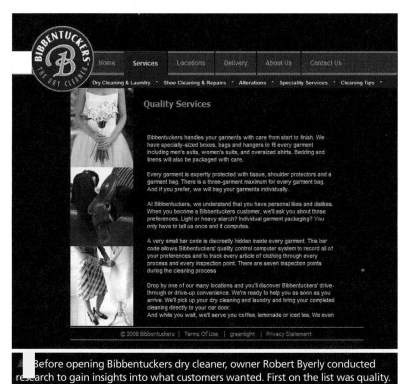

Before opening Bibbentuckers dry cleaner, owner Robert Byerly conducted research to gain insights into what customers wanted. First on the list was quality.

After a string of bad experiences with his local dry cleaner, Robert Byerley decided to open his own dry-cleaning business. But before jumping in, he conducted plenty of market research. He needed a key customer insight: How would he make his cleaners stand out? To start, Byerley spent an entire week in the library and online, researching the dry-cleaning industry. To get input from potential customers, using a marketing firm, Byerley held focus groups on the store's name, look, and brochure. He also took clothes to the 15 best competing cleaners in town and had focus group members critique their work. Based on his research, he made a list of features for his new business. First on his list: quality. His business would stand behind everything it did. Not on the list: cheap prices. Creating the perfect dry-cleaning establishment simply didn't fit with a discount operation.

With his research complete, Byerley opened Bibbentuckers, a high-end dry cleaner positioned on high-quality service and convenience. It featured a bank-like drive-through area with curbside delivery. A computerized bar code system read customer cleaning preferences and tracked clothes all the way through the cleaning process. Byerley added other differentiators, such as decorative awnings, refreshments, and TV screens. "I wanted a place . . . that paired five-star service and quality with an establishment that didn't look like a dry cleaner," he says. The market research yielded results. Today, Bibbentuckers is a thriving three-store operation.

"Too [few] small-business owners have a . . . marketing mind-set," says a small-business consultant. "You have to think like Procter & Gamble. What would they do before launching a new product? They would find out who their customer is and who their competition is."[40]

Managers of small businesses and nonprofit organizations can obtain good marketing insights simply by *observing* things around them and talking with their customers. They can conduct informal *surveys* using small convenience samples. Small organizations can also obtain most of the secondary data available to large businesses. And many associations, local media, chambers of commerce, and government agencies provide special help to small organizations. For example, the U.S. Small Business Administration offers dozens of free publications and a Web site (www.sbaonline.sba.gov) that give advice on topics ranging from starting, financing, and expanding a small business to ordering business cards. Other excellent Web resources for small businesses include the U.S. Census Bureau (www.census.gov) and the Bureau of Economic Analysis (www.bea.gov). Finally, small businesses can collect a considerable amount of information at very little cost on the Internet. They can scour competitor and customer Web sites and use Internet search engines to research specific companies and issues.

In summary, secondary data collection, observation, surveys, and experiments can all be used effectively by small organizations with small budgets. However, although these informal research methods are less complex and less costly, they still must be conducted with care. Managers must think carefully about the objectives of the research, formulate questions in advance, recognize the biases introduced by smaller samples and less skilled researchers, and conduct the research systematically.[41]

International Marketing Research

International marketing research has grown tremendously over the past decade. In 1995, the top 25 global marketing research organizations had total combined revenues of $5.7 billion, with 45 percent of these revenues coming from outside companies' home countries. By 2006, total revenues for these organizations had grown to $15.5 billion, and the out-of-home-country share had grown to more than 55 percent.[42]

International marketing researchers follow the same steps as domestic researchers, from defining the research problem and developing a research plan to interpreting and reporting the results. However, these researchers often face more and different problems. Whereas domestic researchers deal with fairly homogenous markets within a single country, international researchers deal with diverse markets in many different countries. These markets often vary greatly in their levels of economic development, cultures and customs, and buying patterns.

In many foreign markets, the international researcher may have a difficult time finding good secondary data. Whereas U.S. marketing researchers can obtain reliable secondary data from dozens of domestic research services, many countries have almost no research services at all. Some of the largest international research services do operate in many countries. ▲For example, ACNielsen Corporation (owned by The Nielsen Company, the world's largest marketing research company) has offices in more than 100 countries, from Schaumburg, Illinois, to Hong Kong to Nicosia, Cyprus.[43] However, most research firms operate in only a relative handful of countries. Thus, even when secondary information is available, it usually must be obtained from many different sources on a country-by-country basis, making the information difficult to combine or compare.

Because of the scarcity of good secondary data, international researchers often must collect their own primary data. For example, they may find it difficult simply to develop good samples. U.S. researchers can use current telephone directories, e-mail lists, census tract data, and any of several sources of socioeconomic data to construct samples. However, such information is largely lacking in many countries.

Once the sample is drawn, the U.S. researcher usually can reach most respondents easily by telephone, by mail, on the Internet, or in person. Reaching respondents is often not so easy in other parts of the world. Researchers in Mexico cannot rely on telephone, Internet, and mail data collection—most data collection is door to door and concentrated in three or four of the largest cities. In some countries, few people have phones or personal computers. For example, whereas there are 605 main telephone lines, 680 cell phone subscribers, and 762 PCs per thousand people in the United States, there are only 189 phone lines, 460 cell phone subscribers, and 136 PCs per thousand in Mexico. In Kenya, the numbers drop to 8 phone lines, 135 cell

▲ Some of the largest research services firms have large international organizations. ACNielsen has offices in more than 100 countries, here Germany and Japan.

phone subscribers, and 9 PCs per thousand people. In some countries, the postal system is notoriously unreliable. In Brazil, for instance, an estimated 30 percent of the mail is never delivered. In many developing countries, poor roads and transportation systems make certain areas hard to reach, making personal interviews difficult and expensive.[44]

Cultural differences from country to country cause additional problems for international researchers. Language is the most obvious obstacle. For example, questionnaires must be prepared in one language and then translated into the languages of each country researched. Responses then must be translated back into the original language for analysis and interpretation. This adds to research costs and increases the risks of error.

Translating a questionnaire from one language to another is anything but easy. Many idioms, phrases, and statements mean different things in different cultures. For example, a Danish executive noted, "Check this out by having a different translator put back into English what you've translated from English. You'll get the shock of your life. I remember [an example in which] 'out of sight, out of mind' had become 'invisible things are insane.'"[45]

Consumers in different countries also vary in their attitudes toward marketing research. People in one country may be very willing to respond; in other countries, nonresponse can be a major problem. Customs in some countries may prohibit people from talking with strangers. In certain cultures, research questions often are considered too personal. For example, in many Latin American countries, people may feel embarrassed to talk with researchers about their choices of shampoo, deodorant, or other personal care products. Similarly, in most Muslim countries, mixed-gender focus groups are taboo, as is videotaping female-only focus groups. Even when respondents are *willing* to respond, they may not be *able* to because of high functional illiteracy rates.

Despite these problems, as global marketing grows, global companies have little choice but to conduct such international marketing research. Although the costs and problems associated with international research may be high, the costs of not doing it—in terms of missed opportunities and mistakes—might be even higher. Once recognized, many of the problems associated with international marketing research can be overcome or avoided.

Public Policy and Ethics in Marketing Research

Most marketing research benefits both the sponsoring company and its consumers. Through marketing research, companies learn more about consumers' needs, resulting in more satisfying products and services and stronger customer relationships. However, the misuse of marketing research can also harm or annoy consumers. Two major public policy and ethics issues in marketing research are intrusions on consumer privacy and the misuse of research findings.

Intrusions on Consumer Privacy

Many consumers feel positive about marketing research and believe that it serves a useful purpose. Some actually enjoy being interviewed and giving their opinions. However, others strongly resent or even mistrust marketing research. They worry that marketers are building huge databases full of personal information about customers. Or they fear that researchers might use sophisticated techniques to probe our deepest feelings, peek over our shoulders as we shop, or eavesdrop on our conversations and then use this knowledge to manipulate our buying.

There are no easy answers when it comes to marketing research and privacy. For example, is it a good or bad thing that marketers track and analyze consumers' Web clicks and target ads to individuals based on their browsing behavior? (See **Real Marketing 4.2**.) Should we applaud or resent the fact that ConAgra, the giant food company known for its Butterball turkeys and Healthy Choice meals, listens in on consumer Web discussions to learn all it can about diet trends and reactions to its brands?

On the one hand, most online chatter is public information, and listening in helps ConAgra to improve its products and bring more value to customers. On the other hand, although it tracks only public forums, the company does not inform consumers or obtain participants' formal consent. Many consumers would find it disconcerting to learn that ConAgra and other companies are tuning in on their online conversations.

Real MARKETING 4.2

Tracking Consumers on the Web:
Smart Targeting or a Little Creepy?

On the Internet today, everybody knows who you are. In fact, legions of Internet companies also know your gender, your age, the neighborhood you live in, that you like pickup trucks, and that you spent, say, three hours and 43 seconds on a Web site for pet lovers on a rainy day in January. All that data streams through myriad computer networks, where it's sorted, cataloged, analyzed, and then used to deliver ads aimed squarely at you, potentially anywhere you travel on the Web. It's called *behavioral targeting*—tracking consumers' online browsing behavior and using it to target ads to them.

Targeting ads on the Web is nothing new. Sites such as Google and Yahoo! routinely do "contextual targeting"—placing ads related to keyword searches alongside the search results. Most of Google's more than $10 billion in revenues come from search-related advertising. But consider this revealing fact: Internet users spend a mere 5 percent of their time actually searching. The rest of the time, they're trolling the vast expanse of Internet space. To fill that space more effectively, online advertisers are now deploying a new breed of supersmart, supertargeted display ads geared to individual Web-browsing behavior.

Behavioral targeting: Wherever you go on the Internet, marketers are looking over your shoulder, then targeting you with ads based on your Web browsing behavior. Is it smart marketing or just "a little bit creepy"?

What you do when you aren't searching—the other 95 percent of the time you spend online—is pure gold to advertisers. And companies such as Yahoo!, Microsoft's MSN, and AOL are busy mining that gold, helping advertisers to target ads based on just about everything you do on the Internet. Yahoo!, the Web's most visited destination, has an estimated 131 million monthly unique visitors to its sites. By dropping "cookies" onto every Web browser that calls up one of its sites, Yahoo! has amassed a staggering amount of data about its users.

Yahoo!'s head of research and data, Usama Fayyad, rides herd on the 12 terabytes of user information that flow into Yahoo!'s servers every day, more than the entire inventory of the Library of Congress. Fittingly, Fayyad is a former rocket scientist whose resumé includes a seven-year stint at NASA's Jet Propulsion Lab. He's an intense numbers guy who went on to found two data-mining companies, one of which he sold to Yahoo!. Fayyad and his group crunch all that online user data, blend it with information about what people do on Yahoo!'s search engine, and feed it into models that predict consumer behavior. This has led Fayyad to an important conclusion: What you do on the Web reveals far more about you than what you type into a search box.

Interestingly, however, many consumers don't seem to mind. Occasionally, the monitoring of discussion groups itself becomes a topic of online conversation. In one online car forum, a discussion of BuzzMetrics (a Nielsen company that specializes in tracking consumer-generated media, including online exchanges) and its research for General Motors produced no objections—just disbelief that the carmaker could listen to their conversations and still produce such unappealing products. Consumers often moan that companies do not listen to them. Perhaps the monitoring of discussion groups can provide an answer to that problem.[46]

Consumers may also have been taken in by previous "research surveys" that actually turned out to be attempts to sell them something. Still other consumers confuse legitimate marketing research studies with promotional efforts and say "no" before the interviewer can even begin. Most, however, simply resent the intrusion. They dislike mail, telephone, or Web surveys that are too long or too personal or that interrupt them at inconvenient times.

Increasing consumer resentment has become a major problem for the marketing research industry, leading to lower survey response rates in recent years. Just as companies

Armed with this mass of data, Yahoo! often sells ad space based not on a site's content but on an individual consumer's online behavior. Say you spent time at Yahoo! Autos sizing up cars based on fuel efficiency, then clicked over to Yahoo!'s Green Center to read about alternative fuels, then looked at cars on eBay (which has a partnership with Yahoo!). Fayyad can probably predict your next move. In fact, he says he can tell with 75 percent certainty which of the 300,000 monthly visitors to Yahoo! Autos will actually purchase a car within the next three months. And the next time you visit Yahoo! Sports or Finance, you'll likely see ads for hybrid cars.

Also moving quickly into online display advertising are a special breed of behavioral targeting advertising agencies, such as Tacoda (http://tacoda.com) and Revenue Science (http://revenuescience.com). To get an even broader view of what consumers are thinking and doing online, such agencies track consumer behavior across multiple Web sites. These companies "are, in effect, taking the trail of crumbs people leave behind as they move around the Internet, and then analyzing them to anticipate people's next steps," says the analyst. This lets them merge audience data from one group of sites with ad placements on another. So if you surf home lawn and garden sites, don't be surprised to see ads for Scotts lawn products the next time you visit Weather.com. Or if you seek car-buying advice at sites such as Edmunds.com or nadaguides.com, expect to see some ads for the very types of cars you researched the next time you visit your favorite ESPN site to catch up on the latest sports scores.

But what about consumer privacy? Yup. As you've no doubt already considered, that's the downside and the biggest danger to the rapidly expanding world of behavioral targeting. As the practice becomes more common, it faces growing consumer backlash. One observer calls it "the dark art of behavioral ad targeting"—eavesdropping on consumers without their knowledge or consent. "When you start to get into the details, it's scarier than you might suspect," says the director of a consumer privacy rights group. "We're recording preferences, hopes, worries, and fears." A coalition of privacy groups has already asked the Federal Trade Commission to consider a "Do Not Track" list (akin to telephone Do-Not-Call lists) to let consumers opt out of behavioral ad targeting.

Some companies are addressing such privacy issues on their own. For example, AOL recently launched a campaign to educate consumers about online behavioral targeting and promises improved technology for opting out of personalized ads. "We want to make the opt-out process as simple and transparent as possible," sales AOL's chief privacy officer. Google has pledged to make the data it collects anonymous after 18 months and to expire cookie files after two years. Ask.com has gone even further, pledging to make Web searches and cookies anonymous after 18 months and to give users the option of deleting their search histories using a tool called AskEraser.

Despite privacy concerns, proponents claim that behavioral targeting benefits more than abuses consumers. "What we have here is person-centric marketing," says the CEO of Tacoda. "That's been the holy grail of brand advertisers for a long, long time." Behavioral ad targeting takes information from users' Web browsing behavior and feeds back ads that are more relevant to their needs and interests.

Although the practice may seem sinister to some consumers, advertisers like what they see so far. According to one survey, more than half of marketers already use behavioral targeting and another third plan to start this year. U.S. companies spent $350 million on behavioral targeting last year and will spend an estimated $1.65 billion annually by 2009. According to one research firm, dollars spent on behavioral targeting yield a 37 percent return on investment.

Still, it won't be easy to maintain consumer trust while at the same time walking the fine line between personalization and privacy. And as more and more companies enter the behavioral targeting ad space, the chances of the tactic getting a bad name grow. "We have something new and powerful," says Tacoda's CEO, "and there are likely to be people who abuse it." Abusive or beneficial, it'll be a hard sell to consumers. As one analyst observes, following consumers online and stalking them with ads just "feels a little creepy."

Sources: Based on information found in Paul Sloan, "The Quest for the Perfect Online Ad," *Business 2.0,* March 2007, pp. 88–92; Thomas Claburn, "Call Off the Wolves," *InformationWeek,* November 12, 2007; Brian Morissey, "Limits of Search Lead Some to Web Behavior," *Adweek,* March 27, 2006, p. 11; Sam Matthews, "Behavioral Targeting Still Not Appreciated," *New Age Media,* December 14, 2006, p. 2; Brian Morissey, "Aim High: Ad Targeting Moves to the Next Level," *Adweek,* January 14, 2008, pp. 49–50; Louise Story, "To Aim Ads, Web Is Keeping a Closer Eye on You," *New York Times,* March 10, 2008; and Jonothan Lemonnier, "Contextual Targeting Boost Loyal Following," *Advertising Age,* April 14, 2008, p. 7.

face the challenge of unearthing valuable but potentially sensitive consumer data while also maintaining consumer trust, consumers wrestle with the trade-offs between personalization and privacy. Although many consumers willingly exchange personal information for free services, easy credit, discounts, upgrades, points, and all sorts of rewards, they also worry about the growth in online identity theft. One study found that 62 percent of consumers express concern over personal privacy when buying online, an increase of 47 percent over a year earlier. So it's no surprise that they are now less than willing to reveal personal information on Web sites.[47]

The marketing research industry is considering several options for responding to this problem. ▲One example is the Council for Marketing and Opinion Research's "Your Opinion Counts" and "Respondent Bill of Rights" initiatives to educate consumers about the benefits of marketing research and to distinguish it from telephone selling and database building. The industry also has considered adopting broad standards, perhaps based on the International Chamber of Commerce's International Code of Marketing and Social Research Practice. This code outlines researchers' responsibilities to respondents and to the general public. For example, it says that researchers should make their names and addresses available

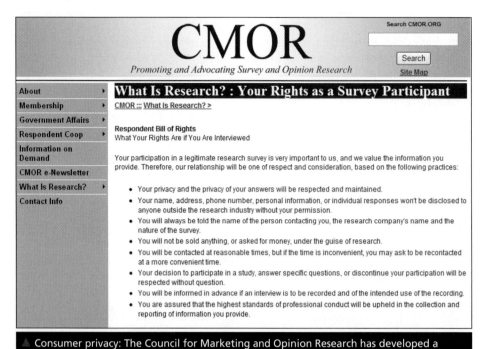

▲ Consumer privacy: The Council for Marketing and Opinion Research has developed a "Respondent Bill of Rights" to help promote responsible marketing research.

to participants. It also bans companies from representing activities such as database compilation or sales and promotional pitches as research.[48]

Most major companies—including IBM, Citigroup, American Express, Eli Lilly, and Microsoft—have now appointed a "chief privacy officer (CPO)," whose job is to safeguard the privacy of consumers who do business with the company. IBM's CPO claims that her job requires "multidisciplinary thinking and attitude." She needs to get all company departments, from technology, legal, and accounting to marketing and communications working together to safeguard customer privacy.[49]

American Express, which deals with a considerable volume of consumer information, has long taken privacy issues seriously. The company developed a set of formal privacy principles in 1991, and in 1998 it became one of the first companies to post privacy policies on its Web site. Its online Internet privacy statement tells customers in clear terms what information American Express collects and how it uses it, how it safeguards the information, and how it uses the information to market to its customers (with instructions on how to opt out).[50]

In the end, if researchers provide value in exchange for information, customers will gladly provide it. For example, Amazon.com's customers do not mind if the firm builds a database of products they buy in order to provide future product recommendations. This saves time and provides value. Similarly, Bizrate users gladly complete surveys rating online seller sites because they can view the overall ratings of others when making purchase decisions. The best approach is for researchers to ask only for the information they need, to use it responsibly to provide customer value, and to avoid sharing information without the customer's permission.

Misuse of Research Findings

Research studies can be powerful persuasion tools; companies often use study results as claims in their advertising and promotion. Today, however, many research studies appear to be little more than vehicles for pitching the sponsor's products. In fact, in some cases, the research surveys appear to have been designed just to produce the intended effect. Few advertisers openly rig their research designs or blatantly misrepresent the findings; most abuses tend to be subtle "stretches."

For example, the choice or wording in a survey can greatly affect the conclusions reached. One Black Flag survey asked: "A roach disk . . . poisons a roach slowly. The dying roach returns to the nest and after it dies is eaten by other roaches. In turn these roaches become poisoned and die. How effective do you think this type of product would be in killing roaches?" Not surprisingly, 79 percent said effective.[51]

Recognizing that surveys can be abused, several associations—including the American Marketing Association, Marketing Research Association, and the Council of American Survey Research Organizations (CASRO)—have developed codes of research ethics and standards of conduct. For example, the CASRO Code of Standards and Ethics for Survey Research outlines researcher responsibilities to respondents, including confidentiality, privacy, and avoidance of harassment. It also outlines major responsibilities in reporting results to clients and the public.[52] In the end, however, unethical or inappropriate actions cannot simply be regulated away. Each company must accept responsibility for policing the conduct and reporting of its own marketing research to protect consumers' best interests and its own.

REVIEWING Objectives AND KEY Terms

To create value for customers and to build meaningful relationships with them, marketers must first gain fresh, deep insights into what customers need and want. Such insights come from good marketing information. As a result of the recent explosion of marketing technology, companies can now obtain great quantities of information, sometimes even too much. The challenge is to transform today's vast volume of consumer information into actionable customer and market insights. A company's marketing research and information system must do more than simply generate lots of information. The real value of marketing research and marketing information lies in how it is used—in the customer insights that it provides.

OBJECTIVE 1 Explain the importance of information in gaining insights about the marketplace and customers. (pp 99–102)

The marketing process starts with a complete understanding of the marketplace and consumer needs and wants. Thus, the company needs sound information in order to produce superior value and satisfaction for customers. The company also requires information on competitors, resellers, and other actors and forces in the marketplace. Increasingly, marketers are viewing information not only as an input for making better decisions but also as an important strategic asset and marketing tool.

OBJECTIVE 2 Define the marketing information system and discuss its parts. (pp 102–105)

The *marketing information system (MIS)* consists of people and procedures for assessing information needs, developing the needed information, and helping decision makers to use the information to generate and validate actionable customer and market insights. A well-designed information system begins and ends with users.

The MIS first *assesses information needs*. The marketing information system primarily serves the company's marketing and other managers, but it may also provide information to external partners. Then, the MIS *develops information* from internal databases, marketing intelligence activities, and marketing research. *Internal databases* provide information on the company's own operations and departments. Such data can be obtained quickly and cheaply but often needs to be adapted for marketing decisions. *Marketing intelligence* activities supply everyday information about developments in the external marketing environment. *Market research* consists of collecting information relevant to a specific marketing problem faced by the company. Lastly, the MIS helps users to analyze and use the information to develop customer insights, make marketing decisions, and manage customer relationships.

OBJECTIVE 3 Outline the steps in the marketing research process. (pp 105–120)

The first step in the marketing research process involves *defining the problem and setting the research objectives,* which may be exploratory, descriptive, or causal research. The second step consists of *developing a research plan* for collecting data from primary and secondary sources. The third step calls for *implementing the marketing research plan* by gathering, processing, and analyzing the information. The fourth step consists of *interpreting and reporting the findings.* Additional information analysis helps marketing managers apply the information and provides them with sophisticated statistical procedures and models from which to develop more rigorous findings.

Both *internal* and *external* secondary data sources often provide information more quickly and at a lower cost than primary data sources, and they can sometimes yield information that a company cannot collect by itself. However, needed information might not exist in secondary sources. Researchers must also evaluate secondary information to ensure that it is *relevant, accurate, current,* and *impartial*. Primary research must also be evaluated for these features. Each primary data collection method— *observational, survey,* and *experimental*—has its own advantages and disadvantages. Similarly, each of the various research contact methods—mail, telephone, personal interview, and online—also has its own advantages and drawbacks.

OBJECTIVE 4 Explain how companies analyze and use marketing information. (pp 120–122)

Information gathered in internal databases and through marketing intelligence and marketing research usually requires more analysis. This may include advanced statistical analysis or the application of analytical models that will help marketers make better decisions. To analyze individual customer data, many companies have now acquired or developed special software and analysis techniques—called *customer relationship management (CRM)*—that integrate, analyze, and apply the mountains of individual customer data contained in their databases.

Marketing information has no value until it is used to make better marketing decisions. Thus, the marketing information system must make the information available to the managers and others who make marketing decisions or deal with customers. In some cases, this means providing regular reports and updates; in other cases it means making nonroutine information available for special situations and on-the-spot decisions. Many firms use company intranets and extranets to facilitate this process. Thanks to modern technology, today's marketing managers can gain direct access to the information system at any time and from virtually any location.

OBJECTIVE 5 Discuss the special issues some marketing researchers face, including public policy and ethics issues. (pp 122–128)

Some marketers face special marketing research situations, such as those conducting research in small business, nonprofit, or international situations. Marketing research can be conducted effectively by small businesses and nonprofit organizations with limited budgets. International marketing researchers follow the same steps as domestic researchers but often face more and different problems. All organizations need to act responsibly to major public policy and ethical issues surrounding marketing research, including issues of intrusions on consumer privacy and misuse of research findings.

KEY Terms

DISCUSSING & APPLYING THE Concepts

Discussing the Concepts

1. Discuss the real value of marketing research and marketing information and how that value is attained. (AACSB: Communication)

2. Which information is more valuable to marketing managers—information from internal databases, from marketing intelligence, or from marketing research? How do these information sources differ? (AACSB: Communication; Reflective Thinking)

3. Explain the differences between primary and secondary data. When is each appropriate and how are they collected? (AACSB: Communication)

4. What are the advantages of Web-based survey research over traditional survey research? (AACSB: Communication)

5. How does customer relationship management (CRM) help companies develop customer insights and deliver superior customer value? (AACSB: Communication)

6. What are the similarities and differences when conducting research in another country versus the domestic market? (AACSB: Communication)

Applying the Concepts

1. Visit www.zoomerang.com or another free online Web survey site. Using the tools at the site, design a five-question survey on the entertainment opportunities in your area. Send the survey to six friends and look at the results. What did you think of the online survey method? (AACSB: Communication; Use of IT; Reflective Thinking)

2. Assume you are interested in opening a children's retail clothing store specializing in upscale children's fashions for newborns through 10-year-olds. You are unsure whether there is enough demand in your area to be profitable. In a small group, discuss what information you need before making this decision and decide on which secondary sources can provide that information. Furthermore, assume you plan to conduct a survey to better estimate demand for this product and describe the best primary data collection method for your needs. (AACSB: Communication; Reflective Thinking)

3. One source of competitive marketing intelligence is a company's Web site. Visit Apple's Web site (www.apple.com) to search for information that might be useful to competitors. Write a brief report of what you found. (AACSB: Communication; Use of IT)

FOCUS ON Technology

If you've ever complained to friends about a bad product or service experience, the marketer probably never heard you. That is, until now. If you complain on a social networking site, you just might get a response. That's what Moosehead, Canada's oldest independent and third largest brewer, did. Moosehead learned of a customer who complained on a blog about purchasing spoiled beer that had not been stored properly at the retail level. The brewer's quick remedy resulted in the blogger posting a "glowing review" of the treatment he received. But how do companies monitor online communications among the millions of consumers worldwide using social media such as blogs, video sharing (YouTube), photo sharing (Flickr), and microblogging (twitter) sites? The key is that users of social media leave clues, such as social bookmarks, friends, followers,

comments, favorites, votes, and so on. Companies could monitor these clues themselves, but most hire experts specializing in social media monitoring to track how people are talking about their brands.

1. Search "social media monitoring" on a search engine to find companies specializing in monitoring social media. Many of these sites discuss examples of how businesses use their service. Discuss two examples in which businesses used social media monitoring successfully. (AACSB: Communication; Use of IT)

2. Monitoring "tagging" is hailed as the way to keep tabs on the Internet. Explain what is meant by a "tag" and explain why monitoring such tags is beneficial for marketers. (AACSB: Communication; Reflective Thinking)

FOCUS ON Ethics

You probably looked at a lot of information before selecting the college or university you are currently attending. Perhaps you even looked at *U.S. News and World Report*'s annual college ranking issue, which is perceived as a trustworthy source of information. There is a wealth of comparative information provided, from standardized test scores to graduation rates. But in 2007, one college president spoke out about the concern over "made up fake" data. It seems that Sarah Lawrence College stopped using SAT scores for entrance requirements. So in its ratings for that school, *U.S. News* planned to use a "made-up" score for that school by taking one standard deviation off the average SAT scores for peer institutions (about 200 points). Many other institutions have changed from requiring SAT scores (in some cases ACT scores as well) to "SAT optional," which means a student can submit a score but it's not required. While "SAT optional" schools still have average scores to report for the rankings, these scores are not necessarily reflective of the entire student body. Critics voiced concerns over how other missing or incomplete information is accounted for in the rankings, lending doubt to the credibility of this influential source.

1. Find an article that provides rankings, such as the college rankings published by *U.S. News* or the ones for business schools, such as that published by *BusinessWeek*. Does the article explain how data are collected and what the values mean? Describe how data are collected and critique the information for usefulness. (AACSB: Communication; Reflective Thinking)

2. In some cases of missing data, it is acceptable to put the average or some variant of that for the missing data. Do you think using fabricated data is appropriate in rankings such as the one published by *U.S. News*? (AACSB: Communication; Ethical Reasoning)

MARKETING BY THE Numbers

"Company X has 34 percent market share," "Brand A is preferred by over 60 percent of consumers," "prices are increasing at a rate of 44 percent," and "the average customer satisfaction rating is 4, satisfied, on a 1–5 scale." These are all conclusions based on statistics. Statistics lend credibility to conclusions and can be very persuasive. But are the conclusions legitimate? Many are survey-based claims, meaning survey research is used to substantiate claims such as those used in advertising. Claiming 60 percent of consumers prefer your brand is powerful but can be misleading if only five consumers were sampled and three preferred that brand (that is, 60 percent). Interpretation of data can vary by who's interpreting it. For example, saying that your average customer is satisfied may not be accurate, as an average rating of 4 could result from half of respondents indicating 5 (extremely satisfied) and the other half rating 3 (neither satisfied nor dissatisfied), which paints a different picture. Market share is the ratio of the company's sales to total market sales, and a 34 percent market share is nice. But how is "market" defined? As you can see, numbers can say almost anything you want them to say. For more discussion of the financial and quantitative implications of marketing decisions, see Appendix 2: Marketing by the Numbers.

1. Using census data on health insurance coverage in the United States (available at http://pubdb3.census.gov/macro/032007/health/h01_001.htm), develop statistics, such as percentages, to support the argument against government reform of the health care industry in the United States. Use any portion of the data you deem important to support your argument. (AACSB: Communication; Use of IT; Analytical Reasoning)

2. Using the same data on that Web site, develop different statistics to support the counterargument to the one above. That is, interpret the data and present it in a way that supports the need for sweeping health care reforms to switch to government-provided health care for all. Again, use any portion of the data you deem important to support your argument. (AACSB: Communication; Use of IT; Analytical Reasoning)

VIDEO Case

ZIBA

How do companies design new products? Quite often, they get someone else to do it for them. That's where design firms such as ZIBA come in. ZIBA is one of a new breed of consultancies whose sole purpose is to help corporations better understand customer needs and turn that understanding in to groundbreaking new products.

The foundation for ZIBA's product development process is market research. That research seeks to understand the brand itself, the competition, and market trends. But most important, ZIBA's research efforts center on getting to know the customer. It has taken a novel approach to market research by utilizing the likes of social anthropologists and cultural ethnographers to get to the heart of what makes consumers tick. Their efforts often include actually following customers around, observing them in their natural environment, and understanding their experiences.

The unique focus that ZIBA takes has earned it contracts with major corporations including P&G, KitchenAid, Logitech, Microsoft, and Intel, as well as with various small start-up companies.

After viewing the video featuring ZIBA, answer the following questions about new-product development:

1. Illustrate some ways in which ZIBA engages in each phase of the marketing research process.

2. Discuss the various ways in which ZIBA's research efforts are focused on customer relationships.

3. Identify evidence of how ZIBA uses the information that it acquires to make marketing decisions.

COMPANY Case

Enterprise Rent-A-Car:
Measuring Service Quality

SURVEYING CUSTOMERS

Kevin Kirkman wheeled his shiny blue BMW coupe into his driveway, put the gearshift into park, set the parking brake, and got out to check his mailbox as he did every day when he returned home. As he flipped through the deluge of catalogs and credit card offers, he noticed a letter from Enterprise Rent-A-Car. He wondered why Enterprise would be writing him.

THE WRECK

Then he remembered. Earlier that month, Kevin had been involved in a wreck. As he was driving to work one rainy morning, another car had been unable to stop on the slick pavement and had plowed into his car as he waited at a stoplight. Thankfully, neither he nor the other driver was hurt, but both cars had sustained considerable damage. In fact, he was not able to drive his car.

Kevin had used his cell phone to call the police, and while he was waiting for the officers to come, he had called his auto insurance agent. The agent had assured Kevin that his policy included coverage to pay for a rental car while he was having his car repaired. He told Kevin to have the car towed to a nearby auto repair shop and gave him the telephone number for the Enterprise Rent-A-Car office that served his area. The agent noted that his company recommended using Enterprise for replacement rentals and that Kevin's policy would cover up to $20 per day of the rental fee.

Once Kevin had checked his car in at the body shop and made the necessary arrangements, he telephoned the Enterprise office. Within 10 minutes, an Enterprise employee had driven to the repair shop and picked him up. They drove back to the Enterprise office, where Kevin completed the paperwork and rented a Ford Taurus. He drove the rental car for 12 days before the repair shop completed work on his car.

"Don't know why Enterprise would be writing me," Kevin thought. "The insurance company paid the $20 per day, and I paid the extra because the Taurus cost more than that. Wonder what the problem could be?"

TRACKING SATISFACTION

Kevin tossed the mail on the passenger's seat and drove up the driveway. Once inside his house, he opened the Enterprise letter to find that it was a survey to determine how satisfied he was with his rental. The survey itself was only one page long and consisted of 13 questions (see exhibit).

Enterprise's executives believed that the company had become the largest rent-a-car company in the United States (in terms of number of cars, rental locations, and revenue) because of its laserlike focus on customer satisfaction and because of its concentration on serving the home-city replacement market. It aimed to serve customers like Kevin who were involved in wrecks and suddenly found themselves without a car. While the more well-known companies like Hertz and Avis battled for business in the cutthroat airport market, Enterprise quietly built its business by cultivating insurance agents and body-shop managers as referral agents so that when one of their clients or customers needed a replacement vehicle, they would recommend Enterprise. Although such replacement rentals accounted for about 80 percent of the company's business, it also served the discretionary

market (leisure/vacation rentals), and the business market (renting cars to businesses for their short-term needs). It had also begun to provide on-site and off-site service at some airports.

Throughout its history, Enterprise had followed founder Jack Taylor's advice. Taylor believed that if the company took care of its customers and employees first, profits would follow. So the company was careful to track customer satisfaction.

About 1 in 20 randomly selected customers received a letter like Kevin's. An independent company mailed the letter and a postage-paid return envelope to the selected customers. Customers who completed the survey used the envelope to return it to the independent company. That company compiled the results and provided them to Enterprise.

CONTINUOUS IMPROVEMENT

Meanwhile, back at Enterprise's St. Louis headquarters, the company's top managers were interested in taking the next steps in their customer satisfaction program. Enterprise had used the percentage of customers who were completely satisfied to develop its Enterprise Service Quality index (ESQi). It used the survey results to calculate an overall average ESQi score for the company and a score for each individual branch. The company's branch managers believed in and supported the process.

However, top management believed that to really "walk the walk" on customer satisfaction, it needed to make the ESQi a key factor in the promotion process. The company wanted to take the ESQi for the branch or branches a manager supervised into consideration when it evaluated that manager for a promotion. Top management believed that such a process would ensure that its managers and all its employees would focus on satisfying Enterprise's customers.

However, the top managers realized they had two problems in taking the next step. First, they wanted a better survey response rate. Although the company got a 25 percent response rate, which was good for this type of survey, it was concerned that it might still be missing important information. Second, it could take up to two months to get results back, and Enterprise believed it needed a process that would get the customer satisfaction information more quickly, at least on a monthly basis, so its branch managers could identify and take action on customer service problems quickly and efficiently.

Enterprise's managers wondered how they could improve the customer-satisfaction-tracking process.

Questions for Discussion

1. Analyze Enterprise's Service Quality Survey. What information is it trying to gather? What are its research objectives?

2. What decisions has Enterprise made with regard to primary data collection—research approach, contact methods, sampling plan, and research instruments?

3. In addition to or instead of the mail survey, what other means could Enterprise use to gather customer satisfaction information?

4. What specific recommendations would you make to Enterprise to improve the response rate and the timeliness of feedback from the process?

Source: Officials at Enterprise Rent-A-Car contributed to and supported the development of this case.

SERVICE QUALITY SURVEY

Please mark the box that best reflects your response to each question.

	Completely Satisfied	Somewhat Satisfied	Neither Satisfied Nor Dissatisfied	Somewhat Dissatisfied	Completely Dissatisfied
1. Overall, how satisfied were you with your recent car rental from Enterprise?	☐	☐	☐	☐	☐

2. What, if anything, could Enterprise have done better? *(Please be specific)* _____

_____

_____

3a. Did you experience any problems during the rental process?   Yes ☐   No ☐

3b. If you mentioned any problems to Enterprise, did they resolve them to your satisfaction?   Yes ☐   No ☐   Did not mention ☐

	Excellent	Good	Fair	Poor	N/A
4. If you personally called Enterprise to reserve a vehicle, how would you rate the telephone reservation process?	☐	☐	☐	☐	☐

	Both at start and end of rental	Just at start of rental	Just at end of rental	Neither time
5. Did you go to the Enterprise office	☐	☐	☐	☐

	Both at start and end of rental	Just at start of rental	Just at end of rental	Neither time
6. Did an Enterprise employee give you a ride to help with your transportation needs	☐	☐	☐	☐

7. After you arrived at the Enterprise office, how long did it take you to:	Less than 5 minutes	5–10 minutes	11–15 minutes	16–20 minutes	21–30 minutes	More than 30 minutes	N/A
• pick up your rental car?	☐	☐	☐	☐	☐	☐	☐
• return your rental car?	☐	☐	☐	☐	☐	☐	☐

8. How would you rate the . . .	Excellent	Good	Fair	Poor	N/A
• timeliness with which you were either picked up at the start of the rental or dropped off afterwards?	☐	☐	☐	☐	☐
• timeliness with which the rental car was either brought to your location and left with you or picked up from your location afterwards?	☐	☐	☐	☐	☐
• Enterprise employee who handled your paperwork . . .					
at the START of the rental?	☐	☐	☐	☐	☐
at the END of the rental?	☐	☐	☐	☐	☐
• mechanical condition of the car?	☐	☐	☐	☐	☐
• cleanliness of the car interior/exterior?	☐	☐	☐	☐	☐

	Yes	No	N/A
9. If you asked for a specific type or size of vehicle, was Enterprise able to meet your needs?	☐	☐	☐

	Car repairs due to accident	All other car repairs/ maintenance	Car was stolen	Business	Leisure/ vacation	Some other reason
10. For what reason did you rent this car?	☐	☐	☐	☐	☐	☐

	Definitely will call	Probably will call	Might or might not call	Probably will not call	Definitely will not call
11. The next time you need to pick up a rental car in the city or area in which you live, how likely are you to call Enterprise?	☐	☐	☐	☐	☐

	Once—this was first time	2 times	3–5 times	6–10 times	11 or more times
12. Approximately how many times in total have you rented from Enterprise (including this rental)?	☐	☐	☐	☐	☐

	0 times	1 time	2 times	3–5 times	6–10 times	11 or more times
13. Considering *all rental companies,* approximately how many times *within the past year* have you rented a car in the city or area in which you live (including this rental)?	☐	☐	☐	☐	☐	☐

Chapter 5

Part 1   Defining Marketing and the Marketing Process (Chapters 1, 2)
Part 2   Understanding the Marketplace and Consumers (Chapters 3, 4, 5, 6)
Part 3   Designing a Customer-Driven Strategy and Mix (Chapters 7, 8, 9, 10, 11, 12, 13, 14, 15, 16, 17)
Part 4   Extending Marketing (Chapters 18, 19, 20)

Consumer Markets and Consumer Buyer Behavior

Chapter **PREVIEW**

In the previous chapter, you studied how marketers obtain, analyze, and use information to understand the marketplace and to assess marketing programs. In this and the next chapter, we'll continue with a closer look at the most important element of the marketplace—customers. The aim of marketing is to affect how customers think and act. To affect the *whats, whens,* and *hows* of buying behavior, marketers must first understand the *whys*. In this chapter, we look at *final*

consumer buying influences and processes. In the next chapter, we'll study the buyer behavior of *business customers*. You'll see that understanding buyer behavior is an essential but very difficult task.

To get a better sense of the importance of understanding consumer behavior, let's look first at Harley-Davidson, maker of the nation's top-selling heavyweight motorcycles. Who rides these big Harley "Hogs"? What moves them to tattoo their bodies with the Harley-Davidson emblem, abandon home and hearth for the open road, and flock to Harley rallies by the hundreds of thousands? *You* might be surprised, but Harley-Davidson knows *very* well.

Few brands engender such intense loyalty as that found in the hearts of Harley-Davidson owners. Harley buyers are granitelike in their devotion to the brand. "You don't see people tattooing Yamaha on their bodies," observes the publisher of *American Iron,* an industry publication. And according to another industry insider, "For a lot of people, it's not that they want a motorcycle; it's that they want a Harley—the brand is that strong."

Each year, in early March, more than 350,000 Harley bikers rumble through the streets of Daytona Beach, Florida, to attend the Daytona Bike Week celebration. Bikers from across the nation lounge on their low-slung Harleys, swap biker tales, and sport T-shirts proclaiming "I'd rather push a Harley than drive a Honda."

Riding such intense emotions, Harley-Davidson has rumbled its way to the top of the heavyweight motorcycle market. Harley's "Hogs" capture 23 percent of all U.S. bike sales and almost 50 percent of the heavyweight segment. For several years running, sales have outstripped supply, with customer waiting lists of up to two years for popular models and street prices running well above suggested list prices. During the past 10 years, annual revenues and earnings have grown at better than 14 percent and 23 percent, respectively. By 2007, Harley-Davidson had experienced 21 straight years of record sales and income, and its stock was at a record high.

Harley-Davidson's marketers spend a great deal of time thinking about customers and their buying behavior. They want to know who their customers are, what they think and how they feel, and why they buy a Harley Fat Boy Softail rather than a

Yamaha or a Kawasaki or a big Honda American Classic. What is it that makes Harley buyers so fiercely loyal? These are difficult questions; even Harley owners themselves don't know exactly what motivates their buying. But Harley management puts top priority on understanding customers and what makes them tick.

Who rides a Harley? You might be surprised. Motorcycles are attracting a new breed of riders—older, more affluent, and better educated. "While the outlaw bad-boy biker image is what we might typically associate with Harley riders," says an analyst, "they're just as likely to be CEOs and investment bankers." "You take off the leathers and the helmet and you'll never know who you'll find," says one hard-core Harley enthusiast, himself a former New York City producer. "We're a varied lot. . . . America, at its very best . . . a melting pot." The average Harley customer is a 47-year-old male with a median income of $82,000. More than 12 percent of Harley purchases today are made by women.

Harley-Davidson makes good bikes, and to keep up with its shifting market, the

> **Few brands engender such intense loyalty as that found in the hearts of Harley-Davidson owners. "You don't see people tattooing Yamaha on their bodies."**

company has upgraded its showrooms and sales approaches. But Harley customers are buying a lot more than just a quality bike and a smooth sales pitch. To a Harley owner, whether it's the guy who sweeps the floors of the factory or the CEO at that factory, it's about something much deeper. To the hard-core Harley fan, it's all about independence, freedom, and power.

"It's much more than a machine," says the analyst. "It is part of their own self-expression and lifestyle." Another analyst suggests that owning a Harley makes you "the toughest, baddest guy on the block. Never mind that [you're] a dentist or an accountant. You [feel] wicked astride all that power." Your Harley renews your spirits and announces your independence.

One Harley owner sums it up this way on the Harley Owners Group Web site: "I believe in the itch that can only be scratched a on motorcycle. I believe in riding alone, with my wife, with a group. I believe in high mountain passes, tunnels of trees, lonely two-lane roads. I believe in family, friends, and God. I believe my Harley-Davidson can get me to all these places." Adds another, "Four wheels move the body . . . two wheels move the soul." The classic look, the throaty sound, the very idea of a Harley—all contribute to its mystique. Owning this "American legend" makes you a part of something bigger, a member of the Harley-Davidson family.

Such strong emotions and motivations are captured in a classic Harley-Davidson advertisement. The ad shows a close-up of an arm, the bicep adorned with a Harley-Davidson tattoo. The headline asks, "When was the last time you felt this strongly about anything?" The ad copy outlines the problem and suggests a solution: "Wake up in the morning and life picks up where it left off. . . . What once seemed exciting has now become part of the numbing routine. It all begins to feel the same. Except when you've got a Harley-Davidson. Something strikes a nerve. The heartfelt thunder rises up, refusing to become part of the background. Suddenly things are different. Clearer. More real. As

they should have been all along. Riding a Harley changes you from within. The effect is permanent. Maybe it's time you started feeling this strongly. Things are different on a Harley."[1]

> Harley-Davidson's marketers put top priority on understanding customers and what makes them tick. Harley customers are buying a lot more than just a quality bike and a smooth sales pitch: "Things are different on a Harley."

> To the hard-core Harley fan, it's all about independence, freedom, and power. Says one Harley owner, "Four wheels move the body . . . two wheels move the soul."

Consumer buyer behavior
The buying behavior of final consumers—individuals and households that buy goods and services for personal consumption.

Consumer market
All the individuals and households who buy or acquire goods and services for personal consumption.

The Harley-Davidson example shows that many different factors affect consumer buying behavior. Buying behavior is never simple, yet understanding it is the essential task of marketing management. **Consumer buyer behavior** refers to the buying behavior of final consumers—individuals and households that buy goods and services for personal consumption. All of these final consumers combine to make up the **consumer market**. The American consumer market consists of more than 300 million people who consume more than $13 trillion worth of goods and services each year, making it one of the most attractive consumer markets in the world. The world consumer market consists of more than 6.6 *billion* people who annually consume an estimated $65 trillion worth of goods and services.[2]

Consumers around the world vary tremendously in age, income, education level, and tastes. They also buy an incredible variety of goods and services. How these diverse consumers relate with each other and with other elements of the world around them impacts their choices among various products, services, and companies. Here we examine the fascinating array of factors that affect consumer behavior.

Objective Outline

Author Comment | Despite the simple-looking model in Figure 5.1, understanding the *whys* of buying behavior is very difficult. Says one expert, "the mind is a whirling, swirling, jumbled mass of neurons bouncing around . . ."

Model of Consumer Behavior (p 136)

Consumers make many buying decisions every day, and the buying decision is the focal point of the marketer's effort. Most large companies research consumer buying decisions in great detail to answer questions about what consumers buy, where they buy, how and how much they buy, when they buy, and why they buy. Marketers can study actual consumer purchases to find out what they buy, where, and how much. But learning about the *whys* of consumer buying behavior is not so easy—the answers are often locked deep within the consumer's mind.

Often, consumers themselves don't know exactly what influences their purchases. "The human mind doesn't work in a linear way," says one marketing expert. "The idea that the mind is a computer with storage compartments where brands or logos or recognizable packages are stored in clearly marked folders that can be accessed by cleverly written ads or commercials simply doesn't exist. Instead, the mind is a whirling, swirling, jumbled mass of neurons bouncing around, colliding and continuously creating new concepts and thoughts and relationships inside every single person's brain all over the world."[3]

The central question for marketers is: How do consumers respond to various marketing efforts the company might use? The starting point is the stimulus-response model of buyer behavior shown in **Figure 5.1**. This figure shows that marketing and other stimuli enter the consumer's "black box" and produce certain responses. Marketers must figure out what is in the buyer's black box.

Marketing stimuli consist of the Four Ps: product, price, place, and promotion. Other stimuli include major forces and events in the buyer's environment: economic, technological, political, and cultural. All these inputs enter the buyer's black box, where they are turned into a set of observable buyer responses: the buyer's brand and company relationship behavior and what he or she buys, when, where, and how often.

The marketer wants to understand how the stimuli are changed into responses inside the consumer's black box, which has two parts. First, the buyer's characteristics influence how he or she perceives and reacts to the stimuli. Second, the buyer's decision process itself affects the buyer's behavior. We look first at buyer characteristics as they affect buyer behavior and then discuss the buyer decision process.

Author Comment | Many, many levels of factors affect our buying behavior—from broad cultural and social influences to motivations, beliefs, and attitudes lying deep within us. For example, why *did* you buy *that* specific cell phone?

Characteristics Affecting Consumer Behavior (pp 137–151)

Consumer purchases are influenced strongly by cultural, social, personal, and psychological characteristics, shown in ✍ **Figure 5.2** on the next page. For the most part, marketers cannot control such factors, but they must take them into account.

Cultural Factors

Cultural factors exert a broad and deep influence on consumer behavior. The marketer needs to understand the role played by the buyer's *culture*, *subculture*, and *social class*.

Culture

Culture
The set of basic values, perceptions, wants, and behaviors learned by a member of society from family and other important institutions.

Culture is the most basic cause of a person's wants and behavior. Human behavior is largely learned. Growing up in a society, a child learns basic values, perceptions, wants, and behaviors from the family and other important institutions. A child in the United States normally learns or is exposed to the following values: achievement and success, activity and involvement, efficiency and practicality, progress, hard work, material comfort, individualism, freedom, humanitarianism, youthfulness, and fitness and health. Every group or society has a culture, and cultural influences on buying behavior may vary greatly from country to country. Failure to adjust to these differences can result in ineffective marketing or embarrassing mistakes.

Marketers are always trying to spot *cultural shifts* in order to discover new products that might be wanted. For example, the cultural shift toward greater concern about health and fitness has created a huge industry for health-and-fitness services, exercise equipment and clothing, organic foods, and a variety of diets. The shift toward informality has resulted in more demand for casual clothing and simpler home furnishings.

Subculture

Subculture
A group of people with shared value systems based on common life experiences and situations.

Each culture contains smaller **subcultures**, or groups of people with shared value systems based on common life experiences and situations. Subcultures include nationalities, religions, racial groups, and geographic regions. Many subcultures make up important market segments, and marketers often design products and marketing programs tailored to their needs. Examples of four such important subculture groups include Hispanic, African American, Asian American, and mature consumers.

Hispanic Consumers. The U.S. *Hispanic market*—Americans of Cuban, Mexican, Central American, South American, and Puerto Rican descent—consists of nearly 45 million consumers. The U.S. Hispanic population has grown fivefold since 1966, making it the fastest growing U.S. subsegment. By 2050, this group will make up nearly one-third of the U.S. population. Hispanic purchasing power now exceeds $850 billion and is expected to top $1.2 trillion by 2012, an 86 percent increase over 2003 levels.[4]

Although Hispanic consumers share many characteristics and behaviors with the mainstream buying pubic, there are also distinct differences. Hispanic consumers tend to buy more branded, higher-quality

We can measure the inputs to consumer buying decisions—for example, Apple introduces a new iTouch device and features it in TV ads. And we can often measure the outputs of consumer buying decisions. For example, 20,000 customers buy the new Apple device at the company's Web site within a week of introduction.

But it's very difficult to "see" inside the consumer's head and figure out the *whys* of buying behavior (that's why it's called the black box). Marketers spend a lot of time and dollars trying to figure out what makes customers tick.

The environment		**Buyer's black box**	**Buyer responses**
Marketing stimuli Other		Buyer's characteristics	Buying attitudes and preferences
Product Economic		Buyer's decision process	Purchase behavior: what the buyer buys, when, where, and how much
Price Technological			Brand and company relationship behavior
Place Social			
Promotion Cultural			

✍ **FIGURE** | **5.1** Model of Buyer Behavior

FIGURE | 5.2
Factors Influencing
Consumer Behavior

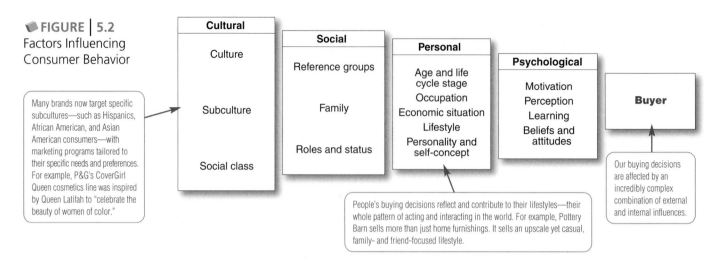

Many brands now target specific subcultures—such as Hispanics, African American, and Asian American consumers—with marketing programs tailored to their specific needs and preferences. For example, P&G's CoverGirl Queen cosmetics line was inspired by Queen Latifah to "celebrate the beauty of women of color."

People's buying decisions reflect and contribute to their lifestyles—their whole pattern of acting and interacting in the world. For example, Pottery Barn sells more than just home furnishings. It sells an upscale yet casual, family- and friend-focused lifestyle.

Our buying decisions are affected by an incredibly complex combination of external and internal influences.

products—generics don't sell well to this group. They tend to be deeply family-oriented and make shopping a family affair—children have a big say in what brands they buy. Perhaps more important, Hispanics, particularly first-generation immigrants, are very brand loyal, and they favor companies who show special interest in them.[5]

Even within the Hispanic market, there exist many distinct subsegments based on nationality, age, income, and other factors. For example, a company's product or message may be more relevant to one nationality over another, such as Mexicans, Costa Ricans, Argentineans, or Cubans. Companies must also vary their pitches across different Hispanic economic segments. Language is another issue. Older, first-generation Hispanics, might prefer Spanish as their primary or only language. Younger second- or third-generation Hispanics might be more comfortable with English.

Thus, companies often target specific subsegments within the larger Hispanic community with different kinds of marketing efforts. Consider two campaigns created by Hispanic agency Conill Advertising of New York for two very different Toyota brands, the full-size Tundra pick-up truck on the one hand and the Lexus on the other.[6]

The Tundra is a high-volume seller among Mexican immigrants in the Southwest who are characterized as *Jefes*, local heroes considered pillars of strength in their communi-

▲ Targeting diverse Hispanic subsegments: Toyota's various brands target different Hispanic markets with very different programs and appeals. This ad for Lexus targets the luxury market in Miami, reaching out to affluent Hispanics who appreciate refinement, art, and culture with a campaign that centers on art and design.

ties. To reach that consumer, Conill devised a campaign that catered to *El Jefe's* penchant for regional Mexican music and the national Mexican sport of *charreadas* (Mexican-style rodeos). The campaign consisted of a series of successful *Tundrazo charreadas* events and a Tundrazo Music Tour, supported by TV and print ads, all emphasizing the Tundra's size, ruggedness, and power. The pitch: The Tundra is as tough as the guy who gets behind the wheel.

▲Conill's campaign for Lexus, couldn't be more different. For Lexus, the agency targeted the luxury market in Miami, reaching out to affluent Hispanics who appreciate refinement, art, and culture with a campaign that centered on art and design. Lexus joined forces with local artists Hector Catá and Christian Duran, asking them to create their view of "the pursuit of perfection in South Florida." The result was a brightly displayed Lexus print campaign placed in the Hispanic lifestyle magazine, *Ocean Drive en Español*. The Miami campaign helped to move Lexus from the fourth-ranked player in the luxury market to market leader in only 18 months.

▲ Procter & Gamble's roots run deep in targeting African American consumers. For example, its CoverGirl Queen Latifah line is specially formulated "to celebrate the beauty of women of color."

African-American Consumers. With annual buying power of $799 billion, estimated to reach $1 trillion by 2012, the nation's 38.7 million *African-American* consumers also attract much marketing attention. The U.S. black population is growing in affluence and sophistication. Although more price conscious than other segments, blacks are also strongly motivated by quality and selection. Brands are important. So is shopping—black consumers seem to enjoy shopping more than other groups, even for something as mundane as groceries. Black consumers are also the most fashion conscious of the ethnic groups.[7]

In recent years, many companies have developed special products, appeals, and marketing programs for African-American consumers. ▲For example, P&G's roots run deep in this market. Procter & Gamble currently spends six times more on media targeting black consumers than it did just five years ago. It has a long history of using black spokespeople in its ads, beginning in 1969 with entertainer Bill Cosby endorsing Crest. Today, you'll see Angela Bassett promoting the benefits of Olay body lotion for black skin, Tiger Woods discussing the virtues of Gillette razors, and Queen Latifah in commercials promoting a CoverGirl line for black women. "The new Queen Collection was inspired by me to celebrate the beauty of women of color," says Latifah, "and it gives women the confidence they are looking for by accentuating our natural features."[8]

P&G has also tailored a number of its products to the special preferences of African-American consumers. For example, when market research showed that blacks prefer more scents and flavors, P&G added new scents to Gain detergent and flavors to Crest Whitening Expressions toothpaste. And the consumer products giant has created a line of Pantene Relaxed and Natural shampoos specially formulated for women of color. Such moves have made P&G an acknowledged leader in serving African-American consumers. Says one industry watcher, "Without question, P&G has to be seen as one of the companies that other companies pattern their behavior after."[9]

Asian-American Consumers. *Asian Americans* are the most affluent U.S. demographic segment. They now number more than 14.4 million and wield more than $450 billion in annual spending power, expected to reach $670 billion in 2012. They are the second-fastest-growing population subsegment after Hispanics. Chinese Americans constitute the largest group, followed by Filipinos, Japanese Americans, Asian Indians, and Korean Americans. The U.S. Asian-American population is expected to more than double by 2050, when it will make up nearly nine percent of the U.S. population.[10]

Asian consumers may be the most tech-savvy segment—more than 90 percent of Asian Americans go online regularly and are most comfortable with Internet technologies such as online banking and instant messaging. As a group, Asian consumers shop frequently and are the most brand conscious of all the ethnic groups. They can be fiercely brand loyal. As a result, many firms are now targeting the Asian-American market, from Verizon, State Farm, Toyota, and FedEx to Southwest Airlines and Wal-Mart. Here's an example:[11]

> ▲PNC Bank builds relationships with Asian Americans through advertising and public relations campaigns that focus on family values and savings, both central to the Asian American culture. Starting with its Lunar New Year campaign, celebrating the most important holiday in many Asian cultures, PNC Bank promotes specific services such as account openings and small business banking tailored specifically to Korean and Chinese customers. The bank sponsors events such as PNC Merry Wind Summer Festival, complete with ethnic food, family entertainment, and free financial consultations. It also provides in-language financial consultants at many branch locations.

Mature Consumers. As the U.S. population ages, *mature consumers* are becoming a very attractive market. By 2015, the entire baby boom generation, the largest and wealthiest demographic cohort in the country for more than half a century, will have moved into the 50-plus age bracket. They will control a larger proportion of wealth, income, and consumption than any other generation. Pharmaceuticals, travel, and

快人一步，確保財運滾滾到！

Keep one step ahead to ensure your wealth
of fortune will arrive again and again!   ◆ PNC BANK
LEADING THE WAY.

▲ Targeting Asian Americans: Because of the segment's affluence and rapidly growing buying power, financial institutions like PNC Bank cater directly to this segment with specially developed ads and marketing programs.

Social class
Relatively permanent and ordered divisions in a society whose members share similar values, interests, and behaviors.

Group
Two or more people who interact to accomplish individual or mutual goals.

financial services companies have long targeted older consumers. But as this group grows in numbers and buying power, companies in all industries—from groceries, beauty products, and clothing to furniture and consumer electronics—are devising new ways to lure aging big spenders.[12]

Contrary to popular belief, mature consumers are not "stuck in their ways." To the contrary, a recent AARP study showed that older consumers for products such as stereos, computers, and mobile phones are more willing to shop around and switch brands than their younger Generation X counterparts. For example, notes one expert, "some 25 percent of Apple's recently released iPhones—the epitome of cool, cutting-edge product—have been bought by people over 50."[13]

The growing cadre of mature consumers creates an attractive market for convenient services. For example, Home Depot and Lowe's now target older consumers who are less enthusiastic about do-it-yourself chores than with "do-it-for-me" handyman services. And their desire to look as young as they feel also makes more-mature consumers good candidates for cosmetics and personal care products, health foods, fitness products, and other items that combat the effects of aging. The best strategy is to appeal to their active, multidimensional lives. For example, Dove's Pro.Age hair and skin care product line claims that "Beauty has no age limit." Pro.Age ads feature active and attractive, real women who seem to be benefiting from the product's promise. Says one ad, "Embrace the best years of your life with Dove Pro.Age, a new line of products for skin and hair created to let women in their best years realize the beautiful potential that lies within. This isn't anti-age, it's pro-age."

Social Class

Almost every society has some form of social class structure. **Social classes** are society's relatively permanent and ordered divisions whose members share similar values, interests, and behaviors. Social scientists have identified the seven American social classes shown in ◤ **Figure 5.3**.

Social class is not determined by a single factor, such as income, but is measured as a combination of occupation, income, education, wealth, and other variables. In some social systems, members of different classes are reared for certain roles and cannot change their social positions. In the United States, however, the lines between social classes are not fixed and rigid; people can move to a higher social class or drop into a lower one.

Marketers are interested in social class because people within a given social class tend to exhibit similar buying behavior. Social classes show distinct product and brand preferences in areas such as clothing, home furnishings, leisure activity, and automobiles.

Social Factors

A consumer's behavior also is influenced by social factors, such as the consumer's *small groups*, *family*, and *social roles* and *status*.

Groups and Social Networks

Many small **groups** influence a person's behavior. Groups that have a direct influence and to which a person belongs are called membership groups. In contrast, reference groups serve as direct (face-to-face) or indirect points of comparison or reference in forming a person's attitudes or behavior. People often are influenced by reference groups to which they do not belong. For example, an aspirational group is one to which the individual wishes to belong, as when a young basketball player hopes to someday emulate basketball star Lebron James and play in the NBA.

FIGURE | 5.3
The Major American
Social Classes

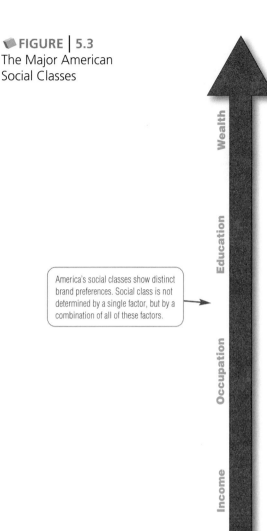

America's social classes show distinct brand preferences. Social class is not determined by a single factor, but by a combination of all of these factors.

Wealth — Education — Occupation — Income

Upper Class
Upper Uppers (1 percent): The social elite who live on inherited wealth. They give large sums to charity, own more than one home, and send their children to the finest schools.

Lower Uppers (2 percent): Americans who have earned high income or wealth through exceptional ability. They are active in social and civic affairs and buy expensive homes, educations, and cars.

Middle Class
Upper Middles (12 percent): Professionals, independent businesspersons, and corporate managers who possess neither family status nor unusual wealth. They believe in education, are joiners and highly civic minded, and want the "better things in life."

Middle Class (32 percent): Average-pay white- and blue-collar workers who live on "the better side of town." They buy popular products to keep up with trends. Better living means owning a nice home in a nice neighborhood with good schools.

Working Class
Working Class (38 percent): Those who lead a "working-class lifestyle," whatever their income, school background, or job. They depend heavily on relatives for economic and emotional support, for advice on purchases, and for assistance in times of trouble.

Lower Class
Upper Lowers (9 percent): The working poor. Although their living standard is just above poverty, they strive toward a higher class. However, they often lack education and are poorly paid for unskilled work.

Lower Lowers (7 percent): Visibly poor, often poorly educated unskilled laborers. They are often out of work and some depend on public assistance. They tend to live a day-to-day existence.

Marketers try to identify the reference groups of their target markets. Reference groups expose a person to new behaviors and lifestyles, influence the person's attitudes and self-concept, and create pressures to conform that may affect the person's product and brand choices. The importance of group influence varies across products and brands. It tends to be strongest when the product is visible to others whom the buyer respects.

Word-of-Mouth Influence and Buzz Marketing. Marketers of brands subjected to strong group influence must figure out how to reach **opinion leaders**—people within a reference group who, because of special skills, knowledge, personality, or other characteristics, exert social influence on others. Some experts call this 10 percent of Americans *the influentials* or *leading adopters*. One recent study found that these influencers are "four times more likely than average consumers to belong to five or more organizations, four times more likely to be considered experts, and twice as likely to recommend a product they like." And when influential friends talk, consumers listen. Another survey found that nearly 78 percent of respondents trusted "recommendations from consumers," 15 percentage points higher than the second most-credible source, newspapers.[14]

Marketers often try to identify opinion leaders for their products and direct marketing efforts toward them. They use *buzz marketing* by enlisting or even creating opinion leaders to serve as "brand ambassadors" who spread the word about their products. Many companies are now creating brand ambassador programs in an attempt to turn influential but everyday customers into brand evangelists (see **Real Marketing 5.1**).

Opinion leader
Person within a reference group who, because of special skills, knowledge, personality, or other characteristics, exerts social influence on others.

Real Marketing 5.1

Brand Ambassadors:
Employing Real Customers to Get Out the Word

People love talking about things that make them happy—including their favorite products and brands. Say you really like JetBlue Airways—they fly with flair and get you there at an affordable price. Or you just plain love your new Sony GPS camera—it's way too cool to keep to yourself. In the old days, you'd have chatted up these brands with a few friends and family members. But these days, thanks to modern technology, armed with little more than a video camera, laptop, and a cell phone, anyone can spread the word about products and brand experiences to thousands, even millions, of other consumers.

In response, marketers are now working to harness the new-found communications power of their everyday customers, turning them into influential brand ambassadors. Companies such as JetBlue, Sony, Unilever, Microsoft, McDonald's, and P&G, among others, are now developing a new breed of brand ambassador programs that organize and supercharge consumer-to-consumer interactions about their brands. These programs employ everyday consumers who are passionate about their products to act as part PR agents, part sales reps, and part evangelists.

Marketers select their brand ambassadors very carefully, based on customers' devotion to a brand and the size of their social circles. They sometimes search blogs and online social networks to identify individuals who are already functioning as brand advocates. Once selected, the ambassadors are trained with real brand knowledge to go along with their passion for the brand. The ambassadors then tap into friends, family, groups, and broader audiences through personal conversations, blogs, live events, and online social media. Their success is measured by things such as online traffic, number of blog posts, reader comments and e-mail responses, and how many people participate in real-world events.

For the ambassadors, it's often a labor of love more than a paying job. Rewards include product samples, gifts, discounts, and token cash payments—anything from $700 worth of free electronics equipment to discounts at local golf courses. Perhaps more important to many brand enthusiasts, they get insider access to company information, such as new products or services in the works.

Brand ambassador programs leverage the power of peer-to-peer communication. Consumers hear about products and brand experiences from others just like themselves— people they trust—rather than from commercial marketing sources. Sony used brand ambassadors to jump-start the launch of its new GPS camera, a high-tech device that draws on satellite tracking technology to let you record the exact location of every picture you take and later map them out online using Google Maps. Sony selected customer ambassadors who like to travel, take pictures, and blog. "This is a product with emerging technology and we really need to let consumers see people using it," says Sony's director of digital imaging.

Out of 2,000 or more online applicants, Sony picked only 25 brand ambassadors. The ambassadors were given a free camera and other equipment along with lessons on how to use them. They were then encouraged to show the camera to friends, associates, and anyone else who asked; hand out discount coupons; and blog weekly about their travel and picture-taking adventures on a dedicated Sony microsite. Sony ambassador and blogger Cheryl Gillet, for instance, described a recent trip to Australia, adding a map of the journey juxtaposed with photos of beach scenes and tanned friends in swimsuits.

College campuses are a traditionally fertile ground for ambassadors. Marketing agency RepNation identifies and manages college student ambassadors for companies as diverse as JetBlue, Microsoft, and Macy's. It solicits potential reps through its own Web site and via classifieds on sites like Craigslist. Over the past few years, it has recruited a small army of ambassadors for JetBlue. JetBlue Ambassador Rebecca Nelson talks about her experiences:

I wasn't looking for a job. But I love perusing the "gigs" section of Craigslist, which was where I saw an ad for JetBlue lovers. I do love the airline (unlimited snacks! low fares!)—and was intrigued by the idea of a flexible 10–15-hour workweek and the possibility of training at JetBlue headquarters in New York City. I applied. In my two phone interviews with RepNation, I talked about my enthusiasm for the brand, my life at Rochester Institute of Technology (RIT), my knowledge of the best venues for events, and my Facebook profile with its over 300 RIT "friends." I was accepted to JetBlue's CrewBlue ambassador program and flown free to New York for a day of training with 41 other reps from 21 campuses. The training covered JetBlue's history, the purpose of the CrewBlue program, the responsibilities of being a rep, and compensation (travel vouchers and gift cards).

There are two parts to being a rep: physical and virtual. The former involves creating events, like JetBlue video game tournaments (RIT's a tech school!). We also partner with clubs to co-sponsor events (for example, a 5k run for charity), which usually means a larger turnout. Each event budget is only $50, so you need to be creative! The virtual part of the job includes managing RIT's JetBlue Facebook group of 1,900 with the creation of new contests and event invitations, and answering student questions. This group management, along with checking the RepNation portal—where reps share ideas, ask questions, and offer tips—was a fun daily job.

Brand ambassadors: Many marketers are now harnessing the new-found communications power of their everyday customers, turning them into influential brand ambassadors. JetBlue's CrewBlue ambassadors help to organize and run events such as JetBlue's BlueDay on campuses across the country.

Continued on next page ▼

Rebecca and JetBlue ambassadors on other campuses help to organize and run events such as JetBlue's BlueDay, now in its third year. Held in the fall on 21 campuses on the East Coast and in Northern California, the event urges students to wear blue costumes (and, on occasion, blue skin and hair), and those with the best costumes are each given a pair of free airline tickets. Rebecca loves BlueDay—"How often do you get to hand someone a round-trip voucher because they painted themselves blue from head to toe?"

According to JetBlue's director of advertising and promotions, the CrewBlue ambassadors are crucial to the success of BlueDay and other campus efforts: "Students know what kinds of activities are important to other kids, what we should say to them in our marketing, and how we should say it. The other side is that we have to not be surprised when

they do something we would not have done, like put an amateur-looking version of our logo on a sheet cake. We have to give up some control of our image." JetBlue's ambassador program doubled in size last year and has "made a big difference" in the brand's strength in the young-adult segment.

The brand ambassador approach has its critics. For example, some view the practice as underhanded or deceptive. However, to avoid charges of deception, most firms advise their ambassadors to openly reveal that they are representatives. Others worry that brand ambassadors will be perceived as hucksters who promote products because they get free stuff—or, worse, as annoying evangelists best

avoided. "To the contrary," says an executive from RepNation. "Our brand ambassadors are seen by their college friends as entrepreneurial, creative people."

What they aren't, he adds, are the super cool kids on campus. "We used to assume the best reps would be the cool kids in any given group. But we learned that most kids are not cool. If marketers want consumers to feel a connection to their ambassadors and to feel that an ambassador is accessible, they have to look beyond the cool customers" who are typically thought of as influentials. The best ambassadors, he says, are "friendly, everyday brand loyalists who love to talk to people."

Sources: Portions adapted from Joan Voigt, "The New Brand Ambassadors," *Adweek*, December 31, 2007, pp. 18–19, 26; and Rebecca Nelson, "A Citizen Marketer Talks," *Adweek*, December 31, 2007, p. 19.

Online social networks
Online social communities—blogs, social networking Web sites, or even virtual worlds—where people socialize or exchange information and opinions.

P&G has created a huge word-of-mouth marketing arm—Vocalpoint—consisting of 350,000 moms. ▲This army of natural-born buzzers leverages the power of peer-to-peer communication to spread the word about brands. Vocalpoint recruits "connectors"—people with vast networks of friends and a gift for gab. They create buzz not just for P&G brands but for those of other client companies as well.[15]

▲ Buzz marketing: The Vocalpoint marketing arm of Procter & Gamble has enlisted an army of buzzers to create word-of-mouth for brands. "We know that the most powerful form of marketing is a message from a trusted friend."

Procter & Gamble couldn't ask for a better salesperson than Vocalpointer Donna Wetherell. The gregarious Columbus, Ohio, mom works at a customer service call center unaffiliated with P&G, where she knows some 300 coworkers by name. Lately, Wetherell has spent so much time at work talking about P&G products and handing out discount coupons that her colleagues have given her a nickname. "I am called the coupon lady," Wetherell says.

Except for educating Vocalpointers about products, the company doesn't coach the moms. The connectors themselves choose whether or not to pitch the product to friends and what to say. What's more, they do the work without pay. What's in it for them? For one thing, they receive a steady flow of coupons and samples. But more important, it makes them insiders, seeing cool new ideas before their friends have them. Second, it gives them a voice. "They're filled with great ideas, and they don't think anybody listens to them," says Vocalpoint's CEO.

Online Social Networks. Over the past few years, a new type of social interaction has exploded onto the scene—online social networking. **Online social networks** are online communities where people socialize or exchange information and opinions. Social networking media range from blogs to social networking Web sites, such as MySpace.com and YouTube, to entire virtual worlds, such as Second Life. This new form of high-tech buzz has big implications for marketers.

> Personal connections—forged through words, pictures, video, and audio posted just for the [heck] of it—are the life of the new Web, bringing together the estimated 60 million bloggers, more than 110 million MySpace.com users (230,000 more sign up every day), and millions more on single-use social networks where people share one category of stuff, like Flickr (photos), Del.icio.us (links), Digg (news stories), Wikipedia (encyclopedia articles), and YouTube (video). . . . It's hard to overstate the coming impact of these new network technologies on business: They hatch trends and build immense waves of interest in specific products. They serve up giant, targeted audiences to advertisers. They edge out old media with the loving labor of amateurs. They effortlessly provide hyperdetailed data to marketers. The new social networking technologies provide an authentic, peer-to-peer channel of communication that is far more credible than any corporate flackery.[16]

Marketers are working to harness the power of these new social networks to promote their products and build closer customer relationships. Instead of throwing more one-way commercial messages at ad-weary consumers, they hope to use social networks to *interact* with consumers and become a part of their conversations and lives. For example, brands ranging from Victoria's Secret to Jack in the Box and Wal-Mart have set up MySpace pages and Facebook groups. Victoria Secret's Facebook group offers free downloads, contests, and printable coupons—the group has more than 300,000 "members." Jack in the Box set up an ultrapopular MySpace profile of Jack, where friends learn that Jack has a wife named Cricket and that his goal is to "rule the fast-food world with an iron fist." And Wal-Mart set up the "Roommate Style Match" Facebook group, aimed at jump-starting college student back-to-school sales. Members take a quiz to determine their decorating style and get a list of "recommended products" they can buy at Wal-Mart to match their style with their roommate's.[17]

A rush of marketers—from Dell and Sears to BMW, Coca-Cola, Adidas, and even CNN—have now set up their brands and are even selling digital goods in Second Life, the Internet-based digital world that is "imagined, created, and owned" by its nearly six million residents. Adidas has sold 21,000 pairs of virtual shoes in Second Life, and the average avatar (your Second Life character) spends 20 minutes in its store. CNN opened a news-gathering outpost in Second Life, staffed by "residents," by which visitors can get the latest news via kiosks throughout the virtual community.[18]

Other companies regularly post ads or custom videos on video-sharing sites such as YouTube. Viewers watch more than 2.5 billion YouTube videos in a single month, making it an attractive marketing outlet. For example, American Eagle Outfitters posts short, entertaining movies on YouTube. Heinz runs the Top This TV Challenge, which invites amateurs to submit homemade Heinz Ketchup commercials with the chance to win a grand prize of $57,000 and have their commercial aired on national television. And Jack in the Box posts specially made, highly irreverent ads on YouTube that draw tens of thousands of page views from its targeted young male audience. Such ads have turned the Jack in the Box character into a cultural icon.[19]

Following the success of large social networking sites such as MySpace and Facebook, thousands of niche sites have popped up that cater to more selective online communities:[20]

There is at least one social networking site for every interest or hobby. ▲Yub.com is for shopaholics; Fuzzster.com is for pet lovers; OnLoq.com is for hip-hop fans; Jango.com lets music fans find others with similar tastes; and PassportStamp.com is one of several sites for avid travelers. Some sites cater to the obscure. Passions Network, with 600,000 members, has 106 groups for special interests, including "Star Trek" fans, truckers, atheists, and people who are shy. The most popular group is a dating site for the overweight. Membership on niche networking sites varies greatly, ranging from a few hundred to a few million. LinkExpats.com, which provides an online haven for U.S. expatriots, opened last month and now has about 200 members. Flixster.com has 40 million members who rate movies and gossip about actors.

These more selective sites often provide richer, more targeted marketing opportunities for brands. "The bigger sites have become so cluttered and overrun with advertisers that members are used to tuning stuff out, even personalized ads," says an analyst. "But on networking sites that have a self-selecting demographic, people tend to trust the content, including ads."[21]

Companies can even create their own social networks. For example, Procter & Gamble set up Capessa (www.capessa.com), "a gathering place for real women to share their stories, offer their personal wisdom and practical advice, improve their lives, and be inspired. The only thing that's missing is the kitchen table." The site gives women a place to express themselves and P&G an opportunity to observe and learn more about their needs and feelings.[22]

But marketers must be careful when tapping into online social networks. Results are difficult to measure and control. Ultimately, the users control the content, so online network marketing attempts can easily backfire. For example, when Chevrolet launched a Web contest inviting folks to create their own ads for its Chevy Tahoe, it quickly lost control. Says one observer, "the entries that got passed around, blogged about, and eventually covered in the mainstream media were all about the SUV's abysmal gas mileage and melting polar ice caps." One user-generated ad proclaimed, "Like this snowy wilderness? Better get your fill of it now. Then say hello to global warming." Another concluded, "$70 to fill up the tank, which will last less than 400 miles. Chevy Tahoe."[23] We will dig deeper into online social networks as a marketing tool in Chapter 17.

▲ Family buying: Family buying roles are changing. For example, men now account for about 40 percent of all food-shopping dollars, while women influence 50 percent of all new technology purchases.

Family

Family members can strongly influence buyer behavior. The family is the most important consumer buying organization in society, and it has been researched extensively. Marketers are interested in the roles and influence of the husband, wife, and children on the purchase of different products and services.

Husband-wife involvement varies widely by product category and by stage in the buying process. Buying roles change with evolving consumer lifestyles. In the United States, the wife traditionally has been the main purchasing agent for the family in the areas of food, household products, and clothing. ▲But with 70 percent of women holding jobs outside the home and the willingness of husbands to do more of the family's purchasing, all this is changing. Men now account for about 40 percent of all food-shopping dollars. Women influence 65 percent of all new car purchases, 91 percent of new home purchases, and 92 percent of vacation purchases. In all, women now make almost 85 percent of all family purchases, spending two-thirds of the nation's GDP.[24]

Such changes suggest that marketers in industries that have sold their products to only men or only women are now courting the opposite sex. For example, after realizing that women today account for 50 percent of all technology purchases, Dell has stepped up its efforts to woo women buyers. It now advertises regularly in female-focused magazines such as

Oprah Winfrey's *O at Home, Ladies' Home Journal, Real Simple,* and *CosmoGIRL* and on woman-centric cable-TV channels such as Oxygen and Lifetime.

Children may also have a strong influence on family buying decisions. The nation's 36 million kids age 3 to 11 wield an estimated $18 billion in disposable income. They also influence an additional $115 billion that their families spend on them in areas such as food, clothing, entertainment, and personal care items. For example, one recent study found that kids significantly influence family decisions about where they take vacations and what cars and cell phones they buy. As a result, marketers of cars, full-service restaurants, cell phones, and travel destinations are now placing ads on networks such as Cartoon Network and Toon Disney.

As part of its efforts to target families, Chrysler recently signed promotional sponsorship and advertising deals with Nickelodeon for its Town & Country minivans. It signed on as a sponsor for Nickelodeon's Slime Across America summer tour and runs ads in Nick's printed publications, Web sites, and TV programs. Nick's boy-genius inventor Jimmy Neutron has appeared prominently in the Chrysler Town & Country advertising.[25]

Roles and Status

A person belongs to many groups—family, clubs, organizations. The person's position in each group can be defined in terms of both role and status. A role consists of the activities people are expected to perform according to the persons around them. Each role carries a status reflecting the general esteem given to it by society.

People usually choose products appropriate to their roles and status. Consider the various roles a working mother plays. In her company, she plays the role of a brand manager; in her family, she plays the role of wife and mother; at her favorite sporting events, she plays the role of avid fan. As a brand manager, she will buy the kind of clothing that reflects her role and status in her company.

Personal Factors

A buyer's decisions also are influenced by personal characteristics such as the buyer's *age and life-cycle stage, occupation, economic situation, lifestyle,* and *personality and self-concept*.

Age and Life-Cycle Stage

People change the goods and services they buy over their lifetimes. Tastes in food, clothes, furniture, and recreation are often age related. Buying is also shaped by the stage of the family life cycle—the stages through which families might pass as they mature over time. Marketers often define their target markets in terms of life-cycle stage and develop appropriate products and marketing plans for each stage.

Traditional family life-cycle stages include young singles and married couples with children. Today, however, marketers are increasingly catering to a growing number of alternative, nontraditional stages such as unmarried couples, singles marrying later in life, childless couples, same-sex couples, single parents, extended parents (those with young adult children returning home), and others.

RBC Royal Bank has identified five life-stage segments. The *Youth* segment includes customers younger than 18. *Getting Started* consists of customers aged 18 to 35 who are going through first experiences, such as their graduation, first credit card, first car, first loan, marriage, and first child. *Builders,* customers aged 35 to 50, are in their peak earning years. As they build careers and family, they tend to borrow more than they invest. *Accumulators,* aged 50 to 60, worry about saving for retirement and investing wisely. Finally, *Preservers,* customers over 60, want to maximize their retirement income to maintain a desired lifestyle. RBC markets different services to the different segments. For example, with *Builders,* who face many expenses, it emphasizes loans and debt-load management services.[26]

Occupation

A person's occupation affects the goods and services bought. Blue-collar workers tend to buy more rugged work clothes, whereas executives buy more business suits. Marketers try to identify the occupational groups that have an above-average interest in their products and services. A company can even specialize in making products needed by a given occupational group.

For example, Spear's Specialty Shoes fills a tiny niche in the shoe world by making high-end shoes for—of all things—clowns (and some team mascots and even store Santas). Founder Gary Spear, a former clown himself, discovered a need for good, comfortable clown shoes with reasonable delivery times. Over the past 25 years his company has built a worldwide reputation. At the company's Web site (www.spearshoes.com), professional clowns can browse different colors and styles and design their own shoes. It's a fun niche but these shoes are no joke. Made for professional clowning around, they are made with lightweight soles and serious padding, at a starting price of $300 a pair.[27]

Economic Situation

A person's economic situation will affect product choice. Marketers of income-sensitive goods watch trends in personal income, savings, and interest rates. If economic indicators point to a recession, marketers can take steps to redesign, reposition, and reprice their products closely. Some marketers target consumers who have lots of money and resources, charging prices to match. For example, Rolex positions its luxury watches as "a tribute to elegance, an object of passion, a symbol for all time." Other marketers target consumers with more modest means. Timex makes more affordable watches that "take a licking and keep on ticking."

Lifestyle

Lifestyle
A person's pattern of living as expressed in his or her activities, interests, and opinions.

People coming from the same subculture, social class, and occupation may have quite different lifestyles. **Lifestyle** is a person's pattern of living as expressed in his or her psychographics. It involves measuring consumers' major AIO dimensions—activities (work, hobbies, shopping, sports, social events), interests (food, fashion, family, recreation), and opinions (about themselves, social issues, business, products). Lifestyle captures something more than the person's social class or personality. It profiles a person's whole pattern of acting and interacting in the world.

When used carefully, the lifestyle concept can help marketers understand changing consumer values and how they affect buying behavior. Consumers don't just buy products, they buy the values and lifestyles those products represent. For example, BMW doesn't just sell convertibles, it sells the convertible lifestyle: "Skies never bluer. Knuckles never whiter." ▲And Georgia Boot sells more than just rugged footwear, it sells a lifestyle to "guys who are comfortable with who they are." Says one marketer, "People's product choices are becoming more and more like value choices. It's not, 'I like this water, the way it tastes.' It's 'I feel like this car, or this show, is more reflective of who I am.'"

For example, Pottery Barn, with its different store formats, sells more than just home furnishings. It sells a lifestyle to which its customers aspire. Pottery Barn Kids offers idyllic scenes of the perfect childhood, whereas PB Teens offer a trendy fashion-forward self-expression. The flagship Pottery Barn stores serve an upscale yet casual, family- and friend-focused lifestyle—affluent but sensibly so.[28]

Shortly after Hadley MacLean got married, she and her husband, Doug, agreed that their old bed had to go. It was a mattress and box spring on a cheap metal frame, a relic of Doug's Harvard days. But Hadley never anticipated how tough it would be to find a new bed. "We couldn't find anything we liked, even though we were willing to spend the money," says Hadley, a 31-year-old marketing director. It turned out to be much more than just finding a piece of furniture at the right price. It was a matter of

▲ Lifestyle: Consumers don't just buy products, they buy the values and lifestyles those products represent. Georgia Boot proudly targets "guys who are comfortable with who they are."

emotion: They needed a bed that meshed with their lifestyle—with who they are and where they are going. The couple finally ended up at the Pottery Barn on Boston's upscale Newbury Street, where Doug fell in love with a mahogany sleigh bed that Hadley had spotted in the store's catalog. The couple was so pleased with how great it looked in their Dutch Colonial home that they hurried back to the store for a set of end tables. And then they bought a quilt. And a mirror for the living room. And some stools for the dining room. "We got kind of addicted," Hadley confesses.

Personality and Self-Concept

Personality

The unique psychological characteristics that lead to relatively consistent and lasting responses to one's own environment.

Each person's distinct personality influences his or her buying behavior. **Personality** refers to the unique psychological characteristics that lead to relatively consistent and lasting responses to one's own environment. Personality is usually described in terms of traits such as self-confidence, dominance, sociability, autonomy, defensiveness, adaptability, and aggressiveness. Personality can be useful in analyzing consumer behavior for certain product or brand choices.

Brand personality

The specific mix of human traits that may be attributed to a particular brand.

The idea is that brands also have personalities, and that consumers are likely to choose brands with personalities that match their own. A **brand personality** is the specific mix of human traits that may be attributed to a particular brand. One researcher identified five brand personality traits:[29]

1. Sincerity (down-to-earth, honest, wholesome, and cheerful)
2. Excitement (daring, spirited, imaginative, and up-to-date)
3. Competence (reliable, intelligent, and successful)
4. Sophistication (upper class and charming)
5. Ruggedness (outdoorsy and tough)

Most well-known brands are strongly associated with one particular trait: Jeep with "ruggedness," Apple with "excitement," CNN with "competence," and Dove with "sincerity." Hence, these brands will attract persons who are high on the same personality traits.

Many marketers use a concept related to personality—a person's *self-concept* (also called *self-image*). The basic self-concept premise is that people's possessions contribute to and reflect their identities—that is, "we are what we have." Thus, in order to understand consumer behavior, the marketer must first understand the relationship between consumer self-concept and possessions.

Apple applies these concepts in a recent series of ads that characterize two people as computers—one guy plays the part of an Apple Mac and the other plays a PC. The two have very different personalities and self-concepts. "Hello, I'm a Mac," says the guy on the right, who's younger and dressed in jeans. "And I'm a PC," says the one on the left, who's wearing dweeby glasses and a jacket and tie. The two men discuss the relative advantages of Macs versus PCs, with the Mac coming out on top. The ads present the Mac brand personality as young, laid back, and hip. The PC is portrayed as buttoned down, corporate, and a bit dorky. The message? If you see yourself as young and with it, you need a Mac.[30]

Psychological Factors

A person's buying choices are further influenced by four major psychological factors: *motivation*, *perception*, *learning*, and *beliefs and attitudes*.

Motivation

Motive (drive)

A need that is sufficiently pressing to direct the person to seek satisfaction of the need.

A person has many needs at any given time. Some are biological, arising from states of tension such as hunger, thirst, or discomfort. Others are psychological, arising from the need for recognition, esteem, or belonging. A need becomes a motive when it is aroused to a sufficient level of intensity. A **motive** (or drive) is a need that is sufficiently pressing to direct the person to seek satisfaction. Psychologists have developed theories of human motivation. Two of the most popular—the theories of Sigmund Freud and Abraham Maslow—have quite different meanings for consumer analysis and marketing.

▲ Motivation: An aging baby boomer who buys a sporty convertible might explain that he or she simply likes the feel of the wind in his or her thinning hair. At a deeper level, the person may be buying the car to feel young and independent again.

Sigmund Freud assumed that people are largely unconscious about the real psychological forces shaping their behavior. He saw the person as growing up and repressing many urges. These urges are never eliminated or under perfect control; they emerge in dreams, in slips of the tongue, in neurotic and obsessive behavior, or ultimately in psychoses.

Freud's theory suggests that a person's buying decisions are affected by subconscious motives that even the buyer may not fully understand. ▲ Thus, an aging baby boomer who buys a sporty BMW 330Ci convertible might explain that he simply likes the feel of the wind in his thinning hair. At a deeper level, he may be trying to impress others with his success. At a still deeper level, he may be buying the car to feel young and independent again.

The term *motivation research* refers to qualitative research designed to probe consumers' hidden, subconscious motivations. Consumers often don't know or can't describe just why they act as they do. Thus, motivation researchers use a variety of probing techniques to uncover underlying emotions and attitudes toward brands and buying situations.

Many companies employ teams of psychologists, anthropologists, and other social scientists to carry out motivation research. One ad agency routinely conducts one-on-one, therapy-like interviews to delve into the inner workings of consumers. Another company asks consumers to describe their favorite brands as animals or cars (say, Cadillacs versus Chevrolets) in order to assess the prestige associated with various brands. Still others rely on hypnosis, dream therapy, or soft lights and mood music to plumb the murky depths of consumer psyches.

Such projective techniques seem pretty goofy, and some marketers dismiss such motivation research as mumbo jumbo. But many marketers use such touchy-feely approaches, now sometimes called *interpretive consumer research,* to dig deeper into consumer psyches and develop better marketing strategies.[31]

Abraham Maslow sought to explain why people are driven by particular needs at particular times. Why does one person spend much time and energy on personal safety and another on gaining the esteem of others? Maslow's answer is that human needs are arranged in a hierarchy, as shown in ◆ **Figure 5.4**, from the most pressing at the bottom to the least pressing at the top.[32] They include *physiological* needs, *safety* needs, *social* needs, *esteem* needs, and *self-actualization* needs.

A person tries to satisfy the most important need first. When that need is satisfied, it will stop being a motivator and the person will then try to satisfy the next most important need. For example, starving people (physiological need) will not take an interest in the latest happenings in the art world (self-actualization needs), nor in how they are seen or esteemed by others (social or esteem needs), nor even in whether they are breathing clean air (safety needs). But as each important need is satisfied, the next most important need will come into play.

◆ FIGURE | 5.4
Maslow's Hierarchy of Needs

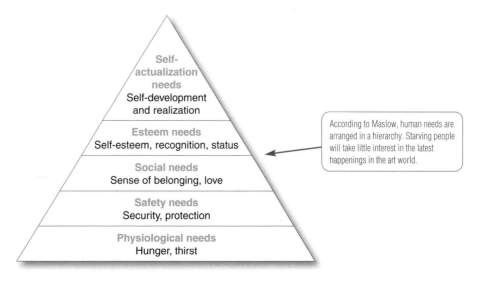

Self-actualization needs
Self-development and realization

Esteem needs
Self-esteem, recognition, status

Social needs
Sense of belonging, love

Safety needs
Security, protection

Physiological needs
Hunger, thirst

According to Maslow, human needs are arranged in a hierarchy. Starving people will take little interest in the latest happenings in the art world.

Perception

Perception
The process by which people select, organize, and interpret information to form a meaningful picture of the world.

A motivated person is ready to act. How the person acts is influenced by his or her own perception of the situation. All of us learn by the flow of information through our five senses: sight, hearing, smell, touch, and taste. However, each of us receives, organizes, and interprets this sensory information in an individual way. **Perception** is the process by which people select, organize, and interpret information to form a meaningful picture of the world.

▲ Selective perception: It's impossible for people to pay attention to the thousands of ads they're exposed to every day, so they screen most of them out.

People can form different perceptions of the same stimulus because of three perceptual processes: selective attention, selective distortion, and selective retention. People are exposed to a great amount of stimuli every day. ▲For example, people are exposed to an estimated 3,000 to 5,000 ad messages every day.[33] It is impossible for a person to pay attention to all these stimuli. *Selective attention*—the tendency for people to screen out most of the information to which they are exposed—means that marketers must work especially hard to attract the consumer's attention.

Even noticed stimuli do not always come across in the intended way. Each person fits incoming information into an existing mind-set. *Selective distortion* describes the tendency of people to interpret information in a way that will support what they already believe. For example, if you distrust a company, you might perceive even honest ads from the company as questionable. Selective distortion means that marketers must try to understand the mind-sets of consumers and how these will affect interpretations of advertising and sales information.

People also will forget much of what they learn. They tend to retain information that supports their attitudes and beliefs. Because of *selective retention*, consumers are likely to remember good points made about a brand they favor and to forget good points made about competing brands. Because of selective attention, distortion, and retention, marketers must work hard to get their messages through. This fact explains why marketers use so much drama and repetition in sending messages to their market.

Interestingly, although most marketers worry about whether their offers will be perceived at all, some consumers worry that they will be affected by marketing messages without even knowing it—through *subliminal advertising*. In 1957, a researcher announced that he had flashed the phrases "Eat popcorn" and "Drink Coca-Cola" on a screen in a New Jersey movie theater every five seconds for 1/300th of a second. He reported that although viewers did not consciously recognize these messages, they absorbed them subconsciously and bought 58 percent more popcorn and 18 percent more Coke. Suddenly advertisers and consumer-protection groups became intensely interested in subliminal perception. People voiced fears of being brainwashed, and California and Canada declared the practice illegal. Although the researcher later admitted to making up the data, the issue has not died. Some consumers still fear that they are being manipulated by subliminal messages.

Numerous studies by psychologists and consumer researchers have found little or no link between subliminal messages and consumer behavior. Recent brain wave studies have found that in certain circumstances, our brains may register subliminal messages. However, it appears that subliminal advertising simply doesn't have the power attributed to it by its critics. Most advertisers scoff at the notion of an industry conspiracy to manipulate consumers through "invisible" messages. Says one industry insider, "[Some consumers believe we are] wizards who can manipulate them at will. Ha! Snort! Oh my sides! As we know, just between us, most of [us] have difficulty getting a 2 percent increase in sales with the help of $50 million in media and extremely *liminal* images of sex, money, power, and other [motivators] of human emotion. The very idea of [us] as puppeteers, cruelly pulling the strings of consumer marionettes, is almost too much to bear."[34]

Learning

Learning

Changes in an individual's behavior arising from experience.

When people act, they learn. **Learning** describes changes in an individual's behavior arising from experience. Learning theorists say that most human behavior is learned. Learning occurs through the interplay of drives, stimuli, cues, responses, and reinforcement.

A *drive* is a strong internal stimulus that calls for action. A drive becomes a motive when it is directed toward a particular *stimulus object*. For example, a person's drive for self-actualization might motivate him or her to look into buying a camera. The consumer's response to the idea of buying a camera is conditioned by the surrounding cues. *Cues* are minor stimuli that determine when, where, and how the person responds. For example, the person might spot several camera brands in a shop window, hear of a special sale price, or discuss cameras with a friend. These are all cues that might influence a consumer's *response* to his or her interest in buying the product.

Suppose the consumer buys a Nikon camera. If the experience is rewarding, the consumer will probably use the camera more and more, and his or her response will be *reinforced*. Then, the next time the consumer shops for a camera, or for binoculars or some similar product, the probability is greater that he or she will buy a Nikon product. The practical significance of learning theory for marketers is that they can build up demand for a product by associating it with strong drives, using motivating cues, and providing positive reinforcement.

Beliefs and Attitudes

Belief

A descriptive thought that a person holds about something.

Attitude

A person's consistently favorable or unfavorable evaluations, feelings, and tendencies toward an object or idea.

Through doing and learning, people acquire beliefs and attitudes. These, in turn, influence their buying behavior. A **belief** is a descriptive thought that a person has about something. Beliefs may be based on real knowledge, opinion, or faith and may or may not carry an emotional charge. Marketers are interested in the beliefs that people formulate about specific products and services, because these beliefs make up product and brand images that affect buying behavior. If some of the beliefs are wrong and prevent purchase, the marketer will want to launch a campaign to correct them.

People have attitudes regarding religion, politics, clothes, music, food, and almost everything else. **Attitude** describes a person's relatively consistent evaluations, feelings, and tendencies toward an object or idea. Attitudes put people into a frame of mind of liking or disliking things, of moving toward or away from them. Our camera buyer may hold attitudes such as "Buy the best," "The Japanese make the best electronics products in the world," and "Creativity and self-expression are among the most important things in life." If so, the Nikon camera would fit well into the consumer's existing attitudes.

Attitudes are difficult to change. A person's attitudes fit into a pattern, and to change one attitude may require difficult adjustments in many others. Thus, a company should usually try to fit its products into existing attitudes rather than attempt to change attitudes. For example, today's beverage marketers now cater to people's new attitudes about health and well-being with drinks that do a lot more than just taste good or quench your thirst. ▲Coca-Cola's Fuze brand, for example, offers a line of "healthy infusion" beverages packed with vitamins, minerals, and antioxidants but without artificial preservatives, sweeteners, or colors. Fuze promises drinks that are good-tasting (with flavors like Blueberry Raspberry, Strawberry Melon, and Dragonfruit Lime) but also good for you—containing only natural ingredients that "help your metabolism work in your favor." By matching today's attitudes about life and healthful living, the Fuze brand has become a leader in the New Age beverage category. Its sales last year grew by more than 50 percent.

▲ Fuze fits well with people's attitudes about health and well-being: Its "healthy infusion" beverages promise drinks that are "good-tasting but also good for you."

We can now appreciate the many forces acting on consumer behavior. The consumer's choice results from the complex interplay of cultural, social, personal, and psychological factors.

Author | Some purchases are
Comment | simple and routine, even
habitual. Others are far more
complex—involving extensive
information gathering and
evaluation—and are subject to
sometimes subtle influences. For
example, think of all that goes into a
new car buying decision.

Types of Buying Decision Behavior
(pp 152–153)

Buying behavior differs greatly for a tube of toothpaste, an iPod, financial services, and a new car. More complex decisions usually involve more buying participants and more buyer deliberation. ⬙ **Figure 5.5** shows types of consumer buying behavior based on the degree of buyer involvement and the degree of differences among brands.

Complex Buying Behavior

Complex buying behavior
Consumer buying behavior in situations characterized by high consumer involvement in a purchase and significant perceived differences among brands.

Consumers undertake **complex buying behavior** when they are highly involved in a purchase and perceive significant differences among brands. Consumers may be highly involved when the product is expensive, risky, purchased infrequently, and highly self-expressive. Typically, the consumer has much to learn about the product category. For example, a PC buyer may not know what attributes to consider. Many product features carry no real meaning: a "3.4GHz Pentium processor," "WUXGA active matrix screen," or "4GB dual-channel DDR2 DRAM memory."

This buyer will pass through a learning process, first developing beliefs about the product, then attitudes, and then making a thoughtful purchase choice. Marketers of high-involvement products must understand the information-gathering and evaluation behavior of high-involvement consumers. They need to help buyers learn about product-class attributes and their relative importance. They need to differentiate their brand's features, perhaps by describing the brand's benefits using print media with long copy. They must motivate store salespeople and the buyer's acquaintances to influence the final brand choice.

Dissonance-Reducing Buying Behavior

Dissonance-reducing buying behavior
Consumer buying behavior in situations characterized by high involvement but few perceived differences among brands.

Dissonance-reducing buying behavior occurs when consumers are highly involved with an expensive, infrequent, or risky purchase, but see little difference among brands. For example, consumers buying carpeting may face a high-involvement decision because carpeting is expensive and self-expressive. Yet buyers may consider most carpet brands in a given price range to be the same. In this case, because perceived brand differences are not large, buyers may shop around to learn what is available, but buy relatively quickly. They may respond primarily to a good price or to purchase convenience.

After the purchase, consumers might experience *postpurchase dissonance* (after-sale discomfort) when they notice certain disadvantages of the purchased carpet brand or hear favorable things about brands not purchased. To counter such dissonance, the marketer's after-sale communications should provide evidence and support to help consumers feel good about their brand choices.

Habitual Buying Behavior

Habitual buying behavior
Consumer buying behavior in situations characterized by low-consumer involvement and few significantly perceived brand differences.

Habitual buying behavior occurs under conditions of low-consumer involvement and little significant brand difference. For example, take salt. Consumers have little involvement in this product category—they simply go to the store and reach for a brand. If they keep

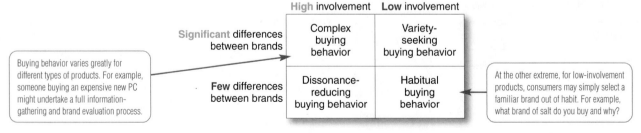

⬙ **FIGURE** | 5.5 Four Types of Buying Behavior

Source: Adapted from Henry Assael, *Consumer Behavior and Marketing Action* (Boston: Kent Publishing Company, 1987), p. 87. Copyright © 1987 by Wadsworth, Inc. Printed by permission of Kent Publishing Company, a division of Wadsworth, Inc.

reaching for the same brand, it is out of habit rather than strong brand loyalty. Consumers appear to have low involvement with most low-cost, frequently purchased products.

In such cases, consumer behavior does not pass through the usual belief-attitude-behavior sequence. Consumers do not search extensively for information about the brands, evaluate brand characteristics, and make weighty decisions about which brands to buy. Instead, they passively receive information as they watch television or read magazines. Ad repetition creates *brand familiarity* rather than *brand conviction*. Consumers do not form strong attitudes toward a brand; they select the brand because it is familiar. Because they are not highly involved with the product, consumers may not evaluate the choice even after purchase. Thus, the buying process involves brand beliefs formed by passive learning, followed by purchase behavior, which may or may not be followed by evaluation.

Because buyers are not highly committed to any brands, marketers of low-involvement products with few brand differences often use price and sales promotions to stimulate product trial. In advertising for a low-involvement product, ad copy should stress only a few key points. Visual symbols and imagery are important because they can be remembered easily and associated with the brand. Ad campaigns should include high repetition of short-duration messages. Television is usually more effective than print media because it is a low-involvement medium suitable for passive learning. Advertising planning should be based on classical conditioning theory, in which buyers learn to identify a certain product by a symbol repeatedly attached to it.

Variety-Seeking Buying Behavior

Variety-seeking buying behavior
Consumer buying behavior in situations characterized by low consumer involvement but significant perceived brand differences.

Consumers undertake **variety-seeking buying behavior** in situations characterized by low consumer involvement but significant perceived brand differences. In such cases, consumers often do a lot of brand switching. For example, when buying cookies, a consumer may hold some beliefs, choose a cookie brand without much evaluation, and then evaluate that brand during consumption. But the next time, the consumer might pick another brand out of boredom or simply to try something different. Brand switching occurs for the sake of variety rather than because of dissatisfaction.

In such product categories, the marketing strategy may differ for the market leader and minor brands. The market leader will try to encourage habitual buying behavior by dominating shelf space, keeping shelves fully stocked, and running frequent reminder advertising. Challenger firms will encourage variety seeking by offering lower prices, special deals, coupons, free samples, and advertising that presents reasons for trying something new.

Author Comment | The actual purchase decision is just part of a much larger buying process—starting with need recognition through how you feel after making the purchase. Marketers want to be involved throughout the buyer decision process.

The Buyer Decision Process (pp 153–157)

Now that we have looked at the influences that affect buyers, we are ready to look at how consumers make buying decisions. **Figure 5.6** shows that the buyer decision process consists of five stages: *need recognition*, *information search*, *evaluation of alternatives*, *purchase decision*, and *postpurchase behavior*. Clearly, the buying process starts long before the actual purchase and continues long after. Marketers need to focus on the entire buying process rather than on just the purchase decision.

The buying process starts long before the actual purchase and continues long after. In fact, it might result in a decision *not* to buy. Therefore, marketers must focus on the entire buying process, not just the purchase decision.

The figure suggests that consumers pass through all five stages with every purchase. But in more routine purchases, consumers often skip or reverse some of these stages. A woman buying her regular brand of toothpaste would recognize the need and go right to the purchase decision, skipping information search and evaluation. However, we use the model in Figure 5.6 because it shows all the considerations that arise when a consumer faces a new and complex purchase situation.

FIGURE | 5.6 Buyer Decision Process

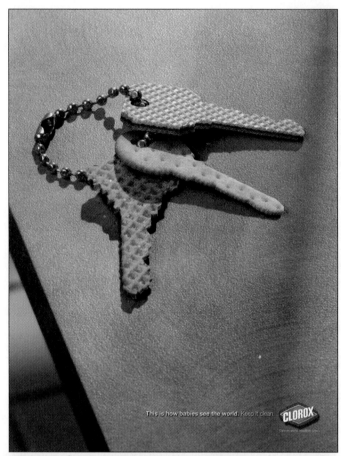

This is how babies see the world. Keep it clean. CLOROX

▲ Need recognition can be triggered by advertising. This innovative ad from Clorox reminds parents that "This is how babies see the world. Keep it clean."

Need Recognition

The buying process starts with **need recognition**—the buyer recognizes a problem or need. The need can be triggered by *internal stimuli* when one of the person's normal needs—hunger, thirst, sex—rises to a level high enough to become a drive. A need can also be triggered by *external stimuli.* ▲For example, an advertisement or a discussion with a friend might get you thinking about buying a new car. At this stage, the marketer should research consumers to find out what kinds of needs or problems arise, what brought them about, and how they led the consumer to this particular product.

Information Search

An interested consumer may or may not search for more information. If the consumer's drive is strong and a satisfying product is near at hand, the consumer is likely to buy it then. If not, the consumer may store the need in memory or undertake an **information search** related to the need. For example, once you've decided you need a new car, at the least, you will probably pay more attention to car ads, cars owned by friends, and car conversations. Or you may actively search the Web, talk with friends, and gather information in other ways. The amount of searching you do will depend on the strength of your drive, the amount of information you start with, the ease of obtaining more information, the value you place on additional information, and the satisfaction you get from searching.

Consumers can obtain information from any of several sources. These include *personal sources* (family, friends, neighbors, acquaintances), *commercial sources* (advertising, salespeople, dealer Web sites, packaging, displays), *public sources* (mass media, consumer rating organizations, Internet searches), and *experiential sources* (handling, examining, using the product). The relative influence of these information sources varies with the product and the buyer.

Generally, the consumer receives the most information about a product from commercial sources—those controlled by the marketer. The most effective sources, however, tend to be personal. Commercial sources normally *inform* the buyer, but personal sources *legitimize* or *evaluate* products for the buyer. A recent Nielsen survey found that 78 percent of consumers found recommendations from others to be the most credible form of endorsement. As one marketer states, "It's rare that an advertising campaign can be as effective as a neighbor leaning over the fence and saying, 'This is a wonderful product.'" Increasingly, that "fence" is a virtual one, as more and more customers pour through the online ratings and reviews of other buyers on sites such as Amazon.com before making a purchase.[35]

As more information is obtained, the consumer's awareness and knowledge of the available brands and features increase. In your car information search, you may learn about the several brands available. The information might also help you to drop certain brands from consideration. A company must design its marketing mix to make prospects aware of and knowledgeable about its brand. It should carefully identify consumers' sources of information and the importance of each source.

Evaluation of Alternatives

We have seen how the consumer uses information to arrive at a set of final brand choices. How does the consumer choose among the alternative brands? The marketer needs to know about **alternative evaluation**—that is, how the consumer processes information to arrive at brand choices. Unfortunately, consumers do not use a simple and single evaluation process in all buying situations. Instead, several evaluation processes are at work.

Need recognition
The first stage of the buyer decision process, in which the consumer recognizes a problem or need.

Information search
The stage of the buyer decision process in which the consumer is aroused to search for more information; the consumer may simply have heightened attention or may go into an active information search.

Alternative evaluation
The stage of the buyer decision process in which the consumer uses information to evaluate alternative brands in the choice set.

The consumer arrives at attitudes toward different brands through some evaluation procedure. How consumers go about evaluating purchase alternatives depends on the individual consumer and the specific buying situation. In some cases, consumers use careful calculations and logical thinking. At other times, the same consumers do little or no evaluating; instead they buy on impulse and rely on intuition. Sometimes consumers make buying decisions on their own; sometimes they turn to friends, consumer guides, or salespeople for buying advice.

Suppose you've narrowed your car choices to three brands. And suppose that you are primarily interested in four attributes—styling, operating economy, warranty, and price. By this time, you've probably formed beliefs about how each brand rates on each attribute. Clearly, if one car rated best on all the attributes, we could predict that you would choose it. However, the brands will no doubt vary in appeal. You might base your buying decision on only one attribute, and your choice would be easy to predict. If you wanted styling above everything else, you would buy the car that you think has the best styling. But most buyers consider several attributes, each with different importance. If we knew the importance that you assigned to each of the four attributes, we could predict your car choice more reliably.

Marketers should study buyers to find out how they actually evaluate brand alternatives. If they know what evaluative processes go on, marketers can take steps to influence the buyer's decision.

Purchase Decision

Purchase decision

The buyer's decision about which brand to purchase.

In the evaluation stage, the consumer ranks brands and forms purchase intentions. Generally, the consumer's **purchase decision** will be to buy the most preferred brand, but two factors can come between the purchase *intention* and the purchase *decision*. The first factor is the *attitudes of others*. If someone important to you thinks that you should buy the lowest-priced car, then the chances of you buying a more expensive car are reduced.

The second factor is *unexpected situational factors*. The consumer may form a purchase intention based on factors such as expected income, expected price, and expected product benefits. However, unexpected events may change the purchase intention. For example, the economy might take a turn for the worse, a close competitor might drop its price, or a friend might report being disappointed in your preferred car. Thus, preferences and even purchase intentions do not always result in actual purchase choice.

Postpurchase Behavior

Postpurchase behavior

The stage of the buyer decision process in which the consumers take further action after purchase, based on their satisfaction or dissatisfaction.

The marketer's job does not end when the product is bought. After purchasing the product, the consumer will be satisfied or dissatisfied and will engage in **postpurchase behavior** of interest to the marketer. What determines whether the buyer is satisfied or dissatisfied with a purchase? The answer lies in the relationship between the *consumer's expectations* and the product's *perceived performance*. If the product falls short of expectations, the consumer is disappointed; if it meets expectations, the consumer is satisfied; if it exceeds expectations, the consumer is delighted. The larger the gap between expectations and performance, the greater the consumer's dissatisfaction. This suggests that sellers should promise only what their brands can deliver so that buyers are satisfied.

Cognitive dissonance

Buyer discomfort caused by postpurchase conflict.

Almost all major purchases, however, result in **cognitive dissonance**, or discomfort caused by postpurchase conflict. After the purchase, consumers are satisfied with the benefits of the chosen brand and are glad to avoid the drawbacks of the brands not bought. However, every purchase involves compromise. So consumers feel uneasy about acquiring the drawbacks of the chosen brand and about losing the benefits of the brands not purchased. Thus, consumers feel at least some postpurchase dissonance for every purchase.[36]

Why is it so important to satisfy the customer? Customer satisfaction is a key to building profitable relationships with consumers—to keeping and growing consumers and reaping their customer lifetime value. Satisfied customers buy a product again, talk favorably to others about the product, pay less attention to competing brands and advertising, and buy other products from the company. Many marketers go beyond merely *meeting* the expectations of customers—they aim to *delight* the customer (see **Real Marketing 5.2**).

Real Marketing 5.2

Lexus:
Delighting Customers After the Sale to Keep Them Coming Back

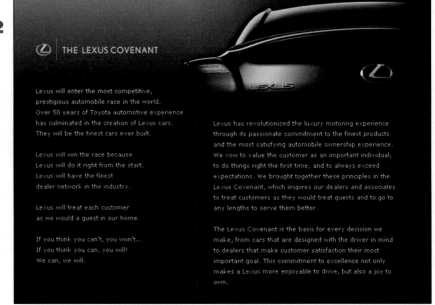

THE LEXUS COVENANT

Lexus will enter the most competitive, prestigious automobile race in the world. Over 50 years of Toyota automotive experience has culminated in the creation of Lexus cars. They will be the finest cars ever built.

Lexus will win the race because Lexus will do it right from the start. Lexus will have the finest dealer network in the industry.

Lexus will treat each customer as we would a guest in our home.

If you think you can't, you won't... If you think you can, you will! We can, we will.

Lexus has revolutionized the luxury motoring experience through its passionate commitment to the finest products and the most satisfying automobile ownership experience. We vow to value the customer as an important individual; to do things right the first time; and to always exceed expectations. We brought together these principles in the Lexus Covenant, which inspires our dealers and associates to treat customers as they would treat guests and to go to any lengths to serve them better.

The Lexus Covenant is the basis for every decision we make, from cars that are designed with the driver in mind to dealers that make customer satisfaction their most important goal. This commitment to excellence not only makes a Lexus more enjoyable to drive, but also a joy to own.

To delight customers and keep them coming back, the Lexus Covenant promises that its dealers will "treat each customer as we would a guest in our home" and "go to any lengths to serve them better."

Close your eyes for a minute and picture a typical car dealership. Not impressed? Talk to a friend who owns a Lexus, and you'll no doubt get a very different picture. The typical Lexus dealership is . . . well, anything but typical. And some Lexus dealers will go to almost any extreme to take care of customers and keep them coming back. Consider the following examples:

Jordan Case has big plans for the ongoing expansion of his business. He's already put in wireless Internet access. He's adding a café. And he's installing a putting green for customers who want to hone their golf skills while waiting for service. Case isn't the manager of a swank hotel or restaurant. He's the president of Park Place Lexus, an auto dealership with two locations in the Dallas area, and he takes pride that his dealership is, well, the anti-dealership. In addition to the café, putting green, and Internet access, customer perks include free car washes and portable DVD players with movies loaned to waiting service clients. Last year, Park Place Lexus's passion for customer service earned it a Malcolm Baldrige National Quality Award, a business-excellence honor bestowed by the U.S. government, making it the first automotive dealership ever in the award's 18-year history to win the Baldrige. "Buying a car doesn't rank up there with the top five things you like to do," Case says. "So we try to make the experience different."

For many people, a trip to the auto dealer means the mind-numbing hour or two in a plastic chair with some tattered magazines and stale coffee. But JM Lexus in Margate, Florida, features four massage chairs, in addition to its Starbucks coffee shop, two putting greens, two customer lounges, plus a library. At another gleaming glass-and-stone Lexus dealership north of Miami, "guests,"

as Lexus calls its customers, leave their cars with a valet and are then guided by a concierge to a European-style coffee bar offering complimentary espresso, cappuccino, and a selection of pastries prepared by a chef trained in Rome. "We have customers checking into world-class hotels," says a dealership executive. "They shop on Fifth Avenue and they expect a certain kind of experience."

Lexus knows that good marketing doesn't stop with making the sale. Keeping customers happy *after* the sale is the key to building lasting relationships. Dealers across the country have a common goal: to delight customers and keep them coming back. Lexus believes that if you "delight the customer, and continue to delight the customer, you will have a customer for life." And Lexus understands just how valuable a customer can be—it estimates that the average lifetime value of a Lexus customer is $600,000.

Despite the amenities, few Lexus customers spend much time hanging around the dealership. Lexus knows that the best dealership visit is the one that you don't have to make at all. So it builds customer-pleasing cars to start with—high-quality cars that need little servicing. In its "Lexus Covenant," the company vows that it will make "the finest cars ever built." In survey after industry survey, Lexus rates at or near the top in quality. Lexus has topped the list in five of the last seven annual J.D. Power and Associates Initial Quality Study ratings.

Still, when a car does need to be serviced, Lexus goes out of its way to make it easy and painless. Most dealers will even pick up the car, and then return it when the maintenance is finished. And the car comes back spotless, thanks to a complimentary cleaning to remove bugs and road grime from the exterior and smudges from the leather interior. You might even be surprised to find that they've touched up a door ding to help restore the car to its fresh-from-the-factory luster. "My wife will never buy another car except a Lexus," says one satisfied Lexus owner. "They come to our house, pick up the car, do an oil change, [spiff it up,] and bring it back. She's sold for life."

And when a customer does bring a car in, Lexus repairs it right the first time, on time. Dealers know that their well-heeled customers have money, "but what they don't have is time." So dealers like Mike Sullivan of California are testing a system that uses three technicians instead of one for 35,000-mile service checkups. The new system will cut a customer's wait in half. "I'm not in the car business," says one dealer. "I'm in the service business."

According to its Web site, from the very start, Lexus set out to "revolutionize the automotive experience with a passionate commitment to the finest products, supported by dealers who create the most satisfying ownership experience the world has ever seen. We

Continued on next page ▼

Real Marketing 5.2 Continued ▼

vow to value the customer as an important individual. To do things right the first time. And to always exceed expectations." Jordan Case of Park Place Lexus fully embraces this philosophy: "You've got to do it right, on time, and make people feel like they are the only one in the room." Proclaims the Lexus Covenant, "Lexus will treat each customer as we would a guest in our own home."

At Lexus, exceeding customer expectations sometimes means fulfilling even seemingly outrageous customer requests. Dave Wilson, owner of several Lexus dealerships in Southern California, tells of a letter he received from an angry Lexus owner who spent $374 to repair her car at his dealership. She'd owned four prior Lexus vehicles without a single problem. She said in her letter that she resented paying to fix her current one. Turns out, she thought they were maintenance free—as in get in and drive . . . and drive and drive. "She didn't think she had to do anything to her Lexus," says Wilson. "She had 60,000 miles on it, and never had the oil changed." Wilson sent back her $374.

By all accounts, Lexus has lived up to its ambitious customer-satisfaction promise. It has created what appear to be the world's most satisfied car owners. Lexus regularly tops not just the J.D. Power quality ratings, but also its customer-satisfaction ratings, and not just in the United States, but worldwide. Last year, for the second consecutive year, Lexus ranked number one in the J.D. Power and Associates Sales Satisfaction Index, which measures customer satisfaction with the new-vehicle sales process. Customer satisfaction translates into sales and customer loyalty. Lexus is the nation's number-one selling luxury car. And once a

Lexus customer, always a Lexus customer—Lexus retains 84 percent of customers who've gone to the dealership for service.

Just ask a Lexus customer. "I'm telling you, this is class, buddy," says customer Barry Speak while reclining in a vibrating massage chair at the Palm Beach Lexus store. Owner of a late-model Lexus LS 4300 sedan, Speak says there is no doubt he will come to the Palm Beach store for a new vehicle in a year or two. "My wife and I are going to be fighting over who gets to take the car in now," he says over the chair's hum. "You're not kidding!" Jane Speak chimes in from the store's other massage chair.

Sources: The examples are adapted from Mac Gordon, "He Runs the Largest Lexus Store," *Ward's Dealer Business,* February 2008, p. 64; Neil E. Boudette, "Luxury Car Sellers Put on the Ritz," *Wall Street Journal,* December 18, 2007, p. B1; and Julia Chang, "At Your Service," *Sales & Marketing Management,* June 2006, pp 42–43. Other information and quotes from Steve Finlay, "At Least She Put Fuel in It," *Ward's Dealer Business,* August 1, 2003; "J.D. Power and Associates Reports: Lexus Ranks Highest in Sales Satisfaction as Industry Achieved Record Highs Sales for a Second Consecutive Year," *PR Newswire,* November 14, 2007; "Toyota Reports 2007 and December Sales," *PR Newswire,* January 3, 2008; and "Lexus Covenant," accessed at www.lexus.com/about/corporate/covenant.html, December 2008.

A dissatisfied consumer responds differently. Bad word of mouth often travels farther and faster than good word of mouth. It can quickly damage consumer attitudes about a company and its products. But companies cannot simply rely on dissatisfied customers to volunteer their complaints when they are dissatisfied. Most unhappy customers never tell the company about their problem. Therefore, a company should measure customer satisfaction regularly. It should set up systems that *encourage* customers to complain. In this way, the company can learn how well it is doing and how it can improve.

By studying the overall buyer decision, marketers may be able to find ways to help consumers move through it. For example, if consumers are not buying a new product because they do not perceive a need for it, marketing might launch advertising messages that trigger the need and show how the product solves customers' problems. If customers know about the product but are not buying because they hold unfavorable attitudes toward it, the marketer must find ways either to change the product or change consumer perceptions.

> **Author Comment** | Here, we look at some special considerations in new-product buying decisions.

The Buyer Decision Process for New Products (pp 157–159)

We have looked at the stages buyers go through in trying to satisfy a need. Buyers may pass quickly or slowly through these stages, and some of the stages may even be reversed. Much depends on the nature of the buyer, the product, and the buying situation.

New product
A good, service, or idea that is perceived by some potential customers as new.

We now look at how buyers approach the purchase of new products. A **new product** is a good, service, or idea that is perceived by some potential customers as new. It may have been around for a while, but our interest is in how consumers learn about products for the first time and make decisions on whether to adopt them. We define the **adoption process** as "the mental process through which an individual passes from first learning about an innovation to final adoption," and *adoption* as the decision by an individual to become a regular user of the product.[37]

Adoption process
The mental process through which an individual passes from first hearing about an innovation to final adoption.

▲ Influencing the adoption process: This Gillette Fusion ad encourages trial of the Gillette Fusion Power Phantom by saving $4 on a Fusion razor.

Stages in the <u>Adoption Process</u>

Consumers go through five stages in the process of adopting a new product:

- *Awareness:* The consumer becomes aware of the new product, but lacks information about it.

- *Interest:* The consumer seeks information about the new product.

- *Evaluation:* The consumer considers whether trying the new product makes sense.

- *Trial:* The consumer tries the new product on a small scale to improve his or her estimate of its value.

- *Adoption:* The consumer decides to make full and regular use of the new product.

This model suggests that the new-product marketer should think about how to help consumers move through these stages. ▲For example, to encourage consumers to try its new Gillette Fusion razor, P&G featured coupons offering substantial savings. Similarly, a luxury car producer might find that many potential customers know about and are interested in its new model but aren't buying because of uncertainty about the model's benefits and the high price. The producer could launch a "take one home for the weekend" promotion to high-value prospects to move them into the trial process and lead them to purchase.

Individual Differences in Innovativeness

People differ greatly in their readiness to try new products. In each product area, there are "consumption pioneers" and early adopters. Other individuals adopt new products much later. People can be classified into the adopter categories shown in ◀**Figure 5.7**. After a slow start, an increasing number of people adopt the new product. The number of adopters reaches a peak and then drops off as fewer nonadopters remain. Innovators are defined as the first 2.5 percent of the buyers to adopt a new idea (those beyond two standard deviations from mean adoption time); the early adopters are the next 13.5 percent (between one and two standard deviations); and so forth.

The five adopter groups have differing values. *Innovators* are venturesome—they try new ideas at some risk. *Early adopters* are guided by respect—they are opinion leaders in their communities and adopt new ideas early but carefully. The *early majority* are deliberate—although they rarely are leaders, they adopt new ideas before the average person. The *late majority* are skeptical—they adopt an innovation only after a majority of people have tried it. Finally, *laggards* are tradition bound—they are suspicious of changes and adopt the innovation only when it has become something of a tradition itself.

This adopter classification suggests that an innovating firm should research the characteristics of innovators and early adopters and should direct marketing efforts toward

◀FIGURE | 5.7

Adopter Categorization on the Basis of Relative Time of Adoption of Innovations

Source: Reprinted with permission of the Free Press, a Division of Simon & Schuster, from *Diffusion of Innovations*, Fifth Edition, by Everett M. Rogers. Copyright © 2003 by the Free Press.

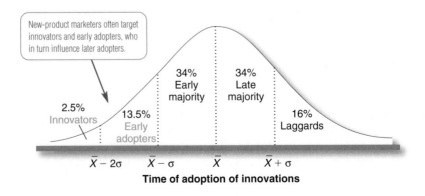

them. In general, innovators tend to be relatively younger, better educated, and higher in income than later adopters and nonadopters. They are more receptive to unfamiliar things, rely more on their own values and judgment, and are more willing to take risks. They are less brand loyal and more likely to take advantage of special promotions such as discounts, coupons, and samples.

Influence of Product Characteristics on Rate of Adoption

The characteristics of the new product affect its rate of adoption. Some products catch on almost overnight—for example, the iPod, which flew off retailers' shelves at an astounding rate from the day it was introduced. Others take a longer time to gain acceptance. For example, the first HDTVs were introduced in the United States in the 1990s, but by 2007 only about 14 percent of U.S. TV households were what Nielsen describes as "HD capable"—equipped with HD televisions and HD tuners capable of receiving HDTV signals.[38]

Five characteristics are especially important in influencing an innovation's rate of adoption. For example, consider the characteristics of HDTV in relation to the rate of adoption:

- *Relative advantage*: the degree to which the innovation appears superior to existing products. HDTV offers substantially improved picture quality. This will speed its rate of adoption.

- *Compatibility*: the degree to which the innovation fits the values and experiences of potential consumers. HDTV, for example, is highly compatible with the lifestyles of the TV-watching public. However, many programs and channels are still not yet available in HD, and this has slowed HDTV adoption.

- *Complexity*: the degree to which the innovation is difficult to understand or use. HDTVs are not very complex and, therefore, once more programming is available and prices come down, they will take less time to penetrate U.S. homes than more complex innovations.

- *Divisibility*: the degree to which the innovation may be tried on a limited basis. Early HDTVs and HD cable and satellite systems were very expensive, slowing the rate of adoption. As prices fall, adoption rates will increase.

- *Communicability*: the degree to which the results of using the innovation can be observed or described to others. Because HDTV lends itself to demonstration and description, its use will spread faster among consumers.

Other characteristics influence the rate of adoption, such as initial and ongoing costs, risk and uncertainty, and social approval. The new-product marketer must research all these factors when developing the new product and its marketing program.

REVIEWING Objectives AND KEY Terms

The American consumer market consists of almost 300 million people who consume more than $13 trillion worth of goods and services each year, making it one of the most attractive consumer markets in the world. The world consumer market consists of more than 6.6 *billion* people. Consumers around the world vary greatly in age, income, education level, and tastes. Understanding how these differences affect *consumer buying behavior* is one of the biggest challenges marketers face.

OBJECTIVE 1 Define the consumer market and construct a simple model of consumer buyer behavior. (p 136)

The *consumer market* consists of all the individuals and households who buy or acquire goods and services for personal consumption. The simplest model of consumer buyer behavior is the stimulus-response model. According to this model, marketing stimuli (the four Ps) and other major forces (economic, technological, political, cultural) enter the consumer's "black box" and produce certain responses. Once in the black box, these inputs produce observable buyer responses, such as product choice, brand choice, purchase timing, and purchase amount.

OBJECTIVE 2 **Name the four major factors that influence consumer buyer behavior.** (pp 137–151)

Consumer buyer behavior is influenced by four key sets of buyer characteristics: cultural, social, personal, and psychological. Although many of these factors cannot be influenced by the marketer, they can be useful in identifying interested buyers and in shaping products and appeals to serve consumer needs better. *Culture* is the most basic determinant of a person's wants and behavior. It includes the basic values, perceptions, preferences, and behaviors that a person learns from family and other important institutions. *Subcultures* are "cultures within cultures" that have distinct values and lifestyles and can be based on anything from age to ethnicity. People with different cultural and subcultural characteristics have different product and brand preferences. As a result, marketers may want to focus their marketing programs on the special needs of certain groups.

Social factors also influence a buyer's behavior. A person's *reference groups*—family, friends, social networks, professional associations—strongly affect product and brand choices. The buyer's age, life-cycle stage, occupation, economic circumstances, lifestyle, personality, and other *personal characteristics* influence his or her buying decisions. Consumer *lifestyles*—the whole pattern of acting and interacting in the world—are also an important influence on purchase decisions. Finally, consumer buying behavior is influenced by four major *psychological factors*—motivation, perception, learning, and beliefs and attitudes. Each of these factors provides a different perspective for understanding the workings of the buyer's black box.

OBJECTIVE 3 **List and define the major types of buying decision behavior and the stages in the buyer decision process.** (pp 152–157)

Buying behavior may vary greatly across different types of products and buying decisions. Consumers undertake *complex buying behavior* when they are highly involved in a purchase and perceive significant differences among brands. *Dissonance-reducing behavior* occurs when consumers are highly involved but see little difference among brands. *Habitual*

buying behavior occurs under conditions of low involvement and little significant brand difference. In situations characterized by low involvement but significant perceived brand differences, consumers engage in *variety-seeking buying behavior.*

When making a purchase, the buyer goes through a decision process consisting of *need recognition, information search, evaluation of alternatives, purchase decision,* and *postpurchase behavior.* The marketer's job is to understand the buyer's behavior at each stage and the influences that are operating. During *need recognition,* the consumer recognizes a problem or need that could be satisfied by a product or service in the market. Once the need is recognized, the consumer is aroused to seek more information and moves into the *information search* stage. With information in hand, the consumer proceeds to *alternative evaluation,* during which the information is used to evaluate brands in the choice set. From there, the consumer makes a *purchase decision* and actually buys the product. In the final stage of the buyer decision process, *postpurchase behavior,* the consumer takes action based on satisfaction or dissatisfaction.

OBJECTIVE 4 **Describe the adoption and diffusion process for new products.** (pp 157–159)

The product adoption process is comprised of five stages: awareness, interest, evaluation, trial, and adoption. Initially, the consumer must become aware of the new product. *Awareness* leads to *interest,* and the consumer seeks information about the new product. Once information has been gathered, the consumer enters the *evaluation* stage and considers buying the new product. Next, in the *trial* stage, the consumer tries the product on a small scale to improve his or her estimate of its value. If the consumer is satisfied with the product, he or she enters the *adoption* stage, deciding to use the new product fully and regularly.

With regard to diffusion of new products, consumers respond at different rates, depending on the consumer's characteristics and the product's characteristics. Consumers may be innovators, early adopters, early majority, late majority, or laggards. *Innovators* are willing to try risky new ideas; *early adopters*—often community opinion leaders—accept new ideas early but carefully; the *early majority*—rarely leaders—decide deliberately to try new ideas, doing so before the average person does; the *late majority* try an innovation only after a majority of people have adopted it; whereas *laggards* adopt an innovation only after it has become a tradition itself. Manufacturers try to bring their new products to the attention of potential early adopters, especially those who are opinion leaders.

KEY Terms

OBJECTIVE 1

Consumer buyer behavior (p 135)
Consumer market (p 135)

OBJECTIVE 2

Culture (p 137)
Subculture (p 137)
Social class (p 140)

Group (p 140)
Opinion leader (p 141)
Online social networks (p 143)
Lifestyle (p 147)
Personality (p 148)
Brand personality (p 148)
Motive (drive) (p 148)
Perception (p 150)

Learning (p 151)
Belief (p 151)
Attitude (p 151)

OBJECTIVE 3

Complex buying behavior (p 152)
Dissonance-reducing buying behavior (p 152)

DISCUSSING & APPLYING THE Concepts

Discussing the Concepts

1. How do consumers respond to various marketing efforts the company might use? List the buyer characteristics that affect buyer behavior and discuss which one(s) influence you most when making a new car purchase decision. (AACSB: Communication; Reflective Thinking)

2. Name and describe the types of consumer buying behavior. Which one would you most likely use if deciding on a laptop computer purchase and which for picking a restaurant for dinner? (AACSB: Communication; Reflective Thinking)

3. Explain the stages of the consumer buyer decision process and describe how you or your family went through this process to make a recent purchase. (AACSB: Communication; Reflective Thinking)

4. How might a marketer influence a consumer's information search through each of the four information sources discussed in the chapter? (AACSB: Communication; Reflective Thinking)

5. What is a "new" product and how do consumers go about deciding whether to adopt a new product? (AACSB: Communication)

6. What product characteristics influence an innovation's rate of adoption? Discuss the characteristics of mobile navigation systems in relation to the rate of adoption. (AACSB: Communication)

Applying the Concepts

1. Marketers often target consumers before, during, or after a trigger event, an event in one's life that triggers change. For example, after having a child, new parents have an increased need for baby furniture, clothes, diapers, car seats, and lots of other baby-related goods. Consumers who never paid attention to marketing efforts for certain products may now be focused on ones related to their life change. In a small group, discuss other trigger events that may provide opportunities to target the right buyer at the right time. (AACSB: Communication; Reflective Thinking)

2. You are the vice president of marketing for a small software company that has developed new and novel spam-blocking software. You are charged with selecting the target market for the product launch. Discuss the adopter groups shown in Figure 5.7 and explain how this knowledge can help you with your targeting decision. (AACSB: Communication; Reflective Thinking)

3. How did you decide on the college or university you are currently attending? Describe the factors that influenced your decision and the decision-making process you followed. (AACSB: Communication; Reflective Thinking)

FOCUS ON Technology

With so many choices available, the decision process for consumers can be daunting, especially for high-risk purchases. Looking for a new digital camera, computer, sunscreen, or coffee maker? Product reviews abound that provide information on products in just about every category. Product reviews and rankings are available from *Consumer Reports* (considered the "gold standard"), *Good Housekeeping*, and *Car & Driver* to *Backpacker Magazine* and Web sites providing consumer reviews. So finding information is not the problem, but sorting it all out is. ConsumerSearch.com has just what consumers need—a service that reviews the reviews. This source is recognized for excellence by the likes of *USAToday*, the *Wall Street Journal*, and Yahoo! Internet Life. It not only reviews the product reviews with respect to credibility, it also consolidates the analyses in its Fast Answers and Full Reports. It also provides a Consensus Report showing the extent of agreement among reviewers regarding the best product.

1. Go to ConsumerSearch.com (www.consumersearch.com), select a product category that interests you, and learn about the best products/brands in that category. Which review is rated the best? Which brand is rated best by the reviews? Based on this analysis, which brand would you select if actually purchasing this product? How useful is this source? Write a brief report with your answers to these questions. (AACSB: Communication; Use of IT; Reflective Thinking)

2. Many Web sites provide consumer reviews, such as Epinions.com (www.epinions.com). Usually, there is a five-star rating, the number of reviews that rating is based on, and the actual written reviews. How influential are these types of reviews for you when deciding on a purchase? (AACSB: Communication; Use of IT; Reflective Thinking)

FOCUS ON Ethics

Apple's iPod revolutionized music listening, with over 100 million iPods sold worldwide. However, iPod and other brands of MP3 players have revolutionized the music industry as well, causing sales of prerecorded CDs to plummet and music file downloading from the Internet—both legal and illegal—to skyrocket. Pay-per-song sites, such as Apple's iTunes, let consumers purchase songs legally and inexpensively. While purchases of songs from these types of sites continue to increase, illegal music file sharing is increasing as well, with hundreds of millions of files downloaded illegally each year. Alarmingly, studies show that college students hold favorable attitudes toward this activity and have little fear of prosecution. Watch out, though, because the Recording Industry Association of America (RIAA) initiates thousands of lawsuits each year, aimed primarily at college students.

1. What is your attitude toward illegal music file downloading? Do you actually view it as an illegal activity? (AACSB: Communication; Ethical Reasoning)
2. Discuss how marketers can combat this problem. (AACSB: Communication; Reflective Thinking)

MARKETING BY THE Numbers

One way that consumers can evaluate alternatives is to decide on important attributes and assess how the alternatives perform on those attributes. Each attribute, such as automobile gas mileage, is given a weight to reflect its level of importance to that consumer. Then, the consumer evaluates each alternative on each attribute. For example, in the table below, gas mileage (weighted at 0.5) is the most important automobile purchase attribute for this consumer. The consumer believes that Brand C performs best on gas mileage, rating it 7 (higher ratings indicate higher performance), Brand B rates worst on gas mileage (rating of 3). Styling and price are the consumer's next two most important attributes; warranty is least important.

A score for each brand can be calculated by multiplying the importance weight for each attribute by the brand's score on that attribute. These weighted scores are then summed to determine the score for that brand. For example, $\text{Score}_{\text{Brand A}} = (0.2 \times 4) + (0.5 \times 6) + (0.1 \times 5) + (0.2 \times 4) = 0.8 + 3.0 + 0.5 + 0.8 = 5.1$. This consumer will select the brand with the highest score. For more discussion of the financial and quantitative implications of marketing decisions, see Appendix 2: Marketing by the Numbers.

1. Determine the scores for brands B and C. Which brand would this consumer likely choose? (AACSB: Communication; Analytic Reasoning)
2. Discuss some other "rules" consumers may use when evaluating alternatives in order to make a purchase decision. (AACSB: Communication; Reflective Thinking)

	Alternative Brands			
Attributes	**Importance Weight**	**A**	**B**	**C**
Styling	0.2	4	6	2
Gas mileage	0.5	6	3	7
Warranty	0.1	5	5	4
Price	0.2	4	6	7

VIDEO Case

Wild Planet

Of the many factors that affect consumer buyer behavior, social responsibility is playing an increasing role. While there have always been companies that have integrated "doing good" with corporate strategy, a new generation of activist entrepreneurs has now taken up the reins. The ones most likely to succeed are those who recognize that beyond just doing good,

social responsibility can provide a powerful means for connecting with consumers.

For example, Wild Planet markets high-quality, nonviolent toys that encourage kids to be imaginative and creative and to explore the world around them. Wild Planet sells more than just toys. It sells positive play experiences. To better understand those experiences, the company conducts a tremendous amount of consumer research through state-of-the-art methods to better understand consumer buyer behavior. Wild Planet even created a Toy Opinion Panel to evaluate current products and develop new product ideas.

After viewing the video featuring Wild Planet, answer the following questions about consumer buyer behavior:

1. Explain how each of the four sets of factors affecting consumer behavior affects the consumer purchase process as it relates to toys from Wild Planet.

2. What demographic segment of consumers is Wild Planet targeting?

3. Visit the Wild Planet Web site at www.wildplanet.com to learn more about the company. How does the Web site help consumers through the buyer decision process?

COMPANY Case

Victoria's Secret Pink:
Keeping the Brand Hip

When most people think of Victoria's Secret, they think of lingerie. Indeed, the Limited Brands division has done a very good job of developing this association by placing images of supermodels donning its signature bras, panties, and "sleepwear" in everything from standard broadcast and print advertising to the controversial prime-time television fashion shows that the company airs each year. Such promotional tactics have paid off for Victoria's Secret, a subsidiary of Limited Brands, which continues to achieve healthy sales and profit growth.

How does a successful company ensure that its hot sales don't cool off? One approach is to sell more to existing customers. Another is to find new customers. Victoria's Secret is doing plenty of both. One key component in its quest to find new customers is the launch and growth of its sub-brand, Pink.

EXPANDING THE TARGET MARKET
Victoria's Secret launched its line of Pink products in 50 test markets in 2003. Based on very positive initial results, the company expanded the sub-brand quickly to a national level. With the Pink introduction, Victoria's Secret hoped to add a new segment to its base: young, hip, and fashionable customers. "Young" in this case means 18 to 30 years of age. More specifically, Pink is geared toward college coeds. According to company spokesman Anthony Hebron, "It's what you see around the dorm. It's the fun, playful stuff she needs, but is still fashionable."

The company classifies the Pink line as "loungewear," a very broad term that includes sweatpants, T-shirts, pajamas, bras and panties, pillows and bedding, and even dog accessories. In keeping with the "young and fun" image, the product line includes bright colors (Pink is not a misnomer) and often incorporates stripes and polka-dots. The garments feature comfortable cuts and mostly soft cotton fabrics. To keep things fresh for the younger segment, stores introduce new Pink products every three or four weeks.

According to those at Victoria's Secret, in sharp contrast to the sexy nature of the core brand, Pink is positioned as cute and playful. "It's spirited and collegiate. It's not necessarily sexy—it's not sexy at all—but young, hip, and casual. It's fashion-forward and accessible," said Mary Beth Wood, a spokeswoman for Victoria's Secret. The Pink line does include underwear that some might consider to be on par with standard Victoria's Secret items. But management is quick to point out that the designs, such as heart-covered thongs, are more cute than racy. Displays of Pink merchandise often incorporate stuffed animals, and many articles display Pink's trademark mascot, a pink dog.

Originally, Pink was considered to be a store-within-a-store concept. But Pink sales have surpassed expectations. To date, Victoria's Secret has opened six stand-alone Pink stores. In 2007, Pink revenues hit $900 million, almost one-sixth of the company's $5.6 billion take for the year. Because of this, the company is giving far more serious consideration to expanding the presence of Pink lifestyle shops in several markets.

A KEY DRIVER OF VICTORIA'S SECRET'S FUTURE GROWTH
Limited Brands has been experiencing good times, and executives have been quick to recognize that Victoria's Secret is a huge part of that success. In fact, the Victoria's Secret and Bath & Body Works divisions have accounted for roughly 70 percent of revenue (Victoria's Secret alone was good for more than 50 percent) and almost all the profit in recent years.

But Limited Brands CEO Les Wexner is not content to let the chain rest. "The Victoria brand is really the power of the business," he says. "We can double the Victoria's Secret business in the next five years." This would mean increasing the division's sales to more than $10 billion. The umbrella strategy for achieving this growth is to continually broaden the customer base. This will include a focus on new and emerging lines, such as IPEX and Angels Secret Embrace (bras), Intimissimi (a line of Italian lingerie for women and men appealing to younger customers), and a new line of fitness apparel called VSX. Pink is a key component of this multibrand strategy.

The future of Victoria's Secret will also include a move toward bigger stores. Currently, the typical Victoria's Secret store is approximately 6,000 square feet. More than 80 percent of Victoria's Secret stores will be remodeled over the next five years, nearly doubling its average store size to 11,000 square feet. Larger stores will allow the company to give more space and attention to the store-within-a-store brands, such as Pink.

BROADENING THE CUSTOMER BASE . . . TOO FAR?
While Victoria's Secret's introduction and expansion of Pink seems well-founded, it has raised some eyebrows. As Pink's young and cute line has expanded rapidly, it has become

apparent that the brand's appeal goes far beyond that of its intended target market. Some women much older than 30 have shown an interest (41-year old Courtney Cox Arquette was photographed wearing Pink sweats). But stronger interest is being shown by girls younger than 18. Girls as young as 11 years old are visiting Victoria's Secret stores to buy Pink items, with and without their mothers.

Two such 11-year-olds, Lily Feingold and Brittany Garrison, were interviewed while shopping at a Victoria's Secret store with Lily's mother. As they browsed exclusively through the Pink merchandise, the two confessed that Victoria's Secret was one of their favorite stores. Passing up cotton lounge pants because each already had multiple pairs, both girls bought $68 pairs of sweatpants with the "Pink" label emblazoned on the derriere. The girls denied buying the items because they wanted to seem more grown up, instead saying that they simply liked the clothes.

The executives at Victoria's Secret are quick to say that they are not targeting girls younger than 18. Perhaps that is due to the backlash that retailer Abercrombie & Fitch experienced not long ago for targeting teens and preteens with sexually charged promotional materials and merchandise. But regardless of Victoria's Secret's intentions, Pink is fast becoming popular among teens and "tweens." Most experts agree that by the time children reach 10, they are rejecting childlike images and aspiring to more mature things associated with being a teenager. Called "age compression," it explains the trend toward preteens leaving their childhoods earlier and giving up traditional toys for more mature interests, such as cell phones, consumer electronics, and fashion products.

Tweens are growing in size and purchasing power. While the 33 million teens (ages 12 to 19) in the United States spend more than $179 billion annually (more than 60 percent have jobs), the 25 million tweens spend $51 billion annually, a number that continues to increase. But perhaps even more telling than the money being spent directly by teens is the $170 billion per year spent by parents and other family members directly for the younger consumers who may not have as much income as their older siblings. "Parents are giving them money or credit cards and children make most of the decisions about whatever purchases are made for them, whether it's toiletries, a bedspread or undergarments," said James McNeal, a former professor of marketing at Texas A&M University and author of *Kids as Customers: A Handbook of Marketing to Children*.

With this kind of purchasing power, as they find revenue for their older target markets leveling off, marketers everywhere are focusing on the teen and tween segments. "Right now, every retailer is looking for growth opportunities," said Marshall Cohen, an industry analyst. And more young women are wearing loungewear, not just at home, but to school and the mall. "Pajamas are streetwear. Slippers are shoes," Cohen continued. "It's amazing how casual we've gotten. This retail segment could get very competitive."

Although executives at Victoria's Secret deny targeting the youth of America, experts disagree. David Morrison, president of marketing research agency Twentysomething, says he is not surprised that Victoria's Secret denies marketing to teens and preteens: "If Victoria's Secret is blatantly catering to seventh and eighth graders, that might be considered exploitative." Morrison also acknowledges that the age group is drawn to the relative maturity and sophistication of the Pink label.

Natalie Weathers, assistant professor of fashion-industry management at Philadelphia University, says that Victoria's Secret is capitalizing on a trend known as co-shopping—mothers and tweens shopping together. "They are advising their daughters about their purchases, and their daughters are advising them," she said. This type of activity may have been strange 20 years ago, but according to Weathers, the preteens of today are more savvy and, therefore, more likely to be shopping partners for moms. "They are not little girls, and they aren't teenagers, but they have a lot of access to sophisticated information about what the media says is beautiful, what is pretty, what is hot and stylish and cool. They are very visually literate."

In general, introducing a brand to younger consumers is considered a sound strategy for growth and for creating long-term relationships. Marketers of everything from packaged foods to shampoo use this strategy. In most cases, it's not considered controversial to engender aspirational motives in young consumers through an entry-level product line. But many critics have questioned the aspirations that Pink engenders in tweens. Specifically, to what does it make them aspire? Based on years of experience working as a creative director for ad agencies in New York, Timothy Matz calls Pink "beginner-level lingerie." Matz does not question the practice of gateway marketing (getting customers to use the brand at an earlier age). But he admits that a "gateway" to a sexy lingerie shop may make parents nervous: "Being a 45-year-old dad, do I want my 10-year-old going to Victoria's Secret?"

Thus far, Victoria's Secret has avoided the negative reactions of the masses who opposed Abercrombie & Fitche's blatant marketing of thong underwear to preteens. Perhaps that's because it adamantly professes its exclusive focus on young adults. But it may also be because Victoria's Secret is not alone in its efforts to capitalize on the second-fastest growing apparel category (loosely defined as "lingerie") by focusing on the younger target market. An almost exhaustive list of retailers are expanding their lingerie lines. Companies that specifically target the same Pink segment include the Gap, Kohl's, Macy's, and J.C. Penney. But the biggest competition comes from fellow mall store American Eagle Outfitters, which has rolled out its own new Aerie line of "fun lingerie." And like Victoria's Secret Pink, the brand has opened stand-alone Aerie stores. In fact, results have been so good for American Eagle that it has opened a whopping 56 new Aerie stores in just a couple of years.

But Victoria's Secret was the first to market with lingerie for young adults and still has the greatest presence. And whether Pink's appeal to the preadult crowd is intentional or unintentional, many critics question the effort. Big tobacco companies have been under fire for years for using childlike imagery to draw the interest of youth to an adult product. Is Pink the Joe Camel of early adolescent sexuality? Are Pink's extreme low-rise string bikini panties the gateway drug to pushup teddies and Pleasure State Geisha thongs? These are questions that Victoria's Secret may have to address more directly at some point in the near future.

Questions for Discussion

1. Analyze the buyer decision process of a typical Pink customer.

2. Apply the concept of aspirational groups to Victoria Secret's Pink line. Should marketers have boundaries with regard to this concept?

3. Explain how both positive and negative consumer attitudes toward a brand like Pink develop? How might someone's attitude toward Pink change?

4. What role does Pink appear to be playing in the self-concept of tweens, teens, and young adults?

Sources: Suzanne Ryan, "Would Hannah Montana Wear It?" *Boston Globe*, January 10, 2008, p. D1; Heather Burke, "Victoria's Secret to Expand Its Stores," *International Herald Tribune,* August 13, 2007, p. F15; Ann Zimmerman, "Retailers' Panty Raid on Victoria's Secret New Lines Target Hot Fashion Lingerie," *Wall Street Journal*, June 20, 2007, p. B1; Fae Goodman, "Lingerie Is Luscious and Lovely—For Grown-Ups," *Chicago Sun Times,* February 19, 2006, p. B02; Vivian McInerny, "Pink Casual Loungewear Brand Nicely Colors Teen Girls' World," *Oregonian,* May 7, 2006, p. O13; Jane M. Von Bergen, "Victoria's Secret? Kids," *Philadelphia Inquirer*, December 22, 2005.

Chapter 6

Part 1   Defining Marketing and the Marketing Process (Chapters 1, 2)
Part 2   Understanding the Marketplace and Consumers (Chapters 3, 4, 5, 6)
Part 3   Designing a Customer-Driven Strategy and Mix (Chapters 7, 8, 9, 10, 11, 12, 13, 14, 15, 16, 17)
Part 4   Extending Marketing (Chapters 18, 19, 20)

Business Markets and Business Buyer Behavior

Chapter PREVIEW

In the previous chapter, you studied *final consumer* buying behavior and factors that influence it. In this chapter, we'll do the same for *business customers*—those that buy goods and services for use in producing their own products and services or for resale to others. As when selling to final buyers, firms marketing to business customers must build profitable relationships with business customers by creating superior customer value.

To start, let's look at another American icon—GE—one of the best-run, most-admired companies in the world. Most of us grew up surrounded by GE consumer products in our homes. But did you know that most of GE's business comes not from consumer products sold to you and me, but from a diverse portfolio of commercial and industrial products sold to large business customers? To succeed in its business-to-business markets, GE must do more than just design good products and make them available to customers. It must work closely and deeply with its business customers to become a strategic, problem-solving partner.

Few brands are more familiar than GE. For more than 130 years, we've packed our homes with GE products—from good ol' GE lightbulbs to refrigerators, ranges, clothes washers and dryers, microwave ovens, dishwashers, coffee makers, room air conditioners, and hundreds of other products bearing the familiar script GE logo. The company's consumer finance unit—GE Money—helps finance these and other purchasers through credit cards, loans, mortgages, and other financial services. GE even entertains us—its NBC Universal division serves up a diverse fare of network and cable television channels, movie entertainment, and even theme parks. In all, GE offers a huge assortment of consumer products and services.

But here's a fact that would startle most consumers. Did you know that GE's consumer products contribute less than one-third of the company's total $173 billion in annual sales? To the surprise of many, most of GE's business comes not from final consumers but from commercial and industrial customers across a wide range of industries. Beyond lightbulbs and electronics, GE sells everything from medical imaging technologies, water processing systems, and security solutions to power generation equipment, aircraft engines, and diesel locomotives.

At a general level, marketing medical imaging technology or diesel locomotives to business customers is like selling refrigerators to final buyers. It requires a deep-down understanding of customer needs and customer-driven marketing strategies that create superior customer value. But that's about where the similarities end. In its business markets, rather than selling to large numbers of small buyers, GE sells to a few very large buyers. Whereas it might be disappointing when a refrigerator buyer chooses a competing brand, losing a single sale to a large business customer can mean the loss of hundreds of millions of dollars in business. Also, with GE's business customers,

buying decisions are much more complex. An average consumer buying a refrigerator might do a little online research and then pop out to the local Best Buy to compare models before buying one. In contrast, buying a batch of jet engines involves a tortuously long buying process, dozens or even hundreds of decision makers from all levels of the buying organization, and layer upon layer of subtle and not-so-subtle buying influences.

To get an idea of the complexities involved in selling one of GE's industrial products, let's dig deeper into the company's GE-Transportation division and one of its bread-and-butter products, diesel locomotives. GE locomotives might not seem glamorous to you, but they are beautiful brutes to those who buy and use them. It's not difficult to identify potential buyers for a 207 ton, 4,400 horsepower GE locomotive with an average list price of $2.2 million. The real challenge is to win buyers' business by building day-in, day-out, year-in, year-out partnerships with them based on superior products and close collaboration.

In the buying decision, locomotive performance plays an important role. In such big-ticket purchases, buyers carefully scrutinize factors such as cost, fuel efficiency, and reliability. By most measures, GE's locomotives

> **Most of GE's business comes not from consumer products sold to you and me, but from commercial and industrial products sold to large business customers.**

outperform competing engines on most of these dimensions. The company's innovative Evolution Series locomotives, part of a broader GE "ecomagination" initiative to build environmentally friendly products, are now the most technically advanced, fuel-efficient, and eco-friendly diesel-electric locomotives in history. Compared with their predecessors, they produce full power but cut fuel consumption by 5 percent and reduce particulate pollution by 40 percent. "If every freight locomotive in North America were as clean as GE's Evolution(R)," notes one expert, "the annual reduction of emissions would compare to removing 48 million cars from the road each year." GE's next-generation Evolution Hybrid diesel-electric engines, scheduled for production in 2010, will reduce fuel consumption by another 15 percent and emissions by as much as 50 percent.

But locomotive performance is only part of the buying equation. GE wins contracts by partnering with business customers to help them translate that performance into moving their passengers and freight more efficiently and reliably. CSX Transportation (CSXT), one of GE-Transportation's largest customers, has purchased more than 300 GE Evolution locomotives since they were launched in 2005. According to a CSXT purchasing executive, the company "evaluates many cost factors before awarding . . . a locomotive contract. Environmental impact, fuel consumption, reliability, serviceability [are] all key elements in this decision." But also important is "the value of our ongoing partnership with GE."

A recent high-stakes international deal involving hundreds of GE locomotives demonstrates the potential importance, scope, and complexity of some business-to-business decisions:

> GE-Transportation recently landed a huge $650 million contract to supply 310 Evolution locomotives to the Kazakhstan National Railway (KTZ)—the largest-ever order for locomotives delivered outside North America. Befitting its importance to not just the companies, but to their countries as well, the deal was inked at the Kazakhstan Embassy in Washington, DC. The signing was attended by high-level executives from both organizations, including the chief executive of GE-Transportation and the president of KTZ.
>
> The buying decision was based on a host of factors. KTZ wanted the very best performance technology available, and GE's Evolution locomotives fit the bill nicely. But the deal also hinged on many factors that had little to do with the engine performance. For example, important matters of international economics and politics came into play as well. Whereas the first 10 locomotives were built at GE's U.S. plant, most of the remaining 300 locomotives will be assembled at a newly built, state-owned plant in Pavlodar, Kazakhstan.
>
> Finally, the current contract was anything but

an impulsive, one-and-done deal. Rather, it represented the culmination of years of smaller steps between the two organizations—the latest episode in a long-running relationship between GE and KTZ that dates back to the mid-1990s. The relationship accelerated in 2003 when GE won the first of several contracts for modernization kits that updated older KTZ locomotives. "I am proud that KTZ and GE are extending our relationship," said the CEO of GE-Transportation, "one that has proven to be very beneficial to both organizations over several years."

GE locomotives might not seem glamorous to you, but they are beautiful brutes to those who buy and use them. In this market, GE's real challenge is to win buyers' business by building day-in, day-out, year-in, year-out partnerships with them.

Thanks to stories like this one, GE-Transportation dominates the worldwide rail locomotive industry, now capturing a phenomenal 80-percent market share. More broadly, people throughout the entire GE organization know that success in business-to-business markets involves more than just developing and selling superior products and technologies. Business customer buying decisions are made within the framework of a strategic, problem-solving partnership. "We love the challenge of a customer's problem," says the company on its GE-Transportation Web site. "Why? It's an opportunity for a true collaborative partnership. We enjoy the exchange of ideas, whether we're developing a brand new technology or applying existing technologies in innovative new ways. [We] go to great lengths to help our customers succeed."

"Customer partnerships are at the center of GE and Ecomagination," confirms GE chairman and CEO Jeffrey Immelt in a recent letter to shareholders. "We are viewed as a technical partner by customers around the world."[1]

> To succeed in its business-to-business markets, GE must do more than just design good products and make them available to customers. It must work closely and deeply with its business customers to become a strategic, problem-solving partner.

Objective Outline

Like GE, in one way or another, most large companies sell to other organizations. Companies such as DuPont, Boeing, IBM, Caterpillar, and countless other firms sell *most* of their products to other businesses. Even large consumer-products companies, which make products used by final consumers, must first sell their products to other businesses. For example, General Mills makes many familiar consumer brands—Big G cereals (Cheerios, Wheaties, Trix, Chex), baking products (Pillsbury, Betty Crocker, Gold Medal flour), snacks (Nature Valley, Pop Secret, Chex Mix), Yoplait yogurt, Häagen-Dazs ice cream, and others. But to sell these products to consumers, General Mills must first sell them to its wholesaler and retailer customers, who in turn serve the consumer market.

Business buyer behavior refers to the buying behavior of the organizations that buy goods and services for use in the production of other products and services that are sold, rented, or supplied to others. It also includes the behavior of retailing and wholesaling firms that acquire goods to resell or rent them to others at a profit. In the **business buying process**, business buyers determine which products and services their organizations need to purchase and then find, evaluate, and choose among alternative suppliers and brands. *Business-to-business (B-to-B) marketers* must do their best to understand business markets and business buyer behavior. Then, like businesses that sell to final buyers, they must build profitable relationships with business customers by creating superior customer value.

Business buyer behavior
The buying behavior of the organizations that buy goods and services for use in the production of other products and services or to resell or rent them to others at a profit.

Business buying process
The decision process by which business buyers determine which products and services their organizations need to purchase, and then find, evaluate, and choose among alternative suppliers and brands.

Author Comment | Business markets operate "behind-the-scenes" to most consumers. Most of the things you buy involve many sets of business purchases before you ever see them.

Business Markets (pp 168–172)

The business market is *huge*. In fact, business markets involve far more dollars and items than do consumer markets. For example, think about the large number of business transactions involved in the production and sale of a single set of Goodyear tires. Various suppliers sell Goodyear the rubber, steel, equipment, and other goods that it needs to produce tires. Goodyear then sells the finished tires to retailers, who in turn sell them to consumers. Thus, many sets of *business* purchases were made for only one set of *consumer* purchases. In addition, Goodyear sells tires as original equipment to manufacturers who install them on new vehicles, and as replacement tires to companies that maintain their own fleets of company cars, trucks, buses, or other vehicles.

In some ways, business markets are similar to consumer markets. Both involve people who assume buying roles and make purchase decisions to satisfy needs. However,

● TABLE | 6.1   Characteristics of Business Markets

Market Structure and Demand

Business markets contain *fewer but larger buyers*.

Business buyer demand is *derived* from final consumer demand.

Demand in many business markets is *more inelastic*—not affected as much in the short run by price changes.

Demand in business markets *fluctuates more*, and more quickly.

Nature of the Buying Unit

Business purchases involve *more buyers*.

Business buying involves a *more professional purchasing effort*.

Types of Decisions and the Decision Process

Business buyers usually face *more complex buying decisions*.

The business buying process is *more formalized*.

In business buying, buyers and sellers work more closely together and build close long-term *relationships*.

business markets differ in many ways from consumer markets. The main differences, shown in ● **Table 6.1**, are in *market structure and demand*, the *nature of the buying unit*, and the *types of decisions and the decision process* involved.

Market Structure and Demand

Derived demand
Business demand that ultimately comes from (derives from) the demand for consumer goods.

The business marketer normally deals with *far fewer but far larger buyers* than the consumer marketer does. Even in large business markets, a few buyers often account for most of the purchasing. For example, when Goodyear sells replacement tires to final consumers, its potential market includes the owners of the millions of cars currently in use in the United States and around the world. But Goodyear's fate in the business market depends on getting orders from one of only a handful of large automakers. Similarly, Black & Decker sells its power tools and outdoor equipment to tens of millions of consumers worldwide. However, it must sell these products through three huge retail customers—Home Depot, Lowe's, and Wal-Mart—which combined account for more than half its sales.

Further, business demand is **derived demand**—it ultimately derives from the demand for consumer goods. Hewlett-Packard and Dell buy Intel microprocessor chips because consumers buy personal computers. If consumer demand for diamond jewelry drops, so will the demand for diamonds. Therefore, B-to-B marketers sometimes promote their products directly to final consumers to increase business demand. ▲ For example, Intel advertises heavily to personal computer buyers, selling them on the virtues of Intel microprocessors. "Multiply your mobility," it tells consumers—"great computing starts with Intel inside." The increased demand for Intel chips boosts demand for the PCs containing them, and both Intel and its business partners win.

Many business markets have *inelastic demand*; that is, total demand for many business products is not affected much by price changes, especially in the short run. A drop in the price of leather will not cause shoe manufacturers to buy much more leather unless it results in lower shoe prices that, in turn, will increase consumer demand for shoes.

Finally, business markets have more *fluctuating demand*. The demand for many business goods and services tends to change more—and more quickly—than the demand for consumer goods and services does. A small percentage increase in consumer demand can cause large increases in business

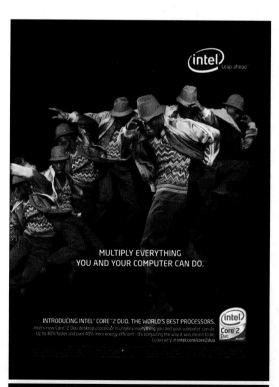

▲ Derived demand: Intel advertises heavily to personal computer buyers, selling them on the virtues of Intel microprocessors—both Intel and its business partners benefit.

demand. Sometimes a rise of only 10 percent in consumer demand can cause as much as a 200 percent rise in business demand during the next period.

Nature of the Buying Unit

Compared with consumer purchases, a business purchase usually involves *more decision participants* and a *more professional purchasing effort*. Often, business buying is done by trained purchasing agents who spend their working lives learning how to buy better. The more complex the purchase, the more likely it is that several people will participate in the decision-making process. Buying committees made up of technical experts and top management are common in the buying of major goods. Beyond this, B-to-B marketers now face a new breed of higher-level, better-trained supply managers. Therefore, companies must have well-trained marketers and salespeople to deal with these well-trained buyers.

Types of Decisions and the Decision Process

Business buyers usually face *more complex* buying decisions than do consumer buyers. Business purchases often involve large sums of money, complex technical and economic considerations, and interactions among many people at many levels of the buyer's organization. Because the purchases are more complex, business buyers may take longer to make their decisions. The business buying process also tends to be *more formalized* than the consumer buying process. Large business purchases usually call for detailed product specifications, written purchase orders, careful supplier searches, and formal approval.

Finally, in the business buying process, the buyer and seller are often much *more dependent* on each other. B-to-B marketers may roll up their sleeves and work closely with their customers during all stages of the buying process—from helping customers define problems, to finding solutions, to supporting after-sale operation. They often customize their offerings to individual customer needs. In the short run, sales go to suppliers who meet buyers' immediate product and service needs. In the long run, however, business-to-business marketers keep a customer's sales and create customer value by meeting current needs *and* by partnering with customers to help them solve their problems. For example, when UPS supplies a broad range of logistics services and resources to its business customers, it asks them "What can Brown do for you?" (See **Real Marketing 6.1**.)

In recent years, relationships between customers and suppliers have been changing from downright adversarial to close and chummy. In fact, many customer companies are now practicing **supplier development**, systematically developing networks of supplier-partners to ensure an appropriate and dependable supply of products and materials that they will use in making their own products or resell to others. For example, Caterpillar no longer calls its buyers "purchasing agents"—they are managers of "purchasing and supplier development." Wal-Mart doesn't have a "Purchasing Department," it has a "Supplier Development Department." ▲ And giant Swedish furniture retailer IKEA doesn't just buy from its suppliers, it involves them deeply in the process of delivering a stylish and affordable lifestyle to IKEA's customers.

Supplier development
Systematic development of networks of supplier-partners to ensure an appropriate and dependable supply of products and materials for use in making products or reselling them to others.

▲ Giant Scandinavian furniture retailer IKEA doesn't just buy from its suppliers. It involves them deeply in the process of designing and making stylish but affordable furniture that keeps customers coming back.

IKEA, the world's largest furniture retailer, is the quintessential global cult brand. Customers from Beijing to Moscow to Middletown, Ohio, flock to the $27 billion Scandinavian retailer's more than 276 huge stores in 36 countries, drawn by IKEA's trendy but simple and practical furniture at affordable prices. But IKEA's biggest obstacle to growth isn't opening new stores and attracting customers. Rather, it's finding enough of the right kinds of *suppliers* to help design and produce the billions of dollars of affordable goods that those customers will carry out of its stores. IKEA currently

Real Marketing 6.1

UPS Partners with Business Customers:
What Can Brown Do for You?

Mention UPS, and most people envision one of those familiar brown trucks with a friendly driver, rumbling around their neighborhood dropping off packages. That makes sense. The company's brown-clad drivers deliver more than 4 billion packages annually, an average of 15.8 million each day. For most of us, seeing a brown UPS truck evokes fond memories of past package deliveries. If you close your eyes and listen, you can probably imagine the sound of the UPS truck pulling up in front of your home.

Even the company's brown color has come to mean something special to customers. UPS has been referred to for years as "Big Brown." "People love our drivers, they love our brown trucks, they love everything we do," says one UPS executive. Thus was born UPS's current "What Can Brown Do for You?" advertising theme.

For most residential customers, the answer to the question "What can Brown do for you?" is pretty simple: "Deliver my package as quickly as possible." But most of UPS's revenues come not from the residential customers who receive the packages, but from the *business* customers who send them. And for these business customers, UPS does more than just get Grandma's holiday package there on time. Whereas residential consumers might look to "Brown" simply for fast, friendly, low-cost package delivery, business customers usually have much more complex needs. For these customers, UPS becomes an ally in finding solutions for a broad range of logistics issues.

For businesses, package delivery is just part of a much more complex logistics process that involves purchase orders, inventory, order status checks, invoices, payments, returned merchandise, and fleets of delivery vehicles. Beyond the physical package flow, companies must also handle the accompanying information and money flows. They need timely information about packages—what's in them, where they're currently located, to whom they are going, when they will get there, how much has been paid, and how much is owed. UPS knows that for many companies, all these work-a-day logistical concerns can be a

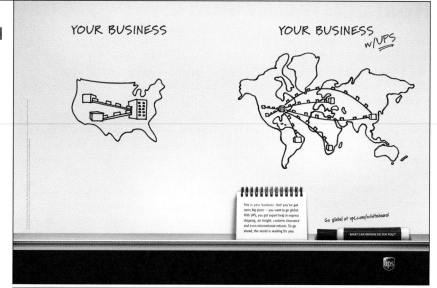

For its business customers, UPS does more than just deliver packages from point A to point B. It becomes a strategic logistics partner, helping customers to solve their complex distribution problems. "What Can Brown Do for You?"

nightmare. Moreover, most companies don't see these activities as strategic competencies that provide competitive advantage.

That's where Big Brown comes in. These are exactly the things that UPS does best. Over the years, UPS has grown to become much more than a small neighborhood package delivery service. It is now a $50 billion corporate giant providing a broad range of logistics solutions. UPS handles the logistics, allowing customers to focus on what they do best. It offers everything from ground and air package distribution, freight delivery (air, ocean, rail, and road), and mail services to inventory management, third-party logistics, international trade management, logistics management software and e-commerce solutions, and even financing. If it has to do with logistics, at home or abroad, UPS can probably do it better than anyone can.

UPS has the resources to handle the logistics needs of just about any size business. It employs 425,300 people, some 93,600 vehicles (package cars, vans, tractors, and motorcycles), 600 owned and chartered aircraft, and more than 1,000 warehouse facilities in 200 countries. UPS now moves an astounding 6 percent of the gross domestic product in the United States, links 1.8 million sellers with 6.1 million buyers every day, and processes more than 460 million electronic transactions every week. It serves 90 percent of the world population and 99 percent of businesses in the Fortune 1000. UPS invests $1 billion a year in information technology to support its highly synchronized,

by-the-clock logistics services and to provide customers with information at every point in the process.

Beyond moving their packages around the United States, UPS can also help business customers to navigate the complexities of international shipping, with some 700 international flights per day to or from 377 international destinations. For example, although most residential customers don't need next-day air service to or from China, many businesses do seek help shipping to and from the burgeoning Asian manufacturing zones. UPS helps ensure the timely flow of crucial business documents, prototypes, high-value goods (such as semiconductors), and emergency repair parts that wing their way across the Pacific every day.

UPS even offers expedited U.S. Customs services, with fast inspection and clearance processes that help get goods into the country quickly. "When you're trading internationally, your entire investment could be hanging on a single clause," says one UPS ad. "We don't get you over oceans, mountains, and deserts only to be delayed by Chapter 3, Part 319, Regulation 40-2 of CFR Title 7. . . . Leave the burden of global compliance to UPS."

In addition to shipping and receiving packages, UPS provides a wide range of financial services for its business customers. For example, its UPS Capital division will handle clients' accounts receivable—UPS shippers can choose to be reimbursed immediately and have UPS collect payment from the recipient.

Continued on next page ▼

Real Marketing 6.1 Continued ▼

Other financial services include credit cards for small businesses and programs to fund inventory, equipment leasing, and asset financing. UPS even bought a bank to underpin UPS Capital's operations.

At a deeper level, UPS can provide the advice and technical resources needed to help business customers large and small improve their own logistics operations. UPS advises companies on redesigning logistics systems to align them better with business strategies. It helps customers to synchronize the flow of goods, funds, and information up and down their supply chains. UPS Logistics Technologies supplies software that improves

customers' distribution efficiency, including street-level route optimization, territory planning, mobile delivery execution, real-time wireless dispatch, and GPS tracking.

So, what can Brown do for you? As it turns out, the answer depends on who you are. For its residential consumers, UPS uses those familiar chugging brown trucks to provide simple and efficient package pickup and delivery services. But in its business-to-business

markets, it develops deeper and more involved customer relationships. For their business customers, UPS employees around the world must do more than just deliver packages from point A to point B. They must roll up their sleeves and work hand in hand with customers to help solve their complex logistics problems. More than just providing shipping services, they must become strategic logistics allies.

Sources: Facts and information from various UPS Web sites, including www.ups-scs.com; www.ups.com/content/us/en/about/facts/worldwide.html; www.upslogisticstech.com; and http://capital.ups.com/contact/; accessed September 2008. UPS®, What Can Brown Do for You®, and UPS Capital® are registered trademarks of United Parcel Service of America, Inc. Big Brown™ is a trademark of United Parcel Service of America, Inc.

relies on about 1,800 suppliers in more than 50 countries to stock its shelves. If the giant retailer continues at its current growth rate, it will need to double its supply network by 2010. IKEA doesn't just rely on spot suppliers who might be available when needed. Instead, it has systematically developed a robust network of supplier-partners that reliably provide the more than 10,000 items it stocks. IKEA's designers start with a basic customer value proposition. Then, they find and work closely with key suppliers to bring that proposition to market. And IKEA does more than just buy from suppliers; it also involves them deeply in the process of designing and making stylish but affordable products to keep IKEA's customers coming back.[2]

> **Author Comment** | Business buying decisions can range from routine to incredibly complex, involving only a few or very many decision makers and buying influences.

Business Buyer Behavior (pp 172–181)

At the most basic level, marketers want to know how business buyers will respond to various marketing stimuli. ◆Figure 6.1 shows a model of business buyer behavior. In this model, marketing and other stimuli affect the buying organization and produce certain buyer responses. These stimuli enter the organization and are turned into buyer responses. In order to design good marketing strategies, the marketer must understand what happens within the organization to turn stimuli into purchase responses.

Within the organization, buying activity consists of two major parts: the buying center, made up of all the people involved in the buying decision, and the buying decision process. The model shows that the buying center and the buying decision process are influenced by internal organizational, interpersonal, and individual factors as well as by external environmental factors.

◆FIGURE | 6.1

The Model of Business Buyer Behavior

In some ways, business markets are similar to consumer markets—this model looks a lot like the model of consumer buyer behavior presented in Figure 5.1. But there are some major differences, especially in the nature of the buying unit, the types of decisions made, and the decision process.

The environment		The buying organization	Buyer responses
Marketing stimuli	**Other stimuli**	**The buying center**	Product or service choice
Product	Economic	**Buying decision process**	Supplier choice
Price	Technological		Order quantities
Place	Political		Delivery terms and times
Promotion	Cultural	(Interpersonal and individual influences)	Service terms
	Competitive	(Organizational influences)	Payment

The model in Figure 6.1 suggests four questions about business buyer behavior: What buying decisions do business buyers make? Who participates in the buying process? What are the major influences on buyers? How do business buyers make their buying decisions?

Major Types of Buying Situations

There are three major types of buying situations.[3] At one extreme is the *straight rebuy*, which is a fairly routine decision. At the other extreme is the *new task*, which may call for thorough research. In the middle is the *modified rebuy*, which requires some research.

Straight rebuy

A business buying situation in which the buyer routinely reorders something without any modifications.

In a **straight rebuy**, the buyer reorders something without any modifications. It is usually handled on a routine basis by the purchasing department. Based on past buying satisfaction, the buyer simply chooses from the various suppliers on its list. "In" suppliers try to maintain product and service quality. They often propose automatic reordering systems so that the purchasing agent will save reordering time. "Out" suppliers try to find new ways to add value or exploit dissatisfaction so that the buyer will consider them.

Modified rebuy

A business buying situation in which the buyer wants to modify product specifications, prices, terms, or suppliers.

In a **modified rebuy**, the buyer wants to modify product specifications, prices, terms, or suppliers. The modified rebuy usually involves more decision participants than does the straight rebuy. The in suppliers may become nervous and feel pressured to put their best foot forward to protect an account. Out suppliers may see the modified rebuy situation as an opportunity to make a better offer and gain new business.

New task

A business buying situation in which the buyer purchases a product or service for the first time.

A company buying a product or service for the first time faces a **new-task** situation. In such cases, the greater the cost or risk, the larger the number of decision participants and the greater their efforts to collect information. The new-task situation is the marketer's greatest opportunity and challenge. The marketer not only tries to reach as many key buying influences as possible but also provides help and information.

The buyer makes the fewest decisions in the straight rebuy and the most in the new-task decision. In the new-task situation, the buyer must decide on product specifications, suppliers, price limits, payment terms, order quantities, delivery times, and service terms. The order of these decisions varies with each situation, and different decision participants influence each choice.

Many business buyers prefer to buy a complete solution to a problem from a single seller instead of buying separate products and services from several suppliers and putting them together. The sale often goes to the firm that provides the most complete *system* for meeting the customer's needs and solving its problems. Such **systems selling** (or **solutions selling**) is often a key business marketing strategy for winning and holding accounts.

Systems selling (or solutions selling)

Buying a packaged solution to a problem from a single seller, thus avoiding all the separate decisions involved in a complex buying situation.

Thus, as we discovered in Real Marketing 6.1, transportation and logistics giant UPS does more than just ship packages for its business customers. It develops entire solutions to customers' transportation and logistics problems. For example, UPS bundles a complete system of services that support Nikon's consumer products supply chain—including logistics, transportation, freight, and customs brokerage services—into one smooth-running system.[4]

When Nikon entered the digital camera market, it decided that it needed an entirely new distribution strategy as well. So it asked transportation and logistics giant UPS to design a complete system for moving its entire electronics product line from its Asian factories to retail stores throughout the United States, Latin America, and the Caribbean. Now, products leave Nikon's Asian manufacturing centers and arrive on American retailers' shelves in as few as two days, with UPS handling everything in between. UPS first manages air and ocean freight and related customs brokerage to bring Nikon products from Korea, Japan, and Indonesia to its Louisville, Kentucky, operations center. There, UPS can either "kit" the Nikon merchandise with accessories such as batteries and chargers or repackage it for in-store display. Finally, UPS distributes the products to thousands of retailers across the United States or exports them to Latin American or Caribbean retail outlets and distributors. Along the way, UPS tracks the goods and provides Nikon with a "snapshot" of the entire supply chain, letting Nikon keep retailers informed of delivery times and adjust them as needed.

Participants in the Business Buying Process

Buying center

All the individuals and units that play a role in the purchase decision-making process.

Who does the buying of the trillions of dollars' worth of goods and services needed by business organizations? The decision-making unit of a buying organization is called its **buying center**—all the individuals and units that play a role in the business purchase decision-making process. This group includes the actual users of the product or service, those who make the buying decision, those who influence the buying decision, those who do the actual buying, and those who control buying information.

The buying center includes all members of the organization who play any of five roles in the purchase decision process.[5]

Users

Members of the buying organization who will actually use the purchased product or service.

Influencers

People in an organization's buying center who affect the buying decision; they often help define specifications and also provide information for evaluating alternatives.

Buyers

The people in the organization's buying center who make an actual purchase.

Deciders

People in the organization's buying center who have formal or informal power to select or approve the final suppliers.

Gatekeepers

People in the organization's buying center who control the flow of information to others.

- **Users** are members of the organization who will use the product or service. In many cases, users initiate the buying proposal and help define product specifications.

- **Influencers** often help define specifications and also provide information for evaluating alternatives. Technical personnel are particularly important influencers.

- **Buyers** have formal authority to select the supplier and arrange terms of purchase. Buyers may help shape product specifications, but their major role is in selecting vendors and negotiating. In more complex purchases, buyers might include high-level officers participating in the negotiations.

- **Deciders** have formal or informal power to select or approve the final suppliers. In routine buying, the buyers are often the deciders, or at least the approvers.

- **Gatekeepers** control the flow of information to others. For example, purchasing agents often have authority to prevent salespersons from seeing users or deciders. Other gatekeepers include technical personnel and even personal secretaries.

The buying center is not a fixed and formally identified unit within the buying organization. It is a set of buying roles assumed by different people for different purchases. Within the organization, the size and makeup of the buying center will vary for different products and for different buying situations. For some routine purchases, one person—say, a purchasing agent—may assume all the buying center roles and serve as the only person involved in the buying decision. For more complex purchases, the buying center may include 20 or 30 people from different levels and departments in the organization.

The buying center concept presents a major marketing challenge. The business marketer must learn who participates in the decision, each participant's relative influence, and what evaluation criteria each decision participant uses. This can be difficult. Says one supplier of healthcare information technology solutions to large hospitals:

▲ Buying center: Cardinal Health deals with a wide range of buying influences, from purchasing executives and hospital administrators to the surgeons who actually use its products.

You have to understand what [doors] to knock on. A lot of salespeople give up on working with hospitals because they don't understand how big the business is, and you have a lot of people you have to deal with. You also have to understand that you're selling to committees, which means 10 or 20 people have to make a decision. For them to make a decision they have to have lots of meetings, and sales can [take] anywhere from six months to two years."[6]

For instance, ▲the medical products and services group of Cardinal Health sells disposable surgical gowns to hospitals. It identifies the hospital personnel involved in this buying decision as the vice president of purchasing, the operating room administrator, and the surgeons. Each participant plays a different role. The vice president of purchasing analyzes whether the hospital should buy disposable gowns or reusable gowns. If analysis favors disposable gowns, then the operating room administrator compares competing products and prices and makes a choice. This administrator considers the gowns' absorbency, antiseptic quality, design, and cost, and normally buys the brand that meets requirements at the lowest cost. Finally, surgeons affect the decision later by reporting their satisfaction or dissatisfaction with the brand.

The buying center usually includes some obvious participants who are involved formally in the buying decision. For example, the decision to buy a corporate jet will probably involve the company's CEO, chief pilot, a purchasing agent, some legal staff, a member of top management, and others formally charged with the buying decision. It may also involve less obvious, informal participants, some of whom may actually make or strongly affect the buying decision. Sometimes, even the people in the buying center are not aware of all the buying participants. For example, the decision about which corporate jet to buy may actually be made by a corporate board member who has an interest in flying and who knows a lot about airplanes. This board member may work behind the scenes to sway the decision. Many business buying decisions result from the complex interactions of ever-changing buying center participants.

Major Influences on Business Buyers

Business buyers are subject to many influences when they make their buying decisions. Some marketers assume that the major influences are economic. They think buyers will favor the supplier who offers the lowest price or the best product or the most service. They concentrate on offering strong economic benefits to buyers. However, business buyers actually respond to both economic and personal factors. Far from being cold, calculating, and impersonal, business buyers are human and social as well. They react to both reason and emotion.

TWO POWERFUL EXPRESSIONS
OF FUEL EFFICIENCY.

Peterbilt

PETERBILT MODELS 386 AND 387
FROM THE INNOVATIVE VERSATILITY OF THE MODEL 386
TO THE SPACIOUS AND ERGONOMIC MODEL 387.
TWO CHOICES OF PREMIUM FUEL EFFICIENCY.

PACCAR FINANCIAL   PACLEASE AND PACCAR FINANCIAL PLANS TAILORED TO YOUR NEEDS.

FOR MORE INFORMATION, CALL 1-800-552-0024. PETERBILT MOTORS COMPANY, A DIVISION OF PACCAR. BUCKLE-UP FOR SAFETY.

Peterbilt
CLASS PAYS
WWW.PETERBILT.COM

▲ Emotions play an important role in business buying. This Peterbilt ad stresses performance factors, such as fuel efficiency. But it also stresses more emotional factors, such as the raw beauty of Peterbilt trucks and the pride of owning and driving one. "Class Pays."

Today, most B-to-B marketers recognize that emotion plays an important role in business buying decisions. For example, you might expect that an advertisement promoting large trucks to corporate fleet buyers or independent owner-operators would stress objective technical, performance, and economic factors. ▲For instance, premium heavy-duty truck maker Peterbilt does stress performance—its dealers and Web site provide plenty of information about factors such as maneuverability, productivity, reliability, comfort, and fuel efficiency. But Peterbilt ads appeal to buyers' emotions as well. They show the raw beauty of the trucks, and the Peterbilt slogan—"Class Pays"—suggests that owning a Peterbilt truck is a matter of pride as well as superior performance. Says the company, "On highways, construction sites, city streets, logging roads—everywhere customers earn their living—Peterbilt's red oval is a familiar symbol of performance, reliability, and pride."

When suppliers' offers are very similar, business buyers have little basis for strictly rational choice. Because they can meet organizational goals with any supplier, buyers can allow personal factors to play a larger role in their decisions. However, when competing products differ greatly, business buyers are more accountable for their choices and tend to pay more attention to economic factors. ▼**Figure 6.2** lists various groups of influences on business buyers—environmental, organizational, interpersonal, and individual.[7]

Environmental Factors

Business buyers are heavily influenced by factors in the current and expected *economic environment*, such as the level of primary demand, the economic outlook, and the cost of money. Another environmental factor is *shortages* in key materials. Many companies now are more willing to buy and hold larger inventories of scarce materials to ensure adequate supply. Business buyers also are affected by technological, political, and competitive developments

FIGURE | 6.2
Major Influences on
Business Buyer Behavior

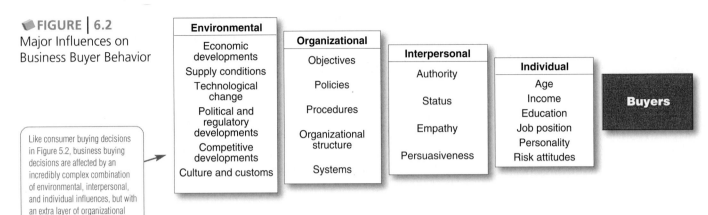

FIGURE | 6.2
Major Influences on
Business Buyer Behavior

Like consumer buying decisions in Figure 5.2, business buying decisions are affected by an incredibly complex combination of environmental, interpersonal, and individual influences, but with an extra layer of organizational factors thrown into the mix.

in the environment. Finally, *culture and customs* can strongly influence business buyer reactions to the marketer's behavior and strategies, especially in the international marketing environment (see **Real Marketing 6.2**). The business buyer must watch these factors, determine how they will affect the buyer, and try to turn these challenges into opportunities.

Organizational Factors

Each buying organization has its own objectives, policies, procedures, structure, and systems, and the business marketer must understand these factors well. Questions such as these arise: How many people are involved in the buying decision? Who are they? What are their evaluative criteria? What are the company's policies and limits on its buyers?

Interpersonal Factors

The buying center usually includes many participants who influence each other, so *interpersonal factors* also influence the business buying process. However, it is often difficult to assess such interpersonal factors and group dynamics. Buying center participants do not wear tags that label them as "key decision maker" or "not influential." Nor do buying center participants with the highest rank always have the most influence. Participants may influence the buying decision because they control rewards and punishments, are well liked, have special expertise, or have a special relationship with other important participants. Interpersonal factors are often very subtle. Whenever possible, business marketers must try to understand these factors and design strategies that take them into account.

Individual Factors

Each participant in the business buying decision process brings in personal motives, perceptions, and preferences. These individual factors are affected by personal characteristics such as age, income, education, professional identification, personality, and attitudes toward risk. Also, buyers have different buying styles. Some may be technical types who make in-depth analyses of competitive proposals before choosing a supplier. Other buyers may be intuitive negotiators who are adept at pitting the sellers against one another for the best deal.

The Business Buying Process

Figure 6.3 lists the eight stages of the business buying process.[8] Buyers who face a new-task buying situation usually go through all stages of the buying process. Buyers making modified or straight rebuys may skip some of the stages. We will examine these steps for the typical new-task buying situation.

Problem Recognition

Problem recognition
The first stage of the business buying process in which someone in the company recognizes a problem or need that can be met by acquiring a good or a service.

The buying process begins when someone in the company recognizes a problem or need that can be met by acquiring a specific product or service. **Problem recognition** can result from internal or external stimuli. Internally, the company may decide to launch a new product that requires new production equipment and materials. Or a machine may break down and need

Problem recognition: Sharp uses ads like this one to alert customers to potential problems and then provide solutions.

new parts. Perhaps a purchasing manager is unhappy with a current supplier's product quality, service, or prices. ▲Externally, the buyer may get some new ideas at a trade show, see an ad, or receive a call from a salesperson who offers a better product or a lower price.

In fact, in their advertising, business marketers often alert customers to potential problems and then show how their products provide solutions. For example, a Sharp ad notes that a multifunction printer can present data security problems and asks "Is your MFP a portal for identity theft?" The solution? Sharp's data security kits "help prevent sensitive information from falling into the wrong hands."

General Need Description

Having recognized a need, the buyer next prepares a **general need description** that describes the characteristics and quantity of the needed item. For standard items, this process presents few problems. For complex items, however, the buyer may need to work with others—engineers, users, consultants—to define the item. The team may want to rank the importance of reliability, durability, price, and other attributes desired in the item. In this phase, the alert business marketer can help the buyers define their needs and provide information about the value of different product characteristics.

Product Specification

The buying organization next develops the item's technical **product specifications**, often with the help of a value analysis engineering team. *Product value analysis* is an approach to cost reduction in which components are studied carefully to determine if they can be redesigned, standardized, or made by less costly methods of production. The team decides on the best product characteristics and specifies them accordingly. Sellers, too, can use value analysis as a tool to help secure a new account. By showing buyers a better way to make an object, outside sellers can turn straight rebuy situations into new-task situations that give them a chance to obtain new business.

Supplier Search

The buyer now conducts a **supplier search** to find the best vendors. The buyer can compile a small list of qualified suppliers by reviewing trade directories, doing computer searches, or phoning other companies for recommendations. Today, more and more companies are turning to the Internet to find suppliers. For marketers, this has leveled the playing field—the Internet gives smaller suppliers many of the same advantages as larger competitors.

The newer the buying task, and the more complex and costly the item, the greater the amount of time the buyer will spend searching for suppliers. The supplier's task is to get listed in major directories and build a good reputation in the marketplace. Salespeople should watch for companies in the process of searching for suppliers and make certain that their firm is considered.

General need description
The stage in the business buying process in which the company describes the general characteristics and quantity of a needed item.

Product specification
The stage of the business buying process in which the buying organization decides on and specifies the best technical product characteristics for a needed item.

Supplier search
The stage of the business buying process in which the buyer tries to find the best vendors.

Buyers facing new, complex buying decisions usually go through all of these stages. Those making rebuys often skip some of the stages. Either way, the business buying process is usually much more complicated than this simple flow diagram suggests.

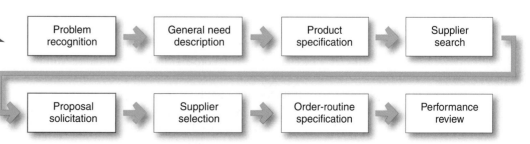

FIGURE | 6.3 Stages of the Business Buying Process

Real Marketing 6.2

International Marketing Manners:
When in Rome, Do as the Romans Do

Picture this: Consolidated Amalgamation, Inc., thinks it's time that the rest of the world enjoyed the same fine products it has offered American consumers for two generations. It dispatches Vice President Harry E. Slicksmile to Europe, Africa, and Asia to explore the territory. Mr. Slicksmile stops first in London, where he makes short work of some bankers—he rings them up on the phone. He handles Parisians with similar ease: After securing a table at La Tour d'Argent, he greets his luncheon guest, the director of an industrial engineering firm, with the words, "Just call me Harry, Jacques."

In Germany, Mr. Slicksmile is a power-house. Whisking through a lavish, state-of-the-art multimedia marketing presentation on his Toshiba tablet laptop, he shows 'em that this Georgia boy *knows* how to make a buck. Heading on to Milan, Harry strikes up a conversation with the Japanese businessman sitting next to him on the plane. He flips his card onto the guy's tray and, when the two say good-bye, shakes hands warmly and clasps the

man's right arm. Later, for his appointment with the owner of an Italian packaging design firm, our hero wears his comfy corduroy sport coat, khaki pants, and Topsiders. Everybody knows Italians are zany and laid back.

Mr. Slicksmile next swings through Saudi Arabia, where he coolly presents a potential client with a multimillion-dollar proposal in a classy pigskin binder. At his next stop in Beijing, China, he talks business over lunch with a group of Chinese executives. After completing the meal, he drops his chopsticks into his bowl of rice and presents each guest with an elegant Tiffany clock as a reminder of his visit. Then, at his final junket in Phuket, Thailand, Mr. Slicksmile wastes no time diving into his business proposal before treating his Thai clients to a first-class lunch.

A great tour, sure to generate a pile of orders, right? Wrong. Six months later, Consolidated Amalgamation has nothing to show for the trip but a stack of bills. Abroad, they weren't wild about Harry.

American companies must help their managers understand international customers and customs. For example, Japanese people revere the business card as an extension of self—they do not hand it out to people, they present it.

This hypothetical case has been exaggerated for emphasis. Americans are seldom such dolts. But experts say success in international business has a lot to do with knowing the territory and its people. By learning English and

---

Proposal Solicitation

In the **proposal solicitation** stage of the business buying process, the buyer invites qualified suppliers to submit proposals. In response, some suppliers will send only a catalog or a salesperson. However, when the item is complex or expensive, the buyer will usually require detailed written proposals or formal presentations from each potential supplier.

Business marketers must be skilled in researching, writing, and presenting proposals in response to buyer proposal solicitations. Proposals should be marketing documents, not just technical documents. Presentations should inspire confidence and should make the marketer's company stand out from the competition.

Supplier Selection

The members of the buying center now review the proposals and select a supplier or suppliers. During **supplier selection**, the buying center often will draw up a list of the desired supplier attributes and their relative importance. Such attributes include product and service quality, reputation, on-time delivery, ethical corporate behavior, honest communication, and competitive prices. The members of the buying center will rate suppliers against these attributes and identify the best suppliers.

Buyers may attempt to negotiate with preferred suppliers for better prices and terms before making the final selections. In the end, they may select a single supplier or a few suppliers. Many buyers prefer multiple sources of supplies to avoid being totally dependent on one supplier and to allow comparisons of prices and performance of several suppliers over

extending themselves in other ways, the world's business leaders have met Americans more than halfway. In contrast, Americans too often do little except assume that others will march to their music. "We want things to be 'American' when we travel. Fast. Convenient. Easy. So we become 'ugly Americans' by demanding that others change," says one American world trade expert. "I think more business would be done if we tried harder."

Poor Harry tried, all right, but in all the wrong ways. The British do not, as a rule, make deals over the phone as much as Americans do. It's not so much a "cultural" difference as a difference in approach. A proper Frenchman neither likes instant familiarity—questions about family, church, or alma mater—nor refers to strangers by their first names. "That poor fellow, Jacques, probably wouldn't show anything, but he'd recoil. He'd *not* be pleased," explains an expert on French business practices. "It's considered poor taste," he continues. "Even after months of business dealings, I'd wait for him or her to make the invitation [to use first names]. . . . You are always right, in Europe, to say 'Mister.'"

Harry's flashy presentation would likely have been a flop with the Germans, who dislike overstatement and showiness. And when Harry grabbed his new Japanese acquaintance by the arm, the executive probably considered him disrespectful and presumptuous. Japan, like many Asian countries, is a "no-contact culture" in which even shaking hands is a strange

experience. Harry made matters worse by tossing his business card. Japanese people revere the business card as an extension of self and as an indicator of rank. They do not *hand* it to people, they *present* it—with both hands. In addition, the Japanese are sticklers about rank. Unlike Americans, they don't heap praise on subordinates in a room; they will praise only the highest-ranking official present.

Hapless Harry also goofed when he assumed that Italians are like Hollywood's stereotypes of them. The flair for design and style that has characterized Italian culture for centuries is embodied in the businesspeople of Milan and Rome. They dress beautifully and admire flair, but they blanch at garishness or impropriety in others' attire.

To the Saudi Arabians, the pigskin binder would have been considered vile. An American salesman who really did present such a binder was unceremoniously tossed out and his company was blacklisted from working with Saudi businesses. In China, Harry's casually dropping his chopsticks could have been misinterpreted as an act of

aggression. Stabbing chopsticks into a bowl of rice and leaving them signifies death to the Chinese. The clocks Harry offered as gifts might have confirmed such dark intentions. To "give a clock" in Chinese sounds the same as "seeing someone off to his end." Finally, not surprisingly, Harry flunked his Phuket junket—in Thailand, it's off limits to speak about business matters until after the meal is served and eaten.

Thus, to compete successfully in global markets, or even to deal effectively with international firms in their home markets, companies must help their managers to understand the needs, customs, and cultures of international business buyers. "When doing business in a foreign country and a foreign culture—particularly a non-Western culture—assume nothing," advises an international business specialist. "Take nothing for granted. Turn every stone. Ask every question. Dig into every detail. Because cultures really are different, and those differences can have a major impact." So the old advice is still good advice: When in Rome, do as the Romans do.

Sources: Portions adapted from Susan Harte, "When in Rome, You Should Learn to Do What the Romans Do," *Atlanta Journal-Constitution*, January 22, 1990, pp. D1, D6. Additional information and examples from James K. Sebenius, "The Hidden Challenge of Cross-Border Negotiatons," *Harvard Business Review*, March 2002, pp. 76–85; Gary Stroller, "Doing Business Abroad? Simple Faux Pas Can Sink You," *USA Today*, August 24, 2007, p. 1B; and Janette S. Martin and Lillian H. Chaney, *Global Business Etiquette: A Guide to International Communication and Customs* (Westport, CT: Greenwood Press, 2008); and information accessed at www.executiveplanet.com, December 2008.

time. Today's supplier development managers want to develop a full network of supplier-partners that can help the company bring more value to its customers.

Order-Routine Specification

Order-routine specification
The stage of the business buying process in which the buyer writes the final order with the chosen supplier(s), listing the technical specifications, quantity needed, expected time of delivery, return policies, and warranties.

The buyer now prepares an **order-routine specification**. It includes the final order with the chosen supplier or suppliers and lists items such as technical specifications, quantity needed, expected time of delivery, return policies, and warranties. In the case of maintenance, repair, and operating items, buyers may use blanket contracts rather than periodic purchase orders. A blanket contract creates a long-term relationship in which the supplier promises to resupply the buyer as needed at agreed prices for a set time period.

Many large buyers now practice *vendor-managed inventory*, in which they turn over ordering and inventory responsibilities to their suppliers. Under such systems, buyers share sales and inventory information directly with key suppliers. The suppliers then monitor inventories and replenish stock automatically as needed. For example, most major suppliers to large retailers such as Wal-Mart, Target, Home Depot, and Lowe's assume vendor-managed inventory responsibilities.

Performance Review

Performance review
The stage of the business buying process in which the buyer assesses the performance of the supplier and decides to continue, modify, or drop the arrangement.

In this stage, the buyer reviews supplier performance. The buyer may contact users and ask them to rate their satisfaction. The **performance review** may lead the buyer to continue, modify, or drop the arrangement. The seller's job is to monitor the same factors used by the buyer to make sure that the seller is giving the expected satisfaction.

The eight-stage buying-process model provides a simple view of the business buying as it might occur in a new-task buying situation. The actual process is usually much more complex. In the modified rebuy or straight rebuy situation, some of these stages would be compressed or bypassed. Each organization buys in its own way, and each buying situation has unique requirements.

Different buying center participants may be involved at different stages of the process. Although certain buying-process steps usually do occur, buyers do not always follow them in the same order, and they may add other steps. Often, buyers will repeat certain stages of the process. Finally, a customer relationship might involve many different types of purchases ongoing at a given time, all in different stages of the buying process. The seller must manage the total customer relationship, not just individual purchases.

E-Procurement: Buying on the Internet

E-procurement

Purchasing through electronic connections between buyers and sellers—usually online.

Advances in information technology have changed the face of the B-to-B marketing process. Electronic purchasing, often called **e-procurement**, has grown rapidly in recent years. Virtually unknown less than a decade ago, online purchasing is standard procedure for most companies today. E-procurement gives buyers access to new suppliers, lowers purchasing costs, and hastens order processing and delivery. In turn, business marketers can connect with customers online to share marketing information, sell products and services, provide customer support services, and maintain ongoing customer relationships.

Companies can do e-procurement in any of several ways. They can conduct *reverse auctions*, in which they put their purchasing requests online and invite suppliers to bid for the business. Or they can engage in online *trading exchanges*, through which companies work collectively to facilitate the trading process. For example, Exostar is an online trading exchange that connects buyers and sellers in the aerospace and defense industry. Its goal is to improve trading efficiency and reduce costs among industry trading partners. Initially a collaboration between five leading aerospace and defense companies—Boeing, Lockheed Martin, Raytheon, BAE Systems, and Rolls-Royce—Exostar has now connected more than 300 procurement systems and 40,000 trading partners in 20 countries around the world.

Companies also can conduct e-procurement by setting up their own *company buying sites*. For example, General Electric operates a company trading site on which it posts its buying needs and invites bids, negotiates terms, and places orders. Or companies can create *extranet links* with key suppliers. For instance, they can create direct procurement accounts with suppliers such as Dell or Office Depot, through which company buyers can purchase equipment, materials, and supplies directly.

B-to-B marketers can help customers who wish to purchase online by creating well-designed, easy-to-use Web sites. ▲ For example, *BtoB* magazine rated the site of Sun Microsystems—a market leader in network computing hardware, software, and services—as one of its "10 great B-to-B Web sites":[9]

A few years ago, Sun Microsystems completely redesigned its Web site. It was most interested in finding a better way to present deep information on its thousands of complex server, storage, and software products and services while also giving the site a more humanistic view. Sun came up with a tab-driven menu design that puts an enormous amount of information within only a few clicks of customers' computers. Action-oriented menu labels—such as Evaluate, Get, Use, and Maintain—leave nothing to the imagination and make navigation a snap. Beyond product pictures and specifications, the site

▲ Online buying: This Sun Microsystems site helps customers who want to purchase online by providing deep information on its thousands of complex products and services. Users who still need help can take advantage of the site's interactive features to request an immediate phone call, an e-mail, or a live online chat with a Sun representative.

provides video walk-throughs of products, along with "success stories" of how other customers have benefited from doing business with Sun.

Customers can even create personalized MySun portals. "We provide you with a customized experience," says Sun's VP-Sun Web Experience. "Maybe you've downloaded software. Based on that download, you'll see a filtered blog, training classes that are available, and a link to unreleased code you can try out. It's integrated support tailored to the type of Sun products you use." Users who still need help can take advantage of the site's interactive features to request an immediate phone call, an e-mail, or a live online chat in English, French, German, or Spanish with a Sun representative.

Business-to-business e-procurement yields many benefits. First, it shaves transaction costs and results in more efficient purchasing for both buyers and suppliers. A Web-powered purchasing program eliminates the paperwork associated with traditional requisition and ordering procedures and helps an organization keep better track of all purchases.

E-procurement reduces the time between order and delivery. Time savings are particularly dramatic for companies with many overseas suppliers. Adaptec, a leading supplier of computer storage, used an extranet to tie all of its Taiwanese chip suppliers together in a kind of virtual family. Now messages from Adaptec flow in seconds from its headquarters to its Asian partners, and Adaptec has reduced the time between the order and delivery of its chips from as long as 16 weeks to just 55 days—the same turnaround time for companies that build their own chips.

Finally, beyond the cost and time savings, e-procurement frees purchasing people to focus on more-strategic issues. For many purchasing professionals, going online means reducing drudgery and paperwork and spending more time managing inventory and working creatively with suppliers. "That is the key," says an HP purchasing executive. "You can now focus people on value-added activities. Procurement professionals can now find different sources and work with suppliers to reduce costs and to develop new products."[10]

The rapidly expanding use of e-procurement, however, also presents some problems. For example, at the same time that the Web makes it possible for suppliers and customers to share business data and even collaborate on product design, it can also erode decades-old customer–supplier relationships. Many buyers now use the power of the Web to pit suppliers against one another and to search out better deals, products, and turnaround times on a purchase-by-purchase basis.

E-procurement can also create potential security disasters. Although e-mail and home banking transactions can be protected through basic encryption, the secure environment that businesses need to carry out confidential interactions is sometimes still lacking. Companies are spending millions for research on defensive strategies to keep hackers at bay. Cisco Systems, for example, specifies the types of routers, firewalls, and security procedures that its partners must use to safeguard extranet connections. In fact, the company goes even further—it sends its own security engineers to examine a partner's defenses and holds the partner liable for any security breach that originates from its computers.

Author Comment | These two nonbusiness organizational markets provide attractive opportunities for many companies. Because of their unique nature, we give them special attention here.

Institutional and Government Markets
(pp 181–184)

So far, our discussion of organizational buying has focused largely on the buying behavior of business buyers. Much of this discussion also applies to the buying practices of institutional and government organizations. However, these two nonbusiness markets have additional characteristics and needs. In this final section, we address the special features of institutional and government markets.

Institutional Markets

Institutional market
Schools, hospitals, nursing homes, prisons, and other institutions that provide goods and services to people in their care.

The **institutional market** consists of schools, hospitals, nursing homes, prisons, and other institutions that provide goods and services to people in their care. Institutions differ from one another in their sponsors and in their objectives. For example, Tenet

Healthcare runs 56 for-profit hospitals in 12 states, generating $8.7 billion in annual revenues. By contrast, the Shriners Hospitals for Children is a 22-hospital nonprofit organization that provides free specialized healthcare for children, whereas the government-run Veteran Affairs Medical Centers located across the country provide special services to veterans.[11] Each institution has different buying needs and resources.

Institutional markets can be huge. Consider the massive and expanding U.S. prisons economy:[12]

> The nation's 2 million inmates and their keepers are the ultimate captive market: a $37 billion economy bulging with opportunity. State prison systems spend more than $30 billion annually, and the federal Bureau of Prisons budgets another $5 billion. That translates into plenty of work for companies looking to break into the prison market. "Our core business touches so many things—security, medicine, education, food service, maintenance, technology—that it presents a unique opportunity for any number of vendors to do business with us," says an executive at Corrections Corporation of America, the largest private prison operator in the country.

Many institutional markets are characterized by low budgets and captive patrons. For example, hospital patients have little choice but to eat whatever food the hospital supplies. A hospital purchasing agent has to decide on the quality of food to buy for patients. Because the food is provided as a part of a total service package, the buying objective is not profit. Nor is strict cost minimization the goal—patients receiving poor-quality food will complain to others and damage the hospital's reputation. Thus, the hospital purchasing agent must search for institutional-food vendors whose quality meets or exceeds a certain minimum standard and whose prices are low.

Many marketers set up separate divisions to meet the special characteristics and needs of institutional buyers. For example, Kellogg's Food Away from Home business unit produces, packages, prices, and markets its broad assortment of cereals, cookies, snacks, and other products to better serve the specific food service requirements of hospitals, colleges, the military, and other institutional markets.[13]

Government Markets

Government market
Governmental units—federal, state, and local—that purchase or rent goods and services for carrying out the main functions of government.

The **government market** offers large opportunities for many companies, both big and small. In most countries, government organizations are major buyers of goods and services. In the United States alone, federal, state, and local governments contain more than 82,000 buying units. Government buying and business buying are similar in many ways. But there are also differences that must be understood by companies that wish to sell products and services to governments. To succeed in the government market, sellers must locate key decision makers, identify the factors that affect buyer behavior, and understand the buying decision process.

Government organizations typically require suppliers to submit bids, and normally they award the contract to the lowest bidder. In some cases, the government unit will make allowances for the supplier's superior quality or reputation for completing contracts on time. Governments will also buy on a negotiated contract basis, primarily in the case of complex projects involving major R&D costs and risks, and in cases where there is little competition.

Government organizations tend to favor domestic suppliers over foreign suppliers. A major complaint of multinationals operating in Europe is that each country shows favoritism toward its nationals in spite of superior offers that are made by foreign firms. The European Economic Commission is gradually removing this bias.

Like consumer and business buyers, government buyers are affected by environmental, organizational, interpersonal, and individual factors. One unique thing about government buying is that it is carefully watched by outside publics, ranging from Congress to a variety of private groups interested in how the government spends taxpayers' money. Because their spending decisions are subject to public review, government organizations require considerable paperwork from suppliers, who often complain about excessive paperwork, bureaucracy, regulations, decision-making delays, and frequent shifts in procurement personnel.

▲ Government markets: The U.S. government is the world's largest buyer of products and services—and its checks don't bounce. The Federal Business Opportunities Web site (FedBizOpps.gov) provides a single point of entry to the entire Federal contracting community.

Given all the red tape, why would any firm want to do business with the U.S. government? The reasons are quite simple: ▲ The U.S. government is the world's largest buyer of products and services—and its checks don't bounce. For example, last year, the federal government spent a whopping $79 billion on information technology alone. The Transportation Security Administration spent more than $690 million just for electronic baggage screening technology.[14]

Most governments provide would-be suppliers with detailed guides describing how to sell to the government. For example, the U.S. Small Business Administration publishes a guide entitled *U.S. Government Purchasing, Specifications, and Sales Directory*, which lists products and services frequently bought by the federal government and the specific agencies most frequently buying them. The U.S. Commerce Department publishes *Business America*, which provides interpretations of government policies and programs and gives concise information on potential worldwide trade opportunities. And the Commerce Department's Web site is loaded with information and advice on international trade opportunities (www.commerce.gov/TradeOpportunities/index.htm).

In several major cities, the General Services Administration operates *Business Service Centers* with staffs to provide a complete education on the way government agencies buy, the steps that suppliers should follow, and the procurement opportunities available. Various trade magazines and associations provide information on how to reach schools, hospitals, highway departments, and other government agencies. And almost all of these government organizations and associations maintain Internet sites offering up-to-date information and advice.

Still, suppliers have to master the system and find ways to cut through the red tape, especially for large government purchases. Consider Envisage Technologies, a small software development company that specializes in Internet-based training applications and human resource management platforms. All of its contracts fall in the government sector; 65 percent are with the federal government. Envisage uses the General Services Administration (GSA) Web site to gain access to smaller procurements, often receiving responses within 14 days. However, it puts the most sweat into seeking large, highly coveted contracts. A comprehensive bid proposal for one of these contracts can easily run from 600 to 700 pages because of federal paperwork requirements. And the company's president estimates that to prepare a single bid proposal the firm has spent as many as 5,000 man-hours over the course of a few years.[15]

Noneconomic criteria also play a growing role in government buying. Government buyers are asked to favor depressed business firms and areas; small business firms; minority-owned firms; and business firms that avoid race, gender, or age discrimination. Sellers need to keep these factors in mind when deciding to seek government business.

Many companies that sell to the government have not been very marketing oriented for a number of reasons. Total government spending is determined by elected officials rather than by any marketing effort to develop this market. Government buying has emphasized price, making suppliers invest their effort in technology to bring costs down. When the product's characteristics are specified carefully, product differentiation is not a marketing factor. Nor do advertising or personal selling matter much in winning bids on an open-bid basis.

Several companies, however, have established separate government marketing departments, including General Electric, CDW, Kodak, and Goodyear. These companies anticipate government needs and projects, participate in the product specification phase, gather competitive intelligence, prepare bids carefully, and produce stronger communications to describe and enhance their companies' reputations.

Other companies have set up customized marketing programs for government buyers. For example, Dell has specific business units tailored to meet the needs of federal as well as state and local government buyers. Dell offers its customers tailor-made Premier Dell.com Web pages that include special pricing, online purchasing, and service and support for each city, state, and federal government entity.

During the past decade, a great deal of the government's buying has gone online. The Federal Business Opportunities Web site (FedBizOpps.gov) provides a single point of entry through which commercial vendors and government buyers can post, search, monitor, and retrieve opportunities solicited by the entire Federal contracting community. The three federal agencies that act as purchasing agents for the rest of government have also launched Web sites supporting online government purchasing activity. The GSA, which influences more than one-quarter of the federal government's total procurement dollars, has set up a GSA Advantage! Web site (www.gsaadvantage.gov). The Defense Logistics Agency (DLA) offers a Procurement Gateway (http://progate.daps.dla.mil/home) for purchases by America's military services. And the Department of Veteran Affairs facilitates e-procurement through its VA Advantage! Web site (https://vaadvantage.gsa.gov).

Such sites allow authorized defense and civilian agencies to buy everything from office supplies, food, and information technology equipment to construction services through online purchasing. The GSA, DAL, and VA not only sell stocked merchandise through their Web sites but also create direct links between buyers and contract suppliers. For example, the branch of the DLA that sells 160,000 types of medical supplies to military forces transmits orders directly to vendors such as Bristol-Myers Squibb. Such Internet systems promise to eliminate much of the hassle sometimes found in dealing with government purchasing.[16]

REVIEWING Objectives AND KEY Terms

Business markets and consumer markets are alike in some key ways. For example, both include people in buying roles who make purchase decisions to satisfy needs. But business markets also differ in many ways from consumer markets. For one thing, the business market is *enormous*, far larger than the consumer market. Within the United States alone, the business market includes organizations that annually purchase trillions of dollars' worth of goods and services.

OBJECTIVE 1 Define the business market and explain how business markets differ from consumer markets. (pp 168–172)

The *business market* comprises all organizations that buy goods and services for use in the production of other products and services or for the purpose of reselling or renting them to others at a profit. As compared to consumer markets, business markets usually have fewer, larger buyers who are more geographically concentrated. Business demand is derived demand, and the business buying decision usually involves more, and more professional, buyers.

OBJECTIVE 2 Identify the major factors that influence business buyer behavior. (pp 172–176)

Business buyers make decisions that vary with the three types of *buying situations*: straight rebuys, modified rebuys, and new tasks. The

decision-making unit of a buying organization—the *buying center*—can consist of many different persons playing many different roles. The business marketer needs to know the following: Who are the major buying center participants? In what decisions do they exercise influence and to what degree? What evaluation criteria does each decision participant use? The business marketer also needs to understand the major environmental, organizational, interpersonal, and individual influences on the buying process.

OBJECTIVE 3 List and define the steps in the business buying decision process. (pp 176–181)

The *business buying decision process* itself can be quite involved, with eight basic stages: problem recognition, general need description, product specification, supplier search, proposal solicitation, supplier selection, order-routine specification, and performance review. Buyers who face a new-task buying situation usually go through all stages of the buying process. Buyers making modified or straight rebuys may skip some of the stages. Companies must manage the overall customer relationship, which often includes many different buying decisions in various stages of the buying decision process.

Recent advances in information technology have given birth to "e-procurement," by which business buyers are purchasing all kinds of products and services online. The Internet gives business buyers access to new suppliers, lowers purchasing costs, and hastens order processing and delivery. However, e-procurement can also erode customer–supplier relationships and create potential security problems. Still, business marketers are increasingly connecting with customers online to share marketing information, sell products and services, provide customer support services, and maintain ongoing customer relationships.

OBJECTIVE 4 Compare the institutional and government markets and explain how institutional and government buyers make their buying decisions. (pp 181-184)

The *institutional market* comprises schools, hospitals, prisons, and other institutions that provide goods and services to people in their care. These markets are characterized by low budgets and captive patrons. The *government market,* which is vast, consists of government units—federal, state, and local—that purchase or rent goods and services for carrying out the main functions of government.

Government buyers purchase products and services for defense, education, public welfare, and other public needs. Government buying practices are highly specialized and specified, with open bidding or negotiated contracts characterizing most of the buying. Government buyers operate under the watchful eye of Congress and many private watchdog groups. Hence, they tend to require more forms and signatures, and to respond more slowly and deliberately when placing orders.

KEY Terms

OBJECTIVE 1

Business buyer behavior (p 168)
Business buying process (p 168)
Derived demand (p 169)
Supplier development (p 170)

OBJECTIVE 2

Straight rebuy (p 173)
Modified rebuy (p 173)
New task (p 173)
Systems selling (solutions selling) (p 173)

Buying center (p 174)
Users (p 174)
Influencers (p 174)
Buyers (p 174)
Deciders (p 174)
Gatekeepers (p 174)

OBJECTIVE 3

Problem recognition (p 176)
General need description (p 177)
Product specification (p 177)

Supplier search (p 177)
Proposal solicitation (p 178)
Supplier selection (p 178)
Order-routine specification (p 179)
Performance review (p 179)
E-procurement (p 180)

OBJECTIVE 4

Institutional market (p 181)
Government market (p 182)

DISCUSSING & APPLYING THE Concepts

Discussing the Concepts

1. Compare and contrast business and consumer markets. (AACSB: Communication)

2. Discuss several ways in which a straight rebuy differs from a new-task situation. (AACSB: Communication)

3. In a buying center purchasing process, which buying center participant is most likely to make each of the following statements? (AACSB: Communication; Reflective Thinking)
- "This bonding agent better be good, because I have to put this product together."
- "I specified this bonding agent on another job, and it worked for them."
- "Without an appointment, no sales rep gets in to see Ms. Johnson."
- "Okay, it's a deal—we'll buy it."
- "I'll place the order first thing tomorrow."

4. List the major influences on business buyer behavior. Why is it important for the business-to-business marketer to understand these major influences? (AACSB: Communication; Reflective Thinking)

5. Name and briefly describe the stages of the business buying process. (AACSB: Communication)

6. How do the institutional and government markets differ from business markets? (AACSB: Communication)

Applying the Concepts

1. Business buying occurs worldwide, so marketers need to be aware of cultural factors influencing business customers. In a small group, select a country and develop a multimedia presentation on proper business etiquette and manners, including appropriate appearance, behavior, and communication. Include a map showing the location of the country as well as a description of the country in terms of demographics, culture, and its economic history. (AACSB: Communication; Multicultural and Diversity; Use of IT)

2. Interview a business person to learn how purchases are made in his or her organization. Ask this person to describe a straight rebuy, a modified rebuy, and a new-task buying situation that took place recently or of which he or she is aware (define them if necessary). Did the buying process differ based on the type of product or purchase situation? Ask the business person to explain the role he or she played in a recent purchase and to discuss the factors that influenced the decision. Write a brief report of your interview by applying the concepts you learned in this chapter regarding business buyer behavior. (AACSB: Communication; Reflective Thinking)

3. A great deal of the government's buying is done online. Go to the Federal Business Opportunities Web site (www.fbo.gov) and watch the general overview demonstration video for vendors. After watching the video, conduct a search for

opportunities using tips you learned in the video. Are there many opportunities in your geographic area? Write a brief report describing the usefulness of this Web site for businesses desiring to sell to the government market. (AACSB: Communication; Reflective Thinking)

FOCUS ON Technology

In today's competitive marketplace, many businesses strive to cut costs. One solution is for business buyers to drive down supplier prices. Online reverse auctions allow businesses to do this more efficiently and effectively. Reverse auctions, often called e-auctions, are conducted online with the buyer and seller roles reversed. Buyers announce auctions months in advance and vendors qualify to participate. During the live online auction, suppliers have a short time in which to bid down their prices anonymously. Such auctions started in the aerospace and automotive industries to reduce costs on commodity parts but have now spread to other industries. Buyers don't always go with the lowest bidder, but the process puts pressure on suppliers to

reduce prices and in turn reduce their own costs to maintain profitability. Although heralded as a "best practices" tool by some, reverse auctions are loathed by others. Some suppliers, bitten by the reverse auctions bug of their customers, turn around and reduce costs by requiring such auctions for their own suppliers.

1. Discuss at least three pros and cons of reverse auctions for buyers. Do the same for suppliers. (AACSB: Communication; Reflective Thinking)

2. How can a supplier succeed in reverse auctions? How can it avoid them altogether? (AACSB: Communication; Reflective Thinking)

FOCUS ON Ethics

China is an emerging economic giant with almost endless potential for business opportunities. *Guan xi*—meaning "connections" or "relationships"—is a Chinese way of doing business and is practically considered an art form there. It involves exchanging "favors" when you need something done. Many Chinese businesspeople see it as a way to solidify relationships, get things done, and cultivate well-being. To Westerners, however, it often looks more like graft in the form of bribery, nepotism, gift giving, and kickbacks. Transparency International, a German-based corruption watchdog, ranks China along with India, Russia, Taiwan, Turkey, Malaysia, and South Africa as the countries with the most rampant corruption. However, China is cracking down

by enacting stricter anticorruption laws and prosecuting violators. In 2007, China's former director of the State Food and Drug Administration was executed for taking bribes.

1. Is it right for Western civilizations to impose their ethical views and behavior on other cultures, such as China? (AACSB: Communication; Multicultural and Diversity; Ethical Reasoning)

2. What are the consequences for U.S. companies that refuse to engage in less-than-ethical practices that foreign businesses or governments expect or that competitors use in foreign markets? (AACSB: Communication; Reflective Thinking)

MARKETING BY THE Numbers

The North American Industry Classification System (NAICS) code is very useful for marketers. It is a relatively new coding system that replaces the old product-based Standard Industrial Classification (SIC) system introduced in the 1930s. The NAICS system classifies businesses by production processes, better reflecting changes in the global economy, especially in the service and technology industries. It was developed jointly by the United States, Canada, and Mexico in 1997 in concert with the North American Free Trade Agreement (NAFTA), providing a common classification system for the three countries and better compatibility with the International Standard Industrial Classification (ISIC)

system. This six-digit number (in some cases, seven or ten digits) is very useful for understanding business markets. For more discussion of the financial and quantitative implications of marketing decisions, see Appendix 2, Marketing by the Numbers.

1. What do the six digits of the NAICS code represent? What industry is represented by the NAICS code 721110? How many businesses comprise this code? (AACSB: Communication)

2. How can marketers use NAICS codes to better deliver customer satisfaction and value? (AACSB: Communication; Reflective Thinking)

VIDEO Case

Eaton

With nearly 60,000 employees doing business in 125 countries and sales last year of more than $11 billion, Eaton is one of the world's largest suppliers of diversified industrial goods. Eaton's products make cars more peppy, 18-wheelers safer to drive, and airliners more fuel efficient. So why haven't you heard of the company? Because Eaton sells its products not to end consumers but to other businesses.

At Eaton, B-to-B marketing means working closely with customers to develop a better product. So the company partners with its sophisticated, knowledgeable clients to create total solutions that meet their needs. Along the way, Eaton maps the decision-making process to better understand the concerns and interests of decision makers. In the end, Eaton's success depends on its ability to provide high-quality, dependable customer service and product support. Through service and support, Eaton develops a clear understanding of consumer needs and builds stronger relationships with clients.

After viewing the video featuring Eaton, answer the following questions about business markets and business buyer behavior:

1. What is Eaton's value proposition?
2. Who are Eaton's customers? Describe Eaton's customer relationships.
3. Discuss the different ways that Eaton provides value beyond that which companies can provide for themselves.

COMPANY Case

Boeing: Selling a Dream(liner)

Think about the biggest purchase that you've ever made. Was it a car? A computer? A piece of furniture or an appliance? Think about the time you put in to researching that decision, all the factors that you considered in making your choice, and how much the purchase ultimately cost.

Now imagine that you are part of a buying team for a major airline considering the purchase of multiple commercial jets, each costing over $100 million. A slightly different situation? Such are the customers that Boeing deals with every day. Selling commercial and military aircraft involves some of the most complicated transactions in the world. At those prices, a single sale can add up to billions of dollars. And beyond initial prices, Boeing's clients must consider numerous factors that affect longer-term operating and maintenance costs. As a result, the airplane purchase process is nerve-rackingly slow, often taking years from the first sales presentation to the day Boeing actually delivers an airplane.

For such purchases, Boeing knows that it takes more than fast talk and a firm handshake to sell expensive aircraft—it takes a lot of relationship building. So Boeing invests heavily in managing customer relationships. Individual salespeople head up an extensive team of company specialists—sales and service technicians, financial analysts, planners, engineers—all dedicated to finding ways to understand and satisfy airline customer needs. These teams work closely with clients through the lengthy buying process. Even after receiving an order, salespeople stay in almost constant contact to keep make certain the customer stays satisfied. The success of customer relationships depends on performance and trust. "When you buy an airplane, it is like getting married," quips Alan Mallaly, the head of Boeing's commercial airplane division. "It is a long-term relationship."

But even with this care in managing customer relationships, Boeing has experienced more than its share of challenges over the past decade. For starters, its only major rival, France-based Airbus, began to overtake Boeing in product innovation during the 1990s. In the wake of September 11, 2001, Boeing lost its industry lead in commercial airplane sales to Airbus. To make matters worse, Boeing soon found itself in the midst of a series of ethical scandals. In the early 2000s, the company faced two separate cases of cheating to win defense contracts with the U.S. Air Force. The scandals resulted in a Department of Justice investigation, the ousting of Boeing's CEO, prison terms for two other executives, and the loss of billions of dollars in business. To make matters even worse, in the face of a scandalous extramarital affair, the next CEO stepped down as well.

AN AIRLINE'S DREAM

With its reputation sullied and its financial situation suffering, Boeing got back to the business of serving its corporate clients. In April 2004, the giant airplane maker announced the program launch of its 787 Dreamliner, Boeing's first all-new aircraft since the 777, launched a decade earlier. The Dreamliner is not the world's biggest passenger jet—Airbus's A380 and even Boeing's own 747 are bigger. But with the 787, Boeing saw more potential in the midsized wide-body market. From the beginning, it set out to create a jet with groundbreaking innovations that would translate into true benefits for its customers, the type of benefits that really stand out to buyers and executives at major airlines.

Some 50 percent of the Dreamliner's fuselage is made from lightweight carbon-fiber materials. The plane is also made in one single piece, eliminating 40,000 to 50,000 fasteners and 1,500 aluminum sheets and putting it in a design class with the B-2 stealth bomber. Combined with other weight-saving design features and advanced engine technologies, the 787 is the world's lightest and most fuel efficient passenger jet, using 20 percent less fuel than comparably sized planes.

Another major benefit that the Boeing 787 Dreamliner brings to its category is flexibility. The 787 line is designed for multiple configurations that carry between 210 and 330 passengers. The plane also offers increased cargo capacity, a fuel range of up to 8,500 nautical miles, and a maximum speed of Mach .85. Thus, the 787 brings big-jet speed, range, and capacity to the midsize market, rivaling the jumbo jets.

The cockpit of the 787 is also loaded with tech toys that will enhance safety and cut departure delays. The advances include a system that self-monitors the plane's vital functions and reports maintenance requirements to ground-based computer systems.

Whereas the airlines will certainly notice all of these improvements, airline passengers will also approve of many new 787 design features. The interior of the Dreamliner is designed to reduce long-haul flying misery and to better imitate life on the ground. The Dreamliner is 60 percent quieter than other planes in its class. It features more legroom, lighting that automatically adjusts to time zone shifts, and higher cabin pressure and humidity, making the flying experience more comfortable and reducing common flying symptoms like headaches, dry mouth, and fatigue. The Dreamliner also boasts the largest-ever overhead storage bins, 19-inch self-dimming windows, and a wireless Internet and entertainment system.

"We looked at every aspect of the flying experience," says Tom Cogan, chief project engineer for the 787. "It's not just an evolutionary step. From my perspective it almost borders on revolutionary." Opinions of industry insiders support Cogan's statement. Many analysts strongly believe that the 787 Dreamliner will one day be regarded as the plane that charted the next age of commercial aviation.

Boeing officially launched the 787 program in April of 2004. Even with the stratospheric list price of $162 million and the fact that Boeing was not promising delivery for at least four years, companies scrambled to place orders. Japan's All-Nippon Airways jumped in first with a record order for 50 Dreamliners. To date, 56 companies from six continents have lined up with orders for 892 of Boeing's newest aeronautic darling. That makes the Dreamliner the most successful new aircraft launch and the fastest selling plane in the history of the industry.

Combined with record sales for its 737 and freighter lines, Boeing's annual sales soared. In 2005, Boeing shattered its records with orders for 1,002 commercial airplanes, edging within inches of Airbus's lead. That number is even more striking considering that Boeing and Airbus combined for a total of 622 orders in 2004. The sales spike was so dramatic that no one in the industry expected the numbers to repeat. But in 2006, Boeing reclaimed its title as the industry sales leader by surpassing Airbus with orders for 1,044 more jets. Even more stunning, 2007 brought the third straight record-breaking year for Boeing with 1,413 orders.

DREAM, OR NIGHTMARE?

As if massive revenue success weren't enough, Boeing was riding high for other reasons as well. In 2005, when Jim McNerney took over as CEO for Boeing, he instituted a massive cost-cutting program that resulted in an 84 percent increase in company earnings on an 8 percent increase in revenue for 2007. Combined with the soaring orders, Boeing's stock price peaked at a record $107 in July of 2007. With over $60 billion in revenue, Boeing once again reigned as the world's biggest aerospace company and the USA's largest exporter. But Mr. McNerney knew better than to revel in the glory of the then-current successes. Across the Atlantic, Airbus had committed severe production blunders resulting in its first jumbo A380s being delivered 22 months late, leading to a major shakeup in management at the French firm. Boeing had projected that it would deliver its first 787 to All Nippon in May of 2008. With that date still more than a year away, McNerney knew that his biggest challenge would be to keep the Dreamliner on track.

McNerney had good reason for concern. The Dreamliner was not only an innovative design, it was being built by an innovative

process that outsourced 70 percent of the work to dozens of partnering firms. Boeing's promises with respect to deadlines and delivery dates could only be met if all the pieces of the puzzle came together as planned. Even though it had so many orders secured, customers were counting on Boeing to make good. The last thing that it needed was for customer relationships to be rocked by delays or other problems.

But by mid-2007, the 787 production process was plagued with problems. Parts shortages and other bottlenecks led suppliers to ship incomplete sections of the first few planes to Boeing's final assembly line in Everett, Washington. By mid-2008, the date of the first 787 delivery had been pushed back three times. All Nippon would not take possession of its first plane until at least 15 months past the original deadline. To make matters worse, Boeing announced that it would only deliver 25 Dreamliners in the first year, rather than the previous estimate of 109.

Months later, Boeing Commercial Airplanes president Scott Carson announced that Boeing had made solid progress in overcoming start-up issues. He apologized and promised that the company would work closely with each customer to minimize the impact of the delays. Boeing also suggested that it would offer incentives and penalty payments as part of that process (some analysts estimate that Boeing could be liable for as much as $4 billion in concessions and penalties). Still, understandably, Boeing's commercial customers quickly grew impatient. The delays began raising havoc with customer relationships. Boeing's biggest customer, All Nippon, stated, "We are extremely disappointed: This is the third delay in the delivery of the first aircraft and we still have no details about the full delivery schedule. We would urge Boeing to provide us with a 120 percent definitive schedule as soon as possible."

As Boeing's customers consider what is happening in the purchase process, it is easy to see how each might become seriously conflicted. On the one hand, they see the promise of a Dreamliner that they believe strongly will provide tremendous benefits, perhaps unlike any previous aircraft. On the other hand, every delay costs them dearly. The delays upset plans to begin new routes and retire old aircraft, events that translate directly into revenue and profits. Customer options are limited—there's only one competitor, and its product in this class is substantially inferior to the Dreamliner. And even if customers switch, Airbus does not have planes sitting on the shelves waiting to be purchased. However, Boeing's customers still have the option of canceling 787 orders and making do with what they have.

RIDING OUT THE STORM

Regardless of what its customers do, the way Boeing handles the 787 crisis will most certainly affect customer relations and *future* orders. Boeing has a lot on its side. The innovativeness of the current product line, expertise in supply chain management, and the strength of its sales teams in managing customer relationships will all help to resolve the problems with the Dreamliner program. But Boeing had these things going for it before the crisis began. The question is, what will Boeing do differently in the future.

In a 2008 memo to employees, CEO McNerney said, "The simple reality is that it's time to get it done—and done right." McNerney has made it very clear that he expects more from everyone involved in the 787 Dreamliner program, from the top down. He has reached deeply into the company's executive roster, plucking a team from Boeing's defense unit to straighten out the Dreamliner process. He is pushing executives to act more aggressively. This includes sticking their noses into suppliers' operations, even stationing Boeing employees on the factory floors of every major supplier.

McNerney himself is more directly involved with the 787 program. He gets daily briefings on the plane's progress. He frequently makes his presence known on factory floors and even visits with assembly line workers. "We've got 240 programs in the company, and there's one that's got more of my attention right now than any one, and that's the 787," Mr. McNerney said. "I hope we are [eventually] defined by the 787. Just not right this instant."

Mr. McNerney took over as CEO well after the Dreamliner program was under way, so the current problems are not being attributed to him. But customers and others throughout the industry are watching him closely to see how he handles the situation. Says Charlie Smith, chief investment officer with Fort Pitt Capital Group, "No matter what other successes Jim McNerney has at Boeing, he will be judged on how he handles the 787. He's either going to win big or lose big," he said. And McNerney's outcome will be directly shared by the Boeing Corporation, including the teams that must deal day in and day out with anxious and frustrated customers.

Questions for Discussion

1. Discuss the nature of the market structure and demand for the Dreamliner. What are the implications of this for Boeing and its customers?

2. What examples of the major types of buying situations do you see in the case? Discuss the implications of each in terms of marketing strategy.

3. List the specific features of the Dreamliner. What customer benefits result from each?

4. Discuss the customer buying process for a Boeing airplane. In what major ways does this process differ from the buying process a passenger might go through in choosing an airline?

5. What marketing recommendations would you make to McNerney as he continues to try to resolve the problems with the 787 Dreamliner program?

Sources: Josh Dean, "Fast 50 2008: Boeing," *Fast Company*, February, 2008, p. 106; Laurence Zuckerman, "Selling Airplanes with a Smile," *New York Times,* February 17, 2002, p. 3.2; J. Lynn Lunsford, "Boeing CEO Fights Headwind," *Wall Street Journal*, April 25, 2008, p. B1; Michael V. Copeland, "Boeing's Big Dream," *Fortune*, April 24, 2008, accessed online at www.money.cnn.com; Marilyn Adams, "Boeing Bounces Back Against Odds," *USA Today*, January 11, 2007, p. 1B.

Chapter 7

Part 1   Defining Marketing and the Marketing Process (Chapters 1, 2)
Part 2   Understanding the Marketplace and Consumers (Chapters 3, 4, 5, 6)
Part 3   Designing a Customer-Driven Strategy and Mix (Chapters 7, 8, 9, 10, 11, 12, 13, 14, 15, 16, 17)
Part 4   Extending Marketing (Chapters 18, 19, 20)

Customer-Driven Marketing
Strategy Creating Value for Target Customers

Chapter PREVIEW

So far, you've learned what marketing is and about the importance of understanding consumers and the marketplace environment. With that as background, you're now ready to delve deeper into marketing strategy and tactics. This chapter looks further into key customer-driven marketing strategy decisions—how to divide up markets into meaningful customer groups (*segmentation*), choose which customer groups to serve (*targeting*), create market offerings that best serve targeted customers (*differentiation*), and position the offerings in the minds of consumers (*positioning*). Then, the chapters that follow explore the tactical marketing tools—the Four Ps—by which marketers bring these strategies to life.

We've talked a lot about premier marketer Procter & Gamble, and we'll start this chapter with another P&G story. When it comes to targeting and positioning, perhaps no company does it better. Here, we'll look at how P&G discovered an important customer segment—college students—and skillfully positioned its fast-growing Febreze brand to meet the special needs of that niche.

One of Procter & Gamble's fastest-growing brands, odor fighter Febreze, is now targeting a new lifestyle segment: college students. How? By zoning in on what stinks about college life—everything from armpits to boyfriends and ever-growing piles of laundry in the corner of a dorm room. The burgeoning $600 million Febreze brand recently kicked off "What Stinks," an online and viral campaign for its fabric-refresher spray aimed at this sometimes hard to reach, often fickle segment.

For most of the brand's existence, Febreze has targeted mostly working adults and soccer moms, positioning itself as a "Breath of Fresh Air" for people looking to remove odors from sweaty gym clothes, soiled furniture, and pet areas. However, P&G realized that this broader targeting and positioning leaves out an entire group of customers—the Millennials, which include college students. "There are 18 million college kids out there and we've never really targeted them," said Martin Hertich, North American marketing director for Febreze. However, despite the fact that Febreze has done little dedicated marketing toward the segment, pockets of students over the years have embraced the odor-fighting spray anyway.

Why is Febreze a natural for college students? "Washing is not a convenient part of the lifestyle at college," says Hettich. And what better for wash-day-reluctant students than products that eliminate the need? So during the past few years, P&G has launched a movement to help students find ways to rewear unwashed clothes rather than doing laundry. For example, it recently introduced a new Swash line of dewrinkling sprays, stain-removing pens, odor-removing sprays, clothes dryer sheets, and lint rollers designed to give students' clothes the look and smell of having been washed without the trouble or expense of actually washing them. Extending the Febreze positioning toward the college student segment is a natural extension of this "rewash movement."

But targeting the potentially huge college-student segment presents some problems. Febreze marketers recognized that the college campus is a far cry from where the brand has thrust its marketing efforts in the past. A mainstream-marketing approach likely would fail to reach and persuade this college-student segment. "Our mainstream media buys are not effective for 18- to 22-year-olds," confirms a P&G advertising agency executive. "P&G had to figure out a clever marketing campaign aimed at these mysterious Millennials," says one analyst. "What better way than to rely on the media already used by this tech-savvy group?"

So Febreze opted for an online and viral approach, built around an interactive Web site, www.WhatStinks.com, linked directly through Facebook. Facebook is a real no-brainer these days when it comes to youth marketing. In a recent brand survey of college students, Facebook beat out MySpace as the most popular social-networking site for that group. It's no surprise, then, that WhatStinks.com is actually housed within Facebook, and that P&G plans to reach its college-student target segment through media buys and banner ads on Facebook.

On the humorous What Stinks? Facebook site, Febreze swaps its broader "Breath of fresh air" positioning for more college-oriented ones such as "Febreze . . . Because surprise! Your parents are visiting!"

> **P&G has launched a movement to help wash-day-reluctant students find ways to rewear unwashed clothes rather than doing laundry.**

and "Febreze . . . Because the laundry room is sooooo far away!" It also adds a mascot in the form of a gigantic Converse-wearing nose.

Other features of the site include the "Dank Game," a video game where players aren't armed with machine guns, but bottles of Febreze to attack dirty socks and boxers, and a "What Stinks?" news feed that gathers news of smells all around the world. Recent posts include an AP wire report about a toilet-paper thief in Wisconsin. Spin the Wheel-O-Stink and get tips on everything from deodorizing the after-air of funky roomies to refreshing that old sweater that smells like grandma's attic. And a Clear the Air link takes visitors to a video of students telling Febreze "what stinks," such as fashion, boyfriends, the real world, and more. As part of the campaign, Febreze is also running a "What Stinks" candid online photo contest with prizes that marry Febreze with another brand college students love—Apple and iTunes.

In step with its humorous tack, Febreze is also invading campuses nationwide with a Febreze-branded comedy tour showcasing the improvisational troupe Upright Citizens Brigade. The tour features interactive performances in which the cast interviews students about what stinks in their lives. Related on-the-ground promotions feature giveaways of dorm-life staples such as marker boards and laundry bags (for fabric items beyond the help of Febreze).

The student-targeted Febreze What Stinks? campaign, along with P&G's other skillful targeting and positioning efforts for the brand, have helped make Febreze the world's leading fabric freshener and deodorizer. It's also one of P&G's fastest-growing brands. That really does make Febreze a breath of fresh air to both the company and its customers.[1]

One of Procter & Gamble's fastest-growing brands, odor fighter Febreze, is now targeting a new lifestyle segment: college students

> When it comes to targeting and positioning, perhaps no company does it better than Procter & Gamble. Such skillful marketing efforts have made Febreze the world's leading fabric freshener and deodorizer.

Companies today recognize that they cannot appeal to all buyers in the marketplace, or at least not to all buyers in the same way. Buyers are too numerous, too widely scattered, and too varied in their needs and buying practices. Moreover, the companies themselves vary widely in their abilities to serve different segments of the market. Instead, like P&G, a company must identify the parts of the market that it can serve best and most profitably. It must design customer-driven marketing strategies that build the *right* relationships with the *right* customers.

Thus, most companies have moved away from mass marketing and toward *target marketing*—identifying market segments, selecting one or more of them, and developing products and marketing programs tailored to each. Instead of scattering their marketing efforts (the "shotgun" approach), firms are focusing on the buyers who have greater interest in the values they create best (the "rifle" approach).

🔋 **Figure 7.1** shows the four major steps in designing a customer-driven marketing strategy. In the first two steps, the company selects the customers that it will serve. **Market segmentation** involves dividing a market into smaller groups of buyers with distinct needs, characteristics, or behaviors that might require separate marketing strategies or mixes. The company identifies different ways to segment the market and develops profiles of the resulting market segments. **Market targeting** (or **targeting**) consists of evaluating each market segment's attractiveness and selecting one or more market segments to enter.

In the final two steps, the company decides on a value proposition—on how it will create value for target customers. **Differentiation** involves actually differentiating the

Market segmentation
Dividing a market into smaller groups with distinct needs, characteristics, or behavior that might require separate marketing strategies or mixes.

Market targeting (targeting)
The process of evaluating each market segment's attractiveness and selecting one or more segments to enter.

Differentiation
Actually differentiating the market offering to create superior customer value.

Objective Outline

Positioning
Arranging for a market offering to occupy a clear, distinctive, and desirable place relative to competing products in the minds of target consumers.

firm's market offering to create superior customer value. **Positioning** consists of arranging for a market offering to occupy a clear, distinctive, and desirable place relative to competing products in the minds of target consumers. We discuss each of these steps in turn.

Author Comment | Market segmentation addresses the first simple-sounding marketing question: What customers will we serve? The answer will be different for each company. For example, The Ritz-Carlton targets the top 5 percent of corporate and leisure travelers. Hampton targets middle Americans traveling on a budget.

Market Segmentation (pp 192–201)

Buyers in any market differ in their wants, resources, locations, buying attitudes, and buying practices. Through market segmentation, companies divide large, heterogeneous markets into smaller segments that can be reached more efficiently and effectively with products and services that match their unique needs. In this section, we discuss four important segmentation topics: segmenting consumer markets, segmenting business markets, segmenting international markets, and requirements for effective segmentation.

Segmenting Consumer Markets

There is no single way to segment a market. A marketer has to try different segmentation variables, alone and in combination, to find the best way to view the market structure. ● **Table 7.1** outlines the major variables that might be used in segmenting consumer markets. Here we look at the major *geographic, demographic, psychographic,* and *behavioral* variables.

● FIGURE | 7.1
Designing a Customer-Driven Marketing Strategy

In concept, marketing boils down to two questions: (1) Which customers will we serve? and (2) How will we serve them? Of course, the tough part is coming up with good answers to these simple-sounding but difficult questions. The goal is to create more value for the customers we serve than competitors do.

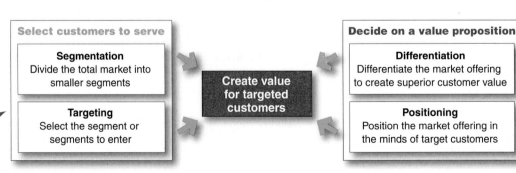

192

● TABLE | 7.1   Major Segmentation Variables for Consumer Markets

Geographic	
World region or country	North America, Western Europe, Middle East, Pacific Rim, China, India, Canada, Mexico
Country region	Pacific, Mountain, West North Central, West South Central, East North Central, East South Central, South Atlantic, Middle Atlantic, New England
City or metro size	Under 5,000; 5,000–20,000; 20,000–50,000; 50,000–100,000; 100,000–250,000; 250,000–500,000; 500,000–1,000,000; 1,000,000–4,000,000; over 4,000,000
Density	Urban, suburban, exurban, rural
Climate	Northern, southern

Demographic	
Age	Under 6, 6–11, 12–19, 20–34, 35–49, 50–64, 65+
Gender	Male, female
Family size	1–2, 3–4, 5+
Family life cycle	Young, single; married, no children; married with children; single parents; unmarried couples; older, married, no children under 18; older, single; other
Income	Under $20,000; $20,000–$30,000; $30,000–$50,000; $50,000–$100,000; $100,000–$250,000; $250,000 and over
Occupation	Professional and technical; managers, officials, and proprietors; clerical; sales; craftspeople; supervisors; farmers; retired; students; homemakers; unemployed
Education	Grade school or less; some high school; high school graduate; some college; college graduate
Religion	Catholic, Protestant, Jewish, Muslim, Hindu, other
Race	Asian, Hispanic, Black, White
Generation	Baby boomer, Generation X, Millennial
Nationality	North American, South American, British, French, German, Italian, Japanese

Psychographic	
Social class	Lower lowers, upper lowers, working class, middle class, upper middles, lower uppers, upper uppers
Lifestyle	Achievers, strivers, survivors
Personality	Compulsive, gregarious, authoritarian, ambitious

Behavioral	
Occasions	Regular occasion; special occasion; holiday; seasonal
Benefits	Quality, service, economy, convenience, speed
User status	Nonuser, ex-user, potential user, first-time user, regular user
User rates	Light user, medium user, heavy user
Loyalty status	None, medium, strong, absolute
Readiness stage	Unaware, aware, informed, interested, desirous, intending to buy
Attitude toward product	Enthusiastic, positive, indifferent, negative, hostile

Geographic Segmentation

Geographic segmentation

Dividing a market into different geographical units such as nations, states, regions, counties, cities, or neighborhoods.

Geographic segmentation calls for dividing the market into different geographical units such as nations, regions, states, counties, cities, or even neighborhoods. A company may decide to operate in one or a few geographical areas, or to operate in all areas but pay attention to geographical differences in needs and wants.

Many companies today are localizing their products, advertising, promotion, and sales efforts to fit the needs of individual regions, cities, and even neighborhoods. For example, one consumer-products company ships additional cases of its low-calorie snack foods to stores in neighborhoods near Weight Watchers clinics. Citibank offers different mixes of branch banking services depending on neighborhood demographics. And Baskin-Robbins practices what it calls "three-mile marketing," emphasizing local events and promotions close to its local store locations. On a global scale, video game companies create different versions of their games depending on the world region in which the game is sold. For example, Capcom sells its *Resident Evil* series as *Biohazard* in most other countries, such as Japan and France, where it is played in local languages.[2]

Other companies are seeking to cultivate as-yet-untapped geographic territory. For example, many large companies are fleeing the fiercely competitive major cities and suburbs to set up shop in small-town America. Home Depot, for instance, is getting ready to unveil a junior version of its stores, roughly half the size of a regular store. These stores, geared toward small markets and vacation areas that can't support a full-size store, are designed to offer a more intimate neighborhood hardware store setting. For example, Georgia will get its first small-scale Home Depot this year, near Lake Hartwell. "We think there's a tremendous opportunity in smaller markets where it's harder to find land for a full-size store, and where they don't need a full-size store," says a Home Depot executive.[3]

In contrast, other retailers are developing new store concepts that will give them access to higher-density urban areas. For example, Wal-Mart has been complementing its supercenters by opening small, supermarket-style Marketside grocery stores in markets where full-size stores are impractical. Marketside stores are a third the size of Wal-Mart's other small-store format, Neighborhood Market supermarkets, and a 10th the size of one of its supercenters.[4]

Demographic Segmentation

Demographic segmentation
Dividing the market into groups based on variables such as age, gender, family size, family life cycle, income, occupation, education, religion, race, generation, and nationality.

Demographic segmentation divides the market into groups based on variables such as age, gender, family size, family life cycle, income, occupation, education, religion, race, generation, and nationality. Demographic factors are the most popular bases for segmenting customer groups. One reason is that consumer needs, wants, and usage rates often vary closely with demographic variables. Another is that demographic variables are easier to measure than most other types of variables. Even when marketers first define segments using other bases, such as benefits sought or behavior, they must know segment demographic characteristics in order to assess the size of the target market and to reach it efficiently.

Age and Life-Cycle Stage. Consumer needs and wants change with age. Some companies use **age and life-cycle segmentation**, offering different products or using different marketing approaches for different age and life-cycle groups. For example, for kids, Oscar Mayer offers Lunchables, full of fun, kid-appealing finger food. For older generations, it markets Deli Creations, everything they need to create a "hot and melty fresh-baked sandwich in a microwave minute."

Age and life-cycle segmentation
Dividing a market into different age and life-cycle groups.

Similarly, whereas HP targets adult buyers with its "The Computer Is Personal Again" campaign, along with Sunday circular ads featuring price and value, it has developed a special "Society for Parental Mind Control" campaign targeting teenagers. Research shows that although parents are the predominant buyers of computers, teens are key recommenders. "It's such an old story, but kids are the arbiters of cool," says one analyst. So HP wants to raise its teen cool quotient. The teen-targeted campaign uses mostly online and viral media. For example, teens can click on to the "Society for Parental Mind Control" site to pick up "fun, new ways to get a sweet computer out of your parents."[5]

Marketers must be careful to guard against stereotypes when using age and life-cycle segmentation. Although some 80-year-olds fit the doddering stereoypes, others play tennis. Similarly, whereas some 40-year-old couples are sending their children off to college, others are just beginning new families. Thus, age is often a poor predictor of a person's life cycle, health, work or family status, needs, and buying power. Companies marketing to mature consumers usually employ positive images and appeals. For example, take the cruise industry, which heavily targets baby boomers at all life stages. One Carnival Cruise Lines ad for its Fun Ships features an older boomer and child riding waterslides, stating "Fun has no age limit."

▲ Gender segmentation: Daisy Rock offers a complete line of smaller, lighter, professional-quality guitars with fun shapes and glossy finishes geared toward women.

Gender segmentation

Dividing a market into different groups based on gender.

Income segmentation

Dividing a market into different income groups.

▲ Marketing to the affluent: For only $100,000, you can experience an extravagant Love at Lake Vegas weekend at The Ritz-Carlton, Lake Las Vegas in Henderson, Nevada. It includes a $50,000 shopping spree at Neiman Marcus.

Gender. **Gender segmentation** has long been used in clothing, cosmetics, toiletries, and magazines. For example, Procter & Gamble was among the first with Secret, a brand specially formulated for a woman's chemistry, packaged and advertised to reinforce the female image. More recently, many mostly women's cosmetics makers have begun marketing men's lines. Nivea markets Nivea for Men, "an advanced line of enriching skincare and soothing aftershave products specially designed for the active, healthy men's lifestyle," and offers a four-step guide to perfect men's care.

A neglected gender segment can offer new opportunities in markets ranging from motorcycles to guitars. For example, 10 years ago, 96 percent of guitars were purchased by and for men. ▲Daisy Rock Guitars, The Girl Guitar Company, is changing that statistic one guitar at a time. Starting with a daisy-shaped guitar with a leafy headstock, Daisy Rock now offers a complete line of smaller, lighter, professional-quality guitars with fun shapes and glossy finishes geared toward women. Guitars range from girly butterfly, heart, and daisy shapes for younger girls to glossy red, black, purple, and pink guitars for women. Daisy Rocks sales have doubled each year since the company was founded in 2000, last year reaching $2.4 million.[6]

Income.   The marketers of products and services such as automobiles, clothing, cosmetics, financial services, and travel have long used **income segmentation**. Many companies target affluent consumers with luxury goods and convenience services. For example, for a price, luxury hotels provide amenities to attract specific groups of affluent travelers, such as families, expectant moms, and even pet owners:[7]

At the Four Seasons Hotel Chicago, guests can buy the Kids in the City package for $520 a night and, among other things, enjoy a visit in their room from the Ice Cream Man, who arrives with all the fixings to make any concoction they desire. At one spa in Scottsdale, Arizona, expectant parents can purchase the "Bundle of Joy" Babymoon package, which includes a 24-hour Cravings-Chef service, a couples massage, and breakfast in bed. The Benjamin Hotel in New York City provides dog beds in a variety of styles and doggie bathrobes, as well as canine room service and DVDs for dogs. And if that isn't decadent of enough, how about dropping $100,000 for an extravagant weekend in Vegas? ▲At The Ritz-Carlton, Lake Las Vegas in Henderson, Nevada, the Love at Lake Las Vegas weekend package includes two nights in the 2,400 square foot presidential suite, helicopter and gondola rides, a champagne-tasting party on a yacht complete with rose petals strewn about and a string trio, use of a luxury car throughout the stay, in-room couples spa treatment, a $5,000 casino line of credit, a $50,000 shopping spree at Neiman Marcus, 14 dozen roses, and a butler-drawn Cristal champagne bath.

However, not all companies that use income segmentation target the affluent. For example, many retailers—such as the Dollar General, Family Dollar, and Dollar Tree store chains—successfully target low- and middle-income groups. The core market for such stores is families with incomes under $30,000. When Family Dollar real-estate experts scout locations for new stores, they look for lower-middle-class neighborhoods where people wear less-expensive shoes and drive old cars that drip a lot of oil.

With their low-income strategies, the dollar stores are now the fastest-growing retailers in the nation. They have been so successful that giant discounters are taking notice. For example, Target has installed a dollar aisle—the "1 Spot"—in its stores. And supermarkets such as Kroger and A&P are launching "10 for $10" promotions. Some experts predict that, to meet the dollar store threat, Wal-Mart will eventually buy one of these chains or start one of its own.[8]

Psychographic Segmentation

Psychographic segmentation
Dividing a market into different groups based on social class, lifestyle, or personality characteristics.

Psychographic segmentation divides buyers into different groups based on social class, lifestyle, or personality characteristics. People in the same demographic group can have very different psychographic makeups.

In Chapter 5, we discussed how the products people buy reflect their *lifestyles*. As a result, marketers often segment their markets by consumer lifestyles and base their marketing strategies on lifestyle appeals. For example, Rockport advertises that its shoes "are meant for a special occasion. It's called life. Live in Rockport." The ads feature people in everyday activities, conveying the wearable nature of Rockport shoes and how they fit into many lifestyles.

Marketers also use *personality* variables to segment markets. For example, cruise lines target adventure seekers. Royal Caribbean appeals to high-energy couples and families with hundreds of activities such as rockwall climbing and ice skating. Its commercials, set to Iggy Pop's "Lust for Life," tells them that "this is more than a cruise" and orders them to "get out there." By contrast, the Regent Seven Seas Cruise Line targets more serene and cerebral adventurers, mature couples seeking a more elegant ambiance and exotic destinations, such as the Orient. Regent invites them to come along as "luxury goes exploring."[9]

Behavioral Segmentation

Behavioral segmentation
Dividing a market into groups based on consumer knowledge, attitudes, uses, or responses to a product.

Behavioral segmentation divides buyers into groups based on their knowledge, attitudes, uses, or responses to a product. Many marketers believe that behavior variables are the best starting point for building market segments.

Occasion segmentation
Dividing the market into groups according to occasions when buyers get the idea to buy, actually make their purchase, or use the purchased item.

Occasions. Buyers can be grouped according to occasions when they get the idea to buy, actually make their purchase, or use the purchased item. **Occasion segmentation** can help firms build up product usage. For example, most consumers drink orange juice in the morning but orange growers have promoted drinking orange juice as a cool, healthful refresher at other times of the day. By contrast, Coca-Cola's "Good Morning" campaign attempts to increase Diet Coke consumption by promoting the soft drink as an early morning pick-me-up.

Some holidays, such as Mother's Day and Father's Day, were originally promoted partly to increase the sale of candy, flowers, cards, and other gifts. And many marketers prepare special offers and ads for holiday occasions. For example, ▲ Peeps creates different shaped sugar-and-fluffy-marshmallow treats for Easter, Valentine's Day, Halloween, and Christmas, when it captures most of its sales, but advertises that Peeps are "Always in Season" to increase the demand for nonholiday occasions.

Benefit segmentation
Dividing the market into groups according to the different benefits that consumers seek from the product.

Benefits Sought. A powerful form of segmentation is to group buyers according to the different *benefits* that they seek from the product. **Benefit segmentation** requires finding the major benefits people look for in the product class, the kinds of people who look for each benefit, and the major brands that deliver each benefit.

▲ Occasion segmentation: Peeps creates different shaped marshmallow treats for special holidays when it captures most of its sales but advertises that Peeps are "Always in Season" to increase the demand for non-holiday occasions.

Champion athletic wear segments its markets according to benefits that different consumers seek from their activewear. For example, "Fit and Polish" consumers seek a balance between function and style—they exercise for results but want to look good doing it. "Serious Sports Competitors" exercise heavily and live in and love their activewear—they seek performance and function. By contrast, "Value-Seeking Moms" have low sports interest and low activewear involvement—they buy for the family and seek durability and value. Thus, each segment seeks a different mix of benefits. Champion must target the benefit segment or segments that it can serve best and most profitably, using appeals that match each segment's benefit preferences.

User Status. Markets can be segmented into nonusers, ex-users, potential users, first-time users, and regular users of a product. Marketers want to reinforce and retain regular users, attract targeted nonusers, and reinvigorate relationships with ex-users.

Included in the potential user group are consumers facing life-stage changes—such as newlyweds and new parents—who can be turned into heavy users. For example, upscale kitchen and cookware retailer Williams-Sonoma actively targets newly engaged couples. Eight-page ad inserts in bridal magazines show a young couple strolling through a park or talking intimately in the kitchen over a glass of wine. The bride-to-be asks, "Now that I've found love, what else do I need?" Pictures of Williams-Sonoma knife sets, toasters, glassware, and pots and pans provide some strong clues. The retailer also offers a bridal registry, of course. But it plans to take its registry a step further next year. Through a program called "The Store Is Yours," it will open its stores early, by appointment, exclusively for individual couples to visit and make their wish lists. This segment is very important to Williams-Sonoma. About half the people who register are new to the brand—and they'll be buying a lot of kitchen and cookware in the future.[10]

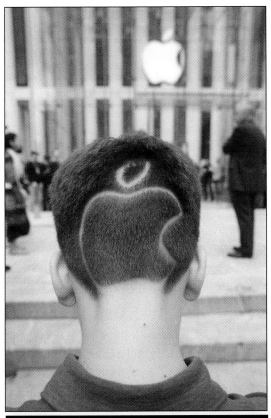

▲ Consumer loyalty: "Mac fanatics"—fanatically loyal Apple users—helped keep Apple afloat during the lean years, and they are now at the forefront of Apple's burgeoning iPod and iTunes empire.

Usage Rate. Markets can also be segmented into light, medium, and heavy product users. Heavy users are often a small percentage of the market but account for a high percentage of total consumption. For example, Burger King targets what it calls "Super Fans," young (age 18 to 34), Whopper-wolfing males who make up 18 percent of the chain's customers but account for almost half of all customer visits. They eat at Burger King an average of 16 times a month.[11] Burger King targets these Super Fans openly with ads that exalt monster burgers containing meat, cheese, and more meat and cheese that can turn "innies into outies."

Loyalty Status. A market can also be segmented by consumer loyalty. Consumers can be loyal to brands (Tide), stores (Target), and companies (Toyota). Buyers can be divided into groups according to their degree of loyalty. Some consumers are completely loyal—they buy one brand all the time. ▲ For example, Apple has an almost cultlike following of loyal users:[12]

There are Mac *users*—folks who happen to own a Mac and use it for e-mailing, blogging, browsing, buying, and social networking. Then there are the Apple *diehards*—the Mac fanatics who buy Apple products and accessories that maximize their Mac lives. Some of these zealots buy two iPhones—one for themselves and the other just to take apart, to see what it looks like on the inside, and maybe, just to marvel at Apple's ingenious ability to cram so much into a tight little elegant package. These Mac fanatics (also called MacHeads or Macolytes) see Apple founder and CEO Steve Jobs as the Walt Disney of technology. Say the word "Apple" in front of Mac fans and they'll go into rhapsodies about the superiority of the brand. Put two MacHeads together and you'll never shut them up. "The Mac [comes] not just as a machine in a box, it [comes] with a whole community," notes one observer. Such fanatically loyal users helped keep Apple afloat during the lean years, and they are now at the forefront of Apple's burgeoning iPod and iTunes empire.

Other consumers are somewhat loyal—they are loyal to two or three brands of a given product or favor one brand while sometimes buying others. Still other buyers show no loyalty to any brand. They either want something different each time they buy or they buy whatever's on sale.

A company can learn a lot by analyzing loyalty patterns in its market. It should start by studying its own loyal customers. For example, by studying Mac fanatics, Apple can better pinpoint its target market and develop marketing appeals. By studying its less-loyal buyers, the company can detect which brands are most competitive with its own. By looking at customers who are shifting away from its brand, the company can learn about its marketing weaknesses.

Using Multiple Segmentation Bases

Marketers rarely limit their segmentation analysis to only one or a few variables. Rather, they often use multiple segmentation bases in an effort to identify smaller, better-defined target groups. Thus, a bank may not only identify a group of wealthy retired adults but also, within that group, distinguish several segments based on their current income, assets, savings and risk preferences, housing, and lifestyles.

Several business information services—such as Claritas, Experian, Acxiom, and MapInfo—provide multivariable segmentation systems that merge geographic, demographic, lifestyle, and behavioral data to help companies segment their markets down to zip codes, neighborhoods, and even households. One of the leading segmentation systems is the PRIZM NE (New Evolution) system by Claritas. ▲PRIZM NE classifies every American household based on a host of demographic factors—such as age, educational level, income, occupation, family composition, ethnicity, and housing—and behavioral and lifestyle factors—such as purchases, free-time activities, and media preferences.

PRIZM NE classifies U.S. households into 66 demographically and behaviorally distinct segments, organized into 14 different social groups. PRIZM NE segments carry such exotic names as "Kids & Cul-de-Sacs," "Gray Power," "Blue Blood Estates," "Mayberry-ville," "Shotguns & Pickups," "Old Glories," "Multi-Culti Mosaic," "Big City Blues," and "Bright Lites L'il City." The colorful names help to bring the clusters to life.[13]

PRIZM NE and other such systems can help marketers to segment people and locations into marketable groups of like-minded consumers. Each cluster has its own pattern of likes, dislikes, lifestyles, and purchase behaviors. For example, "Blue Blood Estates" neighborhoods, part of the Elite Suburbs social group, are suburban areas populated by elite, super-rich families. People in this segment are more likely to own an Audi A8, take a ski vacation, shop at Talbots, and read *Architectural Digest*. In contrast, the "Shotguns & Pickups" segment, part of the Middle America social group, is populated by rural blue-collar workers and families. People in this segment are more likely to go hunting, buy hard rock music, drive a Dodge Ram, watch the Daytona 500 on TV, and read *North American Hunter*.

Such segmentation provides a powerful tool for marketers of all kinds. It can help companies to identify and better understand key customer segments, target them more efficiently, and tailor market offerings and messages to their specific needs.

▲ Using Claritas's PRIZM NE system, marketers can paint a surprisingly precise picture of who you are and what you might buy. PRIZM NE segments carry such exotic names as "Kids & Cul-de-Sacs," "Gray Power," "Blue Blood Estates," "Shotguns & Pickups," and "Bright Lites L'il City."

Segmenting Business Markets

Consumer and business marketers use many of the same variables to segment their markets. Business buyers can be segmented geographically, demographically (industry, company size), or by benefits sought, user status, usage rate, and loyalty status. Yet, business marketers also use some additional variables, such as customer *operating characteristics*, *purchasing approaches*, *situational factors*, and *personal characteristics*. By going after segments instead of the whole market, companies can deliver just the right value proposition to each segment served and capture more value in return.

▲ Segmenting business markets: For small business customers, American Express has created the OPEN: The Small Business Network, "The one place that's all about small business."

Within the image:

BUSINESS

3782 456789 01001

03/04   88
J H MILLER
MILLER AND ASSOCIATES

This helps you buy what your small business needs.

www.OPEN.americanexpress.com

OPEN SMALL BUSINESS NETWORK

This lets you track, organize, categorize, subdivide, examine, break down, cross-reference, combine and archive online what your small business spends.

Now you can access the Expense Management Report and many other online tools. But only if you have the American Express® Business Card. The Card with the savings, rewards and services of OPEN: The Small Business Network℠ behind it. **Apply now and get an instant decision. Visit OPEN.AMERICANEXPRESS.COM.**

Almost every company serves at least some business markets. For example, American Express targets businesses in three segments—merchants, corporations, and small businesses. It has developed distinct marketing programs for each segment. In the merchants segment, American Express focuses on convincing new merchants to accept the card and on managing relationships with those that already do. For larger corporate customers, the company offers a corporate card program, which includes extensive employee expense and travel management services. It also offers this segment a wide range of asset management, retirement planning, and financial education services.

Finally, for small business customers, ▲American Express has created OPEN: The Small Business Network, a system of small business cards and financial services. It includes credit cards and lines of credit, special usage rewards, financial monitoring and spending report features, and 24/7 customized financial support services. "OPEN is how we serve small business," says American Express.[14]

Many companies set up separate systems for dealing with larger or multiple-location customers. For example, Steelcase, a major producer of office furniture, first segments customers into 10 industries, including banking, insurance, and electronics. Next, company salespeople work with independent Steelcase dealers to handle smaller, local, or regional Steelcase customers in each segment. But many national, multiple-location customers, such as ExxonMobile or IBM, have special needs that may reach beyond the scope of individual dealers. So Steelcase uses national account managers to help its dealer networks handle its national accounts.

Within a given target industry and customer size, the company can segment by purchase approaches and criteria. As in consumer segmentation, many marketers believe that *buying behavior* and *benefits* provide the best basis for segmenting business markets.[15]

Segmenting International Markets

Few companies have either the resources or the will to operate in all, or even most, of the countries that dot the globe. Although some large companies, such as Coca-Cola or Sony, sell products in more than 200 countries, most international firms focus on a smaller set. Operating in many countries presents new challenges. Different countries, even those that are close together, can vary greatly in their economic, cultural, and political makeup. Thus, just as they do within their domestic markets, international firms need to group their world markets into segments with distinct buying needs and behaviors.

Companies can segment international markets using one or a combination of several variables. They can segment by *geographic location*, grouping countries by regions such as Western Europe, the Pacific Rim, the Middle East, or Africa. Geographic segmentation assumes that nations close to one another will have many common traits and behaviors. Although this is often the case, there are many exceptions. For example, although the United States and Canada have much in common, both differ culturally and economically from neighboring Mexico. Even within a region, consumers can differ widely. For example, some U.S. marketers lump all Central and South American countries together. However, the Dominican Republic is no more like Brazil than Italy is like Sweden. Many Central and South Americans don't even speak Spanish, including 188 million Portuguese-speaking Brazilians and the millions in other countries who speak a variety of Indian dialects.

World markets can also be segmented on the basis of *economic factors*. For example, countries might be grouped by population income levels or by their overall level of economic development. A country's economic structure shapes its population's product and service needs and, therefore, the marketing opportunities it offers. Countries can be segmented by *political and legal factors* such as the type and stability of government, receptivity to foreign firms, monetary regulations, and amount of bureaucracy. *Cultural factors* can also be used, grouping markets according to common languages, religions, values and attitudes, customs, and behavioral patterns.

Segmenting international markets based on geographic, economic, political, cultural, and other factors assumes that segments should consist of clusters of countries. However, as new communications technologies, such as satellite TV and the Internet, connect consumers around the world, marketers can define and reach segments of like-minded consumers no matter where in the world they are. Using **intermarket segmentation** (also called *cross-market segmentation*), they form segments of consumers who have similar needs and buying behaviors even though they are located in different countries. For example, Lexus targets the world's well-to-do—the "global elite" segment—regardless of their country. Swedish furniture giant IKEA targets the aspiring global middle class—it sells good-quality furniture that ordinary people worldwide can afford. And Coca-Cola creates special programs to target teens, core consumers of its soft drinks the world over.[16]

> Coca-Cola wants to relate to the world's teens. To accomplish that, the global soft drink marketer needed to figure out what the majority of teens finds appealing. The answer: music. So, throughout the world, Coca-Cola links itself with the local pop music scene. For example, in the United States, Coke is the official sponsor of *American Idol*, the country's number-one television show and a teen magnet. In the Middle East, Coca-Cola commercials feature Arab pop stars, such as Nancy Ajram—Coca-Cola even sponsors her world tour. In Europe, Coke has created the Coca-Cola Music Network, which features signed and unsigned musicians online at CokeMusic.com, on stage, and in podcasts. And in Uganda, Coca-Cola sponsored the search for a new MTV VJ. The recent winner, Carol Mugasha, became host of the national weekly music chart show *MTV Coca-Cola Chart Express*.

Intermarket segmentation

Forming segments of consumers who have similar needs and buying behavior even though they are located in different countries.

Requirements for Effective Segmentation

Clearly, there are many ways to segment a market, but not all segmentations are effective. For example, buyers of table salt could be divided into blond and brunette customers. But hair color obviously does not affect the purchase of salt. Furthermore, if all salt buyers bought the same amount of salt each month, believed that all salt is the same, and wanted to pay the same price, the company would not benefit from segmenting this market.

To be useful, market segments must be

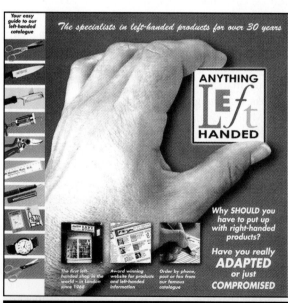

▲ The "Leftie" segment can be hard to identify and measure. As a result, few companies tailor their offers to left-handers. However, some nichers such as Anything Left-Handed in the United Kingdom target this segment.

- *Measurable:* The size, purchasing power, and profiles of the segments can be measured. Certain segmentation variables are difficult to measure. ▲ For example, there are 32.5 million left-handed people in the United States—almost equaling the entire population of Canada. Yet few products are targeted toward this left-handed segment. The major problem may be that the segment is hard to identify and measure. There are no data on the demographics of lefties, and the U.S. Census Bureau does not keep track of left-handedness in its surveys. Private data companies keep reams of statistics on other demographic segments but not on left-handers.

- *Accessible:* The market segments can be effectively reached and served. Suppose a fragrance company finds that heavy users of its brand are single men and women who stay out late and socialize a lot. Unless this group lives or shops at certain places and is exposed to certain media, its members will be difficult to reach.

- *Substantial:* The market segments are large or profitable enough to serve. A segment should be the largest possible homogenous group worth pursuing with a tailored marketing program. It would not pay, for example, for an automobile manufacturer to develop cars especially for people whose height is greater than seven feet.

- *Differentiable:* The segments are conceptually distinguishable and respond differently to different marketing mix elements and programs. If married and unmarried women respond similarly to a sale on perfume, they do not constitute separate segments.

- *Actionable:* Effective programs can be designed for attracting and serving the segments. For example, although one small airline identified seven market segments, its staff was too small to develop separate marketing programs for each segment.

Author Comment | Now that we've divided the market into segments, it's time to answer that first seemingly simple marketing strategy question we raised in Figure 7.1: Which customers will the company serve?

Market Targeting (pp 201–209)

Market segmentation reveals the firm's market segment opportunities. The firm now has to evaluate the various segments and decide how many and which segments it can serve best. We now look at how companies evaluate and select target segments.

Evaluating Market Segments

In evaluating different market segments, a firm must look at three factors: segment size and growth, segment structural attractiveness, and company objectives and resources. The company must first collect and analyze data on current segment sales, growth rates, and expected profitability for various segments. It will be interested in segments that have the right size and growth characteristics.

But "right size and growth" is a relative matter. The largest, fastest-growing segments are not always the most attractive ones for every company. Smaller companies may lack the skills and resources needed to serve the larger segments. Or they may find these segments too competitive. Such companies may target segments that are smaller and less attractive, in an absolute sense, but that are potentially more profitable for them.

The company also needs to examine major structural factors that affect long-run segment attractiveness.[17] For example, a segment is less attractive if it already contains many strong and aggressive *competitors*. The existence of many actual or potential *substitute products* may limit prices and the profits that can be earned in a segment. The relative *power of buyers* also affects segment attractiveness. Buyers with strong bargaining power relative to sellers will try to force prices down, demand more services, and set competitors against one another—all at the expense of seller profitability. Finally, a segment may be less attractive if it contains *powerful suppliers* who can control prices or reduce the quality or quantity of ordered goods and services.

Even if a segment has the right size and growth and is structurally attractive, the company must consider its own objectives and resources. Some attractive segments can be dismissed quickly because they do not mesh with the company's long-run objectives. Or the company may lack the skills and resources needed to succeed in an attractive segment. For example, given current economic conditions, the economy segment of the automobile market is large and growing. But given its objectives and resources, it would make little sense for luxury-performance carmaker BMW to enter this segment. A company should enter only segments in which it can create superior customer value and gain advantages over competitors.

Selecting Target Market Segments

Target market
A set of buyers sharing common needs or characteristics that the company decides to serve.

After evaluating different segments, the company must decide which and how many segments it will target. A **target market** consists of a set of buyers who share common needs or characteristics that the company decides to serve. Market targeting can be carried out at several different levels. **Figure 7.2** shows that companies can target very broadly (undifferentiated marketing), very narrowly (micromarketing), or somewhere in between (differentiated or concentrated marketing).

Undifferentiated (mass) marketing
A market-coverage strategy in which a firm decides to ignore market segment differences and go after the whole market with one offer.

Undifferentiated Marketing

Using an **undifferentiated marketing** (or **mass-marketing**) strategy, a firm might decide to ignore market segment differences and target the whole market with one offer. This mass-marketing strategy focuses on what is *common* in the needs of consumers rather than

FIGURE | 7.2
Marketing Targeting Strategies

This figure covers a pretty broad range of targeting strategies, from mass marketing (virtually no targeting) to individual marketing (customizing products and programs to individual customers). An example of individual marketing: At myMMs.com you can order a batch of M&Ms with your face and personal message printed on each little candy.

Targeting broadly

Targeting narrowly

on what is *different*. The company designs a product and a marketing program that will appeal to the largest number of buyers.

As noted earlier in the chapter, most modern marketers have strong doubts about this strategy. Difficulties arise in developing a product or brand that will satisfy all consumers. Moreover, mass marketers often have trouble competing with more-focused firms that do a better job of satisfying the needs of specific segments and niches.

Differentiated Marketing

Differentiated (segmented) marketing

A market-coverage strategy in which a firm decides to target several market segments and designs separate offers for each.

Using a **differentiated marketing** (or **segmented marketing**) strategy, a firm decides to target several market segments and designs separate offers for each. General Motors tries to produce a car for every "purse, purpose, and personality." Procter & Gamble markets six different laundry detergent brands, which compete with each other on supermarket shelves. ▲ And VF Corporation offers a closet full of more than 30 premium lifestyle brands, each of which "taps into consumer aspirations to fashion, status, and well-being" in a well-defined segment.[18]

VF is the nation's number-one jeans maker, with brands such as Lee, Riders, Rustler, and Wrangler. But jeans are not the only focus for VF. The company's brands are carefully separated into five major segments—Jeanswear, Imagewear (workwear), Outdoor, Sportswear, and Contemporary Brands. The North Face, part of the Outdoor unit, offers top-of-the-line gear and apparel for diehard outdoor enthusiasts, especially those who prefer cold weather activities. From the Sportswear unit, Nautica focuses on people who enjoy high-end casual apparel inspired by sailing and the sea. Vans began as a skate shoe maker, and Reef features surf-inspired footwear and apparel. In the Contemporary Brands unit, Lucy features upscale activewear, whereas 7 for All Mankind supplies premium denim and accessories sold in boutiques and high-end department stores such as Saks and Nordstrom. At the other end of the spectrum, Sentinel, part of the Imagewear unit, markets uniforms for security officers.

By offering product and marketing variations to segments, companies hope for higher sales and a stronger position within each market segment. Developing a stronger position within several segments creates more total sales than undifferentiated marketing across all segments. VF Coporation's combined brands give it a much greater, more stable market share than any single brand could. The four Jeanswear brands alone account for a quarter of all jeans sold in the United States. Similarly, Procter & Gamble's multiple detergent brands capture four times the market share of nearest rival Unilever (see **Real Marketing 7.1**).

But differentiated marketing also increases the costs of doing business. A firm usually finds it more expensive to develop and produce, say, 10 units of 10 different products than 100 units of one product. Developing separate marketing plans for the separate segments requires extra marketing research, forecasting, sales analysis, promotion

▲ Differentiated marketing: VF Corporation offers a closet full of over 30 premium lifestyle brands, each of which "taps into consumer aspirations to fashion, status, and well-being" in a well-defined segment.

Real Marketing 7.1

P&G:
Competing with Itself—and Winning

Differentiated marketing: Procter & Gamble markets six different laundry detergents, including Tide—each with multiple forms and formulations—that compete with each other on store shelves. Yet together, these multiple brands capture four times the market share of nearest rival Unilever.

Procter & Gamble is one of the world's premier consumer-goods companies. Some 99 percent of all U.S. households use at least one of P&G's 86 U.S. brands. Around the world, 156 P&G brands touch the lives of people some three billion times a day.

P&G sells six brands of laundry detergent in the United States (Tide, Cheer, Gain, Era, Dreft, and Ivory). It also sells six brands of bath soap (Ivory, Safeguard, Camay, Olay, Zest, and Old Spice); five brands of shampoo (Pantene, Head & Shoulders, Aussie, Herbal Essences, and Infusium 23); four brands of dishwashing detergent (Dawn, Ivory, Joy, and Cascade); three brands each of tissues and towels (Charmin, Bounty, and Puffs) and skin care products (Olay, Gillette Complete Skincare, and Noxzema); and two brands each of deodorant (Secret and Old Spice), fabric softener (Downy and Bounce), cosmetics (Cover Girl and Max Factor), and disposable diapers (Pampers and Luvs).

Moreover, P&G has many additional brands in each category for different international markets. For example, it sells 16 different laundry product brands in Latin America and 19 in Europe, the Middle East, and Africa. (See P&G's Web site at www.pg.com for a full glimpse of the company's impressive lineup of familiar brands.)

These P&G brands compete with one another on the same supermarket shelves. But why would P&G introduce several brands in one category instead of concentrating its resources on a single leading brand? The answer lies in the fact that different people want different *mixes of benefits* from the products they buy. Take laundry detergents as an example. People use laundry detergents to get their clothes clean. But they also want other things from their detergents—such as economy, strength or mildness, bleaching power, fabric softening, fresh smell, and lots of suds or only a few. We all want *some* of every one of these benefits from our detergent, but we may have different *priorities* for each benefit. To some people, cleaning and bleaching power are most important; to others, fabric softening matters most. Still others want a mild, fresh-scented detergent. Thus,

each segment of laundry detergent buyers seeks a special combination of benefits.

Procter & Gamble has identified at least six important laundry detergent segments, along with numerous subsegments, and has developed a different brand designed to meet the special needs of each. The six brands are positioned for different segments as follows:

- *Tide* "knows fabrics best." It's the all-purpose family detergent that "gets to the bottom of dirt and stains to help keep your whites white and your colors bright."
- *Cheer* is the "color expert." "Dirt goes. Color stays." It helps protect against fading, color transfer, and fabric wear, with or without bleach. *Cheer Free* is "dermatologist tested . . . contains no irritating perfume or dye."
- *Gain*, originally P&G's "enzyme" detergent, was repositioned as the detergent that gives you "excellent cleaning power and a smell that says clean."
- *Era* is "a powerful laundry detergent that is tough on stains." It's "the power tool for stain removal and pretreating that helps combat many stains that families encounter."
- *Ivory* is "Ninety-nine and forty-four one-hundredths percent pure." It provides "mild cleansing benefits for a gentle, pure, and simple clean."
- *Dreft* is specially formulated "to help clean tough baby and toddler stains." It

"rinses out thoroughly, leaving clothes soft next to a baby's delicate skin."

Within each segment, Procter & Gamble has identified even *narrower* niches. For example, you can buy regular Tide (in powder or liquid form) or any of more than 40 different formulations, including the following:

- *Tide Powder* helps keep everyday laundry clean and new. It comes in original and special scents: *Tide Mountain Spring* ("the scent of crisp mountain air and fresh wildflowers"), *Tide Clean Breeze* (the fresh scent of laundry line-dried in a clean breeze), *Tide Tropical Clean* (a fresh tropical scent that soothes, relaxes, and refreshes), and *Tide Free* ("has no scent at all—leaves out the dyes or perfumes").
- *Tide Liquid* combines all the great stain-fighting qualities you've come to expect in Tide powder with the pretreating ease of a liquid detergent. Available in original and Mountain Spring, Clean Breeze, Tropical Clean, and Free scents.
- *Tide with Bleach* helps to "clean even the dirtiest laundry without the damaging effects of chlorine bleach." Keeps "your family's whites white and colors bright." Available in Clean Breeze or Mountain Spring scents.
- *Tide Pure Essentials* contains baking soda, "one of nature's symbols for cleaning,

Continued on next page

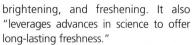

brightening, and freshening. It also "leverages advances in science to offer long-lasting freshness."

- *Tide Liquid with Bleach Alternative* is the "smart alternative to chlorine bleach." It uses active enzymes in pretreating and washing to break down and remove the toughest stains while whitening whites.
- *Tide Simple Pleasures* is a collection of laundry detergents with naturally inspired scents for a "relaxing, refreshing, romantic, or uplifting experience."
- *Tide with a Touch of Downy* provides "outstanding Tide clean with a touch of Downy softness and freshness." Available in April Fresh and Clean Breeze.
- *Tide Coldwater* is specially formulated to help reduce your energy bills by delivering outstanding cleaning, even on the toughest stains, in cold water. Available

in both liquid and powder formulas and in two new cool scents—Fresh Scent and Mountain Spring.

- *Tide HE* is specially formulated to unlock the cleaning potential of high-efficiency washers and provides excellent cleaning with the right level of sudsing. Available in Original, Free, and Clean Breeze scents.
- *2X Ultra Tide* is double-concentrated to provide the same cleaning power as regular Tide. One small capful gets your whole wash clean. P&G now offers 2X Ultra versions of all of its major liquid Tide sub-brands.

By segmenting the market and having several detergent brands, Procter & Gamble has an attractive offering for consumers in all important preference groups. As a result, P&G is really cleaning up in the $3.6 billion U.S. laundry detergent market. Tide, by itself, captures a whopping 44 percent of the detergent market and growing. All P&G brands combined take an impressive 62 percent market share—forcing major competitors Unilever and Colgate to throw in the towel and sell off their laundry detergent brands in the U.S. market.

Sources: See Ellen Byron, "How P&G Led Also-Ran to Sweet Smell of Success; By Focusing on Fragrance, Gain Detergent Developed a Billion-Dollar Following," *Wall Street Journal*, September 4, 2007, p. B2; Jack Neff, "Why Unilever Lost the Laundry War," *Advertising Age*, August 6, 2007, p.1; and information accessed at www.pg. com and www.tide.com, September 2008.

planning, and channel management. And trying to reach different market segments with different advertising campaigns increases promotion costs. Thus, the company must weigh increased sales against increased costs when deciding on a differentiated marketing strategy.

Concentrated Marketing

Concentrated (niche) marketing
A market-coverage strategy in which a firm goes after a large share of one or a few segments or niches.

Using a **concentrated marketing** (or **niche marketing**) strategy, instead of going after a small share of a large market, the firm goes after a large share of one or a few smaller segments or niches. For example, Whole Foods Market has only about 275 stores and $6.5 billion in sales, compared with goliaths such as Kroger (more than 3,000 stores and sales of $66 billion) and Wal-Mart (7,300 stores and sales of $379 billion).[19] Yet the smaller, upscale retailer is growing faster and more profitably than either of its giant rivals. Whole Foods thrives by catering to affluent customers who the Wal-Marts of the world can't serve well, offering them "organic, natural, and gourmet foods, all swaddled in Earth Day politics." In fact, a typical Whole Foods customer is more likely to boycott the local Wal-Mart than to shop at it.

Through concentrated marketing, the firm achieves a strong market position because of its greater knowledge of consumer needs in the niches it serves and the special reputation it acquires. It can market more *effectively* by fine-tuning its products, prices, and programs to the needs of carefully defined segments. It can also market more *efficiently*, targeting its products or services, channels, and communications programs toward only consumers that it can serve best and most profitably.

Whereas segments are fairly large and normally attract several competitors, niches are smaller and may attract only one or a few competitors. Niching lets smaller companies focus their limited resources on serving niches that may be unimportant to or overlooked by larger competitors. Many companies start as nichers to get a foothold against larger, more-resourceful competitors and then grow into broader competitors. For example, Southwest Airlines began by serving intrastate, no-frills commuters in Texas but is now one of the nation's largest airlines. And Enterprise Rent-A-Car began by building a network of neighborhood offices rather competing with Hertz and Avis in airport locations. Enterprise is now the nation's largest car rental company.

In contrast, as markets change, some megamarketers develop niche markets to create sales growth. For example, in recent years, Pepsi has introduced several niche products, such as Sierra Mist, Pepsi Twist, Mountain Dew Code Red, and Mountain Dew LiveWire. Initially, these brands combined accounted for barely 5 percent of Pepsi's overall soft-drink sales. However, Sierra Mist quickly blossomed and now is the number-two lemon-lime soft drink behind Sprite, and Code Red and LiveWire have revitalized the Mountain Dew brand. Says Pepsi-Cola North America's chief marketing officer, "The era of the mass brand has been over for a long time."[20]

Today, the low cost of setting up shop on the Internet makes it even more profitable to serve seemingly miniscule niches. Small businesses, in particular, are realizing riches from serving small niches on the Web. ▲Consider Zappos:

▲ Concentrated marketing: Web niching is paying off handsomely for Zappos and its CEO/Founder Tony Hsieh.

Zappos began by selling shoes online—*only* shoes and *only* online. What gives this online nicher an edge? First, Zappos differentiates itself by its selection: Click to the Zappos site and you can pick through some 3.2 million items representing 950 shoe brands—more inventory than any brick-and-mortar shoe peddler could dream of offering. Zappos also gives you convenience: The warehouse is open 24/7, so you can order as late as 11:00 p.m. and still get next-day delivery. Most important, Zappos has a near-fanatical devotion to pleasing its customers. "We offer the absolute best selection of shoes available anywhere," boasts the company, "but much more important to us is offering the absolute best service." Shipping and return shipping are free and you just can't beat the company's heartfelt returns policy: "If the shoe fits, wear it. If not, ship it back at our expense." All this adds up to a host of satisfied customers. "With Zappos, the shoe store comes to you," says Pamela Leo, a customer in Montclair, New Jersey "I can try the shoes on in the comfort of my own home. I can tell if the shoes I want will really work with a particular suit. It's fabulous." And if the shoes aren't just right, she can click on a Zappos-supplied link to print out a prepaid return shipping label. Web niching is paying off handsomely for Zappos. Although it captures only a small portion of the total $40 billion U.S. shoe market, Zappos is now the Web's number-one shoe seller. Thanks to happy customers like Pamela, sales have soared from "almost nothing" in 1999 to an estimated $1 billion this year. And based on its success in shoes, Zappos is now launching into clothing and other lines.[21]

Concentrated marketing can be highly profitable. At the same time, it involves higher-than-normal risks. Companies that rely on one or a few segments for all of their business will suffer greatly if the segment turns sour. Or larger competitors may decide to enter the same segment with greater resources. For these reasons, many companies prefer to diversify in several market segments.

Micromarketing

Differentiated and concentrated marketers tailor their offers and marketing programs to meet the needs of various market segments and niches. At the same time, however, they do not customize their offers to each individual customer. **Micromarketing** is the practice of tailoring products and marketing programs to suit the tastes of specific individuals and locations. Rather than seeing a customer in every individual, micromarketers see the individual in every customer. Micromarketing includes *local marketing* and *individual marketing*.

Local Marketing. **Local marketing** involves tailoring brands and promotions to the needs and wants of local customer groups—cities, neighborhoods, and even specific stores. For example, Wal-Mart customizes its merchandise store by store to meet the needs of local shoppers. Wal-Mart's store designers create each new store's format according to neighborhood characteristics—stores near office parks, for instance, contain prominent islands featuring ready-made meals for busy workers. Then, using a wealth of customer data on daily sales in every store, Wal-Mart tailors individual store merchandise with similar precision. For example, it uses more than 200 finely tuned planograms (shelf plans) to match soup assortments to each store's demand patterns.[22]

Micromarketing
The practice of tailoring products and marketing programs to the needs and wants of specific individuals and local customer groups—includes *local marketing* and *individual marketing*.

Local marketing
Tailoring brands and promotions to the needs and wants of local customer groups—cities, neighborhoods, and even specific stores.

Advances in communications technology have given rise to a new high-tech version of location-based marketing. By coupling mobile phone services with GPS devices, many marketers are now targeting customers wherever they are with what they want.[23]

▲ Local marketing: By coupling mobile phone services with GPS devices, marketers like Starbucks are now targeting customers wherever they are with what they want.

Location. Location. Location. This is the mantra of the real estate business. But it may not be long before marketers quote it, too. "Location-based technology allows [marketers] to reach people when they're mobile, near their stores, looking to make a decision," says one marketing expert. "When customers get information—even advertising information—linked to their location, research shows that's often perceived as value-added information, not as an advertisement." ▲For example, Starbucks recently launched a store locator service for mobile devices, which allows people to use their phones and in-car GPS systems to search for the nearest Starbucks shop. A consumer sends a text message to "MYSBUX" (697289) including his or her zip code. Within 10 seconds, Starbucks replies with up to three nearby store locations. Starbucks plans to expand the service to include a wider range of text-messaging conversations with local customers that will "showcase Starbucks as a brand that truly listens." Such location-based marketing will grow astronomically as the sales of GPS devices skyrocket.

Local marketing has some drawbacks. It can drive up manufacturing and marketing costs by reducing economies of scale. It can also create logistics problems as companies try to meet the varied requirements of different regional and local markets. Further, a brand's overall image might be diluted if the product and message vary too much in different localities.

Still, as companies face increasingly fragmented markets, and as new supporting technologies develop, the advantages of local marketing often outweigh the drawbacks. Local marketing helps a company to market more effectively in the face of pronounced regional and local differences in demographics and lifestyles. It also meets the needs of the company's first-line customers—retailers—who prefer more finely tuned product assortments for their neighborhoods.

Individual marketing

Tailoring products and marketing programs to the needs and preferences of individual customers—also labeled "one-to-one marketing," "customized marketing," and "markets-of-one marketing."

Individual Marketing. In the extreme, micromarketing becomes **individual marketing**—tailoring products and marketing programs to the needs and preferences of individual customers. Individual marketing has also been labeled *one-to-one marketing*, *mass customization*, and *markets-of-one marketing*.

The widespread use of mass marketing has obscured the fact that for centuries consumers were served as individuals: The tailor custom-made the suit, the cobbler designed shoes for the individual, the cabinetmaker-made furniture to order. Today, however, new technologies are permitting many companies to return to customized marketing. More powerful computers, detailed databases, robotic production and flexible manufacturing, and interactive communication media such as cell phones and the Internet—all have combined to foster "mass customization." *Mass customization* is the process through which firms interact one-to-one with masses of customers to design products and services tailor-made to individual needs.

Dell creates custom-configured computers. Hockey-stick maker Branches Hockey lets customers choose from more than two dozen options—including stick length, blade patterns, and blade curve—and turns out a customized stick in five days. Visitors to Nike's NikeID Web site can personalize their sneakers by choosing from hundreds of colors and putting an embroidered word or phrase on the tongue. At www.myMMs.com, you can upload your photo and order a batch of M&Ms with your face and a personal message printed on each little candy. Toyota even lets Scion owners design their own personal "coat of arms" online, "a piece of owner-generated art that is meant to reflect their own job, hobbies, and—um, okay—Karma." Customers can download their designs and have them made into window decals or professionally airbrushed onto their cars.[24]

Marketers are also finding new ways to personalize promotional messages. For example, plasma screens placed in shopping malls around the country can now analyze shoppers'

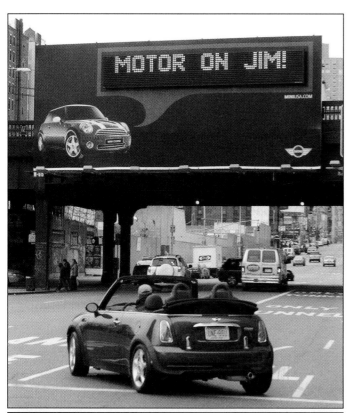

▲ Individual marketing: MINI even uses personalized billboard messages to greet MINI drivers in selected major cities. The messages are triggered by personalized key fobs given to MINI owners.

faces and place ads based on an individual shopper's gender, age, or ethnicity. ▲Last year, MINI USA even began using personalized billboard messages to greet MINI drivers in four major cities. The messages are triggered by personalized key fobs given to new buyers. As the new MINI owner passes by, the fob contacts the billboard database, which then transmits a message such as "Motor on Jim!" or "Great day to be a lawyer in New York, Jim!"[25]

Business-to-business marketers are also finding new ways to customize their offerings. For example, John Deere manufactures seeding equipment that can be configured in more than two million versions to individual customer specifications. The seeders are produced one at a time, in any sequence, on a single production line. Mass customization provides a way to stand out against competitors.

Unlike mass production, which eliminates the need for human interaction, one-to-one marketing has made relationships with customers more important than ever. Just as mass production was the marketing principle of the past century, interactive marketing is becoming a marketing principle for the twenty-first century. The world appears to be coming full circle—from the good old days when customers were treated as individuals, to mass marketing when nobody knew your name, and back again.

The move toward individual marketing mirrors the trend in consumer *self-marketing*. Increasingly, individual customers are taking more responsibility for shaping both the products they buy and the buying experience. Consider two business buyers with two different purchasing styles. The first sees several salespeople, each trying to persuade him to buy his or her product. The second sees no salespeople but rather logs on to the Web. She searches for information on available products; interacts online with various suppliers, users, and product analysts; and then decides which offer is best. The second purchasing agent has taken more responsibility for the buying process, and the marketer has had less influence over the buying decision.

As the trend toward more interactive dialogue and less marketing monologue continues, marketers will need to influence the buying process in new ways. They will need to involve customers more in all phases of the product development and buying processes, increasing opportunities for buyers to practice self-marketing.

Choosing a Targeting Strategy

Companies need to consider many factors when choosing a market-targeting strategy. Which strategy is best depends on *company resources*. When the firm's resources are limited, concentrated marketing makes the most sense. The best strategy also depends on the degree of *product variability*. Undifferentiated marketing is more suited for uniform products such as grapefruit or steel. Products that can vary in design, such as cameras and automobiles, are more suited to differentiation or concentration. The *product's life-cycle stage* also must be considered. When a firm introduces a new product, it may be practical to launch only one version, and undifferentiated marketing or concentrated marketing may make the most sense. In the mature stage of the product life cycle, however, differentiated marketing begins to make more sense.

Another factor is *market variability*. If most buyers have the same tastes, buy the same amounts, and react the same way to marketing efforts, undifferentiated marketing is appropriate. Finally, *competitors' marketing strategies* are important. When competitors use differentiated or concentrated marketing, undifferentiated marketing can be suicidal. Conversely, when competitors use undifferentiated marketing, a firm can gain an advantage by using differentiated or concentrated marketing, focusing on the needs of buyers in specific segments.

Socially Responsible Target Marketing

Smart targeting helps companies to be more efficient and effective by focusing on the segments that they can satisfy best and most profitably. Targeting also benefits consumers—companies serve specific groups of consumers with offers carefully tailored to their needs. However, target marketing sometimes generates controversy and concern. The biggest issues usually involve the targeting of vulnerable or disadvantaged consumers with controversial or potentially harmful products.

For example, over the years, marketers in a wide range of industries—from cereal and toys to fast food and fashion—have been heavily criticized for their marketing efforts directed toward children. Critics worry that premium offers and high-powered advertising appeals presented through the mouths of lovable animated characters will overwhelm children's defenses.

▲ Socially responsible targeting: Victoria's Secret targets its Pink line of young, hip, and sexy clothing to young women 18 to 30 years old. However, critics charge that Pink is now all the rage among girls as young as 11.

Other problems arise when the marketing of adult products spills over into the kid segment—intentionally or unintentionally. ▲For example, Victoria's Secret targets its Pink line of young, hip, and sexy clothing to young women 18 to 30 years old. However, critics charge that Pink is now all the rage among girls as young as 11. Responding to Victoria's Secret's designs and marketing messages, tweens are flocking into stores and buying Pink, with or without their mothers. More broadly, critics worry that marketers of everything from lingerie and cosmetics to Barbie dolls are directly or indirectly targeting young girls with provocative products, promoting a premature focus on sex and appearance.

Ten-year-old girls can slide their low-cut jeans over "eye-candy" panties. French maid costumes, garter belt included, are available in preteen sizes. Barbie now comes in a "bling-bling" style, replete with halter top and go-go boots. And it's not unusual for girls under 12 to sing, "Don't cha wish your girlfriend was hot like me?" American girls, say experts, are increasingly being fed a cultural catnip of products and images that promote looking and acting sexy. "The message we're telling our girls is a simple one," laments one reporter about the Victoria's Secret Pink line. "You'll have a great life if people find you sexually attractive. Grown women struggle enough with this ridiculous standard. Do we really need to start worrying about it at 11?"[26]

The Federal Trade Commission (FTC) and citizen action groups have accused tobacco and beer companies of targeting underage smokers and drinkers. For instance, a recent Adbowl poll found that in the most recent Super Bowl, Bud Light and Budweiser ads ranked first through fourth in popularity among viewers under age 17. Another study found that more than a third of alcohol radio ads are more likely to be heard by underage listeners than adults on a per capita basis.[27] Some critics have even called for a complete ban on advertising to children. To encourage responsible advertising, the Children's Advertising Review Unit, the advertising industry's self-regulatory agency, has published extensive children's advertising guidelines that recognize the special needs of child audiences.

Cigarette, beer, and fast-food marketers have also generated much controversy in recent years by their attempts to target inner-city minority consumers. For example, McDonald's and other chains have drawn criticism for pitching their high-fat, salt-laden fare to low-income, urban residents who are much more likely than suburbanites to be heavy consumers. Similarly, R.J. Reynolds took heavy flak in the early 1990s when it announced plans to market Uptown, a menthol cigarette targeted toward low-income blacks. It quickly dropped the brand in the face of a loud public outcry and heavy pressure from African-American leaders.

The growth of the Internet and other carefully targeted direct media has raised fresh concerns about potential targeting abuses. The Internet allows increasing refinement of audiences and, in turn, more precise targeting. This might help makers of questionable products or deceptive advertisers to more readily victimize the most vulnerable audiences. Unscrupulous marketers can now send tailor-made deceptive messages directly to the computers of millions of unsuspecting consumers. For example, the FBI's Internet Crime Complaint Center Web site alone received more than 207,000 complaints last year.[28]

Not all attempts to target children, minorities, or other special segments draw such criticism. In fact, most provide benefits to targeted consumers. For example, Pantene markets Relaxed and Natural hair products to women of color. Samsung markets the Jitterbug phone directly to seniors who need a simpler cell phone that is bigger and has a louder speaker. And Colgate makes a large selection of toothbrush shapes and toothpaste flavors for children—from Colgate Shrek Bubble Fruit toothpaste to Colgate Bratz character toothbrushes. Such products help make tooth brushing more fun and get children to brush longer and more often.

Thus, in target marketing, the issue is not really *who* is targeted but rather *how* and for *what*. Controversies arise when marketers attempt to profit at the expense of targeted segments—when they unfairly target vulnerable segments or target them with questionable products or tactics. Socially responsible marketing calls for segmentation and targeting that serve not just the interests of the company but also the interests of those targeted.

Author Comment | At the same time that it's answering the first simple-sounding question (Which customers will we serve?), the company must be asking the second question (How will we serve them?). For example, Ritz-Carlton serves the top 5 percent of corporate and leisure travelers. Its value proposition is "The Ritz-Carlton Experience"—one that "enlivens the senses, instills a sense of well-being, and fulfills even the unexpressed wishes and needs of our guests."

Product position

The way the product is defined by consumers on important attributes—the place the product occupies in consumers' minds relative to competing products.

Differentiation and Positioning (pp 209–217)

Beyond deciding which segments of the market it will target, the company must decide on a *value proposition*—on how it will create differentiated value for targeted segments and what positions it wants to occupy in those segments. A **product's position** is the way the product is *defined by consumers* on important attributes—the place the product occupies in consumers' minds relative to competing products. "Products are created in the factory, but brands are created in the mind," says a positioning expert.[29]

Tide is positioned as a powerful, all-purpose family detergent; Ivory is positioned as the gentle detergent for fine washables and baby clothes. At Subway restaurants, you "Eat Fresh"; at Olive Garden, "When You're Here, You're Family"; and at Applebee's you're "Eatin' Good in the Neighborhood." In the automobile market, the Nissan Versa and Honda Fit are positioned on economy, Mercedes and Cadillac on luxury, and Porsche and BMW on performance. Volvo positions powerfully on safety. And Toyota positions its fuel-efficient, hybrid Prius as a high-tech solution to the energy shortage. "How far will you go to save the planet?" it asks.

Consumers are overloaded with information about products and services. They cannot reevaluate products every time they make a buying decision. To simplify the buying process, consumers organize products, services, and companies into categories and "position" them in their minds. A product's position is the complex set of perceptions, impressions, and feelings that consumers have for the product compared with competing products.

Consumers position products with or without the help of marketers. But marketers do not want to leave their products' positions to chance. They must *plan* positions that will give their products the greatest advantage in selected target markets, and they must design marketing mixes to create these planned positions.

Positioning Maps

In planning their differentiation and positioning strategies, marketers often prepare *perceptual positioning maps,* which show consumer perceptions of their brands versus competing products on important buying dimensions. **Figure 7.3** shows a positioning map for the U.S. large luxury sport utility vehicle market.[30] The position of each circle on the map indicates the brand's perceived positioning on two dimensions—price and orientation (luxury versus performance). The size of each circle indicates the brand's relative market share.

Thus, customers view the original Hummer H1 (the little dot in the upper right corner) as a very high-performance SUV with a price tag to match. The market-leading Cadillac Escalade is positioned as a moderately priced large luxury SUV with a balance of luxury and performance. The Escalade is positioned on urban luxury, and in its case, "performance" probably means power and safety performance. You'll find no mention of off-road adventuring in an Escalade ad. By contrast, Range Rover and Land Cruiser are positioned on luxury with nuances of off-road performance.

For example, ▲the Toyota Land Cruiser began in 1951 as a four-wheel drive, Jeep-like vehicle designed to conquer the world's most grueling terrains and climates. In recent years, Land Cruiser has retained this adventure and performance positioning but with luxury

▲ Toyota's Land Cruiser retains some of its adventure and performance positioning but with luxury added.

added. Land Cruiser ads show the vehicle in adventurous settings, suggesting that it still has more trails to forge— "from the Dead Sea to the Himalayas," says the company's Web site. "Its husky VVT-i V8 will remind you of why Land Cruiser is a legend throughout the world." However, the company adds, "its available Bluetooth hands-free technology, DVD entertainment, and a sumptuous interior have softened its edges."

Choosing a Differentiation and Positioning Strategy

Some firms find it easy to choose a differentiation and positioning strategy. For example, a firm well known for quality in certain segments will go for this position in a new segment if there are enough buyers seeking quality. But in many cases, two or more firms will go after the same position. Then, each will have to find other ways to set itself apart. Each firm must differentiate its offer by building a unique bundle of benefits that appeals to a substantial group within the segment.

Above all else, a brand's positioning must serve the needs and preferences of well-defined target markets. For example, although both Dunkin' Donuts and Starbucks are coffee shops, they offer very different product assortments and store atmospheres. Yet each succeeds because it creates just the right value proposition for its unique mix of customers. (See **Real Marketing 7.2**).

The differentiation and positioning task consists of three steps: identifying a set of differentiating competitive advantages upon which to build a position, choosing the right competitive advantages, and selecting an overall positioning strategy. The company must then effectively communicate and deliver the chosen position to the market.

Identifying Possible Value Differences and Competitive Advantages

Competitive advantage
An advantage over competitors gained by offering greater customer value, either through lower prices or by providing more benefits that justify higher prices.

To build profitable relationships with target customers, marketers must understand customer needs better than competitors do and deliver more customer value. To the extent that a company can differentiate and position itself as providing superior customer value, it gains **competitive advantage**.

FIGURE | 7.3
Positioning Map:
Large Luxury SUVs

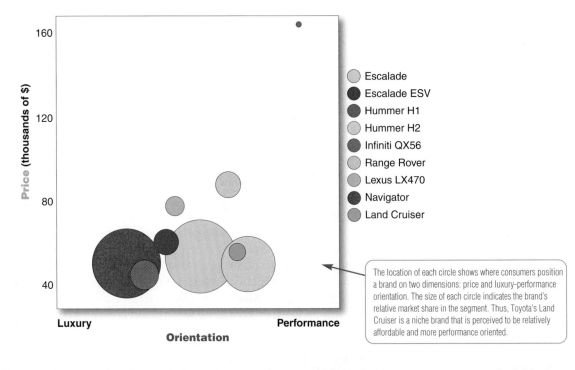

The location of each circle shows where consumers position a brand on two dimensions: price and luxury-performance orientation. The size of each circle indicates the brand's relative market share in the segment. Thus, Toyota's Land Cruiser is a niche brand that is perceived to be relatively affordable and more performance oriented.

Real Marketing 7.2

Dunkin' Donuts:
Positioning for the Average Joe

Dunkin' Donuts recently paid dozens of faithful customers in Phoenix, Chicago, and Charlotte, North Carolina, $100 a week to buy coffee at Starbucks instead. At the same time, the no-frills coffee chain paid Starbucks customers to make the opposite switch. When it later debriefed the two groups, Dunkin' says it found them so polarized that company researchers dubbed them "tribes"—each of whom loathed the very things that made the other tribe loyal to their coffee shop. Dunkin' fans viewed Starbucks as pretentious and trendy, whereas Starbucks loyalists saw Dunkin' as plain and unoriginal. "I don't get it," one Dunkin' regular told researchers after visiting Starbucks. "If I want to sit on a couch, I stay at home."

William Rosenberg opened the first Dunkin' Donuts in Quincy, Massachusetts, in 1950. Residents flocked to his store each morning for the coffee and fresh doughnuts. Rosenberg started franchising the Dunkin' Donuts name and the chain grew rapidly throughout the Midwest and Southeast. By the early 1990s, however, Dunkin' was losing breakfast sales to morning sandwiches at McDonald's and Burger King. Starbucks and other high-end cafés began sprouting up, bringing more competition. Sales slid as the company clung to its strategy of selling sugary doughnuts by the dozen.

In the mid-1990s, however, Dunkin' shifted its focus from doughnuts to coffee in the hope that promoting a more frequently consumed item would drive store traffic. The coffee push worked. Coffee now makes up 64 percent of sales—doughnuts make up a mere 17 percent of sales. Dunkin' sells 2.7 million cups of coffee a day, nearly one billion cups a year. And Dunkin's sales have surged more than 40 percent during the past four years. Based on this recent success, Dunkin' now has ambitious plans to expand into a national coffee powerhouse, on a par with Starbucks, the nation's largest coffee chain. Over the next few years, Dunkin' plans to remake its more than 5,400 U.S. shops in 34 states and to grow to double that number by 2020.

But Dunkin' is not Starbucks. In fact, it doesn't want to be. To succeed, Dunkin' must have its own clear vision of just which cus-

Differentiation and positioning: Starbucks is strongly positioned as a sort of highbrow "third place"; Dunkin' has a decidedly more low-brow, "everyman" kind of positioning. Dunkin is "not going after the Starbucks coffee snob," it's "going after the average Joe."

tomers it wants to serve (what *segments* and *targeting*) and how (what *positioning* or *value proposition*). Dunkin' and Starbucks target very different customers, who want very different things from their favorite coffee shops. Starbucks is strongly positioned as a sort of high-brow "third place"—outside the home and office—featuring couches, eclectic music, wireless Internet access, and art-splashed walls. Dunkin' has a decidedly more low-brow, "everyman" kind of positioning.

With its makeover, Dunkin' plans to move upscale—a bit but not too far—to reposition itself as a quick but appealing alternative to specialty coffee shops and fast-food chains. A prototype Dunkin' store in Euclid, Ohio, outside Cleveland features rounded granite-style coffee bars, where workers make espresso drinks face-to-face with customers. Open-air pastry cases brim with yogurt parfaits and fresh fruit, while a carefully orchestrated pop-music soundtrack is piped throughout.

Yet Dunkin' built itself on serving simple fare to working-class customers. Inching upscale without alienating that base will prove tricky. There will be no couches in the new stores. And Dunkin' renamed a new hot sandwich a "stuffed melt" after customers complained that calling it a "panini" was too fancy. "We're walking that [fine] line," says Regina Lewis, the chain's vice president of consumer insights. "The thing about the Dunkin' tribe is, they see through the hype."

Dunkin's research showed that although loyal Dunkin' customers want nicer stores,

they were bewildered and turned off by the atmosphere at Starbucks. They groused that crowds of laptop users made it difficult to find a seat. They didn't like Starbucks' "tall," "grande," and "venti" lingo for small, medium, and large coffees. And they couldn't understand why anyone would pay so much for a cup of coffee. "It was almost as though they were a group of Martians talking about a group of Earthlings," says an executive from Dunkin's ad agency. The Starbucks customers that Dunkin' paid to switch were equally uneasy in Dunkin' shops. "The Starbucks people couldn't bear that they weren't special anymore," says the ad executive.

Such opposing opinions aren't surprising, given the differences in the two stores' customers. Dunkin's customers include more middle-income blue- and white-collar workers across all age, race, and income demographics. By contrast, Starbucks targets a higher-income, more professional group. But Dunkin' researchers concluded that it wasn't income that set the two tribes apart, as much as an ideal: Dunkin' tribe members want to be part of a crowd, whereas members of the Starbucks tribe want to stand out as individuals. "You could open a Dunkin' Donuts right next to Starbucks and get two completely different types of consumers," says one retailing expert.

Based on such findings, Dunkin' executives have made dozens of store-redesign decisions, big and small, ranging from where to

Continued on next page ▼

Real Marketing 7.2 Continued ▼

put the espresso machines to how much of its signature pink and orange color scheme to retain to where to display its fresh baked goods. Out went the square laminate tables, to be replaced by round imitation-granite tabletops and sleek chairs. Dunkin' covered store walls in espresso brown and dialed down the pink and orange tones. Executives considered but held off on installing wireless Internet access because customers "just don't feel it's Dunkin' Donuts." Executives continue to discuss dropping the word "donuts" from its signs to convey that its menu is now broader.

To grab a bigger share of customer, Dunkin' is expanding its menu beyond breakfast with hearty sweet and savory snacks that can substitute for meals, such as smoothies and personal pizzas. The new Euclid store is doing three times the sales of other stores in its area, partly because more customers are coming after 11 a.m. for new gourmet cookies and flatbread sandwiches. However, whereas customers liked the flatbread sandwiches and smoothies, they balked at tiny pinwheels of dough stuffed with various fillings. Customers said "they felt like

something at a fancy cocktail hour," says Lewis, and they weren't substantial enough.

Stacey Stevens, a 34-year-old Euclid resident who recently visited the new Dunkin' prototype store, said she noticed it felt different than other Dunkin' locations. "I don't remember there being lots of music," she said, while picking up a dozen doughnuts. "I like it in here." She said it felt "more upbeat" than Starbucks. One Euclid store manager even persuaded Richard Wandersleben to upgrade from a regular coffee to a $2.39 latte during a recent visit. The 73-year-old retired tool-and-die maker, who drinks about three cups of coffee a day, says the Dunkin' Donuts latte suited him fine. "It's a little creamier" than regular coffee, he said.

Dunkin' knows that it'll take some time to refresh its positioning. And whatever else

happens, it plans to stay true to the needs and preferences of the Dunkin' tribe. Dunkin is "not going after the Starbucks coffee snob," says one analyst, it's "going after the average Joe." So far, so good. For two years running, Dunkin' Donuts has ranked number one in the coffee category in a leading customer loyalty survey, ahead of number-two Starbucks. According to the survey, Dunkin' Donuts was the top brand for consistently meeting or exceeding customer expectations.

Dunkin's positioning and value proposition are pretty well summed up in its ad slogan "America Runs on Dunkin'." The company's ads show ordinary Americans relying on the chain to get them through their day. Says one ad, "It's where everyday people get things done everyday."

Sources: Adapted from portions of Janet Adamy, "Battle Brewing: Dunkin' Donuts Tries to Go Upscale, but Not Too Far," *Wall Street Journal,* April 8, 2006, p. A1; with quotes and other information from Julie Bosman, "This Joe's for You," *New York Times,* June 8, 2006, p. C1; Chris Reidy, "The New Face of Dunkin' Donuts," *Boston Globe,* March 9, 2007; Scott Olson, "Dunkin' Donuts' Expansion May Create Coffee Clash," *Indianapolis Business Journal,* October 22, 2007, p. 22; "Dunkin' Donuts Invites Coffee Lovers to Enjoy Lattes for Less," *PR Newswire,* February 25, 2008; and www.dunkindonuts.com, September 2008.

But solid positions cannot be built on empty promises. If a company positions its product as *offering* the best quality and service, it must actually differentiate the product so that it *delivers* the promised quality and service. Companies must do much more than simply shout out their positions in ad slogans and taglines. They must first *live* the slogan. ▲For example, when Staples' research revealed that it should differentiate itself on the basis of "an easier shopping experience," the office supply retailer held back its "Staples: That was easy" marketing campaign for more than a year. First, it remade its stores to actually deliver the promised positioning.[31]

Only a few years ago, things weren't so easy for Staples—or for its customers. The ratio of customer complaints to compliments was running an abysmal eight to one at Staples stores. Weeks of focus groups produced an answer: Customers wanted an easier shopping experience. That simple revelation has resulted in one of the most successful marketing campaigns in recent history, built around the now-familiar "Staples: That was easy" tagline. But Staples' positioning turnaround took a lot more than simply bombarding customers with a new slogan. Before it could promise customers a simplified shopping experience, Staples had to actually deliver one. First, it had to *live* the slogan.

So, for more than a year, Staples worked to revamp the customer experience. It remodeled its stores, streamlined its inventory, retrained employees, and even simplified customer communications. Only when all of the customer-experience pieces were in place did Staples begin communicating its new positioning to customers. The "Staples: That was easy" repositioning campaign has met with striking success, helping to make Staples the runaway leader in office retail. And the campaign's easy button has become a pop culture icon. No doubt about it, clever marketing helped. But marketing promises count for little if not backed by the reality of the customer experience. "What has happened at the store has done more to drive the Staples brand than all the marketing in the world," says Staples' vice president of marketing.

Now there's an easy button for your business.

It's called Staples.

Wouldn't it be nice if daily tasks around the office got a little easier? When you shop Staples, it will be as easy as – well – pressing a button. Visit us at staples.com/easy to find out what our Easy Button™ can do for you today.

STAPLES

that was easy.

▲ The "Staples: That was easy" marketing campaign has played a major role in repositioning Staples. But marketing promises count for little if not backed by the reality of the customer experience.

To find points of differentiation, marketers must think through the customer's entire experience with the company's product or service. An alert company can find ways to differentiate itself at every customer contact point. In what specific ways can a company differentiate itself or its market offer? It can differentiate along the lines of *product, services, channels, people,* or *image.*

Through *product differentiation* brands can be differentiated on features, performance, or style and design. Thus, Bose positions its speakers on their striking design and sound characteristics. And Panasonic positions its Toughbook PCs, designed to stand up to rugged use on the road or in the field, as "durable, reliable, wireless—protect your work no matter where you work." The Toughbook Web site offers "Tough Stories," complete with pictures of battered and abused Toughbooks still functioning well.

Beyond differentiating its physical product, a firm can also differentiate the services that accompany the product. Some companies gain *services differentiation* through speedy, convenient, or careful delivery. For example, Commerce Bank has positioned itself as "the most convenient bank in America"—it remains open seven days a week, including evenings, and you can get a debit card while you wait. Others differentiate their service based on high-quality customer care. Lexus makes fine cars but is perhaps even better known for the quality service that creates outstanding ownership experiences for Lexus owners.

Firms that practice *channel differentiation* gain competitive advantage through the way they design their channel's coverage, expertise, and performance. Amazon.com and GEICO set themselves apart with their smooth-functioning direct channels. Companies can also gain a strong competitive advantage through *people differentiation*—hiring and training better people than their competitors do. Disney people are known to be friendly and upbeat. And Singapore Airlines enjoys an excellent reputation, largely because of the grace of its flight attendants. People differentiation requires that a company select its customer-contact people carefully and train them well. For example, Disney trains its theme park people thoroughly to ensure that they are competent, courteous, and friendly—from the hotel check-in agents, to the monorail drivers, to the ride attendants, to the people who sweep Main Street USA. Each employee is carefully trained to understand customers and to "make people happy."

Even when competing offers look the same, buyers may perceive a difference based on company or brand *image differentiation*. A company or brand image should convey the product's distinctive benefits and positioning. Developing a strong and distinctive image calls for creativity and hard work. A company cannot develop an image in the public's mind overnight using only a few advertisements. If Ritz-Carlton means quality, this image must be supported by everything the company says and does.

Symbols—such as the McDonald's golden arches, the red Travelers umbrella, the Nike swoosh, or Google's colorful logo—can provide strong company or brand recognition and image differentiation. The company might build a brand around a famous person, as Nike did with its Air Jordan basketball shoes and Tiger Woods golfing products. Some companies even become associated with colors, such as IBM (blue), UPS (brown), or Coca-Cola (red). The chosen symbols, characters, and other image elements must be communicated through advertising that conveys the company's or brand's personality.

Choosing the Right Competitive Advantages

Suppose a company is fortunate enough to discover several potential differentiations that provide competitive advantages. It now must choose the ones on which it will build its positioning strategy. It must decide *how many* differences to promote and *which ones*.

How Many Differences to Promote. Many marketers think that companies should aggressively promote only one benefit to the target market. Ad man Rosser Reeves, for example, said a company should develop a *unique selling proposition* (USP) for each brand and stick to it. Each brand should pick an attribute and tout itself as "number one" on that attribute. Buyers tend to remember number one better, especially in this overcommunicated society. Thus, Wal-Mart promotes its always low prices and Burger King promotes personal choice—"have it your way."

▲ Pledge Multi Surface is positioned on multiple benefits. The challenge is to convince customers that one brand can do it all.

Other marketers think that companies should position themselves on more than one differentiator. This may be necessary if two or more firms are claiming to be best on the same attribute. Today, in a time when the mass market is fragmenting into many small segments, companies are trying to broaden their positioning strategies to appeal to more segments.

For example, S.C. Johnson recently introduced a new Pledge multi-surface cleaner. Known mainly as a brand for cleaning and dusting wood furniture, the new Pledge is positioned as a cleaner that works on wood, electronics, glass, marble, stainless steel, and other surfaces. ▲Says its Web site, "No need to keep switching products—this multi-surface cleaner is perfect for a quick and easy cleanup of the whole room!" Clearly, many buyers want these multiple benefits. The challenge was to convince them that one brand can do it all. However, as companies increase the number of claims for their brands, they risk disbelief and a loss of clear positioning.

Which Differences to Promote. Not all brand differences are meaningful or worthwhile; not every difference makes a good differentiator. Each difference has the potential to create company costs as well as customer benefits. A difference is worth establishing to the extent that it satisfies the following criteria:

- *Important:* The difference delivers a highly valued benefit to target buyers.

- *Distinctive:* Competitors do not offer the difference, or the company can offer it in a more distinctive way.

- *Superior:* The difference is superior to other ways that customers might obtain the same benefit.

- *Communicable:* The difference is communicable and visible to buyers.

- *Preemptive:* Competitors cannot easily copy the difference.

- *Affordable:* Buyers can afford to pay for the difference.

- *Profitable:* The company can introduce the difference profitably.

Many companies have introduced differentiations that failed one or more of these tests. When the Westin Stamford Hotel in Singapore once advertised that it is the world's tallest hotel, it was a distinction that was not important to most tourists—in fact, it turned many off. Polaroid's Polarvision, which produced instantly developed home movies, bombed too. Although Polarvision was distinctive and even preemptive, it was inferior to another way of capturing motion, namely, camcorders. Thus, choosing competitive advantages upon which to position a product or service can be difficult, yet such choices may be crucial to success.

Selecting an Overall Positioning Strategy

Value proposition
The full positioning of a brand—the full mix of benefits upon which it is positioned.

The full positioning of a brand is called the brand's **value proposition**—the full mix of benefits upon which the brand is differentiated and positioned. It is the answer to the customer's question "Why should I buy your brand?" Volvo's value proposition hinges on safety but also includes reliability, roominess, and styling, all for a price that is higher than average but seems fair for this mix of benefits.

▼**Figure 7.4** shows possible value propositions upon which a company might position its products. In the figure, the five green cells represent winning value propositions—differentiation and positioning that gives the company competitive advantage. The red cells, however, represent losing value propositions. The center yellow cell represents at best a marginal proposition. In the following sections, we discuss the five winning value propositions upon which companies can position their products: more for more, more for the same, the same for less, less for much less, and more for less.

FIGURE | 7.4
Possible Value Propositions

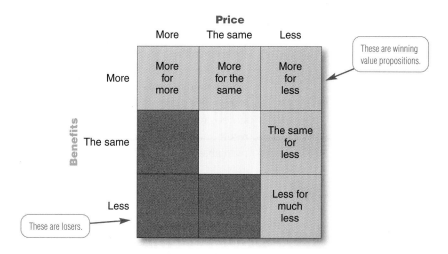

More for More.   "More-for-more" positioning involves providing the most upscale product or service and charging a higher price to cover the higher costs. Ritz-Carlton Hotels, Mont Blanc writing instruments, Mercedes automobiles, Viking appliances—each claims superior quality, craftsmanship, durability, performance, or style and charges a price to match. Not only is the market offering high in quality, it also gives prestige to the buyer. It symbolizes status and a loftier lifestyle. Often, the price difference exceeds the actual increment in quality.

Sellers offering "only the best" can be found in every product and service category, from hotels, restaurants, food, and fashion to cars and household appliances. Consumers are sometimes surprised, even delighted, when a new competitor enters a category with an unusually high-priced brand. Starbucks coffee entered as a very expensive brand in a largely commodity category. When Apple premiered its iPhone, it offered higher-quality features than a traditional cell phone with a hefty price tag to match.

In general, companies should be on the lookout for opportunities to introduce a "more-for-more" brand in any underdeveloped product or service category. Yet "more-for-more" brands can be vulnerable. They often invite imitators who claim the same quality but at a lower price. Luxury goods that sell well during good times may be at risk during economic downturns when buyers become more cautious in their spending.

More for the Same.   Companies can attack a competitor's more-for-more positioning by introducing a brand offering comparable quality but at a lower price. For example, Toyota introduced its Lexus line with a "more-for-the-same" value proposition versus Mercedes and BMW. Its first ad headline read: "Perhaps the first time in history that trading a $72,000 car for a $36,000 car could be considered trading up." It communicated the high quality of its new Lexus through rave reviews in car magazines and through a widely distributed videotape showing side-by-side comparisons of Lexus and Mercedes automobiles. It published surveys showing that Lexus dealers were providing customers with better sales and service experiences than were Mercedes dealerships. Many Mercedes owners switched to Lexus, and the Lexus repurchase rate has been 60 percent, twice the industry average.

The Same for Less.   Offering "the same for less" can be a powerful value proposition—everyone likes a good deal. Discount stores such as Wal-Mart and "category killers" such as Best Buy, Circuit City, and Sportmart also use this positioning. They don't claim to offer different or better products. Instead, they offer many of the same brands as department stores and specialty stores but at deep discounts based on superior purchasing power and lower-cost operations. Other companies develop imitative but lower-priced brands in an effort to lure customers away from the market leader. For example, AMD makes less-expensive versions of Intel's market-leading microprocessor chips.

Less for Much Less.   A market almost always exists for products that offer less and therefore cost less. Few people need, want, or can afford "the very best" in everything they buy. In many cases, consumers will gladly settle for less than optimal performance or give up some of the bells and whistles in exchange for a lower price. For example, many travelers seeking lodgings prefer not to pay for what they consider unnecessary extras, such as a pool, attached restaurant, or mints on the pillow. Hotel chains such as Ramada Limited suspend some of these amenities and charge less accordingly.

"Less-for-much-less" positioning involves meeting consumers' lower performance or quality requirements at a much lower price. For example, Family Dollar and Dollar General stores offer more affordable goods at very low prices. Sam's Club and Costco warehouse stores offer less merchandise selection and consistency and much lower levels of service; as a result, they charge rock-bottom prices. Southwest Airlines, the nation's most consistently profitable air carrier, also practices less-for-much-less positioning.

▲ Less for much less positioning: Southwest has positioned itself firmly as the no-frills, low-price airline. But no frills doesn't mean drudgery—Southwest's cheerful employees go out of their way to amuse, surprise, or somehow entertain passengers.

From the start, ▲Southwest has positioned itself firmly as *the* no-frills, low-price airline. Southwest's passengers have learned to fly without the amenities. For example, the airline provides no meals—just pretzels. It offers no first-class section, only three-across seating in all of its planes. And there's no such thing as a reserved seat on a Southwest flight. Why, then, do so many passengers love Southwest? Perhaps most importantly, Southwest excels at the basics of getting passengers where they want to go on time, and with their luggage. Beyond the basics, however, Southwest offers shockingly low prices. In fact, prices are so low that when Southwest enters a market, it actually increases total air traffic by attracting customers who might otherwise travel by car or bus. No frills and low prices, however, don't mean drudgery. Southwest's cheerful employees go out of their way to amuse, surprise, or somehow entertain passengers. One analyst sums up Southwest's less-for-much-less positioning this way: "It is not luxurious, but it's cheap and it's fun."

More for Less. Of course, the winning value proposition would be to offer "more for less." Many companies claim to do this. And, in the short run, some companies can actually achieve such lofty positions. For example, when it first opened for business, Home Depot had arguably the best product selection, the best service, *and* the lowest prices compared to local hardware stores and other home improvement chains.

Yet in the long run, companies will find it very difficult to sustain such best-of-both positioning. Offering more usually costs more, making it difficult to deliver on the "for-less" promise. Companies that try to deliver both may lose out to more focused competitors. For example, facing determined competition from Lowe's stores, Home Depot must now decide whether it wants to compete primarily on superior service or on lower prices.

All said, each brand must adopt a positioning strategy designed to serve the needs and wants of its target markets. "More for more" will draw one target market, "less for much less" will draw another, and so on. Thus, in any market, there is usually room for many different companies, each successfully occupying different positions. The important thing is that each company must develop its own winning positioning strategy, one that makes it special to its target consumers.

Developing a Positioning Statement

Positioning statement

A statement that summarizes company or brand positioning—it takes this form: *To (target segment and need) our (brand) is (concept) that (point-of-difference).*

Company and brand positioning should be summed up in a **positioning statement**. The statement should follow the form: *To (target segment and need) our (brand) is (concept) that (point of difference).*[32] For example: "To *busy, mobile professionals who need to always be in the loop,* BlackBerry is *a wireless connectivity solution* that *gives you an easier, more reliable way to stay connected to data, people, and resources while on the go.*"[33]

Note that the positioning first states the product's membership in a category (wireless connectivity solution) and then shows its point of difference from other members of the category (easier, more reliable connections to data, people, and resources). Placing a brand in a specific category suggests similarities that it might share with other products in the category. But the case for the brand's superiority is made on its points of difference.

Sometimes marketers put a brand in a surprisingly different category before indicating the points of difference. DiGiorno is a frozen pizza whose crust rises when the pizza is heated. But instead of putting it in the frozen pizza category, the marketers positioned it in the delivered pizza category. DiGiorno ads show delicious pizzas that look like anything but a frozen pizza, proclaiming "No calling. No tipping. No kidding. It's not delivery, its DiGiorno!" Another ad claims that DiGiorno "Makes mouths water. And delivery guys weep." Such positioning helps highlight DiGiorno's fresh quality and superior taste over the normal frozen pizza.

Communicating and Delivering the Chosen Position

Once it has chosen a position, the company must take strong steps to deliver and communicate the desired position to target consumers. All the company's marketing mix efforts must support the positioning strategy.

Positioning the company calls for concrete action, not just talk. If the company decides to build a position on better quality and service, it must first *deliver* that position. Designing the marketing mix—product, price, place, and promotion—involves working out the tactical details of the positioning strategy. Thus, a firm that seizes on a more-for-more position knows that it must produce high-quality products, charge a high price, distribute through high-quality dealers, and advertise in high-quality media. It must hire and train more service people, find retailers who have a good reputation for service, and develop sales and advertising messages that broadcast its superior service. This is the only way to build a consistent and believable more-for-more position.

Companies often find it easier to come up with a good positioning strategy than to implement it. Establishing a position or changing one usually takes a long time. In contrast, positions that have taken years to build can quickly be lost. Once a company has built the desired position, it must take care to maintain the position through consistent performance and communication. It must closely monitor and adapt the position over time to match changes in consumer needs and competitors' strategies. However, the company should avoid abrupt changes that might confuse consumers. Instead, a product's position should evolve gradually as it adapts to the ever-changing marketing environment.

REVIEWING Objectives AND KEY Terms

In this chapter, you've learned about the major elements of a customer-driven marketing strategy: segmentation, targeting, differentiation, and positioning. Marketers know that they cannot appeal to all buyers in their markets, or at least not to all buyers in the same way. Buyers are too numerous, too widely scattered, and too varied in their needs and buying practices. Therefore, most companies today practice *target marketing*—identifying market segments, selecting one or more of them, and developing products and marketing mixes tailored to each.

OBJECTIVE 1 Define the major steps in designing a customer-driven marketing strategy: market segmentation, targeting, differentiation, and positioning. (pp 191–192)

Customer-driven marketing strategy begins with selecting which customers to serve and deciding on a value proposition that best serves the targeted customers. It consists of four steps. *Market segmentation* is the act of dividing a market into distinct groups of buyers with different needs, characteristics, or behaviors who might require separate products or marketing mixes. Once the

groups have been identified, *market targeting* evaluates each market segment's attractiveness and selects one or more segments to serve. Market targeting consists of designing strategies to build the *right relationships* with the *right customers*. *Differentiation* involves actually differentiating the market offering to create superior customer value. *Positioning* consists of positioning the market offering in the minds of target customers.

OBJECTIVE 2 List and discuss the major bases for segmenting consumer and business markets. (pp 192–201)

There is no single way to segment a market. Therefore, the marketer tries different variables to see which give the best segmentation opportunities. For consumer marketing, the major segmentation variables are geographic, demographic, psychographic, and behavioral. In *geographic segmentation*, the market is divided into different geographical units such as nations, regions, states, counties, cities, or neighborhoods. In *demographic segmentation*, the market is divided into groups based on demographic variables, including age, gender, family size, family life cycle, income, occupation, education, religion, race, generation, and nationality. In *psychographic segmentation,* the market is divided into different groups based on social class, lifestyle, or personality characteristics. In *behavioral segmentation,* the market is divided into groups based on consumers' knowledge, attitudes, uses, or responses to a product.

Business marketers use many of the same variables to segment their markets. But business markets also can be segmented by business consumer *demographics* (industry, company size), *operating characteristics, purchasing approaches, situational factors,* and *personal characteristics.* The effectiveness of segmentation analysis depends on finding segments that are *measurable, accessible, substantial, differentiable,* and *actionable.*

OBJECTIVE 3 **Explain how companies identify attractive market segments and choose a market-targeting strategy. (pp 201–209)**

To target the best market segments, the company first evaluates each segment's size and growth characteristics, structural attractiveness, and compatibility with company objectives and resources. It then chooses one of four market-targeting strategies—ranging from very broad to very narrow targeting. The seller can ignore segment differences and target broadly using *undifferentiated (or mass) marketing.* This involves mass producing, mass distributing, and mass promoting about the same product in about the same way to all consumers. Or the seller can adopt *differentiated marketing*—developing different market offers for several segments. *Concentrated marketing* (or *niche marketing*) involves focusing on only one or a few market segments. Finally, *micromarketing* is the practice of tailoring products and marketing programs to suit the tastes of specific individuals and locations. Micromarketing includes *local marketing* and *individual marketing.* Which targeting strategy is best depends on company resources, product variability, product life-cycle stage, market variability, and competitive marketing strategies.

OBJECTIVE 4 **Discuss how companies differentiate and position their products for maximum competitive advantage in the marketplace. (pp 209–217)**

Once a company has decided which segments to enter, it must decide on its *differentiation and positioning strategy.* The differentiation and positioning task consists of three steps: identifying a set of possible differentiations that create competitive advantage, choosing advantages upon which to build a position, and selecting an overall positioning strategy. The brand's full positioning is called its *value proposition*—the full mix of benefits upon which the brand is positioned. In general, companies can choose from one of five winning value propositions upon which to position their products: more for more, more for the same, the same for less, less for much less, or more for less. Company and brand positioning are summarized in positioning statements that state the target segment and need, positioning concept, and specific points of difference. The company must then effectively communicate and deliver the chosen position to the market.

KEY Terms

OBJECTIVE 1

Market segmentation (p 191)
Market targeting (targeting) (p 191)
Differentiation (p 191)
Positioning (p 192)

OBJECTIVE 2

Geographic segmentation (p 193)
Demographic segmentation (p 194)
Age and life-cycle segmentation (p 194)
Gender segmentation (p 195)
Income segmentation (p 195)

Psychographic segmentation (p 196)
Behavioral segmentation (p 196)
Occasion segmentation (p 196)
Benefit segmentation (p 196)
Intermarket segmentation (p 200)

OBJECTIVE 3

Target market (p 201)
Undifferentiated (mass) marketing (p 201)
Differentiated (segmented) marketing (p 202)

Concentrated (niche) marketing (p 204)
Micromarketing (p 205)
Local marketing (p 205)
Individual marketing (p 206)

OBJECTIVE 4

Product position (p 209)
Competitive advantage (p 210)
Value proposition (p 214)
Positioning statement (p 216)

DISCUSSING & APPLYING THE Concepts

Discussing the Concepts

1. Briefly describe the four major steps in designing a customer-driven marketing strategy. (AACSB: Communication)

2. Name and describe the four major sets of variables that might be used in segmenting consumer markets. Which segmenting variable(s) do you think Starbucks is using? (AACSB: Communication; Reflective Thinking)

3. Explain how marketers can segment international markets. (AACSB: Communication)

4. Compare and contrast undifferentiated, differentiated, concentrated, and micromarketing targeting strategies. Which strategy is best? (AACSB: Communication)

5. What is a product's "position" and how do marketers know what it is? (AACSB: Communication)

6. Name and define the five winning value propositions described in the chapter. Which value proposition describes Wal-Mart? Explain your answer. (AACSB: Communication; Reflective Thinking)

Applying the Concepts

1. The chapter described psychographics as one major variable used by marketers when segmenting consumer markets. SRI Consulting has developed a typology of consumers based on values and lifestyles. Go to SRI Consulting's Web site (www.sric-bi.com), click on the VALS survey on the right side of the Web site, and complete the VALS survey. How accurately do your primary and secondary VALS types describe you? How can marketers use this information? Write a brief report of your findings. (AACSB: Communication; Use of IT; Reflective Thinking)

2. Assume you work at a regional state university whose traditional target market, high school students within your region, is shrinking and projections are that this segment will decrease approximately 5 percent per year over the next ten years. Recommend other potential market segments and discuss the criteria you should consider to ensure that the identified segments are effective. (AACSB: Communication; Reflective Thinking)

3. Form a small group and create an idea for a new reality television show. Using the format provided in the chapter, develop a positioning statement for this television show. What competitive advantage does the show have over existing shows? How many and which differences would you promote? (AACSB: Communication; Reflective Thinking)

FOCUS ON Technology

Have you noticed that ads on Web sites seem to reflect your interests? Do you ever wonder if someone is watching your Internet behavior? Well, someone (that is, a computer) probably is watching and tracking you. Marketers use such tracking information to send targeted ads to consumers—it's called behavioral targeting. You've no doubt heard of "cookies," the files deposited on your computer when you visit a Web site. If you've ever given personally identifying information at a site, it remembers you when you return—it's all stored in the cookie file. But even if you don't give personally identifying information on a Web site, Internet protocol addresses (IP addresses) can be tracked to follow where you go and where you've been on the Internet. This tracking lets marketers tailor Web pages, information, offers, and prices to individuals based on their behavioral characteristics. Behavioral targeting is coveted because it allows marketers to implement micromarketing strategies.

1. TACODA is a behavioral targeting ad network. Visit www.tacoda.com to learn more about this company. Explore this Web site to learn how it lets marketers send Internet ads to targeted consumers. Then, write a brief report explaining behavioral targeting and how marketers are using it. (AACSB: Communication; Use of IT)

2. Many individuals are concerned that Internet behavioral tracking violates their privacy. Most Web sites have access to users' IP addresses. Are IP addresses alone "user identifiable" information? Learn more about this issue and write a brief report about it. (AACSB: Communication; Reflective Thinking)

FOCUS ON Ethics

KGOY stands for "kids getting older younger," and marketers are getting much of the blame. Kids today see all types of messages, especially on the Internet, that children would never have seen in the past. Whereas boys may give up G.I. Joe at an earlier age to play war games on their xBox 360s, the greater controversy seems to surround claims of how girls have changed, or rather, how marketers have changed girls. Critics describe clothing designed for young girls aged 8–11 as "floozy" and sexual, with department stores selling youngsters thongs and T-shirts that say "Naughty Girl!" Although Barbie's sexuality has never been subtle, she was originally targeted to girls 9–12 years old. Now, Barbie dolls target primarily girls 3–7 years old! And Barbie's competitor, Bratz dolls, has an "in-your-face" attitude that has some parents complaining that they are too sexual.

1. Do you think marketers are to blame for kids getting older younger? Give some other examples. (AACSB: Communication; Ethical Reasoning)

2. Give an example of a company that is countering this trend by offering age-appropriate products for children. (AACSB: Communication; Reflective Thinking)

MARKETING BY THE Numbers

Americans love their pets. You may have one or more furry, feathery, or scaly friends yourself, so you know how much money you spend each year. Marketers need to know that information to estimate the size of a potential market segment. The National Pet Products Manufacturers Association (NPPMA) conducts a yearly survey of pet owners that provides useful information for estimating market size and potential.

1. Refer to Appendix 2: Marketing by the Numbers and use the information available from the NPPMA survey (www.appma.org/press_industrytrends.asp) to develop an estimate of the market potential for dog food in the United States. (AACSB: Communication; Use of IT; Analytical Reasoning)

2. Using other information from the NPPMA's Web site, evaluate the usefulness of this market segment. (AACSB: Communication; Use of IT; Reflective Thinking)

VIDEO Case

Meredith

The Meredith Corporation has developed an expertise in building customer relationships through segmentation, targeting, and positioning. Amazingly, however, it has done this by focusing on only half of the population—the female half. Meredith has developed the largest database of any U.S. media company and uses that database to meet the specific needs and desires of women.

Meredith is known for leading titles such as *Better Homes and Gardens*, *Family Circle*, and *Ladies' Home Journal*. But that list has grown to a portfolio of 14 magazines and more than 200 special interest publications. Through these magazines alone, Meredith regularly reaches about 30 million readers. By focusing on core categories of home, family, and personal development, Meredith

has developed a product mix designed to meet various needs of women. This creates multiple touch points as individual women engage with more than one magazine, as well as with specialty books and Web sites.

After viewing the video featuring Meredith, answer the following questions about segmenting, targeting, and positioning:

1. On what main variables has Meredith focused in segmenting its markets?

2. Which target marketing strategy best describes Meredith's efforts? Support your choice.

3. How does Meredith use its variety of products to build relationships with the right customers?

COMPANY Case

Saturn: An Image Makeover

Things are changing at Saturn. The General Motors brand had only three iterations of the same compact car for the entire decade of the 1990s. But over the last couple of years, Saturn has introduced an all-new lineup of vehicles that includes a midsized sport sedan, an 8-passenger cross-over vehicle, a 2-seat roadster, a new compact sport sedan, and a compact SUV. Having anticipated the brand's renaissance for years, Saturn executives, employees, and customers are beside themselves with joy.

But with all this change, industry observers wonder whether Saturn will be able to maintain the very characteristics that have distinguished the brand since its inception. Given that Saturn established itself based on a very narrow line of compact vehicles, many believe that the move from targeting one segment of customers to targeting multiple segments will be challenging. Will a newly positioned Saturn still meet the needs of one of the most loyal cadres of customers in the automotive world?

A NEW KIND OF CAR COMPANY

From its beginnings in 1985, Saturn set out to break through the GM bureaucracy and become "A different kind of car. A different kind of company." As the single-most defining characteristic of the new company, Saturn proclaimed that its sole focus would be people: customers, employees, and communities. The company's focus on employees included an unprecedented contract with United Auto Workers (UAW) that focused on progressive work rules, benefits, work teams, and the concept of empowerment. It established a ground-breaking dealer network structure, reversing long-held customer perceptions of dealers as a nemesis. Saturn also received awards and recognition for socially responsible policies that were beneficial to employees, communities, and the environment.

But in addition to establishing an image as a people-oriented company, Saturn put significant resources into product development. The first Saturn cars were made "from scratch," without any allegiance to the GM parts bin or suppliers. The goal was to produce not only a high-quality vehicle, but one known for safety and innovative features that would "wow" the customer.

When the first Saturn vehicles rolled off the assembly line on July 30, 1990, the company offered a sedan, a coupe, and a wagon

in two trim levels each, all based on a single compact vehicle platform. Despite this minimal approach, sales quickly exceeded expectations. By 1992, Saturn had sold 500,000 vehicles. That same year, the company achieved the highest new car sales per retail outlet, something that had not been done by a domestic car company for 15 years.

Indeed, customers were drawn to all the things that Saturn had hoped they would be. They loved the innovations, like dent resistant body panels, the high-tech paint job designed to resist oxidization and chipping longer than any in the industry, and safety features like traction control, anti-lock brakes, and unparalleled body reinforcements. They were overwhelmed by the fresh sales approach that included no-haggle pricing, a 30-day return policy, and no-hassle from the non-commissioned sales associates.

During Saturn's early years of operations, the accolades rolled in. The list included "Best Car" picks from numerous magazines and organizations, along with awards for quality, engineering, safety, and ease-of-maintenance. But the crowning achievement occurred in 1995 as the 1,000,000th Saturn took to the road. That year, Saturn ranked number-one out of all automotive nameplates on the J.D. Power and Associates Sales Satisfaction Index Study, achieving the highest score ever given by the organization. It would be the only company ever to achieve the highest marks in all three categories ranked by the satisfaction index (salesperson performance, delivery activities, and initial product quality). Saturn earned that honor for an astounding four consecutive years, and it was the only non-luxury brand to be at or near the top of J.D. Power's scores for the better part of a decade.

THE HONEYMOON ENDS

Looking back, Saturn unquestionably defied the odds. To launch an all-new automotive company in such a fiercely competitive and barrier-entrenched industry is one thing. To achieve the level of sales, the customer base, and the list of awards that Saturn achieved in such a short period of time is truly remarkable. But despite all of Saturn's initial successes, one thing was always missing from the GM division. Profit. As the new millennium dawned, GM had yet to earn a nickel of return on billions of dollars invested in the brand. Saturn sales peaked early in 1994 at 286,000 and settled in at an average of about 250,000 units per year.

The lack of continued growth may have been due partly to the fact that Saturn released no new models in the 1990s. GM finally introduced the midsized L-series and compact SUV Vue for 2000 and 2002 respectively. It replaced the original S-series with the Ion in 2003. But while these new vehicles addressed the issue of a lack of model options, they brought with them a new concern. Saturn's history of high quality and its long-cherished J.D. Power ratings began to slide. In the early part of the new millennium, not only was Saturn's J.D. Power initial-quality rating not near the top, it fell to below the industry average.

Even with the new models, Saturn's sales did not improve. In fact, they declined. This was partly due to an industrywide downturn in sales wrought by a recession. But Saturn's general manager, Jill Lajdziak, has conceded that, for too long Saturn sold utilitarian vehicles. In 2005, Saturn sales fell to a record low of 213,000 units, only about 1 percent of the overall market. It seems that sales of the L-series and Vue were coming almost entirely from loyal Saturn customers who were trading up to something different, something bigger, and, unfortunately, something not as good.

A NEW KIND OF SATURN

Given the troubles that Saturn was experiencing, it came as a surprise when in 2008, GM executives announced expectations that Saturn would be its growth brand in the ensuing years. GM hoped to perform a makeover similar to the one it achieved with Cadillac earlier in the decade, infusing another $3 billion into its import-fighter nameplate. Given that GM had just experienced a record loss of $38 billion, the world's biggest carmaker was clearly putting faith in one of its smallest brands to help turn the tide.

Jill Lajdziak said "Saturn's initial image as a smart innovation small-car company was blurred by bumps in quality and slow model turnover. We didn't grow the portfolio fast enough, and [now] we're growing it in a huge way." At Vancouver's Pacific International Auto Show in spring 2007, Lajdziak introduced one shiny new model after another: the 2007 Sky two-seat roadster, the 2007 Outlook crossover wagon, the completely redesigned 2008 Vue, the 2007 midsized Aura sedan, and the 2008 Astra. Not a single one of these models had been available in January 2006.

"By the end of this year, the oldest product in a Saturn showroom will be the Sky," said Lajdziak. Of GM's investment, she remarked, "We've asked for beautifully designed products with a level of refinement, interiors, vehicle dynamics—we think we have it all. And we've got that married up with what consumers believe is the best industry experience in the marketplace." Commenting on the magnitude of the changes at Saturn, she continued, "Nobody else has ever tried to grow the portfolio and turn it over as fast as we are, maintain industry-best customer satisfaction, and obviously deliver the [profit] results all at the same time."

At the heart of this makeover is something else all new to Saturn: taking advantage of the GM family of vehicles and parts bins to achieve efficiencies of scale and increase profit margins. In fact, the new Saturn models are largely rebranded Opels, GM's European division. In the future, new product development will be carried out in a joint-venture way between the two divisions. For a company that in the past has been known as making the "car for people who hate cars," this is a 180-degree turnaround.

With a new lineup of European engineered vehicles, Saturn is intent on repositioning its brand image with its "Rethink" campaign. The print and TV ads are designed to change consumers' perceptions of Saturn as a bland, functional, economy car. Saturn may have the advantage of youth in this undertaking. Some industry analysts suggest it can reposition itself more easily than other brands because it is such a young company.

As for the new positioning, GM makes it clear that with Saturn, it's not trying to make another Chevrolet. Chevrolet will remain the only GM brand positioned as "all things to all people." Along with the other GM brands, Saturn will play a niche roll and target a specific market segment. In fact, GM says, it's just trying to help Saturn do more of what it has been doing all along—reach the type of import-buying customer it can't reach with any of its other brands. Indeed, top executives at GM acknowledge that many Saturn owners already believe their car is an Asian brand, not a domestic one. "Saturn has always been the one brand in the GM lineup suitable for attracting import-intenders," commented one GM executive.

SWIMMING, OR SINKING?

GM set a lofty 2007 sales goal for Saturn of 400,000 vehicles, far more than the division had ever sold. However, it didn't even come close to that goal, selling only 240,000 vehicles. With so many new models, it is struggling to create brand awareness for each one. But although Saturn fell short of its goal, unit sales represented a 12 percent increase over the previous year. At a time when the entire industry was struggling, this was a notable achievement. Much more significant, however, was the fact that the average price of a Saturn transaction skyrocketed by a whopping $7,000. This translated into a huge 24 percent increase for dealer profitability.

"We're seeing more cross-shopping than ever," said Lajdziak. "Our retailers are seeing people they've never seen before in their showrooms, in terms of demographics and what they are trading in." And better yet, Saturn is not cannibalizing other GM brands. Saturn sales appear to be increasing at the expense of Honda, Nissan, and Toyota. In fact, not a single GM model ranks among the top ten vehicles cross-shopped by potential Saturn buyers.

The new Saturn strategy is a big change: new positioning, new vehicles, even a new advertising agency. But despite all this change, Saturn is remaining focused on the core elements that have always made Saturn a different kind of car company: innovation, social responsibility, a focus on employees, and creating and maintaining strong customer relationships. This unique combination of change and consistency may just result in Saturn fulfilling GM's expectations of a growth brand.

Questions for Discussion

1. Using the full spectrum of segmentation variables, describe how GM has segmented the automobile market.

2. What segment(s) is Saturn now targeting? How is GM now positioning Saturn? How do these strategies differ from those employed with the original Saturn S-series?

3. Describe the role that social responsibility plays in Saturn's targeting strategy.

4. Do you think that GM will accomplish its goals with the "new Saturn"? Why or why not?

5. What segmentation, targeting, and positioning recommendations would you make to GM for future Saturn models?

Sources: Jamie LaReau, "Saturn Is Expected to Be GM's Growth Brand," *Automotive News*, February 18, 2008, p. 52; Frank Aukofer, "Resurgent Saturn Has Appealing Vue," *Washington Times*, April 18, 2008, p. G01; Gregory Solman, "Saturn Asks Americans to 'Rethink' Its Brand," *Adweek*, May 21, 2007, accessed online at www.adweek.com; Jeremy Cato, "Saturn's Revival Shows What the 'New GM' Can Do," *Globe and Mail*, April 5, 2007, p. G10; Barbara Powell, "GM's Saturn Seeks to Shake Up Humdrum Image," *Ottawa Citizen*, April 12, 2006, p. F7; and "Our Story," accessed at www.saturn.com, November 2008.

Chapter 8

Part 1   Defining Marketing and the Marketing Process (Chapters 1, 2)
Part 2   Understanding the Marketplace and Consumers (Chapters 3, 4, 5, 6)
Part 3   Designing a Customer-Driven Strategy and Mix (Chapters 7, 8, 9, 10, 11, 12, 13, 14, 15, 16, 17)
Part 4   Extending Marketing (Chapters 18, 19, 20)

Products, Services, and Brands
Building Customer Value

Chapter PREVIEW

Now that you've had a good look at customer-driven marketing strategy, we'll take a deeper look at the marketing mix—the tactical tools that marketers use to implement their strategies and deliver superior customer value. In this and the next chapter, we'll study how companies develop and manage products and brands. Then, in the chapters that follow, we'll look at pricing, distribution, and marketing communication tools.

The product is usually the first and most basic marketing consideration. We'll start with a seemingly simple question: What *is* a product? As it turns out, however, the answer is not so simple.

Before starting the chapter, let's look at an interesting branding story. Brands may be the most important tools for creating customer value and profitable customer relationships. Marketing is all about building brands that connect deeply with customers. So, when you think of top brands, which ones pop up first? Here's a tale about one strong brand you may not have considered.

When you think of today's "hottest brands," what names come to mind? Coca-Cola? Nike? Google? Target? Maybe Starbucks? But scan last year's list of hottest brands, prepared by respected brand consultancy Landor Associates, and you'll find an unlikely entry—Las Vegas. That's right, Las Vegas. Most people wouldn't even think of Vegas as a "product," let alone as a brand. But there it is, number two on the list of the nation's hottest brands, right behind Google.

Many old-timers still think of Las Vegas as "Sin City"—an anything-goes gambling town built on smoke-filled casinos, bawdy all-girl revues, all-you-can-eat buffets, Elvis impersonators, and no-wait weddings on the Vegas Strip. But that's the old Las Vegas. The new Vegas has reinvented itself as a luxury destination. Casinos and gaming now account for less than half of the city's revenues. Instead, the new Las Vegas brims with classy resort hotel/casinos, expansive shopping malls filled with luxury goods, first-run entertainment, and restaurants bearing the names of world-renowned chefs.

However, to the nearly 40 million visitors who flock to Las Vegas each year, the town is much more than just an assortment of facilities and amenities. To visitors, Vegas is an emotional connection, and a total brand experience. What *is* the "Las Vegas experience"? To answer that question, the city conducted extensive consumer research. "We talked to old customers and new customers to determine the essence of the brand of Las Vegas" says Rossi Ralenkotter, CEO of the Las Vegas Convention and Visitors Authority (LVCVA).

The research showed that when people come to Las Vegas, they're a little naughtier—a little less inhibited. They stay out longer, eat more, do some gambling, and spend more on shopping and dining. "We found that [the Las Vegas experience] centered on adult freedom," says Ralenkotter. "People could stay up all night and do things they wouldn't normally do in their own towns."

Based on these customer insights, the LVCVA coined a now-familiar catchphrase—"Only Vegas: What happens here, stays here." The phrase captures the essence of the Las Vegas experience—that it's okay to be a little naughty in Vegas. Now the centerpiece of what has become one of the most successful tourism campaigns in history, that simple phrase has helped transform Las Vegas's brand image from one of a down-and-dirty "Sin City" to an enticing and luxurious "Only Vegas."

In 2003 the LVCVA launched its innovative $75 million "What happens here, stays here" ad campaign. Early ads were based on 2,500 real stories culled from visitors through the market research. True to the brand's positioning, the award-winning campaign showed the naughty nature of people once they arrive in Las Vegas.

In one ad, a woman spontaneously married a visibly younger man in a Las Vegas wedding chapel. Then, ignoring his ardent pleas, she kissed him goodbye and pulled herself away, insisting that she had to get back to her business convention. In another ad, a suave young man tested different identities on the various women he met during a night on the town. "I'm a hand model," he declared—or a lifeguard, or a big-game hunter, or a brain doctor. In still another ad, a young woman lounged by the pool with friends at a Vegas hotel, preoccupied with her cell phone. "Okay, what's with the phone?" asked one of the friends.

> Las Vegas is number two on a recent list of the nation's hottest brands, right behind Google.

"You had that out all last night." To the friend's chagrin, the woman announced, "Oh, it's not just a phone. It takes photos with this little camera, and it also records little video clips." When she dived into the pool, the phone was shown sinking slowly behind her. At the end, each ad reminded us that, "What happens here, stays here."

The LVCVA is still investing heavily in the bold and provocative campaign. The most recent version extends the now-classic "What happens here" theme with a subtler "Your Vegas is showing" twist. This latest campaign keeps the Only Vegas naughtiness intact. However, it also highlights some of the town's tamer features—high fashion, extravagant shows, and gourmet dining, making these events seem decadent in themselves:

One ad begins by panning portraits of chefs Mario Batali, Wolfgang Puck, and Emeril Lagasse on the wall in a fine restaurant before settling on three girlfriends chatting at a table. The voice-over says, "Three celebrity chefs in three days—you could write a thesis on gourmet delights." One of the women drifts off, imagining that she is being hand-fed by a handsome male attendant. "And yet," says the announcer, "what exactly does it say that you've developed a taste for such exotic delicacies, at least to those back home?" The woman is snapped back to reality by a mental image of "Mom" holding a chicken casserole. Concludes the voice-over: "People might begin to wonder what else you've developed a taste for in this epicurean fantasyland. Hey, cuisine curator, your Vegas is showing."

In another ad, a man decides to buy albino crocodile loafers, imagining himself as an international spy with multiple passports and an exploding pen. Back home, when he wears the shoes in the backyard, his friends eye him suspiciously: "People might start wondering just what kind of double life have you been leading," says the narrator. "Because who really knows what a guy with an outfit like that is capable of? Hey fashion-istador, your Vegas is showing."

The "Your Vegas is showing" campaign conveys the notion that you can be naughtier in Vegas, then bring just a little of that attitude back to your day-to-day lifestyle. "We want you to bring Vegas home with you," says the LVCVA's marketing vice president.

Since the first LVCVA campaign began, the "What happens here, stays here" slogan has become a part of the national vernacular, strongly positioning Las Vegas in the minds of potential visitors and setting it apart from the rapidly growing list of competing destinations. "It's all about branding," says CEO Ralenkotter. "The slogan captures the city's experiences rather than amenities, the image that Las Vegas represents freedom."

Thus, thanks to smart marketing and brand building, Las Vegas really does belong among the ranks of the world's hottest brands. Vegas tourism is booming, with a hotel occupancy rate hovering at an incredible 90 percent. By 2011, an estimated 45 million tourists will overindulge in the naughtiness that Vegas affords, secure in the promise that "What happens here, stays here."[1]

> To visitors, Las Vegas is an emotional connection a total brand experience. When people come to Vegas, they're a little naughtier—a little less inhibited.

> Brands may be the most important tools for creating value and profitable customer relationships. Marketing is all about building brands that connect deeply with customers.

As the Las Vegas example shows, in their quest to create customer relationships, marketers must build and manage products and brands that connect with customers. This chapter begins with a deceptively simple question: *What is a product*? After addressing this question, we look at ways to classify products in consumer and business markets. Then we discuss the important decisions that marketers make regarding individual products, product lines, and product mixes. Next, we look into the critically important issue of how marketers build and manage brands. Finally, we examine the characteristics and marketing requirements of a special form of product—services.

Objective Outline

Author Comment | As you'll see, this is a deceptively simple question with a very complex answer. For example, think back to our opening Las Vegas story. What is the Las Vegas "product"?

Product
Anything that can be offered to a market for attention, acquisition, use, or consumption that might satisfy a want or need.

Service
Any activity or benefit that one party can offer to another that is essentially intangible and does not result in the ownership of anything.

What Is a Product? (pp 224–229)

We define a **product** as anything that can be offered to a market for attention, acquisition, use, or consumption that might satisfy a want or need. Products include more than just tangible objects, such as cars, computers, or cell phones. Broadly defined, "products" also include services, events, persons, places, organizations, ideas, or mixes of these. Throughout this text, we use the term *product* broadly to include any or all of these entities. Thus, an Apple iPod, a Toyota Camry, and a Caffé Mocha at Starbucks are products. But so are a trip to Las Vegas, Fidelity online investment services, and advice from your family doctor.

Because of their importance in the world economy, we give special attention to services. **Services** are a form of product that consists of activities, benefits, or satisfactions offered for sale that are essentially intangible and do not result in the ownership of anything. Examples are banking, hotel, airline, retail, wireless communication, and home-repair services. We will look at services more closely later in this chapter.

Products, Services, and Experiences

Product is a key element in the overall *market offering*. Marketing-mix planning begins with building an offering that brings value to target customers. This offering becomes the basis upon which the company builds profitable customer relationships.

A company's market offering often includes both tangible goods and services. At one extreme, the offer may consist of a *pure tangible good*, such as soap, toothpaste, or salt—no services accompany the product. At the other extreme are *pure services*, for which the offer consists primarily of a service. Examples include a doctor's exam or financial services. Between these two extremes, however, many goods-and-services combinations are possible.

Today, as products and services become more commoditized, many companies are moving to a new level in creating value for their customers. To differentiate their offers, beyond simply making products and delivering services they are creating and managing customer *experiences* with their brands or company.

Experiences have always been an important part of marketing for some companies. Disney has long manufactured dreams and memories through its movies and theme parks. And Nike has long declared, "It's not so much the shoes but where they take you." Today, however, all kinds of firms are recasting their traditional goods and services to

▲ Creating experiences: Umpqua Bank's "stores" are designed to make banking a pleasurable experience. "Customers aren't just doing transactions . . . they're paying admission to a club—one that delivers something to satisfy the soul."

create experiences. ▲For example, a visit to Umpqua bank involves a lot more than just loans and deposits:[2]

> Most customers would never describe a bank transaction as soul satisfying, but Oregon-based Umpqua Bank isn't your average bank. Umpqua feels more like a café—think bank crossed with your local Starbucks. Umpqua's "stores" are designed to make banking a pleasurable experience that will cause customers to stick around and maybe buy something. Customers sit at a cozy coffee bar, sip Umpqua-branded coffee, read the morning paper, watch investment news on big-screen TVs, pay bills online via WiFi access, and don headphones to check out local bands at the bank's online music store. After-hours activities such as movies, knitting, and yoga classes are encouraged just as much as financial events. Turning bank services into a rewarding experience has been good for Umpqua's business. The company has grown from only $140 million in assets in 1994 to more than $8.3 billion last year. Customers aren't just . . . doing transactions at Umpqua Bank," says an analyst. "They're paying admission to a club—one that delivers something to satisfy the soul."

Companies that market experiences realize that customers are really buying much more than just products and services. They are buying what those offers will *do* for them.

Levels of Product and Services

Product planners need to think about products and services on three levels (see 📖 **Figure 8.1**). Each level adds more customer value. The most basic level is the *core customer value*, which addresses the question *What is the buyer really buying?* When designing products, marketers must first define the core, problem-solving benefits or services that consumers seek. A woman buying lipstick buys more than lip color. Charles Revson of Revlon saw this early: "In the factory, we make cosmetics; in the store, we sell hope." ▲And people who buy a BlackBerry smartphone are buying more than a cell phone, e-mail device, or personal organizer. They are buying freedom and on-the-go connectivity to people and resources.

At the second level, product planners must turn the core benefit into an *actual product*. They need to develop product and service features, design, a quality level, a brand name, and packaging. For example, the BlackBerry is an actual product. Its name, parts, styling, features, packaging, and other attributes have all been combined carefully to deliver the core customer value of staying connected.

▲ Core, actual, and augmented product: People who buy a BlackBerry are buying more than a cell phone, e-mail device, or organizer. They are buying freedom and on-the-go connectivity to people and resources.

Finally, product planners must build an *augmented product* around the core benefit and actual product by offering additional consumer services and benefits. The BlackBerry solution offers more than just a communications device. It provides consumers with a complete solution to mobile connectivity problems. Thus, when consumers buy a BlackBerry, the company and its dealers also might give buyers a warranty on parts and workmanship, instructions on how to use the device, quick repair services when needed, and a toll-free telephone number and Web site to use if they have problems or questions.

Consumers see products as complex bundles of benefits that satisfy their needs. When developing products, marketers first must identify the *core customer value* that consumers seek from the product. They must then design the *actual* product and find ways to *augment* it in order to create this customer value and the most satisfying customer experience.

FIGURE | 8.1
Three Levels of Product

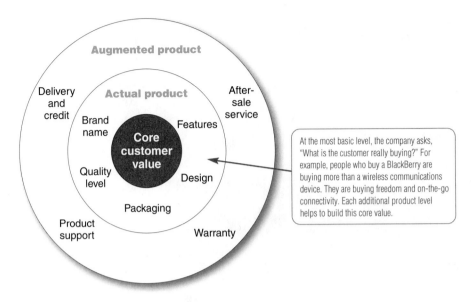

At the most basic level, the company asks, "What is the customer really buying?" For example, people who buy a BlackBerry are buying more than a wireless communications device. They are buying freedom and on-the-go connectivity. Each additional product level helps to build this core value.

Product and Service Classifications

Products and services fall into two broad classes based on the types of consumers that use them—*consumer products* and *industrial products*. Broadly defined, products also include other marketable entities such as experiences, organizations, persons, places, and ideas.

Consumer Products

Consumer product

A product bought by final consumer for personal consumption.

Consumer products are products and services bought by final consumers for personal consumption. Marketers usually classify these products and services further based on how consumers go about buying them. Consumer products include *convenience products, shopping products, specialty products,* and *unsought products.* These products differ in the ways consumers buy them and, therefore, in how they are marketed (see ● **Table 8.1**).

Convenience product

A consumer product that customers usually buy frequently, immediately, and with a minimum of comparison and buying effort.

Convenience products are consumer products and services that customers usually buy frequently, immediately, and with a minimum of comparison and buying effort. Examples include laundry detergent, candy, magazines, and fast food. Convenience products are usually low priced, and marketers place them in many locations to make them readily available when customers need them.

Shopping product

A consumer product that the customer, in the process of selection and purchase, usually compares on such bases as suitability, quality, price, and style.

Shopping products are less frequently purchased consumer products and services that customers compare carefully on suitability, quality, price, and style. When buying shopping products and services, consumers spend much time and effort in gathering information and making comparisons. Examples include furniture, clothing, used cars, major appliances, and hotel and airline services. Shopping products marketers usually distribute their products through fewer outlets but provide deeper sales support to help customers in their comparison efforts.

Specialty product

A consumer product with unique characteristics or brand identification for which a significant group of buyers is willing to make a special purchase effort.

Specialty products are consumer products and services with unique characteristics or brand identification for which a significant group of buyers is willing to make a special purchase effort. Examples include specific brands of cars, high-priced photographic equipment, designer clothes, and the services of medical or legal specialists. A Lamborghini automobile, for example, is a specialty product because buyers are usually willing to travel great distances to buy one. Buyers normally do not compare specialty products. They invest only the time needed to reach dealers carrying the wanted products.

Unsought product

A consumer product that the consumer either does not know about or knows about but does not normally think of buying.

Unsought products are consumer products that the consumer either does not know about or knows about but does not normally think of buying. Most major new innovations are unsought until the consumer becomes aware of them through advertising. Classic examples of known but unsought products and services are life insurance, preplanned funeral services, and blood donations to the Red Cross. By their very nature, unsought products require a lot of advertising, personal selling, and other marketing efforts.

● TABLE | 8.1   Marketing Considerations for Consumer Products

Marketing Considerations	Type of Consumer Product			
	Convenience	**Shopping**	**Specialty**	**Unsought**
Customer buying behavior	Frequent purchase, little planning, little comparison or shopping effort, low customer involvement	Less frequent purchase, much planning and shopping effort, comparison of brands on price, quality, style	Strong brand preference and loyalty, special purchase effort, little comparison of brands, low price sensitivity	Little product awareness, knowledge (or, if aware, little or even negative interest)
Price	Low price	Higher price	High price	Varies
Distribution	Widespread distribution, convenient locations	Selective distribution in fewer outlets	Exclusive distribution in only one or a few outlets per market area	Varies
Promotion	Mass promotion by the producer	Advertising and personal selling by both producer and resellers	More carefully targeted promotion by both producer and resellers	Aggressive advertising and personal selling by producer and resellers
Examples	Toothpaste, magazines, laundry detergent	Major appliances, televisions, furniture, clothing	Luxury goods, such as Rolex watches or fine crystal	Life insurance, Red Cross blood donations

Industrial Products

Industrial product

A product bought by individuals and organizations for further processing or for use in conducting a business.

Industrial products are those purchased for further processing or for use in conducting a business. Thus, the distinction between a consumer product and an industrial product is based on the *purpose* for which the product is bought. If a consumer buys a lawn mower for use around home, the lawn mower is a consumer product. If the same consumer buys the same lawn mower for use in a landscaping business, the lawn mower is an industrial product.

The three groups of industrial products and services include materials and parts, capital items, and supplies and services. *Materials and parts* include raw materials and manufactured materials and parts. Raw materials consist of farm products (wheat, cotton, livestock, fruits, vegetables) and natural products (fish, lumber, crude petroleum, iron ore). Manufactured materials and parts consist of component materials (iron, yarn, cement, wires) and component parts (small motors, tires, castings). Most manufactured materials and parts are sold directly to industrial users. Price and service are the major marketing factors; branding and advertising tend to be less important.

Capital items are industrial products that aid in the buyer's production or operations, including installations and accessory equipment. Installations consist of major purchases such as buildings (factories, offices) and fixed equipment (generators, drill presses, large computer systems, elevators). Accessory equipment includes portable factory equipment and tools (hand tools, lift trucks) and office equipment (computers, fax machines, desks). They have a shorter life than installations and simply aid in the production process.

The final group of industrial products is *supplies and services*. Supplies include operating supplies (lubricants, coal, paper, pencils) and repair and maintenance items (paint, nails, brooms). Supplies are the convenience products of the industrial field because they are usually purchased with a minimum of effort or comparison. Business services include maintenance and repair services (window cleaning, computer repair) and business advisory services (legal, management consulting, advertising). Such services are usually supplied under contract.

Organizations, Persons, Places, and Ideas

In addition to tangible products and services, marketers have broadened the concept of a product to include other market offerings—organizations, persons, places, and ideas.

Organizations often carry out activities to "sell" the organization itself. *Organization marketing* consists of activities undertaken to create, maintain, or change the attitudes and behavior of target consumers toward an organization. Both profit and not-for-profit organizations practice organization marketing. Business firms sponsor public relations or *corporate image advertising* campaigns to market themselves and polish their images. For example, chemical giant BASF markets itself to the general public as a company whose "invisible contributions" result in "visible success." Its ads show how BASF works behind the scenes with its industrial customers to bring the world visible success in everything from water treatment and agricultural productivity to outdoor clothing, sun protection, and sports and leisure equipment. Similarly, not-for-profit organizations, such as churches, colleges, charities, museums, and performing arts groups, market their organizations in order to raise funds and attract members or patrons.

People can also be thought of as products. *Person marketing* consists of activities undertaken to create, maintain, or change attitudes or behavior toward particular people. People ranging from presidents, entertainers, and sports figures to professionals such as doctors, lawyers, and architects use person marketing to build their reputations. And businesses, charities, and other organizations use well-known personalities to help sell their products or causes. For example, more than a dozen big-name companies—including Nike, Buick, Accenture, EA Sports, American Express, Gillette, Gatorade, and Apple—combine to pay more than $100 million a year to link themselves with golf superstar Tiger Woods.[3]

The skillful use of marketing can turn a person's name into a powerhouse brand. Carefully managed and well-known names such as Oprah Winfrey, Martha Stewart, and businessman Donald Trump now adorn everything from sports apparel, housewares, and magazines to book clubs and casinos. Trump, who describes himself as "the hottest brand on the planet," has skillfully made his life a nonstop media event. Says a friend, "He's a skillful marketer, and what he markets is his name."[4]

Such well-known, well-marketed names hold substantial branding power. ▲Consider Rachael Ray:

> Not unlike Oprah or Martha Stewart, Rachael Ray has become a one-woman marketing phenomenon: In less than a decade, she's zipped from nobody to pop-culture icon. Beginning with her 30-Minute Meals cookbooks, followed later by a Food Network TV show, Ray won her way into the hearts of America by demystifying cooking and dishing out a ton of energy. Thanks to her perky personality, which has a dollop of upstate New York twang and a sprinkling of catch phrases such as "yum-o" and "sammies," Rachael Ray has moved far beyond quick meals. Bearing her name are more than a dozen best-selling cookbooks (the latest is *Yum-o! The Family Cookbook*), a monthly lifestyle magazine, three Food Network shows, a syndicated daytime talk show, and assorted licensing deals that have stamped her name on kitchen essentials from knives to her own "E.V.O.O." (extra virgin olive oil for those not familiar with Rayisms). There are even Ray-branded music CDs and ring tones. Ultimately, Ray's brand power derives from all that she has come to represent. Her brands "begin with food and move briskly on to the emotional, social, and cultural benefits that food gives us." Ray's persona—and hence her brand—is a "celebration of why food matters."[5]

▲ Person marketing: Rachael Ray has become a one-woman marketing phenomenon.

Place marketing involves activities undertaken to create, maintain, or change attitudes or behavior toward particular places. Cities, states, regions, and even entire nations compete to attract tourists, new residents, conventions, and company offices and factories. Texas advertises that "It's like a whole other country" and California urges you to "Find yourself here." The Chinese National Tourist Office (CNTO) invites travelers from around the world to "Discover China now!" The CNTO has 15 overseas tourist offices, including 2 in the United States. Tourism in China has been booming as more and more travelers discover the treasures of China's ancient civilization alongside the towering skylines of modern cities such as Shanghai and Beijing (site of the 2008 Summer Olympics). At its Web site, the CNTO offers information about the country and its attractions, travel tips, lists of tour operators, and much more information that makes it easier to say "yes" to China travel.[6]

Ideas can also be marketed. In one sense, all marketing is the marketing of an idea, whether it is the general idea of brushing your teeth or the specific idea that Crest toothpastes create "healthy, beautiful smiles for life." Here, however, we narrow our focus to the marketing of *social ideas*. This area has been called **social marketing**, defined by the Social Marketing Institute as the use of commercial marketing concepts and tools in programs designed to influence individuals' behavior to improve their well-being and that of society.[7]

Social marketing programs include public health campaigns to reduce smoking, alcoholism, drug abuse, and obesity. Other social marketing efforts include environmental campaigns to promote wilderness protection, clean air, and conservation. Still others address issues such as family planning, human rights, and racial equality. The Ad Council of America (www.adcouncil.org) has developed dozens of social advertising campaigns, involving issues ranging from preventive health, education, and personal safety to environmental preservation.

But social marketing involves much more than just advertising—the Social Marketing Institute (SMI) encourages the use of a broad range of marketing tools. "Social marketing goes well beyond the promotional '*P*' of the marketing mix to include every other element to achieve its social change objectives," says the SMI's executive director.[8]

Social marketing

The use of commercial marketing concepts and tools in programs designed to influence individuals' behavior to improve their well-being and that of society.

Product and Service Decisions (pp 229–235)

Author Comment | Now that we've answered the "What is a product?" question, let's dig into the specific decisions that companies must make when designing and marketing products and services.

Marketers make product and service decisions at three levels: individual product decisions, product line decisions, and product mix decisions. We discuss each in turn.

Individual Product and Service Decisions

Figure 8.2 shows the important decisions in the development and marketing of individual products and services. We will focus on decisions about *product attributes, branding, packaging, labeling,* and *product support services*.

Product and Service Attributes

Developing a product or service involves defining the benefits that it will offer. These benefits are communicated and delivered by product attributes such as *quality, features,* and *style and design*.

Product quality

The characteristics of a product or service that bear on its ability to satisfy stated or implied customer needs.

Product Quality. **Product quality** is one of the marketer's major positioning tools. Quality has a direct impact on product or service performance; thus, it is closely linked to customer value and satisfaction. In the narrowest sense, quality can be defined as "freedom from defects." But most customer-centered companies go beyond this narrow definition. Instead, they define quality in terms of creating customer value and satisfaction. The American Society for Quality defines quality as the characteristics of a product or service that bear on its ability to satisfy stated or implied customer needs. Similarly, Siemens defines quality this way: "Quality is when our customers come back and our products don't."[9]

Don't forget Figure 8.1! The focus of all of these decisions is to create core customer value.

FIGURE | 8.2
Individual Product Decisions

Total quality management (TQM) is an approach in which all the company's people are involved in constantly improving the quality of products, services, and business processes. For most top companies, customer-driven quality has become a way of doing business. Today, companies are taking a "return on quality" approach, viewing quality as an investment and holding quality efforts accountable for bottom-line results.

Product quality has two dimensions—level and consistency. In developing a product, the marketer must first choose a *quality level* that will support the product's positioning. Here, product quality means *performance quality*—the ability of a product to perform its functions. For example, a Rolls-Royce provides higher performance quality than a Chevrolet: It has a smoother ride, provides more "creature comforts," and lasts longer. Companies rarely try to offer the highest possible performance quality level—few customers want or can afford the high levels of quality offered in products such as a Rolls-Royce automobile, a Viking range, or a Rolex watch. Instead, companies choose a quality level that matches target market needs and the quality levels of competing products.

Beyond quality level, high quality also can mean high levels of quality consistency. Here, product quality means *conformance quality*—freedom from defects and *consistency* in delivering a targeted level of performance. All companies should strive for high levels of conformance quality. In this sense, a Chevrolet can have just as much quality as a Rolls-Royce. Although a Chevy doesn't perform at the same level as a Rolls-Royce, it can deliver as consistently the quality that customers pay for and expect.

Product Features. A product can be offered with varying features. A stripped-down model, one without any extras, is the starting point. The company can create higher-level models by adding more features. Features are a competitive tool for differentiating the company's product from competitors' products. Being the first producer to introduce a valued new feature is one of the most effective ways to compete.

How can a company identify new features and decide which ones to add to its product? The company should periodically survey buyers who have used the product and ask these questions: How do you like the product? Which specific features of the product do you like most? Which features could we add to improve the product? The answers provide the company with a rich list of feature ideas. The company can then assess each feature's *value* to customers versus its *cost* to the company. Features that customers value highly in relation to costs should be added.

Product Style and Design. Another way to add customer value is through distinctive *product style and design*. Design is a larger concept than style. *Style* simply describes the appearance of a product. Styles can be eye-catching or yawn producing. A sensational style may grab attention and produce pleasing aesthetics, but it does not necessarily make the product *perform* better. Unlike style, *design* is more than skin deep—it goes to the very heart of a product. Good design contributes to a product's usefulness as well as to its looks.

Design begins with a deep understanding of customer needs. More than simply creating product or service attributes, it involves shaping the customer's product-use experience. ▲Consider OXO's outstanding design philosophy and process:[10]

OXO's uniquely designed kitchen and gardening gadgets look pretty cool. But to OXO, good design means a lot more than good looks. It means that OXO tools work—*really* work—for anyone and everyone. For OXO, design means a salad spinner that can be used with one hand; tools with pressure-absorbing, nonslip handles that make them more efficient; or a watering can with a spout that rotates back toward the body, allowing for easier filling and storing. Ever since it came out with its supereffective Good Grips vegetable peeler in 1990, OXO has been known for its clever designs that make everyday living easier.

Much of OXO's design inspiration comes directly from users. "We . . . do a lot of talking to consumers and chefs . . . we do a lot of surveys, we talk to people we know . . . all over the country," says an OXO executive. OXO use-tests its product ideas exhaustively—in the OXO kitchen, in employees' homes, at a cooking school, or by just corralling casual

We've remodeled the most important parts of your kitchen.

We've remodeled the peeler. We've remodeled the garlic press, the can opener and the wooden spoon. And we didn't stop there. Any kitchen tools that weren't comfortable or easy to use were fair game. The idea isn't to make the old tools obsolete, it's to make them better. If we can't make them better, we don't make them at all. Pick up OXO Good Grips® and you'll feel what we mean. They're easy to hold, easy to use and easy to love. In fact, they might just change the way you feel about your kitchen.

OXO GOOD GRIPS

For information call 1-800-545-4411

▲ Product design: OXO focuses on the desired end-user experience, and then translates its pie-cutter-in-the-sky notions into eminently usable gadgets.

Brand
A name, term, sign, symbol, design, or a combination of these that identifies the products or services of one seller or group of sellers and differentiates them from those of competitors.

Packaging
The activities of designing and producing the container or wrapper for a product.

shoppers outside its location near Manhattan's Chelsea Market. For example, after watching people struggle with the traditional Pyrex measuring cup, OXO discovered a critical flaw: You can't tell how full it is without lifting it up to eye level. The resulting OXO measuring cups have markings down the *inside* that can be read from above, big enough to read without glasses.

Interestingly, although OXO offers more than 500 really well-designed products, it doesn't actually do its own designs. Instead, OXOnians focus on the desired end-user experience, and then work with design firms to translate their pie-cutter-in-the-sky notions into eminently usable gadgets.

Thus, product designers should think less about product attributes and technical specifications and more about how customers will use and benefit from the product.

Branding

Perhaps the most distinctive skill of professional marketers is their ability to build and manage brands. A **brand** is a name, term, sign, symbol, or design, or a combination of these, that identifies the maker or seller of a product or service. Consumers view a brand as an important part of a product and branding can add value to a product. Customers attach meanings to brands and develop brand relationships. For example, most consumers would perceive a bottle of White Linen perfume as a high-quality, expensive product. But the same perfume in an unmarked bottle would likely be viewed as lower in quality, even if the fragrance was identical.

Branding has become so strong that today hardly anything goes unbranded. Salt is packaged in branded containers, common nuts and bolts are packaged with a distributor's label, and automobile parts—spark plugs, tires, filters—bear brand names that differ from those of the automakers. Even fruits, vegetables, dairy products, and poultry are branded—Sunkist oranges, Dole Classic iceberg salads, Horizon Organic milk, and Perdue chickens.

Branding helps buyers in many ways. Brand names help consumers identify products that might benefit them. Brands also say something about product quality and consistency—buyers who always buy the same brand know that they will get the same features, benefits, and quality each time they buy. Branding also gives the seller several advantages. The brand name becomes the basis on which a whole story can be built about a product's special qualities. The seller's brand name and trademark provide legal protection for unique product features that otherwise might be copied by competitors. And branding helps the seller to segment markets. For example, Toyota Motor Corporation can offer the major Lexus, Toyota, and Scion brands, each with numerous sub-brands—such as Camry, Prius, Matrix, Yaris, Tundra, Land Cruiser, and others—not just one general product for all consumers.

Building and managing brands are perhaps the marketer's most important tasks. We will discuss branding strategy in more detail later in the chapter.

Packaging

Packaging involves designing and producing the container or wrapper for a product. Traditionally, the primary function of the package was to hold and protect the product. In recent times, however, numerous factors have made packaging an important marketing tool as well. Increased competition and clutter on retail store shelves means that packages must now perform many sales tasks—from attracting attention, to describing the product, to making the sale.

Companies are realizing the power of good packaging to create immediate consumer recognition of a brand. For example, an average supermarket stocks 45,000 items; the

average Wal-Mart supercenter carries 142,000 items. The typical shopper passes by some 300 items per minute, and more than 70 percent of all purchase decisions are made in stores. In this highly competitive environment, the package may be the seller's last and best chance to influence buyers. Thus, for many companies, the package itself has become an important promotional medium.[11]

Poorly designed packages can cause headaches for consumers and lost sales for the company. *Consumer Reports* even has an award for the most difficult to open packages, fittingly named the "Oyster Awards" (as in trying to pry open a tight-jawed oyster). One recent winner was packaging for the Bratz Sisterz dolls, which contained some 50 packaging restraints, from rubber bands to molded plastic covers. It took one test subject, a seven-year-old girl, eight minutes to free the dolls. Says one reporter, after wrestling with the packaging, the child was "noticeably agitated and breathing heavily," and the dolls "looked as if they'd just returned from a rough night on the town."[12]

By contrast, innovative packaging can give a company an advantage over competitors and boost sales. Sometimes even seemingly small packaging improvements can make a big difference. ▲For example, Heinz revolutionized the 170-year-old condiments industry by inverting the good old ketchup bottle, letting customers quickly squeeze out even the last bit of ketchup. At the same time, it adopted a "fridge-door-fit" shape that not only slots into shelves more easily but also has a cap that is simpler for children to open. In the four months following the introduction of the new package, sales jumped 12 percent. What's more, the new package does double duty as a promotional tool. Says a packaging analyst, "When consumers see the Heinz logo on the fridge door every time they open it, it's taking marketing inside homes."[13]

In recent years, product safety has also become a major packaging concern. We have all learned to deal with hard-to-open "childproof" packaging. And after the rash of product tampering scares during the 1980s, most drug producers and food makers now put their products in tamper-resistant packages. In making packaging decisions, the company also must heed growing environmental concerns. Fortunately, many companies have gone "green" by reducing their packaging and using environmentally responsible packaging materials.

Labeling

Labels range from simple tags attached to products to complex graphics that are part of the package. They perform several functions. At the very least, the label *identifies* the product or brand, such as the name Sunkist stamped on oranges. The label might also *describe* several things about the product—who made it, where it was made, when it was made, its contents, how it is to be used, and how to use it safely. Finally, the label might help to *promote* the brand, support its positioning, and connect with customers. For many companies, labels have become an important element in broader marketing campaigns.

For example, ▲Pepsi recently recrafted the graphics on its soft drink cans as part of a broader effort to give the brand more meaning and social relevance to its youth audience.[14]

In its quest for a refreshing, more relevant new look, Pepsi created no less than 35 new domestic and international can designs. The first wave of eight new U.S. designs—featuring such exotic names as "Emoticons" and "Groovy"—was timed to coincide with the start of Pepsi's broader "More Happy" ad campaign. Additional new cans were then rolled out about every three weeks. Beyond eye-catching artwork, each Pepsi design carried a unique Web address that linked customers to a microsite created specifically for that design. The first microsites, aptly named "This Is the Beginning," allowed users from

GROOVY

around the world to gather in real time to collectively design the next *Pepsi* billboard in Times Square. Additional experiences, such as the music-oriented "Move the Crowd," went live every few weeks in tandem with the can releases, all of which were cataloged at the "Pepsi Can Gallery" Web site. "What we did with the [can designs] and sites is create custom experiences that users discover on their own," said a Pepsi marketing executive. "Every time a consumer buys a Pepsi, they're getting a new experience."

Along with the positives, labeling also raises concerns. There has been a long history of legal concerns about packaging and labels. The Federal Trade Commission Act of 1914 held that false, misleading, or deceptive labels or packages constitute unfair competition. Labels can mislead customers, fail to describe important ingredients, or fail to include needed safety warnings. As a result, several federal and state laws regulate labeling. The most prominent is the Fair Packaging and Labeling Act of 1966, which set mandatory labeling requirements, encouraged voluntary industry packaging standards, and allowed federal agencies to set packaging regulations in specific industries.

Labeling has been affected in recent times by *unit pricing* (stating the price per unit of standard measure), *open dating* (stating the expected shelf life of the product), and *nutritional labeling* (stating the nutritional values in the product). The Nutritional Labeling and Educational Act of 1990 requires sellers to provide detailed nutritional information on food products, and recent sweeping actions by the Food and Drug Administration regulate the use of health-related terms such as *low fat*, *light*, and *high fiber*. Sellers must ensure that their labels contain all the required information.

Product Support Services

Customer service is another element of product strategy. A company's offer usually includes some support services, which can be a minor or a major part of the total offering. Later in the chapter, we will discuss services as products in themselves. Here, we discuss services that augment actual products.

The first step is to survey customers periodically to assess the value of current services and to obtain ideas for new ones. For example, Cadillac holds regular focus group interviews with owners and carefully watches complaints that come into its dealerships. From this careful monitoring, Cadillac has learned that buyers are very upset by repairs that are not done correctly the first time. GM research indicates that customers who experience good service are five times more likely to repurchase the same brand then those who have had a bad service experience.

Once the company has assessed the quality of various support services to customers, it can take steps to fix problems and add new services that will both delight customers and yield profits to the company. For instance, Cadillac tracks repair data to find out if certain dealerships or even individual technicians are frequently making the same repair mistakes. Then, to promote good first-time repairs, it informs dealers and rewards those that have high customer-service ratings. And to keep customers happier after the sale, Cadillac also offers as a standard feature an early-warning system for mechanical problems, built into the onboard OnStar system.[15]

Many companies are now using a sophisticated mix of phone, e-mail, fax, Internet, and interactive voice and data technologies to provide support services that were not possible before. ▲For example, HP offers a complete set of sales and after-sale services. It promises "HP Total Care—expert help for every stage of your computer's life. From choosing it, to configuring it, to protecting it, to tuning it up—all the way to recycling it." Customers can click onto the HP Total Care

▲ Product support services: HP promises "HP Total Care—expert help for every stage of your computer's life. From choosing it, to configuring it, to protecting it, to tuning it up—all the way to recycling it."

service portal that offers online resources for HP products and 24/7 tech support, which can be accessed via e-mail, instant online chat, and telephone.[16]

Product Line Decisions

Beyond decisions about individual products and services, product strategy also calls for building a product line. A **product line** is a group of products that are closely related because they function in a similar manner, are sold to the same customer groups, are marketed through the same types of outlets, or fall within given price ranges. For example, Nike produces several lines of athletic shoes and apparel, and Marriott offers several lines of hotels.

The major product line decision involves *product line length*—the number of items in the product line. The line is too short if the manager can increase profits by adding items; the line is too long if the manager can increase profits by dropping items. Managers need to analyze their product lines periodically to assess each product item's sales and profits and to understand how each item contributes to the line's overall performance.

Product line length is influenced by company objectives and resources. For example, one objective might be to allow for upselling. Thus BMW wants to move customers up from its 3-series models to 5- and 7-series models. Another objective might be to allow cross-selling: Hewlett-Packard sells printers as well as cartridges. Still another objective might be to protect against economic swings: Gap runs several clothing-store chains (Gap, Old Navy, and Banana Republic) covering different price points.

A company can expand its product line in two ways: by *line filling* or by *line stretching*. *Product line filling* involves adding more items within the present range of the line. There are several reasons for product line filling: reaching for extra profits, satisfying dealers, using excess capacity, being the leading full-line company, and plugging holes to keep out competitors. However, line filling is overdone if it results in cannibalization and customer confusion. The company should ensure that new items are noticeably different from existing ones.

Product line stretching occurs when a company lengthens its product line beyond its current range. The company can stretch its line downward, upward, or both ways. Companies located at the upper end of the market can stretch their lines *downward*. A company may stretch downward to plug a market hole that otherwise would attract a new competitor or to respond to a competitor's attack on the upper end. Or it may add low-end products because it finds faster growth taking place in the low-end segments. Honda stretched downward for all of these reasons by adding its thrifty little Honda Fit to its line. The Fit, economical to drive and priced in the $12,000 to $13,000 range, met increasing consumer demands for more frugal cars and preempted competitors in the new-generation minicar segment.

Companies can also stretch their product lines *upward*. Sometimes, companies stretch upward in order to add prestige to their current products. Or they may be attracted by a faster growth rate or higher margins at the higher end. For example, some years ago, each of the leading Japanese auto companies introduced an upmarket automobile: Honda launched Acura; Toyota launched Lexus; and Nissan launched Infiniti. They used entirely new names rather than their own names.

Companies in the middle range of the market may decide to stretch their lines in *both directions*. Marriott did this with its hotel product line. Along with regular Marriott hotels, it added eight new branded hotel lines to serve both the upper and lower ends of the market. For example, Renaissance Hotels & Resorts aims to attract and please top executives; Fairfield Inn by Marriott, vacationers and business travelers on a tight travel budget; and Courtyard by Marriott, salespeople and other "road warriors."[17] The major risk with this strategy is that some travelers will trade down after finding that the lower-price hotels in the Marriott chain give them pretty much everything they want. However, Marriott would rather capture its customers who move downward than lose them to competitors.

Product Mix Decisions

An organization with several product lines has a product mix. A **product mix** (or **product portfolio**) consists of all the product lines and items that a particular seller offers for sale. Some companies manage very complex product portfolios. ▲For example, Sony's

---

Product line
A group of products that are closely related because they function in a similar manner, are sold to the same customer groups, are marketed through the same types of outlets, or fall within given price ranges.

Product mix (or product portfolio)
The set of all product lines and items that a particular seller offers for sale.

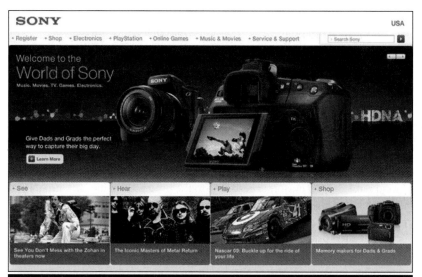

▲ Product mix decisions: Sony has a large and diverse product portfolio, divided into four primary product businesses, each containing hundreds of products. "Welcome to the world of Sony."

diverse portfolio consists of four primary product businesses worldwide: Sony Electronics, Sony Computer Entertainment (games), Sony Pictures Entertainment (movies, TV shows, music, DVDs), and Sony Financial Services (life insurance, banking, and other offerings).

Each major Sony business consists of several product lines. For example, Sony Electronics includes cameras and camcorders, computers, TV and home entertainment products, mobile electronics, and others. In turn, each of these lines contains many individual items. Sony's TV and home entertainment line includes TVs, DVD players, home audio components, digital home products, and more. Altogether, Sony's product mix includes a diverse collection of hundreds and hundreds of products.

A company's product mix has four important dimensions: width, length, depth, and consistency. Product mix *width* refers to the number of different product lines the company carries. Sony markets a wide range of consumer and industrial products around the world, from TVs and PlayStation consoles to semiconductors. Product mix *length* refers to the total number of items the company carries within its product lines. Sony typically carries many products within each line. The camera and camcorder line, for instance, includes digital cameras, camcorders, photo printers, memory media, and tons of accessories.

Product mix *depth* refers to the number of versions offered of each product in the line. Sony has a very deep product mix. For example, it makes and markets about any kind of TV you'd ever want to buy—tube, flat panel, rear projection, front projection, HD or low resolution—each in almost any imaginable size. Finally, the *consistency* of the product mix refers to how closely related the various product lines are in end use, production requirements, distribution channels, or some other way. Within each major business, Sony's product lines are fairly consistent in that they perform similar functions for buyers and go through the same distribution channels. Companywide, however, Sony markets a very diverse mix of products. Managing such a broad and diverse product portfolio requires much skill.

These product mix dimensions provide the handles for defining the company's product strategy. The company can increase its business in four ways. It can add new product lines, widening its product mix. In this way, its new lines build on the company's reputation in its other lines. The company can lengthen its existing product lines to become a more full-line company. Or it can add more versions of each product and thus deepen its product mix. Finally, the company can pursue more product line consistency—or less—depending on whether it wants to have a strong reputation in a single field or in several fields.

Author Comment | A brand represents everything that a product or service *means* to consumers. As such, brands are valuable assets to a company. For example, when you hear someone say "Coca-Cola," what do you think, feel, or remember? What about "Harley-Davidson"? Or "Google"?

Branding Strategy: Building Strong Brands (pp 235–244)

Some analysts see brands as *the* major enduring asset of a company, outlasting the company's specific products and facilities. John Stewart, former CEO of Quaker Oats, once said, "If this business were split up, I would give you the land and bricks and mortar, and I would keep the brands and trademarks, and I would fare better than you." A former CEO of McDonald's declared, "If every asset we own, every building, and every piece of equipment were destroyed in a terrible natural disaster, we would be able to borrow all the money to replace it very quickly because of the value of our brand. . . . The brand is more valuable than the totality of all these assets."[18]

Thus, brands are powerful assets that must be carefully developed and managed. In this section, we examine the key strategies for building and managing brands.

Brand Equity

Brands are more than just names and symbols. They are a key element in the company's relationships with consumers. Brands represent consumers' perceptions and feelings about a product and its performance—everything that the product or service *means* to consumers. In the final analysis, brands exist in the heads of consumers. As one well-respected marketer once said, "Products are created in the factory, but brands are created in the mind."[19]

Brand equity

The differential effect that knowing the brand name has on customer response to the product or its marketing.

A powerful brand has high *brand equity*. **Brand equity** is the differential effect that knowing the brand name has on customer response to the product and its marketing. It's a measure of the brand's ability to capture consumer preference and loyalty. A brand has positive brand equity when consumers react more favorably to it than to a generic or unbranded version of the same product. It has negative brand equity if consumers react less favorably than to an unbranded version.

Brands vary in the amount of power and value they hold in the marketplace. Some brands—such as Coca-Cola, Nike, Disney, GE, McDonald's, Harley-Davidson, and others—become larger-than-life icons that maintain their power in the market for years, even generations. Other brands create fresh consumer excitement and loyalty, brands such as Google, YouTube, Apple, eBay, and Wikipedia. These brands win in the marketplace not simply because they deliver unique benefits or reliable service. Rather, they succeed because they forge deep connections with customers.

Ad agency Young & Rubicam's Brand Asset Valuator measures brand strength along four consumer perception dimensions: *differentiation* (what makes the brand stand out), *relevance* (how consumers feel it meets their needs), *knowledge* (how much consumers know about the brand), and *esteem* (how highly consumers regard and respect the brand). Brands with strong brand equity rate high on all of these dimensions. A brand must be distinct, or consumers will have no reason to choose it over other brands. But the fact that a brand is highly differentiated doesn't necessarily mean that consumers will buy it. The brand must stand out in ways that are relevant to consumers' needs. But even a differentiated, relevant brand is far from a shoe-in. Before consumers will respond to the brand, they must first know about and understand it. And that familiarity must lead to a strong, positive consumer-brand connection (see **Real Marketing 8.1**).[20]

Thus, positive brand equity derives from consumer feelings about and connections with a brand. Consumers sometimes bond *very* closely with specific brands. ▲ For example, one Michigan couple had such a passion for Black & Decker's DeWalt power tool brand that they designed their entire wedding around it. They wore trademark DeWalt black-and-yellow T-shirts, made their way to a wooden chapel that they'd built with their DeWalt gear, exchanged vows and power tools, and even cut cake with a power saw. Joked the wife about her husband (a carpenter by trade), "He loves DeWalt nearly as much as he loves me."[21]

A brand with high brand equity is a very valuable asset. *Brand valuation* is the process of estimating the total financial value of a brand. Measuring such value is difficult. However, according to one estimate, the brand value of Google is a whopping $86 billion, with GE and Microsoft close behind at $71 billion and Coca-Cola at $58 billion. Other brands rating among the world's most valuable include China Mobile, Nokia, IBM, Apple, McDonald's, and Toyota.[22]

High brand equity provides a company with many competitive advantages. A powerful brand enjoys a high level of consumer brand

▲ Consumers sometimes bond very closely with specific brands. Jokes the bride at this wedding: "He loves DeWalt nearly as much as he loves me."

Real Marketing 8.1

Breakaway Brands:
Connecting with Customers

"Big blue-chip companies like General Electric and Microsoft do many things well," notes a brand analyst, "but showing up on lists of the hottest brands is typically not one of them. Yet these two lumbering giants both made their way onto brand consultancy Landor Associates' annual Breakaway Brands ranking—a comprehensive survey that measures consumer sizzle."

Each year, brand consultancy Landor Associates, an arm of ad agency Young & Rubicam, conducts a "Top Ten Breakaway Brands" survey in which it identifies the ten brands with the greatest percentage gains in brand health and business value as a result of superb brand strategy and execution over a three-year period. The survey taps Young & Rubicam's Brand Asset Valuator, a database of responses from 9,000 consumers evaluating 2,500 brands measured across 56 metrics. Landor looks at brand factors such as differentiation, relevance, esteem, and knowledge. At the same time, another consultancy, BrandEconomics, assesses the financial performance of the brand ("Economic Value Added"). Combined, the Brand Asset Valuator and Economic Value Added models provide a brand valuation based on both consumer and financial measures.

Ideas about achieving brand strength, that elusive blend of awareness and trust, have changed in the past decade. "It's no longer, What can we blast out there about ourselves?" says another branding expert. "Brand theory now asks, How can we connect with the community in a really meaningful way?" It's a big question. Armed with information about price and quality, today's consumer is a tough challenge. But, says the expert, "if you're willing to talk directly and deeply to your audience, you can become a strong brand without a lot of fanfare."

The most recent Breakaway Brands list includes a strange agglomeration, from hot technology brands such as iPod and BlackBerry to blue chips such as GE and Microsoft to down-and-dirty discount retailers such as TJ Maxx and Costco.

Breakaway brand BlackBerry has perfected a truly unique community-building tool. Today, it is becoming increasingly difficult within the business community to imagine life before BlackBerry.

Top Ten Breakaway Brands

1. TJ Maxx
2. iPod
3. BlackBerry
4. Stonyfield Farm
5. Samsung
6. Costco
7. Propel
8. Barnes & Noble
9. GE
10. Microsoft

Missing are some brand titans such as Coca-Cola (big but not growing very fast) and fresh-faced young brands like MySpace (the consumer panel consists of adults 18 and older, so the youth-centric sensation doesn't show up yet). But Landor found that each brand that did make the list embraced one or more of three themes. "Today it's all about *trust, community*, and creating a *dialogue* with your customer that shares real knowledge," says Landor's chief marketing officer. That is, all of the brands really connect with customers.

So, how are dinosaurs Microsoft and GE connecting with consumers? Microsoft's resurrection from its corporate-bad-guy status of past years results from several factors. More consumer-connecting products such as its Xbox game console now give Microsoft a cachet that even dominant office-related brands such as a PowerPoint and Word never could. And the good works of the Bill & Melinda Gates Foundation have also helped to boost consumer trust and community, helping

to foster perceptions of a kinder, gentler Microsoft. Finally, as new corporate bogeymen like Google and MySpace owner News Corp. begin throwing their weight around, Microsoft now "comes off as an underdog even though it is a behemoth," says the brand expert.

General Electric's appearance on the breakaway brands list derives almost entirely from its "ecomagination" environmental efforts. Between 2005 and 2010, the company aims to more than double its annual research budget for cleaner technologies—like energy-efficient refrigerators and wind turbines. Last year, GE's increasing connections with customer and community concerns about the environment generated $12 billion in revenues from 45 ecomagination products and services. "They are trying to turn that entire ship into the ecovessel of the future," says Landor's chief marketing executive.

iPod and BlackBerry—that's more like it! These are brands that you'd expect to see on a Breakaway Brands list. Among brands that foster customer community, the iPod is an obvious winner by virtue of its ability to create an online music ecosystem virtually overnight. With each new product introduction, iPod and Apple advance the causes of democratizing technology and approachable innovation.

Continued on next page

Real Marketing 8.1 Continued ▼

Similarly, BlackBerry maker Research In Motion perfected a truly unique community-building tool: a user-friendly device that lets business people stay connected to their jobs and to each other. Jokes about "crackberry addicts" and the appearance of BlackBerry smart-phones in the hands of celebrities from Oprah to Madonna illustrate the brand's rapid rise. "Today, virtually the world over," says a Landor analyst, "it is becoming increasingly difficult among the business community to imagine life 'BB' (Before BlackBerry)."

If iPod and BlackBerry seem like naturals for a Breakaway Brands list, an unlikely pair of retailers—TJ Maxx and Costco—just don't seem to fit. Yet in these difficult days of rising costs and spiraling economics, the two fast-growing discounters are creating treasure-hunt experiences that build strong emotional bonds with customers. TJ Maxx—at

number-one, no less—fulfills the fantasy of luxury for less. At TJ Maxx, saving is no longer a priority reserved for the lower- and middle-income consumers. Now, even the most affluent shopper can experience the "thrill of the save" and the euphoria of a great "Maxx Moment." Similarly, Costco helps customers to save on everyday purchases while also experiencing great deals on high-end products. Says the Landor analyst, Costco has "perfected the art of understanding not only what customers need, but also what they fantasize about, and putting both at their fingertips."

As proves true each year, Landor's breakaway brands list includes some old standbys

and a number of pleasant surprises. As the analyst concludes:

In today's uncertain world it is no wonder that organizations have to work harder and harder to gain the trust of their [customers] in order to be successful. What's more, [with brands], as in life, trust must be earned, not bought, and it must be constantly validated. The . . . marketers at the helm of this year's Top Ten Breakaway Brands understand not only the need to connect with their customers and instill trust, they also understand that brand is one of the most powerful tools available for making those coveted relationships a reality.

Sources: Based on information from Matthew Boyle, "Microsoft and GE: Not Old and in the Way," *Fortune,* November 12, 2007, p. 28; Ellen McGirt, "Breakaway Brands," *Fortune,* September 18, 2006, p. 27; and Chelsea Greene, "Using Brands to Drive Business Results," Landor Brands, November 2008, accessed at www.wpp.com/WPP/Marketing/ReportsStudies/Usingbrandstodrivebusinessresults.htm.

awareness and loyalty. Because consumers expect stores to carry the brand, the company has more leverage in bargaining with resellers. Because the brand name carries high credibility, the company can more easily launch line and brand extensions. A powerful brand offers the company some defense against fierce price competition.

Above all, however, a powerful brand forms the basis for building strong and profitable customer relationships. The fundamental asset underlying brand equity is *customer equity*—the value of the customer relationships that the brand creates. A powerful brand is important, but what it really represents is a profitable set of loyal customers. The proper focus of marketing is building customer equity, with brand management serving as a major marketing tool. Companies need to think of themselves not as portfolios of products, but as portfolios of customers.

Building Strong Brands

Branding poses challenging decisions to the marketer. ◀ **Figure 8.3** shows that the major brand strategy decisions involve brand positioning, brand name selection, brand sponsorship, and brand development.

Brand Positioning

Marketers need to position their brands clearly in target customers' minds. They can position brands at any of three levels.[23] At the lowest level, they can position the brand on *product attributes*. For example, P&G invented the disposable diaper category with its Pampers brand. Early Pampers marketing focused on attributes such as fluid absorption, fit, and disposability. In general, however, attributes are the least desirable level for brand positioning. Competitors can easily copy attributes. More importantly, customers are not interested in attributes as such; they are interested in what the attributes will do for them.

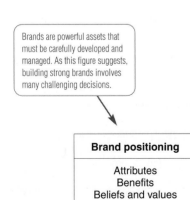

Brands are powerful assets that must be carefully developed and managed. As this figure suggests, building strong brands involves many challenging decisions.

Brand positioning	Brand name selection	Brand sponsorship	Brand development
Attributes Benefits Beliefs and values	Selection Protection	Manufacturer's brand Private brand Licensing Co-branding	Line extensions Brand extensions Multibrands New brands

◀ **FIGURE** | **8.3** Major Brand Strategy Decisions

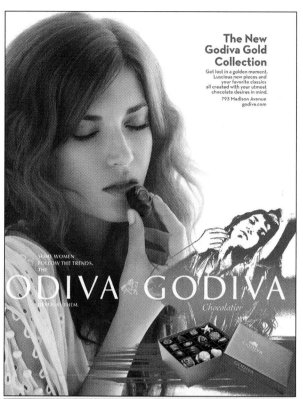

The New
Godiva Gold
Collection

Get lost in a golden moment.
Luscious new pieces and
your favorite classics
all created with your utmost
chocolate desires in mind.
793 Madison Avenue
godiva.com

▲ Brand positioning: The strongest brands go beyond attribute or benefit positioning. Godiva engages customers on a deeper level, touching universal emotions.

A brand can be better positioned by associating its name with a desirable *benefit*. Thus, Pampers can go beyond technical product attributes and talk about the resulting containment and skin-health benefits from dryness. "There are fewer wet bottoms in the world because of us," says Jim Stengel, P&G's global marketing officer. Some successful brands positioned on benefits are Volvo (safety), FedEx (guaranteed on-time delivery), Nike (performance), and Lexus (quality).

The strongest brands go beyond attribute or benefit positioning. They are positioned on strong *beliefs and values*. These brands pack an emotional wallop. ▲Brands such as Godiva, Starbucks, Apple, and Victoria's Secret rely less on a product's tangible attributes and more on creating surprise, passion, and excitement surrounding a brand. Successful brands engage customers on a deep, emotional level. Thus, P&G knows that, to parents, Pampers mean much more than just containment and dryness. According to P&G's Stengel:[24]

> If you go back, we often thought of our brands in terms of functional benefits. But when we began listening very closely to customers, they told us Pampers meant much more to them—Pampers are more about parent-child relationships and total baby care. So we started to say, "We want to be a brand experience; we want to be there to help support parents and babies as they grow and develop." In the initial days people thought we were nuts. How can a diaper help a baby's development? But babies wear diapers 24/7 for almost three years. It actually reorients R&D to ask a question like "How can we help babies sleep better?" Why are we concerned about babies sleeping better? Because sleep is important to brain development. It helps relationship skills. Thinking like that, we're able to

help improve life for our consumers. The equity of great brands has to be something that a consumer finds inspirational and the organization finds inspirational. You know, our baby care business didn't start growing aggressively until we changed Pampers from being about dryness to being about helping mom with her baby's development.

When positioning a brand, the marketer should establish a mission for the brand and a vision of what the brand must be and do. A brand is the company's promise to deliver a specific set of features, benefits, services, and experiences consistently to the buyers. The brand promise must be simple and honest. Motel 6, for example, offers clean rooms, low prices, and good service but does not promise expensive furniture or large bathrooms. In contrast, The Ritz-Carlton offers luxurious rooms and a truly memorable experience but does not promise low prices.

Brand Name Selection

A good name can add greatly to a product's success. However, finding the best brand name is a difficult task. It begins with a careful review of the product and its benefits, the target market, and proposed marketing strategies. After that, naming a brand becomes part science, part art, and a measure of instinct.

Desirable qualities for a brand name include the following: (1) It should suggest something about the product's benefits and qualities. Examples: Beautyrest, Die Hard, Intensive Care, Curves (women's fitness centers). (2) It should be easy to pronounce, recognize, and remember: Tide, Silk, iPod Touch, JetBlue. (3) The brand name should be distinctive: Lexus, Zappos. (4) It should be extendable: Amazon.com began as an online bookseller but chose a name that would allow expansion into other categories. (5) The name should translate easily into foreign languages. Before changing its name to Exxon, Standard Oil of New Jersey rejected the name Enco, which it learned meant a stalled engine when pronounced in Japanese. (6) It should be capable of registration and legal protection. A brand name cannot be registered if it infringes on existing brand names.

Choosing a new brand name is hard work. After a decade of choosing quirky names (Yahoo!, Google) or trademark-proof made-up names (Novartis, Aventis, Lycos), today's style is to build brands around names that have real meaning. For example, names like Silk (soy milk), Method (home products), Smartwater (beverages), and Blackboard (school software) are simple and make intuitive sense. But with trademark applications soaring, *available* new names can be hard to find. Try it yourself. Pick a product and see if you can come up with a better name for it. How about Moonshot? Tickle? Vanilla? Treehugger? Simplicity? Google them and you'll find that they're already taken.

Once chosen, the brand name must be protected. Many firms try to build a brand name that will eventually become identified with the product category. Brand names such as Kleenex, Levi's, JELL-O, BAND-AID, Scotch Tape, Formica, and Ziploc have succeeded in this way. However, their very success may threaten the company's rights to the name. Many originally protected brand names—such as cellophane, aspirin, nylon, kerosene, linoleum, yo-yo, trampoline, escalator, thermos, and shredded wheat—are now generic names that any seller can use. To protect their brands, marketers present them carefully using the word "brand" and the registered trademark symbol, as in "BAND-AID® Brand Adhesive Bandages." Even the long-standing "I am stuck on BAND-AID and BAND AID's stuck on me" jingle has now become "I am stuck on BAND AID *brand* and BAND AID's stuck on me."

Brand Sponsorship

A manufacturer has four sponsorship options. The product may be launched as a *national brand* (or *manufacturer's brand*), as when Sony and Kellogg sell their output under their own brand names (Sony Bravia HDTV or Kellogg's Frosted Flakes). Or the manufacturer may sell to resellers who give the product a *private brand* (also called a *store brand* or *distributor brand*). Although most manufacturers create their own brand names, others market *licensed brands*. Finally, two companies can join forces and *co-brand* a product.

Store brand (or private brand)
A brand created and owned by a reseller of a product or service.

National Brands Versus Store Brands.   National brands (or manufacturers' brands) have long dominated the retail scene. In recent times, however, an increasing number of retailers and wholesalers have created their own **store brands** (or *private brands*). Store brand sales are soaring. In fact, they are growing much faster than national brands. In all, private brands now capture more than 20 percent of all North American supermarket sales, and sales of private-label foods, drinks, and personal care products will increase by 20 percent by 2010. Private-label apparel, such as Gap, The Limited, Arizona Jeans (JCPenney), and Liz Lange (Target), captures a 45 percent share of all U.S. apparel sales.[25]

Once known as "generic" or "no-name" brands, today's store brands are a far cry from the early no-frills generics. Store brands now offer much greater selection and higher quality. Rather than simply creating low-end generic brands that offer a low-price alternative to national brands, retailers are now moving toward higher-end private brands that boost both the store's revenues and its image. As store brand selection and quality have improved, so have consumer confidence and acceptance. Some 40 percent of U.S. consumers now identify themselves as frequent buyers of store brands, up from just 12 percent in the early 1990s.[26]

It seems that almost every retailer now carries its own store brands. Wal-Mart's private brands account for a whopping 40 percent of its sales: brands such as Sam's Choice beverages and food products; Equate pharmacy, health, and beauty products; and White Cloud brand toilet tissue, diapers, detergent, and fabric softener. Its private label brands alone generate nearly twice the sales of all P&G brands.[27] Grocery giant Kroger markets some 8,000 items under a variety of private brands, such as Private Selection, Kroger Brand, F.M.V. (For Maximum Value), Naturally Preferred, and Everyday Living. ▲And Costco, the world's largest warehouse club, offers a staggering array of goods and services under its

▲ Store brands: Costco offers a staggering array of goods and services under its Kirkland Signature brand—anything from Kirkland Signature rotisserie chickens to a $3,439-per-person Kirkland Signature Tahitian cruise package.

Kirkland Signature brand. Costco customers can buy anything from Kirkland Signature rotisserie chickens to a $3,439-per-person Kirkland Signature Tahitian cruise package. At the other end of the spectrum, upscale retailer Saks Fifth Avenue carries its own clothing line, which features $98 men's ties, $200 halter-tops, and $250 cotton dress shirts.

In the so-called *battle of the brands* between national and private brands, retailers have many advantages. They control what products they stock, where they go on the shelf, what prices they charge, and which ones they will feature in local circulars. Retailers often price their store brands lower than comparable national brands, thereby appealing to the budget-conscious shopper in all of us. Although store brands can be hard to establish and costly to stock and promote, they also yield higher profit margins for the reseller. And they give resellers exclusive products that cannot be bought from competitors, resulting in greater store traffic and loyalty. Fast-growing retailer Trader Joe's, which carries 80 percent store brands, began creating its own brands so that "we could put our destiny in our own hands," says the company's president.[28]

To compete with store brands, leading brand marketers must invest in R&D to bring out new brands, new features, and continuous quality improvements. They must design strong advertising programs to maintain high awareness and preference. And they must find ways to "partner" with major distributors in a search for distribution economies and improved joint performance.

Licensing. Most manufacturers take years and spend millions to create their own brand names. However, some companies license names or symbols previously created by other manufacturers, names of well-known celebrities, or characters from popular movies and books. For a fee, any of these can provide an instant and proven brand name.

Apparel and accessories sellers pay large royalties to adorn their products—from blouses to ties, and linens to luggage—with the names or initials of well-known fashion innovators such as Calvin Klein, Tommy Hilfiger, Gucci, or Armani. Sellers of children's products attach an almost endless list of character names to clothing, toys, school supplies, linens, dolls, lunch boxes, cereals, and other items. Licensed character names range from classics such as *Sesame Street*, Disney, Peanuts, Winnie the Pooh, the Muppets, Scooby Doo, and Dr. Seuss characters to the more recent *Dora the Explorer*, *Powerpuff Girls*, *Rugrats*, *Blue's Clues*, and *Harry Potter* characters. And currently a number of top-selling retail toys are products based on television shows and movies, such as the Spiderman Deluxe Spinning Web Blaster and the Talking Friendship Adventures Dora.

Name and character licensing has grown rapidly in recent years. Annual retail sales of licensed products in the United States and Canada have grown from only $4 billion in 1977 to $55 billion in 1987 and more than $187 billion today. Licensing can be a highly profitable business for many companies. ▲ For example, Nickelodeon has developed a stable full of hugely popular characters, such as Dora the Explorer, Go, Diego, Go!, and SpongeBob SquarePants. Dora alone has generated more than $5.3 billion in retail sales in under five years. "When it comes to licensing its brands for consumer products, Nickelodeon has proved that it has the Midas touch," states a brand licensing expert.[29]

Co-branding. Although companies have been **co-branding** products for many years, there has been a recent resurgence in co-branding. Co-branding occurs when two established brand names of different companies are used on the same product. For example, financial services firms often partner with other companies to create co-branded credit cards, such as when Chase and United Airlines joined forces to create the Chase United Travel Card. Similarly, Costco teamed with mattress maker Stearns & Foster to market a line of Kirkland Signature by Stearns & Foster mattress sets. And Nike and Apple co-branded the Nike+iPod Sport Kit, which lets runners link their Nike shoes with their iPod Nanos to track and enhance running performance

Co-branding
The practice of using the established brand names of two different companies on the same product.

Most fashions only last a season. These pants never go out of style.

RECORD BREAKING
SpongeBob SquarePants has become an enduring, revolutionary pop icon, inspiring nautical nonsense in millions of people worldwide while generating record-breaking ratings and retail sales.

NICKELODEON
SpongeBob SquarePants

▲ Licensing: Nickelodeon has developed a stable full of hugely popular characters—such as SpongeBob SquarePants—that generate billions of dollars of retail sales each year.

in real time. "Thanks to a unique partnership between Nike and Apple, your iPod nano becomes your coach. Your personal trainer. Your favorite workout companion."[30]

In most co-branding situations, one company licenses another company's well-known brand to use in combination with its own. Co-branding offers many advantages. Because each brand dominates in a different category, the combined brands create broader consumer appeal and greater brand equity. Co-branding also allows a company to expand its existing brand into a category it might otherwise have difficulty entering alone. For example, Nickelodeon Family Suites by Holiday Inn gives Nickelodeon yet another opportunity to become a deeper part of viewers' lives. And it provides Holiday Inn with a shot at a new, younger travel market made up of young parents who grew up watching Nick. Similarly, the Nike + iPod arrangement gives Apple a presence in the sports and fitness market. At the same time, it helps Nike to bring new value to its customers.[31]

Co-branding also has limitations. Such relationships usually involve complex legal contracts and licenses. Co-branding partners must carefully coordinate their advertising, sales promotion, and other marketing efforts. Finally, when co-branding, each partner must trust that the other will take good care of its brand. For example, consider the marriage between Kmart and the Martha Stewart Everyday housewares brand. When Kmart declared bankruptcy before being acquired by Sears, it cast a shadow on the Martha Stewart brand. In turn, when Martha Stewart was convicted and jailed for illegal financial dealings, it created negative associations for Kmart. Finally, Kmart was further embarrassed when Martha Stewart Living Omnimedia recently struck major licensing agreements with Macy's and Lowe's, announcing that it would separate from Kmart when the current contract ends in 2009. Thus, as one manager puts it, "Giving away your brand is a lot like giving away your child—you want to make sure everything is perfect."[32]

Brand Development

A company has four choices when it comes to developing brands (see ▸ **Figure 8.4**). It can introduce *line extensions*, *brand extensions*, *multibrands*, or *new brands*.

Line Extensions. **Line extensions** occur when a company extends existing brand names to new forms, colors, sizes, ingredients, or flavors of an existing product category. Thus, Morton Salt has expanded its line to include regular iodized salt plus Morton Coarse Kosher Salt, Morton Sea Salt, Morton Lite Salt (low in sodium), Morton Popcorn Salt, Morton Salt Substitute, and several others. The vast majority of all new-product activity consists of line extensions.

A company might introduce line extensions as a low-cost, low-risk way to introduce new products. Or it might want to meet consumer desires for variety, to use excess capacity, or simply to command more shelf space from resellers. However, line extensions involve some risks. An overextended brand name might lose its specific meaning. For example, you can now pick from an array of seven different Jeep SUV models—Commander, Grand Cherokee, Compass, Patriot, Liberty, Wrangler, and Wrangler Unlimited. It's unlikely that many customers will fully appreciate the differences across the many similar models, and such "Jeep creep" can cause consumer confusion or even frustration.

Another risk is that sales of an extension may come at the expense of other items in the line. ▲For example, the original Doritos Tortilla Chips have now morphed into a full line of 20 different types and flavors of chips, including such high-decibel flavors as

Line extension
Extending an existing brand name to new forms, colors, sizes, ingredients, or flavors of an existing product category.

▸**FIGURE | 8.4**
Brand Development Strategies

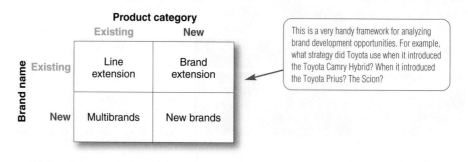

Product category

	Existing	New
Existing	Line extension	Brand extension
New	Multibrands	New brands

Brand name

This is a very handy framework for analyzing brand development opportunities. For example, what strategy did Toyota use when it introduced the Toyota Camry Hybrid? When it introduced the Toyota Prius? The Scion?

▲ Line extensions: An overextended brand name might cause consumer confusion or frustration. The original Doritos Tortilla Chips have now morphed into a full line of 20 different types and flavors of chips, making the original Doritos seem like just another flavor.

Brand extension

Extending an existing brand name to new product categories.

Blazin' Buffalo Ranch, Black Pepper Jack, and Fiery Habanero. Although the line seems to be doing well, the original Doritos chips seem like just another flavor. A line extension works best when it takes sales away from competing brands, not when it "cannibalizes" the company's other items.

Brand Extensions. A **brand extension** extends a current brand name to new or modified products in a new category. For example, Kimberly-Clark extended its market-leading Huggies brand from disposable diapers to a full line of toiletries for tots, from shampoos, lotions, and diaper-rash ointments to baby wash, disposable wash-cloths, and disposable changing pads. Victorinox extended its venerable Swiss Army brand from multitool knives to products ranging from cutlery and ballpoint pens to watches, luggage, and apparel. And P&G has leveraged the strength of its Mr. Clean household cleaner brand to launch several new lines: cleaning pads (Magic Eraser), bathroom cleaning tools (Magic Reach), and home auto cleaning kits (Mr. Clean AutoDry). It's even launching Mr. Clean-branded car washes.

A brand extension gives a new product instant recognition and faster acceptance. It also saves the high advertising costs usually required to build a new brand name. At the same time, a brand extension strategy involves some risk. Brand extensions such as Bic panty-hose, Heinz pet food, Life Savers gum, and Clorox laundry detergent met early deaths. The extension may confuse the image of the main brand. And if a brand extension fails, it may harm consumer attitudes toward the other products carrying the same brand name.

Furthermore, a brand name may not be appropriate to a particular new product, even if it is well made and satisfying—would you consider flying on Hooters Air or drinking Hooters energy drink? How about Donald Trump steaks or an Evian water-filled padded bra? All of these products failed. Companies that are tempted to transfer a brand name must research how well the brand's associations fit the new product.[33]

Multibrands. Companies often introduce additional brands in the same category. Thus, Procter & Gamble markets many different brands in each of its product categories. *Multibranding* offers a way to establish different features and appeal to different buying motives. It also allows a company to lock up more reseller shelf space.

A major drawback of multibranding is that each brand might obtain only a small market share, and none may be very profitable. The company may end up spreading its resources over many brands instead of building a few brands to a highly profitable level. These companies should reduce the number of brands they sell in a given category and set up tighter screening procedures for new brands.

New Brands. A company might believe that the power of its existing brand name is waning and a new brand name is needed. Or it may create a new brand name when it enters a new product category for which none of the company's current brand names are appropriate. For example, Toyota created the separate Scion brand, targeted toward Millennial consumers.

As with multibranding, offering too many new brands can result in a company spreading its resources too thin. And in some industries, such as consumer packaged goods, consumers and retailers have become concerned that there are already too many brands, with too few differences between them. Thus, Procter & Gamble, Frito-Lay, Kraft, and other large consumer-product marketers are now pursuing *megabrand* strategies—weeding out weaker or slower-growing brands and focusing their marketing dollars only on brands that can achieve the number-one or number-two market share positions with good growth prospects in their categories.

Managing Brands

Companies must manage their brands carefully. First, the brand's positioning must be continuously communicated to consumers. Major brand marketers often spend huge amounts on advertising to create brand awareness and to build preference and loyalty. For example, Verizon spends more than $2.8 billion annually to promote its brand. McDonald's spends more than $1.7 billion.[34]

Such advertising campaigns can help to create name recognition, brand knowledge, and maybe even some brand preference. However, the fact is that brands are not maintained by advertising but by the *brand experience*. Today, customers come to know a brand through a wide range of contacts and touch points. These include advertising, but also personal experience with the brand, word of mouth, company Web pages, and many others. The company must put as much care into managing these touch points as it does into producing its ads. "Managing each customer's experience is perhaps the most important ingredient in building [brand] loyalty," states one branding expert. "Every memorable interaction . . . must be completed with excellence and . . . must reinforce your brand essence." ▲ A former Disney executive agrees: "A brand is a living entity, and it is enriched or undermined cumulatively over time, the product of a thousand small gestures."[35]

The brand's positioning will not take hold fully unless everyone in the company lives the brand. Therefore the company needs to train its people to be customer centered. Even better, the company should carry on internal brand building to help employees understand and be enthusiastic about the brand promise. Many companies go even further by training and encouraging their distributors and dealers to serve their customers well.

Finally, companies need to periodically audit their brands' strengths and weaknesses.[36] They should ask: Does our brand excel at delivering benefits that consumers truly value? Is the brand properly positioned? Do all of our consumer touch points support the brand's positioning? Do the brand's managers understand what the brand means to consumers? Does the brand receive proper, sustained support? The brand audit may turn up brands that need more support, brands that need to be dropped, or brands that must be rebranded or repositioned because of changing customer preferences or new competitors.

▲ Managing brands requires managing "touch points." Says a former Disney executive: "A brand is a living entity, and it is enriched or undermined cumulatively over time, the product of a thousand small gestures."

Author Comment | As noted at the start of the chapter, services are "products," too—just intangible ones. So all of the product topics we've discussed so far apply to services as well as to physical products. However, in this final section, we'll focus in on the special characteristics and marketing needs that set services apart.

Services Marketing (pp 244–251)

Services have grown dramatically in recent years. Services now account for close to 79 percent of U.S. gross domestic product. And the service industry is growing. By 2014, it is estimated that nearly four out of five jobs in the United States will be in service industries. Services are growing even faster in the world economy, making up 64 percent of gross world product.[37]

Service industries vary greatly. *Governments* offer services through courts, employment services, hospitals, military services, police and fire departments, postal service, and schools. *Private not-for-profit organizations* offer services through museums, charities, churches, colleges, foundations, and hospitals. A large number of *business organizations* offer services—airlines, banks, hotels, insurance companies, consulting firms, medical and legal practices, entertainment companies, real-estate firms, retailers, and others.

Nature and Characteristics of a Service

A company must consider four special service characteristics when designing marketing programs: *intangibility, inseparability, variability,* and *perishability* (see ◉ **Figure 8.5**).

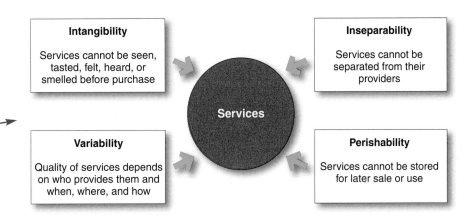

FIGURE | 8.5
Four Service Characteristics

Although services are "products" in a general sense, they have special characteristics and marketing needs. The biggest differences come from the fact that services are essentially intangible and that they are created through direct interactions with customers. Think about your experiences with an airline versus Nike or Apple.

Service intangibility
A major characteristic of services—they cannot be seen, tasted, felt, heard, or smelled before they are bought.

Service intangibility means that services cannot be seen, tasted, felt, heard, or smelled before they are bought. For example, people undergoing cosmetic surgery cannot see the result before the purchase. Airline passengers have nothing but a ticket and the promise that they and their luggage will arrive safely at the intended destination, hopefully at the same time. To reduce uncertainty, buyers look for "signals" of service quality. They draw conclusions about quality from the place, people, price, equipment, and communications that they can see.

Therefore, the service provider's task is to make the service tangible in one or more ways and to send the right signals about quality. One analyst calls this *evidence management*, in which the service organization presents its customers with organized, honest evidence of its capabilities. The Mayo Clinic practices good evidence management:[38]

> When it comes to hospitals, it's very hard for the average patient to judge the quality of the "product." You can't try it on, you can't return it if you don't like it, and you need an advanced degree to understand it. And so, when we're considering a medical facility, most of us unconsciously turn detective, looking for evidence of competence, caring, and integrity. The Mayo Clinic doesn't leave that evidence to chance. By carefully managing a set of visual and experiential clues, Mayo offers patients and their families concrete evidence of its strengths and values. For example, staff people at the clinic are trained to act in a way that clearly signals its patient-first focus. "My doctor calls me at home to check on how I am doing," marvels one patient. "She wants to work with what is best for my schedule." Mayo's physical facilities also send the right signals. They've been carefully designed to relieve stress, offer a place of refuge, create positive distractions, convey caring and respect, signal competence, accommodate families, and make it easy to find your way around. The result? Exceptionally positive word of mouth and abiding customer loyalty have allowed Mayo Clinic to build what is arguably the most powerful brand in health care with very little advertising. Ninety-five percent of Mayo Clinic patients report that they voluntarily praise the clinic to others.

Service inseparability
A major characteristic of services—they are produced and consumed at the same time and cannot be separated from their providers.

Service variability
A major characteristic of services—their quality may vary greatly, depending on who provides them and when, where, and how.

Physical goods are produced, then stored, later sold, and still later consumed. In contrast, services are first sold, then produced and consumed at the same time. In services marketing, the service provider is the product. **Service inseparability** means that services cannot be separated from their providers, whether the providers are people or machines. If a service employee provides the service, then the employee becomes a part of the service. Because the customer is also present as the service is produced, *provider–customer interaction* is a special feature of services marketing. Both the provider and the customer affect the service outcome.

Service variability means that the quality of services depends on who provides them as well as when, where, and how they are provided. For example, some hotels—say, Marriott—have reputations for providing better service than others. Still, within a given Marriott hotel, one registration-counter employee may be cheerful and efficient, whereas another standing just a few feet away may be unpleasant and slow. Even the quality of a single Marriott employee's service varies according to his or her energy and frame of mind at the time of each customer encounter.

Service perishability
A major characteristic of services—they cannot be stored for later sale or use.

Service perishability means that services cannot be stored for later sale or use. Some doctors charge patients for missed appointments because the service value existed only at that point and disappeared when the patient did not show up. The perishability of services is not a problem when demand is steady. However, when demand fluctuates, service firms often have difficult problems. For example, because of rush-hour demand, public transportation companies have to own much more equipment than they would if demand were even throughout the day. Thus, service firms often design strategies for producing a better match between demand and supply. Hotels and resorts charge lower prices in the off-season to attract more guests. And restaurants hire part-time employees to serve during peak periods.

Marketing Strategies for Service Firms

Just like manufacturing businesses, good service firms use marketing to position themselves strongly in chosen target markets. JetBlue promises "Happy Jetting"; Target says "Expect more, pay less." At Hampton, "We love having you here. A great stay. A great Value. That's 100% Hampton." And St. Jude Children's Hospital is "Finding cures. Saving children." These and other service firms establish their positions through traditional marketing mix activities. However, because services differ from tangible products, they often require additional marketing approaches.

The Service-Profit Chain

In a service business, the customer and front-line service employee *interact* to create the service. Effective interaction, in turn, depends on the skills of front-line service employees and on the support processes backing these employees. Thus, successful service companies focus their attention on *both* their customers and their employees. They understand the **service-profit chain**, which links service firm profits with employee and customer satisfaction. This chain consists of five links:[39]

Service-profit chain
The chain that links service firm profits with employee and customer satisfaction.

- *Internal service quality:* superior employee selection and training, a quality work environment, and strong support for those dealing with customers, which results in . . .

- *Satisfied and productive service employees:* more satisfied, loyal, and hardworking employees, which results in . . .

- *Greater service value:* more effective and efficient customer value creation and service delivery, which results in . . .

- *Satisfied and loyal customers:* satisfied customers who remain loyal, repeat purchase, and refer other customers, which results in . . .

- *Healthy service profits and growth:* superior service firm performance

Therefore, reaching service profits and growth goals begins with taking care of those who take care of customers. In fact, legendary founder and former CEO of Southwest Airlines Herb Kelleher always put employees first, not customers. His reasons? "If they're happy, satisfied, dedicated, and energetic, they'll take good care of customers," he says. "When the customers are happy, they come back, and that makes shareholders happy."[40] Consider ▲Four Seasons Hotels and Resorts, a chain legendary for outstanding service:[41]

At Four Seasons, every guest is a somebody. Other exclusive resorts pamper their guests, but Four Seasons offers a subtler brand of doting: helpful rather than subservient; instinctive rather than programmed. So it's easy to understand why Four Seasons has a cult-like clientele. As one Four Seasons Maui guest recently told a manager, "If there's a heaven, I hope it's run by Four Seasons." What makes the Four Seasons so special? It's the staff. The chain knows that happy, satisfied employees make for happy, satisfied customers. "Personal service is not something you can dictate as a policy," says the company's founder and CEO. "It comes from the culture. How you treat your employees is how you expect them to treat the customer."

▲ The service-profit chain: Happy employees make for happy customers. At Four Seasons, employees feel as important and pampered as the guests.

And Four Seasons treats its employees well. Compared with the competition, Four Seasons salaries are in the 75th to 90th percentile, with generous retirement and profit sharing plans. All employees—seamstresses, valets, the ski concierge, the general manager—eat together regularly, free, in the hotel cafeteria. Another killer perk: free rooms. After six months, any staffer can stay three nights free per year at any Four Seasons hotel or resort. That number increases to six nights after a year and steadily thereafter. The room stays make employees feel as important and pampered as the guests. Says a Four Seasons Maui pool attendant about his free stays, "You walk in and you say, 'Yeah, I'm somebody.'" Says another Maui employee, "You come back from those trips on fire. You want to do so much for the guest." As a result, the Four Seasons staff loves the hotel just as much as customers do. Although guests can check out anytime they like, employees never want to leave. The yearly turnover for full-time employees is around 18 percent, half the industry average. And that's the biggest secret to Four Seasons' success.

Thus, service marketing requires more than just traditional external marketing using the Four Ps. 🔖 **Figure 8.6** shows that service marketing also requires *internal marketing* and *interactive marketing*. **Internal marketing** means that the service firm must orient and motivate its customer-contact employees and supporting service people to work as a *team* to provide customer satisfaction. Marketers must get everyone in the organization to be customer centered. In fact, internal marketing must *precede* external marketing.

For example, Four Seasons hires the right people, orients them carefully, instills in them a sense of pride, and motivates them by recognizing and rewarding outstanding service deeds. Says one analysts, "Every job applicant, whether hoping to fold laundry or teach yoga, goes through at least four interviews. "We look for people who say 'I'd be proud to be a doorman,'" says the CEO. Once hired, the training never stops. The most important guideline, contends the CEO, is "the golden rule: Do unto others . . . . That's not a gimmick," he says. "In the hiring process, we're looking for people who are very comfortable with this idea."[42] As a result, Four Seasons employees know what good service is and are highly motivated to give it.

Interactive marketing means that service quality depends heavily on the quality of the buyer–seller interaction during the service encounter. In product marketing, product quality often depends little on how the product is obtained. But in services marketing, service quality depends on both the service deliverer and the quality of the delivery. Service marketers, therefore, have to master interactive marketing skills. Thus, Four Seasons selects only people

Internal marketing
Orienting and motivating customer-contact employees and supporting service people to work as a team to provide customer satisfaction.

Interactive marketing
Training service employees in the fine art of interacting with customers to satisfy their needs.

🔖 **FIGURE** | **8.6**
Three Types of Service Marketing

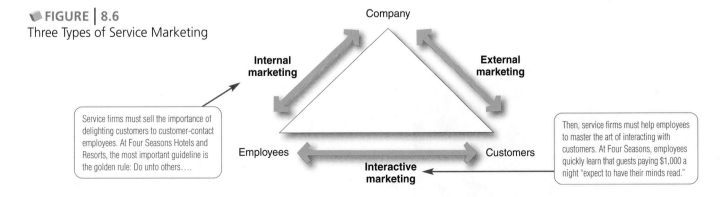

Service firms must sell the importance of delighting customers to customer-contact employees. At Four Seasons Hotels and Resorts, the most important guideline is the golden rule: Do unto others....

Then, service firms must help employees to master the art of interacting with customers. At Four Seasons, employees quickly learn that guests paying $1,000 a night "expect to have their minds read."

Company

Internal marketing

External marketing

Employees

Customers

Interactive marketing

with an innate "passion to serve" and instructs them carefully in the fine art of interacting with customers to satisfy their every need. Employees learn quickly that guests paying $1,000 a night "expect to have their [minds] read." All new hires complete a three-month training regimen that includes improvisation exercises to help them anticipate guest behavior.

In today's marketplace, companies must know how to deliver interactions that are not only "high-touch" but also "high-tech." For example, customers can log onto the Charles Schwab Web site and access account information, investment research, real-time quotes, after-hours trading, and the Schwab learning center. They can also participate in live online events and chat online with customer-service representatives. Customers seeking more-personal interactions can contact service representatives by phone or visit a local Schwab branch office to "talk with Chuck." Thus, Schwab has mastered interactive marketing at all three levels—calls, clicks, *and* personal visits.

Today, as competition and costs increase, and as productivity and quality decrease, more service marketing sophistication is needed. Service companies face three major marketing tasks: They want to increase their *service differentiation, service quality*, and *service productivity*.

Managing Service Differentiation

In these days of intense price competition, service marketers often complain about the difficulty of differentiating their services from those of competitors. To the extent that customers view the services of different providers as similar, they care less about the provider than the price.

The solution to price competition is to develop a differentiated offer, delivery, and image. The *offer* can include innovative features that set one company's offer apart from competitors' offers. Some hotels offer car-rental, banking, and business-center services in their lobbies and free high-speed Internet connections in their rooms. Airlines differentiate their offers though frequent-flyer award programs and special services. For example, ▲British Airways offers spa services at its Arrivals Lounge at Heathrow airport and softer in-flight beds, plumper pillows, and cozier blankets. Says one ad: "Our simple goal is to deliver the best service you could ask for, without you having to ask."

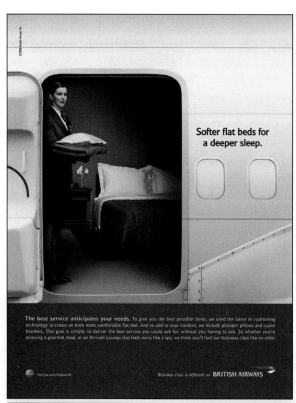

Softer flat beds for a deeper sleep.

The best service anticipates your needs. To give you the best possible sleep, we used the latest in cushioning technology to create an even more comfortable flat bed. And to add to your comfort, we include plumper pillows and cozier blankets. Our goal is simple: to deliver the best service you could ask for, without you having to ask. So whether you're enjoying a gourmet meal, or an Arrivals Lounge that feels more like a spa, we think you'll find our business class like no other.

Visit ba.com/clubworld   *Business class is different on* BRITISH AIRWAYS ✈

▲ Service differentiation: At British Airways, says this ad, "Our goal is simple: to deliver the best service you can ask for, without you having to ask."

Service companies can differentiate their service *delivery* by having more able and reliable customer-contact people, by developing a superior physical environment in which the service product is delivered, or by designing a superior delivery process. For example, many grocery chains now offer online shopping and home delivery as a better way to shop than having to drive, park, wait in line, and tote groceries home.

Finally, service companies also can work on differentiating their *images* through symbols and branding. Aflac adopted the duck as its symbol in its advertising, and even as stuffed animals, golf club covers, and free ring tones and screensavers. The well-known Aflac duck, with the familiar voice of comedian Gilbert Gottfried, helped make the big but previously unknown insurance company memorable and approachable. Other well-known service symbols include Merrill Lynch's bull, MGM's lion, McDonald's golden arches, Allstate's "good hands," and The Travelers red umbrella.

Managing Service Quality

A service firm can differentiate itself by delivering consistently higher quality than its competitors provide. Like manufacturers before them, most service industries have now joined the customer-driven quality movement. And like product marketers, service providers need to identify what target customers expect in regards to service quality.

Unfortunately, service quality is harder to define and judge than product quality. For instance, it is harder to agree on the quality of a haircut than on the quality of a hair dryer. Customer retention is perhaps the best measure of quality—a service firm's ability to hang onto its customers depends on how consistently it delivers value to them.

Top service companies set high service-quality standards. They watch service performance closely, both their own and that of competitors. They do not settle for merely good service; they aim for 100 percent defect-free service. A 98 percent performance standard may sound good, but using this standard, UPS would lose or misdirect 316,000 packages each day and U.S. pharmacists would misfill close to 1.4 million prescriptions each week.[43]

Unlike product manufacturers who can adjust their machinery and inputs until everything is perfect, service quality will always vary, depending on the interactions between employees and customers. As hard as they try, even the best companies will have an occasional late delivery, burned steak, or grumpy employee. However, good *service recovery* can turn angry customers into loyal ones. In fact, good recovery can win more customer purchasing and loyalty than if things had gone well in the first place. Therefore, companies should take steps not only to provide good service every time but also to recover from service mistakes when they do occur (see **Real Marketing 8.2**).

The first step is to *empower* front-line service employees—to give them the authority, responsibility, and incentives they need to recognize, care about, and tend to customer needs. For example, Nordstrom, the department store chain long known for extraordinary service, gives its employees the autonomy they need to create outstanding customer-service experiences. Here's an example:[44]

In Portland, Oregon, a man walked into Nordstrom asking for an Armani tuxedo to wear to his daughter's wedding. The sales representative took his measurements but said she'd need time to work on his request. She called later to say that the tuxedo would be ready the next day. As it turned out, Nordstrom did not carry Armani tuxedos at the time. The sales representative had found the tux through a distributor in New York, then had it rushed to Portland and altered to fit the customer in time for the wedding. At Nordstrom, such employee empowerment is built into the process. "It is not a thing of the day," says a Nordstrom store manager, "it is part of our culture."

Managing Service Productivity

With their costs rising rapidly, service firms are under great pressure to increase service productivity. They can do so in several ways. They can train current employees better or hire new ones who will work harder or more skillfully. Or they can increase the quantity of their service by giving up some quality. The provider can "industrialize the service" by adding equipment and standardizing production, as in McDonald's assembly-line approach to fast-food retailing. Finally, the service provider can harness the power of technology. Although we often think of technology's power to save time and costs in manufacturing companies, it also has great—and often untapped—potential to make service workers more productive.

However, companies must avoid pushing productivity so hard that doing so reduces quality. Attempts to industrialize a service or to cut costs can make a service company more efficient in the short run. But they can also reduce its longer-run ability to innovate, maintain service quality, or respond to consumer needs and desires. Many airlines are learning this lesson the hard way as they attempt to streamline and economize in the face of rising costs.

Over the past year, Northwest Airlines has stopped offering free magazines, pillows, movies, and even minibags of pretzels on its domestic flights. Passengers can still get an in-flight snack of raisins and nuts, but it costs $1. The airline is also charging a $15 fee for a roomier seat on the aisle or in an exit row. Combine that with higher fares and a sharply curtailed schedule, and it's little wonder that flyers rate Northwest dead last among the nation's major airlines. "If at all possible, I don't fly Northwest," says one veteran traveler. "I have found a lack of interest in the customer." A services marketing expert agrees: "The upshot is that some companies, in their passion to drive down costs, have mangled their relationships with customers."[45]

Thus, in attempting to improve service productivity, companies must be mindful of how they create and deliver customer value. In short, they should be careful not to take the "service" out of service.

Real Marketing 8.2

Service Recovery: Doing Things Right when Service Goes Wrong

Southwest Airlines and JetBlue Airways are both great service companies. For more than three decades, Southwest has set the airline industry standard for efficient service, low fares, and fun flying. And since first taking off in 2000, JetBlue has amassed a soaring list of service honors, including Readers' Choice Awards from discerning *Condé Nast Traveler* magazine for five years running and high rankings in every measured category in the airline satisfaction ratings by J.D. Power & Associates. As a result, Southwest and JetBlue have been the only consistently profitable air carriers in the otherwise troubled U.S. airline industry.

But all service companies, even the great ones, make mistakes once in a while. Perhaps the truest test of good customer service is how well companies do when things go *wrong*. Consider the following tales in which Southwest and JetBlue committed similar service blunders—but with dramatically different outcomes.

Southwest. Bob Emig was flying home from St. Louis on Southwest Airlines this past December when an all-too-familiar travel nightmare began to unfold. After his airplane backed away from the gate, he and his fellow passengers were told that the plane would need to be de-iced. When the aircraft was ready to fly two and a half hours later, the pilot had reached the hour limit set by the Federal Aviation Administration, and a new pilot was required. By that time, the plane had to be de-iced again. Five hours after the scheduled departure time, Emig's flight was finally ready for takeoff.

A customer-service disaster, right? Not to hear Emig tell it. The pilot walked the aisles, answering questions and offering constant updates. Flight attendants, who Emig says "really seemed like they cared," kept up with the news on connecting flights. And within a couple of days of arriving home, Emig, who travels frequently, received a letter from Southwest that included two free round-trip ticket vouchers. "I could not believe they acknowledged the situation and apologized," says Emig. "Then they gave me

a gift, for all intents and purposes, to make up for the time spent sitting on the runway."

Emig's "gift" from Southwest was not the result of an unusually kind customer-service agent who took pity on his plight. Nor was it a scramble to make amends after a disastrous operational fiasco. Rather, it was standard service-recovery procedure for Southwest Airlines. Almost six years ago, Southwest created a new high-level group that oversees all proactive communications with customers. Southwest carefully coordinates information that is sent to all frontline reps in the event of major flight disruptions. It also sends out letters, and in many cases flight vouchers, to customers caught up in flight delays or cancellations, customer bumping incidents, baggage problems, or other travel messes—even those beyond Southwest's control. "It's not something we have to do," says a Southwest executive. "It's just something we feel our customers deserve." Thanks to such caring service recovery, Southwest doesn't just appease wronged customers like Bob Emig, it turns them into even more loyal customers.

JetBlue. On February 14, 2007—Valentine's Day—a devastating ice storm struck JetBlue's main hub at New York's John F. Kennedy International Airport. The resulting disastrous

mix of closed runways, aircraft congestion, and frozen equipment kept many JetBlue customers stranded for hours in grounded planes. So far, this sounds a lot like the Southwest Airlines example just discussed. But rather than recovering with Southwest-like efficiency and caring customer communications, JetBlue experienced a startling, near-total customer-service collapse.

A series of bad decisions resulted in chaos on the tarmac. In a fruitless attempt to eventually get planes off the ground, JetBlue waited too long to cancel flights and to bus enplaned passengers back to the terminal. Many passengers were trapped in planes for as long as 11 hours, as the tires of their planes literally froze to the runway. All the while, increasingly furious customers—both on the stranded planes and in the terminal—were kept pretty much in the dark about what was going to happen and why.

Even after passengers were returned to the terminal, the nightmare continued. Unlike Southwest, the relatively new and rapidly growing JetBlue simply hadn't built the customer-service and operational infrastructure needed to deal with such a crisis. JetBlue flight crews and terminal agents were befuddled and disorganized in helping passengers.

Over the next six days, JetBlue experienced major disruptions throughout its entire

Service recovery: Following its Valentine's Day customer-service meltdown, JetBlue announced a host of actions to repair its bond with customers. "We've learned from this," said JetBlue CEO David Needleman, shown here. "That's why it's never going to happen again."

system, canceling more than 1,000 flights and leaving customers fuming over rough handling and lost vacations. During that critical week, JetBlue struggled just to get operations back to normal. The airline did little by way of responding to customers' seething emotions. Whereas Southwest's smooth and immediate service recovery created even stronger customer relationships, JetBlue's meltdown created a serious crisis of customer trust.

In the weeks following the six-day disaster, JetBlue went into long-term service recovery mode. JetBlue's chairman seemed to pop up everywhere—*The New York Times*, *The Late Show with David Letterman*, NPR, even YouTube—accepting responsibility, apologizing repeatedly, and promising refunds and credits to wronged customers. He quickly announced a new Customer Bill of Rights, a unique document that outlines policies for notifying customers about delays and cancellations, sets a limit before ground-delayed passengers must be deplaned, and provides for generous customer compensation for all types of service missteps.

But even more important than apologies, refunds, and guarantees, JetBlue later made sweeping systems changes that will prevent future customer-service debacles. "We should have acted quicker. We should have had contingency plans that were better [tested] to be able to [unload] customers," says the chairman. "We've learned from this," he declares. "That's why it's never going to happen again."

How much damage did the Valentine's Day service disaster do to JetBlue's hard-earned customer-service reputation? As it turns out, thanks to a ton of previously earned goodwill and a solid longer-term recovery effort, this single incident has not undone years of good customer relationships. Says one analyst, "[JetBlue's] customers largely accept that it cares, because it has demonstrated that

it does, flight after flight." In fact, by mid-2007, for the third year running, JetBlue was awarded highest honors in customer satisfaction among low-cost airlines by J.D. Power and Associates. And in 2008, the airline was ranked number seven among *BusinessWeek's* Customer Service Champs across all industries.

But the message is clear. Even good service companies screw up from time to time. Good service recovery, however, can turn such screw ups into opportunities to actually strengthen bonds with customers. Companies must think ahead and plan for good service recovery. In these two examples, Southwest was well prepared, while JetBlue wasn't. In the future, JetBlue's reputation will hinge on its ability to make the right moves when things go wrong.

Sources: Portions adapted from Jena McGregor, "Customer Service Champs," *BusinessWeek*, March 5, 2007, pp. 52–64. Quotes and other information from Justin Bachman, "JetBlue's Fiasco Could Improve Flying," *BusinessWeek*, February 21, 2007, p. 10; Chuck Salter, "Lessons from the Tarmac," *Fast Company,* May 2007, pp. 31–32; Mel Duvall and Doug Bartholomew, "What Really Happened at JetBlue?" *Baseline,* April 2007, pp. 53–59; Melissa Waite, "Managing Under Crisis: The Source of Atonement at JetBlue Airways," *The Business Review, Cambridge,* December 2007, pp. 187+; and Jena McGregor, "Customer Service Champs," *BusinessWeek*, March 3, 2008, p. 37.

REVIEWING Objectives AND KEY Terms

A product is more than a simple set of tangible features. Each product or service offered to customers can be viewed on three levels. The *core customer value* consists of the core problem-solving benefits that consumers seek when they buy a product. The *actual product* exists around the core and includes the quality level, features, design, brand name, and packaging. The *augmented product* is the actual product plus the various services and benefits offered with it, such as a warranty, free delivery, installation, and maintenance.

OBJECTIVE 1 Define *product* and the major classifications of products and services. (pp 224–229)

Broadly defined, a *product* is anything that can be offered to a market for attention, acquisition, use, or consumption that might satisfy a want or need. Products include physical objects but also services, events, persons, places, organizations, ideas, or mixes of these entities. *Services* are products that consist of activities, benefits, or satisfactions offered for sale that are essentially intangible, such as banking, hotel, tax preparation, and home-repair services.

Products and services fall into two broad classes based on the types of consumers that use them. *Consumer products*—those bought by final consumers—are usually classified according to consumer shopping habits (convenience products, shopping products, specialty products, and unsought products). *Industrial products*—purchased for further processing or for use in conducting a business—include materials and parts, capital items, and supplies and services. Other marketable entities—such as

organizations, persons, places, and ideas—can also be thought of as products.

OBJECTIVE 2 Describe the decisions companies make regarding their individual products and services, product lines, and product mixes. (pp 229–235)

Individual product decisions involve product attributes, branding, packaging, labeling, and product support services. *Product attribute* decisions involve product quality, features, and style and design. *Branding* decisions include selecting a brand name and developing a brand strategy. *Packaging* provides many key benefits, such as protection, economy, convenience, and promotion. Package decisions often include designing *labels,* which identify, describe, and possibly promote the product. Companies also develop *product support services* that enhance customer service and satisfaction and safeguard against competitors.

Most companies produce a product line rather than a single product. A *product line* is a group of products that are related in function, customer-purchase needs, or distribution channels. *Line stretching* involves extending a line downward, upward, or in both directions to occupy a gap that might otherwise be filled by a competitor. In contrast, *line filling* involves adding items within the present range of the line. All product lines and items offered to customers by a particular seller make up the *product mix.* The mix can be described by four dimensions: width, length, depth, and consistency. These dimensions are the tools for developing the company's product strategy.

OBJECTIVE 3 **Discuss branding strategy—the decisions companies make in building and managing their brands.** (pp 235–244)

Some analysts see brands as *the* major enduring asset of a company. Brands are more than just names and symbols—they embody everything that the product or service *means* to consumers. *Brand equity* is the positive differential effect that knowing the brand name has on customer response to the product or service. A brand with strong brand equity is a very valuable asset.

In building brands, companies need to make decisions about brand positioning, brand name selection, brand sponsorship, and brand development. The most powerful *brand positioning* builds around strong consumer beliefs and values. *Brand name selection* involves finding the best brand name based on a careful review of product benefits, the target market, and proposed marketing strategies. A manufacturer has four *brand sponsorship* options: it can launch a *manufacturer's brand* (or national brand), sell to resellers who use a *private brand*, market *licensed brands*, or join forces with another company to *cobrand* a product. A company also has four choices when it comes to developing brands. It can introduce *line extensions, brand extensions, multibrands,* or *new brands*.

Companies must build and manage their brands carefully. The brand's positioning must be continuously communicated to consumers. Advertising can help. However, brands are not maintained by advertising but by the *brand experience*. Customers come to know a brand through a wide range of contacts and interactions. The company must put as much care into managing these touch points as it does into producing its ads. Thus, managing a company's brand assets can no longer be left only to brand managers. Some companies are now setting up brand asset management teams to manage their major brands. Finally, companies must periodically audit their brands' strengths and weaknesses. In some cases, brands may need to be repositioned because of changing customer preferences or new competitors.

OBJECTIVE 4 **Identify the four characteristics that affect the marketing of a service and the additional marketing considerations that services require.** (pp 244–251)

Services are characterized by four key characteristics: they are *intangible, inseparable, variable,* and *perishable*. Each characteristic poses problems and marketing requirements. Marketers work to find ways to make the service more tangible, to increase the productivity of providers who are inseparable from their products, to standardize the quality in the face of variability, and to improve demand movements and supply capacities in the face of service perishability.

Good service companies focus attention on *both* customers and employees. They understand the *service-profit chain*, which links service firm profits with employee and customer satisfaction. Services marketing strategy calls not only for external marketing but also for *internal marketing* to motivate employees and *interactive marketing* to create service delivery skills among service providers. To succeed, service marketers must create *competitive differentiation*, offer high *service quality*, and find ways to increase *service productivity.*

KEY Terms

OBJECTIVE 1

Product (p 224)
Service (p 224)
Consumer product (p 226)
Convenience product (p 226)
Shopping product (p 226)
Specialty product (p 226)
Unsought product (p 226)
Industrial product (p 227)
Social marketing (p 229)

OBJECTIVE 2

Product quality (p 229)
Brand (p 231)
Packaging (p 231)
Product line (p 234)
Product mix (product portfolio) (p 234)

OBJECTIVE 3

Brand equity (p 236)
Store brand (private brand) (p 240)
Co-branding (p 241)

Line extension (p 242)
Brand extension (p 243)

OBJECTIVE 4

Service intangibility (p 245)
Service inseparability (p 245)
Service variability (p 245)
Service perishability (p 246)
Service-profit chain (p 246)
Internal marketing (p 247)
Interactive marketing (p 247)

DISCUSSING & APPLYING THE Concepts

Discussing the Concepts

1. What is a product and how can product planners build customer value? (AACSB: Communication)

2. How does an industrial product differ from a consumer product? Discuss the types of industrial products and provide an example of each. (AACSB: Communication; Reflective Thinking)

3. Discuss the product attributes through which benefits are communicated and delivered to customers. (AACSB: Communication)

4. Define brand equity. What competitive advantages does high brand equity provide a company? (AACSB: Communication)

5. Discuss the brand development strategies marketers use to develop brands. Provide an example of each strategy. (AACSB: Communication; Reflective Thinking)

6. Describe the four characteristics of services that marketers must consider when designing marketing programs. How do the services offered by a dentist differ from those offered by a drug store regarding these characteristics? (AACSB: Communication, Reflective Thinking)

Application Questions

1. What do Betty Crocker, Pillsbury, Cheerios, and Hamburger Helper have in common? They are all familiar brands that are

part of the General Mills product mix. Visit the General Mills Web site (www.generalmills.com) and examine its list of brands. Name and define the four dimensions of a company's product mix and describe General Mills' product mix on these dimensions. (AACSB: Communication; Reflective Thinking; Use of IT)

2. Using the six qualities that a good brand name should possess, create a brand name for a personal care product that has the following positioning statement: "Intended for X-Games

sports participants and enthusiasts, _____ is a deodorant that combines effective odor protection with an enduring and seductive fragrance that will enhance your romantic fortunes." (AACSB: Communication; Reflective Thinking)

3. List the names of the store brands found in the following stores: Wal-Mart, JCPenney, and Whole Foods. Identify the private label brands of another retailer of your choice. (AACSB: Communication; Reflective Thinking)

FOCUS ON Technology

With the magazine industry's circulation and ad sales suffering, Time Inc. is offering a new Internet service, called Maghound that allows customers the "convenience of subscriptions with the flexibility of newsstand sales." Instead of paying a fixed-term subscription fee for one magazine, customers pay a monthly fee for home delivery of a wanted publication plus with the added benefit of being able to go online when desired and change to a different publication. The Maghound new service is beginning with 300 consumer magazines, including Time's popular titles, such as *People*, *Fortune*, and *Sports Illustrated*. Magazines from several other publishers are also available. Customer can get three magazines for about $5 a month, five magazines for $8, or seven magazines for $10, with each additional magazine costing

another $1. Maghound lets a reader who enjoys golfing or fishing to read about that in the summer and then switch to winter sports, such as skiing, in the winter. Moreover, gone are the "renew now" nuisance offers and being locked into a subscription for a long time. The only drawback is that changes will not take effect immediately, so customers may not receive a specific issue of a magazine they're interested in.

1. Explain the core, actual, and augmented levels of this service. (AACSB: Communication; Reflective Thinking)

2. Does this service have the potential to deliver customer value? Explain your answer. (AACSB: Communication; Reflective Thinking)

FOCUS ON Ethics

The date February 17, 2009 is significant because, as part of the Deficit Reduction Act of 2005, Congress mandated that by then all full-power broadcast stations must have switched to digital signals. This may or may not affect you, but as of mid-2008 an estimated 20 million households would be affected and an estimated 70 million televisions would be at risk of losing their signal. That's the number of analog sets owned by viewers who use antennas to receive free television signals rather than subscribing to cable, satellite, or another pay-TV service. What options do these consumers have? They can subscribe to cable, satellite, or other pay-television services, which will complete the conversion for customers. Alternatively, they can buy new digital televisions and still receive digital signals with an antenna, as they did with the old analog televisions. Finally, they can purchase a converter box for only $40 to $70, but each set affected will need a converter box. The government is allowing each affected household

to apply for two $40 coupons to help defray costs of converter boxes. The bottom line, though, is that affected consumers will have to pay something if they want to keep watching television.

1. Learn more about the switch to digital programming by visiting the Federal Communication Commission's information Web site (www.dtv.gov). What is the reason for the switch to digit programming? Write a brief report of what you learned about this transition and how it is going. (AACSB: Communication; Use of IT; Reflective Thinking)

2. Television stations and many consumers have already incurred costs related to the switchover mandated by Congress. Is it right for Congress to mandate actions that will require businesses and consumers to pay money for new equipment or services to continue receiving free television over the airways? (AACSB: Communication; Ethical Reasoning)

MARKETING BY THE Numbers

Mars, maker of the famous M&M's candy brand, recently introduced M&M Premiums. The new candies include flavors such as mint chocolate, mocha, chocolate almond, and raspberry-almond with white chocolate. They are wrapped in iridescent colors and sold in reclosable cartons. Mars also plans new offerings with its Snickers and Dove brands. Although the new M&M Premiums will garner a higher wholesale price for the company ($0.48 per ounce for the new product versus $0.30 per ounce for the original product), they also come with higher variable

costs ($0.35 per ounce for the new product versus $0.15 per ounce for the original product).

1. What brand development strategy is Mars undertaking? (AACSB: Communication; Reflective Thinking)

2. Assume the company expects to sell 300 million ounces of M&M Premiums within the first year after introduction but expects that half of those sales will come from buyers who would normally purchase M&M regular candies (that is,

cannibalized sales). Assuming the sales of regular M&M candies are normally 1 billion ounces per year and that the company will incur an increase in fixed costs of $5 million during the first year of production for M&M Premiums, will

the new product be profitable for the company? Refer to the discussion of cannibalization in Appendix 2: Marketing by the Numbers for an explanation regarding how to conduct this analysis. (AACSB: Communication; Analytical Reasoning)

VIDEO Case

Swiss Army Brands

It seems appropriate that Swiss Army Brands, maker of multifunction knives, has become a multiproduct brand. Victorinox Swiss Army Inc. has made its famous knives for more than 100 years. Former product line extensions included different variations of the standard Swiss Army Knife for applications such as fishing, golf, and an accessory for women's purses.

But the popularity of the Swiss Army Knife has enabled the company to expand into all manner of consumer goods, including watches, luggage, apparel, and other lines. These brand extensions have been based on consumer research to ensure that each fits within the concept that consumers hold for the brand.

The success that Swiss Army Brands has achieved through expansion has even allowed it to open its own retail stores.

After viewing the video featuring Swiss Army Brands, answer the following questions about product and branding strategies:

1. How might brand extensions affect Swiss Army Brands, in both positive and negative ways?

2. Why did Swiss Army Brands open retail stores? How do these stores help the company build its brand?

3. Do you think Swiss Army Brands could extend its brand to any type of product? What additional products and lines might Swiss Army Brands consider?

COMPANY Case

ESPN: The Evolution of an Entertainment Brand

In the 2004 movie *Anchorman* character Ron Burgundy (Will Ferrell) auditions for a position on *SportsCenter* with the very new and little known network, ESPN (Entertainment and Sports Programming Network). The year was 1979. After pronouncing the name of the network "Espen," he then is shocked to find out that ESPN is a round-the-clock sports network. Through his laughter, he asserts that the concept is as ridiculous as a 24-hour cooking network or an all-music channel. "Seriously," he shouts. "This thing is going to be a financial and cultural disaster. *SportsCenter* . . . that's just dumb!"

While this comical sketch is fictitious, when a young college graduate named George Bodenheimer took a job in the mailroom at ESPN it 1981, it was for real. Today, Mr. Bodenheimer is president of the network that has become one of the biggest franchises in sports, not to mention one of the most successful and envied brands in the entertainment world. As a cable network, ESPN commands $2.91 from cable operators for each subscriber every month. Compare that to $1.67 for Fox Sports, 89 cents for TNT, and only 40 cents for CNN. The core ESPN channel alone is currently in more than 96 million homes. With that kind of premium power, it's no wonder that ESPN shocked the world in 2006 by becoming the first cable network to land the coveted TV contract for Monday Night Football, which went on to become the highest rated cable series ever.

But even with its three sibling channels (ESPN2, ESPNEWS, and ESPN Classic), the ESPN cable network is only one piece of a bigger brand puzzle that has become Bodenheimer's $6 billion sports empire. Through very savvy strategic planning, Bodenheimer is realizing his vision of taking quality sports content across the widest possible collection of media assets to reach sports fans wherever they may be. Employing a hands-off management style, Bodenheimer has cultivated a brand that is brash, tech savvy, creative, and innovative. He tells employees that ESPN belongs to all of them. He gives them the freedom to come up with their own ideas and push them forward. His only rule is that every new idea

must focus on fulfilling ESPN's mission of reaching sports fans and making them happy. In the process, ESPN has become as recognized and revered by its customers as other megabrands such as Tide, Nike, and Coca-Cola are to theirs.

Bodenheimer's career-spanning dedication has grown ESPN to well over 50 businesses. The all-sports network has become a truly multiplatform brand, a rarity for any TV network. This growth has given ESPN tremendous reach. ESPN.com alone reaches 22.4 million viewers a week. But even more stunning is the fact that during any seven-day period, 120 million people ages 12 to 64 interact with some ESPN medium. Here's a rundown of ESPN's portfolio of brands:

Television: ESPN has sprawled into six cable channels and other TV divisions that give it both a local (ESPN Regional Television) and global (ESPN International and ESPN Deportes) presence. It was one of the first networks to break new ground in HDTV with simulcast service for ESPN and ESPN2 and it still maintains the most HD programming content and highest level of HD viewership in sports. Cable operators and viewers alike consistently rank ESPN, ESPN2 and ESPN Classic above all other channels with respect to perceived value and programming quality.

But perhaps one of the most innovative moves in all of television sports occurred in 2003, when ESPN content was integrated into its sibling network ABC. *ESPN on ABC* is now the home for the NBA Finals, NASCAR, NCAA football, NCAA basketball, World Cup Soccer, British Open, and the IndyCar Series.

Although ESPN has numerous cable channel brands, one program stands out as a brand in its own right. *SportsCenter* was ESPN's first program. And with as many as 93 million viewers each month, it remains the network's flagship studio show. *SportsCenter* is the only nightly, full-hour sports news program. And whereas, in the past, ESPN has rebroadcast taped episodes of *SportsCenter* during the day, a new schedule incorporating nine straight hours of live *SportsCenter* everyday from 6 a.m. to 3 p.m. will begin in the fall of 2008. Outside the United States, ESPN airs 14 local versions of *SportsCenter* broadcast in eight languages.

Radio: Whereas many radio formats are suffering, sports radio is thriving. And ESPN Radio is the nation's largest sports radio network with 750 U.S. affiliates and more than 335 full-time stations. In addition to college and major league sports events, the network broadcasts syndicated sports talk shows, providing more than 9,000 hours of content annually.

Publishing: *ESPN The Magazine* launched in 1998 and immediately began carving out market share with its bold look, bright colors, and unconventional type, a combination consistent with its content. With the dominance of *Sports Illustrated*, many didn't give ESPN's magazine venture much of a chance. Within its first year, *ESPN The Magazine* was circulating 800,000 copies. Today, that number has ballooned two-and-a-half times to 2 million, whereas *Sports Illustrated* has remained at a stagnant 3.3 million.

At the same time, ESPN is making headway into one of the oldest of all media: books. Although ESPN Books is still waiting for a megaseller, because of the cross-marketing opportunities with the other arms of ESPN, this small division has considerable marketing clout in a struggling industry. "If they didn't have the TV stuff and everything else, they'd be as hardpressed as other publishers to make these books into major events," said Rick Wolff, executive editor at Warner Books.

Internet: ESPN.com is the leading sports Web site, and ESPNRadio.com is the most listened to online sports destination, boasting live streaming and 32 original podcasts each week. But the rising star in ESPN's online portfolio is ESPN360.com, a subscription-based broadband offering that delivers high-quality, customized, on-demand video content. Not only can fans access content carried on ESPN's other networks, but they also get exclusive content and sports video games. For the true sports fan, there's nothing like it—it allows viewers to watch up to six different events at the same time choosing from live events for all major professional and college sports. Since ESPN360.com began service in 2006, this broadband effort has doubled its distribution and now reaches 20 million homes.

Beyond working through its own Web sites, ESPN is exploring the limits of the Internet through an open distribution venture with AOL. By providing ESPN content via a branded ESPN video player in AOL's portal, viewers have more access to ESPN's content. But advertisers also benefit from a larger online audience than ever before.

Mobile: In 2005, ESPN ventured in to one of its trickiest and riskiest brand extensions to date. Mobile ESPN was designed as ESPN's own cell phone network, putting content into sports fans' pockets 24/7. But after a year, the venture was far from breaking even and ESPN shut it down. However, even though Mobile ESPN is down, it's not out. ESPN has capitalized on the lessons learned and started over with a different strategy. Today, ESPN provides real-time scores, stats, news, highlights, and even programming through every major U.S. carrier, with premium content available through Verizon Wireless and Qualcomm. Mobile ESPN also reaches an international audience of mobile customers through more than 35 international carriers.

ESPN's mission with its mobile venture is to "serve the sports fan any time, anywhere, and from any device." In fall 2007, it reached a major milestone in that goal when more people sought NFL content from its mobile-phone Web site than from its PC Web site. "We're having extraordinary growth on ESPN.com's NFL pages, but we're also seeing extraordinary usage with mobile devices as well," said Ed Erhardt, president of ESPN Sports customer marketing and sales. Mr. Erhardt sees great potential in mobile, saying that it is "a big part of the future as it relates to how fans are going to consume sports."

Bodehnheimer and his team see no limit to how far they can take the ESPN brand. In addition to the above ventures, ESPN extends its reach through event management (X Games, Winter X Games, ESPN Outdoors & Bass), consumer products (CDs, DVDs, ESPN Video Games, ESPN Golf Schools), and even a chain of ESPN Zone restaurants and SportsCenter Studio stores. ESPN content is now reaching viewers through agencies that place it in airports and on planes, in health clubs, and even in gas stations. "Now you're not going to be bored when you fill up your tank. It gives new meaning to pulling into a full-service station," says Bodenheimer. "I've been on flights where people are watching our content and don't want to get off the flight."

A powerful media brand results not only in direct revenues from selling products but also in advertising revenues. Advertising accounts for about 40 percent of ESPN's overall revenues. With so many ways to reach the customer, ESPN offers very creative and flexible package deals for any marketer trying to reach the coveted and illusive 18–34 year old male demographic. "Nobody attracts more men than we do," asserts Bodenheimer. "We've got a product and we know how to cater to advertisers' needs. The merchandising opportunities we provide, whether it's working with Home Depot, Wal-Mart, or Dick's Sporting Goods, we want to partner if you want young men."

As amazing as the ESPN brand portfolio is, it is even more amazing when you consider that it is part of the mammoth ABC portfolio, which in turn is a part of The Walt Disney Company portfolio. However, it is no small piece of the Disney pie. ESPN revenues alone accounted for about 18 percent of Disney's total in 2007. Since obtaining ESPN as part of the 1995 ABC acquisition, because ESPN has delivered on the numbers, Disney has allowed ESPN to do pretty much whatever it wants to do. Just a few years after the acquisition, Disney's then-CEO Michael Eisner told investors, "We bought ABC media network and ESPN for $19 billion in 1995. ESPN is worth substantially more than we paid for the entire acquisition." And Disney leverages that value every way that it can, from Mouse House advertising package deals to conditionally attaching its cable channels to the ESPN networks through cable operators.

Questions for Discussion

1. In a succinct manner, describe what the ESPN brand means to consumers.

2. What is ESPN selling? Discuss this in terms of the core benefit, actual product, and augmented product levels of ESPN.

3. Does ESPN have strong brand equity? How does its brand equity relate to its brand value?

4. Cite as many examples as you can of co-branding efforts involving the ESPN brand. For each of these cases, what are the benefits and possible risks to ESPN?

5. Analyze EPSN according to the brand development strategies from the text. What have they done in the past? What would you recommend to ESPN for future brand development?

Sources: Alice Cuneo, "More Football Fans Hit ESPN's Mobile Site Than Its PC Pages," *Advertising Age*, January 7, 2008, p. 17; Mike Shields, "ESPN, AOL Strike Web Video Deal," *Brandweek*, April 8, 2008, accessed online at www.brandweek.com; Andrew Hampp, "ESPN Makes Jump to Major League," *Advertising Age*, May 14, 2007, p. 32; Ronald Grover, "Comcast's C-TV: Channeling Disney," *BusinessWeek.com*, December 1, 2006; Jeffrey Trachtenberg, "ESPN's Next Hurdle: Selling Its Audience on Books," *Wall Street Journal*, February 13, 2007; Jason Brown, "Out-of-Home TV Ads Finally Coming of Age," *Television Week*, January 28, 2008, p.12; also see www.espnmediazone.com.

New-Product Development and Product Life-Cycle Strategies

Chapter PREVIEW

In the previous chapter, you learned how marketers manage and develop products and brands. In this chapter, we'll look into two additional product topics: developing new products and managing products through their life cycles. New products are the lifeblood of an organization. However, new-product development is risky, and many new products fail. So, the first part of this chapter lays out a process for finding and growing successful new products. Once introduced, marketers want their products to enjoy long and happy lives. In the second part of the chapter, you'll see that every product passes through several life-cycle stages and that each stage poses new challenges requiring different marketing strategies and tactics. Finally, we'll wrap up our product discussion by looking at two additional considerations, social responsibility in product decisions and international product and services marketing.

For openers, consider Apple. More than two decades ago, as an early new-product innovator, Apple got off to a fast and impressive start. But only a decade later, as its creative fires cooled, Apple found itself on the brink of extinction. That set the stage for one of the most remarkable turnarounds in corporate history. Read on to see how Apple's cofounder, Steve Jobs, used lots of innovation and creative new products to first start the company and then to remake it again 20 years later.

From the very start, the tale of Apple is a tale of dazzling creativity and customer-driven innovation. Under the leadership of its cofounder and creative genius, Steve Jobs, Apple's very first personal computers, introduced in the late 1970s, stood apart because of their user-friendly look and feel. The company's Macintosh computer, unveiled in 1984, and its LazerWriter printers blazed new trails in desktop computing and publishing, making Apple an early industry leader in both innovation and market share.

But then things took an ugly turn for Apple. In 1985, after tumultuous struggles with the new president he'd hired only a year earlier, Steve Jobs left Apple. With Jobs gone, Apple's creative fires cooled. By the late 1980s, the company's fortunes dwindled as a new wave of PC machines, sporting Intel chips and Microsoft software, swept the market. By the mid- to late-1990s, Apple's sales had plunged to $5 billion, 50 percent off previous highs. And its once-commanding share of the personal-computer market had dropped to a tiny 2 percent. Even the most ardent Apple fans—the "MacHeads"—wavered, and the company's days seemed numbered.

Yet Apple has engineered a remarkable turnaround. Last year's sales soared to a record $24 billion, almost triple the sales just three years earlier. Profits rose a stunning 13-fold in that same three-year period. "To say Apple Computer is hot just doesn't do the company justice," said one analyst. "Apple is smoking, searing, blisteringly hot, not to mention hip, with a side order of funky. . . . Gadget geeks around the world have crowned Apple the keeper of all things cool."

What caused this breathtaking turnaround? Apple rediscovered the magic that had made the company so successful in the first place: customer-driven creativity and new-product innovation. The remarkable makeover began with the return of Steve Jobs in 1997. Since leaving Apple, Jobs had started a new computer company, NeXT. He'd then bought out Pixar Animation Studios, turning it into an entertainment-industry powerhouse. Jobs returned to Apple determined to breathe new creative life and customer focus into the company he'd cofounded 20 years earlier.

Jobs' first task was to revitalize Apple's computer business. For starters, in 1998 Apple launched the iMac personal computer, which featured a sleek, egg-shaped monitor and hard drive, all in one unit, in a futuristic translucent turquoise casing. With its one-button Internet access, this machine was designed specifically for cruising the Internet (hence the "i" in "iMac"). The dramatic

> "Apple is smoking, searing, blisteringly hot, not to mention hip, with a side order of funky—it's the keeper of all things cool."

iMac won raves for design and lured buyers in droves. Within a year, it had sold more than a million units.

Jobs next unleashed Mac OS X, a ground-breaking new Apple operating system that one observer called "the equivalent of a cross between a Porsche and an Abram's tank." OS X served as the launching pad for a new generation of Apple computers and software products. Consider iLife, a bundle of lifestyle applications that comes with every new Mac. It includes applications such as iMovie (for video editing), iDVD (for recording movies, digital-photo slide shows, and music onto TV-playable DVDs), iPhoto (for managing and touching up digital pictures), GarageBand (for making and mixing your own music), iWeb (for creating Web sites and blogs and getting them online), and iWork (for making presentations and newsletters).

The iMac and Mac OS X put Apple back on the map in personal computing. But Jobs knew that Apple, still a nicher claiming just a 6 percent share of the U.S. market, would never catch up in computers with dominant competitors such as Dell and HP. Real growth and stardom would require even more creative thinking. And it just doesn't get much more creative than iPod and iTunes, innovations that would utterly change the way people acquire and listen to music.

A music buff himself, Jobs noticed that kids by the millions were using computers and CD writers to download digital songs from then-illegal online services such as Napster, and then burning their own music CDs. He moved quickly to make CD burners standard equipment on all Macs. Then, to help users download music and manage their music databases, Apple's programmers created state-of-the-art jukebox software called iTunes.

Even before iTunes hit the streets, according to Apple watcher Brent Schendler, Jobs "recognized that although storing and playing music on your computer was pretty cool, wouldn't it be even cooler if there was a portable, Walkman-type player that could hold all your digital music so that you could listen to it anywhere?" Less than nine months later, Apple introduced the sleek and sexy iPod. In another 18 months, the Apple iTunes Music Store opened on the Web, enabling consumers to legally download CDs and individual songs.

The results, of course, have been astonishing. The iPod now ranks as one of the greatest consumer electronics hits of all time. By March of 2008, Apple had sold more than 119 million iPods, and more than four billion songs had been downloaded from the iTunes Store. "We had hoped to sell a million songs in the first six months, but we did that in the first six days," notes an Apple spokesman. The iPod captures more than 70 percent of the music player market; and Apple's iTunes Store is currently the number-two music store—online or offline—in the world (Wal-Mart is number one).

Apple's success is attracting a horde of large, resourceful competitors. To stay ahead, the company must keep its eye on the consumer and continue to innovate. So, Apple isn't standing still. Following the debut of its incredibly popular iPhone, Apple has introduced movie rentals via iTunes, which can be

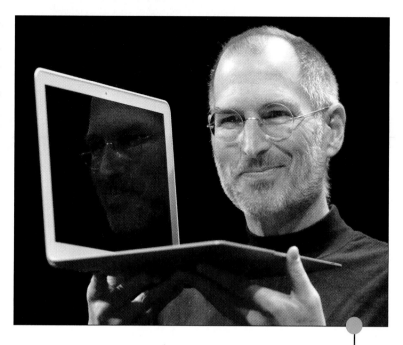

Apple's cofounder, Steve Jobs, used lots of innovation and creative new products to first start the company and then to remake it again 20 years later.

watched on an iPod, iPhone, PC, or via Apple TV; MacBook Air, the world's thinnest notebook computer; and Time Capsule, an appliance that automatically and wirelessly backs up everything on your Mac. Apple has also opened more than 200 chic and gleaming Apple Stores, now the world's fastest-growing retail chain. And observers see a host of new products just on or just over the horizon, such as iHome (a magical device that powers all your digital home entertainment devices) and an iPod on Wheels (a digital hub that integrates your iPod with your car's entertainment system).

For the third straight year, Apple was named the world's most innovative company in Boston Consulting Group's "Most Innovative Company" survey of 2,500 senior executives worldwide. Apple received an amazing 25 percent of the votes, twice the number of runner-up 3M and three times that of third-place Microsoft. The innovative company also topped the most recent *Fortune* magazine list of America's most admired companies.

Thus, almost overnight, it seems, Steve Jobs has transformed Apple from a failing niche computer maker to a major force in consumer electronics, digital music and video, and who knows what else in the future. And he's done it through innovation—by helping those around him to "Think Different" (Apple's motto) in their quest to bring value to customers. *Fortune* sums it up this way: "Apple has demonstrated how to create real, breathtaking growth by dreaming up products so new and ingenious that they have upended one industry after another. Jobs' utter dedication to discovery and excellence has created a culture that has made Apple a symbol of innovation. There, innovation is a way of life."[1]

Through dazzling creativity and customer-driven new-product innovation, Apple has engineered a remarkable turnaround in recent years. At Apple, innovation is a way of life.

Objective Outline

As the Apple story suggests, companies that excel at developing and managing new products reap big rewards. Every product seems to go through a life cycle—it is born, goes through several phases, and eventually dies as newer products come along that create greater value for customers. This product life cycle presents two major challenges: First, because all products eventually decline, a firm must be good at developing new products to replace aging ones (the challenge of *new-product development*). Second, the firm must be good at adapting its marketing strategies in the face of changing tastes, technologies, and competition as products pass through life-cycle stages (the challenge of *product life-cycle strategies*). We first look at the problem of finding and developing new products and then at the problem of managing them successfully over their life cycles.

> **Author Comment** | New products are the lifeblood of a company. As old products mature and fade away, companies must develop new ones to take their place. For example, only seven years after it unveiled its first iPod, half of Apple's revenues come from iPods and iTunes.

New-Product Development Strategy
(pp 258–259)

A firm can obtain new products in two ways. One is through *acquisition*—by buying a whole company, a patent, or a license to produce someone else's product. The other is through the firm's own **new-product development** efforts. By *new products* we mean original products, product improvements, product modifications, and new brands that the firm develops through its own research-and-development efforts. In this chapter, we concentrate on new-product development.

New-product development
The development of original products, product improvements, product modifications, and new brands through the firm's own product-development efforts.

New products are important—to both customers and the marketers who serve them. For companies, new products are a key source of growth. For customers, they bring new solutions and variety to their lives. Yet innovation can be very expensive and very risky. New products face tough odds. According to one estimate, 90 percent of all new products in America fail. Each year, companies lose an estimated $20 billion to $30 billion on failed food products alone.[2]

Why do so many new products fail? There are several reasons. Although an idea may be good, the company may overestimate market size. The actual product may be poorly designed. Or it might be incorrectly positioned, launched at the wrong time, priced too high, or poorly advertised. A high-level executive might push a favorite idea despite poor marketing research findings. Sometimes the costs of product development are higher than expected, and sometimes competitors fight back harder than expected. However, the

▲ Visiting the NewProductWorks is like finding yourself in some nightmare version of a supermarket. Each product failure represents squandered dollars and hopes.

reasons behind some new-product failures seem pretty obvious. Try the following on for size:[3]

▲Strolling the aisles at NewProductWorks is like finding yourself in some nightmare version of a supermarket. Most of the over 110,000 products on display were abject flops. Behind each of them are squandered dollars and hopes and the classic question, "What were they thinking?" Some products failed because they simply failed to bring value to customers—for example, Look of Buttermilk Shampoo, Cucumber antiperspirant spray, or Premier smokeless cigarettes. *Smokeless* cigarettes? What were they thinking? Other companies failed because they attached trusted brand names to something totally out of character. Can you imagine swallowing Ben-Gay aspirin? Or how about Gerber Singles food for adults (perhaps the tasty pureed sweet-and-sour pork or chicken Madeira)? Other misbegotten attempts to stretch a good name include Cracker Jack cereal, Exxon fruit punch, Smucker's premium ketchup, Fruit of the Loom laundry detergent, and Harley-Davidson cake-decorating kits. Really, what were they thinking?

> **Author Comment** | Companies can't just hope that they'll stumble across good new products. Instead, they must develop a systematic new-product development process.

The New-Product Development Process (pp 259–268)

Companies face a problem—they must develop new products, but the odds weigh heavily against success. In all, to create successful new products, a company must understand its consumers, markets, and competitors and develop products that deliver superior value to customers. It must carry out strong new-product planning and set up a systematic, customer-driven *new-product development process* for finding and growing new products. ◣**Figure 9.1** shows the eight major steps in this process.

Idea Generation

Idea generation
The systematic search for new-product ideas.

New-product development starts with **idea generation**—the systematic search for new-product ideas. A company typically generates hundreds of ideas, even thousands, in order to find a few good ones. For example, IBM recently held an "Innovation Jam"—a kind of online suggestion box—in which it invited IBM and customer employees worldwide to submit ideas for new products and services. The mammoth brainstorming session generated some 46,000 ideas from 150,000 people in more than 160 countries over three days. Since the jam fest, however, IBM has whittled down this surge of ideas to only 10 products, businesses, and services that it plans to develop.[4]

> New-product development starts with good new-product ideas—*lots* of them. For example, a recent IBM online "Innovation Jam" generated 46,000 ideas, of which IBM planned to develop only 10.

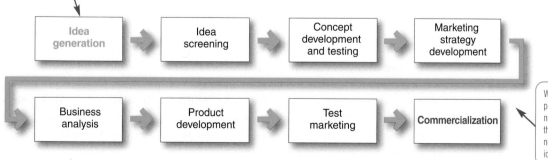

> Whereas the first step of this process generates a large number of new-product ideas, the remaining steps reduce that number and develop the best ideas into profitable products.

◣**FIGURE | 9.1** Major Stages in New-Product Development

Major sources of new-product ideas include internal sources and external sources such as customers, competitors, distributors and suppliers, and others.

Internal Idea Sources

Using *internal sources*, the company can find new ideas through formal research and development. However, in one recent survey, 750 global CEOs reported that only 14 percent of their innovation ideas came from traditional R&D. Instead, 41 percent said employees and 36 percent said customers.[5]

Thus, companies can pick the brains of employees—from executives to scientists, engineers, and manufacturing staff to salespeople. Using today's new Web 2.0 technology, many companies are making it everybody's business to come up with great ideas. For example, Cisco has set up an internal wiki called Idea Zone or I-Zone, through which any Cisco employee can propose an idea for a new product or comment on or modify someone else's proposed idea. Since its inception, I-Zone has generated more than 400 business ideas, and another 10,000 people have added to those ideas. Cisco selects ideas that draw the most activity for further development. So far 12 I-Zone ideas have reached the project stage and four new Cisco business units have been formed.[6]

Some companies have developed successful "intrapreneurial" programs that encourage employees to think up and develop new-product ideas. For example, ▲Samsung built a special Value Innovation Program (VIP) Center in Suwon, South Korea, to encourage and support internal new-product innovation.

The VIP Center is the total opposite of Samsung's typical office facilities—which feature gray computers on gray desks inside gray walls—where workers adhere to strict Confucian traditions and would never dream of questioning a superior or making a wacky suggestion. Instead, the VIP Center features workrooms, dorm rooms, training rooms, a kitchen, and a basement filled with games, a gym, and sauna. Grass sprouts from the ceilings, doors are covered with funhouse mirrors, and walls are covered with chalk drawings of ideas. Inside the center, Samsung researchers, engineers, and designers sport Viking and bumblebee hats, play with Elmo toys and inflatable dolphins, and throw around ideas without regard to rank. Recent ideas sprouting from the VIP Center include a 102-inch plasma HDTV and a process to reduce material costs on a multifunction printer by 30 percent. The center has helped Samsung, once know as the maker of cheap knock-off products, become one of the world's most innovative and profitable consumer electronics companies.[7]

▲ Internal new-product idea sources: Samsung built a special Value Innovation Program Center in which company researchers, engineers, and designers comingle to come up with creative new-product ideas.

External Idea Sources

Companies can also obtain good new-product ideas from any of a number of external sources. For example, *distributors and suppliers* can contribute ideas. Distributors are close to the market and can pass along information about consumer problems and new-product possibilities. Suppliers can tell the company about new concepts, techniques, and materials that can be used to develop new products. *Competitors* are another important source. Companies watch competitors' ads to get clues about their new products. They buy competing new products, take them apart to see how they work, analyze their sales, and decide whether they should bring out a new product of their own. Other idea sources include trade magazines, shows, and seminars; government agencies; advertising agencies; marketing research firms; university and commercial laboratories; and inventors.

Some companies seek the help of outside new-product consultancies and design firms, such as ZIBA, Frog Design, or IDEO, for new-product ideas and designs. For example, when Cranium needed innovative new ideas for extending its popular family board game, it turned to award-winning design firm IDEO. A team of IDEO and Cranium designers worked together to develop a suite of games focused on Cranium's four iconic characters: Word Worm, Creative Cat, Data Head, and Star Performer. The design team began with the core premise that the games should focus on laughter, togetherness, and creativity rather than competition. For inspiration, the team observed people who exemplified the Cranium characters, and then tested prototypes in actual game-playing sessions with families. Based on customer insights gained from these observations and interactions, the IDEO-Cranium team developed four popular new character-based games: Tune Twister (Star Performer), Super Showdown (Data Head), Doodle Tales (Creative Cat), and Wacky Words (Word Worm).[8]

Many companies are also turning to online collaborative communities to help solve new-product problems. For example, collaborative network InnoCentive puts its corporate clients ("seekers") in touch with its global network of more than 100,000 scientists ("solvers"). The seeker companies post "challenges," and solvers can earn up to $100,000 for providing solutions. For instance, P&G used InnoCentive to find a cost-effective way to print the trivia questions on Pringles Prints, snack chips with messages printed on them, dramatically reducing the time and expense of launching its new product.[9]

Says P&G's CEO, "Someone outside your organization today knows how to answer your specific question, solve your specific problem, or take advantage of your current opportunity better than you do. You need to find them and find a way to work collaboratively and productively with them." It is estimated that 35 percent of P&G's new products today have elements that originated outside the company, up from 15 percent in 2000.[10]

Perhaps the most important source of new-product ideas is *customers* themselves. The company can analyze customer questions and complaints to find new products that better solve consumer problems. For example, Staples developed its Easy Rebate program in response to concerns expressed by small-business customers that lost rebates were one of their biggest frustrations.[11]

Company engineers or salespeople can meet with and work alongside customers to get suggestions and ideas. ▲LEGO did just that when it invited 250 LEGO train-set enthusiasts to visit its New York office to assess new designs. "We pooh-poohed them all," says one LEGO fan, an Intel engineer from Portland. But the group gave LEGO lots of new ideas, and the company put them to good use. The result was the Santa Fe Super Chief set. Thanks to word-of-mouth endorsements from the 250 enthusiasts, LEGO sold out the first 10,000 units in less than two weeks with no additional marketing.[12]

Other companies actively solicit ideas from customers and turn customers into cocreators. For example, Dell set up an interactive Web site forum called IdeaStorm that asks consumers for insights on how to improve its product offering. Users post suggestions, the community votes, and the most popular ideas rise to the top. Only two months after launch, the site had received some 3,850 ideas and 236,000 votes. Michael Dell sees such customer-driven innovation as a key to reenergizing Dell. "We are our best when we are hearing directly from customers," says Dell. "We listened, learn, and then improve and innovate based on what our customers want."[13]

Finally, customers often create new products and uses on their own, and companies can benefit by putting them on the market. For example, for years customers were spreading the word that Avon Skin-So-Soft bath oil and moisturizer was also a terrific bug repellent. Whereas some consumers were content simply to bathe in water scented with the fragrant oil, others carried it in their backpacks to mosquito-infested campsites or kept a bottle on the decks of their beach houses. Avon turned the idea into a complete line of Skin-So-Soft Bug Guard products,

▲ Product ideas from customers: Advice from 250 train-set enthusiasts resulted in the LEGO Santa Fe Super Chief set, a blockbuster new product that sold out in less than two weeks.

including Bug Guard Mosquito Repellant Moisturizing Towelettes and Bug Guard Plus, a combination moisturizer, insect repellent, and sunscreen.[14]

Although customer input on new products yields many benefits, companies must be careful not to rely *too* heavily on what customers say. For some products, especially highly technical ones, customers may not know what they need. "You can't ask people what they want if it's around the next corner," says Apple CEO Steve Jobs. And even when they think they know what they want, adds an innovation management consultant, "Merely giving people what they want isn't always enough. People want to be surprised; they want something that's better than they imagined, something that stretches them in what they like."[15]

Idea Screening

Idea screening

Screening new-product ideas in order to spot good ideas and drop poor ones as soon as possible.

The purpose of idea generation is to create a large number of ideas. The purpose of the succeeding stages is to *reduce* that number. The first idea-reducing stage is **idea screening**, which helps spot good ideas and drop poor ones as soon as possible. Product development costs rise greatly in later stages, so the company wants to go ahead only with the product ideas that will turn into profitable products.

Many companies require their executives to write up new-product ideas in a standard format that can be reviewed by a new-product committee. The write-up describes the product or service, the proposed customer value proposition, the target market, and the competition. It makes some rough estimates of market size, product price, development time and costs, manufacturing costs, and rate of return. The committee then evaluates the idea against a set of general criteria.

One marketing expert proposes an R-W-W ("real, win, worth it") new-product screening framework that asks three questions. First, *Is it real?* Is there a real need and desire for the product and will customers buy it? Is there a clear product concept and will the product satisfy the market? Second, *Can we win?* Does the product offer a sustainable competitive advantage? Does the company have the resources to make the product a success? Finally, *Is it worth doing?* Does the product set the company's overall growth strategy? Does it offer sufficient profit potential? The company should be able to answer yes to all three R-W-W questions before developing the new-product idea further.[16]

Concept Development and Testing

Product concept

A detailed version of the new-product idea stated in meaningful consumer terms.

An attractive idea must be developed into a **product concept**. It is important to distinguish between a product idea, a product concept, and a product image. A *product idea* is an idea for a possible product that the company can see itself offering to the market. A *product concept* is a detailed version of the idea stated in meaningful consumer terms. A *product image* is the way consumers perceive an actual or potential product.

Concept Development

Suppose that a car manufacturer has developed a practical battery-powered all-electric car. ▲ Its initial prototype is a sleek, sporty convertible that sells for about $100,000.[17] However, later this decade, it plans to introduce more-affordable, mass-market models that will complete with today's hybrid-powered cars. This 100 percent electric car will accelerate from 0 to 60 in 4 seconds, travel more than 250 miles on a single charge, recharge from a normal 120-volt electrical outlet, and cost about one penny per mile to power.

Looking ahead, the marketer's task is to develop this new product into alternative product concepts, find out how attractive each concept is to customers, and choose the best one. It might create the following product concepts for the electric car:

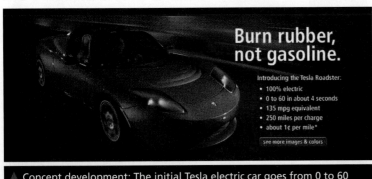

Burn rubber, not gasoline.

Introducing the Tesla Roadster:
- 100% electric
- 0 to 60 in about 4 seconds
- 135 mpg equivalent
- 250 miles per charge
- about 1¢ per mile*

see more images & colors

▲ Concept development: The initial Tesla electric car goes from 0 to 60 mph in 4 seconds, travels 250 miles on a single charge, and costs about a penny a mile to power.

- *Concept 1* An affordably priced midsize car designed as a second family car to be used around town for running errands and visiting friends.

- *Concept 2* A midpriced sporty compact appealing to young singles and couples.

- *Concept 3* A "green" car appealing to environmentally conscious people who want practical, low-polluting transportation.

- *Concept 4* A high-end midsize utility vehicle appealing to those who love the space SUVs provide but lament the poor gas mileage.

Concept Testing

Concept testing

Testing new-product concepts with a group of target consumers to find out if the concepts have strong consumer appeal.

Concept testing calls for testing new-product concepts with groups of target consumers. The concepts may be presented to consumers symbolically or physically. Here, in words, is concept 3:

> An efficient, fun-to-drive, battery-powered compact car that seats four. This 100 percent electric wonder provides practical and reliable transportation with no pollution. It goes more than 250 miles on a single charge and costs pennies per mile to operate. It's a sensible, responsible alternative to today's pollution-producing gas-guzzlers. It's priced, fully equipped, at $25,000.

Many firms routinely test new-product concepts with consumers before attempting to turn them into actual new products. For some concept tests, a word or picture description might be sufficient. However, a more concrete and physical presentation of the concept will increase the reliability of the concept test. After being exposed to the concept, consumers then may be asked to react to it by answering questions such as those in ● **Table 9.1**.

The answers to such questions will help the company decide which concept has the strongest appeal. For example, the last question asks about the consumer's intention to buy. Suppose 2 percent of consumers say they "definitely" would buy, and another 5 percent say "probably." The company could project these figures to the full population in this target group to estimate sales volume. Even then, the estimate is uncertain because people do not always carry out their stated intentions.

Marketing Strategy Development

Marketing strategy development

Designing an initial marketing strategy for a new product based on the product concept.

Suppose the car maker finds that concept 3 for the fuel-cell-powered electric car tests best. The next step is **marketing strategy development**, designing an initial marketing strategy for introducing this car to the market.

The *marketing strategy statement* consists of three parts. The first part describes the target market; the planned value proposition; and the sales, market share, and profit goals for the first few years. Thus:

> The target market is younger, well-educated, moderate- to high-income individuals, couples, or small families seeking practical, environmentally responsible transportation. The car will be positioned as more fun to drive and less polluting than today's internal combustion engine or hybrid cars. The company will aim to sell 100,000 cars in the first year, at a loss of not more than $15 million. In the second year, the company will aim for sales of 120,000 cars and a profit of $25 million.

● TABLE | 9.1
Questions for Battery-Powered Electric Car Concept Test

1. Do you understand the concept of a battery-powered electric car?
2. Do you believe the claims about the car's performance?
3. What are the major benefits of the battery-powered electric car compared with a conventional car?
4. What are its advantages compared with a gas-electric hybrid car?
5. What improvements in the car's features would you suggest?
6. For what uses would you prefer a battery-powered electric car to a conventional car?
7. What would be a reasonable price to charge for the car?
8. Who would be involved in your decision to buy such a car? Who would drive it?
9. Would you buy such a car (definitely, probably, probably not, definitely not)?

The second part of the marketing strategy statement outlines the product's planned price, distribution, and marketing budget for the first year:

The battery-powered electric car will be offered in three colors—red, white, and blue—and will have a full set of accessories as standard features. It will sell at a retail price of $25,000—with 15 percent off the list price to dealers. Dealers who sell more than 10 cars per month will get an additional discount of 5 percent on each car sold that month. A marketing budget of $50 million will be split 50–50 between a national media campaign and local event marketing. Advertising and Web site will emphasize the car's fun spirit and low emissions. During the first year, $100,000 will be spent on marketing research to find out who is buying the car and their satisfaction levels.

The third part of the marketing strategy statement describes the planned long-run sales, profit goals, and marketing mix strategy:

We intend to capture a 3 percent long-run share of the total auto market and realize an after-tax return on investment of 15 percent. To achieve this, product quality will start high and be improved over time. Price will be raised in the second and third years if competition permits. The total marketing budget will be raised each year by about 10 percent. Marketing research will be reduced to $60,000 per year after the first year.

Business Analysis

Business analysis

A review of the sales, costs, and profit projections for a new product to find out whether these factors satisfy the company's objectives.

Once management has decided on its product concept and marketing strategy, it can evaluate the business attractiveness of the proposal. **Business analysis** involves a review of the sales, costs, and profit projections for a new product to find out whether they satisfy the company's objectives. If they do, the product can move to the product development stage.

To estimate sales, the company might look at the sales history of similar products and conduct market surveys. It can then estimate minimum and maximum sales to assess the range of risk. After preparing the sales forecast, management can estimate the expected costs and profits for the product, including marketing, R&D, operations, accounting, and finance costs. The company then uses the sales and costs figures to analyze the new product's financial attractiveness.

Product Development

Product development

Developing the product concept into a physical product in order to ensure that the product idea can be turned into a workable market offering.

So far, for many new-product concepts, the product may have existed only as a word description, a drawing, or perhaps a crude mock-up. If the product concept passes the business test, it moves into **product development**. Here, R&D or engineering develops the product concept into a physical product. The product development step, however, now calls for a large jump in investment. It will show whether the product idea can be turned into a workable product.

The R&D department will develop and test one or more physical versions of the product concept. R&D hopes to design a prototype that will satisfy and excite consumers and that can be produced quickly and at budgeted costs. Developing a successful prototype can take days, weeks, months, or even years depending on the product and prototype methods.

Often, products undergo rigorous tests to make sure that they perform safely and effectively, or that consumers will find value in them. Companies can do their own product testing or outsource testing to other firms that specialize in testing. Here are some examples of such product tests:[18]

Thunk. Thunk. Thunk. Behind a locked door in the basement of Louis Vuitton's elegant Paris headquarters, a mechanical arm hoists a brown-and-tan handbag a half-meter off the floor—then drops it. The bag, loaded with an 8-pound weight, will be lifted and dropped, over and over again, for four days. This is Vuitton's test laboratory, a high-tech torture chamber for its fabled luxury goods. Another piece of lab equipment bombards handbags with ultraviolet rays to test resistance to fading. Still another tests zippers by tugging them open and shutting them 5,000 times. There's even a mechanized mannequin hand, with a Vuitton charm bracelet around its wrist, being shaken vigorously to make sure none of the charms fall off.

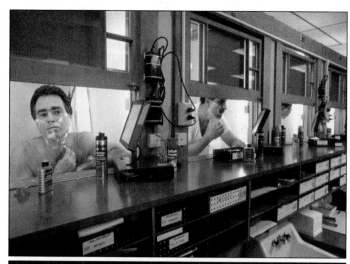

At Gillette, almost everyone gets involved in new-product testing. ▲Every working day at Gillette, 200 volunteers from various departments come to work unshaven, troop to the second floor of the company's gritty South Boston plant, and enter small booths with a sink and mirror. There they take instructions from technicians on the other side of a small window as to which razor, shaving cream, or aftershave to use. The volunteers evaluate razors for sharpness of blade, smoothness of glide, and ease of handling. In a nearby shower room, women perform the same ritual on their legs, underarms, and what the company delicately refers to as the "bikini area." "We bleed so you'll get a good shave at home," says one Gillette employee.

A new product must have the required functional features and also convey the intended psychological characteristics. The battery-powered electric car, for example, should strike consumers as being well built, comfortable, and safe. Management must learn what makes consumers decide that a car is well built. To some consumers, this means that the car has "solid-sounding" doors. To others, it means that the car is able to withstand heavy impact in crash tests. Consumer tests are conducted in which consumers test-drive the car and rate its attributes.

Test Marketing

Test marketing
The stage of new-product development in which the product and marketing program are tested in realistic market settings.

If the product passes concept and product tests, the next step is **test marketing**, the stage at which the product and marketing program are introduced into realistic market settings. Test marketing gives the marketer experience with marketing the product before going to the great expense of full introduction. It lets the company test the product and its entire marketing program—targeting and positioning strategy, advertising, distribution, pricing, branding and packaging, and budget levels.

The amount of test marketing needed varies with each new product. Test marketing costs can be high, and it takes time that may allow competitors to gain advantages. When the costs of developing and introducing the product are low, or when management is already confident about the new product, the company may do little or no test marketing. In fact, test marketing by consumer-goods firms has been declining in recent years. Companies often do not test-market simple line extensions or copies of successful competitor products.

However, when introducing a new product requires a big investment, when the risks are high, or when management is not sure of the product or marketing program, a company may do a lot of test marketing. ▲For instance, KFC will soon introduce a major new product—Kentucky Grilled Chicken. Although the fast-food chain built its legacy on serving crispy, seasoned fried chicken, it hopes that the new product will lure back health-conscious consumers who dropped fried chicken from their diets. "This is transformational for our brand," says KFC's chief food innovation officer. Given the importance of the decision, KFC will have conducted more than three years of product and market testing before rolling Kentucky Grilled Chicken out nationally. "You might say, 'what took you so long,'" says the chain's president. "I've asked that question a couple of times myself. The answer is we had to get it right."[19]

Although test-marketing costs can be high, they are often small when compared with the costs of making a major mistake. Still, test marketing doesn't guarantee success. For example, Procter & Gamble tested its Fit produce rinse heavily for five years. Although market tests suggested the product would be successful, P&G pulled the plug on it shortly after its introduction.[20]

When using test marketing, consumer products companies usually choose one of three approaches—standard test markets, controlled test markets, or simulated test markets.

Standard Test Markets

Using standard test markets, the company finds a small number of representative test cities, conducts a full marketing campaign in these cities, and uses store audits, consumer and distributor surveys, and other measures to gauge product performance. The results are used to forecast national sales and profits, discover potential product problems, and fine-tune the marketing program. KFC used standard test markets for its new Kentucky Grilled Chicken in cities such as Indianapolis, Colorado Springs, San Diego, Oklahoma City, and Austin, Texas. At these sites, KFC tested both the new product and its full marketing program, including new store signage and a series of ads.

Standard test markets have some drawbacks. They can be very costly and they may take a long time. Moreover, competitors can monitor test market results or interfere with them by cutting their prices in test cities, increasing their promotion, or even buying up the product being tested. Finally, test markets give competitors a look at the company's new product well before it is introduced nationally. Thus, competitors may have time to develop defensive strategies, and may even beat the company's product to the market.

Despite these disadvantages, standard test markets are still the most widely used approach for major in-market testing. However, many companies today are shifting toward quicker and cheaper controlled and simulated test marketing methods.

Controlled Test Markets

Several research firms keep controlled panels of stores that have agreed to carry new products for a fee. Controlled test marketing systems such as ACNielsen's Scantrack and Information Resources, Inc.'s (IRI) BehaviorScan track individual consumer behavior for new products from the television set to the checkout counter.

In each BehaviorScan market, IRI maintains a panel of shoppers who report all of their purchases by showing an identification card at checkout in participating stores and by using a handheld scanner at home to record purchases at non-participating stores. Within test stores, IRI controls such factors as shelf placement, price, and in-store promotions for the product being tested. IRI also measures TV viewing in each panel household and sends special commercials to panel member television sets to test their affect on shopping decisions. Direct mail promotions can also be tested.[21]

Detailed scanner information on each consumer's purchases is fed into a central computer, where it is combined with the consumer's demographic and TV viewing information and reported daily. Thus, BehaviorScan can provide store-by-store, week-by-week reports on the sales of tested products. Such panel purchasing data enables in-depth diagnostics not possible with retail point-of-sale data alone, including repeat purchase analysis, buyer demographics, and earlier, more accurate sales forecasts after just 12 to 24 weeks in market. Most importantly, the system allows companies to evaluate their specific marketing efforts.

Controlled test markets, such as BehaviorScan, usually cost less than standard test markets. Also, because retail distribution is "forced" in the first week of the test, controlled test markets can be completed much more quickly than standard test markets. As in standard test markets, controlled test markets allow competitors to get a look at the company's new product. And some companies are concerned that the limited number of controlled test markets used by the research services may not be representative of their products' markets or target consumers. However, the research firms are experienced in projecting test market results to broader markets and can usually account for biases in the test markets used.

Simulated Test Markets

Companies can also test new products in a simulated shopping environment. The company or research firm shows ads and promotions for a variety of products, including the new product being tested, to a sample of consumers. It gives consumers a small amount of money and invites them to a real or laboratory store where they may keep the money or use it to buy items. The researchers note how many consumers buy the new product and competing brands.

This simulation provides a measure of trial and the commercial's effectiveness against competing commercials. The researchers then ask consumers the reasons for their purchase or nonpurchase. Some weeks later, they interview the consumers by phone to determine product attitudes, usage, satisfaction, and repurchase intentions. Using sophisticated computer models, the researchers then project national sales from results of the simulated test market. Recently, some marketers have begun to use interesting new high-tech approaches, such as virtual reality and the Internet, to simulated test market research.

Simulated test markets overcome some of the disadvantages of standard and controlled test markets. They usually cost much less, can be run in eight weeks, and keep the new product out of competitors' view. Yet, because of their small samples and simulated shopping environments, many marketers do not think that simulated test markets are as accurate or reliable as larger, real-world tests. Still, simulated test markets are used widely, often as "pretest" markets. Because they are fast and inexpensive, they can be run to quickly assess a new product or its marketing program.

Many marketers are now using new simulated marketing technologies to reduce the costs of test marketing and to speed up the process. ▲For example, Frito-Lay worked with research firm Decision Insight to create an online virtual convenience store in which to test new products and marketing ideas.[22]

> Decision Insight's SimuShop online shopping environment lets Frito-Lay's marketers test shopper reactions to different extensions, shelf placements, pricing, and packaging of its Lay's, Doritos, Cheetos, and Fritos brands in a variety of store setups without investing huge amounts of time and money on actual in-store research in different locations. Recruited shoppers visit the online store, browse realistic virtual shelves featuring Frito-Lay's and competing products, click on individual products to view them in more detail, and select products to put in their carts. When the shopping is done, selected customers are questioned in one-on-one, on-screen interviews about why they chose the products they did. Watching the entire decision process unfold gives Frito-Lay marketers reams of information about what would happen in the real world. With 200-some bags of Frito-Lay products sitting on a typical store shelf, the company doesn't have the luxury of test marketing in actual market settings. "For us, that can only really be done virtually," says a Frito-Lay marketer. The SimuShop tests produce a 90 percent or better correlation to real shopper behavior when compared with later real-world data.

▲ New test marketing technologies: Frito-Lay worked with research firm Decision Insight to create an online virtual convenience store in which to test new products and marketing ideas.

Commercialization

Commercialization
Introducing a new product into the market.

Test marketing gives management the information needed to make a final decision about whether to launch the new product. If the company goes ahead with **commercialization**—introducing the new product into the market—it will face high costs. The company may need to build or rent a manufacturing facility. And, in the case of a major new consumer packaged good, it may spend hundreds of millions of dollars for advertising, sales promotion, and other marketing efforts in the first year. For example, when Unilever introduced its Sunsilk hair care line, it spent $200 million in the United States alone, including $30 million for nontraditional media such as MySpace ads and profiles, mall displays that used audio to catch passersby, 3-D ads in tavern bathrooms, and cinema ads.[23]

The company launching a new product must first decide on introduction *timing*. If the car maker's new battery-powered electric car will eat into the sales of the company's other cars, its introduction may be delayed. If the car can be improved further, or if the economy is down, the company may wait until the following year to launch it. However, if competitors are ready to introduce their own battery-powered models, the company may push to introduce its car sooner.

Next, the company must decide *where* to launch the new product—in a single location, a region, the national market, or the international market. Few companies have the confidence, capital, and capacity to launch new products into full national or international distribution right away. Instead, they develop a planned *market rollout* over time. For example, when Miller introduced Miller Chill, a lighter Mexican-style lager flavored with lime and salt, it started in selected southwestern states, such as Arizona, New Mexico, and Texas, supported by local TV commercials. Based on strong sales in these initial markets, the company then rolled out Miller Chill nationally, supported by $30 million worth of TV commercials, print ads, and a live in-show ad on *Late Night with Conan O'Brien*. Finally, based on the brand's U.S. success, Miller is now rolling out Miller Chill internationally, starting with Australia.[24]

Some companies, however, may quickly introduce new models into the full national market. Companies with international distribution systems may introduce new products through swift global rollouts. ▲ Microsoft recently did this with its Windows Vista operating system. Microsoft used a mammoth advertising blitz to launch Vista simultaneously in more than 30 markets worldwide. The campaign targeted 6.6 billion global impressions in just its first two months. "There won't be a PC sold anywhere in the world that doesn't have Vista within the next six months," said an industry analyst at the start of the campaign.[25]

▲ Commercialization: Microsoft launched its new Windows Vista operating system in a swift global rollout. Its mammoth "Wow!" advertising blitz hit more than 30 markets worldwide simultaneously, creating some 6.6 billion global impressions in just its first two months.

Author Comment | Above all else, new-product development must focus on creating customer value. Apple's Steve Jobs is obsessed with the Apple user's experience. For every new product that Apple introduces, it's clear that someone actually asked, "how can we make life better for our customers?"

Managing New-Product Development
(pp 268–272)

The new-product development process shown in Figure 9.1 highlights the important activities needed to find, develop, and introduce new products. However, new-product development involves more than just going through a set of steps. Companies must take a holistic approach to managing this process. Successful new-product development requires a customer-centered, team-based, and systematic effort.

Customer-Centered New-Product Development

Above all else, new-product development must be customer-centered. When looking for and developing new products, companies often rely too heavily on technical research in their R&D labs. But like everything else in marketing, successful new-product development begins with a thorough understanding of what consumers need and value. **Customer-centered new-product development** focuses on finding new ways to solve customer problems and create more customer-satisfying experiences.

Customer-centered new-product development

New-product development that focuses on finding new ways to solve customer problems and create more customer-satisfying experiences.

One recent study found that the most successful new products are ones that are differentiated, solve major customer problems, and offer a compelling customer value proposition. Another study showed that companies that directly engage their customers in the new-product innovation process had twice the return on assets and triple the growth in operating income of firms that don't.[26]

For products ranging from consumer package goods to power tools, today's innovative companies are getting out of the research lab and mingling with customers in the search for new customer value. Consider this example:[27]

Engineers and marketers from Black & Decker's DeWalt division—the division that makes power tools used by professional contractors—spend a great deal of time at job sites, generating ideas by talking to end users and observing how they work. Then, once prototypes of new products have been completed, those same people take them directly to the same job sites, leave the tools, and come back a week or so later to collect information on how they perform. Thanks to its strong customer focus, DeWalt now captures a more than 50 percent share of the U.S. professional power tool market.

John Schiech, president of the DeWalt division, tells a valuable story about the importance of paying close attention to customers. "The best-selling miter saws on the market in the early 1990s cost about $199, and they all had 10-inch blades. Our guys went out and did some research and found a lot of people building big colonial-style homes with big moldings. Saw blades cut only half way through those big pieces of trim, so they had to pass a 16-foot piece of molding out the window, flip it around, pass it back in, and make the rest of the cut. We realized that if we moved to a 12-inch blade, which required a completely different, much bigger saw, they could make these cuts in one pass. So we developed and launched a 12-inch miter saw, and charged $399. It became the number one-selling miter saw by a huge margin, and remains so to this day." When asked what makes his company so successful, Schiech summarized: "It's engineers and marketing product managers spending hours and hours on job sites talking to the guys who are trying to make their living with these tools."

Thus, customer-centered new-product development begins and ends with solving customer problems (see **Real Marketing 9.1** for a great example). As one expert asks: "What is innovation after all, if not products and services that offer fresh thinking in a way that meets the needs of customers?"[28] Says another expert, "Getting consumer insights at the beginning of the process, using those insights consistently and respectfully throughout the process, and communicating them in a compelling form when you go to market is critical to a product's success in the market these days."[29]

Team-Based New-Product Development

Good new-product development also requires a total-company, cross-functional effort. Some companies organize their new-product development process into the orderly sequence of steps shown in Figure 9.1, starting with idea generation and ending with commercialization. Under this *sequential product development* approach, one company department works individually to complete its stage of the process before passing the new product along to the next department and stage. This orderly, step-by-step process can help bring control to complex and risky projects. But it also can be dangerously slow. In fast-changing, highly competitive markets, such slow-but-sure product development can result in product failures, lost sales and profits, and crumbling market positions.

Real Marketing 9.1

IDEO's Design Approach:

Putting Customers First

IDEO, the nation's hottest industrial design firm, has won countless awards for innovative product design. Its diverse roster of clients has included companies ranging from Apple, Microsoft, Marriott, Caterpillar, and Procter & Gamble to Boston Beer, Lufthansa, Mayo Clinic, and the Red Cross. IDEO's design teams came up with the first laptop computer, the first Apple mouse, the industry-changing, sleek and elegant Palm V PDA, and even Crest's first standup toothpaste tube.

But it's not so much IDEO's innovative designs that make it stand out. It's IDEO's design *process*. In designing new products, IDEO doesn't start with engineers working in design labs. It starts with customers. And it doesn't just design products, it designs customer product *experiences*. At the start of every design project, IDEO's "human factors" teams conduct "deep dives" into consumer behavior. The design teams shadow customers, get to know them deeply, and analyze the intricacies of their product-use experiences. "Tech companies design from the inside out," says an IDEO executive. "We design from the outside in so that we can put customers first."

IDEO's work with bicycle components maker Shimano illustrates its customer-centered design approach. Shimano sells bike parts—such as gears, crank arms, and derailleurs—to most of the world's major bicycle manufacturers. If you own a high-end bike, chances are good that it contains several

Customer-centered new-product development: With the help of design firm IDEO, Shimano and bicycle makers like Trek learned that people didn't want better bikes, they wanted better biking experiences. The result: Industry-changing "coasting" bikes that are simple, comfortable, and fun to use.

Shimano parts. But in 2006, Shimano faced a problem. Bicycle manufacturers were selling fewer bikes, so Shimano was selling fewer parts.

U.S. bicycle sales had been flat for nearly a decade. Worse, the number of people riding bikes was actually declining. The proportion of American bike riders over the age of seven who rode a bike at least six times per year plunged more than 17 percent in 2006 versus 2005, part of a more than 33 percent drop over the prior decade. About the only thing propping up the bicycle industry was the blip in sales of high-margin, top-of-the-line bikes following Lance Armstrong's incredible string of seven Tour de France victories. The industry began to focus more heavily on developing the ever-more sophisticated—and ever-more expensive—bikes coveted by hard-core cycling enthusiasts. But Shimano knew that the surge in top-end sales couldn't last. The industry

had to find a way to get more of America's non-bikers back in the saddle.

So Shimano turned to IDEO for help. IDEO's challenge? Design a premium bike that would get Americans—especially baby boomers and older Gen Xers—riding again. But IDEO didn't follow the usual industry design process—using computer models to turn out great-looking new high-tech marvels and then testing them out on bike riding enthusiasts. Instead, IDEO began by sending its design team into the homes of people who *don't* ride bikes.

IDEO's social scientists and designers, accompanied by Shimano's marketers and engineers, spent months observing and meeting with non-riders in Atlanta, Chicago, Phoenix, and San Francisco, talking in depth about their leisure activities and their thoughts about biking. These deep customer interactions yielded rich insights into why

---

Team-based new-product development
An approach to developing new products in which various company departments work closely together, overlapping the steps in the product development process to save time and increase effectiveness.

In order to get their new products to market more quickly, many companies use a **team-based new-product development** approach. Under this approach, company departments work closely together in cross-functional teams, overlapping the steps in the product development process to save time and increase effectiveness. Instead of passing the new product from department to department, the company assembles a team of people from various departments that stays with the new product from start to finish. Such teams usually include people from the marketing, finance, design, manufacturing, and legal departments, and even supplier and customer companies. In the sequential process, a bottleneck at one phase can seriously slow the entire project. In the team-based approach, if one area hits snags, it works to resolve them while the team moves on.

The team-based approach does have some limitations. For example, it sometimes creates more organizational tension and confusion than the more orderly sequential approach.

people have stopped riding bikes. According to one account:

It wasn't so much that they were out of shape, or too busy or lazy. It was because cycling had become intimidating, something for hard-core athletes who love all the technical minutiae. "Everything had changed in bicycling," says a senior Shimano marketing executive. "It had gone from fun to being a sport, and no one [in the industry] had noticed." For boomers, bikes changed from the 10-speed rides on steel frame bikes to 30-speed carbon fiber and titanium machines. Costs rose from a few hundred dollars to thousands. Handlebars, pedals, tires, even seats came in so many varieties that consumers got overwhelmed. Expensive helmets, special shoes, and tight-fitting spandex clothes simply didn't appeal to recreational riders. And bike shops, filled with workers who fawned over gear, had little time for customers interested in just plain bikes.

Still, IDEO concluded, there was hope for Shimano and the bicycle manufacturers. "Everyone we talked to, as soon as we talked about bikes, a [nostalgic] smile came to their face," says an IDEO researcher. That nostalgia gave IDEO and Shimano an opening. People didn't want better bikes. They wanted a better biking experience, one that took them back to their memories of riding a bike as a kid.

Based on these customer insights, IDEO and Shimano came up with the concept of a "coasting" bike—a bicycle with a classic look that is simple, comfortable, and fun to use. Shimano built a prototype and sold the concept to three top bike manufacturers—Giant, Raleigh, and Trek. Coasting bikes are designed to create the ideal casual biking experience. They feature a traditional heads-up riding position, wide and comfortable

seats, a chain guard to keep grease off the cyclist's pants, and old-fashioned coaster brakes that stop when you peddle backwards. The coasting bikes are high-tech—for example, they come equipped with computer-controlled automatic gear shifting. But the technology remains hidden behind soft and familiar contours.

At first, it took some selling to convince the big bike makers to buy into the coasting concept:

The first Shimano prototype was unlike anything on the market, with rounded chrome hubs on the wheels, a swoopy curved frame, and handlebars with loops in them big enough to set a coffee cup inside. The cushy seat flipped up to reveal a mini-trunk to store a cell phone. "It was kind of like Audi meets Dr. Seuss," says a Raleigh executive. "Shimano thought this was the next big thing, and we were like, 'Is it?'"

However, Trek, Raleigh, and Giant soon embraced the idea and rolled out their first lines of coasting bikes in the spring of 2007, supported by a 15-city Shimano marketing campaign. The launch created more excitement than anything most industry insiders can remember. Surprised bicycle retailers soon found noncyclists making their way into their stores, and the three manufacturers quickly sold out of their 2007 inventories. By 2008, seven additional bicycle manufacturers had added the new old-fashioned coasting bikes to their lines.

The new designs appear to have hit the high-end casual biking market spot-on. "The automatic shifting [has really resonated] with customers," says one bicycle shop owner.

"Shimano is onto something." Importantly, coasting bikes may help to reinvigorate the stagnant bicycle industry by pulling new types of buyers in the door—recreational buyers like Alice Wilkes:

This summer, cyclists in skintight shorts raced through the French countryside in the annual Tour de France. The winner rode to victory on a Trek Madone 6.9 Pro that would cost consumers $8,249.99. Alice Wilkes also bought a Trek bike this summer, but she had a very different experience. Wilkes bought a Trek Lime, which shifts automatically so riders don't have to fuss with gears, stops when cyclists pedal backwards (like in the old days), and has a big, comfy seat. It retails for $589.99. With her new bike, the first one she has owned in 40 years, Wilkes hits the trails near her Lynchburg, Virginia, home. For Wilkes, it's not about speed and performance. "Tight cycling clothes—that's not my world," says the 55-year-old grandmother. "I like to feel free, with the wind flying up my sleeves."

Despite their initial success, it remains to be seen whether coasting bikes will be real industry-changers or just a passing fad. But whatever happens, IDEO's customer-driven design ideas are opening eyes in the traditionally myopic bicycle industry. IDEO knows that bike riding has never really been about the bikes themselves. In the end, it's about customer biking experiences. For the past decade, the Lance Armstrongs of the world have had theirs. And now, thanks to IDEO and Shimano, the Alice Wilkeses have theirs as well.

Sources: Extracts, quotes, and other information from Matt Wiebe, "Retailers Worry over Future Coasting Sales," *Bicycle Retailer and Industry News*, March 15, 2008, pp. 1,2; Jay Green, "Return of the Easy Rider," *BusinessWeek*, September 17, 2007, p. 78; Philip Kotler and Kevin Lane Keller, *Marketing Management*, 13th edition (Upper Saddle River, NJ: Prentice Hall, 2008), pp. 105; Jessi Hempel, "Bringing Design to Blue Chips," *Fortune*, November 12, 2007, p. 32; and www.coasting.com, October 2008.

However, in rapidly changing industries facing increasingly shorter product life cycles, the rewards of fast and flexible product development far exceed the risks. Companies that combine a customer-centered approach with team-based new-product development gain a big competitive edge by getting the right new products to market faster.

Systematic New-Product Development

Finally, the new-product development process should be holistic and systematic rather than compartmentalized and haphazard. Otherwise, few new ideas will surface, and many good ideas will sputter and die. To avoid these problems, a company can install an *innovation management system* to collect, review, evaluate, and manage new-product ideas.

The company can appoint a respected senior person to be the company's innovation manager. It can set up Web-based idea management software and encourage all company stakeholders—employees, suppliers, distributors, dealers—to become involved in finding and developing new products. It can assign a cross-functional innovation management committee to evaluate proposed new-product ideas and help bring good ideas to market. It can create recognition programs to reward those who contribute the best ideas.

The innovation management system approach yields two favorable outcomes. First, it helps create an innovation-oriented company culture. It shows that top management supports, encourages, and rewards innovation. Second, it will yield a larger number of new-product ideas, among which will be found some especially good ones. The good new ideas will be more systematically developed, producing more new-product successes. No longer will good ideas wither for the lack of a sounding board or a senior product advocate.

Thus, new-product success requires more than simply thinking up a few good ideas, turning them into products, and finding customers for them. It requires a holistic approach for finding new ways to create valued customer experiences, from generating and screening new-product ideas to creating and rolling out want-satisfying products to customers.

▲ Google is both spectacularly successful and wildly innovative. At Google, innovation is more than just a process. It's in the air, in the spirit of the place.

More than this, successful new-product development requires a whole-company commitment. At companies known for their new-product prowess—such as Google, Apple, IDEO, 3M, Procter & Gamble, and General Electric—the entire culture encourages, supports, and rewards innovation. ▲Consider Google, which recently topped *Fast Company* magazine's list of the world's most innovative companies, and which regularly ranks among everyone else's top two or three innovators. Google is spectacularly successful. Despite formidable competition from giants such as Microsoft and Yahoo!, Google's share in its core business—online search—has climbed to a decisive 56 percent. Google is also wildly innovative. But at Google, innovation is more than a process—it's part of the company's DNA:[30]

Google's famously chaotic innovation process has unleashed a flurry of diverse products, ranging from a blog search engine (Google Blog Search), an e-mail service (Gmail), an online payment service (Google Checkout), and a news portal (Google News) to a universal platform for mobile-phone applications (Google Android) and projects for mapping and exploring the world (Google Maps and Google Earth). Talk to Googlers at various levels and departments, and one powerful theme emerges: Whether they're designing search engines for the blind or preparing meals for their colleagues, these people feel that their work can change the world. The marvel of Google is its ability to continue to instill a sense of creative fearlessness and ambition in its employees. Prospective hires are often asked, "If you could change the world using Google's resources, what would you build?" But here, this isn't a goofy or even theoretical question: Google wants to know, because thinking—and building—on that scale is what Google does. This, after all, is the company that wants to make available online every page of every book ever published. Smaller-gauge ideas die of disinterest. When it comes to innovation, Google *is* different. But the difference isn't tangible. It's in the air, in the spirit of the place.

Author Comment | A company's products are born, grow, mature, and then decline, just as living things do. To remain vital, the firm must continually develop new products and manage them effectively through their life cycles.

Product Life-Cycle Strategies (pp 272–279)

After launching the new product, management wants the product to enjoy a long and happy life. Although it does not expect the product to sell forever, the company wants to earn a decent profit to cover all the effort and risk that went into launching it.

FIGURE | 9.2
Sales and Profits over the Product's Life from Inception to Decline

Some products die quickly; others stay in the mature stage for a long, long time. For example, TABASCO sauce has been around for more than 130 years. Even then, to keep the product young, the company has added a full line of flavors (such as Sweet & Spicy and Chipotle) and a kitchen cabinet full of new TABASCO products (such as spicy beans, a chili mix, and jalapeno nacho slices).

Sales and profits ($)

Sales

Profits

0 — Time

Product development   Introduction   Growth   Maturity   Decline

Losses/ investment ($)

Product life cycle

The course of a product's sales and profits over its lifetime. It involves five distinct stages: product development, introduction, growth, maturity, and decline.

Management is aware that each product will have a life cycle, although its exact shape and length is not known in advance.

Figure 9.2 shows a typical **product life cycle** (PLC), the course that a product's sales and profits take over its lifetime. The product life cycle has five distinct stages:

1. *Product development* begins when the company finds and develops a new-product idea. During product development, sales are zero and the company's investment costs mount.

2. *Introduction* is a period of slow sales growth as the product is introduced in the market. Profits are nonexistent in this stage because of the heavy expenses of product introduction.

3. *Growth* is a period of rapid market acceptance and increasing profits.

4. *Maturity* is a period of slowdown in sales growth because the product has achieved acceptance by most potential buyers. Profits level off or decline because of increased marketing outlays to defend the product against competition.

5. *Decline* is the period when sales fall off and profits drop.

Not all products follow this product life cycle. Some products are introduced and die quickly; others stay in the mature stage for a long, long time. Some enter the decline stage and are then cycled back into the growth stage through strong promotion or repositioning. It seems that a well-managed brand could live forever. ▲Such venerable brands as Coca-Cola, Gillette, Budweiser, American Express, Wells-Fargo, Kikkoman, and TABASCO, for instance, are still going strong after more than 100 years.

The PLC concept can describe a *product class* (gasoline-powered automobiles), a *product form* (SUVs), or a *brand* (the Ford Escape). The PLC concept applies differently in each case. Product classes have the longest life cycles—the sales of many product classes stay in the mature stage for a long time. Product forms, in contrast, tend to have the standard PLC shape. Product forms such as "dial telephones" and "VHS tapes" passed through a regular history of introduction, rapid growth, maturity, and decline.

A specific brand's life cycle can change quickly because of changing competitive attacks and responses. For example, although laundry soaps (product class) and powdered detergents (product form) have enjoyed fairly long life cycles, the life cycles of specific brands have tended to be much shorter. Today's leading brands of powdered laundry soap are Tide and Cheer; the leading brands 75 years ago were Fels-Naptha, Octagon, and Kirkman.

IT'S OVER 130 YEARS OLD AND YET STILL ABLE TO TOTALLY WHUP YOUR BUTT.™ ORIGINAL TABASCO® PEPPER SAUCE TABASCO.com

▲ Product life cycle: Some products die quickly; others stay in the mature stage for a long, long time. TABASCO sauce is "over 130 years old and yet still able to totally whup your butt!"

Style

A basic and distinctive mode of expression.

Fashion

A currently accepted or popular style in a given field.

Fad

A temporary period of unusually high sales driven by consumer enthusiasm and immediate product or brand popularity.

The PLC concept also can be applied to what are known as styles, fashions, and fads. Their special life cycles are shown in 🔹 **Figure 9.3**. A **style** is a basic and distinctive mode of expression. For example, styles appear in homes (colonial, ranch, transitional), clothing (formal, casual), and art (realist, surrealist, abstract). Once a style is invented, it may last for generations, passing in and out of vogue. A style has a cycle showing several periods of renewed interest. A **fashion** is a currently accepted or popular style in a given field. For example, the more formal "business attire" look of corporate dress of the 1980s and 1990s gave way to the "business casual" look of today. Fashions tend to grow slowly, remain popular for a while, and then decline slowly.

Fads are temporary periods of unusually high sales driven by consumer enthusiasm and immediate product or brand popularity.[31] A fad may be part of an otherwise normal life cycle, as in the case of recent surges in the sales of poker chips and accessories. Or the fad may comprise a brand's or product's entire life cycle. "Pet rocks" are a classic example. Upon hearing his friends complain about how expensive it was to care for their dogs, advertising copywriter Gary Dahl joked about his pet rock. He soon wrote a spoof of a dog-training manual for it, titled "The Care and Training of Your Pet Rock." Soon Dahl was selling some 1.5 million ordinary beach pebbles at $4 a pop. Yet the fad, which broke one October, had sunk like a stone by the next February. Dahl's advice to those who want to succeed with a fad: "Enjoy it while it lasts." Other examples of such fads include the Rubik's Cube and low-carb diets.[32]

The PLC concept can be applied by marketers as a useful framework for describing how products and markets work. And when used carefully, the PLC concept can help in developing good marketing strategies for different stages of the product life cycle. But using the PLC concept for forecasting product performance or for developing marketing strategies presents some practical problems. For example, in practice, it is difficult to forecast the sales level at each PLC stage, the length of each stage, and the shape of the PLC curve. Using the PLC concept to develop marketing strategy also can be difficult because strategy is both a cause and a result of the product's life cycle. The product's current PLC position suggests the best marketing strategies, and the resulting marketing strategies affect product performance in later life-cycle stages.

Moreover, marketers should not blindly push products through the traditional stages of the product life cycle. "As marketers instinctively embrace the old life-cycle paradigm, they needlessly consign their products to following the curve into maturity and decline," notes one marketing professor. Instead, marketers often defy the "rules" of the life cycle and position their products in unexpected ways. By doing this, "companies can rescue products foundering in the maturity phase of their life cycles and return them to the growth phase. And they can catapult new products forward into the growth phase, leapfrogging obstacles that could slow consumers' acceptance."[33]

The moral of the product life cycle is that companies must continually innovate or they risk extinction. No matter how successful its current product lineup, for future success, a company must skillfully manage the life cycles of existing products. And to grow, it must develop a steady stream of new products that bring new value to customers (see **Real Marketing 9.2**).

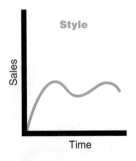

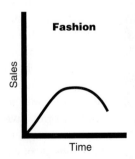

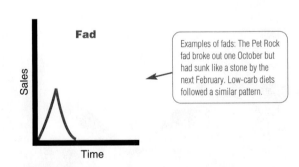

Examples of fads: The Pet Rock fad broke out one October but had sunk like a stone by the next February. Low-carb diets followed a similar pattern.

🔹 **FIGURE | 9.3** Styles, Fashions, and Fads

Real Marketing 9.2

Kraft:
Lots of Good Old Products; Too Few Good New Ones?

Kraft makes and markets an incredible portfolio of known and trusted brands, including half a dozen $1 billion brands and another 50 that top $100 million in sales. Beyond the Kraft label of cheeses, snacks, dips, and dressings, its megabrands include the likes of Oscar Mayer, Post cereals, DiGiorno pizza, Maxwell House coffee, JELL-O, Cool Whip, Kool-Aid, A1 sauce, Velveeta, Planters, Miracle Whip, Light 'n Lively, Grey Poupon, CapriSun, and Nabisco (Oreo, Chips Ahoy!, Triscuit, SnackWells, and a whole lot more). Search America's pantries and you'll find at least one Kraft product in 199 of every 200 households.

However, despite its long list of familiar brands, Kraft hasn't done very well in recent years. Over the past six years, its sales and profits have stagnated and its stock price has flat-lined. Investors would have made a better return on bank certificates of deposit than on their investments in Kraft stock. The problem? Until just recently, Kraft has done a poor job of managing the product life cycle. Although it's had a slew of good *old* products, it's had far too few good *new* products.

Many of Kraft's venerable old brands—such as Maxwell House, Velveeta, and JELL-O—have been showing their age. Other brands have been extended about as far as they can go—for instance, Kraft now markets more than 20 varieties of Oreos, from the original sandwich cookies, Oreo Double Stuf, Oreo Double Double Stuf, Chocolate-Covered Oreos, and Double Delight Chocolate Mint'n Crème Oreos to Oreo Mini Bites, Oreo Snack Cakes, and even Oreo ice cream cones. How much pop would yet one more variety provide?

Over the years, competitors such as P&G have invested dollars and energy in their mature or declining brands, such as Mr. Clean and Old Spice, moving them back into the growth stage of the product life cycle. In contrast, Kraft has focused on cost-cutting, leaving its mature brands to wither. Whereas rival P&G has developed a constant stream of really new products—even inventing all new product categories, with products such as Swiffer and Febreze—Kraft has been slow to innovate. And while P&G has been intensely

Welcome to the **new Kraft**

**Chairman and CEO
Irene Rosenfeld**

Managing the product life cycle: Kraft CEO Irene Rosenfeld announces, "We are about to take this great portfolio of ours in a new direction that's more consistent with the reality of consumers' lives today. Welcome to the new Kraft."

customer-focused, bringing innovative new solutions to its customers, Kraft has slowly lost touch with its customers.

In 2006, however, under pressure from investors, Kraft installed a brand-new leadership team, including a new CEO, a first-ever chief marketing officer, and a leader of consumer innovation and marketing services. Under the leadership of CEO Irene Rosenfeld, the new leadership team laid out an ambitious turnaround plan to restore Kraft's sales and profit growth.

For starters, the team announced that it would make heavy investments to reconnect with customers and to improve product quality. To better understand what customers think and want, "We're going to connect with the consumer wherever she is," said Rosenfeld. "On the quality side, [we need to] shift from 'good enough' to 'truly delicious,' turning brands that [our] consumers have lived with for years into brands they can't live without." Most importantly, pronounced Rosenfeld, Kraft would invest heavily in innovation and new-product development. Simply put, she said, "We need to rebuild our new-product pipeline."

Rosenfeld and her team began their new-product development efforts not in the test kitchens but by visiting consumer homes, viewing the world through customers' eyes rather than through a company's lens. "We are about to take this great portfolio of ours in a new direction that's more consistent with the reality of consumers' lives today," she declared. We need "customer-focused innovation!" The team discovered the simple truth that with the way customers live their

lives today, they want high-quality but convenient and healthy foods. "Wouldn't it be a whole lot easier if you could have restaurant-quality food at home for a fraction of the cost?" asked Rosenfeld.

The team also realized that Kraft already had all the fixings it needed to complete this mission. It needed only to reframe its offerings in ways that fit customers' changing lifestyles. For example, Kraft developed the highly successful "Deli Creations" brand—a build-your-own premium sandwich kit that includes bread, Oscar Mayer meats, Kraft cheeses, and condiments such as A1 steak sauce and Grey Poupon mustard. Customers can quickly assemble the sandwiches, pop them into the microwave for one minute, and wrap their mouths around a hot, restaurant-style sandwich. In a similar fashion, Kraft rolled out "Fresh Creations" salads, complete with Oscar Mayer meat, Kraft cheese, Good Season's salad dressing, and Planter's nuts, a move that took its product portfolio into a whole new section of the grocery store, the produce section.

In addition to creating new brands and categories, Kraft quickly launched a pantry full of new products under the old familiar brand names. For example, it introduced DiGiorno Ultimate, its best-yet alternative to delivery pizza, featuring premium vine-ripened tomatoes, whole-milk mozzarella cheese, specialty meats, and julienne vegetables. Under previous management, this project had been black-balled because the premium ingredients were considered too

Continued on next page

Real Marketing 9.2 Continued ▼

hard to get and too expensive. With Rosenfeld's blessing, DiGiorno Ultimate was on the shelves in just 18 months.

Dozens of other new products ranged from higher-quality Oscar Mayer Deli Fresh cold cuts and an entirely rejuvenated line of Kraft salad dressings with no artificial preservatives to Kraft Bagel-Fuls handheld breakfast sandwiches, Cakesters snack cakes, healthy LiveActive products with probiotic cultures and prebiotic fiber, and Oscar Mayer Fast Franks prepackaged microwavable stadium-style hotdogs.

Kraft even invested to reinvigorate some of its old brands. For example, it added four bold new flavors to the Grey Poupon brand, a name that had retained 70 percent consumer awareness even without much investment. The new flavors will be supported by a fresh version of the old and much-liked Grey Poupon "Pardon me" ad campaign. Kraft is also infusing new life into existing brands such

as Knudsen and Breakstone by co-marketing them with the LiveActive health brand. And, to get the word out about all its new products, Kraft invested an additional $400 million on a new marketing program designed to better tell the Kraft story. "We [are] telling the consumer that Kraft is back," said Rosenfeld.

And it appears that Kraft *is* back—or at least heading in the right direction. Although profits are still languishing, sales are now growing at a healthy clip. Rosenfeld and her team are optimistic. "Our brands are getting stronger every day," she says. "Our insights about consumers are deeper and richer than ever before. And our new product pipeline is flowing with

exciting ideas that will accelerate our growth and improve our margins. I'm pleased to tell you, the new Kraft is taking shape."

Kraft has learned that a company can't just sit back, basking in the glory of today's successful brands. Continued success requires skillful management of the product life cycle. But Rosenfeld knows that Kraft still has a long way to go in serving up a tastier investment to shareholders. "It's time to grow. Our investors have told us that, and I would agree with them," she says. "But this is not *Extreme Makeover: Home Edition* that'll get fixed in 60 minutes. We've [still] got some fundamental work to do."

Sources: Quotes and other information from Michael Arndt, "It Just Got Hotter in Kraft's Kitchen," *BusinessWeek*, February 12, 2007; "Kraft Highlights Growth Strategy, Reconfirms 2008 Guidelines and Unveils Product Innovations at CAGNY Conference," *Business Wire*, February 19, 2008; John Schmeltzer, "Foodmaker Whips Up Plan For a Comeback," *Chicago Tribune*, February 21, 2007, p. 1; and Kraft annual reports and other information from www.kraft.com, accessed September 2008.

We looked at the product-development stage of the product life cycle in the first part of the chapter. We now look at strategies for each of the other life-cycle stages.

Introduction Stage

Introduction stage
The product life-cycle stage in which the new product is first distributed and made available for purchase.

The **introduction stage** starts when the new product is first launched. Introduction takes time, and sales growth is apt to be slow. Well-known products such as instant coffee, frozen foods, and HDTVs lingered for many years before they entered a stage of more rapid growth.

In this stage, as compared to other stages, profits are negative or low because of the low sales and high distribution and promotion expenses. Much money is needed to attract distributors and build their inventories. Promotion spending is relatively high to inform consumers of the new product and get them to try it. Because the market is not generally ready for product refinements at this stage, the company and its few competitors produce basic versions of the product. These firms focus their selling on those buyers who are the most ready to buy.

A company, especially the *market pioneer*, must choose a launch strategy that is consistent with the intended product positioning. It should realize that the initial strategy is just the first step in a grander marketing plan for the product's entire life cycle. If the pioneer chooses its launch strategy to make a "killing," it may be sacrificing long-run revenue for the sake of short-run gain. As the pioneer moves through later stages of the life cycle, it must continuously formulate new pricing, promotion, and other marketing strategies. It has the best chance of building and retaining market leadership if it plays its cards correctly from the start.

Growth Stage

Growth stage
The product life-cycle stage in which a product's sales start climbing quickly.

If the new product satisfies the market, it will enter a **growth stage**, in which sales will start climbing quickly. The early adopters will continue to buy, and later buyers will start following their lead, especially if they hear favorable word of mouth. Attracted by the opportunities for profit, new competitors will enter the market. They will introduce new product features, and the market will expand. The increase in competitors leads to an increase in the number of distribution outlets, and sales jump just to build reseller inventories. Prices remain where they are or fall only slightly. Companies keep their promotion spending at the same or a slightly higher level. Educating the market remains a goal, but now the company must also meet the competition.

Profits increase during the growth stage as promotion costs are spread over a large volume and as unit manufacturing costs fall. The firm uses several strategies to sustain rapid market growth as long as possible. It improves product quality and adds new product features and models. It enters new market segments and new distribution channels. It shifts some advertising from building product awareness to building product conviction and purchase, and it lowers prices at the right time to attract more buyers.

In the growth stage, the firm faces a trade-off between high market share and high current profit. By spending a lot of money on product improvement, promotion, and distribution, the company can capture a dominant position. In doing so, however, it gives up maximum current profit, which it hopes to make up in the next stage.

Maturity Stage

Maturity stage

The product life-cycle stage in which sales growth slows or levels off.

At some point, a product's sales growth will slow down, and the product will enter a **maturity stage**. This maturity stage normally lasts longer than the previous stages, and it poses strong challenges to marketing management. Most products are in the maturity stage of the life cycle, and therefore most of marketing management deals with the mature product.

The slowdown in sales growth results in many producers with many products to sell. In turn, this overcapacity leads to greater competition. Competitors begin marking down prices, increasing their advertising and sales promotions, and upping their product development budgets to find better versions of the product. These steps lead to a drop in profit. Some of the weaker competitors start dropping out, and the industry eventually contains only well-established competitors.

Although many products in the mature stage appear to remain unchanged for long periods, most successful ones are actually evolving to meet changing consumer needs. Product managers should do more than simply ride along with or defend their mature products—a good offense is the best defense. They should consider modifying the market, product, and marketing mix.

In *modifying the market*, the company tries to increase the consumption of the current product. It may look for new users and new market segments, as when John Deere targeted the retiring baby-boomer market with the Gator, a vehicle traditionally used on a farm. For this new market, Deere has repositioned the Gator, promising that it can "take you from a do-it-yourselfer to a do-it-a-lot-easier." As one ad for the Gator XUV puts it, "When your plans include landscaping, gardening, or transporting people and materials on your property, the XUV provides a smooth, comfortable ride with heavy-duty performance."

The manager may also look for ways to increase usage among present customers. ▲For example, Glad

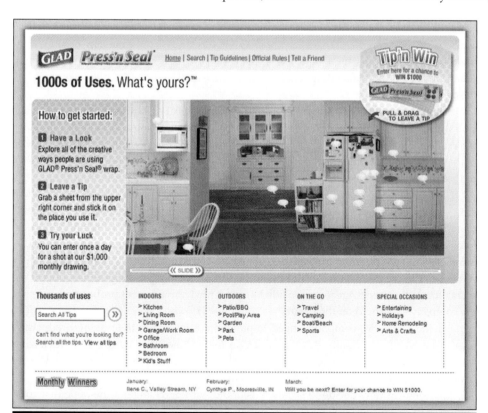

▲ Modifying the market: Glad helps customers to swap new uses for its Press'n Seal wrap on it's "1000s of Uses. What's Yours?" Web site.

Products Company helps customers to find new uses for its Press'n Seal wrap, the plastic wrap that creates a Tupperware-like seal. As more and more customers contacted the company about alternative uses for the product, Glad set up a special "1000s of Uses. What's Yours?" Web site (www.1000uses.com) at which customers can swap usage tips. "We found out our heavy users use it for a lot more than just covering food," says a Glad brand manager. "And they all became heavy users when they had an 'aha' moment with Press'n Seal." Suggested uses for Press'n Seal range from protecting a computer keyboard from dirt and spills and keeping garden seeds fresh to use by soccer moms sitting on damp benches while watching their tykes play. "We just roll out the Glad Press'n Seal over the long benches," says the mom who shared the tip, "and everyone's bottom stays nice and dry."[34]

The company might also try *modifying the product*—changing characteristics such as quality, features, style, or packaging to attract new users and to inspire more usage. It can improve the product's styling and attractiveness. It might improve the product's quality and performance—its durability, reliability, speed, and taste. Thus, makers of consumer food and household products introduce new flavors, colors, scents, ingredients, or packages to enhance performance and revitalize consumer buying. For example, TABASCO pepper sauce may have been around for more than 130 years, but to keep the brand young, the company has added a full line of flavors (such as Garlic, Sweet & Spicy, and Chipotle) and a kitchen cabinet full of new products under the TABASCO name (such as steak sauces, spicy beans, a chili mix, jalapeno nacho slices, and even a TABASCO lollipop).

Finally, the company can try *modifying the marketing mix*—improving sales by changing one or more marketing mix elements. The company can offer new or improved services to buyers. It can cut prices to attract new users and competitors' customers. It can launch a better advertising campaign or use aggressive sales promotions—trade deals, cents-off, premiums, and contests. In addition to pricing and promotion, the company can also move into new marketing channels to help serve new users.

Decline Stage

The sales of most product forms and brands eventually dip. The decline may be slow, as in the case of oatmeal cereal, or rapid, as in the cases of cassette and VHS tapes. Sales may plunge to zero, or they may drop to a low level where they continue for many years. This is the **decline stage**.

Decline stage
The product life-cycle stage in which a product's sales decline.

Sales decline for many reasons, including technological advances, shifts in consumer tastes, and increased competition. As sales and profits decline, some firms withdraw from the market. Those remaining may prune their product offerings. They may drop smaller market segments and marginal trade channels, or they may cut the promotion budget and reduce their prices further.

Carrying a weak product can be very costly to a firm, and not just in profit terms. There are many hidden costs. A weak product may take up too much of management's time. It often requires frequent price and inventory adjustments. It requires advertising and sales-force attention that might be better used to make "healthy" products more profitable. A product's failing reputation can cause customer concerns about the company and its other products. The biggest cost may well lie in the future. Keeping weak products delays the search for replacements, creates a lopsided product mix, hurts current profits, and weakens the company's foothold on the future.

For these reasons, companies need to pay more attention to their aging products. A firm's first task is to identify those products in the decline stage by regularly reviewing sales, market shares, costs, and profit trends. Then, management must decide whether to maintain, harvest, or drop each of these declining products.

Management may decide to *maintain* its brand without change in the hope that competitors will leave the industry. For example, Procter & Gamble made good profits by remaining in the declining liquid soap business as others withdrew. Or management may decide to reposition or reinvigorate the brand in hopes of moving it back into the growth stage of the product life cycle. Procter & Gamble has done this with several brands, including Mr. Clean and Old Spice.

Management may decide to *harvest* the product, which means reducing various costs (plant and equipment, maintenance, R&D, advertising, sales force) and hoping that sales hold up. If successful, harvesting will increase the company's profits in the short run. Or management may decide to *drop* the product from the line. It can sell it to another firm or simply liquidate it at salvage value. In recent years, P&G has sold off a number of lesser or declining brands such as Crisco oil, Comet cleanser, Sure deodorant, Duncan Hines cake mixes, and Jif peanut butter. If the company plans to find a buyer, it will not want to run down the product through harvesting.

● **Table 9.2** summarizes the key characteristics of each stage of the product life cycle. The table also lists the marketing objectives and strategies for each stage.[35]

● TABLE | 9.2   Summary of Product Life-Cycle Characteristics, Objectives, and Strategies

Characteristics	Introduction	Growth	Maturity	Decline
Sales	Low sales	Rapidly rising sales	Peak sales	Declining sales
Costs	High cost per customer	Average cost per customer	Low cost per customer	Low cost per customer
Profits	Negative	Rising profits	High profits	Declining profits
Customers	Innovators	Early adopters	Middle majority	Laggards
Competitors	Few	Growing number	Stable number beginning to decline	Declining number
Marketing Objectives				
	Create product awareness and trial	Maximize market share	Maximize profit while defending market share	Reduce expenditure and milk the brand
Strategies				
Product	Offer a basic product	Offer product extensions, service, warranty	Diversify brand and models	Phase out weak items
Price	Use cost-plus	Price to penetrate market	Price to match or beat competitors	Cut price
Distribution	Build selective distribution	Build intensive distribution	Build more intensive distribution	Go selective: phase out unprofitable outlets
Advertising	Build product awareness among early adopters and dealers	Build awareness and interest in the mass market	Stress brand differences and benefits	Reduce to level needed to retain hard-core loyals
Sales Promotion	Use heavy sales promotion to entice trial	Reduce to take advantage of heavy consumer demand	Increase to encourage brand switching	Reduce to minimal level

Source: Philip Kotler and Kevin Lane Keller, *Marketing Management*, 13th ed. (Upper Saddle River, NJ: Prentice Hall, 2009), p. 288.

Additional Product and Service Considerations (pp 280–282)

Here, we'll wrap up our discussion of products and services with two additional considerations: social responsibility in product decisions and issues of international product and service marketing.

Product Decisions and Social Responsibility

Product decisions have attracted much public attention. Marketers should carefully consider public policy issues and regulations regarding acquiring or dropping products, patent protection, product quality and safety, and product warranties.

Regarding new products, the government may prevent companies from adding products through acquisitions if the effect threatens to lessen competition. Companies dropping products must be aware that they have legal obligations, written or implied, to their suppliers, dealers, and customers who have a stake in the dropped product. Companies must also obey U.S. patent laws when developing new products. A company cannot make its product illegally similar to another company's established product.

Manufacturers must comply with specific laws regarding product quality and safety. The Federal Food, Drug, and Cosmetic Act protects consumers from unsafe and adulterated food, drugs, and cosmetics. Various acts provide for the inspection of sanitary conditions in the meat- and poultry-processing industries. Safety legislation has been passed to regulate fabrics, chemical substances, automobiles, toys, and drugs and poisons. The Consumer Product Safety Act of 1972 established a Consumer Product Safety Commission, which has the authority to ban or seize potentially harmful products and set severe penalties for violation of the law.

If consumers have been injured by a product that has a defective design, they can sue manufacturers or dealers. A recent survey of manufacturing companies found that product liability was the second-largest litigation concern, behind only labor and employment matters. Product liability suits are now occurring in federal courts at the rate of almost 24,000 per year. Although manufacturers are found at fault in only 6 percent of all product liability cases, when they are found guilty, the median jury award is $1.5 million and individual awards can run into the tens or even hundreds of millions of dollars. For example, in 2005 a jury ordered Merck to pay $253 million to the widow of a man who died from a heart attack after using the painkiller Vioxx for his arthritis. The judge later reduced the award to a "mere" $26.1 million. However, this was only the first of more than 60,000 Vioxx claims against the company and an eventual proposed settlement of nearly $5 billion that deeply crippled the company.[36]

This litigation phenomenon has resulted in huge increases in product liability insurance premiums, causing big problems in some industries. Some companies pass these higher rates along to consumers by raising prices. Others are forced to discontinue high-risk product lines. Some companies are now appointing "product stewards," whose job is to protect consumers from harm and the company from liability by proactively ferreting out potential product problems.

Many manufacturers offer written product warranties to convince customers of their products' quality. To protect consumers, Congress passed the Magnuson-Moss Warranty Act in 1975. The act requires that full warranties meet certain minimum standards, including repair "within a reasonable time and without charge" or a replacement or full refund if the product does not work "after a reasonable number of attempts" at repair. Otherwise, the company must make it clear that it is offering only a limited warranty. The law has led several manufacturers to switch from full to limited warranties and others to drop warranties altogether.

International Product and Services Marketing

International product and service marketers face special challenges. First, they must figure out what products and services to introduce and in which countries. Then, they must decide how much to standardize or adapt their products and services for world markets.

On the one hand, companies would like to standardize their offerings. Standardization helps a company to develop a consistent worldwide image. It also lowers the product design, manufacturing, and marketing costs of offering a large variety of products. On the other hand, markets and consumers around the world differ widely. Companies must usually respond to these differences by adapting their product offerings. ▲ For example, Nestlé sells a variety of very popular Kit Kat flavors in Japan that might make the average Western chocolate-lover's stomach turn, such as green tea, red bean, and red wine. Beyond taste, Kit Kat's strong following in Japan may also be the result of some unintended cultural factors:

▲ Nestlé Kit Kat chocolate bar in Japan benefits from the coincidental similarity between the bar's name and the Japanese phrase *kitto katsu*, which roughly translates to "You will surely win!" The brand's innovative "May cherries blossom" campaign has turned the Kit Kat bar and logo into national good luck charms.

In recent years, Kit Kat—the world's number two chocolate bar behind Snickers—has become very popular in Japan. Some of this popularity, no doubt, derives from the fact that the notoriously sweet-toothed Japanese love the bar's taste. But part of the bar's appeal may also be attributed to the coincidental similarity between its name and the Japanese phrase *kitto katsu*, which roughly translates in Japanese as "You will surely win!" Spotting this opportunity, marketers for Nestlé Japan developed an innovative Juken (college entrance exam) Kit Kat campaign. The multimedia campaign positions the Kit Kat bar and logo as good luck charms during the highly stressful university entrance exam season. Nestlé even developed a cherry flavored Kit Kat bar in packaging containing the message "May cherries blossom," wishing students luck in achieving their dreams. The campaign has been such a hit in Japan that it has led to a nationwide social movement to cheer up students for Juken. Kit Kat has also become an even broader national good luck charm. For example, a large flag featuring the Kit Kat logo and the phrase "Kitto Katsu!" has been used by fans of professional football team Jubilo IWATA, which is sponsored by Nestlé Japan. Since the Juken campaign began six years ago, Kit Kat sales in Japan have increased more than 250 percent.[37]

Packaging also presents new challenges for international marketers. Packaging issues can be subtle. For example, names, labels, and colors may not translate easily from one country to another. A firm using yellow flowers in its logo might fare well in the United States but meet with disaster in Mexico, where a yellow flower symbolizes death or disrespect. Similarly, although Nature's Gift might be an appealing name for gourmet mushrooms in America, it would be deadly in Germany, where *gift* means poison. Packaging may also need to be tailored to meet the physical characteristics of consumers in various parts of the world. For instance, soft drinks are sold in smaller cans in Japan to fit the smaller Japanese hand better. Thus, although product and package standardization can produce benefits, companies must usually adapt their offerings to the unique needs of specific international markets.

Service marketers also face special challenges when going global. Some service industries have a long history of international operations. For example, the commercial banking industry was one of the first to grow internationally. Banks had to provide global services in order to meet the foreign exchange and credit needs of their home country clients wanting to sell overseas. In recent years, many banks have become truly global. Germany's Deutsche Bank, for example, serves more than 13 million customers through 1,868 branches in 73 countries. For its clients around the world who wish to grow globally, Deutsche Bank can raise money not only in Frankfurt but also in Zurich, London, Paris, Tokyo, and Moscow.[38]

Professional and business services industries such as accounting, management consulting, and advertising have also globalized. The international growth of these firms followed the globalization of the client companies they serve. For example, as more clients employ worldwide marketing and advertising strategies, advertising agencies have responded by globalizing their own operations. McCann Worldgroup, a large U.S.-based advertising and marketing services agency, operates in more than 130 countries. It serves international clients such as Coca-Cola, General Motors, ExxonMobil, Microsoft, MasterCard, Johnson & Johnson, and Unilever in markets ranging from the United States and Canada to Korea and Kazakhstan. Moreover, McCann Worldgroup is one company in the Interpublic Group of Companies, an immense, worldwide network of advertising and marketing services companies.[39]

Retailers are among the latest service businesses to go global. As their home markets become saturated, American retailers such as Wal-Mart, Office Depot, and Saks Fifth Avenue are expanding into faster-growing markets abroad. For example, since 1995, Wal-Mart has entered 13 countries; its international division's sales grew nearly 18 percent last year, skyrocketing to more than $90.6 billion. Foreign retailers are making similar moves. Asian shoppers can now buy American products in French-owned Carrefour stores. Carrefour, the world's second-largest retailer behind Wal-Mart, now operates more than 12,500 stores in more than 30 countries. It is the leading retailer in Europe, Brazil, and Argentina and the largest foreign retailer in China.[40]

The trend toward growth of global service companies will continue, especially in banking, airlines, telecommunications, and professional services. Today, service firms are no longer simply following their manufacturing customers. Instead, they are taking the lead in international expansion.

REVIEWING Objectives AND KEY Terms

A company's current products face limited lifespans and must be replaced by newer products. But new products can fail—the risks of innovation are as great as the rewards. The key to successful innovation lies in a total-company effort, strong planning, and a systematic *new-product development* process.

OBJECTIVE 1 Explain how companies find and develop new-product ideas. (pp 258–259)

Companies find and develop new-product ideas from a variety of sources. Many new-product ideas stem from *internal sources.* Companies conduct formal research and development, pick the brains of their employees, and brainstorm at executive meetings. Other ideas come from *external sources.* By conducting surveys and focus groups and analyzing *customer* questions and complaints, companies can generate new-product ideas that will meet specific consumer needs. Companies track *competitors'* offerings and inspect new products, dismantling them, analyzing their performance, and deciding whether to introduce a similar or improved product. *Distributors and suppliers* are close to the market and can pass along information about consumer problems and new-product possibilities.

OBJECTIVE 2 List and define the steps in the new-product development process and the major considerations in managing this process. (pp 259–272)

The new-product development process consists of eight sequential stages. The process starts with *idea generation.* Next

comes *idea screening,* which reduces the number of ideas based on the company's own criteria. Ideas that pass the screening stage continue through *product concept development,* in which a detailed version of the new-product idea is stated in meaningful consumer terms. In the next stage, *concept testing,* new-product concepts are tested with a group of target consumers to determine whether the concepts have strong consumer appeal. Strong concepts proceed to *marketing strategy development,* in which an initial marketing strategy for the new product is developed from the product concept. In the *business-analysis* stage, a review of the sales, costs, and profit projections for a new product is conducted to determine whether the new product is likely to satisfy the company's objectives. With positive results here, the ideas become more concrete through *product development* and *test marketing* and finally are launched during *commercialization.*

New-product development involves more than just going through a set of steps. Companies must take a systematic, holistic approach to managing this process. Successful new-product development requires a customer-centered, team-based, systematic effort.

OBJECTIVE 3 Describe the stages of the product life cycle and how marketing strategies change during the product life cycle. (pp 272–279)

Each product has a *life cycle* marked by a changing set of problems and opportunities. The sales of the typical product follow an S-shaped curve made up of five stages. The cycle begins with the *product development stage* in which the company finds and develops a new-product idea. The *introduction stage* is marked by slow growth and low profits as the product is distributed to the market. If successful, the product enters a *growth stage,* which offers rapid sales growth and increasing profits. Next comes a *maturity stage* in which sales growth slows down and profits stabilize. Finally, the product enters a *decline stage* in which sales and profits dwindle. The company's task during this stage is to recognize the decline and to decide whether it should maintain, harvest, or drop the product.

In the *introduction stage*, the company must choose a launch strategy consistent with its intended product positioning. Much money is needed to attract distributors and build their inventories and to inform consumers of the new product and achieve trial. In the *growth stage,* companies continue to educate potential consumers and distributors. In addition, the company works to stay ahead of the competition and sustain rapid market growth by improving product quality, adding new product features and models, entering new market segments and distribution channels, shifting advertising from building product awareness to building product conviction and purchase, and lowering prices at the right time to attract new buyers.

In the *maturity stage,* companies continue to invest in maturing products and consider modifying the market, the product, and the marketing mix. When *modifying the market,* the company attempts to increase the consumption of the current product. When *modifying the product,* the company changes some of the product's characteristics—such as quality, features, or style—to attract new users or inspire more usage. When *modifying the marketing mix,* the company works to improve sales by changing one or more of the marketing-mix elements. Once the company recognizes that a product has entered the *decline stage,* management must decide whether to *maintain* the brand without change, hoping that competitors will drop out of the market; *harvest* the product, reducing costs and trying to maintain sales; or *drop* the product, selling it to another firm or liquidating it at salvage value.

OBJECTIVE 4 **Discuss two additional product issues: socially responsible product decisions and international product and services marketing.** (pp 280–282)

Marketers must consider two additional product issues. The first is *social responsibility*. This includes public policy issues and regulations involving acquiring or dropping products, patent protection, product quality and safety, and product warranties. The second involves the special challenges facing international product and service marketers. International marketers must decide how much to standardize or adapt their offerings for world markets.

KEY Terms

OBJECTIVE 1

New-product development (p 258)

OBJECTIVE 2

Idea generation (p 259)
Idea screening (p 262)
Product concept (p 262)
Concept testing (p 263)
Marketing strategy development (p 263)

Business analysis (p 264)
Product development (p 264)
Test marketing (p 265)
Commercialization (p 268)
Customer-centered new-product development (p 269)
Team-based new-product development (p 270)

OBJECTIVE 3

Product life cycle (p 273)
Style (p 274)
Fad (p 274)
Fashion (p 274)
Introduction stage (p 276)
Growth stage (p 276)
Maturity stage (p 277)
Decline stage (p 278)

DISCUSSING & APPLYING THE Concepts

Discussing the Concepts

1. Name and describe the major steps in the new-product development process. (AACSB: Communication)

2. Discuss the benefits and drawbacks of test marketing and explain why some companies do or do not use test marketing for new products. Name and describe the three approaches to test marketing. (AACSB: Communication)

3. Explain why successful new-product development requires a customer-centered, team-based, and systematic effort. (AACSB: Communication)

4. Name and describe the five stages of the product life cycle. Identify a product class, product form, or brand that is in each stage. (AACSB: Communication; Reflective Thinking)

5. Explain the differences among styles, fashions, and fads and give an example of each. (AACSB: Communication; Reflective Thinking)

6. Discuss the special challenges facing international product and service marketers. (AACSB: Communication)

Applying the Concepts

1. Think of a problem that really bugs you or a need you have that is not satisfied by current market offerings. In a small group, brainstorm ideas for a new product or service that solves this problem or satisfies this need. (AACSB: Communication; Reflective Thinking)

2. Coca-Cola has sustained success in the maturity stage of the product life cycle for many years. Visit Coca-Cola's Web site (www.thecoca-colacompany.com/heritage/ourheritage.html)

and discuss how Coca-Cola has evolved over the years. Identify ways that Coca-Cola can continue to evolve to meet changing consumer needs and wants. (AACSB: Communication; Use of IT; Reflective Thinking)

3. Write a marketing strategy statement for a new full-functioning but folding bicycle. (AACSB: Communication; Reflective Thinking)

FOCUS ON Technology

If you think the flash-memory chip found in digital cameras and music players is small, wait until you see what's coming next. Researchers at Hewlett-Packard have developed a new kind of electronic circuit that could revolutionize computer data storage, making it smaller and more energy-efficient than current memory chip technology. The part is call a memory resistor, or "memristor," and it allows storage of information on memory chips for long periods of time without electrical current. The theory behind the circuit is not new—it dates back to an electrical engineering professor from the University of California at Berkley in 1971. Most consumers don't realize that flash chips lose data after a year or so. But with the memrister, the atomic structure is actually changed, allowing for permanent storage of data. This isn't

the only revolutionary change on the horizon. In a joint venture called Numonyx, Intel Corporation and STMicroelectronics are betting on a new technology known as phase-change memory. One thing is for sure, big change is on the way for computers and handheld devices.

1. What stage of the product life cycle are these products currently in? (AACSB: Communication; Reflective Thinking)

2. Discuss the factors HP Hewlett-Packard and other tech companies should consider when conducting the business analysis for a product such as the "memristor." How will it add value for customers? (AACSB: Communication; Reflective Thinking)

FOCUS ON Ethics

Does your computer have a floppy disk drive or use the DOS operating system? Do you listen to music on a cassette deck? How about recording movies on a VCR tape? You probably answered no. In fact, you may not even be aware of these products. All are examples of obsolete products. But did marketers plan it that way? Many companies have been accused of using planned obsolescence as a strategy to make more money. However, new products often provide greater value for customers, especially in fast-changing industries such as computers and electronics. But what happens to the old products? This creates a growing concern over electronic waste, called *e-waste*. Although e-waste represents only 2 percent of the trash in our landfills, some analysts estimate that it accounts for 70 percent of overall toxic waste. The February 2009 digital programming mandate will generate a tidal wave of old TVs that will require disposal. Cathode ray tube (CRT) televisions contain several pounds of lead as well as other

toxic materials. Although recycling programs are increasing and are required by law in some states, the waste is often shipped for recycling or disposal to landfills in China, Kenya, India, and other developing countries, where concerns over worker and environmental welfare are more lax.

1. Who should be responsible for properly disposing of electronic products no longer needed—consumers or manufacturers? Is it appropriate to ship e-waste to developing countries? Discuss alternative solutions. (AACSB: Communication; Ethical Reasoning; Reflective Thinking)

2. Visit several electronics manufacturers' Web sites to learn if they offer electronic recycling programs. Are manufacturers doing enough? Write a brief report on what you learned. (AACSB: Communication; Ethical Reasoning; Reflective Thinking)

MARKETING BY THE Numbers

When introducing new products, some manufacturers set a high initial price and then reduce the price later. However, reducing price also reduces contribution margins, which in turn impacts profitability. To be profitable, the reduced price must sufficiently increase sales. For example, a company with a contribution margin of 30 percent on sales of $60,000,000 realizes a total contribution to fixed costs and profits of $18 million ($60 million × 0.30 = $18 million). If this company decreases price, the contribution margin will also decrease. So to maintain or increase profitability, the price reduction must increase sales considerably.

1. Refer to Appendix 2, Marketing by the Numbers, and calculate the new contribution margin for the company discussed here if it reduces price by 10 percent. Assume that unit variable costs are $70 and the original price was $100. (AACSB: Communication; Analytic Reasoning)

2. What level of total sales must a company capture at the new price to maintain the same level of total contribution as before the price reduction (that is, total contribution = $18 million)? (AACSB: Communication; Analytic Reasoning)

VIDEO Case

Electrolux

Since the 1920s, Swedish company Electrolux has been making and selling home appliances worldwide. Decade after decade, the company, originally known for its vacuum cleaners, has been turning out innovative products in a way that seems to magically predict what will work for consumers. The success of Electrolux's new-product development process results from more than just technological and design expertise. More importantly, it is rooted in what the company calls "consumer insight."

The concept of consumer insight is integrated into the Electrolux marketing strategy. It involves starting with the customer and working backward to design the product. Electrolux employs various methods to get deeply into the consumer's mind and to understand consumer needs. It then boils down that information to form concepts and, from concepts, it designs products. Because of its customer-centric approach, Electrolux refers to itself as the "thoughtful" design innovator and has for years stood behind the slogan "Thinking of you."

After viewing the video featuring Electrolux, answer the following questions about the company's new product development process:

1. What is consumer insight? What are some ways in which Electrolux develops consumer insight?

2. Describe how Electrolux might go about developing products if it were focused solely on engineering and technology. What might be the result of this product-development process?

3. With household appliances in mind, identify some consumer trends from the video, as well as any others that you can think of. Explain how new products could take advantage of each trend.

COMPANY Case

Nintendo: Reviving a Company, Transforming a Market

In the world of video games, Nintendo has been a household name for nearly three decades. After all, it was one of the pioneers of home video game consoles with the Nintendo Entertainment System in the early 1980s. It continued as the market leader with its Super Nintendo and Nintendo 64 systems. But in the mid-1990s, all that began to change. Along came Sony with its Playstation and Playstation 2, and Microsoft introduced the Xbox. Before long, Nintendo was reduced to a fraction of its former glory, running a distant third in a highly competitive market.

What happened? In certain respects, Nintendo fell prey to the industry model that it had created. More advanced technology led to the creation of more powerful gaming consoles, which in turn paved the road for more sophisticated games with more realistic graphics. As each new generation of product hit the market, Nintendo found that it could not keep up with more technologically advanced rivals. While more than 120 million Sony PS2s became fixtures in homes, apartments, and dorm rooms around the world, Nintendo moved just slightly more than 20 million GameCubes. As the most recent generation of gaming platforms from the gaming industry's "big three" came to market, many industry insiders figured Nintendo was destined to continue its downward path. Sony's PS3 and Microsoft's Xbox 360 were so advanced that it looked like Nintendo was due for another drubbing.

Oh what a difference a couple of years makes. For Nintendo, everything is now coming up Super Mario Bros. Last year, revenues and profits were up by 73 percent and 67 percent, respectively. In the last couple of years, during a time in which the Nikkei Stock Average fell nearly 25 percent, Nintendo's stock price tripled. In fact, Nintendo's stock price rose so high during 2007 that its market capitalization exceeded that of the Sony Corporation. On that measure alone, Nintendo became the second largest corporation in Japan, trailing only Toyota Motor Company. How did this struggling number three player go from product loser to product leader in such a short time?

FROM PRODUCT LOSER TO PRODUCT LEADER

Most people probably don't know that Nintendo was founded way back in 1889. Obviously, Nintendo did not make video games back then. It began as a playing cards manufacturer. But it also found success in hotels, packaged foods, and toys. When it came time to revive itself as a veteran in the video game industry, Nintendo did something that it had done time and time again. It focused on customers to find true opportunities.

For the video game industry, "the customer" typically means one of two groups: the 18- to 35-year-old hard-core gamers and the children/teenagers. The industry earns most of its revenue and profits from these core consumers who spend a great deal of time and money enhancing their virtual skills. Over the years, as hardware became more sophisticated and games more realistic, these tech junkies were all the more pleased.

In the process, Nintendo watched its revenues slide and its rivals strengthen. It realized that it could not compete against technologically superior products. So when it set out to develop the Wii console, it didn't even try. Instead, it focused on something the others were ignoring. It set its sights on the masses. "Nintendo took a step back from the technology arms race and chose to focus on the fun of playing rather than cold tech specs," said Reggie Fils-Aimé, president and COO of Nintendo of America. "We took a more intuitive approach and developed something that could be fun for every member of the family."

For the Wii, this meant that Nintendo had to do more with less. The Wii boasts a humble combination of low-powered processors and a standard optical disc drive. Compared to the powerful, state-of-the-art chips and high-definition lasers contained in the PS3 and Xbox 360, the Wii's graphics are outright scrawny.

But at the core of the Wii's broad appeal lies a revolutionary motion-sensing wireless technology that forces the once sedentary gamer to get up off the couch and get into the game. The Wii controller resembles a television remote. This feature was no accident as Wii designers correctly speculated that the familiarity of a TV remote would be more inviting than the more typical and complex video game controllers. The Wii's basic software also allows users to custom design avatars from a seemingly infinite combination of characteristics. With this configuration, users play tennis, go bowling, and hit the links by swinging the controller like a racket, ball, or golf club, all with characters resembling themselves.

The Wii met with immediate and drastic success. Entering the market *after* the release of the Xbox 360 and the PS3, Wii consoles flew off the shelves. Not only did the Wii contain an enticing combination of features, it also had a cost advantage. Microsoft and Sony had priced their offerings in the stratosphere. And even at $599 for the top and most popular PS3 model, Sony was still losing hundreds of dollars on each unit that it sold! Nintendo's low-tech approach allowed it to earn a hefty profit *and* be the low-price leader at only $250. With such a favorable benefit-to-cost ratio, the Wii easily won the launch phase, outselling each of the two competing consoles by nearly two-to-one in the first few months.

NOT JUST A FAD

Although the Wii was an instant smash hit, many analysts wondered whether or not its appeal would hold up. That speculation began to subside when retailers were still having trouble keeping the Wii in stock more than a year after it was introduced. In its first 18 months, Nintendo moved more than 24 million Wiis. Even though the Xbox 360 had been on the market a full year longer, it had sold only 19 million units. And Sony, once the undisputed industry champ, placed only 12 million PS3s.

Nintendo's willingness to reinvent what a video gaming system can mean continues to drive Wii sales. For example, the Wii can scan weather, news, and Web sites through a wireless Internet connection. Through the Wii Shop Channel, an iTunes-style store, customers can download classic Nintendo games as well as games from independent developers.

But in its pursuit to break gaming boundaries, Nintendo has also relentlessly pursued new applications for the basic motion-sensing technology. A plastic rifle contraption allows users to realistically play shooting gallery games. Snapping the Wii controller into a steering wheel has made driving games all the more electrifying. And tiny in-controller speakers add touches like the sound of an arrow being shot while the TV makes the "thwack" of that arrow hitting its target.

But perhaps one of the greatest strokes of creative genius in Nintendo's continuing stream of new applications is the Wii Fit, an add-on device targeted directly at women wanting to lose weight or keep in shape. The idea for the Wii Fit came to Takao Sawano, general manager of development for Nintendo, as he watched sumo wrestlers being weighed in for a television match. The tubby athletes were so heavy that they had to have each foot placed on a separate scale. The lightbulb went on as Sawano thought about the possibility of tracking a user's shifting weight on a game pad as he or she shimmied and twisted his or her way through virtual worlds.

That game pad is now called the Balance Board and lies at the heart (or rather the foot) of the Wii Fit's portfolio of exercise applications. Users can do aerobic, strength training, balancing, and yoga exercises all in realistic virtual settings. "It is now possible to go beyond the fingertip controls of past games and now use your whole body," Sawano told a crowd of game developers. The Wii Fit also facilitates exercise programs as it tracks and analyzes individual performance over time as well as keeping track of stats like weight and body-mass index.

Perhaps the most promising part of the Wii Fit is not that it continues to broaden an ever-growing market segment. In addition, the Balance Board component has the potential to be integrated into a nearly limitless number of applications. Already, Nintendo has developed ski jump and slalom games. It's only a matter of time before Nintendo develops a Balance Board version for just about every sport imaginable.

Releasing hit after hit, Nintendo has vaulted to the top of *The Wall Street Journal*'s latest Asia 200 survey. Placing first in the "Innovative in Responding to Customer Needs" category, the company placed second overall, trailing only Toyota. For a company that hadn't placed in the top 10 since 2002, the sudden turnaround is a telling demonstration of consumer confidence.

SECURING THE FUTURE

Although the success of the Wii has largely been attributed to attracting non-traditional gamers, hard-core gamers have hardly been absent. In fact, many of the industry faithful saw the Wii as a relatively cheap second gaming platform—as a nice diversion from more graphic-intensive games. The Wii also has the nostalgic advantage of appealing to the gaming elite with characters they grew up with, such as those from the Mario and Zelda franchises.

But developers and executives at Nintendo are not content to sit back and risk having hard-core gamers lose interest. Part of Nintendo's future strategy includes games focused on more serious gamers. CEO Satoru Iwata shocked the industry last year when he announced that Nintendo would soon add games from two Sony allies: Capcom's *Monster Hunter* series and Square Enix's *Final Fantasy Crystal Chronicles*. The release of these titles will do more than appeal to traditional gamers. It will elevate the Wii's image from that of a machine with little firepower to one that will run the industry's most advanced games. Said one game industry analyst at a tradeshow sneak preview, "It's symbolic. I didn't think the Wii could handle this type of game. Everyone in the room today saw that it can."

As Nintendo has successfully attracted an untapped audience of gamers over the past few years, it has done more than revive its business. It has transformed a market. The competitors that once trounced Nintendo now find that they must play catch-up. Both Sony and Microsoft are now developing easier-to-play games that depart from their usual fast-action fare. Game publishers, including powerhouses such as Electronic Arts Inc., have started putting more resources into developing games for the Wii. And even small, independent shops are getting into the action as Nintendo's download channel reduces barriers to entry. All this is causing an already huge $30 billion industry to swell.

Simon Jeffery, president and COO of Sega of America, summarizes why Nintendo has been successful and why the rest of the industry must keep up.

The fundamental interface in games has always been a controller, and Nintendo is bringing opportunities to developers to think about how interactions use motion. That has opened doors of creativity throughout the video game business. Nintendo's success is about creative leadership and the willingness to do things differently.

As long as Nintendo can stay focused on these elements that have returned it to its throne, it will reign for a long time to come.

Questions for Discussion

1. Was Nintendo just lucky, or does the Wii's success have strategic merit?

2. Has Nintendo put the "fad" question to rest? State a case as to why the Wii is or is not here to stay.

3. In which stage of the product life cycle is the Wii? Based on that stage, is Nintendo employing good marketing mix strategies?

4. Develop a strategy for the Wii's next product life cycle phase.

5. Discuss the potential threats to Nintendo's future success. What will help Nintendo avoid a premature decline for the Wii?

Sources: Robert Levine, "Fast 50 2008: Nintendo," *Fast Company*, February 19, 2008, accessed online at www.fastcompany.com; Yukari Iwatani Kane, "Nintendo Captures Top Spot in Japan for Innovation," *Wall Street Journal*, June 27, 2008, accessed online at www.wsj.com; Yukari Iwatani Kane, "Nintendo Is Ahead of the Game, But Sustaining May Be Hard," *Wall Street Journal*, April 15, 2008, p. C3; Yukari Iwatani Kane, "Wii Sales Help Nintendo Net Rise 48 Percent," *Wall Street Journal*, April 25, 2008, p. B8; Kenji Hall, "Nintendo: Calling All Players," *BusinessWeek*, October 10, 2007, accessed online at www.businessweek.com; Brian Caulfield, "Nintendo's Sumo-Inspired Hit," *Forbes*, February 21, 2008, accessed online at www.forbes.com.

Chapter 10

Part 1   Defining Marketing and the Marketing Process (Chapters 1, 2)
Part 2   Understanding the Marketplace and Consumers (Chapters 3, 4, 5, 6)
Part 3   Designing a Customer-Driven Strategy and Mix (Chapters 7, 8, 9, 10, 11, 12, 13, 14, 15, 16, 17)
Part 4   Extending Marketing (Chapters 18, 19, 20)

Pricing Understanding
and **Capturing Customer Value**

Chapter
PREVIEW

Next, we look at a second major marketing mix tool—pricing. If effective product development, promotion, and distribution sow the seeds of business success, effective pricing is the harvest. Firms successful at creating customer value with the other marketing mix activities must still capture some of this value in the prices they earn. Yet, despite its importance, many firms do not handle pricing well. In this chapter, we'll look at internal and external considerations that affect pricing

decisions and examine general pricing approaches. In the next chapter, we dig into pricing strategies.

For openers, let's look at Trader Joe's, whose unique price and value strategy has made it one of the nation's fastest-growing, most popular food stores. Trader Joe's understands that success comes not just from what products you offer customers, or from the prices you charge. It comes from offering the combination of products and prices that produces the greatest customer *value*—what customers get for the prices they pay.

As they prepared to open the new Trader Joe's store in Chapel Hill, North Carolina, manager Greg Fort (the "captain") and his Hawaiian-shirt-clad employees (the "crew") scurried about, stocking shelves, hanging plastic lobsters, and posting hand-painted signs in preparation for the expected tidal wave of 5,000 customers who would descend on the store on opening day. A veteran of two other store openings, Fort knew that customers would soon be lined up 10 deep at checkouts with carts full of Trader Joe's exclusive $2.99 Charles Shaw wine—a.k.a. "Two-Buck Chuck"—and an assortment of other exclusive gourmet products at impossibly low prices. Fort also knew that he would have to spend time explaining Trader Joe's prices to new customers. "These are our everyday prices, not grand-opening specials," he'd tell them. "There's no need to buy a year's worth in one visit!"

Trader Joe's isn't really a gourmet food store. Then again, it's not a discount food store either. It's actually a bit of both. One of America's hottest retailers, Trader Joe's has put its own special twist on the food price-value equation—call it "cheap gourmet." It offers gourmet-caliber, one-of-a-kind products at bargain prices, all served up in a festive, vacation-like atmosphere that makes shopping fun. "When you look at food retailers, there is the low end, the big middle, and then there is the cool edge—that's Trader Joe's," says one food marketing expert. Whatever you call it, Trader Joe's inventive price-value positioning has earned it an almost cult-like following of devoted customers who love what they get from Trader Joe's for the prices they pay.

Trader Joe's describes itself as an "island paradise" where "value, adventure, and tasty treasures are discovered, every day." Shoppers bustle and buzz amid cedar-plank-lined walls and fake

palm trees as a ship's bell rings out occasionally at checkout alerting them to special announcements. Unfailingly helpful and cheery associates in Aloha shirts chat with customers about everything from the weather to menu suggestions for dinner parties. Customers don't just shop at Trader Joe's, they experience it.

Shelves bristle with an eclectic assortment of gourmet-quality grocery items. Trader Joe's stocks only a limited assortment of about 2,000 specialty products (compared with the 45,000 items found in an average Safeway). However, the assortment is uniquely Trader Joe's, including special concoctions of gourmet packaged foods and sauces, ready-to-eat soups, fresh and frozen entrees, snacks, and desserts, all free of artificial colors, flavors, and preservatives. Trader Joe's is a gourmet foodie's delight, featuring everything from wasabi peas, organic strawberry lemonade, organic mango fruit spread, dark-chocolate-dipped orange candy, and fair trade coffees to chile lime chicken burgers and triple-ginger ginger snaps. "Where else can you find Soy & Flax Cereal clusters, Ginger Cats Cookies, and Jalapeño Blue Cornbread Mix?" asks one shopper.

Another thing that makes Trader Joe's products so special is

> Trader Joe's has put its own special twist on the food price-value equation—call it "cheap gourmet."

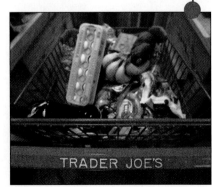

that you simply can't get them anywhere else. More than 80 percent of the store's brands are private label goods, sold exclusively by Trader Joe's. If asked, almost any customer can tick off a ready list of Trader Joe's favorites that they just can't live without, a list that quickly grows. "People get hooked on something and they keep coming back for it. That's how it starts," says a Trader Joe's store captain. "They end up filling up their baskets, then entire carts. That's the most common complaint that we hear. They came in for one or two things, and ended up with a whole cart full of stuff."

A special store atmosphere, exclusive gourmet products, helpful and attentive associates—this all sounds like a recipe for high prices. Not so at Trader Joe's. Whereas upscale competitors such as Whole Foods Market charge upscale prices to match their wares ("Whole Foods, whole paycheck"), Trader Joe's amazes customers with its relatively frugal prices. The prices aren't all that low in absolute terms, but they're a real bargain compared with what you'd pay for the same quality and coolness elsewhere.

How does Trader Joe's keep its gourmet prices so low? It all starts with lean operations and a near-fanatical focus on saving money. To keep costs down, Trader Joe's typically locates its stores in low-rent, out-of-the-way locations, such as suburban strip malls. Its small store size and limited product assortment results in reduced facilities and inventory costs. Trader Joe's stores save money by eliminating large produce sections and expensive on-site bakery, butcher, deli, and seafood shops. And for its private label brands, Trader Joe's buys directly from suppliers and negotiates hard on price. "We buy in huge quantities straight from our distributors, which cuts out the middle man and lets us offer the lowest possible prices," says the store manager.

Finally, the frugal retailer saves money by spending almost nothing on advertising. Trader Joe's unique combination of quirky products and low prices produces so much word-of-mouth promotion that the company doesn't really need to advertise. The closest thing to an official promotion is the company's Web site or a newsletter mailed out to people who opt in to receive it. Trader Joe's most potent promotional weapon is its army of faithful followers. Trader Joe's customers have even started their own fan Web site, www.traderjoesfan.com,

where they discuss new products and stores, trade recipes, and swap their favorite Trader Joe's stories.

Trader Joe's unique price-value strategy has earned it an almost cult-like following of devoted customers who love what they get for the prices they pay.

Thus, finding the right price-value formula has made Trader Joe's one of the nation's fastest-growing and most popular food stores. Its 310 stores in 25 states now reap annual sales of more than $6.5 billion, up almost 45 percent in just the previous two years. Trader Joe's stores pull in an amazing $1,440 per square foot, more than twice the supermarket industry average. *Consumer Reports* recently ranked the company as the second-best supermarket chain in the nation, behind only Wegmans.

It's all about value and price—what you get for what you pay. Just ask Trader Joe's regular Chrissi Wright, found early one Friday morning browsing her local Trader Joe's in Bend, Oregon.

Chrissi expects she'll leave Trader Joe's with eight bottles of the popular Charles Shaw wine priced at $2.99 each tucked under her arms. "I love Trader Joe's because they let me eat like a yuppie without taking all my money," says Wright. "Their products are gourmet, often environmentally conscientious and beautiful ... and, of course, there's Two-Buck Chuck—possibly the greatest innovation of our time."[1]

> Trader Joe's understands that success comes not just from what products you offer customers or from the prices you charge. It comes from offering the combination of products and prices that produces the greatest customer value.

Companies today face a fierce and fast-changing pricing environment. Value-seeking customers have put increased pricing pressure on many companies. "Thank the Wal-Mart phenomenon," says one analyst. "These days, we're all cheapskates in search of a spend-less strategy." In response, it seems that almost every company is looking for ways to slash prices.[2]

Yet, cutting prices is often not the best answer. Reducing prices unnecessarily can lead to lost profits and damaging price wars. It can signal to customers that the price is more important than the customer value a brand delivers. Instead, companies should sell value, not price.

Objective Outline

They should persuade customers that paying a higher price for the company's brand is justified by the greater value they gain. The challenge is to find the price that will let the company make a fair profit by getting paid for the customer value it creates. ▲ "Give people something of value," says Ronald Shaich, CEO of Panera Bread Company, "and they'll happily pay for it."[3]

What Is a Price? (pp 290–291)

Price

The amount of money charged for a product or service, or the sum of the values that customers exchange for the benefits of having or using the product or service.

In the narrowest sense, **price** is the amount of money charged for a product or service. More broadly, price is the sum of all the values that customers give up in order to gain the benefits of having or using a product or service. Historically, price has been the major factor affecting buyer choice. In recent decades, nonprice factors have gained increasing importance. However, price still remains one of the most important elements determining a firm's market share and profitability.

Price is the only element in the marketing mix that produces revenue; all other elements represent costs. Price is also one of the most flexible marketing mix elements. Unlike product features and channel commitments, prices can be changed quickly. At the same time, pricing is the number-one problem facing many marketing executives, and many companies do not handle pricing well. One frequent problem is that companies are too quick to reduce prices in order to get a sale rather than convincing buyers that their product's greater value is worth a higher price. Other common mistakes include pricing that is too cost oriented rather than customer-value oriented, and pricing that does not take the rest of the marketing mix into account.

Some managers view pricing as a big headache, preferring instead to focus on the other marketing mix elements. However, smart managers treat pricing as a key strategic tool for creating and capturing customer value. Prices have a direct impact on a firm's bottom line. A small percentage improvement in price can generate a large percentage in profitability. More importantly, as

▲ Pricing: The challenge is to harvest the customer value the company creates. Says Panera's CEO, Ronald Shaich, pictured here, "Give people something of value, and they'll happily pay for it."

a part of a company's overall value proposition, price plays a key role in creating customer value and building customer relationships. "Instead of running away from pricing," says the expert, "savvy marketers are embracing it."[4]

Author Comment | Setting the right price is one of the marketer's most difficult tasks. A host of factors come into play. But finding and implementing the right pricing strategy is critical to success.

Factors to Consider When Setting Prices (pp 291–305)

The price the company charges will fall somewhere between one that is too high to produce any demand and one that is too low to produce a profit. Figure 10.1 summarizes the major considerations in setting price. Customer perceptions of the product's value set the ceiling for prices. If customers perceive that the price is greater than the product's value, they will not buy the product. Product costs set the floor for prices. If the company prices the product below its costs, company profits will suffer. In setting its price between these two extremes, the company must consider a number of other internal and external factors, including its overall marketing strategy and mix, the nature of the market and demand, and competitors' strategies and prices.

Customer Perceptions of Value

In the end, the customer will decide whether a product's price is right. Pricing decisions, like other marketing mix decisions, must start with customer value. When customers buy a product, they exchange something of value (the price) in order to get something of value (the benefits of having or using the product). Effective, customer-oriented pricing involves understanding how much value consumers place on the benefits they receive from the product and setting a price that captures this value.

Value-Based Pricing

Value-based pricing

Setting price based on buyers' perceptions of value rather than on the seller's cost.

Good pricing begins with a complete understanding of the value that a product or service creates for customers. **Value-based pricing** uses buyers' perceptions of value, not the seller's cost, as the key to pricing. Value-based pricing means that the marketer cannot design a product and marketing program and then set the price. Price is considered along with the other marketing mix variables *before* the marketing program is set.

Figure 10.2 compares value-based pricing with cost-based pricing. Cost-based pricing is product driven. The company designs what it considers to be a good product, adds up the costs of making the product, and sets a price that covers costs plus a target profit. Marketing must then convince buyers that the product's value at that price justifies its purchase. If the price turns out to be too high, the company must settle for lower markups or lower sales, both resulting in disappointing profits.

Value-based pricing reverses this process. The company first assesses customer needs and value perceptions. It then sets its target price based on customer perceptions of value. The targeted value and price then drive decisions about what costs can be incurred and the resulting product design. As a result, pricing begins with analyzing consumer needs and value perceptions, and price is set to match consumers' perceived value.

FIGURE | 10.1
Considerations in Setting Price

If customers perceive that a product's price is greater than its value, they won't buy it. If the company prices a product below its costs, profits will suffer. Between the two extremes, the "right" pricing strategy is one that delivers both value to the customer and profits to the company.

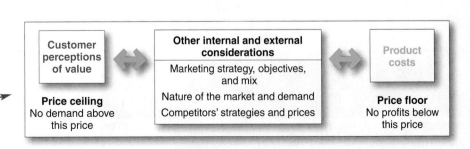

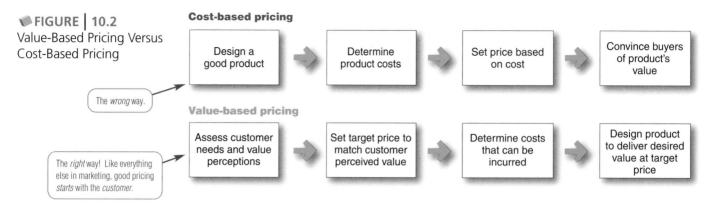

FIGURE | 10.2

Value-Based Pricing Versus
Cost-Based Pricing

Cost-based pricing

| Design a good product | → | Determine product costs | → | Set price based on cost | → | Convince buyers of product's value |

The wrong way.

Value-based pricing

| Assess customer needs and value perceptions | → | Set target price to match customer perceived value | → | Determine costs that can be incurred | → | Design product to deliver desired value at target price |

The right way! Like everything else in marketing, good pricing starts with the customer.

It's important to remember that "good value" is not the same as "low price." ▲For example, some car buyers consider the luxurious Bentley Continental GT automobile a real value, even at an eye-popping price of $175,000:[5]

Stay with me here, because I'm about to [tell you why] a certain automobile costing $175,000 is not actually expensive, but is in fact a tremendous value. Every Bentley GT is built by hand, an Old World bit of automaking requiring 160 hours per vehicle. Craftsmen spend 18 hours simply stitching the perfectly joined leather of the GT's steering wheel, almost as long as it takes to assemble an entire VW Golf. The results are impressive: Dash and doors are mirrored with walnut veneer, floor pedals are carved from aluminum, window and seat toggles are cut from actual metal rather than plastic, and every air vent is perfectly chromed. . . . The sum of all this is a fitted cabin that approximates that of a $300,000 vehicle, matched to an engine the equal of a $200,000 automobile, within a car that has brilliantly incorporated . . . technological sophistication. As I said, the GT is a bargain. [Just ask anyone on the lengthy waiting list.] The waiting time to bring home your very own GT is currently half a year.

A company using value-based pricing must find out what value buyers assign to different competitive offers. However, companies often find it hard to measure the value customers will attach to its product. For example, calculating the cost of ingredients in a meal at a fancy restaurant is relatively easy. But assigning a value to other satisfactions such as taste, environment, relaxation, conversation, and status is very hard. And these values will vary both for different consumers and different situations.

Still, consumers will use these perceived values to evaluate a product's price, so the company must work to measure them. Sometimes, companies ask consumers how much they would pay for a basic product and for each benefit added to the offer. Or a company might conduct experiments to test the perceived value of different product offers. According to an old Russian proverb, there are two fools in every market—one who asks too much and one who asks too little. If the seller charges more than the buyers' perceived value, the company's sales will suffer. If the seller charges less, its products sell very well. But they produce less revenue than they would if they were priced at the level of perceived value.

CONTINENTAL GTC.
WHAT IS BUILT BY HAND CAN TOUCH THE HEART.

Be moved by hand-craftsmanship at its finest. Book your test drive today.

BENTLEY

www.bentleymotors.com

▲ Value-based pricing: "Good value" is not the same as "low price." Some car buyers consider the luxurious Bentley Continental GT automobile a real value, even at an eye-popping price of $175,000.

We now examine two types of value-based pricing: *good-value pricing* and *value-added pricing*.

Good-value pricing

Offering just the right combination of quality and good service at a fair price.

Good-Value Pricing. During the past decade, marketers have noted a fundamental shift in consumer attitudes toward price and quality. Many companies have changed their pricing approaches to bring them into line with changing economic conditions and consumer price perceptions. More and more, marketers have adopted **good-value pricing** strategies—offering just the right combination of quality and good service at a fair price.

In many cases, this has involved introducing less-expensive versions of established, brand-name products. To meet the tougher economic times and more frugal consumer spending habits, fast-food restaurants such as Taco Bell and McDonald's offer "value menus." Armani offers the less-expensive, more-casual Armani Exchange fashion line. Alberto-Culver's TRESemmé hair care line promises "Curls you'll love. A price you'll adore." And Volkswagen recently reintroduced the Rabbit, an economical car with a base price under $16,000, because "The people want an entry-level price and top-level features."[6]

In other cases, good-value pricing has involved redesigning existing brands to offer more quality for a given price or the same quality for less. Some companies even succeed by offering less value but at rock-bottom prices. For example, passengers flying low-cost European airline Ryanair won't get much in the way of free amenities, but they'll like the airline's unbelievably low prices (see **Real Marketing 10.1**).

An important type of good-value pricing at the retail level is *everyday low pricing (EDLP)*. EDLP involves charging a constant, everyday low price with few or no temporary price discounts. In contrast, *high-low pricing* involves charging higher prices on an everyday basis but running frequent promotions to lower prices temporarily on selected items. In recent years, high-low pricing has given way to EDLP in retail settings ranging from Saturn car dealerships to Costco warehouse clubs to furniture stores such as Room & Board. The king of EDLP is Wal-Mart, which practically defined the concept. Except for a few sale items every month, Wal-Mart promises everyday low prices on everything it sells.

Value-added pricing

Attaching value-added features and services to differentiate a company's offers and charging higher prices.

Value-Added Pricing. Value-based pricing doesn't mean simply charging what customers want to pay or setting low prices to meet the competition. In many marketing situations, the challenge is to build the company's *pricing power*—its power to escape price competition and to justify higher prices and margin. To increase pricing power, a firm must retain or build the value of its market offering. This is especially true for suppliers of commodity products, which are characterized by little differentiation and intense price competition.

To increase their pricing power, many companies adopt **value-added pricing** strategies. Rather than cutting prices to match competitors, they attach value-added features and services to differentiate their offers and thus support higher prices. ▲Consider this example:

▲ Value-added pricing: Rather than dropping prices for its venerable Stag umbrella brand to match cheaper imports, Currims successfully launched umbrellas with funky designs, cool colors, and value-added features and sold them at even higher prices.

The monsoon season in Mumbai, India, is three months of near-nonstop rain. For 147 years, most Mumbaikars protected themselves with a Stag umbrella from venerable Ebrahim Currim & Sons. Like Ford's Model T, the basic Stag was sturdy, affordable, and of any color, as long as it was black. By the end of the twentieth century, however, the Stag was threatened by cheaper imports from China. Stag responded by dropping prices and scrimping on quality. It was a bad move: For the first time since the 1940s, the brand began losing money. Finally, however, the company came to its senses. It abandoned the price war and vowed to improve quality. Surprisingly, even at higher prices, sales of the improved Stag umbrellas actually increased.

Real Marketing 10.1

Ryanair:
Pricing Low and Proud of It

The major airlines are facing very difficult pricing strategy decisions in these tough air-travel times. Pricing strategies vary widely. Some airlines offer no-frills flights and charge rock-bottom prices (Southwest, JetBlue, Frontier, Skybus). Others offer luxury and charge higher prices to match (Virgin, Silverjet, Eos, Singapore Airlines). But most airlines haven't yet figured pricing out, leaving air-travel passengers generally grumpy when it comes to the topic of airline ticket prices.

One airline, however, appears to have found a radical new pricing solution, one that customers are sure to love: Make flying *free!* According to a *Business 2.0* magazine analyst:

That's right, Michael O'Leary, chief executive of Ireland's Ryanair, Europe's most profitable airline, wants to make air travel free. Not free as in free from regulation, but free as in zero cost. By the end of the decade, he promises, "more than half of our passengers will fly free." The remarkable thing is, few analysts think his prediction is far-fetched: Ryanair already offers free fares to a quarter of its customers.

Even without free flights, Ryanair has become one of Europe's most popular carriers. Last year it flew 42.5 million passengers to more than 100 European destinations. The airline's sales of more than $3.6 billion were up 32 percent over the previous year, and profits surged 33 percent. And although its average fare is just $87 compared with U.S. low-cost leader Southwest's $107, Ryanair's net margins are 21 percent, triple Southwest's 7 percent. Given the prospects of rising fuel costs, economic dips, and other troubled times ahead for the airline industry, Ryanair seems well positioned to weather the storm.

What's the secret? Ryanair's frugal cost structure makes even cost-conscious Southwest look like a reckless spender. In addition, the Irish airline charges for virtually everything except tickets, from baggage check-in to seat-back advertising space. "[Ryanair] thinks like a retailer and charges for absolutely every little thing, except the seat itself," says another analyst. "Imagine the seat as akin to a cell phone: It comes free, or nearly free, but its

Good-value pricing: Ryanair appears to have found a radical new pricing solution, one that customers are sure to love: Make flying free!

owner winds up spending on all sorts of services."

Ryanair's low-cost strategy is modeled after Southwest's. In 1991, when Ryanair was just another struggling European carrier, CEO O'Leary went to Dallas to meet with Southwest executives and see what he could learn. The result was a wholesale revamping of the Irish carrier's business model. Following Southwest's lead, to economize, Ryanair began employing

Then the company started innovating. Noting the new fashion consciousness of Indian men, it launched designer umbrellas in funky designs and cool colors. Teenagers and young adults lapped them up. Stag then launched umbrellas with a built-in high-power flashlight for those who walk unlit roads at night, and models with prerecorded tunes for music lovers. For women who walk secluded streets after dark, there's Stag's Bodyguard model, armed with glare lights, emergency blinkers, and an alarm. Customers willingly pay up to a 100 percent premium for the new products. Under the new value-added strategy, the Stag brand has now returned to profitability. Come the monsoon in June, the grand old black Stags still reappear on the streets of Mumbai—but now priced 15 percent higher than the imports.[7]

The Stag example illustrates once again that customers are motivated not by price, but by what they get for what they paid. "If consumers thought the best deal was simply a question of money saved, we'd all be shopping in one big discount store," says one pricing expert. "Customers want value and are willing to pay for it. Savvy marketers price their products accordingly."[8]

only a single type of aircraft—the good old Boeing 737. Also like Southwest, it began focusing on smaller, secondary airports and offering unassigned passenger seating.

But Ryanair has since taken Southwest's low-cost pricing model even further. When it comes to keeping costs down, O'Leary is an absolute fanatic. "We want to be known as the Wal-Mart of flying," he says. Like the giant retailer, Ryanair is constantly on the lookout for new ways to cut costs—for example, by removing seat-back pockets to reduce weight and cleaning expense. Passengers reap the benefits of such savings in the form of lower fares. Ryanair also sells more than 98 percent of its tickets online, cutting down on administration costs and travel agent commissions. Flight crews even buy their own uniforms and headquarters staff supply their own pens.

The penny-pinching airline also charges passengers for virtually every optional amenity they consume. There's no such thing as a free beverage or bag of pretzels on Ryanair; the airline was first to begin charging passengers for in-flight refreshments, a move that generates tens of millions of dollars in revenues each year. It was also first to charge a bag-checking fee, which it offset by cutting ticket prices an equivalent amount. That move resulted in tens of millions of dollars of savings by reducing fuel and handling costs. The airline is just as aggressive in its efforts to develop new sources of revenue.

Ryanair has turned its planes into giant billboards, displaying ads for such companies as Vodafone Group, Jaguar, and Hertz. Soon, ads will also stare each passenger in the eye when his or her seat back trays are up. Once in the air, flight attendants hawk everything from scratch-card games to perfume and digital cameras to their captive audience. Upon arrival at some out-of-the-way airport, Ryanair will sell you a bus or train ticket into town. Ryanair uses its Web site, with 15 million unique visitors each month, to boost related revenues. The company gets commissions from sales of Hertz rental cars, hotel rooms, ski packages, and travel insurance. Last year, such ancillary revenues rose 36 percent, to $332 million. "Every chance they get, Ryanair tries to squeeze just that little bit of extra margin out of its passengers," says an industry consultant.

About Ryanair's outrageously low prices, customers aren't complaining, especially because the additional purchases are discretionary. Moreover, many are entertaining or make life a little easier:

For passengers seeking extra distractions, Ryanair even intends to offer in-flight gambling in the near future, with the airline earning a tiny cut off of each wager. O'Leary thinks gambling could double Ryanair's profits over the next decade, but he's not stopping there. He also envisions a day when the airline can charge passengers for the ability to use their cell phones at 35,000 feet. And he's expressed interest in partnering with operators of airport parking lots and concession stands to capture a bigger slice of the cash that passengers spend on the ground getting to and from his planes.

The *Business 2.0* analyst concludes: "Add it all up—relentless cost cutting on the operations side, combined with innovative efforts to extract more revenue from each traveler—and O'Leary's plan to give away half of Ryanair's seats by 2010 starts to look quite sane. Sure, taking to the skies on Ryanair may feel more like riding in a subway car than an airplane, but you can't beat the prices. And financially strapped U.S. carriers should take note: Flying people from here to there for free could truly be liberating." For Ryanair, not even the sky's the limit.

Sources: Quotes and excerpts from or adapted from Matthew Maier, "A Radical Fix for Airlines: Make Flying Free," *Business 2.0,* April 2006, pp. 32–34; and Kerry Capell, "Wal-Mart with Wings," *BusinessWeek,* November 27, 2006, pp. 44–46. Also see "Ryanair Offers Gambling Web Site," *Associated Press,* November 1, 2006; Will Sullivan, "Flying on the Cheap," *U.S. News & World Report,* March 26, 2007, p. 47; "Ryanair Offers Ad Space in Planes," *Marketing,* February 28, 2007; Mark Tatge, "Nightmare at 30,000 Feet," *Forbes,* June 4, 2007, p. 56; Kevin Done, "Ryanair Warns of Perfect Storm Damage," *Financial Times,* February 5, 2008, p. 17; Kerry Capell, "Fasten Your Seatbelt, Ryanair," *BusinessWeek,* February 18, 2008, p. 16; and www.southwest.com and www.ryanair.com, accessed November 2008.

> **Author Comment** | Costs set the floor for price but the goal isn't always to *minimize* costs. In fact, many firms invest in higher costs so that they can claim higher prices and margins (think about Bentley automobiles). The key is to manage the *spread* between costs and prices—how much the company makes for the customer value it delivers.

Cost-based pricing

Setting prices based on the costs for producing, distributing, and selling the product plus a fair rate of return for effort and risk.

Fixed costs (overhead)

Costs that do not vary with production or sales level.

Company and Product Costs

Whereas customer-value perceptions set the price ceiling, costs set the floor for the price that the company can charge. **Cost-based pricing** involves setting prices based on the costs for producing, distributing, and selling the product plus a fair rate of return for its effort and risk. A company's costs may be an important element in its pricing strategy.

Some companies, such as Southwest Airlines, Wal-Mart, and Dell, work to become the "low-cost producers" in their industries. Companies with lower costs can set lower prices that result in smaller margins but greater sales and profits. Other companies, however, intentionally pay higher costs so that they can claim higher prices and margins. For example, it costs more to make a "built by hand" Bentley than a Toyota Camry. But the higher costs result in higher quality, justifying that eye-popping $175,000 price. The key is to manage the spread between costs and prices—how much the company makes for the customer value it delivers.

Types of Costs

A company's costs take two forms, fixed and variable. **Fixed costs** (also known as **overhead**) are costs that do not vary with production or sales level. For example, a company must pay each month's bills for rent, heat, interest, and executive salaries, whatever the

Variable costs
Costs that vary directly with the level of production.

Total costs
The sum of the fixed and variable costs for any given level of production.

company's output. **Variable costs** vary directly with the level of production. Each PC produced by Hewlett-Packard involves a cost of computer chips, wires, plastic, packaging, and other inputs. These costs tend to be the same for each unit produced. They are called variable because their total varies with the number of units produced. **Total costs** are the sum of the fixed and variable costs for any given level of production. Management wants to charge a price that will at least cover the total production costs at a given level of production.

The company must watch its costs carefully. If it costs the company more than competitors to produce and sell its product, the company will need to charge a higher price or make less profit, putting it at a competitive disadvantage.

Costs at Different Levels of Production

To price wisely, management needs to know how its costs vary with different levels of production. For example, suppose Texas Instruments (TI) has built a plant to produce 1,000 calculators per day. **Figure 10.3A** shows the typical short-run average cost curve (SRAC). It shows that the cost per calculator is high if TI's factory produces only a few per day. But as production moves up to 1,000 calculators per day, average cost falls. This is because fixed costs are spread over more units, with each one bearing a smaller share of the fixed cost. TI can try to produce more than 1,000 calculators per day, but average costs will increase because the plant becomes inefficient. Workers have to wait for machines, the machines break down more often, and workers get in each other's way.

If TI believed it could sell 2,000 calculators a day, it should consider building a larger plant. The plant would use more efficient machinery and work arrangements. Also, the unit cost of producing 2,000 calculators per day would be lower than the unit cost of producing 1,000 units per day, as shown in the long-run average cost (LRAC) curve (Figure 10.3B). In fact, a 3,000-capacity plant would even be more efficient, according to Figure 10.3B. But a 4,000-daily production plant would be less efficient because of increasing diseconomies of scale—too many workers to manage, paperwork slowing things down, and so on. Figure 10.3B shows that a 3,000-daily production plant is the best size to build if demand is strong enough to support this level of production.

Costs as a Function of Production Experience

Suppose TI runs a plant that produces 3,000 calculators per day. As TI gains experience in producing calculators, it learns how to do it better. Workers learn shortcuts and become more familiar with their equipment. With practice, the work becomes better organized, and TI finds better equipment and production processes. With higher volume, TI becomes more efficient and gains economies of scale. As a result, average cost tends to fall with accumulated production experience. This is shown in **Figure 10.4.**[9] Thus, the average cost of producing the first 100,000 calculators is $10 per calculator. When the company has produced the first 200,000 calculators, the average cost has fallen to $9. After its accumulated production experience doubles again to 400,000, the average cost is $7. This drop in the average cost with accumulated production experience is called the **experience curve** (or the **learning curve**).

Experience curve (learning curve)
The drop in the average per-unit production cost that comes with accumulated production experience.

FIGURE | 10.3
Cost Per Unit at Different Levels of Production Per Period

> What's the point of all the cost curves in this and the next few figures? Costs are an important factor in setting price, and companies must understand them well!

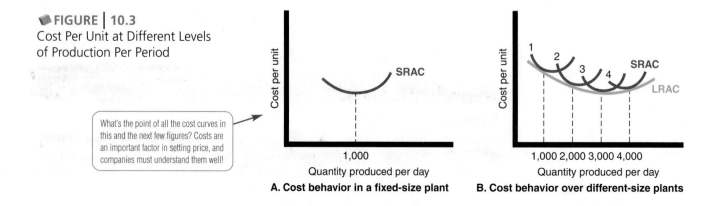

A. Cost behavior in a fixed-size plant

B. Cost behavior over different-size plants

FIGURE | 10.4
Cost Per Unit as a Function of Accumulated Production: The Experience Curve

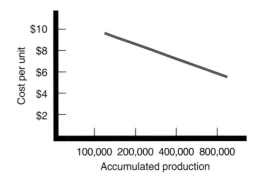

If a downward-sloping experience curve exists, this is highly significant for the company. Not only will the company's unit production cost fall, but it will fall faster if the company makes and sells more during a given time period. But the market has to stand ready to buy the higher output. And to take advantage of the experience curve, TI must get a large market share early in the product's life cycle. This suggests the following pricing strategy: TI should price its calculators low; its sales will then increase, and its costs will decrease through gaining more experience, and then it can lower its prices further.

Some companies have built successful strategies around the experience curve. For example, Bausch & Lomb solidified its position in the soft contact lens market by using computerized lens design and steadily expanding its one SofLens plant. As a result, its market share climbed steadily to 65 percent.

However, a single-minded focus on reducing costs and exploiting the experience curve will not always work. Experience-curve pricing carries some major risks. The aggressive pricing might give the product a cheap image. The strategy also assumes that competitors are weak and not willing to fight it out by meeting the company's price cuts. Finally, while the company is building volume under one technology, a competitor may find a lower-cost technology that lets it start at prices lower than those of the market leader, who still operates on the old experience curve.

Cost-Plus Pricing

Cost-plus pricing
Adding a standard markup to the cost of the product.

The simplest pricing method is **cost-plus pricing**—adding a standard markup to the cost of the product. Construction companies, for example, submit job bids by estimating the total project cost and adding a standard markup for profit. Lawyers, accountants, and other professionals typically price by adding a standard markup to their costs. Some sellers tell their customers they will charge cost plus a specified markup; for example, aerospace companies price this way to the government.

To illustrate markup pricing, suppose a toaster manufacturer had the following costs and expected sales:

Variable cost	$10
Fixed costs	$300,000
Expected unit sales	50,000

Then the manufacturer's cost per toaster is given by the following:

$$\text{Unit Cost} = \text{Variable Cost} + \frac{\text{Fixed Costs}}{\text{Unit Sales}} = \$10 + \frac{\$300,000}{50,000} = \$16$$

Now suppose the manufacturer wants to earn a 20 percent markup on sales. The manufacturer's markup price is given by the following:[10]

$$\text{Markup Price} = \frac{\text{Unit Cost}}{(1 - \text{Desired Return on Sales})} = \frac{\$16}{1 - .2} = \$20$$

The manufacturer would charge dealers $20 per toaster and make a profit of $4 per unit. The dealers, in turn, will mark up the toaster. If dealers want to earn 50 percent on the sales price, they will mark up the toaster to $40 ($20 + 50% of $40). This number is equivalent to a *markup on cost* of 100 percent ($20/$20).

Does using standard markups to set prices make sense? Generally, no. Any pricing method that ignores demand and competitor prices is not likely to lead to the best price. Still, markup pricing remains popular for many reasons. First, sellers are more certain about costs than about demand. By tying the price to cost, sellers simplify pricing—they do not need to make frequent adjustments as demand changes. Second, when all firms in the industry use this pricing method, prices tend to be similar and price competition is thus minimized. Third, many people feel that cost-plus pricing is fairer to both buyers and sellers. Sellers earn a fair return on their investment but do not take advantage of buyers when buyers' demand becomes great.

Still, markup pricing remains popular for many reasons. First, sellers are more certain about costs than about demand. By tying the price to cost, sellers simplify pricing—they do not have to make frequent adjustments as demand changes. Second, when all firms in the industry use this pricing method, prices tend to be similar and price competition is thus minimized. Third, many people feel that cost-plus pricing is fairer to both buyers and sellers. Sellers earn a fair return on their investment but do not take advantage of buyers when buyers' demand becomes great.

Break-Even Analysis and Target Profit Pricing

Break-even pricing (target profit pricing)

Setting price to break even on the costs of making and marketing a product, or setting price to make a target profit.

Another cost-oriented pricing approach is **break-even pricing** (or a variation called **target profit pricing**). The firm tries to determine the price at which it will break even or make the target profit it is seeking. Such pricing is used by General Motors, which prices its automobiles to achieve a 15 to 20 percent profit on its investment. This pricing method is also used by public utilities, which are constrained to make a fair return on their investment.

Target pricing uses the concept of a *break-even chart*, which shows the total cost and total revenue expected at different sales volume levels. 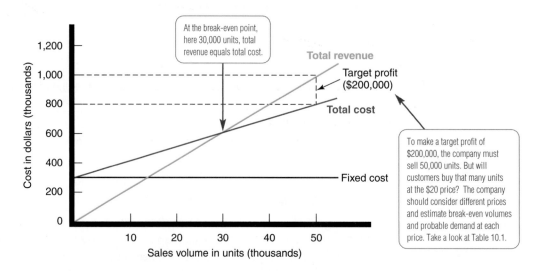**Figure 10.5** shows a break-even chart for the toaster manufacturer discussed here. Fixed costs are $300,000 regardless of sales volume. Variable costs are added to fixed costs to form total costs, which rise with volume. The total revenue curve starts at zero and rises with each unit sold. The slope of the total revenue curve reflects the price of $20 per unit.

The total revenue and total cost curves cross at 30,000 units. This is the *break-even volume*. At $20, the company must sell at least 30,000 units to break even, that is, for total revenue to cover total cost. Break-even volume can be calculated using the following formula:

$$\text{Break-Even Volume} = \frac{\text{Fixed Cost}}{\text{Price} - \text{Variable Cost}} = \frac{\$300,000}{\$20 - \$10} = 30,000$$

If the company wants to make a target profit, it must sell more than 30,000 units at $20 each. Suppose the toaster manufacturer has invested $1,000,000 in the business and wants to set price to earn a 20 percent return, or $200,000. In that case, it must sell at least 50,000 units at $20 each. If the company charges a higher price, it will not need to sell as many toasters to achieve its target return. But the market may not buy even this lower volume at the higher price. Much depends on the price elasticity and competitors' prices.

FIGURE | 10.5
Break-Even Chart for
Determining Target Price

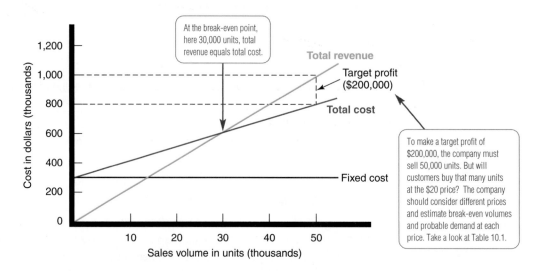

The manufacturer should consider different prices and estimate break-even volumes, probable demand, and profits for each. This is done in ● **Table 10.1**. The table shows that as price increases, break-even volume drops (column 2). But as price increases, demand for the toasters also falls off (column 3). At the $14 price, because the manufacturer clears only $4 per toaster ($14 less $10 in variable costs), it must sell a very high volume to break even. Even though the low price attracts many buyers, demand still falls below the high break-even point, and the manufacturer loses money. At the other extreme, with a $22 price the manufacturer clears $12 per toaster and must sell only 25,000 units to break even. But at this high price, consumers buy too few toasters, and profits are negative. The table shows that a price of $18 yields the highest profits. Note that none of the prices produce the manufacturer's target profit of $200,000. To achieve this target return, the manufacturer will have to search for ways to lower fixed or variable costs, thus lowering the break-even volume.

Other Internal and External Considerations Affecting Price Decisions

Customer perceptions of value set the upper limit for prices and costs set the lower limit. However, in setting prices within these limits, the company must consider a number of other internal and external factors. Internal factors affecting pricing include the company's overall marketing strategy, objectives, and marketing mix, as well as other organizational considerations. External factors include the nature of the market and demand, competitors' strategies and prices, and other environmental factors.

Overall Marketing Strategy, Objectives, and Mix

Price is only one element of the company's broader marketing strategy. Thus, before setting price, the company must decide on its overall marketing strategy for the product or service. If the company has selected its target market and positioning carefully, then its marketing mix strategy, including price, will be fairly straightforward. For example, when Honda developed its Acura brand to compete with European luxury-performance cars in the higher-income segment, this required charging a high price. In contrast, when it introduced the Honda Fit model—billed as "a pint-sized fuel miser with feisty giddy up"—this positioning required charging a low price. Thus, pricing strategy is largely determined by decisions on market positioning.

Pricing may play an important role in helping to accomplish company objectives at many levels. A firm can set prices to attract new customers or to profitably retain existing ones. It can set prices low to prevent competition from entering the market or set prices at competitors' levels to stabilize the market. It can price to keep the loyalty and support of resellers or to avoid government intervention. Prices can be reduced temporarily to create excitement for a brand. Or one product may be priced to help the sales of other products in the company's line.

Price is only one of the marketing mix tools that a company uses to achieve its marketing objectives. Price decisions must be coordinated with product design, distribution, and promotion decisions to form a consistent and effective integrated marketing program. Decisions

● TABLE | 10.1   **Break-Even Volume and Profits at Different Prices**

(1)	(2)	(3)	(4)	(5)	(6)
Price	Unit Demand Needed to Break Even	Expected Unit Demand at Given Price	Total Revenue (1) × (3)	Total Costs*	Profit (4) – (5)
$14	75,000	71,000	$ 994,000	$1,010,000	–$16,000
16	50,000	67,000	1,072,000	970,000	102,000
18	37,500	60,000	1,080,000	900,000	180,000
20	30,000	42,000	840,000	720,000	120,000
22	25,000	23,000	506,000	530,000	– 24,000

*Assumes fixed costs of $300,000 and constant unit variable costs of $10.

made for other marketing mix variables may affect pricing decisions. For example, a decision to position the product on high-performance quality will mean that the seller must charge a higher price to cover higher costs. And producers whose resellers are expected to support and promote their products may have to build larger reseller margins into their prices.

Companies often position their products on price and then tailor other marketing mix decisions to the prices they want to charge. Here, price is a crucial product-positioning factor that defines the product's market, competition, and design. Many firms support such price-positioning strategies with a technique called **target costing**, a potent strategic weapon. Target costing reverses the usual process of first designing a new product, determining its cost, and then asking, "Can we sell it for that?" Instead, it starts with an ideal selling price based on customer-value considerations and then targets costs that will ensure that the price is met. For example, when Honda set out to design the Fit, it began with a $13,950 starting price point and 34-mpg operating efficiency firmly in mind. It then designed a stylish, peppy little car with costs that allowed it to give target customers those values.

Other companies deemphasize price and use other marketing mix tools to create *nonprice* positions. Often, the best strategy is not to charge the lowest price but rather to differentiate the marketing offer to make it worth a higher price. For example, Bang & Olufsen—known for its cutting-edge consumer electronics—builds more value into its products and charges sky-high prices. For example, a B&O 50-inch BeoVision 4 HDTV will cost you $7,500; a 65-inch model runs $13,500. A complete B&O sound system? Well, you don't really want to know. But target customers recognize Bang & Olufsen's very high quality and are willing to pay more to get it.

Some marketers even position their products on *high* prices, featuring high prices as part of their product's allure (see **Real Marketing 10.2**). For example, Grand Marnier offers a $225 bottle of Cuvée du Cent Cinquantenaire that's marketed with the tagline "Hard to find, impossible to pronounce, and prohibitively expensive." ▲ And Titus Cycles, a premium bicycle manufacturer, features its high prices and its advertising. One ad humorously shows a man giving his girlfriend a "cubic zirconia" engagement ring so that he can purchase a Titus Solera for himself. Suggested retail price: $7,750.00.

Target costing
Pricing that starts with an ideal selling price, then targets costs that will ensure that the price is met.

▲ Positioning on high price: Titus features its lofty prices in its advertising— "suggested retail price: $7,750.00."

Thus, marketers must consider the total marketing strategy and mix when setting prices. If the product is positioned on nonprice factors, then decisions about quality, promotion, and distribution will strongly affect price. If price is a crucial positioning factor, then price will strongly affect decisions made about the other marketing mix elements. But even when featuring price, marketers need to remember that customers rarely buy on price alone. Instead, they seek products that give them the best value in terms of benefits received for the prices paid.

Organizational Considerations

Management must decide who within the organization should set prices. Companies handle pricing in a variety of ways. In small companies, prices are often set by top management rather than by the marketing or sales departments. In large companies, pricing is typically handled by divisional or product line managers. In industrial markets, salespeople may be allowed to negotiate with customers within certain price ranges. Even so, top management sets the pricing objectives and policies, and it often approves the prices proposed by lower-level management or salespeople.

In industries in which pricing is a key factor (airlines, aerospace, steel, railroads, oil companies), companies often have pricing departments to set the best prices or to help others in setting them. These departments report to the marketing department or top management. Others who have an influence on pricing include sales managers, production managers, finance managers, and accountants.

Real Marketing 10.2

Pricing High and Proud of It

Whereas some companies work to achieve irresistibly low prices that will pull in the masses, others take just the opposite tack. They proudly pronounce *higher* prices on brands that appeal to a more select few. The higher prices actually add value, helping to position the brand—and the owner—as something special. Consider the following examples.

Ferraris are anything but cheap. But owners like this one will tell you that when it comes to a Ferrari, price is nothing. The Ferrari experience is everything.

Ferrari. Ferraris are anything but cheap. Prices run from a mere $190,000 for the sleek Ferrari F430 to $280,000 for the 599 GTB. These prices don't include the lengthy list of expensive options or the typical markups over list price by dealers. And these are just the street models. For the real Ferrari fanatic, there's the ultralimited-edition FXX that can be driven only on race tracks. It goes out the door for around $2 million, give or take a few tens of thousands. And you don't need to worry too much about depreciation. At a recent auction, a 1959 Ferrari 250 GT LWB California Spider sold for a show-stopping $3.3 million.

How can any car be worth such high-octane prices? Part of it's the deeply rooted Ferrari racing heritage, which has established the brand as one of the world's fastest cars. "Racing is in our DNA," says a Ferrari spokesperson. Ferraris also feature some of the most beautiful automotive designs on the planet. These cars are thoroughbreds through and through. Still, there are plenty of other fast and stylish cars—Corvettes, Vipers, Porsches, Maseratis, Lotuses, and even some Mercedes and BMWs. These cars play in the same performance neighborhood as Ferraris but can be had for a lot less money.

One pillar of Ferrari's special positioning is its exclusivity. People want what they can't get and it's not easy to get a Ferrari. Ferrari made just 5,700 cars worldwide last year (Porsche made about 100,000). Each new Ferrari rolls off the assembly line presold, and the average buyer waits one year to take delivery. Buyers can wait as long as three years depending on the model, options, and location. "It's [part of] the value of the brand," says an investment banker who owns a Ferrari. "It's the cachet of being not easy to obtain."

But what really sets Ferrari apart from less-spendy rivals is what owners sum up as "the Ferrari experience." When you own a Ferrari, you become a part of something bigger, something special. Ferrari spends millions of dollars annually on managing relationships with its small, elite core of customers. "We have 20,000 owners in the United States and we need to know them by name," says Marco Mattiacci, vice president of marketing in North America. The company knows that its millionaire, even billionaire, customers "are looking for more unique things with more adrenaline than a golf game on Sunday." So Ferrari sponsors several owner-only events that fuel owners' driving passions while at the same time making them feel very special.

For example, the automaker sponsors the Ferrari Challenge, a series of six owners-only U.S. races, with the finals held in Italy. And for $5,925, owners can enter the Ferrari Challenge Rally, three-day touring trips on scenic back roads with stays at fine hotels. But the ultimate for owners and their spouses is the Ferrari Driving Experience. For an undisclosed amount, participants are coddled for two-and-a-half days at a five-star hotel. Ferrari loans each participant a sleek and powerful F430. Professional drivers school owners on the technical details of the car and how to get the best performance out of it. Then, Ferrari lets the owners loose on a Formula One race track to apply what they learned in the classroom.

Add it all up and it's not so surprising that Ferrari commands such high prices. Most owners will tell you that when it comes to a Ferrari, price is nothing. The Ferrari experience is everything.

Stella Artois. Positioning an exclusive, high-performance car on high price is one thing, but can such a strategy work for a more ordinary product—say, beer? Indeed it can. Consider Stella Artois. As a premium lager, Stella Artois has long been positioned as a high-end brew, with a price to match. In its advertising and other promotions, Stella doesn't hide its higher price; it flaunts it. For

more than two decades, Stella advertising has carried the tagline, "reassuringly expensive." Years of artful, critically acclaimed television ads featuring this tagline have become a Stella trademark, establishing the brand as something beyond the ordinary.

Stella Artois has even run an award-winning negative-savings coupon campaign featuring a series of authentic-looking Stella Artois coupons. Rather than offering discounts to coupon clippers, the coupons boast deals such as "$1.25 extra," "20% more," and "$4.00, regularly $2.75." The headline in each coupon affirms that Stella is "reassuringly expensive."

To further support the Stella Artois drinking experience, the brewer also promotes its well-known Nine-Step Pouring Ritual in ads and live pub appearances. Under the tutelage of a Stella Artois brewmaster, bar patrons learn important pouring steps, such as "The Purification" (cleansing and rinsing the trademark Stella Artois chalice), "The Liquid Alchemy" (the chalice glass is held at a 45-degree angle during filling), "The Beheading" (while the head is flowing over the edge of the glass, it is gently cut with a knife held at a 45-degree angle), and "The Judgment" (the foam is checked to insure two-finger thickness).

You can practice this ritual yourself in a classy, European-style virtual bar—Le Cercle Bar et Brasserie—located at the Stella Artois Web site (www.stellaartois.com). There, you become the star in an interactive drama that begins when you order a Stella and ends when you've completed the nine-step ritual and proven yourself worthy of drinking such a perfect beer. "When you've spent over 600 years crafting the perfect beer," says the company, "you become very fastidious about the way it's served."

Continued on next page ▼

Real Marketing 10.2 Continued ▼

Premium pricing has worked well for Stella Artois. Over the years, the company has managed to convince a host of loyal beer drinkers around the globe that its high prices are a good thing, not a bad thing. Although not well-known in the United States, Stella Artois is the number-one selling premium lager in most of the 80 countries in which it's distributed. The brand has been the number-one premium beer in the United Kingdom for years. U.S. sales have grown more than 60 percent over the past five years. Based on this success, Anheuser-Busch recently acquired

U.S. distribution rights for the Stella Artois brand and other U.S. rivals are adopting Stella-like strategies for their premium brands.

What is it that makes Stella Artois worth the premium price to so many beer drinkers?

Like Ferrari buyers (okay, maybe with a little less conviction), Stella Artois loyalists will tell you this: It's not the price, it's the Stella experience. Or, maybe the higher price helps to create that experience.

Sources: Harry Hodge, "Stella Artois' 9-Step Ritual," *24 Hours*, April 18, 2007, p. 12; Mike Beirne, "Rivals Crib from Stella's Stellar Marketing Plan," *Brandweek*, January 2, 2007, accessed at www.brandweek.com; "Stella Artois: The Beater or the Beaten?" *Marketing Week*, February 7, 2008, p. 18; Michael Taylor, "'Red Mist—The Ferrari Mystique," *San Francisco Chronicle*, June 25, 2006, p. J1; Jean Halliday, "For $2M, They Throw in the Sheets," *Advertising Age*, February 6, 2006, p. 14; Gabriel Kahn, "How to Slow Down a Ferrari: Buy It," *Wall Street Journal*, May 8, 2007; "Gooding & Company Announces $21+ Million Results from First-Ever Scottsdale Auction," *PR Newswire*, January 19, 2008; and information from www.stellaartois.com, September 2008.

The Market and Demand

As noted earlier, good pricing starts with an understanding of how customers' perceptions of value affect the prices they are willing to pay. Both consumer and industrial buyers balance the price of a product or service against the benefits of owning it. Thus, before setting prices, the marketer must understand the relationship between price and demand for the company's product. In this section, we take a deeper look at the price-demand relationship and how it varies for different types of markets. We then discuss methods for analyzing the price-demand relationship.

Pricing in Different Types of Markets. The seller's pricing freedom varies with different types of markets. Economists recognize four types of markets, each presenting a different pricing challenge.

Under *pure competition*, the market consists of many buyers and sellers trading in a uniform commodity such as wheat, copper, or financial securities. No single buyer or seller has much effect on the going market price. A seller cannot charge more than the going price, because buyers can obtain as much as they need at that price. Nor would sellers charge less than the market price, because they can sell all they want at this price. If price and profits rise, new sellers can easily enter the market. In a purely competitive market, marketing research, product development, pricing, advertising, and sales promotion play little or no role. Thus, sellers in these markets do not spend much time on marketing strategy.

Under *monopolistic competition*, the market consists of many buyers and sellers who trade over a range of prices rather than a single market price. A range of prices occurs because sellers can differentiate their offers to buyers. Either the physical product can be varied in quality, features, or style, or the accompanying services can be varied. Buyers see differences in sellers' products and will pay different prices for them. Sellers try to develop differentiated offers for different customer segments and, in addition to price, freely use branding, advertising, and personal selling to set their offers apart. ▲ Thus, Kohler differentiates itself from dozens of other kitchen and bath fixture brands through strong branding and advertising. Its ad campaign—"The Bold Look of Kohler"—emphasizes the brand's passion for design and craftsmanship, reducing the impact of price. Because there are many competitors in such markets, each firm is less affected by competitors' pricing strategies than in oligopolistic markets.

Under *oligopolistic competition*, the market consists of a few sellers who are highly sensitive to each other's pricing and

▲ Monopolistic competition: Kohler sets its brand apart through strong branding and advertising, reducing the impact of price.

FIGURE | 10.6
Demand Curves

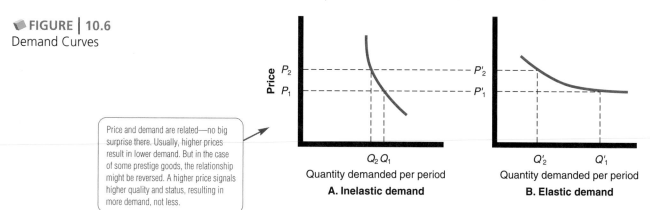

A. Inelastic demand

B. Elastic demand

marketing strategies. The product can be uniform (steel, aluminum) or nonuniform (cars, computers). There are few sellers because it is difficult for new sellers to enter the market. Each seller is alert to competitors' strategies and moves. If a steel company slashes its price by 10 percent, buyers will quickly switch to this supplier. The other steelmakers must respond by lowering their prices or increasing their services.

In a *pure monopoly*, the market consists of one seller. The seller may be a government monopoly (the U.S. Postal Service), a private regulated monopoly (a power company), or a private nonregulated monopoly (DuPont when it introduced nylon). Pricing is handled differently in each case. In a regulated monopoly, the government permits the company to set rates that will yield a "fair return." Nonregulated monopolies are free to price at what the market will bear. However, they do not always charge the full price for a number of reasons: a desire not to attract competition, a desire to penetrate the market faster with a low price, or a fear of government regulation.

Analyzing the Price-Demand Relationship. Each price the company might charge will lead to a different level of demand. The relationship between the price charged and the resulting demand level is shown in the **demand curve** in **Figure 10.6**. The demand curve shows the number of units the market will buy in a given time period at different prices that might be charged. In the normal case, demand and price are inversely related; that is, the higher price, the lower the demand. Thus, the company would sell less if it raised its price from P_1 to P_2. In short, consumers with limited budgets probably will buy less of something if its price is too high.

In the case of prestige goods, the demand curve sometimes slopes upward. Consumers think that higher prices mean more quality. ▲For example, Gibson Guitar Corporation once toyed with the idea of lowering its prices to compete more effectively with Japanese rivals such

Demand curve

A curve that shows the number of units the market will buy in a given time period, at different prices that might be charged.

CAN YOU GET RICH AND FAMOUS PLAYING A GIBSON? HOW DO YOU DEFINE RICH AND FAMOUS?

▲ The demand curve sometimes slopes upward: Gibson was surprised to learn that its high-quality instruments didn't sell as well at lower prices.

as Yamaha and Ibanez. To its surprise, Gibson found that its instruments didn't sell as well at lower prices. "We had an inverse [price-demand relationship]," noted Gibson's chief executive. "The more we charged, the more product we sold." At a time when other guitar manufacturers have chosen to build their instruments more quickly, cheaply, and in greater numbers, Gibson still promises guitars that "are made one-at-a-time, by hand. No shortcuts. No substitutions." It turns out that low prices simply aren't consistent with "Gibson's century-old tradition of creating investment-quality instruments that represent the highest standards of imaginative design and masterful craftsmanship."[11]

Most companies try to measure their demand curves by estimating demand at different prices. The type of market makes a difference. In a monopoly, the demand curve shows the total market demand resulting from different prices. If the company faces competition, its demand at different prices will depend on whether competitors' prices stay constant or change with the company's own prices.

Price elasticity

A measure of the sensitivity of demand to changes in price.

Price Elasticity of Demand. Marketers also need to know **price elasticity**—how responsive demand will be to a change in price. Consider the two demand curves in Figure 10.6. In Figure 10.6A, a price increase from P_1 to P_2 leads to a relatively small drop in demand from Q_1 to Q_2. In Figure 10.6B, however, the same price increase leads to a large drop in demand from Q'_1 to Q'_2. If demand hardly changes with a small change in price, we say the demand is *inelastic*. If demand changes greatly, we say the demand is *elastic*. The price elasticity of demand is given by the following formula:

$$\text{Price Elasticity of Demand} = \frac{\% \text{ Change in Quantity Demanded}}{\% \text{ Change in Price}}$$

Suppose demand falls by 10 percent when a seller raises its price by 2 percent. Price elasticity of demand is therefore –5 (the minus sign confirms the inverse relation between price and demand) and demand is elastic. If demand falls by 2 percent with a 2 percent increase in price, then elasticity is –1. In this case, the seller's total revenue stays the same: The seller sells fewer items but at a higher price that preserves the same total revenue. If demand falls by 1 percent when price is increased by 2 percent, then elasticity is –1/2 and demand is inelastic. The less elastic the demand, the more it pays for the seller to raise the price.

What determines the price elasticity of demand? Buyers are less price sensitive when the product they are buying is unique or when it is high in quality, prestige, or exclusiveness. They are also less price sensitive when substitute products are hard to find or when they cannot easily compare the quality of substitutes. Finally, buyers are less price sensitive when the total expenditure for a product is low relative to their income or when the cost is shared by another party.[12]

If demand is elastic rather than inelastic, sellers will consider lowering their prices. A lower price will produce more total revenue. This practice makes sense as long as the extra costs of producing and selling more do not exceed the extra revenue. At the same time, most firms want to avoid pricing that turns their products into commodities. In recent years, forces such as deregulation, dips in the economy, and the instant price comparisons afforded by the Internet and other technologies have increased consumer price sensitivity, turning products ranging from telephones and computers to new automobiles into commodities in some consumers' eyes.

Marketers need to work harder than ever to differentiate their offerings when a dozen competitors are selling virtually the same product at a comparable or lower price. More than ever, companies need to understand the price sensitivity of their customers and the trade-offs people are willing to make between price and product characteristics. In the words of marketing consultant Kevin Clancy, those who target only the price sensitive are "leaving money on the table."

Competitors' Strategies and Prices

In setting its prices, the company must also consider competitors' costs, prices, and market offerings. Consumers will base their judgments of a product's value on the prices that competitors charge for similar products. A consumer who is thinking about buying a Canon digital camera will evaluate Canon's customer value and price against the value and prices of comparable products made by Kodak, Nikon, Sony, and others.

In addition, the company's pricing strategy may affect the nature of the competition it faces. If Canon follows a high-price, high-margin strategy, it may attract competition. A low-price, low-margin strategy, however, may stop competitors or drive them out of the market. Canon needs to benchmark its costs and value against competitors' costs and value. It can then use these benchmarks as a starting point for its own pricing.

In assessing competitors' pricing strategies, the company should ask several questions. First, how does the company's market offering compare with competitors' offerings in terms of customer value? If consumers perceive that the company's product or service provides greater value, the company can charge a higher price. If consumers perceive less value relative to competing products, the company must either charge a lower price or change customer perceptions to justify a higher price.

Next, how strong are current competitors and what are their current pricing strategies? If the company faces a host of smaller competitors charging high prices relative to the value they deliver, it might charge lower prices to drive weaker competitors out of the market. If the market is dominated by larger, low-price competitors, the company may decide to target unserved market niches with value-added products at higher prices.

For example, ▲ Annie Bloom's Books, an independent bookseller in Portland, Oregon, isn't likely to win a price war against Amazon.com or Barnes & Noble—it doesn't even try. Instead, the shop relies on its personal approach, cozy atmosphere, and friendly and knowledgeable staff to turn local book lovers into loyal patrons, even if they have to pay a little more. Customers writing on a consumer review Web site recently gave Annie Bloom's straight five-star ratings, supported by the kinds of comments you likely wouldn't see for Barnes & Noble:[13]

▲ Pricing against larger, low-price competitors: Independent bookstore Annie Bloom's Books isn't likely to win a price war against Amazon.com or Barnes & Noble. Instead, it relies on outstanding customer service and a cozy atmosphere to turn book lovers into loyal customers.

A good bookstore can feel like a sacred place to me. Annie Bloom's is one of those places. This place radiates love. Their fine selection of books is arranged in a way that lets you know the people who work here are very interested in books, too. The air is cool and has a certain literary smell. I can't explain it. This is a bookstore where you could spend all afternoon just browsing, getting swept up into different stories and ways of thinking.

Annie Bloom's is not the biggest bookstore, nor the most convenient to park at, nor are the prices incredibly discounted, nor is the bathroom easy to find. . . . However, it is one of the friendliest bookstores in town. It is just big enough for a solid hour of browsing. And it has a talented, smart, and long-term staff with incredible taste. You'll find common best sellers here, but you'll also find all those cool books you heard about on NPR or in *Vanity Fair* that you never see featured at Barnes & Noble. [It's a] bookstore for the book crowd. Good customer service here! Also, be nice to the cat. PS: [It] has a kid's play area in the back.

Finally, the company should ask, How does the competitive landscape influence customer price sensitivity?[14] For example, customers will be more price sensitive if they see few differences between competing products. They will buy whichever product costs the least. The more information customers have about competing products and prices before buying, the more price sensitive they will be. Easy product comparisons help customers to assess the value of different options and to decide what prices they are willing to pay. Finally, customers will be more price sensitive if they can switch easily from one product alternative to another.

What principle should guide decisions about what price to charge relative to those of competitors? The answer is simple in concept but often difficult in practice: No matter what price you charge—high, low, or in between—be certain to give customers superior value for that price.

Other External Factors

When setting prices, the company also must consider a number of other factors in its external environment. *Economic conditions* can have a strong impact on the firm's pricing strategies. Economic factors such as boom or recession, inflation, and interest rates affect pricing decisions because they affect both consumer perceptions of the product's price and value and the costs of producing a product.

The company must also consider what impact its prices will have on other parties in its environment. How will *resellers* react to various prices? The company should set prices that give resellers a fair profit, encourage their support, and help them to sell the product effectively. The *government* is another important external influence on pricing decisions. Finally, *social concerns* may need to be taken into account. In setting prices, a company's short-term sales, market share, and profit goals may need to be tempered by broader societal considerations. We will examine public policy issues in pricing in the next chapter.

REVIEWING Objectives AND KEY Terms

Companies today face a fierce and fast-changing pricing environment. Firms successful at creating customer value with the other marketing mix activities must still capture some of this value in the prices they earn. This chapter looks at internal and external considerations that affect pricing decisions and examines general pricing approaches.

OBJECTIVE 1   Answer the question "What is price?" and discuss the importance of pricing in today's fast-changing environment. (pp 290–291)

Price can be defined narrowly as the amount of money charged for a product or service. Or it can be defined more broadly as the sum of the values that consumers exchange for the benefits of having and using the product or service. The pricing challenge is to find the price that will let the company make a fair profit by getting paid for the customer value it creates.

Despite the increased role of nonprice factors in the modern marketing process, price remains an important element in the marketing mix. It is the only marketing mix element that produces revenue; all other elements represent costs. Price is also one of the most flexible elements of the marketing mix. Unlike product features and channel commitments, price can be raised or lowered quickly. Even so, many companies are not good at handling pricing—pricing decisions and price competition are major problems for many marketing executives. Pricing problems often arise because managers are too quick to reduce prices, prices are too cost oriented rather than customer-value oriented, or prices are not consistent with the rest of the marketing mix.

OBJECTIVE 2   Discuss the importance of understanding customer value perceptions when setting prices. (pp 291–295)

Good pricing begins with a complete understanding of the value that a product or service creates for customers and setting a price that captures that value. Customer perceptions of the product's value set the ceiling for prices. If customers perceive that the price is greater than the product's value, they will not buy the product. *Value-based pricing* uses buyers' perceptions of value, not the seller's cost, as the key to pricing.

Companies can pursue either of two types of value-based pricing. *Good-value pricing* involves offering just the right combination of quality and good service at a fair price. Everyday low pricing (EDLP) is an example of this strategy. *Value-added pricing* involves attaching value-added features and services to differentiate the company's offers and support charging higher prices.

OBJECTIVE 3   Discuss the importance of company and product costs in setting prices. (pp 295–299)

The price the company charges will fall somewhere between one that is too high to produce any demand and one that is too low to produce a profit. Whereas customer perceptions of value set the ceiling for prices, company and product costs set the floor. If the company prices the product below its costs, its profits will suffer. *Cost-based pricing* involves setting prices based on the costs for producing, distributing, and selling the product plus a fair rate of return for effort and risk.

Costs are an important consideration in setting prices. However, cost-based pricing is product-driven rather than customer-driven. The company designs what it considers to be a good product and sets a price that covers costs plus a target profit. If the price turns out to be too high, the company must settle for lower markups or lower sales, both resulting in disappointing profits. The company must watch its costs carefully. If it costs the company more than it costs competitors to produce and sell its product, the company must charge a higher price or make less profit, putting it at a competitive disadvantage.

Total costs are the sum of the fixed and variable costs for any given level of production. Management wants to charge a price that will at least cover the total costs at a given level of production. To price wisely, management also needs to know how its costs vary with different levels of production and accumulated production experience. Cost-based pricing approaches include *cost-plus pricing* and *break-even pricing* (or target profit pricing).

OBJECTIVE 4   Identify and define the other important external and internal factors affecting a firm's pricing decisions. (pp 299–305)

Other *internal* factors that influence pricing decisions include the company's overall marketing strategy, objectives, mix, and organization for pricing. Price is only one element of the company's broader marketing strategy. If the company has selected its target market and positioning carefully, then its marketing mix strategy, including price, will be fairly straightforward. Some companies position their products on price and then tailor other marketing mix decisions to the prices they want to charge. Other companies deemphasize price and use other marketing mix tools to create *nonprice* positions.

Common pricing objectives might include survival, current profit maximization, market share leadership, or customer retention and relationship building. Price decisions must be coordinated with product design, distribution, and promotion decisions to form a consistent and effective marketing program. Finally, in order to coordinate pricing goals and decisions, management must decide who within the organization is responsible for setting price.

Other *external* pricing considerations include the nature of the market and demand, competitors' strategies and prices, and environmental factors such as the economy, reseller needs, and government actions. The seller's pricing freedom varies with different types of markets. Ultimately, the customer decides whether the company has set the right price. The customer weighs the price against the perceived values of using the product—if the price exceeds the sum of the values, consumers will not buy. So the company must understand concepts like demand curves (the price-demand relationship) and price elasticity (consumer sensitivity to prices). Consumers also compare a product's price to the prices of competitors' products. A company therefore must learn the customer value and prices of competitors' offers.

KEY Terms

OBJECTIVE 1
Price (p 290)

OBJECTIVE 2
Value-based pricing (p 291)
Good-value pricing (p 293)
Value-added pricing (p 293)

OBJECTIVE 3
Cost-based pricing (p 295)
Fixed costs (overhead) (p 295)
Variable costs (p 296)
Total costs (p 296)
Experience curve (learning curve) (p 296)

Cost-plus pricing (p 297)
Break-even pricing (target profit pricing) (p 298)

OBJECTIVE 4
Target costing (p 300)
Demand curve (p 303)
Price elasticity (p 304)

DISCUSSING & APPLYING THE Concepts

Discussing the Concepts

1. What is price? List five other words that mean the same thing as price (for example, tuition). (AACSB: Communication; Reflective Thinking)

2. Explain the differences between value-based pricing and cost-based pricing. (AACSB: Communication)

3. Name and describe the two types of value-based pricing methods. (AACSB: Communication)

4. Compare and contrast fixed and variable costs and give an example of each. (AACSB: Communication)

5. Discuss other internal and external considerations besides cost and customer perceptions of value that affect pricing decisions. (AACSB: Communication)

6. Name and describe the four types of markets recognized by economists and discuss the pricing challenges posed by each. (AACSB: Communication)

Applying the Concepts

1. In a small group, discuss your perceptions of value and how much you are willing to pay for the following products: automobiles, frozen dinners, jeans, and athletic shoes. Are there differences among members of your group? Explain why those differences exist. Discuss some examples of brands of these products that are positioned to deliver different value to consumers. (AACSB: Communication; Reflective Thinking)

2. Find estimates of price elasticity for a variety of consumer goods and services. Explain what price elasticities of 0.5 and 2.4 mean. (Note: these are absolute values, as price elasticity is usually negative.) (AACSB: Communication; Reflective Thinking)

3. What does the following positioning statement suggest about the firm's marketing objectives, marketing mix strategy, and costs? "No one beats our prices. We crush the competition." (AACSB: Communication; Reflective Thinking)

FOCUS ON Technology

It seems a day doesn't go by without some talk about gas prices. Consumers are more keenly aware of the price now that it costs $40 to $100 to fill up the tank. And many consumers are using technology to help find the lowest prices in their area. The Internet is making it much easier to get price comparisons from Web sites such as GasBuddy.com (www.gasbuddy.com) and GasPriceWatch.com (www.gaspricewatch.com). These sites give price information on maps for a consumer's zip code area. Consumers can download programs, called widgets, which continually update this information on users' computers. If you're not at your computer, you can get this information on your cell phone from www.getmobio.com/learn/cheapgas/. Most of the Web sites rely on volunteers to update prices.

1. Visit some of these Web sites and evaluate their usefulness to consumers. Recommend some other applications that would enable consumers to find the best gas prices. (AACSB: Communication; Use of IT; Reflective Thinking)

2. Why are consumers so concerned about the price of gas and why are they willing to search out stations with lower prices? (AACSB: Communication; Reflective Thinking)

FOCUS ON Ethics

You've heard of a monopoly, but have you ever heard of a *monopsony*? A monopsony involves one powerful buyer and many sellers. The buyer is so powerful that it can drive prices down. An example is Wal-Mart, the world's largest retailer. Wal-Mart's power allows it to get the lowest possible prices from its suppliers. Similarly, wine-making giant E. & J. Gallo has so much power buying grapes that growers have to concede to the wine maker's demands for lower prices.

1. Is it fair that a buyer can exert so much power over a supplier? Are there any benefits to consumers? (AACSB: Communication; Ethical Reasoning)

2. Should the government step in and set minimum price levels? Discuss the consequences of your answer. (AACSB: Communication; Reflective Thinking)

MARKETING BY THE Numbers

One external factor manufacturers must consider when setting prices is reseller margins. Manufacturers do not have the final say concerning the price to consumers—retailers do. So, manufacturers must start with their suggested retail prices and work back, subtracting out the markups required by resellers that sell the product to consumers. Once that is considered, manufacturers know at what price to sell their products to resellers, and they can determine what volume they must sell to break even at that price and cost combination. To answer the following questions, refer to Appendix 2, Marketing by the Numbers.

1. A consumer purchases a flat iron to straighten her hair for $150 from a salon at which she gets her hair cut. If the salon's markup is 40 percent and the wholesaler's markup is 15 percent, both based on their selling prices, for what price does the manufacturer sell the product to the wholesaler? (AACSB: Communication; Analytical Reasoning)

2. If the unit variable costs for each flat iron are $40 and the manufacturer has fixed costs totaling $200,000, how many flat irons must this manufacturer sell to break even? How many must it sell to realize a profit of $800,000? (AACSB: Communication; Analytical Reasoning)

VIDEO Case

IKEA

Lots of companies have idealistic missions. But IKEA's vision, "To create a better everyday life for the many people," seems somewhat implausible. How can a company that makes furniture improve everyday life for the masses? Interestingly, the most important part of that strategy is price. For every product that it designs, from leather sofas to plastic mugs, IKEA starts with a target price. The target price is one that's deemed affordable, making the product accessible to the masses.

Only then does IKEA begin the grueling process of creating a high-quality, stylish, and innovative product that can be delivered to the customer for that target price. As IKEA points out, anyone can make high-quality goods for a high price or poor-quality goods for a low price. The real challenge is making high-quality products at a low price. To do so requires a relentless focus on costs combined with a thirst for innovation. That has been IKEA's quest for more than 65 years.

After viewing the video featuring IKEA, answer the following questions about the company's pricing strategy:

1. What is IKEA's promise of value?

2. Referring to the Klippan sofa, illustrate how IKEA delivers its promise of value to consumers.

3. Based on the concepts from the text, does IKEA employ a value-based pricing approach or a cost-based pricing approach? Support your answer.

COMPANY Case

Southwest Airlines: Staying Ahead in the Pricing Game

In the early 1970s, when Herb Kelleher and a partner sketched a business plan on a cocktail napkin, they had no idea that Southwest Airlines would become the most successful U.S. airline. In 2003, the company earned $442 million—more than *all* the other U.S. airlines *combined*. From 1972 through 2002, *Money* magazine indicated that Southwest was the nation's best-performing stock—growing at a compound annual rate of 26 percent over the period! It has been profitable every year since its founding, something no other U.S. airline can claim. By 2008, Southwest had 35,000 employees and $9.1 billion in revenue. It has never laid off employees or cut wages in an industry plagued by mergers, downsizing, labor squabbles, and bankruptcies.

Most people didn't give upstart Southwest Airlines much of a chance. Southwest's strategy was the complete opposite of the industry's conventional wisdom. Its planes flew from "point-to-point" rather than using the major airlines' "hub-and-spoke" pattern. This gave it more flexibility to move planes around based on demand. Southwest did not serve the major airports dominated by the major airlines, preferring instead to serve second-tier destinations where costs were lower. Southwest served no meals, only snacks. It did not charge passengers a fee to change same-fare tickets. It had no assigned seats. It had no electronic entertainment, relying on humorous flight attendants to entertain passengers. The airline did not offer a retirement plan; rather, it offered its employees a profit-sharing plan, thus keeping its fixed costs low.

Because of all these factors, Southwest had much lower costs than its competitors and was able to crush the competition with its low-price strategy. Moreover, it consistently stuck with its strategy. That is, until 2004.

In July 2004, Gary Kelly, a 21-year Southwest veteran, took over the CEO role from Mr. Kelleher. Despite Southwest's success, Kelly told analysts that it was "time for a little remodeling" of its strategy. He realized Southwest would no longer be able to cruise above the turbulent storm clouds buffeting the U.S. airline industry. In fact, as one analyst noted, it appeared to be "boxed in by its strategy of frequent flights and rapid growth in a weak domestic market."

In early 2004, Southwest had already ditched its strategy of not attacking the major carriers in their main hubs as it launched service to Philadelphia, the home of US Airways. It also began service to other higher-cost airports such as Denver. At the same time, other discount airlines, such as JetBlue, were tearing pages out of Southwest's playbook by offering low prices and enhanced services, such as in-flight television, thereby eating into its market share.

Further, Southwest was losing its cost advantage. Many major airlines had declared bankruptcy and restructured or had merged with other airlines and emerged with lower cost structures that allowed them to challenge Southwest's fares. Southwest's aging workforce had become one of the highest paid in the industry. To make matters worse, rapidly escalating fuel prices were making its fuel-price hedging strategy, a key factor in its cost advantage since 1999, less effective.

To respond, Kelly entered Southwest's first code-sharing agreement with discount carrier ATA Airlines. The agreement allowed the two carriers to expand their networks by selling tickets on each other's flights and earned Southwest millions of dollars of additional revenue. Furthermore, although Southwest had built customer loyalty by offering frequent flights between many of the 63 cities it served in 32 states, Kelly began to evaluate underperforming routes and developed new software to shift planes to more profitable routes. At the same time, he also announced that Southwest would curb its expansion plans. Kelly also began to raise prices aggressively—increasing prices six times in 2006, an 11.4 percent average fare increase.

Perhaps Kelly's boldest move yet was the decision to target business travelers. Although 40 percent to 50 percent of Southwest's customers were bargain-hunting businesspeople, other airlines were being more successful catering to business travelers who were often willing to pay higher prices if an airline offered last-minute tickets, assigned seating, first-class cabins, and private airport lounges—none of which Southwest had. To grow revenue in the increasingly competitive industry, Kelly realized that he needed more business travelers but that these customers would be harder to attract.

To implement the new strategy, Southwest announced a new fare category, Business Select, in late 2007. These fares are $30 to $50 higher for a round-trip ticket. The tickets, however, offer the customer preferential boarding, bonus frequent-flier credits, and a free cocktail on each flight. Business Select customers board first, ahead of the regular-fare customers herded in the airline's famous A, B, and C queuing stalls.

Southwest changed its Web site, which used to offer five fare categories with headings like "refundable anytime" and "discount fare," to offer only three fares: "Business Select," "Business," and "Wanna Get Away." Southwest will also offer more nonstop routes and more frequent flights that work with business travelers' schedules. It is renovating boarding areas and installing roomier seats, power outlets, workstation counters, and flat-screen TVs broadcasting CNN.

To encourage companies to begin to use Southwest, the airline increased its business sales force from 5 to 15 members who meet with corporate travel managers to promote the new offerings. The staff points out that Southwest maintains one of the industry's best customer-service and on-time performance records—important considerations for business travelers. The company has also begun to make its tickets available through computer systems that the travel managers use to book tickets, counter to its long-standing strategy of only selling tickets directly through its Web site and toll-free number. It has also begun to negotiate discounted contracts with businesses, something it had always avoided.

The strategic question for Southwest becomes how its traditional customers will react to all this change. Will those customers who logged on its Web site 24 hours before a flight to get a low boarding number be upset when they see business customers boarding first and taking all the good seats? Will budget-minded leisure travelers be upset when they see that two of the three ticket classes target business travelers? Will loyal customers who liked Southwest's egalitarian, democratic system like all these changes?

Southwest wants to use its new business-focused strategy to generate $100 million of the $1 billion it wants to add to its revenue by 2010. It is also considering international flights and in-flight Internet service. And, like other airlines, it is beginning to charge extra fees for things, such as extra luggage, that airlines used to include in the basic airfare.

Southwest's vice president of marketing notes that, "We have changed, and the environment we are in has changed. There are a lot of times where that one-size approach is appropriate. When it comes to customers, it becomes more difficult."

Perhaps *Advertising Age* best sums up the challenges Southwest, Wal-Mart, and other "power discounters" face:

> If one thing defined the marketing landscape of the 1990s, it was the power of cheap. . . . The power discounters are paying the price for their own success. They have reached the end of the frontier for easy growth and made their rivals stronger. Now they are all trying . . . to adapt their marketing and business models to the new, tougher competitive landscape they've helped spawn.

One thing Southwest has learned is that no matter how successful, the only constant in marketing and pricing strategy is change.

Questions for Discussion

1. What has been Southwest's traditional pricing strategy? Why has this pricing strategy been so successful throughout the airline's first three decades?

2. What values do airline customers—both business and leisure travelers—seek when they buy air travel tickets? Has Southwest done a better job than competitors of meeting the needs of these air travelers? In what ways?

3. What internal and external factors affect airline pricing decisions? What impact are these factors now having on airline pricing and profitability?

4. What is Southwest's current pricing strategy? Does this strategy differentiate Southwest from its competitors? Is the strategy sustainable?

5. What marketing recommendations, including pricing recommendations, would you make to Southwest as it moves into the next decade?

Sources: Excerpts and quotes from: Scott McCartney, "Unusual Route: Discount Airlines Woo Business Set," *Wall Street Journal*, February 19, 2008, p.D1; Jack Neff, "How the Discounters Hurt Themselves," *Advertising Age*, December 10, 2007, p.12; Melanie Trottman, "New Route: As Competition Rebounds, Southwest Faces Squeeze," *Wall Street Journal*, June 27, 2007, p. A1. See also: Melanie Trottman, "Southwest's New Flight Plan: Win More Business Travelers," *Wall Street Journal*, November 27, 2007, p. B1.

Chapter 11

Part 1　Defining Marketing and the Marketing Process (Chapters 1, 2)
Part 2　Understanding the Marketplace and Consumers (Chapters 3, 4, 5, 6)
Part 3　Designing a Customer-Driven Strategy and Mix (Chapters 7, 8, 9, 10, 11, 12, 13, 14, 15, 16, 17)
Part 4　Extending Marketing (Chapters 18, 19, 20)

Pricing Strategies

Chapter
PREVIEW

In the last chapter, you learned that price is an important marketing mix tool for both creating and capturing customer value. You explored the many internal and external factors that affect a firm's pricing decisions and examined three general approaches to setting prices. In this chapter, we'll look at pricing strategies available to marketers—new-product pricing strategies, product mix pricing strategies, price adjustment strategies, and price reaction strategies.

Let's start with a look at Kodak and its revolutionary new pricing strategy for inkjet printers: Are you tired of buying a reasonably priced printer, then paying scandalous prices for replacement ink cartridges? Kodak may have the answer. In a move that promises to turn the printer industry on its head, Kodak sells its EasyShare printers for more but charges you less for replacement ink.

HP, Epson, Canon, and Lexmark have long dominated the $50 billion printer industry with a maddening "razor-and-blades" pricing strategy (as in give away the razor, then make your profits on the blades). They sell printers at little or no profit. But once you own the printer, you're stuck buying their grossly overpriced, high-margin replacement ink cartridges. For example, you can pick up a nifty little HP multifunction inkjet printer for only $69.99. But the HP tricolor inkjet cartridge that goes with it costs $24.99. And a 100-count pack of HP 4-by-6-inch photo paper costs another $14.49. The price per ounce of inkjet printer ink can exceed the per-ounce price of an expensive perfume, premium champagne, or even caviar.

The big manufacturers seem content with this captive-product pricing strategy. In fact, they pull in four times more revenues from ink cartridges and paper than from the printers themselves. Customers don't like being held hostage and having to pay through the nose for ink and paper—some are outraged by it. But what can they do? Only HP cartridges work with HP printers. Buying another brand isn't the answer, either—all of the manufacturers pursue the same pricing strategy. Besides, it's difficult to compare long-term per-print prices across manufacturers. Few of us know or go to the trouble to figure out in advance how many cartridges we'll use or what future ink prices will be.

Enter Kodak—with a unique solution. Kodak recently introduced its first line of printers—EasyShare All-in-One printers—with a revolutionary pricing strategy that threatens to turn the entire inkjet printer industry upside-down. In a twist on typical industry practice, Kodak sells its printers at premium prices with no discounts, and then sells the ink cartridges for less. EasyShare printers sell for $149.99 to $299.99, depending on features, about $50 higher than comparable printers sold by competitors. However, EasyShare black and color ink cartridges go for just $9.99 and

$14.99, respectively, about half the prevailing competitor prices. It's a whole new concept in printer pricing and economics.

To make the strategy work, Kodak first had to create a new kind of inkjet printer. It developed an innovative technology that uses tiny nozzles to squirt pigment ink drops that are just a few atoms in size. EasyShare printers take about 55 seconds to produce a 4-by-6-inch print, longer than some competitive printers that do it in 32 seconds. But the resulting photos take up to 90 years to fade versus dye-based inks that can begin to fade in as little as a year.

Moreover, Kodak found a way to contain all of the printing electronics within the EasyShare printer itself, whereas rivals include some of the electronics in the cartridges. This lets Kodak charge less for the cartridges. As a result, according to one independent lab study, Kodak's new printers "whomped" rival's printers in price per printout. The study showed that consumers using an EasyShare printer and buying specially priced packages of photo paper and an ink cartridge can print 4-by-6-inch photos for only 10 cents each, compared with about 29 cents each for typical home printers and 19 cents each at retail store photo services.

Thus, Kodak has the right printer and the right ink prices. Now, all it has to do is to re-educate consumers about printer pricing—about the benefits of paying more up front in order to reduce long-run printing costs. To do this, Kodak launched a

Kodak launched a "Think Ink" marketing campaign, built around the visual "think" image, with the first two letters in black and the last three in gold.

"Think Ink" marketing campaign, built around the visual image "ThINK," with the first two letters in black and the last three in gold. The campaign asks the pivotal question: "Is it smarter to save money on a printer or save money on ink? (Hint: You only buy the printer once.)"

The ThINK campaign began with online viral efforts, centered on a series of popular "Inkisit" videos, featuring two dorky guys, Nathan and Max, who love to print photos but who don't like ink's high cost. In the videos, they ask enthusiastically, "Have you ever thought about what life would be like if ink was cheaper?" Kodak posted the videos on YouTube and MySpace and set up an entertaining and informative microsite, www.inkisit.com.

Then came the bread-and-butter "ThINK" media campaign, targeting budget-conscious consumers who want to print at home but have limited this activity because of high ink costs. Kodak's research showed that more than 70 percent of all families restrict their children's printing because of cost concerns. So the campaign targets "enterprising parents" who want to empower their kids' creativity and not have to worry about "silly economics."

The ThINK campaign tackles the very difficult task of shifting consumer value perceptions away from initial printer prices and toward prices per print. "Our strategy," says a Kodak marketing executive, "is to crystallize for consumers that they're not only buying a printer today but also buying into three to four years of ink purchases." The campaign has sent shockwaves through the inkjet printer industry and its "razor-and-blades" pricing mentality. Says one analyst, Kodak is "plastering their costs per printed page all over the place. No one has ever done that before in this market. [The others] don't want to remind consumers how much it costs." Another analyst agrees:

> This is not your usual printer introduction. Kodak completely changes the game . . . and [these printers] will not be welcomed by competition. Competing openly on cost-per-print puts the profits of the printing industry in grave danger. To compete with Kodak, competitors will have to reveal their own printing costs and ultimately lower [their ink] prices. While this is great for consumers, it is bad for printer manufacturers' bottom lines. Kodak's [EasyShare printers] will take the market by storm.

It's still too soon to tell whether Kodak's revolutionary pricing strategy is working, but the early results are promising. The company sold 520,000 EasyShare printers in 2007, exceeding forecasts, and expected to sell as many as 1.5 million in 2008. Competitors are now scrambling to introduce their own lower-priced cartridges and longer lasting inks. But Kodak

claims that EasyShare printers will still save customers up to 50 percent on everything they print.

As one observer concludes, Kodak "Has its priorities straight: Great-looking photos that last a lifetime," with affordable per-print prices in the bargain. "It makes a world-rocking point about the razor-blades model that's lined the coffers of the inkjet industry for years. If you're mad as hell, you don't have to take it anymore."[1]

Kodak recently introduced its first line of printers with a revolutionary pricing strategy that threatens to turn the entire inkjet printer industry upside-down—charge more for the printers but less for replacement ink. It's a whole new concept in printer pricing and economics

Kodak has the right printer and the right ink prices. Now, all it has to do is to re-educate consumers about the benefits of paying more up front in order to reduce long-run printing costs.

As the Kodak story illustrates, pricing decisions are subject to a complex array of company, environmental, and competitive forces. To make things even more complex, a company sets not a single price but rather a *pricing structure* that covers different items in its line. This pricing structure changes over time as products move through their life cycles. The company adjusts its prices to reflect changes in costs and demand and to account for variations in buyers and situations. As the competitive environment changes, the company considers when to initiate price changes and when to respond to them.

Objective Outline

This chapter examines the major pricing strategies available to marketers. We look in turn at *new-product pricing strategies* for products in the introductory stage of the product life cycle, *product mix pricing strategies* for related products in the product mix, *price adjustment strategies* that account for customer differences and changing situations, and strategies for initiating and responding to *price changes.*[2]

Author Comment | Pricing new products can be especially challenging. Just think about all the things you'd have to consider in pricing a new cell phone, say the first Apple iPhone. What's more, you'd have to start thinking about the price—along with many other marketing considerations—at the very beginning of the design process.

New-Product Pricing Strategies (pp 312-313)

Pricing strategies usually change as the product passes through its life cycle. The introductory stage is especially challenging. Companies bringing out a new product face the challenge of setting prices for the first time. They can choose between two broad strategies: *market-skimming pricing* and *market-penetration pricing*.

Market-Skimming Pricing

Market-skimming pricing

Setting a high price for a new product to skim maximum revenues layer by layer from the segments willing to pay the high price; the company makes fewer but more profitable sales.

Many companies that invent new products set high initial prices to "skim" revenues layer by layer from the market. Sony frequently uses this strategy, called **market-skimming pricing** (or **price skimming**). When Sony introduced the world's first high-definition television (HDTV) to the Japanese market in 1990, the high-tech sets cost $43,000. These televisions were purchased only by customers who really wanted the new technology and could afford to pay a high price for it. Sony rapidly reduced the price over the next several years to attract new buyers. By 1993 a 28-inch HDTV cost a Japanese buyer just over $6,000. In 2001, a Japanese consumer could buy a 40-inch HDTV for about $2,000, a price that many more customers could afford. An entry-level HDTV set now sells for less than $500 in the United States, and prices continue to fall. In this way, Sony skimmed the maximum amount of revenue from the various segments of the market.[3]

Market skimming makes sense only under certain conditions. First, the product's quality and image must support its higher price and enough buyers must want the product at that price. Second, the costs of producing a smaller volume cannot be so high that they cancel the advantage of charging more. Finally, competitors should not be able to enter the market easily and undercut the high price.

Market-Penetration Pricing

Market-penetration pricing
Setting a low price for a new product in order to attract a large number of buyers and a large market share.

Rather than setting a high initial price to skim off small but profitable market segments, some companies use **market-penetration pricing**. They set a low initial price in order to *penetrate* the market quickly and deeply—to attract a large number of buyers quickly and win a large market share. The high sales volume results in falling costs, allowing the companies to cut their prices even further. For example, Dell used penetration pricing to enter the personal computer market, selling high-quality computer products through lower-cost direct channels. Its sales soared when HP, Apple, and other competitors selling through retail stores could not match its prices. ▲And giant Swedish retailer IKEA used penetration pricing to boost its success in the Chinese market:[4]

▲ Penetration pricing: To lure famously frugal Chinese customers, IKEA slashed its prices. The strategy worked. Weekend crowds at its cavernous Beijing store are so big that employees need to use megaphones to keep them in control.

When IKEA first opened stores in China in 2002, people crowded in, but not to buy home furnishings. Instead, they came to take advantage of the freebies—air conditioning, clean toilets, and even decorating ideas. Chinese consumers are famously frugal. When it came time to actually buy, they shopped instead at local stores just down the street that offered knockoffs of IKEA's designs at a fraction of the price. So to lure the finicky Chinese customers, IKEA slashed its prices in China to the lowest in the world, the opposite approach of many Western retailers there. By increasingly stocking its Chinese stores with China-made products, the retailer pushed prices on some items as low as 70 percent below prices in IKEA's outlets outside China. The penetration pricing strategy worked. IKEA now captures a 43 percent market share of China's fast-growing home wares market alone, and the sales of its four mammoth Chinese stores surged 38 percent last year. The cavernous Beijing store draws nearly 6 million visitors annually. Weekend crowds are so big that employees need to use megaphones to keep them in control.

Several conditions must be met for this low-price strategy to work. First, the market must be highly price sensitive so that a low price produces more market growth. Second, production and distribution costs must fall as sales volume increases. Finally, the low price must help keep out the competition, and the penetration pricer must maintain its low-price position—otherwise, the price advantage may be only temporary.

Author Comment | Most individual products are part of a broader product mix and must be priced accordingly. For example, Gillette prices its Fusion razors low. But once you buy the razor, you're a captive customer for its higher-margin replacement cartridges

Product Mix Pricing Strategies (pp 313–315)

The strategy for setting a product's price often has to be changed when the product is part of a product mix. In this case, the firm looks for a set of prices that maximizes the profits on the total product mix. Pricing is difficult because the various products have related demand and costs and face different degrees of competition. We now take a closer look at the five product mix pricing situations summarized in ● **Table 11.1**: *product line pricing, optional-product pricing, captive-product pricing, by-product pricing,* and *product bundle pricing.*

Product Line Pricing

Product line pricing
Setting the price steps between various products in a product line based on cost differences between the products, customer evaluations of different features, and competitors' prices.

Companies usually develop product lines rather than single products. For example, Samsonite offers some 20 different collections of bags of all shapes and sizes at prices that range from under $50 for a Sammie's child's backpack to more than $1,250 for a bag from its Black Label Vintage Collection.[5] In **product line pricing**, management must decide on the price steps to set between the various products in a line.

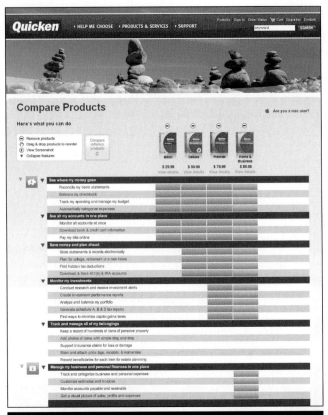

▲ Product line pricing: Quicken offers an entire line of financial management software, including Basic, Deluxe, Premier, and Home & Business versions priced at $29.99, $59.99, $79.99, and $89.99. Quicken's task is to establish perceived value differences that support the price differences.

Optional-product pricing
The pricing of optional or accessory products along with a main product.

Captive-product pricing
Setting a price for products that must be used along with a main product, such as blades for a razor and film for a camera.

The price steps should take into account cost differences between the products in the line. More importantly, they should account for differences in customer perceptions of the value of different features. ▲For example, Quicken offers an entire line of financial management software, including Basic, Deluxe, Premier, and Home & Business versions priced at $29.99, $59.99, $79.99, and $89.99. Although it costs Quicken no more to produce the CD containing the Premier version than the CD containing the Basic version, many buyers happily pay more to obtain additional Premier features, such as financial-planning and investment-monitoring tools. Quicken's task is to establish perceived value differences that support the price differences.

Optional-Product Pricing

Many companies use **optional-product pricing**—offering to sell optional or accessory products along with their main product. For example, a car buyer may choose to order a GPS navigation system and Bluetooth wireless communication. Refrigerators come with optional ice makers. And when you order a new PC, you can select from a bewildering array of hard drives, docking systems, software options, service plans, and carrying cases.

Pricing these options is a sticky problem. Automobile companies must decide which items to include in the base price and which to offer as options. Until recent years, General Motors' normal pricing strategy was to advertise a stripped-down model at a base price to pull people into showrooms and then to devote most of the showroom space to showing option-loaded cars at higher prices. The economy model was stripped of so many comforts and conveniences that most buyers rejected it. Then, GM and other U.S. automakers followed the examples of the Japanese and German companies and included in the sticker price many useful items previously sold only as options. Thus, most advertised prices today represent well-equipped cars.

Captive-Product Pricing

Companies that make products that must be used along with a main product are using **captive-product pricing**. Examples of captive products are razor blade cartridges, video games, and printer cartridges. Producers of the main products (razors, video game consoles, and printers) often price them low and set high markups on the supplies. For example, Gillette sells low-priced razors but makes money on the replacement cartridges. You can buy a Gillette Fusion razor with a replacement cartridge and storage case for under $12. But once you've bought the razor, you're committed to buying replacement cartridges at $24.95 an eight-pack. Companies that use captive-product pricing must be careful—consumers trapped into buying expensive supplies may come to resent the brand that ensnared them.

● TABLE | 11.1   Product Mix Pricing Strategies

Strategy	Description
Product line pricing	Setting prices across an entire product line
Optional-product pricing	Pricing optional or accessory products sold with the main product
Captive-product pricing	Pricing products that must be used with the main product
By-product pricing	Pricing low-value by-products to get rid of them
Product bundle pricing	Pricing bundles of products sold together

▲ Captive-product pricing: At Six Flags, you pay a daily ticket or season charge plus additional fees for food and other in-park features.

In the case of services, this captive-product pricing is called *two-part pricing*. The price of the service is broken into a *fixed fee* plus a *variable usage rate*. ▲ Thus, at Six Flags and other amusement parks, you pay a daily ticket or season pass charge plus additional fees for food and other in-park features. Theaters charge admission and then generate additional revenues from concessions. And cell phone companies charge a flat rate for a basic calling plan, then charge for minutes over what the plan allows. The service firm must decide how much to charge for the basic service and how much for the variable usage. The fixed amount should be low enough to induce usage of the service; profit can be made on the variable fees.

By-Product Pricing

By-product pricing

Setting a price for by-products in order to make the main product's price more competitive.

Producing products and services often generates by-products. If the by-products have no value and if getting rid of them is costly, this will affect the pricing of the main product. Using **by-product pricing**, the company seeks a market for these by-products to help offset the costs of disposing of them and to help make the price of the main product more competitive. The by-products themselves can even turn out to be profitable. For example, papermaker MeadWestvaco has turned what was once considered chemical waste into profit-making products.

> MeadWestvaco created a separate company, Asphalt Innovations, which creates useful chemicals entirely from the by-products of MeadWestvaco's wood-processing activities. In fact, Asphalt Innovations has grown to become the world's biggest supplier of specialty chemicals for the paving industry. Using the salvaged chemicals, paving companies can pave roads at a lower temperature, create longer-lasting roads, and more easily recycle road materials when roads need to be replaced. What's more, salvaging the by-product chemicals eliminates the costs and environmental hazards once associated with disposing of them.[6]

Product Bundle Pricing

Product bundle pricing

Combining several products and offering the bundle at a reduced price.

Using **product bundle pricing**, sellers often combine several of their products and offer the bundle at a reduced price. For example, fast-food restaurants bundle a burger, fries, and a soft drink at a "combo" price. Resorts sell specially priced vacation packages that include airfare, accommodations, meals, and entertainment. And Comcast, Time Warner, and other cable companies bundle cable service, phone service, and high-speed Internet connections at a low combined price. Price bundling can promote the sales of products consumers might not otherwise buy, but the combined price must be low enough to get them to buy the bundle.[7]

> **Author Comment** | Setting the base price for a product is only the start. The company must then adjust the price to adjust for customer and situational differences. When was the last time you paid full suggested retail price for something?

Price-Adjustment Strategies (pp 315–324)

Companies usually adjust their basic prices to account for various customer differences and changing situations. Here we examine the seven price adjustment strategies summarized in ● **Table 11.2**: *discount and allowance pricing, segmented pricing, psychological pricing, promotional pricing, geographical pricing, dynamic pricing,* and *international pricing.*

Discount and Allowance Pricing

Most companies adjust their basic price to reward customers for certain responses, such as early payment of bills, volume purchases, and off-season buying. These price adjustments—called *discounts* and *allowances*—can take many forms.

● TABLE | 11.2   Price Adjustment Strategies

Strategy	Description
Discount and allowance pricing	Reducing prices to reward customer responses such as paying early or promoting the product
Segmented pricing	Adjusting prices to allow for differences in customers, products, or locations
Psychological pricing	Adjusting prices for psychological effect
Promotional pricing	Temporarily reducing prices to increase short-run sales
Geographical pricing	Adjusting prices to account for the geographic location of customers
Dynamic pricing	Adjusting prices continually to meet the characteristics and needs of individual customers and situations
International pricing	Adjusting prices for international markets

Discount
A straight reduction in price on purchases during a stated period of time.

The many forms of **discounts** include a *cash discount*, a price reduction to buyers who pay their bills promptly. A typical example is "2/10, net 30," which means that although payment is due within 30 days, the buyer can deduct 2 percent if the bill is paid within 10 days. A *quantity discount* is a price reduction to buyers who buy large volumes. Such discounts provide an incentive to the customer to buy more from one given seller, rather than from many different sources.

A *functional discount* (also called a *trade discount*) is offered by the seller to trade-channel members who perform certain functions, such as selling, storing, and record keeping. A *seasonal discount* is a price reduction to buyers who buy merchandise or services out of season. For example, lawn and garden equipment manufacturers offer seasonal discounts to retailers during the fall and winter months to encourage early ordering in anticipation of the heavy spring and summer selling seasons. Seasonal discounts allow the seller to keep production steady during an entire year.

Allowance
Promotional money paid by manufacturers to retailers in return for an agreement to feature the manufacturer's products in some way.

Allowances are another type of reduction from the list price. For example, *trade-in allowances* are price reductions given for turning in an old item when buying a new one. Trade-in allowances are most common in the automobile industry but are also given for other durable goods. *Promotional allowances* are payments or price reductions to reward dealers for participating in advertising and sales support programs.

Segmented Pricing

Segmented pricing
Selling a product or service at two or more prices, where the difference in prices is not based on differences in costs.

Companies will often adjust their basic prices to allow for differences in customers, products, and locations. In **segmented pricing**, the company sells a product or service at two or more prices, even though the difference in prices is not based on differences in costs.

Segmented pricing takes several forms. Under *customer-segment* pricing, different customers pay different prices for the same product or service. Museums, for example, may charge a lower admission for students and senior citizens. Under *product-form pricing*, different versions of the product are priced differently but not according to differences in their costs. ▲ For instance, a 1-liter bottle (about 34 ounces) of Evian mineral water may cost $1.59 at your local supermarket. But a 5-ounce aerosol can of Evian Brumisateur Mineral Water Spray sells for a suggested retail price of $11.39 at beauty boutiques and spas. The water is all from the same source in the French Alps and the aerosol packaging costs little more than the plastic bottles. Yet you pay about 5 cents an ounce for one form and $2.28 an ounce for the other.

Using *location pricing*, a company charges different prices for different locations, even though the cost of offering each location is the same. For instance, theaters vary their seat prices because of audience preferences for certain locations and state universities charge higher tuition for out-of-state students. Finally, using *time pricing*, a firm varies its price by the season, the month, the day, and even the hour. Some public utilities vary their prices to commercial users by time of day and weekend versus weekday. Resorts give weekend and seasonal discounts.

▲ Product-form pricing: Evian water in a 1 liter bottle might cost you 5 cents an ounce at your local supermarket, whereas the same water might run $2.28 an ounce when sold in 5-ounce aerosol cans as Evian Brumisateur Mineral Water Spray moisturizer.

Psychological pricing

A pricing approach that considers the psychology of prices and not simply the economics; the price is used to say something about the product.

Segmented pricing goes by many names. Robert Cross, a longtime consultant to the airlines, calls it *revenue management*. According to Cross, the practice ensures that "companies will sell the right product to the right consumer at the right time for the right price." Airlines, hotels, and restaurants call it *yield management* and practice it religiously.

The airlines, for example, routinely set prices hour-by-hour—even minute-by-minute—depending on seat availability, demand, and competitor price changes. Thus, the price you pay for a given seat on a given flight might vary greatly depending not just on class of service, but also on when and where you buy the ticket. Furthermore, the person sitting next to you might have paid half that price or twice as much. If these widely varying prices puzzle or infuriate you, imagine the pricing headaches they give an airline's revenue management team. Continental Airlines launches more than 2,900 flights every day, each with between 10 and 20 prices. As a result, at any given moment, Continental may have nearly 7 million prices in the market.[8]

For segmented pricing to be an effective strategy, certain conditions must exist. The market must be segmentable, and the segments must show different degrees of demand. The costs of segmenting and watching the market cannot exceed the extra revenue obtained from the price difference. Of course, the segmented pricing must also be legal.

Most importantly, segmented prices should reflect real differences in customers' perceived value. Consumers in higher price tiers must feel that they're getting their extra money's worth for the higher prices paid. By the same token, companies must be careful not to treat customers in lower price tiers as second-class citizens. Otherwise, in the long run, the practice will lead to customer resentment and ill will. For example, in recent years, the airlines have incurred the wrath of frustrated customers at both ends of the airplane. Passengers paying full fare for business or first class seats often feel that they are being gouged. At the same time, passengers in lower-priced coach seats feel that they're being ignored or abused. In all, as we discussed in the Ryanair example in the previous chapter, the airlines today face many very difficult pricing issues (see **Real Marketing 11.1**).

Psychological Pricing

Price says something about the product. For example, many consumers use price to judge quality. A $100 bottle of perfume may contain only $3 worth of scent, but some people are willing to pay the $100 because this price indicates something special.

In using **psychological pricing**, sellers consider the psychology of prices and not simply the economics. For example, consumers usually perceive higher-priced products as having higher quality. When they can judge the quality of a product by examining it or by calling on past experience with it, they use price less to judge quality. But when they cannot judge quality because they lack the information or skill, price becomes an important quality signal:

Some years ago, Heublein produced Smirnoff, then America's leading vodka brand. Smirnoff was attacked by another brand, Wolfschmidt, which claimed to have the same quality as Smirnoff but was priced at one dollar less per bottle. To hold on to market share, Heublein considered either lowering Smirnoff's price by one dollar or holding Smirnoff's price but increasing advertising and promotion expenditures. Either strategy would lead to lower profits and it seemed that Heublein faced a no-win situation. At this point, however, Heublein's marketers thought of a third strategy. They *raised* the price of Smirnoff by one dollar! Heublein then introduced a new brand, Relska, to compete with Wolfschmidt. Moreover, it introduced yet another brand, Popov, priced even *lower* than Wolfschmidt. This clever strategy positioned Smirnoff as the elite brand and Wolfschmidt as an ordinary brand, producing a large increase in Heublein's overall profits. The irony is that Heublein's three brands were pretty much the same in taste and manufacturing costs. Heublein knew that a product's price signals its quality. Using price as a signal, Heublein sold roughly the same product at three different quality positions.

Real Marketing 11.1

Airline Pricing:
Balancing The Price-Value Equation

The price-value equation: These days, when it comes to airline pricing, almost nobody's very happy with what they get for what they pay. Back in coach, tempers are flaring over rising prices coupled with cattle-car service or fewer amenities.

It's the same plane going to the same place at exactly the same time. But these days, not all airline passengers are equal. Nor do they all pay equally. No matter where they sit, however, it seems that all passengers have one thing in common: Almost nobody's very happy with what they get for what they pay. At the front of the plane, first class or business class passengers—who might pay as much as three to six times the fare paid by economy class passengers at the back of the plane—are wondering whether it's worth it. At the same time, back in coach, tempers are flaring over rising air travel prices coupled with fewer amenities and less attentive customer service. Something is just not right with the airline price-value equation.

Flying in coach has become an increasingly miserable experience. Legroom is practically nonexistent. Passengers are more tightly packed together. Hot meals have been eliminated. Ditto pillows and blankets. And the next time that guy in front of you leans his seat back directly into your face, few of your fellow passengers are likely to blame you if you feel a brief, murderous urge to strike back.

Most of us have had experiences like those of Doug Fesler, an executive at a medical research group in Washington. He wasn't expecting much in the way of amenities on his American Airlines flight to Honolulu in September. In fact, knowing the airline no longer served free meals, he had packed his own lunch for the second leg of his flight from Dallas to Honolulu. But he said he was shocked at the lack of basic services and the overall condition of the cabin. On that flight, the audio for the movie was broken. The light that indicated when the bathroom was occupied was squirrelly, causing confusion and, in some cases, embarrassingly long waits for passengers in need of the lavatory. And though food was available for purchase, it ran out before the flight attendants could serve the entire cabin, leaving some fellow passengers looking longingly at the snack he had packed.

His return flight was just as disappointing. This time the audio for the movie worked—but only in Spanish—and his seat refused to stay in the upright position. "I was just appalled," said Fesler. "You pay $500 or $600 for a seat, and you expect it to be functional." He said he has considered refusing to fly airlines with such poor service, but added that "if you did that with every airline that made you mad, you'd never get anywhere in this country."

The story is much different in the front of the plane—and it's not just things like the four-course meal (served on china, with real utensils, and with a choice of four wines) that American now serves its business-class passengers on overseas flights and the fact that, yes, a pillow and a blanket still await you. Passengers flying business class on United from Washington Dulles to Frankfurt, for example, are now offered "180-degree lie-flat" seats. The seats transform into 6-foot-4-inch beds and feature larger personal TV screens, iPod adapters, and noise-canceling headphones. American and other airlines are also upgrading their upper-class cabins on international flights with such features as in-flight entertainment and new food options.

What with all these privileges and the impeccable service that comes with them, you'd think that upper-class passengers would be delighted, but that's often not so. Premium passengers *get* more. But, of course, they also *pay* a lot more—some think *too much* more. Many upper-class passengers complain that they're picking up an unfair share of the bill for those who fly cheaply in the back. And they may be right. United says just 8 percent of its customers—the ones paying a premium for first and business class—generate 36 percent of passenger revenue.

But it's the folks back in coach who are grumbling the most. Why, they ask, has the quality of their flying experience degraded so quickly, even as prices have risen? The fact is that airlines, flying so close to full capacity today, have realized that they really don't have to cater to economy passengers—most of whom are booking on price alone and who increasingly have no real airline loyalty. The cost of pampering low-fare passengers would never be worth it in pure bottom-line terms. Thus airlines are increasingly cutting back services in coach or charging passengers for things that used to be free, like meals ($5 for a snack box on United) or drinks ($2 for a 16-fluid-ounce bottle of water on Spirit) or, in the case of Delta, US Airways, Northwest, and Continental, starting to use narrow-body planes more frequently on trans-Atlantic flights, making those long-haul flights more cost-effective, even if it is at the expense of passenger comfort.

It's all simple economics. For example, Northwest claims it saves $2 million a year by cutting pretzels from the economy section of flights. Meanwhile, American estimates that it pares $30 million a year by eliminating free meal service in coach. Last September, in a move that extinguished any hope of hot meals returning to coach, the airline removed the rear galleys—including the oven—from its MD-80 aircraft and replaced them with four seats. That change, says American, will be worth an additional $34 million a year. And wonder why it's almost impossible to get a pillow anymore? Again, it comes down to money. American

Continued on next page ▼

Real Marketing 11.1 Continued ▼

claims that removing pillows saves it almost $1 million a year. It seems like the airlines are always finding new ways to dig deeper into the pockets of coach passengers—say by charging an extra $5 or $10 for reserving an aisle or window seat or $25 for checking a second bag.

The major airlines insist they want to please all their passengers but concede that it all comes down to the bottom line. "The passenger who is buying a ticket from us based on price sensitivity—we want to make sure they have a comfortable flight," says an executive at American. "But the way we chiefly derive a profit from any given flight is the passenger willing to pay the premium."

In the short run, the restructured pricing scheme seems to have helped the airline industry's finances. After losing a combined $35 billion between 2001 and 2005, the U.S. airlines posted profits in 2006 and 2007, even in the face of soaring fuel prices. Still, hauling plane loads of increasingly grumpy passengers can't be good for the airlines in

the long run. With the industry once again headed into turbulent economic skies, it will need all the lift it can get from customer goodwill. Any airline that gets pricing right will surely reap the rewards.

The airlines do acknowledge that while their finances have improved, they must do a better job of managing the price-value equation. "We recognize we have missed some opportunities in the last couple of years to do the right thing for the customer experience," says Mark Mitchell, American's managing director of customer experience, a newly created position. "We have fallen off," he concedes. Mitchell says he was hired to "work on the broken pieces of our airline," including how American handles delays, the boarding process, cabin cleaning, baggage handling, and flight attendant interactions with customers.

More broadly, perhaps it's just a matter of adjusting passenger expectations. Some passengers seem to feel that the airlines should just acknowledge that the flying experience is no longer a glamorous or, at times, even tolerable one—especially back in coach—and that it's something passengers are going to have to accept. Low-cost carriers such as Southwest and JetBlue have long managed to keep costs down while at the same time keeping customers delighted.

"I actually have more respect for Southwest Airlines in this area," says one experienced traveler, referring to that historically no-frills airline. "They've never pretended to have more than they do."

Sources: Adapted from portions of Michelle Higgins, "Aboard Planes, Class Conflict," *New York Times*, November 25, 2007; with information from Jefferson George, "Want an Aisle Window? Get Ready to Pay for It," *McClatchy-Tribune Business News*, April 17, 2008.

Reference prices

Prices that buyers carry in their minds and refer to when they look at a given product.

Another aspect of psychological pricing is **reference prices**—prices that buyers carry in their minds and refer to when looking at a given product. The reference price might be formed by noting current prices, remembering past prices, or assessing the buying situation. Sellers can influence or use these consumers' reference prices when setting price. For example, a company could display its product next to more expensive ones in order to imply that it belongs in the same class. Department stores often sell women's clothing in separate departments differentiated by price: Clothing found in the more expensive department is assumed to be of better quality.

For most purchases, consumers don't have all the skill or information they need to figure out whether they are paying a good price. They don't have the time, ability, or inclination to research different brands or stores, compare prices, and get the best deals. ▲Instead, they may rely on certain cues that signal whether a price is high or low. Interestingly, such pricing cues are often provided by sellers:[9]

It's Saturday morning and you stop by your local supermarket to pick up a few items for tonight's backyard barbeque. Cruising the aisles, you're bombarded with prices. But are they good prices? If you're like most shoppers, you don't really know. So to help you out, retailers themselves give you a host of subtle and not-so-subtle signals telling you whether a given price is relatively high or low. For example, *sales signs* shout out "Sale!" "Reduced" "Price after rebate!" or "Now 2 for only . . .!" *Prices ending in 9* let you know that the product has to be a bargain. Another good clue is *signpost pricing* (also called *loss-leader pricing*)—low prices on products for which you have accurate price knowledge. You probably know a good price on a 12-pack of Coke when you see one, so a low price there suggests that the store's other prices must be low as well. A *price-matching guarantee* also suggests that one store's prices are lower than another's—how else could they make such a promise?

Are such pricing signals really helpful hints, or are they just retailer ploys? These tactics certainly work for the retailer. For example, research shows that the word *sale* beside a price (even without actually varying the price) can increase demand

▲ Psychological pricing: What do the prices marked on this tag suggest about the product and buying solution?

by more than 50 percent. But do these signals really help customers? The answer, often, is yes—careful buyers really can take advantage of such cues to find good buys. And if used properly, retailers can use such tactics to provide useful price information to their customers, building more solid customer relationships. Used improperly, however, they can mislead consumers, tarnishing a brand and damaging customer relationships.

Even small differences in price can signal product differences. Consider a stereo receiver priced at $300 compared to one priced at $299.99. The actual price difference is only 1 cent, but the psychological difference can be much greater. For example, some consumers will see the $299.99 as a price in the $200 range rather than the $300 range. The $299.99 will more likely be seen as a bargain price, whereas the $300 price suggests more quality. Some psychologists argue that each digit has symbolic and visual qualities that should be considered in pricing. Thus, 8 is round and even and creates a soothing effect, whereas 7 is angular and creates a jarring effect.[10]

Promotional Pricing

Promotional pricing

Temporarily pricing products below the list price, and sometimes even below cost, to increase short-run sales.

▲With **promotional pricing**, companies will temporarily price their products below list price and sometimes even below cost to create buying excitement and urgency. Promotional pricing takes several forms. A seller may simply offer *discounts* from normal prices to increase sales and reduce inventories. Sellers also use *special-event pricing* in certain seasons to draw more customers. Thus, linens are promotionally priced every January to attract weary Christmas shoppers back into stores. Manufacturers sometimes offer *cash rebates* to consumers who buy the product from dealers within a specified time; the manufacturer sends the rebate directly to the customer. Rebates have been popular with automakers and producers of durable goods and small appliances, but they are also used with consumer packaged goods. Some manufacturers offer *low-interest financing, longer warranties,* or *free maintenance* to reduce the consumer's "price." This practice has become another favorite of the auto industry.

Promotional pricing, however, can have adverse effects. Used too frequently and copied by competitors, price promotions can create "deal-prone" customers who wait until brands go on sale before buying them. Or, constantly reduced prices can erode a brand's value in the eyes of customers. Marketers sometimes become addicted to promotional pricing, using price promotions as a quick fix instead of sweating through the difficult process of developing effective longer-term strategies for building their brands. The use of promotional pricing can also lead to industry price wars. Such price wars usually play into the hands of only one or a few competitors—those with the most efficient operations. For example, in the face of intense competition with Intel, computer chip maker Advanced Micro Devices (AMD) began to aggressively reduce its prices. Intel retaliated with even lower prices. In the resulting price war, AMD has seen its margins and profits skid against those of its larger rival.[11]

The point is that promotional pricing can be an effective means of generating sales for some companies in certain circumstances. But it can be damaging for other companies or if taken as a steady diet.

Geographical Pricing

A company also must decide how to price its products for customers located in different parts of the country or world. Should the company risk losing the business of

▲ Promotional pricing: Companies offer promotional prices to create buying excitement and urgency.

Geographical pricing

Setting prices for customers located in different parts of the country or world.

more-distant customers by charging them higher prices to cover the higher shipping costs? Or should the company charge all customers the same prices regardless of location? We will look at five **geographical pricing** strategies for the following hypothetical situation:

The Peerless Paper Company is located in Atlanta, Georgia, and sells paper products to customers all over the United States. The cost of freight is high and affects the companies from whom customers buy their paper. Peerless wants to establish a geographical pricing policy. It is trying to determine how to price a $10,000 order to three specific customers: Customer A (Atlanta), Customer B (Bloomington, Indiana), and Customer C (Compton, California).

One option is for Peerless to ask each customer to pay the shipping cost from the Atlanta factory to the customer's location. All three customers would pay the same factory price of $100, with Customer A paying, say, $100 for shipping; Customer B, $150; and Customer C, $250. Called **FOB-origin pricing**, this practice means that the goods are placed *free on board* (hence, *FOB*) a carrier. At that point the title and responsibility pass to the customer, who pays the freight from the factory to the destination. Because each customer picks up its own cost, supporters of FOB pricing feel that this is the fairest way to assess freight charges. The disadvantage, however, is that Peerless will be a high-cost firm to distant customers.

Uniform-delivered pricing is the opposite of FOB pricing. Here, the company charges the same price plus freight to all customers, regardless of their location. The freight charge is set at the average freight cost. Suppose this is $150. Uniform-delivered pricing therefore results in a higher charge to the Atlanta customer (who pays $150 freight instead of $100) and a lower charge to the Compton customer (who pays $150 instead of $250). Although the Atlanta customer would prefer to buy paper from another local paper company that uses FOB-origin pricing, Peerless has a better chance of winning over the California customer. Other advantages of uniform-delivered pricing are that it is fairly easy to administer and it lets the firm advertise its price nationally.

Zone pricing falls between FOB-origin pricing and uniform-delivered pricing. The company sets up two or more zones. All customers within a given zone pay a single total price; the more distant the zone, the higher the price. For example, Peerless might set up an East Zone and charge $100 freight to all customers in this zone, a Midwest Zone in which it charges $150, and a West Zone in which it charges $250. In this way, the customers within a given price zone receive no price advantage from the company. For example, customers in Atlanta and Boston pay the same total price to Peerless. The complaint, however, is that the Atlanta customer is paying part of the Boston customer's freight cost.

Using **basing-point pricing**, the seller selects a given city as a "basing point" and charges all customers the freight cost from that city to the customer location, regardless of the city from which the goods are actually shipped. For example, Peerless might set Chicago as the basing point and charge all customers $100 plus the freight from Chicago to their locations. This means that an Atlanta customer pays the freight cost from Chicago to Atlanta, even though the goods may be shipped from Atlanta. If all sellers used the same basing-point city, delivered prices would be the same for all customers and price competition would be eliminated. Industries such as sugar, cement, steel, and automobiles used basing-point pricing for years, but this method has become less popular today. Some companies set up multiple basing points to create more flexibility: They quote freight charges from the basing-point city nearest to the customer.

Finally, the seller who is anxious to do business with a certain customer or geographical area might use **freight-absorption pricing**. Using this strategy, the seller absorbs all or part of the actual freight charges in order to get the desired business. The seller might reason that if it can get more business, its average costs will fall and more than compensate for its extra freight cost. Freight-absorption pricing is used for market penetration and to hold on to increasingly competitive markets.

FOB-origin pricing

A geographical pricing strategy in which goods are placed free on board a carrier; the customer pays the freight from the factory to the destination.

Uniform-delivered pricing

A geographical pricing strategy in which the company charges the same price plus freight to all customers, regardless of their location.

Zone pricing

A geographical pricing strategy in which the company sets up two or more zones. All customers within a zone pay the same total price; the more distant the zone, the higher the price.

Basing-point pricing

A geographical pricing strategy in which the seller designates some city as a basing point and charges all customers the freight cost from that city to the customer

Freight-absorption pricing

A geographical pricing strategy in which the seller absorbs all or part of the freight charges in order to get the desired business.

Dynamic Pricing

Throughout most of history, prices were set by negotiation between buyers and sellers. *Fixed price* policies—setting one price for all buyers—is a relatively modern idea that arose with the development of large-scale retailing at the end of the nineteenth century. Today, most prices are set this way. However, some companies are now reversing the fixed pricing trend. They are using **dynamic pricing**—adjusting prices continually to meet the characteristics and needs of individual customers and situations.

Dynamic pricing
Adjusting prices continually to meet the characteristics and needs of individual customers and situations.

For example, think about how the Internet has affected pricing. From the mostly fixed pricing practices of the past century, the Web seems now to be taking us back—into a new age of fluid pricing. The flexibility of the Internet allows Web sellers to instantly and constantly adjust prices on a wide range of goods based on demand dynamics. In many cases, this involves regular changes in the prices that Web sellers set for their goods. In others, such as eBay or Priceline, consumers negotiate the final prices they pay. Still other companies customize their offers based on the characteristics and behaviors of specific customers:[12]

▲ Dynamic pricing: Alaska Airlines creates unique prices and advertisements for people as they surf the Web.

It's an offer you can't resist: fly ▲Alaska Airlines to Honolulu for $200 round trip. But what you might not know is that the offer was designed especially for you. Alaska Airlines is introducing a system that creates unique prices and advertisements for people as they surf the Web. The system identifies consumers by their computers, using a small piece of code known as a cookie. It then combines detailed data from several sources to paint a picture of who's sitting on the other side of the screen. When the person clicks on an ad, the system quickly analyzes the data to assess how price-sensitive customers seem to be. Then, in an instant, one customer gets an offer for a flight from Seattle to Portland for $99 and another is quoted $109. Or someone who had visited Alaska Airlines' site frequently but then abruptly stopped visiting might be greeted with the $200 Hawaii offer. "I guarantee you there are a lot of people who will say yes to that," says Marston Gould, director of customer relationship management and online marketing for Alaska Airlines.

Dynamic pricing offers many advantages for marketers. For example, Internet sellers such as Amazon.com can mine their databases to gauge a specific shopper's desires, measure his or her means, instantaneously tailor products to fit that shopper's behavior, and price products accordingly. Catalog retailers such as L.L.Bean or Spiegel can change prices on the fly according to changes in demand or costs, changing prices for specific items on a day-by-day or even hour-by-hour basis.

Many direct marketers monitor inventories, costs, and demand at any given moment and adjust prices instantly. For example, Dell uses dynamic pricing to achieve real-time balancing of supply and demand for computer components. By raising prices on components in short supply and dropping prices for oversupplied items, Dell actually reshapes demand on the go to meet supply conditions.

Buyers also benefit from the Web and dynamic pricing. A wealth of price comparison sites—such as Yahoo! Shopping, Bizrate.com, NexTag.com, Epinions.com, PriceGrabber.com, mySimon.com, and PriceScan.com—offer instant product and price comparisons from thousands of vendors. Epinions.com, for instance, lets shoppers browse by category or search for specific products and brands. It then searches the Web and reports back links to sellers offering the best prices along with customer reviews. In addition to simply finding the best product and the vendor with the best price for that product, customers armed with price information can often negotiate lower prices.

Buyers can also negotiate prices at online auction sites and exchanges. Suddenly the centuries-old art of haggling is back in vogue. Want to sell that antique pickle jar that's been collecting dust for generations? Post it on eBay, the world's biggest online flea market. Want to name your own price for a hotel room or rental car? Visit Priceline.com or another reverse auction site. Want to bid on a ticket to a Coldplay show? Check out Ticketmaster. com, which now offers an online auction service for concert tickets.

Dynamic pricing can also be controversial. Most customers would find it galling to learn that the person in the next seat on that flight from Gainesville to Galveston paid 10 percent less just because he or she happened to call at the right time or buy through the right sales channel. Amazon.com learned this some years ago when it experimented with lowering prices to new customers in order to woo their business. When regular customers learned through Internet chatter that they were paying generally higher prices than first-timers, they protested loudly. An embarrassed Amazon.com halted the experiments.

Dynamic pricing makes sense in many contexts—it adjusts prices according to market forces, and it often works to the benefit of the customer. But marketers need to be careful not to use dynamic pricing to take advantage of certain customer groups, damaging important customer relationships.

International Pricing

Companies that market their products internationally must decide what prices to charge in the different countries in which they operate. In some cases, a company can set a uniform worldwide price. For example, Boeing sells its jetliners at about the same price everywhere, whether in the United States, Europe, or a third-world country. However, most companies adjust their prices to reflect local market conditions and cost considerations.

The price that a company should charge in a specific country depends on many factors, including economic conditions, competitive situations, laws and regulations, and development of the wholesaling and retailing system. Consumer perceptions and preferences also may vary from country to country, calling for different prices. Or the company may have different marketing objectives in various world markets, which require changes in pricing strategy. For example, Samsung might introduce a new product into mature markets in highly developed countries with the goal of quickly gaining mass-market share—this would call for a penetration-pricing strategy. In contrast, it might enter a less-developed market by targeting smaller, less price-sensitive segments; in this case, market-skimming pricing makes sense.

Costs play an important role in setting international prices. Travelers abroad are often surprised to find that goods that are relatively inexpensive at home may carry outrageously higher price tags in other countries. A pair of Levi's selling for $30 in the United States might go for $63 in Tokyo and $88 in Paris. A McDonald's Big Mac selling for a modest $3.50 here might cost $7.50 in Reykjavik, Iceland, and an Oral-B toothbrush selling for $2.49 at home may cost $10 in China. Conversely, a Gucci handbag going for only $140 in Milan, Italy, might fetch $240 in the United States. In some cases, such *price escalation* may result from differences in selling strategies or market conditions. In most instances, however, it is simply a result of the higher costs of selling in another country—the additional costs of product modifications, shipping and insurance, import tariffs and taxes, exchange-rate fluctuations, and physical distribution.

Price has become a key element in the international marketing strategies of companies attempting to enter emerging markets, such as China, India, and Brazil. Consider ▲ Dell's current China strategy:

It seems that every personal computer maker now wants a piece of China, where PC sales grew at a dazzling 21 percent rate last year, compared with just a 2.6 percent U.S. growth rate. By 2013, China will overtake the United States as the world's largest PC market. To gain a stronger foothold in China, Dell is pursuing a penetration pricing strategy. It recently launched a new, low-priced computer designed especially for the still-developing, less-affluent Chinese market. The $340 Dell EC280 uses

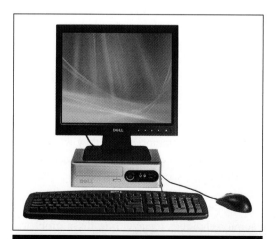

▲ International pricing: Smart pricing plays a key role in Dell's marketing in China and other emerging markets.

only about a quarter of the power of a conventional desktop and has been simplified for first-time computer buyers. "We said to ourselves: 'Let's design something that doesn't have things that people don't use,'" says a Dell international marketing executive. "Those things cost money and add [unneeded] complexity." Smart pricing has helped Dell to increase its share of the Chinese market by almost 30 percent in just the past four years. The PC maker is now adapting the low-cost China PC to Brazil, India, and other emerging markets.[13]

Thus, international pricing presents some special problems and complexities. We discuss international pricing issues in more detail in Chapter 19.

Author Comment | When and how should a company change its price? What if costs rise, putting the squeeze on profits? What if the economy sags and customers become more price-sensitive? Or what if a major competitor raises or drops its prices? As Figure 11.1 suggests, companies face many price-changing options.

Price Changes (pp 324–327)

After developing their pricing structures and strategies, companies often face situations in which they must initiate price changes or respond to price changes by competitors.

Initiating Price Changes

In some cases, the company may find it desirable to initiate either a price cut or a price increase. In both cases, it must anticipate possible buyer and competitor reactions.

Initiating Price Cuts

Several situations may lead a firm to consider cutting its price. One such circumstance is excess capacity. Another is falling demand in the face of strong price competition. In such cases, the firm may aggressively cut prices to boost sales and share. But as the airline, fast-food, automobile, and other industries have learned in recent years, cutting prices in an industry loaded with excess capacity may lead to price wars as competitors try to hold on to market share.

A company may also cut prices in a drive to dominate the market through lower costs. Either the company starts with lower costs than its competitors, or it cuts prices in the hope of gaining market share that will further cut costs through larger volume. Bausch & Lomb used an aggressive low-cost, low-price strategy to become an early leader in the competitive soft contact lens market. Costco used this strategy to become the world's largest warehouse retailer.

Initiating Price Increases

A successful price increase can greatly improve profits. For example, if the company's profit margin is 3 percent of sales, a 1 percent price increase will boost profits by 33 percent if sales volume is unaffected. A major factor in price increases is cost inflation. Rising costs squeeze profit margins and lead companies to pass cost increases along to customers. Another factor leading to price increases is overdemand: When a company cannot supply all that its customers need, it may raise its prices, ration products to customers, or both. Consider today's worldwide oil and gas industry.

When raising prices, the company must avoid being perceived as a price gouger. ▲For example, facing rapidly rising gasoline prices, angry customers are accusing the major oil companies of enriching themselves at the expense of consumers. Customers have long memories, and they will eventually turn away from companies or even whole industries that they perceive as charging excessive prices. In the extreme, claims of price gouging may even bring about increased government regulation.

There are some techniques for avoiding these problems. One is to maintain a sense of fairness surrounding any price increase. Price increases should be supported by company communications telling customers why prices are being raised.

▲ Initiating price increases: Rising crude oil prices and overdemand have led to rapidly rising gasoline prices, resulting in charges that the major oil companies are enriching themselves by gouging customers.

Making low-visibility price moves first is also a good technique: Some examples include dropping discounts, increasing minimum order sizes, and curtailing production of low-margin products. The company sales force should help business customers find ways to economize.

Wherever possible, the company should consider ways to meet higher costs or demand without raising prices. For example, it can consider more cost-effective ways to produce or distribute its products. It can shrink the product or substitute less-expensive ingredients instead of raising the price, as candy bar manufacturers often do. Or it can "unbundle" its market offering, removing features, packaging, or services and separately pricing elements that were formerly part of the offer. For example, to keep fares down, most major U.S. airlines now charge separately for once-complimentary services such as curb-side luggage check-in, checking more than one piece of luggage, and food served on flights.

Buyer Reactions to Price Changes

Customers do not always interpret price changes in a straightforward way. A price *increase*, which would normally lower sales, may have some positive meanings for buyers. For example, what would you think if Rolex *raised* the price of its latest watch model? On the one hand, you might think that the watch is even more exclusive or better made. On the other hand, you might think that Rolex is simply being greedy by charging what the traffic will bear.

Similarly, consumers may view a price *cut* in several ways. For example, what would you think if Rolex were to suddenly cut its prices? You might think that you are getting a better deal on an exclusive product. More likely, however, you'd think that quality had been reduced, and the brand's luxury image might be tarnished.

A brand's price and image are often closely linked. A price change, especially a drop in price, can adversely affect how consumers view the brand. ▲Tiffany found this out when it attempted to broaden its appeal by offering a line of more affordable jewelry:[14]

Tiffany is all about luxury and the cachet of its blue boxes. However, in the late 1990s, the high-end jeweler responded to the "affordable luxuries" craze with a new "Return to Tiffany" line of less expensive silver jewelry. The "Return to Tiffany" silver charm bracelet quickly became a must-have item, as teens jammed Tiffany's hushed stores clamoring for the $110 silver bauble. Sales skyrocketed. But despite this early success, Tiffany's bosses grew worried that the bracelet fad could alienate the firm's older, wealthier, and more conservative clientele. Worse, it could forever damage Tiffany's reputation for luxury. So, in 2002, to chase away the teeny-boppers, the firm began hiking prices on the fast-growing, highly profitable line of cheaper silver jewelry. At the same time, it introduced pricier jewelry collections, renovated its stores, and showed off its craftsmanship by highlighting spectacular gems like a $2.5 million pink diamond ring. However, the jury is still out on whether Tiffany can fully regain its exclusivity. Although high-end jewelry has once again replaced silver as Tiffany's fastest growing business, the company's profit margins and stock price have suffered in recent years. Say's one well-heeled customer: "You used to aspire to be able to buy something at Tiffany, but now it's not that special anymore."

▲ Price changes: A brand's price and image are often closely linked and a change in price can adversely affect how consumers view the brand. Tiffany found this out when it attempted to broaden its appeal by offering a line of more affordable jewelry.

Competitor Reactions to Price Changes

A firm considering a price change must worry about the reactions of its competitors as well as those of its customers. Competitors are most likely to react when the number of firms involved is small, when the product is uniform, and when the buyers are well informed about products and prices.

How can the firm anticipate the likely reactions of its competitors? The problem is complex because, like the customer, the competitor can interpret a company price cut in many ways. It might think the company is trying to grab a larger market share, or that it's doing poorly and trying to boost its sales. Or it might think that the company wants the whole industry to cut prices to increase total demand.

The company must guess each competitor's likely reaction. If all competitors behave alike, this amounts to analyzing only a typical competitor. In contrast, if the competitors do not behave alike—perhaps because of differences in size, market shares, or policies—then separate analyses are necessary. However, if some competitors will match the price change, there is good reason to expect that the rest will also match it.

Responding to Price Changes

Here we reverse the question and ask how a firm should respond to a price change by a competitor. The firm needs to consider several issues: Why did the competitor change the price? Is the price change temporary or permanent? What will happen to the company's market share and profits if it does not respond? Are other competitors going to respond? Besides these issues, the company must also consider its own situation and strategy and possible customer reactions to price changes.

🖢 **Figure 11.1** shows the ways a company might assess and respond to a competitor's price cut. Suppose the company learns that a competitor has cut its price and decides that this price cut is likely to harm company sales and profits. It might simply decide to hold its current price and profit margin. The company might believe that it will not lose too much market share, or that it would lose too much profit if it reduced its own price. Or it might decide that it should wait and respond when it has more information on the effects of the competitor's price change. However, waiting too long to act might let the competitor get stronger and more confident as its sales increase.

If the company decides that effective action can and should be taken, it might make any of four responses. First, it could *reduce its price* to match the competitor's price. It may decide that the market is price sensitive and that it would lose too much market share to the lower-priced competitor. Cutting the price will reduce the company's profits in the short run. Some companies might also reduce their product quality, services, and marketing communications to retain profit margins, but this will ultimately hurt long-run market share. The company should try to maintain its quality as it cuts prices.

Alternatively, the company might maintain its price but *raise the perceived value* of its offer. It could improve its communications, stressing the relative value of its product

🖢 FIGURE | 11.1
Assessing and Responding to
Competitor Price Changes

When a competitor cuts prices, a company's first reaction may be to drop its prices as well. But that is often the wrong response. Instead, the firm may want to emphasize the "value" side of the price-value equation.

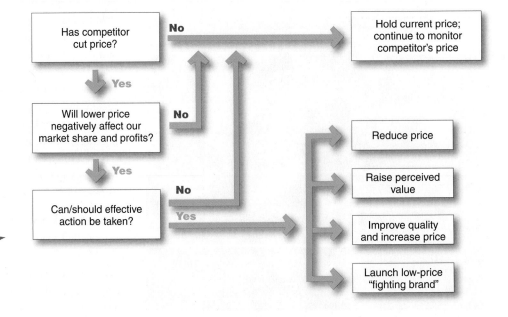

▲ Fighting brands: P&G offers popular budget-priced Basic versions of several of its major brands. For example, Bounty Basic is "practical, not pricey."

over that of the lower-price competitor. The firm may find it cheaper to maintain price and spend money to improve its perceived value than to cut price and operate at a lower margin. Or, the company might *improve quality and increase price*, moving its brand into a higher price-value position. The higher quality creates greater customer value, which justifies the higher price. In turn, the higher price preserves the company's higher margins.

Finally, the company might *launch a low-price "fighting brand"*—adding a lower-price item to the line or creating a separate lower-price brand. This is necessary if the particular market segment being lost is price sensitive and will not respond to arguments of higher quality. Thus, to counter store brands and other low-price entrants, Procter & Gamble turned a number of its brands into fighting brands. Luvs disposable diapers give parents "premium leakage protection for less than pricier brands." ▲ And P&G offers popular budget-priced Basic versions of several of its major brands. For example, Charmin Basic is "the quality toilet tissue at a price you'll love." And Bounty Basic is "practical, not pricey." It offers "great strength at a great price—the paper towel that can take care of business without costing a bundle." In all, the Bounty brand claims an astounding 42.5 percent share of the paper towel market, and Bounty Basic has accounted for much of the brand's recent growth.[15]

> **Author Comment** | Pricing decisions are often constrained by social and legal issues. For example, think about the oil industry. Are rapidly rising gas prices justified? Or are the oil companies unfairly lining their pockets by gouging consumers who have few alternatives? Should the government step in?

Public Policy and Pricing (pp 327–330)

Price competition is a core element of our free-market economy. In setting prices, companies usually are not free to charge whatever prices they wish. Many federal, state, and even local laws govern the rules of fair play in pricing. In addition, companies must consider broader societal pricing concerns (see **Real Marketing 11.2**). The most important pieces of legislation affecting pricing are the Sherman, Clayton, and Robinson-Patman acts, initially adopted to curb the formation of monopolies and to regulate business practices that might unfairly restrain trade. Because these federal statutes can be applied only to interstate commerce, some states have adopted similar provisions for companies that operate locally.

Figure 11.2 shows the major public policy issues in pricing. These include potentially damaging pricing practices within a given level of the channel (price-fixing and predatory pricing) and across levels of the channel (retail price maintenance, discriminatory pricing, and deceptive pricing).[16]

> Major public policy issues in pricing take place at two levels: Pricing practices within a given channel level...

> ...and pricing practices across channel levels.

FIGURE | 11.2
Public Policy Issues in Pricing

Producer A
↕
Price-fixing
Predatory pricing
↕
Producer B

Retail price maintenance
Discriminatory pricing

Retailer 1
↕
Price-fixing
Predatory pricing
↕
Retailer 2

Deceptive pricing

Consumers

Deceptive pricing

Real Marketing 11.2

GlaxoSmithKline: Pricing for More Than Sales and Profits

Most consumers appreciate the steady stream of beneficial drugs produced by pharmaceutical companies like GlaxoSmithKline. However, with the prices of many of the most important drugs skyrocketing, others protest that the industry's huge success may be coming at their own expense—literally.

The U.S. pharmaceutical industry has historically been one of the nation's most profitable industries. Annual drug industry revenues have grown 33 percent in just the past five years, a growth rate that few industries can match. As the world's second-largest pharmaceuticals company, GlaxoSmithKline (GSK) has played a large role in the industry's success. It produces a medicine cabinet full of well-known prescription drugs that combat infections, depression, skin conditions, asthma, heart and circulatory disease, and cancer. It also makes dozens of familiar over-the-counter remedies, from Contac, Nicorette, Aquafresh, and Sensodyne to Tagamet and Tums.

GlaxoSmithKline is doing very well in a high-performing industry. Around the world, more than 1,100 prescriptions are written for GSK products every minute. In most situations, we applaud companies for strong performance. However, when it comes to pharmaceutical firms, critics claim, healthy sales and profits may not be so healthy for consumers. Learning that companies like GlaxoSmithKline are reaping big profits leaves a bad taste in the mouths of many consumers. It's like learning that the oil companies are profiting as gas prices soar. Although most consumers appreciate the steady stream

of beneficial drugs produced by pharmaceutical companies, they sense that the industry's huge success may be coming at their own expense—literally.

Americans spend more than $230 billion a year on prescription medications, nearly half of worldwide spending, and this spending is expected to exceed $515 billion by 2017. Prescription prices have risen rapidly over the years and healthcare costs continue to jump. Last year, prices of the 50 top-selling prescription drugs in the United States surged almost 8 percent, nearly twice the nation's annual inflation rate. High drug prices have sent many consumers, especially those with limited budgets

and fixed incomes, to Mexico or Canada in search of cheaper alternatives. Says one senior after a visit to Mexico, "If we couldn't get cheap meds, I wouldn't live."

The critics claim that competitive forces don't operate well in the pharmaceutical market, allowing GSK and other companies to charge excessive prices. Unlike purchases of other consumer products, drug purchases cannot be postponed. And consumers don't usually shop for the best deals on medicines—they simply take what the doctor orders. Because physicians who write the prescriptions don't pay for the medicines they recommend, they have little incentive to be price conscious. Finally, because of patents and FDA

Pricing Within Channel Levels

Federal legislation on *price-fixing* states that sellers must set prices without talking to competitors. Otherwise, price collusion is suspected. Price-fixing is illegal per se—that is, the government does not accept any excuses for price-fixing. Companies found guilty of such practices can receive heavy fines.

Recently, governments at the state and national levels have been aggressively enforcing price-fixing regulations in industries ranging from gasoline, insurance, and concrete to credit cards, CDs, and computer chips. For example, the United States, Canada, and the European Union are investigating charges by major retailers that candy makers such as Hershey, Nestlé, Mars, Kraft, and Cadbury colluded with one another to raise candy prices higher than justified by recent increases in the price of raw materials. If the companies are found guilty, they could face fines up to 10 percent of their annual profits.[17]

Sellers are also prohibited from using *predatory pricing*—selling below cost with the intention of punishing a competitor or gaining higher long-run profits by putting competitors out

approvals, few competing brands exist to force lower prices, and existing brands don't go on sale.

The critics claim that these market factors leave pharmaceutical companies free to practice monopoly pricing resulting in unfair practices and price gouging. To add insult to injury, the critics say, drug companies pour more than $5 billion a year into direct-to-consumer advertising and another $16 billion into sampling. These marketing efforts dictate higher prices at the same time that they build demand for more expensive remedies.

As a pharmaceutical industry leader, GlaxoSmithKline has borne its share of the criticism. For example, as the largest producer of AIDS-fighting antiretroviral drugs, GSK has been accused of pricing its drugs out of the reach of the poor people who need them the most. And the company recently settled claims by the U.S. Department of Justice and 40 states alleging that it had inflated the wholesale prices of drugs used by cancer patients and others. Thus, the severest critics say, GSK may be profiting unfairly—or even at the expense of human life.

But there's another side to the drug-pricing issue. Industry proponents point out that, over the years, GSK has developed a steady stream of medicines that transform people's lives. Developing such new drugs is a risky and expensive endeavor, involving legions of scientists, expensive technology, and years of effort with no certainty of success. The pharmaceutical industry invests nearly $50 billion a year in R&D—GSK alone invested $7 billion last year. GSK now has 157 vaccines or other drug projects under development. On average, each new drug takes 12 to 15 years to develop at a

cost of close to $990 million. Even then, 70 percent of new drugs never generate enough revenue to recover the cost of development. Although the prices of prescription drugs seem high, they're needed to fund the development of important future drugs.

A recent GlaxoSmithKline ad notes that it took 15 years to complete all the tests and to find the exact right compound for a new heart medicine, at a cost of more than the price of a space shuttle mission. Profits from the heart drug will help to fund critical research on diseases such as multiple sclerosis and Alzheimer's. The ad concludes: "Inventing new medicines isn't easy, but it's worth it. . . . Today's medicines finance tomorrow's miracles."

What about all that expensive prescription drug advertising? The industry argues that the ads have considerable information value—that they help educate people about treatments and encourage them to get help for conditions of which they might not otherwise have been aware.

And so the controversy continues. As drug prices climb, GSK and the industry are facing pressures from the federal government, insurance companies, managed-care providers, and advocacy groups to exercise restraint in setting prices. Rather than waiting for tougher legislation on prices—or simply because it's the

right thing to do—GSK has undertaken several initiatives to make drugs available to those who need but can't afford them. For some years now, it has priced its HIV/AIDS and malaria medicines at cost to customers and not-for-profit organizations in developing countries. And the company recently launched tiered-pricing experiments in the developing world, selling its medicines to patients at different prices linked to their ability to pay. In the United States and other developed countries, GSK sponsors patient assistance programs and discount cards that provide prescription medicines to low-income, uninsured patients free or at minimal cost. And GSK regularly donates free medicines in response to disaster relief efforts around the globe.

The pharmaceutical pricing controversy will no doubt continue. For GlaxoSmithKline, it's more than a matter of sales and profits. In setting prices, short-term financial goals must be tempered by broader societal considerations. GSK's heartfelt mission is "to improve the quality of human life by enabling people to do more, feel better, and live longer." Accomplishing this mission won't come cheap. Most consumers understand that one way or another they'll have to pay the price. All they really ask is that they be treated fairly in the process.

Sources: Heather Won Tesoriero, "Drug Prices Surged Despite Criticisms on Campaign Trail," *Wall Street Journal*, February 21, 2008, p. B1; Rich Tomaselli, "Pharma Biz Cops to $5 Billion Drug Problem," *Advertising Age*, January 28, 2008, p. 3; Joel Millman, "Not Your Generic Smugglers—American Seniors Flock to Border Town for Cheap Prescriptions," *Wall Street Journal*, March 20, 2003, p. D3; "GSK to Settle Pricing Claims," *News & Observer*, August 11, 2006, p. 2D; "GSK to Cut Prices of HIV Medicines," *McClatchy-Tribune Business News*, February 21, 2008; Andrew Jack, "GSK Varies Prices to Raise Sales," *Financial Times*, March 17, 2008, p. 18; Mark Dolliver, "The Consumer: Seeing Good Side Effects to Drug Ads," *Adweek*, April 7–April 14, 2008, p. 42; and information from www.gsk.com, accessed November 2008.

of business. This protects small sellers from larger ones who might sell items below cost temporarily or in a specific locale to drive them out of business. The biggest problem is determining just what constitutes predatory pricing behavior. Selling below cost to unload excess inventory is not considered predatory; selling below cost to drive out competitors is. Thus, the same action may or may not be predatory depending on intent, and intent can be very difficult to determine or prove.

In recent years, several large and powerful companies have been accused of predatory pricing. For example, Wal-Mart has been sued by dozens of small competitors charging that it lowered prices in their specific geographic areas or on specific products—such as gasoline and generic drugs—to drive them out of business. In fact, the state of New York passed a bill requiring companies to price gas at or above 98 percent of cost to "address the more extreme cases of predatory pricing by big-box stores" such as Wal-Mart. Yet, in North Dakota, the same gas pricing proposal was rejected because state representatives did not view the practice as predatory pricing. And in Colorado, a bill was passed that allowed below-cost fuel.[18]

Pricing Across Channel Levels

The Robinson-Patman Act seeks to prevent unfair *price discrimination* by ensuring that sellers offer the same price terms to customers at a given level of trade. For example, every retailer is entitled to the same price terms from a given manufacturer, whether the retailer is Sears or your local bicycle shop. However, price discrimination is allowed if the seller can prove that its costs are different when selling to different retailers—for example, that it costs less per unit to sell a large volume of bicycles to Sears than to sell a few bicycles to the local dealer.

The seller can also discriminate in its pricing if the seller manufactures different qualities of the same product for different retailers. The seller has to prove that these differences are proportional. Price differentials may also be used to "match competition" in "good faith," provided the price discrimination is temporary, localized, and defensive rather than offensive.

Laws also prohibit *retail (or resale) price maintenance*—a manufacturer cannot require dealers to charge a specified retail price for its product. Although the seller can propose a manufacturer's *suggested* retail price to dealers, it cannot refuse to sell to a dealer who takes independent pricing action, nor can it punish the dealer by shipping late or denying advertising allowances. For example, the Florida attorney general's office investigated Nike for allegedly fixing the retail price of its shoes and clothing. It was concerned that Nike might be withholding items from retailers who were not selling its most expensive shoes at prices the company considered suitable.

Deceptive pricing occurs when a seller states prices or price savings that mislead consumers or are not actually available to consumers. This might involve bogus reference or comparison prices, as when a retailer sets artificially high "regular" prices then announces "sale" prices close to its previous everyday prices. For example, Overstock.com recently came under scrutiny for inaccurately listing manufacturer's suggested retail prices, often quoting them higher than the actual price. Such comparison pricing is widespread.

Comparison pricing claims are legal if they are truthful. However, the FTC's *Guides Against Deceptive Pricing* warns sellers not to advertise a price reduction unless it is a saving from the usual retail price, not to advertise "factory" or "wholesale" prices unless such prices are what they are claimed to be, and not to advertise comparable value prices on imperfect goods.[19]

Other deceptive pricing issues include *scanner fraud* and price confusion. ▲The widespread use of scanner-based computer checkouts has led to increasing complaints of retailers overcharging their customers. Most of these overcharges result from poor management—from a failure to enter current or sale prices into the system. Other cases, however, involve intentional overcharges. *Price confusion* results when firms employ pricing methods that make it difficult for consumers to understand just what price they are really paying. For example, consumers are sometimes misled regarding the real price of a home mortgage or car leasing agreement. In other cases, important pricing details may be buried in the "fine print."

Many federal and state statutes regulate against deceptive pricing practices. For example, the Automobile Information Disclosure Act requires automakers to attach a statement to new-car windows stating the manufacturer's suggested retail price, the prices of optional equipment, and the dealer's transportation charges. However, reputable sellers go beyond what is required by law. Treating customers fairly and making certain that they fully understand prices and pricing terms is an important part of building strong and lasting customer relationships.

▲ Deceptive pricing concerns: The widespread use of checkout scanners has led to increasing complaints of retailers overcharging their customers.

REVIEWING Objectives AND KEY Terms

Pricing decisions are subject to an incredibly complex array of environmental and competitive forces. A company sets not a single price, but rather a *pricing structure* that covers different items in its line. This pricing structure changes over time as products move through their life cycles. The company adjusts product prices to reflect changes in costs and demand and to account for variations in buyers and situations. As the competitive environment changes, the company considers when to initiate price changes and when to respond to them.

OBJECTIVE 1 **Describe the major strategies for pricing imitative and new products.** (pp 312–313)

Pricing is a dynamic process. Companies design a *pricing structure* that covers all their products. They change this structure over time and adjust it to account for different customers and situations. Pricing strategies usually change as a product passes through its life cycle. The company can decide on one of several price-quality strategies for introducing an imitative product, including premium pricing, economy pricing, good value, or overcharging. In pricing innovative new products, it can use *market-skimming pricing* by initially setting high prices to "skim" the maximum amount of revenue from various segments of the market. Or it can use *market-penetrating pricing* by setting a low initial price to penetrate the market deeply and win a large market share.

OBJECTIVE 2 **Explain how companies find a set of prices that maximizes the profits from the total product mix.** (pp 313–315)

When the product is part of a product mix, the firm searches for a set of prices that will maximize the profits from the total mix. In *product line pricing*, the company decides on price steps for the entire set of products it offers. In addition, the company must set prices for *optional products* (optional or accessory products included with the main product), *captive products* (products that are required for use of the main product), *by-products* (waste or residual products produced when making the main product), and *product bundles* (combinations of products at a reduced price).

OBJECTIVE 3 **Discuss how companies adjust their prices to take into account different types of customers and situations.** (pp 315–324)

Companies apply a variety of *price adjustment strategies* to account for differences in consumer segments and situations. One is *discount and allowance pricing*, whereby the company establishes cash, quantity, functional, or seasonal discounts, or varying types of allowances. A second strategy is *segmented pricing*, where the company sells a product at two or more prices to accommodate different customers, product forms, locations, or times. Sometimes companies consider more than economics in their pricing decisions, using *psychological pricing* to better communicate a product's intended position. In *promotional pricing*, a company offers discounts or temporarily sells a product below list price as a special event, sometimes even selling below cost as a loss leader. Another approach is *geographical pricing*, whereby the company decides how to price to distant customers, choosing from such alternatives as FOB-origin pricing pricing, uniform-delivered pricing, zone pricing, basing-point pricing, and freight-absorption pricing. Finally, *international pricing* means that the company adjusts its price to meet different conditions and expectations in different world markets.

OBJECTIVE 4 **Discuss the key issues related to initiating and responding to price changes.** (pp 324–330)

When a firm considers initiating a *price change*, it must consider customers' and competitors' reactions. There are different implications to *initiating price cuts* and *initiating price increases*. Buyer reactions to price changes are influenced by the meaning customers see in the price change. Competitors' reactions flow from a set reaction policy or a fresh analysis of each situation.

There are also many factors to consider in responding to a competitor's price changes. The company that faces a price change initiated by a competitor must try to understand the competitor's intent as well as the likely duration and impact of the change. If a swift reaction is desirable, the firm should preplan its reactions to different possible price actions by competitors. When facing a competitor's price change, the company might sit tight, reduce its own price, raise perceived quality, improve quality and raise price, or launch a fighting brand.

KEY Terms

OBJECTIVE 1

Market-skimming pricing (p 312)
Market-penetration pricing (p 313)

OBJECTIVE 2

Product line pricing (p 313)
Optional-product pricing (p 314)
Captive-product pricing (p 314)

By-product pricing (p 315)
Product bundle pricing (p 315)

OBJECTIVE 3

Discount (p 316)
Allowance (p 316)
Segmented pricing (p 316)
Psychological pricing (p 317)
Reference prices (p 319)

Promotional pricing (p 320)
Geographic pricing (p 321)
FOB-origin pricing (p 321)
Uniform-delivered pricing (p 321)
Zone pricing (p 321)
Basing-point pricing (p 321)
Freight-absorption pricing (p 321)
Dynamic pricing (p 322)

DISCUSSING & APPLYING THE Concepts

Discussing the Concepts

1. Explain market-skimming and market-penetration pricing strategies. Why would a marketer of innovative high-tech products choose market-skimming pricing rather than market-penetration pricing when launching a new product? (AACSB: Communication; Reflective Thinking)

2. Name and briefly describe the five product mix pricing decisions. (AACSB: Communication)

3. Retailers often use psychological pricing as a price-adjustment strategy. Explain this pricing strategy. How do reference prices affect psychological pricing decisions? (AACSB: Communication; Reflective Thinking)

4. Compare and contrast the geographic pricing strategies companies use for customers located in different parts of the country or world. Which strategy is best? (AACSB: Communication; Reflective Thinking)

5. What factors influence the price a company charges in different countries? (AACSB: Communication)

6. Why would a company consider cutting its price? (AACSB: Communication)

Applying the Concepts

1. Identify three price-comparison shopping Web sites and shop for an MP3 player of your choice. Compare the price ranges given at these three Web sites. (AACSB: Communication; Use of IT)

2. Convert US $1.00 to the currencies of five other countries (you can do this at www.xe.com/ucc/). What implications do currency exchange rates hold for setting prices in other countries? (AACSB: Communication; Use of IT; Reflective Thinking)

3. You are an owner of a small independent chain of coffeehouses competing head-to-head with Starbucks. The retail price your customers pay for coffee is exactly the same as at Starbucks. The wholesale price you pay for roasted coffee beans has increased by 25 percent. You know that you cannot absorb this increase and that you must pass it on to your customers. However, you are concerned about the consequences of an open price increase. Discuss three alternative price-increase strategies that address these concerns. (AACSB: Communication; Reflective Thinking)

FOCUS ON Technology

Most high-tech products are introduced at a high price, and consumers know that the price will come down eventually. However, Apple slashed $200 off the price of its 8GB iPhone to $399 just two months after introducing the product in 2007. Apple's CEO Steve Jobs apologized to customers and said "this is life in the technology lane." To pacify customers who purchased the $599 iPhone, Apple gave them $100 in Apple store credit. Just one year later, the new iPhone 3G, priced at $199, was launched and was touted as twice as much for half the price.

1. Why did Apple reduce the price of the iPhone so soon? Was it a smart move? (AACSB: Communication; Reflective Thinking)

2. Give examples of other recent high-tech products that have come down in price over a relatively short period of time. (AACSB: Communication; Reflective Thinking)

FOCUS ON Ethics

Businesses often charge different prices to different customers. For example, movie theaters charge less to students and senior citizens, and prices vary across times of the day. Women are charged more for dry cleaning and haircuts. Business flyers pay more than leisure travelers. And that person sitting next to you on the airplane may have paid more or less than you did—the same goes for hotel rooms. Consumers with arthritis pay more per milligram of pain relief when they buy the Tylenol Arthritis product than when they buy regular Tylenol, even though the active ingredient, acetaminophen, and dosage over an 8-hour period are identical. Technology offers marketers the ability to price-discriminate in various ways. For example, in 2000, Coca-Cola experimented with vending machines that raised prices at higher outdoor temperatures.

Electronic shelf labels allow retailers to change prices based on supply and demand. Moreover, the Internet provides the capability for businesses to charge different prices on their Web sites to different customers of the same product.

1. Is it fair for businesses to charge different prices to different customers? (AACSB: Communication; Ethical Reasoning; Reflective Thinking)

2. Go to www.answers.com/topic/price-discrimination?cat=biz-fin and research the "three degrees of price discrimination." Does this discussion impact your opinion stated in question 1 regarding the fairness of this practice? Explain. (AACSB: Communication; Ethical Reasoning; Reflective Thinking)

MARKETING BY THE Numbers

Have you noticed that you're getting fewer chips in a bag of Lay's potato chips? Or less ice cream in a tub of Breyer's ice cream? Well, that's because you are. Frito-Lay cut the number of chips in bags and some 12-ounce bags are now 10 ounces. And the traditional half-gallon tub (that is, two quarts) of Breyer's ice cream is now 1.75 quarts and soon to be 1.5 quarts. All for the same price! Several consumer-packaged goods manufacturers are using this tactic instead of raising prices in the face of rising costs. Normally, manufacturers would just raise prices, but right now consumers are very price sensitive.

1. Because of rising costs, Frito-Lay's contribution margin has decreased to 30 percent. Refer to Appendix 2, Marketing by the Numbers, and calculate the contribution per ounce Frito-Lay realizes if it sells a 12-ounce bag of chips to resellers for $3.00 per bag. What is the contribution per ounce if Frito-Lay reduces the package size to 10 ounces but does not change the price? (AACSB: Communication; Analytical Reasoning)

2. What price per 12-ounce bag would Frito-Lay have to charge in order to realize the same contribution per ounce as reducing the package size without changing price? (AACSB: Communication; Analytical Reasoning)

VIDEO Case

General Electric

Several years ago, GE found its appliance business in decline. Prices were dropping and GE's brands stood largely undifferentiated from others on the market. In response, GE applied its considerable marketing muscle to revamp, rebrand, and reprice its entire appliances line.

Through market research, GE learned that even though appliance prices were dropping overall, a segment of customers was willing to pay considerably higher prices for better performance, innovative features, and a distinctive look. To deliver on these factors, the GE Monogram and GE Profile lines received a full makeover. As a result, the average retail price paid for GE appliance products increased more than 15 percent. At the same time, GE's appliances business delivered five years of double-digit earnings growth.

After viewing the video featuring GE, answer the following questions about pricing strategies:

1. Which pricing approach and pricing mix strategy does GE follow with its appliance lines? Support your response.

2. In order for GE to raise the price of its Monogram and Profile lines, what adjustments did it have to make to the other marketing mix variables?

3. How did the new positioning strategies for the Monogram and Profile lines affect pricing decisions for the standard GE line?

COMPANY Case

Payless ShoeSource: Paying Less for Fashion

When you think of New York's Fifth Avenue, what retailers come to mind? Tiffany? Gucci? Armani? One name that probably *doesn't* come to mind is Payless. But for the past few years, Payless ShoeSource has been operating one of its low-priced shoe stores on this avenue of luxury retailing. In fact, Payless is now well on its way to placing stores in more than 100 higher-end malls around the country.

Although the discount shoe peddler still focuses on selling inexpensive shoes to the masses, Payless is now moving upscale. It's on a mission to "democratize fashion"—to make truly fashionable products more accessible by applying its cost-effective model to a product portfolio infused with well-known brand labels and some of the hottest high-end designers in the business. Sound like a hair-brained scheme? Well, you might change your mind after hearing the whole story.

Founded in 1956 in Topeka, Kansas, Payless grew rapidly based on what was then a revolutionary idea: selling shoes in a self-service environment. Fifty years later, Payless had become the largest shoe retailer in the Western Hemisphere, with over 4,500 stores in all 50 states and throughout the Americas. Targeting budget-minded families, Payless was serving up more than 150 million pairs of shoes each year, roughly 1 in every 10 pairs of shoes purchased in America.

However, although all seemed rosy for the choose-it-yourself shoe store, by 2005, Payless was losing market share and closing stores. The retail landscape had changed, and giant discount one-stop shops like Wal-Mart, Target, and Kohl's had become the vendors of choice for budget conscious shoppers buying shoes. Said one industry insider, "You can no longer produce the same boring shoes year after year and hope that price alone will get customers to your door." With thrift as its only positioning point, Payless had lost its edge.

NEW IMAGE, HIGHER PRICES

So in June of 2005, Payless made its first move to turn things around. It hired a new CEO, Matt Rubel. Rubel knew that to regain its market leadership, Payless would have to design shoes that *Sex in the City's* Carrie Bradshaw would drool over but at prices that Roseanne could afford. It had to change its image from the dusty dungeon of cheap footwear into the fun, hip merchant of fashion. "We have the ability to make shoes at the most affordable prices anywhere in the world, and we want to marry that with the greatest creativity," Rubel said in a statement reflecting the company's new strategy.

Rubel wasted no time in making big changes. To reflect the new image and communicate change to consumers, Payless redesigned its logo for the first time in 20 years. It then launched new "Fashion Lab" and "Hot Zone" store formats. Both were a drastic improvement, making the stores more open, light, and airy, with a more satisfying consumer experience built around style and design rather than price. Of the new store atmosphere, Rubel said, "It makes the $12 shoe look like a $20 shoe." Rubel hopes that the new formats will not only attract more customers, but that customers will be willing to pay a little bit more than they have in the past. All new Payless stores now have one of the two new formats and old stores are being progressively remodeled.

A FASHION REVOLUTION

Beyond these changes in presentation, Rubel focused on the ultimate product. He implemented a "House of Brands" strategy, shifting the Payless product line from one comprised almost entirely of store brands to one dominated by well-known national brands. Payless now sells shoes under numerous brand names that it either owns or licenses, including Airwalk, Champion, Spalding, Dexter, Shaquille O'Neal-endorsed Dunkman, and various Disney brands. Rubel also acquired the Stride Rite chain and all its associated brands. To organize the new corporate structure and keep track of all the brands, he created a holding company (Collective Brands) as an umbrella over Payless, Stride Rite, and all the licensing activities for the company's brands.

To develop products that would resonate better with consumers, Payless stepped up its emphasis on fashion. The Payless Design Team, an in-house design group, dedicated itself to developing original footwear and accessory designs to keep new styles on target with changing fashion trends. Top designers from Kenneth Cole and Michael Kors were hired as full-time employees to head the new team.

But in perhaps the biggest move to raise the caché of the brand, Rubel started what it calls "Designer Collections." Aiming for the highest levels of haute couture, Payless has forged relationships with four top New York-based designers—Laura Poretzky, Lela Rose, Stacey Bendet, and Patricia Field. The four are designing everything from pumps to boots to handbags for Payless under the brands Abaete, Lela Rose, alice + olivia, and Patricia Field.

To support this design effort and the new Fashion Lab store format, Payless has done something really out of character. After signing its first designer, Laura Poretzky, Payless took its designs to the runway of New York's Fashion Week, the invitation-only event where designers debut fall fashions for the industry. In another first, Payless began running full-page ads in *Elle*, *Vogue*, and *W*, featuring the tagline, "Look Again."

Can Payless's luxury-meets-low-price strategy work? Or will this go down as a disaster of two drastically different worlds that collided, crashed, and burned? "There's nothing cool about shopping at Payless," says skeptic Marian Salzman, a trends forecaster at a major ad firm. "It gets the cash-strapped working girl." But Rubel refutes this view, quickly pointing out that Payless shoppers have median household incomes that are higher than those of both Wal-Mart and Target. "All we've done is bring Payless into the twenty-first century. We're . . . speaking with greater clarity to who our customer already is."

Maxine Clark, former president of Payless and now CEO of Build-A-Bear Workshop, also recognizes the potential of the new strategy. "The customer who wants to buy Prada will not come to Payless. But this will energize the old customers who they lost and attract new ones." Mardi Larson, head of public relations for Payless, claims that the trendy new image is perfect for existing customers. "We target the 24-year-old demographic, because women in their 40s who shop for their family are nostalgic about that time in their lives, while [at the same time] teenagers aspire to that age group."

But what about that potential new customer? Does this risky venture into high fashion stand a chance of appealing to those who have never crossed the threshold of a Payless store? Rubel admits going after new customers. The "cheap chic" approach is attempting to lure 20-to-30-year-old women who are looking for something trendy. Given that such fashion-conscious females buy 50 percent more shoes than most current Payless customers, going after new customers make sense.

Perhaps Lela Rose's experience in 2007 best illustrates why Payless might just succeed in attracting this previously out-of-reach customer:

> When actresses Sophia Bush (*One Tree Hill*) and Brittany Snow (*Hairspray*) landed backstage in Lela Rose's showroom at New York Fashion Week, they swooned over the designer's new shoe collection that was about to debut on the runway. Rose, best known for $1,500 frocks, happily handed pairs of navy peep-toe pumps and polka-dot round-toe pumps over to the young celebs, who would soon be flaunting them on the sidelines of the catwalk. "Did they know they were Payless shoes?" says Rose, who's now designing her fifth exclusive line for the discounter. "Absolutely. They didn't care. They looked cute to them and that's all that mattered."

Additionally, Payless is not the first to try this new direction. In fact, co-branded designer lines for retailers date back decades. But in recent years, the trend is proliferating. Karl Lagerfeld has designed for Britain's H&M, Vera Wang has teamed up with Kohl's, Ralph Lauren has put store brands on JCPenney's shelves, and Todd Oldham has stepped out with Old Navy, to name just a few.

Although many ventures such as these have failed miserably, some have been wildly successful. Lela Rose claims that she would never have considered her arrangement with Payless if it hadn't been for the success of Target's alliance with Isaac Mizrahi. Mizrahi's couture career was pretty much on the rocks. Then, he started designing preppy cashmere sweaters, cheerful jersey dresses, and trendy trench coats for Target, all priced at under $40. With the low-rent strategy, Mizrahi became more popular and famous than ever. After that, he once again had high-end retailers knocking on his door. Since Mizrahi's successful entry to the mainstream in 2003, more than two dozen designers have co-branded with mass retailers.

PAYING LESS OR PAYING MORE?

There's more in it for Payless than just making the brand more attractive to both old and new customers. The company is looking to move its average price point up a notch or two. Whereas "higher price" is a relative term when most of a store's product line is priced below $15, higher margins are higher margins. Rubel has suggested that in many cases, price increases may be as little as 50 cents per pair of shoes. But the expansion of its brand portfolio to include famous labels will certainly give Payless greater pricing flexibility. And the designer collections will allow for some of the highest priced products that have ever graced its shelves—think $25 for pumps and up to $45 for boots. Whereas that is a substantial price increase from Payless's average, it's a bargain for fashion-conscious consumers.

One industry insider declares, "Fashion isn't a luxury, it's a right." With Rubel's mission to democratize fashion, it seems that this right is becoming a reality in the shoe world. The benefits of such democracy are plentiful. The designers get tremendous exposure, a large customer base, and the power and budget of a mass retailer. Payless gets brand caché, almost certain to transform its outdated image. And consumers get runway styles they can afford. Payless is banking that making everyone happy will ring up the sales and profits it needs.

Questions for Discussion

1. Which of the different product mix pricing strategies discussed in the text applies best to Payless's new strategy? Discuss this in detail.

2. How do concepts such as psychological pricing and reference pricing apply to the Payless strategy? In what ways does Payless's strategy deviate from these concepts?

3. Discuss the benefits and risks of the new Payless strategy for both Payless and the designers. Which of these two stands to lose the most?

4. Consider the scale on which Payless operates. How much of a price increase does Payless need to achieve in order to make this venture worthwhile?

Sources: Danielle Sacks, "The Fast 50 Companies," *Fast Company*, March 2008, p. 112; Maria Puente, "Top Designers Go Down-Market," *USA Today*, September 26, 2007, p. 11B; Eric Wilson, "The Big Brand Theory," *New York Times Magazine*, September 9, 2007, p. 74; Bruce Horovitz, "Payless Is Determined to Put a Fashionably Shod Foot Forward," *USA Today*, July 28, 2006, p. 1B; Nicole Zerillo, "Payless Launches 'I Love Shoes.'" *PR Week*, March 10, 2008, p. 3; and www.paylessinfo.com, accessed September 2008.

Chapter 12

Part 1   Defining Marketing and the Marketing Process (Chapters 1, 2)
Part 2   Understanding the Marketplace and Consumers (Chapters 3, 4, 5, 6)
Part 3   Designing a Customer-Driven Strategy and Mix (Chapters 7, 8, 9, 10, 11, 12, 13, 14, 15, 16, 17)
Part 4   Extending Marketing (Chapters 18, 19, 20)

Marketing Channels
Delivering Customer Value

Chapter **PREVIEW**

We now arrive at the third marketing mix tool—distribution. Firms rarely work alone in creating value for customers and building profitable customer relationships. Instead, most are only a single link in a larger supply chain and marketing channel. As such, an individual firm's success depends not only on how well *it* performs but also on how well its *entire marketing channel* competes with competitors' channels. To be good at customer relationship management, a company must also be good at partner relationship management. The first part of this chapter explores the nature of marketing channels and the marketer's channel design and management decisions. We then examine physical distribution—or logistics—an area that is growing dramatically in importance and sophistication. In the next chapter, we'll look more closely at two major channel intermediaries—retailers and wholesalers.

We'll start with a look at a company whose groundbreaking, customer-centered distribution strategy took it to the top of its industry.

Quick, which rental-car company is number one? Chances are good that you said Hertz. Okay, who's number two? That must be Avis, you say. After all, for years Avis advertising has said, "We're #2, so we try harder!" But if you said Hertz or Avis, you're about to be surprised. By any measure—most locations, revenues, profits, or number of cars—the number-one U.S. rental-car company is Enterprise Rent-A-Car. What's more, this is no recent development. Enterprise left number-two Hertz in its rearview mirror in the late 1990s and has never looked back.

What may have fooled you is that for a long time, Hertz was number one in airport car rentals. However, with estimated revenues of $9.5 billion and growing, Enterprise now has 30 percent more overall car-rental sales than Hertz. What's more, analysts estimate that the privately owned Enterprise is twice as profitable as Hertz.

How did Enterprise become such a dominating industry leader? The company might argue that it was through better prices or better marketing. But what contributed most to Enterprise taking the lead was an industry-changing, customer-driven distribution strategy. While competitors such as Hertz and Avis focused on serving travelers at airports, Enterprise developed a new distribution doorway to a large and untapped segment. It opened off-airport, neighborhood locations that provided short-term car-replacement rentals for people whose cars were wrecked, stolen, or being serviced, or for people who simply wanted a different car for a short trip or special occasion.

It all started more than half a century ago when Enterprise founder Jack Taylor discovered an unmet customer need. He was working at a St. Louis auto dealership, and customers often asked him where they could get a replacement car when theirs was in the shop for repairs or body work. To meet this need, Taylor opened a car-leasing business. But rather than competing head-on with the likes of Hertz and Avis serving travelers at airports, Taylor located his rental offices in center-city and neighborhood areas, closer to his replacement-car target customers. These locations also gave Taylor a cost advantage—property rents were lower and he didn't have to pay airport taxes and fees.

Taylor's groundbreaking distribution strategy worked and the business grew quickly. As he opened multiple locations in St. Louis and other cities, he renamed his business Enterprise Rent-A-Car after the U.S. Navy aircraft carrier on which he had served as a naval aviator. Enterprise continued to focus steadfastly on what it called the "home-city" market, primarily serving customers who'd been in wrecks or whose cars were being serviced. Enterprise branch managers developed strong relationships with local auto insurance adjusters, dealership sales and service personnel, and body shops and service garages, making Enterprise their preferred neighborhood rental-car provider.

Customers in the home-city market had special needs. Often, they were at the scene of a wreck or at a repair shop and had no way to get to an Enterprise office to pick up a rental car. So the company came up with another game-changing idea—picking customers up wherever they happen to be and bringing them back to the rental office. Hence, the tagline: "Pick Enterprise. We'll Pick

> The tagline "Pick Enterprise. We'll Pick You Up" remains the company's main value proposition.

We'll pick you up.

You Up," which remains the company's main value proposition to this day.

By the late 1980s, Enterprise had a large nationwide network of company-owned off-airport locations and a virtual lock on the home-city market. From this strong base, in the mid-1990s Enterprise began expanding its distribution system by directly challenging Hertz and Avis in the on-airport market. A decade later, it had set up operations in 230 airports in North America and Europe. Then, in late 2007, Enterprise purchased the Vanguard Car Rental Group, which owned the National and Alamo brands. National focused on the corporate negotiated rental market while Alamo served primarily the leisure traveler airport market.

With the Vanguard acquisition, Enterprise now captures a 27.4 percent share of the airport market, putting it neck-and-neck with Hertz at 28.5 percent and jointly owned Avis/Budget at 30.1 percent. That, combined with its more than 55 percent share of the off-airport market, makes Enterprise the runaway leader in overall car rental. Enterprise owns a stunning one-half of all U.S. rental cars and is the world's largest automobile buyer. Last year, it purchased 800,000 cars to support its 7,900 locations in the United States and four other countries.

However, rather than resting on its laurels, Enterprise continues to seek better ways to get its cars where customers want them. The enterprising company is now motoring into yet another innovative distribution venue—"car sharing" and hourly rentals. Car-sharing was pioneered in the late 1990s by Zipcar, which operates on parking-starved college campuses and in congested urban areas, where it rents cars on an hourly or daily basis to people who want to run errands or make short trips.

Enterprise has now revved up its own car-sharing program, WeCar. This new operation will park automobiles at convenient locations in densely populated urban areas, where residents often don't own cars and where business commuters would like to have occasional car access. Enterprise will also target businesses that want to have WeCar vehicles available in their parking lots for commuting employees to use. WeCar members pay a $35 annual membership fee. They can then rent conveniently located, fuel-efficient cars (mostly Toyota Prius hybrids) for $10 per hour or

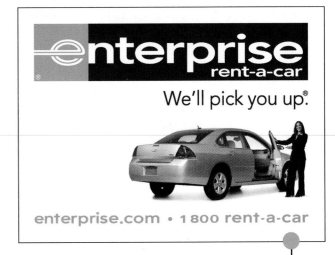

$30 overnight—the rate includes gas and a 200-mile allotment. Renting a WeCar vehicle is a simple get-in-and-go operation. Just pass your member key fob over a sensor to unlock the car, then open the glove box and enter a PIN to release the car key. Although the car sharing market now belongs to tiny Zipcar, a $100 million company that has cars on more than 70 college campuses in several large metropolitan areas, look for giant Enterprise to perfect and expand the new distribution concept.

Thus, Enterprise continues to move ahead aggressively with its winning distribution strategy. Says Andy Taylor, founder Jack's son and now long-time Enterprise CEO, "We own the high ground in this business and we aren't going to give it up. As the dynamics of our industry continue to evolve, it's clear to us that the future belongs to the service providers who offer the broadest array of services for anyone who needs or wants to rent a car." The company intends to make cars available wherever, whenever, and however customers want them.[1]

> While competitors Hertz and Avis focused on serving travelers at airports, Enterprise opened off-airport, neighborhood locations that provided short-term car-replacement rentals for people whose cars were wrecked, stolen, or being serviced.

> Thanks to an industry-changing, customer-driven distribution strategy, Enterprise Rent-A-Car left number-two Hertz in its rearview mirror more than a decade ago and has never looked back.

As the Enterprise story shows, good distribution strategies can contribute strongly to customer value and create competitive advantage for both a firm and its channel partners. It demonstrates that firms cannot bring value to customers by themselves. Instead, they must work closely with other firms in a larger value delivery network.

> **Author Comment** | These are pretty hefty terms for what's really a simple concept: A company can't go it alone in creating customer value. It must work within an entire network of partners to accomplish this task. Individual companies and brands don't compete, their entire value delivery networks do.

Supply Chains and the Value Delivery Network (pp 337–339)

Producing a product or service and making it available to buyers requires building relationships not just with customers, but also with key suppliers and resellers in the company's *supply chain*. This supply chain consists of "upstream" and "downstream" partners. Upstream from the company is the set of firms that supply the raw materials, components, parts, information, finances, and expertise needed to create a product or service. Marketers,

Objective Outline

▲ Value delivery network: In making and marketing iPod Touch products, Apple manages an entire network of people within Apple plus suppliers and resellers outside the company who work effectively together to give final customers "So much to touch."

however, have traditionally focused on the "downstream" side of the supply chain—on the *marketing channels* (or *distribution channels*) that look toward the customer. Downstream marketing channel partners, such as wholesalers and retailers, form a vital connection between the firm and its customers.

The term *supply chain* may be too limited—it takes a *make-and-sell* view of the business. It suggests that raw materials, productive inputs, and factory capacity should serve as the starting point for market planning. A better term would be *demand chain* because it suggests a *sense-and-respond* view of the market. Under this view, planning starts with the needs of target customers, to which the company responds by organizing a chain of resources and activities with the goal of creating customer value.

Even a demand chain view of a business may be too limited, because it takes a step-by-step, linear view of purchase-production-consumption activities. With the advent of the Internet and other technologies, however, companies are forming more numerous and complex relationships with other firms. For example, Ford manages numerous supply chains. It also sponsors or transacts on many B-to-B Web sites and online purchasing exchanges as needs arise. Like Ford, most large companies today are engaged in building and managing a continuously evolving *value delivery network*.

As defined in Chapter 2, a **value delivery network** is made up of the company, suppliers, distributors, and ultimately customers who "partner" with each other to improve the performance of the entire system. ▲For example, in making and marketing its iPod Touch products, Apple manages an entire network of people within Apple plus suppliers and resellers outside the company who work together effectively to give final customers "So much to touch."

This chapter focuses on marketing channels—on the downstream side of the value delivery network. We examine four major questions concerning marketing channels:

Value delivery network

The network made up of the company, suppliers, distributors, and ultimately customers who "partner" with each other to improve the performance of the entire system in delivering customer value.

What is the nature of marketing channels and why are they important? How do channel firms interact and organize to do the work of the channel? What problems do companies face in designing and managing their channels? What role do physical distribution and supply chain management play in attracting and satisfying customers? In Chapter 13, we will look at marketing channel issues from the viewpoint of retailers and wholesalers.

Author Comment | In this section, we look at the "downstream" side of the value delivery network—the marketing channel organizations that connect the company and its customers. To understand their value, imagine life without retailers—say, grocery stores or department stores.

The Nature and Importance of Marketing Channels (pp 339–341)

Marketing channel (or distribution channel)

A set of interdependent organizations that help make a product or service available for use or consumption by the consumer or business user.

Few producers sell their goods directly to the final users. Instead, most use intermediaries to bring their products to market. They try to forge a **marketing channel** (or **distribution channel**)—a set of interdependent organizations that help make a product or service available for use or consumption by the consumer or business user.

A company's channel decisions directly affect every other marketing decision. Pricing depends on whether the company works with national discount chains, uses high-quality specialty stores, or sells directly to consumers via the Web. The firm's sales force and communications decisions depend on how much persuasion, training, motivation, and support its channel partners need. Whether a company develops or acquires certain new products may depend on how well those products fit the capabilities of its channel members. For example, Kodak initially sold its EasyShare printers only in Best Buy stores to take advantage of the retailer's on-the-floor sales staff and their ability to educate buyers on the economics of paying higher initial prices but lower long-term ink costs.

Companies often pay too little attention to their distribution channels, sometimes with damaging results. In contrast, many companies have used imaginative distribution systems to *gain* a competitive advantage. FedEx's creative and imposing distribution system made it a leader in express delivery. Enterprise revolutionized the car-rental business by setting up off-airport rental offices. And Calyx & Corolla led the way in selling fresh flowers and plants direct to consumers by phone and from its Web site, cutting a week or more off the time it takes flowers to reach consumers through conventional retail channels.

Distribution channel decisions often involve long-term commitments to other firms. For example, companies such as Ford, HP, or McDonald's can easily change their advertising, pricing, or promotion programs. They can scrap old products and introduce new ones as market tastes demand. But when they set up distribution channels through contracts with franchisees, independent dealers, or large retailers, they cannot readily replace these channels with company-owned stores or Web sites if conditions change. Therefore, management must design its channels carefully, with an eye on tomorrow's likely selling environment as well as today's.

How Channel Members Add Value

Why do producers give some of the selling job to channel partners? After all, doing so means giving up some control over how and to whom they sell their products. Producers use intermediaries because they create greater efficiency in making goods available to target markets. Through their contacts, experience, specialization, and scale of operation, intermediaries usually offer the firm more than it can achieve on its own.

 Figure 12.1 shows how using intermediaries can provide economies. Figure 12.1A shows three manufacturers, each using direct marketing to reach three customers. This system requires nine different contacts. Figure 12.1B shows the three manufacturers working through one distributor, which contacts the three customers. This system requires only six contacts. In this way, intermediaries reduce the amount of work that must be done by both producers and consumers.

FIGURE | 12.1
How Adding a Distributor Reduces the Number of Channel Transactions

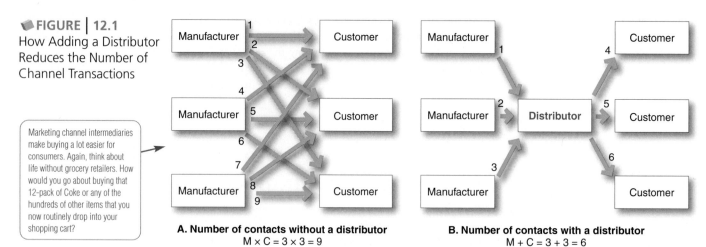

A. Number of contacts without a distributor
$M \times C = 3 \times 3 = 9$

B. Number of contacts with a distributor
$M + C = 3 + 3 = 6$

From the economic system's point of view, the role of marketing intermediaries is to transform the assortments of products made by producers into the assortments wanted by consumers. Producers make narrow assortments of products in large quantities, but consumers want broad assortments of products in small quantities. Marketing channel members buy large quantities from many producers and break them down into the smaller quantities and broader assortments wanted by consumers.

For example, Unilever makes millions of bars of Lever 2000 hand soap each day, but you want to buy only a few bars at a time. So big food, drug, and discount retailers, such as Kroger, Walgreens, and Wal-Mart, buy Lever 2000 by the truckload and stock it on their stores' shelves. In turn, you can buy a single bar of Lever 2000, along with a shopping cart full of small quantities of toothpaste, shampoo, and other related products as you need them. Thus, intermediaries play an important role in matching supply and demand.

In making products and services available to consumers, channel members add value by bridging the major time, place, and possession gaps that separate goods and services from those who would use them. Members of the marketing channel perform many key functions. Some help to complete transactions:

- *Information:* Gathering and distributing marketing research and intelligence information about actors and forces in the marketing environment needed for planning and aiding exchange.

- *Promotion:* Developing and spreading persuasive communications about an offer.

- *Contact:* Finding and communicating with prospective buyers.

- *Matching:* Shaping and fitting the offer to the buyer's needs, including activities such as manufacturing, grading, assembling, and packaging.

- *Negotiation:* Reaching an agreement on price and other terms of the offer so that ownership or possession can be transferred.

Others help to fulfill the completed transactions:

- *Physical distribution:* Transporting and storing goods.

- *Financing:* Acquiring and using funds to cover the costs of the channel work.

- *Risk taking:* Assuming the risks of carrying out the channel work.

The question is not *whether* these functions need to be performed—they must be—but rather *who* will perform them. To the extent that the manufacturer performs these functions, its costs go up and its prices must be higher. When some of these functions are shifted to intermediaries, the producer's costs and prices may be lower, but the intermediaries must charge more to cover the costs of their work. In dividing the work of the channel, the various functions should be assigned to the channel members who can add the most value for the cost.

Number of Channel Levels

Channel level

A layer of intermediaries that performs some work in bringing the product and its ownership closer to the final buyer.

Direct marketing channel

A marketing channel that has no intermediary levels.

Indirect marketing channel

Channel containing one or more intermediary levels.

Companies can design their distribution channels to make products and services available to customers in different ways. Each layer of marketing intermediaries that performs some work in bringing the product and its ownership closer to the final buyer is a **channel level**. Because the producer and the final consumer both perform some work, they are part of every channel.

The *number of intermediary levels* indicates the *length* of a channel. 🔖**Figure 12.2A** shows several consumer distribution channels of different lengths. Channel 1, called a **direct marketing channel**, has no intermediary levels; the company sells directly to consumers. For example, Mary Kay and Amway sell their products door-to-door, through home and office sales parties, and on the Web; GEICO sells direct via the telephone and the Internet. The remaining channels in Figure 12.2A are **indirect marketing channels**, containing one or more intermediaries.

🔖**Figure 12.2B** shows some common business distribution channels. The business marketer can use its own sales force to sell directly to business customers. Or it can sell to various types of intermediaries, who in turn sell to these customers. Consumer and business marketing channels with even more levels can sometimes be found, but less often. From the producer's point of view, a greater number of levels means less control and greater channel complexity. Moreover, all of the institutions in the channel are connected by several types of *flows*. These include the *physical flow* of products, the *flow of ownership*, the *payment flow*, the *information flow*, and the *promotion flow*. These flows can make even channels with only one or a few levels very complex.

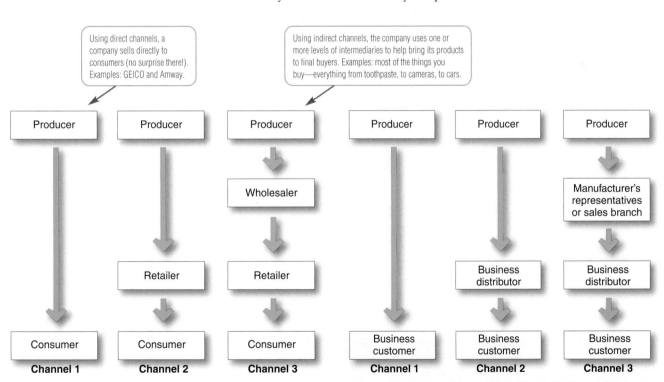

A. Customer marketing channels   **B. Business marketing channels**

🔖**FIGURE** | **12.2** Consumer and Business Marketing Channels

Channel Behavior and Organization
(pp 342–348)

Distribution channels are more than simple collections of firms tied together by various flows. They are complex behavioral systems in which people and companies interact to accomplish individual, company, and channel goals. Some channel systems consist only of informal interactions among loosely organized firms. Others consist of formal interactions guided by strong organizational structures. Moreover, channel systems do not stand still—new types of intermediaries emerge and whole new channel systems evolve. Here we look at channel behavior and at how members organize to do the work of the channel.

Channel Behavior

A marketing channel consists of firms that have partnered for their common good. Each channel member depends on the others. For example, a Ford dealer depends on Ford to design cars that meet consumer needs. In turn, Ford depends on the dealer to attract consumers, persuade them to buy Ford cars, and service cars after the sale. Each Ford dealer also depends on other dealers to provide good sales and service that will uphold the brand's reputation. In fact, the success of individual Ford dealers depends on how well the entire Ford marketing channel competes with the channels of other auto manufacturers.

Each channel member plays a specialized role in the channel. For example, consumer electronics maker Samsung's role is to produce electronics products that consumers will like and to create demand through national advertising. Best Buy's role is to display these Samsung products in convenient locations, to answer buyers' questions, and to complete sales. The channel will be most effective when each member assumes the tasks it can do best.

Channel conflict

Disagreement among marketing channel members on goals and roles—who should do what and for what rewards.

Ideally, because the success of individual channel members depends on overall channel success, all channel firms should work together smoothly. They should understand and accept their roles, coordinate their activities, and cooperate to attain overall channel goals. However, individual channel members rarely take such a broad view. Cooperating to achieve overall channel goals sometimes means giving up individual company goals. Although channel members depend on one another, they often act alone in their own short-run best interests. They often disagree on who should do what and for what rewards. Such disagreements over goals, roles, and rewards generate **channel conflict**.

Horizontal conflict occurs among firms at the same level of the channel. For instance, some Ford dealers in Chicago might complain that the other dealers in the city steal sales from them by pricing too low or by advertising outside their assigned territories. Or Holiday Inn franchisees might complain about other Holiday Inn operators overcharging guests or giving poor service, hurting the overall Holiday Inn image.

Vertical conflict, conflicts between different levels of the same channel, is even more common. ▲For example, Goodyear created hard feelings and conflict with its premier independent-dealer channel when it began selling through mass-merchant retailers:[2]

For more than 60 years, Goodyear sold replacement tires exclusively through its premier network of independent Goodyear dealers. Then, in the 1990s, Goodyear shattered

▲ Channel conflict: Goodyear created conflict with its premiere independent-dealer channel when it began selling through mass-merchant retailers. Fractured dealer relations weakened the Goodyear name and dropped the company into a more than a decade-long profit funk.

tradition and jolted its dealers by agreeing to sell its tires through mass-merchants such as Sears, Wal-Mart, and Sam's Club, placing dealers in direct competition with the nation's most potent retailers. It even opened its own no-frills, quick-serve Just Tires discount stores designed to fend off low-priced competitors. Goodyear claimed that value-minded tire buyers were increasingly buying from cheaper, multibrand discount outlets and department stores, and that it simply had to put its tires where many consumers were going to buy them.

Not surprisingly, Goodyear's aggressive moves into new channels set off a surge of channel conflict, and dealer relations deteriorated rapidly. Some of Goodyear's best dealers defected to competitors. Other angry dealers struck back by taking on competing brands of cheaper private-label tires. Such dealer actions weakened the Goodyear name, and the company's replacement tire sales—which make up 71 percent of its revenues—went flat, dropping the company into a more than decade-long profit funk. Although Goodyear has since actively set about repairing fractured dealer relations, it still has not fully recovered. "We lost sight of the fact that it's in our interest that our dealers succeed," admits a Goodyear executive.

Some conflict in the channel takes the form of healthy competition. Such competition can be good for the channel—without it, the channel could become passive and noninnovative. But severe or prolonged conflict, as in the case of Goodyear, can disrupt channel effectiveness and cause lasting harm to channel relationships. Companies should manage channel conflict to keep it from getting out of hand.

Vertical Marketing Systems

For the channel as a whole to perform well, each channel member's role must be specified and channel conflict must be managed. The channel will perform better if it includes a firm, agency, or mechanism that provides leadership and has the power to assign roles and manage conflict.

Historically, *conventional distribution channels* have lacked such leadership and power, often resulting in damaging conflict and poor performance. One of the biggest channel developments over the years has been the emergence of *vertical marketing systems* that provide channel leadership. **Figure 12.3** contrasts the two types of channel arrangements.

FIGURE | 12.3
Comparison of Conventional Distribution Channel with Vertical Marketing System

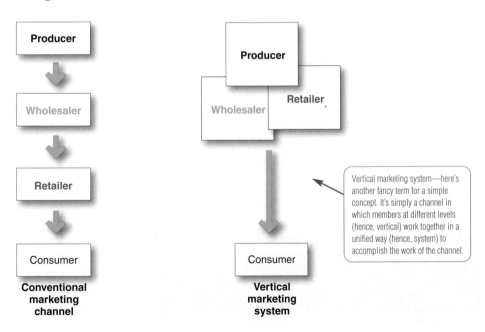

Producer → Wholesaler → Retailer → Consumer
Conventional marketing channel

Producer / Wholesaler / Retailer → Consumer
Vertical marketing system

Vertical marketing system—here's another fancy term for a simple concept. It's simply a channel in which members at different levels (hence, vertical) work together in a unified way (hence, system) to accomplish the work of the channel.

Conventional distribution channel
A channel consisting of one or more independent producers, wholesalers, and retailers, each a separate business seeking to maximize its own profits, even at the expense of profits for the system as a whole.

Vertical marketing system (VMS)
A distribution channel structure in which producers, wholesalers, and retailers act as a unified system. One channel member owns the others, has contracts with them, or has so much power that they all cooperate.

Corporate VMS
A vertical marketing system that combines successive stages of production and distribution under single ownership—channel leadership is established through common ownership.

A **conventional distribution channel** consists of one or more independent producers, wholesalers, and retailers. Each is a separate business seeking to maximize its own profits, perhaps even at the expense of the system as a whole. No channel member has much control over the other members, and no formal means exists for assigning roles and resolving channel conflict.

In contrast, a **vertical marketing system (VMS)** consists of producers, wholesalers, and retailers acting as a unified system. One channel member owns the others, has contracts with them, or wields so much power that they must all cooperate. The VMS can be dominated by the producer, wholesaler, or retailer.

We look now at three major types of VMSs: *corporate, contractual,* and *administered.* Each uses a different means for setting up leadership and power in the channel.

Corporate VMS

A **corporate VMS** integrates successive stages of production and distribution under single ownership. Coordination and conflict management are attained through regular organizational channels. For example, grocery giant Kroger owns and operates 42 factories that crank out more than 8,000 private label items found on its store shelves. Similarly, to help supply products for its 1,760 grocery stores, Safeway owns and operates nine milk plants, eight bakery plants, four ice cream plants, four soft drink bottling plants, and four fruit and vegetable processing plants. And little-known Italian eyewear maker Luxottica produces many famous eyewear brands—including its own Ray-Ban brand and licensed brands such as Polo Ralph Lauren, Dolce & Gabbana, Prada, Versace, and Bvlgari. It then sells these brands through two of the world's largest optical chains, LensCrafters and Sunglass Hut, which it also owns.[3]

Controlling the entire distribution chain has turned ▲Spanish clothing chain Zara into the world's fastest-growing fashion retailer.

The secret to Zara's success is its control over almost every aspect of the supply chain, from design and production to its own worldwide distribution network. Zara makes 40 percent of its own fabrics and produces more than half of its own clothes, rather than relying on a hodgepodge of slow-moving suppliers. New designs feed into Zara manufacturing centers, which ship finished products directly to 1,161 Zara stores in 68 countries, saving time, eliminating the need for warehouses, and keeping inventories low. Effective vertical integration makes Zara faster, more flexible, and more efficient than international competitors such as Gap, Benetton, and H&M. And Zara's low costs let it offer midmarket chic at downmarket prices.

A couple of summers ago, Zara managed to latch onto one of the season's hottest trends in just four weeks (versus an industry average of nine months). The process started when trend-spotters spread the word back to headquarters: White eyelet—cotton with tiny holes in it—was set to become white-hot. A quick telephone survey of Zara store managers confirmed that the fabric could be a winner, so in-house designers got down to work. They zapped patterns electronically to Zara's factory across the street, and the fabric was cut. Local subcontractors stitched white-eyelet V-neck belted dresses—think Jackie Kennedy, circa 1960—and finished them in less than a week. The $129 dresses were inspected, tagged, and transported through a tunnel under the street to a distribution center. From there, they were quickly dispatched to Zara stores from New

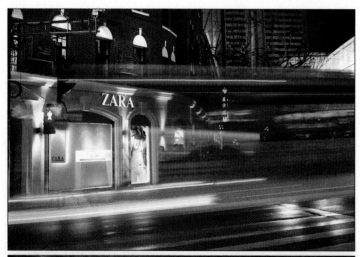

▲ Corporate VMS: Effective vertical integration makes Zara more flexible, and more efficient—a virtual blur compared with competitors. It can take a new line from design to production to worldwide distribution in its own stores in less than a month (versus an industry average of nine months).

York to Tokyo—where they were flying off the racks just two days later. In all, the company's stylish but affordable offerings have attracted a cult following. Zara store sales grew almost 40 percent last year to nearly $9.8 billion.[4]

Contractual VMS

Contractual VMS
A vertical marketing system in which independent firms at different levels of production and distribution join together through contracts to obtain more economies or sales impact than they could achieve alone.

A **contractual VMS** consists of independent firms at different levels of production and distribution who join together through contracts to obtain more economies or sales impact than each could achieve alone. Channel members coordinate their activities and manage conflict through contractual agreements.

Franchise organization
A contractual vertical marketing system in which a channel member, called a franchisor, links several stages in the production-distribution process.

The **franchise organization** is the most common type of contractual relationship—a channel member called a *franchisor* links several stages in the production-distribution process. In the United States alone, some 1,500 franchise businesses and 750,000 franchise outlets account for more than $1.5 trillion in annual sales. Industry analysts estimate that a new franchise outlet opens somewhere in the United States every eight minutes and that about one out of every 12 retail business outlets is a franchised business.[5] Almost every kind of business has been franchised—from motels and fast-food restaurants to dental centers and dating services, from wedding consultants and maid services to fitness centers and funeral homes.

There are three types of franchises. The first type is the *manufacturer-sponsored retailer franchise system*—for example, Ford and its network of independent franchised dealers. The second type is the *manufacturer-sponsored wholesaler franchise system*—Coca-Cola licenses bottlers (wholesalers) in various markets who buy Coca-Cola syrup concentrate and then bottle and sell the finished product to retailers in local markets. The third type is the *service-firm-sponsored retailer franchise system*—examples are found in the auto-rental business (Hertz, Avis), the fast-food service business (McDonald's, Burger King), and the motel business (Holiday Inn, Ramada Inn).

The fact that most consumers cannot tell the difference between contractual and corporate VMSs shows how successfully the contractual organizations compete with corporate chains. Chapter 13 presents a fuller discussion of the various contractual VMSs.

Administered VMS

Administered VMS
A vertical marketing system that coordinates successive stages of production and distribution, not through common ownership or contractual ties, but through the size and power of one of the parties.

In an **administered VMS**, leadership is assumed not through common ownership or contractual ties but through the size and power of one or a few dominant channel members. Manufacturers of a top brand can obtain strong trade cooperation and support from resellers. For example, General Electric, Procter & Gamble, and Kraft can command unusual cooperation from resellers regarding displays, shelf space, promotions, and price policies. Large retailers such as Wal-Mart, Home Depot, and Barnes & Noble can exert strong influence on the manufacturers that supply the products they sell.

Horizontal Marketing Systems

Horizontal marketing system
A channel arrangement in which two or more companies at one level join together to follow a new marketing opportunity.

Another channel development is the **horizontal marketing system**, in which two or more companies at one level join together to follow a new marketing opportunity. By working together, companies can combine their financial, production, or marketing resources to accomplish more than any one company could alone.

Companies might join forces with competitors or noncompetitors. They might work with each other on a temporary or permanent basis, or they may create a separate company. For example, McDonald's now places "express" versions of its restaurants in Wal-Mart stores. McDonald's benefits from Wal-Mart's heavy store traffic, and Wal-Mart keeps hungry shoppers from needing to go elsewhere to eat.

Such channel arrangements also work well globally. ▲For example, McDonald's recently joined forces with Sinopec, China's largest gasoline retailer, to place drive-through restaurants at Sinopec's more than 31,000 gas stations. The move greatly speeds McDonald's expansion into China while at the same time pulling hungry motorists into Sinopec gas stations.[6] As another example, Coca-Cola and Nestlé formed a joint distribution venture,

▲ Horizontal marketing systems: McDonald's recently joined forces with Sinopec, China's largest gasoline retailer, to place restaurants at its more than 30,000 gas stations. Here, the presidents of the two companies shake hands while announcing the partnership.

Multichannel distribution system

A distribution system in which a single firm sets up two or more marketing channels to reach one or more customer segments.

Beverage Partners Worldwide, to market ready-to-drink coffees, teas, and flavored milks in more than 40 countries worldwide. Coke provides worldwide experience in marketing and distributing beverages, and Nestlé contributes two established brand names—Nescafé and Nestea.[7]

Multichannel Distribution Systems

In the past, many companies used a single channel to sell to a single market or market segment. Today, with the proliferation of customer segments and channel possibilities, more and more companies have adopted **multichannel distribution systems**—often called *hybrid marketing channels*. Such multichannel marketing occurs when a single firm sets up two or more marketing channels to reach one or more customer segments. The use of multichannel systems has increased greatly in recent years.

⬗ **Figure 12.4** shows a multichannel marketing system. In the figure, the producer sells directly to consumer segment 1 using direct-mail catalogs, telemarketing, and the Internet and reaches consumer segment 2 through retailers. It sells indirectly to business segment 1 through distributors and dealers and to business segment 2 through its own sales force.

These days, almost every large company and many small ones distribute through multiple channels. For example, John Deere sells its familiar green and yellow lawn and garden tractors, mowers, and outdoor power products to consumers and commercial users through several channels, including John Deere retailers, Lowe's home improvement stores, and online. It sells and services its tractors, combines, planters, and other agricultural equipment through its premium John Deere dealer network. And it sells large construction and forestry equipment through selected large, full-service dealers and their sales forces.

Multichannel distribution systems offer many advantages to companies facing large and complex markets. With each new channel, the company expands its sales and market coverage and gains opportunities to tailor its products and services to the specific needs of diverse customer segments. But such multichannel systems are harder to control, and they generate conflict as more channels compete for customers and sales. For example, when

⬗**FIGURE** | **12.4**
Multichannel Distribution System

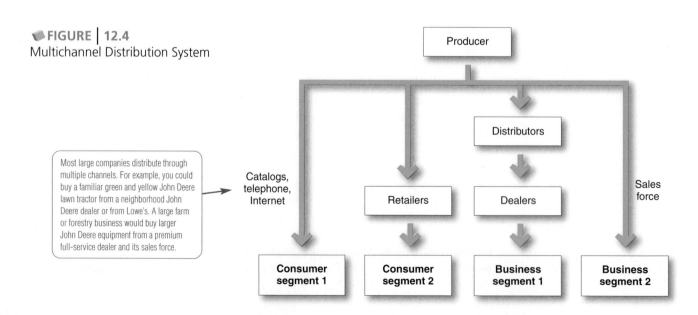

Most large companies distribute through multiple channels. For example, you could buy a familiar green and yellow John Deere lawn tractor from a neighborhood John Deere dealer or from Lowe's. A large farm or forestry business would buy larger John Deere equipment from a premium full-service dealer and its sales force.

John Deere began selling selected consumer products through Lowe's home improvement stores, many of its dealers complained loudly. To avoid such conflicts in its Internet marketing channels, the company routes all of its Web site sales to John Deere dealers.

Changing Channel Organization

Changes in technology and the explosive growth of direct and online marketing are having a profound impact on the nature and design of marketing channels. One major trend is toward **disintermediation**—a big term with a clear message and important consequences. Disintermediation occurs when product or service producers cut out intermediaries and go directly to final buyers, or when radically new types of channel intermediaries displace traditional ones.

Thus, in many industries, traditional intermediaries are dropping by the wayside. For example, companies such as Southwest and other airlines sell directly to final buyers, cutting travel agents from their marketing channels altogether. In other cases, new forms of resellers are displacing traditional intermediaries. For example, online marketing is growing rapidly, taking business from traditional brick-and-mortar retailers. Consumers can buy airline tickets and hotel rooms from Expedia.com and Travelocity.com; electronics from Sonystyle.com; clothes and accessories from Bluefly.com; and books, videos, toys, jewelry, sports, consumer electronics, home and garden items, and almost anything else from Amazon.com; all without ever stepping into a traditional retail store. Online music download services such as iTunes and Yahoo! Music are threatening the very existence of traditional music-store retailers. In fact, once-dominant music retailer Tower Records declared bankruptcy and closed its doors for good.

Disintermediation presents both opportunities and problems for producers and resellers. Channel innovators who find new ways to add value in the channel can sweep aside traditional resellers and reap the rewards. In turn, traditional intermediaries must continue to innovate in order to avoid being swept aside. For example, when Netflix pioneered online video rentals, it sent traditional brick-and-mortar video-rental stores such as Blockbuster reeling. To meet the threat, Blockbuster developed its own online DVD-rental service. Now, both Netflix and Blockbuster face disintermediation threats from an even hotter channel—digital video distribution (see **Real Marketing 12.1**)

Similarly, to remain competitive, product and service producers must develop new channel opportunities, such as the Internet and other direct channels. However, developing these new channels often brings them into direct competition with their established channels, resulting in conflict.

Disintermediation

The cutting out of marketing channel intermediaries by product or service producers, or the displacement of traditional resellers by radical new types of intermediaries.

▲ Avoiding disintermediation problems: Black & Decker's Web site provides detailed information, but you can't buy any of the company's products there. Instead, Black & Decker refers you to resellers' Web sites and stores.

To ease this problem, companies often look for ways to make going direct a plus for the entire channel. ▲For example, Black & Decker knows that many customers would prefer to buy its power tools and outdoor power equipment online. But selling directly through its Web site would create conflicts with important and powerful retail partners, such as Home Depot, Lowe's, Target, Wal-Mart, and Amazon.com. So, although Black & Decker's Web site provides detailed information about the company's products, you can't buy a new Black & Decker cordless drill, laser level, or leaf blower there. Instead, the Black & Decker Web site refers you to resellers' Web sites and stores. Thus, Black & Decker's direct marketing helps both the company and its channel partners.

Real Marketing 12.1

Netflix:
Disintermediator or Disintermediated?

Baseball great Yogi Berra, known more for his mangled phrasing than for his baseball prowess, once said, "The future ain't what it used to be." For Netflix, the world's largest online movie-rental service, no matter how you say it, figuring out the future is challenging and a bit scary. Netflix faces dramatic changes in how movies and other entertainment content will be distributed. The question: Will Netflix be among the disintermediat*ors* or among the disintermediat*ed*?

Less than a decade ago, if you wanted to watch a movie in the comfort of your own home, your only choice was to roust yourself out of that easy chair and trot down to the local Blockbuster or another neighborhood movie-rental store. In fact, that's how most people still do it. Blockbuster has grown to become the world's largest store-rental chain, with more than 7,800 outlets worldwide and more than $5.5 billion in annual sales.

But now, thanks to Netflix, that distribution model is changing quickly. In the late 1990s, Netflix pioneered a new way to rent movies—via the Web and direct mail. With Netflix, you pay a monthly subscription fee and create a movie wish list online. Netflix mails you a set number of DVDs from your list at a given time, which you can keep for as long as you like. As you return the DVDs in

Netflix faces dramatic changes in how movies and other entertainment content will be distributed. Instead of simply watching the developments, Netflix intends to lead them.

prepaid return envelopes, Netflix automatically sends you new ones from your list.

Netflix offers lots of advantages over the traditional Blockbuster brick-and-mortar system. With store video rentals, you have to make a special trip whenever you want a movie, and if you don't plan ahead, you'll probably find the latest hot releases out of stock. As for finding copies of oldies but goodies, or an old documentary or independent film, forget it—stores can hold only a limited selection of DVDs. Finally, many consumers are frustrated by short due dates and those dreaded late return fees. In contrast, Netflix isn't bound by store-space limitations. It offers a huge selection of more than 90,000 titles and 40 million DVDs total.

The Netflix system eliminates store trips—you always have a stack of DVDs on hand. And there are no per-movie charges, no due dates, and no late fees.

Since first opening its virtual doors, Netflix has continued to add innovative features. Its "dynamic queue" lets customers select as many movie titles as they wish and rank them by preference. Netflix has also developed an online recommendation system, called Cinematch, to help customers find movies they'll love based on their own past ratings, member and critic reviews, and top-rented lists.

As a result, more and more customers are signing up with Netflix. Membership has grown to more than 7.5 million subscribers, and in just the past two years, sales and profits have

---

Author Comment | Like everything else in marketing, good channel design begins with analyzing customer needs. Remember, marketing channels are really *customer-value delivery networks*.

Channel Design Decisions (pp 348–352)

We now look at several channel decisions manufacturers face. In designing marketing channels, manufacturers struggle between what is ideal and what is practical. A new firm with limited capital usually starts by selling in a limited market area. Deciding on the best channels might not be a problem: The problem might simply be how to convince one or a few good intermediaries to handle the line.

If successful, the new firm can branch out to new markets through the existing intermediaries. In smaller markets, the firm might sell directly to retailers; in larger markets, it might sell through distributors. In one part of the country, it might grant exclusive franchises; in another, it might sell through all available outlets. Then, it might add a Web store that sells directly to hard-to-reach customers. In this way, channel systems often evolve to meet market opportunities and conditions.

Marketing channel design
Designing effective marketing channels by analyzing consumer needs, setting channel objectives, identifying major channel alternatives, and evaluating them.

For maximum effectiveness, however, channel analysis and decision making should be more purposeful. **Marketing channel design** calls for analyzing consumer needs, setting channel objectives, identifying major channel alternatives, and evaluating them.

surged 77 percent and 60 percent, respectively. Meanwhile, Netflix's success has sent Blockbuster and other video-rental stores reeling. As Netflix sales and profits have soared, Blockbuster's sales have lagged and losses have mounted. The video rental giant has lost money in 10 of the last 11 years. Although the traditional brick-and-mortar video-rental market is still alive and kicking, it's stagnating as the red-hot online channel gains momentum.

To meet the disintermediation threat, Blockbuster introduced its own online video-rental service. In fact, Blockbuster Total Access takes the new distribution model one step further. Total Access customers can order videos online and then return or exchange them either through the mail or at their local Blockbuster store. Blockbuster's online business grew quickly to over 2 million subscribers before leveling off. However, for the most part, Blockbuster is still struggling to find the right formula.

And so the video-rental channels battle continues. Blockbuster claims the advantages of a click-and-mortar model that offers both online and store services. In contrast, Netflix sees physical stores as an unnecessary and costly limitation. Says Netflix founder and CEO Reed Hastings, "For people who'd love never to go into a Blockbuster store ever again, we offer better selection, better tools for choosing movies, and more consistent overnight delivery." Either way, there's no going back to the past—the two competitors are rapidly disintermediating store-only video-rental outfits.

But just as the present isn't what it used to be, neither is the future. At the same time that Netflix is displacing traditional store channels, it faces its own disintermediation threat from a potentially even hotter channel—digital video distribution in the form of digital downloads and video on demand (VOD). Digital distribution is a fact of life in the music industry, where music download services are fast making traditional CD retailers obsolete. Most experts agree that it's only a matter of time until digital video distribution displaces DVD video sales and rentals.

In fact, it's already begun. These days, you can download all kinds of video entertainment—from movies and TV shows to ads and amateur videos—to your computer, iPod, or even your cell phone. Satellite and cable TV companies are promising VOD services that will let you view movies and other video entertainment on television whenever and wherever you wish. And video-rental download services such as CinemaNow are already offering a growing list of downloadable titles via the Web.

Digital video downloads and video on demand create obvious cost, distribution, and customer convenience advantages over physically producing and distributing DVDs. For sure, the digital video distribution industry still faces problems. Downloading videos can take a lot of time and yields less-than-DVD quality. Perhaps the biggest barrier so far—Hollywood has been cautious about granting video distribution rights, severely limiting the number of available titles. In time, however, all these limitations will likely dissipate. When

that happens, it could be lights out for the DVD sales and rental industry.

Netflix CEO Hastings understands the future challenges. "We're sure that we're going to be buying cars in 25 years, whereas renting DVDs through the mail in 25 years—for sure that's not going to exist," he says. The solution? Keep innovating. Instead of simply watching digital video distribution developments, Netflix intends to lead them. Netflix has already added a "watch instantly" feature to its Web site that allows subscribers to instantly stream near-DVD quality video for a limited but growing list of movie titles and TV programs. "Our intention," says Hasting, "is to get [our watch instantly] service to every Internet-connected screen, from cell phones to laptops to Wi-Fi-enabled plasma screens." In this way, Netflix plans to disintermediate its own distribution model before others can do it.

To Hastings, the key to the future is all in how Netflix defines itself. "If [you] think of Netflix as a DVD rental business, [you're] right to be scared," he says. But "if [you] think of Netflix as an online movie service with multiple different delivery models, then [you're] a lot less scared. We're only now starting to deliver [on] that second vision." When asked what Netflix will be like in five years, Hasting responds, "We hope to be much larger, have more subscribers, and be successfully expanding into online video."

Sources: Quotes and other information from Matthew Boyle, "Reed Hastings," *Fortune*, May 28, 2007, p. 30; Nick Wingfield, "Netflix vs. Naysayers," *Wall Street Journal*, March 27, 2007, p. B1; Yuval Rosenberg, "What's Next for Netflix?" *Fortune*, November 29, 2006, p. 172; Paul R. La Monica, "DVD or Download?" *CNNMoney.com*, June 26, 2006; Nancy Macdonald, "Blockbuster Proves It's Not Dead Yet," *Maclean's*, March 17, 2008, p. 36; Michael V. Copeland, "Netflix Lives!" *Fortune*, April 28, 2008, p. 40; "Netflix, Inc.," *Hoover's Company Records*, April 15, 2008, p.100752; and information from www.netflix.com and www.blockbuster.com, accessed November 2008.

Analyzing Consumer Needs

As noted previously, marketing channels are part of the overall *customer-value delivery network*. Each channel member and level adds value for the customer. Thus, designing the marketing channel starts with finding out what target consumers want from the channel. Do consumers want to buy from nearby locations or are they willing to travel to more distant centralized locations? Would they rather buy in person, by phone, or online? Do they value breadth of assortment or do they prefer specialization? Do consumers want many add-on services (delivery, repairs, installation), or will they obtain these elsewhere? The faster the delivery, the greater the assortment provided, and the more add-on services supplied, the greater the channel's service level.

Providing the fastest delivery, greatest assortment, and most services may not be possible or practical. The company and its channel members may not have the resources or skills needed to provide all the desired services. Also, providing higher levels of service results in higher costs for the channel and higher prices for consumers. The company must balance consumer needs not only against the feasibility and costs of meeting these needs but also against customer price preferences. The success of discount retailing shows that consumers will often accept lower service levels in exchange for lower prices.

Setting Channel Objectives

Companies should state their marketing channel objectives in terms of targeted levels of customer service. Usually, a company can identify several segments wanting different levels of service. The company should decide which segments to serve and the best channels to use in each case. In each segment, the company wants to minimize the total channel cost of meeting customer-service requirements.

The company's channel objectives are also influenced by the nature of the company, its products, its marketing intermediaries, its competitors, and the environment. For example, the company's size and financial situation determine which marketing functions it can handle itself and which it must give to intermediaries. Companies selling perishable products may require more direct marketing to avoid delays and too much handling.

In some cases, a company may want to compete in or near the same outlets that carry competitors' products. In other cases, companies may avoid the channels used by competitors. Mary Kay Cosmetics, for example, sells direct to consumers through its corps of more than one million independent beauty consultants in 34 markets worldwide rather than going head-to-head with other cosmetics makers for scarce positions in retail stores. And GEICO primarily markets auto and homeowner's insurance directly to consumers via the telephone and Web rather than through agents.

Finally, environmental factors such as economic conditions and legal constraints may affect channel objectives and design. For example, in a depressed economy, producers want to distribute their goods in the most economical way, using shorter channels and dropping unneeded services that add to the final price of the goods.

Identifying Major Alternatives

When the company has defined its channel objectives, it should next identify its major channel alternatives in terms of *types* of intermediaries, the *number* of intermediaries, and the *responsibilities* of each channel member.

Types of Intermediaries

A firm should identify the types of channel members available to carry out its channel work. Most companies face many channel member choices. For example, until recently, Dell sold directly to final consumers and business buyers only through its sophisticated phone and Internet marketing channel. It also sold directly to large corporate, institutional, and government buyers using its direct sales force. However, to reach more consumers and to match competitors such as HP, Dell now sells indirectly through retailers such as Best Buy and Wal-Mart. It also sells indirectly through "value-added resellers," independent distributors and dealers who develop computer systems and applications tailored to the special needs of small and medium-sized business customers.

Using many types of resellers in a channel provides both benefits and drawbacks. For example, by selling through retailers and value-added resellers in addition to its own direct channels, Dell can reach more and different kinds of buyers. However, the new channels will be more difficult to manage and control. And the direct and indirect channels will compete with each other for many of the same customers, causing potential conflict. In fact, Dell is already finding itself "stuck in the middle," with its direct sales reps complaining about new competition from retail stores, while at the same time value-added resellers complain that the direct sales reps are undercutting their business.[8]

Number of Marketing Intermediaries

Companies must also determine the number of channel members to use at each level. Three strategies are available: intensive distribution, exclusive distribution, and selective distribution. Producers of convenience products and common raw materials typically seek

Intensive distribution

Stocking the product in as many outlets as possible.

Exclusive distribution

Giving a limited number of dealers the exclusive right to distribute the company's products in their territories.

▲ Exclusive distribution: Rolex sells its watches exclusively through only a handful of authorized dealers in any given market. Such limited distribution enhances the brand's image and generates stronger retailer support.

Selective distribution

The use of more than one, but fewer than all, of the intermediaries who are willing to carry the company's products.

intensive distribution—a strategy in which they stock their products in as many outlets as possible. These products must be available where and when consumers want them. For example, toothpaste, candy, and other similar items are sold in millions of outlets to provide maximum brand exposure and consumer convenience. Kraft, Coca-Cola, Kimberly-Clark, and other consumer-goods companies distribute their products in this way.

By contrast, some producers purposely limit the number of intermediaries handling their products. The extreme form of this practice is **exclusive distribution**, in which the producer gives only a limited number of dealers the exclusive right to distribute its products in their territories. Exclusive distribution is often found in the distribution of luxury automobiles and prestige women's clothing. ▲ For example, exclusive Rolex watches are typically sold by only a handful of authorized dealers in any given market area. By granting exclusive distribution, Rolex gains stronger dealer selling support and more control over dealer prices, promotion, and services. Exclusive distribution also enhances the brand's image and allows for higher markups.

Between intensive and exclusive distribution lies **selective distribution**—the use of more than one, but fewer than all, of the intermediaries who are willing to carry a company's products. Most television, furniture, and home appliance brands are distributed in this manner. For example, Whirlpool and General Electric sell their major appliances through dealer networks and selected large retailers. By using selective distribution, they can develop good working relationships with selected channel members and expect a better-than-average selling effort. Selective distribution gives producers good market coverage with more control and less cost than does intensive distribution.

Responsibilities of Channel Members

The producer and intermediaries need to agree on the terms and responsibilities of each channel member. They should agree on price policies, conditions of sale, territorial rights, and specific services to be performed by each party. The producer should establish a list price and a fair set of discounts for intermediaries. It must define each channel member's territory, and it should be careful about where it places new resellers.

Mutual services and duties need to be spelled out carefully, especially in franchise and exclusive distribution channels. For example, McDonald's provides franchisees with promotional support, a record-keeping system, training at Hamburger University, and general management assistance. In turn, franchisees must meet company standards for physical facilities and food quality, cooperate with new promotion programs, provide requested information, and buy specified food products.

Evaluating the Major Alternatives

Suppose a company has identified several channel alternatives and wants to select the one that will best satisfy its long-run objectives. Each alternative should be evaluated against economic, control, and adaptive criteria.

Using *economic criteria*, a company compares the likely sales, costs, and profitability of different channel alternatives. What will be the investment required by each channel alternative, and what returns will result? The company must also consider *control issues*. Using intermediaries usually means giving them some control over the marketing of the product, and some intermediaries take more control than others. Other things being equal, the company prefers to keep as much control as possible. Finally, the company must apply *adaptive criteria*. Channels often involve long-term commitments, yet the company wants to keep the channel flexible so that it can adapt to environmental changes. Thus, to be considered, a channel involving long-term commitments should be greatly superior on economic and control grounds.

Designing International Distribution Channels

International marketers face many additional complexities in designing their channels. Each country has its own unique distribution system that has evolved over time and changes very slowly. These channel systems can vary widely from country to country. Thus, global marketers must usually adapt their channel strategies to the existing structures within each country.

In some markets, the distribution system is complex and hard to penetrate, consisting of many layers and large numbers of intermediaries. At the other extreme, distribution systems in developing countries may be scattered, inefficient, or altogether lacking. For example, China and India are huge markets, each with populations well over one billion people. However, because of inadequate distribution systems, most companies can profitably access only a small portion of the population located in each country's most affluent cities. "China is a very decentralized market," notes a China trade expert. "[It's] made up of two dozen distinct markets sprawling across 2,000 cities. Each has its own culture. . . . It's like operating in an asteroid belt." China's distribution system is so fragmented that logistics costs amount to 15 percent of the nation's GDP, far higher than in most other countries. After years of effort, even Wal-Mart executives admit that they have been unable to assemble an efficient supply chain in China.[9]

▲ International channel complexities: When the Chinese government banned door-to-door selling, Avon had to abandon its traditional direct marketing approach and sell through retail shops.

Sometimes customs or government regulation can greatly restrict how a company distributes products in global markets. ▲For example, it wasn't an inefficient distribution structure that caused problems for Avon in China—it was restrictive government regulations. Fearing the growth of multilevel marketing schemes, the Chinese government banned door-to-door selling altogether in 1998, forcing Avon to abandon its traditional direct marketing approach and sell through retail shops. The Chinese government recently gave Avon and other direct sellers permission to sell door-to-door again, but that permission is tangled in a web of restrictions. Fortunately for Avon, its earlier focus on store sales is helping it weather the restrictions better than most other direct sellers.[10]

International marketers face a wide range of channel alternatives. Designing efficient and effective channel systems between and within various country markets poses a difficult challenge. We discuss international distribution decisions further in Chapter 19.

Author Comment | Now it's time to implement the chosen channel design and to work with selected channel members to manage and motivate them.

Channel Management Decisions (pp 352–355)

Once the company has reviewed its channel alternatives and decided on the best channel design, it must implement and manage the chosen channel. **Marketing channel management** calls for selecting, managing, and motivating individual channel members and evaluating their performance over time.

Marketing channel management
Selecting, managing, and motivating individual channel members and evaluating their performance over time.

Selecting Channel Members

Producers vary in their ability to attract qualified marketing intermediaries. Some producers have no trouble signing up channel members. For example, when Toyota first introduced its Lexus line in the United States, it had no trouble attracting new dealers. In fact, it had to turn down many would-be resellers.

At the other extreme are producers who have to work hard to line up enough qualified intermediaries. For example, when Timex first tried to sell its inexpensive watches through regular jewelry stores, most jewelry stores refused to carry them. The company then managed to get its watches into mass-merchandise outlets. This turned out to be a wise decision because of the rapid growth of mass-merchandising.

When selecting intermediaries, the company should determine what characteristics distinguish the better ones. It will want to evaluate each channel member's years in business, other lines carried, growth and profit record, cooperativeness, and reputation. If the intermediaries are sales agents, the company will want to evaluate the number and character of other lines carried and the size and quality of the sales force. If the intermediary is a retail store that wants exclusive or selective distribution, the company will want to evaluate the store's customers, location, and future growth potential.

Managing and Motivating Channel Members

Once selected, channel members must be continuously managed and motivated to do their best. The company must sell not only *through* the intermediaries but *to* and *with* them. Most companies see their intermediaries as first-line customers and partners. They practice strong *partner relationship management (PRM)* to forge long-term partnerships with channel members. This creates a value delivery system that meets the needs of both the company *and* its marketing partners. For example, heavy-equipment manufacturer Caterpillar and its worldwide network of independent dealers work in close harmony to find better ways to bring value to customers. Dealers play a vital role in almost every aspect of Caterpillar's operations (see **Real Marketing 12.2**).

In managing its channels, a company must convince distributors that they can succeed better by working together as a part of a cohesive value delivery system. Thus, Procter & Gamble works closely with Wal-Mart to create superior value for final consumers. The two jointly plan merchandising goals and strategies, inventory levels, and advertising and promotion programs. ▲Similarly, Samsung's Information Technology Division works closely with value-added resellers through the industry-leading Samsung Power Partner Program (P3).

The Samsung P3 program creates close partnerships with important value-added resellers (VARs)—channel firms that assemble IT solutions for their own customers using products from Samsung and other manufacturers. Through the Power Partner Program, Samsung provides extensive presale, selling, and postsale tools and support to some 17,255 registered North America VAR partners at one of three levels— silver, gold, or platinum. For example, platinum-level partners—those selling $500,000 or more of Samsung IT products per year—receive access to a searchable online product and pricing database and downloadable marketing materials. They can tap into partner-only Samsung training programs, special seminars, and conferences. A dedicated Samsung P3 team helps partners to find good sales prospects and initiate sales. Then, a dedicated Samsung field sales rep works with each partner to close deals, and inside sales reps provide the partner with information and technical support. Platinum partners even participate in Samsung's Reseller Council. Finally, the P3 program rewards high-performing reseller-partners with rebates, discount promotions, bonuses, and sales awards. In all, the Power Partner Program turns important resellers into strong, motivated marketing partners by helping them to be more effective and profitable at selling Samsung.[11]

▲ Partnering with marketing channel members: The Samsung Power Partner Program turns important resellers into strong, motivated marketing partners by helping them to be more effective and profitable at selling Samsung.

Real Marketing 12.2

With the Help of Its Dealer Network, the Big Cat Is Purring

For more than eight decades, Caterpillar has dominated the world's markets for heavy construction, mining, and logging equipment. Its familiar yellow tractors, crawlers, loaders, bulldozers, and trucks are a common sight at any construction area around the world. Caterpillar sells more than 300 products in nearly 200 countries, with sales of more than $45 billion annually. Over the past four years, sales have nearly doubled and profits have more than tripled. The big Cat captures some 40 percent of the worldwide heavy-equipment business, twice that of number-two Komatsu. The waiting line for some of Caterpillar's biggest equipment is three years long.

Many factors contribute to Caterpillar's enduring success—high-quality products, flexible and efficient manufacturing, and a steady stream of innovative new products. Yet these are not the most important reasons for Caterpillar's dominance. Instead, Caterpillar credits its focus on customers and its distribution network of 181 outstanding independent dealers worldwide, who work with Caterpillar to do a superb job of taking care of every customer need. According to a former Caterpillar CEO:

After the product leaves our door, the dealers take over. They are the ones on the front line. They're the ones who live with the product for its lifetime. They're the ones customers see. . . . They're out there making sure that when a machine is

Caterpillar works closely with its worldwide network of independent dealers to find better ways to bring value to customers. When a big piece of CAT equipment breaks down, customers know they can count on Caterpillar and its outstanding dealer network for support.

delivered, it's in the condition it's supposed to be in. They're out there training a customer's operators. They service a product frequently throughout its life, carefully monitoring a machine's health and scheduling repairs to prevent costly downtime. The customer . . . knows that there is a [$45-billion-plus] company called Caterpillar. But the dealers create the image of a company that doesn't stand just *behind* its products but *with* its products, anywhere in the world. Our dealers are the reason that our motto—Buy the Iron, Get the Company—is not an empty slogan.

"Buy the Iron, Get the Company"—that's a powerful value proposition. It means that when you buy Cat equipment, you

become a member of the Caterpillar family. Caterpillar and its dealers work in close harmony to find better ways to bring value to customers. Dealers play a vital role in almost every aspect of Caterpillar's operations, from product design and delivery, to product service and support, to market intelligence and customer feedback.

In the heavy-equipment industry, in which equipment downtime can mean big losses, Caterpillar's exceptional service gives it a huge advantage in winning and keeping customers. Consider BHP Billiton, a Caterpillar customer that operates the huge Antamina mine in Peru:

More than a mile in length, the Antamina mine sits 14,100 oxygen-deprived feet

Many companies are now installing integrated high-tech partner relationship management systems to coordinate their whole-channel marketing efforts. Just as they use customer relationship management (CRM) software systems to help manage relationships with important customers, companies can now use PRM and supply chain management (SCM) software to help recruit, train, organize, manage, motivate, and evaluate relationships with channel partners.

Evaluating Channel Members

The producer must regularly check channel member performance against standards such as sales quotas, average inventory levels, customer delivery time, treatment of damaged and lost goods, cooperation in company promotion and training programs, and services to the customer. The company should recognize and reward intermediaries who are performing well and adding good value for consumers. Those who are performing poorly should be assisted or, as a last resort, replaced.

above sea level in the Peruvian Andes. From the rim of the vast open pit, huge mechanized beasts of burden below look like scuttling yellow insects. Descend the dirt ramps to the floor of the pit, however, and those bugs are transformed into Caterpillars. The industrial ballet goes on every hour of every day here, as Cat machines—giant trucks, mechanical shovels, scrapers, and other brutes—carve out massive amounts of copper and zinc from the earth. Forty-nine of those yellow bugs are mammoth 200- to 250-ton Caterpillar 793C and 793D trucks, 43-foot-high machines, costing millions of dollars each, which are powered by a diesel engine with more oomph than a tank. Made in Decatur, Illinois, each truck is shipped in pieces to Lima, hauled to the job site in nine tractor-trailers, and then assembled. Like sharks pursued by pilot fish, the big trucks are surrounded by a bevy of smaller Caterpillar equipment—wheel loaders to fill them, motor graders to keep the roads cleared, and bulldozers to clean up the spills. All told, BHP uses more than $200 million worth of Caterpillar machinery at Antamina—and it will spend another $200 million servicing them over their working life.

When equipment breaks down, BHP loses money fast. It gladly pays a premium price for machines and service it can count on. In fact, Caterpillar's reputation for gold-standard quality and service allows it to charge 10 percent to 20 percent more than its competitors. Customers know that they can count on Caterpillar and its outstanding dealer network for superb support.

The close working relationship between Caterpillar and its dealers comes down to more than just formal contracts and business agreements. Caterpillar really knows its dealers

and cares about their success. It closely monitors each dealership's sales, market position, service capability, financial situation, and other performance measures. When it sees a problem, it jumps in to help. As a result, Caterpillar dealerships, many of which are long-standing family businesses, tend to be stable and profitable.

Caterpillar believes that it should "share the gain as well as the pain." When times are good, Caterpillar shares the bounty with its dealers rather than trying to grab all the riches for itself. When times are bad, Caterpillar protects its dealers. In the mid-1980s, facing a depressed global construction-equipment market and cutthroat competition, Caterpillar sheltered its dealers by absorbing much of the economic damage. It lost almost $1 billion in just three years but didn't lose a single dealer. In contrast, competitors' dealers struggled and many failed. As a result, Caterpillar emerged with its distribution partnerships intact and its competitive position stronger than ever.

Caterpillar provides extraordinary dealer support. Nowhere is this support more apparent than in the company's parts delivery system, the fastest and most reliable in the industry. Caterpillar maintains 23 distribution centers and 1,500 service facilities around the world, which stock more than 150,000 different parts and ship 84,000 items per day, every day of the year. In turn, dealers have made huge investments in inventory, warehouses, fleets of trucks, service bays, diagnostic and service equipment, and information technology. Together, Caterpillar

and its dealers guarantee parts delivery within 48 hours anywhere in the world, from the Alaskan tundra to the deserts of Timbuktu. The company ships 80 percent of parts orders immediately and 99 percent on the same day the order is received. In contrast, it's not unusual for competitors' customers to wait four or five costly days for a part.

Finally, in addition to more formal business ties, Cat forms close personal ties with its dealers in a kind of family relationship. One Caterpillar executive relates the following example: "When I see Chappy Chapman, a retired executive vice-president . . . out on the golf course, he always asks about particular dealers or about their children, who may be running the business now. And every time I see those dealers, they inquire, 'How's Chappy?' That's the sort of relationship we have. . . . I consider the majority of dealers personal friends."

Thus, Caterpillar's superb integrated distribution system serves as a major source of competitive advantage, for both the company and its independent dealers. The system is built on a firm base of mutual trust and shared dreams. Caterpillar and its dealers feel a deep pride in what they are accomplishing together. As the former CEO puts it, "There's a camaraderie among our dealers around the world that really makes it more than just a financial arrangement. They feel that what they're doing is good for the world because they are part of an organization that makes, sells, and tends to the machines that make the world work."

Sources: Quotes, examples, and other information from Alex Taylor III, "Caterpillar," *Fortune*, August 20, 2007, pp. 48–54; Donald V. Fites, "Make Your Dealers Your Partners," *Harvard Business Review*, March–April 1996, pp. 84–95; Tony Reid, "Caterpillar Predicts Record Sales, Profits," *McClatchy Tribune Business News*, March 19, 2008; and information accessed at www.caterpillar.com, accessed November 2008.

Finally, manufacturers need to be sensitive to their dealers. Those who treat their dealers poorly risk not only losing dealer support but also causing some legal problems. The next section describes various rights and duties pertaining to manufacturers and their channel members.

Public Policy and Distribution Decisions (pp 355–356)

For the most part, companies are legally free to develop whatever channel arrangements suit them. In fact, the laws affecting channels seek to prevent the exclusionary tactics of some companies that might keep another company from using a desired channel. Most channel law deals with the mutual rights and duties of the channel members once they have formed a relationship.

Many producers and wholesalers like to develop exclusive channels for their products. When the seller allows only certain outlets to carry its products, this strategy is called *exclusive distribution*. When the seller requires that these dealers not handle competitors' products, its strategy is called *exclusive dealing*. Both parties can benefit from exclusive arrangements: The seller obtains more loyal and dependable outlets, and the dealers obtain a steady source of supply and stronger seller support. But exclusive arrangements also exclude other producers from selling to these dealers. This situation brings exclusive dealing contracts under the scope of the Clayton Act of 1914. They are legal as long as they do not substantially lessen competition or tend to create a monopoly and as long as both parties enter into the agreement voluntarily.

Exclusive dealing often includes *exclusive territorial agreements*. The producer may agree not to sell to other dealers in a given area, or the buyer may agree to sell only in its own territory. The first practice is normal under franchise systems as a way to increase dealer enthusiasm and commitment. It is also perfectly legal—a seller has no legal obligation to sell through more outlets than it wishes. The second practice, whereby the producer tries to keep a dealer from selling outside its territory, has become a major legal issue.

Producers of a strong brand sometimes sell it to dealers only if the dealers will take some or all of the rest of the line. This is called full-line forcing. Such *tying agreements* are not necessarily illegal, but they do violate the Clayton Act if they tend to lessen competition substantially. The practice may prevent consumers from freely choosing among competing suppliers of these other brands.

Finally, producers are free to select their dealers, but their right to terminate dealers is somewhat restricted. In general, sellers can drop dealers "for cause." However, they cannot drop dealers if, for example, the dealers refuse to cooperate in a doubtful legal arrangement, such as exclusive dealing or tying agreements.[12]

<table>
<tr><td>**Author Comment**</td><td>Markers used to call this plain old "physical distribution." But as these titles suggest, the topic has grown in importance, complexity, and sophistication.</td></tr>
</table>

Marketing Logistics and Supply Chain Management (pp 356–363)

In today's global marketplace, selling a product is sometimes easier than getting it to customers. Companies must decide on the best way to store, handle, and move their products and services so that they are available to customers in the right assortments, at the right time, and in the right place. Logistics effectiveness has a major impact on both customer satisfaction and company costs. Here we consider the nature and importance of logistics management in the supply chain, goals of the logistics system, major logistics functions, and the need for integrated supply chain management.

Nature and Importance of Marketing Logistics

Marketing logistics (or physical distribution)

Planning, implementing, and controlling the physical flow of materials, final goods, and related information from points of origin to points of consumption to meet customer requirements at a profit.

To some managers, marketing logistics means only trucks and warehouses. But modern logistics is much more than this. **Marketing logistics**—also called **physical distribution**—involves planning, implementing, and controlling the physical flow of goods, services, and related information from points of origin to points of consumption to meet customer requirements at a profit. In short, it involves getting the right product to the right customer in the right place at the right time.

In the past, physical distribution planners typically started with products at the plant and then tried to find low-cost solutions to get them to customers. However, today's marketers prefer *customer-centered* logistics thinking, which starts with the marketplace and works backward to the factory, or even to sources of supply. Marketing logistics involves not only *outbound distribution* (moving products from the factory to resellers and ultimately to customers) but also *inbound distribution* (moving products and materials from suppliers to the factory) and *reverse distribution* (moving broken, unwanted, or excess products returned by consumers or resellers). That is, it involves entire **supply chain management**—managing upstream and downstream value-added flows of materials, final goods, and related information among suppliers, the company, resellers, and final consumers, as shown in ◆ **Figure 12.5**.

Supply chain management

Managing upstream and downstream value-added flows of materials, final goods, and related information among suppliers, the company, resellers, and final consumers.

The logistics manager's task is to coordinate activities of suppliers, purchasing agents, marketers, channel members, and customers. These activities include forecasting,

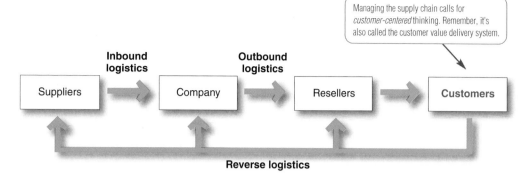

FIGURE | 12.5
Supply Chain Management

information systems, purchasing, production planning, order processing, inventory, warehousing, and transportation planning.

Companies today are placing greater emphasis on logistics for several reasons. First, companies can gain a powerful competitive advantage by using improved logistics to give customers better service or lower prices. Second, improved logistics can yield tremendous cost savings to both the company and its customers. As much as 20 percent of an average product's price is accounted for by shipping and transport alone. This far exceeds the cost of advertising and many other marketing costs. American companies spent over $1.3 trillion last year—almost 10 percent of gross domestic product—to wrap, bundle, load, unload, sort, reload, and transport goods. That's more than the national GDPs of all but 12 countries worldwide. What's more, these costs have risen more than 50 percent over the past decade. By itself, ▲ Ford has more than 500 million tons of finished vehicles, production parts, and aftermarket parts in transit at any given time, running up an annual logistics bill of around $4 billion.[13] Shaving off even a small fraction of these costs can mean substantial savings.

Third, the explosion in product variety has created a need for improved logistics management. For example, in 1911 the typical A&P grocery store carried only 270 items. The store manager could keep track of this inventory on about 10 pages of notebook paper stuffed in a shirt pocket. Today, the average A&P carries a bewildering stock of more than 25,000 items. A Wal-Mart Supercenter store carries more than 100,000 products, 30,000 of which are grocery products.[14] Ordering, shipping, stocking, and controlling such a variety of products presents a sizable logistics challenge.

Improvements in information technology have also created opportunities for major gains in distribution efficiency. Today's companies are using sophisticated supply chain management software, Web-based logistics systems, point-of-sale scanners, uniform product codes, satellite tracking, and electronic transfer of order and payment data. Such technology lets them quickly and efficiently manage the flow of goods, information, and finances through the supply chain.

Finally, more than almost any other marketing function, logistics affects the environment and a firm's environmental sustainability efforts. Transportation, warehousing, packaging, and other logistics functions are typically the biggest supply chain contributors to the company's environmental footprint. At the same time, they also provide one of the most fertile areas for cost savings. So developing a *green supply chain* is not only environmentally responsible, it can also be profitable. "Your CO2 footprint of transportation and your cost of fuel are permanently linked," says one logistics manager. "The good news is if you can reduce logistics costs you can write an environmental story about it."[15]

Goals of the Logistics System

Some companies state their logistics objective as providing maximum customer service at the least cost. Unfortunately, no logistics system can *both* maximize customer service *and* minimize distribution costs. Maximum customer service implies rapid delivery, large inventories, flexible assortments,

▲ The importance of logistics: At any given time, Ford has more than 500 million tons of finished vehicles, production parts, and aftermarket parts in transit, running up an annual logistics bill of around $4 billion.

liberal returns policies, and other services—all of which raise distribution costs. In contrast, minimum distribution costs imply slower delivery, smaller inventories, and larger shipping lots—which represent a lower level of overall customer service.

The goal of marketing logistics should be to provide a *targeted* level of customer service at the least cost. A company must first research the importance of various distribution services to customers and then set desired service levels for each segment. The objective is to maximize *profits*, not sales. Therefore, the company must weigh the benefits of providing higher levels of service against the costs. Some companies offer less service than their competitors and charge a lower price. Other companies offer more service and charge higher prices to cover higher costs.

Major Logistics Functions

Given a set of logistics objectives, the company is ready to design a logistics system that will minimize the cost of attaining these objectives. The major logistics functions include *warehousing, inventory management, transportation,* and *logistics information management.*

Warehousing

Production and consumption cycles rarely match. So most companies must store their goods while they wait to be sold. For example, Snapper, Toro, and other lawn mower manufacturers run their factories all year long and store up products for the heavy spring and summer buying seasons. The storage function overcomes differences in needed quantities and timing, ensuring that products are available when customers are ready to buy them.

A company must decide on *how many* and *what types* of warehouses it needs and *where* they will be located. The company might use either *storage warehouses* or *distribution centers.* Storage warehouses store goods for moderate to long periods. **Distribution centers** are designed to move goods rather than just store them. They are large and highly automated warehouses designed to receive goods from various plants and suppliers, take orders, fill them efficiently, and deliver goods to customers as quickly as possible.

For example, Wal-Mart operates a network of 112 huge U.S. distribution centers and another 57 around the globe. A single center, serving the daily needs of 75 to 100 Wal-Mart stores, typically contains some 1 million square feet of space (about 20 football fields) under a single roof. At a typical center, laser scanners route as many as 190,000 cases of goods per day along 5 miles of conveyer belts, and the center's 1,000 workers load or unload some 500 trucks daily. Wal-Mart's Monroe, Georgia, distribution center contains a 127,000-square-foot freezer (that's about 2½ football fields) that can hold 10,000 pallets—room enough for 58 million Popsicles.[16]

Like almost everything else these days, warehousing has seen dramatic changes in technology in recent years. Outdated materials-handling methods are steadily being replaced by newer, computer-controlled systems requiring few employees. Computers and scanners read orders and direct lift trucks, electric hoists, or robots to gather goods, move them to loading docks, and issue invoices. ▲For example, office supplies retailer Staples now employs "a team of super-retrievers—in day-glo orange—that keep its warehouse humming":[17]

Imagine a team of employees that works 16 hours a day, seven days a week. They never call in sick or show up late, because they never leave the building. They demand no benefits, require no health insurance, and receive no pay checks. And they never complain. Sounds like a bunch of robots, huh? They are, in fact, robots—and they're dramatically changing the way Staples delivers notepads, pens, and paper clips to its customers. Every day, Staples' huge Chambersburg, Pennsylvania, distribution center receives thousands of customer orders, each containing a wide range of office supply items. Having people run around a

Distribution center

A large, highly automated warehouse designed to receive goods from various plants and suppliers, take orders, fill them efficiently, and deliver goods to customers as quickly as possible.

▲ High-tech distribution centers: Staples employs a team of super-retrievers—in day-glo orange—to keep its warehouse humming.

warehouse looking for those items is expensive, especially when the company has promised to delight customers by delivering orders the next day.

Enter the robots. On the distribution center floor, the 150 robots most resemble a well-trained breed of working dogs, say, golden retrievers. When orders come in, a centralized computer tells the robots where to find racks with the appropriate items. The robots retrieve the racks and carry them to picking stations, then wait patiently as humans pull the correct products and place them in boxes. When orders are filled, the robots neatly park the racks back among the rest. The robots pretty much take care of themselves. When they run low on power, they head to battery-charging terminals, or, as warehouse personnel say, "They get themselves a drink of water." The robots now run 50 percent of the Chambersburg facility, where average daily output is up 60 percent since they arrived on the scene.

Inventory Management

Inventory management also affects customer satisfaction. Here, managers must maintain the delicate balance between carrying too little inventory and carrying too much. With too little stock, the firm risks not having products when customers want to buy. To remedy this, the firm may need costly emergency shipments or production. Carrying too much inventory results in higher-than-necessary inventory-carrying costs and stock obsolescence. Thus, in managing inventory, firms must balance the costs of carrying larger inventories against resulting sales and profits.

Many companies have greatly reduced their inventories and related costs through *just-in-time* logistics systems. With such systems, producers and retailers carry only small inventories of parts or merchandise, often only enough for a few days of operations. New stock arrives exactly when needed, rather than being stored in inventory until being used. Just-in-time systems require accurate forecasting along with fast, frequent, and flexible delivery so that new supplies will be available when needed. However, these systems result in substantial savings in inventory-carrying and handling costs.

Marketers are always looking for new ways to make inventory management more efficient. In the not-too-distant future, handling inventory might even become fully automated. For example, in Chapter 3 we discussed RFID or "smart tag" technology, by which small transmitter chips are embedded in or placed on products and packaging on everything from flowers and razors to tires. "Smart" products could make the entire supply chain—which accounts for nearly 75 percent of a product's cost—intelligent and automated.

Companies using RFID would know, at any time, exactly where a product is located physically within the supply chain. "Smart shelves" would not only tell them when it's time to reorder, but would also place the order automatically with their suppliers. Such exciting new information technology applications will revolutionize distribution as we know it. Many large and resourceful marketing companies, such as Wal-Mart, Procter & Gamble, Kraft, IBM, HP, and Best Buy, are investing heavily to make the full use of RFID technology a reality.[18]

Transportation

The choice of transportation carriers affects the pricing of products, delivery performance, and condition of the goods when they arrive—all of which will affect customer satisfaction. In shipping goods to its warehouses, dealers, and customers, the company can choose among five main transportation modes: truck, rail, water, pipeline, and air, along with an alternative mode for digital products—the Internet.

Trucks have increased their share of transportation steadily and now account for nearly 35 percent of total cargo ton-miles (more than 60 percent of actual tonnage).[19] Each year in the United States, trucks travel more than 216 billion miles—a distance that has more than doubled over the past 20 years—carrying 11 billion tons of freight worth over $9 trillion. Trucks are highly flexible in their routing and time schedules, and they can usually offer faster service than railroads. They are efficient for short hauls of high-value merchandise.

Trucking firms have evolved in recent years to become full-service providers of global transportation services. ▲For example, Roadway now offers services for next-day,

▲ Roadway Customer Care Teams focus on specific customers' needs: "With the Roadway team in your corner, you get transportation solutions that are simple, smart, and effective.

Intermodal transportation
Combining two or more modes of transportation.

second-day, expedited, and time-definite transcontinental and international shipping with specialized services ranging from patented shipment protection to personal border-clearance assistance to Web-based shipment management. ▲The Roadway Customer Care Teams focus on specific customer's needs: "With the entire Roadway team in your corner, you get transportation solutions that are simple, smart, and effective. And that makes everything better for you."

Railroads account for 31 percent of total cargo ton-miles moved. They are one of the most cost-effective modes for shipping large amounts of bulk products—coal, sand, minerals, and farm and forest products—over long distances. In recent years, railroads have increased their customer services by designing new equipment to handle special categories of goods, providing flatcars for carrying truck trailers by rail (piggyback), and providing in-transit services such as the diversion of shipped goods to other destinations en route and the processing of goods en route.

Water carriers, which account for about 11 percent of cargo ton-miles, transport large amounts of goods by ships and barges on U.S. coastal and inland waterways. Although the cost of water transportation is very low for shipping bulky, low-value, nonperishable products such as sand, coal, grain, oil, and metallic ores, water transportation is the slowest mode and may be affected by the weather. *Pipelines*, which also account for about 16 percent of cargo ton-miles, are a specialized means of shipping petroleum, natural gas, and chemicals from sources to markets. Most pipelines are used by their owners to ship their own products.

Although *air* carriers transport less than 5 percent of the nation's goods, they are an important transportation mode. Airfreight rates are much higher than rail or truck rates, but airfreight is ideal when speed is needed or distant markets have to be reached. Among the most frequently airfreighted products are perishables (fresh fish, cut flowers) and high-value, low-bulk items (technical instruments, jewelry). Companies find that airfreight also reduces inventory levels, packaging costs, and the number of warehouses needed.

The *Internet* carries digital products from producer to customer via satellite, cable, or phone wire. Software firms, the media, music companies, and education all make use of the Internet to transport digital products. Although these firms primarily use traditional transportation to distribute DVDs, newspapers, and more, the Internet holds the potential for lower product distribution costs. Whereas planes, trucks, and trains move freight and packages, digital technology moves information bits.

Shippers also use **intermodal transportation**—combining two or more modes of transportation. *Piggyback* describes the use of rail and trucks; *fishyback*, water and trucks; *trainship*, water and rail; and *airtruck*, air and trucks. Combining modes provides advantages that no single mode can deliver. Each combination offers advantages to the shipper. For example, not only is piggyback cheaper than trucking alone but it also provides flexibility and convenience.

In choosing a transportation mode for a product, shippers must balance many considerations: speed, dependability, availability, cost, and others. Thus, if a shipper needs speed, air and truck are the prime choices. If the goal is low cost, then water or pipeline might be best.

Logistics Information Management

Companies manage their supply chains through information. Channel partners often link up to share information and to make better joint logistics decisions. From a logistics perspective, information flows such as customer transactions, billing, shipment and inventory levels, and even customer data are closely linked to channel performance. The company wants to design a simple, accessible, fast, and accurate process for capturing, processing, and sharing channel information.

Information can be shared and managed in many ways but most sharing takes place through traditional or Internet-based *electronic data interchange (EDI)*, the computerized exchange of data between organizations. Wal-Mart, for example, maintains EDI links with almost all of its 91,000 suppliers. And where it once took eight weeks using EDI, Krispy Kreme can now turn around 1,000 supplier invoices and process the checks in only a single week.[20]

In some cases, suppliers might actually be asked to generate orders and arrange deliveries for their customers. Many large retailers—such as Wal-Mart and Home Depot—work closely with major suppliers such as Procter & Gamble or Black & Decker to set up *vendor-managed inventory* (VMI) systems or *continuous inventory replenishment* systems. Using VMI, the customer shares real-time data on sales and current inventory levels with the supplier. The supplier then takes full responsibility for managing inventories and deliveries. Some retailers even go so far as to shift inventory and delivery costs to the supplier. Such systems require close cooperation between the buyer and seller.

Integrated Logistics Management

Integrated logistics management
The logistics concept that emphasizes teamwork, both inside the company and among all the marketing channel organizations, to maximize the performance of the entire distribution system.

Today, more and more companies are adopting the concept of **integrated logistics management**. This concept recognizes that providing better customer service and trimming distribution costs require *teamwork*, both inside the company and among all the marketing channel organizations. Inside, the company's various departments must work closely together to maximize the company's own logistics performance. Outside, the company must integrate its logistics system with those of its suppliers and customers to maximize the performance of the entire distribution network.

Cross-Functional Teamwork Inside the Company

Most companies assign responsibility for various logistics activities to many different departments—marketing, sales, finance, operations, and purchasing. Too often, each function tries to optimize its own logistics performance without regard for the activities of the other functions. However, transportation, inventory, warehousing, and information management activities interact, often in an inverse way. Lower inventory levels reduce inventory-carrying costs. But they may also reduce customer service and increase costs from stockouts, back orders, special production runs, and costly fast-freight shipments. Because distribution activities involve strong trade-offs, decisions by different functions must be coordinated to achieve better overall logistics performance.

The goal of integrated supply chain management is to harmonize all of the company's logistics decisions. Close working relationships among departments can be achieved in several ways. Some companies have created permanent logistics committees made up of managers responsible for different physical distribution activities. Companies can also create supply chain manager positions that link the logistics activities of functional areas. For example, Procter & Gamble has created supply managers, who manage all of the supply chain activities for each of its product categories. Many companies have a vice president of logistics with cross-functional authority.

Finally, companies can employ sophisticated, systemwide supply chain management software, now available from a wide range of software enterprises large and small, from SAP and Oracle to Infor and ▲Logility. The worldwide market for supply chain management software topped an estimated $6.5 billion last year and will reach an estimated $11.6 billion by 2013.[21] The important thing is that the company must coordinate its logistics and marketing activities to create high market satisfaction at a reasonable cost.

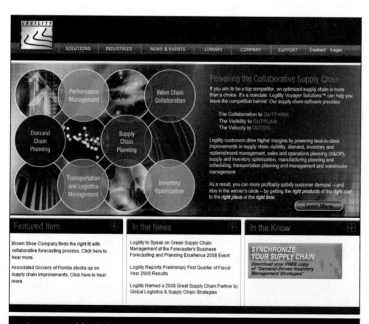

Integrated logistics management: Many companies now employ sophisticated, systemwide supply chain management software, available from companies such as Logility.

Building Logistics Partnerships

Companies must do more than improve their own logistics. They must also work with other channel partners to improve whole-channel distribution. The members of a marketing channel are linked closely in creating customer value and building customer relationships. One company's distribution system is another company's supply system. The success of each channel member depends on the performance of the entire supply chain. For example, IKEA can create its stylish but affordable furniture and deliver the "IKEA lifestyle" only if its entire supply chain—consisting of thousands of merchandise designers and suppliers, transport companies, warehouses, and service providers—operates at maximum efficiency and customer-focused effectiveness.

Smart companies coordinate their logistics strategies and forge strong partnerships with suppliers and customers to improve customer service and reduce channel costs. Many companies have created *cross-functional, cross-company teams*. For example, Procter & Gamble has a team of more than 200 people working in Bentonville, Arkansas, home of Wal-Mart. The P&Gers work jointly with their counterparts at Wal-Mart to find ways to squeeze costs out of their distribution system. Working together benefits not only P&G and Wal-Mart but also their shared final consumers.

Other companies partner through *shared projects*. For example, many large retailers conduct joint in-store programs with suppliers. Home Depot allows key suppliers to use its stores as a testing ground for new merchandising programs. The suppliers spend time at Home Depot stores watching how their product sells and how customers relate to it. They then create programs specially tailored to Home Depot and its customers. Clearly, both the supplier and the customer benefit from such partnerships. The point is that all supply chain members must work together in the cause of bringing value to final consumers.

Third-Party Logistics

Most big companies love to make and sell their products. But many loathe the associated logistics "grunt work." They detest the bundling, loading, unloading, sorting, storing, reloading, transporting, customs clearing, and tracking required to supply their factories and get products out to customers. They hate it so much that a growing number of firms now outsource some or all of their logistics to **third-party logistics (3PL) providers**. Here's an example:[22]

Third-party logistics (3PL) provider

An independent logistics provider that performs any or all of the functions required to get its client's product to market.

Whirlpool's ultimate goal is to create loyal customers who continue to buy its brands over their lifetimes. One key loyalty factor is good repair service, which in turn depends on fast and reliable parts distribution. Only a few years ago, however, Whirlpool's replacement parts distribution system was fragmented and ineffective, often causing frustrating customer service delays. "Whirlpool is the world's largest manufacturer and marketer of appliances, but we're not necessarily experts in parts warehousing and distribution," says Whirlpool's national director of parts operations. So to help fix the problem, ▲Whirlpool turned the entire job over to third-party logistics supplier Ryder, which quickly streamlined Whirlpool's service parts distribution system. Ryder now provides order fulfillment and worldwide distribution of Whirlpool's service parts across six continents to hundreds of customers that include, in addition to end-consumers, the Sears service network, authorized repair centers, and independent parts distributors that in turn ship parts out to a network of service companies and technicians. "Through our partnership with Ryder, we are now operating at our highest service level ever," says the Whirlpool executive. "We've . . . dramatically reduced [our parts distribution] costs. Our order cycle time has improved, and our customers are getting their parts more quickly."

These "3PLs"—companies such as Ryder, UPS Supply Chain Solutions, Penske Logistics, BAX Global, DHL Logistics, FedEx Logistics, or Roadway Logistics Services—help clients to tighten up sluggish, overstuffed supply chains, slash inventories, and get products to customers more quickly and reliably. For example, as we saw in Chapter 6, UPS's Supply Chain Solutions unit provides clients with a wide range of logistics services, from inventory control, warehousing, and transportation management to customer service and fulfillment. According to a survey of chief logistics executives at *Fortune* 500 companies, 82 percent of these companies use third-party

YOU NAME IT

We'll Customize A Supply Chain Solution For It

Ryder

SUPPLY CHAIN, WAREHOUSING & TRANSPORTATION SOLUTIONS

▲ Third-party logistics (3PL): Companies such as Ryder help clients to tighten up sluggish, overstuffed supply chains, slash inventories, and get products to customers more quickly and reliably.

logistics (also called *3PL, outsourced logistics,* or *contract logistics*) services. In just the past ten years, the revenues for 3PL companies in the United States has tripled in size to more than $110 billion.[23]

Companies use third-party logistics providers for several reasons. First, because getting the product to market is their main focus, these providers can often do it more efficiently and at lower cost. Outsourcing typically results in 15 percent to 30 percent cost savings. Second, outsourcing logistics frees a company to focus more intensely on its core business. Finally, integrated logistics companies understand increasingly complex logistics environments.

Third-party logistics partners can be especially helpful to companies attempting to expand their global market coverage. For example, companies distributing their products across Europe face a bewildering array of environmental restrictions that affect logistics, including packaging standards, truck size and weight limits, and noise and emissions pollution controls. By outsourcing its logistics, a company can gain a complete pan-European distribution system without incurring the costs, delays, and risks associated with setting up its own system.

REVIEWING Objectives AND KEY Terms

Marketing channel decisions are among the most important decisions that management faces. A company's channel decisions directly affect every other marketing decision. Management must make channel decisions carefully, incorporating today's needs with tomorrow's likely selling environment. Some companies pay too little attention to their distribution channels, but others have used imaginative distribution systems to gain competitive advantage.

OBJECTIVE 1 Explain why companies use marketing channels and discuss the functions these channels perform. (pp 337–341)

Most producers use intermediaries to bring their products to market. They try to forge a *marketing channel* (or *distribution channel*)—a set of interdependent organizations involved in the process of making a product or service available for use or consumption by the consumer or business user. Through their contacts, experience, specialization, and scale of operation, intermediaries usually offer the firm more than it can achieve on its own.

Marketing channels perform many key functions. Some help *complete* transactions by gathering and distributing *information* needed for planning and aiding exchange, by developing and spreading persuasive *communications* about an offer, by performing *contact* work—finding and communicating with prospective buyers, by *matching*—shaping and fitting the offer to the buyer's needs, and by entering into *negotiation* to reach an agreement on price and other terms of the offer so that ownership can be transferred. Other functions help to *fulfill* the completed transactions by offering *physical distribution*—transporting and storing goods, *financing*—acquiring and using funds to cover the costs of the channel work, and *risk taking*—assuming the risks of carrying out the channel work.

OBJECTIVE 2 Discuss how channel members interact and how they organize to perform the work of the channel. (pp 342–348)

The channel will be most effective when each member is assigned the tasks it can do best. Ideally, because the success of individual

channel members depends on overall channel success, all channel firms should work together smoothly. They should understand and accept their roles, coordinate their goals and activities, and cooperate to attain overall channel goals. By cooperating, they can more effectively sense, serve, and satisfy the target market.

In a large company, the formal organization structure assigns roles and provides needed leadership. But in a distribution channel made up of independent firms, leadership and power are not formally set. Traditionally, distribution channels have lacked the leadership needed to assign roles and manage conflict. In recent years, however, new types of channel organizations have appeared that provide stronger leadership and improved performance.

OBJECTIVE 3 Identify the major channel alternatives open to a company. (pp 348–352)

Each firm identifies alternative ways to reach its market. Available means vary from direct selling to using one, two, three, or more intermediary *channel levels*. Marketing channels face continuous and sometimes dramatic change. Three of the most important trends are the growth of *vertical, horizontal,* and *multichannel marketing systems*. These trends affect channel cooperation, conflict, and competition.

Channel design begins with assessing customer channel service needs and company channel objectives and constraints. The company then identifies the major channel alternatives in terms of the *types* of intermediaries, the *number* of intermediaries, and the *channel responsibilities* of each. Each channel alternative must be evaluated according to economic, control, and adaptive criteria. *Channel management* calls for selecting qualified intermediaries and motivating them. Individual channel members must be evaluated regularly.

OBJECTIVE 4 Explain how companies select, motivate, and evaluate channel members. (pp 352–356)

Producers vary in their ability to attract qualified marketing intermediaries. Some producers have no trouble signing up channel members. Others have to work hard to line up enough qualified intermediaries. When selecting intermediaries, the company should evaluate each channel member's qualifications and select those who best fit its channel objectives.

Once selected, channel members must be continuously motivated to do their best. The company must sell not only *through* the intermediaries but *with* them. It should work to forge strong partnerships with channel members to create a marketing system that meets the needs of both the manufacturer *and* the partners. The company must also regularly check channel member performance against established performance standards, rewarding intermediaries who are performing well and assisting or replacing weaker ones.

OBJECTIVE 5 **Discuss the nature and importance of marketing logistics and integrated supply chain management.** (pp 356–363)

Just as firms are giving the marketing concept increased recognition, more business firms are paying attention to *marketing logistics* (or *physical distribution*). Logistics is an area of potentially high cost savings and improved customer satisfaction.

Marketing logistics addresses not only *outbound distribution* but also *inbound distribution* and *reverse distribution*. That is, it involves entire *supply chain management*—managing value-added flows between suppliers, the company, resellers, and final users. No logistics system can both maximize customer service and minimize distribution costs. Instead, the goal of logistics management is to provide a *targeted* level of service at the least cost. The major logistics functions include *warehousing, inventory management, transportation*, and *logistics information management*.

The *integrated supply chain management concept* recognizes that improved logistics requires teamwork in the form of close working relationships across functional areas inside the company and across various organizations in the supply chain. Companies can achieve logistics harmony among functions by creating cross-functional logistics teams, integrative supply manager positions, and senior-level logistics executives with cross-functional authority. Channel partnerships can take the form of cross-company teams, shared projects, and information-sharing systems. Today, some companies are outsourcing their logistics functions to third-party logistics (3PL) providers to save costs, increase efficiency, and gain faster and more effective access to global markets.

KEY Terms

OBJECTIVE 1

Value delivery network (p 338)
Marketing channel (distribution channel (p 339)
Channel level (p 341)
Direct marketing channel (p 341)
Indirect marketing channel (p 341)

OBJECTIVE 2

Channel conflict (p 342)
Conventional distribution channel (p 344)
Vertical marketing system (VMS) (p 344)
Corporate VMS (p 344)

Contractual VMS (p 345)
Franchise organization (p 345)
Administered VMS (p 345)
Horizontal marketing system (p 345)
Multichannel distribution system (p 346)
Disintermediation (p 347)

OBJECTIVE 3

Marketing channel design (p 348)
Intensive distribution (p 351)
Exclusive distribution (p 351)
Selective distribution (p 351)

OBJECTIVE 4

Marketing channel management (p 352)

OBJECTIVE 5

Marketing logistics (physical distribution) (p 356)
Supply chain management (p 356)
Distribution center (p 358)
Intermodal transportation (p 360)
Integrated logistics management (p 361)
Third-party logistics (3PL) provider (p 362)

DISCUSSING & APPLYING THE Concepts

Discussing the Concepts

1. Explain how channel members add value for manufacturers and consumers. (AACSB: Communication)

2. Discuss the various types of conflict that may arise in the channel of distribution. Is all channel conflict bad? (AACSB: Communication; Reflective Thinking)

3. What factors does a cosmetics company need to consider when designing its marketing channel for a new low-priced line of cosmetics? (AACSB: Communication; Reflective Thinking)

4. Describe the major types of vertical marketing systems and provide an example of each. (AACSB: Communication; Reflective Thinking)

5. Discuss the complexities international marketers face when designing channels in other countries. (AACSB: Communication)

6. List and briefly describe the major logistics functions. Provide an example of a decision a logistics manager would make for each major function. (AACSB: Communication; Reflective Thinking)

Applying the Concepts

1. ExerWise, a new company marketing a high-end ab toner exercise machine, is considering direct marketing versus selling through Strongs, a national sporting goods retailer. As the buyer for Strongs, explain the functions your retail chain can offer to ExerWise. (AACSB: Communication; Reflective Thinking)

2. Ward's Berry Farm specializes in fresh strawberries, which it sells to a variety of retailers through a produce wholesale distributor. Form a small group and have each member assume one of the following roles: berry farmer, wholesaler, and grocery retailer. In your role, discuss three things that might have recently angered you about the other channel members. Take turns voicing your gripes and attempting to resolve the conflict. (AACSB: Communication; Reflective Thinking)

3. Visit http://electronics.howstuffworks.com/rfid.htm# and watch the video "How UPS Smart Labels Work." You can also learn more about RFID technology from this site. What impact will RFID tags have on each of the major logistical functions? What are the biggest current obstacles to adopting this technology? (AACSB: Communication; Use of IT; Reflective Thinking)

FOCUS ON Technology

If you're eager to get the latest movie released on DVD, you don't have to go any farther than your iTunes account on your computer. Normally, these movies weren't available from Apple's iTunes until several weeks after they were released, but major movie studios are allowing Apple to sell movies the day they are released. Consumers have been able to get movies on the same day as the DVD release from services such as CinemaNow and MovieLink for a few years, but those e-tailers don't have the same clout as iTunes, which is now the biggest retailer of music in the United States. Although movie studios get less revenue than selling through traditional retail channels, their profits will be bigger due to lower costs.

1. What costs are movie studios reducing by using this alternative channel of distribution? (AACSB: Communication; Reflective Thinking)

2. Is this an example of disintermediation? Will electronic distribution displace traditional distribution channels for movies? (AACSB: Communication; Reflective Thinking)

FOCUS ON Ethics

Parallel imports, *gray products*, and *price diversion* all represent the same activity—diverting imported products meant for one market at lower prices and reselling them at higher profits in other markets. This happens in many industries, including pharmaceuticals, apparel, high-tech electronics, auto parts, luxury goods, cosmetics, and tobacco. The textbook you're using now might be a gray product if it was intended for an international market but you purchased it from Amazon.com for much less than what you'd pay at your bookstore or the publisher's Web site. And the designer sweater you bought at Marshalls or TJ Maxx most likely got into those stores through gray market trading. Although U.S. federal law prohibits importing prescription drugs from abroad, the same is not true in other countries.

For example, gray traders purchase pharmaceutical drugs in poorer countries, such as Greece and Spain, and resell them in the United Kingdom or Sweden, where higher prices garner profits for the traders. In fact, parallel importing of most products is legal, and some experts claim that it's just the free market working. In some cases, though, counterfeit goods are mixed in with the legitimate brands.

1. Learn more about this phenomenon. Who receives value in such transactions? Who loses value? (AACSB: Communication; Ethical Reasoning)

2. How are manufacturers dealing with this problem? (AACSB: Communication; Reflective Thinking)

MARKETING BY THE Numbers

Lightco, Inc., is a manufacturer of decorative lighting fixtures sold primarily in the eastern United States. Lightco wants to expand to the Midwest and Southern United States and intends to hire ten new sales representatives to secure distribution for its products. Sales reps will acquire new retail accounts and manage those accounts after acquisition. Each sales rep earns a salary of $50,000 plus 2 percent commission. Each retailer generates an average $50,000 in revenue for Lightco. Refer to Appendix 2, Marketing by the Numbers, to answer the following questions:

1. If Lightco's contribution margin is 40 percent, what increase in sales will it need to break even on the increase in fixed costs to hire the new sales reps? (AACSB: Communication; Analytical Reasoning)

2. How many new retail accounts must the company acquire to break even on this tactic? What average number of accounts must each new rep acquire? (AACSB: Communication; Analytical Reasoning)

VIDEO Case

Progressive

Progressive has attained top-tier status in the insurance industry by focusing on innovation. Progressive was the first company to offer drive-in claims services, installment payment of premiums, and 24/7 customer service. But some of Progressive's most innovative moves involve its channels of distribution. Whereas most insurance companies distribute their products to consumers via intermediary agents or direct-to-consumer methods, Progressive was one of the first companies to recognize the value in doing both. In the late 1980s, it augmented its agency distribution with a direct 800-number channel.

In 1995, Progressive moved into the future by becoming the first major insurer in the world to launch a Web site. In 1997, customers could buy auto insurance policies online in real time.

Today, at Progressive's Web site, customers can do everything from managing their own account information to reporting claims directly. Progressive even offers one-stop concierge claim service.

After viewing the Progressive video, answer the following questions about marketing channels:

1. Apply the concept of the supply chain to Progressive.

2. Using the model of consumer and business channels found in the chapter, sketch out as many channels for Progressive as you can. How does each of these channels meet distinct customer needs?

3. Discuss the various ways that Progressive has had an impact on the insurance industry.

COMPANY Case

Zara: The Technology Giant of the Fashion World

One global retailer is expanding at a dizzying pace. It's on track for what appears to be world domination of its industry. Having built its own state-of-the art distribution network, the company is leaving the competition in the dust in terms of sales and profits, not to mention speed of inventory management and turnover. Wal-Mart you might think? Dell possibly? Although these two retail giants definitely fit the description, we're talking here about Zara, the flagship specialty chain of Spain-based clothing conglomerate, Inditex.

This dynamic retailer is known for selling stylish designs that resemble those of big-name fashion houses, but at moderate prices. "We sell the latest trends at low prices, but our clients value our design, quality, and constant innovation," a company spokesman said. "That gives us the advantage even in highly competitive, developed markets, including Britain." More interesting is the way that Zara achieves its mission.

FAST-FASHION—THE NEWEST WAVE

A handful of European specialty clothing retailers are taking the fashion world by storm with a business model that has come to be known as "fast-fashion." In short, these companies can recognize and respond to fashion trends very quickly, create products that mirror the trends, and get those products onto shelves much faster and more frequently than the industry norm. Fast-fashion retailers include Sweden's Hennes & Mauritz (H&M), Britain's Top Shop, Spain's Mango, and the Netherland's Mexx. Although all of these companies are successfully employing the fast-fashion concept, Zara leads the pack on virtually every level.

For example, "fast" at Zara means that it can take a product from concept through design, manufacturing, and store-shelf placement in as little as two weeks, much quicker than any of its fast-fashion competitors. For more mainstream clothing chains, such as the United States' Gap and Abercrombie & Fitch, the process takes months.

This gives Zara the advantage of virtually copying fashions from the pages of *Vogue* and having them on the streets in dozens of countries before the next issue of the magazine even hits the newsstands! When Spain's Crown Prince Felipe and Letizia Ortiz Rocasolano announced their engagement, the bride-to-be wore a stylish white trouser suit. This raised some eyebrows, given that it violated royal protocol. But European women loved it and within a few weeks, hundreds of them were wearing a nearly identical outfit they had purchased from Zara.

But Zara is more than just fast. It's also prolific. In a typical year, Zara launches about 11,000 new items. Compare that to the 2,000 to 4,000 items introduced by both H&M and Gap. In the fashion world, this difference is huge. Zara stores receive new merchandise two to three times each week, whereas most clothing retailers get large shipments on a seasonal basis, four to six times per year.

As part of its strategy to introduce more new items with greater frequency, Zara also produces items in smaller batches. Thus, it assumes less risk if an item doesn't sell well. But smaller batches also means exclusivity, a unique benefit from a mass-market retailer that draws young fashionistas through Zara's doors like a magnet. When items sell out, they are not restocked with another shipment. Instead, the next Zara shipment contains something new, something different. Popular items can appear and disappear within a week. Consumers know that if they like something, they have to buy it or miss out. Customers are enticed to check out store stock more often, leading to very high levels of repeat patronage. But it also means that Zara doesn't have to follow the industry pattern of marking products down as the season progresses. Thus, Zara reaps the benefit of prices that average much closer to the list price.

THE VERTICAL SECRET TO ZARA'S SUCCESS

Just how does Zara achieve such mind-blowing responsiveness? The answer lies in its distribution system. In 1975, Amancio Ortega opened the first Zara store in Spain's remote northwest town of La Coruña, home to Zara's headquarters. Having already worked in the textile industry for two decades, his experience led him to design a system in which he could control every aspect of the supply chain, from design and production to distribution and retailing. He knew, for example, that in the textile business, the biggest mark-ups were made by wholesalers and retailers. He was determined to maintain control over these activities.

Ortega's original philosophy forms the heart of Zara's unique, rapid-fire supply chain today. But it's Zara's high-tech information system that has taken vertical integration in the company to an unprecedented level. According to CEO Pablo Isla, "Our information system is absolutely avant-guard. It's what links the shop to our designers and our distribution system."

Zara's vertically integrated system makes the starting point of a product concept hard to nail down. At Zara's headquarters, creative teams of more than 300 professionals carry out the design process. But they act on information fed to them from the stores. This goes far beyond typical point-of-sales data. Store managers act as trend spotters. Every day they report hot fads to headquarters, enabling popular lines to be tweaked and slow movers to be whisked away within hours. If customers are asking for a rounded neck on a vest rather than a V neck, such an item can be in stores in seven to ten days. This process would take traditional retailers months.

Managers also consult a personal digital assistant every evening to check what new designs are available and place their orders according to what they think will sell best to their customers. Thus, store managers help shape designs by ensuring that the creative teams have real-time information based on the observed tastes of actual consumers. Mr. Ortega refers to this as the democratization of fashion.

When it comes to sourcing, Zara's supply chain is unique as well. Current conventional wisdom calls for manufacturers in all industries to outsource their goods globally to the cheapest provider. Thus, most of Zara's competitors contract manufacturing out to low-wage countries, notably Asia. But Zara makes 40 percent of its own fabrics and produces more than half of its own clothes, rather than relying on a hodgepodge of slow-moving suppliers. Even things that are farmed out are done locally in order to maximize time efficiency. Nearly all Zara clothes for its stores worldwide are produced in its remote northeast corner of Spain.

As it completes designs, Zara cuts fabric in-house. It then sends the designs to one of several hundred local co-operatives for sewing, minimizing the time for raw material distribution. When items return to Zara's facilities, they are ironed by an assembly line of workers who specialize in a specific task (lapels, shoulders, and so on). Clothing items are wrapped in plastic and transported on conveyor belts to a group of giant warehouses.

Zara's warehouses are a vision of modern automation as swift and efficient as any automotive or consumer electronics plant. Human labor is a rare sight in these cavernous buildings. Customized machines patterned after the equipment used by overnight parcel services process up to 80,000 items an hour. The computerized system sorts, packs, labels, and allocates clothing items to every one of Zara's 1,495 stores. For stores within a 24-hour drive, Zara delivers goods by truck, whereas it ships merchandise via cargo jet to stores farther away.

DOMESTIC MANUFACTURING PAYS OFF

The same philosophy that has produced such good results for Zara has led parent company Inditex to diversify. Its other chains now include underwear retailer Oysho, teen-oriented Bershka and Stradivarius, children's Kiddy's Class, menswear Massimo Duti, and casual and sportswear chain Pull & Bear. Recently, Inditex opened its first nonclothing chain, Zara Home. Each chain operates under the same style of vertical integration perfected at Zara.

Making speed the main goal of its supply chain has really paid off for Inditex. In only three years, its sales and profits more than doubled. Last year, revenues increased over 15 percent over the previous year to $14.5 billion. Not bad considering retail revenue growth worldwide averages single digits, and many major retailers were feeling the effects of slowing economies worldwide. Perhaps more importantly, Inditex's total profits grew by 25 percent last year to $1.8 billion. Most of this performance was driven by Zara, now ranked number 64 on Interbrand's list of top 100 most valuable worldwide brands.

Although Inditex has grown rapidly, it wants more. Last year it opened 560 new stores worldwide (most of those were Zara stores) and plans to do the same this year. That's even considering an entry into the fast-growing Indian market. Global retailers are pushing into India in droves in response to India's thirst for premium brands. Zara can really capitalize on this trend. With more than one ribbon-cutting ceremony per day, Inditex could increase its number of stores from the current 3,890 to more than 5,000 stores in more than 70 countries by the end of this decade.

European fast-fashion retailers have thus far expanded cautiously in the United States (Zara has only 32 stores stateside). But the threat has U.S. clothing retailers rethinking the models they have relied on for years. According to one analyst, the industry may soon experience a reversal from outsourcing to China to "Made in the USA":

> U.S. retailers are finally looking at lost sales as lost revenue. They know that in order to capture maximum sales they need to turn their inventory much quicker. The disadvantage of importing from China is that it requires a longer lead time of between three to six months from the time an order is placed to when the inventory is stocked in stores. By then the trends may have changed and you're stuck with all the unsold inventory. If retailers want to refresh their merchandise quicker, they will have to consider sourcing at least some of the merchandise locally.

So being the fastest of the fast-fashion retailers has not only paid off for Zara, the model has reconfigured the fashion landscape everywhere. Zara has blazed a trail for cheaper and cheaper fashion-led mass-retailers, has put the squeeze on mid-priced fashion, and has forced luxury brands to scramble to find ways to set themselves apart from Zara's look-alike designs. Leadership certainly has its perks.

Questions for Discussion

1. As completely as possible, sketch the supply chain for Zara from raw materials to consumer purchase.

2. Discuss the concepts of horizontal and vertical conflict as they relate to Zara.

3. Which type of vertical marketing system does Zara employ? List all the benefits that Zara receives by having adopted this system.

4. Does Zara experience disadvantages from its "fast-fashion" distribution system? Are these disadvantages offset by the advantages?

5. How does Zara add value for the customer through major logistics functions?

Sources: James Hall, "Zara Helps Fashion Profit for Inditex," *Daily Telegraph*, April 1, 2008, p. 12; Christopher Bjork, "New Stores Boost Inditex's Results," *Wall Street Journal*, June 12, 2008, p. B4; "The Future of Fast-Fashion," *The Economist*, June 18, 2005, accessed online at www.economist.com; John Tagliabue, "A Rival to Gap that Operates Like Dell," *New York Times*, May 30, 2003, p. W1; Elizabeth Nash, "Dressed For Success," *Independent*, March 31, 2006, p. 22; Sarah Mower, "The Zara Phenomenon," *Evening Standard*, January 13, 2006, p. 30; also see www.inditex.com, accessed November 2008.

Chapter 13	Part 1	Defining Marketing and the Marketing Process (Chapters 1, 2)
	Part 2	Understanding the Marketplace and Consumers (Chapters 3, 4, 5, 6)
	Part 3	Designing a Customer-Driven Strategy and Mix (Chapters 7, 8, 9, 10, 11, 12, 13, 14, 15, 16, 17)
	Part 4	Extending Marketing (Chapters 18, 19, 20)

Retailing and Wholesaling

Chapter **PREVIEW**

In the previous chapter, you learned the basics of delivering customer value through good distribution channel design and management. Now, we'll look more deeply into the two major intermediary channel functions, retailing and wholesaling. You already know something about retailing—you're served every day by retailers of all shapes and sizes. However, you probably know much less about the hoard of wholesalers that work behind the scenes. In this chapter, we'll examine the characteristics of different kinds of retailers and wholesalers, the marketing decisions they make, and trends for the future.

When it comes to retailers, everyone always talks about Wal-Mart, the $379 billion behemoth whose "always low prices" strategy has made it not only the nation's largest retailer but also the world's largest company. But we'll start the chapter with a story about the nation's *fourth*-largest retailer, Costco. Surprisingly, although it captures only about one-sixth the sales of Wal-Mart, in warehouse retailing, Costco is trouncing Wal-Mart at its own low-price game.

Giant Wal-Mart is used to beating up on competitors. It outsells Toys"R"Us in the toy market, gives Blockbuster headaches in DVD sales, and puts a big dent in Best Buy's consumer electronics business. With 23 percent of the grocery market, it sells far more groceries than the number-two grocery retailer, Kroger. Almost every retailer, no matter what the category, has its hands full devising strategies by which it can compete with Wal-Mart and survive.

But this isn't a story about Wal-Mart. It's about Costco, the red-hot warehouse retailer that competes head-on with Wal-Mart's Sam's Club. Sam's Club is huge. With almost 600 stores and $44 billion in revenues, if Sam's Club were a separate company, it would be the seventh-largest U.S. retailer. But when it comes to warehouse retailing, it's Costco that's the bully, not the other way around.

With about the same number of members but 60 fewer stores, Costco outsells Sam's Club by 50 percent. Its $64 billion in sales makes Costco the nation's fourth-largest retailer, behind only Wal-Mart, Home Depot, and Kroger, and one step ahead of Target. And unlike Wal-Mart and Sam's Club, Costco is growing at a torrid pace. In just the past four years, Costco's sales have surged 51 percent; profits are up 50 percent. Costco's same-store sales are growing at more than twice the rate of Wal-Mart's. How is Costco beating Sam's Club at its own low-price game? The two retailers are very similar in many ways. But inside the store, Costco adds a certain merchandising magic that Sam's Club just can't match.

Let's start with the similarities. Both Costco and Sam's Club are warehouse retailers. They offer a limited selection of nationally branded and private-label products in a wide range of categories at very low prices to shoppers who pay an annual membership fee. Both retailers stock about 4,000 items, often only jumbo sizes (a typical supermarket stocks 40,000 items; a Wal-Mart supercenter

about 150,000). And to keep costs and prices low, both operate out of big, drafty, bare-bones stores and use their substantial buying power to wring low prices from suppliers.

Price is an important part of the equation, and Costco seems addicted to selling every item at the lowest possible price, regardless of competitors' prices. It refuses to mark up any item more than 14 percent above costs. According to Costco founder and CEO Jim Sinegal (shown in the picture), "Many retailers look at an item and say, 'I'm selling this for 10 bucks. How can I sell it for 11?' We look at it and say, 'How can we get it to 9 bucks?' And then, 'How can we get it to 8?' It is contrary to the thinking of [most retailers]. But once you start doing that, it's like heroin." Costco's operating profit margins average just 2.8 percent; Sam's Club's margins are only 3.5 percent.

Thus, both Costco and Sam's Club excel at low-cost operations and low prices. What is it, then, that sets Costco apart? It has to do with Costco's differentiated value proposition—with the

> In many ways, retailing boils down to the unglamorous art of getting the right product in the right place at the right time at the right price. But, says Costco founder and CEO Jim Sinegal, "Do that without being boring. That's the trick."

products it carries and sense of urgency that it builds into the Costco shopper's store experience. Alongside the gallon jars of peanut butter and 2,250-count packs of Q-Tips that make other warehouse clubs popular, Costco offers an ever-changing assortment of high-quality products—even luxuries—all at tantalizingly low margins. As one industry analyst puts it, "While Wal-Mart stands for low prices, Costco is a retail treasure hunt, where one's shopping cart could contain a $50,000 diamond ring resting on top of a vat of mayonnaise."

Costco brings flair to an otherwise dreary setting. It has managed to make discount shopping fashionable, even for affluent Americans. It's the place where high-end products meet deep-discount prices. In just one year, Costco sold 63 million hot dog and soda combinations (still only $1.50). At the same time, it sold more than 96,000 carats of diamonds at up to $100,000 per item. It's the nation's biggest baster of poultry (77,000 rotisserie chickens a day) but also the country's biggest seller of fine wines (including the likes of a Chateau Cheval Blanc Premier Grand Cru Classe at $1,750 a bottle). It once even offered a Pablo Picasso drawing at Costco.com for only $129,999.99!

Mixed in with its regular stock of staples, Costco features a glittering, constantly shifting array of one-time specials such as discounted Prada bags, Calloway golf clubs, or Kenneth Cole bags—deals you just won't find at Sam's Club. In fact, of the 4,000 items at Costco carries, 1,000 are designated as "treasure items" (Costco's words). The changing assortment and great prices keep people coming back, wallets in hand. Says CEO Sinegal, "a customer knows they'd better buy because it will not be there next time, like Waterford crystal. We try to get that sense of urgency in our customers."

There was a time when only the great unwashed masses shopped at off-price retailers. But Costco has changed all that. Even people who don't have to pinch pennies shop there. Not by accident, Costco's stores tend to be located in more affluent locations than Sam's Clubs. One-third of Costco's members have household incomes over $75,000; one-fourth over $100,000.

[Costco] attracts a breed of urban sophisticates attuned to what one retail consultant calls the "new luxury." These shoppers shun Seiko watches for TAG Heuer; Jack Nicklaus golf clubs for Callaway; Maxwell House coffee (it goes without saying) for Starbucks. They "trade up," eagerly spending more for items that make their hearts pound and for which they don't have to pay full price. Then they "trade down" to private labels for things like paper towels, detergent, and vitamins. Catering to this fast-growing segment, Costco has exploded. "It's the ultimate concept in trading up and trading down," says the consultant. "It's a brilliant innovation for the new luxury."

> Whereas Wal-Mart stands for low prices, Costco is a retail treasure hunt, where one's shopping cart could contain a $50,000 diamond ring resting on top of a vat of mayonnaise.

Costco's flair even extends to its store brand—Kirkland Signature. Whereas the Sam's Club Member's Mark store brand covers a limited assortment of generic-priced food, household, and apparel lines, Costco puts the Kirkland Signature brand on a wider range of goods—330 items accounting for 15 percent of its sales. Customers seek out Kirkland Signature products not just for price but also for quality. Costco customers can buy anything from a $20 bottle of Kirkland Signature Tierra de Chile Chilean red wine to a $1,299 Kirkland Signature stainless steel outdoor grill to a $6,330-per-person, 10-day package vacation to South Africa promising "luxury" accommodations.

So, in its own warehouse retailing backyard, it's Costco, not Wal-Mart, that's beating up on competitors. In fact, a mighty but frustrated Wal-Mart is even considering selling off its perennial runner-up Sam's Club division. Costco is more than a big box store that "stacks 'em high and sells 'em cheap"—more than just a place to load up on large sizes of consumer staples. Each Costco store is a theater of retail that creates buying urgency and excitement for customers. In many ways, retailing boils down to the unglamorous art of getting the right product in the right place at the right time at the right price. But there's a lot more than that to Costco's value proposition. Says Sinegal: "Do that without being boring. That's the trick."[1]

> Giant Wal-Mart is used to beating up on competitors. But when it comes to warehouse retailing, it's Costco that's the bully, not the other way around. Costco adds a certain merchandising magic that Wal-Mart's Sam's Club just can't match.

The Costco story sets the stage for examining the fast-changing world of today's resellers. This chapter looks at *retailing* and *wholesaling*. In the first section, we look at the nature and importance of retailing, major types of store and nonstore retailers, the decisions retailers make, and the future of retailing. In the second section, we discuss these same topics as they relate to wholesalers.

Objective Outline

Author Comment | You already know a lot about retailers. You deal with them every day—store retailers, service retailers, online retailers, and others.

Retailing
All activities involved in selling goods or services directly to final consumers for their personal, nonbusiness use.

Retailer
A business whose sales come *primarily* from retailing.

Retailing (pp 370–389)

What is retailing? We all know that Costco, Home Depot, Macy's, and Target are retailers, but so are Avon representatives, Amazon.com, the local Hampton Inn, and a doctor seeing patients. **Retailing** includes all the activities involved in selling products or services directly to final consumers for their personal, nonbusiness use. Many institutions—manufacturers, wholesalers, and retailers—do retailing. But most retailing is done by **retailers**: businesses whose sales come *primarily* from retailing.

Retailing plays a very important role in most marketing channels. Each year, retailers account for more than $4.5 trillion of sales to final consumers. They connect brands to consumers in what marketing agency OgilvyAction calls "the last mile"—the final stop in the consumer's path to purchase. It's the "distance a consumer travels between an attitude and an action," explains OgilvyAction's CEO. "Nearly 70 percent of purchase decisions are made near or in the store." Thus, retailers "reach consumers at key moments of truth, ultimately [influencing] their actions at the point of purchase."[2]

In fact, many marketers are now embracing the concept of *shopper marketing*, the idea that the retail store itself is an important marketing medium. Shopper marketing involves focusing the entire marketing process—from product and brand development to logistics, promotion, and merchandising—toward turning shoppers into buyers at the point of sale. Of course, every well-designed marketing effort focuses on customer buying behavior. But the concept of shopper marketing suggests that these efforts should be coordinated around the shopping process itself. Shopper marketing emphasizes the importance of the retail environment on customer buying.[3]

Although most retailing is done in retail stores, in recent years *nonstore retailing* has been growing much faster than has store retailing. Nonstore retailing includes selling to final consumers through the Internet, direct mail, catalogs, the telephone, and other direct-selling approaches. We discuss such direct-marketing approaches in detail in Chapter 17. In this chapter, we focus on store retailing.

Types of Retailers

Retail stores come in all shapes and sizes—from your local hairstyling salon or family-owned restaurant to national specialty chain retailers such as REI or Williams-Sonoma to megadiscounters such as Costco or Wal-Mart. The most important types of retail stores are described in ● **Table 13.1** and discussed in the following sections. They can be classified in terms of several characteristics, including the *amount of service* they offer, the breadth and depth of their *product lines*, the *relative prices* they charge, and how they are *organized*.

Amount of Service

Different types of customers and products require different amounts of service. To meet these varying service needs, retailers may offer one of three service levels—self-service, limited service, and full service.

Self-service retailers serve customers who are willing to perform their own "locate-compare-select" process to save time or money. Self-service is the basis of all discount operations and is typically used by retailers selling convenience goods (such as super-markets) and nationally branded, fast-moving shopping goods (such as Wal-Mart or Kohl's). *Limited-service retailers,* such as Sears or JCPenney, provide more sales assistance because they carry more shopping goods about which customers need information. Their increased operating costs result in higher prices.

● TABLE | 13.1   Major Store Retailer Types

Type	Description	Examples
Specialty stores	Carry a narrow product line with a deep assortment, such as apparel stores, sporting-goods stores, furniture stores, florists, and bookstores. A clothing store would be a *single-line* store, a men's clothing store would be a *limited-line store,* and a men's custom-shirt store would be a *superspecialty* store.	REI, Tiffany, Radio Shack, Williams-Sonoma
Department stores	Carry several product lines—typically clothing, home furnishings, and household goods—with each line operated as a separate department managed by specialist buyers or merchandisers.	Macy's, Sears, Neiman Marcus
Supermarkets	A relatively large, low-cost, low-margin, high-volume, self-service operation designed to serve the consumer's total needs for grocery and household products.	Kroger, Safeway, Supervalu, Publix
Convenience stores	Relatively small stores located near residential areas, open long hours seven days a week, and carrying a limited line of high-turnover convenience products at slightly higher prices.	7-Eleven, Stop-N-Go, Circle K
Discount stores	Carry standard merchandise sold at lower prices with lower margins and higher volumes.	Wal-Mart, Target, Kohl's
Off-price retailers	Sell merchandise bought at less-than-regular wholesale prices and sold at less than retail, often leftover goods, overruns, and irregulars obtained at reduced prices from manufacturers or other retailers. These include *factory outlets* owned and operated by manufacturers; *independent off-price retailers* owned and run by entrepreneurs or by divisions of larger retail corporations; and *warehouse (or wholesale) clubs* selling a limited selection of brand-name groceries, appliances, clothing, and other goods at deep discounts to consumers who pay membership fees.	Mikasa (factory outlet); TJ Maxx (independent off-price retailer); Costco, Sam's Club, BJ's Wholesale Club (warehouse clubs)
Superstores	Very large stores traditionally aimed at meeting consumers' total needs for routinely purchased food and nonfood items. Includes *supercenters,* combined supermarket and discount stores, and *category killers,* which carry a deep assortment in a particular category and have a knowledgeable staff.	Wal-Mart Supercenter, SuperTarget, Kmart Super Center, Meijer (discount stores); Best Buy, PetSmart, Staples, Barnes & Noble (category killers)

In *full-service retailers*, such as high-end specialty stores (for example, Tiffany or Williams-Sonoma) and first-class department stores (such as Nordstrom or Neiman Marcus), salespeople assist customers in every phase of the shopping process. Full-service stores usually carry more specialty goods for which customers need or want assistance or advice. They provide more services resulting in much higher operating costs, which are passed along to customers as higher prices.

Product Line

Retailers can also be classified by the length and breadth of their product assortments. Some retailers, such as **specialty stores**, carry narrow product lines with deep assortments within those lines. Today, specialty stores are flourishing. The increasing use of market segmentation, market targeting, and product specialization has resulted in a greater need for stores that focus on specific products and segments.

In contrast, **department stores** carry a wide variety of product lines. In recent years, department stores have been squeezed between more focused and flexible specialty stores on the one hand, and more efficient, lower-priced discounters on the other. In response, many have added promotional pricing to meet the discount threat. Others have stepped up the use of store brands and single-brand "designer shops" to compete with specialty stores. Still others are trying catalog, telephone, and Web selling. Service remains the key differentiating factor. Retailers such as Nordstrom, Saks, Neiman Marcus, and other high-end department stores are doing well by emphasizing exclusive merchandise and high-quality service.

Supermarkets are the most frequently shopped type of retail store. Today, however, they are facing slow sales growth because of slower population growth and an increase in competition from discount supercenters (Wal-Mart) on the one hand and upscale specialty food stores (Whole Foods, Trader Joe's) on the other. Supermarkets also have been hit hard by the rapid growth of out-of-home eating. In fact, supermarkets' share of the groceries and consumables market plunged from 89 percent in 1989 to less than 50 percent in 2008.[4] Thus, many traditional supermarkets are facing hard times.

In the battle for "share of stomachs," some supermarkets are cutting costs, establishing more-efficient operations, lowering prices, and attempting to compete more effectively with food discounters. However, they are finding it difficult to profitably match the low prices of superlow-cost operators such as Wal-Mart, now the nation's largest grocery retailer. In contrast, many other large supermarkets have moved upscale, providing improved store environments and higher-quality food offerings, such as from-scratch bakeries, gourmet deli counters, natural foods, and fresh seafood departments. ▲For example, consider Safeway's "lifestyle store" strategy:[5]

> To raise itself above the cutthroat low-price food frenzy, during the past four years Safeway has built more than 50 new "lifestyle" stores and remodeled nearly two-thirds of its existing stores under the lifestyle store concept. The lifestyle stores feature upscale touches, such as soft lighting and hardwood floors, along with higher-quality fare, including gourmet and organic foods and premium brands. The restyled stores are supported by a $100 million "Ingredients for Life" marketing campaign, which assures customers that Safeway's food offerings are designed for the way people live today. The strategy has resulted in increased customer loyalty and a 55 percent growth in earnings last year. Safeway plans to remodel all of its stores under the lifestyle concept by 2009.

Convenience stores are small stores that carry a limited line of high-turnover convenience goods. After several years of stagnant sales, convenience stores are now experiencing healthy growth. Last year, U.S. convenience stores posted sales of $579 billion, a 15 percent increase over the previous year. More than 70 percent of convenience store revenues come from sales of gasoline; a majority of in-store sales are from tobacco products (39 percent) and beer and other beverages (26 percent).[6]

In recent years, convenience store chains have tried to expand beyond their primary market of young, blue-collar men, redesigning their stores to attract female shoppers. They are shedding the image of a "truck stop" where men go to buy beer, cigarettes, or shriveled

---

Specialty store
A retail store that carries a narrow product line with a deep assortment within that line.

Department store
A retail organization that carries a wide variety of product lines—each line is operated as a separate department managed by specialist buyers or merchandisers.

Supermarket
A large, low-cost, low-margin, high-volume, self-service store that carries a wide variety of grocery and household products.

Convenience store
A small store, located near a residential area, that is open long hours seven days a week and carries a limited line of high-turnover convenience goods.

▲ Facing increased competition, many supermarkets are moving upscale. For example, Safeway is converting to "lifestyle" stores, supported by a big-budget "Ingredients for Life" marketing campaign.

hotdogs on a roller grill and are instead offering freshly prepared foods and cleaner, safer, more-upscale environments. ▲For example, consider Sheetz, widely recognized as one of the nation's top convenience stores. Driven by its Total Customer Focus mission and the motto—"Life's a Trip. Every Day"—Sheetz aims to provide "kicked-up convenience while being more than just a convenience store."[7]

Whether it's for road warriors, construction workers, or soccer moms, Sheetz offers "a mecca for people on the go"—fast, friendly service and quality products in clean and convenient locations. "We really care about our customers," says the company. "If you need to refuel your car or refresh your body, . . . Sheetz has what you need, when you need it. And, we're here 24/7/365." Sheetz certainly isn't your run-of-the-mill convenience store operation. Stores offer up a menu of made-to-order cold and toasted subs, sandwiches, and salads, along with hot fries, onion rings, chicken fingers, and burgers—all ordered through touch-screen terminals. Locations feature Sheetz Bros. Coffeez, a full-service espresso bar staffed by a trained barista. Frozen fruit smoothies round out the menu. To help make paying easier, Sheetz was the first chain in the nation to install system-wide MasterCard PayPass, allowing customers to quickly tap their credit cards and go. Sheetz also partnered with M&T Bank to offer ATM services at any Sheetz without a surcharge. Some analysts say that Sheetz aims to become the Wal-Mart of convenience stores, and it just might get there. The average Sheetz store is nearly twice the size of the average 7-Eleven. And although the privately held company now operates in only six states, it generates sales of more than $3.3 billion. Founder Stan Sheetz was recently named by *Chain Store Age* on its list of the top 25 people who have completely changed the way the world does business.

Superstore
A store much larger than a regular supermarket that offers a large assortment of routinely purchased food products, nonfood items, and services.

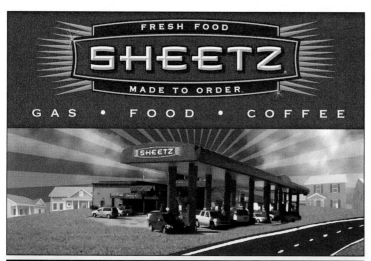

▲ Convenience stores: Sheetz provides kicked-up convenience while being more than just a convenience store. "If you need to refuel your car or refresh your body, . . . Sheetz has what you need, when you need it. And, we're here 24/7/365."

Superstores are much larger than regular supermarkets and offer a large assortment of routinely purchased food products, nonfood items, and services. Wal-Mart, Target, Meijer, and other discount retailers offer *supercenters*, very large combination food and discount stores. Whereas a traditional grocery store brings in about $270,000 a week in sales, a supercenter brings in about

Category killer
A giant specialty store that carries a very deep assortment of a particular line and is staffed by knowledgeable employees.

Service retailer
A retailer whose product line is actually a service, including hotels, airlines, banks, colleges, and many others.

Discount store
A retail operation that sells standard merchandise at lower prices by accepting lower margins and selling at higher volume.

Off-price retailer
A retailer that buys at less-than-regular wholesale prices and sells at less than retail. Examples are factory outlets, independents, and warehouse clubs.

Independent off-price retailer
An off-price retailer that is either independently owned and run or is a division of a larger retail corporation.

Factory outlet
An off-price retailing operation that is owned and operated by a manufacturer and that normally carries the manufacturer's surplus, discontinued, or irregular goods.

$1.5 million a week. Wal-Mart, which opened its first supercenter in 1988, now has more than 2,200 supercenters worldwide and is opening new ones at a rate of 170 per year.[8]

Recent years have also seen the explosive growth of superstores that are actually giant specialty stores, the so-called **category killers**. They feature stores the size of airplane hangars that carry a very deep assortment of a particular line with a knowledgeable staff. Category killers are prevalent in a wide range of categories, including books, baby gear, toys, electronics, home-improvement products, linens and towels, party goods, sporting goods, and even pet supplies.

Finally, for many retailers, the product line is actually a service. **Service retailers** include hotels and motels, banks, airlines, colleges, hospitals, movie theaters, tennis clubs, bowling alleys, restaurants, repair services, hair salons, and dry cleaners. Service retailers in the United States are growing faster than product retailers.

Relative Prices

Retailers can also be classified according to the prices they charge (see Table 13.1). Most retailers charge regular prices and offer normal-quality goods and customer service. Others offer higher-quality goods and service at higher prices. The retailers that feature low prices are discount stores and "off-price" retailers.

Discount Stores. A **discount store** sells standard merchandise at lower prices by accepting lower margins and selling higher volume. The early discount stores cut expenses by offering few services and operating in warehouse-like facilities in low-rent, heavily traveled districts. Today's discounters have improved their store environments and increased their services, while at the same time keeping prices low through lean, efficient operations. Leading discounters now dominate the retail scene, and world-leading retailer Wal-Mart—what one financial guru calls "the retailing machine of all time"—dominates the discounters (see **Real Marketing 13.1**).[9]

Off-Price Retailers. As the major discount stores traded up, a new wave of **off-price retailers** moved in to fill the ultralow-price, high-volume gap. Ordinary discounters buy at regular wholesale prices and accept lower margins to keep prices down. In contrast, off-price retailers buy at less-than-regular wholesale prices and charge consumers less than retail. Off-price retailers can be found in all areas, from food, clothing, and electronics to no-frills banking and discount brokerages.

The three main types of off-price retailers are *independents, factory outlets*, and *warehouse clubs*. **Independent off-price retailers** either are independently owned and run or are divisions of larger retail corporations. Although many off-price operations are run by smaller independents, most large off-price retailer operations are owned by bigger retail chains. Examples include store retailers such as TJ Maxx and Marshalls, owned by TJX Companies, and Web sellers such as Overstock.com.

Factory outlets—manufacturer-owned and operated stores by firms such as Liz Claiborne, Carters, Levi Strauss, and others—sometimes group together in *factory outlet malls* and *value-retail centers*, where dozens of outlet stores offer prices as low as 50 percent below retail on a wide range of mostly surplus, discounted, or irregular goods. Whereas outlet malls consist primarily of manufacturers' outlets, value-retail centers combine manufacturers' outlets with off-price retail stores and department store clearance outlets, such as Nordstrom Rack, Neiman Marcus Last Call Clearance Centers, and Off 5th (Saks Fifth Avenue outlets). Factory outlet malls have become one of the hottest growth areas in retailing.

The malls now are moving upscale—and even dropping "factory" from their descriptions—narrowing the gap between factory outlet and more traditional forms of retailers. As the gap narrows, the discounts offered by outlets are getting smaller. However, a growing number of outlet malls now feature brands such as Coach, Polo Ralph Lauren, Dolce & Gabbana, Giorgio Armani, Gucci, and Versace, causing department stores to protest to the manufacturers of these brands. Given their higher costs, the department stores must charge more than the off-price outlets. Manufacturers counter

Real Marketing 13.1

Wal-Mart:
Almost Unimaginably Big

Wal-Mart is almost unimaginably big. It's the world's largest retailer—the world's largest *company*. It rang up an incredible $379 billion in sales last year—that's 1.75 times the sales of competitors Costco, Target, Sears/Kmart, JCPenney, and Kohl's *combined*.

Wal-Mart is the number-one seller in several categories of consumer products, including groceries, clothing, toys, CDs, and pet care products. It sells twice as many groceries as Kroger, the leading grocery-only food retailer, and its clothing and shoe sales alone last year exceeded the total revenues of Macy's Inc., parent of Macy's and Bloomingdale's department stores. Incredibly, Wal-Mart sells 30 percent of the disposable diapers purchased in the United States each year, 30 percent of the hair care products, 30 percent of all health and beauty products, 26 percent of the toothpaste, and 20 percent of the pet food. On average, more than 180 million people around the globe visit Wal-Mart stores each week.

It's also hard to fathom Wal-Mart's impact on the U.S. economy. It's the nation's largest employer—one out of every 234 men, women, and children in the United States is a Wal-Mart associate. Its sales of $1.52 billion on one day in 2003 exceeded the GDPs of 26 countries. According to one study, Wal-Mart was responsible for some 25 percent of the nation's astonishing productivity gains during the 1990s. Another study found that—through its own low prices and through its impact on competitors' prices—Wal-Mart saves the average American household $2,500 each year, equivalent to more than six months worth of groceries for the average family.

What's behind this spectacular success? First and foremost, Wal-Mart is passionately dedicated to its long-time low-price value proposition and what its low prices mean to customers: "Save money. Live better." Its mission is to "lower the world's cost of living." To accomplish this mission, Wal-Mart offers a broad selection of carefully selected goods at unbeatable prices. No other retailer has come nearly so close to mastering the concepts of everyday low prices and one-stop shopping. As one analyst puts it, "The company gospel . . . is relatively simple: Be an agent for customers—find out what they want, and sell it to them for

Wal-Mart, the world's largest retailer, is passionately dedicated to its long-time low-price value proposition and what its low prices mean to customers—"Save money. Live better."

the lowest possible price." Says Wal-Mart's president and chief executive, "We're obsessed with delivering value to customers."

How does Wal-Mart make money with such low prices? Wal-Mart is a lean, mean, distribution machine—it has the lowest cost structure in the industry. Low costs let the giant retailer charge lower prices but still reap higher profits. For example, grocery prices drop an average of 10 to 15 percent in markets Wal-Mart has entered, and Wal-Mart's food prices average 20 percent less than its grocery store rivals. Lower prices attract more shoppers, producing more sales, making the company more efficient, and enabling it to lower prices even more.

Wal-Mart's low costs result in part from superior management and more sophisticated technology. Its Bentonville, Arkansas, headquarters contains a computer communications system that the U.S. Defense Department would envy, giving managers around the country instant access to sales and operating information. And its huge, fully automated distribution centers employ the latest technology to supply stores efficiently.

Wal-Mart also keeps costs down through good old "tough buying." The company is known for the calculated way it wrings low prices from suppliers. "Don't expect a greeter and don't expect friendly," says one supplier's sales executive after a visit to Wal-Mart's buying offices. "Once you are ushered into one of the spartan little buyers' rooms, expect a steely eye across the table and be prepared to cut your price. They are very, very focused

people, and they use their buying power more forcefully than anyone else in America."

Some critics argue that Wal-Mart squeezes its suppliers too hard, driving some out of business. Wal-Mart proponents counter, however, that it is simply acting in its customers' interests by forcing suppliers to be more efficient. "Wal-Mart is tough, but totally honest and straightforward in its dealings with vendors," says an industry consultant. "Wal-Mart has forced manufacturers to get their acts together."

Despite its incredible success over the past four decades, some analysts are noting chinks in the once seemingly invincible Wal-Mart's armor. True, Wal-Mart's sales are huge, and through new-store and international expansion, Wal-Mart has kept its sales growing at a respectable 9 to 11 percent annually. However, Wal-Mart seems now to be facing a midlife crisis. Profit growth has slowed and Wal-Mart's stock has slumped a bit over the past few years.

Having grown so big, the maturing giant is having difficulty maintaining the speedy growth rates of its youth. "The glory days [of exploding sales and profits] are over," says an analyst. To reignite growth, the megaretailer is pushing into new, faster-growing product and service lines, including organic foods, in-store health clinics, and consumer financial services.

Wal-Mart has also had to grapple with an aging image. To many mid-to-high income consumers, Wal-Mart seems downright dowdy

Continued on next page ▼

Real Marketing 13.1 Continued ▼

compared with the younger, hipper Target. "Many of its upscale customers . . . come into the store for vegetables, cereal, detergent, and the like—but turn up their noses at higher-margin items like apparel and electronics," says an analyst. So, in an attempt to capture a larger share of wallet from higher-income consumers, Wal-Mart has recently been giving itself a modest image face-lift.

For example, it's sprucing up its stores and adding new, higher-quality merchandise. Many urban Wal-Marts now carry a slew of higher-end consumer electronics products, from Sony plasma televisions to Dell and Toshiba laptops to Apple iPods. The retailer has also dressed up its apparel racks with more stylish fashion lines under brand names such as Metro 7, George by designer Mark Eisen, and a new lifestyle brand by designer

Norma Kamali. Finally, Wal-Mart's new "Save money. Live better." slogan and supporting advertising have a softer, more refined feel than the old "Always low prices. *Always*" pitch. In some ways, Wal-Mart is looking decidedly more like Target. Maybe that's because Wal-Mart's chief marketing officer and the architect of the image makeover, John Fleming, is a 20-year Target marketing veteran.

But don't expect Wal-Mart to try to out-Target Target. Even with its slightly more upscale image, in no way will Wal-Mart ever give up its core low price value proposition. After all, Wal-Mart is and always will be a discount store. "I don't think Wal-Mart's . . . ever going to be edgy," says Fleming. "I don't think that fits our brand. Our brand is about saving people money" so that they can live better.

Sources: Quotes and other information from Anthony Bianco, "Wal-Mart's Midlife Crisis," *BusinessWeek*, April 30, 2007, p. 46; "The Fortune 500," *Fortune*, May 5, 2008, pp. F1–F3; Michael Barbaro and Stuart Elliot, "Clinging to Its Roots, Wal-Mart Steps Back from an Edgy, New Image," *International Herald Tribune*, December 10, 2006, accessed at www.iht.com/articles/2006/12/10/business/walmart.php; Elizabeth Woyke, "Buffett, the Wal-Mart Shopper," *BusinessWeek*, May 14, 2007, pp. 66–67; David Kiley, "Wal-Mart Is Out to Change Its Story with New Ads," *BusinessWeek*, September 13, 2007, accessed at www.businessweek.com; Ann Zimmerman and Cheryl Lu-Lien Tan, "After Misstep, Wal-Mart Revisits Fashion," *Wall Street Journal*, April 24, 2008, p. B1; and various fact sheets found at www.walmartstores.com, accessed November 2008.

that they send last year's merchandise and seconds to the factory outlet malls, not the new merchandise that they supply to the department stores. Still, the department stores are concerned about the growing number of shoppers willing to make weekend trips to stock up on branded merchandise at substantial savings.

Warehouse club

An off-price retailer that sells a limited selection of brand name grocery items, appliances, clothing, and a hodgepodge of other goods at deep discounts to members who pay annual membership fees.

Warehouse clubs (or *wholesale clubs* or *membership warehouses*), such as Costco, Sam's Club, and BJ's, operate in huge, drafty, warehouse-like facilities and offer few frills. Customers themselves must wrestle furniture, heavy appliances, and other large items to the checkout line. Such clubs make no home deliveries and often accept no credit cards. However, they do offer ultralow prices and surprise deals on selected branded merchandise.

Although they account for only about 8 percent of total U.S. retail sales, warehouse clubs have grown rapidly in recent years. As we learned in the opening Costco story, these retailers appeal not just to low-income consumers seeking bargains on bare-bones products. They appeal to all kinds of customers shopping for a wide range of goods, from necessities to extravagances.

Organizational Approach

Although many retail stores are independently owned, others band together under some form of corporate or contractual organization. The major types of retail organizations—*corporate chains, voluntary chains* and *retailer cooperatives, franchise organizations*, and *merchandising conglomerates*—are described in ● **Table 13.2**.

Chain stores

Two or more outlets that are commonly owned and controlled.

Chain stores are two or more outlets that are commonly owned and controlled. They have many advantages over independents. Their size allows them to buy in large quantities at lower prices and gain promotional economies. They can hire specialists to deal with areas such as pricing, promotion, merchandising, inventory control, and sales forecasting.

The great success of corporate chains caused many independents to band together in one of two forms of contractual associations. One is the *voluntary chain*—a wholesaler-sponsored group of independent retailers that engages in group buying and common merchandising—which we discussed in Chapter 12. Examples include Independent Grocers Alliance (IGA), Western Auto, and Do-It Best hardware. The other type of contractual association is the *retailer cooperative*—a group of independent retailers that band together to set up a jointly owned, central wholesale operation and conduct joint merchandising and promotion efforts. Examples are Associated Grocers and Ace Hardware.

● TABLE | 13.2   Major Types of Retail Organizations

Type	Description	Examples
Corporate chain store	Two or more outlets that are commonly owned and controlled. Corporate chains appear in all types of retailing, but they are strongest in department stores, food stores, drug stores, shoe stores, and women's clothing stores.	Sears, Kroger (grocery stores), CVS (drug stores), Williams-Sonoma (cookware and housewares)
Voluntary chain	Wholesaler-sponsored group of independent retailers engaged in group buying and merchandising.	Independent Grocers Alliance (IGA), Do-It Best hardware, Western Auto, True Value
Retailer cooperative	Group of independent retailers who set up a central buying organization and conduct joint promotion efforts.	Associated Grocers (groceries), Ace (hardware)
Franchise organization	Contractual association between a franchisor (a manufacturer, wholesaler, or service organization) and franchisees (independent businesspeople who buy the right to own and operate one or more units in the franchise system). Franchise organizations are normally based on some unique product or service, on a method of doing business, or on a trade name, goodwill, or patent that the franchisor has developed.	McDonald's, Subway, Pizza Hut, Jiffy Lube, Meineke Mufflers, 7-Eleven
Merchandising conglomerate	A free-form corporation that combines several diversified retailing lines and forms under central ownership, along with some integration of their distribution and management functions.	Limited Brands

These organizations give independents the buying and promotion economies they need to meet the prices of corporate chains.

Another form of contractual retail organization is a **franchise**. The main difference between franchise organizations and other contractual systems (voluntary chains and retail cooperatives) is that franchise systems are normally based on some unique product or service; on a method of doing business; or on the trade name, goodwill, or patent that the franchisor has developed. Franchising has been prominent in fast food and restaurants, motels, health and fitness centers, auto sales and service, and real estate.

But franchising covers a lot more than just burger joints and fitness centers. Franchises have sprung up to meet about any need. For example, Mad Science Group franchisees put on science programs for schools, scout troops, and birthday parties. And Mr. Handyman provides repair services for homeowners, while Merry Maids tidies up their houses.

Once considered upstarts among independent businesses, franchises now command 40 percent of all retail sales in the United States. ▲These days, it's nearly impossible to stroll down a city block or drive on a city street without seeing a McDonald's, Subway, Jiffy Lube, or Holiday Inn. One of the best-known and most successful franchisers, McDonald's, now has nearly 31,000 stores in 118 countries. It serves nearly 52 million customers a day and racks up nearly $47 billion in annual systemwide sales. More than 78 percent of McDonald's restaurants worldwide are owned and operated by franchisees. Gaining fast is Subway, one of the fastest-growing franchises, with more than 29,000 shops in 86 countries, including almost 21,000 in the United States.[10]

Finally, *merchandising conglomerates* are corporations that combine several different retailing forms under central ownership. An example is Limited

Franchise
A contractual association between a manufacturer, wholesaler, or service organization (a franchisor) and independent businesspeople (franchisees) who buy the right to own and operate one or more units in the franchise system.

▲ Franchising: These days, it's nearly impossible to stroll down a city block or drive on a suburban street without seeing a McDonald's, Jiffy Lube, Subway, or Holiday Inn.

Brands, which operates The Limited (fashion-forward women's clothing), Express (trendy private-label women's and men's apparel), Victoria's Secret (glamorous lingerie and beauty products), Bath & Body Works (natural but luxurious beauty and body care products), and The White Barn Candle Company (home fragrance and décor items). Such diversified retailing, similar to a multibranding strategy, provides superior management systems and economies that benefit all the separate retail operations.

Retailer Marketing Decisions

Retailers are always searching for new marketing strategies to attract and hold customers. In the past, retailers attracted customers with unique product assortments and more or better services. Today, retail assortments and services are looking more and more alike. Many national-brand manufacturers, in their drive for volume, have placed their brands almost everywhere. You can find most consumer brands not only in department stores but also in mass-merchandise discount stores, off-price discount stores, and on the Web. Thus, it's now more difficult for any one retailer to offer exclusive merchandise.

Service differentiation among retailers has also eroded. Many department stores have trimmed their services, whereas discounters have increased theirs. Customers have become smarter and more price sensitive. They see no reason to pay more for identical brands, especially when service differences are shrinking. For all these reasons, many retailers today are rethinking their marketing strategies.

As shown in ◆ **Figure 13.1**, retailers face major marketing decisions about *segmentation and targeting, store differentiation and positioning*, and the *retail marketing mix*.

Segmentation, Targeting, Differentiation, and Positioning Decisions

Retailers must first segment and define their target markets and then decide how they will differentiate and position themselves in these markets. Should the store focus on upscale, midscale, or downscale shoppers? Do target shoppers want variety, depth of assortment, convenience, or low prices? Until they define and profile their markets, retailers cannot make consistent decisions about product assortment, services, pricing, advertising, store décor, or any of the other decisions that must support their positions.

Too many retailers, even big ones, fail to define their target markets and positions clearly. They tried to have "something for everyone" and end up satisfying no market well. For example, what market does Sears target? What is its value proposition? For years now, the venerable $50 billion retailer has struggled unsuccessfully to answer these questions well, resulting in customer apathy and stagnant sales and profits. "We

◆FIGURE | 13.1
Retailer Marketing Strategy

have a lot of lapsed customers," says Sears's new chief marketing officer. "Sears is a great brand in people's minds. We've become just a little less top of mind." The answer? "We have to make sure that the overall customer experience—merchandise, in-store [environment], service, and marketing—are the best that they can be and working together to create a differentiated proposition that makes someone come to Sears versus going somewhere else."[11]

In contrast, successful retailers define their target markets well and position themselves strongly. For example, Wal-Mart positions itself strongly on low prices. For decades, it consistently promised "Always low prices. *Always*." Recently, it successfully extended this positioning to include what those always low prices mean to its customers. It now promises that customers will "Save money. Live better."

If Wal-Mart owns the low-price position, how can other discounters hope to compete? Again, the answer is good targeting and positioning. For example, rather than facing Wal-Mart head-on, Target—or Tar-*zhay* as many fans call it—thrives by aiming at a seemingly oxymoronic "upscale discount" niche. It has become the nation's number-two discount chain by offering low prices but rising above the discount fray with upmarket style and design and higher-grade service. Target's "Expect more, pay less" positioning sets it apart and helps insulate it from Wal-Mart.

Similarly, ▲Whole Foods Market has only 275 stores and less than $7 billion in sales versus Wal-Mart's more than 6,800 stores worldwide and sales of $379 billion. How does this small grocery chain complete with giant Wal-Mart? It doesn't—at least not directly. Whole Foods Market thrives by carefully positioning itself *away* from Wal-Mart. It targets a select group of upscale customers and offers them "organic, natural, and gourmet foods, all swaddled in Earth Day politics." In fact, a devoted Whole Foods customer is more likely to boycott the local Wal-Mart than to shop at it. One analyst sums up the Whole Foods shopping experience this way:[12]

▲ Retail targeting and positioning: By positioning itself strongly away from Wal-Mart and other discounters, Whole Foods Market has made itself one of the nation's fastest-growing and most profitable food retailers.

Counters groan with creamy hunks of artisanal cheese. Medjool dates beckon amid rows of exotic fruit. Savory breads rest near fruit-drenched pastries, and prepared dishes like sesame-encrusted tuna rival what's sold in fine restaurants. In keeping with the company's positioning, most of the store's goods carry labels proclaiming "organic," "100% natural," and "contains no additives." Staff people smile, happy to suggest wines that go with a particular cheese, or pause to debate the virtues of peanut butter maltballs. And it's all done against a backdrop of eye-pleasing earth-toned hues and soft lighting. This is grocery shopping? Well, not as most people know it. Whole Foods Market has cultivated its mystique with shoppers . . . by being anything but a regular supermarket chain. Whole Foods is, well, special.

Whole Foods can't match Wal-Mart's massive economies of scale, incredible volume purchasing power, ultraefficient logistics, wide selection, and hard-to-beat prices. But then again, it doesn't even try. By positioning itself strongly away from Wal-Mart and other discounters, Whole Foods Market has made itself one of the nation's fastest-growing and most profitable food retailers.

Product Assortment and Services Decision

Retailers must decide on three major product variables: *product assortment*, *services mix*, and *store atmosphere*.

The retailer's *product assortment* should differentiate the retailer while matching target shoppers' expectations. One strategy is to offer merchandise that no other competitor carries, such as store brands or national brands on which it holds exclusives. For example, Saks gets exclusive rights to carry a well-known designer's labels. It also offers its own private-label lines—the Saks Fifth Avenue Signature, Classic, and Sport collections. At JCPenney, private-label brands account for 45 percent of sales.[13]

Another strategy is to feature blockbuster merchandising events—Bloomingdale's is known for running spectacular shows featuring goods from a certain country, such as India or China. Or the retailer can offer surprise merchandise, as when Costco offers surprise assortments of seconds, overstocks, and closeouts. Finally, the retailer can differentiate itself by offering a highly targeted product assortment—Lane Bryant carries plus-size clothing; Brookstone offers an unusual assortment of gadgets in what amounts to an adult toy store.

The *services mix* can also help set one retailer apart from another. For example, some retailers invite customers to ask questions or consult service representatives in person or via phone or keyboard. Home Depot offers a diverse mix of services to do-it-yourselfers, from "how-to" classes to a proprietary credit card. Nordstrom promises to "take care of the customer, no matter what it takes."

The *store's atmosphere* is another important element in the reseller's product arsenal. The retailer wants to create a unique store experience, one that suits the target market and moves customers to buy. ▲For example, Apple's retail stores are very seductive places. The store design is clean, simple, and just oozing with style—much like an Apple iPod or iPhone. The stores invite shoppers to stay a while, use the equipment, and soak up all of the exciting new technology:[14]

It was 2 o'clock in the morning but in the subterranean retailing mecca in Midtown Manhattan, otherwise known as the Apple store, it might as well have been midafternoon. Late one night shortly before Christmas, parents pushed strollers and tourists straight off the plane mingled with nocturnal New Yorkers, clicking through iPod playlists, cruising the Internet on MacBooks, and touch-padding their way around iPhones. And through the night, cheerful sales staff stayed busy, ringing up customers at the main checkout counter and on hand-held devices in an uninterrupted stream of brick-and-mortar commerce. Not only has the company made many of its stores feel like gathering places, but the bright lights and equally bright acoustics create a buzz that makes customers feel more like they are at an event than a retail store. Apple stores encourage a lot of purchasing, to be sure. But they also encourage lingering, with dozens of fully functioning computers, iPods and iPhones for visitors to try—for hours on end. The policy has given some stores, especially those in urban neighborhoods, the feel of a community center. "Whenever we ask consumers to cite a great retail experience, the Apple store is the first store they mention," says a retail research consultant. "Basically, everything about it works.

Apple stores are going gangbusters. They attract, on average, 13,800 visitors per week, per store and average an incredible $4,000 in sales per square foot a year. By comparison, Saks generates $362 per square foot; Best Buy stores turn $930—tops for electronics retailers.[15]

Today's successful retailers carefully orchestrate virtually every aspect of the consumer store experience,

▲ Store atmosphere: Apple's retail stores are very seductive places—real consumer meccas. The bright lights and equally bright acoustics create a buzz that makes customers feel more like they are at an event than a retail store.

down to the music, lighting, and even the smells (see **Real Marketing 13.2**). Such "experiential retailing" confirms that retail stores are much more than simply assortments of goods. They are environments to be experienced by the people who shop in them. Store atmospheres offer a powerful tool by which retailers can differentiate their stores from those of competitors.

Price Decision

A retailer's price policy must fit its target market and positioning, product and service assortment, and competition. All retailers would like to charge high markups and achieve high volume, but the two seldom go together. Most retailers seek *either* high markups on lower volume (most specialty stores) *or* low markups on higher volume (mass merchandisers and discount stores).

www.bijan.com

bijan
America on Rodeo
by Appointment
menswear, jewelry, perfume

▲ Bijan's boutique on Rodeo Drive in Beverly Hills sells $375 silk ties and $19,000 ostrich-skin vests. Its "by appointment only" policy makes wealthy, high-profile clients comfortable with these prices.

Thus, ▲ Bijan's boutique, with locations in New York City and on Rodeo Drive in Beverly Hills, designs and sells "the most expensive menswear in the world" to "men of substance." Its million-dollar wardrobes include $1,000 silk tie sets, each one presented in a matching silk box, numbered and signed, and $75,000 crocodile-skin jackets. Customers must make appointments in advance just to shop at Bijan's. On a typical visit, wealthy, high-profile clients spend in the neighborhood of $100,000 on men's fashions.[16] Since every item is one-of-a-kind and surrounded by personal pampering, Bijan's sells a low volume but reaps a healthy margin on each sale. At the other extreme, TJ Maxx sells brand-name clothing at discount prices, settling for a lower margin on each sale but selling at a much higher volume.

Retailers must also decide on the extent to which they will use sales and other price promotions. Some retailers use no price promotions at all, competing instead on product and service quality rather than on price. For example, it's difficult to imagine Bijan's holding a two-for-the-price-of-one sale. Other retailers practice *"high-low" pricing*—charging higher prices on an everyday basis, coupled with frequent sales and other price promotions to increase store traffic, create a low-price image, or attract customers who will buy other goods at full prices. Still others—such as Wal-Mart, Costco, Family Dollar, and other mass retailers—practice *everyday low pricing (EDLP)*, charging constant, everyday low prices with few sales or discounts. Which strategy is best depends on the retailer's marketing strategy and the pricing approaches of competitors.

Promotion Decision

Retailers use any or all of the promotion tools—advertising, personal selling, sales promotion, public relations, and direct marketing—to reach consumers. They advertise in newspapers, magazines, radio, television, and on the Internet. Advertising may be supported by newspaper inserts, catalogs, and direct mail. Personal selling requires careful training of salespeople in how to greet customers, meet their needs, and handle their complaints. Sales promotions may include in-store demonstrations, displays, contests, and visiting celebrities. Public relations activities, such as press conferences and speeches, store openings, special events, newsletters, magazines, and public service activities, are always available to retailers. Most retailers have also set up Web sites, offering customers information and other features and often selling merchandise directly.

Real Marketing 13.2

Orchestrating the Retail Experience

The next time that you step into a retail store—whether it sells consumer electronics, hardware, or high fashion—stop and carefully consider your surroundings. Think about the store's layout and displays. Listen to the background sounds. Smell the smells. Chances are good that everything in the store, from the layout and lighting to the music and even the smells, has been carefully orchestrated to help shape your shopping experience—and to open your wallet. In most cases, you're probably being affected in ways so subtle that you don't even realize what's happening to you.

It all starts at the store entrance. According to one reporter, "what's in the entrance is the spring on the trap"—it pulls you in and puts you in the mood to buy. "The entrance is important because it hints at what's inside that you must have."

At a JCPenney, a "decompression area" at the front of the store lets shoppers get acclimated and calm down from the noise in the mall or on the street. Dressed mannequins offer a taste of the season's hot trends and set up a line of sight to the shopping ahead. "We're trying to give [shoppers] ideas right as [they're] walking into the store," says J.C. Penney's vice president of store design. In other department stores, the key items that draw women—the high-volume, high-profit goods—are right up front: handbags, cosmetics, jewelry, and sometimes intimate apparel.

At a new Home Depot in the Atlanta suburb of Buckhead, the entrance-way lures shoppers in with an open floor plan so they get a better "vista" of the store. Floor-to-ceiling racks of goods, long the signature of the warehouse store, are now further back. Lower-down displays of expensive goods—riding lawn mowers, upscale porch furniture, and a home design center for redecorating kitchen, bath, and flooring—are clustered so they're visible from the front door. All are ways to engage you in the store and draw you in.

Once inside a store, "how you as a shopper move in and around a store is not, really, up to you," continues the reporter.

Next time you shop, stop, look, and listen. Successful retailers like Sony Style orchestrate every aspect of the shopper store experience, down to the music, lighting, and even the smells (a subtle fragrance of vanilla and mandarin orange).

In a department store, you're funneled from the entrance past the store's most expensive goods through a maze of aisles and into departments that are set up as stores-within-a-store. Then you find yourself on "the racetrack," an oval aisle that carries you around the entire building to get a look at everything. Mini-displays

Place Decision

Retailers often point to three critical factors in retailing success: *location, location,* and *location*! It's very important that retailers select locations that are accessible to the target market in areas that are consistent with the retailer's positioning. For example, Apple locates its stores in high-end malls and trendy shopping districts—such as the "Miracle Mile" on Chicago's Michigan Avenue or Fifth Avenue in Manhattan—not low-rent strip malls on the edge of town. Small retailers may have to settle for whatever locations they can find or afford. Large retailers, however, usually employ specialists who select locations using advanced methods.

Most stores today cluster together to increase their customer pulling power and to give consumers the convenience of one-stop shopping. *Central business districts* were the main form of retail cluster until the 1950s. Every large city and town had a central business district with department stores, specialty stores, banks, and movie theaters. When people began to move to the suburbs, however, these central business districts, with their traffic, parking, and crime problems, began to lose business. Downtown merchants opened branches in suburban shopping centers, and the decline of the central business districts continued. In recent years, many cities have joined with merchants to try to revive downtown shopping areas by building malls and providing underground parking.

called "trend stations" are parked in the middle of aisles to stop shoppers' progress and entice them to look and buy.

Meanwhile, everything in a well-designed store is carefully constructed to create just the right moods and actions. At a Sony Style store, for instance, it's all designed to encourage touch, from the silk wallpaper to the smooth maple wood cabinets, to the etched-glass countertops. Products are displayed like museum pieces and set up for you to touch and try. Once you touch something, Sony figures, you'll buy it. Sony Style even has mini-living rooms set up to showcase what its 40-inch flat-panel TV would look like over a fireplace. "We've had customers bring in their architect and say, 'Re-create this in my house. I want the whole setup,'" says a Sony retail executive.

A store's lighting can affect anything from your moods to the pace at which you move and shop. Bright lighting can create excitement, whereas softer lighting can create a mellow mood. Many retailers adjust lighting to regulate shoppers' "blink rates"—the slower you blink, they reason, the more likely you are to browse, pause, and eventually buy.

Sound is another important element of the retail experience. "Music has been used by retailers for decades as a way to identify their stores and affect a shopper's mood, to make you feel happy, nostalgic, or relaxed so that you linger," notes the reporter. "Think of '50s cocktail bar music in a Pottery Barn.

But retailers are becoming more sophisticated in how they use music." They now hire "audio architects" to develop music and sounds that fit their unique positioning. "What does your business sound like?" asks background music provider Muzak. "A bikini and coconut oil or an oil change and a new set of tires? Muzak can create the ultimate music experience designed specifically for your business."

Perhaps the hottest store environment frontier these days is scent—that's right, the way the store smells:

Anyone who's walked into a mall has been enticed by the smell of cinnamon buns or chocolate chip cookies. Now, most large retailers are developing "signature scents" that you smell only in their stores. Luxury shirtmaker Thomas Pink pipes the smell of clean, pressed shirts into its stores—its signature "line-dried linen" scent. The essence of lavender wafts out of L'Occitane skin-care stores. Bloomingdale's uses different essences in different departments: baby powder in the baby store; suntan lotion in the bathing suit area; lilacs in lingerie; cinnamon and pine scent during the holiday season. Last year, it pumped a sugar-cookie scent into its Christmas shop.

At a Sony Style store, the subtle fragrance of vanilla and mandarin orange—designed exclusively for Sony—wafts down on shoppers, relaxing them and helping them believe that this is a very nice place to be. Sony decided to create its own store scent as one way to make the consumer electronics it sells less intimidating, particularly to women. At Sony's Madison Avenue store in New York, the scent is even pumped onto the street. "From research, we found that scent is closest to the brain and will evoke the most emotion, even faster than the eye," says the Sony retail executive. "Our scent helps us create an environment like no other." A scents expert agrees: "Scent is so closely aligned with your emotions, it's so primitive."

Thus, in their quest to orchestrate the optimal shopper experience, today's successful retailers leave no store environment stone unturned. The next time you visit a store, stop, look, and listen. See if you can spot the subtle and not-so-subtle things that retailers do to affect what you feel, think, and buy in their stores. "Most people know they are being influenced subliminally when they shop," says a retail consumer behavior expert. "They just may not realize how much."

Sources: Extracts, quotes, and other information are from or adapted from Mindy Fetterman and Jayne O'Donnall, "Just Browsing at the Mall? That's What You Think," *USA Today*, September 1, 2006, accessed at www.usatoday.com; Ylan Q. Mui, "Dollars and Scents," *Washington Post*, December 19, 2006, p. D01, and Denise Power, "Something Is in the Air: Panel Says Scent Sells," *WWD*, March 25, 2008, p. 14.

Shopping center
A group of retail businesses planned, developed, owned, and managed as a unit.

A **shopping center** is a group of retail businesses planned, developed, owned, and managed as a unit. A *regional shopping center*, or *regional shopping mall*, the largest and most dramatic shopping center, contains from 40 to over 200 stores, including 2 or more full-line department stores. It is like a covered mini-downtown and attracts customers from a wide area. A *community shopping center* contains between 15 and 40 retail stores. It normally contains a branch of a department store or variety store, a supermarket, specialty stores, professional offices, and sometimes a bank. Most shopping centers are *neighborhood shopping centers* or *strip malls* that generally contain between 5 and 15 stores. They are close and convenient for consumers. They usually contain a supermarket, perhaps a discount store, and several service stores—dry cleaner, drugstore, video-rental store, barber or beauty shop, hardware store, local restaurant, or other stores.[17]

Combined, the nation's nearly 48,500 shopping centers now account for about 75 percent of U.S. retail activity (not counting cars and gasoline). The average American makes three trips to the mall a month, shopping for an average of 82 minutes per trip and spending about $90. However, many experts suggest that America is now "over-malled." During the 1990s, mall shopping space grew at about twice the rate of population growth. As a result, almost 20 percent of America's traditional shopping centers are either dead or dying.[18]

▲ Shopping centers: The current trend is toward large "power centers" on the one hand and smaller "lifestyle centers" on the other—or a hybrid version of the two called a power-lifestyle center. In all, today's centers are more about creating places to be rather than just places to buy.

Thus, despite the recent development of many new "megamalls," the current trend is toward the so-called *power centers,* huge unenclosed shopping centers consisting of a long strip of retail stores, including large, freestanding anchors such as Wal-Mart, Home Depot, Costco, Best Buy, Michaels, Office Max. Each store has its own entrance with parking directly in front for shoppers who wish to visit only one store. Power centers have increased rapidly during the past few years to challenge traditional indoor malls.

In contrast, ▲ *lifestyle centers* are smaller malls with upscale stores, convenient locations, and nonretail activities such as dining and a movie theater. They are usually located near affluent residential neighborhoods and cater to the retail needs of consumers in their areas. "Think of lifestyle centers as part Main Street and part Fifth Avenue," comments an industry observer. In fact, the original power center and lifestyle center concepts are now morphing into hybrid lifestyle-power centers. "The idea is to combine the hominess and community of an old-time village square with the cachet of fashionable urban stores; the smell and feel of a neighborhood park with the brute convenience of a strip center." In all, today's centers are more about "creating places to be rather than just places to buy."[19]

The Future of Retailing

Retailers operate in a harsh and fast-changing environment, which offers threats as well as opportunities. For example, the industry suffers from chronic overcapacity, resulting in fierce competition for customer dollars, especially in tough economic times. Consumer demographics, lifestyles, and shopping patterns are changing rapidly, as are retailing technologies. To be successful, then, retailers will need to choose target segments carefully and position themselves strongly. They will need to take the following retailing developments into account as they plan and execute their competitive strategies.

New Retail Forms and Shortening Retail Life Cycles

New retail forms continue to emerge to meet new situations and consumer needs, but the life cycle of new retail forms is getting shorter. Department stores took about 100 years to reach the mature stage of the life cycle; more recent forms, such as warehouse stores, reached maturity in about 10 years. In such an environment, seemingly solid retail positions can crumble quickly. Of the top 10 discount retailers in 1962 (the year that Wal-Mart and Kmart began), not one still exists today.

Consider the Price Club, the original warehouse store chain. When Sol Price pioneered his first warehouse store outside San Diego in 1976, he launched a retailing revolution. Selling everything from tires and office supplies to five-pound tubs of peanut butter at super low prices, his store chain was generating $2.6 billion a year in sales within 10 years. But as the industry quickly matured, Price ran headlong into wholesale clubs run by such retail giants as Wal-Mart and Kmart. (In his autobiography, Sam Walton confesses: "I guess I've stolen—I actually prefer the word 'borrowed'—as many ideas from Sol Price as from anybody else in the business.") Only 17 years later, in a stunning reversal of fortune, a faltering Price sold out to competitor Costco. Price's rapid rise and fall shows that even the most successful retailers can't sit back with a winning formula. To remain successful, they must keep adapting.[20]

Many retailing innovations are partially explained by the **wheel-of-retailing concept**. According to this concept, many new types of retailing forms begin as low-margin, low-price, low-status operations. They challenge established retailers that have become "fat" by letting their costs and margins increase. The new retailers' success leads them to upgrade their facilities and offer more services. In turn, their costs increase, forcing them to increase their prices.

Wheel-of-retailing concept
A concept that states that new types of retailers usually begin as low-margin, low-price, low-status operations but later evolve into higher-priced, higher-service operations, eventually becoming like the conventional retailers they replaced.

Eventually, the new retailers become like the conventional retailers they replaced. The cycle begins again when still newer types of retailers evolve with lower costs and prices. The wheel-of-retailing concept seems to explain the initial success and later troubles of department stores, supermarkets, and discount stores and the recent success of off-price retailers.

Growth of Nonstore Retailing

Most of us still make most of our purchases the old-fashioned way: We go to the store, find what we want, wait patiently in line to plunk down our cash or credit card, and bring home the goods. However, consumers now have a broad array of alternatives, including mail-order, television, phone, and online shopping. Americans are increasingly avoiding the hassles and crowds at malls by doing more of their shopping by phone or computer. As we'll discuss in Chapter 17, direct and online marketing are now the fastest-growing forms of marketing.

Only a few years ago, prospects for online retailing were soaring. As more and more consumers flocked to the Web, some experts even saw a day when consumers would bypass stodgy "old economy" store retailers and do almost all of their shopping via the Internet. However, the dot-com meltdown of 2000 dashed these overblown expectations. Many once-brash Web sellers crashed and burned and expectations reversed almost overnight. The experts began to predict that online retailing was destined to be little more than a tag-on to in-store retailing.

However, today's online retailing is alive and thriving. With easier-to-use and more-enticing Web sites, improved online service, and the increasing sophistication of search technologies, online business is booming. In fact, although it currently accounts for only 6 percent of total U.S. retail sales, online buying is growing at a much brisker pace than retail buying as a whole. This year's U.S. online retail sales will reach an estimated $204 billion, a 17 percent leap over the last year's.[21]

Retailer online sites also influence a large amount of in-store buying. Here are some surprising statistics: 69 percent of shoppers research products online before going to a store to make a purchase; 62 percent have looked at least once at online peer reviews before making a purchase; and 39 percent have compared a product's features and price across retail outlets online before buying.[22] So it's no longer a matter of customers deciding to shop in the store *or* to shop online. Increasingly, customers are merging store and online outlets into a single shopping process.

All types of retailers now employ direct and online channels. The online sales of large brick-and-mortar retailers, such as Sears, Staples, Wal-Mart, and Best Buy, are increasing rapidly. Several large online-only retailers—Amazon.com, online auction site eBay, online travel companies such as Travelocity.com and Expedia.com, and others—are now making it big on the Web. At the other extreme, hordes of niche marketers are using the Web to reach new markets and expand their sales. Today's more-sophisticated search engines (Google, Yahoo!) and comparison-shopping sites (Shopping.com, Buy.com, Shopzilla.com, and others) put almost any online retailer within a mouse click or two's reach of millions of customers.

Still, much of the anticipated growth in online sales will go to multichannel retailers—the click-and-brick marketers who can successfully merge the virtual and physical worlds. In a recent ranking of the top 500 online retail sites, 55 percent were multichannel retailers.[23] ▲For example, consider Macy's, the nation's largest department store chain:[24]

> Macy's is beefing up its online and direct-to-consumer channel to complement its more than 800 Macy's stores around the country. The retailer's new feature-rich Web site offers a bigger merchandise selection, backed by two big new high-tech distribution facilities that ensure faster delivery. But the Web site aims to do more than just sell products online. "We see Macys.com as far more than a selling site," says Peter Sachse, chairman of Macys.com. "We see it as the online hub of the Macy's brand." While some customers make purchases online, the site offers a range of features—from customer reviews and side-by-side item comparisons to listings of in-store events and credit card bill payment—designed to build loyalty to Macy's and to pull customers

Online retailing: Macy's feature-rich Web site does more than just sell products online. It serves as "the online hub of the Macy's brand" and pulls customers into stores.

into stores. Like many retailers, Macy's has discovered that its best customers shop both online and offline. "When our customers shop online and in stores they spend 20 percent more in stores than the average in-store shopper and 60 percent more online than the average online shopper at Macys.com," says Sachse. "Our core woman shopper, like the rest of us, is spending a larger and larger part of her media day online," adds Macy's chief marketing officer. "We need to increase our time there, just as she increases her time there."

Retail Convergence

Today's retailers are increasingly selling the same products at the same prices to the same consumers in competition with a wider variety of other retailers. For example, you can buy books at outlets ranging from independent local bookstores to warehouse clubs such as Costco, superstores such as Barnes & Noble, or Web sites such as Amazon.com. When it comes to brand-name appliances, department stores, discount stores, home improvement stores, off-price retailers, electronics superstores, and a slew of Web sites all compete for the same customers. So if you can't find the microwave oven you want at Sears, step across the street and find one for a better price at Lowe's or Best Buy—or just order one online from Amazon.com or even RitzCamera.com.

This merging of consumers, products, prices, and retailers is called *retail convergence*. Such convergence means greater competition for retailers and greater difficulty in differentiating offerings. The competition between chain superstores and smaller, independently owned stores has become particularly heated. Because of their bulk-buying power and high sales volume, chains can buy at lower costs and thrive on smaller margins. The arrival of a superstore can quickly force nearby independents out of business. For example, the decision by electronics superstore Best Buy to sell CDs as loss leaders at rock-bottom prices pushed a number of specialty record-store chains into bankruptcy. And with its everyday low prices, Wal-Mart has been accused of destroying independents in countless small towns around the country who sell the same merchandise.

Yet the news is not all bad for smaller companies. Many small, independent retailers are thriving. They are finding that sheer size and marketing muscle are often no match for the personal touch small stores can provide or the specialty merchandise niches that small stores fill for a devoted customer base. Remember Annie Bloom's Books, the cozy independent book store we discussed in Chapter 10, whose personal approach turns local book lovers into loyal patrons, even if they have to pay a little more?

The Rise of Megaretailers

The rise of huge mass merchandisers and specialty superstores, the formation of vertical marketing systems, and a rash of retail mergers and acquisitions have created a core of superpower megaretailers. Through their superior information systems and buying power, these giant retailers can offer better merchandise selections, good service, and strong price savings to consumers. As a result, they grow even larger by squeezing out their smaller, weaker competitors.

The megaretailers have shifted the balance of power between retailers and producers. A relative handful of retailers now control access to enormous numbers of consumers, giving them the upper hand in their dealings with manufacturers. For example, in the United States, Home Depot's sales of $84.7 billion are close to 13 times those of major supplier Black & Decker, and Home Depot generates well over 20 percent of Black & Decker's $6.5 billion in revenues. Home Depot can, and often does, use this power to wring concessions from Black & Decker and other suppliers.[25]

Growing Importance of Retail Technology

Retail technologies have become critically important as competitive tools. Progressive retailers are using advanced information technology and software systems to produce better forecasts, control inventory costs, interact electronically with suppliers, send information between stores, and even sell to customers within stores. They have adopted sophisticated systems for checkout scanning, RFID inventory tracking, merchandise handling, information sharing, and interacting with customers.

Perhaps the most startling advances in retailing technology concern the ways in which retailers are connecting with consumers. Today's customers have gotten used to the speed and convenience of buying online and to the control that the Internet gives them over the buying process. "The Web provides shopping when you like it, where you like it, with access to gobs of research—from a product's attributes to where it's cheapest," says one retail technology expert. "No real-world store can replicate all that."

But increasingly, retailers are attempting to meet these new consumer expectations by bringing Web-style technologies into their stores. Many retailers now routinely use technologies ranging from touch-screen kiosks, handheld shopping assistants, customer-loyalty cards, and self-scanning checkout systems to in-store access to store inventory databases. Consider the following examples:[26]

Today's customer doesn't always have the patience for traipsing around for the perfect cashmere scarf or obscure French novel. So Barnes & Noble and other retailers are installing in-store kiosks that allow people to search inventory, locate merchandise, and order out-of-stock items. For impatient online customers who don't want to wait for the UPS truck, many retailers now offer in-store pickup. Circuit City promises that online purchases will be available for pickup in 24 minutes. If the item isn't ready, shoppers get a $24 gift card. Circuit City reports that 50 percent of its online orders are now picked up in stores. Importantly, getting people to show up at stores gives the retailer the opportunity to sell them more stuff.

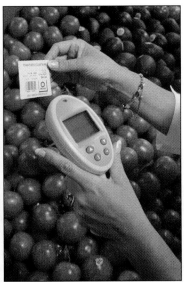

▲ Retail technology: In its new pilot store—Bloom—southeastern grocery chain Food Lion is using technology to make shopping easier for its customers.

▲ Bloom supermarkets, owned by Food Lion, have poured money into a sophisticated system that allows shoppers to pick up a scanner and grocery bag at the front of the store, keep track of the bill as they shop, download the scanner and grocery bag at the self-service checkout, and pay. Voilà—the weekly food run with fewer hassles, in Internet time. Along the way, a computerized kiosk in the wine section lets shoppers scan a bottle and get serving suggestions. The kiosk, and a second one in the meat section, lets them print recipes off the screen. And if shoppers drop off a prescription, the pharmacy can send a message to the scanner when their order is ready. Visitors to Shopbloom.com can even key in a shopping list before going to the store to get a printout of aisles they need to hit.

Global Expansion of Major Retailers

Retailers with unique formats and strong brand positioning are increasingly moving into other countries. Many are expanding internationally to escape mature and saturated home markets. Over the years, some giant U.S. retailers, such as McDonald's, have become globally prominent as a result of their marketing prowess. Others, such as Wal-Mart, are rapidly establishing a global presence. Wal-Mart, which now operates more than 3,000 stores in 13 countries abroad, sees exciting global potential. Its international division alone last year racked up sales of more than $90 billion, an increase of almost 18 percent over the previous year and 42 percent more than rival Target's *total* sales of $63.4.[27]

However, most U.S retailers are still significantly behind Europe and Asia when it comes to global expansion. Ten of the world's top 20 retailers are U.S. companies; only 3 of these retailers have set up stores outside of North America (Wal-Mart, Home Depot, and Costco). Of the 10 non-U.S. retailers in the world's top 20, 7 have stores in at least 10 countries. Among foreign retailers that have gone global are France's Carrefour and Auchan chains, Germany's Metro and Aldi chains, and Britain's Tesco.[28]

French discount retailer Carrefour, the world's second-largest retailer after Wal-Mart, has embarked on an aggressive mission to extend its role as a leading international retailer:

> The Carrefour Group has an interest in more than 14,576 stores in over 30 countries in Europe, Asia, and the Americas, including 1,108 hypermarkets (supercenters). It leads Europe in supermarkets and the world in hypermarkets. Carrefour is outpacing Wal-Mart in several emerging markets, including South America, China, and the Pacific Rim. It's the leading retailer in Brazil and Argentina, where it operates more than 900 stores, compared to Wal-Mart's 336 units in those two countries. Carrefour is the largest foreign retailer in China, where it operates more than 350 stores versus Wal-Mart's 203. In short, although Wal-Mart has more than three times Carrefour's overall sales, Carrefour is forging ahead of Wal-Mart in most markets outside North America. The only question: Can the French retailer hold its lead? Although no one retailer can safely claim to be in the same league with Wal-Mart as an overall retail presence, Carrefour stands a better chance than most to hold its own in global retailing.[29]

Retail Stores as "Communities" or "Hangouts"

With the rise in the number of people living alone, working at home, or living in isolated and sprawling suburbs, there has been a resurgence of establishments that, regardless of the product or service they offer, also provide a place for people to get together. These places include coffee shops and cafés, shopping malls, bookstores, children's play spaces, superstores, and urban greenmarkets. For example, today's bookstores have become part bookstore, part library, part living room, and part coffeehouse. On an early evening at your local Barnes & Noble, you'll likely find backpack-toting high school students doing homework with friends in the coffee bar. Nearby, retirees sit in cushy chairs thumbing through travel or gardening books while parents read aloud to their children. Barnes & Noble sells more than just books, it sells comfort, relaxation, and community.

Retailers don't create communities only in their brick-and-mortar stores. Many also build virtual communities on the Internet. ▲For example, Fiskars sells scissors, along with scrapbooking and crafting tools and supplies. A few years ago, Fiskars learned that its image was lackluster. In focus groups, respondents told the company that if Fiskars were a color, it would be beige; if it were a food, it would be saltines. So, to light a fire under the brand, the company created Fiskateers, an exclusive online community of crafters:[30]

> Crafting is a very high-involvement product category for the women who love it. As one enthusiast put it: "Crafting isn't a matter of life and death. It's much more important than that." So, to light a fire under the Fiskars brand, the company created Fiskateers, an exclusive community of crafters. You have to be invited to get in. When you join up, you

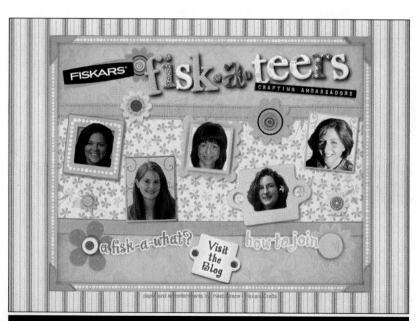

▲ Retail communities: Scissors and crafting supplies maker Fiskars has created an online community of more than 4,000 crafting enthusiasts.

get a box that includes crafting supplies plus unique two-tone scissors available only to members. But, most importantly, you get to connect online at Fiskateers.com to draw ideas and support from fellow crafters. Crafting enthusiasts couldn't wait to join. In just over a year, Fiskars has grown the community to include more than 4,000 members, 20 times its original goal. In that time, mentions of Fiskars in online chatter has surged by a factor of six. Fiskars has found that building relationships with and between the crafting enthusiasts is more important than the week's sales numbers. More than creating sales, the Fiskateers community creates collaboration between the company and important customers. "We are actually listening to them," says the president of Fiskars' School, Office, and Craft Division, "and they are listening to us."[31]

<table>
<tr><td>**Author Comment** | Whereas retailers primarily sell goods and services directly to final consumers for personal use, wholesalers sell primarily to those buying for resale or business use. Because wholesalers operate behind the scenes, they are largely unknown to final consumers. But they are very important to their business customers.</td></tr>
</table>

Wholesaling

All activities involved in selling goods and services to those buying for resale or business use.

Wholesaler

A firm engaged *primarily* in wholesaling activities.

Wholesaling (pp 389–394)

Wholesaling includes all activities involved in selling goods and services to those buying for resale or business use. We call **wholesalers** those firms engaged *primarily* in wholesaling activities.

Wholesalers buy mostly from producers and sell mostly to retailers, industrial consumers, and other wholesalers. As a result, many of the nation's largest and most important wholesalers are largely unknown to final consumers. ▲For example, you may never have heard of Grainger, even though it's very well known and much valued by its more than 1.8 million business and institutional customers across North America.

Grainger may be the biggest market leader you've never heard of. It's a $6.4 billion business that offers more than 800,000 maintenance, repair, and operating (MRO) products to more than 1.8 million customers. Through its branch network, service centers, sales reps, catalog, and Web site, Grainger links customers with the supplies they need to keep their facilities running smoothly—everything from light bulbs, cleaners, and display cases to nuts and bolts, motors, valves, power tools, and test equipment. Grainger's 606 North American branches, 18 strategically located distribution centers, more than 17,000 employees, and innovative Web site handle more than 115,000 transactions a day. Its customers include organizations ranging from factories, garages, and grocers to schools and military bases. Most American businesses are located within 20 minutes of a Grainger branch. Customers include notables such as Abbott Laboratories, General Motors, Campbell Soup, American Airlines, Chrysler, and the U.S. Postal Service.

Grainger operates on a simple value proposition: to make it easier and less costly for customers to find and buy MRO supplies. It starts by acting as a one-stop shop for products needed to maintain facilities. On a broader level, it builds lasting relationships with customers by helping them find *solutions* to their overall MRO problems. Acting as consultants, Grainger sales reps help buyers with everything from improving their supply chain management to reducing inventories and streamlining warehousing operations. So, how come you've never heard of Grainger? Maybe it's because the company operates in the not-so-glamorous world of MRO supplies, which are important to every business but not so important to consumers. More likely, it's because Grainger is a wholesaler. And like most wholesalers, it operates behind the scenes, selling only to other businesses.[32]

▲ Wholesaling: Many of the nation's largest and most important wholesalers—like Grainger—are largely unknown to final consumers. But they are very well known and much valued by the business customers they serve.

Why are wholesalers important to sellers? For example, why would a producer use wholesalers rather than selling directly to retailers or consumers? Simply put, wholesalers add value by performing one or more of the following channel functions:

- *Selling and promoting:* Wholesalers' sales forces help manufacturers reach many small customers at a low cost. The wholesaler has more contacts and is often more trusted by the buyer than the distant manufacturer.

- *Buying and assortment building:* Wholesalers can select items and build assortments needed by their customers, thereby saving the consumers much work.

- *Bulk breaking:* Wholesalers save their customers money by buying in carload lots and breaking bulk (breaking large lots into small quantities).

- *Warehousing:* Wholesalers hold inventories, thereby reducing the inventory costs and risks of suppliers and customers.

- *Transportation:* Wholesalers can provide quicker delivery to buyers because they are closer than the producers.

- *Financing:* Wholesalers finance their customers by giving credit, and they finance their suppliers by ordering early and paying bills on time.

- *Risk bearing:* Wholesalers absorb risk by taking title and bearing the cost of theft, damage, spoilage, and obsolescence.

- *Market information:* Wholesalers give information to suppliers and customers about competitors, new products, and price developments.

- *Management services and advice:* Wholesalers often help retailers train their salesclerks, improve store layouts and displays, and set up accounting and inventory control systems.

Types of Wholesalers

Merchant wholesaler
An independently owned business that takes title to the merchandise it handles.

Wholesalers fall into three major groups (see ● **Table 13.3**): *merchant wholesalers, agents and broker,* and *manufacturers' sales branches and offices.* **Merchant wholesalers** are the largest single group of wholesalers, accounting for roughly 50 percent of all wholesaling. Merchant wholesalers include two broad types: full-service wholesalers and limited-service wholesalers. *Full-service wholesalers* provide a full set of services, whereas the various *limited-service wholesalers* offer fewer services to their suppliers and customers. The several different types of limited-service wholesalers perform varied specialized functions in the distribution channel.

Broker
A wholesaler who does not take title to goods and whose function is to bring buyers and sellers together and assist in negotiation.

Brokers and *agents* differ from merchant wholesalers in two ways: They do not take title to goods, and they perform only a few functions. Like merchant wholesalers, they generally specialize by product line or customer type. A **broker** brings buyers and sellers together and assists in negotiation. **Agents** represent buyers or sellers on a more permanent basis. *Manufacturers' agents* (also called manufacturers' representatives) are the most common type of agent wholesaler. The third major type of wholesaling is that done in **manufacturers' sales branches and offices** by sellers or buyers themselves rather than through independent wholesalers.

Agent
A wholesaler who represents buyers or sellers on a relatively permanent basis, performs only a few functions, and does not take title to goods.

Wholesaler Marketing Decisions

Manufacturers' sales branches and offices
Wholesaling by sellers or buyers themselves rather than through independent wholesalers.

Wholesalers now face growing competitive pressures, more-demanding customers, new technologies, and more direct-buying programs on the part of large industrial, institutional, and retail buyers. As a result, they have taken a fresh look at their marketing strategies. As with retailers, their marketing decisions include choices of segmentation and targeting, differentiation and positioning, and the marketing mix—product and service assortments, price, promotion, and distribution (see ▼**Figure 13.2** on page 392).

Segmentation, Targeting, Differentiation, and Positioning Decisions

Like retailers, wholesalers must segment and define their target markets and differentiate and position themselves effectively—they cannot serve everyone. They can choose a target group by size of customer (only large retailers), type of customer (convenience stores

● **TABLE** | **13.3**   Major Types of Wholesalers

Type	Description
Merchant wholesalers	Independently owned businesses that take title to the merchandise they handle. In different trades they are called *jobbers, distributors,* or *mill supply houses.* They include *full-service wholesalers* and *limited-service wholesalers.*
Full-service wholesalers	Provide a full line of services: carrying stock, maintaining a sales force, offering credit, making deliveries, and providing management assistance. There are two types:
Wholesale merchants	Sell primarily to retailers and provide a full range of services. *General merchandise wholesalers* carry several merchandise lines, whereas *general line wholesalers* carry one or two lines in great depth. *Specialty wholesalers* specialize in carrying only part of a line. Examples: health food wholesalers, seafood wholesalers.
Industrial distributors	Sell to manufacturers rather than to retailers. Provide several services, such as carrying stock, offering credit, and providing delivery. May carry a broad range of merchandise, a general line, or a specialty line.
Limited-service wholesalers	Offer fewer services than full-service wholesalers. Limited-service wholesalers are of several types:
Cash-and-carry wholesalers	Carry a limited line of fast-moving goods and sell to small retailers for cash. Normally do not deliver. Example: A small fish store retailer may drive to a cash-and-carry fish wholesaler, buy fish for cash, and bring the merchandise back to the store.
Truck wholesalers (or truck jobbers)	Perform primarily a selling and delivery function. Carry a limited a line of semiperishable merchandise (such as milk, bread, snack foods), which they sell for cash as they make their rounds to supermarkets, small groceries, hospitals, restaurants, factory cafeterias, and hotels.
Drop shippers	Do not carry inventory or handle the product. On receiving an order, they select a manufacturer, who ships the merchandise directly to the customer. The drop shipper assumes title and risk from the time the order is accepted to its delivery to the customer. They operate in bulk industries, such as coal, lumber, and heavy equipment.
Rack jobbers	Serve grocery and drug retailers, mostly in nonfood items. They send delivery trucks to stores, where the delivery people set up toys, paperbacks, hardware items, health and beauty aids, or other items. They price the goods, keep them fresh, set up point-of-purchase displays, and keep inventory records. Rack jobbers retain title to the goods and bill the retailers only for the goods sold to consumers.
Producers' cooperatives	Are owned by farmer members and assemble farm produce to sell in local markets. The co-op's profits are distributed to members at the end of the year. They often attempt to improve product quality and promote a co-op brand name, such as Sun-Maid raisins, Sunkist oranges, or Diamond walnuts.
Mail-order wholesalers	Send catalogs to retail, industrial, and institutional customers featuring jewelry, cosmetics, specialty foods, and other small items. Maintain no outside sales force. Main customers are businesses in small outlying areas. Orders are filled and sent by mail, truck, or other transportation.
Brokers and agents	Do not take title to goods. Main function is to facilitate buying and selling, for which they earn a commission on the selling price. Generally specialize by product line or customer type.
Brokers	Chief function is bringing buyers and sellers together and assisting in negotiation. They are paid by the party who hired them and do not carry inventory, get involved in financing, or assume risk. Examples: food brokers, real estate brokers, insurance brokers, and security brokers.
Agents	Represent either buyers or sellers on a more permanent basis than brokers do. There are several types:
Manufacturers' agents	Represent two or more manufacturers of complementary lines. A formal written agreement with each manufacturer covers pricing, territories, order handling, delivery service and warranties, and commission rates. Often used in such lines as apparel, furniture, and electrical goods. Most manufacturers' agents are small businesses with only a few skilled salespeople as employees. They are hired by small manufacturers who cannot afford their own field sales forces and by large manufacturers who use agents to open new territories or to cover territories that cannot support full-time salespeople.
Selling agents	Have contractual authority to sell a manufacturer's entire output. The manufacturer either is not interested in the selling function or feels unqualified. The selling agent serves as a sales department and has significant influence over prices, terms, and conditions of sale. Found in product areas such as textiles, industrial machinery and equipment, coal and coke, chemicals, and metals.

● TABLE | 13.3   Major Types of Wholesalers—*continued*

Type	Description
Purchasing agents	Generally have a long-term relationship with buyers and make purchases for them, often receiving, inspecting, warehousing, and shipping the merchandise to the buyers. They provide helpful market information to clients and help them obtain the best goods and prices available.
Commission merchants	Take physical possession of products and negotiate sales. Normally, they are not employed on a long-term basis. Used most often in agricultural marketing by farmers who do not want to sell their own output and do not belong to producers' cooperatives. The commission merchant takes a truckload of commodities to a central market, sells it for the best price, deducts a commission and expenses, and remits the balance to the producers.
Manufacturers' and retailers' branches and offices	Wholesaling operations conducted by sellers or buyers themselves rather than through independent wholesalers. Separate branches and offices can be dedicated to either sales or purchasing.
Sales branches and offices	Set up by manufacturers to improve inventory control, selling, and promotion. *Sales branches* carry inventory and are found in industries such as lumber and automotive equipment and parts. *Sales offices* do not carry inventory and are most prominent in dry-goods and notions industries.
Purchasing officers	Perform a role similar to that of brokers or agents but are part of the buyer's organization. Many retailers set up purchasing offices in major market centers such as New York and Chicago.

only), need for service (customers who need credit), or other factors. Within the target group, they can identify the more profitable customers, design stronger offers, and build better relationships with them. They can propose automatic reordering systems, set up management-training and advising systems, or even sponsor a voluntary chain. They can discourage less-profitable customers by requiring larger orders or adding service charges to smaller ones.

Marketing Mix Decisions

Like retailers, wholesalers must decide on product and service assortments, prices, promotion, and place. Wholesalers add customer value though the *products and services* they offer. They are often under great pressure to carry a full line and to stock enough for immediate delivery. But this practice can damage profits. Wholesalers today are cutting down on the number of lines they carry, choosing to carry only the more-profitable ones. They are also rethinking which services count most in building strong customer relationships and which should be dropped or paid for by the customer. The key is to find the mix of services most valued by their target customers.

📦 FIGURE | 13.2
Wholesaler Marketing Strategy

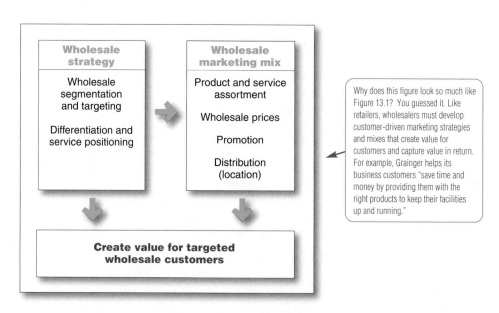

Why does this figure look so much like Figure 13.1? You guessed it. Like retailers, wholesalers must develop customer-driven marketing strategies and mixes that create value for customers and capture value in return. For example, Grainger helps its business customers "save time and money by providing them with the right products to keep their facilities up and running."

Price is also an important wholesaler decision. Wholesalers usually mark up the cost of goods by a standard percentage—say, 20 percent. Expenses may run 17 percent of the gross margin, leaving a profit margin of 3 percent. In grocery wholesaling, the average profit margin is often less than 2 percent. Wholesalers are trying new pricing approaches. They may cut their margin on some lines in order to win important new customers. They may ask suppliers for special price breaks when they can turn them into an increase in the supplier's sales.

Although *promotion* can be critical to wholesaler success, most wholesalers are not promotion minded. They use largely scattered and unplanned trade advertising, sales promotion, personal selling, and public relations. Many are behind the times in personal selling—they still see selling as a single salesperson talking to a single customer instead of as a team effort to sell, build, and service major accounts. Wholesalers also need to adopt some of the nonpersonal promotion techniques used by retailers. They need to develop an overall promotion strategy and to make greater use of supplier promotion materials and programs.

Finally, *distribution* (location) is important—wholesalers must choose their locations, facilities, and Web locations carefully. There was a time when wholesalers could locate in low-rent, low-tax areas and invest little money in their buildings, equipment, and systems. Today, however, as technology zooms forward, such behavior results in outdated materials-handling, order-processing, and delivery systems.

Instead, today's large and progressive wholesalers have reacted to rising costs by investing in automated warehouses and information technology systems. Orders are fed from the retailer's information system directly into the wholesaler's, and the items are picked up by mechanical devices and automatically taken to a shipping platform where they are assembled. Most large wholesalers are using technology to carry out accounting, billing, inventory control, and forecasting. Modern wholesalers are adapting their services to the needs of target customers and finding cost-reducing methods of doing business.

Trends in Wholesaling

Today's wholesalers face considerable challenges. The industry remains vulnerable to one of the most enduring trends of the last decade—fierce resistance to price increases and the winnowing out of suppliers who are not adding value based on cost and quality. Progressive wholesalers constantly watch for better ways to meet the changing needs of their suppliers and target customers. They recognize that, in the long run, their only reason for existence comes from adding value by increasing the efficiency and effectiveness of the entire marketing channel. As with other types of marketers, the goal is to build value-adding customer relationships. For example, Grainger succeeds by making life easier and more efficient for the commercial and institutional buyers and sellers it serves:

> Beyond making it easier for customers to find the products they need, Grainger also helps them streamline their acquisition processes. For most companies, acquiring MRO supplies is a very costly process. In fact, 40 percent of the cost of MRO supplies stems from the purchase process, including finding a supplier, negotiating the best deal, placing the order, receiving the order, and paying the invoice. Grainger constantly seeks ways to reduce the costs associated with MRO supplies acquisition, both internally and externally. One company found that working with Grainger cut MRO requisition time by more than 60 percent; lead times went from days to hours. Its supply chain dropped from 12,000 suppliers to 560—significantly reducing expenses. Similarly, a large timber and paper-products company has come to appreciate Grainger's selection and streamlined ordering process. It orders two-thirds of its supplies from Grainger's Web site at an annual acquisition cost of only $300,000. By comparison, for the remainder of its needs, this company deals with more than 1,300 small distributors at an acquisition cost of $2.4 million each year—eight times the cost of dealing with Grainger for half of the volume. The company is now looking

MCKESSON
Empowering Healthcare

You have the power to drive results

McKesson has the right solution for your pharmacy

▲ Pharmaceuticals wholesaler McKesson helps its retail pharmacist customers be more efficient by offering a wide range of online resources. Retail pharmacists can even use the McKesson system to maintain medical profiles on their customers.

for ways to buy all of its MRO supplies from Grainger. As one Grainger branch manager puts it, "If we don't save [customers] time and money every time they come [to us], they won't come back."[33]

▲McKesson, the nation's leading wholesaler of pharmaceuticals, health and beauty care, home health care, and medical supply and equipment products, provides another example of progressive, value-adding wholesaling. To survive, McKesson has to remain more cost effective than manufacturers' sales branches. Thus, the company has built efficient automated warehouses, established direct computer links with drug manufacturers, and set up extensive online supply management and accounts receivable systems for customers. It offers retail pharmacists a wide range of online resources, including supply-management assistance, catalog searches, real-time order tracking, and an account-management system. It has also created solutions such as automated pharmaceutical-dispensing machines that assist pharmacists by reducing costs and improving accuracy. Retailers can even use the McKesson system to maintain medical profiles on their customers.

McKesson's medical-surgical supply and equipment customers receive a rich assortment of online solutions and supply management tools, including an online order management system and real-time information on products and pricing, inventory availability, and order status. According to McKesson, it adds value in the channel by providing "supply, information, and health care management products and services designed to reduce costs and improve quality across healthcare."[34]

The distinction between large retailers and large wholesalers continues to blur. Many retailers now operate formats such as wholesale clubs and supercenters that perform many wholesale functions. In return, many large wholesalers are setting up their own retailing operations. For example, until recently, SuperValu was classified as a food wholesaler, with a majority of its business derived from supplying grocery products to independent grocery retailers. However, over the past decade, SuperValu has started or acquired several retail food chains of its own—including Albertsons, Jewel-Osco, Save-A-Lot, Cub Foods, Acme, and others—to become the nation's third-largest food retailer. Thus, even though it remains the country's largest food wholesaler, SuperValu is now classified as a retailer because 75 percent of its $37 billion in sales come from retailing.[35]

Wholesalers will continue to increase the services they provide to retailers—retail pricing, cooperative advertising, marketing and management information reports, accounting services, online transactions, and others. Rising costs on the one hand, and the demand for increased services on the other, will put the squeeze on wholesaler profits. Wholesalers who do not find efficient ways to deliver value to their customers will soon drop by the wayside. However, the increased use of computerized, automated, and Web-based systems will help wholesalers to contain the costs of ordering, shipping, and inventory holding, boosting their productivity.

Finally, facing slow growth in their domestic markets and such developments as the North American Free Trade Agreement, many large wholesalers are now going global. For example, McKesson now derives more than 7 percent of its revenues from Canadian and other international operations, up 28 percent in just the past two years. Its Information Solutions group operates widely throughout North America, the United Kingdom, and other European countries.[36]

REVIEWING Objectives AND KEY Terms

Retailing and wholesaling consist of many organizations bringing goods and services from the point of production to the point of use. In this chapter, we first looked at the nature and importance of retailing, major types of retailers, the decisions retailers make, and the future of retailing. We then examined these same topics for wholesalers.

OBJECTIVE 1 Explain the role of retailers in the distribution channel and describe the major types of retailers. (pp 370–378)

Retailing includes all activities involved in selling goods or services directly to final consumers for their personal, nonbusiness use. Retail stores come in all shapes and sizes, and new retail types keep emerging. Store retailers can be classified by the *amount of service* they provide (self-service, limited service, or full service), *product line sold* (specialty stores, department stores, supermarkets, convenience stores, superstores, and service businesses), and *relative prices* (discount stores and off-price retailers). Today, many retailers are banding together in corporate and contractual *retail organizations* (corporate chains, voluntary chains and retailer cooperatives, franchise organizations, and merchandising conglomerates).

OBJECTIVE 2 Describe the major retailer marketing decisions. (pp 378–384)

Retailers are always searching for new marketing strategies to attract and hold customers. They face major marketing decisions about segmentation and targeting, store differentiation and positioning, and the retail marketing mix.

Retailers must first segment and define their target markets and then decide how they will differentiate and position themselves in these markets. Those that try to offer "something for everyone" end up satisfying no market well. In contrast, successful retailers define their target markets well and position themselves strongly.

Guided by strong targeting and positioning, retailers must decide on a retail marketing mix—product and services assortment, price, promotion, and place. Retail stores are much more than simply an assortment of goods—beyond the products and services they offer, today's successful retailers carefully orchestrate virtually every aspect of the consumer store experience. A retailer's price policy must fit its target market and positioning, products and services assortment, and competition. Retailers use any or all of the promotion tools—advertising, personal selling, sales

promotion, public relations, and direct marketing—to reach consumers. Finally, it's very important that retailers select locations that are accessible to the target market in areas that are consistent with the retailer's positioning.

OBJECTIVE 3 Discuss the future of retailing. (pp 384–389)

Retailers operate in a harsh and fast-changing environment, which offers threats as well as opportunities. New retail forms continue to emerge to meet new situations and consumer needs, but the life cycle of new retail forms is getting shorter—retailers must pay attention to the wheel-of-retailing concept. Other trends in retailing include the rapid growth of nonstore retailing, retail convergence (the merging of consumers, products, prices, and retailers), the rise of megaretailers, the growing importance of retail technology, the global expansion of major retailers, and the resurgence of retail stores as consumer "communities" or "hangouts."

OBJECTIVE 4 Explain the major types of wholesalers and their marketing decisions. (pp 389–394)

Wholesaling includes all the activities involved in selling goods or services to those who are buying for the purpose of resale or for business use. Wholesalers fall into three groups. First, *merchant wholesalers* take possession of the goods. They include *full-service wholesalers* (wholesale merchants, industrial distributors) and *limited-service wholesalers* (cash-and-carry wholesalers, truck wholesalers, drop shippers, rack jobbers, producers' cooperatives, and mail-order wholesalers). Second, *brokers* and *agents* do not take possession of the goods but are paid a commission for aiding buying and selling. Finally, *manufacturers' sales branches and offices* are wholesaling operations conducted by nonwholesalers to bypass the wholesalers.

Like retailers, wholesalers must target carefully and position themselves strongly. And, like retailers, wholesalers must decide on product and service assortments, prices, promotion, and place. Progressive wholesalers constantly watch for better ways to meet the changing needs of their suppliers and target customers. They recognize that, in the long run, their only reason for existence comes from adding value by increasing the efficiency and effectiveness of the entire marketing channel. As with other types of marketers, the goal was to build value-adding customer relationships.

KEY Terms

OBJECTIVE 1

Retailing (p 370)
Retailer (p 370)
Specialty store (p 372)
Department store (p 372)

Supermarket (p 372)
Convenience store (p 372)
Superstore (p 373)
Category killer (p 374)
Service retailer (p 374)
Discount store (p 374)

Off-price retailer (p 374)
Independent off-price retailer (p 374)
Factory outlet (p 374)
Warehouse club (p 376)
Chain stores (p 376)
Franchise (p 377)

OBJECTIVE 2
Shopping center (p 383)

OBJECTIVE 3
Wheel-of-retailing concept (p 384)

OBJECTIVE 4
Wholesaling (p 389)
Wholesaler (p 389)
Merchant wholesaler (p 390)

Broker (p 390)
Agent (p 390)
Manufacturers' sales branches and offices (p 390)

DISCUSSING & APPLYING THE Concepts

Discussing the Concepts

1. Discuss how retailers and wholesalers add value to the marketing system. Explain why marketers are embracing the concept of *shopper marketing*. (AACSB: Communication; Reflective Thinking)

2. Different types of customers and products require different amounts of service. Discuss the different levels of retailer service and give one example of each. (AASCB: Communication; Reflective Thinking)

3. Discuss the different organizational approaches for retailers and provide an example of each. (AACSB: Communication; Reflective Thinking)

4. What is the wheel-of-retailing concept? Does it apply to online retailing? (AACSB: Communication; Reflective Thinking)

5. What is retail convergence? Has it helped or harmed small retailers? (AACSB: Communication; Reflective Thinking)

6. Explain how wholesalers add value in the channel of distribution. (AACSB: Communication)

Applying the Concepts

1. Choose three retailers that you buy from often. Classify these retailers in terms of the characteristics presented in the chapter. Next, use Table 13.1 to categorize each retailer. (AACSB: Communication; Reflective Thinking)

2. Deciding on a target market and positioning for a retail store are very important marketing decisions. In a small group, develop the concept for a new retail store. Who is the target market for your store? How is your store positioned? What retail atmospherics will enhance this positioning effectively to attract and satisfy your target market? (AACSB: Communication; Reflective Thinking)

3. Suppose that you are a manufacturer's agent for three lines of complementary women's apparel. Discuss what types of marketing mix decisions you will be making. (AACSB: Communication; Reflective Thinking)

FOCUS ON Technology

Thanks to today's shaky economy, many luxury goods are going unsold and are piling up in storerooms. However, this creates an opportunity for a whole new breed of online sellers, such as Gilt.com, Ideeli.com, and HauteLook.com. Within six months of launch, HauteLook.com had more that 100,000 members and was growing 10 percent per week. These members-only sites announce limited-time "flash sales" of designer goods discounted up to 70 percent. You can get $250 Rag & Bone jeans for $118 or Nina Ricci sunglasses for a fraction of the retail price. But you have to act fast because sales typically last only a few days, with digital clocks ticking down the time. Gilt.com reports unloading 600 dresses within six minutes and

members buying within 45 seconds of logging on! Some sites offer free membership, whereas others are by invitation only. For $100, Ideeli.com offers members cell phone invitations to private sales.

1. Visit www.hautelook.com to learn more about this online retailer. In what ways does it provide value for manufacturers and consumers? (AACSB: Communication; Use of IT; Reflective Thinking)

2. Do sites like these create conflicts between manufacturers and retailers within the traditional channel of distribution? (AACSB: Communication; Reflective)

FOCUS ON Ethics

If not for a stroke of luck, consumers might never have enjoyed some of the best tortilla products sold in retail stores—the Tamxico and Wrap-Itz brands. In 2008, La Bonita Ole, maker of these brands (www.tamxicos.com), was named "Tortilla Manufacturer of the Year" by *Snack & Wholesale Bakery* magazine and one of the "100 Best Packaged Foods for Women"

by *Women's Health* magazine. But back in 1992, founder Tammy Young couldn't afford the slotting fees required to get her brands into large retail stores or to get good shelf placement in available stores. The stroke of luck came when a high school friend's wealthy husband become her benefactor in 1996. Now, with both brands available in major retail stores in the eastern United

States—10 stockkeeping units (SKUs) of Tamxico and 12 SKUs of Wrap-Itz—La Bonita Ole is a $20 million a year company. Slotting fees, also called slotting allowances, are fees that retailers charge manufacturers to get onto retail shelves. In their early days, small manufacturers such as La Bonita Ole usually couldn't ante up these fees, which average $10,000 per chain for each new product according to the Federal Trade Commission. Big consumer goods makers report total slotting fees in the $1 million to $2 million range per new brand. Tammy was lucky—she had a wealthy friend who helped her get started. But you have to wonder how

many small manufacturers of outstanding products are denied entry into retail stores.

1. Is it fair for retailers to charge manufacturers to get onto store shelves? Discuss both points of view on this issue. (AACSB: Communication; Ethical Reasoning; Reflective Thinking)

2. Go to www.ftc.gov/opa/2003/11/slottingallowance.shtm to read the FTC's report on slotting fees. What did you learn from this report and what is the FTC's position on slotting fees? (AACSB: Communication; Use of IT; Reflective Thinking)

MARKETING BY THE Numbers

Retailers need merchandise to make sales. In fact, a retailer's inventory is its biggest asset. Not stocking enough merchandise can result in lost sales, but carrying too much inventory increases costs and lowers margins. Both circumstances reduce profits. One measure of a reseller's inventory management effectiveness is its *stockturn rate* (also called *inventory turnover rate* for manufacturers). The key to success in retailing is realizing a large volume of sales on as little inventory as possible while maintaining enough stock to meet customer demands.

1. Refer to Appendix 2, Marketing by the Numbers, and determine the stockturn rate of a retailer carrying an average inventory at cost of $350,000, with a cost of goods sold of $800,000. (AACSB: Communication; Analytical Reasoning)

2. If this company's stockturn rate was 3.5 last year, is the stockturn rate calculated above better or worse? Explain. (AACSB: Communication; Reflective Thinking)

VIDEO Case

Wellbeing

In 2003, Dan Wales and Matt Lennox opened their first Wellbeing restaurant. As a retail concept, the team identified a gap in the market and developed a strong point of differentiation. "There are few truly healthy fast food chains," says Wales. "People have been desperate for healthy options." With this perspective on the market, their goal was to offer consumers a healthy alternative to typical fast-food options. Working with fresh ingredients, bright and open stores, and a well-crafted, healthy menu, the new chain clearly offered something new. So it came as no surprise that customers responded with enthusiasm to Wellbeing's new choices as they gobbled up sandwiches, salads, soups, juices, smoothies, and fruit salads. In only a few years, the chain

has expanded to 18 stores. Within the next two years, it expects to nearly double that number.

After viewing the video featuring Wellbeing, answer the following questions about retailing:

1. Categorize Wellbeing according to the four characteristics of retailers discussed in the chapter.

2. How is Wellbeing positioned in the marketplace? Which consumers does the chain target? Are its product assortment, pricing, promotion, and place decisions consistent with this targeting and positioning?

3. Which trend affecting the future of retailing do you think will most impact Wellbeing in the coming years?

COMPANY Case

Whole Foods: A Whole-istic Strategy

It's tough to compete in the grocery business these days. What was once a landscape littered with hundreds of local and regional players has now become an industry dominated by the mega-chains. Wal-Mart, Kroger, and Safeway have each taken their own approach to expanding as far and wide as possible with one goal: sell massive amounts of groceries to mainstream consumers at the lowest possible prices. Sure, there are still some small, regional grocers. But they

exist mostly because some segment of customers wants to support local businesses. It's getting harder and harder for such grocers to stay alive or avoid getting gobbled up by the big dogs on the block.

So how does a smaller chain not only survive but thrive in such a dog-eat-dog environment? Perhaps the worst strategy is trying to out-Wal-Mart Wal-Mart. Instead of competing head-to-head, smart competitors choose their turf carefully. Rather than competing directly with the volume and price leaders, some have succeeded by reducing emphasis on price and focusing instead on providing something that the low-price, high-volume competitors simply can't supply.

The grocer that's doing the best job of this is Whole Foods Market. Growing from a single store in 1980, Whole Foods has gone far beyond the status of "regional player." It now operates more than 270 stores in 36 states, Canada, and the United Kingdom. Although that's tiny compared to Kroger's 2,500 stores or Wal-Mart's 7,300, Whole Foods is thriving and expanding.

How does Whole Foods do it? Through careful positioning—specifically, by positioning *away* from the industry giants. Rather than pursuing mass-market sales volume and razor-thin margins, Whole Foods targets a select group of upscale customers and offers them "organic, natural, and gourmet foods, all swaddled in Earth Day politics." As one analyst puts it, "While other grocers are looking over their shoulder, watching and worrying about Wal-Mart, Whole Foods is going about business as usual. The tofu is still selling; the organic eggs are fresh in the back dairy cooler; and meats are still hormone free." The value package that Whole Foods offers to its unique customers is best summed up in its motto: "Whole Foods, Whole People, Whole Planet."

WHOLE FOODS

Customers that enter Whole Foods' doors are looking for the highest quality, least processed, most flavorful, and naturally preserved foods. Whole Foods claims that "Food in its purest state is the best tasting and most nutritious food available." One journalist captures the essence of Whole Foods' mission based on her own experience:

Counters groan with creamy hunks of artisanal cheese. Medjool dates beckon amid rows of exotic fruit. Savory breads rest near fruit-drenched pastries, and prepared dishes like sesame-encrusted tuna rival what's sold in fine restaurants. In keeping with the company's positioning, most of the store's goods carry labels proclaiming "organic," "100% natural," and "contains no additives." Staff people smile, happy to suggest wines that go with a particular cheese, or pause to debate the virtues of peanut butter maltballs. And it's all done against a backdrop of eye-pleasing earth-toned hues and soft lighting. This is grocery shopping? Well, not as most people know it. Whole Foods Market has cultivated its mystique with shoppers . . . by being anything but a regular supermarket chain. Whole Foods is, well, special.

The Whole Foods Web site reinforces the company's positioning. The site offers up recipes for healthy and gourmet eating, such as "Sweet Potato Pancakes with Creamy Dill Sauce," "Baked Basmati & Currant Stuffed Trout," and "Beginner's Tips for Tofu, Tempeh, and Other Soy Foods."

One aspect of Whole Foods' strategy that allows it to deliver products that foodies love might seem like a step back in time in the supply chain driven grocery industry. The bigger chains are centralized, sourcing their products from all over the world in identical batches through various distribution centers. But Whole Foods uses a more local approach. Each geographic division, headed by its own president, handles its own store network. Thus, in addition to gathering some foods globally, Whole Foods obtains a significant portion of its goods locally, often from small, uniquely dedicated food artisans. The company backs its talk with action on this issue. Its Local Producer Loan Program doles out $10 million annually in long-term, low-interest loans to local suppliers.

WHOLE PEOPLE

Whole Foods' customers appreciate the fact that the store's quality commitment reaches far beyond what's on its shelves. In its "Declaration of Interdependence," the company recognizes that living up to its "Whole Foods, Whole People, Whole Planet" motto means doing more than simply selling food. It means caring about the well-being and quality of life of everyone associated with the business, from customers and employees, to suppliers, to the broader communities in which it operates.

Nowhere is this more evident than in the way that Whole Foods treats employees. For 11 consecutive years, Whole Foods has been listed among *Fortune* magazine's "Top 100 Companies to Work for in America." Ranked as high as fifth, it is 1 of only 14 companies ranked every year since the list's inception. Said Whole Foods CEO and cofounder, John Mackey:

To be among only 14 companies in the nation to be named as one of the Best Companies to Work For since the listing began is an amazing achievement and a validation that we are honoring our core value of "Supporting Team Member Excellence and Happiness" by creating an empowering work environment.

"Empowering work environment," "self-directed teams," and "self-responsibility" all sound like corporate catch phrases that get tossed around by management without permeating the culture. But at Whole Foods, employees believe in these pillars of the company's mission. In fact, two-thirds of *Fortune*'s ranking is based on survey responses from randomly selected employees. Just ask Shateema Dillard, who after two years as an employee is a supervisor and proud owner of two stock option grants. Even though these grants are worth less than $200, Dillard feels "well-paid and confident that opportunities for growth are phenomenal."

Whole Foods is one of a shrinking number of companies that still pay 100 percent of their employees' health-care premiums. It also ranks very high on the diversity of its employee team. Out of a sense of teamwork and fairness, it caps the salaries of its highest-paid team members at 19 times the average total compensation of all full-time team members in the company.

WHOLE PLANET

"We believe companies, like individuals, must assume their share of responsibility as tenants of Planet Earth," professes the company's value statement. While this might seem simple, the extensiveness of Whole Foods' environmental program illustrates just how complex a genuine "Earth first" philosophy can be.

For starters, Whole Foods actively supports organic farming on a global basis. This, it believes, is the best way to promote sustainable agriculture and protect both the environment and farm workers. This policy supports Whole Foods' core product offering, but it's just the tip of the company's sustainability iceberg.

In January of 2006, Whole Foods became the first *Fortune* 500 company to offset 100 percent of its electricity use with the purchase of wind energy credits. The credits cover its stores, bakehouses, distributions centers, offices, and every other facility. Beyond energy conservation, Whole Foods has committed to completely eliminating disposable plastic grocery bags, not only conserving resources but also reducing non-biodegradable wastes. No other U.S. grocer has made this commitment.

Such efforts represents a tremendous corporatewide commitment to environmental protection. However, the Whole Planet culture reaches right down to the store level. Each and every store has a Green Mission Team, a task force comprised of team members who meet often to improve environmental actions for their stores. This has led many Whole Foods stores to serve as collection points for plastic bag recycling. Most stores also participate in composting programs for food waste and compostable paper goods. One store in Berkeley, California, even gets most of its electrical power from roof-top solar panels.

Under the Whole Planet mantra, Whole Foods also supports the local communities in which it operates. It believes that local efforts will create healthier and more productive societies at the micro level, resulting in less need to ship products and waste long distances. This, in turn, lowers pollution and carbon emissions. Whole Foods supports food banks, sponsors neighborhood events, and even provides financial support for employees doing voluntary community service. Perhaps most telling of Whole Foods' community commitment: It donates 5 percent of its after-tax profits to not-for-profit organizations.

A WHOLE LOT OF CUSTOMERS

Each element of the three-part philosophy underlying the Whole Foods strategy just happens to appeal strongly to a carefully targeted segment of consumers. Whole Foods is not for everyone—intentionally. Whole Foods customers are affluent, liberal, educated people living in university towns such as Austin, Texas, Boulder, Colorado, and Ann Arbor, Michigan. Their median annual household income exceeds the U.S. average by almost $8,000. Whole Foods customers live a health-conscious lifestyle, care about the food they eat, and worry about the environment. They tend to be social do-gooders who abhor soulless corporate greed. Whole Foods doesn't really need to compete with mass merchandisers such as Wal-Mart for these customers. In fact, a Whole Foods customer is more likely to boycott the local Wal-Mart than to shop at it.

But something beyond great food, environmental conscience, and human rights draws these people to Whole Foods. A store visit is more than just a shopping trip—it's an experience. And the experience is anything but what you'd find at Kroger. "We create store environments that are inviting, fun, unique, informal, comfortable, attractive, nurturing, and educational," the company claims. "We want our stores to become community meeting places where our customers come to join their friends and to make new ones." Whole Foods' concern for customers runs deep. "We go to extraordinary lengths to satisfy and delight our customers," says a company spokesperson. "We want to meet or exceed their expectations on every shopping trip."

Such commitment, along with strong targeting and positioning, have made Whole Foods one of the nation's fastest growing and most profitable food retailers. After acquiring nearly 100 stores in its 2007 merger with Wild Oats, a growing chain with a similar positioning strategy, Whole Foods is now the world's number-one natural food chain. Its upscale stores ring up an average of $689 in sales per square foot, almost twice that of a traditional grocer. And the chain reaps 35 percent gross margins, half again as large as those of traditional competitors such as Kroger. Whereas other grocers have faced limited sales and profit growth or even declines in the face of the withering Wal-Mart assault, Whole Foods' sales and profits have more than doubled over the past four years.

So, Whole Foods can't compete directly with the Wal-Marts of the world. It can't match Wal-Mart's massive economies of scale, incredible volume purchasing power, ultraefficient logistics, wide selection, and hard-to-beat prices. But then again, it doesn't even try. Instead, it targets customers that Wal-Mart can't serve, offering them value that Wal-Mart can't deliver. And while Whole Foods' future is not without challenges, it has found its own very profitable place in the world by positioning away from the grocery behemoths. Says Whole Foods' chief executive, "Not everyone is concerned with getting mediocre food at the lowest price."

Questions for Discussion

1. Define Whole Foods' "product." How does it deliver value to customers?

2. Organic food are becoming very popular. Many chains, including Wal-Mart, have begun offering and expanding their selection of organics. Does this pose a competitive threat to Whole Foods?

3. With respect to Whole Foods' targeting and positioning strategies, what challenges will the company face in the future as it continues to grow and expand?

4. In some places, Whole Foods is commonly known as "Whole Paycheck." While the firm has clearly positioned itself away from pricing issues, can it avoid this element of the marketing mix forever? Why or why not?

5. What other trends in the future of retailing do you think will have an impact on Whole Foods?

Sources: David Kesmodel, "Whole Foods Net Falls," *Wall Street Journal*, May 14, 2008, p. B5; Staff writer, "The Fast 50 Companies," *Fast Company*, March 2008, p. 111; Diane Brady, "Eating Too Fast at Whole Foods," *BusinessWeek*, October 24, 2005, p. 82; Samantha Thompson Smith, "Grocer's Success Seems Entirely Natural," *News & Observer*, May 21, 2004, p. D1; Marianne Wilson, "Retail as Theater, Naturally," *Chain Store Age*, May 25, 2005, p. 182; Carl Gutierrez, "Court Frees Whole Foods to Swallow Wild Oats," *Forbes*, August 23, 2007, accessed online at www.forbes.com; also see www.wholefoodsmarket.com.

Chapter 14

Part 1   Defining Marketing and the Marketing Process (Chapters 1, 2)
Part 2   Understanding the Marketplace and Consumers (Chapters 3, 4, 5, 6)
Part 3   Designing a Customer-Driven Strategy and Mix (Chapters 7, 8, 9, 10, 11, 12, 13, 14, 15, 16, 17)
Part 4   Extending Marketing (Chapters 18, 19, 20)

Communicating
Customer Value   Integrated Marketing Communications Strategy

Chapter PREVIEW

In this and the next four chapters, we'll examine the last of the marketing mix tools—promotion. Companies must do more than just create customer value. They must also use promotion to clearly and persuasively communicate that value. Promotion is not a single tool but, rather, a mix of several tools. Under the concept of *integrated marketing communications,* the company must carefully coordinate these promotion elements to deliver a clear, consistent, and compelling message about the organization and its brands. We'll begin by introducing you to the various promotion mix tools. Next, we'll examine the rapidly changing communications environment and the need for integrated marketing communications. Finally, we'll discuss the steps in developing marketing communications and the promotion budgeting process. In the next three chapters, we'll visit the specific marketing communications tools.

To start this chapter, let's look at one of the world's biggest marketers—Unilever—and at one of today's biggest marketing communication issues—the impact of the digital revolution on how marketers communicate with customers. More than most other companies, Unilever has mastered the digital marketing space. However, Unilever's marketers will tell you that they don't really do "digital campaigns" as such. Instead, they do *integrated* marketing communications campaigns.

These days, most advertisers are scrambling to make sense of the Web and other digital media, everything from Web sites and online social networks to Webisodes and viral video. The digital revolution has created a kind of "media divide," pitting traditional media such as television and magazines against the new-age digital media. Consumer goods giant Unilever, however, appears to have mastered the new digital space. In fact, Unilever was recently anointed Digital Marketer of the Year by *Advertising Age.*

But here's the funny thing about Unilever being Digital Marketer of the Year: The company doesn't really do "digital campaigns" as such. For Unilever, it's not an either-or proposition—either traditional media or digital media. Instead, Unilever has made Web and digital tactics just another important part of its mainstream marketing, seamlessly blending the old and the new into fully integrated communications campaigns.

Sure, Unilever does plenty of stand-out digital. It creates innovative Web sites for its bevy of familiar brands, ranging from Dove, Suave, Axe, Lever 2000, and Vaseline to Hellmann's, Knorr, Lipton, Ragú, and Slim-Fast to Breyers, Bertolli, and Ben & Jerry's. And Unilever has made headlines for numerous Web and viral video successes. For example, its Dove brand won a cyber Grand Prix award at Cannes last year for its spectacularly successful "Evolution" viral video. And Suave developed a series of "In the Motherhood" webisodes—the Web's version of TV soap operas—that drew more than 5.5 million viewers.

It seems that every Unilever brand has something big going digitally. At one extreme, Axe holds an online "World's Dirtiest Film" competition, which asks young male customers to create films so dirty that you'll beg for a shower when it's done—with Axe Shower Gel, of course. At the other extreme, comparatively stodgy Hellmann's produces an online "Real Food Summer School" program, which features recipes and cooking demos by celebrity chefs such as the Food Network's Bobby Flay. During its first season, about a million unique visitors visited the Real Food site, and more than 5,000 visitors signed up to be a part of the Real Food online community. After Hellmann's aired the show, Web searches for "Hellmann's" and related words jumped 50 percent on Yahoo!.

Although these and other Unilever digital efforts were highly successful in their own right, none was a purely digital campaign. Instead, each digital effort was carefully integrated with other media and marketing tactics, such as TV and print ads and broader PR initiatives. "Digital is [not] done in isolation," says Rob Master, Unilever's North American media director. "It's part of a

> Suave's "In the Motherhood" Webisodes are only a small part of a much larger integrated communications campaign for the brand.

Is motherhood messing with your hair?

Motherhood Isn't Always Pretty.
Meet the women who got themselves back. Roll over for more.

Suave's TV and other ads pull customers onto two nicely integrated Web sites, which create a "sisterhood" of moms and deliver the brand's "Say yes to beauty" positioning in more detail.

broader campaign. In many cases now it's the centerpiece of a broader campaign. I think that's become a real integral part of how we use the Web, moving beyond just promoting Web addresses in TV spots or print ads to really making them a critical part of the storytelling for the brands."

Unilever certainly has not abandoned traditional media in favor of digital—anything but. The world's number two advertiser (behind only Procter & Gamble) still devotes a sizable majority of its huge $7.8 billion global advertising and promotion spending to television and print media. But whereas its television budget increased by only 3 percent last year, its overall promotion budget soared 11 percent, with most of those extra dollars pouring into online and digital. The real secret behind Unilever's digital success is its skillful blending of new media with old to build and extend customer involvement and the brand experience. "What I push for is to understand the space," says Master, "so when you're doing your [broader] campaigns, you make [digital] a part of it."

For example, Suave's "In the Motherhood" webisodes are only a small part of a much larger integrated communications campaign for the brand. It starts with television spots featuring real mothers sharing their experiences, including beauty experiences. "Is motherhood messing with your hair?" the commercials ask. "Say yes to beautiful without paying the price."

The TV ads pull customers onto two related Web sites. Suave.com confirms that "Motherhood Isn't Always Pretty" and lets visitors dig more deeply into the lives and trials of mothers featured in the TV ads. The other site, inthemotherhood.com, presents entertaining and engaging webisodes created "For Moms. By Moms. About Moms" based on true-life experiences of motherhood. Each site is loaded with links to other Suave-related content.

Public relations has also played a role in the Suave campaign. When "In the Motherhood" was just starting, clips or even whole 5-minute episodes aired on *The Ellen DeGeneres Show*, whose host called on moms to submit their real-life stories and to vote on the best entries. Thus, the entire Suave campaign—television, digital, and public relations—is all wonderfully integrated to create a "sisterhood" of moms and to deliver the brand's "Say yes to beauty" positioning.

The degree to which digital is integrated into the mainstream of Unilever's marketing is clear in how the efforts are managed. "We don't have a digital-media person in the media organization," Master says. "But all of us are very fluent in digital." Unlike many other advertisers today, Unilever doesn't hand its online promotional efforts off to digital shops. Instead, online efforts are handled by Unilever's mainstream advertising agencies, further helping to integrate digital with more traditional promotional tactics.

One powerful result of integrating digital with traditional media is what Master

calls "superdistribution," the idea of getting Web programs, most often video, picked up by other media—most often for free. One of the best examples is Dove's "Evolution" video created as part of its "Real Beauty" campaign. "Evolution" shows an ordinary young woman being transformed into a beautiful poster model with a lot of help from a make-up artist and photo-editing software. The end line: "It's no wonder our perception of beauty is distorted." "Evolution" has racked up an impressive 20 million views on YouTube and other video sites. But throw in viewership via everything from TV news and talk shows to classrooms and general word-of-Web, and global viewership has exceeded 400 million. To put that in perspective, that level of distribution equates with some $150 million worth of free media coverage.

"Really, for us, superdistribution means [asking], 'Is the core of what you're doing big enough that it's going to be picked up in other channels such as PR, television, print, [and] radio ... and be repurposed and replayed in those other channels?'" Master says. "We used to repurpose things from television for the Internet. Now the ideas we have are so rich and creative ... we're able to feed that into all these other channels from digital." Again, we're talking about *integrated* marketing communications.

In all, Unilever—Digital Marketer of the Year and all—understands that the growing shift to digital doesn't really change the fundamentals much. If anything, says Master, it means brand managers have to be more firmly grounded in what their brands are about in order to clearly and consistently define the brands across an exploding array of old and new media. But "almost inherent in what we do, I think, is the importance of storytelling for our brands," he says. "A 30-second ad is a story we pull together for consumers on TV. Digital is an extension of that storytelling in a typically longer format." The richness of the story and the resulting brand experience depend on everything communicating well together.[1]

Digital Marketer of the Year Unilever has mastered the digital marketing space. However, Unilever's marketers will tell you that they don't really do "digital campaigns" as such. Instead, they do complete *integrated marketing communications* campaigns.

Objective Outline

Building good customer relationships calls for more than just developing a good product, pricing it attractively, and making it available to target customers. Companies must also *communicate* their value propositions to customers, and what they communicate should not be left to chance. All of their communications must be planned and blended into carefully integrated marketing communications programs. Just as good communication is important in building and maintaining any kind of relationship, it is a crucial element in a company's efforts to build profitable customer relationships.

Author Comment | The promotion mix is the marketer's bag of tools for communicating with customers and other stakeholders. All of these many tools must be carefully coordinated under the concept of *integrated marketing communications* in order to deliver a clear and compelling message.

The Promotion Mix (pp 402–403)

A company's total **promotion mix**—also called its **marketing communications mix**—consists of the specific blend of advertising, public relations, personal selling, sales promotion, and direct-marketing tools that the company uses to persuasively communicate customer value and build customer relationships. Definitions of the five major promotion tools follow:[2]

Promotion mix (or marketing communications mix)
The specific blend of promotion tools that the company uses to persuasively communicate customer value and build customer relationships.

Advertising
Any paid form of nonpersonal presentation and promotion of ideas, goods, or services by an identified sponsor.

Sales promotion
Short-term incentives to encourage the purchase or sale of a product or service.

- **Advertising**: Any paid form of nonpersonal presentation and promotion of ideas, goods, or services by an identified sponsor.

- **Sales promotion**: Short-term incentives to encourage the purchase or sale of a product or service.

- **Personal selling**: Personal presentation by the firm's sales force for the purpose of making sales and building customer relationships.

- **Public relations**: Building good relations with the company's various publics by obtaining favorable publicity, building up a good corporate image, and handling or heading off unfavorable rumors, stories, and events.

- **Direct marketing**: Direct connections with carefully targeted individual consumers to both obtain an immediate response and cultivate lasting customer relationships—the use of direct mail, the telephone, direct-response television, e-mail, the Internet, and other tools to communicate directly with specific consumers.

Personal selling

Personal presentation by the firm's sales force for the purpose of making sales and building customer relationships.

Public relations

Building good relations with the company's various publics by obtaining favorable publicity, building up a good corporate image, and handling or heading off unfavorable rumors, stories, and events.

> **Author Comment** | This is a really hot marketing topic these days. Perhaps no other area of marketing is changing so profoundly as marketing communications.

Direct marketing

Direct connections with carefully targeted individual consumers to both obtain an immediate response and cultivate lasting customer relationships.

Each category involves specific promotional tools used to communicate with consumers. For example, advertising includes broadcast, print, Internet, outdoor, and other forms. Sales promotion includes discounts, coupons, displays, and demonstrations. Personal selling includes sales presentations, trade shows, and incentive programs. Public relations includes press releases, sponsorships, special events, and Web pages. And direct marketing includes catalogs, telephone marketing, kiosks, the Internet, mobile, and more.

At the same time, marketing communication goes beyond these specific promotion tools. The product's design, its price, the shape and color of its package, and the stores that sell it *all* communicate something to buyers. Thus, although the promotion mix is the company's primary communication activity, the entire marketing mix—promotion *and* product, price, and place—must be coordinated for greatest communication impact.

Integrated Marketing Communications (pp 403–407)

In past decades, marketers perfected the art of mass marketing—selling highly standardized products to masses of customers. In the process, they developed effective mass-media communications techniques to support these strategies. Large companies now routinely invest millions or even billions of dollars in television, magazine, or other mass-media advertising, reaching tens of millions of customers with a single ad. Today, however, marketing managers face some new marketing communications realities. Perhaps no other area of marketing is changing so profoundly as marketing communications, creating both exciting and scary times for marketing communicators.

The New Marketing Communications Landscape

Several major factors are changing the face of today's marketing communications. First, consumers are changing. In this digital, wireless age, they are better informed and more communications empowered. Rather than relying on marketer-supplied information, they can use the Internet and other technologies to seek out information on their own. More than that, they can more easily connect with other consumers to exchange brand-related information or even to create their own marketing messages.

Second, marketing strategies are changing. As mass markets have fragmented, marketers are shifting away from mass marketing. More and more, they are developing focused marketing programs designed to build closer relationships with customers in more narrowly defined micromarkets. Vast improvements in information technology are speeding the movement toward segmented marketing. Today's marketers can amass detailed customer information, keep closer track of customer needs, and tailor their offerings to narrowly target groups.

Finally, sweeping changes in communications technology are causing remarkable changes in the ways in which companies and customers communicate with each other. ▲ The digital age has spawned a host of new information and communication tools—from cell phones and iPods to satellite and cable television systems to the many faces of the Internet (e-mail, social networks, brand Web sites, and so much more). The new communications technologies give companies exciting new media for interacting with targeted consumers. At the same time, they give consumers more control over the nature and timing of messages they choose to send and receive.

▲ The new marketing communications landscape: The digital age has spawned a host of new information and communication tools—from cell phones and iPods to the Internet and satellite and cable television systems.

The Shifting Marketing Communications Model

The explosive developments in communications technology and changes in marketer and customer communication strategies have had a dramatic impact on marketing communications. Just as mass marketing once gave rise to a new generation of mass-media communications, the new digital media have given birth to a new marketing communications model.

Although television, magazines, and other mass media remain very important, their dominance is declining. Advertisers are now adding a broad selection of more-specialized and highly targeted media to reach smaller customer segments with more-personalized, interactive messages. The new media range from specialty magazines, cable television channels, and video on demand (VOD) to Internet catalogs, e-mail, podcasts, cell phones, and online social networks. In all, companies are doing less *broadcasting* and more *narrowcasting*.

Some advertising industry experts even predict a doom-and-gloom "chaos scenario," in which the old mass-media communications model will collapse entirely. They believe that marketers will increasingly abandon traditional mass media in favor of new digital technologies. These new technologies will let marketers "reach—and have a conversation with—small clusters of consumers who are consuming not what is force-fed to them, but exactly what they want."[3]

Maybe you'd better lean forward. . . . Consider something barely imaginable: a post-apocalyptic media world substantially devoid of brand advertising as we have long known it. It's a world in which . . . consumer engagement occurs without consumer interruption, in which listening trumps dictating. Perhaps you believe that the TV commercial and magazine spread—and radio spot and newspaper classified—are forever and immutable, like the planets orbiting the sun. Good for you. [But] the pillars of old media [will] soon be tumbling down. [Instead, imagine] a digital landscape in which marketing achieves hitherto unimaginable effectiveness, but in which traditional advertising's main goal will be too quickly, straightforwardly, and informatively draw you into a broader brand experience. Welcome to the chaos scenario.

For example, just think about what's happening to television viewing these days. "Adjust your set," says one reporter, "television is changing as quickly as the channels. It's on cell phones. It's on digital music players. It's on almost anything with a screen. Shows can be seen at their regular times or when you want [with or without the commercials]. Some 'TV' programs aren't even on cable or network or satellite; they're being created just for Internet viewing."[4]

As mass media costs rise, audiences shrink, ad clutter increases, and viewers use video on demand and TiVo-like systems to skip past disruptive television commercials; many skeptics even predict the demise of the old mass-media mainstays—30-second television commercials and glossy magazine advertisements. It will be a world, says a major "chaos scenario" proponent, "in which marketing—and even branding—are conducted without much reliance on [those traditional media] because nobody is much interested in seeing them and because soon they will be largely unnecessary."[5]

Thus, many large advertisers are shifting their advertising budgets away from network television in favor of more targeted, cost-effective, interactive, and engaging media. "The ad industry's plotline used to be a lot simpler: Audiences are splintering off in dozens of new directions, watching TV shows on iPods, watching movies on video game players, and listening to radio on the Internet," observes one analyst. So marketers must "start planning how to reach consumers in new and unexpected ways." Says the CEO and creative director of one large ad agency, "There's no medium we don't perform in."[6]

Rather than a "chaos scenario," however, other industry insiders see a more gradual shift to the new marketing communications model. They note that broadcast television and other mass media still capture a lion's share of the promotion budgets of most major marketing firms, a fact that isn't likely to change quickly. Although some may question the future of the 30-second spot, it's still very much in use today. Last year, more than 43 percent of advertising dollars are spent on national and local television commercials versus

7.6 percent on Internet advertising. "So if you think that TV is an aging dinosaur," says one media expert, "maybe you should think again." Another expert agrees: "Does TV work? Of course it does. It's just not the only game in town anymore."[7]

Thus, it seems likely that the new marketing communications model will consist of a shifting mix of both traditional mass media and a wide array of exciting, new, more-targeted, more-personalized media. The challenge for traditional advertisers is to bridge the "media divide" that too often separates traditional creative and media approaches from new interactive and digital ones. Many established Madison Avenue advertising agencies are struggling with this transition (see **Real Marketing 14.1**). Says one analyst, "advertisers need to look at old media and new media as just plain media. The real-world demands that advertisers use a new cocktail of . . . media tools." Says another "The whole landscape has changed. . . . Marketers have to be savvy enough [to understand] what to do with all this stuff."[8]

The Need for *Integrated* Marketing Communications

The shift toward a richer mix of media and communication approaches poses a problem for marketers. Consumers today are bombarded by commercial messages from a broad range of sources. But consumers don't distinguish between message sources the way marketers do. In the consumer's mind, messages from different media and promotional approaches all become part of a single message about the company. Conflicting messages from these different sources can result in confused company images, brand positions, and customer relationships.

All too often, companies fail to integrate their various communications channels. The result is a hodgepodge of communications to consumers. Mass-media advertisements say one thing, while a price promotion sends a different signal, and a product label creates still another message. Company sales literature says something altogether different and the company's Web site seems out of sync with everything else.

The problem is that these communications often come from different parts of the company. Advertising messages are planned and implemented by the advertising department or an advertising agency. Personal selling communications are developed by sales management. Other company specialists are responsible for public relations, sales promotion events, Internet marketing, and other forms of marketing communications. However, whereas these companies have separated their communications tools, customers won't. Mixed communications from these sources will results in blurred consumer brand perceptions.

Today, more companies are adopting the concept of **integrated marketing communications (IMC)**. Under this concept, as illustrated in ⬡ **Figure 14.1**, the company carefully integrates its many communications channels to deliver a clear, consistent, and compelling message about the organization and its brands.

Integrated marketing communications (IMC)
Carefully integrating and coordinating the company's many communications channels to deliver a clear, consistent, and compelling message about the organization and its products.

⬡ **FIGURE | 14.1**
Integrated Marketing Communications

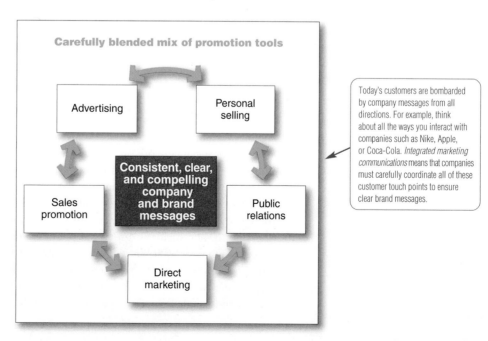

Carefully blended mix of promotion tools

Advertising

Personal selling

Consistent, clear, and compelling company and brand messages

Sales promotion

Public relations

Direct marketing

Today's customers are bombarded by company messages from all directions. For example, think about all the ways you interact with companies such as Nike, Apple, or Coca-Cola. *Integrated marketing communications* means that companies must carefully coordinate all of these customer touch points to ensure clear brand messages.

Real Marketing 14.1

Staying Relevant in a Shifting Advertising Universe:
The Old Versus the New

In today's splintering advertising universe, advertising agency Saatchi & Saatchi Worldwide is scrambling to stay relevant. As of now, the old-line Madison Avenue agency is one of the ad industry's brightest stars. It's still signing up blue-chip clients at an impressive rate and scooping up awards for its creative work. Yet Saatchi CEO Kevin Roberts worries that at a time when there are more new places than ever to stick ads—online, on cell phones, in all places digital and interactive—Saatchi may not be ready for this new universe.

Saatchi & Saatchi is a traditional Madison Avenue creative agency. It cut its teeth on developing creative ads for big-budget, mostly television and magazine campaigns. But the ad landscape is now shifting. Here is the universe as CEO Roberts sees it:

TV viewers are using DVRs to blast through the very commercials that are Saatchi's

SAATCHI & SAATCHI

In today's splintered advertising universe, Saatchi & Saatchi Worldwide's CEO Kevin Roberts is scrambling to keep his advertising agency relevant. To become a Web-era player, "'We've got to reinvent and transform the way we work."

bread and butter. Marketers are stampeding online, where Saatchi lacks the tools and talent to compete. Digital boutiques are proliferating, staffed with tech vets and Gen Y video artists dedicated to making ads for video-sharing and social-networking sites and whatever comes after them.

These days, Saatchi often finds itself outmaneuvered by nimbler new-age rivals. Traditional agencies like Saatchi still have a long way to go to match the new-media prowess of today's digital, interactive, and media agencies. The traditional agencies didn't predict how dramatically the industry would

IMC calls for recognizing all touch points where the customer may encounter the company and its brands. Each *brand contact* will deliver a message, whether good, bad, or indifferent. Says one advertising executive, "the world has evolved to a place where brands that need to speak to their audience have to understand that everything they do is media."[9] The company wants to deliver a consistent and positive message with each contact. IMC leads to a total marketing communication strategy aimed at building strong customer relationships by showing how the company and its products can help customers solve their problems.

IMC ties together all of the company's messages and images. The company's television and print advertisements have the same message, look, and feel as its e-mail and personal selling communications. And its public relations materials project the same image as its Web site or social network presence. Often, different media play unique roles in attracting, informing, and persuading consumers, and these roles must be carefully coordinated under the overall marketing communications plan.

For example, Nikon used a carefully coordinated mix of media in a recent campaign designed to demonstrate that even ordinary people can take amazing digital pictures with its Nikon D40 camera. To prove the point, Nikon gave 200 of the cameras to people in Georgetown, South Carolina, and then featured the people and their photos in TV and print ads. The ads delivered the brand message and referred consumers to a specially constructed supporting Web site (www.stunningnikon.com/picturetown), where they could explore the stories and people behind the pictures, learn more about the Nikon D40 camera, and find

go digital, and they must now struggle to catch up.

For most of the twentieth century the so-called creatives ruled the industry. They didn't worry about where or how an ad ran. They were about Big Ideas that would connect a brand emotionally with millions of consumers. Today, you might say, the Small Idea is ascendant. Ads are targeted at individuals or communities of consumers rather than to the masses. The media universe is now so fragmented—into blogs, social networks, television, magazines, and so on—that finding the right medium is fast becoming more important than the creative message itself. And the people best equipped to deal with this new world are not the big creative agencies. Instead, it is the direct marketers who are now perfect for the Web—the folks who've always interacted directly with individual consumers. And as the media fragment and reform, media buyers—once consigned by the creative agencies to back-office obscurity—are playing a much bigger role in helping clients figure out where they should spend their advertising budgets. More and more, these media buyers are steering advertisers into new digital and direct media, a powerful threat to the venerable 30-second TV spot that has always been at the heart and soul of traditional creative agencies like Saatchi.

Saatchi's CEO Roberts still believes in the power of creative—the emotional connection to the customer. But the truth is that creative and media feed off of one another, and media is shifting into a new realm that Saatchi has yet to master. Most clients still believe in creating an emotional bond with consumers. But in today's fragmented media universe, advertisers are looking for agencies that can help them create an integrated customer experience across multiple media, including both the traditional mass media that Saatchi knows so well and the new digital and direct media that remain a bit beyond Saatchi's comfort zone.

To fill the widening gap between traditional and digital, Saatchi is now hiring its own corps of Web ad makers, direct marketers, and digital media specialists. In fact, a while back, Saatchi tried to buy an existing digital agency, Blast Radius, known for building Web sites and creating passionate online communities for with-it companies such as Nike and game maker Electronic Arts. However, in a deeply troubling development, Blast Radius declined Saatchi's proposal. Instead, it merged with Wunderman, one of the world's largest direct-marketing agencies. Said Blast Radius's CEO at the time, "As an interactive agency, . . . we saw a big chasm between us . . . versus the more traditional

agencies. The traditional agencies were still very much about [messages and creativity]."

Interestingly, Publicis Groupe, the mammoth holding company that owns Saatchi & Saatchi along with dozens of other communications agencies, appears not to be counting on Saatchi and its other traditional agencies to lead the digital transformation. Instead, Publicis invested heavily to purchase an existing interactive agency, Digitas, and to bankroll the creation of another, Droga5. Publicis's CEO sees these interactive agencies as defining the very future of both his company and the entire advertising industry. His goal is to make Publicis the industry's premier digital-marketing outfit—to create a blueprint of the agency of the future. "It's not about cosmetic changes," he says, "it's about profound and unsettling changes."

Such actions and thinking have created an undercurrent of near-panic at some traditional creative agencies, including large and successful ones such as Saatchi & Saatchi. The question is clear: With digital and direct agencies muscling onto Saatchi's turf, is it "too late for an old-school creative shop to transform itself into a Web-era player"? CEO Roberts doesn't think so. But it won't be an easy transition for Saatchi and the other traditional agencies. "We've got to reinvent and transform the way we work," he says.

Sources: Excerpts and quotes adapted from Burt Helm, "Struggles of a Mad Man," *BusinessWeek*, December 3, 2007, pp. 44–49; and Linda Tischler, "A Mad Man Gets His Head Together," *Fast Company*, January 2008, pp. 90–97.

out where to buy one. The ads, Web site, supporting PR, and even the event itself were carefully integrated to deliver a unified message.

In the past, no one person or department was responsible for thinking through the communication roles of the various promotion tools and coordinating the promotion mix. To help implement integrated marketing communications, some companies appoint a marketing communications director who has overall responsibility for the company's communications efforts. This helps to produce better communications consistency and greater sales impact. It places the responsibility in someone's hands—where none existed before—to unify the company's image as it is shaped by thousands of company activities.

> **Author Comment** | To develop effective marketing communications, you must first understand the general communication process.

A View of the Communication Process (pp 407–409)

Integrated marketing communications involves identifying the target audience and shaping a well-coordinated promotional program to obtain the desired audience response. Too often, marketing communications focus on immediate awareness, image, or preference goals in the target market. But this approach to communication is too shortsighted. Today, marketers are moving toward viewing communications as *managing the customer relationship over time*.

Because customers differ, communications programs need to be developed for specific segments, niches, and even individuals. And, given the new interactive communications technologies, companies must ask not only, "How can we reach our customers?" but also, "How can we find ways to let our customers reach us?"

Thus, the communications process should start with an audit of all the potential touch points that target customers may have with the company and its brands. For example, someone purchasing a new kitchen appliance may talk to others, see television ads, read articles and ads in newspapers and magazines, visit various Web sites for prices and reviews, and check out appliances in one or more stores. The marketer needs to assess what influence each of these communications experiences will have at different stages of the buying process. This understanding will help marketers allocate their communication dollars more efficiently and effectively.

To communicate effectively, marketers need to understand how communication works. Communication involves the nine elements shown in ◗ **Figure 14.2**. Two of these elements are the major parties in a communication—the *sender* and the *receiver*. Another two are the major communication tools—the *message* and the *media*. Four more are major communication functions—*encoding, decoding, response,* and *feedback*. The last element is *noise* in the system. Definitions of these elements follow and are applied to a McDonald's "I'm lovin' it" television commercial.

- *Sender:* The *party sending the message* to another party—here, McDonald's.

- *Encoding:* The process of *putting thought into symbolic form*—McDonald's advertising agency assembles words, sounds, and illustrations into an advertisement that will convey the intended message.

- *Message:* The *set of symbols* that the sender transmits—the actual McDonald's ad.

- *Media:* The *communication channels* through which the message moves from sender to receiver—in this case, television and the specific television programs that McDonald's selects.

- *Decoding:* The process by which the receiver *assigns meaning to the symbols* encoded by the sender—a consumer watches the McDonald's ad and interprets the words and images it contains.

◗ FIGURE | 14.2
Elements in the
Communication Process

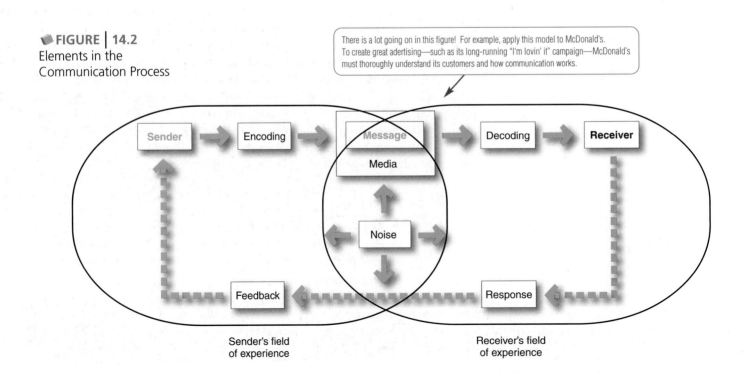

There is a lot going on in this figure! For example, apply this model to McDonald's. To create great adertising—such as its long-running "I'm lovin' it" campaign—McDonald's must thoroughly understand its customers and how communication works.

Sender's field of experience

Receiver's field of experience

- *Receiver:* The *party receiving the message* sent by another party—the customer who watches the McDonald's ad.

- *Response:* The *reactions of the receiver* after being exposed to the message—any of hundreds of possible responses, such as the consumer likes McDonald's better, is more likely to eat at McDonald's next time, hums the "I'm lovin' it" jingle, or does nothing.

- *Feedback:* The part of the *receiver's response communicated back to the sender*—McDonald's research shows that consumers are struck by and remember the ad, or consumers write or call McDonald's praising or criticizing the ad or products.

- *Noise:* The *unplanned static or distortion* during the communication process, which results in the receiver's getting a different message than the one the sender sent—the consumer it distracted while watching the commercial misses its key points.

For a message to be effective, the sender's encoding process must mesh with the receiver's decoding process. The best messages consist of words and other symbols that are familiar to the receiver. The more the sender's field of experience overlaps with that of the receiver, the more effective the message is likely to be. Marketing communicators may not always *share* their consumer's field of experience. For example, an advertising copywriter from one socioeconomic stratum might create ads for consumers from another stratum— say, wealthy business owners. However, to communicate effectively, the marketing communicator must *understand* the consumer's field of experience.

This model points out several key factors in good communication. Senders need to know what audiences they wish to reach and what responses they want. They must be good at encoding messages that take into account how the target audience decodes them. They must send messages through media that reach target audiences, and they must develop feedback channels so that they can assess the audience's response to the message.

Author Comment | Now that we understand how communication works, it's time to turn all of those promotion mix elements into an actual marketing communications program.

Steps in Developing Effective Marketing Communication (pp 409–414)

We now examine the steps in developing an effective integrated communications and promotion program. Marketers must do the following: Identify the target audience, determine the communication objectives, design a message, choose the media through which to send the message, select the message source, and collect feedback.

Identifying the Target Audience

A marketing communicator starts with a clear target audience in mind. The audience may be current users or potential buyers, those who make the buying decision or those who influence it. The audience may be individuals, groups, special publics, or the general public. The target audience will heavily affect the communicator's decisions on *what* will be said, *how* it will be said, *when* it will be said, *where* it will be said, and *who* will say it.

Determining the Communication Objectives

Once the target audience has been defined, the marketers must decide what response they seek. Of course, in many cases, they will seek a *purchase* response. But purchase may be only the result of a long consumer decision-making process. The marketing communicator needs to know where the target audience now stands and to what stage it needs to be moved. The target audience may be in any of six **buyer-readiness stages**, the stages consumers normally pass through on their way to making a purchase. These stages include *awareness, knowledge, liking, preference, conviction,* and *purchase* (see **Figure 14.3**).

The marketing communicator's target market may be totally unaware of the product, know only its name, or know only a few things about it. The communicator must first build *awareness* and *knowledge*. For example, when Apple launched the iPhone in mid-2007, it first ran a teaser ad during the Oscars to create initial awareness and curiosity. The Oscars teaser

Buyer-readiness stages
The stages consumers normally pass through on their way to purchase, including awareness, knowledge, liking, preference, conviction, and purchase.

▲ Moving customers through the buyer-readiness stages: IBM used teaser ads to peak interest in its new BladeCenter server technology. The ads never mentioned IBM BladeCenter, instead driving curious users to a Web site (ibm.com/outwithcables) for answers.

commercial featured clips of characters from famous movies and television shows answering the phone with "Hello" (to check it out, go to YouTube and search "iPhone Oscars Teaser"). At the end came a rotating image of the new iPhone with only the simple text "Hello" and "Coming in June."

Similarly, as in a business-to-business context, ▲IBM used teaser ads to peak interest in its new BladeCenter server technology, which integrates servers, storage, and networking applications into one system, consolidating space and eliminating cables. BladeCenter print ads in IT magazines and videos released through YouTube made no mention at all of either IBM or BladeCenter. Instead, they showed a large, mysterious ball of cables and drove curious users to a Web site—www.ibm.com/outwithcables—for answers.

Assuming that target consumers *know* about the product, how do they *feel* about it? Once potential buyers knew about the iPhone, Apple's marketers wanted to move them through successively stronger stages of feelings toward the innovative phone. These stages included *liking* (feeling favorable about the phone), *preference* (preferring iPhone to other cell phone brands), and *conviction* (believing that iPhone is the best cell phone for them). Apple marketers used a combination of the promotion mix tools to create positive feelings and conviction. Advertising built an emotional brand connection and illustrated the iPhone's design and features. Press releases and other public relations activities helped build up anticipation for the release of the iPhone. And a packed Web site informed potential buyers about technical specs, FAQs, software updates, and rate plans with partner AT&T.

Finally, some members of the target market might be convinced about the product, but not quite get around to making the *purchase*. Potential iPhone buyers might have decided to wait for more information or for the price to drop. The communicator must lead these consumers to take the final step. Actions might include offering special promotional prices, add-ons, rebates, or premiums. Apple might send out e-mails to customers of other Apple products urging them to add the eye-catching iPhone to their collection of Apple goodies.

Of course, marketing communications alone could not create positive feelings and purchases for the iPhone. The cell phone itself must provide superior value for the customer. In fact, outstanding marketing communications can actually speed the demise of a poor product. The more quickly potential buyers learn about the poor product, the more quickly they become aware of its faults. Thus, good marketing communication calls for "good deeds followed by good words."

Designing a Message

Having defined the desired audience response, the communicator turns to developing an effective message. Ideally, the message should get *Attention*, hold *Interest*, arouse *Desire*, and obtain *Action* (a framework known as the *AIDA model*). In practice, few messages take the consumer all the way from awareness to purchase, but the AIDA framework suggests the desirable qualities of a good message.

A goal of marketing in general, and of marketing communications in particular, is to move target customers through the buying process. Once again, it all starts with understanding customer needs and wants.

| Awareness | Knowledge | Liking | Preference | Conviction | Purchase |

FIGURE | 14.3 Buyer-Readiness Stages

When putting the message together, the marketing communicator must decide what to say (*message content*) and how to say it (*message structure* and *format*).

Message Content

The marketer has to figure out an appeal or theme that will produce the desired response. There are three types of appeals: rational, emotional, and moral. *Rational appeals* relate to the audience's self-interest. They show that the product will produce the desired benefits. Examples are messages showing a product's quality, economy, value, or performance. Thus, in one ad, natural foods marketer Kashi proclaims "7 whole grains on a mission" and asks consumers "why use fake flavors and additives when you can use lemongrass and coconut?" And a Weight Watchers' ad states this simple fact: "The diet secret to end all diet secrets is that there is no diet secret."

Emotional appeals attempt to stir up either negative or positive emotions that can motivate purchase. Communicators may use emotional appeals ranging from love, joy, and humor to fear and guilt. Advocates of emotional messages claim that they attract more attention and create more belief in the sponsor and brand. "Brain science has proved [that] consumers feel before they think, and feelings happen fast," says one expert. "Real persuasion is emotional in nature."[10] Thus, Michelin sells tires using mild fear appeals, showing families riding in cars and telling parents "Michelin: Because so much is riding on your tires." And the Diamond Trading Company runs emotional ads showing men surprising the women they love with diamond jewelry. Concludes one commercial, "With every waking moment love grows. A diamond is forever."

These days, it seems as though every company is using humor in its advertising, from consumer product firms such as Anheuser-Busch to the scholarly American Heritage Dictionary. For example, 13 of the top 15 most popular ads in *USA Today*'s ad meter consumer rankings of last year's Super Bowl advertisements used humor. Properly used, humor can capture attention, make people feel good, and give a brand personality. However, advertisers must be careful when using humor. Used poorly, it can detract from comprehension, wear out its welcome fast, overshadow the product, or even irritate consumers.

Moral appeals are directed to the audience's sense of what is "right" and "proper." They are often used to urge people to support social causes such as a cleaner environment or aid to the disadvantaged. ▲For example, the United Way's Live United campaign urges people to give back to their communities—to "Live United. Make a difference. Help create opportunities for everyone in your community." An Earthshare ad urges environmental involvement by reminding people that "Every decision we make has consequences. We choose the world we live in, so let's make the right choices. We live in the house we all build."

Message Structure

Marketers must also decide how to handle three message structure issues. The first is whether to draw a conclusion or leave it to the audience. Research suggests that in many cases, rather than drawing a conclusion, the advertiser is better off asking questions and letting buyers come to their own conclusions. The second message structure issue is whether to present the strongest arguments first or last. Presenting them first gets strong attention but may lead to an anticlimactic ending.

The third message structure issue is whether to present a one-sided argument (mentioning only the product's strengths) or a two-sided argument (touting the product's strengths while also admitting its shortcomings). Usually, a one-sided argument is

▲ Ad message content: United Way uses moral appeals—urging people to "Live United. Make a difference. Help create opportunities for everyone in your community."

▲ Message format: To attract attention, advertisers can use novelty and contrast, eye-catching pictures and headlines, and distinctive formats, as in this National Aquarium in Baltimore print ad.

more effective in sales presentations—except when audiences are highly educated or likely to hear opposing claims, or when the communicator has a negative association to overcome. In this spirit, Heinz ran the message "Heinz Ketchup is slow good" and Listerine ran the message "Listerine tastes bad twice a day." In such cases, two-sided messages can enhance the advertiser's credibility and make buyers more resistant to competitor attacks.

Message Format

The marketing communicator also needs a strong *format* for the message. ▲In a print ad, the communicator has to decide on the headline, copy, illustration, and color. To attract attention, advertisers can use novelty and contrast; eye-catching pictures and headlines; distinctive formats; message size and position; and color, shape, and movement. If the message is to be carried over the radio, the communicator has to choose words, sounds, and voices. The "sound" of an ad promoting banking services should be different from one promoting an iPod.

If the message is to be carried on television or in person, then all these elements plus body language have to be planned. Presenters plan every detail—their facial expressions, gestures, dress, posture, and hairstyles. If the message is carried on the product or its package, the communicator has to watch texture, scent, color, size, and shape. For example, one study revealed that people make subconscious judgments about an item within 90 seconds of initial viewing and that up to 90 percent of that assessment is based on color. Another study suggests that color increases brand recognition by up to 80 percent. Thus, in designing effective marketing communications, marketers must consider color and other seemingly unimportant details carefully.[11]

Choosing Media

The communicator must now select *channels of communication*. There are two broad types of communication channels—*personal* and *nonpersonal*.

Personal Communication Channels

Personal communication channels

Channels through which two or more people communicate directly with each other, including face to face, on the phone, through mail or e-mail, or even through an Internet "chat."

In **personal communication channels**, two or more people communicate directly with each other. They might communicate face to face, on the phone, through mail or e-mail, or even through an Internet "chat." Personal communication channels are effective because they allow for personal addressing and feedback.

Some personal communication channels are controlled directly by the company. For example, company salespeople contact target buyers. But other personal communications about the product may reach buyers through channels not directly controlled by the company. These channels might include independent experts—consumer advocates, online buying guides, and others—making statements to buyers. Or they might be neighbors, friends, family members, and associates talking to target buyers. This last channel, **word-of-mouth influence**, has considerable effect in many product areas.

Word-of-mouth influence

Personal communication about a product between target buyers and neighbors, friends, family members, and associates.

Personal influence carries great weight for products that are expensive, risky, or highly visible. Consider the power of simple customer reviews on Amazon.com:

> It doesn't matter how loud or often you tell consumers your "truth," few today are buying a big-ticket item before they know what existing users have to say about the product. This is a low-trust world. That's why "recommendation by a relative or friend" comes out on top in just about every survey of purchasing influences. A recent study

found that more than 90 percent of customers trust "recommendations from consumers," whereas trust in ads runs from a high of about 40 percent to less than 10 percent. It's also a major reason for Amazon's success in growing sales per customer. Who hasn't made an Amazon purchase based on another customer's review or the "Customers who bought this also bought . . ." section? And it explains what a recent Shop.org survey found—that 96 percent of retailers find ratings and reviews to be an effective tactic in lifting online sales.[12]

Companies can take steps to put personal communication channels to work for them. For example, they can create *opinion leaders* for their brands—people whose opinions are sought by others—by supplying influencers with the product on attractive terms or by educating them so that they can inform others. **Buzz marketing** involves cultivating opinion leaders and getting them to spread information about a product or service to others in their communities. ▲Consider BzzAgent, a Boston marketing firm that creates word-of-mouth campaigns for many of the country's best-known companies.[13]

Buzz marketing
Cultivating opinion leaders and getting them to spread information about a product or service to others in their communities.

BzzAgent has assembled a nationwide volunteer army of over 600,000 natural-born buzzers that channel their chatter toward products and services they deem authentically worth talking about. Last year, more than 34 million consumers were reached through 119 word-of-mouth programs. "Our goal is to find a way to capture honest word of mouth," says David Baiter, BzzAgent's founder, "and to build a network that will turn passionate customers into brand evangelists." Once a client signs on, BzzAgent searches its database for "agents" matching the demographic and psychographic profile of target customers of the product or service. Selected volunteers receive a sample product and a training manual for buzz-creating strategies. These volunteers aren't just chatty teenagers on cell phones. Some 65 percent are over 25, 60 percent are women, and 40 percent are in managerial positions or above. The average campaign size use about 10,000 agents, creating some 600,000 communications at an average cost of about $300,000. BzzAgent has buzzed products as diverse as Estée Lauder facial masks, *TV Guide*, Rock Bottom Restaurants, and The March of Dimes. In Alabama, BzzAgent ArnoldGinger123 even buttonholed her probation officer to chat up a tush-flattering new brand of jeans. The service's appeal is its authenticity. "What I like is that BzzAgents aren't scripted," says Steve Cook, vice president of worldwide strategic marketing at Coca-Cola. "[The company tells its agents,] 'Here's the information; if you believe in it, say whatever you think.' It's . . . genuine."

▲ Personal communications channels: BzzAgent's army of 600,000 natural born buzzers creates word-of-mouth chatter for many of the world's best-known brands.

Nonpersonal Communication Channels

Nonpersonal communication channels
Media that carry messages without personal contact or feedback, including major media, atmospheres, and events.

Nonpersonal communication channels are media that carry messages without personal contact or feedback. They include major media, atmospheres, and events. Major *media* include print media (newspapers, magazines, direct-mail), broadcast media (radio, television), display media (billboards, signs, posters), and online media (e-mail, company Web sites, online social and sharing networks). *Atmospheres* are designed environments that create or reinforce the buyer's leanings toward buying a product. Thus, lawyers' offices and banks are designed to communicate confidence and other qualities that might be valued by clients. *Events* are staged occurrences that communicate messages to target audiences. For example, public relations departments arrange press conferences, grand openings, shows and exhibits, public tours, and other events.

Nonpersonal communication affects buyers directly. In addition, using mass media often affects buyers indirectly by causing more personal communication. Communications first flow from television, magazines, and other mass media to opinion leaders and then from these opinion leaders to others. Thus, opinion leaders step between the mass media and their audiences and carry messages to people who are less exposed to media. This suggests that mass communicators should aim their messages directly at opinion leaders, letting them carry the message to others. Interestingly, marketers often use nonpersonal communications channels to replace or stimulate personal communications by embedding consumer endorsements or word-of-mouth testimonials in their ads and other promotions.

Selecting the Message Source

In either personal or nonpersonal communication, the message's impact on the target audience is also affected by how the audience views the communicator. Messages delivered by highly credible sources are more persuasive. Thus, many food companies promote to doctors, dentists, and other health care providers to motivate these professionals to recommend their products to patients. And marketers hire celebrity endorsers—well-known athletes, actors, musicians, and even cartoon characters—to deliver their messages. ▲Golfer Tiger Woods speaks for Nike, Accenture, Buick, and a dozen other brands and Michelle Wie lends her image to brands such as Nike and Sony. Sarah Jessica Parker poses for Garnier and Keith Richards endorses Louis Vuitton.[14]

But companies must be careful when selecting celebrities to represent their brands. Picking the wrong spokesperson can result in embarrassment and a tarnished image. TrimSpa found this out when Anna Nicole Smith lost her life to a drug overdose. H&M, Chanel, and Burberry had to publicly dismiss supermodel Kate Moss after she was reportedly photographed using cocaine. And Nike, Coca-Cola, and Kraft faced embarrassment when Michael Vick was convicted in an illegal dog fighting case. "Arranged marriages between brands and celebrities are inherently risky," notes an expert. "Today it's standard practice to sign a celeb only after an extensive background check. But accidents still happen."[15]

Collecting Feedback

After sending the message, the communicator must research its effect on the target audience. This involves asking the target audience members whether they remember the message, how many times they saw it, what points they recall, how they felt about the message, and their past and present attitudes toward the product and company. The communicator would also like to measure behavior resulting from the message—how many people bought a product, talked to others about it, or visited the store.

Feedback on marketing communications may suggest changes in the promotion program or in the product offer itself. For example, AirTran Airway uses television and newspaper advertising to inform area consumers about the airline, its routes, and its fares. Suppose feedback research shows that 80 percent of all fliers in an area recall seeing the airline's ads and are aware of its flights and prices. Sixty percent of these aware fliers have flown AirTran but only 20 percent of those who tried it were satisfied. These results suggest that although promotion is creating *awareness*, the airline isn't giving consumers the *satisfaction* they expect. Therefore, AirTran needs to improve its service while staying with the successful communication program. In contrast, suppose the research shows that only 40 percent of area consumers are aware of the airline, only 30 percent of those aware have tried it, but 80 percent of those who have tried it return. In this case, AirTran needs to strengthen its promotion program to take advantage of its power to create customer satisfaction.

seeing things simply
50%

seeing things fully
50%

We know what it takes to be a Tiger.
High performers combine razor-sharp strategic focus with a thorough command of the details. For a deeper look at our research and experience with the world's most successful companies, including our landmark study of over 500 high performers, visit accenture.com/research

• Consulting • Technology • Outsourcing

accenture
High performance. Delivered.

▲ Marketers hire celebrity endorsers to deliver their messages. Here, Tiger Woods represents Accenture, symbolizing "High Performance. Delivered."

Author Comment | In this section, we'll look at the promotion budget-setting process and at how marketers blend the various marketing communication tools into a smooth-functioning integrated promotion mix.

Setting the Total Promotion Budget and Mix (pp 415–421)

We have looked at the steps in planning and sending communications to a target audience. But how does the company decide on the total *promotion budget* and its division among the major promotional tools to create the *promotion mix*? By what process does it blend the tools to create integrated marketing communications? We now look at these questions.

Setting the Total Promotion Budget

One of the hardest marketing decisions facing a company is how much to spend on promotion. ▲John Wanamaker, the department store magnate, once said, "I know that half of my advertising is wasted, but I don't know which half. I spent $2 million for advertising, and I don't know if that is half enough or twice too much." Thus, it is not surprising that industries and companies vary widely in how much they spend on promotion. Promotion spending may be 10 to 12 percent of sales for consumer packaged goods, 14 percent for cosmetics, and only 1 percent for industrial machinery products. Within a given industry, both low and high spenders can be found.[16]

How does a company decide on its promotion budget? Here, we look at four common methods used to set the total budget for advertising: the *affordable method*, the *percentage-of-sales method*, the *competitive-parity method*, and the *objective-and-task method*.[17]

Affordable Method

Affordable method
Setting the promotion budget at the level management thinks the company can afford.

Percentage-of-sales method
Setting the promotion budget at a certain percentage of current or forecasted sales or as a percentage of the unit sales price.

Some companies use the **affordable method**: They set the promotion budget at the level they think the company can afford. Small businesses often use this method, reasoning that the company cannot spend more on advertising than it has. They start with total revenues, deduct operating expenses and capital outlays, and then devote some portion of the remaining funds to advertising.

Unfortunately, this method of setting budgets completely ignores the effects of promotion on sales. It tends to place promotion last among spending priorities, even in situations in which advertising is critical to the firm's success. It leads to an uncertain annual promotion budget, which makes long-range market planning difficult. Although the affordable method can result in overspending on advertising, it more often results in underspending.

Percentage-of-Sales Method

Other companies use the **percentage-of-sales method**, setting their promotion budget at a certain percentage of current or forecasted sales. Or they budget a percentage of the unit sales price. The percentage-of-sales method has advantages. It is simple to use and helps management think about the relationships between promotion spending, selling price, and profit per unit.

Despite these claimed advantages, however, the percentage-of-sales method has little to justify it. It wrongly views sales as the *cause* of promotion rather than as the *result*. Although studies have found a positive correlation between promotional spending and brand strength, this relationship often turns out to be effect and cause, not cause and effect. Stronger brands with higher sales can afford the biggest ad budgets.

The Blackberry Pearl is now faster than ever.

verion wireless

▲ Setting the promotion budget is one of the hardest decisions facing the company. Verizon Wireless spends more than $450 million annually on advertising, but is that "half enough or twice too much"?

Thus, the percentage-of-sales budget is based on availability of funds rather than on opportunities. It may prevent the increased spending sometimes needed to turn around falling sales. Because the budget varies with year-to-year sales, long-range planning is difficult. Finally, the method does not provide any basis for choosing a *specific* percentage, except what has been done in the past or what competitors are doing.

Competitive-Parity Method

Competitive-parity method
Setting the promotion budget to match competitors' outlays.

Still other companies use the **competitive-parity method**, setting their promotion budgets to match competitors' outlays. They monitor competitors' advertising or get industry promotion spending estimates from publications or trade associations, and then set their budgets based on the industry average.

Two arguments support this method. First, competitors' budgets represent the collective wisdom of the industry. Second, spending what competitors spend helps prevent promotion wars. Unfortunately, neither argument is valid. There are no grounds for believing that the competition has a better idea of what a company should be spending on promotion than does the company itself. Companies differ greatly, and each has its own special promotion needs. Finally, there is no evidence that budgets based on competitive parity prevent promotion wars.

Objective-and-Task Method

Objective-and-task method
Developing the promotion budget by (1) defining specific objectives, (2) determining the tasks that must be performed to achieve these objectives, and (3) estimating the costs of performing these tasks. The sum of these costs is the proposed promotion budget.

The most logical budget-setting method is the **objective-and-task method**, whereby the company sets its promotion budget based on what it wants to accomplish with promotion. This budgeting method entails (1) defining specific promotion objectives, (2) determining the tasks needed to achieve these objectives, and (3) estimating the costs of performing these tasks. The sum of these costs is the proposed promotion budget.

The advantage of the objective-and-task method is that it forces management to spell out its assumptions about the relationship between dollars spent and promotion results. But it is also the most difficult method to use. Often, it is hard to figure out which specific tasks will achieve stated objectives. For example, suppose Sony wants 95 percent awareness for its latest camcorder model during the six-month introductory period. What specific advertising messages and media schedules should Sony use to attain this objective? How much would these messages and media schedules cost? Sony management must consider such questions, even though they are hard to answer.

Shaping the Overall Promotion Mix

The concept of integrated marketing communications suggests that the company must blend the promotion tools carefully into a coordinated *promotion mix*. But how does the company determine what mix of promotion tools it will use? Companies within the same industry differ greatly in the design of their promotion mixes. For example, Mary Kay spends most of its promotion funds on personal selling and direct marketing, whereas competitor CoverGirl spends heavily on consumer advertising. We now look at factors that influence the marketer's choice of promotion tools.

The Nature of Each Promotion Tool

Each promotion tool has unique characteristics and costs. Marketers must understand these characteristics in shaping the promotion mix.

Advertising. Advertising can reach masses of geographically dispersed buyers at a low cost per exposure, and it enables the seller to repeat a message many times. For example, television advertising can reach huge audiences. An estimated 97.5 million Americans tuned in to watch the most recent Super Bowl, about 32 million people watched at least part of the last Academy Awards broadcast, and 33.4 million fans tuned in to watch the debut episode of the fourth season of *American Idol*. For companies that want to reach a mass audience, TV is the place to be.[18]

Beyond its reach, large-scale advertising says something positive about the seller's size, popularity, and success. Because of advertising's public nature, consumers tend to view advertised products as more legitimate. Advertising is also very expressive—it allows the company to dramatize its products through the artful use of visuals, print, sound, and color. On the one hand, advertising can be used to build up a long-term image for a product (such as Coca-Cola ads). On the other hand, advertising can trigger quick sales (as when Kohl's advertises weekend specials).

Advertising also has some shortcomings. Although it reaches many people quickly, advertising is impersonal and cannot be as directly persuasive as can company salespeople. For the most part, advertising can carry on only a one-way communication with the audience, and the audience does not feel that it has to pay attention or respond. In addition, advertising can be very costly. Although some advertising forms, such as newspaper and radio advertising, can be done on smaller budgets, other forms, such as network TV advertising, require very large budgets.

Personal Selling.   Personal selling is the most effective tool at certain stages of the buying process, particularly in building up buyers' preferences, convictions, and actions. It involves personal interaction between two or more people, so each person can observe the other's needs and characteristics and make quick adjustments. Personal selling also allows all kinds of customer relationships to spring up, ranging from matter-of-fact selling relationships to personal friendships. An effective salesperson keeps the customer's interests at heart in order to build a long-term relationship by solving customer problems. ▲ Finally, with personal selling, the buyer usually feels a greater need to listen and respond, even if the response is a polite "No thank you."

These unique qualities come at a cost, however. A sales force requires a longer-term commitment than does advertising—advertising can be turned on and off, but sales force size is harder to change. Personal selling is also the company's most expensive promotion tool, costing companies $329 on average per sales call. In some industries, the average cost of a sales call reaches $452.[19] U.S. firms spend up to three times as much on personal selling as they do on advertising.

Sales Promotion.   Sales promotion includes a wide assortment of tools—coupons, contests, cents-off deals, premiums, and others—all of which have many unique qualities. They attract consumer attention, offer strong incentives to purchase, and can be used to dramatize product offers and to boost sagging sales. Sales promotions invite and reward quick response—whereas advertising says, "Buy our product," sales promotion says, "Buy it now." Sales promotion effects are often short-lived, however, and often are not as effective as advertising or personal selling in building long-run brand preference and customer relationships.

Public Relations.   Public relations is very believable—news stories, features, sponsorships, and events seem more real and believable to readers than ads do. Public relations can also reach many prospects who avoid salespeople and advertisements—the message gets to the buyers as "news" rather than as a sales-directed communication. And, as with advertising, public relations can dramatize a company or product. Marketers tend to underuse public relations or to use it as an

▲ With personal selling, the customer feels a greater need to listen and respond, even if the response is a polite "no thank you."

afterthought. Yet a well-thought-out public relations campaign used with other promotion mix elements can be very effective and economical.

Direct Marketing. Although there are many forms of direct marketing—direct mail and catalogs, telephone marketing, online marketing, and others—they all share four distinctive characteristics. Direct marketing is *less public*: The message is normally directed to a specific person. Direct marketing is *immediate* and *customized*: Messages can be prepared very quickly and can be tailored to appeal to specific consumers. Finally, direct marketing is *interactive*: It allows a dialogue between the marketing team and the consumer, and messages can be altered depending on the consumer's response. Thus, direct marketing is well suited to highly targeted marketing efforts and to building one-to-one customer relationships.

Promotion Mix Strategies

Marketers can choose from two basic promotion mix strategies—*push* promotion or *pull* promotion. ◆ **Figure 14.4** contrasts the two strategies. The relative emphasis on the specific promotion tools differs for push and pull strategies. A **push strategy** involves "pushing" the product through marketing channels to final consumers. The producer directs its marketing activities (primarily personal selling and trade promotion) toward channel members to induce them to carry the product and to promote it to final consumers.

Using a **pull strategy**, the producer directs its marketing activities (primarily advertising and consumer promotion) toward final consumers to induce them to buy the product. If the pull strategy is effective, consumers will then demand the product from channel members, who will in turn demand it from producers. Thus, under a pull strategy, consumer demand "pulls" the product through the channels.

Some industrial-goods companies use only push strategies; some direct-marketing companies use only pull. However, most large companies use some combination of both. For example, Kraft uses mass-media advertising and consumer promotions to pull its products and a large sales force and trade promotions to push its products through the channels. In recent years, consumer-goods companies have been decreasing the pull portions of their mixes in favor of more push. This has caused concern that they may be driving short-run sales at the expense of long-term brand equity (see **Real Marketing 14.2**).

Companies consider many factors when designing their promotion mix strategies, including *type of product/market* and the *product life-cycle stage*. For example, the importance of different promotion tools varies between consumer and business markets. Business-to-consumer companies usually "pull" more, putting more of their funds into

Push strategy

A promotion strategy that calls for using the sales force and trade promotion to push the product through channels. The producer promotes the product to channel members who in turn promote it to final consumers.

Pull strategy

A promotion strategy that calls for spending a lot on advertising and consumer promotion to induce final consumers to buy the product, creating a demand vacuum that "pulls" the product through the channel.

◆**FIGURE** | **14.4** Push versus Pull Promotion Strategy

In a pull strategy, the company promotes directly to final consumers, creating a demand vacuum that "pulls" the product through the channel. Most companies use some combination of push and pull.

In a push strategy, the company "pushes" the product to resellers, who in turn "push" it to consumers.

Producer → Producer marketing activities (personal selling, trade promotion, other) → Retailers and wholesalers → Reseller marketing activities (personal selling, advertising, sales promotion, other) → Consumers

Push strategy

Producer ← Demand ← Retailers and wholesalers ← Demand ← Consumers

Producer marketing activities (consumer advertising, sales promotion, other)

Pull strategy

Real Marketing 14.2

Are Consumer Goods Companies Too Pushy?

Consumer packaged-goods companies such as Procter & Gamble, Kraft Foods, Kellogg, and General Mills grew into giants by using mostly pull promotion strategies. They used massive doses of national advertising to differentiate their products, gain market share, and build brand equity and customer loyalty. But during the past few decades, such companies have gotten more "pushy," deemphasizing national advertising and putting more of their marketing budgets into trade and consumer sales promotions.

General trade promotions (trade allowances, displays, cooperative advertising, slotting fees aimed at retailers) now account for 60 percent of total marketing spending by consumer product companies. That represents a seven-percentage-point increase in trade spending in just the past six years. Consumer promotions (coupons, discounts, premiums) account for another 14 percent of the typical marketing budget. That leaves less than 26 percent of total marketing spending for advertising, down from 42 percent 20 years ago.

Why have these companies shifted so heavily toward push strategies? One reason is that mass-media campaigns have become more expensive and less effective in recent years. Network television costs have risen sharply while audiences have fallen off, making national advertising less cost effective. Companies are also tailoring their marketing programs more narrowly, making national advertising less suitable than localized retailer promotions. And in these days of brand extensions and me-too products, companies sometimes have trouble finding meaningful product differences to feature in advertising. So they have differentiated their products through price reductions, premium offers, coupons, and other push techniques.

Another factor speeding the shift from pull to push has been the growing strength of retailers. Retail giants such as Wal-Mart, Target, Kroger, and Safeway now have the power to demand and get what they want— and what they want is more push. Whereas national advertising bypasses them on its way to the masses, push promotion benefits them directly. Thus, producers must often use push

Too pushy? Some categories tend to self-destruct by always being on sale. For example, when automakers get promotion happy, the market just sits back and waits for a deal while the car companies lose money on profit-eating incentives.

just to obtain good shelf space and other support from important retailers.

However, many marketers are concerned that the reckless use of push will lead to fierce price competition and a never-ending spiral of price slashing and deal making. If used improperly, push promotion can mortgage a brand's future for short-term gains. Sales promotion buys short-run reseller support and consumer sales, but advertising builds long-run brand equity and consumer preference. By robbing the media advertising budget to pay for more sales promotion, companies might win the battle for short-run earnings but lose the war for long-run brand equity, consumer loyalty, and market share. "If brands are built over years, why are they managed over quarters?" laments one analyst.

Of special concern is the overuse of short-term price promotions. The regular use of price as a selling tool can destroy brand equity by encouraging consumers to seek value though price rather than through the benefits of the brand. In fact, some analysts blame the surge in promotions for a recent two-decade-long drop in the percentage of consumers who buy only well-known brands. And according to one source, consumers are now 50 percent more price sensitive than they were 25 years ago. In recent surveys, consumer goods managers pointed to pricing pressures and declining shopper loyalty as their primary concerns.

In cases where price is a key part of the brand's positioning, featuring price makes sense. But for brands where price does not underlie value, "price promotions are really

desperate acts by brands that have their backs against the wall," says one marketing executive. "Generally speaking, it is better to stick to your guns with price and invest in advertising to drive sales."

Jack Trout, a well-known marketing consultant, cautions that some categories tend to self-destruct by always being on sale. Furniture, automobile tires, airline tickets, and many other categories of goods are rarely sold at anything near list price. And when automakers get rebate happy, the market just sits back and waits for a deal while the car companies lose money on profit-eating incentives. For example, General Motors has chopped $1 billion out of its advertising budget over the past four years while doling out billions of dollars in sales incentives—discounted prices, rebates, low-cost financing, gas price guarantees—to move cars out of its showrooms. Such promotion tactics have done little to win profits or customer loyalty over the years. Over the past three years alone, GM has lost a staggering $46 billion, and its domestic market share has dwindled to less than 25 percent, down from 44.5 percent in 1980.

Trout offers several "Commandments of Discounting," such as "Thou shalt not offer discounts because everyone else does," "Thou shalt be creative with your discounting," "Thou shalt put time limits on the deal," and "Thou shalt stop discounting as soon as you can."

Continued on next page ▼

Real Marketing 14.2 Continued ▼

Thus, many consumer companies are now rethinking their promotion strategies and reversing the trend by shifting their promotion budgets back toward advertising. They realize that it's not a question of sales promotion versus advertising, or of push versus pull. Success lies in finding the best mix of the two: consistent advertising to build long-run brand value and consumer preference, and sales promotion to create

short-run trade support and consumer excitement. The company needs to blend both push and pull elements into an integrated

marketing communications program that meets immediate consumer and retailer needs as well as long-run strategic needs.

Sources: Promotion spending statistics from *Shopper-Centric Trade: The Future of Trade Promotion* (Cannondale Associates: Wilton, CT, October 2007), p. 15. Other information and quotes from Jack Trout, "Prices: Simple Guidelines to Get Them Right," *Journal of Business Strategy*, November–December 1998, pp. 13–16; Jean Halliday, "GM Bleeds as Incentives Undermine Brand Value," *Advertising Age*, March 21, 2005, pp. 1, 37; Leonard M. Lodish and Carl F. Mela, "If Brands Are Built over Years, Why Are They Managed over Quarters?" *Harvard Business Review*, July–August 2007, pp. 107–112; John D. Stoll, "GM Is Still Facing Tricky Curves," *Wall Street Journal*, February 5, 2008, p. C3; and "General Motors Corporation," *Hoover's Company Records*, April 2008, p. 10640.

advertising, followed by sales promotion, personal selling, and then public relations. In contrast, business-to-business marketers tend to "push" more, putting more of their funds into personal selling, followed by sales promotion, advertising, and public relations. In general, personal selling is used more heavily with expensive and risky goods and in markets with fewer and larger sellers.

The effects of different promotion tools also vary with stages of the product life cycle. In the introduction stage, advertising and public relations are good for producing high awareness, and sales promotion is useful in promoting early trial. Personal selling must be used to get the trade to carry the product. In the growth stage, advertising and public relations continue to be powerful influences, whereas sales promotion can be reduced because fewer incentives are needed. In the mature stage, sales promotion again becomes important relative to advertising. Buyers know the brands, and advertising is needed only to remind them of the product. In the decline stage, advertising is kept at a reminder level, public relations is dropped, and salespeople give the product only a little attention. Sales promotion, however, might continue to be strong.

Integrating the Promotion Mix

Having set the promotion budget and mix, the company must now take steps to see that all of the promotion mix elements are smoothly integrated. Here is a checklist for integrating the firm's marketing communications.[20]

- *Start with customers.* Identify all customer touch points for the company and its brands. Work to ensure that communications at each touch point are consistent with the overall communications strategy and that communications efforts are occurring when, where, and how *customers* want them.

- *Analyze trends—internal and external—that can affect the company's ability to do business.* Look for areas where communications can help the most. Determine the strengths and weaknesses of each communications function. Develop a combination of promotional tactics based on these strengths and weaknesses.

- *Audit the pockets of communications spending throughout the organization.* Itemize the communications budgets and tasks and consolidate these into a single budgeting process. Reassess all communications expenditures by product, promotional tool, stage of the life cycle, and observed effect.

- *Team up in communications planning.* Engage all communications functions in joint planning. Include customers, suppliers, and other stakeholders at every stage of communications planning.

- *Create compatible themes, tones, and quality across all communications media.* Make sure each element carries the company's unique primary messages and selling points. This consistency achieves greater impact and prevents the unnecessary duplication of work across functions.

- *Create performance measures that are shared by all communications elements.* Develop systems to evaluate the combined impact of all communications activities.

- *Appoint a director responsible for the company's persuasive communications efforts.* This move encourages efficiency by centralizing planning and creating shared performance measures.

Author Comment | Marketers should go beyond what's "legal" and communicate openly and responsibly with customers. Good customer relationships are built on honesty and trust.

Socially Responsible Marketing Communication (pp 421–422)

In shaping its promotion mix, a company must be aware of the large body of legal and ethical issues surrounding marketing communications. Most marketers work hard to communicate openly and honestly with consumers and resellers. Still, abuses may occur, and public policy makers have developed a substantial body of laws and regulations to govern advertising, sales promotion, personal selling, and direct-marketing activities. In this section, we discuss issues regarding advertising, sales promotion, and personal selling. We discuss issues regarding direct marketing in Chapter 17.

Advertising and Sales Promotion

By law, companies must avoid false or deceptive advertising. Advertisers must not make false claims, such as suggesting that a product cures something when it does not. They must avoid ads that have the capacity to deceive, even though no one actually may be deceived. An automobile cannot be advertised as getting 32 miles per gallon unless it does so under typical conditions, and a diet bread cannot be advertised as having fewer calories simply because its slices are thinner.

Sellers must avoid bait-and-switch advertising that attracts buyers under false pretenses. For example, a large retailer advertised a sewing machine at $179. However, when consumers tried to buy the advertised machine, the seller downplayed its features, placed faulty machines on showroom floors, understated the machine's performance, and took other actions in an attempt to switch buyers to a more expensive machine. Such actions are both unethical and illegal.

A company's trade promotion activities also are closely regulated. For example, under the Robinson-Patman Act, sellers cannot favor certain customers through their use of trade promotions. They must make promotional allowances and services available to all resellers on proportionately equal terms.

Beyond simply avoiding legal pitfalls, such as deceptive or bait-and-switch advertising, companies can use advertising and other forms of promotion to encourage and promote socially responsible programs and actions. For example, Caterpillar is one of several companies and environmental groups forming the Tropical Forest Foundation, which is working to save the great Amazon rain forest. Caterpillar promotes the cause through advertising and pages on its Web site. ▲Similarly, Häagen-Dazs launched an interactive Web site in

▲ Many companies use promotion to encourage socially responsible actions. Häagen-Dazs launched an interactive Web site in the United States to promote awareness of the current honey bee crisis.

the United States to promote awareness of the current honey bee crisis (www. helpthehoneybees.com). It also created the Vanilla Honey Bee flavor and donates money to support honey bee and sustainable pollination research programs.

Personal Selling

A company's salespeople must follow the rules of "fair competition." Most states have enacted deceptive sales acts that spell out what is not allowed. For example, salespeople may not lie to consumers or mislead them about the advantages of buying a product. To avoid bait-and-switch practices, salespeople's statements must match advertising claims.

Different rules apply to consumers who are called on at home versus those who go to a store in search of a product. Because people called on at home may be taken by surprise and may be especially vulnerable to high-pressure selling techniques, the Federal Trade Commission (FTC) has adopted a *three-day cooling-off rule* to give special protection to customers who are not seeking products. Under this rule, customers who agree in their own homes to buy something costing more than $25 have 72 hours in which to cancel a contract or return merchandise and get their money back, no questions asked.

Much personal selling involves business-to-business trade. In selling to businesses, salespeople may not offer bribes to purchasing agents or to others who can influence a sale. They may not obtain or use technical or trade secrets of competitors through bribery or industrial espionage. Finally, salespeople must not disparage competitors or competing products by suggesting things that are not true.[21]

REVIEWING Objectives AND KEY Terms

In this chapter, you've learned how companies use integrated marketing communications (IMC) to communicate customer value. Modern marketing calls for more than just creating customer value by developing a good product, pricing it attractively, and making it available to target customers. Companies also must clearly and persuasively *communicate* that value to current and prospective customers. To do this, they must blend five promotion mix tools, guided by a well-designed and implemented integrated marketing communications strategy.

OBJECTIVE 1 Define the five promotion mix tools for communicating customer value. (pp 402–403)

A company's total *promotion mix*—also called its *marketing communications mix*—consists of the specific blend of *advertising, personal selling, sales promotion, public relations,* and *direct-marketing* tools that the company uses to persuasively communicate customer value and build customer relationships. Advertising includes any paid form of nonpersonal presentation and promotion of ideas, goods, or services by an identified sponsor. In contrast, public relations focuses on building good relations with the company's various publics by obtaining favorable unpaid publicity. Personal selling is any form of personal presentation by the firm's sales force for the purpose of making sales and building

customer relationships. Firms use sales promotion to provide short-term incentives to encourage the purchase or sale of a product or service. Finally, firms seeking immediate response from targeted individual customers use nonpersonal direct-marketing tools to communicate with customers.

OBJECTIVE 2 Discuss the changing communications landscape and the need for integrated marketing communications. (pp 403–407)

Recent shifts toward targeted or one-to-one marketing, coupled with advances in information and communication technology, have had a dramatic impact on marketing communications. As marketing communicators adopt richer but more fragmented media and promotion mixes to reach their diverse markets, they risk creating a communications hodgepodge for consumers. To prevent this, more companies are adopting the concept of *integrated marketing communications (IMC)*. Guided by an overall IMC strategy, the company works out the roles that the various promotional tools will play and the extent to which each will be used. It carefully coordinates the promotional activities and the timing of when major campaigns take place. Finally, to help implement its integrated marketing strategy, the company appoints a marketing communications director who has overall responsibility for the company's communications efforts.

OBJECTIVE 3 Outline the communications process and the steps in developing effective marketing communications. (pp 407–414)

The communication process involves nine elements—two major parties (sender, receiver), two communication tools (message, media), four communication functions (encoding, decoding, response, and feedback), and noise. To communicate effectively, marketers must understand how these elements combine to communicate value to target customers.

In preparing marketing communications, the communicator's first task is to *identify the target audience* and its characteristics. Next, the communicator has to determine the *communication objectives* and define the response sought, whether it be *awareness*, *knowledge*, *liking*, *preference*, *conviction*, or *purchase*. Then a *message* should be constructed with an effective content and structure. *Media* must be selected, both for personal and nonpersonal communication. The communicator must find highly credible sources to deliver messages. Finally, the communicator must collect *feedback* by watching how much of the market becomes aware, tries the product, and is satisfied in the process.

OBJECTIVE 4 Explain the methods for setting the promotion budget and factors that affect the design of the promotion mix. (pp 415–422)

The company has to decide how much to spend for promotion. The most popular approaches are to spend what the company can afford, to use a percentage of sales, to base promotion on competitors' spending, or to base it on an analysis and costing of the communication objectives and tasks. The company has to divide the *promotion budget* among the major tools to create the *promotion mix*. Companies can pursue a *push* or a *pull* promotional strategy, or a combination of the two. The best specific blend of promotion tools depends on the type of product/market, the buyer's readiness stage, and the product life-cycle stage. People at all levels of the organization must be aware of the many legal and ethical issues surrounding marketing communications. Companies must work hard and proactively at communicating openly, honestly, and agreeably with their customers and resellers.

KEY Terms

OBJECTIVE 1

Promotion mix (marketing communications mix) (p 402)
Advertising (p 402)
Sales promotion (p 402)
Personal selling (p 402)
Public relations (p 402)
Direct marketing (p 402)

OBJECTIVE 2

Integrated marketing communications (IMC) (p 405)

OBJECTIVE 3

Buyer-readiness stages (p 409)
Personal communication channels (p 412)
Word-of-mouth influence (p 412)
Buzz marketing (p 413)
Nonpersonal communication channels (p 413)

OBJECTIVE 4

Affordable method (p 415)
Percent-of-sales method (p 415)
Competitive-parity method (p 416)
Objective-and-task method (p 416)
Push strategy (p 418)
Pull strategy (p 418)

DISCUSSING & APPLYING THE Concepts

Discussing the Concepts

1. List and briefly describe the five major promotion mix tools. (AASCB: Communication)

2. Discuss the three major factors changing the face of today's marketing communications. (AACSB: Communication)

3. Name and briefly describe the nine elements of the communications process. Why do marketers need to understand these elements? (AACSB: Communication; Reflective Thinking)

4. List the steps in developing effective marketing communications. (AACSB: Communication)

5. Name and describe the common methods for setting promotion budgets. (AACSB: Communication)

6. Compare and contrast push and pull promotion strategies. Which promotion tools are most effective in each? (AACSB: Communication)

Applying the Concepts

1. Describe the three types of appeals used in marketing communications messages and develop three different advertisements for the same brand of a product of your choice, each using a different appeal. (AACSB: Communication; Reflective Thinking)

2. Energizer is introducing a new line of batteries that provide a longer life than its existing models. The brand manager for the new line believes most of the promotion budget should be spent on consumer and trade promotions, but the assistant brand manager thinks that the promotion mix should emphasize television advertising. Partner with another student. Play the roles of the brand manager and assistant brand manager and debate their opposing views on advertising versus promotion. (AACSB: Communication; Reflective Thinking)

3. Visit www.ftc.gov/bcp/edu/pubs/consumer/products/pro03.pdf to learn more about the FTC's three-day cooling-off rule. Name at least five types of sales that are exempt from this rule. (AACSB: Communication; Use of IT; Reflective Thinking)

FOCUS ON Technology

Businesses spend an estimated $290 billion vying for consumers' attention to their advertising messages. And that's just in the United States. Procter & Gamble alone spends $8.5 billion worldwide on advertising. Add spending on other promotional elements to that and the figure grows much higher. That's a lot of money! Marketers need to be accountable for these expenditures, so audience measurement is crucial. Technological solutions abound to help marketers assess how many people might see, read, or hear their marketing messages. For example, Nielsen Media Research, the goliath of television audience measurement, uses written diary and People Meter technology. But new upstarts are now entering the ring with other measurement tools that reflect the changing landscape of television viewing—live viewing, timeshift viewing, video-on-demand, online viewing, and mobile viewing. The

rapid shift to digital advertising media leaves marketers with a dizzying array of measurement options but no industry standard, creating somewhat of a "wild west" phenomenon. Even once low-tech magazine audience measurement is getting a high-tech upgrade through radio frequency identification (RFID) tags embedded in individual magazines to measure each time they are opened or closed.

1. Research media audience measurement methods for electronic and print media and discuss how technology is changing the way media audiences are measured. (AACSB: Communication; Reflective Thinking)

2. Are these audience measurement techniques adequate when accounting for return on promotional expenditures? Explain. (AACSB: Communication; Reflective Thinking)

FOCUS ON Ethics

An automobile purchase is a high-involvement one for consumers wanting to make a smart decision. That's why many car advertisements use rational appeals to relate to the audience's self-interest. The ads show that the product will produce the desired benefits in terms of quality, economy, value, or performance. Consumers pay attention to this information when deciding which automobile to purchase. For example, a recent television commercial for Mercury's Mariner SUV claimed that it could go "429 miles on a tank of gas, . . . more than a Honda CRV." Now, this is technically correct, because the CRV's fuel tank capacity is smaller (it can go

413 miles on a tank of gas). However, what the ad didn't say is that, in reality, the CRV's gas mileage rating is slightly higher than the Mariner's (27 miles per gallon versus Mariner's 26 miles per gallon).

1. Was Mercury guilty of deceptive advertising with its Mariner commercial? (AACSB: Communication; Ethical Reasoning)

2. Check the "truth in advertising" guidelines at the FTC Web site (www.ftc.gov/bcp/edu/pubs/business/adv/bus35.shtm). Has Mercury followed these guidelines? (AACSB: Communication; Use of IT; Ethical Reasoning)

MARKETING BY THE Numbers

Using the percent of sales method, an advertiser sets its budget at a certain percentage of current or forecasted sales. However, determining what percentage to use is not always clear. Many marketers look at industry averages and competitor spending for comparisons. Trade publications, such as *Advertising Age*, publish data regarding industry averages as well as advertising-to-sales ratios for top advertisers. For more discussion of the financial and quantitative implications of marketing decisions, see Appendix 2, Marketing by the Numbers.

1. Using information regarding industry and leading advertisers' advertising-to-sales ratios (see http://company.news-record.com/advertising/advertising/ratio.html and http://adage.com/datacenter/datapopup.php?article_id=127916),

recommend percentages of sales that advertisers for the following businesses should use to set next year's advertising budget: beverage company, bicycle dealer, furniture store, jeweler, women's clothing store, and automobile manufacturer. (AACSB: Communication; Use of IT; Analytical Reasoning)

2. If a women's clothing store forecasted $100 million in sales next year, what amount would you recommend it spend on advertising? How useful are the percentages found above for this business? How might the percent of sales figure be adjusted given this particular advertiser's situation? (AACSB: Communication; Analytical Reasoning; Reflective Thinking)

VIDEO Case

Crispin Porter + Bogusky

Crispin Porter + Bogusky (Crispin) may not be the oldest advertising agency in the world. It isn't the biggest either. But it has been working over time to prove that it is the most innovative firm at integrating marketing promotions. In fact, Crispin relies very little on the king of all advertising channels, broadcast TV. Instead, Crispin has worked miracles for companies such as Virgin Atlantic Airways, BMW's MINI Cooper, and Burger King by employing nontraditional campaigns on limited budgets.

Crispin attributes its success to the fact that it redefined what an advertisement is. Customer appropriate messages, Crispin discovered, could be delivered in many different ways. So its realm of "ad space" includes things as obscure as the side of a mailbox or an oversized phone booth in an airport. By communicating a message in many different ways, Crispin has developed a reputation for truly integrating marketing communications.

After viewing the video featuring Crispin, answer the following questions about advertising and promotions:

1. Alex Bogusky once said, "Anything and everything is an ad." What does this means? How is Crispin demonstrating this mantra?

2. In what ways has Crispin differentiated itself from other advertising agencies?

3. Give some examples as to how Crispin balances strategy with creativity.

COMPANY Case

Burger King: Promoting a Food Fight

CHALLENGING CONVENTIONAL WISDOM

In early 2004, as Burger King's CEO Brad Blum reviewed the company's 2003 outcomes, he decided once again that he had to do something to spice up BK's bland performance. Industry leader McDonald's had just reported a 9 percent sales jump in 2003 to a total of $22.1 billion while number-two BK's U.S. sales had *slipped* about 5 percent to $7.9 billion. Further, number-three Wendy's sales had spiked 11 percent to $7.4 billion, putting it in a position to overtake BK.

Blum surprised the fast-food industry by abruptly firing the firm's advertising agency, Young & Rubicam (Y&R), and awarding its global creative account to a small, Miami-based, upstart firm Crispin Porter + Bogusky (Crispin). The switch marked the fifth time in four years that BK had moved its account! Ad agency Y&R had gotten the $350 million BK account only 10 months earlier. To help revive BK's sales, it had developed a campaign with the theme "The Fire's Ready," which focused on BK's flame-broiled cooking method versus frying. However, observers found the message to be flat and uninspiring, and the declining sales sealed Y&R's fate.

With the move to Crispin, there was no shortage of speculation that the fickle Burger King would soon move again. Many saw BK as a bad client, impossible to work for. Others predicted that the "win" of this account would ruin Crispin's quirky culture. But in announcing the Crispin selection, Blum indicated he had challenged the firm to develop "groundbreaking, next-level, results-oriented, and innovative advertising that strongly connects with our core customers." BK automatically became the small firm's largest client, but Crispin was not without an impressive track record. The creative shop was known for its offbeat, unorthodox, and even irreverent promotions. Because its clients often had little money for advertising, Crispin found inexpensive ways to gain attention, veering away from the traditional mass media.

Crispin had produced award-winning, low-budget campaigns for BMW's MINI Cooper, IKEA furniture, Sunglass Hut, and Virgin Atlantic Airways, forging a reputation as an out-of-the-box, results-oriented agency. Along the way, Crispin developed some loose "rules." Among them were the following:

- zero in on the product
- kick the TV commercial habit
- find the sweet spot (the overlap between product characteristics and customer needs)
- surprise = buzz = exposure
- don't be timid
- think of advertising as a product rather than a service

HIT AFTER HIT FOR THE KING

It was these rules that guided Crispin's work for BK. Within a month of getting the burger giant's account, Crispin recommended going back to the firm's "Have It Your Way" tagline, developed by BK's second advertising agency, BBDO, way back in 1974. Crispin argued that it could take that old phrase and make it relevant to today's customers. Although Crispin's pitch may have initially seemed "same-old," it was anything but. Uncharacteristic of its past campaigns, Crispin kicked off the new BK campaign with TV commercials. In a series of offbeat ads that were a takeoff on the comedy series *The Office*, office workers competed and compared their "made my way" BK burgers, reinforcing the message that each customer could have a custom-made burger—no matter how unusual it might be. Crispin planned an entire package of promotions around the new-old theme, including everything from in-store signage to messages on cups.

Although *The Office* ads were unusual and catchy, they were also mainstream media. However, the TV campaign created an environment for the real Crispin approach to emerge. To promote BK's TenderCrisp chicken, Crispin launched a microsite, www.subservientchicken.com. Among other things, the site featured a man dressed in a chicken suit who would respond by performing any commands that visitors typed in to a text box. The only indication that the site was sponsored by Burger King was a small icon marked, "BK Tendercrisp." When Crispin launched the site, it told only 20 people—all of whom were friends of people who worked at the agency. Within the first 10 days, 20 million people visited the site, with the average visitor spending more than seven minutes.

As a follow-up to the Subservient Chicken promotion, Crispin created a campaign to launch a new BK product, chicken fries. The promotion was based on a faux heavy metal band called Coq Roq (the lead singer's name was Fowl Mouth). The whole idea was to create the charade of a real band, complete with songs, videos, cell phone ring tones, and promotional merchandise. Crispin targeted this campaign squarely at what it perceived to be the main BK target market—young men. Whatever those young men thought of Coq Roq, it led them to buy more than 100 million orders of chicken fries in the first four weeks of the new product launch.

Crispin clearly demonstrated with both the Subservient Chicken and Cog Roq campaigns that it was a master at viral marketing—using unusual methods to get attention and to generate buzz and word of mouth. Despite the success of these campaigns in producing lots of Web site hits, many analysts wondered if they would turn around BK's sliding market share. There was also speculation as to whether or not Crispin could continue to produce ideas that would keep BK strong in the fast-food fights.

A VIRAL TURNAROUND

Largely because of years of poor performance, tension had been mounting between Burger King's franchisees and the corporation. Initially, the new direction of its ad campaigns didn't help. Franchisees hated the viral Web campaigns, as they did an earlier Crispin campaign featuring an eerie bobblehead-looking King with a gargantuan ceramic head.

But at Burger King's 2006 annual franchisee convention, the feeling in the air was "long live the king." CEO Blum debuted a new Crispin ad entitled, "Manthem." A parody of the Helen Reddy Song, "I Am Woman," the spot was yet another example of BK's strategy to unapologetically embrace the young, male, fast-food "super fan." "Manthem's" lyrics spurned "chick food" and gleefully exalted the meat, cheese, and more meat and cheese combos that turn "innies into outies," all the while showing guys burning their briefs and pushing a minivan off a bridge.

After openly revolting at the convention the year before, BK's restaurant operators rose to their feet in a thunderous ovation, demanding an encore. They now embraced the kind of uncomfortably edgy advertising that they had rejected not so long before. Why this sudden change of heart?

Perhaps it was because Burger King was on the verge of a public offering. Or maybe it was because sales and profits go a long way in healing wounds. "I feel much better this year than I have in the last three, four, or five years," said Mahendra Nath, owner/operator of 90 stores in the upper Midwest and Florida. With sales up multiple years in a row, another franchisee, Alex Salgueiro, said, "I think our competitors are scared of the King ... they should be. They say, 'What's with the King?' and my answer is 'It's better than clowns.'"

With BK's fortunes apparently changing, franchisees were much less likely to question the irreverent Crispin promotional tactics, whether they liked them or not. And why would they? With the young male demographic providing nearly half of all Burger King visits, Mr. Salguiero said it best: "All opinions boil

down to traffic and sales. Once that happens, everybody has to shut up with their opinion. We have a very old franchisee base at this point and some of us don't understand our customers. We have a lot of gray hair."

NO END IN SIGHT

The creative ads have continued to flow, including the humorous series to promote the Western Whopper. The spots, based on the tagline, "Bring out your inner cowboy," featured people from all walks of life developing huge handlebar mustaches after eating Burger King fare. The ads were accompanied by a link to www.petmoustache.com, where people could register, upload a photo, and design a custom mustache. The mustache would then take on a life of its own. "It sends you e-mails that say, 'Hey, I miss you and why haven't you waxed me?' If you neglect it, it grows willy-nilly and wild," explained Rob Reilly, a creative director for Crispin.

But the most recent BK/Crispin promotional tactic took things to a whole new level. For the 50th anniversary of the Whopper, Crispin created the "Whopper Freakout" campaign. In doing so, Crispin did something it had never done before. Mr. Reilly explained the reasoning behind what can only be described as Whopper deprivation:

> If you really want to prove [that the Whopper is still America's favorite burger] put your money where your mouth is and let's take it off the menu and film natural reactions from people. We knew technically we could pull it off, but this is really a social experiment, that's the new ground we're breaking, using a social experiment as marketing. There's no fake dialogue, no fake customers. We were really testing this: If you deprive people of a thing they love, even down to a hamburger, will they react with a thing that's visceral?

Visceral is truly what they got. The eight-minute film is taken from the perspective of hidden cameras in a real Burger King restaurant. After being told by employees that the Whopper had been discontinued, customers revolt in a way that only truly distraught brand-loyal fans could. In the movie, customers scoff, twitch, roll their heads, demand to speak to managers, and even yell. Some of the more wistful subjects give folksy anecdotes about family bonding and passage into manhood, all based on the Whopper.

Crispin plugged the film's Web site with 30-second spot ads and then let the viral marketing forces take over. The results were nothing short of astounding. The microsite received more than one million visits at an average logged time of 8:33. But what really stood out was that visitors watched the video in its entirety four million times, meaning that most visitors watched several times. Multiple parodies of the ad emerged on the Web, including one based on an animated Michael Jackson and an R-rated version called "Ghetto Freakout" (which racked up more than three million views on YouTube). The campaign won a 2008 *Creativity* magazine award and IAG research found recall of the campaign to be the highest of any it had seen in its six-year history.

But all these measures amount to very little if the overall objective is not achieved. On that score, Crispin has delivered in spades for the flame-broiler. Burger King is in its fourth consecutive year of same-store sales growth. Not only is it growing, but BK is currently delivering a solid thrashing to McDonald's and Wendy's, who are blaming the recession, housing crisis, and fuel prices for sluggish growth. BK 2007 systemwide revenue reached $13.2 billion, up nearly 60 percent since Crispin assumed the account. Burger King is also showing healthy profits, rising stock prices, and strong international growth.

Many analysts are giving Crispin's promotional efforts a lion's share of the credit for Burger King's success. "They're doing a super job on the advertising front," said UBS analyst David Palmer. "They're clearly connecting with the super fan that is the young, hungry male." Despite the previous speculation that Crispin would fail, the firm is now into its fifth year as Burger King's promotional agency, with no sign of being shown the door. As long as Crispin continues to hit home runs with its creative promotions, its franchisees, shareholders, and customers alike will continue to shout, "Long live the King!"

Questions for Discussion

1. What are Burger King's communication objectives for its target audience?

2. With its focus on the "super fan," does BK risk alienating other customers? What are the implications of this?

3. Why is viral or buzz marketing effective? Analyze the design of the Subservient Chicken Web site's message, including content, structure, and format. What can you conclude from this analysis?

4. Do the TV and viral elements of BK's campaigns work well together? What additional elements and media might Crispin add to the integrated marketing communications campaign?

5. What other recommendations would you make to BK and Crispin to help them improve the integration of Burger King's promotion mix?

Sources: Emily Bryson York, "Economy, Rivals, No Match for BK's Marketing," *Advertising Age*, May 5, 2008, p.4; "Burger King: Whopper Freakout," *Creativity*, May 1, 2008, p. 76; Kevin, Kingsbury, "Burger King Swings to Net Profit," *Wall Street Journal*, August 24, 2007, accessed online at www.wsj.com; Barbara Lippert, "King of All Media," *Adweek*, November 20, 2006, accessed online at www.adweek.com; Kamau High, "BK Intros 'Inner Cowboy,'" *Adweek*, June 5, 2007, accessed online at www.adweek.com; Kate Macarthur, "BK Rebels Fall in Love with King," *Advertising Age*, May 1, 2006, p. 1; Elaine Walker, "Franchisees, Burger King Work to Mend Rift," *Miami Herald*, March 27, 2006.

Chapter 15

Part 1   Defining Marketing and the Marketing Process (Chapters 1, 2)
Part 2   Understanding the Marketplace and Consumers (Chapters 3, 4, 5, 6)
Part 3   Designing a Customer-Driven Strategy and Mix (Chapters 7, 8, 9, 10, 11, 12, 13, 14, 15, 16, 17)
Part 4   Extending Marketing (Chapters 18, 19, 20)

Advertising and Public Relations

Chapter PREVIEW

Now that we've looked at overall integrated marketing communications planning, let's dig more deeply into the specific marketing communications tools. In this chapter, we'll explore advertising and public relations. Advertising involves communicating the company's or brand's value proposition by using paid media to inform, persuade, and remind consumers. Public relations involves building good relations with various company publics—from consumers and the general public to the media, investor, donor, and government publics. As with all of the promotion mix tools, advertising and public relations must be blended into the overall integrated marketing communications program. In the two chapters that follow, we'll discuss the remaining promotion mix tools: personal selling, sales promotion, and direct marketing.

Let's start by looking at an outstanding advertising campaign. Until about 10 years ago, GEICO was a little-known nicher in the auto insurance industry. But now, thanks in large part to an industry-changing advertising campaign featuring a likable spokes-lizard, an indignant clan of cavemen, and an enduring tagline, GEICO has grown to become a major industry player. Here's the story.

Founded in 1936, GEICO initially targeted a select customer group of government employees and the top three grades of noncommissioned military officers with exceptional driving records. Unlike its much larger competitors, for the most part, GEICO markets directly to customers. Founder Leo Goodwin believed that by marketing directly, he could lower costs and pass on the savings in the form of lower premiums. For nearly 60 years, little GEICO relied almost entirely on direct-mail advertising and the telephone to market its services to its select clientele.

When GEICO decided to expand its customer base, it knew that it must also expand its marketing. So it hired The Martin Agency, an advertising firm located in Richmond, Virginia. Together, they launched their very first national spot and created the tagline "15 minutes could save you 15 percent or more on car insurance." GEICO's advertising adventure began modestly. In 1995, the company spent a paltry $3 million to launch its first national TV and radio spots, part of the total marketing budget of only $25 million. Then, in 1996, billionaire investor Warren Buffet bought GEICO, making it a wholly-owned subsidiary of Berkshire Hathaway. Over the next 10 years, GEICO's ad spending jumped 50-fold, to more than $500 million.

By now you probably know a lot about GEICO and its smooth-talking Gecko. But at the start, The Martin Agency faced a tough task—introducing a little-known company with a funny name to a national audience. Like all good advertising, the GEICO campaign began with a simple but enduring theme, one that highlights the convenience and savings advantages of GEICO's direct-to-customers system. Every single one of the more than 150 commercials produced in the campaign so far drives home the now-familiar tagline: "15 minutes could save you 15 percent or more on car insurance."

But what really set GEICO's advertising apart was the inspired way the company chose to bring its value proposition to life. At the time, competitors were using serious and sentimental pitches— "You're in good hands with Allstate" or "Like a good neighbor, State Farm is there." To help make its advertising stand out, GEICO decided to deliver its punch line with humor. The creative approach worked and sales began to climb.

As the brand grew, it became apparent that customers had difficulty pronouncing the GEICO name (which stands for Government Employees Insurance Company). Too often, GEICO became "gecko." Enter the charismatic green lizard. In 1999, GEICO ran a 15-second spot in which the now-famous, British-accented Gecko calls a press conference and pleads: "I am a gecko, not to be confused with GEICO, which could save you hundreds on car insurance. So stop calling me." The ad was supposed to be a "throwaway." "It was an odd

> Most important, GEICO's innovative ad campaign relentlessly drives home the company's value proposition: "15 minutes could save you 15 percent or more on car insurance."

spot that didn't fit," says Ted Ward, GEICO vice president of marketing, "but we thought it was funny." Consumers agreed. They quickly flooded the company with calls and letters begging to see more of the Gecko. The rest, as they say, is history.

Not only has the Gecko helped people to pronounce and remember GEICO's name, it's become a pop culture icon. The unlikely lizard has become so well known that it was recently voted one of America's top two favorite icons by public vote as part of Advertising Week in New York, one of the ad industry's largest and most important gatherings.

Although the Gecko ads remain a fixture, one lizard could take the company only so far. Over the past eight years, to keep its advertising fresh and entertaining, GEICO has added several new minicampaigns. Each new campaign has emphasized a different dimension of the brand's positioning. The first new campaign was "Good News," which addressed the difficulties of getting drivers to switch insurance companies. The humorous spots appeared to be about other products or TV programming, say a soap opera or a home improvement program, until one of the characters unexpectedly announced, "I have good news. I just saved a bunch of money on my car insurance by switching to GEICO."

Then came the cavemen. GEICO told The Martin Agency, "Make people understand that GEICO.com is simple." The agency responded with the Caveman minicampaign, designed to bring younger buyers to the GEICO Web site by showing them how easy it is to purchase insurance online. In the campaign, notes one observer, "a clutch of metrosexual cavemen, having somehow eluded extinction while developing a taste for racquet sports, plasma TVs, and 'duck with mango salsa,' is insulted by the company's advertising" slogan, "so easy to use GEICO.com, even a caveman could do it."

The indignant cavemen have taken on a cult status all their own. They've starred in a host of ads and have their own award-winning GEICO-created Web site (cavemanscrib.com) where you can visit one of the urbane hominids at home with his "iPod docking stations, glossy fashion mags, and hors d'oeuvres on toothpicks." ABC even had its own cavemen sitcom based on the GEICO campaign.

To open yet another front in its quest to expand customer relationships, GEICO launched its "Testimonials" campaign, in which real customers recount how GEICO helped them out in tough situations. But the testimonials have been GEICO-ized. Each ad notes that the real customers "aren't paid celebrities, so GEICO paid a real celebrity to help them tell their stories." The result is a set of hilarious commercials in which celebrities such as Little Richard, Peter Graves, and Burt Bacharach deliver their own unique simultaneous translations of the otherwise plain testimonials (remember Little Richard's "mashed potatoes, gravy, and cranberry sauce—wooooooo!").

Not only has the Gecko helped people to pronounce and remember GEICO's name, it's become a pop culture icon.

Although different, all of the minicampaigns have a distinctly GEICO flavor. And each closes strongly with the crucial "15 minutes could save you 15 percent" tagline. Also, as we've come to expect, "the ads are fun," says a branding expert. "What makes GEICO so good is that the ads entertain, deliver a message, *and* satisfy a need."

Just how good *is* GEICO's advertising? It helped earned The Martin Agency Advertising Age's "Top 5 Agency A-List" designation two years ago and GEICO an *Advertising Age* runner-up "Marketer of the Year" honor last year. And the Caveman and Testimonials ad series were named by *Adweek* as two of the year's top three ad campaigns. More importantly, 91 percent of shoppers today say that they've seen or heard at least one GEICO message, and GEICO leads the insurance industry in new customer acquisition. And for the last two years, GEICO earned the top spot among car insurance companies for its ability to create loyal customers in the respected Brand Keys Customer Loyalty Engagement Index. Rising from relative obscurity only a dozen years ago, the upstart direct marketer now serves more than eight million customers, making it the third-largest private passenger auto insurance company, behind State Farm and Allstate, based on the last 12 months written premium.

Not only have the Gecko and cavemen helped GEICO grow, they've changed the face of the auto insurance industry. Many analysts credit GEICO with changing the way insurance companies market their products in this traditionally boring category. "GEICO is spicing it up, and other companies are having to respond," says a communications consultant. "GEICO is exponentially ahead of its competitors in this category." Says another industry observer, "When your advertising has become part of the [contemporary culture], you have hit a home run."[1]

> Thanks in large part to an industry-changing advertising campaign featuring a likable spokes-lizard, an indignant clan of cavemen, and an enduring tagline, GEICO has grown to become a major industry player.

Objective Outline

As we discussed in the previous chapter, companies must do more than simply create customer value. They must also clearly and persuasively communicate that value to target consumers. In this chapter, we'll take a closer look at two marketing communications tools, *advertising* and *public relations*.

Advertising (pp 430–447)

Author Comment | You already know a lot about advertising—you are exposed to it every day. But here we'll look behind the scenes at how companies make advertising decisions.

Advertising
Any paid form of nonpersonal presentation and promotion of ideas, goods, or services by an identified sponsor.

Advertising can be traced back to the very beginnings of recorded history. Archaeologists working in the countries around the Mediterranean Sea have dug up signs announcing various events and offers. The Romans painted walls to announce gladiator fights, and the Phoenicians painted pictures promoting their wares on large rocks along parade routes. During the golden age in Greece, town criers announced the sale of cattle, crafted items, and even cosmetics. An early "singing commercial" went as follows: "For eyes that are shining, for cheeks like the dawn / For beauty that lasts after girlhood is gone / For prices in reason, the woman who knows / Will buy her cosmetics from Aesclyptos."

Modern advertising, however, is a far cry from these early efforts. U.S. advertisers now run up an estimated annual advertising bill of more than $290 billion; worldwide ad spending exceeds an estimated $604 billion. Procter & Gamble, the world's largest advertiser, last year spent $5.2 billion on U.S. advertising and $8.5 billion worldwide.[2]

Although advertising is used mostly by business firms, a wide range of not-for-profit organizations, professionals, and social agencies also use advertising to promote their causes to various target publics. In fact, the 34th largest advertising spender is a not-for-profit organization—the U.S. government. Advertising is a good way to inform and persuade, whether the purpose is to sell Coca-Cola worldwide or to get consumers in a developing nation to use birth control.

Marketing management must make four important decisions when developing an advertising program (see **Figure 15.1**): *setting advertising objectives, setting the advertising*

FIGURE | 15.1
Major Advertising Decisions

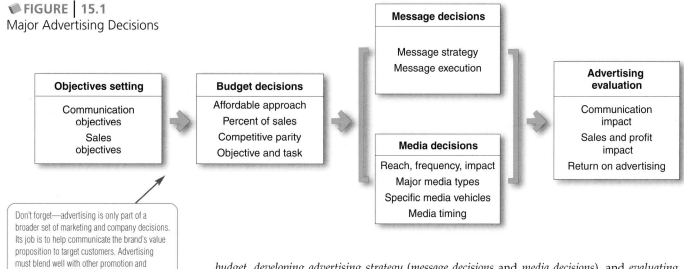

Don't forget—advertising is only part of a broader set of marketing and company decisions. Its job is to help communicate the brand's value proposition to target customers. Advertising must blend well with other promotion and marketing mix decisions.

budget, developing advertising strategy (*message decisions* and *media decisions*), and *evaluating advertising campaigns*.

Setting Advertising Objectives

The first step is to set *advertising objectives*. These objectives should be based on past decisions about the target market, positioning, and the marketing mix, which define the job that advertising must do in the total marketing program. The overall advertising objective is to help build customer relationships by communicating customer value. Here, we discuss specific advertising objectives.

Advertising objective
A specific communication *task* to be accomplished with a specific *target* audience during a specific period of *time*.

An **advertising objective** is a specific communication *task* to be accomplished with a specific *target* audience during a specific period of *time*. Advertising objectives can be classified by primary purpose—whether the aim is to *inform*, *persuade*, or *remind*. ● **Table 15.1** lists examples of each of these specific objectives.

Informative advertising is used heavily when introducing a new product category. In this case, the objective is to build primary demand. Thus, early producers of DVD players first had to inform consumers of the image quality and convenience benefits of the new product. *Persuasive advertising* becomes more important as competition increases. Here,

● **TABLE | 15.1** Possible Advertising Objectives

The overall advertising goal is to help build customer relationships by communicating customer value.

Informative Advertising	
Communicating customer value	Suggesting new uses for a product
Building a brand and company image	Informing the market of a price change
Telling the market about a new product	Describing available services and support
Explaining how the product works	Correcting false impressions

Persuasive Advertising	
Building brand preference	Persuading customers to purchase now
Encouraging switching to your brand	Persuading customers to receive a sales call
Changing customer's perception of product value	Convincing customers to tell others about the brand

Reminder Advertising	
Maintaining customer relationships	Reminding consumers where to buy the product
Reminding consumers that the product may be needed in the near future	Keeping the brand in customer's mind during off-seasons

the company's objective is to build selective demand. For example, once DVD players became established, Sony began trying to persuade consumers that *its* brand offered the best quality for their money.

Some persuasive advertising has become *comparative advertising*, in which a company directly or indirectly compares its brand with one or more other brands. Comparative advertising has been used for products ranging from soft drinks, beer, and pain relievers to computers, batteries, car rentals, and credit cards. For example, in its classic comparative campaign, Avis positioned itself against market-leading Hertz by claiming, "We try harder." And Apple's familiar "I'm a Mac; I'm a PC" ads take jabs at rival Windows-based computers.

You see examples of comparative advertising in almost every product category. ▲For example, Gatorade recently ran ads comparing the 25 calories in its Propel fitness beverage to the 125 calories found in Glacéau's Vitaminwater, asking "How Fit Is Your Water?" And Pizza Hut has reignited its long-running rivalry with Papa John's and Domino's with a comparative ad in which delivery drivers from the three chains gather around a table to dig into a Pizza Hut pizza. "Now this is real pizza," one driver tells the others. "Sure tastes better than Domino's," adds another. "And Papa John's," says a third. The announcer confirms that "Americans preferred Pizza Hut's pan pizza almost two to one in a national taste test."[3] Advertisers should use comparative advertising with caution. All too often, such ads invite competitor responses, resulting in an advertising war that neither competitor can win.

Reminder advertising is important for mature products—it helps to maintain customer relationships and keep consumers thinking about the product. Expensive Coca-Cola television ads primarily build and maintain the Coca-Cola brand relationship rather than inform or persuade customers to buy in the short run.

Advertising's goal is to help move consumers through the buying process. Some advertising is designed to move people to immediate action. For example, a direct-response television ad by The Sharper Image for its Ionic Breeze air purifier urges consumers to pick up the phone and order right away, and a Sears newspaper ad for a weekend sale encourages immediate store visits. However, many of the other ads focus on building or strengthening long-term customer relationships. For example, a Nike television ad in which well-known athletes working through extreme challenges in their Nike gear never directly asks for a sale. Instead, the goal is to somehow change the way the customers think or feel about the brand.

▲ Comparative advertising: Gatorade ran ads comparing the 25 calories in its Propel fitness beverage to the 125 calories in Glacéau's Vitaminwater, asking "How Fit Is Your Water?"

Setting the Advertising Budget

Advertising budget
The dollars and other resources allocated to a product or company advertising program.

After determining its advertising objectives, the company next sets its **advertising budget** for each product. Four commonly used methods for setting promotion budgets are discussed in Chapter 14. Here we discuss some specific factors that should be considered when setting the advertising budget.

A brand's advertising budget often depends on its *stage in the product life cycle.* For example, new products typically need large advertising budgets to build awareness and to gain consumer trial. In contrast, mature brands usually require lower budgets as a ratio to sales. *Market share* also impacts the amount of advertising needed: Because building the market or taking market share from competitors requires larger advertising spending than does simply maintaining current share, low-share brands usually need more advertising spending as a percentage of sales. Also, brands in a market with many competitors and high advertising clutter must be advertised more heavily to be noticed above the noise in the market. Undifferentiated brands—those that closely resemble other brands in their product class (soft drinks, laundry detergents)—may require heavy advertising to set them apart. When the product differs greatly from competitors, advertising can be used to point out the differences to consumers.

No matter what method is used, setting the advertising budget is no easy task. How does a company know if it is spending the right amount? Some critics charge that large consumer packaged-goods firms tend to spend too much on advertising and that business-to-business marketers generally underspend on advertising. They claim that, on the one hand, the large consumer companies use lots of image advertising without really knowing its effects. They overspend as a form of "insurance" against not spending enough. On the other hand, business advertisers tend to rely too heavily on their sales forces to bring in orders. They underestimate the power of company and product image in preselling industrial customers. Thus, they do not spend enough on advertising to build customer awareness and knowledge.

Companies such as Coca-Cola and Kraft have built sophisticated statistical models to determine the relationship between promotional spending and brand sales, and to help determine the "optimal investment" across various media. Still, because so many factors affect advertising effectiveness, some controllable and others not, measuring the results of advertising spending remains an inexact science. In most cases, managers must rely on large doses of judgment along with more quantitative analysis when setting advertising budgets.[4]

Developing Advertising Strategy

Advertising strategy

The strategy by which the company accomplishes its advertising objectives. It consists of two major elements: creating advertising messages and selecting advertising media.

Advertising strategy consists of two major elements: creating advertising *messages* and selecting advertising *media*. In the past, companies often viewed media planning as secondary to the message-creation process. The creative department first created good advertisements, and then the media department selected and purchased the best media for carrying these advertisements to desired target audiences. This often caused friction between creatives and media planners.

Today, however, soaring media costs, more-focused target marketing strategies, and the blizzard of new media have promoted the importance of the media-planning function. The decision about which media to use for an ad campaign—television, magazines, cell phones, a Web site, or e-mail—is now sometimes more critical than the creative elements of the campaign. As a result, more and more, advertisers are orchestrating a closer harmony between their messages and the media that deliver them.[5]

In fact, in a really good ad campaign, you often have to ask "Is that a media idea or a creative idea?" ▲For example, BMW created a huge buzz for its quirky, anything-but-ordinary little British-made MINI car with an anything-but-ordinary Let's Motor campaign.

The Let's Motor campaign employed a rich mix of unconventional media, carefully integrated to create personality for the car and a tremendous buzz of excitement among consumers. To create buzz, the company put MINIs in all kinds of imaginative places. It mounted them atop Ford Excursion SUVs and drove them around 22 major cities, highlighting the car's sensible size. It set up "MINI Ride" displays outside department stores, featuring an actual MINI that looked like a children's ride. "Rides $16,850. Quarters only," the sign said. Displays in airport terminals featured oversize newspaper vending machines and pay phones next to billboards showing the undersized MINI and proclaiming,

▲ Close media-creative partnerships: The MINI Let's Motor campaign used a rich mix of conventional and unconventional media, carefully integrated to create personality for the car and a tremendous buzz of excitement among consumers.

"Makes everything else seem a little too big." The car was also promoted on the Internet, in ads painted on city buildings, and on baseball-type cards handed out at auto shows. In addition, BMW created MINI games, MINI booklets, MINI suitcases, and MINI placements in movies. It worked closely with selected magazines to create memorable print ads. For example, ads in *Wired* magazine contained a cardboard fold-out of a MINI, suggesting that readers assemble it and drive it around their desks making "putt-putt" noises. The Let's Motor campaign has been a smashing success, creating an almost cult-like following for the personable little car. Were these clever media ideas or clever creative ideas? They were both, the product of a tight media-creative partnership.

Creating the Advertising Message

No matter how big the budget, advertising can succeed only if advertisements gain attention and communicate well. Good advertising messages are especially important in today's costly and cluttered advertising environment. In 1950, the average U.S. household received just three network television channels and a handful of major national magazines. Today, there are seven networks and 263 subscription channels, and consumers have more than 22,600 magazines from which to choose.[6] Add the countless radio stations and a continuous barrage of catalogs, direct mail, e-mail and online ads, and out-of-home media, and consumers are being bombarded with ads at home, at work, and at all points in between. As a result, consumers are exposed to as many as 3,000 to 5,000 commercial messages every day.[7]

Breaking through the Clutter. If all this advertising clutter bothers some consumers, it also causes huge headaches for advertisers. Take the situation facing network television advertisers. They pay an average of $381,000 to make a single 30-second commercial. Then, each time they show it, they regularly pay $250,000 or more for 30 seconds of advertising time during a popular prime-time program. They pay even more if it's an especially popular program such as *Grey's Anatomy* ($419,000), *The Simpsons* ($315,000), *American Idol* (up to $750,000 for one commercial spot; more than $1.3 million for the season finale), or a mega-event such as the Super Bowl ($3 million per 30 seconds!).[8]

Then, their ads are sandwiched in with a clutter of other commercials, announcements, and network promotions, totaling more than nearly 20 minutes of nonprogram material per prime-time hour with commercial breaks coming every 6 minutes on average. Such clutter in television and other ad media has created an increasingly hostile advertising environment. According to one recent study, 63 percent of Americans believe there are too many ads, and 47 percent say ads spoil their . . . viewing enjoyment.[9]

Until recently, television viewers were pretty much a captive audience for advertisers. But today's digital wizardry has given consumers a rich new set of information and entertainment choices. With the growth in cable and satellite TV, the Internet, video on demand (VOD), video downloads, and DVD rentals, today's viewers have many more options. ▲Digital technology has also armed consumers with an arsenal of weapons for choosing what they watch or don't watch. Increasingly, consumers are choosing *not* to watch ads. They "zap" commercials by fast-forwarding though recorded programs. With the remote control, they mute the sound during a commercial or "zip" around the channels to see what else is on. A recent study found that 40 percent of all television viewers now switch channels when the commercial break starts.[10]

Adding to the problem is the rapid growth of DVR (digital video recorder) systems. Almost 25 percent of American homes now have DVR technology, and an estimated 39 percent will have it by 2011. Although DVRs increase total TV

▲ Advertising clutter: Today's consumers, armed with an arsenal of weapons, can choose what they watch and don't watch. Advertising messages must be better planned, more imaginative, more entertaining, and more rewarding to consumers.

watching, research shows that 86 percent of DVR owners fast-forward through all or most commercials. As a result, according to one study, about 20 percent of brands experienced lower sales in ad-skipping households. One ad agency executive calls DVR systems "electronic weedwhackers." "In time, the number of people using them to obliterate commercials will totally erode faith in the 30-second commercial," he declares. Similarly, the number of VOD viewers is expected to quadruple during the next five years. These viewers will be able to watch programming on their own time terms, with or without commercials.[11]

Thus, advertisers can no longer force-feed the same old cookie-cutter ad messages to captive consumers through traditional media. Just to gain and hold attention, today's advertising messages must be better planned, more imaginative, more entertaining, and more rewarding to consumers. "Interruption or disruption as the fundamental premise of marketing" no longer works, says one advertising executive. Instead, "you have to create content that is interesting, useful, or entertaining enough to invite [consumers]." According to another, "Everything is about control. If an ad is interesting to you, you'll have a conversation with the brand. If it's not, it's a waste of time."[12]

In fact, many marketers are now subscribing to a new merging of advertising and entertainment, dubbed "**Madison & Vine**." You've probably heard of Madison Avenue. It's the New York City street that houses the headquarters of many of the nation's largest advertising agencies. You may also have heard of Hollywood & Vine, the intersection of Hollywood Avenue and Vine Street in Hollywood, California, long the symbolic heart of the U.S. entertainment industry. Now, Madison Avenue and Hollywood & Vine are coming together to form a new intersection—*Madison & Vine*—that represents the merging of advertising and entertainment in an effort to break through the clutter and create new avenues for reaching consumers with more engaging messages (see **Real Marketing 15.1**).

Message Strategy.   The first step in creating effective advertising messages is to plan a *message strategy*—to decide what general message will be communicated to consumers. The purpose of advertising is to get consumers to think about or react to the product or company in a certain way. People will react only if they believe that they will benefit from doing so. Thus, developing an effective message strategy begins with identifying customer *benefits* that can be used as advertising appeals. Ideally, advertising message strategy will follow directly from the company's broader positioning and customer value strategies.

Message strategy statements tend to be plain, straightforward outlines of benefits and positioning points that the advertiser wants to stress. The advertiser must next develop a compelling **creative concept**—or *"big idea"*—that will bring the message strategy to life in a distinctive and memorable way. At this stage, simple message ideas become great ad campaigns. Usually, a copywriter and art director will team up to generate many creative concepts, hoping that one of these concepts will turn out to be the big idea. The creative concept may emerge as a visualization, a phrase, or a combination of the two.

The creative concept will guide the choice of specific appeals to be used in an advertising campaign. *Advertising appeals* should have three characteristics. First, they should be *meaningful*, pointing out benefits that make the product more desirable or interesting to consumers. Second, appeals must be *believable*—consumers must believe that the product or service will deliver the promised benefits.

However, the most meaningful and believable benefits may not be the best ones to feature. Appeals should also be *distinctive*—they should tell how the product is better than the competing brands. For example, the most meaningful benefit of owning a wristwatch is that it keeps accurate time, yet few watch ads feature this benefit. Instead, based on the distinctive benefits they offer, watch advertisers might select any of a number of advertising themes. For years, Timex has been the affordable watch that "Takes a lickin' and keeps on tickin'." In contrast, Fossil has featured style and fashion, whereas Rolex stresses luxury and status.

Madison & Vine

A term that has come to represent the merging of advertising and entertainment in an effort to break through the clutter and create new avenues for reaching consumers with more engaging messages.

Creative concept

The compelling "big idea" that will bring the advertising message strategy to life in a distinctive and memorable way.

Real Marketing 15.1

Madison & Vine:
The New Intersection of Advertising and Entertainment

Welcome to the ever-busier intersection of Madison & Vine, where the advertising industry meets the entertainment industry. In today's cluttered advertising environment, Madison Avenue knows that it must find new ways to engage ad-weary consumers with more-compelling messages. The answer? Entertainment! And who knows more about entertainment than the folks at Hollywood & Vine? The term "Madison & Vine" has come to represent the merging of advertising and entertainment. It takes one of two primary forms: *advertainment* or *branded entertainment*.

The aim of *advertainment* is to make ads themselves so entertaining, or so useful, that people *want* to watch them. It's advertising by invitation rather than by intrusion. There's no chance that you'd watch ads on purpose, you say? Think again. For example, the Super Bowl has become an annual advertainment showcase. Tens of millions of people tune in to the Super Bowl each year, as much to watch the entertaining ads as to see the game.

In fact, rather than bemoaning TiVo and other DVR systems, many advertisers are now realizing that the devices can actually *improve* viewership of a really good ad. For example, one study showed that most Super Bowl ads last year were viewed more in DVR households than non-DVR households. Rather than zipping past the ads, many people were rewinding to watch them again and again.

Interestingly, this dynamic extends beyond Super Bowl ads. Although DVRs contribute to lower overall ad viewership, studies show that DVR users don't necessarily skip all the ads. According to one study, 55 percent of DVR users take their finger off the fast-forward button to watch a commercial that is entertaining or relevant, sometimes even watching it again. "If advertising is really entertaining [or informative], you don't zap it," notes an industry observer. "You might even go out of your way to see it."

Beyond making their regular ads more entertaining, advertisers are also creating new advertising forms that look less like ads and more like short films or shows. Online "webisodes" spending is now growing faster (45 percent per year) than any other form of promotion. For example, American Eagle Outfitters has embraced the concept whole-heartedly. The clothing marketer has gone way beyond 30-second spots by introducing its own dedicated media channel, dubbed 77e, on its Web site. The channel's biggest hit thus far is the webisode series, "It's a Mall World." Featuring heartthrob Milo Ventimiglia from the NBC TV series *Heroes*, the 2- to 5-minute video shorts have racked up more than 150 million views. On nights when a new episode debuts, traffic on the main AEO site jumps 20 percent. More astounding, 75 percent of those who watch the episode make a purchase.

Branded entertainment (or *brand integrations*) involves making the brand an inseparable part of some other form of

Welcome to Madison & Vine. As this book cover suggests, in today's cluttered advertising environment, Madison Avenue must find new ways to engage ad-weary consumers with more compelling messages. The answer? Entertainment!

entertainment. The most common form of branded entertainment is product placements—imbedding brands as props within other programming. In all, U.S. advertisers shelled out an estimated $10 billion on product placements last year, more than the GDP of Paraguay. In only the first three months of this year alone, America's top 11 TV channels produced a massive 117,976 product placements.

The nature of these placements can vary widely. It might be a brief glimpse of a

---

Message Execution.   The advertiser now has to turn the big idea into an actual ad execution that will capture the target market's attention and interest. The creative team must find the best approach, style, tone, words, and format for executing the message. Any message can be presented in different **execution styles**, such as the following:

Execution style
The approach, style, tone, words, and format used for executing an advertising message.

- *Slice of life:* This style shows one or more "typical" people using the product in a normal setting. For example, a Silk soymilk "Rise and Shine" ad shows a young professional starting the day with a healthier breakfast and high hopes.

- *Lifestyle:* This style shows how a product fits in with a particular lifestyle. For example, an ad for Liquidlogic kayaks shows kayakers challenging some serious white water and states, "2/3 of the earth is covered in playground—live wet."

Motorola phone on the ABC hit show *Lost,* or *24*'s Cloe clicking away at a Cisco terminal. Or it might involve actually scripting products into the theme of the program. For example, the boss of *The Office* frequents Chili's restaurant and orders his "awesome blossom, extra awesome"—in one episode, he even breaks into the restaurant's catchy "baby back ribs" jingle while entertaining a client there. In another, he sings the praises of Sandals resort in Jamaica—literally. "I've got two tickets to paradise. Pack your bags, we'll leave day after tomorrow," he croons.

These days, you'd be hard-pressed to find any TV show that doesn't feature some kind of product placement. But the practice is particularly prevalent on reality TV. Last year, NBC's *The Biggest Loser* was responsible for almost 4,000 different placements from companies ranging from Quaker Oats and Wrigley's chewing gum to Subway. Fox's *American Idol*, the nation's highest rated show, shoehorned in more than 3,000 placements. Old Navy dressed the contestants while Clairol did their hair, and Ford supplied the winners with new cars.

Reality shows are big hits with advertisers because they top the charts in placement effectiveness as well as in ratings.

Giving away products on a feel-good show like ABC's *Extreme Makeover: Home Edition* or having Donald Trump praise a brand on *The Apprentice* has a huge impact on product awareness. Just ask the folks at Tyson Foods, which topped IAG's list of products with the greatest number of TV viewers who recalled the brand from shows and thought better of it afterward. Tyson gave 20,000 pounds of meat to a community and a year's worth of food to a family featured on *Extreme Makeover: Home Edition*. The brand's appearance on the show—which included mentions by name, plus a visual of a Tyson truck—was

nearly four times more effective than the average TV show product placement. Matching the brand to the program is key. For example, Kraft got a good bump from being on Bravo's *Top Chef* and Propel fitness beverage got a boost from mentions from Bravo's *Work Out*. "On average, product placements are breaking through better in terms of recall than traditional commercials," says an industry executive.

Originally created with TV in mind, branded entertainment has spread quickly into other sectors of the entertainment industry. It's widely used in movies (remember all those GM vehicles in *Transformers* or the billboard of brands on Ricky Bobby's racing outfit in *Talladega Nights*?). If you look carefully, you'll also see subtle and not-so-subtle product placements in video games, comic books, Broadway musicals, and even pop music. A single mention of the new energy drink Fever in a music video by rapper Ludacris sent sales skyrocketing. One San Francisco firm even gauges brand equity by the number of mentions received in Billboard's top 100 (Nike, Mercedes, and Cadillac are typically at the top of that heap).

How much advertisers pay for a product placement depends on the magnitude of the placement, the size of the audience, and whether or not the deal is packaged with other stuff. More and more, the best placements are being sold with strings attached. "It's no longer, 'Here's $50,000, get my car in a

background shot,'" says an analyst. "Now you negotiate a package of advertising, marketing, space on your Web site, and, in exchange, the product is in the picture." AT&T is rumored to have paid $50 million for an *American Idol* deal that mixes traditional ads with frequent product placements.

So, Madison & Vine is *the* new meeting place for the advertising and entertainment industries. When done right, advertainment and branded entertainment can pay big dividends. However, experts caution that Madison & Vine can also be a dangerous crossing. They worry that making ads too entertaining might detract from the seller's brand message—consumers will remember the clever ad but forget the brand or advertiser. And they note that the intersection is getting pretty congested. With all these new ad formats and product placements, Madison & Vine threatens to create even more of the very clutter that it's designed to break through. At what point will consumers decide that the intersection of Madison & Vine is just too congested and take yet a different route?

But a spokesperson for *American Idol* says that show's having no such placement-overload problems. "We haven't heard [any complaints] from our focus groups, and the advertisers are pleased with the results. [In fact], we spend most of our time turning [advertisers] away." Ford's general marketing manager agrees. "If we didn't [re-sign, our slot] would be snapped up by a competitor in a heartbeat."

Sources: Quotes and information from Steve McClellan, "TiVo Helps Super Bowl Ad Ratings," *Adweek*, January 31, 2008, accessed online at www.adweek.com; Elizabeth Olson, "Practicing the Subtle Sell of Placing Products on Webisodes," *New York Times*, January 3, 2008, p. C3; Richard Huff, "Product Placement Outsells Ads," *Daily News*, December 27, 2007, p. 73; Phil Rosenthal, "'Office' Makes Pitch to Viewers: Watch and Buy," *Chicago Tribune*, December 10, 2007; Louise Story, "Viewers Fast-Forwarding Pat Ads? Not Always," *New York Times*, February 16, 2007, p. 1; Ravi Somaiya, "Product Placement: 'Cloe, It's Jack. Who Does Our Phones?'" *The Guardian*, June 16, 2008, p. 3; Ken Bensinger, "Carmakers Stretch Mileage of Product Placement Deals," *Los Angeles Times*, June 14, 2008, p. C1; Ronald Grover, "American Idol's Ads Infinitum," *BusinessWeek*, June 2, 2008, p. 38; Alana Semuels, "Advertising's Matchmaker," *Los Angeles Times*, June 2, 2008, p. C1.

- *Fantasy:* This style creates a fantasy around the product or its use. For example. one Travelers Insurance commercial features a gentleman carrying a giant red umbrella (the company's brand symbol). The man helps groups of people by using the umbrella to protect them from the rain, sail them across a flooded river, and fly home. The ad closes with "Travelers Insurance. There when you need it."

- *Mood or image:* This style builds a mood or image around the product or service, such as beauty, love, or serenity. Few claims are made about the product except through suggestion. For example, ads for Singapore Airlines feature soft lighting and refined flight attendants pampering relaxed and happy customers.

- *Musical:* This style shows people or cartoon characters singing about the product. For example, one of the most famous ads in history was a Coca-Cola ad built around the song "I'd Like to Teach the World to Sing." Similarly, Oscar Mayer has long run ads showing children singing its now-classic "I wish I were an Oscar Mayer wiener ..." jingle. And is there anyone who doesn't know the Chili's advertising song, "I love my baby-back, baby-back, baby-back, ... baby-back ribs"?

- *Personality symbol:* This style creates a character that represents the product. The character might be *animated* (Mr. Clean, Tony the Tiger, the GEICO Gecko) or *real* (Ol' Lonely the Maytag repairman, the GEICO cavemen, or the Aflac duck).

- *Technical expertise:* This style shows the company's expertise in making the product. Thus, Maxwell House shows one of its buyers carefully selecting coffee beans, and Jim Koch of the Boston Beer Company tells about his many years of experience in brewing Samuel Adams beer.

- *Scientific evidence:* This style presents survey or scientific evidence that the brand is better or better liked than one or more other brands. For years, Crest toothpaste has used scientific evidence to convince buyers that Crest is better than other brands at fighting cavities.

- *Testimonial evidence or endorsement:* This style features a highly believable or likable source endorsing the product. It could be ordinary people saying how much they like a given product. For example, Subway uses spokesman Jared, a customer who lost 245 pounds on a diet of Subway heroes. Or it might be a celebrity presenting the product, such as Vanessa Williams and Jessica Simpson speaking for Proactiv Solution.

The advertiser also must choose a *tone* for the ad. Procter & Gamble always uses a positive tone: Its ads say something very positive about its products. Other advertisers now use edgy humor to break through the commercial clutter. Bud Light commercials are famous for this.

The advertiser must use memorable and attention-getting *words* in the ad. For example, rather than claiming simply that "a BMW is a well-engineered automobile," BMW uses more creative and higher-impact phrasing: "The ultimate driving machine." Microsoft's Zune isn't just a "programmable digital media device." With Zune, "you make it you." The World Wildlife Fund doesn't say, "We need your money to help save nature." Instead, it says "We share the sky. We share the future. Together, we can be a force of nature."

Finally, ▲*format* elements make a difference in an ad's impact as well as in its cost. A small change in ad design can make a big difference in its effect. In a print ad, the *illustration* is the first thing the reader notices—it must be strong enough to draw attention. Next, the *headline* must effectively entice the right people to read the copy. Finally, the *copy*—the main block of text in the ad—must be simple but strong and convincing. Moreover, these three elements must effectively work *together* to persuasively present customer value.

Consumer-Generated Messages. Taking advantage of today's interactive technologies, many companies are now tapping consumers for message ideas or actual ads. They are searching existing video sites, setting up their own sites, and sponsoring ad-creation contests and other promotions.

Sometimes, marketers capitalize on consumer videos that are already posted on sites hosted by YouTube, MySpace,

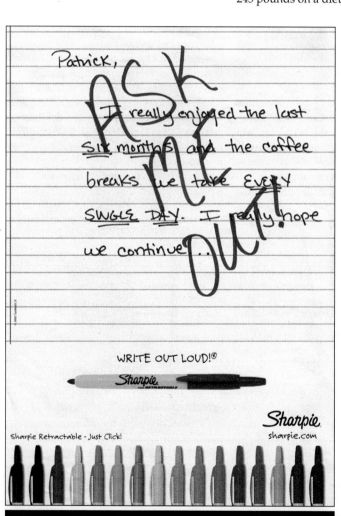

▲ Ad format and design: In this ad, Sharpie uses humor along with an attention-getting layout to highlight the benefits of its colorful markers.

Google, and Yahoo!. For example, one of the most viewed amateur videos on the Web last year showed Diet Coke mixed with Mentos candies to produce shooting fountains of soda. The video produced a windfall of free buzz for Coca-Cola. To gain even more mileage, Coca-Cola hired the amateur videographers—a professional juggler and a lawyer—to create another video and to star in a 30-second Coke ad.[13]

created by
Dale Backus
Cary, NC

live the flavor.
SnackStrongProductions.com

▲ Consumer-generated messages: The Doritos' "Crash the Super Bowl Challenge" contest invited consumers to create their own video ads. Frito-Lay showed the winning ad during the Super Bowl.

Other marketers hold contests or develop brand Web sites of their own that invite consumers to submit ad message ideas and videos. ▲ For example, PepsiCo's Doritos brand held a "Crash the Super Bowl Challenge" contest that invited consumers to create their own video ads about the tasty triangular corn chips. Doritos received 1,080 user-generated videos and posted the top five on the contest Web site, where consumers could view the ads and vote for a winner. The five finalists received a $10,000 prize and PepsiCo showed the winning ad during the Super Bowl. The campaign was a smashing success. The user-generated Doritos ad placed fifth in *USA Today* Ad Meter's most popular Super Bowl ad ratings and Doritos received a heap of pre- and post-Super Bowl buzz surrounding the contest and the finalist ads. The campaign was so successful that Frito-Lay followed up in 2008 by inviting consumers to submit original songs at www.snackstrongproductions.com—its *Second Life*–inspired Doritos Web environment. Frito-Lay then gave winner Kina Grannis the stage of a lifetime by airing a 60-second music video featuring her winning song on the Super Bowl.[14]

Not all consumer-generated advertising efforts are so successful. In fact, it can be downright dangerous to give consumers too much creative freedom and control. For example, Quiznos, the toasted-sandwich chain, recently invited the public to submit homemade commercials in a contest designed to attack rival Subway. The rules for its "Quiznos vs. Subway TV Ad Challenge" made it clear that the ads should depict Quiznos sandwiches as superior to Subway's. Subway promptly sued Quiznos, claiming that the submitted videos made false claims and portrayed Subway in a derogatory way.[15]

In another case, when Chevrolet ran a promotion for its Tahoe SUV allowing consumers to write their own text for video clips of the vehicle, it got some unexpected negative results. Many of the user-created ads contained critical gibes about the big SUV's poor gas mileage, high operating costs, and harmful environmental impact. Thus, marketers should be cautious when inviting consumer creative inputs.[16]

If used carefully, however, consumer-generated advertising efforts can produce big benefits. First, for relatively little expense, companies can collect new creative ideas, as well as fresh perspectives on the brand and what it actually means to consumers. "Companies have [their own] vision of what they want their brand to be," says the founder of Adcandy.com, a Web site that solicits consumer ideas for product and company taglines. "But if everyone is saying your brand is something else, it may be a battle. Powerful things come from the street, from the people who use the product."[17]

Second, consumer-generated message campaigns can boost consumer involvement and get consumers talking and thinking about a brand and its value to them. Not only do marketers get "a peek into the public's consciousness and what they are thinking, . . . [but] by participating and interacting, [consumers] develop a vested interest in your brand," says the Adcandy.com founder. Adds another marketer, "Engage a satisfied customer in a dialogue about a product—and give them a forum to express their creative aspirations for that product—and you will have a brand advocate who speaks from the heart."[18]

Selecting Advertising Media

Advertising media

The vehicles through which advertising messages are delivered to their intended audiences.

The major steps in **advertising media** selection are (1) deciding on *reach, frequency,* and *impact*; (2) choosing among major *media types*; (3) selecting specific *media vehicles*; and (4) deciding on *media timing*.

Deciding on Reach, Frequency, and Impact. To select media, the advertiser must decide on the reach and frequency needed to achieve advertising objectives. *Reach* is a measure of the *percentage* of people in the target market who are exposed to the ad campaign during a given period of time. For example, the advertiser might try to reach 70 percent of the target market during the first three months of the campaign. *Frequency* is a measure of how many *times* the average person in the target market is exposed to the message. For example, the advertiser might want an average exposure frequency of three.

But advertisers want to do more than just reach a given number of consumers a specific number of times. The advertiser also must decide on the desired *media impact*—the *qualitative value* of a message exposure through a given medium. For example, the same message in one magazine (say, *Newsweek*) may be more believable than in another (say, the *National Enquirer*). For products that need to be demonstrated, messages on television may have more impact than messages on radio because television uses sight *and* sound. Products for which consumers provide input on design or features might be better promoted at an interactive Web site than in a direct mailing.

More generally, the advertiser wants to choose media that will *engage* consumers rather than simply reach them. For example, for television advertising, "how relevant a program is for its audience and where the ads are inserted are likely to be much more important than whether the program was a Nielsen winner" numbers-wise, says one expert. "This is about 'lean to' TV rather than 'lean back.'"

Although Nielsen is beginning to measure levels of television *media engagement*, such measures are hard to come by for most media. "All the measurements we have now are media metrics: ratings, readership, listenership, click-through rates," says an executive of the Advertising Research Foundation, but engagement "happens inside the consumer, not inside the medium. What we need is a way to determine how the targeted prospect connected with, got engaged with, the brand idea. With engagement, you're on your way to a relationship. . . ."[19]

Choosing Among Major Media Types. The media planner has to know the reach, frequency, and impact of each of the major media types. As summarized in ● **Table 15.2**, the major media types are television, the Internet, newspapers, direct mail, magazines, radio, and outdoor. Advertisers can also choose from a wide array of new digital media, such as cell phones and other digital devices, which reach consumers directly. Each medium has advantages and limitations. Media planners consider many factors when making their media choices. They want to choose media that will effectively and efficiently present the advertising message to target customers. Thus, they must consider each medium's impact, message effectiveness, and cost.

The mix of media must be reexamined regularly. For a long time, television and magazines dominated in the media mixes of national advertisers, with other media often neglected. However, as discussed previously, the media mix appears to be shifting. As mass-media costs rise, audiences shrink, and exciting new digital media emerge, many advertisers are finding new ways to reach consumers. They are supplementing the traditional mass media with more-specialized and highly targeted media that cost less, target more effectively, and engage consumers more fully.

For example, cable television and satellite television systems are booming. Such systems allow narrow programming formats such as all sports, all news, nutrition, arts, home improvement and gardening, cooking, travel, history, finance, and others that target select groups. Time Warner, Comcast, and other cable operators are even testing systems that will let them target specific types of ads to specific neighborhoods or individually to specific types of customers. For example, ads for a Spanish-language channel would run only in Hispanic neighborhoods, or only pet owners would see ads from pet food companies.

Advertisers can take advantage of such "narrowcasting" to "rifle in" on special market segments rather than use the "shotgun" approach offered by network broadcasting. Cable and satellite television media seem to make good sense. But, increasingly, ads are

● TABLE | 15.2   Profiles of Major Media Types

Medium	Advantages	Limitations
Television	Good mass-marketing coverage; low cost per exposure; combines sight, sound, and motion; appealing to the senses	High absolute costs; high clutter; fleeting exposure; less audience selectivity
The Internet	High selectivity; low cost; immediacy; interactive capabilities	Relatively low impact; the audience controls exposure
Newspapers	Flexibility; timeliness; good local market coverage; broad acceptability; high believability	Short life; poor reproduction quality; small pass-along audience
Direct mail	High audience selectivity; flexibility; no ad competition within the same medium; allows personalization	Relatively high cost per exposure, "junk mail" image
Magazines	High geographic and demographic selectivity; credibility and prestige; high-quality reproduction; long life and good pass-along readership	Long ad purchase lead time; high cost; no guarantee of position
Radio	Good local acceptance; high geographic and demographic selectivity; low cost	Audio only, fleeting exposure; low attention ("the half-heard" medium); fragmented audiences
Outdoor	Flexibility; high repeat exposure; low cost; low message competition; good positional selectivity	Little audience selectivity; creative limitations

> Typically, its not a question of which one medium to use. Rather, the advertiser selects a *mix* of media and blends them into a fully integrated marketing communications campaign. Each medium plays a specific role.

popping up in far-less-likely places. In their efforts to find less-costly and more-highly targeted ways to reach consumers, advertisers have discovered a dazzling collection of "alternative media." ▲These days, no matter where you go or what you do, you will probably run into some new form of advertising.[20]

Tiny billboards attached to shopping carts, ads on shopping bags, and advertising decals on supermarket floors urge you to buy JELL-O Pudding Pops or Pampers, while ads roll by on the store's checkout conveyor touting your local Volvo dealer. Even supermarket eggs are stamped with the names of CBS television shows. At the local laundromat, you load your laundry through a clever Pepto-Bismol ad plastered on the front of the washing machine. Step outside and there goes a city trash truck sporting an ad for Glad trash bags. You escape to the ballpark, only to find billboard-size video screens running Budweiser ads while a blimp with an electronic message board circles lazily overhead. How about a quiet trip in the country? Sorry—you find an enterprising farmer using his milk cows as four-legged billboards mounted with ads for Ben & Jerry's ice cream.

These days, you're likely to find ads—well, anywhere. Boats cruise along public beaches flashing advertising messages for Sundown Sunscreen as sunbathers spread their towels over ads for Snapple pressed into the sand. Taxi cabs sport electronic messaging signs tied to GPS location sensors that can pitch local stores and restaurants wherever they roam. Ad space is being sold on DVD cases, parking-lot tickets, subway turnstiles, golf scorecards, delivery trucks, pizza boxes, gas pumps, ATMs, municipal garbage cans, police cars, doctors' examining tables, and church bulletins. One agency even leases space on the foreheads of college students for temporary advertising tattoos. And the group meeting at the

▲ Marketers have discovered a dazzling array of "alternative media."

office water cooler has a new member—a "coolertising" ad sitting on top of the water cooler jug trying to start up a conversation about the latest episode of *American Idol.*

Such alternative media seem a bit far-fetched, and they sometimes irritate consumers who resent it all as "ad nauseam." But for many marketers, these media can save money and provide a way to hit selected consumers where they live, shop, work, and play. Of course, all this may leave you wondering if there are any commercial-free havens remaining for ad-weary consumers. Public elevators, perhaps, or stalls in a public restroom? Forget it! Each has already been invaded by innovative marketers.

Another important trend affecting media selection is the rapid growth in the number of "media multitaskers," people who absorb more than one medium at a time:[21]

It looks like people who aren't satisfied with "just watching TV" are in good company. According to a recent survey, three-fourths of U.S. TV viewers read the newspaper while they watch TV, and two-thirds of them go online during their TV time. Another study indicates that the tasks now carried out in a typical day would have taken 31 hours to do 10 years ago with more primitive systems. What's more, if today's kids are any indication, media multitasking is on the rise. Americans aged 8 to 18 are managing to cram an average 8.5 hours of media consumption into 6.5 hours. What's more, 73 percent of multitasking kids are engaged in "active multitasking," with the content in one medium influencing concurrent behavior in another. It's not uncommon to find a teenage boy chasing down photos of Keira Knightly on Google, IMing several friends at once, listening to a mix of music on iTunes, and talking on the cell phone to a friend—all while, in the midst of the multimedia chaos, trying to complete an essay he's got open in a Word file a few layers down on his desktop.

Media planners need to take such media interactions into account when selecting the types of media they will use.

Selecting Specific Media Vehicles. The media planner now must choose the best *media vehicles*—specific media within each general media type. For example, television vehicles include *30 Rock* and *ABC World News Tonight.* Magazine vehicles include *Newsweek, Vogue,* and *ESPN the Magazine.*

Media planners must compute the cost per thousand persons reached by a vehicle. For example, if a full-page, four-color advertisement in the U.S. national edition of *Newsweek* costs $215,800 and *Newsweek's* readership is 2.6 million people, the cost of reaching each group of 1,000 persons is about $83. The same advertisement in *BusinessWeek* may cost only $108,000 but reach only 900,000 persons—at a cost per thousand of about $120. The media planner ranks each magazine by cost per thousand and favors those magazines with the lower cost per thousand for reaching target consumers.[22]

The media planner must also consider the costs of producing ads for different media. Whereas newspaper ads may cost very little to produce, flashy television ads can be very costly. For example, a typical television commercial might cost $500,000 to $1 million or more to produce. Guinness recently filmed a commercial titled "Tipping Point" in a tiny town of just 2,000 people high in the mountains of northern Argentina, where you can't even get a pint of the stout. The cost to create the ad? An almost unimaginable $20 million. Interestingly, the mentioned consumer-generated Doritos Super Bowl ad cost just $12.79, mostly spent on the bags of Doritos used in the ad.[23] There must be a lesson there somewhere for professional ad makers.

In selecting specific media vehicles, the media planner must balance media costs against several media effectiveness factors. First, the planner should evaluate the media vehicle's *audience quality.* For a Huggies disposable diapers advertisement, for example, *Parenting* magazine would have a high exposure value; *Maxim* would have a low-exposure value. Second, the media planner should consider *audience engagement.* Readers of *Vogue,* for example, typically pay more attention to ads than do *Newsweek* readers. Third, the planner should assess the vehicle's *editorial quality*—*Time* and *The Wall Street Journal* are more believable and prestigious than *Star* or the *National Enquirer.*

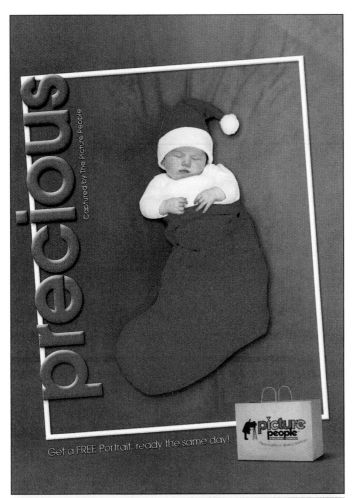

Captured by The Picture People

precious

Get a FREE Portrait, ready the same day!

▲ Media timing: The Picture People, the national chain of family portrait studios, advertises more heavily before special holidays.

Deciding on Media Timing. The advertiser must also decide how to schedule the advertising over the course of a year. Suppose sales of a product peak in December and drop in March. The firm can vary its advertising to follow the seasonal pattern, to oppose the seasonal pattern, or to be the same all year. Most firms do some seasonal advertising. ▲For example, The Picture People, the national chain of portraits studios, advertises more heavily before major holidays such as Christmas, Easter, and Valentine's Day. Some marketers do *only* seasonal advertising: For instance, Hallmark advertises its greeting cards only before major holidays.

Finally, the advertiser has to choose the pattern of the ads. *Continuity* means scheduling ads evenly within a given period. *Pulsing* means scheduling ads unevenly over a given time period. Thus, 52 ads could either be scheduled at 1 per week during the year or pulsed in several bursts. The idea behind pulsing is to advertise heavily for a short period to build awareness that carries over to the next advertising period. Those who favor pulsing feel that it can be used to achieve the same impact as a steady schedule but at a much lower cost. However, some media planners believe that although pulsing achieves minimal awareness, it sacrifices depth of advertising communications.

Evaluating Advertising Effectiveness and Return on Advertising Investment

Return on advertising investment

The net return on advertising investment divided by the costs of the advertising investment.

Advertising accountability and **return on advertising investment** have become hot issues for most companies. Two separate recent studies show that advertising effectiveness has fallen 40 percent over the past decade and that 37.3 percent of advertising budgets are wasted. This leaves top management and many companies asking their marketing managers, "How do we know that we're spending the right amount on advertising?" and "What return are we getting on our advertising investment?" According to a recent survey by the Association of National Advertisers (ANA), measuring advertising's efficiency and effectiveness is the number-one issue in the minds of today's advertisers.[24]

Advertisers should regularly evaluate two types of advertising results: the communication effects and the sales and profit effects. Measuring the *communication effects* of an ad or ad campaign tells whether the ads and media are communicating the ad message well. Individual ads can be tested before or after they are run. Before an ad is placed, the advertiser can show it to consumers, ask how they like it, and measure message recall or attitude changes resulting from it. After an ad is run, the advertiser can measure how the ad affected consumer recall or product awareness, knowledge, and preference. Pre- and post-evaluations of communication effects can be made for entire advertising campaigns as well.

Advertisers have gotten pretty good at measuring the communication effects of their ads and ad campaigns. However, *sales and profit* effects of advertising are often much harder to measure. For example, what sales and profits are produced by an ad campaign that increases brand awareness by 20 percent and brand preference by 10 percent? Sales and profits are affected by many factors other than advertising—such as product features, price, and availability.

One way to measure the sales and profit effects of advertising is to compare past sales and profits with past advertising expenditures. Another way is through experiments. For example, to test the effects of different advertising spending levels, Coca-Cola could vary the amount it spends on advertising in different market areas and measure the differences in the resulting sales and profit levels. More complex experiments could be designed to include other variables, such as differences in the ads or media used.

However, because so many factors affect advertising effectiveness, some controllable and others not, measuring the results of advertising spending remains an inexact science. For example, dozens of advertisers spend lavishly on high-profile Super Bowl ads each year. Although they sense that the returns are worth the sizable investment, few could actually measure or prove it (see **Real Marketing 15.2**). A recent survey of marketing and advertising agency executives concluded that over 80 percent of marketers don't measure return on investment because it's just too difficult to measure.[25] The ANA study cited earlier asked advertising managers if they would be able to "forecast the impact on sales" of a 10 percent cut in advertising spending—63 percent said no.

"Marketers are tracking all kinds of data and they still can't answer basic questions" about advertising accountability, says a marketing analyst, "because they don't have real models and metrics by which to make sense of it." Advertisers are measuring "everything they can, and that ranges from how many people respond to an ad to how many sales are closed and then trying to hook up those two end pieces," says another analyst. "The tough part is, my goodness, we've got so much data. How do we sift through it?"[26] Thus, although the situation is improving as marketers seek more answers, managers often must rely on large doses of judgment along with quantitative analysis when assessing advertising performance.

Other Advertising Considerations

In developing advertising strategies and programs, the company must address two additional questions. First, how will the company organize its advertising function—who will perform which advertising tasks? Second, how will the company adapt its advertising strategies and programs to the complexities of international markets?

Organizing for Advertising

Different companies organize in different ways to handle advertising. In small companies, advertising might be handled by someone in the sales department. Large companies set up advertising departments whose job it is to set the advertising budget, work with the ad agency, and handle other advertising not done by the agency. Most large companies use outside advertising agencies because they offer several advantages.

How does an **advertising agency** work? Advertising agencies were started in the mid- to late-1800s by salespeople and brokers who worked for the media and received a commission for selling advertising space to companies. As time passed, the salespeople began to help customers prepare their ads. Eventually, they formed agencies and grew closer to the advertisers than to the media.

Today's agencies employ specialists who can often perform advertising tasks better than the company's own staff can. Agencies also bring an outside point of view to solving the company's problems, along with lots of experience from working with different clients and situations. So, today, even companies with strong advertising departments of their own use advertising agencies.

Some ad agencies are huge—the largest U.S. agency, BBDO Worldwide, has worldwide annual gross revenue of more than $1.9 billion. In recent years, many agencies have grown by gobbling up other agencies, thus creating huge agency holding companies. The largest of these agency "megagroups," Omnicom Group, includes several large advertising, public relations, and promotion agencies with combined worldwide revenues of almost $12.7 billion.[27] Most large advertising agencies have the staff and resources to handle all phases of an advertising campaign for their clients, from creating a marketing plan to developing ad campaigns and preparing, placing, and evaluating ads.

International Advertising Decisions

International advertisers face many complexities not encountered by domestic advertisers. The most basic issue concerns the degree to which global advertising should be adapted to the unique characteristics of various country markets. Some large advertisers

Advertising agency
A marketing services firm that assists companies in planning, preparing, implementing, and evaluating all or portions of their advertising programs.

Real Marketing 15.2

The Super Bowl:
The Mother of All Advertising Events—But Is It Worth It?

The Super Bowl is the mother of all advertising events. Each year, dozens of blue chip advertisers showcase some of their best work to huge audiences around the world. But all this doesn't come cheap. Last year, major advertisers plunked down an average of $2.7 million per 30-second spot and will top $3 million in 2009. Over the past two decades, they've spent over $2 *billion* on just 11.5 hours of Super Bowl advertising time. But that's just for the air time. Throw in ad production costs—often $1 million or more per showcase commercial—and running even a single Super Bowl ad becomes a super-expensive proposition. Anheuser-Busch ran *seven* spots last year.

So every year, as the Super Bowl season nears, up pops the BIG QUESTION: Is Super Bowl advertising worth all that money? Does it deliver a high advertising ROI? As it turns out, there's no easy answer to the question.

Advertiser and industry expert opinion varies widely. Super Bowl stalwarts such as Anheuser-Busch, FedEx, General Motors, CareerBuilder, and the Frito-Lay, Gatorade, and Pepsi-Cola divisions of PepsiCo must think it's a good investment—they come back year after year. But what about savvy marketers such as Unilever, who opted out last year? In a survey of board members of the National Sports Marketing Network, 31 percent said they would recommend Super Bowl ads. But 41 percent said no—Super Bowl ads just aren't worth the money.

The naysayers make some pretty good arguments. Super Bowl advertising is outrageously expensive. Advertisers pay 85 percent more per viewer than they'd pay using prime-time network programming. And that $2.7 million would buy a lot of alternative media—for example, 50 different product placements in movies, TV shows, and video games; or two massive billboards in New York's Times Square that would be seen by a million people each day for a year. Beyond the cost, the competition for attention during the Super Bowl is fierce. Every single ad represents the best efforts of a major marketer trying to design a knock-your-socks-off spectacular

Super Bowl ROI: The Super Bowl plays to a huge and receptive audience—90 million viewers who put away their DVR remotes and watch it live, glued to their screens, ads and all. But is the advertising worth the huge cost?

that will reap high ratings from both critics and consumers. Many advertisers feel they can get more for their advertising dollar in venues that aren't so crowded with bigger-than-life commercials.

Then there's the question of strategic fit. Whereas the Super Bowl might be a perfect advertising event for big-budget companies selling beer, snacks, soft drinks, or sporting goods, it simply doesn't fit the pocketbooks or creative strategies of many other companies and their brands. One media executive likens a Super Bowl ad to a trophy wife: "It makes sense if you are an advertiser with a huge budget," he says. "But if you're an advertiser with a modest budget, that would not be the best use of your money."

As for creative fit, consider Unilever's Dove. Three years ago, the company ran a sentimental 45-second commercial from the Dove "Campaign for Real Beauty." The ad was highly rated by consumers and it created considerable buzz—some 400 million impressions of the ad before and after its single

appearance on the Super Bowl. But much of that buzz came from publicity surrounding the issue of girls' self-esteem rather than the product. And research showed that the ad produced low levels of involvement with the brand message.

Dove got almost equal exposure numbers and more engagement for a lot less money from an outdoor campaign that it ran that same year, and it got a much larger online response from its viral "Dove Evolution" and "Onslaught" films, which incurred no media cost at all. "The Super Bowl really isn't the right environment for Dove," says a Unilever executive. The past two years, instead, Dove opted to run consumer-generated ads during the more-female-oriented Academy Awards, an event where beauty brands thrive.

Still, the Super Bowl has a lot to offer to the right advertisers. It's the most-watched TV event of the year. It plays to a huge and

Continued on next page ▼

Real Marketing 15.2 Continued ▼

receptive audience—97.5 million viewers who put away their DVR remotes and watch it live, glued to their screens, ads and all. In fact, to many viewers, the Super Bowl ads are more important than what happens on the gridiron. Last year, the game itself drew an average 41.6 rating; the ads drew 41.22.

"There is no other platform quite like the Super Bowl," says the chief creative officer at Anheuser-Busch. "It's worth it. When you can touch that many households [with that kind of impact] in one sitting, it's actually efficient." In terms of dollars and cents, a study by one research firm found that consumer package-goods firms get a return of $1.25 to $2.74 for every dollar invested in Super Bowl advertising and one Super Bowl ad is as effective as 250 regular TV spots.

What's more, for most advertisers, the Super Bowl ad itself is only the centerpiece of something much bigger. Long after the game is over, ad critics, media pundits, and consumers are still reviewing, rehashing, and rating the commercials. It's one of the few sports-related events where "it ain't over when it's over." Thus, measuring the effectiveness of Super Bowl advertising involves a lot more than just measuring eyeballs and reach. "Those 30 seconds of fame are only the tip of the iceberg," says the analyst, "with online views, water-cooler chatter, blog buzz, and *USA Today*'s ratings all below the surface."

"The Super Bowl is the only media property where the advertising is as big a story as the content of the show," says Steven Schreibman, vice president of advertising and brand management for Nationwide Financial, "so you want to see how much you can leverage it." Schreibman is still agog over the response to Nationwide's Super Bowl spot two years ago that featured the hunk Fabio demonstrating that "life comes at you fast." Months afterward, consumers were still visiting Web sites such as ifilm.com to watch the commercial. "We got 1.8 million downloads on [just] that one site," says Schreibman. "Fabio himself keeps me apprised of that."

Advertisers don't usually sit back and just hope that consumers will talk about their ads. They build events that help to boost the buzz. For example, year before last, leading up to the Super Bowl at least three advertisers—GM's Chevrolet Division, the NFL, and Doritos—held contests inviting consumers to create their own Super Bowl ads. As noted previously, Doritos' "Crash the Super Bowl Challenge" contest produced more than 1,000 quality

entries, considerable media attention, and a bunch of online consumer interest. The winning ad topped the IAG Top 10 Best-Liked Super Bowl Ads list and came in fourth in the *USA Today* Ad Meter rankings.

The Super Bowl's largest advertiser, Anheuser-Busch, extends the festivities far beyond game day. It follows up with a postgame e-mail campaign to keep the fires burning. It also hosts a designated Web site, where consumers can view all of the company's Super Bowl ads and vote for their favorites via the Web site or text messages.

So—back to the original question. Is the Super Bowl advertising really worth the huge investment? It seems that there's no definitive answer—for some advertisers it's "yes"; for others, "no." The real trick is in trying to measure the returns. As the title of one recent article asserts, "Measuring Bowl Return? Good Luck!" The writer's conclusion: "For all the time, energy, and angst marketers spend crafting the perfect Super Bowl spot, [that's] a relative breeze compared to trying to prove its return on investment."

Sources: Quotes and other information from Claire Atkinson, "Measuring Bowl ROI? Good Luck," *Advertising Age*, January 29, 2007, p. 9; Lacey Rose, "Is a Super Bowl Ad a Super Deal?" *Forbes*, January 30, 2007, accessed at www.forbes.com; Jack Neff, "P&G, Unilever Sit Out the Super Bowl," *Advertising Age*, January 29, 2007, pp. 1, 36; Stuart Elliott, "Multiplying the Payoffs from a Super Bowl Spot," *New York Times*, January 26, 2007, p. C2; Stuart Elliott, "Tide to Make Its Super Bowl Debut," *New York Times*, January 11, 2008, p. 5; "20th Annual Super Bowl Ad Results," *USA Today*, February 4, 2008; Brian Steinberg, "Super Bowl Busts Ratings Record on 'the Greatest Day Ever' for Fox," *Advertising Age*, February 11, 2008, p. 21; and Brian Steinberg, "Super Bowl Spots Hit $3 Million," *Advertising Age*, May 12, 2008, p. 4.

have attempted to support their global brands with highly standardized worldwide advertising, with campaigns that work as well in Bangkok as they do in Baltimore. For example, McDonald's now unifies its creative elements and brand presentation under the familiar "I'm lovin' it" theme in all of its 100-plus markets worldwide. Coca-Cola coordinates worldwide advertising for its flagship brand under the theme, "The Coke Side of Life." ▲ And the Mr. Clean you see in a French ad is the same guy you see in U.S. ads, but with the name translated to "Mr. Propre."

In recent years, the increased popularity of online social networks and video sharing has boosted the need for advertising standardization for global brands. Most big marketing and advertising campaigns include a large online presence. Connected consumers can now zip easily across borders via the Internet, making it difficult for advertisers to roll out adapted campaigns in a controlled, orderly fashion. As a result, at the very least, most global consumer brands coordinate their Web sites internationally. For example, check out the McDonald's Web sites from Germany to Jordan to China and you'll find the golden arches logo, the "I'm lovin it" logo and jingle, a Big Mac equivalent, and maybe even Ronald McDonald himself.

Standardization produces many benefits—lower advertising costs, greater global advertising coordination, and a more consistent worldwide image. But it also has drawbacks. Most importantly, it ignores the fact that country markets differ greatly in their cultures, demographics, and economic conditions. Thus, most international advertisers "think globally but act locally." They develop global advertising *strategies* that make their worldwide advertising efforts more efficient and consistent. Then they adapt their

▲ Standardized worldwide advertising: The Mr. Clean you see in this French ad is the same guy you see in U.S. ads, but with the name translated to Mr. Propre. And in France, as in the United States, he'll get your floors clean enough that you can eat off of them.

advertising *programs* to make them more responsive to consumer needs and expectations within local markets.

For example, Apple uses "I'm a Mac; I'm a PC" commercials in many countries. In some markets, such as Spain, France, Germany, and Italy, it uses U.S. versions of the ads dubbed in the local language. However, it rescripts and reshoots the ads to fit the Japanese culture.

What's funny in one culture can seem ill-mannered in another. In the American ads, a nerdy PC guy keeps getting trumped by his hip Mac counterpart, who uses pointed banter that demonstrates how Macs are better. But in Japanese culture, where direct-comparison ads have long been frowned upon, it's rude to brag about one's strengths. So Japanese versions of the ads include subtle changes to emphasize that Macs and PCs are not that different. Instead of clothes that cast PC clearly as a nerd and Mac as a hipster, PC wears plain office attire and Mac weekend fashion, highlighting the work/home divide between the devices more than personality differences. In the first ad of the series, Mac even gives PC a nickname: *waaku*—a playful Japanese version of the word "work." PC's body language is a big source of the humor in Japan: Mac looks embarrassed when PC touches his shoulder or hides behind Mac's legs to avoid viruses. "PC constantly makes friendship-level approaches that Mac rejects in a friendly-irritated way," says a Tokyo brand consultant. "The Western Mac ads would backfire in Japan, because the Mac would appear to lack class." In fact, the jury is still out on whether even the toned-down comparative ads will work there.[28]

Global advertisers face several special problems. For instance, advertising media costs and availability differ vastly from country to country. Countries also differ in the extent to which they regulate advertising practices. Many countries have extensive systems of laws restricting how much a company can spend on advertising, the media used, the nature of advertising claims, and other aspects of the advertising program. Such restrictions often require advertisers to adapt their campaigns from country to country.

For example, alcoholic products cannot be advertised in India or in Muslim countries. In many countries, Sweden and Canada, for example, junk food ads are banned from kids' TV. To play it safe, McDonald's advertises itself as a family restaurant in Sweden. Comparative ads, although acceptable and even common in the United States and Canada, are less commonly used in the United Kingdom and illegal in India and Brazil. China bans sending e-mail for advertising purposes to people without their permission and all advertising e-mail that is sent must be titled "advertisement."

China also has restrictive censorship rules for TV and radio advertising; for example, the words *the best* are banned, as are ads that "violate social customs" or present women in "improper ways." McDonald's once avoided government sanctions there by publicly apologizing for an ad that crossed cultural norms by showing a customer begging for a discount. Similarly, Coca-Cola's Indian subsidiary was forced to end a promotion that offered prizes, such as a trip to Hollywood, because it violated India's established trade practices by encouraging customers to buy in order to "gamble."[29]

Thus, although advertisers may develop global strategies to guide their overall advertising efforts, specific advertising programs must usually be adapted to meet local cultures and customs, media characteristics, and advertising regulations.

Author Comment | Not long ago, public relations was considered a marketing stepchild because of its limited marketing use. That situation is changing fast, however, as more marketers recognize PR's brand-building power.

Public relations

Building good relations with the company's various publics by obtaining favorable publicity, building up a good corporate image, and handling or heading off unfavorable rumors, stories, and events.

Public Relations (pp 448–451)

Another major mass-promotion tool is **public relations**—building good relations with the company's various publics by obtaining favorable publicity, building up a good corporate image, and handling or heading off unfavorable rumors, stories, and events. Public relations departments may perform any or all of the following functions:[30]

- *Press relations or press agency:* Creating and placing newsworthy information in the news media to attract attention to a person, product, or service.

- *Product publicity:* Publicizing specific products.

- *Public affairs:* Building and maintaining national or local community relations.

- *Lobbying:* Building and maintaining relations with legislators and government officials to influence legislation and regulation.

- *Investor relations:* Maintaining relationships with shareholders and others in the financial community.

- *Development:* Public relations with donors or members of nonprofit organizations to gain financial or volunteer support.

Public relations is used to promote products, people, places, ideas, activities, organizations, and even nations. Companies use public relations to build good relations with consumers, investors, the media, and their communities. The state of New York turned its image around when its "I ♥ New York!" publicity and advertising campaign took root, bringing in millions more tourists. Trade associations have used public relations to rebuild interest in declining commodities such as eggs, apples, potatoes, and milk. For example, the milk industry's popular "Got Milk?" public relations campaign featuring celebrities with milk mustaches reversed a long-standing decline in milk consumption.[31]

> By 1994, milk consumption had been in decline for 20 years. The general perception was that milk was unhealthy, outdated, just for kids, or good only with cookies and cake. To counter these notions, the National Fluid Milk Processors Education Program (MilkPEP) began a public relations campaign featuring milk be-mustached celebrities and the tagline "Got Milk?" The campaign has not only been wildly popular, it has been successful as well—not only did it stop the decline, milk consumption actually increased. The campaign is still running.

> Although initially targeted at women in their twenties, the campaign has been expanded to other target markets and has gained cult status with teens, much to their parents' delight. Starting with basic print ads featuring a musician (Kelly Clarkson), actor (Jessica Alba), or sports idol (Tracy McGrady), the campaign has naturally spread to the Internet. One Web site (www.whymilk.com) appeals to Moms in a search for America's first "Chief Health Officer." Another (www.bodybymilk.com) targets young people, who can bid on gear using saved milk UPCs, go behind the scenes of the latest "Got Milk?" photo shoot, or get facts about "everything you ever need to know about milk." There are milk moustache MySpace pages of celebrities such as David Beckham. The milk marketers even created the world's first branded emoticon—the milk moustache :-{).

The Role and Impact of Public Relations

Public relations can have a strong impact on public awareness at a much lower cost than advertising can. The company does not pay for the space or time in the media. Rather, it pays for a staff to develop and circulate information and to manage events. If the company develops an interesting story or event, it could be picked up by several different media, having the same effect as advertising that would cost millions of dollars. And it would have more credibility than advertising.

▲ Public relations results can sometimes be spectacular. Starting with preview events like this one, Nintendo's award-winning PR campaign for its new Wii game produced nonstop stock-outs for more than two years.

Public relations results can sometimes be spectacular. ▲Consider the launch of Nintendo's Wii game console:[32]

By 2006, once-dominant Nintendo had dropped to third place in the video-game industry behind Sony and Microsoft. To get back on top, Nintendo's newest offering, the amazing Wii, needed to soar. The Wii's motion-sensitive controller makes it fun for almost anyone to play. This let Nintendo target the core gaming audience but also "dabblers," "lapsed gamers," and "non-gamers," including girls, women, and seniors. But rather than investing millions in media advertising, Nintendo took advantage of Wii's natural appeal to create a results-producing PR campaign. Pre-launch, Nintendo held preview events at which industry analysts and the media spent time with the amazing Wii. The company targeted consumers on MySpace, where the "How Wii Play" profile made more than 60,000 friends. Nintendo also launched an ambassador program that got the game into the hands of gamers, moms, and large inter-generational families, who spread information about the system through blogs and word of mouth.

On launch day, Nintendo midnight events, held in New York and Los Angeles, were attended by thousands of consumers, with coverage by media ranging from AP to MTV and *Good Morning America*. In the end, the Wii PR campaign earned a whopping 10 billion audience impressions over just three months, including 14 *Today Show* appearances and a stint on *South Park*. Despite early surveys showing that only 11 percent of consumers intended to buy it, Wii sales sizzled. Stores experienced two years of nonstop stock-outs and the Wii outsold the Xbox 360 by two to one and the newly introduced Playstation 3 by three to one. As a result, the Wii public relations effort was named *PRWeek's* 2008 Consumer Launch Campaign of the Year.

Despite its potential strengths, public relations is sometimes described as a marketing stepchild because of its often limited and scattered use. The public relations department is often located at corporate headquarters or handled by a third-party agency. Its staff is so busy dealing with various publics—stockholders, employees, legislators, the press—that public relations programs to support product marketing objectives may be ignored. Moreover, marketing managers and public relations practitioners do not always speak the same language. Whereas many public relations practitioners see their jobs as simply communicating, marketing managers tend to be much more interested in how advertising and public relations affect brand building, sales and profits, and customer relationships.

This situation is changing, however. Although public relations still captures only a small portion of the overall marketing budgets of most firms, PR can be a powerful brand-building tool. Two well-known marketing consultants even go so far as to conclude that advertising doesn't build brands, PR does. In their book *The Fall of Advertising & the Rise of PR*, the consultants proclaim that the dominance of advertising is over, and that public relations is quietly becoming the most powerful marketing communications tools.

The birth of a brand is usually accomplished with [public relations], not advertising. Our general rule is [PR] first, advertising second. [Public relations] is the nail, advertising the hammer. [PR] creates the credentials that provide the credibility for advertising.... Anita Roddick built The Body Shop into a major brand with no advertising at all. Instead, she traveled the world on a relentless quest for publicity.... Until recently Starbucks Coffee didn't spend a hill of beans on advertising, either. In 10 years, the company spent less than $10 million on advertising, a trivial amount for a brand that delivers annual sales [in the billions]. Wal-Mart stores became the world's largest retailer . . . with very little advertising. . . . On the Internet, Amazon.com became a powerhouse brand with virtually no advertising.[33]

Although the book created much controversy, and most advertisers wouldn't agree about the "fall of advertising" part of the title, the point is a good one. Advertising and public relations should work hand in hand within an integrated marketing communications program to build brands and customer relationships.

Major Public Relations Tools

Public relations uses several tools. One of the major tools is *news*. PR professionals find or create favorable news about the company and its products or people. Sometimes news stories occur naturally, and sometimes the PR person can suggest events or activities that would create news. *Speeches* can also create product and company publicity. Increasingly, company executives must field questions from the media or give talks at trade associations or sales meetings, and these events can either build or hurt the company's image. Another common PR tool is *special events*, ranging from news conferences, press tours, grand openings, and fireworks displays to laser shows, hot air balloon releases, multimedia presentations, or educational programs designed to reach and interest target publics.

Public relations people also prepare *written materials* to reach and influence their target markets. These materials include annual reports, brochures, articles, and company newsletters and magazines. *Audiovisual materials*, such as slide-and-sound programs, DVDs, and online videos are being used increasingly as communication tools. *Corporate identity materials* can also help create a corporate identity that the public immediately recognizes. Logos, stationery, brochures, signs, business forms, business cards, buildings, uniforms, and company cars and trucks—all become marketing tools when they are attractive, distinctive, and memorable. Finally, companies can improve public goodwill by contributing money and time to *public service activities*.

As we discussed in Chapter 5, many marketers are now also designing *buzz marketing* campaigns to generate excitement and favorable word of mouth for their brands. Buzz marketing takes advantage of *social networking* processes by getting consumers themselves to spread information about a product or service to others in their communities. ▲For example, Johnson & Johnson used buzz marketing to launch its Aveeno Positively Ageless product line:

▲ Buzz marketing: Aveeno used social networking processes to get consumers to spread the word about its new product line. This YouTube video has captured over 1.2 million views.

To build buzz for its new line, Johnson & Johnson employed talented street artist Julian Beever—the "Pavement Picasso"—to create a 3D "Fountain of Youth" chalk drawing on a sidewalk in the heart of New York City. Although the drawing captivated thousands of passersby, Aveeno turned "Fountain of Youth" into an online event via a four-minute, time-lapse video of the artist at work posted on YouTube (www.youtube.com/watch?v=hfn8Dz_13Ms). In addition the brand distributed the video to more than 50 blogs, with 21 responding by promoting the YouTube posting. With a soft "Aveeno Presents" slate at the beginning of the video and a closeup of the Fountain of Youth artwork showing the Aveeno logo at the end, the spot was well branded but without appearing to be commercial. The video reverberated through video sites and the blogosphere via strong word of mouth. Within two weeks, on YouTube alone, the video was viewed more than 65,000 times and grew to reach 121,346 views within one month. As of November 2008, the YouTube video had been viewed close to 1 million times.[34]

A company's Web site is another important public relations vehicle. Consumers and members of other publics often visit Web sites for information or entertainment. Such sites can be extremely popular. For example, Butterball's site (www.butterball.com), which features cooking and carving tips, once received 550,000 visitors in one day during Thanksgiving week. The Web site supplements the Butterball Turkey Talk-Line (1-800-BUTTERBALL)—called by some the "granddaddy of all help lines—staffed by 50 home economists and nutritionists who respond to more than 100,000 questions each November and December. Visitors to the site can even download a series of "Turkey Talk" podcasts containing tips on holiday food preparation.[35]

Web sites can also be ideal for handling crisis situations. For example, when several bottles of Odwalla apple juice sold on the West Coast were found to contain E. coli bacteria, Odwalla initiated a massive product recall. Within only three hours, it set up a Web site laden with information about the crisis and Odwalla's response. Company staffers also combed the Internet looking for newsgroups discussing Odwalla and posted links to the site. In all, in this age where "it's easier to disseminate information through e-mail marketing, blogs, and online chat," notes an analyst, "public relations is becoming a valuable part of doing business in a digital world."[36]

As with the other promotion tools, in considering when and how to use product public relations, management should set PR objectives, choose the PR messages and vehicles, implement the PR plan, and evaluate the results. The firm's public relations should be blended smoothly with other promotion activities within the company's overall integrated marketing communications effort.

REVIEWING Objectives AND KEY Terms

Companies must do more than make good products—they have to inform consumers about product benefits and carefully position products in consumers' minds. To do this, they must master *advertising* and *public relations*.

OBJECTIVE 1 Define the role of advertising in the promotion mix. (pp 430–431)

Advertising—the use of paid media by a seller to inform, persuade, and remind buyers about its products or organization—is an important promotion tool for communicating the value that marketers create for their customers. American marketers spend more than $264 billion each year on advertising, and worldwide ad spending exceeds $600 billion. Advertising takes many forms and has many uses. Although advertising is used mostly by business firms, a wide range of not-for-profit organizations, professionals, and social agencies also use advertising to promote their causes to various target publics. *Public relations*—gaining favorable publicity and creating a favorable company image—is the least used of the major promotion tools, although it has great potential for building consumer awareness and preference.

OBJECTIVE 2 Describe the major decisions involved in developing an advertising program. (pp 431–447)

Advertising decision making involves decisions about the advertising objectives, the budget, the message, the media, and, finally, the evaluation of results. Advertisers should set clear target, task,

and timing *objectives,* whether the aim is to inform, persuade, or remind buyers. Advertising's goal is to move consumers through the buyer-readiness stages discussed in the previous chapter. Some advertising is designed to move people to immediate action. However, many of the ads you see today focus on building or strengthening long-term customer relationships. The advertising *budget* can be based on sales, on competitors' spending, or on the objectives and tasks of the advertising program. The size and allocation of the budget depends on many factors.

Advertising strategy consists of two major elements: creating advertising *messages* and selecting advertising *media*. The *message decision* calls for planning a message strategy and executing it effectively. Good advertising messages are especially important in today's costly and cluttered advertising environment. Just to gain and hold attention, today's advertising messages must be better planned, more imaginative, more entertaining, and more rewarding to consumers. In fact, many marketers are now subscribing to a new merging of advertising and entertainment, dubbed "Madison & Vine." The *media decision* involves defining reach, frequency, and impact goals; choosing major media types; selecting media vehicles; and deciding on media timing. Message and media decisions must be closely coordinated for maximum campaign effectiveness.

Finally, *evaluation* calls for evaluating the communication and sales effects of advertising before, during, and after the advertising is placed. Advertising accountability has become a hot issue for most companies. Increasingly, top management is asking: "What return are we getting on our advertising investment?" and "How do we know that we're spending the right amount?" Other important advertising issues involve *organizing* for advertising and dealing with the complexities of international advertising.

OBJECTIVE 3 **Define the role of public relations in the promotion mix. (pp 448–450)**

Public relations—gaining favorable publicity and creating a favorable company image—is the least used of the major promotion tools, although it has great potential for building consumer awareness and preference. Public relations is used to promote products, people, places, ideas, activities, organizations, and even nations. Companies use public relations to build good relations with consumers, investors, the media, and their communities. Public relations can have a strong impact on public awareness at a much lower cost than advertising can, and public relations results can sometimes be spectacular. Although public relations still captures only a small portion of the overall marketing budgets of most firms, PR is playing an increasingly important brand-building role.

OBJECTIVE 4 **Explain how companies use public relations to communicate with their publics.** (pp 450–451)

Companies use public relations to communicate with their publics by setting PR objectives, choosing PR messages and vehicles, implementing the PR plan, and evaluating PR results. To accomplish these goals, public relations professionals use several tools such as *news, speeches,* and *special events.* They also prepare *written, audiovisual,* and *corporate identity materials* and contribute money and time to *public service activities. Buzz marketing* is a form of public relations that gets consumers themselves to spread word-of-mouth information about the company and its brands. The Internet has also become a major public relations tool.

KEY Terms

OBJECTIVE 1

Advertising (p 430)

OBJECTIVE 2

Advertising objective (p 431)
Advertising budget (p 432)

Advertising strategy (p 433)
Madison & Vine (p 435)
Creative concept (p 435)
Execution style (p 436)
Advertising media (p 439)

Return on advertising investment
(p 443)
Advertising agency (p 444)

OBJECTIVE 3

Public relations (p 448)

DISCUSSING & APPLYING THE Concepts

Discussing the Concepts

1. List and briefly describe the four important decisions marketing managers must make when developing an advertising program. (AASCB: Communication)

2. Why is it important that the advertising media and creative departments work closely together? (AACSB: Communication)

3. How do an advertisement's appeals differ from its execution style? (AACSB: Communication)

4. Define the terms *reach, frequency*, and *impact*. (AACSB: Communication)

5. What are the role and functions of public relations within an organization? (AACSB: Communication)

6. Discuss the tools used by public relations professionals. (AACSB: Communication)

Applying the Concepts

1. Any message can be presented using different execution styles. Select a brand and target audience and design two advertisements, each using a different execution style to deliver the same message to the target audience but in a different way. Identify the types of execution styles you are using and present your advertisements. (AACSB: Communication; Reflective Thinking)

2. Recommend three advertising media for a campaign to introduce a new line of men's personal care products under a LeBron James label. (AACSB: Communication; Reflective Thinking)

3. In a small group, discuss the major public relations tools and develop three public relations items for each of the following: a hospital, a restaurant, and any brand of your choice. (AACSB: Communication; Reflective Thinking)

FOCUS ON Technology

Have you ever watched your favorite television program and wished you could immediately buy the clothes your favorite character was wearing or learn more about the car he or she was driving? Or how about ordering a pizza while watching an ad? Well, now you can—with interactive television. Marketers are increasingly using this vehicle to interact with consumers. For example, Unilever, one of the largest consumer packaged-goods companies, is banking on consumers wanting more information and interactivity from their televisions and is planning several interactive TV-ad deals with DIRECTV and Comcast cable. Interactive TV works by providing links, known as triggers, that when clicked take viewers into a longer advertisement. These longer ads, called long-form or long-tail advertising, provide opportunities for deeper interaction.

1. Will interactive television catch on with consumers? What might be slowing the adoption of this innovative advertising technique? (AACSB: Communication; Reflective Thinking)

2. Discuss the types of products or services that would benefit most from interactive television advertising. (AACSB: Communication; Reflective Thinking)

FOCUS ON Ethics

Word-of-mouth communications can be very persuasive. You're more likely to see a movie or buy a clothing brand because your friends recommended them. Marketers are harnessing the power of word-of-mouth with creative tactics. However, some tactics are criticized because consumers don't know they are being marketed to. For example, Sony Ericsson came under fire when it became known that it hired actors to pose as tourists asking strangers to take their picture with the cool T68i phone. Wal-Mart was criticized for a blog about Laura and Jim RVing around America, stopping at Wal-Marts across the country and writing glowing things about the retailer. Wal-Mart never disclosed that it was sponsoring the trip. Procter & Gamble, while not paying moms to talk about its products, provides samples and coupons to these influential people recruited into their Vocalpoint network in hopes that they say positive things about them to others.

1. These types of activities are often called "stealth marketing" because they are not openly presented as promotional tactics. Learn more about this practice and decide if it is ethical. (AACSB: Communication; Ethical Reasoning; Reflective Thinking)

2. Can some of the tools used in public relations be considered stealth marketing? How about product placement in movies or television shows? Others? (AACSB: Communication; Ethical Reasoning)

MARKETING BY THE Numbers

AARP Magazine and *Reader's Digest* are the top two magazines with regard to circulation. They also attract similar audiences. Although consumers aged 50+ are plugged in online like younger consumers, they still like print media, making these two magazines valuable media vehicles in which to reach seniors with their advertising.

1. Using advertising rate information for these magazines (see www.aarpmedia.org/atm-rates.html and www. rdglobaladvertising.com/rates/rates.shtml?united_states_english), determine the cost per thousand of a full page, 4-color advertisement. Which magazine is more cost effective for advertisers? (AACSB: Communication; Use of IT; Analytical Reasoning)

2. Suppose a manufacturer of a diabetes testing monitor wants to advertise in *AARP Magazine*. Refer to Appendix 2, Marketing by the Numbers, to determine by how much the manufacturer's sales must increase to break even on the purchase of 10 full-page, 4-color advertisements in *AARP Magazine*. Assume that the company has a 40 percent contribution margin. Should the advertiser purchase this advertising space? (AACSB: Communication; Analytical Reasoning)

VIDEO Case

E*TRADE

Super Bowl XXXIV, the first of the new millennium, was known as the Dot-com Bowl for the glut of Internet companies that plopped down an average of $2.2 million per 30-second spot ad. Today, most of the companies that defined the dot-com glory days are gone. But one darling of the dot-com era, E*TRADE, remains one of the few survivors. Although E*TRADE has experienced challenges since the turn of the century, it has also turned profits.

Advertising on the big game hasn't worked out well for everyone. But for E*TRADE, Super Bowl ads have been part of a larger advertising effort that played a role in its survival. In this video, E*TRADE reports on its advertising strategy as well as the advantages and disadvantages of Super Bowl advertising.

After viewing the video featuring E*TRADE, answer the following questions about advertising and promotions:

1. What makes E*TRADE different from now-defunct dot-coms?

2. What has been the role of advertising at E*TRADE?

3. Discuss the factors in E*TRADE's decision to advertise during the Super Bowl.

COMPANY Case

Coca-Cola: Another Advertising Hit

When you think of Coca-Cola, what comes to mind? It wouldn't be surprising if you thought first of Coke ads. In the history of advertising, perhaps no other company has had such a strong and continuous impact on society through advertising. Not only have Coke's ads been successful at selling its soft drinks, but decade after decade Coca-Cola's ads and campaigns have influenced our very culture by making their way into the hearts and minds of consumers.

A BRIEF AD HISTORY

In the 1920s, Coca-Cola shifted its advertising strategy, focusing for the first time on creating brand loyalty. It began advertising the soft drink as fun and refreshing. Coke's 1929 campaign slogan was, "The Pause that Refreshes." To this day, that slogan remains number two on *Advertising Age*'s top 100 slogans of all time.

How about those famous Coca-Cola Santa Clause print ads? Most people probably have seen an example of such. What most people don't realize is that our modern-day vision of Santa as a jolly old man with a white beard in a red suit and hat is to some extent a result of those Coke ads that began emerging in popular magazines in 1931. Before that, the world's image of Santa was fragmented, with physical portrayals of the legendary holiday visitor ranging from a pixie to a leprechaun to even a frightening gnome! But Coca-Cola's long-running series of ads solidified what was becoming a common U.S. image, making our beloved Santa Clause recognizable around the world.

Those Coca-Cola campaigns were probably a little before your time. But what about Coca-Cola's 1971 "Hilltop" campaign. Perhaps you remember its lyrics, "I'd like to teach the world to sing, in perfect harmony. I'd like to buy the world a Coke, and keep it company." The song was sung by a choir of young people from all over the world, perched high on a hilltop, each holding an iconic hourglass-shaped bottle of Coke. Within months, Coca-Cola and its bottlers received more than a hundred thousand letters about the ad. The ad actually received requests at radio stations; so many in fact, that a version of the song was released as a pop-music single. The jingle's tagline, "It's the real thing," served as the foundation for Coke ads for years.

Still too long ago for you? Maybe you've heard of Coke's ad showing a bruised and battered Mean Joe Green tossing his shirt to a young fan after the boy shares his Coke with the pro football player. The ad appears consistently at the top of "Best Super Bowl Ads" lists. Or how about "Coke is it?" "Can't Beat the Feeling?" Certainly you would remember the jingle made famous in the 1990s, "Always Coca-Cola." And who doesn't make some association between the sweet, dark, bubbly beverage and polar bears? Innovative animation technology put those lovable creatures in only a handful of ads, but they are forever etched in the memories of consumers everywhere.

These are only some highlights of Coca-Cola's long advertising history, stretching back to the company's origin in 1886. With so many hits and such a huge impact on consumers, it's hard to imagine that the beverage giant ever gets into an advertising rut. But as the new millennium began to unfold, many considered that Coke had lost its advertising sizzle. The company was struggling to create ads that resonated with younger folks while at the same time appealing to older consumers. And the company's ads we're routinely out-pointed by those of rival Pepsi. Coca-Cola needed some new advertising fizz.

BACK TO THE BOWL

Where does a company turn when it wants to make a big ad splash? For Coca-Cola, its thoughts turned to the marquee of all advertising events—the Super Bowl. The company had certainly had success with the ad venue before. But scoring big with a Super Bowl ad isn't guaranteed. In fact, many cynics view the ad venue as a waste of money. One team of researchers found that average brand recall one week after the 2008 Super Bowl was an unimpressive 7 percent. Recall for specific commercials and the brand represented therein was even worse at only 4 percent. That doesn't speak very highly for a 30-second ad that cost $2.7 million to air, and perhaps even more to produce. The Super Bowl has its share of critics who think it is far too costly for a single event, regardless of how many people tune in.

But for all the misses, there have been plenty of hits. In 1999, HotJobs.com blew half of its $4 million advertising budget for the year on a single 30-second spot. The result? Traffic on its Web site immediately shot up 120 percent, choking its network and server system. Monster.com saw similar results that same year. And hundreds of advertisers throughout the Super Bowl's history have been very satisfied with the results of their ads.

For its 2008 campaign debut, Coca-Cola was confident that the Super Bowl was just right for its broad target market. It assigned Wieden + Kennedy the task of crafting a 60-second commercial. Hal Curtis, one of the top creative directors for the agency, took charge of the project. Two years before, Mr. Curtis had come up with an idea for an ad while working on a different campaign. He thought the idea was perfect for Coke.

By now, you've probably seen the ad. Titled "It's Mine," the spot is set at Macy's Thanksgiving Day Parade in New York City, a parade famous for its blimp-sized balloons marched through the Central Park area on long tethers. The Coke ad focuses on two particular characters, Stewie Griffin from Fox's *Family Guy* and the classic cartoon character Underdog. Both balloons sidle up to a huge Coke balloon. The two characters begin fighting over the Coke, bouncing around in a kind of slow-motion ballet against the New York skyline, bumping up against buildings. As the scuffle progresses above the streets, moving higher and higher, New Yorkers look on from hot dog stands, cabs, and even inside buildings. At the story's climactic moment, a giant Charlie Brown balloon emerges from nowhere, swooping in and claiming the giant Coke, leaving Stewie and Underdog empty-handed.

The spot cost Coca-Cola $2.3 million to make and more than double that to air. It was also the most difficult ad that Mr. Curtis had ever produced. For starters, he encountered mounds of red tape in negotiating the rights to use the well-known cartoon characters in the ad. Choreographing and shooting footage of giant balloons in one of the world's biggest cities brought its own set of challenges. At one point, bad weather forced the project indoors and all the way across the country to the Paramount studios on the West Coast. The post-shoot animation was considered yet a third shoot for the ad. It all added up to four months of production and postproduction.

When asked about the challenge of simultaneously reaching consumers of all ages with an advertisement, Mr. Curtis responded, "A good story appeals to everyone. And a story that is well told appeals to young and old. Certainly, there are times where we want to skew a message younger, but for this spot that wasn't part of the thinking." Pio Schunker, Coca-Cola's head of creative excellence, added, "We are at our best when we speak to universal values that appeal to everyone rather than try and skew it to specific segments."

According to Mr. Schunker, the universal value referred to here was that "Good really wins in the end," a point that he thought was made strongly with the contrast of Charlie Brown over a character like Stewie. In fact, Curtis originally pitched the ad with an ending that had the Coke bottle getting punctured on a flagpole and neither balloon getting it. But Coca-Cola wanted something that was emotionally more positive, something that expressed optimism. "I felt it was such a downer of an

ending to have these characters chase the Coke and not get it," stated Mr. Schunker. It was Curtis's 12-year-old son, Will, who gave him the idea for what became the ending when he said, "Why can't another balloon get it?" For Hal Curtis, the next logical step was Charlie Brown.

Everyone was happy with the end result. Both Coca-Cola and Wieden + Kennedy felt that the ad communicated the desired message perfectly while bringing out the kind of warm emotions that had emanated from Coca-Cola ads for decades.

The hunches of these ad veterans proved correct. The day after the game, Coke's balloon ad had 350 blog posts while Pepsi's ads had only 250. A week after that, the "It's Mine" ad was the most talked about ad online. SuperBowl-Ads.com had it rated as the top ad of the dozens that aired on the 2008 gridiron matchup. And later in the year, the spot won a Silver Lion at the Cannes Lions festival, the most prestigious award event in the industry.

There's no doubt that the "It's Mine" ad achieved more buzz and more sizzle than Coca-Cola's ads in recent history. But that's only a first step to advertising success. In the end, the only result that really matters is whether or not the ad has the intended effect on consumers. Although the impact of Coca-Cola's "It's Mine" ad or its history of other outstanding ads on actual beverage sales may never be known, one broader conclusion is clear. Every year, Interbrand publishes the premier ranking of global brands based on monetary value. And every year since Interbrand began publishing the list in 2001, Coca-Cola has held the top spot. At $65 billion, Coca-Cola is the world's most valuable brand. Thus, it's pretty easy to make the connection between Coca-Cola's brand value and more than 100 years of stellar advertising.

Questions for Discussion

1. Consider Coca-Cola's advertising throughout its history. Identify as many commonalities as possible for its various ads and campaigns. (For a list of Coca-Cola slogans over the years, check out http://en.wikipedia.org/wiki/Coca-Cola_slogans.)

2. Analyze the "It's Mine" ad based on the process of creating an advertising message as outlined in the text.

3. Discuss issues of selecting advertising media for the "It's Mine" ad. How might this process differ from that of other Coca-Cola campaigns? From other campaigns for other companies?

4. Based on the information in this case, how might Coca-Cola measure the effectiveness of the "It's Mine" ad? What else might Coca-Cola want to measure?

Sources: Lucinda Watrous, "The History of Coca-Cola's Advertising," *Associated Content*, January 14, 2008, accessed online at www.associatedcontent.com; Suzanne Vranica, "Coca-Cola Ad Scores Big," *Wall Street Journal*, March 12, 2008, p. B3A; G. Michael Maddock and Raphael Louis Vitón, "Super Bowl Ads: A Big Fumble," *BusinessWeek*, March 27, 2008, accessed online at www.businessweek.com; "Celebrating 75 Years of the Coca-Cola Santa," October 2006 press release, accessed online at www.thecoca-colacompany.com.

Chapter 16

Part 1   Defining Marketing and the Marketing Process (Chapters 1, 2)
Part 2   Understanding the Marketplace and Consumers (Chapters 3, 4, 5, 6)
Part 3   Designing a Customer-Driven Strategy and Mix (Chapters 7, 8, 9, 10, 11, 12, 13, 14, 15, 16, 17)
Part 4   Extending Marketing (Chapters 18, 19, 20)

Personal Selling and Sales Promotion

Chapter PREVIEW

In the previous chapter, you learned about communicating customer value through integrated marketing communications (IMC) and about two elements of the promotion mix—advertising and public relations. In this chapter, we'll look at two more IMC elements—personal selling and sales promotion. Personal selling is the interpersonal arm of marketing communications, in which the sales force interacts with customers and prospects to build relationships and make sales. Sales promotion consists of short-term incentives to encourage purchase or sale of a product or service. As you read on, remember that although this chapter examines personal selling and sales promotion as separate tools, they must be carefully integrated with other elements of the promotion mix.

When someone says "salesperson," what image comes to mind? Perhaps you think about a stereotypical glad-hander who's out to lighten your wallet by selling you something you don't really need. Think again. Today, for most companies, personal selling plays an important role in building profitable customer relationships. Consider CDW Corporation, whose customer-focused sales strategy has helped it grow rapidly while competitors have faltered.

CDW Corporation, a leading provider of multibrand technology products and services, is thriving. In only 24 years since founder Michael Krasny started the business at his kitchen table, CDW has grown to become a high-tech heavyweight in its highly volatile and competitive industry. In just the past five years, CDW has increased its sales by 75 percent, to $8.1 billion annually. And CDW recently ranked first in the Wholesalers: Electronics category on *Fortune*'s 2008 list of America's Most Admired Companies.

How has CDW managed to grow so profitably? The company owes its success to good old-fashioned high-touch personal selling that builds lasting one-to-one customer relationships. The strategy is fueled by a genuine passion for solving customer problems. Under CDW's "Circle of Service" philosophy, "everything revolves around the customer."

CDW sells a complex assortment of more than 100,000 technology products and advanced technology services—computers, software, accessories, and networking products. Many of CDW's competitors chase after a relative handful of very large customers. However, although CDW serves customers of all sizes, one of the company's core customer segments is small and midsize businesses (SMBs). These smaller customers often need lots of advice and support. "Many of our clients don't have IT departments," says one CDW executive, "so they look to us for expertise."

That's where CDW's sales force comes in. The major responsibility for building and managing customer relationships falls to CDW's sales force of over 2,500 account managers. Each customer is assigned an account manager, who helps the customer select the right products and technologies and keep them running smoothly. "The server room can be a cold and lonely place," notes one CDW advertisement. "We can definitely help with the lonely part. At CDW, we provide you with a personal account manager who knows your business and the IT challenges you face."

Account managers orchestrate the efforts of a team of CDW specialists who help customers select the best mix of products, services, and support. But they do more than just sell technology products and services. They work closely with customers to find solutions to their technology problems. "This is a big deal to us," says Jim Grass, CDW's senior director of state and local sales. "We want to go beyond fulfilling the order and become the trusted adviser for them. We [want to] talk . . . about what a customer is trying to accomplish and really add value to the sale, as opposed to just sending out a box."

To become trusted advisers and effective customer-relationship builders, CDW account managers really have to know their stuff. And CDW boasts some of the most knowledgeable salespeople in the industry. Before they make a single sales call, new account managers complete a

> The major responsibility for managing customer relationships falls to CDW's energetic and passionately customer-focused account managers. "We want to become the trusted adviser for [customers]."

six-week orientation and then a six-month training program. CDW University's College of Sales offers intensive schooling in the science behind the company's products and in the art of consultative selling. But that's just the beginning—the training never ends. Tenured account managers receive ongoing training to enhance their relationship-selling skills. Each year, CDW's sales force completes a whopping 339,000 hours of sales-specific training. John Edwardson, chairman and CEO of CDW and former head of United Airlines, likes to point out that CDW reps get more training than some pilots.

To further support salespeople's customer problem-solving efforts, the company's technology specialists help design customized solutions, while its advanced technology engineers help customers implement and manage those solutions. Account managers can draw on these teams to design customer-specific solutions in technology areas such as notebooks, desktops, printers, servers and storage, unified communications, security, wireless, power and cooling, networking, software licensing, and mobile wireless solutions.

Customers who want to access CDW's products and expertise without going through their account manager can do so easily at any of several CDW Web sites. Better yet, CDW will create a free personalized CDW@work extranet site that reflects a given customer's pricing, order status, account history, and special considerations. The extranet site serves as a 24-hour extension of the customer's account manager. But even here, the ever-present account managers are likely to add personal guidance. Account managers receive immediate notification of their customers' online activities. So if a blurry-eyed SMB manager makes a mistake on an emergency order placed in the middle of the night, chances are good that the account manager will find and correct the error first thing in the morning.

Beyond being knowledgeable and ever-present, CDW's account managers are energetic and passionately customer focused. Much of the energy has passed down from CDW founder and former CEO Michael Krasny. Selling has always been a top priority for Krasny, not surprising given that he began the company by selling used personal computers out of his home through classified ads. Krasny's most important legacy is the "Circle of Service" culture that he created—a culture that focuses on taking care of customers, and on the CDW employees who serve them.

So when someone says "salesperson," you may still think of the stereotypical "traveling salesman"—the fast-talking, ever-smiling peddler who travels his territory foisting his wares on reluctant customers. Such stereotypes, however, are out of date. Today, like CDW's account managers, most professional salespeople are well-educated, well-trained men and women who work to build valued customer relationships. They succeed not by taking customers in, but by helping them out—by assessing customer needs and solving customer problems.

CDW's sales force instills loyalty in what are traditionally very price-conscious SMB customers. The company wants to create customer satisfaction at every touch point. Says a former CDW marketing executive, "We're competitively priced, but what's most important is the service and the customers' relationships with their account managers. It's how we actually touch people that creates our most long-lasting [success]."[1]

The server room can be a cold and lonely place. We can definitely help with the lonely part.

As you sit there among the humming and buzzing of servers, the miles of cables and the flashing of tiny little lights, know this—you are not alone. At CDW, we provide you with a personal account manager who knows your business and the IT challenges you face. We make sure your most difficult questions get answered by highly trained technology specialists who, quite frankly, are ridiculously smart. And we offer a full range of custom configuration services that can save you valuable time and money. With all this, plus an unfathomable number of products from the top names in the industry, you should feel quite comfortable knowing CDW has everything you need, when you need it. And as always, we're only a phone call away.

CDW.com | 800.399.4CDW

CDW

The Right Technology. Right Away.

CDW's good old-fashioned high-touch personal selling strategy is fueled by a genuine passion for solving customer problems.

Personal selling plays an important role in building profitable customer relationships. Technology products and services firm CDW's customer-focused sales strategy has helped it grow rapidly while competitors have faltered.

In this chapter, we examine two more promotion mix tools—*personal selling* and *sales promotion.* Personal selling consists of interpersonal interactions with customers and prospects to make sales and maintain customer relationships. Sales promotion involves using short-term incentives to encourage customer purchasing, reseller support, and sales force efforts.

Objective Outline

Author Comment | Personal selling is the interpersonal arm of the promotion mix. A company's salespeople create and communicate customer value through personal interactions with customers.

Personal Selling (pp 458–461)

Robert Louis Stevenson once noted that "everyone lives by selling something." Companies all around the world use sales forces to sell products and services to business customers and final consumers. But sales forces are also found in many other kinds of organizations. For example, colleges use recruiters to attract new students and churches use membership committees to attract new members. Museums and fine arts organizations use fund-raisers to contact donors and raise money. Even governments use sales forces. The U.S. Postal Service, for instance, uses a sales force to sell Express Mail and other services to corporate customers. In the first part of this chapter, we examine personal selling's role in the organization, sales force management decisions, and the personal selling process.

The Nature of Personal Selling

Personal selling
Personal presentation by the firm's sales force for the purpose of making sales and building customer relationships.

Personal selling is one of the oldest professions in the world. The people who do the selling go by many names: salespeople, sales representatives, district managers, account executives, sales consultants, sales engineers, agents, and account development reps to name just a few.

People hold many stereotypes of salespeople—including some unfavorable ones. "Salesman" may bring to mind the image of Arthur Miller's pitiable Willy Loman in *Death of a Salesman* or Meredith Willson's cigar-smoking, backslapping, joke-telling Harold Hill in *The Music Man*. These examples depict salespeople as loners, traveling their territories, trying to foist their wares on unsuspecting or unwilling buyers.

However, modern salespeople are a far cry from these unfortunate stereotypes. Today, most salespeople are well-educated, well-trained professionals who add value for customers and maintain long-term customer relationships. They listen to their customers, assess customer needs, and organize the company's efforts to solve customer problems.[2]

Sales is no longer the avenue of choice for washouts from other fields or for the glad-handers who anticipate doing business over steaks and a three-martini lunch. In today's hypercompetitive markets, "buying is not about transactions any more," says one sales expert. "Salespeople must know their customers' businesses better than customers do and align themselves with customers' strategies." That creates an entirely new role for salespeople. These days, "salespeople must have a wheelbarrow full of business savvy, combined with the credibility to sell to [empowered, well-informed buying] executives," says another expert. Today, sales is about building customer relationships through a "focus on differentiation and linking those differences to the customer's realization of value."

▲ Professional selling: It takes more than fast talk and a warm smile to sell high-tech aircraft, a single big sale can easily run into billions of dollars. Success depends on building solid, long-term relationships with customers.

Salesperson

An individual representing a company to customers by performing one or more of the following activities: prospecting, communicating, selling, servicing, information gathering, and relationship building.

Consider Boeing, the aerospace giant competing in the rough-and-tumble worldwide commercial aircraft market. ▲ It takes more than fast talk and a warm smile to sell expensive high-tech aircraft. A single big sale can easily run into billions of dollars. Boeing salespeople head up an extensive team of company specialists—sales and service technicians, financial analysts, planners, engineers—all dedicated to finding ways to satisfy airline customer needs. The selling process is nerve-rackingly slow—it can take two or three years from the first sales presentation to the day the sale is announced. After getting the order, salespeople then must stay in almost constant touch to make certain the customer stays satisfied. Success depends on building solid, long-term relationships with customers, based on performance and trust.

The term **salesperson** covers a wide range of positions. At one extreme, a salesperson might be largely an *order taker*, such as the department store salesperson standing behind the counter. At the other extreme are *order getters*, whose positions demand *creative selling* and *relationship building* for products and services ranging from appliances, industrial equipment, and airplanes to insurance and information technology services. Here, we focus on the more creative types of selling and on the process of building and managing an effective sales force.

The Role of the Sales Force

Personal selling is the interpersonal arm of the promotion mix. Advertising consists largely of nonpersonal communication with target consumer groups. In contrast, personal selling involves interpersonal interactions between salespeople and individual customers—whether face-to-face, by telephone, via e-mail, through video or Web conferences, or by other means. Personal selling can be more effective than advertising in more complex selling situations. Salespeople can probe customers to learn more about their problems and then adjust the marketing offer and presentation to fit the special needs of each customer.

The role of personal selling varies from company to company. Some firms have no salespeople at all—for example, companies that sell only online or through catalogs, or companies that sell through manufacturer's reps, sales agents, or brokers. In most firms, however, the sales force plays a major role. In companies that sell business products and services, such as IBM or DuPont, the company's salespeople work directly with customers. In consumer product companies such as Procter & Gamble and Nike, the sales force plays an important behind-the-scenes role. It works with wholesalers and retailers to gain their support and to help them be more effective in selling the company's products.

Linking the Company with Its Customers

The sales force serves as a critical link between a company and its customers. ▲ In many cases, salespeople serve both masters—the seller and the buyer. First, they *represent the company to customers*. They find and develop new customers and communicate information about the

▲ Salespeople link the company with its customers. To many customers, the salesperson is the company.

company's products and services. They sell products by approaching customers, presenting their products, answering objections, negotiating prices and terms, and closing sales. In addition, salespeople provide customer service and carry out market research and intelligence work.

At the same time, salespeople *represent customers to the company*, acting inside the firm as "champions" of customers' interests and managing the buyer–seller relationship. Salespeople relay customer concerns about company products and actions back inside to those who can handle them. They learn about customer needs and work with other marketing and nonmarketing people in the company to develop greater customer value.

In fact, to many customers, the salesperson *is* the company—the only tangible manifestation of the company that they see. Hence, customers may become loyal to salespeople as well as to the companies and products they represent. This concept of "salesperson-owned loyalty" lends even more importance to the salesperson's customer relationship building abilities. Strong relationships with the salesperson will result in strong relationships with the company and its products. Conversely, poor salesperson relationships will probably result in poor company and product relationships.[3]

Coordinating Marketing and Sales

Ideally, the sales force and the firm's other marketing functions should work together closely to jointly create value for both customers and the company. Unfortunately, however, some companies still treat "marketing" and "sales" as separate functions. When this happens, the separated marketing and sales functions often don't get along well. When things go wrong, the marketers (marketing planners, brand managers, and researchers) blame the sales force for its poor execution of an otherwise splendid strategy. In turn, the sales team blames the marketers for being out of touch with what's really going on with customers. The marketers sometimes feel that salespeople have their "feet stuck in the mud" whereas salespeople feel that the marketers have their "heads stuck in the clouds." Neither group fully values the other's contributions. If not repaired, such disconnects between marketing and sales can damage customer relationships and company performance.

A company can take several actions to help bring its marketing and sales functions closer together. At the most basic level, it can *increase communications* between the two groups by arranging joint meetings and by spelling out when and with whom each group should communicate. The company can create *joint assignments*.[4]

It's important to create opportunities for marketers and salespeople to work together. This will make them more familiar with each other's ways of thinking and acting. It's useful for marketers, particularly brand managers and researchers, to occasionally go along on sales calls. They should also sit in on important account-planning sessions. Salespeople, in turn, should help to develop marketing plans. They should sit in on product-planning reviews and share their deep knowledge about customers' purchasing habits. They should preview ad and sales-promotion campaigns. Jointly, marketers and salespeople should generate a playbook for expanding business with the top 10 accounts in each market segment. They should also plan events and conferences together.

A company can also create *joint objectives and reward systems* for sales and marketing or appoint *marketing-sales liaisons*—people from marketing who "live with the sales force" and help to coordinate marketing and sales force programs and efforts. Finally, the firm can appoint a *chief revenue officer* (or *chief customer officer*)—a high-level marketing executive who oversees both marketing and sales. Such a person can help infuse marketing and sales with the common goal of creating value for customers in order to capture value in return.

Author | Here's another definition
Comment | of sales force
management: Planning, organizing, leading, and controlling personal contact programs designed to achieve profitable customer relationships. Here again, the goal of every marketing activity is to create customer value and build customer relationships.

Managing the Sales Force (pp 461–472)

We define **sales force management** as the analysis, planning, implementation, and control of sales force activities. It includes designing sales force strategy and structure and recruiting, selecting, training, compensating, supervising, and evaluating the firm's salespeople. These major sales force management decisions are shown in ▼ **Figure 16.1** and are discussed in the following sections.

Designing Sales Force Strategy and Structure

Marketing managers face several sales force strategy and design questions. How should salespeople and their tasks be structured? How big should the sales force be? Should salespeople sell alone or work in teams with other people in the company? Should they sell in the field or by telephone or on the Web? We address these issues next.

Sales Force Structure

Sales force management
The analysis, planning, implementation, and control of sales force activities. It includes designing sales force strategy and structure and recruiting, selecting, training, supervising, compensating, and evaluating the firm's salespeople.

A company can divide sales responsibilities along any of several lines. The decision is simple if the company sells only one product line to one industry with customers in many locations. In that case the company would use a *territorial sales force structure*. However, if the company sells many products to many types of customers, it might need either a *product sales force structure*, a *customer sales force structure*, or a combination of the two.

Territorial Sales Force Structure. In the **territorial sales force structure**, each salesperson is assigned to an exclusive geographic area and sells the company's full line of products or services to all customers in that territory. This organization clearly defines each salesperson's job and fixes accountability. It also increases the salesperson's desire to build local customer relationships that, in turn, improve selling effectiveness. Finally, because each salesperson travels within a limited geographic area, travel expenses are relatively small.

Territorial sales force structure
A sales force organization that assigns each salesperson to an exclusive geographic territory in which that salesperson sells the company's full line.

A territorial sales organization is often supported by many levels of sales management positions. For example, Campbell Soup Company uses a territorial structure in which each salesperson is responsible for selling all Campbell products. Starting at the bottom of the organization, *sales merchandisers* report to *sales representatives*, who report to *retail supervisors*, who report to *directors of retail sales operations*, who report to 1 of 22 *regional sales managers*. Regional sales managers, in turn, report to 1 of 4 *general sales managers* (West, Central, South, and East), who report to a *vice president and general sales manager*.

Product Sales Force Structure. Salespeople must know their products—especially when the products are numerous and complex. This need, together with the growth of product management, has led many companies to adopt a **product sales force structure**, in which the sales force sells along product lines. For example, GE employs different sales forces within different product and service divisions of its major businesses. Within GE Infrastructure, for instance, the company has separate sales forces for aviation, energy, transportation, and water processing products and technologies. Within GE Healthcare, it employs different sales forces for diagnostic imaging, life sciences, and integrated IT solu-

Product sales force structure
A sales force organization under which salespeople specialize in selling only a portion of the company's products or lines.

▼ **FIGURE | 16.1**
Major Steps in Sales Force Management

The goal? You guessed it! The company wants to build a skilled and motivated sales team that will help to create customer value and build strong customer relationships.

Designing sales force strategy and structure → Recruiting and selecting salespeople → Training salespeople → Compensating salespeople → Supervising salespeople → Evaluating salespeople

tions products and services. In all, a company as large and complex as GE might have dozens of separate sales forces serving its diverse product and service portfolio.

The product structure can lead to problems, however, if a single large customer buys many different company products. For example, Cardinal Health, the large health care products and services company, has several product divisions, each with a separate sales force. Using a product sales force structure might mean that several Cardinal salespeople end up calling on the same hospital on the same day. This means that they travel over the same routes and wait to see the same customer's purchasing agents. These extra costs must be compared with the benefits of better product knowledge and attention to individual products.

Customer sales force structure
A sales force organization under which salespeople specialize in selling only to certain customers or industries.

Customer Sales Force Structure. More and more companies are now using a **customer sales force structure**, in which they organize the sales force along customer or industry lines. Separate sales forces may be set up for different industries, for serving current customers versus finding new ones, and for major accounts versus regular accounts. Many companies even have special sales forces set up to handle the needs of individual large customers. For example, Black & Decker has a Home Depot sales organization and a Lowe's sales organization.

Organizing the sales force around customers can help a company to build closer relationships with important customers. Consider Lear Corporation, one of the largest automotive suppliers in the world.

> Each year, Lear Corporation produces almost $16 billion worth of automotive seating systems, electrical distribution systems, and related automotive electronics products. Its customers include all of the world's leading automotive companies, from Ford, General Motors, Chrysler, Toyota, and Volvo to BMW, Ferrari, Rolls-Royce, and more than a dozen others. Perhaps more than any other part of the organization, it's Lear's outstanding 145-person sales force that brings to life the company's credo, "Consumer driven. Customer focused." Lear salespeople work hard at relationship building and doing what's best for the customer. "Our salespeople don't really close deals," notes a senior marketing executive. "They consult and work with customers to learn exactly what's needed and when."

> Lear organizes its sales force around major customers. More than that, the company itself is broken up into separate divisions dedicated to specific customers. For example, there's a Ford division, a General Motors division, and a Fiat division. This organization lets Lear's sales teams get very close to their customers. In fact, Lear often locates its sales offices in customers' facilities. For instance, the team that handles GM's light truck division works at GM's truck operation campus. "We can't just be there to give quotes and ask for orders," says the marketing executive. "We need to be involved with customers every step of the way—from vehicle concept through launch."[5]

Complex Sales Force Structures. When a company sells a wide variety of products to many types of customers over a broad geographic area, it often combines several types of sales force structures. Salespeople can be specialized by customer and territory, by product and territory, by product and customer, or by territory, product, and customer. No single structure is best for all companies and situations. Each company should select a sales force structure that best serves the needs of its customers and fits its overall marketing strategy.

A good sales structure can mean the difference between success and failure. Companies should periodically review their sales force organizations to be certain that they serve the needs of the company and its customers. Over time, sales force structures can grow complex, inefficient, and unresponsive to customers' needs. This happened recently to technology giant Hewlett-Packard. To correct the problem, the company's new CEO took dramatic steps to restructure HP's corporate sales force (see **Real Marketing 16.1**).

Real Marketing 16.1

Hewlett-Packard Overhauls Its Vast Corporate Sales Force

Imagine this scenario: You need a new digital camera. You're not sure which one to buy or even what features you need. So you visit your nearest electronics superstore to talk with a salesperson. You walk through the camera section but can't find anyone to help you. When you finally find a salesperson, he yawns and tells you that he's responsible for selling all the products in the store, so he doesn't really know all that much about cameras—maybe you should talk to someone else. You finally find a camera-savvy salesperson. However, after answering a few questions, she disappears to handle some other task, handing you off to someone new. And the new salesperson seems to contradict what the first salesperson said, even quoting different prices on a couple of models you like.

As incredible as it seems, at least until recently, this is the kind of situation that many large business buyers faced when they attempted to buy from technology giant Hewlett-Packard. Before Mark Hurd took over as HP's new CEO in spring 2005, the company's revenues and profits had flattened and its stock price had plummeted. To find out why, Hurd first talked directly with 400 corporate customers. Mostly what he heard was gripes about HP's corporate sales force.

Customers complained that they had to deal with too many salespeople, and that HP's confusing management layers made it hard to figure out whom to call. They had trouble tracking down HP sales representatives. And once found, the reps often came across as apathetic, leaving the customer to take the initiative. HP reps were responsible for a broad range of complex products, so they sometimes lacked the needed depth of knowledge on any subset of them. Customers grumbled that they received varying price quotes from different sales reps, and that it often took weeks for reps to respond to seemingly simple requests. In all, HP's corporate customers were frustrated, not a happy circumstance for a company that gets more than 70 percent of its revenues from businesses.

But customers weren't the only ones frustrated by HP's unwieldy and unresponsive sales force structure. HP was organized into

One of CEO Mark Hurd's biggest challenges: Overhauling HP's vast corporate sales force. The new HP sales force structure has reduced salesperson frustration and helped salespeople to create better value for customers.

three main product divisions: the Personal Systems Group (PSG), the Technology Solutions Group (TSG), and the Image and Printing Group (IPG). However, these divisions had little control over the sales process. Instead, HP's corporate sales force was housed in a fourth division, the Customer Sales Group (CSG). All salespeople reported directly to the CSG and were responsible for selling products from all three product divisions. To make matters worse, the CSG was bloated and underperforming. According to one reporter, "of the 17,000 people working in HP's corporate sales, only around 10,000 directly sold to customers. The rest were support staff or in management."

HP division executives were frustrated by the CSG structure. They complained that they had little or no direct control over the salespeople who sold their products. And multiple layers of management slowed sales force decision making and customer responsiveness. Finally, salespeople themselves were frustrated by the structure. They weren't being given the time and support they needed to serve their customers well. Burdened with administrative tasks and bureaucratic red tape, they were spending less than a third of their time with customers. And they had to work through multiple layers of bureaucracy to get price quotes and sample products for customers. "The customer focus was lacking," says an HP sales vice president. "Trying to navigate inside HP was difficult. It was unacceptable."

As CEO Mark Hurd peeled back the layers, it became apparent that HP's organizational

problems went deeper than the sales force. The entire company had become so centralized, with so many layers of management, that it was unresponsive and out of touch with customers. Thus began what one observer called "one of Hurd's biggest management challenges: overhauling HP's vast corporate sales force."

For starters, Hurd eliminated the CSG division, instead assigning salespeople directly to the three product divisions. He also did away with three layers of management and cut hundreds of unproductive sales workers. This move gave divisional marketing and sales executives direct control over a leaner, more efficient sales process, resulting in speedier sales decisions and quicker market response.

Hurd also took steps to reduce salesperson and customer frustrations. Eliminating the CSG meant that each salesperson was responsible for selling a smaller number of products and was able to develop expertise in a specific product area. Hurd urged sales managers to cut back on salesperson administrative requirements and to improve sales support so that salespeople could spend more quality time with customers. As a result, salespeople now spend more than 40 percent of their time with customers, up from just 30 percent last year. And HP salespeople are noticing big changes in the sales support they receive:

Salesman Richard Ditucci began noticing some of the changes late last year. At the time, Ditucci was trying to sell computer servers to Staples. As part of the process,

Continued on next page ▼

Real Marketing 16.1 Continued ▼

Staples had asked him to provide a sample server for the company to evaluate. In the past, such requests typically took two to three weeks to fulfill because of HP's bureaucracy. This time, Ditucci got the server he needed within three days. The quick turnaround helped him win the contract, valued at several million dollars.

To ensure that important customers are carefully tended, HP assigned each salesperson three or fewer accounts. The top 2,000 accounts were assigned just one salesperson—"so they'll always know whom to contact." Customers are noticing differences in the attention that they get from HP salespeople:

James Farris, a senior technology executive at Staples, says HP has freed up its salesman to drop by Staples at least twice a month instead of about once a month as before.

The extra face time has enabled the HP salesman to create more valuable interactions, such as recently arranging a workshop to explain HP's technology to Staples executives. As a result, Farris says he is planning to send more business HP's way. Similarly, Keith Morrow, chief information officer of convenience-store chain 7-Eleven, says his HP sales representative is now "here all the time," and has been more knowledgeable in pitching products tailored to his business. As a result, last October, 7-Eleven began deploying in its U.S. stores 10,000 HP pen pads—a mobile device that helps 7-Eleven workers on the sales floor.

So HP's sales force restructuring appears to be paying off. Since Mr. Hurd's arrival, HP has become a much leaner and more efficient sales organization. Last year, revenues rose 14 percent to $104 billion and profits jumped 17 percent. More importantly, salespeople are happier and more productive, resulting in happier customers, suggesting that more good news is yet to come for the company. CEO Hurd knows that there's still much more work to be done. But step by step, through restructuring, HP is fixing its sales force to create better value for its business customers. Now, if your local electronics superstore would only do the same for you. . . .

Sources: Quotes and adapted examples from Pui-Wing Tam, "System Reboot: Hurd's Big Challenge at HP: Overhauling Corporate Sales," *Wall Street Journal*, April 3, 2006, p. A1. Other information from "HP Restructures, Putting More Assignments In Play," *Adweek*, March 27, 2006, accessed at www.adweek.com; Christopher Hosford, "Rebooting Hewlett-Packard," *Sales & Marketing Management*, July–August 2006, pp. 32–35; Mike McCue, "Solutions that Make a Difference," *Sales & Marketing Management*, October 2007, pp. 19–21; Louise Lee, "HP's Hurd Is About to Be Tested," *BusinessWeek*, February 28, 2008, p. 59; and www.hp.com, accessed November 2008.

Sales Force Size

Once the company has set its structure, it is ready to consider *sales force size*. Sales forces may range in size from only a few salespeople to tens of thousands. ▲Some sales forces are huge—for example, Xerox employs 16,000 U.S. salespeople; American Express, 23,400; PepsiCo, 36,000; and Aflac, 56,000.[6] Salespeople constitute one of the company's most productive—and most expensive—assets. Therefore, increasing their number will increase both sales and costs.

Many companies use some form of *workload approach* to set sales force size. Using this approach, a company first groups accounts into different classes according to size, account status, or other factors related to the amount of effort required to maintain them. It then determines the number of salespeople needed to call on each class of accounts the desired number of times.

The company might think as follows: Suppose we have 1,000 Type-A accounts and 2,000 Type-B accounts. Type-A accounts require 36 calls a year and Type-B accounts require 12 calls a year. In this case, the sales force's *workload*—the number of calls it must make per year—is 60,000 calls [(1,000 × 36) + (2,000 × 12) = 36,000 + 24,000 = 60,000]. Suppose our average salesperson can make 1,000 calls a year. Thus, we need 60 salespeople (60,000 ÷ 1,000).[7]

▲ Some sales forces are huge—for example, Xerox employs 16,000 salespeople; American Express, 23,400; PepsiCo, 36,000; and Aflac, 56,000.

Other Sales Force Strategy and Structure Issues

Sales management must also decide who will be involved in the selling effort and how various sales and sales support people will work together.

Outside and Inside Sales Forces. The company may have an **outside sales force** (or *field sales force*), an **inside sales force**, or both. Outside salespeople travel to call on customers in the field. Inside salespeople conduct business from their offices via telephone, the Internet, or visits from buyers.

Some inside salespeople provide support for the outside sales force, freeing them to spend more time selling to major accounts and finding new prospects. For example,

Outside sales force (or *field sales force*)
Outside salespeople who travel to call on customers in the field.

Inside sales force
Inside salespeople who conduct business from their offices via telephone, the Internet, or visits from prospective buyers.

technical sales support people provide technical information and answers to customers' questions. *Sales assistants* provide administrative backup for outside salespeople. They call ahead and confirm appointments, follow up on deliveries, and answer customers' questions when outside salespeople cannot be reached. Using such combinations of inside and outside salespeople can help to serve important customers better. As one sales manager notes, "You have the support and easy access to the inside rep and the face-to-face relationship building of the outside rep."[8]

Other inside salespeople do more than just provide support. *Telemarketers* and *Web sellers* use the phone and Internet to find new leads and qualify prospects or to sell and service accounts directly. Telemarketing and Web selling can be very effective, less costly ways to sell to smaller, harder-to-reach customers. Depending on the complexity of the product and customer, for example, a telemarketer can make from 20 to 33 decision-maker contacts a day, compared to the average of 4 that an outside salesperson can make. And whereas an average business-to-business field sales call costs $329 or more, a routine industrial telemarketing call costs only about $5 and a complex call about $20.[9]

Although the federal government's Do Not Call Registry put a dent in telephone sales to consumers, telemarketing remains a vital tool for many business-to-business marketers. For some smaller companies, telephone and Web selling may be the primary sales approaches. However, larger companies also use these tactics, either to sell directly to small and midsize customers or to help out with larger ones. For example, Avaya, a $5 billion global telecommunications firm, formed a telemarketing sales force to service its smaller, more routine, less complex accounts. Not only did the telesales force do a better job of selling to these smaller accounts, it freed Avaya's outside salespeople to focus their attention on the company's highest-value customers and prospects. As a result, the company has experienced 40 percent higher sales in areas where the telesales model is being used.[10]

For many types of products and selling situations, phone or Web selling can be as effective as a personal sales call. Notes a DuPont telemarketer: "I'm more effective on the phone. [When you're in the field], if some guy's not in his office, you lose an hour. On the phone, you lose 15 seconds. . . . Through my phone calls, I'm in the field as much as the rep is." There are other advantages. "Customers can't throw things at you," quips the rep, "and you don't have to outrun dogs."[11]

What's more, although they may seem impersonal, the phone and Internet can be surprisingly personal when it comes to building customer relationships. Remember CDW from our chapter-opening story?

> ▲ If you're one of CDW Account Manager Ron Kelly's regular customers, you probably know that he's 35 and has a wife named Michelle, a 9-year-old son named Andrew, and a German shepherd named Bones. You know that he majored in journalism and political science at SIU (that's Southern Illinois University) and was supposed to attend Northwestern's law school, but instead came to work at CDW. You know that he bleeds red and black for the Chicago Blackhawks. You also know that he knows as much, if not more, about you. Kelly, an affable account manager, is a master at relationship-based selling, CDW's specialty. Customers love it. "He's my sales rep, but he's also my friend," says Todd Greenwald, director of operations for Heartland Computers, which sells barcode scanners. "Most of the time we don't even talk about price. I trust Ron."

What's particularly impressive is that, for the most part, the interaction occurs over the phone and Internet. Despite the lack of face time, CDW account managers forge close ties. One customer invited his CDW contact to his wedding. Kelly and Greenwald share Blackhawks season tickets. It's not uncommon to find customers and reps whose partnership has outlasted job changes, budget cuts, and marriages. Of course, the relationships aren't based solely on being likable. They're grounded in helping customers succeed. Account managers

▲ Inside sales force: The phone and Internet can be surprisingly personal in building customer relationships. "He's my business partner," says one CDW customer about her account manager, who manages account relationships almost entirely by phone.

think like the customer and try to anticipate problems. For instance, before storms rocked Florida one summer, some account managers called or e-mailed clients there with battery and backup-storage solutions. "Instead of just sending a purchase order, we want to ask, 'Why are you buying [that product]?' says a CDW executive. "That's how you identify customers' needs." In this way, to their customers, CDW account managers are much more than just peddlers. When asked if she thinks of her CDW rep as a salesperson anymore, one customer replied "Never. He's my business partner." And it all happens over the phone or the Web—both supposedly "arms-length" media.[12]

Team Selling. As products become more complex, and as customers grow larger and more demanding, a single salesperson simply can't handle all of a large customer's needs. Instead, most companies now use **team selling** to service large, complex accounts. Sales teams can unearth problems, solutions, and sales opportunities that no individual salesperson could. Such teams might include experts from any area or level of the selling firm—sales, marketing, technical and support services, R&D, engineering, operations, finance, and others. In team selling situations, the salesperson shifts from "soloist" to "orchestrator."

Team selling
Using teams of people from sales, marketing, engineering, finance, technical support, and even upper management to service large, complex accounts.

In many cases, the move to team selling mirrors similar changes in customers' buying organizations. "Buyers implementing team-based purchasing decisions have necessitated the equal and opposite creation of team-based selling—a completely new way of doing business for many independent, self-motivated salespeople," says a sales force analyst. "Today, we're calling on teams of buying people, and that requires more firepower on our side," agrees one sales vice president. "One salesperson just can't do it all—can't be an expert in everything we're bringing to the customer. We have strategic account teams, led by customer business managers, who basically are our quarterbacks."[13]

Some companies, such as IBM, Xerox, and Procter & Gamble, have used teams for a long time. P&G sales reps are organized into "customer business development (CBD) teams." Each CBD team is assigned to a major P&G customer, such as Wal-Mart, Safeway, or CVS Pharmacy. Teams consist of a customer business development manager, several account executives (each responsible for a specific category of P&G products), and specialists in marketing strategy, operations, information systems, logistics, and finance. This organization places the focus on serving the complete needs of each important customer. It lets P&G "grow business by working as a 'strategic partner' with our accounts, not just as a supplier. Our goal: to grow their business, which also results in growing ours."[14]

Team selling does have some pitfalls. For example, salespeople are by nature competitive and have often been trained and rewarded for outstanding individual performance. Salespeople who are used to having customers all to themselves may have trouble learning to work with and trust others on a team. In addition, selling teams can confuse or overwhelm customers who are used to working with only one salesperson. Finally, difficulties in evaluating individual contributions to the team selling effort can create some sticky compensation issues.

Recruiting and Selecting Salespeople

At the heart of any successful sales force operation is the recruitment and selection of good salespeople. The performance difference between an average salesperson and a top salesperson can be substantial. In a typical sales force, the top 30 percent of the salespeople might bring in 60 percent of the sales. Thus, careful salesperson selection can greatly increase overall sales force performance. Beyond the differences in sales performance, poor selection results in costly turnover. When a salesperson quits, the costs of finding and training a new salesperson—plus the costs of lost sales—can be very high. Also, a sales force with many new people is less productive, and turnover disrupts important customer relationships.

What sets great salespeople apart from all the rest? In an effort to profile top sales performers, Gallup Management Consulting Group, a division of the well-known Gallup polling

▲ Great salespeople: The best salespeople, such as Jennifer Hansen of 3M, possess intrinsic motivation, disciplined work style, the ability to close a sale, and perhaps most important, the ability to build relationships with customers.

organization, has interviewed hundreds of thousands of salespeople. ▲Its research suggests that the best salespeople possess four key talents: intrinsic motivation, disciplined work style, the ability to close a sale, and perhaps most important, the ability to build relationships with customers.[15]

Super salespeople are motivated from within—they have an unrelenting drive to excel. Some salespeople are driven by money, a desire for recognition, or the satisfaction of competing and winning. Others are driven by the desire to provide service and to build relationships. The best salespeople possess some of each of these motivations. They also have a disciplined work style. They lay out detailed, organized plans and then follow through in a timely way.

But motivation and discipline mean little unless they result in closing more sales and building better customer relationships. Super salespeople build the skills and knowledge they need to get the job done. Perhaps most important, top salespeople are excellent customer problem solvers and relationship builders. They understand their customers' needs. Talk to sales executives and they'll describe top performers in these terms: Empathetic. Patient. Caring. Responsive. Good listeners. Top performers can put themselves on the buyer's side of the desk and see the world through their customers' eyes. They don't want just to be liked, they want to add value for their customers.

When recruiting, a company should analyze the sales job itself and the characteristics of its most successful salespeople to identify the traits needed by a successful salesperson in their industry. Then, it must recruit the right salespeople. The human resources department looks for applicants by getting names from current salespeople, using employment agencies, placing classified ads, searching the Web, and working through college placement services. Another source is to attract top salespeople from other companies. Proven salespeople need less training and can be productive immediately.

Recruiting will attract many applicants from whom the company must select the best. The selection procedure can vary from a single informal interview to lengthy testing and interviewing. Many companies give formal tests to sales applicants. Tests typically measure sales aptitude, analytical and organizational skills, personality traits, and other characteristics. But test scores provide only one piece of information in a set that includes personal characteristics, references, past employment history, and interviewer reactions.

Training Salespeople

New salespeople may spend anywhere from a few weeks or months to a year or more in training. Then, most companies provide continuing sales training via seminars, sales meetings, and Web e-learning throughout the salesperson's career. In all, U.S. companies spend more than $7 billion annually on training salespeople. Although training can be expensive, it can also yield dramatic returns. For example, one recent study showed that sales training conducted by a major telecommunications firm paid for itself in 16 days and resulted in a six-month return on investment of 812 percent.[16]

Training programs have several goals. First, salespeople need to know about customers and how to build relationships with them. So the training program must teach them about different types of customers and their needs, buying motives, and buying habits. And it must teach them how to sell effectively and train them in the basics of the selling process. Salespeople also need to know and identify with the company, its products, and its competitors. So an effective training program teaches them about the company's objectives, organization, and chief products and markets, and about the strategies of major competitors.

Today, many companies are adding e-learning to their sales training programs. Most e-learning is Web-based but many companies now offer on-demand training for PDAs, cell phones, and even video iPods. Online and other e-learning approaches cut training costs and make training more efficient. One recent study estimates that companies spend 40 cents of every sales training dollar on travel and lodging. Such costs can be greatly reduced through Web-based training. As a result, last year, companies did 33 percent of their corporate training online, up from 24 percent two years earlier.[17]

Online training may range from simple text-based product information to Internet-based sales exercises that build sales skills to sophisticated simulations that re-create the dynamics of real-life sales calls. ▲International Rectifier, a global manufacturer of power management semiconductors, has learned that using the Internet to train salespeople offers many advantages.

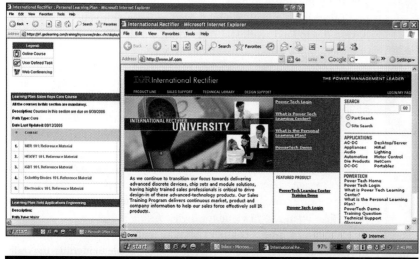

▲ Training salespeople: International Rectifier created the online IR University to help keep its hundreds of global sales reps, internal sales staffers, and others trained on the constant stream of new products it introduces.

To stay competitive in its complex, fast-changing industry, International Rectifier must continually retrain its sales and support people. For example, IR introduces an average of three or more major new products each month. For each new product, the company must coordinate and train hundreds of sales reps, internal sales staffers, field engineers, key executives, and independent inside sales reps across a variety of time zones in 17 locations around the world.

The answer: International Rectifier's online IR University, which provides timely training in advance of new product launches, along with ongoing training on other company and industry developments. The e-learning center provides enhanced presentations, complete with creative animation and streamlined text, to share knowledge accurately but in a way that excites and captures attention. The center also allows for "real-time" visual and audio communications with the presenter via live chat and conference calls. Beyond learning about new products, salespeople can refresh their memories and sharpen their knowledge on almost any topic before meeting with customers. And evaluation diagnostics help sales managers to identify the skill and knowledge levels of each individual salesperson for ongoing support and training.

The sales force is thrilled about being able to "attend" training sessions at times convenient for them, without leaving their home offices. And online training results in significant cost savings. Approximately 500 IR sales and support people have completed more than 5,500 online courses during the past nine months. The cost? Just an estimated $12 per trainee per course. Compared to the costs associated with onsite training, the online learning system has saved the company approximately $250,000 during the past year. In all, online training has reduced IR's training costs by 75 percent.[18]

Compensating Salespeople

To attract good salespeople, a company must have an appealing compensation plan. Compensation is made up of several elements—a fixed amount, a variable amount, expenses, and fringe benefits. The fixed amount, usually a salary, gives the salesperson some stable income. The variable amount, which might be commissions or bonuses based on sales performance, rewards the salesperson for greater effort and success.

Management must decide what *mix* of these compensation elements makes the most sense for each sales job. Different combinations of fixed and variable compensation give rise to four basic types of compensation plans—straight salary, straight commission, salary plus bonus, and salary plus commission. A recent study of sales force compensation showed that the average salesperson's pay consists of about 67 percent salary and 33 percent incentive pay.[19]

The sales force compensation plan can both motivate salespeople and direct their activities. Compensation should direct salespeople toward activities that are consistent with overall sales force and marketing objectives. For example, if the strategy is to acquire new business, grow rapidly, and gain market share, the compensation plan might include a larger commission component, coupled with a new-account bonus to encourage high sales performance and new-account development. In contrast, if the goal is to maximize current account profitability, the compensation plan might contain a larger base-salary component with additional incentives for current account sales or customer satisfaction.

In fact, more and more companies are moving away from high commission plans that may drive salespeople to make short-term grabs for business. They worry that a salesperson who is pushing too hard to close a deal may ruin the customer relationship. Instead, companies are designing compensation plans that reward salespeople for building customer relationships and growing the long-run value of each customer.

Supervising and Motivating Salespeople

New salespeople need more than a territory, compensation, and training—they need supervision and motivation. The goal of *supervision* is to help salespeople "work smart" by doing the right things in the right ways. The goal of *motivation* is to encourage salespeople to "work hard" and energetically toward sales force goals. If salespeople work smart and work hard, they will realize their full potential, to their own and the company's benefit.

Supervising Salespeople

Companies vary in how closely they supervise their salespeople. Many help their salespeople to identify target customers and set call norms. Some may also specify how much time the sales force should spend prospecting for new accounts and set other time management priorities. One tool is the weekly, monthly, or annual *call plan* that shows which customers and prospects to call on and which activities to carry out. Another tool is *time-and-duty analysis*. In addition to time spent selling, the salesperson spends time traveling, waiting, taking breaks, and doing administrative chores.

Figure 16.2 shows how salespeople spend their time. On average, active selling time accounts for only 10 percent of total working time! If selling time could be raised from 10 percent to 30 percent, this would triple the time spent selling.[20] Companies always are looking for ways to save time—simplifying administrative duties, developing better sales-call and routing plans, supplying more and better customer information, and using phones, e-mail, or video conferencing instead of traveling. Consider the changes GE made to increase its sales force's face-to-face selling time.[21]

When Jeff Immelt became General Electric's new chairman, he was dismayed to find that members of the sales team were spending far more time on deskbound administrative chores than in face-to-face meetings with customers and prospects. "He said

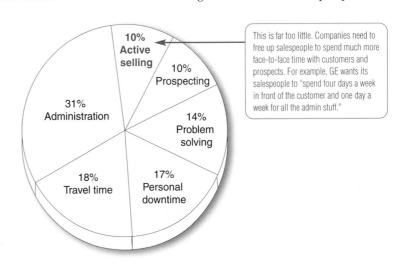

FIGURE | 16.2
How Salespeople Spend
Their Time
Source: Proudfoot Consulting. Data used with permission

we needed to turn that around," recalls Venki Rao, an IT leader in global sales and marketing at GE Power Systems, a division focused on energy systems and products. "[We need] to spend four days a week in front of the customer and one day for all the admin stuff." GE Power's salespeople spent much of their time at their desks because they had to go to many sources for the information needed to sell multimillion-dollar turbines, turbine parts, and services to energy companies worldwide. To fix the problem, GE created a new sales portal, a kind of "one-stop shop" for just about everything they need. The sales portal connects the vast array of existing GE databases, providing everything from sales tracking and customer data to parts pricing and information on planned outages. GE also added external data, such as news feeds. "Before, you were randomly searching for things," says Bill Snook, a GE sales manager. Now, he says, "I have the sales portal as my home page, and I use it as the gateway to all the applications that I have." The sales portal has freed Snook and 2,500 other users around the globe from once time-consuming administrative tasks, greatly increasing their face time with customers.

Many firms have adopted *sales force automation systems*—computerized, digitized sales force operations that let salespeople work more effectively anytime, anywhere. ▲Companies now routinely equip their salespeople with technologies such as laptops, smart phones, wireless Web connections, Webcams for videoconferencing, and customer-contact and relationship management software. Armed with these technologies, salespeople can more effectively and efficiently profile customers and prospects, analyze and forecast sales, schedule sales calls, make presentations, prepare sales and expense reports, and manage account relationships. The result is better time management, improved customer service, lower sales costs, and higher sales performance.[22]

▲ Sales force automation: Many sales forces have gone high tech, equipping salespeople with everything from smart phones, wireless Web connections, and videoconferencing tools to customer-contact and relationship management software that helps them to be more effective and efficient.

Selling and the Internet

Perhaps the fastest-growing technology tool is the Internet. The Internet offers explosive potential for conducting sales operations and for interacting with and serving customers. More and more companies are now using the Internet to support their personal selling efforts—not just for selling but for everything from training salespeople to conducting sales meetings and servicing accounts.

Sales organizations around the world are now saving money and time by using a host of Web approaches to train reps, hold sales meetings, and even conduct live sales presentations. The Web can be a good tool for selling to hard-to-reach customers. For example, consider the U.S. pharmaceuticals industry:[23]

The big U.S. pharmaceutical companies currently employ some 87,000 sales reps (often called "detailers") to reach roughly 600,000 practicing physicians. However, these reps are finding it harder than ever to get through to the busy doctors. "Doctors need immense amounts of medical information, but their patient loads limit their ability to see pharmaceutical reps or attend outside conferences," says an industry researcher. As a result, the average call lasts only 4.6 minutes and only 24 percent of sales calls on doctors result in quality, two-way discussions. The answer: Increasingly, it's the Web. The pharmaceutical companies now regularly use product Web sites, e-mail marketing, and video conferencing to help reps deliver useful information to physicians on their home or office PCs. One study found that last year more than 200,000 physicians participated in "e-detailing"—the process of receiving drug marketing information via the Web—a 400 percent jump in only three years.

More than 20 percent have now substituted e-detailing for face-to-face meetings with reps entirely. Using direct-to-doctor Web conferences, pharmaceuticals reps can make live, interactive medical sales presentations to any physician with a PC and Web access, saving both the customer's and the rep's time.

Web-based technologies can produce big organizational benefits for sales forces. They help conserve salespeople's valuable time, save travel dollars, and give salespeople a new vehicle for selling and servicing accounts. But the technologies also have some drawbacks. For starters, they're not cheap. And such systems can intimidate low-tech salespeople or clients. What's more, Web tools are susceptible to server crashes and other network difficulties, not a happy event when you're in the midst of an important sales meeting or presentation. Finally, there are some things you just can't do or teach via the Web, things that require personal interactions.

For these reasons, some high-tech experts recommend that sales executives use Web technologies to supplement training, sales meetings, and preliminary client sales presentations, but resort to old-fashioned, face-to-face meetings when the time draws near to close the deal.

Motivating Salespeople

Beyond directing salespeople, sales managers must also motivate them. Some salespeople will do their best without any special urging from management. To them, selling may be the most fascinating job in the world. But selling can also be frustrating. Salespeople often work alone and they must sometimes travel away from home. They may face aggressive competing salespeople and difficult customers. Therefore, salespeople often need special encouragement to do their best.

Management can boost sales force morale and performance through its organizational climate, sales quotas, and positive incentives. *Organizational climate* describes the feeling that salespeople have about their opportunities, value, and rewards for a good performance. Some companies treat salespeople as if they are not very important and performance suffers accordingly. Other companies treat their salespeople as valued contributors and allow virtually unlimited opportunity for income and promotion. Not surprisingly, these companies enjoy higher sales force performance and less turnover.

Sales quota

A standard that states the amount a salesperson should sell and how sales should be divided among the company's products.

Many companies motivate their salespeople by setting **sales quotas**—standards stating the amount they should sell and how sales should be divided among the company's products. Compensation is often related to how well salespeople meet their quotas. Companies also use various *positive incentives* to increase sales force effort. *Sales meetings* provide social occasions, breaks from routine, chances to meet and talk with "company brass," and opportunities to air feelings and to identify with a larger group. Companies also sponsor *sales contests* to spur the sales force to make a selling effort above what would normally be expected. Other incentives include honors, merchandise and cash awards, trips, and profit-sharing plans.

Evaluating Salespeople and Sales-Force Performance

We have thus far described how management communicates what salespeople should be doing and how it motivates them to do it. This process requires good feedback. And good feedback means getting regular information about salespeople to evaluate their performance.

Management gets information about its salespeople in several ways. The most important source is *sales reports,* including weekly or monthly work plans and longer-term territory marketing plans. Salespeople also write up their completed activities on *call reports* and turn in *expense reports* for which they are partly or wholly repaid. The company can also monitor the sales and profit performance data in the salesperson's territory. Additional information comes from personal observation, customer surveys, and talks with other salespeople.

Using various sales force reports and other information, sales management evaluates members of the sales force. It evaluates salespeople on their ability to "plan their work and work their plan." Formal evaluation forces management to develop and communicate clear standards for judging performance. It also provides salespeople with constructive feedback and motivates them to perform well.

On a broader level, management should evaluate the performance of the sales force as a whole. Is the sales force accomplishing its customer relationship, sales, and profit objectives? Is it working well with other areas of the marketing and company organization? Are sales-force costs in line with outcomes? As with other marketing activities, the company wants to measure its *return on sales investment*.

<table>
<tr><td>**Author Comment**</td><td>So far, we've examined how sales management develops and implements overall sales force strategies and programs. In this section, we'll look at how individual salespeople and sales teams sell to customers and build relationships with them.</td></tr>
</table>

The Personal Selling Process (pp 472–475)

We now turn from designing and managing a sales force to the actual personal selling process. The **selling process** consists of several steps that the salesperson must master. These steps focus on the goal of getting new customers and obtaining orders from them. However, most salespeople spend much of their time maintaining existing accounts and building long-term customer *relationships*. We discuss the relationship aspect of the personal selling process in a later section.

Steps in the Selling Process

As shown in ● **Figure 16.3**, the selling process consists of seven steps: prospecting and qualifying, preapproach, approach, presentation and demonstration, handling objections, closing, and follow-up.

Selling process
The steps that the salesperson follows when selling, which include prospecting and qualifying, preapproach, approach, presentation and demonstration, handling objections, closing, and follow-up.

Prospecting and Qualifying

The first step in the selling process is **prospecting**—identifying qualified potential customers. Approaching the right potential customers is crucial to selling success. As one sales expert puts it, "If the sales force starts chasing anyone who is breathing and seems to have a budget, you risk accumulating a roster of expensive-to-serve, hard-to-satisfy customers who never respond to whatever value proposition you have." He continues, "The solution to this isn't rocket science. [You must] train salespeople to actively scout the right prospects." Another expert concludes, "Increasing your prospecting effectiveness is the fastest single way to boost your sales."[24]

Prospecting
The step in the selling process in which the salesperson or company identifies qualified potential customers.

The salesperson must often approach many prospects to get just a few sales. Although the company supplies some leads, salespeople need skill in finding their own. The best source is referrals. Salespeople can ask current customers for referrals and cultivate other referral sources, such as suppliers, dealers, noncompeting salespeople, and bankers. They can also search for prospects in directories or on the Web and track down leads using the telephone and direct-mail. Or they can drop in unannounced on various offices (a practice known as "cold calling").

Salespeople also need to know how to *qualify* leads—that is, how to identify the good ones and screen out the poor ones. Prospects can be qualified by looking at their financial ability, volume of business, special needs, location, and possibilities for growth.

● **FIGURE** | **16.3**
Steps in the Selling Process

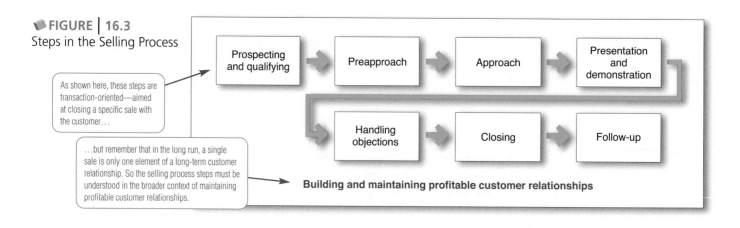

As shown here, these steps are transaction-oriented—aimed at closing a specific sale with the customer...

...but remember that in the long run, a single sale is only one element of a long-term customer relationship. So the selling process steps must be understood in the broader context of maintaining profitable customer relationships.

Building and maintaining profitable customer relationships

Preapproach

Preapproach
The step in the selling process in which the salesperson learns as much as possible about a prospective customer before making a sales call.

Before calling on a prospect, the salesperson should learn as much as possible about the organization (what it needs, who is involved in the buying) and its buyers (their characteristics and buying styles). This step is known as the **preapproach**. "Revving up your sales starts with your preparation," says one sales consultant. "A successful sale begins long before you set foot in the prospect's office." Preapproach begins with good research. The salesperson can consult standard industry and online sources, acquaintances, and others to learn about the company. Then, the salesperson must apply the research to develop a customer strategy. "Being able to recite the prospect's product line in your sleep isn't enough," says the consultant. "You need to translate the data into something useful for your client."[25]

The salesperson should set *call objectives*, which may be to qualify the prospect, to gather information, or to make an immediate sale. Another task is to decide on the best approach, which might be a personal visit, a phone call, or a letter or e-mail. The best timing should be considered carefully because many prospects are busiest at certain times. Finally, the salesperson should give thought to an overall sales strategy for the account.

Approach

Approach
The step in the selling process in which the salesperson meets the customer for the first time.

During the **approach** step, the salesperson should know how to meet and greet the buyer and get the relationship off to a good start. This step involves the salesperson's appearance, opening lines, and the follow-up remarks. The opening lines should be positive to build goodwill from the beginning of the relationship. This opening might be followed by some key questions to learn more about the customer's needs or by showing a display or sample to attract the buyer's attention and curiosity. As in all stages of the selling process, listening to the customer is crucial.

Presentation and Demonstration

Presentation
The step in the selling process in which the salesperson tells the "value story" to the buyer, showing how the company's offer solves the customer's problems.

During the **presentation** step of the selling process, the salesperson tells the "value story" to the buyer, showing how the company's offer solves the customer's problems. The *customer-solution approach* fits better with today's relationship marketing focus than does a hard-sell or glad-handing approach. Buyers today want answers, not smiles; results, not razzle-dazzle. Moreover, they don't want just products—they want to know how those products will add value to their businesses. They want salespeople who listen to their concerns, understand their needs, and respond with the right products and services.

But before salespeople can *present* customer solutions, they must *develop* solutions to present. Many companies now train their salespeople to go beyond "product thinking." ▲Weyerhaeuser, the $21 billion U.S. forest products company, reorganized its entire sales force around customer-solutions selling:

Weyerhaeuser, long a product-driven company, undertook an extreme makeover, creating a customer-solutions-focused sales organization called iLevel. Rather than selling wood products piecemeal, Weyerhaeuser wants to be considered the one-stop location for all of the innovation and products required to construct residential home frames—joists, beams, floors and all. The new iLevel organization assigns a single salesperson to each major builder or dealer. The sales rep leads a coordinated sales team that serves all of the customer's needs. To implement iLevel, Weyerhaeuser retrained its 250 salespeople to present customers with solutions, not products. "It is a consultative selling approach," says a Weyerhaeuser executive. Never again will salespeople merely sell orders of lumber. "What we want [our sales reps] to do is help our customers find solutions that make them [and us] money."[26]

▲ Weyerhaeuser created a customer-solutions-focused sales organization called iLevel. It promises customers "a coordinated sales team that gives you access to all the products, logistics, tech services, and software you need [to] quickly resolve issues."

The solutions approach calls for good listening and problem-solving skills. One study revealed that 74 percent of 200 purchasers surveyed at companies nationwide said they would be much more likely to buy from a salesperson if the seller would simply listen to them. Says one experienced salesperson, "That typecast chatty character may be the kind of person who's most often drawn to sales, but it's not often the one who's most successful at it. Unless you listen to what your customer is saying, you won't understand his deeper wants and needs. And you'll find that the more you listen to others, the more they'll listen to you. As the old saying goes, 'God gave us two ears and only one mouth, to use in that proportion.'"[27]

The qualities that buyers *dislike most* in salespeople include being pushy, late, deceitful, and unprepared or disorganized. The qualities they *value most* include good listening, empathy, honesty, dependability, thoroughness, and follow-through. Great salespeople know how to sell, but more importantly they know how to listen and to build strong customer relationships. Says one professional, "Salespeople must have the right answers, certainly, but they also have to learn how to ask those questions and listen."[28]

Finally, salespeople must also plan their presentation methods. Good interpersonal communication skills count when it comes to making effective sales presentations. However, today's media-rich and cluttered communications environment presents many new challenges for sales presenters:[29]

The goal of a sales presentation is to deliver a clear, concise, and consistent message to your prospects about your product and your brand, as well as why you are better than the competition. Doing that and keeping your audience's attention for longer than 30 minutes is the real challenge. Today's information-overloaded prospects demand a richer presentation experience. And sales presenters must now overcome multiple distractions from cell phones, text messaging, and portable Internet viewers during a presentation. Sales presentations today take creativity, careful planning, and the application of the hottest technologies available. You can't fill your prospects' heads with unnecessary, useless information, and you have to capture their interest fast or risk losing them forever. So you must deliver your message in a more engaging and compelling way than your competition does, and you must deliver more information in less time.

▲ Presentation technology: Today's salespeople are employing advanced presentation technologies that allow for full multimedia presentations—in person, online, or both.

Thus, ▲today's salespeople are employing advanced presentation technologies that allow for full multimedia presentations to only one or a few people. The venerable old flip chart has been replaced by CDs and DVDs, online presentation technologies, interactive white boards, and handheld and laptop computers with sophisticated presentation software.

Handling Objections

Handling objections
The step in the selling process in which the salesperson seeks out, clarifies, and overcomes customer objections to buying.

Customers almost always have objections during the presentation or when asked to place an order. The problem can be either logical or psychological, and objections are often unspoken. In **handling objections**, the salesperson should use a positive approach, seek out hidden objections, ask the buyer to clarify any objections, take objections as opportunities to provide more information, and turn the objections into reasons for buying. Every salesperson needs training in the skills of handling objections.

Closing

Closing
The step in the selling process in which the salesperson asks the customer for an order.

After handling the prospect's objections, the salesperson now tries to close the sale. Some salespeople do not get around to **closing** or do not handle it well. They may lack confidence, feel guilty about asking for the order, or fail to recognize the right moment to close the sale. Salespeople should know how to recognize closing signals from the buyer, including physical actions, comments, and questions. For example, the customer might sit forward and nod approvingly or ask about prices and credit terms.

Salespeople can use one of several closing techniques. They can ask for the order, review points of agreement, offer to help write up the order, ask whether the buyer wants this model or that one, or note that the buyer will lose out if the order is not placed now. The salesperson may offer the buyer special reasons to close, such as a lower price or an extra quantity at no charge.

Follow-Up

Follow-up

The last step in the selling process in which the salesperson follows up after the sale to ensure customer satisfaction and repeat business.

The last step in the selling process—**follow-up**—is necessary if the salesperson wants to ensure customer satisfaction and repeat business. Right after closing, the salesperson should complete any details on delivery time, purchase terms, and other matters. The salesperson then should schedule a follow-up call when the initial order is received to make sure there is proper installation, instruction, and servicing. This visit would reveal any problems, assure the buyer of the salesperson's interest, and reduce any buyer concerns that might have arisen since the sale.

Personal Selling and Managing Customer Relationships

The steps in the selling process as just described are *transaction oriented*—their aim is to help salespeople close a specific sale with a customer. But in most cases, the company is not simply seeking a sale: It has targeted a major customer that it would like to win and keep. The company would like to show that it has the capabilities to serve the customer over the long haul in a mutually profitable *relationship*. The sales force usually plays an important role in building and managing profitable customer relationships. Thus, as shown in Figure 16.3, the selling process must be understood in the context of building and maintaining profitable customer relationships.

Today's large customers favor suppliers who can sell and deliver a coordinated set of products and services to many locations, and who can work closely with customer teams to improve products and processes. For these customers, the first sale is only the beginning of the relationship. Unfortunately, some companies ignore these relationship realities. They sell their products through separate sales forces, each working independently to close sales. Their technical people may not be willing to lend time to educate a customer. Their engineering, design, and manufacturing people may have the attitude that "it's our job to make good products and the salesperson's to sell them to customers." Their salespeople focus on pushing products toward customers rather than listening to customers and providing solutions.

Other companies, however, recognize that winning and keeping accounts requires more than making good products and directing the sales force to close lots of sales. If the company wishes only to close sales and capture short-term business, it can do this by simply slashing its prices to meet or beat those of competitors. Instead, most companies want their salespeople to practice value selling—demonstrating and delivering superior customer value and capturing a return on that value that's fair for both the customer and the company (see **Real Marketing 16.2**). Value selling requires listening to customers, understanding their needs, and carefully coordinating the whole company's efforts to create lasting relationships based on customer value.

Author Comment | Sales promotion is the most short-term of the promotion mix tools. Whereas advertising or personal selling says "buy," sales promotions says "by now."

Sales Promotion (pp 475–482)

Personal selling and advertising often work closely with another promotion tool, sales promotion. **Sales promotion** consists of short-term incentives to encourage purchase or sales of a product or service. Whereas advertising offers reasons to buy a product or service, sales promotion offers reasons to buy *now*.

Sales promotion

Short-term incentives to encourage the purchase or sale of a product or service.

▲ Examples of sales promotions are found everywhere. A freestanding insert in the Sunday newspaper contains a coupon offering $1 off Folgers coffee. An e-mail from

Real Marketing 16.2

Value-Selling: Value Merchants versus Value Spendthrifts

It's the company's job to create a compelling value proposition for customers. Then, it's the salesperson's job to build profitable customer relationships based on that value proposition. Unfortunately, in the heat of closing sales, salespeople too often take the easy way out by cutting prices rather than selling value. It's usually much easier to win a sale by matching competitors' lower prices than by working to convince a customer that your product's greater value justifies its higher price.

In their book *Value Merchants: Demonstrating and Documenting Superior Value in Business Markets*, three marketing professors define two types of salespeople: *value spendthrifts* and *value merchants*. Value spendthrifts give value away, emphasizing low prices while getting little from customers in return. By contrast, value merchants emphasize customer value. They recognize the value that the company's offer gives the customer and work to obtain a return on that value that's fair for both the customer and company. Rather than simply dropping prices to get or keep short-term sales, value-merchant salespeople document and demonstrate superior value in order to capture a customer's long-term business.

How can a company tell whether it has value spendthrift or value merchant salespeople? The following table compares the behaviors of the two salesperson types. For example, value spendthrifts prefer to give quick price concessions in order to close deals; value merchants "hang tough" in negotiations to capture profits in line with the value their market offering provides. Value spendthrifts complain to the company that its prices are too high, keeping them from winning a customer's business; value merchants explain that they need more proof of superior customer value in order to win a customer's business. Value-spendthrift salespeople give services away for free to close a deal, whereas value merchant-salespeople employ services strategically to generate additional business.

The challenge for sales managers is to transform value spendthrifts into value merchants. Compensation plays an important role. To encourage salespeople to seek return on value rather than simply cutting price to gain or retain business, the sales compensation plan should reward value-selling behaviors and profitable outcomes rather than just short-term sales outcomes. Beyond compensation, management must install a value-selling process—one that starts with communicating the company's value proposition and ends with measures of actual value delivered. Finally, the company must equip salespeople with specific value-selling tools that they can use to forcefully demonstrate the value of the firm's offerings to target customers. These tools include value data, value calculators, and value case histories that provide evidence to customers about value gained versus competitors.

Here are examples of two companies that have applied value-merchant thinking to transform their salespeople from customer advocates for price cuts into company advocates for value provided.

Applied Industrial Technologies. Bearings and industrial supplies reseller Applied Industrial Technologies has implemented a Documented Value Added (DVA) program, which requires salespeople to prepare formal DVA reports in which they record all of their efforts to provide value for individual customers. Importantly, customer managers must sign off on these reports, confirming that the value claimed has actually been delivered. Since its inception, the DVA program has documented more than $1 billion in savings for Applied's customers.

Applied salespeople use DVA as an integral part of their everyday selling activities in a number of ways. They use DVA reports to build customer loyalty and gain future sales. DVA enables the salesperson to

Value-Merchant versus Value-Spendthrift Salespeople	
Value Spendthrifts	**Value Merchants**
• Prefer to give quick price concessions to close deals and move on to other business	• "Hang tough" in the negotiations to gain better profitability out of each deal based on customer value
• Give price concessions without changes in the market offering	• Only give price concessions in exchange for cost-saving reductions in the market offering
• Routinely trade more business for lower prices	• Routinely gain more business at the same price
• Give services away for free to close a deal	• Strategically employ services to generate additional business
• Sell primarily on price comparisons with competitors	• Sell primarily on cost of ownership comparisons versus competitors
• Complain to the company that its prices are too high	• Explain to the company that they need more proof of superior value
• Believe management pursues a volume-driven strategy	• Believe management pursues a value-driven strategy
• Tell the company that customers are only interested in price	• Provide customer insights to improve the value of the company's offerings
• Make token, unsupported claims about superior value to customers	• Demonstrate and document claims about superior value in monetary terms to customers
• Focus on revenue and volume components of their compensation plan	• Concentrate on gross margins and profitability component of their compensation plan

Real Marketing 16.2 Continued ▼

make compelling statements to a customer, such as "Last year, the $200,000 worth of products you purchased from Applied gained you more than $85,000 in documented cost savings." Applied's salespeople report that such statements not only take the sting out of a 3 percent to 4 percent price increase, they also enable the reps to capture a sale even when competitors have undercut Applied's prices. The DVA program itself even adds value for customers. It provides customer purchasing managers with documentation that shows their managers how they have met their firm's cost reduction goals. Thus, the DVA program helps Applied's salespeople to build profitable relationships with buyers based on mutual benefit.

Rockwell Automation. Facing considerable pressure from Wal-Mart to lower its prices, a condiment producer hastily summoned several competing supplier representatives—including Rockwell Automation sales rep Jeff Policicchio—to participate in a "Continuous Improvement Conference" at one of its major plant sites. Policicchio and the competing sales

reps were given full access to the plant for one day and asked to find ways to dramatically reduce the customer's operating costs. From discussions with plant personnel, Policicchio quickly learned that a major problem stemmed from lost production and down time due to poorly performing pumps on 32 huge condiment tanks. Policicchio gathered relevant cost and usage data. Then, he used a Rockwell Automation laptop value-assessment tool to analyze the data, find potential cost savings, and construct the best pump solution for the customer.

The next day, Policicchio and the competing reps presented their solutions to plant management. Policicchio offered this specific value proposition: "With this Rockwell Automation pump solution, through the elimination of downtime, reduced administrative costs associated with procurement, and lower spending on repair parts, your company will save at least $16,268 per

pump—on up to 32 pumps—relative to our best competitor's solution." Soon after the presentations, Policicchio learned that he was the only rep to demonstrate tangible cost savings for his proposed solution. Everyone else made fuzzy promises about possible benefits, and many competing reps offered to save the customer money by simply shaving their prices.

The plant managers were so impressed with Policicchio's value proposition that—despite its higher initial price—they immediately purchased one Rockwell Automation pump solution for a trial. When they discovered that the actual savings were even better than predicted, they placed orders for the remaining pumps, which will be installed as the existing pumps wear out. Thus, Policicchio's value-selling approach not only landed the initial sale but also provided the basis for a profitable long-term relationship with the customer.

Sources: The examples and table are adapted from James C. Anderson, Nirmalya Kumar, and James A. Narus, "Be a Value Merchant," *Sales & Marketing Management,* May 6, 2008; and "Business Market Value Merchants," *Marketing Management,* March/April 2008, pp. 31+. They can also be found in Anderson, Kumar, and Narus, *Value Merchants: Demonstrating and Documenting Superior Value in Business Markets* (Boston: Harvard Business School Press, 2007).

EddieBauer.com offers free shipping on your next purchase over $100. The end-of-the-aisle display in the local supermarket tempts impulse buyers with a wall of Coke cases. An executive buys a new Sony laptop and gets a free carrying case, or a family buys a new Ford Escape and receives a factory rebate of $1,000. A hardware store chain receives a 10 percent discount on selected Black & Decker portable power tools if it agrees to advertise them in local newspapers. Sales promotion includes a wide variety of promotion tools designed to stimulate earlier or stronger market response.

Rapid Growth of Sales Promotion

Sales promotion tools are used by most organizations, including manufacturers, distributors, retailers, and not-for-profit institutions. They are targeted toward final buyers (*consumer promotions*), retailers and wholesalers (*trade promotions*), business customers (*business promotions*), and members of the sales force (*sales force promotions*). Today, in the average consumer packaged-goods company, sales promotion accounts for 74 percent of all marketing expenditures.[30]

Several factors have contributed to the rapid growth of sales promotion, particularly in consumer markets. First, inside the company, product managers face greater pressures to increase their current sales, and promotion is viewed as an effective short-run sales tool. Second,

▲ Sales promotions are found everywhere. For example, your Sunday newspaper is loaded with freestanding inserts that promote strong and immediate market response.

externally, the company faces more competition and competing brands are less differentiated. Increasingly, competitors are using sales promotion to help differentiate their offers. Third, advertising efficiency has declined because of rising costs, media clutter, and legal restraints. Finally, consumers have become more deal oriented, and ever-larger retailers are demanding more deals from manufacturers.

The growing use of sales promotion has resulted in *promotion clutter*, similar to advertising clutter. Consumers are increasingly tuning out promotions, weakening their ability to trigger immediate purchase. Manufacturers are now searching for ways to rise above the clutter, such as offering larger coupon values, creating more dramatic point-of-purchase displays, or delivering promotions through new interactive media, such as the Internet or cell phones.

In developing a sales promotion program, a company must first set sales promotion objectives and then select the best tools for accomplishing these objectives.

Sales Promotion Objectives

Sales promotion objectives vary widely. Sellers may use *consumer promotions* to urge short-term customer buying or to enhance customer brand involvement. Objectives for *trade promotions* include getting retailers to carry new items and more inventory, buy ahead, or promote the company's products and give them more shelf space. For the *sales force*, objectives include getting more sales force support for current or new products or getting salespeople to sign up new accounts.

Sales promotions are usually used together with advertising, personal selling, direct marketing, or other promotion mix tools. Consumer promotions must usually be advertised and can add excitement and pulling power to ads. Trade and sales force promotions support the firm's personal selling process.

In general, rather than creating only short-term sales or temporary brand switching, sales promotions should help to reinforce the product's position and build long-term *customer relationships*. If properly designed, every sales promotion tool has the potential to build both short-term excitement and long-term consumer relationships. Increasingly, marketers are avoiding "quick fix," price-only promotions in favor of promotions designed to build brand equity.

Examples include all of the "frequency marketing programs" and loyalty clubs that have mushroomed in recent years. Most hotels, supermarkets, and airlines offer frequent-guest/buyer/flyer programs giving rewards to regular customers. ▲All kinds of companies offer rewards programs, even *The Washington Post*:[31]

▲ Customer-relationship building programs: The *Washington Post's* PostPoints rewards program strengthens the three-way relationship between the newspaper, its customers, and its advertisers.

Washington Post readers can now opt to join the newspaper's new PostPoints rewards program, designed to boost reader involvement and advertiser support. Home-delivery and online customers earn PostPoints by reading and interacting with Post columns and features, supplying information about themselves and their interests, or even by helping the community through activities such as giving blood or participating in charity fundraising events. They can also earn points by shopping at partnering retail stores—called PostPoints Spots. These retail partners are limited to *Washington Post* advertisers. Once earned, PostPoints can be redeemed for everything from gift cards, merchandise, and event tickets to major appliances and dream trips. Other benefits of membership include invitations to exclusive PostPoints partner events and meet and greets with *Washington Post* writers. In all, the PostPoints loyalty program strengthens the three-way relationship between the newspaper, its customers, and its advertisers. "The innovation is in . . . how this approach relates to [both] customers and advertisers," says a marketing executive at CVS Pharmacy, a PostPoints partner with over 300 stores in the Washington, D.C., area. "It's a new dialogue based on community ties and trust."

Major Sales Promotion Tools

Many tools can be used to accomplish sales promotion objectives. Descriptions of the main consumer, trade, and business promotion tools follow.

Consumer Promotions

Consumer promotions

Sales promotion tools used to boost short-term customer buying and involvement or to enhance long-term customer relationships.

The **consumer promotions** include a wide range of tools—from samples, coupons, refunds, premiums, and point-of-purchase displays to contests, sweepstakes, and event sponsorships.

Samples are offers of a trial amount of a product. Sampling is the most effective—but most expensive—way to introduce a new product or to create new excitement for an existing one. Some samples are free; for others, the company charges a small amount to offset its cost. The sample might be delivered door-to-door, sent by mail, handed out in a store or kiosk, attached to another product, or featured in an ad. Sometimes, samples are combined into sample packs, which can then be used to promote other products and services. Sampling can be a powerful promotional tool.

Coupons are certificates that give buyers a saving when they purchase specified products. Most consumers love coupons. U.S. package-goods companies distributed more than 286 billion coupons last year with an average face value of over $1.25. Consumers redeemed more than 2.6 billion of them for a total savings of about $3.25 billion.[32] Coupons can promote early trial of a new brand or stimulate sales of a mature brand. However, as a result of coupon clutter, redemption rates have been declining in recent years. Thus, most major consumer-goods companies are issuing fewer coupons and targeting them more carefully.

Marketers are also cultivating new outlets for distributing coupons, such as supermarket shelf dispensers, electronic point-of-sale coupon printers, e-mail and online media, or even mobile text-messaging systems. Mobile couponing is very popular in Europe, India, and Japan, and it's now gaining popularity in the United States. ▲For example, consider Cellfire, a mobile couponing company in California:[33]

Cellfire (cellfire.com) distributes digital coupons to the cell phones of consumers nationwide who sign up for its free service. Cellfire's growing list of clients ranges from Domino's Pizza, T.G.I. Friday's, and Hardee's and Carl's Jr. restaurants to Kimberly-Clark, Supercuts, Hollywood Video, 1-800-FLOWERS.COM, and Enterprise Rent-A-Car. Cellfire sends an ever-changing assortment of digital coupons to users' cell phones. To use the coupons, users simply call up the stored coupon list, navigate to the coupon they want, press the "Use Now" button, and show the digital coupon to the store cashier. Domino's even permits consumers holding the mobile coupons to simply click on a link to have their cell phones dial the nearest Domino's store to place an order. To date, Cellfire users have redeemed more than $28 million in coupon savings.

Coupons distributed through Cellfire offer distinct advantages to both consumers and marketers. Consumers don't have to find and clip paper coupons or print out Web coupons and

▲ New forms of coupons: Cellfire distributes digital coupons to the cell phones of consumers who sign up for its free service.

bring them along when they shop. They always have their cell phone coupons with them. For marketers, mobile coupons allow more careful targeting and eliminate the costs of printing and distributing paper coupons. "We don't pay for distribution of digital coupons," says one client. "We pay on redemptions." And the redemption rates can be dazzling. According to Cellfire's chief executive, "We're seeing redemption rates as high as 10 to 15 percent, while the industry average paper response is . . . less than 1 percent."

Cash refunds (or *rebates*) are like coupons except that the price reduction occurs after the purchase rather than at the retail outlet. The consumer sends a "proof of purchase" to the manufacturer, who then refunds part of the purchase price by mail. For example, Toro ran a clever preseason promotion on some of its snowblower models, offering a rebate if the snowfall in the buyer's market area turned out to be below average. Competitors were not able to match this offer on such short notice, and the promotion was very successful.

Price packs (also called *cents-off deals*) offer consumers savings off the regular price of a product. The producer marks the reduced prices directly on the label or package. Price packs can be single packages sold at a reduced price (such as two for the price of one), or two related products banded together (such as a toothbrush and toothpaste). Price packs are very effective—even more so than coupons—in stimulating short-term sales.

Premiums are goods offered either free or at low cost as an incentive to buy a product, ranging from toys included with kids' products to phone cards and DVDs. A premium may come inside the package (in-pack), outside the package (on-pack), or through the mail. For example, over the years, McDonald's has offered a variety of premiums in its Happy Meals—from Teeny Beanie Babies to Speed Racers. For the past two years, the fast feeder has featured *American Idol*-inspired musical toy characters in its Happy Meals, each representing a favorite music genre. Customers can visit www.happymeal.com to choose their favorite character, whether it's Rockin' Riley, Lil' Hip Hop, Country Clay, Soulful Selma, or Punky Pete. The promotion also includes a chance to win a trip to see the season finale of *American Idol* live in Los Angeles.[34]

Advertising specialties, also called *promotional products*, are useful articles imprinted with an advertiser's name, logo, or message that are given as gifts to consumers. Typical items include T-shirts and other apparel, pens, coffee mugs, calendars, key rings, mouse pads, matches, tote bags, coolers, golf balls, and caps. U.S. marketers spent almost $19 billion on advertising specialties last year. Such items can be very effective. The "best of them stick around for months, subtly burning a brand name into a user's brain," notes a promotional products expert.[35]

Point-of-purchase (POP) promotions include displays and demonstrations that take place at the point of sale. Think of your last visit to the local Safeway, Costco, CVS, or Bed Bath & Beyond. Chances are good that you were tripping over aisle displays, promotional signs, "shelf talkers," or demonstrators offering free tastes of featured food products. Unfortunately, many retailers do not like to handle the hundreds of displays, signs, and posters they receive from manufacturers each year. Manufacturers have responded by offering better POP materials, offering to set them up, and tying them in with television, print, or online messages.

Contests, sweepstakes, and games give consumers the chance to win something, such as cash, trips, or goods, by luck or through extra effort. A *contest* calls for consumers to submit an entry—a jingle, guess, suggestion—to be judged by a panel that will select the best entries. A *sweepstakes* calls for consumers to submit their names for a drawing. A *game* presents consumers with something—bingo numbers, missing letters—every time they buy, which may or may not help them win a prize. Such promotions can create considerable brand attention and consumer involvement.[36]

Doritos recently ran a "Get It. Taste It. Name It" sweepstakes asking consumers to taste its newest flavor, initially labeled X-13D, and then suggest a name and write an ad for it. Those who submitted a name or ad were entered into the sweeps to become one of 100 Doritos Flavor Masters. Winners were selected through a random drawing. As Flavor Masters, the 100 grand-prize winners got the chance to take part in Doritos research and development, giving feedback on future flavor ideas. Each also got a year's supply of Doritos, 52 coupons good for one bag per week. The X-13D chips, packaged in a black bag with a label that looked like it's lifted from a science lab, built a lot of buzz. The promotion pulled in more than 100,000 entries within only a month of launch. And the promotion sparked considerable online chatter as bloggers wrote about stumbling upon the distinctive bag in convenience stores and tackled the question of what the flavor really was.

Event marketing
Creating a brand-marketing event or serving as a sole or participating sponsor of events created by others.

Finally, marketers can promote their brands through **event marketing** (or *event sponsorships*). They can create their own brand-marketing events or serve as sole or participating sponsors of events created by others. The events might include anything from mobile brand tours to festivals, reunions, marathons, concerts, or other sponsored gatherings. Event marketing is huge, and it may be the fastest-growing area of promotion. Consumer event-marketing spending in the United States reached $19 billion last year, up 12 percent from a year earlier.[37]

Most companies sponsor brand events. Harley-Davidson holds "HOG Rallies" and Harley biker reunions that draw hundreds of thousands of bikers each year. Sprint is paying $700 million over 10 years to sponsor the NASCAR Sprint Cup Series. And Coca-Cola, Anheuser-Busch, Nickelodeon, and others jointly sponsor Carnival Miami's culminating event, Calle Ocho, said to be the largest annual celebration of Hispanic culture in the United States. ▲Procter & Gamble creates numerous events for its major brands. Consider this example:

> P&G recently sponsored a holiday event promotion for its Charmin brand in New York's Times Square, where it can be very difficult to find a public restroom. For the second year running, P&G set up 20 sparkling clean Charmin-themed mini-bathrooms, each with its own sink and a bountiful supply of Charmin. The event turned out to be the ultimate in experiential marketing—touching people in places advertising wouldn't dare to go. More than 420,000 people gratefully used the facilities and privately voted for the Charmin they preferred (Charmin Ultra Soft or Ultra Strong).[38]

▲ Event marketing: P&G recently sponsored a holiday event promotion for its Charmin brand in New York's Times Square, where it can be very difficult to find a public restroom. P&G set up 20 sparkling clean Charmin-themed mini-bathrooms, each with its own sink and a bountiful supply of Charmin.

Trade Promotions

Trade promotions
Sales promotion tools used to persuade resellers to carry a brand, give it shelf space, promote it in advertising, and push it to consumers.

Manufacturers direct more sales promotion dollars toward retailers and wholesalers (81 percent) than to final consumers (19 percent).[39] **Trade promotions** can persuade resellers to carry a brand, give it shelf space, promote it in advertising, and push it to consumers. Shelf space is so scarce these days that manufacturers often have to offer price-offs, allowances, buy-back guarantees, or free goods to retailers and wholesalers to get products on the shelf and, once there, to keep them on it.

Manufacturers use several trade promotion tools. Many of the tools used for consumer promotions—contests, premiums, displays—can also be used as trade promotions. Or the manufacturer may offer a straight *discount* off the list price on each case purchased during a stated period of time (also called a *price-off, off-invoice,* or *off-list*). Manufacturers also may offer an *allowance* (usually so much off per case) in return for the retailer's agreement to feature the manufacturer's products in some way. An advertising allowance compensates retailers for advertising the product. A display allowance compensates them for using special displays.

Manufacturers may offer *free goods,* which are extra cases of merchandise, to resellers who buy a certain quantity or who feature a certain flavor or size. They may offer *push money*—cash or gifts to dealers or their sales forces to "push" the manufacturer's goods. Manufacturers may give retailers free *specialty advertising items* that carry the company's name, such as pens, pencils, calendars, paperweights, matchbooks, memo pads, and yardsticks.

Business Promotions

Business promotions
Sales promotion tools used to generate business leads, stimulate purchases, reward customers, and motivate salespeople.

Companies spend billions of dollars each year on promotion to industrial customers. **Business promotions** are used to generate business leads, stimulate purchases, reward customers, and motivate salespeople. Business promotions include many of the same tools used for consumer or trade promotions. Here, we focus on two additional major business promotion tools—conventions and trade shows, and sales contests.

Many companies and trade associations organize *conventions and trade shows* to promote their products. Firms selling to the industry show their products at the trade show. Vendors receive many benefits, such as opportunities to find new sales leads, contact customers, introduce new products, meet new customers, sell more to present customers, and educate customers with publications and audiovisual materials. Trade shows also help companies reach many prospects not reached through their sales forces.

Some trade shows are huge. ▲ For example, at this year's International Consumer Electronics Show, 2,700 exhibitors attracted more than 141,000 professional visitors. Even more impressive, at the BAUMA mining and construction equipment trade show in Munich, Germany, some 3,000 exhibitors from 49 countries presented their latest product innovations to more than 500,000 attendees from 190 countries.[40]

A *sales contest* is a contest for salespeople or dealers to motivate them to increase their sales performance over a given period. Sales contests motivate and recognize good company performers, who may receive trips, cash prizes, or other gifts. Some companies award points for performance, which the receiver can turn in for any of a variety of prizes. Sales contests work best when they are tied to measurable and achievable sales objectives (such as finding new accounts, reviving old accounts, or increasing account profitability).

▲ Some trade shows are huge: At this year's International Consumer Electronics Show, 2,700 exhibitors attracted more than 141,000 professional visitors.

Developing the Sales Promotion Program

Beyond selecting the types of promotions to use, marketers must make several other decisions in designing the full sales promotion program. First, they must decide on the *size of the incentive*. A certain minimum incentive is necessary if the promotion is to succeed; a larger incentive will produce more sales response. The marketer also must set *conditions for participation*. Incentives might be offered to everyone or only to select groups.

Marketers must decide how to *promote and distribute the promotion* program itself. A $2-off coupon could be given out in a package, at the store, via the Internet, or in an advertisement. Each distribution method involves a different level of reach and cost. Increasingly, marketers are blending several media into a total campaign concept. The *length of the promotion* is also important. If the sales promotion period is too short, many prospects (who may not be buying during that time) will miss it. If the promotion runs too long, the deal will lose some of its "act now" force.

Evaluation is also very important. Many companies fail to evaluate their sales promotion programs, and others evaluate them only superficially. Yet marketers should work to measure the returns on their sales promotion investments, just as they should seek to assess the returns on other marketing activities. The most common evaluation method is to compare sales before, during, and after a promotion. Marketers should ask, Did the promotion attract new customers or more purchasing from current customers? Can we hold onto these new customers and purchases? Will the long-run customer relationship and sales gains from the promotion justify its costs?

Clearly, sales promotion plays an important role in the total promotion mix. To use it well, the marketer must define the sales promotion objectives, select the best tools, design the sales promotion program, implement the program, and evaluate the results. Moreover, sales promotion must be coordinated carefully with other promotion mix elements within the overall integrated marketing communications program.

REVIEWING Objectives AND KEY Terms

This chapter is the second of three chapters covering the final marketing mix element—promotion. The previous chapter dealt with overall integrated marketing communications and with advertising and public relations. This one investigates personal selling and sales promotion. Personal selling is the interpersonal arm of the communications mix. Sales promotion consists of short-term incentives to encourage the purchase or sale of a product or service.

OBJECTIVE 1 Discuss the role of a company's salespeople in creating value for customers and building customer relationships. (pp 458-461)

Most companies use salespeople and many companies assign them an important role in the marketing mix. For companies selling business products, the firm's salespeople work directly with customers. Often, the sales force is the customer's only direct contact with the company and therefore may be viewed by customers as representing the company itself. In contrast, for consumer-product companies that sell through intermediaries, consumers usually do not meet salespeople or even know about them. The sales force works behind the scenes, dealing with wholesalers and retailers to obtain their support and helping them become effective in selling the firm's products.

As an element of the promotion mix, the sales force is very effective in achieving certain marketing objectives and carrying out such activities as prospecting, communicating, selling and servicing, and information gathering. But with companies becoming more market oriented, a customer-focused sales force also works to produce both *customer satisfaction* and *company profit*. The sales force plays a key role in developing and managing profitable *customer relationships*.

OBJECTIVE 2 Identify and explain the six major sales force management steps. (pp 461-472)

High sales force costs necessitate an effective sales management process consisting of six steps: designing sales force strategy and structure, recruiting and selecting, training, compensating, supervising, and evaluating salespeople and sales force performance.

In designing a sales force, sales management must address strategy issues such as what type of sales force structure will work best (territorial, product, customer, or complex structure); how large the sales force should be; who will be involved in the selling effort; and how its various salespeople and sales-support people will work together (inside or outside sales forces and team selling).

To hold down the high costs of hiring the wrong people, salespeople must be recruited and selected carefully. In recruiting salespeople, a company may look to job duties and the characteristics of its most successful salespeople to suggest the traits it wants in its salespeople. It must then look for applicants through recommendations of current salespeople, employment agencies, classified ads, the Internet, and contacting college students. In the selection process, the procedure can vary from a single informal interview to lengthy testing and interviewing. After the selection process is complete, training programs familiarize new salespeople not only with the art of selling but also with the company's history, its products and policies, and the characteristics of its market and competitors.

The sales force compensation system helps to reward, motivate, and direct salespeople. In compensating salespeople, companies try to have an appealing plan, usually close to the going rate for the type of sales job and needed skills. In addition to compensation, all salespeople need supervision, and many need continuous encouragement because they must make many decisions and face many frustrations. Periodically, the company must evaluate their performance to help them do a better job. In evaluating salespeople, the company relies on getting regular information gathered through sales reports, personal observations, customers' letters and complaints, customer surveys, and conversations with other salespeople.

OBJECTIVE 3 Discuss the personal selling process, distinguishing between transaction-oriented marketing and relationship marketing. (pp 472-475)

The art of selling involves a seven-step *selling process: prospecting and qualifying, preapproach, approach, presentation and demonstration, handling objections, closing,* and *follow-up.* These steps help marketers close a specific sale and as such are *transaction oriented.* However, a seller's dealings with customers should be guided by the larger concept of *relationship marketing.* The company's sales force should help to orchestrate a whole-company effort to develop profitable long-term relationships with key customers based on superior customer value and satisfaction.

OBJECTIVE 4 Explain how sales promotion campaigns are developed and implemented. (pp 475-482)

Sales promotion campaigns call for setting sales promotions objectives (in general, sales promotions should be *consumer relationship building*); selecting tools; and developing and implementing the sales promotion program by using *consumer promotion tools* (from coupons, refunds, premiums, and point-of-purchase promotions to contests, sweepstakes, and events), *trade promotion tools* (discounts, allowances, free goods, push money) and *business promotion tools* (conventions, trade shows, sales contests), as well as deciding on such things as the size of the incentive, the conditions for participation, how to promote and distribute the promotion package, and the length of the promotion. After this process is completed, the company evaluates its sales promotion results.

KEY Terms

OBJECTIVE 1

Personal selling (p 458)
Salesperson (p 459)

OBJECTIVE 2

Sales force management (p 461)
Territorial sales force structure (p 461)
Product sales force structure (p 461)
Customer sales force structure (p 462)
Outside sales force (*field sales force*)
(p 464)

Inside sales force (p 464)
Team selling (p 466)
Sales quota (p 471)

OBJECTIVE 3

Selling process (p 472)
Prospecting (p 472)
Preapproach (p 473)
Approach (p 473)
Presentation (p 473)

Handling objections (p 474)
Closing (p 474)
Follow-up (p 475)

OBJECTIVE 4

Sales promotion (p 475)
Consumer promotions (p 479)
Event marketing (p 481)
Trade promotions (p 481)
Business promotions (p 481)

DISCUSSING & APPLYING THE Concepts

Discussing the Concepts

1. Discuss the role of personal selling in the promotion mix. In what situations is it more effective than advertising? (AASCB: Communication; Reflective Thinking)

2. Briefly describe the activities involved in sales force management. (AACSB: Communication)

3. List and briefly describe the three sales force structures outlined in the chapter. What sales force structure does CDW employ? (AACSB: Communication)

4. Define *sales promotion* and discuss its objectives. (AACSB: Communication)

5. Name and describe the types of trade sales promotions. (AACSB: Communication)

Applying the Concepts

1. Work in pairs to describe the stages in the selling process for a small company in your community that sells cleaning services to owners of small businesses, such as hair salons, dentists' offices, and clothing stores. Role-play the actual selling process, from approach to close, with one team member acting as the salesperson. The other member of the team should act as a customer and raise at least three objections. (AACSB: Communication; Reflective Thinking)

2. Suppose you are the marketing coordinator responsible for recommending the sales promotion plan for the market launch of a new brand of energy drink sold in supermarkets. What promotional tools would you consider for this task and what decisions must be made? (AACSB: Communication; Reflective Thinking)

3. Find examples of five different types of consumer promotions and present them to your class. (AACSB: Communication; Reflective Thinking)

FOCUS ON Technology

Consumers love saving money, especially during economic downturns. That makes coupons a very attractive promotional tool. And what better way to deliver coupons than via the Internet? After a slowdown following counterfeit Internet coupon problems between 2001 and 2003, manufacturers and retailers are now coming back to online printable coupons—and consumers are responding. Scarborough Research reports Internet coupon usage among U.S. households has increased 83 percent since 2005. Coupon, Inc., is the leading provider of printable coupons for more than 600 consumer package-goods retailers and manufacturers, distributing coupons through 2,000 Web sites. You can find coupons available just about everywhere on the Internet. Delta Airlines has even launched online boarding-pass ads containing coupons for discounts at fliers' destinations. However, Bud Miller, executive director of the Coupon Information Corporation warns that counterfeit coupons are once again on the rise.

1. Find and print 10 coupons from the Internet for products you normally purchase. Use some of these coupons on your next purchase. Did all of the retailers accept your coupons? If not, explain why not. (AACSB: Communication; Use of IT; Reflective Thinking)

2. How can consumers be certain that a coupon obtained from the Internet is legitimate? How can manufacturers and retailers ensure the coupons are not counterfeited? Go to the Coupon Information Corporation's Web site to learn more about this problem (www.cents-off.com/index.htm). (AACSB: Communication; Use of IT; Reflective Thinking)

FOCUS ON Ethics

Free samples, gifts, expensive trips, dinners, and entertainment—these tools have been, and in some cases still are, widely used by pharmaceutical companies to influence doctors' prescribing behavior. Physicians control the majority of health care expenditures through their prescription writing authority. Although direct-to-consumer advertising expenditures have grown exponentially over the past decade, an estimated 90 percent of pharmaceutical marketing dollars are directed at physicians. More than 90,000 pharmaceutical sales representatives in the United States, called "physician detailers," vie for health care professionals' attention to pitch their drugs. Research has shown that pharmaceutical companies' marketing tactics do influence physicians, causing them to prescribe more expensive drugs over less expensive alternatives. Critics proclaim that these tactics are unethical. However, the pharmaceutical companies claim that their sales representatives help keep health care professionals well informed in this rapidly changing industry.

1. Is it ethical for pharmaceutical sales representatives to influence physicians' prescribing behavior using free samples and promotional gifts? (AACSB: Communication; Ethical Reasoning)

2. National and international trade associations in the pharmaceuticals industry have codes of conduct regarding interactions with health care professionals. Visit the Web sites of the Pharmaceutical Research and Manufacturers of America (PhRMA) (www.phrma.org) and the International Federation of Pharmaceutical Manufacturers Association (IFPMA) (http://ifpma.org/) and examine their codes of ethics regarding sales activities. Write a brief report on what you learn. (AACSB: Communication; Use of IT; Reflective Thinking)

MARKETING BY THE Numbers

Salespeople do more than just sell products and services—they manage relationships with customers to deliver value to both the customer and their company. Thus, for many companies, sales reps visit customers several times per year—often for hours at a time. Thus, sales managers must ensure that their companies have enough salespeople to adequately deliver value to customers.

1. Refer to Appendix 2, Marketing by the Numbers, to determine the number of salespeople a company needs if it has 3,000 customers who need to be called on 10 times per year. Each sales call lasts approximately 2 1/2 hours, and each sales rep has approximately 1,250 hours per year to devote to customers. (AACSB: Communication; Analytical Reasoning)

2. If each sales representative earns a salary of $60,000 per year, what sales are necessary to break even on the sales force costs if the company has a contribution margin of 40 percent? What effect will adding each additional sales representative have on the break-even sales? (AACSB: Communication; Analytical Reasoning)

VIDEO Case

The Principal Financial Group

The Principal Financial Group delivered strong growth in its first six years as a public company. Operating earnings grew from $577 million in 2001 to $1.06 billion in 2007 alone. In that same year, total assets under management soared from $98 billion to $311 billion. The Principal also achieved a 16.4 percent return on equity for 2007, compared to 8.9 percent for 2001. As a result, its stock price increased 236 percent from its opening price at the October 2001 initial public offering (IPO) through its closing price at year-end 2007.

One of the biggest reasons for this success is The Principal Financial Group's strongly customer-centered sales force. The company's varied and complex product line (from retirement products to insurance) demands the one-on-one attention of a salesperson who understands how to build customer relationships. The company's sales force has helped make The Principal a global player in the financial services industry.

After viewing the video featuring The Principal Financial Group, answer the following questions:

1. How is the sales force at The Principal Financial Group structured?

2. Identify the selling process of the company. Give evidence of each step.

3. How does The Principal build long-term customer relationships through its sales force?

COMPANY Case

Procter & Gamble: Selling Through Customer Business Development

It seems that when it comes to personal selling, the term "win-win" gets thrown around so much that it has become a cliché. But at Procter & Gamble, the sales concept that the company benefits only as much as the customer benefits is a way of life. Since William Procter and James Gamble formed a family-operated soap and candle company in 1837, P&G has understood that if the customer doesn't do well, neither will the company.

That's why even though P&G boasts a massive sales force of more than 12,000 employees worldwide, P&G people rarely utter the term "sales." At P&G, it's called "customer business development," or CBD. The title alone pretty much says it all. Rather than just selling detergent or toothpaste, P&G's philosophy is to grow its own business by growing the business of its customers. In this case, customers are the thousands of retailers and wholesalers that distribute P&G's brands throughout the world. P&G isn't just a supplier. It's a strategic business partner with its customers. "We depend on them as much as they depend on us," says Jeff Weedman, a CBD manager.

THE CORE COMPETENCY OF CUSTOMER BUSINESS DEVELOPMENT

As the big-box retailers get bigger and bigger, they also grow more complex. Take companies such as Wal-Mart or Target. How can a vendor like P&G ever fully understand such a customer? These complex organizations have so many arms and legs that it becomes nearly impossible to get a full and firm grasp on their operations and needs.

To deal with such customer complexities, P&G organizes its sales representatives into customer business development teams. Rather than assigning reps to specific geographic regions or products, it assigns each CBD team to a P&G customer. For the company's biggest customer, Wal-Mart (which tallies a massive 20 percent of all P&G sales) the CBD team consists of some 350 employees. For a customer like Family Dollar, the nation's second-largest dollar store chain, the CBD team has only about 30 employees.

Regardless of the team's size, the strength of the CBD concept derives from the fact that each team, in and of itself, is a complete customer-service unit, containing at least one support specialist for every important business function. In addition to a general CBD manager and several sales account executives (each responsible for a specific category of P&G products), each CBD team includes a marketing strategy, operations, information systems, logistics, finance, and human resources specialist. This "multifunctional" structure enables each team to meet the multiple and vast needs of its customer, whether the needs revolve around those of a chief finance officer or an entire IT department.

A real strength of the CBD teams is that team members function as a collaborative whole, rather than as individuals performing their own tasks in isolation. Team members share information, organizational capabilities, and technologies. "I have all the resources I need right here," says Amy Fuschino, a HealthCare and Cosmetics account executive. "If I need to, I can go right down the hall and talk with someone in marketing about doing some kind of promotional deal. It's that simple."

But the multifunctional nature of the CBD team also means that collaboration extends far beyond internal interactions. Each time a CBD team member contacts the customer, he or she represents the entire team. For example, if during a customer call a CBD account executive receives a question about a promotional, logistical, or financial matter, the account executive acts as the liaison with the appropriate CBD specialist. So, although not each CBD member has specialized knowledge in every area, the CBD team as a unit does.

Competitors have attempted to implement some aspects of P&G's multifunctional approach. However, P&G pioneered the CBD structure. And it has built in some unique characteristics that have allowed it to leverage more power from its team structure than its rivals can.

THE TRUE ADVANTAGE

For starters, P&G's CBD structure is broader and more comprehensive, making it more multifunctional than similar team structures employed by other companies. But perhaps more important, P&G's structure is designed to accomplish four key objectives. So important are these objectives that they are referred to internally as the "core work" of CBD. These four objectives are:

- Align Strategy—to create opportunities for both P&G and the customer to benefit by collaborating in strategy development.
- Create Demand—to build profitable sales volume for P&G and the customer through consumer value and shopper satisfaction.
- Optimize Supply—to maximize the efficiency of the supply chain from P&G to the point of purchase to optimize cost and responsiveness.
- Enable the Organization—to develop capabilities to maximize business results by creating the capacity for frequent breakthrough.

More than just corporate catch-phrases jotted down in an employee handbook, for CBD employees, these are words to live by. P&G trains sales employees in methods of achieving each objective and evaluates their effectiveness in meeting the objectives.

In fact, the CBD concept came about through the recognition that, in order to develop true win-win relationships with each customer, P&G would need to accomplish the first objective. According to Bill Warren, a CBD senior account executive, "The true competitive advantage is achieved by taking a multi-functional approach from basic selling to strategic customer collaboration!"

Strategic collaboration starts with annual joint business planning. Both the P&G team and the customer come to the table focused on the most important thing: How can each best provide value for the final consumer? The team and customer give much attention during this planning phase to how products can best be presented and placed in the retail setting. This is because P&G and its customers know that the end consumer assesses value within the first three to seven seconds of seeing that product on the shelf. At P&G, this is known as "winning the first moment of truth." If customers quickly perceive that a product will meet their needs, they will likely purchase it.

CBD team members are very good at demonstrating to the retailer that the best way to win the first moment of truth is most often with a P&G product. But P&G is so committed to the principle of developing the *customer's* business as a means of developing its own, it is open to the possibility that the best way to serve the customer may be through a competitor's product. The CBD team's primary goal is to help the customer win in each product category. Sometimes, analysis shows that the best solution for the customer is "the other guy's product." For P&G, that's okay. P&G knows that creating the best situation for the retailer ultimately brings in more customer traffic, which in turn will likely result in increased sales for other P&G products in the same category. Because most of P&G's brands are market leaders, it stands to benefit more from the increased traffic than competitors. Again, it's a win-win situation. This type of honesty also helps to build trust and strengthen the company–customer relationship.

The collaborative efforts between P&G and each of its customers do not only involve planning and the sharing of information. They may also involve cooperative efforts to share the costs of different activities. "We'll help customers run these commercials or do those merchandising events, but there has to be a return-on-investment," explains Amy Fuschino. "Maybe it's helping us with a new distribution or increasing space for fabric care. We're very willing if the effort creates value for us in addition to creating value for the customer and the consumer."

An example of such a joint effort is the recent rollout of Prism. P&G partnered with Wal-Mart to implement this system of infrared sensors that counts the number of times shoppers are exposed to product displays, banners, and video monitors. The goal with Prism is to improve the effectiveness of in-store marketing, making consumers more aware of the value provided by P&G's products.

If the CBD team can effectively accomplish the first objective of aligning strategy and collaborating on strategic development, accomplishing the other three objectives will follow more easily. For example, if strategic planning leads to winning the first moment of truth, not only does the consumer benefit, but both the retailer and P&G achieve higher revenues and profits as well. Through proper strategic planning, it is also more likely that both P&G and the customer will create greater efficiencies in the supply chain.

IT'S BETTER TO GIVE . . . THAN TO RECEIVE

As a result of collaborating with customers, P&G receives as much or more than it gives. Among other things, P&G receives information that helps in achieving the fourth CBD objective, enabling the organization to achieve innovation. Where the research and development process is concerned, this means creating better products. This is one reason why, at the 2007 Product of the Year awards held in London, P&G cleaned up, winning 10 of the 32 categories and

taking home a special prize for "most innovative company." P&G's dominance in innovation is no one-time fluke. Gianni Ciserani, vice president and managing director of P&G UK & Ireland, claims that some of P&G's strongest innovations are yet to come. "We have shared this portfolio with the key retailers and got strong collaboration on how we can drive these ideas forward."

In the five years leading up to 2008, P&G's profits doubled, revenues nearly doubled, and stock price increased by more than 50 percent. Not only is P&G the world's largest consumer products firm with $76 billion in revenues, it ranks 23rd among all U.S. companies in the most recent *Fortune* 500 ranking. P&G manages a whopping 23 brands that *each* bring in over $1 billion every year. Last year, Pampers sales exceeded $7 billion, a figure that would have placed the leading diaper brand all by itself as number 350 on *Fortune*'s prestigious list.

Many factors have contributed to P&G's growth and success. But the role that CBD plays can't be overestimated. And as P&G moves forward, Mr. Weedman's words that "We depend on them as much as they depend on us" ring ever truer. As P&G's megacustomers grow in size and power, developing P&G's business means first developing its customers' business. And the CBD sales organization lies at the heart of that effort.

Questions for Discussion

1. Which of the sales force structures discussed in the text best describes P&G's CBD structure?

2. From the perspective of team selling, discuss the positive as well as some possible negative aspects to the customer business development sales organization.

3. Visit www.mypgcareer.com/activity/customer.html to learn more about the P&G CBD organization. Based on information on this Web site and information in this case, discuss the importance of recruiting, training, and compensation in making the CBD structure more effective.

4. Discuss some ways that the CBD structure may be more effective than a single sales rep for each step in the personal selling process.

5. It seems that P&G has the most effective sales force structure of any company in its industry. Why have competitors not been able to match it?

Sources: Officials at Procter & Gamble contributed to and supported development of this case; with other information from www.pg.com, accessed July 2008. Also see Craig Smith, "P&G Tops List for Innovation," *Marketing*, January 31, 2007, p. 6; and "Will She, Won't She?—Procter & Gamble," *Economist*, August 11, 2007, accessed at www.economist.com.

Chapter 17

Part 1   Defining Marketing and the Marketing Process (Chapters 1, 2)
Part 2   Understanding the Marketplace and Consumers (Chapters 3, 4, 5, 6)
Part 3   Designing a Customer-Driven Strategy and Mix (Chapters 7, 8, 9, 10, 11, 12, 13, 14, 15, 16, 17)
Part 4   Extending Marketing (Chapters 18, 19, 20)

Direct and Online

Marketing Building Direct
Customer Relationships

Chapter PREVIEW In the previous three chapters, you learned about communicating customer value through integrated marketing communication (IMC) and about four specific elements of the marketing communications mix—advertising, publicity, personal selling, and sales promotion. In this chapter, we'll look at the final IMC element, direct marketing, and at its fastest-growing form, online marketing. Actually, direct marketing can be viewed as more than just a communications tool. In many ways it constitutes an overall marketing approach—a blend of communication and distribution channels all rolled into one. As you read on, remember that although this chapter examines direct marketing as a separate tool, it must be carefully integrated with other elements of the promotion mix.

For starters, let's first look at Amazon.com. In less than 15 years, Amazon.com has blossomed from an obscure dot-com upstart into one of the best-known names on the Internet. According to one estimate, 52 percent of people who shopped the Internet last year started at Amazon.com. How has Amazon.com become such an incredibly successful direct and online marketer in such a short time? It's all about creating direct, personal, satisfying customer experience. Few direct marketers do that as well as Amazon.com.

When you think of shopping on the Web, chances are good that you think first of Amazon.com. Amazon.com first opened its virtual doors in 1995, selling books out of founder Jeff Bezos's garage in suburban Seattle. The online pioneer still sells books—*lots and lots* of books. But it now sells just about everything else as well, from music, videos, electronics, tools, housewares, apparel, groceries, and kids' products to loose diamonds and Maine lobsters. "We have the Earth's Biggest Selection," declares the company's Web site.

In little more than a decade, Amazon.com has become one of the best-known names on the Web. In perfecting the art of online selling, it has also rewritten the rules of marketing. Many analysts view Amazon.com as *the* model for businesses in the digital age. They predict that it will one day become the Wal-Mart of the Internet.

From the start, Amazon.com has grown explosively. Its annual sales have rocketed from a modest $15 million in 1996 to more than $15 *billion* today. In only the past five years, its sales have nearly quadrupled. Although it took Amazon.com eight years to turn its first full-year profit in 2003, profits have since surged more than 13-fold. Last year the company ranked fifth in the nation in return to shareholders, two ranks above Apple. More than 72 million active customers now spend an average of $184 a year at Amazon.com. One study estimates that 52 percent of all consumers who went to the Internet to shop last year started at Amazon.com. Fifty percent of Amazon.com's sales come from overseas.

What has made Amazon.com one of the world's premier direct marketers? To its core, the company is relentlessly customer driven. "The thing that drives everything is creating genuine value for customers," says founder Jeff Bezos. "If you focus on what customers want and build a relationship, they will allow you to make money." In one promotion in Japan, for example, Bezos donned a delivery driver's uniform and went house to house with packages. His point: Everything at Amazon—from top to bottom—begins and ends with the customer.

Anyone at Amazon.com will tell you that the company wants to do much more than just sell books or DVDs or digital cameras. It wants to deliver a special *experience* to every customer. "The customer experience really matters," says Bezos. "We've focused on just having a better store, where it's easier to shop, where you can learn more about the products, where you have a bigger selection, and where you have the lowest prices. You combine all of that stuff together and people say, 'Hey, these guys really get it.'"

And customers do get it. Most

Says Amazon founder and CEO Jeff Bezos. "We are not great advertisers. So we start with customers, figure out what they want, and figure out how to get it to them."

Amazon.com regulars feel a surprisingly strong relationship with the company, especially given the almost complete lack of actual human interaction. Amazon.com obsesses over making each customer's experience uniquely personal. For example, the Amazon.com Web site greets customers with their very own personalized home pages, and the site's "Recommended for you" feature prepares personalized product recommendations. Amazon.com was first to use "collaborative filtering" technology, which sifts through each customer's past purchases and the purchasing patterns of customers with similar profiles to come up with personalized site content. "We want Amazon.com to be the right store for you as an individual," says Bezos. "If we have 72 million customers, we should have 72 million stores."

Visitors to Amazon.com's Web site receive a unique blend of benefits: huge selection, good value, convenience, and what the company calls "discovery." In books alone, for example, Amazon.com offers an easily searchable virtual selection of more than 3 million titles, 15 times more than in any physical bookstore. Good value comes in the form of reasonable prices, plus free delivery on orders over $25. And at Amazon.com, it's irresistibly convenient to buy. You can log on, find anything and everything you want, and order with a single mouse click, all in less time than it takes to find a parking space at the local mall.

But it's the "discovery" factor that makes the Amazon.com marketing experience really special. Once on the Web site, you're compelled to stay for a while—looking, learning, and discovering. Amazon.com has become a kind of online community, in which customers can browse for products, research purchase alternatives, share opinions and reviews with other visitors, and chat online with authors and experts. In this way, Amazon.com does much more than just sell goods on the Web. It creates direct, personalized customer relationships and satisfying online experiences. Year after year, Amazon.com comes in number one or number two on the University of Michigan's American Customer Satisfaction Index, regardless of industry.

In fact, Amazon.com has become so good at managing online relationships that many traditional "brick-and-mortar" retailers are turning to Amazon for help in adding more "clicks" to their "bricks." For example, Amazon.com now partners with well-known retailers such as Target and Bebe to help them run their Web interfaces. And to create even greater selection and convenience for customers, Amazon.com allows competing retailers—from mom-and-pop operations to Marks & Spencer—to offer their products on its Web site, creating a virtual shopping mall of incredible proportions. It even encourages customers to sell used items on the site.

Amazon.com is constantly on the lookout for innovative new ways to use the power of the Web and direct marketing to create more shopping selection, value, convenience, and discovery for customers. For example, it started Amazon Prime, a program by which members pay $79 per year and get free two-day shipping on all orders and next-day shipping for $3.99 on any order.

Amazon.com now offers music downloading, with the music files not restricted by digital rights management software (DRM), which means that (unlike iTunes) you can freely and conveniently copy the songs. All four major music labels promptly signed on. The Web merchant also launched Amazon Giver and Amazon Grapevine, applications for social-networking Web site Facebook. These features allow Facebook users to see and purchase what their friends want via wish lists and to view recent public activity on the retail site.

And late last year, Amazon.com took another bold customer-convenience and personalization step. It introduced the Kindle, a $399 wireless reading device for downloading books, blogs, magazines, newspapers, and other matter. Lighter and thinner than a typical paperback book, the Kindle wireless reader connects like a cell phone, letting customers buy and download content of personal interest—from the *Wall Street Journal* or *Time* magazine to the latest *New York Times* bestsellers—from home or on the go in less than 60 seconds. The Kindle has a paper-like electronic-ink display that's easy to read even in bright daylight. In all, Amazon.com is betting that the Kindle will prove to be an ultimate direct-marketing device.

So, what do you think? Will Amazon.com become the Wal-Mart of the Web? That remains to be seen. But whatever its fate, the direct and online pioneer has forever changed the face of marketing. Most importantly, Amazon.com has set a very high bar for the online customer experience. "The reason I'm so obsessed with ... the customer experience is that I believe [that our success] has been driven exclusively by that experience," says Jeff Bezos. "We are not great advertisers. So we start with customers, figure out what they want, and figure out how to get it to them."[1]

> Amazon.com obsesses over making each customer's experience uniquely personal. "If we have 72 million customers, we should have 72 million stores."

> In perfecting the art of online selling, Amazon.com has rewritten the rules of marketing. The Web pioneer excels at creating personal, satisfying direct marketing customer experiences.

Objective Outline

Many of the marketing and promotion tools that we've examined in previous chapters were developed in the context of *mass marketing*: targeting broad markets with standardized messages and offers distributed through intermediaries. Today, however, with the trend toward more narrowly targeted marketing, many companies are adopting *direct marketing*, either as a primary marketing approach, as in Amazon.com's case, or as a supplement to other approaches. In this section, we explore the exploding world of direct marketing.

Direct marketing consists of connecting directly with carefully targeted individual consumers to both obtain an immediate response and cultivate lasting customer relationships. Direct marketers communicate directly with customers, often on a one-to-one, interactive basis. Using detailed databases, they tailor their marketing offers and communications to the needs of narrowly defined segments or even individual buyers.

Beyond brand and relationship building, direct marketers usually seek a direct, immediate, and measurable consumer response. For example, as we learned in the chapter-opening story, Amazon.com interacts directly with customers on its Web site to help them discover and buy almost anything and everything on the Internet, with only a few clicks of the mouse button. Similarly, Dell interacts directly with customers, by telephone or through its Web site, to design built-to-order systems that meet customers' individual needs. Buyers can order directly from Dell, and Dell quickly and efficiently delivers the new computers to their homes or offices.

Direct marketing
Connecting directly with carefully targeted individual consumers to both obtain an immediate response and cultivate lasting customer relationships.

Author Comment | For most companies, direct marketing is a supplemental channel or medium. But for many other companies today—such as Amazon.com, eBay, or GEICO—direct marketing is a complete way of doing business.

The New Direct Marketing Model (pp 490–491)

Early direct marketers—catalog companies, direct mailers, and telemarketers—gathered customer names and sold goods mainly by mail and telephone. Today, however, fired by rapid advances in database technologies and new marketing media—especially the Internet—direct marketing has undergone a dramatic transformation.

490

In previous chapters, we've discussed direct marketing as direct distribution—as marketing channels that contain no intermediaries. We also include direct marketing as one element of the promotion mix—as an approach for communicating directly with consumers. In actuality, direct marketing is both these things and more.

Most companies still use direct marketing as a supplementary channel or medium. Thus, Lexus markets mostly through mass-media advertising and its high-quality dealer network but also supplements these channels with direct marketing. Its direct marketing includes promotional DVDs and other materials mailed directly to prospective buyers and a Web page (www.lexus.com) that provides consumers with information about various models, competitive comparisons, financing, and dealer locations. Similarly, most department stores such as Sears or Macy's sell the majority of their merchandise off their store shelves but also sell through direct mail and online catalogs.

However, for many companies today, direct marketing is more than just a supplementary channel or advertising medium. For these companies, direct marketing—especially in its most recent transformation, online marketing—constitutes a complete model for doing business. Rather than using direct marketing and the Internet only as supplemental approaches, firms employing this new *direct model* use it as the *only* approach. ▲Companies such as Amazon.com, eBay, and GEICO have built their entire approach to the marketplace around direct marketing. The direct model is rapidly changing the way that companies think about building relationships with customers.

▲ The new direct marketing model: Companies such as GEICO have built their entire approach to the marketplace around direct marketing. Just visit www.geico.com or call 1-800-947-AUTO.

Author Comment | Direct marketing—especially online marketing—is growing explosively. It's at the heart of the trend toward building closer, more interactive customer relationships.

Growth and Benefits of Direct Marketing (pp 491–493)

Direct marketing has become the fastest-growing form of marketing. According to the Direct Marketing Association, U.S. companies spent $173.2 billion on direct marketing last year. These expenditures generated an estimated $2 trillion in direct marketing sales, or about 10 percent of total sales in the U.S. economy. And direct marketing-driven sales are growing rapidly. The DMA estimates that direct marketing sales will grow 6.6 percent annually through 2012, compared with a projected 5.7 percent annual growth for total U.S. sales.[2]

Direct marketing continues to become more Web-oriented, and Internet marketing is claiming a fast-growing share of direct marketing spending and sales. The Internet now accounts for only about 20 percent of direct marketing-driven sales. However, the DMA predicts that over the next five years Internet marketing expenditures will grow at a blistering 16 percent a year, more than three times faster than expenditures in other direct marketing media. Internet-driven sales will grow by almost 15 percent.

Whether employed as a complete business model or as a supplement to a broader integrated marketing mix, direct marketing brings many benefits to both buyers and sellers.

Benefits to Buyers

For buyers, direct marketing is convenient, easy, and private. Direct marketers never close their doors, and customers don't have to battle traffic, find parking spaces, and trek through stores to find products. From the comfort of their homes or offices, they can browse catalogs or company Web sites at any time of the day or night. Business buyers can learn about products and services without tying up time with salespeople.

Direct marketing gives buyers ready access to a wealth of products. For example, unrestrained by physical boundaries, direct marketers can offer an almost unlimited selection to consumers almost anywhere in the world. Just compare the huge selections offered by many Web merchants to the more meager assortments of their brick-and-mortar counterparts. For instance, log onto Bulbs.com, "the Web's number-one light bulb superstore," and you'll have instant access to every imaginable kind of light bulb or lamp—incandescent bulbs, fluorescent bulbs, projection bulbs, surgical bulbs, automotive bulbs—you name it. Similarly, Web shoes and accessories retailer Zappos.com stocks more than 3 million shoes, handbags, clothing items, and accessories from more than 1,100 brands. No physical store could offer handy access to such vast selections.

Direct marketing channels also give buyers access to a wealth of comparative information about companies, products, and competitors. Good catalogs or Web sites often provide more information in more useful forms than even the most helpful retail salesperson can. For example, the Amazon.com site offers more information than most of us can digest, ranging from top-10 product lists, extensive product descriptions, and expert and user product reviews to recommendations based on customers' previous purchases. And Sears catalogs offer a treasure trove of information about the store's merchandise and services. In fact, you probably wouldn't think it strange to see a Sears salesperson referring to a catalog in the store for more detailed information while trying to advise a customer on a specific product or offer.

Finally, direct marketing is interactive and immediate—buyers can interact with sellers by phone or on the seller's Web site to create exactly the configuration of information, products, or services they desire, and then order them on the spot. Moreover, direct marketing gives consumers a greater measure of control. Consumers decide which catalogs they will browse and which Web sites they will visit.

Benefits to Sellers

For sellers, direct marketing is a powerful tool for building customer relationships. Using database marketing, today's marketers can target small groups or individual consumers and promote their offers through personalized communications. Because of the one-to-one nature of direct marketing, companies can interact with customers by phone or online, learn more about their needs, and tailor products and services to specific customer tastes. In turn, customers can ask questions and volunteer feedback.

Direct marketing also offers sellers a low-cost, efficient, speedy alternative for reaching their markets. Direct marketing has grown rapidly in business-to-business marketing, partly in response to the ever-increasing costs of marketing through the sales force. When personal sales calls cost an average of more than $320 per contact, they should be made only when necessary and to high-potential customers and prospects.[3] Lower-cost-per-contact media—such as telemarketing, direct mail, and company Web sites—often prove more cost effective.

Similarly, online direct marketing results in lower costs, improved efficiencies, and speedier handling of channel and logistics functions, such as order processing, inventory handling, and delivery. Direct marketers such as Amazon.com or Netflix also avoid the expense of maintaining a store and the related costs of rent, insurance, and utilities, passing the savings along to customers.

Direct marketing can also offer greater flexibility. It allows marketers to make ongoing adjustments to its prices and programs, or to make immediate, timely, and personal announcements and offers. ▲For example, in its signature folksy manner, Southwest

Southwest Airlines uses techie direct marketing tools—including a widget and a blog— to inject itself directly into customers' everyday lives. Its Nuts About Southwest blog builds direct, interactive customer relationships that media advertising simply can't achieve.

Airlines uses techie direct marketing tools—including a widget and a blog—to inject itself directly into customers' everyday lives:[4]

The widget—called DING!—is a computer application that consumers can download to their personal computer desktop. Whenever exclusive discount fares are offered, the program emits the familiar in-flight seatbelt-light bell dinging sound. The deep discounts last only 6–12 hours and can only be accessed online by clicking on the application. DING! lets Southwest bypass the reservations system and pass bargain fares directly to interested customers. Eventually, DING! may even allow Southwest to customize fare offers based on each customer's unique characteristics and travel preferences. In its first two years, the DING! application was downloaded by about 2 million consumers and generated more than $150 million in ticket sales. Forty-five percent of its DING! users come back to book again compared to the industry average of just 27 percent.

Based in part on the success of DING!, Southwest launched a "Nuts About Southwest" blog. Written by employees, the blog lets Southwest talk directly with and solicit comments from customers. In turn, it gives customers an inside look at the company and access to 30 cross-department employee bloggers. The blog generates a decisive response from Southwest loyalists. Last year, the blog attracted more than 100,000 total visits and more than 40,000 unique visitors. A blog post by CEO Gary Kelly about the airline's consideration of assigned seating drew more than 600 comments, mainly in support of the current non-assigned seating practice. In all, the low-key blog builds direct, interactive customer relationships that media advertising simply can't achieve.

Finally, direct marketing gives sellers access to buyers that they could not reach through other channels. Smaller firms can mail catalogs to customers outside their local markets and post 1-800 telephone numbers to handle orders and inquiries. Internet marketing is a truly global medium that allows buyers and sellers to click from one country to another in seconds. A Web user from Paris or Istanbul can access an online L.L.Bean catalog as easily as someone living in Freeport, Maine, the direct retailer's hometown. Even small marketers find that they have ready access to global markets.

> **Author Comment** | Direct marketing begins with a good customer database. A company is no better than what it knows about its customers.

Customer Databases and Direct Marketing (pp 493–495)

Customer database

An organized collection of comprehensive data about individual customers or prospects, including geographic, demographic, psychographic, and behavioral data.

Effective direct marketing begins with a good customer database. A **customer database** is an organized collection of comprehensive data about individual customers or prospects, including geographic, demographic, psychographic, and behavioral data. A good customer database can be a potent relationship-building tool. The database gives companies a 360-degree view of its customers and how they behave. A company is no better than what it knows about its customers.

In consumer marketing, the customer database might contain a customer's demographics (age, income, family members, birthdays), psychographics (activities, interests, and opinions), and buying behavior (buying preferences and the recency, frequency, and monetary value— RFM—of past purchases). In business-to-business marketing, the customer profile might contain

▲ Direct marketing databases: Casino operator Harrah's Entertainment's customer information database contains roughly three times the number of printed characters found in the Library of Congress. It uses this data to create special customer experiences.

the products and services the customer has bought, past volumes and prices, key contacts (and their ages, birthdays, hobbies, and favorite foods), competing suppliers, status of current contracts, estimated customer spending for the next few years, and assessments of competitive strengths and weaknesses in selling and servicing the account.

Some of these databases are huge. ▲For example, casino operator Harrah's Entertainment has built a customer database containing 30 terabytes worth of customer information, roughly three times the number of printed characters in the Library of Congress. It uses this data to create special customer experiences. Similarly, Internet portal Yahoo! records every click made by every visitor, adding some 400 billion bytes of data per day to its database—the equivalent of 800,000 books. And Wal-Mart captures data on every item, for every customer, for every store, every day. Its database contains more than 1 petabyte of data—that's a quadrillion bytes, far greater than the storage capacity of 250,000 4-gigabyte flash drives.[5]

Companies use their databases in many ways. They use databases to locate good potential customers and to generate sales leads. They can mine their databases to learn about customers in detail, and then fine-tune their market offerings and communications to the special preferences and behaviors of target segments or individuals. In all, a company's database can be an important tool for building stronger long-term customer relationships.

For example, ▲financial services provider USAA uses its database to find ways to serve the long-term needs of customers, regardless of immediate sales impact, creating an incredibly loyal customer base:

USAA provides financial services to U.S. military personnel and their families, largely through direct marketing via the telephone and Internet. It maintains a customer database built from customer purchasing histories and from information collected directly from customers. To keep the database fresh, the organization regularly surveys its more than 6 million customers worldwide to learn such things as whether they have children (and if so, how old they are), if they have moved recently, and when they plan to retire. USAA uses the database to tailor direct marketing offers to the specific needs of individual customers. For example, for customers looking toward retirement, it sends information on estate planning. If the family has college-age children, USAA sends those children information on how to manage their credit cards. If the family has younger children, it sends booklets on things such as financing a child's education.

▲ Financial services provider USAA uses its extensive database to tailor its services to the specific needs of individual customers, creating incredible customer loyalty.

One delighted reporter, a USAA customer, recounts how USAA even helped him teach his 16-year-old daughter to drive. Just before her birthday, but before she received her driver's license, USAA mailed a "package of materials, backed by research, to help me teach my daughter how to drive, help her practice, and help us find ways to agree on what constitutes safe driving later on, when she gets her license." What's more, marvels the reporter, "USAA didn't try to sell me a thing. My take-away: that USAA is investing in me for the long term, that it defines profitability not just by what it sells today." Through such skillful use of its database, USAA serves each customer uniquely, resulting in high levels of customer loyalty and sales growth. The average customer household owns almost five USAA products, and the $13.4 billion company retains 97 percent of its customers. For four years running, USAA has received the top score of any insurance company in Forrester Research, Inc.'s respected customer advocacy survey, as measured by percentage of customers who agree with the statement: "My financial provider does what's best for me, not just its own bottom line."[6]

Like many other marketing tools, database marketing requires a special investment. Companies must invest in computer hardware, database software, analytical programs, communication links, and skilled personnel. The database system must be user-friendly and available to various marketing groups, including those in product and brand management, new-product development, advertising and promotion, direct mail, telemarketing, Web marketing, field sales, order fulfillment, and customer service. However, a well-managed database should lead to sales and customer-relationship gains that will more than cover its costs.

<table>
<tr><td>**Author Comment**</td><td>Direct marketing is rich in tools, from traditional old favorites such as direct mail, catalogs, and telemarketing to the Internet and other new digital approaches.</td></tr>
</table>

Forms of Direct Marketing (pp 495–504)

The major forms of direct marketing—as shown in ❧ **Figure 17.1**—include personal selling, direct-mail marketing, catalog marketing, telephone marketing, direct-response television marketing, kiosk marketing, new digital direct marketing technologies, and online marketing. We examined personal selling in depth in Chapter 16. Here, we examine the other direct-marketing forms.

Direct-Mail Marketing

Direct-mail marketing
Direct marketing by sending an offer, announcement, reminder, or other item to a person at a particular physical or virtual address.

Direct-mail marketing involves sending an offer, announcement, reminder, or other item to a person at a particular physical or virtual address. Using highly selective mailing lists, direct marketers send out millions of mail pieces each year—letters, catalogs, ads, brochures, samples, CDs and DVDs, and other "salespeople with wings." Direct mail is by far the largest direct marketing medium. The DMA reports that direct mail (including both catalog and non-catalog mail) drives more than a third of all U.S. direct marketing sales.[7]

❧ **FIGURE | 17.1**
Forms of Direct Marketing

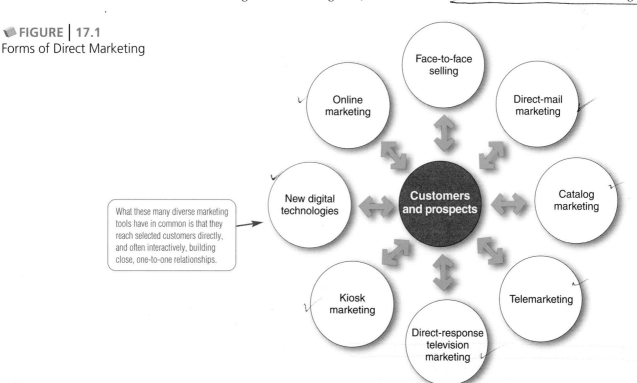

What these many diverse marketing tools have in common is that they reach selected customers directly, and often interactively, building close, one-to-one relationships.

Direct mail is well suited to direct, one-to-one communication. It permits high target-market selectivity, can be personalized, is flexible, and allows easy measurement of results. Although direct mail costs more per thousand people reached than mass media such as television or magazines, the people it reaches are much better prospects. Direct mail has proved successful in promoting all kinds of products, from books, music, DVDs, and magazine subscriptions to insurance, gift items, clothing, gourmet foods, and industrial products. Charities also use direct mail heavily to raise billions of dollars each year.

The direct mail industry constantly seeks new methods and approaches. For example, CDs and DVDs are now among the fastest-growing direct mail media. One study showed that including a CD or DVD in a marketing offer generates responses between 50 to 1,000 percent greater than traditional direct mail.[8] New forms of delivery have also become popular, such as *voice mail, text messaging,* and *e-mail.* Voice mail is subject to the same do-not-call restrictions as telemarketing, so its use has been limited in recent years. However, permission-based mobile marketing (via cell phones) is growing rapidly and e-mail is booming as a direct marketing tool. Today's e-mail messages have moved far beyond the drab text-only messages of old. The new breed of e-mail ad uses animation, interactive links, streaming video, and personalized audio messages to reach out and grab attention.

E-mail, mobile, and other new forms deliver direct mail at incredible speeds compared to the post office's "snail mail" pace. Yet, much like mail delivered through traditional channels, they may be resented as "junk mail" or spam if sent to people who have no interest in them. For this reason, smart marketers are targeting their direct mail carefully so as not to waste their money and recipients' time. They are designing permission-based programs, sending e-mail and mobile ads only to those who want to receive them. We will discuss e-mail and mobile marketing in more detail later in the chapter.

Although the new digital direct mail forms are gaining popularity, the traditional form is still by far the most widely used. Despite the clutter, traditional direct mail can be highly effective, especially for reaching certain segments that don't get as much direct mail as the general population. For example, direct mail plays a big role in pitches by P&G's Tremor buzz-marketing unit to teens:[9]

> You'd expect any marketing program for teens in the twenty-first century to be heavy on digital and light on most forms of old media. But P&G's Tremor found direct mail works particularly well with teens. "What we found was that teens don't get much mail," says a Tremor executive. "So they actually appreciate it when they get it." As a result, Tremor has made direct-mail product information, offers, and samples a cornerstone of its program, although the online component remains substantial as well.

Catalog Marketing

Catalog marketing
Direct marketing through print, video, or digital catalogs that are mailed to select customers, made available in stores, or presented online.

Advances in technology, along with the move toward personalized, one-to-one marketing have resulted in exciting changes in **catalog marketing**. *Catalog Age* magazine used to define a *catalog* as "a printed, bound piece of at least eight pages, selling multiple products, and offering a direct ordering mechanism." Today, only a few years later, this definition is sadly out of date.

With the stampede to the Internet, more and more catalogs are going digital. A variety of Web-only catalogers have emerged, and most print catalogers have added Web-based catalogs to their marketing mixes. For example, click on the Shop by Catalog link at www.llbean.com and you can flip through the latest L.L.Bean catalog page by page online. Web-based catalogs eliminate production, printing, and mailing costs. And whereas print-catalog space is limited, online catalogs can offer an almost unlimited amount of merchandise. Finally, online catalogs allow real-time merchandising—products and features can be added or removed as needed and prices can be adjusted instantly to match demand.

However, despite the advantages of Web-based catalogs, as your overstuffed mailbox may suggest, printed catalogs are still thriving. Why aren't companies ditching their old-fashioned paper catalogs in this new digital era? It turns out that printed catalogs are one of the best ways to drive online sales. "Our catalog is itself an advertising vehicle, and it is

▲ Catalog marketing has grown explosively. There are 8,000 to 10,000 unique catalog titles in the United States alone.

an effective way to drive traffic to our Web site," says an L.L.Bean marketer. In a recent study, 66 percent of retailers surveyed said that they measure a catalog's success by its ability to boost Web sales. Even online-only retailers, such as eBay and UncommonGoods, have started producing catalogs with the hopes of driving online sales. The retailers said that 13 percent of new online customers last year resulted from catalog mailings, and about 43 percent of catalog customers also buy online.[10]

In addition, paper catalogs can also create emotional connections with customers that Web-based sales spaces simply can't (see **Real Marketing 17.1**). For example, Sears recently brought back its holiday Wish Book after a 14-year hiatus. According to Sears' chief marketing officer, many customers were nostalgic for the catalog, reminiscing about the days when they would fold over pages and hope that Santa would notice.[11]

In all, ▲ catalog marketing—printed and online—has grown explosively during the past 25 years. According to one study, there are 8,000 to 10,000 unique catalog titles in the United States. Annual catalog sales amounted to about $150 billion last year and are expected to top $200 billion by 2011.[12]

These days, consumers can buy just about anything from a catalog. Each year Lillian Vernon sends out 17 editions of its 3 catalogs with total circulation of 80 million copies to its 20-million-person database, selling more than 700 products in each catalog, ranging from shoes to decorative lawn birds and monogrammed oven mitts.[13] Specialty department stores, such as Neiman Marcus, Bloomingdale's, and Saks Fifth Avenue, use catalogs to cultivate upper-middle-class markets for high-priced, often exotic, merchandise. Want to buy a rocket trip into outer space? It's featured in the latest Neiman Marcus catalog for only $1.7 million.

Telephone Marketing

Telephone marketing
Using the telephone to sell directly to customers.

Telephone marketing involves using the telephone to sell directly to consumers and business customers. Telephone marketing now accounts for nearly 20 percent of all direct marketing-driven sales. We're all familiar with telephone marketing directed toward consumers, but business-to-business marketers also use telephone marketing extensively, accounting for more than 55 percent of all telephone marketing sales.[14]

Marketers use *outbound* telephone marketing to sell directly to consumers and businesses. ▲ They use *inbound* toll-free 800 numbers to receive orders from television and print ads, direct mail, or catalogs. The use of 800 numbers has taken off in recent years as more and more companies have begun using them, and as current users have added new features such as toll-free fax numbers. To accommodate this rapid growth, new toll-free area codes, such as 888, 877, and 866, have been added.

Properly designed and targeted telemarketing provides many benefits, including purchasing convenience and increased product and service information. However, the explosion in unsolicited outbound telephone marketing over the years annoyed many consumers, who objected to the almost daily "junk phone calls" that pulled them away from the dinner table or filled the answering machine.

In 2003, U.S. lawmakers responded with a National Do Not Call Registry, managed by the Federal Trade Commission. The legislation bans most telemarketing calls to registered phone numbers (although people can still receive calls from nonprofit groups, politicians, and companies with which they have recently done business). Delighted consumers have responded enthusiastically. To date, nearly three-fourths of Americans have registered their phone numbers at www.donotcall.gov or by calling 888-382-1222. Businesses that break do-not-call laws can be

*Careful...*you might sprain a taste bud.

Don't wait another day! Call now to place an order or request a catalog. Also, go on line at **www.carolinacookie.com** to place an order, request a catalog or view our entire selection of products.

1-800-447-5797

▲ Inbound telephone marketing: The Carolina Cookie Company urges, "Don't wait another day. Call now to place an order or request a catalog."

Real Marketing 17.1

Catalogs, Catalogs—
Everywhere!

For outdoor furniture and garden accessories seller Smith & Hawken, the future lies in cyberspace. Sales of flower pots and gardening gadgets on the company's Web site are blossoming, accounting for 20 percent of its total sales. Meanwhile, catalog sales are wilting, declining to 15 percent of total sales last year, from 19 percent the year before. So why not just ditch the paper catalog? Not a chance, says Felix Carbullido, senior vice president for marketing. Rather than becoming obsolete in the online age, he says, the old-fashioned catalog is the most effective way to make an emotional appeal to the consumer. And ultimately, he argues, the catalog is the best method to convince customers to go online.

Thanks to e-commerce, as well as rising printing and mailing costs, catalogs were supposed to be dead by now. In fact, some of the classic "big books," such as Bloomingdale's mail order catalog, are being phased out. But a quick visit to the mailbox will confirm that predictions of death of catalogs have been vastly exaggerated. In fact, catalogs are more popular than ever—and thriving because of the limitations of shopping by pointing and clicking. Unlike the bulky books of yore, such as the venerable Sears catalog, which at times ran to 1,000 pages, the new breed of catalog is a glossy, magazine-like statement meant to convey to consumers the look and feel of a

brand. That's a task that the typical home PC just isn't up to, no matter how good the resolution of the monitor. The prototypical new catalogs don't attempt to list everything in the product line. Rather, they simply show a carefully selected and dramatically photographed selection. "We're promoting an entire lifestyle in the garden or patio, not just items," says Carbullido.

Sure, consumers may complain about the stacks of catalogs stuffing their mailboxes. But they're using them anyway, and their actions are speaking louder than their words to retailers. That's why companies are sending out more and more catalogs—the number mailed grew by 5.5 percent last year to 19.2 billion. A big mass-mailer like Victoria's Secret ships 400 million of them annually, or 1.33 for every American citizen. What can Victoria's Secret possibly get out of those 400 million catalogs? Plenty. Last year

its catalog and online orders accounted for nearly 28 percent of its overall revenues. And catalog sales grew by 10 percent, more than double the 4 percent increase in store sales.

Even companies that started life on the Web appreciate the allure of a well-designed catalog. Zappos.com, the online shoe and accessories giant, now includes its Zappos Life catalog with orders. And tiny candy company JohnandKiras.com started a catalog in October after operating for more than four years only on the Web. The e-commerce site itself is an efficient way to place an order, says co-owner John Doyle, but "it's not a good way to attract attention, especially with new customers." Marketing through electronic mail, although cheap, often gets caught in spam filters, he says.

Thus, net shopping isn't rendering print catalogs obsolete, it's just changing their mission. In their new roles as brand-building

---

fined up to $11,000 per violation. As a result, reports an FTC spokesperson, the program "has been exceptionally successful."[15]

Do-not-call legislation has hurt the telemarketing industry, but not all that much. Two major forms of telemarketing—inbound consumer telemarketing and outbound business-to-business telemarketing—remain strong and growing. Telemarketing also remains a major fund-raising tool for nonprofit groups. However, many telemarketers are shifting to alternative methods for capturing new customers and sales, from direct mail, direct-response TV, and live-chat Web technology to sweepstakes that prompt customers to call in.

For example, ServiceMaster's TruGreen lawn-care service used to generate about 90 percent of its sales through telemarketing. It now uses more direct mail, as well as having employees go door-to-door in neighborhoods where it already has customers. The new approach appears to be working even better than the old cold-calling one. The company's sales have grown under the new methods, and less than 50 percent of sales come from telemarketing. "We were nervous, but were thrilled with what we've accomplished," says ServiceMaster's chief executive.[16]

In fact, do-not-call appears to be helping most direct marketers more than it's hurting them. Many of these marketers are shifting their call-center activity from making cold calls on often resentful customers to managing existing customer relationships. They are developing

devices, catalogs are meant only to give consumers ideas instead of listing every product, so they can be smaller and punchier. And in their roles as lures to draw consumers to the Web, paper catalogs are sprinkled throughout with online come-ons. In the current L.L.Bean outdoor gear catalog, page 3, a prominent spot in any catalog, features a blurb about a sales rep's climb up Mt. Everest. "Read about his trip and see his remarkable photographs" at the Bean Web site, it says. Indeed, almost every spread in the Williams-Sonoma catalog tells readers to go online for information ranging from sample Thanksgiving menus to recipes for Brussels sprouts.

Even as they try to drive people to the Web, companies are also working harder to tap into a desire of consumers to have something to touch and hold. "Catalogs are a tangible connection in an intangible, online, all-in-the-ether world," says a retail strategist. For instance, the cover of L.L.Bean's clothing catalog this season features an actual fabric swatch for its Fitness Fleece Pullovers. "Feel the softness and the quality," the cover copy says. Try doing that online.

To fire shoppers' imaginations, high-end retailers from Saks Fifth Avenue to Neiman Marcus are upping the number of over-the-top fantasy gifts they're offering, such as Neiman's $1.7 million rocket trip into space. Lavish descriptions of these offerings are more than sales tools. They also make good reading material. "People like to receive a beautifully produced catalog. It's entertaining," says a catalog consultant.

Beyond entertainment, a well-designed catalog can be an effective relationship builder. A recent study conducted by Frank About Women, a marketing-to-women communications company, found that a majority of women who receive catalogs are actively engaged with them.

Eighty-nine percent of the participants revealed that they do more than just browse through the catalogs they receive in the mail. They circle or "tab" the items that they want, fold over the corners of pages, and tear pages out. Some 69 percent save their catalogs to look through again. More than just a buying tool, many women view catalogs as a source of entertainment and inspiration. Women claim to love perusing catalogs almost like reading a woman's magazine, looking for ideas for everything from decorating, to fashion, to that extraspecial gift. More than one-third of women surveyed greet their catalogs with enthusiasm, stating they are the first things they look at when they get their mail. Seventy-five percent of women find catalog browsing really enjoyable, fun, and relaxing, with 74 percent agreeing that they get excited when a new catalog arrives.

To enhance such consumer connections, Smith & Hawken recently completed a top-to-bottom revamping of its catalog design approach. Previously, the typical layout in a Smith & Hawken catalog had as many as six items, each shown in photos of roughly equal size. Lighting was stark. Copy focused heavily on the attributes of the products themselves. In the spread showing the Hadley Peak line of wooden furniture, for instance, the main 5-inch-by-7-inch photo of the furniture was on one page and surrounded by six photos of other products. The lighting in the main photo casts hard shadows of chair legs onto a brick patio. Folded napkins and glasses on the table are unused. The spread, says company creative director Sam Osher, "was item specific. The imagery was based just on the product."

Fast-forward a year to the new design. Using a practice known as "heroing," or blowing up an item so it overshadows everything else in the layout, Smith & Hawken now promotes the same Hadley Peak furniture using a 6-inch-by-11-inch photo spread over the layout. It's surrounded by only three other items in far smaller photos, making the furniture the clear focal point. The table is set with actual food and glasses of beer, one half-consumed to show that "there's life in there. Someone was using this napkin," says Osher.

Patio furniture that tugs at the heartstrings? That's exactly the point. "We're showcasing an environment to be aspirational, inspirational," Osher says. "We want to build a scene that makes you say: 'I want to be there.'"

Sources: Adapted from portions of Louise Lee, "Catalogs, Catalogs, Everywhere," *BusinessWeek*, December 4, 2006, pp. 32–34; with additional information from Janie Curtis, "Catalogs as Portals: Why You Should Keep On Mailing," *Multichannel Merchant*, November 30, 2005, accessed at http://multichannelmerchant.com/news/catalogs_portal_1130/index.html; Ylan Q. Mui, "Paging Through the Holidays," *Washington Post*, December 1, 2007, p. D1; and "Digital: Farewell to Mail Order Catalogues," *Precision Marketing*, June 27, 2008, p. 6.

"opt-in" calling systems, in which they provide useful information and offers to customers who have invited the company to contact them by phone or e-mail. These "sales tactics have [produced] results as good—or even better—than telemarketing," declares one analyst. "The opt-in model is proving [more] valuable for marketers [than] the old invasive one."[17]

Direct-Response Television Marketing

Direct-response television marketing takes one of two major forms. The first is *direct-response television advertising* (DRTV). Direct marketers air television spots, often 60 or 120 seconds long, which persuasively describe a product and give customers a toll-free number or Web site for ordering. Television viewers also often encounter full 30-minute or longer advertising programs, or *infomercials*, for a single product.

Some successful direct-response ads run for years and become classics. For example, Dial Media's classic ads for Ginsu knives ran for seven years and sold almost three million sets of knives worth more than $40 million in sales. Bowflex has grossed more than $1.3 billion in infomercial sales. And little-known infomercial maker Guthy-Renker has helped propel Proactiv Solution acne treatment into a power brand that pulls in $850 million in sales annually to five million active customers (compare that to annual American drugstore sales of acne

Direct-response television marketing
Direct marketing via television, including direct-response television advertising (or infomercials) and home shopping channels.

products of only about $150 million). Proactiv's incredible success derives from powerful, formulaic infomercials in which celebrities and average Joes gush about how Proactiv cleared their skin. "My skin is now clear and beautiful," says Serena Williams. "Yours can be too!"[18]

For years, infomercials have been associated with somewhat questionable pitches for juicers and other kitchen gadgets, get-rich-quick schemes, and nifty ways to stay in shape without working very hard at it. In recent years, however, a number of large companies—from Procter & Gamble, Dell, Sears, Disney, Bose, and Revlon to Apple, Land Rover, Anheuser-Busch, and even AARP and the U.S. Navy—have begun using infomercials to sell their wares, refer customers to retailers, send out product information, recruit members, or attract buyers to their Web sites. For example, P&G has used DRTV to market more than a dozen brands, including Dryel, Mr. Clean, CoverGirl, Iams pet food, and Old Spice. An estimated 20 percent of all new infomercials now come to you courtesy of *Fortune* 1000 companies.[19]

Direct-response TV commercials are usually cheaper to make and the media purchase is less costly. Moreover, unlike most media campaigns, direct-response ads always include a 1-800 number or Web address, making it easier for marketers to track the impact of their pitches. For these reasons, DRTV is growing more quickly than traditional broadcast and cable advertising. Some DRTV experts even predict that in 5 or 10 years, as marketers seek greater returns on their advertising investments, all television advertising will be some form of direct-response advertising. "In a business environment where marketers are obsessed with return on investment," notes one such expert, "direct response is tailor-made—[marketers can] track phone calls and Web-site hits generated by the ads. [They can] use DRTV to build brand awareness while simultaneously generating leads and sales."[20]

Home shopping channels, another form of direct-response television marketing, are television programs or entire channels dedicated to selling goods and services. Some home shopping channels, such as the Quality Value Channel (QVC), Home Shopping Network (HSN), and ShopNBC, broadcast 24 hours a day. Program hosts chat with viewers by phone and offer products ranging from jewelry, lamps, collectible dolls, and clothing to power tools and consumer electronics. Viewers call a toll-free number or go online to order goods. With widespread distribution on cable and satellite television, the top three shopping networks combined now reach 248 million homes worldwide.

Despite their lowbrow images, home shopping channels have evolved into highly sophisticated, very successful marketing operations. ▲Consider QVC:

> *Wired* magazine once described QVC as a place appealing to "trailer-park housewives frantically phoning for another ceramic clown." But look past QVC's reputation and you'll find one of the world's most successful and innovative retailers. Last year, the company rang up $7.4 billion in sales. It sits along side NBC and ABC as being one of the largest U.S. broadcasters in terms of revenues. And thanks to shrewd coordination with TV programming that drives buyers online, the company's Web site, QVC.com, is now one of the largest general merchandise Internet retailers. Moreover, QVC isn't just a place where little-known marketers hawk trinkets and trash at bare-bones prices. Prominent manufacturers such as Estée Lauder, Nextel, and Tourneau now sell through QVC. Even high-fashion designers such as John Bartlett and Marc Bouwer now sell lines on QVC.
>
> QVC has honed the art and science of TV retailing. Its producers react in real time, adjusting offers, camera angles, lighting, and dialogue to maximize sales and profits. QVC has become the gold standard of "retailtainment"—the blending of retailing

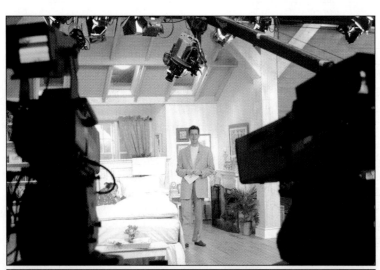

▲ Despite its lowbrow image, QVC is a highly sophisticated marketing operation. The network once sold $65 million worth of Dell computers in 24 hours. When Michael Dell later appeared on the network, QVC did $48,000 in sales every minute he chatted on the air.

and entertainment. QVC folks call it the "backyard fence" sell—the feeling that the merchants are neighbors visiting from next door. But according to QVC's president for U.S. commerce, "we aren't really in the business of selling." Instead, QVC uses products to build relationships with customers.[21]

Kiosk Marketing

As consumers become more and more comfortable with computer and digital technologies, many companies are placing information and ordering machines—called *kiosks* (in contrast to vending machines, which dispense actual products)—in stores, airports, and other locations. Kiosks are popping up everywhere these days, from self-service hotel and airline check-in devices to in-store ordering kiosks that let you order merchandise not carried in the store.

In-store Kodak, Fuji, and HP kiosks let customers transfer pictures from memory sticks, mobile phones, and other digital storage devices, edit them, and make high-quality color prints. Kiosks in Hilton hotel lobbies let guests view their reservations, get room keys, view prearrival messages, check in and out, and even change seat assignments and print boarding passes for flights on any of 18 airlines. ▲And Redbox operates more than 8,000 DVD rental kiosks in supermarkets and fast-food outlets. Customers make their selections on a touch screen, then swipe a credit or debit card to rent DVDs at $1 a day. Customers can even pre-reserve DVDs online to ensure that their trip to the kiosk will not be a wasted one.[22]

▲ Kiosk marketing: Redbox operates more than 8,000 DVD rental kiosks in supermarkets and fast-food outlets nationwide.

Business marketers also use kiosks. For example, Dow Plastics places kiosks at trade shows to collect sales leads and to provide information on its 700 products. The kiosk system reads customer data from encoded registration badges and produces technical data sheets that can be printed at the kiosk or faxed or mailed to the customer. The system has resulted in a 400 percent increase in qualified sales leads.[23]

New Digital Direct Marketing Technologies

Today, thanks to a wealth of new digital technologies, direct marketers can reach and interact with consumers just about anywhere, at anytime, about almost anything. Here, we look into several exciting new digital direct marketing technologies: mobile phone marketing, podcasts and vodcasts, and interactive TV (ITV).

Mobile Phone Marketing

With more than 260 million Americans now subscribing to wireless services, many marketers view mobile phones as the next big direct marketing medium. About 80 percent of consumers in the United States use cell phones and about 60 percent of those people also text message. Within five years, an estimated 40 percent of cell phone subscribers will use their phones to access the Web. Some 23 percent of cell phone users have seen advertising on their phones in the last 30 days and about half of them responded to the ads.[24]

A growing number of consumers—especially younger ones—are using their cell phones as a "third screen" for text messaging, surfing the wireless Web, watching downloaded videos and shows, and checking e-mail. According to one expert, "the cell phone, which makes on-the-go conversing so convenient, is morphing into a content device, a kind of digital Swiss Army knife with the capability of filling its owner's every spare minute with games, music, live and on-demand TV, Web browsing, and, oh yes, advertising." Cell phones allow "marketers to reach consumers anytime, anywhere, on a device they love."[25]

▲ Mobile marketing: Mobile phones and wireless devices have quietly become the newest, hottest frontier for big brand messages.

A recent study estimated that spending on mobile marketing will grow from $1.8 billion in 2007 to as much as $24 billion worldwide by 2013.[26]

▲Mobile phones and wireless devices have quietly become the newest, hottest frontier for big brands, especially those itching to reach the coveted 18- to 34-year-old set. TV networks are prodding viewers to send text messages to vote for their favorite reality TV character. Wireless Web sites are lacing sports scores and news digests with banner ads for Lexus, Burger King, and Sheraton. A few companies are even customizing 10-second video ads for short, TV-style episodes that are edging their way onto mobile phones. For advertisers, the young audience is just one selling point. Wireless gadgets are always-on, ever-present accessories. The fact that a phone is tethered to an individual means that ads can be targeted. And users can respond instantly to time-sensitive offers. The mobile phone is very personal and it's always with you.

Marketers of all kinds—from Pepsi and Nike to P&G, Burger King, Toyota, McDonald's, and Nordstrom—are now integrating mobile phones into their direct marketing. Cell phone promotions include everything from ring-tone giveaways, mobile games, text-in contests, and ad-supported content to retailer announcements of discounts, specials sales, and gift suggestions. For example, McDonald's recently put a promotion code on 20 million Big Mac packages in a joint sweepstakes contest with the House of Blues, urging participants to enter to win prizes and to text in from concerts. Some 40 percent of contest entries came via text messaging, resulting in a 3 percent sales gain for McDonald's. More important, 24 percent of those entering via cell phones opted in to receive future promotions and messages.[27]

 As with other forms of direct marketing, however, companies must use mobile marketing responsibly or risk angering already ad-weary consumers. Most people are initially skeptical about receiving cell phone ad messages. But they often change their minds if the ads deliver value in the form of lower cell phone bills, useful information, entertaining content, or discounted prices and coupons for their favorite products and services. A recent study found that 42 percent of cell phone users are open to mobile advertising if it's relevant.[28] When used properly, mobile marketing can greatly enrich the buyer's experience. For example, Broadway Marketplace, an upscale Cambridge, Massachusetts, grocery store, successfully replaced its card-based loyalty program with one based on mobile phones:[29]

> The new mobile marketing approach lets Broadway Marketplace deliver promotions directly to each shopper's cell phone based on the shopper's purchase history. Customers sign up for the loyalty program and mobile alerts while they're in the store. Then, a few days before a special sale, discount, or in-store event, the grocer sends an e-mail to enrolled customers, followed by a text-message alert the day of the event. The mobile marketing campaign has been successful from day one. Eighty-two percent of the store's shoppers have enlisted in the program and 64 percent use it actively. Broadway Marketplace's sales, which had been flat for the previous few years, grew 10 percent in the first year of the mobile marketing campaign. For more than a decade, Broadway promoted itself with local cable-TV spots, direct-mail campaigns, in-store fliers, and community outreach. These methods alone, however, failed to bring many customers into the store for scheduled food and cooking demonstrations. "We couldn't get the word out," says owner Charlie Bougas. But "now we can," thanks to mobile marketing.

Podcasts and Vodcasts

Podcasting and vodcasting are the latest on-the-go, on-demand technologies. The name *podcast* derives from Apple's now-everywhere iPod. ▲With podcasting, consumers can download audio files (podcasts) or video files (vodcasts) via the Internet to an iPod or other handheld device and then listen to or view them whenever and wherever they wish. They can search for podcast topics through sites such as iTunes or through podcast networks such as PodTrac, Podbridge, or PodShow. These days, you can download podcasts or vodcasts on an exploding array of topics, everything from your favorite National Public Radio show, a recent sitcom episode, or current sports features to the latest music video or Bud Light commercial.

One recent study predicts that the U.S. podcast audience will reach 65 million by 2012, up from 6 million in 2005.[30] As a result, this new medium is drawing much attention from marketers. Many are now integrating podcasts and vodcasts into their direct marketing programs in the form of ad-supported podcasts, downloadable ads and informational features, and other promotions.

▲ With podcasting, consumers can download files via the Internet to an iPod or other handheld device and listen to or view them whenever and wherever they wish.

For example, Volvo sponsors podcasts on Autoblog and Absolut vodka buys ads on PodShow programs. Hot Topic sponsors its own new music podcast featuring underground bands. The Walt Disney World Resort offers weekly podcasts on a mix of topics, including behind-the-scenes tours, interviews, upcoming events, and news about new attractions. New podcasts automatically download to subscribers' computers, where they can transfer them to portable media players to enjoy and share them. And Nestlé Purina publishes podcasts on animal training and behavioral issues. It invites customers to "Take these shows on the road—from serious discussions with veterinarians about pet health to wacky animal videos featuring dogs and cats, Purina has a podcast for you."[31]

Interactive TV (ITV)

Interactive TV (ITV) lets viewers interact with television programming and advertising using their remote controls. In the past, ITV has been slow to catch on. However, the technology now appears poised take off as a direct marketing medium. A recent poll indicated that 66 percent of viewers would be "very interested" in interacting with commercials that piqued their interest.[32] And satellite broadcasting systems such as DIRECTV, EchoStar, and Time Warner are now offering ITV capabilities.

Interactive TV gives marketers an opportunity to reach targeted audiences in an interactive, more involving way. For example, shopping channel HSN recently developed a "Shop by Remote" interactive TV service that allows viewers to immediately purchase any item on HSN using their remote. Procter & Gamble ran interactive ads for its Tide to Go brand. The 30-second TV spots contained remote control links giving interested consumers instant access to more information about the product, as well as coupons and the opportunity to enter a sweepstakes to win a trip to an amusement park. Similarly, Nike's "Quick Is Deadly" campaign for its Zoom training-shoe line included more than 20 minutes of interactive content accessible to Dish Network subscribers with DVRs.[33]

Dish DVR users were able to click into 30- and 60-second TV spots starring San Diego Chargers running back LaDanian Tomlinson and other fleet-footed Nike athletes. Nike gave them the option to view interview footage of the football star discussing his exhaustive training regimen, footage of Tomlinson's signature spin move in different speeds, a Nike-branded game designed to test viewers' remote-control reflexes, and a three-dimensional demo of the Zoom shoe. Nike made similar interactive content available in ads featuring several other Nike endorsers, including basketball's Steve

Nash, runner Lauren Fleshman, Olympic sprinters Asafa Powell and Sanya Richards, and tennis player Rafael Nadal. Using zip-code information in each Dish unit, users were also able to find stores carrying the shoe at the click of a button. The campaign stopped short of actually letting viewers buy the shoes directly from their sets, although the technology enables that function. Research shows that the level of viewer engagement with interactive TV is much higher than with 30-second spots. "We've gotten to the point where all media needs to be interactive," says a creative director at Nike's advertising agency.

Mobile phone marketing, podcasts and vodcasts, and interactive TV offer exciting direct marketing opportunities. But marketers must be careful to use these new direct marketing approaches wisely. As with other direct marketing forms, marketers who use them risk backlash from consumers who may resent such marketing as an invasion of their privacy. Marketers must target their direct marketing offers carefully, bringing real value to customers rather than making unwanted intrusions into their lives.

> **Author Comment** │ Online direct marketing spending is growing at a blistering pace—about 16 percent a year. The Web now accounts for about 20 percent of direct marketing-driven sales.

Online Marketing (pp 504-517)

As noted earlier, **online marketing** is the fastest-growing form of direct marketing. Recent technological advances have created a digital age. Widespread use of the Internet is having a dramatic impact on both buyers and the marketers who serve them. In this section, we examine how marketing strategy and practice are changing to take advantage of today's Internet technologies.

Marketing and the Internet

Much of the world's business today is carried out over digital networks that connect people and companies. The **Internet**, a vast public web of computer networks, connects users of all types all around the world to each other and to an amazingly large information repository. The Web has fundamentally changed customers' notions of convenience, speed, price, product information, and service. As a result, it has given marketers a whole new way to create value for customers and build relationships with them.

Online marketing
Company efforts to market products and services and build customer relationships over the Internet.

Internet
A vast public web of computer networks that connects users of all types all around the world to each other and to an amazingly large "information repository."

Internet usage and impact continues to grow steadily. Last year, Internet household penetration in the United States reached 72 percent, with more than 221 million people now using the Internet at home or at work. The average U.S. Internet user spends some 70 hours a month surfing the Web at home and at work. Worldwide, more than 540 million people now have Internet access.[34] Moreover, in a recent survey, 33 percent of American consumers chose the Internet as the second-most-essential medium in their lives (close behind TV at 36 percent). However, the Internet came in first as the "most cool and exciting medium."[35]

Click-only companies
The so-called dot-coms, which operate only online without any brick-and-mortar market presence.

All kinds of companies now market online. **Click-only companies** operate only on the Internet. They include a wide array of firms, from *e-tailers* such as Amazon.com and Expedia.com that sell products and services directly to final buyers via the Internet to *search engines and portals* (such as Yahoo!, Google, and MSN), *transaction sites* (eBay), and *content sites* (*New York Times* on the Web, ESPN.com, and Encyclopaedia Britannica Online). After a frenzied and rocky start in the 1990s, many click-only dot-coms are now prospering in today's online marketspace.

As the Internet grew, the success of the dot-coms caused existing *brick-and-mortar* manufacturers and retailers to reexamine how they served their markets. Now, almost all of these traditional companies have set up their own online sales and communications channels, becoming **click-and-mortar companies**. It's hard to find a company today that doesn't have a substantial Web presence.

Click-and-mortar companies
Traditional brick-and-mortar companies that have added online marketing to their operations.

In fact, many click-and-mortar companies are now having more online success than their click-only competitors. In a recent ranking of the top 10 online retail sites, only two were click-only retailers. All of the others were multichannel retailers.[36] ▲ For example, Office Depot's more than 1,000 office-supply superstores rack up annual sales of $15.5 billion in more than 42 countries. But you might be surprised to learn that Office Depot's fastest recent growth has

▲ Click-and-mortar marketing: No click-only or brick-only seller can match the call, click, or visit convenience and support afforded by Office Depot's "4 easy ways to shop."

come not from its traditional "brick-and-mortar" channels, but from the Internet.[37]

Office Depot's online sales have soared in recent years, now accounting for 31 percent of total sales. Selling on the Web lets Office Depot build deeper, more personalized relationships with customers large and small. For example, a large customer such as GE or P&G can create lists of approved office products at discount prices and then let company departments or even individuals do their own online purchasing. This reduces ordering costs, cuts through the red tape, and speeds up the ordering process for customers. At the same time, it encourages companies to use Office Depot as a sole source for office supplies. Even the smallest companies find 24-hour-a-day online ordering easier and more efficient.

Importantly, Office Depot's Web operations don't steal from store sales. Instead, the OfficeDepot.com site actually builds store traffic by helping customers find a local store and check stock. In return, the local store promotes the Web site through in-store kiosks. If customers don't find what they need on the shelves, they can quickly order it via the Web from the kiosk. Thus, Office Depot now offers a full range of contact points and delivery modes—online, by phone or fax, and in the store. No click-only or brick-only seller can match the call, click, or visit convenience and support afforded by Office Depot's click-and-mortar model.

Online Marketing Domains

 The four major online marketing domains are shown in ◆ **Figure 17.2**. They include B2C (business-to-consumer), B2B (business-to-business), C2C (consumer-to-consumer), and C2B (consumer-to-business).

Business-to-Consumer (B2C)

Business-to-consumer (B2C) online marketing
Businesses selling goods and services online to final consumers.

The popular press has paid the most attention to **business-to-consumer (B2C) online marketing**—businesses selling goods and services online to final consumers. Today's consumers can buy almost anything online—from clothing, kitchen gadgets, and airline tickets to computers and cars. Online consumer buying continues to grow at a healthy rate. More than half of all U.S. households now regularly shop online. Last year, U.S. consumers generated $175 billion in online retail sales, up 22 percent from the previous year.[38]

Perhaps more importantly, the Internet now influences 35 percent of total retail sales—sales transacted online plus those carried out offline but encouraged by online research. By 2010, the Internet will influence a staggering 50 percent of total retail sales.[39] Thus, smart marketers are employing integrated multichannel strategies that use the Web to drive sales to other marketing channels.

◆ FIGURE | 17.2
Online Marketing Domains

Online marketing can be classified by who initiates it and to whom it's targeted. As consumers, we're most familiar with B2C and C2C, but B2B is also flourishing.

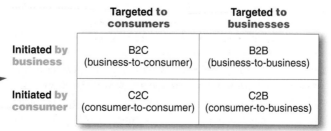

	Targeted to consumers	Targeted to businesses
Initiated by business	B2C (business-to-consumer)	B2B (business-to-business)
Initiated by consumer	C2C (consumer-to-consumer)	C2B (consumer-to-business)

As more and more people find their way onto the Web, the population of online consumers is becoming more mainstream and diverse. The Web now offers marketers a palette of different kinds of consumers seeking different kinds of online experiences. However, Internet consumers still differ from traditional offline consumers in their approaches to buying and in their responses to marketing. In the Internet exchange process, customers initiate and control the contact. Traditional marketing targets a somewhat passive audience. In contrast, online marketing targets people who actively select which Web sites they will visit and what marketing information they will receive about which products and under what conditions. Thus, the new world of online marketing requires new marketing approaches.

People now go online to order a wide range of goods—clothing from Gap or L.L.Bean, books or electronics or about anything else from Amazon.com, furniture from Ethan Allen, major appliances from Sears, flowers from Calyx & Corolla, ▲or even home mortgages from Quicken Loans.[40]

At Quicken Loans (www.QuickenLoans.com), prospective borrowers receive a high-tech, high-touch, one-stop mortgage experience. At the site, customers can research a wide variety of home-financing and refinancing options, apply for a mortgage, and receive quick loan approval—all without leaving the comfort and security of their homes. The site provides useful interactive tools that help borrowers decide how much house they can afford, whether to rent or buy, whether to refinance a current mortgage, the economics of fixing up their current homes rather than moving, and much more. Customers can receive advice by phone or by chatting online with one of several thousand mortgage experts and sign up for later e-mail rate updates. Quicken Loans augments its main site with two other online resources—Quizzle.com and Qtopia.com. Quizzle helps give customers a better picture of their overall financial situation, including their credit score, debt, home value and equity, and monthly budget. Qtopia is a virtual world that lets Quicken Loans work with customers beyond the loan's closing, providing them with access to educational tools, their loan documents, real estate listings, and exclusive discounts on partner companies' products and services—all with the goal of remaining the customer's lender for life.

▲ B2C Web sites: People now go online to order a wide range of goods and services, even home mortgages.

Business-to-Business (B2B)

Business-to-business (B2B) online marketing

Businesses using B2B Web sites, e-mail, online catalogs, online trading networks, and other online resources to reach new business customers, serve current customers more effectively, and obtain buying efficiencies and better prices.

Although the popular press has given the most attention to B2C Web sites, **business-to-business (B2B) online marketing** is also flourishing. B2B marketers use B2B Web sites, e-mail, online product catalogs, online trading networks, and other online resources to reach new business customers, serve current customers more effectively, and obtain buying efficiencies and better prices.

Most major business-to-business marketers now offer product information, customer purchasing, and customer-support services online. For example, corporate buyers can visit Sun Microsystems' Web site (www.sun.com), select detailed descriptions of Sun's products and solutions, request sales and service information, and interact with staff members. Some major companies conduct almost all of their business on the Web. Networking equipment and software maker Cisco Systems takes more than 80 percent of its orders over the Internet.

Beyond simply selling their products and services online, companies can use the Internet to build stronger relationships with important business customers. For example, Dell has set up customized Web sites for more than 113,000 business and institutional customers worldwide.

These individualized Premier/Dell.com sites help business customers to more efficiently manage all phases of their Dell computer buying and ownership. Each customer's Premier.Dell.com Web site can include a customized online computer store, purchasing and asset management reports and tools, system-specific technical information, links to useful information throughout Dell's extensive Web site, and more. The site makes all the information a customer needs in order to do business with Dell available in one place, 24 hours a day, 7 days a week.[41]

Consumer-to-Consumer (C2C)

Much **consumer-to-consumer (C2C) online marketing** and communication occurs on the Web between interested parties over a wide range of products and subjects. In some cases, the Internet provides an excellent means by which consumers can buy or exchange goods or information directly with one another. For example, eBay, Amazon.com Auctions, Overstock.com, and other auction sites offer popular market spaces for displaying and selling almost anything, from art and antiques, coins and stamps, and jewelry to computers and consumer electronics.

eBay's C2C online trading community of more than 275 million registered users worldwide (greater than the combined populations of France, Germany, Italy, and Britain!) transacted some $60 billion in trades last year. At any given time, the company's Web site lists more than 115 million items up for auction in more than 50,000 categories. Such C2C sites give people access to much larger audiences than the local flea market or newspaper classifieds (which, by the way, have also gone online at Web sites such as Craigslist.com and eBay's Kijiji.com). Interestingly, based on its huge success in the C2C market, eBay has now attracted more than 500,000 B2C sellers, ranging from small businesses peddling their regular wares to large businesses liquidating excess inventory at auction.[42]

In other cases, C2C involves interchanges of information through Internet forums that appeal to specific special-interest groups. Such activities may be organized for commercial or noncommercial purposes. An example is Web logs, or *blogs*, online journals where people post their thoughts, usually on a narrowly defined topic. Blogs can be about anything, from politics or baseball to haiku, car repair, or the latest television series. There are currently about 15 million active blogs read by 57 million people. Such numbers give blogs—especially those with large and devoted followings—substantial influence.[43]

Many marketers are now tapping into blogs as a medium for reaching carefully targeted consumers. One way is to advertise on an existing blog or to influence content there. Consider this example:[44]

When Nescafé launched its Dolce Gusto coffee maker in France last year, it turned to bloggers. It placed an ad on French Web site BlogBang.com, which has a community of more than 2,000 bloggers. The site sent a message to its members telling them about the ad campaign, which came in the form of an interactive game. The bloggers were asked to put a link to the game on their sites. In return, Dolce Gusto's home page posted links to the blogs that joined up. "The advantage of using blogs is that the message gets around very quickly," says the Dolce Gusto brand manager, "and it focuses on our target audience" of 25- to 35-year-olds. "It really created a marketing buzz." Within three weeks of its launch, Dolce Gusto's ad was displayed on 500 blogs, and 320,000 people had played the online game.

Other companies set up their own blogs. ▲For example, GM maintains a blog called FastLane that helps it connect with its core consumers in a virtual grassroots kind of way. The log is penned by GM executives, including Vice Chairman Bob Lutz, who some claim is the big reason for its popularity. The company says it wants all kinds of feedback—so the blog includes both positive and negative comments from readers. Says Lutz, "I'd say the biggest surprise is the passion in which people respond and comment on the blogs. You're getting the real deal there. There is so much passion that even the negative comments are palatable, and indeed, often helpful." The FastLane blog receives about 3,000 visitors a day, helping GM build or rebuild relationships with customers. "If there is a gap between GM's excellence and people's perception of it, we believe blogs are a

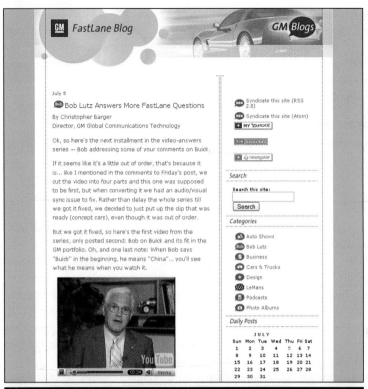

July 5

Bob Lutz Answers More FastLane Questions
By Christopher Barger
Director, GM Global Communications Technology

Ok, so here's the next installment in the video-answers series — Bob addressing some of your comments on Buick.

If it seems like it's a little out of order, that's because it is... like I mentioned in the comments to Friday's post, we cut the video into four parts and this one was supposed to be first, but when converting it we had an audio/visual sync issue to fix. Rather than delay the whole series till we got it fixed, we decided to just put up the clip that was ready (concept cars), even though it was out of order.

But we got it fixed, so here's the first video from the series, only posted second: Bob on Buick and its fit in the GM portfolio. Oh, and one last note: When Bob says "Buick" in the beginning, he means "China"... you'll see what he means when you watch it.

▲ Many marketers are now tapping into consumer-to-consumer Web communications by setting up their own blogs. GM's FastLane blog—penned primarily by Vice Chairman Bob Lutz—helps GM connect with its core consumers in a virtual grassroots kind of way.

great opportunity to change those perceptions," says GM's digital marketing chief.[45]

As a marketing tool, blogs offer some advantages. They can offer a fresh, original, personal, and cheap way to reach today's fragmented audiences. However, the blogosphere is cluttered and difficult to control. "Blogs may help companies bond with consumers in exciting new ways, but they won't help them control the relationship," says a blog expert. Such Web journals remain largely a C2C medium. "That isn't to suggest companies can't influence the relationship or leverage blogs to engage in a meaningful relationship," says the expert, "but the consumer will remain in control."[46]

Whether or not they actively participate in the blogosphere, companies should show up, monitor, and listen to them. For example, Starbucks sponsors its own blog (www.MyStarbucksIdea.com) but also closely follows consumer dialogue on the 30 or more other third-party online sites devoted to the brand. It then uses the customer insights it gains from all of these proprietary and third party blogs to adjust its marketing programs. For instance, it recently altered the remaining installments of a four-part podcast based on the negative blog feedback it gleaned on the first one.[47]

In all, C2C means that online buyers don't just consume product information—increasingly, they create it. As a result, "word of Web" is joining "word of mouth" as an important buying influence.

Consumer to Business (C2B)

Consumer-to-business (C2B) online marketing

Online exchanges in which consumers search out sellers, learn about their offers, and initiate purchases, sometimes even driving transaction terms.

The final online marketing domain is **consumer-to-business (C2B) online marketing**. Thanks to the Internet, today's consumers are finding it easier to communicate with companies. Most companies now invite prospects and customers to send in suggestions and questions via company Web sites. Beyond this, rather than waiting for an invitation, consumers can search out sellers on the Web, learn about their offers, initiate purchases, and give feedback. Using the Web, consumers can even drive transactions with businesses, rather than the other way around. For example, using Priceline.com, would-be buyers can bid for airline tickets, hotel rooms, rental cars, cruises, and vacation packages, leaving the sellers to decide whether to accept their offers.

Consumers can also use Web sites such as GetSatisfaction.com, Complaints.com, and PlanetFeedback.com to ask questions, offer suggestions, lodge complaints, or deliver compliments to companies. GetSatisfaction.com provides "people-powered customer service" by creating a user-driven customer-service community. The site provides forums where customers discuss problems they're having with the products and services of 2,500 companies—from Apple to Zappos.com—whether the company participates or not. GetSatisfaction.com also provides tools by which companies can adopt GetSatisfaction.com as an official customer service resource. Since launching in 2007, the site has drawn more than a million unique visitors.[48]

Setting up an Online Marketing Presence

Clearly, all companies need to consider moving online. Companies can conduct online marketing in any of the four ways shown in ▶ **Figure 17.3**: creating a Web site, placing ads and promotions online, setting up or participating in online social networks, or using e-mail.

Creating a Web Site

For most companies, the first step in conducting online marketing is to create a Web site. However, beyond simply creating a Web site, marketers must design an attractive site and find ways to get consumers to visit the site, stay around, and come back often.

FIGURE | 17.3
Setting Up for Online Marketing

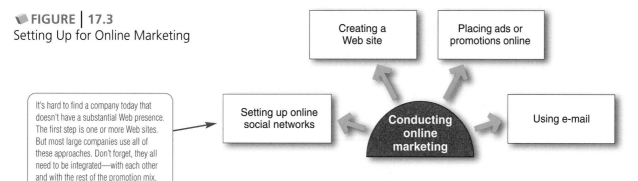

It's hard to find a company today that doesn't have a substantial Web presence. The first step is one or more Web sites. But most large companies use all of these approaches. Don't forget, they all need to be integrated—with each other and with the rest of the promotion mix.

Corporate (or brand) Web site
A Web site designed to build customer goodwill, collect customer feedback, and supplement other sales channels, rather than to sell the company's products directly.

Marketing Web site
A Web site that engages consumers in interactions that will move them closer to a direct purchase or other marketing outcome.

Types of Web Sites. Web sites vary greatly in purpose and content. The most basic type is a **corporate (or brand) Web site**. These sites are designed to build customer goodwill, collect customer feedback, and supplement other sales channels, rather than to sell the company's products directly. They typically offer a rich variety of information and other features in an effort to answer customer questions, build closer customer relationships, and generate excitement about the company or brand.

For example, you can't buy anything at P&G's Tide to Go brand site, but you can learn how to use the handy stain remover stick (including a video demo), watch recent ads, and share "Tide to Go saves the day!" stories with others. And Unilever's campaignforrealbeauty.com site doesn't sell Dove soaps and lotions. But it does provide a place for people interested in the cause of women and girl's self-esteem to share their thoughts, view ads and viral videos such as "Dove Evolution" or "Onslaught," and download self-esteem assessment tools and workbooks. They can even register for a free training guide to become a Dove Real Beauty Workshop for Girls facilitator. Such Web sites, once brushed aside as digital "brochureware," are now attracting consumers in numbers that vie with flashier consumer sites and even traditional mass media.[49]

Believe it or not, those boring corporate Web sites are pulling in more eyeballs—and more influencers—than flashy prime time TV shows, print magazines, and general-interest sites. Package-goods marketers such as P&G and Unilever don't sell many products directly online. Their low-cost, low-involvement brands tend not to generate much search. Yet P&G and Unilever Web sites now reach nearly 6 million and 3 million unique visitors, respectively, in the United States each month, easily swamping the audiences of many magazines and cable and syndicated TV shows where the companies advertise. But more important than the volume may be who the visitors are. Corporate and brand Web site visitors are much more likely to influence others and to recommend brands to them. Of all options for influencing the online influencers, brand Web sites rank highest both in consumer acceptance and marketer control.

Other companies create a **marketing Web site**. These sites engage consumers in an interaction that will move them closer to a direct purchase or other marketing outcome. For example, visitors to SonyStyle.com can search through dozens of categories of Sony products, learn more about specific items, and read expert product reviews. They can check out the latest hot deals, place orders online, and pay by credit card, all with a few mouse clicks.

MINI USA operates a marketing Web site at www.MINIUSA.com. Once a potential customer clicks in, the carmaker wastes no time trying to turn the inquiry into a sale, and then into a long-term relationship. ▲The site offers a garage full of useful information and interactive selling features, including detailed and fun descriptions of current MINI models, tools for designing your very own MINI, information on dealer locations and services, and even tools for tracking your new MINI from factory to delivery.

Before Angela DiFabio bought her MINI Cooper last September, she spent untold hours on the company's Web site, playing with dozens of possibilities before coming up with the perfect combination: a chili-pepper-red exterior, white racing stripes on the hood, and a "custom rally badge bar" on the grill. When DiFabio placed her order with her dealer, the same build-your-own tool—and all the price and product details it provided—left her

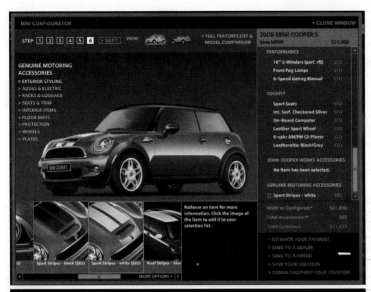

▲ The MINI marketing Web site does more than just provide information or sell cars; it keeps customers engaged, from designing their very own MINI to tracking it from factory to delivery.

feeling like she was getting a fair deal. "He even used the site to order my car," she says. While she waited for her MINI to arrive, DiFabio logged on to MINI's Web site every day, this time using its "Where's My Baby?" tracking tool to follow her car, like an expensive FedEx package, from the factory in Britain to its delivery. The Web site does more than just provide information or sell products or services. It makes an impact on the customer experience: It's fun, it's individual, it makes users feel like part of the clan.[50]

Designing Effective Web Sites. Creating a Web site is one thing; getting people to *visit* the site is another. To attract visitors, companies aggressively promote their Web sites in offline print and broadcast advertising and through ads and links on other sites. But today's Web users are quick to abandon any Web site that doesn't measure up. The key is to create enough value and excitement to get consumers who come to the site to stick around and come back again. This means that companies must constantly update their sites to keep them current, fresh, and useful.

For some types of products, attracting visitors is easy. Consumers buying new cars, computers, or financial services will be open to information and marketing initiatives from sellers. Marketers of lower-involvement products, however, may face a difficult challenge in attracting Web site visitors. If you're in the market for a computer and you see a banner ad that says, "The top 10 PCs under $800," you'll likely click on the banner. But what kind of ad would get you to visit a site like dentalfloss.com?

A key challenge is designing a Web site that is attractive on first view and interesting enough to encourage repeat visits. Many marketers create colorful, graphically sophisticated Web sites that combine text, sound, and animation to capture and hold attention (for examples, see www.looneytunes.com or www.nike.com). ▲To attract new visitors and to encourage revisits, suggests one expert, online marketers should pay close attention to the seven Cs of effective Web site design:[51]

- *Context:* the site's layout and design

- *Content:* the text, pictures, sound, and video that the Web site contains

- *Community:* the ways that the site enables user-to-user communication

- *Customization:* the site's ability to tailor itself to different users or to allow users to personalize the site

- *Communication:* the ways the site enables site-to-user, user-to-site, or two-way communication

- *Connection:* the degree that the site is linked to other sites

- *Commerce:* the site's capabilities to enable commercial transactions

And to keep customers coming back to the site, companies need to embrace yet another "C"—constant change.

At the very least, a Web site should be easy to use, professional looking, and physically attractive. Ultimately, however, Web sites must also be *useful*. When it comes to Web surfing and shopping, most people prefer substance over style and function over flash. ▲Thus, effective Web sites contain deep and useful information, interactive tools that help buyers find and evaluate products of interest, links to other related sites, changing promotional offers, and entertaining features that lend relevant excitement.

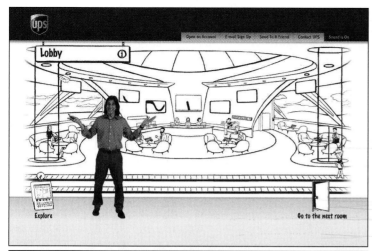

▲ Effective Web sites: Check out the above UPS Web site at http://whiteboard.ups.com/. The Web Marketing Association judged this as one of last year's two best Web sites. Applying the seven Cs of effective Web site design, do you agree?

Maintaining a top Web site is a complex and ongoing task. For example, The Walt Disney Company recently overhauled its marquee Disney.com site for the second time in only two years:[52]

The changes to Disney.com will introduce more free videos (including full-length movies like *Finding Nemo*) as well as more games and things for visitors to do with their cell phones. For instance, little girls (or bigger ones) who create fairy avatars in a virtual world called Pixie Hollow will be able to use their cell phones to create pet butterflies for their fairies. "I'm going to want to use my phone to feed and love my butterfly all the time," said Disney's executive vice president for mobile content. "That kind of emotional vesting is what we're after." With the changes, Disney is trying to position its Web site more as a place that entertains and less of one that exists to promote Disney wares. No longer will the site ask youngsters to navigate through categories like "Movies," "TV," and "Live Events." New options will include "Games," "Videos" and "Characters" and will emphasize how to find immediate entertainment. "It's a repositioning of our digital front door," says another Disney Online executive. The constant changes reflect the whiplash-fast pace at which online is evolving. The previous site overhaul increased unique visitors to Disney.com by about 40 percent to nearly 30 million a month, making it the number-one Web destination for children and family-oriented Web sites. The average user spends 45 minutes per visit. But refreshing the site is an ongoing process. "Our initial instincts [have been] right," says the executive. "We just need to take it much further."

Placing Ads and Promotions Online

Online advertising

Advertising that appears while consumers are surfing the Web, including display ads, search-related ads, online classifieds, and other forms.

As consumers spend more and more time on the Internet, many companies are shifting more of their marketing dollars to **online advertising** to build their brands or to attract visitors to their Web sites. Online advertising is becoming a major medium. Last year, U.S. companies spent more than $21 billion on online advertising, up an incredible 26 percent over the previous year, and more than they spent on newspaper, outdoor, or radio advertising. Online ad spending will jump to more than $42 billion by 2011, rivaling or surpassing the amount spent on magazines and even television.[53] Here, we discuss forms of online advertising and promotion and their future.

Forms of Online Advertising. The major forms of online advertising include display ads, search-related ads, and online classifieds. Online display ads might appear anywhere on an Internet user's screen. The most common form is *banners*, banner-shaped ads found at the top, bottom, left, right, or center of a Web page. For instance, a Web surfer looking up airline schedules or fares might encounter a flashing banner that screams, "Rent a car from Alamo and get up to two days free!" Clicking on the ad takes consumers to the Alamo Web site, where they can redeem the promotion.

Interstitials are online display ads that appear between screen changes on a Web site, especially while a new screen is loading. For example, visit www.marketwatch.com and you'll probably see a 10-second ad for Visa, Verizon, Dell, or another sponsor before the home page loads. *Pop-ups* are online ads that appear suddenly in a new window in front of the window being viewed. Such ads can multiply out of control, creating a major annoyance. As a result, Internet services and Web browser providers have developed applications that let users block most pop-ups. But not to worry. Many advertisers have now developed pop-*unders*, new windows that evade pop-up blockers by appearing behind the page you're viewing.

With the increase in broadband Internet access in American homes, many companies are developing exciting new *rich media* display ads, which incorporate animation, video, sound, and interactivity. Rich media ads attract and hold consumer attention better than traditional banner ads. They employ techniques such as float, fly, and snapback—animations that jump out and sail over the Web page before retreating to their original space.

But many rich media ads do more than create a little bit of jumping animation—they also create interactivity. Many of today's rich media ads provide consumers with product information, a brand experience, and even local or online buying options without taking them away from the site they are viewing. For example, to attract would-be commodity traders to its Web site, the Chicago Board of Trade runs a small rich media banner ad that explodes into a small site when the user's mouse rolls over it. The mouse-over site features a "tasting" of the site—free streaming quotes, sample research, and a virtual trading account, all of which would never fit into a traditional static ad.[54]

Another hot growth area for online advertising is *search-related ads* (or *contextual advertising*), in which text-based ads and links appear alongside search engine results on sites such as Google and Yahoo!. For example, search Google for "HDTV." At the top and side of the resulting search list, you'll see inconspicuous ads for 10 or more advertisers, ranging from Circuit City, Best Buy, and Amazon.com to Dish Network, Nextag.com, and TigerDirect.com. Nearly all of Google's $16.59 billion in revenues come from ad sales. An advertiser buys search terms from the search site and pays only if consumers click through to its site. Search-related ads account for some 41 percent of all online advertising expenditures, more than any other category of online advertising.[55]

Search ads can be an effective way to link consumers to other forms of online promotion. For example, Diageo uses keyword searches to lure Web surfers to sites promoting its Smirnoff Raw Tea and Ice products:[56]

> In the summer season of 2006, Diageo wanted to create brand awareness and engagement for its two brands, Smirnoff Ice and Smirnoff Raw Tea. The goal was to drive visitors to the brands' Web sites, where they could enter a sweepstake competition and see a goofy video called "Tea Partay." The video featured wanna-be rappers, called the Prep Unit, who live in the suburbs, wear Docksiders and polos, and brag about drinking Raw Tea and eating finger sandwiches. From Yahoo!, Diageo purchased keywords such as "Smirnoff Ice," and then extended to terms such as "finger sandwiches," "preppy," "hilarious video," and "hip-hop music" to drive more traffic to the viral video. ("Finger sandwiches" had one of the campaign's highest click-through rates.) Overall, the campaign generated nearly 15 million search impressions in only four months, with the integrated search and display campaign delivering 600 million impressions and 2 million clicks. The "Tea Partay" videos had more than 5 million views and even prompted a second video release the following summer—"Green Tea Partay"—to help introduce the new Smirnoff Raw Tea flavor, Green Tea Smirnoff.

Other Forms of Online Promotion.   Other forms of online promotions include content sponsorships, alliances and affiliate programs, and viral advertising.

Using *content sponsorships*, companies gain name exposure on the Internet by sponsoring special content on various Web sites, such as news or financial information or special-interest topics. For example, Scotts, the lawn-and-garden products company, sponsors the Local Forecast section on WeatherChannel.com, and David Sunflower Seeds sponsors the ESPN Fantasy Baseball site at ESPN.com. Sponsorships are best placed in carefully targeted sites where they can offer relevant information or service to the audience. Internet companies can also develop *alliances and affiliate programs*, in which they work with other companies, online and offline, to "promote each other." For example, through its Amazon Associates Program, Amazon.com has more than 900,000 affiliates who post Amazon.com banners on their Web sites.

Finally, online marketers use **viral marketing**, the Internet version of word-of-mouth marketing. Viral marketing involves creating a Web site, video, e-mail message, or other marketing event that is so infectious that customers will want to pass it along to their friends. One observer describes viral marketing as "addictive, self-propagating advertisement

Viral marketing
The Internet version of word-of-mouth marketing—Web sites, videos, e-mail messages, or other marketing events that are so infectious that customers will want to pass them along to friends.

that lives on Web sites, blogs, cell phones, message boards, and even in real-world stunts."[57] Because customers pass the message or promotion along to others, viral marketing can be very inexpensive. And when the information comes from a friend, the recipient is much more likely to open and read it.

Although marketers usually have little control over where their viral messages end up, a well-concocted viral campaign can gain vast exposure. ▲Consider OfficeMax's wacky ElfYourself.com seasonal viral Web site, which lets visitors paste images of their own faces onto dancing elves, along with a personal message.[58]

▲ Viral marketing: OfficeMax's ElfYourself.com viral Web site has propelled itself into the digital record books. With no promotion at all, the site logged more than 193 million visits between late November and early January last year. One-third of those visiting the site were influenced to shop at OfficeMax.

OfficeMax's holiday ElfYourself.com viral Web site has propelled itself into the digital record books, all with no hint of promotion. Between late November 2007 and early January 2008, ElfYourself.com logged more than 193 million site visits and a whopping 123 million elves were created, with 53 percent of visitors returning for additional visits. The elves were publicity magnets for OfficeMax, drawing fawning coverage from CNN, *ABC World News Tonight*, Fox News, the *New York Times*, *The Today Show*, and *Good Morning America*. Popular in more than 50 countries, the elves even popped up dancing on the Jumbo Tron overlooking Times Square in New York City. OfficeMax executives even joke about the elves replacing Frosty and Rudolph as holiday icons for this generation. More important, one-third of those who visited the ElfYourself.com site were influenced to shop at OfficeMax, and another one-third said the holiday treat improved their perception of the retailer.

However, achieving such success isn't as easy as it might seem. In its first season, ElfYourself.com was just one of 20 holiday-themed viral Web sites developed by OfficeMax, which hoped that at least one would catch fire among bored office workers looking for things to share online over the holidays. (All 20 sites were built at less than the cost of producing just one television commercial—generally about $350,000.) ElfYourself.com was the only one that blossomed. "There's a lot of luck to this stuff," says one of the site's creators. Companies "don't make things viral, consumers do. We were lucky enough to land on something that worked very well."

Creating or Participating in Online Social Networks

Online social networks

Online social communities—blogs, social networking Web sites, or even virtual worlds—where people socialize or exchange information and opinions.

As we discussed in Chapter 5, the popularity of the Internet has resulted in a rash of **online social networks** or *Web communities*. Countless independent and commercial Web sites have arisen that give consumers online places to congregate, socialize, and exchange views and information. These days, it seems, almost everyone is buddying up on MySpace or Facebook, tuning into the day's hottest videos at YouTube, or even living a surprisingly real fantasy life as an avatar on *Second Life*. And, of course, wherever consumers congregate, marketers will surely follow. More and more marketers are now starting to ride the huge social networking wave.

Marketers can engage in online communities in two ways: They can participate in existing Web communities or they can set up their own. Joining existing networks seems easiest. Thus, many major brands—from Burger King, Honda, and Motorola to Estée Lauder and Victoria's Secret—have set up MySpace pages and profiles. Burger King, for instance, has amassed more than 120,000 MySpace "friends," fellow users who have chosen to associate themselves with this profile. Similarly, the Apple Students group on Facebook, which offers information and deals on Apple products, has more than

Real Marketing 17.2

Online Social Networks:
Targeting Niches of Like-Minded People

Marketers who think bigger is better may want to reconsider, at least when it comes to online social networks. Although giant networks such as MySpace and Facebook get all the attention these days, social networks focused on topics as remote as knitting or bird watching can present marketers with strong targeting opportunities:

When jet-setters began flocking to an exclusive social-networking Web site reserved for the rich, they got the attention of an online community's most valuable ally: advertisers. The invitation-only site, ASmallWorld.net, has 300,000 select members who have become a magnet for companies that make luxury goods and are trying to reach people who can afford them. The site's biggest advertisers include Burberry, Cartier, and Land Rover. Cognac maker Remy Martin last month threw a tasting party for the site's elite members, at which its top-shelf, $1,800-a-bottle liquor flowed freely.

Thousands of social-networking sites have popped up to cater to specific interests,

When it comes to marketing through online social-networking sites, smaller might be better. Niche site imeem.com works with sponsors such as Burger King, which target its younger and edgier membership community. "Relevance trumps size," says one expert.

backgrounds, professions, and age groups. Nightclub frequenters can converge at DontStayIn.com. Wine connoisseurs have formed Snooth.com, and people going through divorce can commiserate at Divorce360.com.

More and more, marketers are taking a chance on smaller sites that could be more relevant to their products. AT&T, for example, recently promoted one of its global cell phones on WAYN.com (short for "Where are you now?"), a social network for international travelers. While

AT&T advertises on the bigger sites like MySpace to reach a large audience quickly, the wireless carrier is also turning to niche networks, "where your ads are more meaningful—those are the real gems," says a social networking expert.

There's at least one social network for just about every interest or hobby. Yub.com is for shopoholics, Fuzzster.com is for pet lovers, OnLoq.com is for hip-hop fans, Jango.com lets music fans find others with similar tastes, and PassportStamp.com is one of several sites for avid travelers.

500,000 members. And companies by the dozens are now hanging up virtual shingles in *Second Life*—from Nike and Coca-Cola to Dell, Toyota, IBM, 1-800-FLOWERS.COM, and H&R Block.

Although the large online social networks such as MySpace and Facebook have grabbed most of the headlines, a new breed of more focused niche networks has recently emerged. These more focused networks cater to the needs of smaller communities of like-minded people, making them ideal vehicles for marketers who want to target special interest groups (see **Real Marketing 17.2**).

But participating successfully in existing online social networks presents challenges. First, online social networks are new and results are hard to measure. Most companies are still experimenting with how to use them effectively. Second, such Web communities are largely user controlled. The company's goal is to make the brand a part of consumers' conversations and their lives. However, marketers can't simply muscle their way into consumers' online interactions—they need to earn the right to be there. "You're talking about conversations between groups of friends," says one analyst. "And in those conversations a brand has no right to be there, unless the conversation is already about that brand." Says another expert, "Being force-fed irrelevant content, or feeling tricked into taking in a brand,

Some cater to the obscure. Passions Network, with 600,000 members, has 106 groups for specific interests, including "Star Trek" fans, truckers, atheists, and people who are shy. The most popular group is a dating site for the overweight. Membership on niche networking sites varies greatly, ranging from a few hundred to a few million. LinkExpats.com, which provides an online haven for U.S. expatriates, launched last month and has about 200 members. Flixster.com has 40 million members who rate movies and gossip about actors.

According to e-marketer, by 2011, half of all adults in the United States and 84 percent of online teens will use social networks. A running tally of emerging social networks, now upward of 7,000 by one estimate, suggests an explosive market. That's both a golden opportunity and a colossal headache for brands trying to nail down the best new network for their campaigns.

Although the niche sites have many fewer members than mega-sites such as MySpace (more than 110 million active profiles) and Facebook (59 million), they contain dedicated communities of like-minded people. And as on the bigger networks, members can build personalized pages and use them to share information, photos, and news with friends. That makes the niche sites ideal vehicles for marketers who want to target special interest groups.

The niche sites often provide a better marketing message environment. "Because members of niche social networks share common interests and experiences, they tend to spend more time on the site and contribute to the group by chatting and posting comments," notes an online consultant. On bigger sites, "members tend to be less involved . . . and are therefore less appealing to advertisers." Also, "the bigger sites have become so cluttered and overrun with advertisers that members are used to tuning stuff out, even personalized ads. . . . But on networking sites that have a self-selecting demographic, people tend to trust the content, including ads."

Not all niche networks welcome marketers. Sermo.com—a social-networking site at which some 65,000 licensed physicians consult with colleagues specializing in areas ranging from dermatology to psychiatry—allows no marketing. However, for a fee, companies can gain access to Sermo.com data and member discussions. "They can monitor online discussions, with the doctors' names omitted, or see a tally of topics being discussed at the site to determine what's rising or falling in popularity," notes a health care industry analyst.

Still, most of the niche sites offer unique campaign opportunities to brands. Sites like imeem.com—a social network where "fans and artists discover new music, videos, and photos, and share their tastes with friends"—are carving out their niches and actively soliciting advertising dollars. "We tend to skew younger and edgier," with a demographic of 13–24, says imeem's chief marketer. An ever-growing niche of more than 100 million users interact with imeem, helping it to attract big-name sponsors such as Burger King, Scion, Nokia, and T-Mobile, which sponsor special features and events. For example, one promotion involved artist J. Holiday texting his thoughts on tour to imeem.com members through his T-Mobile sidekick.

The more focused audiences offered by such niche networks are increasingly popular with brands because "relevance," says the consultant, "trumps size." But how brands execute social-networking campaigns is as important as where they do it. Marketers must be careful not to become too commercial or too intrusive. Keeping sites hip and unencumbered by advertising is a balancing act for both the brands and the social networks. The best approach is not to *market* to network members but to *interact* with them on topics of mutual interest. Says one online marketer, "The real way of getting into social media is you don't advertise, you participate in the community."

Sources: Portions adapted from Betsey Cummings, "Why Marketers Love Small Social Networks," *Brandweek*, April 27, 2008, accessed at www.brandweek.com; with adapted extracts, quotes, and other information from Kim Hart, "Online Networking Goes Small, and Sponsors Follow," *Washington Post*, December 29, 2007; p. D1; and Jessica E. Vascellaro, "Social Networking Goes Professional," *Wall Street Journal*, August 28, 2007, p. D1. Also see Heather Green, "Arts and Crafts Find New Life Online," *BusinessWeek*, January 14, 2008, pp. 60–61; and Paula Lehman, "Social Networks That Break a Sweat," *BusinessWeek*, February 4, 2008, p. 68.

is a major turn-off." Rather than intruding, marketers must learn to become a valued part of the online experience.[59]

When it comes to online networks, it's not enough just to be there. For example, when Toyota's Scion first opened a *Second Life* showroom last year, it quickly became a top destination. But only a few months later, *Second Life* residents had largely deserted the showroom. Toyota's mistake? It failed to understand that driving adds little value in a virtual world where *Second Life* avatars can walk underwater, fly, and "beam" themselves around. Instead, as in any other marketing endeavor, companies participating in Web communities must learn how to add value for consumers in order to capture value in return.

To avoid the mysteries and challenges of building a presence on existing online social networks, many companies are now launching their own targeted Web communities. For example, Coca-Cola has developed a Sprite Yard cell phone network—available to Web-ready phones—where members can set up profiles, post pictures, and meet new friends. On Nike's Nike Plus Web site, some 200,000 runners upload, track, and compare their performances. More than half visit the site as least four times a week, and Nike plans eventually to have 15 percent or more of the world's 100 million runners actively participating in the Nike Plus online community.

Using E-Mail

E-mail is an important and growing online marketing tool. A recent study of ad, brand, and marketing managers found that nearly half of all the companies surveyed use e-mail marketing to reach customers. U.S. companies spent about $1.2 billion a year on e-mail marketing, up from just $164 million in 1999. And this spending is estimated to grow to $2.1 billion in 2012.[60]

To compete effectively in this ever-more-cluttered e-mail environment, marketers are designing "enriched" e-mail messages—animated, interactive, and personalized messages full of streaming audio and video. Then, they are targeting these attention-grabbers more carefully to those who want them and will act upon them.

Spam
Unsolicited, unwanted commercial e-mail messages.

But there's a dark side to the growing use of e-mail marketing. The explosion of **spam**—unsolicited, unwanted commercial e-mail messages that clog up our e-mailboxes—has produced consumer irritation and frustration. Last year, for the first time, the total number of spam e-mails sent worldwide surpassed the number of person-to-person e-mails. According to one research company, spam now accounts for between 80 to 95 percent of all e-mail sent.[61] E-mail marketers walk a fine line between adding value for consumers and being intrusive.

To address these concerns, most legitimate marketers now practice *permission-based e-mail marketing,* sending e-mail pitches only to customers who "opt in." Financial services firms such as Charles Schwab use configurable e-mail systems that let customers choose what they want to get. Others, such as Yahoo! or Amazon.com, include long lists of opt-in boxes for different categories of marketing material. Amazon.com targets opt-in customers with a limited number of helpful "we thought you'd like to know" messages based on their expressed preferences and previous purchases. Few customers object and many actually welcome such promotional messages.

When used properly, e-mail can be the ultimate direct marketing medium. Blue-chip marketers such as Amazon.com, Dell, L.L.Bean, Office Depot, Charles Schwab, and others use it regularly, and with great success. E-mail lets these marketers send highly targeted, tightly personalized, relationship-building messages to consumers who actually *want* to receive them. Consider Scotts:

> Scotts, the plant, lawn, and garden products company, designs its e-mail marketing around the customer preferences, season of the year, and the region of the recipient. When individuals sign up for the e-mail program, Scotts asks them a series of questions about where they live and their particular plant and garden interests. It then uses this information to create content and offers that resonate with each recipient. For example, a city dweller, who may not even have a lawn, gets advice and tips on the care and feeding of houseplants and terrace shrubs, whereas a homeowner in the southwest receives information on maintaining a lawn or garden in a hot and arid climate. To deliver this level of customization, Scotts has developed an e-mail template that allows it to incorporate appropriate, personal content into an otherwise mass e-mailing. Far from thinking of the Scotts' online missives as irritating spam, recipients grow to rely on them as a valuable problem-solving tool.[62]

Given its targeting effectiveness and low costs, e-mail can be an outstanding marketing investment. According to the Direct Marketing Association, e-mail marketing produces a return on investment 40 to 50 percent higher than other forms of direct-marketing media.[63]

The Promise and Challenges of Online Marketing

Online marketing continues to offer both great promise and many challenges for the future. Its most ardent apostles still envision a time when the Internet and online marketing will replace magazines, newspapers, and even stores as sources for information and buying. Most marketers, however, hold a more realistic view. To be sure, online marketing will become a successful business model for some companies—Internet firms such as Amazon.com, eBay, and Google; and direct marketing companies such as Dell. However, for most companies, online marketing will remain just one important approach to the marketplace that works alongside other approaches in a fully integrated marketing mix.

Despite the many challenges, companies large and small are quickly integrating online marketing into their marketing strategies and mixes. As it continues to grow, online marketing will prove to be a powerful direct marketing tool for improving sales, communicating company and product information, delivering products and services, and building deeper customer relationships.

Author Comment	Although we mostly benefit from direct marketing, like most other things in life, it has its dark side as well. Marketers and customers alike must guard against irritating or harmful direct marketing practices.

Public Policy Issues in Direct Marketing (pp 517–519)

Direct marketers and their customers usually enjoy mutually rewarding relationships. Occasionally, however, a darker side emerges. The aggressive and sometimes shady tactics of a few direct marketers can bother or harm consumers, giving the entire industry a black eye. Abuses range from simple excesses that irritate consumers to instances of unfair practices or even outright deception and fraud. The direct marketing industry has also faced growing invasion-of-privacy concerns, and online marketers must deal with Internet security issues.

Irritation, Unfairness, Deception, and Fraud

Direct marketing excesses sometimes annoy or offend consumers. Most of us dislike direct-response TV commercials that are too loud, too long, and too insistent. Our mailboxes fill up with unwanted junk mail, our e-mailboxes bulge with unwanted spam, and our computer screens flash with unwanted banner or pop-under ads.

Beyond irritating consumers, some direct marketers have been accused of taking unfair advantage of impulsive or less-sophisticated buyers. TV shopping channels and program-long "infomercials" targeting television-addicted shoppers seem to be the worst culprits. They feature smooth-talking hosts, elaborately staged demonstrations, claims of drastic price reductions, "while they last" time limitations, and unequaled ease of purchase to inflame buyers who have low sales resistance.

Worse yet, so-called heat merchants design mailers and write copy intended to mislead buyers. Even well-known direct mailers have been accused of deceiving consumers. A few years back, sweepstakes promoter Publishers Clearing House paid $52 million to settle accusations that its high-pressure mailings confused or misled consumers, especially the elderly, into believing that they had won prizes or would win if they bought the company's magazines. Even the venerable *Reader's Digest* has had to pay restitution to consumers for alleged deceptive marketing in its sweepstakes contests.[64]

Fraudulent schemes, such as investment scams or phony collections for charity, have also multiplied in recent years. Internet fraud, including identity theft and financial scams, has become a serious problem. ▲Last year alone, the Federal Internet Crime Complaint Center (IC3) received more than 90,000 complaints related to Internet fraud involving monetary loss, with a total dollar loss of $239 million.[65]

One common form of Internet fraud is *phishing*, a type of identity theft that uses deceptive e-mails and fraudulent Web sites to fool users into divulging their personal data. According to e-mail security firm MessageLabs, 1 in 87 e-mails is now tagged as a phishing scam, compared with 1 in 500 a year ago. Although many consumers are now aware of such schemes, phishing can be extremely costly to those caught in the net. It also damages the brand identities of legitimate online marketers who have worked to build user confidence in Web and e-mail transactions.[66]

Many consumers also worry about *online security*. They fear that unscrupulous snoopers will eavesdrop on their online transactions,

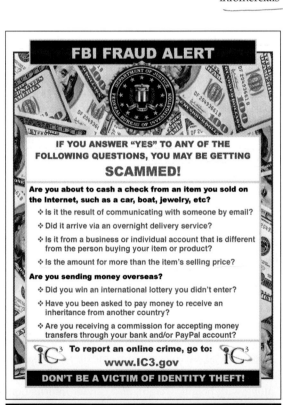

▲ Internet fraud has multiplied in recent years. The FBI's Internet Crime Complaint Center provides consumers with a convenient way to alert authorities to suspected violations.

picking up personal information or intercepting credit and debit card numbers. In a recent survey, 68 percent of participants said they were concerned that their credit or debit card information will be stolen if they use their cards for online purchases. More than one-third also see the Internet as the medium most likely to result in identity theft.[67] Internet shoppers are also concerned about contracting annoying or harmful viruses, spyware, and other "malware" (malicious software). A recent Google study of 4.5 million Web sites found that 10 percent of them were downloading malware:[68]

> Spyware programs track where you go on the Internet and clutter your screen with annoying pop-up advertisements for everything from pornography to wireless phone plans. Spyware can get stuck in your computer's hard drive as you shop, chat, or download a song. It might arrive attached to that clever video you just nabbed at no charge. Web security company McAfee estimates that nearly three-quarters of all sites listed in response to Internet searches for popular phrases like "free screen savers" or "digital music" attempt to install some form of advertising software in visitors' computers. Once lodged there, spyware can sap a PC's processing power, slow its functioning, and even cause it to crash.

Another Internet marketing concern is that of *access by vulnerable or unauthorized groups.* For example, marketers of adult-oriented materials have found it difficult to restrict access by minors. For example, 13 percent of the respondents in a recent *Consumer Reports* survey had children in their household registered as MySpace users who were under the online community's official minimum age of 14. The survey also indicated that many parents haven't prepared their children for potential online risks.[69]

Invasion of Privacy

Invasion of privacy is perhaps the toughest public policy issue now confronting the direct marketing industry. Consumers often benefit from database marketing—they receive more offers that are closely matched to their interests. However, many critics worry that marketers may know *too* much about consumers' lives and that they may use this knowledge to take unfair advantage of consumers. At some point, they claim, the extensive use of databases intrudes on consumer privacy.

These days, it seems that almost every time consumers enter a sweepstakes, apply for a credit card, visit a Web site, or order products by mail, telephone, or the Internet, their names enter some company's already bulging database. Using sophisticated computer technologies, direct marketers can use these databases to "microtarget" their selling efforts. *Online privacy* causes special concerns. Most online marketers have become skilled at collecting and analyzing detailed consumer information. For example, behavioral tracking systems use data about consumers' Web travels to deliver relevant ads to them. As Web tracking technology grows in sophistication, digital privacy experts worry that unscrupulous marketers will use such information to take unfair advantage of unknowing customers.

Some consumers and policy makers worry that the ready availability of information may leave consumers open to abuse if companies make unauthorized use of the information in marketing their products or exchanging databases with other companies. For example, they ask, should phone companies be allowed to sell marketers the names of customers who frequently call the 800 numbers of catalog companies? Should credit card companies be allowed to make data on their millions of cardholders worldwide available to merchants who accept their cards? Is it right for credit bureaus to compile and sell lists of people who have recently applied for credit cards—people who are considered prime direct marketing targets because of their spending behavior? Or is it right for states to sell the names and addresses of driver's license holders, along with height, weight, and gender information, allowing apparel retailers to target tall or overweight people with special clothing offers?

In their drives to build databases, companies sometimes get carried away. For example, Microsoft caused substantial privacy concerns when one version of its

Windows software used a "Registration Wizard" that snooped into users computers. When users went online to register, without their knowledge, Microsoft "read" the configurations of their PCs to learn about the major software products they were running. Users protested loudly and Microsoft abandoned the practice.

A Need for Action

All of this calls for strong actions by marketers to prevent privacy abuses before legislators step in to do it for them. For example, to curb direct marketing excesses, various government agencies are investigating not only do-not-call lists but also "do-not-mail" lists, "do-not-track" lists, and "Can Spam" legislation. And in response to online privacy and security concerns, the federal government has considered numerous legislative actions to regulate how Web operators obtain and use consumer information. State governments are also stepping in. In 2003, California enacted the California Online Privacy Protection Act (OPPA), under which any online business that collects personally identifiable information from California residents must take steps such as posting its privacy policy and notifying consumers about what data will be gathered and how it will be used.[70]

Of special concern are the privacy rights of children. In 1998, the Federal Trade Commission surveyed 212 Web sites directed toward children. It found that 89 percent of the sites collected personal information from children. However, 46 percent of them did not include any disclosure of their collection and use of such information. As a result, Congress passed the Children's Online Privacy Protection Act (COPPA), which requires Web site operators targeting children to post privacy policies on their sites. They must also notify parents about the information they're gathering and obtain parental consent before collecting personal information from children under age 13. Under this act, teen social networking site Xanga.com was fined $1 million for collecting, using, and disclosing personal information from 1.7 million children under the age of 13 without first notifying parents and obtaining their consent.[71]

Many companies have responded to consumer privacy and security concerns with actions of their own. Still others are taking an industrywide approach. For example, TRUSTe, a nonprofit self-regulatory organization, works with many large corporate sponsors, including Microsoft, AT&T, and Intuit, to audit companies' privacy and security measures and help consumers navigate the Web safely. According to the company's Web site, "TRUSTe believes that an environment of mutual trust and openness will help make and keep the Internet a free, comfortable, and richly diverse community for everyone." To reassure consumers, the company lends its "trustmark" stamp of approval to Web sites that meet its privacy and security standards.[72]

The direct marketing industry as a whole is also addressing public policy issues. For example, in an effort to build consumer confidence in shopping direct, the Direct Marketing Association (DMA)—the largest association for businesses practicing direct, database, and interactive marketing, with more than 4,800 member companies—launched a "Privacy Promise to American Consumers." The Privacy Promise requires that all DMA members adhere to a carefully developed set of consumer privacy rules. Members must agree to notify customers when any personal information is rented, sold, or exchanged with others. They must also honor consumer requests to "opt out" of receiving further solicitations or having their contact information transferred to other marketers. Finally, they must abide by the DMA's Preference Service by removing the names of consumers who wish not to receive mail, telephone, or e-mail offers.[73]

Direct marketers know that, left untended, such direct marketing abuses will lead to increasingly negative consumer attitudes, lower response rates, and calls for more restrictive state and federal legislation. Most direct marketers want the same things that consumers want: honest and well-designed marketing offers targeted only toward consumers who will appreciate and respond to them. Direct marketing is just too expensive to waste on consumers who don't want it.

REVIEWING Objectives AND KEY Terms

Let's revisit this chapter's key concepts. This chapter is the last of four chapters covering the final marketing mix element—promotion. The previous chapters dealt with advertising, publicity, personal selling, and sales promotion. This one investigates the burgeoning field of direct and online marketing.

OBJECTIVE 1 **Define direct marketing and discuss its benefits to customers and companies.** (pp 490–495)

Direct marketing consists of direct connections with carefully targeted individual consumers to both obtain an immediate response and cultivate lasting customer relationships. Using detailed databases, direct marketers tailor their offers and communications to the needs of narrowly defined segments or even individual buyers.

For buyers, direct marketing is convenient, easy to use, and private. It gives buyers ready access to a wealth of products and information, at home and around the globe. Direct marketing is also immediate and interactive, allowing buyers to create exactly the configuration of information, products, or services they desire, then order them on the spot. For sellers, direct marketing is a powerful tool for building customer relationships. Using database marketing, today's marketers can target small groups or individual consumers, tailor offers to individual needs, and promote these offers through personalized communications. It also offers them a low-cost, efficient alternative for reaching their markets. As a result of these advantages to both buyers and sellers, direct marketing has become the fastest-growing form of marketing.

OBJECTIVE 2 **Identify and discuss the major forms of direct marketing.** (pp 495–504)

The main forms of direct marketing include personal selling, direct-mail marketing, catalog marketing, telephone marketing, direct-response television marketing, kiosk marketing, and online marketing. We discussed personal selling in the previous chapter.

Direct-mail marketing, the largest form of direct marketing, consists of the company sending an offer, announcement, reminder, or other item to a person at a specific address. Recently, new forms of "mail delivery" have become popular, such as e-mail and text message marketing. Some marketers rely on catalog marketing—selling through catalogs mailed to a select list of customers, made available in stores, or accessed on the Web. Telephone marketing consists of using the telephone to sell directly to consumers. Direct-response television marketing has two forms: direct-response advertising (or infomercials) and home shopping channels. Kiosks are information and ordering machines that direct marketers place in stores, airports, and other locations. In recent years, a number of new digital direct marketing technologies have emerged, including mobile marketing, podcasts and vodcasts, and interactive TV. Online marketing involves online channels that digitally link sellers with consumers.

OBJECTIVE 3 **Explain how companies have responded to the Internet and other powerful new technologies with online marketing strategies.** (pp 504–508)

Online marketing is the fastest-growing form of direct marketing. The Internet enables consumers and companies to access and share huge amounts of information with just a few mouse clicks. In turn, the Internet has given marketers a whole new way to create value for customers and build customer relationships. It's hard to find a company today that doesn't have a substantial Web marketing presence.

Online consumer buying continues to grow at a healthy rate. Most American online users now use the Internet to shop. Perhaps more importantly, the Internet influences offline shopping. Thus, smart marketers are employing integrated multichannel strategies that use the Web to drive sales to other marketing channels.

OBJECTIVE 4 **Discuss how companies go about conducting online marketing to profitably deliver more value to customers.** (pp 508–517)

Companies of all types are now engaged in online marketing. The Internet gave birth to the *click-only* dot-coms, which operate only online. In addition, many traditional brick-and-mortar companies have now added online marketing operations, transforming themselves into *click-and-mortar* competitors. Many click-and-mortar companies are now having more online success than their click-only competitors.

Companies can conduct online marketing in any of the four ways: creating a Web site, placing ads and promotions online, setting up or participating in Web communities and online social networks, or using e-mail. The first step typically is to set up a Web site. Beyond simply setting up a site, however, companies must make their sites engaging, easy to use, and useful in order to attract visitors, hold them, and bring them back again.

Online marketers can use various forms of online advertising and promotion to build their Internet brands or to attract visitors to their Web sites. Forms of online promotion include online display advertising, search-related advertising, content sponsorships, alliances and affiliate programs, and viral marketing, the Internet version of word-of-mouth marketing. Online marketers can also participate in online social networks and other Web communities, which take advantage of the C2C properties of the Web. Finally, e-mail marketing has become a fast-growing tool for both B2C and B2B marketers. Whatever direct marketing tools they use, marketers must work hard to integrate them into a cohesive marketing effort.

OBJECTIVE 5 **Overview the public policy and ethical issues presented by direct marketing.** (pp 517–519)

Direct marketers and their customers usually enjoy mutually rewarding relationships. Sometimes, however, direct marketing presents a darker side. The aggressive and sometimes shady tactics of a few direct marketers can bother or harm consumers, giving the entire industry a black eye. Abuses range from simple excesses that irritate consumers to instances of unfair practices or even outright deception and fraud. The direct marketing industry has also faced growing concerns about invasion-of-privacy and Internet security issues. Such concerns call for strong action by marketers and public policy makers to curb direct marketing abuses. In the end, most direct marketers want the same things that consumers want: honest and well-designed marketing offers targeted only toward consumers who will appreciate and respond to them.

KEY Terms

OBJECTIVE 1

Direct marketing (p 490)
Customer database (p 493)

OBJECTIVE 2

Direct-mail marketing (p 495)
Catalog marketing (p 496)
Telephone marketing (p 497)
Direct-response television marketing (p 499)

OBJECTIVE 3

Online marketing (p 504)
Internet (p 504)
Click-only companies (p 504)
Click-and-mortar companies (p 504)
Business-to-consumer (B2C) online marketing (p 505)
Business-to business (B2B) online marketing (p 506)
Consumer-to-consumer (C2C) online marketing (p 507)

Consumer-to-business (C2B) online marketing (p 508)

OBJECTIVE 4

Corporate (brand) Web site (p 509)
Marketing Web site (p 509)
Online advertising (p 511)
Viral marketing (p 512)
Online social networks (p 513)
Spam (p 516)

DISCUSSING & APPLYING THE Concepts

Discussing the Concepts

1. Discuss the benefits of direct marketing to both buyers and sellers. (AASCB: Communication)

2. A local oriental rug cleaning company has contacted you for advice on setting up its customer database. It needs this database for customer-relationship management and for direct marketing of new products and services. Describe the qualities and features it must consider for an effective database and how it might go about creating one. (AACSB: Communication)

3. Name and describe the major forms of direct marketing. (AACSB: Communication)

4. Explain the ways in which companies can conduct online marketing. (AACSB: Communication)

5. Compare and contrast the different forms of online advertising. What factors should a company consider in deciding among these different forms? (AACSB: Communication)

6. Why is privacy a tough public policy issue confronting the direct marketing industry and what is being done to address this issue? (AACSB: Communication; Reflective Thinking)

Applying the Concepts

1. Visit your favorite retail Web site and evaluate the site according to the seven Cs of effective Web site design. (AACSB: Communication; Use of IT; Reflective Thinking)

2. Visit Nike's Web site at http://nikeid.nike.com and design your own shoe. Print out your shoe design and bring it to class. Do you think the price is appropriate for the value received from being able to customize your shoe? Identify and describe two other Web sites that allow buyers to customize products. (AACSB: Communication; Use of IT; Reflective Thinking)

3. Consumers can register with the Do Not Call Registry to avoid unwanted phone solicitations from marketers. But what can consumers do to reduce unsolicited mail and e-mail? Find out how consumers can do this and report your findings. (AACSB: Communication; Reflective Thinking)

FOCUS ON Technology

Electronic payment systems and databases are essential for today's competitive marketplace. Databases are essential for government and not-for-profit entities, too. But they can also create problems for organizations and individuals. Individuals ranging from military veterans to TJ Maxx shoppers may suffer from identity theft following significant security breaches. Some data security breaches occur from sloppy security practices, ranging from laptops being stolen to high-tech electronic capture of information from companies' data systems. While you've no doubt seen headlines of large security breaches involving millions of personal and financial files, small business are just as vulnerable. A recent examination of 500 security breach cases concluded that more than half occurred in the retail and food-and-beverage industries. The same study concluded that in 90 percent of the cases, data breaches could have been prevented by using adequate security measures.

1. Find articles about two data security breaches in the news. How did the breaches occur, and who is potentially affected by them? (AACSB: Communication; Reflective Thinking)

2. What can organizations and businesses do to ensure adequate data security for their members and customers? What can consumers do to protect themselves if their personal information has been compromised? (AACSB: Communication; Reflective Thinking)

FOCUS ON Ethics

"Six books for 99¢," "12 CDs for $1.00," or "7 DVDs for FREE!" We've all seen these offers—but are they too good to be true? The Book-of-the-Month Club and Columbia House are just two well-known examples of the many buying clubs. These clubs can cause problems for consumers who do not always fully understand what they are getting themselves into. By accepting such offers, consumers may unwittingly join a "prenotification negative option plan." Under these plans, if you don't tell the marketer that you don't want additional merchandise sent to you it is sent automatically and you are billed for it. Some clubs require a minimum number of purchases at regular prices before you can cancel membership. Critics claim that marketers offer enticing incentives to lure consumers but are deceptive about the membership obligations.

1. Search the Internet for a book club, a music club, and a movie club that offer negative option plans. Describe the incentives offered to get consumers to join, the obligations of membership, and the mechanism by which members can deny future merchandise. Does that club give adequate information for consumers to understand their obligations or is some part of the offer deceiving? (AACSB: Communication; Ethical Reasoning)

2. Learn about the Federal Trade Commission's (FTC) Negative Option Rule at www.ftc.gov/bcp/edu/pubs/consumer/products/pro09.shtm and discuss concerns the government and consumers have with this direct marketing tactic (Note: search "negative option" at www.ftc.gov for more information). (AACSB: Communication; Reflective Thinking)

MARKETING BY THE Numbers

Many companies are realizing the efficiency of telemarketing in the face of soaring sales force costs. Whereas an average cost of a business-to-business sales call by an outside salesperson costs more than $300, the cost of a telemarketing sales call can be as little as $5 to $20. And telemarketers can make 20 to 33 decision-maker contacts per day to a salesperson's 4 per day. This has gotten the attention of many business-to-business marketers—where telemarketing can be very effective.

1. Refer to Appendix 2, Marketing by the Numbers, to determine the marketing return on sales (marketing ROS) and return on marketing investment (marketing ROI) for Company A and Company B in the chart below. Which company is performing better? Explain. (AACSB: Communication; Analytical Reasoning; Reflective Thinking)

2. Should all companies consider reducing their sales forces in favor of telemarketing? Discuss the pros and cons of this action. (AACSB: Communication; Reflective Thinking)

	Company A (sales force only)	Company B (telemarketing only)
Net sales	$1,000,000	$850,000
Cost of goods sold	$ 500,000	$425,000
Sales expenses	$ 300,000	$100,000

VIDEO Case

Google

It's mind-boggling to think that only 15 years ago, a company like Google was not within the realm of possibility. Yet when the World Wide Web went online, the foundation was set for Google's mission: to organize the world's information and make it universally accessible and useful.

Google was not the first search engine. But it has become the most successful. Its primary reason for success has been its customer-focused strategy. For Google, there are two basic types of customers. For the Internet search services customer, Google has been relentless in developing products that are both innovative and user-friendly. Google now offers dozens of services, including foreign language translation, stock quotes, maps, phone book listings, images, video, and news headlines. And the most amazing thing about these services? They are all free.

Google can offer all of its services free of charge because of its second customer, advertisers. Google has turned Internet advertising upside down. Today, products such as AdWords (keyword search advertising) and AdSense (a method that generates only the most relevant ads for client Web sites) are breaking new ground because they result in ads that are actually useful and helpful to consumers.

After viewing the Google video, answer the following online marketing questions:

1. Brainstorm the many benefits that Google provides for consumers.

2. Brainstorm the many benefits that Google provides for online marketers.

3. Visit www.google.com. For each of the four major e-marketing domains, discuss Google's presence.

COMPANY Case

StubHub: Ticket Scalping, a Respectable Endeavor?

As the rock band KISS returned to the United States for the final performances of its "Alive/35" tour in the summer of 2008, Roger felt like reliving some old memories. Just because he was in his 50s didn't mean he was too old to rock. After all, he was an original KISS fan dating back to the 70s. It had been years since he had gone to a concert for any band. But on the day the KISS tickets went on sale, he grabbed a lawn chair and headed to his local Ticketmaster outlet to "camp out" in line. Roger knew that the terminal, located inside a large chain music store, wouldn't open until 10 a.m. when tickets went on sale. He got to the store at 6 a.m. to find only three people ahead of him. "Fantastic," Roger thought. With so few people in front of him, getting good seats would be a snap. Maybe he would even score something close to the stage.

By the time the three people in front of him had their tickets, it was 10:13. As the clerk typed away on the Ticketmaster computer terminal, Roger couldn't believe what he heard. No tickets were available. The show at the Palms Resort in Las Vegas was sold out. Dejected, Roger turned to leave. As he made his way out the door, another customer said, "You can always try StubHub." As the fellow KISS fan explained what StubHub was, it occurred to Roger that the world had become a very different place with respect to buying concert tickets.

Indeed, in this Internet age, buying tickets for live events has changed dramatically since Roger's concert-going days. Originators such as Ticketmaster now sell tickets online for everything from Broadway shows to sporting events. Increasingly, however, event tickets are resold through Web sites such as eBay, RazorGator, TicketsNow, Craigslist, and StubHub, the fastest growing company in the business. Various industry observers estimate that as many as 30 percent of all event tickets are resold. This secondary market for online sports and entertainment tickets has grown to billions of dollars in annual revenues.

And although prices are all over the map, tickets for sold-out hot events routinely sell for double or triple their face value. In some cases, the markup is astronomical. The nationwide average price for kids to see Miley Cyrus was $249, up from about $50 for the highest face value seat. A pair of tickets to see Bruce Springsteen at Washington, D.C.'s Verizon Center set some back as much as $2,000. Prices for a seat at Superbowl XLII in Phoenix, one of the hottest ticket resale events of all time, sold for as high as $13,000. And one U.K. Led Zeppelin fan with obviously far too much money on his hands paid over $160,000 for a pair of Led Zeppelin tickets, close enough to see a geriatric Robert Plant perspire. Extreme cases? Yes. But not uncommon.

When most people think of buying a ticket from a reseller, they probably envision a seedy scalper standing in the shadows near an event venue. But scalping is moving mainstream. While the Internet and other technologies have allowed professional ticket agents to purchase event tickets in larger numbers, anyone with a computer and broadband connection can instantly become a scalper. And regular folks, even fans, are routinely doing so. "Because we allowed people to buy four [tickets], if they only need two they put the other two up for sale," said Dave Holmes, manager for Coldplay. This dynamic, occurring for events across the board, has dramatically increased the number of ticket resellers.

STUBHUB ENTERS THE GAME

With the ticket resale market booming, StubHub started operations in 2000 as Liquid Seats. It all started with an idea by two first-year students at the Stanford Graduate School of Business. Eric Baker and Jeff Fluhr had been observing the hysteria on the ticket resale market. In their opinion, the market was highly fragmented and rampant with fraud and distorted pricing. Two buyers sitting side-by-side at the same event might find they'd paid wildly different prices for essentially the same product. Even with heavy hitter eBay as the biggest ticket reseller at the time, Baker and Fluhr saw an opportunity to create a system that would bring buyers and sellers together in a more efficient manner.

They entered their proposal in a new-business plan competition. Fluhr was utterly convinced the concept would work—so much so that he withdrew the proposal from the competition and dropped out of school in order to launch the business. At a time when dot-coms were dropping like flies, this might have seemed like a very poor decision. But Fluhr ultimately became CEO of StubHub, the leader and fastest-growing company of a $10 billion-a-year industry.

Home to over 300 employees, StubHub utilizes 20,000 square feet of prime office space in San Francisco's pricey financial district, seven satellite offices, and two call centers. Even more telling is the company's growth. In November of 2006, a little over six years after starting, StubHub sold its five millionth ticket. Just over one year later, it sold its 10 millionth. And six months after that in June of 2008, StubHub rewarded the buyer and seller of the 15 millionth ticket sold with a pair of $5,000 gift certificates for its Web site. In its first few years of operations, StubHub posted a staggering growth rate of more than

3,200 percent. According to comScore Networks, a firm that tracks Web traffic, StubHub.com is the leading site among more than a dozen competitors in the ticket-resale category.

THE DEVIL IS IN THE DETAILS

StubHub's model is showing that buying a ticket on the aftermarket doesn't have to mean paying a huge price premium. Sharing his own experience, a *New York Times* writer provides his own StubHub experience:

To test the system I started with the New York Yankees. A series with the Seattle Mariners was coming up, just before the Yankees left town for a long road trip. Good tickets would be scarce. I went to StubHub. Lots of tickets there, many priced stratospherically. I settled on two Main Box seats in Section 313, Row G. They were in the right-field corner, just one section above field level. The price was $35 each, or face price for a season ticketholder. This was tremendous value for a sold-out game. I registered with StubHub, creating a user name and password, ordered the tickets, then sealed the deal by providing my credit card number. An e-mail message arrived soon after, confirming the order and informing me that StubHub was contacting the seller to arrange for shipment. My card would not be charged until the seller had confirmed to StubHub the time and method of delivery. A second e-mail message arrived a day later giving the delivery details. The tickets arrived on the Thursday before the game, and the seller was paid by StubHub on confirmation of delivery. On Saturday, under a clear, sunny sky, the Yankees were sending a steady stream of screaming line drives into the right-field corner.

From the beginning, Baker and Fluhr set out to provide better options for both buyers and sellers by making StubHub different. Like eBay, StubHub has no ticket inventory of its own, reducing its risk. It simply provides the venue that gives buyers and sellers the opportunity to come together. But it's the differences, perhaps, that have allowed StubHub to achieve such success in such a short period of time.

One of the first differences noticed by buyers and sellers is StubHub's ticket-listing procedure. Sellers can list tickets by auction or at a fixed price, a price that declines as the event gets closer. Whereas some sites charge fees just to list tickets, StubHub lists them for free. Thus, initially, the seller has no risk whatsoever. StubHub's system is simpler than most, splitting the fee burden between buyer and seller. It charges sellers a 15-percent commission and buyers a 10-percent fee.

StubHub's Web site structure also creates a marketplace that comes closer to pure competition than any other reseller's Web site. All sellers are equal on StubHub, as ticket listings are identical in appearance and seller identify is kept anonymous. StubHub even holds the shipping method constant, via FedEx. This makes the purchase process much more transparent for buyers. They can browse tickets by event, venue, and section. Comparison shopping is very easy as shoppers can simultaneously view different pairs of tickets in the same section, even in the same row.

Although prices still vary, this system makes tickets more of a commodity and allows market forces to narrow the gap considerably from one seller to another. In fact, while tickets often sell for high prices, this reselling model can also have the effect of pushing ticket prices down below face value. Many experts believe that the emergence of Internet resellers such as StubHub is having an equalizing effect, often resulting in fair prices determined by market forces.

Unlike eBay, StubHub provides around-the-clock customer service via a toll-free number. But perhaps the biggest and most important difference between StubHub and competitors is the company's 100 percent FanProtect guarantee. Initially, it might seem more risky buying from a seller whose identity is unknown. But StubHub puts the burden of responsibility on the seller, remaining involved after the purchase where competing sites bow out. Buyers aren't charged until they confirm receipt of the tickets. "If you open the package and it contains two squares of toilet paper instead of the tickets," Baker explains, "then we debit the seller's credit card for the amount of the purchase." StubHub will also revoke site privileges for fraudulent or unreliable sellers. In contrast, the eBay system is largely self-policing and does not monitor the shipment or verification of the purchased items.

WHAT THE FUTURE HOLDS

When StubHub was formed, it targeted professional ticket brokers and ordinary consumers. In examining individuals as sellers, Baker and Fluhr capitalized on the underexploited assets of sport team season ticket holders. "If you have season tickets to the Yankees, that's 81 games," Mr. Baker said. "Unless you're unemployed or especially passionate, there's no way you're going to attend every game." StubHub entered the equation, not only giving ticket holders a way to recoup some of their investment, but allowing them to have complete control over the process rather than selling to a ticket agent.

It quickly became apparent to StubHub's founders that the benefits of season ticket holders selling off unused tickets extended to the sports franchises as well. Being able to sell unwanted tickets encourages season ticket holders to buy again. It also puts customers in seats that would otherwise go empty—customers who buy hot dogs, souvenirs, and programs. Thus, StubHub began entering into signed agreements with professional sports teams. The company has signed agreements with numerous NFL, NBA, and NHL teams to be their official secondary marketplace for season ticket holders.

But most recently, StubHub scored a huge breakthrough deal by becoming the official online ticket reseller for Major League Baseball and its 30 teams. Given that an estimated $10 billion worth of baseball tickets are resold each year, this single move will likely bring tremendous growth to StubHub. "This is the final vindication for the secondary ticketing market," StubHub spokesman Sean Pate said. "That really puts the final stamp of approval on StubHub."

Revenues from sporting events account for more than half of all StubHub sales. So it's not surprising that the company continues to pursue new partnerships with collegiate sports organizations and even media organizations, such as AOL, Sporting News, and CBS Sportsline. However, it has arranged similar contractual agreements with big-name performers such as Madonna, Coldplay, the Dixie Chicks, Justin Timberlake, Jessica Simpson, and country music's rising star, Bobby Pinson. Arrangements allow StubHub to offer exclusive event packages with a portion of the proceeds supporting charities designated by the performer.

The reselling of event tickets is here to stay. With the rise of safe and legal reseller Web sites and the repeal of long-standing antiscalping laws in many states, aftermarket ticket reselling continues to gain legitimacy. There are numerous hands in the fast-growing cookie jar that is the secondary ticket market. StubHub founder Eric Baker left the company and formed Viagogo, a European ticket reseller site that is entering the U.S. market. Even

Ticketmaster—the longstanding dominant force in primary ticket sales—has jumped into the act. Not only has the ticket power-house turned to auctioning a certain portion of premium tickets to the highest bidders, but it has its own resale arm, TicketExchange.

Although there is more than one channel to buy or sell, StubHub's future looks bright. The company's model of entering into partnerships with event-producing organizations is establishing it as "the official" ticket reseller. In fact, in an "if you can't beat 'em, join 'em," move, rival reseller eBay bought StubHub last year for over $300 million, allowing it to continue to function as its own entity. At this point, there is no end in sight to StubHub's growth curve. Who knows—at some point, ticket-seeking consumers may even think of StubHub before thinking of Ticketmaster.

Questions for Discussion

1. Conduct a brief analysis of the marketing environment and the forces shaping the development of StubHub.

2. Discuss StubHub's business model. What general benefits does it afford to buyers and sellers? Which benefits are most important in terms of creating value for buyers and sellers?

3. Discuss StubHub as a new intermediary. What effects has this new type of intermediary had on the ticket industry?

4. Apply the text's e-marketing domains framework to StubHub's business model. How has each domain played a role in the company's success?

5. What recommendations can you make for improving StubHub's future growth and success?

6. What are the legal or ethical issues, if any, for ticket-reselling Web sites?

Sources: Ethan Smith, "StubHub Enlisted in Resale of Madonna Concert Tickets," *Wall Street Journal*, May 9, 2008, p. B6; Neil Best, "Want Super Bowl Tickets? Sell or Rent the House," *Newsday*, January 25, 2008, p. A70; Joe Nocera, "Internet Puts a Sugarcoat on Scalping," *New York Times*, January 19, 2008, p. C1; Amy Feldman, "Hot Tickets," *Fast Company*, September 1, 2007, p. 44; "Ticket Reseller StubHub Hits a Home Run," *Reuters*, August 2, 2007; William Grimes, "That Invisible Hand Guides the Game of Ticket Hunting," *New York Times*, June 18, 2004, p. E1; Steve Stecklow, "Can't Get No . . . Tickets?" *Wall Street Journal*, January 7, 2006, p. P1; Steve Stecklow, "StubHub's Ticket to Ride," *Wall Street Journal*, January 17, 2006, p. B1; and information from www.stubhub.com, accessed November 2008.

Chapter 18	Part 1 Defining Marketing and the Marketing Process (Chapters 1, 2)
	Part 2 Understanding the Marketplace and Consumers (Chapters 3, 4, 5, 6)
	Part 3 Designing a Customer-Driven Strategy and Mix (Chapters 7, 8, 9, 10, 11, 12, 13, 14, 15, 16, 17)
	Part 4 **Extending Marketing** (Chapters 18, 19, 20)

Creating Competitive Advantage

Chapter PREVIEW

In previous chapters, you explored the basics of marketing. You've learned that the aim of marketing is to create value *for* customers in order to capture value *from* consumers in return. Good marketing companies win, keep, and grow customers by understanding customer needs, designing customer-driven marketing strategies, constructing value-delivering marketing programs, and building customer and marketing partner relationships. In the final three chapters, we'll extend this concept to three special areas—creating competitive advantage, global marketing, and marketing ethics and social responsibility.

In this chapter, we pull all of the marketing basics together. Understanding customers is an important first step in developing profitable customer relationships, but it's not enough. To gain competitive advantage, companies must use this understanding to design market offers that deliver more value than the offers of *competitors* seeking to win the same customers. In this chapter, we look first at competitor analysis, the process companies use to identify and analyze competitors. Then, we examine competitive marketing strategies by which companies position themselves against competitors to gain the greatest possible competitive advantage.

Let's look first at Nike. During the past several decades, Nike has forever changed the rules of sports marketing strategy. In the process, it has built the Nike swoosh into one of the world's best-known brand symbols. But to stay on top in the intensely competitive sports apparel business, Nike will have to keep a keen eye on both customers and competitors, finding fresh ways to beat rivals at bringing value to its customers.

The Nike "swoosh"—it's everywhere! Just for fun, try counting the swooshes whenever you pick up the sports pages or watch a pickup basketball game or tune into a televised golf match. Through innovative marketing, Nike has built the ever-present swoosh into one of the best-known brand symbols on the planet.

Some 45 years ago, when young CPA Phil Knight and college track coach Bill Bowerman cofounded the company, Nike was just a brash, young upstart in the athletic footwear industry. In 1964, the pair chipped in $500 apiece to start Blue Ribbon Sports. In 1970, Bowerman dreamed up a new sneaker tread by stuffing a piece of rubber into his wife's waffle iron. The Waffle Trainer quickly became the nation's best-selling training shoe. In 1972, the company became Nike, named after the Greek goddess of victory. The swoosh was designed by a graduate student for a fee of $35. By 1979, Nike had sprinted ahead of the competition, owning 50 percent of the U.S. running shoe market. It all seemed easy then. Running was in, sneakers were hot, and Nike had the right stuff.

During the 1980s, under Phil Knight's leadership, Nike revolutionized sports marketing. To build its brand image and market share, Nike lavishly outspent its competitors on big-name endorsements, splashy promotional events, and in-your-face "Just Do It" ads. At Nike, however, good marketing meant more than just promotional hype and promises—it meant consistently building strong relationships with customers based on real value.

Nike's initial success resulted from the technical superiority of its running and basketball shoes. To this day, Nike leads the industry in research-and-development spending. But Nike gave customers much more than just good athletic gear. Customers didn't just wear their Nikes, they experienced them. As the company stated on its Web page (www.nike.com), "Nike has always known the truth—it's not so much the shoes but where they take you." Beyond shoes, apparel, and equipment, Nike marketed a way of life, a sports culture, a just-do-it attitude. As Phil Knight said at the time, "Basically, our culture and our style is to be a rebel." The company was built on a genuine passion for sports, a maverick disregard for convention, and a belief in hard work and serious sports performance.

Throughout the 1980s and 1990s, still playing the role of the upstart underdog, Nike solidified its position as the dominant market leader. It leveraged its brand strength, moving aggressively into new product categories,

> Nike has built the swoosh into one of the world's best-known brand symbols, signifying the very close bond between customers and the Nike brand.

sports, and regions of the world. The company slapped its familiar swoosh logo on everything from sunglasses and soccer balls to batting gloves and golf clubs. Nike invaded a dozen new sports, including baseball, golf, skateboarding, wall climbing, bicycling, and hiking. It seemed that things couldn't be going any better.

In the late 1990s, however, Nike stumbled as a new breed of competitor arose and the company's sales slipped. The whole industry suffered a setback, as a "brown shoe" craze for hiking and outdoor shoe styles ate into the athletic sneaker business. Moreover, Nike's creative juices seemed to run dry. Ho-hum new sneaker designs collected dust on retailer shelves as buyers seeking a new look switched to competing brands.

But Nike's biggest obstacle may have been its own incredible success. The brand appeared to suffer from big-brand backlash, and the swoosh may have become too common to be cool. As sales moved past the $10 billion mark, market leader Nike moved from maverick to mainstream. Rooting for Nike was like rooting for Microsoft. Instead of antiestablishment, Nike *was* the establishment. Once the brat of sports marketing, Nike now had to grow up and act its age.

And grow up it did. The company still spends hundreds of millions of dollars each year on very creative advertising, innovative brand-building promotions, and big-name endorsers. But behind the bright lights, Nike now focuses on the important marketing basics: customer relationships, new-product innovation, and leaving competitors in its dust. When it comes to the competition, Nike is ruthless but a little paranoid. "As the industry gets bigger, as Nike gets bigger, it has to be even faster," says Knight. "That's an enormous challenge and always has been." Nike president and CEO Mark Parker agrees. ""I don't fear any competitor, but I respect them all," he says. "Anybody who takes their competition for granted ends up watching them from behind."

With Nike's deep pockets, it can outspend most competitors on marketing by a wide margin. But where today's Nike really out-points its competitors is in its cutting-edge efforts to build a deep community with customers. Nike's mission is "to bring inspiration and innovation to every athlete* in the world (*if you have a body, you are an athlete.)" And whether customers come to know Nike through ads, in its Niketown stores, through a local Nike running club, or at one of the company's many community Web sites— NikePlus.com, Joga.com, or another—the sports giant's customers build very close bonds with the Nike brand.

As a result, the modern-day Nike is once again

Nike gives consumers more than just good athletic gear. It markets a way of life, a sports culture, and a just-do-it attitude.

achieving stunning results. In the past four years, as many competitors have struggled, Nike's sales have grown 53 percent to $16.3 billion; profits have more than tripled. Nike captures an eye-popping 45 percent of the U.S. athletic footwear market; next-biggest competitor Adidas captures less than half that figure. For four years running, Nike's return on invested capital has exceeded 20 percent. Nike is growing even faster abroad than at home, with international revenues now accounting for 57 percent of total Nike brand sales. Nike is now the fastest growing running brand in Germany. In Russia, it has doubled its revenue in the last three years. Nike is the number-one athletic brand in China, a market that will be Nike's second largest within three years.

To stay ahead of competitors, however, Nike will have to keep its marketing strategy fresh, finding new ways to deliver the kind of innovation and value that built the brand so powerfully in the past. Nike will have to act more like a fresh, young start-up than like an aging market leader, constantly reassessing its competitive standing and rekindling its meaning to customers. Says Knight, "The spirit of entrepreneurship is key to our success. It certainly defined Nike when we started the company. And it's what keeps us nimble in this industry today."[1]

> To stay ahead of competitors, Nike must find new ways to deliver the kind of innovation and value that built the brand so powerfully in the past. It will have to act more like a fresh, young start-up than like an aging market leader, constantly rekindling its meaning to customers.

Today's companies face their toughest competition ever. In previous chapters, we argued that to succeed in today's fiercely competitive marketplace, companies will have to move from a product-and-selling philosophy to a customer-and-marketing philosophy. Guerrino De Luca, president and CEO of Logitech, puts it well: "It is now more critical than

Objective Outline

Competitive advantage
An advantage over competitors gained by offering consumers greater value than competitors do.

Competitor analysis
The process of identifying key competitors; assessing their objectives, strategies, strengths and weaknesses, and reaction patterns; and selecting which competitors to attack or avoid.

Competitive marketing strategies
Strategies that strongly position the company against competitors and that give the company the strongest possible strategic advantage.

ever to keep the people who buy and use our products at the center of our focus—for all our customers to be delighted by their experience with our products."[2]

This chapter spells out in more detail how companies can go about outperforming competitors in order to win, keep, and grow customers. To win in today's marketplace, companies must become adept not just in *managing products*, but in *managing customer relationships* in the face of determined competition. Understanding customers is crucial, but it's not enough. Building profitable customer relationships and gaining **competitive advantage** requires delivering *more* value and satisfaction to target consumers than *competitors* do. Customers will see competitive advantages as *customer advantages*, giving the company an edge over its competitors.

In this chapter, we examine *competitive marketing strategies*—how companies analyze their competitors and develop successful, value-based strategies for building and maintaining profitable customer relationships. The first step is **competitor analysis**, the process of identifying, assessing, and selecting key competitors. The second step is developing **competitive marketing strategies** that strongly position the company against competitors and give it the greatest possible competitive advantage.

Author Comment | Creating competitive advantage begins with a thorough understanding of competitors' strategies. But before a company can analyze its competitors, it must first identify them—a task that's not as simple as it seems.

Competitor Analysis (pp 528–534)

To plan effective marketing strategies, the company needs to find out all it can about its competitors. It must constantly compare its marketing strategies, products, prices, channels, and promotions with those of close competitors. In this way the company can find areas of potential competitive advantage and disadvantage. As shown in Figure 18.1, competitor analysis involves first identifying and assessing competitors and then selecting which competitors to attack or avoid.

Identifying Competitors

Normally, identifying competitors would seem a simple task. At the narrowest level, a company can define its competitors as other companies offering similar products and services to the same customers at similar prices. Thus, Abercrombie & Fitch might see Gap as a major competitor, but not Macy's or Target. Ritz-Carlton might see Four Seasons hotels as a major competitor, but not Holiday Inn Hotels, the Hampton Inn, or any of the thousands of bed-and-breakfasts that dot the nation.

FIGURE | 18.1

Steps in Analyzing Competitors

Identifying competitors isn't as easy as it seems. For example, when film cameras dominated, Kodak saw Fujifilm as its only major competitor. But its real competitor turned out to be digital imaging, including other digital camera makers and a host of digital image developers and online image-sharing services.

| Identifying the company's competitors | → | Assessing competitors' objectives, strategies, strengths and weaknesses, and reaction patterns | → | Selecting which competitors to attack or avoid |

But companies actually face a much wider range of competitors. The company might define competitors as all firms making the same product or class of products. Thus, Ritz-Carlton would see itself as competing against all other hotels. Even more broadly, competitors might include all companies making products that supply the same service. Here Ritz-Carlton would see itself competing not only against other hotels but also against anyone who supplies rooms for weary travelers. Finally, and still more broadly, competitors might include all companies that compete for the same consumer dollars. Here Ritz-Carlton would see itself competing with travel and leisure services, from cruises and summer homes to vacations abroad.

Companies must avoid "competitor myopia." A company is more likely to be "buried" by its latent competitors than its current ones. For example, it wasn't direct competitors that put an end to Western Union's telegram businesses after 161 years; it was cell phones and the Internet. And Kodak's film business didn't suffer at the hands of direct competitor Fujifilm; it lost out to competitors that Kodak didn't see coming—Sony, Canon, and other digital camera makers, along with a host of digital image developers and online image-sharing services. Perhaps the classic example of competitor myopia is Encyclopaedia Britannica:[3]

> For more than 200 years, Encyclopaedia Britannica saw itself as competing with other publishers of printed reference books and encyclopedia sets selling for as much as $2,200 per set. However, it learned a hard lesson when the world went digital in the 1990s. Microsoft introduced *Encarta*, a CD-ROM encyclopedia that sold for only $50. *Encarta* and other digital encyclopedias took the market by storm, followed quickly by Web-based encyclopedias and reference sources. As a result, Britannica's sales plunged 50 percent during the next seven years. As it turns out, Britannica's real competitors weren't other print publishers, they were the computer, the Internet, and digital content. Britannica still publishes its flagship 32-volume *Encyclopedia Britannica* and several other printed reference sets. However, it also offers popular DVD and Web versions of its information services. Britannica recognizes competitors ranging from World Book to Microsoft to free Web upstarts such as Wikipedia, the bottom-up, dynamic, nonprofit, Internet-based encyclopedia "that anyone can edit."

Companies can identify their competitors from the *industry* point of view. They might see themselves as being in the oil industry, the pharmaceutical industry, or the beverage industry. A company must understand the competitive patterns in its industry if it hopes to be an effective "player" in that industry. Companies can also identify competitors from a *market* point of view. Here they define competitors as companies that are trying to satisfy the same customer need or build relationships with the same customer group.

From an industry point of view, Pepsi might see its competition as Coca-Cola, Dr Pepper, 7UP, and the makers of other soft drink brands. From a market point of view, however, the customer really wants "thirst quenching." This need can be satisfied by bottled water, energy drinks, fruit juice, iced tea, or many other fluids. Similarly, Hallmark's Binney & Smith, maker of Crayola crayons, might define its competitors as other makers of crayons and children's drawing supplies. But from a market point of view, it would include all firms making recreational and educational products for children. In general, the market concept of competition opens the company's eyes to a broader set of actual and potential competitors.

Assessing Competitors

Having identified the main competitors, marketing management now asks: What are competitors' objectives—what does each seek in the marketplace? What is each competitor's strategy? What are various competitor's strengths and weaknesses, and how will each react to actions the company might take?

Determining Competitors' Objectives

Each competitor has a mix of objectives. The company wants to know the relative importance that a competitor places on current profitability, market share growth, cash flow, technological leadership, service leadership, and other goals. Knowing a competitor's mix of objectives reveals whether the competitor is satisfied with its current situation and how it might react to different competitive actions. For example, a company that pursues low-cost leadership will react much more strongly to a competitor's cost-reducing manufacturing breakthrough than to the same competitor's advertising increase.

A company also must monitor its competitors' objectives for various segments. If the company finds that a competitor has discovered a new segment, this might be an opportunity. If it finds that competitors plan new moves into segments now served by the company, it will be forewarned and, hopefully, forearmed.

Identifying Competitors' Strategies

Strategic group
A group of firms in an industry following the same or a similar strategy.

The more that one firm's strategy resembles another firm's strategy, the more the two firms compete. In most industries, the competitors can be sorted into groups that pursue different strategies. A **strategic group** is a group of firms in an industry following the same or a similar strategy in a given target market. For example, in the major appliance industry, GE, and Whirlpool belong to the same strategic group. Each produces a full line of medium-price appliances supported by good service. ▲In contrast, Sub-Zero and Viking belong to a different strategic group. They produce a narrower line of higher-quality appliances, offer a higher level of service, and charge a premium price.

Some important insights emerge from identifying strategic groups. For example, if a company enters one of the groups, the members of that group become its key competitors. Thus, if the company enters the first group, against GE and Whirlpool, it can succeed only if it develops strategic advantages over these competitors.

Although competition is most intense within a strategic group, there is also rivalry among groups. First, some of the strategic groups may appeal to overlapping customer segments. For example, no matter what their strategy, all major appliance manufacturers will go after the apartment and homebuilders segment. Second, the customers may not see much difference in the offers of different groups—they may see little difference in quality between GE and Whirlpool. Finally, members of one strategic group might expand into new strategy segments. Thus, GE's Monogram and Profile lines of appliances compete in the premium-quality, premium-price line with Viking and Sub-Zero.

The company needs to look at all of the dimensions that identify strategic groups within the industry. It must understand how each competitor delivers value to its customers. It needs to know each competitor's product quality, features, and mix; customer services; pricing policy; distribution coverage; sales force strategy; and advertising and sales promotion programs. And it must study the details of each competitor's R&D, manufacturing, purchasing, financial, and other strategies.

IMAGINE YOUR LIFE IN A VIKING KITCHEN. VIKING 1-888-845-4641 vikingrange.com

▲ Strategic groups: Viking belongs to the appliance industry strategic group offering a narrow line of higher-quality appliances supported by good service.

Assessing Competitors' Strengths and Weaknesses

Marketers need to assess each competitor's strengths and weaknesses carefully in order to answer a critical question: What *can* our competitors do? As a first step, companies can gather data on each competitor's goals, strategies, and performance over the past few years. Admittedly, some of this information will be hard to obtain. For example, business-to-business marketers find it hard to estimate competitors' market shares because they do not have the same syndicated data services that are available to consumer packaged-goods companies.

Companies normally learn about their competitors' strengths and weaknesses through secondary data, personal experience, and word of mouth. They can also conduct primary marketing research with customers, suppliers, and dealers. Or they can **benchmark** themselves against other firms, comparing the company's products and processes to those of competitors or leading firms in other industries to identify "best practices" and find ways to improve quality and performance. Benchmarking has become a powerful tool for increasing a company's competitiveness.

Benchmarking
The process of comparing the company's products and processes to those of competitors or leading firms in other industries to identify "best practices" and find ways to improve quality and performance.

Estimating Competitors' Reactions

Next, the company wants to know: What *will* our competitors do? A competitor's objectives, strategies, and strengths and weaknesses go a long way toward explaining its likely actions. They also suggest its likely reactions to company moves such as price cuts, promotion increases, or new-product introductions. In addition, each competitor has a certain philosophy of doing business, a certain internal culture and guiding beliefs. Marketing managers need a deep understanding of a given competitor's mentality if they want to anticipate how the competitor will act or react.

Each competitor reacts differently. Some do not react quickly or strongly to a competitor's move. They may feel their customers are loyal, they may be slow in noticing the move, or they may lack the funds to react. Some competitors react only to certain types of moves and not to others. Other competitors react swiftly and strongly to any action. Thus, Procter & Gamble does not let a new detergent come easily into the market. Many firms avoid direct competition with P&G and look for easier prey, knowing that P&G will react fiercely if challenged.

In some industries, competitors live in relative harmony; in others, they fight constantly. Knowing how major competitors react gives the company clues on how best to attack competitors or how best to defend the company's current positions.

Selecting Competitors to Attack and Avoid

A company has already largely selected its major competitors through prior decisions on customer targets, distribution channels, and marketing-mix strategy. Management now must decide which competitors to compete against most vigorously.

Strong or Weak Competitors

The company can focus on one of several classes of competitors. Most companies prefer to compete against *weak competitors*. This requires fewer resources and less time. But in the process, the firm may gain little. You could argue that the firm also should compete with *strong competitors* in order to sharpen its abilities. Moreover, even strong competitors have some weaknesses, and succeeding against them often provides greater returns.

A useful tool for assessing competitor strengths and weaknesses is **customer value analysis**. The aim of customer value analysis is to determine the benefits that target customers value and how customers rate the relative value of various competitors' offers. In conducting a customer value analysis, the company first identifies the major attributes that customers value and the importance customers place on these attributes. Next, it assesses the company's and competitors' performance on the valued attributes.

Customer value analysis
Analysis conducted to determine what benefits target customers value and how they rate the relative value of various competitors' offers.

The key to gaining competitive advantage is to take each customer segment and examine how the company's offer compares to that of its major competitors. As shown in **Figure 18.2**, the company wants to find the "strategic sweet spot"—the place where it meets customers' needs in a way that rivals can't. If the company's offer delivers greater value by exceeding the competitor's offer on important attributes, the company can charge a higher price and earn higher profits, or it can charge the same price and gain more market share. But if the company is seen as performing at a lower level than its major competitor on some important attributes, it must invest in strengthening those attributes or finding other important attributes where it can build a lead on the competitor.

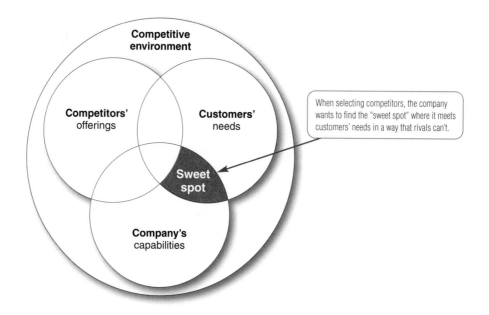

FIGURE | 18.2

Strategic Sweet Spot versus Competitors

Source: Adapted from David J. Collins and Michael G. Rukstad, "Can You Say What Your Strategy Is?" *Harvard Business Review*, April 2008, p. 89. Copyright © 2008 by the President and Fellows of Harvard College; all rights reserved.

Close or Distant Competitors

Most companies will compete with *close competitors*—those that resemble them most—rather than *distant competitors*. Thus, Nike competes more against Adidas than against Timberland or Keen. And Target competes against Wal-Mart rather than Neiman Marcus or Nordstrom.

At the same time, the company may want to avoid trying to "destroy" a close competitor. ▲For example, in the late 1970s, Bausch & Lomb moved aggressively against other soft lens manufacturers with great success. However, this forced weak competitors to sell out to larger firms such as Johnson & Johnson. As a result, Bausch & Lomb then faced much larger competitors—and it suffered the consequences. Johnson & Johnson acquired Vistakon, a small nicher with only $20 million in annual sales. Backed by Johnson & Johnson's deep pockets, the small but nimble Vistakon developed and introduced its innovative Acuvue disposable lenses. With Vistakon leading the way, Johnson & Johnson is now the top U.S. contact lens maker, while Bausch & Lomb lags in fourth place. In this case, success in hurting a close rival brought in tougher competitors.

▲ After driving smaller competitors from the market, Bausch & Lomb faces larger, more resourceful ones, such as Johnson & Johnson's Vistakon division. With Vistakon's Acuvue lenses leading the way, J&J is now the top U.S. contact lens maker.

"Good" or "Bad" Competitors

A company really needs and benefits from competitors. The existence of competitors results in several strategic benefits. Competitors may share the costs of market and product development and help to legitimize new technologies. They may serve less-attractive segments or lead to more product differentiation. Finally, competitors may help increase total demand. For example, you might think that an independent coffeehouse surrounded by Starbucks stores might have trouble staying in business. But that's often not the case:[4]

Coffee-shop owners around the country have discovered that the corporate steamroller known as Starbucks is actually good for their business. It turns out that when a Starbucks comes to the neighborhood, the result is new converts to the latte-drinking fold. When all those converts overrun the local Starbucks, the independents are there to catch the spillover. In fact, some independent storeowners now actually try to open their stores near a Starbucks if they can. That's certainly not how the coffee behemoth planned it. "Starbucks is actually *trying* to be ruthless," says the owner of a small coffeehouse chain in Los Angeles. But "in its predatory store-placement strategy, Starbucks has been about as lethal a killer as a fluffy bunny rabbit."

However, a company may not view all of its competitors as beneficial. An industry often contains *"good"* competitors and *"bad"* competitors.[5] Good competitors play by the rules of the industry. Bad competitors, in contrast, break the rules. They try to buy share rather than earn it, take large risks, and play by their own rules.

For example, Yahoo! Music Unlimited sees Napster, Rhapsody, AOL Music, Amazon.com, and most other digital music download services as good competitors. They share a common platform, so that music bought from any of these competitors can be played on almost any playback device. However, it sees Apple's iTunes Music Store as a bad competitor, one that plays by its own rules at the expense of the industry as a whole.[6]

With the iPod, Apple initially created a closed system with mass-appeal. In 2003, when the iPod was the only game in town, Apple cut deals with the four major music labels that locked up its device. The music companies wanted to sell songs on iTunes, but they were afraid of Internet piracy. So Apple promised to wrap their songs in its FairPlay digital rights management (DRM) technology—the only copy-protection encryption that is compatible with iPods and iPhones. Other digital music services such as Yahoo! Music Unlimited and Napster reached similar deals with the big music labels. When Apple refused to license FairPlay to them, those companies turned to Microsoft for DRM technology. But that meant that none of the songs sold by those services could be played on the wildly popular iPod and vice versa. The situation has been a disaster for Apple's competitors. Although some recording labels, notably EMI and Universal Music Group, are now foregoing DMR technology in an effort to weaken the bargaining power they gave to Apple by first insisting on it, iTunes still holds a commanding 80 percent of the digital music market. It recently sold its four billionth song.

The implication is that "good" companies would like to shape an industry that consists of only well-behaved competitors. A company might be smart to support good competitors, aiming its attacks at bad competitors. Thus, Yahoo! Music Unlimited, Napster, and other digital music competitors will no doubt support one another in trying to break Apple's stranglehold on the market.

Finding Uncontested Market Spaces

Rather than competing head to head with established competitors, many companies seek out unoccupied positions in uncontested market spaces. They try to create products and services for which there are *no* direct competitors. Called a "blue ocean strategy," the goal is to make competition irrelevant:[7]

Companies have long engaged in head-to-head competition in search of profitable growth. They have flocked for competitive advantage, battled over market share, and struggled for differentiation. Yet in today's overcrowded industries, competing head-on results in nothing but a bloody "red ocean" of rivals fighting over a shrinking profit pool. In their book *Blue Ocean Strategy*, two marketing professors contend that although most companies compete within such red oceans, the strategy isn't likely to create profitable growth in the future. Tomorrow's leading companies will succeed not by battling competitors but by creating "blue oceans" of uncontested market space. Such strategic moves—termed "value innovation"—create powerful leaps in value for both the firm and its buyers, creating all new demand and rendering rivals obsolete. By creating and capturing blue oceans, companies can largely take rivals out of the picture.

▲ "Blue-ocean" strategies: Cirque du Soleil reinvented the circus, finding an uncontested new market space that created new demand and rendered rivals irrelevant.

An example of a company exhibiting blue-ocean thinking is ▲Cirque du Soleil, which reinvented the circus as a higher form of modern entertainment. At a time when the circus industry was declining, Cirque du Soleil innovated by eliminating high cost and controversial elements such as animal acts and instead focused on the theatrical experience. Cirque du Soleil did not compete with then market leader Ringling Bros. and Barnum & Bailey—it was altogether different from anything that preceded it. Instead, it created an uncontested new market space that made existing competitors irrelevant. The results have been spectacular. Thanks to its blue-ocean strategy, in only its first 20 years, Cirque du Soleil achieved more revenues than Ringling Brothers and Barnum & Bailey achieved in its first 100 years.

Designing a Competitive Intelligence System

We have described the main types of information that companies need about their competitors. This information must be collected, interpreted, distributed, and used. The cost in money and time of gathering competitive intelligence is high, and the company must design its competitive intelligence system in a cost-effective way.

The competitive intelligence system first identifies the vital types of competitive information needed and the best sources of this information. Then, the system continuously collects information from the field (sales force, channels, suppliers, market research firms, trade associations, Web sites) and from published data (government publications, speeches, articles). Next the system checks the information for validity and reliability, interprets it, and organizes it in an appropriate way. Finally, it sends key information to relevant decision makers and responds to inquiries from managers about competitors.

With this system, company managers will receive timely intelligence information about competitors in the form of phone calls, e-mails, bulletins, newsletters, and reports. In addition, managers can connect with the system when they need an interpretation of a competitor's sudden move, or when they want to know a competitor's weaknesses and strengths, or when they need to know how a competitor will respond to a planned company move.

Smaller companies that cannot afford to set up formal competitive intelligence offices can assign specific executives to watch specific competitors. Thus, a manager who used to work for a competitor might follow that competitor closely; he or she would be the "in-house expert" on that competitor. Any manager needing to know the thinking of a given competitor could contact the assigned in-house expert.

Author Comment | Now that we've identified competitors and know all about them, it's time to design a strategy for gaining competitive advantage.

Competitive Strategies (pp 534–546)

Having identified and evaluated its major competitors, the company now must design broad competitive marketing strategies by which it can gain competitive advantage through superior customer value. But what broad marketing strategies might the company use? Which ones are best for a particular company, or for the company's different divisions and products?

Approaches to Marketing Strategy

No one strategy is best for all companies. Each company must determine what makes the most sense given its position in the industry and its objectives, opportunities, and resources. Even within a company, different strategies may be required for different businesses or products. Johnson & Johnson uses one marketing strategy for its leading brands in stable consumer markets—such as BAND-AID, Tylenol, or Johnson's baby products—and a different marketing strategy for its high-tech health-care businesses and products—such as Monocryl surgical sutures or NeuFlex finger joint implants.

Companies also differ in how they approach the strategy-planning process. Many large firms develop formal competitive marketing strategies and implement them religiously. However, other companies develop strategy in a less formal and orderly fashion. Some companies, such as Harley-Davidson, Virgin Atlantic Airways, and BMW's MINI Cooper unit succeed by breaking many of the "rules" of marketing strategy. Such companies don't operate large marketing departments, conduct expensive marketing research, spell out elaborate competitive strategies, and spend huge sums on advertising. Instead, they sketch out strategies on the fly, stretch their limited resources, live close to their customers, and create more satisfying solutions to customer needs. They form buyer's clubs, use buzz marketing, and focus on winning customer loyalty. It seems that not all marketing must follow in the footsteps of marketing giants such as IBM and Procter & Gamble.

In fact, approaches to marketing strategy and practice often pass through three stages: entrepreneurial marketing, formulated marketing, and intrepreneurial marketing.

- *Entrepreneurial marketing:* Most companies are started by individuals who live by their wits. They visualize an opportunity, construct flexible strategies on the backs of envelopes, and knock on every door to gain attention. ▲Gary Hirshberg, who started the Stonyfield Farm yogurt company, will tell you that it's not about dumping millions of dollars into marketing and advertising. For Stonyfield, it's about company blogs, snappy packaging, environmental responsibility, and handing out free yogurt. And it's about telling the company story to the media. Hirshberg, known for wearing khakis and a vest, started making yogurt in Wilton, New Hampshire, with seven cows and a dream. His marketing strategy: building a strong connection with customers using guerilla marketing. His idea is that "companies can do better with less advertising, less marketing research, more guerilla marketing, and more acting from the gut." Using this strategy, Hirshberg has built Stonyfield Farm into a $320 million company.[8]

▲ Entrepreneurial marketing: Stonyfield Farm's idea of marketing strategy—"companies can do better with less advertising, less marketing research, more guerilla marketing, and more acting from the gut."

- *Formulated marketing:* As small companies achieve success, they inevitably move toward more-formulated marketing. They develop formal marketing strategies and adhere to them closely. With 85 percent of the company now owned by Groupe Danone (which also makes Dannon yogurt), Stonyfield Farm has now developed a formal marketing department that carries out market research and plans strategy. Although Stonyfield may remain less formal in its strategy than the P&Gs of the marketing world, it employs many of the tools used in these more-developed marketing companies.

- *Intrepreneurial marketing:* Many large and mature companies get stuck in formulated marketing. They pore over the latest Nielsen numbers, scan market research reports, and try to fine-tune their competitive strategies and programs. These companies sometimes lose the marketing creativity and passion that they had at the start. They now need to reestablish within their companies the entrepreneurial spirit and actions that made them successful in the first place. They need to encourage more initiative and "intrepreneurship" at the local level. They need to refresh their marketing strategies and try new approaches. Their brand and product managers need to get out of the office, start living with their customers, and visualize new and creative ways to add value to their customers' lives.

The bottom line is that there are many approaches to developing effective competitive marketing strategy. There will be a constant tension between the formulated side of marketing and the creative side. It is easier to learn the formulated side of marketing, which has occupied most of our attention in this book. But we have also seen how marketing creativity and passion in the strategies of many of the companies we've studied—whether small or large, new or mature—have helped to build and maintain success in the marketplace. With this in mind, we now look at broad competitive marketing strategies companies can use.

Basic Competitive Strategies

Almost three decades ago, Michael Porter suggested four basic competitive positioning strategies that companies can follow—three winning strategies and one losing one.[9] The three winning strategies include:

- *Overall cost leadership:* Here the company works hard to achieve the lowest production and distribution costs. Low costs let it price lower than its competitors and win a large market share. Texas Instruments, Dell, and Wal-Mart are leading practitioners of this strategy.

- *Differentiation:* Here the company concentrates on creating a highly differentiated product line and marketing program so that it comes across as the class leader in the industry. Most customers would prefer to own this brand if its price is not too high. IBM and Caterpillar follow this strategy in information technology and services and heavy construction equipment, respectively.

- *Focus:* Here the company focuses its effort on serving a few market segments well rather than going after the whole market. For example, Ritz-Carlton focuses on the top 5 percent of corporate and leisure travelers. Tetra Food supplies 80 percent of pet tropical fish food. Similarly, Hohner owns a stunning 85 percent of the harmonica market.[10]

Companies that pursue a clear strategy—one of the above—will likely perform well. The firm that carries out that strategy best will make the most profits. But firms that do not pursue a clear strategy—*middle-of-the-roaders*—do the worst. Sears and Holiday Inn encountered difficult times because they did not stand out as the lowest in cost, highest in perceived value, or best in serving some market segment. Middle-of-the-roaders try to be good on all strategic counts, but end up being not very good at anything.

Two marketing consultants, Michael Treacy and Fred Wiersema, offer a more customer-centered classification of competitive marketing strategies.[11] They suggest that companies gain leadership positions by delivering superior value to their customers. Companies can pursue any of three strategies—called *value disciplines*—for delivering superior customer value. These are:

- *Operational excellence:* The company provides superior value by leading its industry in price and convenience. It works to reduce costs and to create a lean and efficient value-delivery system. It serves customers who want reliable, good-quality products or services, but who want them cheaply and easily. Examples include Wal-Mart, Southwest Airlines, and Dell.

- *Customer intimacy:* The company provides superior value by precisely segmenting its markets and tailoring its products or services to match exactly the needs of targeted customers. It specializes in satisfying unique customer needs through a close relationship with and intimate knowledge of the customer. It builds detailed customer databases for segmenting and targeting, and empowers its marketing people to respond quickly to customer needs. Customer-intimate companies serve customers who are willing to pay a premium to get precisely what they want. They will do almost anything to build long-term customer loyalty and to capture customer lifetime value. Examples include Nordstrom, Lexus, American Express, British Airways, and Ritz-Carlton hotels.

- *Product leadership:* The company provides superior value by offering a continuous stream of leading-edge products or services. It aims to make its own and competing products obsolete. Product leaders are open to new ideas, relentlessly pursue new solutions, and work to get new products to market quickly. They serve customers who want state-of-the-art products and services, regardless of the costs in terms of price or inconvenience. Examples include Nokia and Apple.

Some companies successfully pursue more than one value discipline at the same time. For example, FedEx excels at both operational excellence and customer intimacy. However, such companies are rare—few firms can be the best at more than one of these disciplines. By trying to be *good at all* of the value disciplines, a company usually ends up being *best at none.*

Treacy and Wiersema found that leading companies focus on and excel at a single value discipline, while meeting industry standards on the other two. Such companies design their entire value delivery network to single-mindedly support the chosen discipline. For example, Wal-Mart knows that customer intimacy and product leadership are important. Compared with other discounters, it offers very good customer service and an excellent product assortment. Still, it purposely offers less customer service and less product depth than do Nordstrom or Williams-Sonoma, which pursue customer intimacy. Instead, Wal-Mart focuses obsessively on operational excellence—on reducing costs and streamlining its order-to-delivery process in order to make it convenient for customers to buy just the right products at the lowest prices.

By the same token, Ritz-Carlton Hotels wants to be efficient and to employ the latest technologies. But what really sets the luxury hotel chain apart is its customer intimacy. Ritz-Carlton creates custom-designed experiences to coddle its customers (see **Real Marketing 18.1**).

Classifying competitive strategies as value disciplines is appealing. It defines marketing strategy in terms of the single-minded pursuit of delivering superior value to customers. Each value discipline defines a specific way to build lasting customer relationships.

Competitive Positions

Firms competing in a given target market, at any point in time, differ in their objectives and resources. Some firms are large, others small. Some have many resources, others are strapped for funds. Some are mature and established, others new and fresh. Some strive for rapid market share growth, others for long-term profits. And the firms occupy different competitive positions in the target market.

We now examine competitive strategies based on the roles firms play in the target market—leader, challenger, follower, or nicher. Suppose that an industry contains the firms shown in ◗ **Figure 18.3**. Forty percent of the market is in the hands of the **market leader**, the firm with the largest market share. Another 30 percent is in the hands of **market challengers**, runner-up firms that are fighting hard to increase their market share. Another 20 percent is in the hands of **market followers**, other runner-up firms that want to hold their share without rocking the boat. The remaining 10 percent is in the hands of **market nichers**, firms that serve small segments not being pursued by other firms.

Market leader
The firm in an industry with the largest market share.

Market challenger
A runner-up firm that is fighting hard to increase its market share in an industry.

Market follower
A runner-up firm that wants to hold its share in an industry without rocking the boat.

Market nicher
A firm that serves small segments that the other firms in an industry overlook or ignore.

◗ **FIGURE** | **18.3**
Competitive Market Positions and Roles

Each market position calls for a different competitive strategy. For example, the market leader wants to expand total demand and protect or expand its share. Market nichers seek market segments that are big enough to be profitable but small enough to be of little interest to major competitors.

Market leader	Market challengers	Market followers	Market nichers
40%	30%	20%	10%

Real Marketing 18.1

Ritz-Carlton:
Creating Customer Intimacy

Ritz-Carlton, a chain of luxury hotels renowned for outstanding service, caters to the top 5 percent of corporate and leisure travelers. The company's Credo sets lofty customer-service goals: "The Ritz-Carlton is a place where the genuine care and comfort of our guests is our highest mission. . . . The Ritz-Carlton experience enlivens the senses, instills well-being, and fulfills even the unexpressed wishes and needs of our guests."

The Credo is more than just words on paper—Ritz-Carlton delivers on its promises. In surveys of departing guests, some 95 percent report that they've had a truly memorable experience. In fact, at Ritz-Carlton, exceptional service encounters have become almost commonplace. Take the experiences of Nancy and Harvey Heffner of Manhattan, who stayed at The Ritz-Carlton Naples, in Naples, Florida (rated the best hotel in the United States and fourth best in the world, by *Travel + Leisure* magazine).

"The hotel is elegant and beautiful," Mrs. Heffner said, "but more important is the beauty expressed by the staff. They can't do enough to please you." When the couple's son became sick last year in Naples, the hotel staff brought him hot tea

When it comes to creating customer intimacy, Ritz-Carlton sets the gold standard. "It's all about providing a unique, personal, memorable experience."

with honey at all hours of the night, she said. When Mr. Heffner had to fly home on business for a day and his return flight was delayed, a driver for the hotel waited in the lobby most of the night.

Such personal, high-quality service has also made The Ritz-Carlton a favorite among conventioneers. For seven of the last nine years, the luxury hotel came out on top in *Business Travel News*'s Top U.S. Hotel Chain Survey of business travel buyers. "They not only treat us like kings when we hold our top-level meetings in their hotels, but we just never get any complaints," comments one convention planner. Says another, who had recently held a meeting at The Ritz-Carlton Half Moon Bay, "The first-rate catering and convention services staff

[and] The Ritz-Carlton's ambiance and beauty—the elegant, Grand Dame-style lodge, nestled on a bluff between two championship golf courses overlooking the Pacific Ocean—makes a day's work there seem anything but."

Since its incorporation in 1983, Ritz-Carlton has received virtually every major award that the hospitality industry bestows. In addition, it's the only hotel company ever to win the prestigious Malcolm Baldrige National Quality Award and one of only two companies from any industry to win the award twice. A recent *Consumer Reports* hotels issue ranked Ritz-Carlton the number-one luxury hotel company in all areas, including value, service, upkeep, and problem resolution. More than 90 percent of Ritz-Carlton customers return. And despite its hefty room

● **Table 18.1** shows specific marketing strategies that are available to market leaders, challengers, followers, and nichers.[12] Remember, however, that these classifications often do not apply to a whole company, but only to its position in a specific industry. Large companies such as GE, Microsoft, Procter & Gamble, or Disney might be leaders in some markets and nichers in others. For example, Procter & Gamble leads in many segments, such as laundry detergents and shampoo. But it challenges Unilever in hand soaps and Kimberly-Clark in facial tissues. Such companies often use different strategies for different business units or products, depending on the competitive situations of each.

● TABLE | 18.1   Strategies for Market Leaders, Challengers, Followers, and Nichers

Market Leader Strategies	Market Challenger Strategies	Market Follower Strategies	Market Nicher Strategies
Expand total market	Full frontal attack	Follow closely	By customer, market, quality-price, service
Protect market share	Indirect attack	Follow at a distance	Multiple niching
Expand market share			

rates, the chain enjoys a 70 percent occupancy rate, almost nine points above the industry average.

Most of the responsibility for keeping guests satisfied falls to Ritz-Carlton's customer-contact employees. Thus, the hotel chain takes great care in finding just the right personnel—"people who care about people." Then, Ritz-Carlton goes to great lengths to rigorously—even fanatically—train employees in the art of coddling customers. New employees attend a two-day orientation, in which top management drums into them the "12 Ritz-Carlton Service Values." Service Value number one: "I build strong relationships and create Ritz-Carlton guests for life." Ritz-Carlton trains every single employee worldwide every day, using a start-of-shift 15-minute meeting called "the lineup" to remind them of its service values.

Employees are taught to do everything they can to avoid never losing a guest. "There's no negotiating at Ritz-Carlton when it comes to solving customer problems," says a quality executive. Staff learn that *anyone* who receives a customer complaint *owns* that complaint until it's resolved (Ritz-Carlton Service Value number six). They are trained to drop whatever they're doing to help a customer—no matter what they're doing or what their department. Ritz-Carlton employees are empowered to handle problems on the spot. Each employee can spend up to $2,000 to redress a guest grievance without consulting higher-ups.

Beyond just fixing problems, Ritz-Carlton staff at all levels are "empowered to create unique, memorable, and personal experiences for our guests" (Ritz-Carlton Service Value

number three). The company expects employees to use their own good judgment rather than telling them what to do. "We are managing to outcomes, and the outcome is a happy guest," says Ritz-Carlton's vice president of global learning. "We don't care how you get there—as long as it's moral, legal, and ethical—but we want you to use your genuine talent, we want you to do what we call 'radar on, antenna up,' which means staying in the moment so you can read what a guest wants."

As a result, almost everyone who frequents The Ritz-Carlton has a "you won't believe this" story to tell about their experiences there. Employee heroics seem almost commonplace. For example, an administrative assistant at The Ritz-Carlton Philadelphia once overheard a guest lamenting that he'd forgotten to pack a pair of formal shoes and would have to wear hiking boots to an important meeting. Early the next morning, she delivered to the awestruck man a new pair in his size and favorite color.

In another case, a business traveler arrived at The Ritz-Carlton Atlanta late on a cold, rainy December night, tired to the bone and suffering from a bad head cold. To her surprise and relief, hotel staff met her at the door, greeted her by name, and, seeing her condition, escorted her directly to her room. When she arrived at her room, to her amazement, she found fresh flowers, two boxes of cough drops, and a personally addressed get-well card awaiting her. Such "Wow!" stories of service are read aloud every Monday to give Ritz-Carlton employees an understanding that they work among extraordinary people who do extraordinary things when the opportunity presents itself.

Ritz-Carlton instills a sense of pride in its employees. "You serve," they are told, "but you are not servants." The company motto states, "We are ladies and gentlemen serving ladies and gentlemen." "When you invite guests to your house," it tells them, "you want everything to be perfect." As a result, Ritz-Carlton's employees appear to be just as satisfied as its customers. Employee turnover is less than 25 percent a year, compared an 85 percent industry average.

Thus, when it comes to creating customer intimacy, Ritz-Carlton sets the gold standard. The key is ensuring that guests don't feel like just another nameless face walking through the door. "It's all about personalization," says the Ritz-Carlton executive. "It's about providing a unique, personal, memorable experience, and what each person can do within your own environment to make that happen."

Sources: Quotes and other information from Julio Barker, "Power to the People," *Incentive*, February 2008, p. 34; "The World's Best Hotels 2007—Where Luxury Lives," *Institutional Investor*, November 2007, p. 1; Edwin McDowell, "Ritz-Carlton's Keys to Good Service," *New York Times*, March 31, 1993, p. D1; "The Ritz-Carlton, Half Moon Bay," *Successful Meetings*, November 2001, p. 40; Bruce Serlen, "Ritz-Carlton Retains Hold on Corporate Deluxe Buyers," *Business Travel News*, February 7, 2005, pp. 15–17; Michael B. Baker, Four Seasons, Ritz-Carlton Tie as Deluxe Tier Leads Rate Growth," March 24, 2008, pp. 12–14; Margery Weinstein, "Service with a Smile," *Training*, March–April 2008, p. 40; and www.ritzcarlton.com, accessed October 2008.

Market Leader Strategies

Most industries contain an acknowledged market leader. The leader has the largest market share and usually leads the other firms in price changes, new-product introductions, distribution coverage, and promotion spending. The leader may or may not be admired or respected, but other firms concede its dominance. Competitors focus on the leader as a company to challenge, imitate, or avoid. Some of the best-known market leaders are Wal-Mart (retailing), Microsoft (computer software), Caterpillar (earth-moving equipment), Anheuser-Busch (beer), McDonald's (fast food), Nike (athletic footwear and apparel), and Google (Internet search services).

A leader's life is not easy. It must maintain a constant watch. Other firms keep challenging its strengths or trying to take advantage of its weaknesses. The market leader can easily miss a turn in the market and plunge into second or third place. A product innovation may come along and hurt the leader (as when Apple developed the iPod and took the market lead from Sony's Walkman portable audio devices). The leader might grow arrogant or complacent and misjudge the competition (as when Sears lost its lead to Wal-Mart). Or the leader might look old-fashioned against new and peppier rivals (as when Levi's lost serious ground to more current or stylish brands like Gap, Tommy Hilfiger, DKNY, or GUESS).

To remain number one, leading firms can take any of three actions. First, they can find ways to expand total demand. Second, they can protect their current market share through good defensive and offensive actions. Third, they can try to expand their market share further, even if market size remains constant.

Expanding the Total Demand

The leading firm normally gains the most when the total market expands. If Americans eat more fast food, McDonald's stands to gain the most because it holds more than three times the fast-food market share of nearest competitor Burger King. If McDonald's can convince more Americans that fast food is the best eating-out choice in these economic times, it will benefit more than its competitors.

Market leaders can expand the market by developing new users, new uses, and more usage of its products. They usually can find *new users* or untapped market segments in many places. For example, NutriSystem has typically targeted its weight loss programs toward women. Recently, however, it stepped up its efforts to attract male customers.[13]

Prior to 2006, NutriSystem featured only a few men in its customer testimonials. However, it now directly targets men with its NutriSystem Advanced Men's Program. The weight-management company advertises regularly in male-skewing media such as ESPN TV and radio, *Sports Illustrated*, and *Men's Health*. NutriSystem spends nearly one-third of its television advertising budget on male-oriented networks. The men's program offers pretty much the same types of meals offered to women. Ads feature sports legends such as Dan Marino (who lost 22 pounds on the NutriSystem program) and Don Schula (who lost 32 pounds). They focus on what men want most: not having to think about losing weight, no group meetings, and prepackaged "man foods." In one commercial, Marino proclaims, "With NutriSystem, I got to eat the foods I grew up with back in Pittsburgh—burgers, hot dogs, lasagna, pancakes, pot roast, meatballs—foods that guys love to eat. . . . Thanks to NutriSystem, I ate like a man and still lost weight." The result? Since hiring the spokesmen and adding men's chat rooms to its Web site, the male share of NutriSystem customers rose from 13 percent to 30, fueling substantial growth. Company sales increased 37 percent last year.

Marketers can expand markets by discovering and promoting *new uses* for the product. For example, Arm & Hammer baking soda, whose sales had flattened after 125 years, discovered that consumers were using baking soda as a refrigerator deodorizer. It launched a heavy advertising and publicity campaign focusing on this use and persuaded consumers in half of America's homes to place an open box of baking soda in their refrigerators and to replace it every few months. Today, its Web site (www.armandhammer.com) features new uses—"Solutions for my home, my family, my body"—ranging from removing residue left behind by hairstyling products and sweetening garbage disposals, laundry hampers, refrigerators, and trash cans to creating a home spa in your bathroom.

Finally, market leaders can encourage *more usage* by convincing people to use the product more often or to use more per occasion. ▲For example, Campbell urges people to eat soup and other Campbell's products more often by running ads containing new recipes. It also offers a toll-free hotline (1-888-MM-MM-GOOD), staffed by live "recipe representatives" who offer recipes to last-minute cooks at a loss for meal ideas. And the Campbell's Kitchen section of the company's Web site (www.campbellsoup.com) lets visitors search for or exchange recipes, set up their own personal recipe box, sign up for a daily or weekly Meal Mail program, and even watch online video clips of guest chefs cooking any of 27 recipes on Campbell's Kitchen TV.

▲ Creating more usage: Campbell urges people to eat its soups and other products more often by running ads containing new recipes. It even offers online video clips of guest chefs cooking any of 27 recipes on Campbell's Kitchen TV.

Protecting Market Share

While trying to expand total market size, the leading firm also must protect its current business against competitors' attacks. Wal-Mart must also constantly guard against Target; Caterpillar against Komatsu; and McDonald's against Burger King.

What can the market leader do to protect its position? First, it must prevent or fix weaknesses that provide opportunities for competitors. It must always fulfill its value promise. Its prices must remain consistent with the value that customers see in the brand. It must work tirelessly to keep strong relationships with valued customers. The leader should "plug holes" so that competitors do not jump in.

But the best defense is a good offense, and the best response is *continuous innovation*. The leader refuses to be content with the way things are and leads the industry in new products, customer services, distribution effectiveness, promotion, and cost cutting. It keeps increasing its competitive effectiveness and value to customers. And when attacked by challengers, the market leader reacts decisively. ▲For example, in the laundry products category, market leader P&G has been relentless in its offense against challengers such as Unilever.

▲ Protecting market share: In the face of market leader P&G's relentless assault in the laundry war, Unilever recently threw in the towel by putting its U.S. detergents business up for sale.

In one of the most fabled marketing battles of the past century, P&G won the laundry war because it was bigger, better, more focused, and more aggressive than challenger Unilever. Last year alone, P&G outgunned Unilever on U.S. media spending for laundry brands by $218 million to $25 million. Entering this millennium, even though its U.S. laundry detergent market share was well over 50 percent, P&G kept raining blows on Unilever and all other comers with stepped-up product launches. Such products as Tide with Downey, Tide Coldwater, and the scent-focused Simple Pleasures lineup for Tide and Downey helped P&G steadily gain a share point or two per year in recent years, so that it now owns a 62.5 percent share of the $3.6 billion laundry-detergent market to Unilever's 12.9 percent (including Unilever's All and Wisk brands). It has an even bigger lead in fabric softeners—66 percent to Unilever's 8.4 percent (Unilever's Snuggle brand). Globally, P&G has gone from being the number-two laundry player in the early 1990s to dominant market leader today, with a global market share of 34 percent to Unilever's 17 percent. In the face of P&G's relentless assault, Unilever finally threw in the towel and recently put its U.S. detergents business up for sale.[14]

Expanding Market Share

Market leaders also can grow by increasing their market shares further. In many markets, small market share increases mean very large sales increases. For example, in the U.S. digital camera market, a 1 percent increase in market share is worth $90 million; in carbonated soft drinks, $720 million![15]

Studies have shown that, on average, profitability rises with increasing market share. Because of these findings, many companies have sought expanded market shares to improve profitability. GE, for example, declared that it wants to be at least number one or two in each of its markets or else get out. GE shed its computer, air-conditioning, small appliances, and television businesses because it could not achieve top-dog position in these industries.

However, some studies have found that many industries contain one or a few highly profitable large firms, several profitable and more focused firms, and a large number of medium-sized firms with poorer profit performance. It appears that profitability increases as a business gains share relative to competitors in its *served market*. For example, Lexus holds only a small share of the total car market, but it earns a high profit because it is the leading brand in the luxury-performance car segment. And it has achieved this high share in its served market because it does other things right, such as producing high-quality products, creating good service experiences, and building close customer relationships.

Companies must not think, however, that gaining increased market share will automatically improve profitability. Much depends on their strategy for gaining increased share. There are many high-share companies with low profitability and many low-share companies with high profitability. The cost of buying higher market share may far exceed the returns. Higher shares tend to produce higher profits only when unit costs fall with increased market share, or when the company offers a superior-quality product and charges a premium price that more than covers the cost of offering higher quality.

Market Challenger Strategies

Firms that are second, third, or lower in an industry are sometimes quite large, such as Colgate, Ford, Lowe's, Avis, and Verizon. These runner-up firms can adopt one of two competitive strategies: They can challenge the leader and other competitors in an aggressive bid for more market share (market challengers). Or they can play along with competitors and not rock the boat (market followers).

A market challenger must first define which competitors to challenge and its strategic objective. The challenger can attack the market leader, a high-risk but potentially high-gain strategy. Its goal might be to take over market leadership. Or the challenger's objective may simply be to wrest more market share.

Although it might seem that the market leader has the most going for it, challengers often have what some strategists call a "second-mover advantage." The challenger observes what has made the leader successful and improves upon it. For example, Home Depot invented the home-improvement superstore. However, after observing Home Depot's success, number two Lowe's, with its brighter stores, wider aisles, and arguably more helpful salespeople, has positioned itself as the friendly alternative to Big Bad Orange. For Lowe's, the advantage has been profitable. Although it still captures only 58 percent of Home Depot's revenues, over the past 10 years Lowe's has earned average annual returns of 14.7 compared with Home Depot's 4.1 percent.[16]

Alternatively, the challenger can avoid the leader and instead challenge firms its own size, or smaller local and regional firms. These smaller firms may be underfinanced and not serving their customers well. Several of the major beer companies grew to their present size not by challenging large competitors, but by gobbling up small local or regional competitors. If the company goes after a small local company, its objective may be to put that company out of business. The important point remains: The challenger must choose its opponents carefully and have a clearly defined and attainable objective.

How can the market challenger best attack the chosen competitor and achieve its strategic objectives? It may launch a full *frontal attack*, matching the competitor's product, advertising, price, and distribution efforts. It attacks the competitor's strengths rather than its weaknesses. The outcome depends on who has the greater strength and endurance.

If the market challenger has fewer resources than the competitor, however, a frontal attack makes little sense. Thus, many new market entrants avoid frontal attacks, knowing that the market leaders can head them off with ad blitzes, price wars, and other retaliations. Rather than challenging head-on, the challenger can make an *indirect attack* on the competitor's weaknesses or on gaps in the competitor's market coverage. It can carve out toeholds using tactics that the established leaders have trouble responding to or choose to ignore. ▲ For example, compare the vastly different strategies of two different European challengers— Virgin Drinks and Red Bull—when they entered the U.S. soft drink market in the late 1990s against market leaders Coca-Cola and PepsiCo.[17]

Virgin Drinks took on the leaders head-on, launching its own cola, advertising heavily, and trying to get into all the same retail outlets that stocked the leading brands. At Virgin Cola's launch, Virgin CEO Richard Branson even drove a tank through a wall of rivals' cans in New York's Times Square to symbolize the war he wished to wage on the big, established rivals. However, Coke's and Pepsi's viselike grip on U.S. shelf space proved impossible for Virgin Drinks to break. Although Virgin Drinks is still around, it has never gained more than a 1 percent share of the U.S. cola market.

Market challenger strategies: Virgin Drinks mounted a full frontal attack on Coca-Cola and PepsiCo but couldn't break the leaders' viselike grip on U.S. shelf space.

Red Bull, by contrast, tackled the leaders indirectly. It entered the U.S. soft drink market with a niche product: a carbonated energy drink retailing at about twice what you would pay for a Coke or Pepsi. It started by selling Red Bull through unconventional outlets not dominated by the market leaders, such as bars and nightclubs, where twenty-somethings gulped down the caffeine-rich drink so they could dance all night. After gaining a loyal following, Red Bull used the pull of high margins to elbow its way into the corner store, where it now sits in refrigerated bins within arm's length of Coke and Pepsi. In the United States, where Red Bull enjoys a 65 percent share of the energy drink market, its sales are growing at about 35 percent a year.

Market Follower Strategies

Not all runner-up companies want to challenge the market leader. Challenges are never taken lightly by the leader. If the challenger's lure is lower prices, improved service, or additional product features, the leader can quickly match these to defuse the attack. The leader probably has more staying power in an all-out battle for customers. For example, a few years ago, when Kmart launched its renewed low-price "bluelight special" campaign, directly challenging Wal-Mart's everyday low prices, it started a price war that it couldn't win. Wal-Mart had little trouble fending off Kmart's challenge, leaving Kmart worse off for the attempt. Thus, many firms prefer to follow rather than challenge the leader.

A follower can gain many advantages. The market leader often bears the huge expenses of developing new products and markets, expanding distribution, and educating the market. By contrast, as with challengers, the market follower can learn from the leader's experience. It can copy or improve on the leader's products and programs, usually with much less investment. Although the follower will probably not overtake the leader, it often can be as profitable.

Following is not the same as being passive or a carbon copy of the leader. A market follower must know how to hold current customers and win a fair share of new ones. It must find the right balance between following closely enough to win customers from the market leader but following at enough of a distance to avoid retaliation. Each follower tries to bring distinctive advantages to its target market—location, services, financing. The follower is often a major target of attack by challengers. Therefore, the market follower must keep its manufacturing costs and prices low or its product quality and services high. It must also enter new markets as they open up.

Market Nicher Strategies

Almost every industry includes firms that specialize in serving market niches. Instead of pursuing the whole market, or even large segments, these firms target subsegments. Nichers are often smaller firms with limited resources. But smaller divisions of larger firms also may pursue niching strategies. Firms with low shares of the total market can be highly successful and profitable through smart niching.

Why is niching profitable? The main reason is that the market nicher ends up knowing the target customer group so well that it meets their needs better than other firms that casually sell to that niche. As a result, the nicher can charge a substantial markup over costs because of the added value. Whereas the mass-marketer achieves high volume, the nicher achieves high margins.

Nichers try to find one or more market niches that are safe and profitable. An ideal market niche is big enough to be profitable and has growth potential. It is one that the firm can serve effectively. Perhaps most importantly, the niche is of little interest to major competitors. And the firm can build the skills and customer goodwill to defend itself against a major competitor as the niche grows and becomes more attractive. For example, computer mouse and interface device maker Logitech is only a fraction the size of giant Microsoft. Yet, through skillful niching, it dominates the PC mouse market, with Microsoft as its runner-up (see **Real Marketing 18.2**). ▲Here's another example of a profitable nicher:

R.A.B. Food Group is no Kraft. Then again, it doesn't aspire to be. Giant Kraft, with sales of more than $37 billion, makes foods for all occasions, targeting broadly. In contrast, R.A.B. Food Group, with sales of little more the $100 million, targets a narrow segment of consumers who want to cook kosher. R.A.B. is the nation's leading marketer of kosher foods, fielding brands such as Manischewitz, Horiwitz Margareten, Goodman's, and Rokeach. Kosher is a very attractive niche, and a profitable one. During the past five years, whereas Kraft has struggled for single-digit growth, R.A.B. Food Group's sales have grown nearly 50 percent. And the future looks bright for this profitable nicher. Fueled by the boom in ethnic foods and an intensified interest in nutrition and food ingredient quality, kosher foods are now going mainstream. Research shows that consumers perceive kosher foods, made in accordance with centuries-old dietary laws, to be cleaner, purer, and higher in quality. Today, only one in five buyers of kosher foods is the traditional Jewish customer. In an effort to push its brands out of the smaller kosher sections of stores and into more heavily trafficked aisles, R.A.B. Food Group recently launched a Simply Manischewitz ad campaign (the Manischewitz brand accounts for some 54 percent of sales). Says the company's chief executive, "[Although] kosher foods are clearly our heritage and our anchor, we're reasserting our kosher credentials and positioning ourselves for broader growth."[18]

▲ Profitable niching: R.A.B. Food Group—with its Manischewitz and other brands—is the nation's leading marketer of kosher foods. Although small, the company is growing faster and more profitably than Kraft and the other food giants.

The key idea in niching is specialization. A market nicher can specialize along any of several market, customer, product, or marketing mix lines. For example, it can specialize in serving one type of *end user*, as when a law firm specializes in the criminal, civil, or business law markets. The nicher can specialize in serving a given *customer-size* group. Many nichers specialize in serving small and midsize customers who are neglected by the majors.

Some nichers focus on one or a few *specific customers*, selling their entire output to a single company, such as Wal-Mart or General Motors. Still other nichers specialize by *geographic market*, selling only in a certain locality, region, or area of the world. *Quality-price* nichers operate at the low or high end of the market. For example, HP specializes in the high-quality, high-price end of the hand-calculator market. Finally, *service nichers* offer services not available from other firms. For example, LendingTree provides online lending and realty services, connecting home buyers and sellers with national networks of mortgage lenders and realtors who compete for the customer's business. "When lenders compete," it proclaims, "you win."

Niching carries some major risks. For example, the market niche may dry up, or it might grow to the point that it attracts larger competitors. That is why many companies practice *multiple niching*. By developing two or more niches, a company increases its chances for survival. Even some large firms prefer a multiple niche strategy to serving the total market. For example, Alberto-Culver is a $1.5 billion company that has used a multiple niching strategy to grow profitably without incurring the wrath of a market leader. The company, known mainly for its Alberto VO5 hair products, has focused its marketing muscle on acquiring a stable of smaller niche brands. It niches in hair, skin,

Real Marketing 18.2

Nicher Logitech:
The Little Mouse that Roars

Among the big tech companies, market leader Microsoft is the king of the jungle. When giant Microsoft looms, even large competitors quake. But when it comes to dominating specific market niches, overall size isn't always the most important thing. For example, in its own corner of the high-tech jungle, Logitech International is the little mouse that roars. In its niches, small but mighty Logitech is the undisputed market leader.

Logitech focuses on human interface devices—computer mice, keyboards, game controllers, remote controls, Webcams, PC speakers, headsets, and other accessories. Logitech makes every variation of mouse imaginable. Over the years, it has flooded the world with more than 700 million computer mice of all varieties, mice for left- and right-handed people, wireless mice, travel mice, mini mice, 3-D mice, mice shaped like real mice for children, and even an "air mouse" that uses motion sensors to let you navigate your computer from a distance.

In the PC mouse market, Logitech competes head-on with Microsoft. At first glance it looks like an unfair contest. With more than $51 billion in sales, Microsoft is nearly 25 times bigger than $2.4 billion Logitech. But when it comes to mice, Logitech has a depth of focus and knowledge that no other company in the world—including Microsoft—can match. Whereas mice and other computer interface devices are pretty much a sideline for software maker Microsoft—almost a distraction—they are the main attraction for Logitech. As a result, each new generation of Logitech mouse is a true work of both art and science. Logitech's mice received raves from designers, expert reviewers, and users alike.

A *BusinessWeek* analyst gives us a behind-the-scenes look at Logitech's deep design and development prowess:

One engineer, given the moniker "Teflon Tim" by amused colleagues, spent three months scouring the Far East to find just the right nonstick coatings and sound-deadening foam. Another spent hours taking apart wind-up toys. Others pored over the contours of luxury BMW motorcycles, searching for designs to crib. They were members of a most unusual team that spent thousands of hours during the past two years on a single goal: to build a better mouse. The result: Logitech's revolutionary MX Revolution, the next-generation mouse that hit consumer electronics shelves about two years ago. It represented the company's most ambitious attempt yet to refashion the lowly computer mouse into a kind of control center for a host of PC applications. The sheer scope of the secret mission—which crammed 420 components, including a tiny motor, into a palm-sized device that usually holds about 20—brought together nearly three dozen engineers, designers, and marketers from around the globe.

Part of Logitech's product-development strategy is defensive. Once content to design mice and other peripherals for PC makers to slap their own names on, Logitech over the past half-decade has increasingly focused on selling its branded add-on equipment directly to consumers. Some 89 percent of Logitech's annual sales now come from retail. That forces Logitech to deliver regular improvements to entice new shoppers and purchases. "We think of mice as pretty simple," says one industry analyst, "but there's a pretty aggressive technology battle going on to prove what the mouse can do." Logitech's latest feat of cutting-edge wizardry is its MX Air, which promises to change the very definition of the computer mouse as we know it. More like an airborne remote control than a traditional mouse, you can surf the Web, play games, and control your home theater PC from up to 30 feet away. There's also a cool-factor at play. Wielding the MX Air is like holding a work of art.

Breeding mice has been very good for nicher Logitech. Thanks to its single-minded market focus and its dedication to creating the next best mouse, Logitech dominates the

WANDERFUL

The world is your office. Anywhere you are, open your laptop and your cordless mouse is ready to go. The Logitech® VX Nano Cordless Laser Mouse for Notebooks. Its plug-and-forget nano receiver is the world's smallest USB receiver.® So small, it can stay plugged into your laptop. That means the ultra-slim mouse is ready to use in no time flat. Now, no layover is too short to get some work done. Sorry about that. To simplify your mobile life, go to Logitech.com

Logitech
Designed to move you®

Breeding mice has been so successful for nicher Logitech that it dominates the world mouse market, with giant Microsoft as its runner-up.

world mouse market, with giant Microsoft as its runner-up. Logitech mice have accompanied an estimated 55 percent of desktop PCs shipped out over the past two decades. And although Logitech isn't nearly as big as Microsoft, pound for pound and mouse for mouse it's even more profitable. In just the past five years, even as PC growth has slowed, Logitech's sales have more than doubled and profits have surged 225 percent.

"Our business is about the last inch between people and content and technology, and the mouse has always been the icon of that last inch," explains Logitech CEO Guerrino De Luca. And nobody spans that last inch better than Logitech. The next time that you sit at your desktop PC, it's a pretty good bet that you'll have your hand on a Logitech mouse (regardless of the brand name on the outside). It's also a good bet that you'll really like the way it works and feels. "The goal [is] passing the 'ooooh' test," says a Logitech project leader, "creating a visceral experience that communicates both performance and luxury."

Sources: Quotes and other information from "Logitech Delivers Tenth Consecutive Record Year with Strongest Q4 Ever," Logitech press release, April 22, 2008, accessed at www.logitech.com; Cliff Edwards, "Here Comes Mighty Mouse," *BusinessWeek,* September 4, 2006, p. 76; Cliff Edwards, "The Mouse That Soars," *BusinessWeek,* August 20, 2007, p. 22; "Logitech International S.A.," *Hoover's Company Records,* May 15, 2008, p. 42459; and annual reports and other information from www.logitech.com, accessed October 2008.

and personal care products (Alberto VO5, St. Ives, Motions, Just for Me, Pro-Line, TRESemmé, and Consort men's hair products), seasonings and sweeteners (Molly McButter, Mrs. Dash, SugarTwin, Baker's Joy), and home products (static-cling fighter Static Guard). Most of its brands are number one in their niches. Alberto Culver's CEO explains the company's philosophy this way: "We know who we are and, perhaps more importantly, we know who we are not. We know that if we try to out-Procter Procter, we will fall flat on our face."[19]

Balancing Customer and Competitor Orientations (p 546)

Whether a company is a market leader, challenger, follower, or nicher, it must watch its competitors closely and find the competitive marketing strategy that positions it most effectively. And it must continually adapt its strategies to the fast-changing competitive environment. This question now arises: Can the company spend *too* much time and energy tracking competitors, damaging its customer orientation? The answer is yes! A company can become so competitor centered that it loses its even more important focus on maintaining profitable customer relationships.

Competitor-centered company

A company whose moves are mainly based on competitors' actions and reactions.

A **competitor-centered company** is one that spends most of its time tracking competitors' moves and market shares and trying to find strategies to counter them. This approach has some pluses and minuses. On the positive side, the company develops a fighter orientation, watches for weaknesses in its own position, and searches out competitors' weaknesses. On the negative side, the company becomes too reactive. Rather than carrying out its own customer relationship strategy, it bases its own moves on competitors' moves. As a result, it may end up simply matching or extending industry practices rather than seeking innovative new ways to create more value for customers.

Customer-centered company

A company that focuses on customer developments in designing its marketing strategies and on delivering superior value to its target customers.

A **customer-centered company**, by contrast, focuses more on customer developments in designing its strategies. Clearly, the customer-centered company is in a better position to identify new opportunities and set long-run strategies that make sense. By watching customer needs evolve, it can decide what customer groups and what emerging needs are the most important to serve. Then it can concentrate its resources on delivering superior value to target customers. In practice, today's companies must be **market-centered companies**, watching both their customers and their competitors. But they must not let competitor watching blind them to customer focusing.

Market-centered company

A company that pays balanced attention to both customers and competitors in designing its marketing strategies.

Figure 18.4 shows that companies have moved through four orientations over the years. In the first stage, they were product oriented, paying little attention to either customers or competitors. In the second stage, they became customer oriented and started to pay attention to customers. In the third stage, when they started to pay attention to competitors, they became competitor oriented. Today, companies need to be market oriented, paying balanced attention to both customers and competitors. Rather than simply watching competitors and trying to beat them on current ways of doing business, they need to watch customers and find innovative ways to build profitable customer relationships by delivering more customer value than competitors do. As noted previously, marketing begins with a good understanding of consumers and the marketplace.

FIGURE | 18.4

Evolving Company Orientations

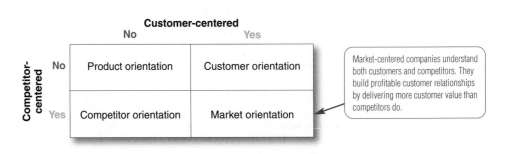

	Customer-centered	
	No	**Yes**
Competitor-centered **No**	Product orientation	Customer orientation
Competitor-centered **Yes**	Competitor orientation	Market orientation

Market-centered companies understand both customers and competitors. They build profitable customer relationships by delivering more customer value than competitors do.

REVIEWING Objectives AND KEY Terms

Today's companies face their toughest competition ever. Understanding customers is an important first step in developing strong customer relationships, but it's not enough. To gain competitive advantage, companies must use this understanding to design market offers that deliver more value than the offers of *competitors* seeking to win over the same customers. This chapter examines how firms analyze their competitors and design effective competitive marketing strategies.

OBJECTIVE 1 Discuss the need to understand competitors as well as customers through competitor analysis. (pp 528-534)

In order to prepare an effective marketing strategy, a company must consider its competitors as well as its customers. Building profitable customer relationships requires satisfying target consumer needs *better than competitors do*. A company must continuously analyze competitors and develop *competitive marketing strategies* that position it effectively against competitors and give it the strongest possible *competitive advantage*.

Competitor analysis first involves identifying the company's major competitors, using both an industry-based and a market-based analysis. The company then gathers information on competitors' objectives, strategies, strengths and weaknesses, and reaction patterns. With this information in hand, it can select competitors to attack or avoid. Competitive intelligence must be collected, interpreted, and distributed continuously. Company marketing managers should be able to obtain full and reliable information about any competitor affecting their decisions.

OBJECTIVE 2 Explain the fundamentals of competitive marketing strategies based on creating value for customers. (pp 534-546)

Which *competitive marketing strategy* makes the most sense depends on the company's industry, and on whether it is a market leader, challenger, follower, or nicher. A *market leader* has to mount strategies to expand the total market, protect market share, and expand market share. A *market challenger* is a firm that tries aggressively to expand its market share by attacking the leader, other runner-up companies, or smaller firms in the industry. The challenger can select from a variety of direct or indirect attack strategies.

A *market follower* is a runner-up firm that chooses not to rock the boat, usually from fear that it stands to lose more than it might gain. But the follower is not without a strategy and seeks to use its particular skills to gain market growth. Some followers enjoy a higher rate of return than the leaders in their industry. A *market nicher* is a smaller firm that is unlikely to attract the attention of larger firms. Market nichers often become specialists in some end use, customer size, specific customer, geographic area, or service.

OBJECTIVE 3 Illustrate the need for balancing customer and competitor orientations in becoming a truly market-centered organization. (p 546)

A competitive orientation is important in today's markets, but companies should not overdo their focus on competitors. Companies are more likely to be hurt by emerging consumer needs and new competitors than by existing competitors. *Market-centered companies* that balance consumer and competitor considerations are practicing a true market orientation.

KEY Terms

OBJECTIVE 1

Competitive advantage (p 528)
Competitor analysis (p 528)
Competitive marketing strategies (p 528)
Strategic group (p 530)

Benchmarking (p 531)
Customer value analysis (p 531)

OBJECTIVE 2

Market leader (p 537)
Market challenger (p 537)

Market follower (p 537)
Market nicher (p 537)

OBJECTIVE 3

Competitor-centered company (p 546)
Customer-centered company (p 546)
Market-centered company (p 546)

DISCUSSING & APPLYING THE Concepts

Discussing the Concepts

1. Which point of view is best for identifying competitors—industry or market? (AASCB: Communication)

2. Explain how having strong competitors can benefit a company. (AACSB: Communication; Reflective Thinking)

3. What is the difference between entrepreneurial, intrepreneurial, and formulated marketing? What are the advantages and disadvantages of each? (AACSB: Communication)

4. Describe the three value disciplines for delivering superior customer value and explain why classifying competitive strategies in this way is appealing. (AACSB: Communication)

5. Discuss the strategies available to market leaders. (AACSB: Communication)

6. What are the advantages and disadvantages of a market-nicher competitive strategy? (AACSB: Communication)

Applying the Concepts

1. Form a small group and conduct a customer value analysis for five local restaurants. Who are the strong and weak competitors? For the strong competitors, what are their vulnerabilities? (AACSB: Communication; Reflective Thinking)

2. Research "blue ocean strategy" and discuss examples of companies that have succeeded in pursuing this strategy. Do companies succeeding in developing uncontested marketspaces necessarily have to be innovative upstarts? (AACSB: Communication; Reflective Thinking)

3. Identify a company following a market niche strategy in each of the following industries: automobiles, restaurants, airlines, and golf equipment. (AACSB: Communication; Reflective Thinking)

FOCUS ON Technology

Apple is the leader in MP3 players and wants to lead in the mobile smart phone segment, too. In 2008, only one in every 200 mobile phone users in the United States owned an iPhone, but the recent introduction of the iPhone 3G is likely to change that. Unlike other phone applications, Apple opened up its heralded App Store, where iPhone owners can find thousands of applications developed by third parties for their phones—everything from ring tones to games to accounting software and global positioning applications. Many of them are free because they display ads that produce revenues for developers. So far, Apple is not taking a cut of the ad revenues, and developers keep 70 percent of the money that they take in from paid for consumer applications. This is a higher percentage than developers get from other applications markets in the cell phone industry. As a result, iPhone applications can be priced cheaper than similar applications for rivals BlackBerry and Windows Mobile smart phones. And these competitors offer fewer applications on their Web sites than Apple does. Within a month of the iPhone 3G's release, more than 500 applications were available from Apple's App Store. An estimated 20 million applications will be downloaded by the end of 2008, followed by 110 million in 2009 and another 210 million in 2010.

1. What position does Apple hold in the smart phone industry? What competitive strategy is Apple using? (AACSB: Communication; Reflective Thinking)

2. Why is Apple virtually giving away this platform to third-party applications developers? Wouldn't it be more profitable for Apple to generate more revenue from its App Store? (AACSB: Communication; Reflective Thinking)

FOCUS ON Ethics

After more than a year following the announcement of a potential merger between Sirius Satellite Radio and XM Satellite Radio, the United States Department of Justice and the Federal Communication Commission have now approved it. Since the January 2007 announcement, critics have voiced many concerns regarding programming redundancy and equipment compatibility, but the major issue was the effect the merger will have on competition. Sirius and XM are the only two providers of satellite radio, so a merger would create a monopoly with more than 17 million subscribers. The controversy was fueled by fears of consumer price increases unabated by competitive pressures.

1. The U.S. Justice Department determined that the merger was not anticompetitive because forms of competition exist in the audio entertainment market. Discuss the competitors in this market. (AACSB: Communication; Reflective Thinking)

2. Will this merger harm or benefit consumers? (AACSB: Communication; Ethical Reasoning; Reflective Thinking)

MARKETING BY THE Numbers

Bottled water, consisting of still and sparkling unflavored and flavored waters, is a hot industry—sales grew by 8.8 percent between 2001 and 2006 and are expected to grow another 48.5 percent by 2011. The bottled water industry in the United States totaled 31.4 billion liters valued at $15.6 billion in 2006—that's an average of $0.50 in revenue per liter. Big players in this industry include Nestlé, PepsiCo, and Coca-Cola. Nestlé is the market leader, selling 9.58 billion liters, followed by PepsiCo's 4.33 billion liters and Coca-Cola's 3.74 billion liters.

1. Refer to Appendix 2, Marketing by the Numbers, and calculate 2006 market shares by volume for Nestlé, PepsiCo, and Coca-Cola in the bottled water market. (AACSB: Communication; Analytical Reasoning)

2. How much revenue did one market share point represent in 2006? How much will it represent in 2011? (AACSB: Communication; Reflective Thinking)

VIDEO Case

Umpqua Bank

The retail banking industry has become very competitive. And with a few powerhouses dominating the market, how is a small bank to thrive? By differentiating itself through a competitive advantage that the big guys can't touch.

That's exactly what Umpqua has done. Step inside a branch of this Oregon-based community bank and you'll see immediately that this is not your typical Christmas club savings account/free toaster bank. Umpqua's business model has transformed banking from retail drudgery into a holistic experience. Umpqua has created an environment in which people just love to hang out. It not only has its own music download service featuring local artists, it even has its own blend of coffee.

But beneath all these bells and whistles lies the core of what makes Umpqua so different—a rigorous service culture where every branch and employee gets measured on how well they serve customers. That's why every customer feels like they get the help and attention they need from employees.

After viewing the video featuring Umpqua Bank, answer the following questions about creating competitive advantage:

1. With what companies does Umpqua compete?

2. What is Umpqua's competitive advantage?

3. Will Umpqua be able to maintain this advantage in the long run? Why or why not?

COMPANY Case

Bose: Competing by Being Truly Different

Recently, Forrester Research announced the results of its semi-annual survey ranking consumer electronics and personal computer companies on consumer trust. Based on a poll of more than 4,700 customers as to their opinions of 22 of the best-known consumer technology brands, the company drew this conclusion: "Americans' trust in consumer technology companies is eroding."

Why is consumer trust important? Forrester vice president Ted Schadler answers that question this way: "Trust is a powerful way to measure a brand's value and its ability to command a premium price or drive consumers into a higher-profit direct channel. A decline in trust causes brand erosion and price-driven purchase decisions, which in turn correlates with low market growth."

But despite the decline in trust for most technology companies, Forrester made another surprising finding. Consumer trust in the Bose Corporation is riding high. In fact, Bose far outscored all other companies in Forrester's survey. That's not bad, considering that it was the first time the company had been included in the survey. Forrester points out that these results are no fluke, noting that Bose has 10 million regular users but more than 17 million consumers who aspire to use the brand (compared to 7 million for next highest, Apple).

These high levels of consumer trust result from philosophies that have guided Bose for nearly 50 years. Most companies today focus heavily on building revenue, profits, and stock price. They try to outdo the competition by differentiating product lines with features and attributes that other companies do not have. While Bose doesn't exactly ignore such factors, its true competitive advantage is rooted in the company's unique corporate philosophy. Bose president Bob Maresca provides insights on that philosophy: "We are not in it strictly to make money," he says. Pointing to the company's focus on research and product innovation, he continues, "The business is almost a secondary consideration."

THE BOSE PHILOSOPHY

You can't understand Bose the company without taking a look at Bose the man. Amar Bose, the company's founder and still its CEO, has been in charge from the start. In the 1950s, Mr. Bose was working on his third degree at the Massachusetts Institute of Technology. He had a keen interest in research and studied various areas of electrical engineering. He also had a strong interest in music. When he purchased his first hi-fi system—a model that he believed had the best specifications—he was very disappointed in the system's ability to reproduce realistic sound. So he set out to find his own solution. Thus began a stream of research that would ultimately lead to the founding of the Bose Corporation in 1964.

From those early days, Amar Bose worked around certain core principles that have guided the philosophy of the company. In conducting his first research on speakers and sound, he did something that has since been repeated time and time again at Bose. He ignored existing technologies and started entirely from scratch, something not very common in product development strategies.

In another departure from typical corporate strategies, Amar Bose plows all of the privately held company's profits back into research. This practice reflects his avid love of research and his belief that it will produce the highest quality products. But he also does this because he can. Bose has been quoted many times saying, "if I worked for another company, I would have been fired a long time ago," pointing to the fact that publicly held companies have long lists of constraints that don't apply to his privately held company. For this reason, Bose has always vowed that he will never take the company public. "Going public for me would have been the equivalent of losing the company. My real interest is research—that's the excitement—and I wouldn't have been able to do long-term projects with Wall Street breathing down my neck."

This commitment to research and development has led to the high level of trust that Bose customers have for the company. It also explains their almost cult-like loyalty. Customers know that the company cares more about their best interests—about making the best product—than about maximizing profits. But for a company not driven by the bottom line, Bose does just fine. According to market information firm NPD Group, Bose leads the market in home speakers with a 12.6 percent share. And that market share translates into financial performance. Although figures are tightly held by the private corporation, the most recent known estimate of company revenue was $1.8 billion for 2006. While that number doesn't come close to the $88 billion that Sony reported last year, it does represent a 38 percent gain in just two years.

GROUNDBREAKING PRODUCTS

The company that started so humbly now has a breadth of product lines beyond its core home audio line. Additional lines target a variety of applications that have captured Amar Bose's creative attention over the years, including military, automotive, homebuilding/remodeling, aviation, and professional and commercial sound systems. It even has a division that markets testing equipment to research institutions, universities, medical device companies, and engineering companies worldwide. The following are just a few of the products that illustrate the innovative breakthroughs produced by the company.

Speakers. Bose's first product, introduced in 1965, was a speaker. Expecting to sell $1 million worth of speakers that first year, Bose made 60 but sold only 40. The original Bose speaker evolved into the 901 Direct/Reflecting speaker system launched in 1968. The speaker was so technologically advanced that the company still sells it today.

The system was designed around the concept that live sound reaches the human ear via direct as well as reflected channels (off walls, ceilings, and other objects). The configuration of the speakers was completely unorthodox. They were shaped like an eighth of a sphere and mounted facing into a room's corner. The speakers had no woofers or tweeters and were very small compared to the high-end speakers of the day. The design came much closer to the essence and emotional impact of live music than anything else on the market and won immediate industry acclaim.

However, Bose had a hard time convincing customers of the merits of these innovative speakers. At a time when woofers, tweeters, and size were everything, the 901 series initially flopped. In 1968, a retail salesman explained to Amar Bose why the speakers weren't selling:

Look, I love your speaker but I cannot sell it because it makes me lose all my credibility as a salesman. I can't explain to anyone why the 901 doesn't have any woofers or tweeters. A man came in and saw the small size, and he started looking in the drawers for the speaker cabinets. I walked over to him, and he said, "Where are you hiding the woofer?" I said to him, "There is no woofer." So he said, "You're a liar," and he walked out.

Bose eventually worked through the challenges of communicating the virtues of the 901 series to customers through innovative display and demonstration tactics. The product became so successful that Amar Bose now credits the 901 series for building the company.

The list of major speaker innovations at Bose is a long one. In 1975, the company introduced concert-like sound in the bookshelf-size 301 Direct/Reflecting speaker system. Fourteen years of research lead to the 1984 development of acoustic waveguide speaker technology, a technology today found in the award-winning Wave radio, Wave music system, and Acoustic Wave music system. In 1986, the company again changed conventional thinking about the relationship between speaker size

and sound. The Acoustimass system enabled palm-size speakers to produce audio quality equivalent to that of high-end systems many times their size. And most recently, Bose has again introduced the state-of-the-art with the MusicMonitor, a pair of compact computer speakers that rival the sound of three-piece subwoofer systems. It may sound simple, but at $399, it's anything but.

Headphones. Bob Maresca recalls that, "Bose invested tens of million of dollars over 19 years developing headset technology before making a profit. Now, headsets are a major part of the business." Initially, Bose focused on noise reduction technologies to make headphones for pilots that would block out the high level of noise interference from planes. Bose headphones didn't just muffle noise, they electronically cancelled ambient noise so that pilots wearing them heard nothing but the sound coming through the phones. Bose quickly discovered that airline passengers could benefit as much as pilots from its headphone technology. Today, the Bose QuietComfort series, used in a variety of consumer applications, is the benchmark in noise canceling headphones. One journalist considers this product to be so significant that it made his list of "101 gadgets that changed the world" (some of the other inventions on the list included aspirin, paper, and the light bulb).

Automotive suspensions. Another major innovation from Bose has yet to be introduced. The company has been conducting research since 1980 on a product outside of its known areas of expertise: automotive suspensions. Amar Bose's interest in suspensions dates back to the 1950s when he bought both a Citroën DS-19 C and a Pontiac Bonneville, each riding on unconventional air suspension systems. Since that time, he has been obsessed with the engineering challenge of achieving good cornering capabilities without sacrificing a smooth ride. "In cars today, there's always a compromise between softness over bumps and roll and pitch during maneuvering," Bose said in a recent interview. The Bose Corporation is now on the verge of introducing a suspension that it believes eliminates that compromise.

The basics of the system include an electromagnetic motor installed at each wheel. Based on inputs from road sensing monitors, the motor can retract and extend almost instantaneously. If there is a bump in the road, the suspension reacts by "jumping" over it. If there is a pothole, the suspension allows the wheel to extend downward, but then retracts it quickly enough that the pothole is not felt. In addition to these comfort producing capabilities, the wheel motors are strong enough to keep a car completely level during an aggressive maneuver such as cornering or stopping. In a recent interview about this system, Dr. Bose said, "This system provides absolutely better handling than any sports car, and the most comfortable ride imaginable."

Thus far, Bose has invested more than $100 million and 27 years in its groundbreaking suspension. And while it is ready to take the product to market, it is staying true to its philosophy by not rushing things. Bose plans first to partner with one automotive manufacturer in the near future. The cost of the system will put it in the class of higher-end luxury automobiles. But eventually, Bose anticipates that wider adoption and higher volume will bring the price down to the point where the suspension could be found in all but the least expensive cars.

At an age when most people have long since retired, 78-year-old Amar Bose still works every day, either at the company's headquarters in Framingham, Massachusetts, or at his home in nearby Wayland. "He's got more energy than an 18-year-old," says Maresca. "Every one of the naysayers only strengthens his resolve." This work ethic illustrates the passion of the man who has shaped one of today's most innovative and yet most trusted companies. His philosophies have produced Bose's long list of groundbreaking innovations. Even now, as the company prepares to enter the world of automotive suspensions, it continues to achieve success by following another one of Dr. Bose's basic philosophies: "The potential size of the market? We really have no idea. We just know that we have a technology that's so different and so much better that many people will want it."

Questions for Discussion

1. Based on the business philosophies of Amar Bose, how do you think the Bose Corporation goes about analyzing its competition?

2. Which of the text's three approaches to marketing strategy best describes Bose's approach?

3. Using the Michael Porter and Treacy and Wiersema frameworks presented in the text, which basic competitive marketing strategies does Bose pursue?

4. What is Bose's competitive position in its industry? Do its marketing strategies match this position?

5. In your opinion, is Bose a customer-centric company?

6. What will happen when Amar Bose leaves the company?

Sources: Jeffrey Krasner, "Shocks and Awe," *Boston Globe*, December 3, 2007, p. E1; Simon Usborne, "101 Gadgets That Changed the World," *Belfast Telegraph*, November 5, 2007, accessed online at www.belfasttelegraph.co.uk; Brian Dumaine, "Amar Bose," *Fortune Small Business*, September 1, 2004, accessed online at www.money.cnn.com/magazines/fsb/; Olga Kharif, "Selling Sound: Bose Knows," *BusinessWeek Online*, May 15, 2006, accessed online at www.businessweek.com; Mark Jewell, "Bose Tries to Shake Up Auto Industry," *Associated Press*, November 27, 2005; "Bose Introduces New QuietComfort 3 Acoustic Noise Cancelling Headphones," *Business Wire*, June 8, 2006; "Forrester Research Reveals The Most Trusted Consumer Technology Brands," press release accessed online at www.forrester.com; also see, "About Bose," accessed online at www.bose.com, June 2008.

Chapter 19

Part 1   Defining Marketing and the Marketing Process (Chapters 1, 2)
Part 2   Understanding the Marketplace and Consumers (Chapters 3, 4, 5, 6)
Part 3   Designing a Customer-Driven Strategy and Mix (Chapters 7, 8, 9, 10, 11, 12, 13, 14, 15, 16, 17)
Part 4   Extending Marketing (Chapters 18, 19, 20)

The Global Marketplace

Chapter PREVIEW

You've now learned the fundamentals of how companies develop competitive marketing strategies to create customer value and build lasting customer relationships. In this chapter, we extend these fundamentals to global marketing. We've visited global topics in each previous chapter—it's difficult to find an area of marketing that doesn't contain at least some international issues. Here, however, we'll focus on special considerations that companies face when they market their brands globally. Advances in communication, transportation, and other technologies have made the world a much smaller place. Today, almost every firm, large or small, faces international marketing issues. In this chapter, we will examine six major decisions marketers make in going global.

To start things off, let's look at good old McDonald's. Despite its homegrown American roots, McDonald's is a truly global enterprise. Over the years, the company has learned many important lessons about adapting locally in global markets. Here, we'll examine McDonald's odyssey into Russia, now one of the crown jewels in its global empire.

Most Americans think of McDonald's as their very own. The first McDonald's stand popped up in California in 1954, and what could be more American than burger-and-fries fast food? But as it turns out, the quintessentially all-American company now sells more burgers and fries outside the country than within. Nearly 65 percent of McDonald's $22.8 billion of sales last year came from outside the United States, and its international sales grew at close to twice the rate of domestic sales growth.

McDonald's today is a truly global enterprise. Its 30,000 restaurants serve more than 52 million people in more than 100 countries each day. Few firms have more international marketing experience than McDonald's. But going global hasn't always been easy, and McDonald's has learned many important lessons in its journeys overseas. To see how far McDonald's has come, consider its experiences in Russia, a market that's very different culturally, economically, and politically from our own.

McDonald's first set its sights on Russia (then a part of the Soviet Union) in 1976, when George Cohon, head of McDonald's in Canada, took a group of Soviet Olympics officials to a McDonald's while they visited for the Montreal Olympic Games. Cohon was struck by how much the Soviets liked McDonald's hamburgers, fries, and other fare. Over the next 14 years, Cohon flew to Russia more than 100 times, first to get Soviet permission for McDonald's to provide food for the 1980 Moscow Olympics, and later to be allowed to open McDonald's restaurants in the country. He quickly learned that no one in Russia had any idea what a McDonald's was. The Soviets turned Cohon down flat on both requests.

Finally in 1988, as Premier Mikhail Gorbachev began to open the Russian economy, Cohon forged a deal with the city of Moscow to launch the first Russian McDonald's in Moscow's Pushkin Square. But obtaining permission was only the first step. Actually opening the restaurant brought a fresh set of challenges. Thanks to Russia's large and bureaucratic government structure, McDonald's had to obtain some 200 separate signatures just to open the single location. It had difficulty finding reliable suppliers for even such basics as hamburgers and buns. So McDonald's forked over $45 million to build a facility to produce these things itself. It even brought in technical experts from Canada with special strains of disease-resistant seed to teach Russian farmers how to grow Russet Burbank potatoes for

> The Pushkin Square McDonald's is huge—26 cash registers and 900 seats.

french fries, and it built its own pasteurizing plant to ensure a plentiful supply of fresh milk.

When the Moscow McDonald's at Pushkin Square finally opened its doors in January 1990, it quickly won the hearts of Russian consumers. However, the company faced still more hurdles. The Pushkin Square restaurant is huge—26 cash registers (more than you'll find in a typical Wal-Mart supercenter) and 900 seats (compared with 40–50 seats in a typical U.S. McDonald's). The logistics of serving customers on such a scale was daunting, made even more difficult by the fact that few employees or customers understood the fast-food concept.

Although American consumers were well acquainted with McDonald's, the Russian's were clueless. So, in order to meet its high standards for customer satisfaction in this new market, the U.S. fast feeder had to educate employees about the time-tested McDonald's way of doing things. It trained Russian managers at Hamburger University and subjected each of 630 new employees (most of whom didn't know a chicken McNugget from an Egg McMuffin) to 16 to 20 hours of training on such essentials as cooking meat patties, assembling Fillet-O-Fish sandwiches, and giving service with a smile. Back in those days, McDonald's even had to train consumers—most Muscovites had never seen a fast-food restaurant. Customers waiting in line were shown videos telling them everything from how to order and pay at the counter, to how to put their coats over the backs of their seats, to how to handle a Big Mac.

However, the new Moscow McDonald's got off to a spectacular start. An incredible 50,000 customers swarmed the restaurant during its first day of business. And in its usual way, McDonald's began immediately to build community involvement. On opening day, it held a kickoff party for 700 Muscovite orphans and then donated all opening-day proceeds to the Moscow children's fund.

Today, less than 20 years after opening its first restaurant there, McDonald's is thriving in Russia. The Pushkin Square location is now the busiest McDonald's in the world, and Russia is the crown jewel in McDonald's global empire. The company's 180 restaurants in 40 Russian cities each serve an average of 850,000 diners a year—twice the per-store traffic of any of the other 117 countries in which McDonald's operates.

Despite the long lines of customers, McDonald's has been careful about how rapidly it expands in Russia. In recent years, it has reined in its rapid growth strategy and focused instead on improving profitability and product and service quality. The goal is to squeeze more business out of existing restaurants and to grow slowly but profitably. One way to do that is to add new menu items to draw in consumers at different times of the day. So, as it did many years ago in the United States, McDonald's in Russia is now adding breakfast items.

Although only about 5 percent of Russians eat breakfast outside the home, more commuters in the big cities are leaving home earlier to avoid heavy traffic. The company hopes that the new breakfast menu will encourage commuters to stop off at McDonald's on their way to work. However, when the fast-food chain added breakfast items, it stopped offering its traditional hamburger fare during the morning hours. When many customers complained of "hamburger withdrawal," McDonald's introduced the Fresh McMuffin, an English muffin with a sausage patty topped with cheese, lettuce, tomato, and special sauce. The new sandwich became an instant hit.

To reduce the lines inside restaurants and to attract motorists, McDonald's is also introducing Russian consumers to drive-thru windows. At first, many Russians just didn't get the concept. Instead, they treated the drive-thru window as just another line, purchasing their food there, parking, and going inside to eat. Also, Russian cars often don't have cupholders, so drive-thru customers bought fewer drinks. However, as more customers get used to the concept, McDonald's is putting drive-thru and walk-up windows in about half of its new stores.

So, that's a look at McDonald's in Russia. But just as McDonald's has tweaked its formula in Russia, it also adjusts its marketing and operations to meet the special needs of local consumers in other major global markets. To be sure, McDonald's is a global brand. Its restaurants around the world employ a common global strategy—convenient food at affordable prices. And no matter where you go in the world—from Moscow to Montréal or Shanghai to Cheboygan, Michigan—you'll find those good old golden arches and a menu full of Quarter Pounders, Big Macs, fries, milkshakes, and other familiar items. But within that general strategic framework, McDonald's adapts to the subtleties of each local market. Says a McDonald's Europe executive, "Across Europe with 40 different markets, there are 40 sets of tastes. There are also differences within each market. We are a local market but a global brand."[1]

Moscow's Pushkin Square location is the busiest McDonald's in the world, and Russia is the crown jewel in McDonald's global empire.

McDonald's is a truly global enterprise. The quintessentially all-American company now sells more burgers and fries outside the United States than within.

Objective Outline

In the past, U.S. companies paid little attention to international trade. If they could pick up some extra sales through exporting, that was fine. But the big market was at home, and it teemed with opportunities. The home market was also much safer. Managers did not need to learn other languages, deal with strange and changing currencies, face political and legal uncertainties, or adapt their products to different customer needs and expectations. Today, however, the situation is much different. Organizations of all kinds, from Coca-Cola, IBM, and Google to MTV and even the NBA, have gone global.

| **Author Comment** | The rapidly changing global environment provides both opportunities and threats. It's difficult to find a marketer today that isn't affected in some way by global developments. |

Global Marketing Today (pp 554–555)

The world is shrinking rapidly with the advent of faster communication, transportation, and financial flows. Products developed in one country—Gucci purses, Sony electronics, McDonald's hamburgers, Japanese sushi, German BMWs—have found enthusiastic acceptance in other countries. We would not be surprised to hear about a German businessman wearing an Italian suit meeting an English friend at a Japanese restaurant who later returns home to drink Russian vodka and watch *American Idol* on TV.

International trade is booming. Since 1990, the number of multinational corporations in the world has grown from 30,000 to more than 60,000. Some of these multinationals are true giants. In fact, of the largest 150 "economies" in the world, only 76 are countries. The remaining 74 are multinational corporations. Wal-Mart, the world's largest company, has annual revenues greater than the gross domestic product of all but the world's 24 largest-GDP countries.[2]

Since 2003, total world trade has been growing at 4.5 to 11 percent annually, whereas global gross domestic product has grown at only 2.5 to 5 percent annually. World trade of products and services was valued at over $16.9 trillion last year, which accounted for about 25 percent of GDP worldwide.[3]

▲Many U.S. companies have long been successful at international marketing: Coca-Cola, GE, IBM, Colgate, Caterpillar, Ford, Boeing, McDonald's, and dozens of other

▲ Many American companies have made the world their market.

Global firm

A firm that, by operating in more than one country, gains R&D, production, marketing, and financial advantages in its costs and reputation that are not available to purely domestic competitors.

American firms have made the world their market. And in the United States, names such as Sony, Toyota, BP, IKEA, Nestlé, Nokia, and Prudential have become household words. Other products and services that appear to be American are in fact produced or owned by foreign companies: Bantam books, Baskin-Robbins ice cream, GE and RCA televisions, Carnation milk, Universal Studios, and Motel 6, to name just a few. Michelin, the oh-so-French tire manufacturer, now does 32 percent of its business in North America; Johnson & Johnson, the maker of quintessentially all-American products such as BAND-AIDs and Johnson's Baby Shampoo, does 45 percent of its business abroad. And America's own Caterpillar belongs more to the wider world, with 63 percent of its sales coming from outside the United States.[4]

But while global trade is growing, global competition is intensifying. Foreign firms are expanding aggressively into new international markets, and home markets are no longer as rich in opportunity. Few industries are now safe from foreign competition. If companies delay taking steps toward internationalizing, they risk being shut out of growing markets in western and eastern Europe, China and the Pacific Rim, Russia, and elsewhere. Firms that stay at home to play it safe might not only lose their chances to enter other markets but also risk losing their home markets. Domestic companies that never thought about foreign competitors suddenly find these competitors in their own backyards.

Ironically, although the need for companies to go abroad is greater today than in the past, so are the risks. Companies that go global may face highly unstable governments and currencies, restrictive government policies and regulations, and high trade barriers. Corruption is also an increasing problem—officials in several countries often award business not to the best bidder but to the highest briber.

A **global firm** is one that, by operating in more than one country, gains marketing, production, R&D, and financial advantages that are not available to purely domestic competitors. The global company sees the world as one market. It minimizes the importance of national boundaries and develops "transnational" brands. It raises capital, obtains materials and components, and manufactures and markets its goods wherever it can do the best job. For example, Otis Elevator, the world's largest elevator maker, achieves four-fifths of its sales from outside the United States. It gets its elevators' door systems from France, small geared parts from Spain, electronics from Germany, and special motor drives from Japan. It uses the United States only for systems integration. "Borders are so 20th century," says one global marketing expert. "Transnationals take 'stateless' to the next level."[5]

This does not mean that small and medium-size firms must operate in a dozen countries to succeed. These firms can practice global niching. But the world is becoming smaller, and every company operating in a global industry—whether large or small—must assess and establish its place in world markets.

The rapid move toward globalization means that all companies will have to answer some basic questions: What market position should we try to establish in our country, in our economic region, and globally? Who will our global competitors be and what are their strategies and resources? Where should we produce or source our products? What strategic alliances should we form with other firms around the world?

As shown in ▶ **Figure 19.1**, a company faces six major decisions in international marketing. We will discuss each decision in detail in this chapter.

Author Comment | As if operating within a company's own borders wasn't difficult enough, going global adds many layers of complexities. For example, Coca-Cola markets its products in hundreds of countries around the globe. It must understand the varying trade, economic, cultural, and political environments in each market.

Looking at the Global Marketing Environment (pp 556–563)

Before deciding whether to operate internationally, a company must understand the international marketing environment. That environment has changed a great deal in the past two decades, creating both new opportunities and new problems.

The International Trade System

U.S. companies looking abroad must start by understanding the international *trade system*. When selling to another country, a firm may face restrictions on trade between nations. Foreign governments may charge *tariffs*, taxes on certain imported products designed to raise revenue or to protect domestic firms. For example, China slaps a 25 percent tariff on U.S. and other imported autos. Or they may set *quotas*, limits on the amount of foreign imports that they will accept in certain product categories. The purpose of a quota is to conserve on foreign exchange and to protect local industry and employment. American firms may also face *exchange controls*, which limit the amount of foreign exchange and the exchange rate against other currencies.

The company also may face *nontariff trade barriers*, such as biases against U.S. company bids, restrictive product standards, or excessive regulations. ▲For example, U.S. foreign policy makers have criticized China for protectionist regulations and other actions that restrict access to several Chinese markets, including banking services.

For years U.S. financial houses have dreamed of the day when they'll be allowed to offer banking services to individual Chinese savers. But critics complain that, despite China's promises to the World Trade Organization, Western banks are effectively fenced out by investment caps and regulations that make going solo frightfully expensive. In theory, foreign banks can open branches from Hainan to Harbin. But in reality, they can open only one branch a year, and each branch must have operating capital of $50 million, a burden local banks don't face. Committing $500 million to open 10 branches in a decade doesn't make a lot of sense, so foreign banks instead have bought stakes in local banks. But Beijing limits total foreign ownership in any Chinese bank to just 25 percent, leaving the foreign investors little say in strategy. Last year, for instance, Bank of America spent $3 billion for 9 percent of China Construction Bank Corp. But the Americans have only one seat on the board and had to abandon their own mainland retail effort as part of the deal. Beijing denies any effort to block access to its market. True, foreigners control just 2 percent of assets in the banking system, notes a Chinese trade expert. "The problem is, the U.S. banking sector is not patient."[6]

▲ Trade barriers: U.S. and other Western banks have been effectively fenced out of China's huge retail banking market by protectionist regulations.

At the same time, certain forces *help* trade between nations. Examples include the General Agreement on Tariffs and Trade (GATT) and various regional free trade agreements.

It's a big and beautiful but threatening world out there for marketers! Most large American firms have made the world their market. For example, once all-American McDonald's now captures 65 percent of its sales from outside the United States.

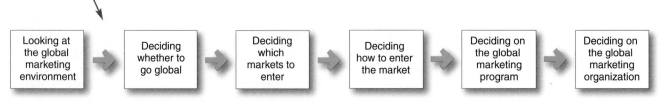

| Looking at the global marketing environment | → | Deciding whether to go global | → | Deciding which markets to enter | → | Deciding how to enter the market | → | Deciding on the global marketing program | → | Deciding on the global marketing organization |

◥**FIGURE** | **19.1** Major International Marketing Decisions

▲ The WTO and GATT: The General Agreement on Tariffs and Trade (GATT) promotes world trade by reducing tariffs and other international trade barriers. The WTO oversees GATT, imposes trade sanctions, and mediates global disputes.

The World Trade Organization and GATT

The General Agreement on Tariffs and Trade (GATT) is a 61-year-old treaty designed to promote world trade by reducing tariffs and other international trade barriers. ▲Since the treaty's inception in 1947, member nations (currently numbering 152) have met in eight rounds of GATT negotiations to reassess trade barriers and set new rules for international trade. The first seven rounds of negotiations reduced the average worldwide tariffs on manufactured goods from 45 percent to just 5 percent.[7]

The most recently completed GATT negotiations, dubbed the Uruguay Round, dragged on for seven long years before concluding in 1994. The benefits of the Uruguay Round will be felt for many years as the accord promotes long-term global trade growth. It reduced the world's remaining merchandise tariffs by 30 percent. The agreement also extended GATT to cover trade in agriculture and a wide range of services, and it toughened international protection of copyrights, patents, trademarks, and other intellectual property. Although the financial impact of such an agreement is difficult to measure, research suggests that cutting agriculture, manufacturing, and services trade barriers by one-third would boost the world economy by $613 billion, the equivalent of adding another Turkey to the world economy.[8]

Beyond reducing trade barriers and setting global standards for trade, the Uruguay Round set up the World Trade Organization (WTO) to enforce GATT rules. In general, the WTO acts as an umbrella organization, overseeing GATT, mediating global disputes, and imposing trade sanctions. The previous GATT organization never possessed such authorities. A new round of GATT negotiations, the Doha round, began in Doha, Qatar, in late 2001 and was set to conclude in 2005, but the discussions continue.[9]

Regional Free Trade Zones

Economic community
A group of nations organized to work toward common goals in the regulation of international trade.

Certain countries have formed *free trade zones* or **economic communities**. These are groups of nations organized to work toward common goals in the regulation of international trade. ▲One such community is the *European Union (EU)*. Formed in 1957, the EU set out to create a single European market by reducing barriers to the free flow of products, services, finances, and labor among member countries and developing policies on trade with nonmember nations. Today, the EU represents one of the world's single largest markets. Currently, it has 27 member countries containing close to half a billion consumers and accounts for more than 20 percent of the world's exports.[10]

European unification offers tremendous trade opportunities for U.S. and other non-European firms. However, it also poses threats. As a result of increased unification, European companies have grown bigger and more competitive. Perhaps an even greater concern, however, is that lower barriers *inside* Europe will create only thicker *outside* walls. Some observers envision a "Fortress Europe" that heaps favors on firms from EU countries but hinders outsiders by imposing obstacles.

Progress toward European unification has been slow—many doubt that complete unification will ever be achieved. In recent years, 13 member nations have taken a significant step toward unification by adopting the euro as a common currency. Many other countries are expected to follow within the next few years. Widespread adoption of the euro will decrease much of the currency risk associated with doing business in Europe, making member countries with previously weak currencies more attractive markets.[11]

However, even with the adoption of the euro, it is unlikely that the EU will ever go against 2,000 years of tradition and become the "United States of Europe." A community with two dozen different languages and cultures will always have difficulty coming together and acting as a single entity. For example, efforts to forge a single European constitution appear to have failed following French and Dutch "no" votes in mid-2005. And economic disputes between member nations have stalled long-term budget negotiations. Still,

▲ Economic communities: The European Union represents one of the world's single largest markets. Its current member countries contain more than half a billion consumers and account for 20 percent of the world's exports.

although only partly successful so far, unification has made Europe a global force with which to reckon, with a combined annual GDP of more than $14.5 trillion.[12]

In 1994, the *North American Free Trade Agreement (NAFTA)* established a free trade zone among the United States, Mexico, and Canada. The agreement created a single market of 447 million people who produce and consume over $16 trillion worth of goods and services annually. As it is implemented over a 15-year period, NAFTA will eliminate all trade barriers and investment restrictions among the three countries. Thus far, the agreement has allowed trade between the countries to flourish. In the dozen years following its establishment, trade among the NAFTA nations has risen 198 percent. U.S. merchandise exports to NAFTA partners grew 157 percent, compared with exports to the rest of the world at 108 percent. Canada and Mexico are now the nation's first and second-largest trading partners.[13]

Following the apparent success of NAFTA, in 2005 the Central American Free Trade Agreement (CAFTA) established a free trade zone between the United States and Costa Rica, the Dominican Republic, El Salvador, Guatemala, Honduras, and Nicaragua. And talks have been underway since 1994 to investigate establishing a Free Trade Area of the Americas (FTAA). This mammoth free trade zone would include 34 countries stretching from the Bering Strait to Cape Horn, with a population of more than 800 million and a combined GDP of about $18.5 trillion.[14]

Other free trade areas have formed in Latin America and South America. For example, Mercosur links 11 Latin America and South America countries, and the Andean Community (CAN, for its Spanish initials) links 4 more. In late 2004, Mercosur and CAN agreed to unite, creating the Union of South American Nations (Unasur), which is modeled after the EU. Complete integration between the two trade blocs was expected by mid-2008 and all tariffs between the nations are to be eliminated by 2019. With a population of more than 361 million, a combined economy of more than $2.65 trillion a year, and exports worth $181 billion, Unasur will make up the largest trading bloc after NAFTA and the EU.[15]

Each nation has unique features that must be understood. A nation's readiness for different products and services and its attractiveness as a market to foreign firms depend on its economic, political-legal, and cultural environments.

Economic Environment

The international marketer must study each country's economy. Two economic factors reflect the country's attractiveness as a market: the country's industrial structure and its income distribution.

The country's *industrial structure* shapes its product and service needs, income levels, and employment levels. The four types of industrial structures are as follows:

- *Subsistence economies:* In a subsistence economy, the vast majority of people engage in simple agriculture. They consume most of their output and barter the rest for simple goods and services. They offer few market opportunities.

- *Raw material exporting economies:* These economies are rich in one or more natural resources but poor in other ways. Much of their revenue comes from exporting these resources. Examples are Chile (tin and copper), the Democratic Republic of the Congo (copper, cobalt, and coffee), and Saudi Arabia (oil). These countries are good markets for large equipment, tools and supplies, and trucks. If there are many foreign residents and a wealthy upper class, they are also a market for luxury goods.

- *Industrializing economies:* In an industrializing economy, manufacturing accounts for 10 to 20 percent of the country's economy. Examples include Egypt, India, and Brazil. As manufacturing increases, the country needs more imports of raw textile materials, steel, and heavy machinery, and fewer imports of finished textiles, paper products, and automobiles. Industrialization typically creates a new rich class and a small but growing middle class, both demanding new types of imported goods.

- *Industrial economies:* Industrial economies are major exporters of manufactured goods, services, and investment funds. They trade goods among themselves and also export them to other types of economies for raw materials and semifinished goods. The varied manufacturing activities of these industrial nations and their large middle class make them rich markets for all sorts of goods.

The second economic factor is the country's *income distribution*. Industrialized nations may have low-, medium-, and high-income households. In contrast, countries with subsistence economies may consist mostly of households with very low family incomes. Still other countries may have households with only either very low or very high incomes. However, even poor or developing economies may be attractive markets for all kinds of goods, including luxuries. ▲For example, many luxury-brand marketers are rushing to take advantage of China's rapidly developing consumer markets:[16]

More than half of China's 1.3 billion consumers can barely afford rice, let alone luxuries. According to the World Bank, more than 400 million Chinese live on less than $2 a day. Yet posh brands—from Gucci and Cartier to Lexus and Bentley—are descending on China in force. How can purveyors of $2,000 handbags, $20,000 watches, and $1 million limousines thrive in a developing economy? Easy, says a Cartier executive. "Remember, even medium-sized cities in China . . . have populations larger than Switzerland's. So it doesn't matter if the percentage of people in those cities who can afford our products is very small." Thus, even though China has only 0.2 millionaires per 1,000 residents (compared with 8.4 per 1,000 in the United States), it trails only the United States, Germany, and the United Kingdom in the total number of millionaires. In 2005, China's luxury-goods consumption accounted for 12 percent of the world's total, slightly under half of that of America's and Japan's. By 2014, however, the figure is expected to jump to 23 percent, making China the world's largest consumer of luxury goods. Dazzled by the pace at which China's booming economy is minting millionaires and swelling the ranks of the middle class, luxury brands are rushing to stake out shop space and tout their wares. "The Chinese are a natural audience for luxury goods," notes one analyst. After decades of socialism and poverty, China's elite are suddenly "keen to show off their newfound wealth."

▲ Economic environment: Many luxury brand marketers are rushing to take advantage of China's rapidly developing consumer markets.

Thus, country and regional economic environments will affect an international marketer's decisions about which global markets to enter and how.

Political-Legal Environment

Nations differ greatly in their political-legal environments. In considering whether to do business in a given country, a company should consider factors such as the country's attitudes toward international buying, government bureaucracy, political stability, and monetary regulations.

Some nations are very receptive to foreign firms; others are less accommodating. For example, India has tended to bother foreign businesses with import quotas, currency restrictions, and other limitations that make operating there a challenge. In contrast, neighboring Asian countries such as Singapore and Thailand court foreign investors and shower them with incentives and favorable operating conditions. Political and regulatory stability is another issue. For example, Venezuela's government is notoriously volatile—due to economic factors such as inflation and steep public spending—increasing the risk of doing business there. Although most international marketers still find the Venezuela market attractive, the unstable political and regulatory situation will affect how they handle business and financial matters.[17]

Companies must also consider a country's monetary regulations. Sellers want to take their profits in a currency of value to them. Ideally, the buyer can pay in the seller's currency or in other world currencies. Short of this, sellers might accept a blocked currency— one whose removal from the country is restricted by the buyer's government—if they can buy other goods in that country that they need themselves or can sell elsewhere for a needed currency. In addition to currency limits, a changing exchange rate also creates high risks for the seller.

Most international trade involves cash transactions. Yet many nations have too little hard currency to pay for their purchases from other countries. They may want to pay with other items instead of cash, which has led to a growing practice called **countertrade**. Countertrade takes several forms: *Barter* involves the direct exchange of goods or services, as when Azerbaijan imported wheat from Romania in exchange for crude oil and Vietnam exchanged rice for Philippine fertilizer and coconuts. Another form is *compensation* (or *buyback*), whereby the seller sells a plant, equipment, or technology to another country and agrees to take payment in the resulting products. Thus, Japan's Fukusuke Corporation sold knitting machines and raw textile materials to Shanghai clothing manufacturer Chinatex in exchange for finished textiles produced on the machines. The most common form of countertrade is *counterpurchase*, in which the seller receives full payment in cash but agrees to spend some of the money in the other country. For example, Boeing sells aircraft to India and agrees to buy Indian coffee, rice, castor oil, and other goods and sell them elsewhere.[18]

Countertrade deals can be very complex. For example, a few years back, DaimlerChrysler agreed to sell 30 trucks to Romania in exchange for 150 Romanian jeeps, which it then sold Ecuador for bananas, which were in turn sold to a German supermarket chain for German currency. Through this roundabout process, DaimlerChrysler finally obtained payment in German money.

Cultural Environment

Each country has its own folkways, norms, and taboos. When designing global marketing strategies, companies must understand how culture affects consumer reactions in each of its world markets. In turn, they must also understand how their strategies affect local cultures.

The Impact of Culture on Marketing Strategy

The seller must understand the ways that consumers in different countries think about and use certain products before planning a marketing program. There are often surprises. For example, the average French man uses almost twice as many cosmetics and grooming aids as his wife. The Germans and the French eat more packaged, branded spaghetti than do Italians. Some 49 percent of Chinese eat on the way to work. Most American women let down their hair and take off makeup at bedtime, whereas 15 percent of Chinese women style their hair at bedtime and 11 percent put *on* makeup.[19]

Companies that ignore cultural norms and differences can make some very expensive and embarrassing mistakes. Here are examples:

Nike inadvertently offended Chinese officials when it ran an advertisement featuring LeBron James crushing a number of culturally revered Chinese figures in a kung-fu-themed TV spot. ▲The Chinese government found that the ad violated

Countertrade
International trade involving the direct or indirect exchange of goods for other goods instead of cash.

▲ Overlooking cultural differences can result in embarrassing mistakes. China imposed a nationwide ban on a "blasphemous" kung fu–themed TV spot featuring LeBron James crushing a number of culturally revered Chinese figures.

regulations to uphold national dignity and respect of the "motherland's culture" and yanked the multimillion-dollar campaign. With egg on its face, Nike released a formal apology. Distiller Brown-Forman made a similar mistake when it created a window display in an Athens, Greece, bar showing Hindu Goddess Durga sitting on a tiger holding bottles of its Southern Comfort brand in all eight of her hands. Infuriated Hindus worldwide sent mail and e-mail messages decrying the defamation of their goddess—consuming alcohol is a sin to Hindus. An embarrassed Brown-Forman quickly removed the display, stating "we didn't realize it was the image of a Hindu goddess. It was human error and a violation of our marketing code" (which prohibits the use of religious images in the promotion of the company's alcoholic beverages).[20]

Business norms and behavior also vary from country to country. For example, American executives like to get right down to business and engage in fast and tough face-to-face bargaining. However, Japanese and other Asian businesspeople often find this behavior offensive. They prefer to start with polite conversation, and they rarely say no in face-to-face conversations. As another example, South Americans like to sit or stand very close to each other when they talk business—in fact, almost nose-to-nose. The American business executive tends to keep backing away as the South American moves closer. Both may end up being offended. American business executives need to be briefed on these kinds of factors before conducting business in another country.[21]

By the same token, companies that understand cultural nuances can use them to their advantage when positioning products and preparing campaigns internationally. Consider LG Electronics, the $60 billion South Korean electronics, telecommunications, and appliance powerhouse. LG now operates in more than 39 countries and captures 86 percent of its sales from markets outside its home country. LG's global success rests on understanding and catering to the unique characteristics of each local market through in-country research, manufacturing, and marketing.[22]

If you've got kimchi in your fridge, it's hard to keep it a secret. Made from fermented cabbage seasoned with garlic and chili, kimchi is served with most meals in Korea. But when it's stored inside a normal refrigerator, its pungent odor taints nearby foods. That's why, two decades ago, LG introduced the kimchi refrigerator, featuring a dedicated compartment that isolates smelly kimchi from other foods. Kimchi refrigerators now have become a fixture in 65 percent of Korean homes, and LG is the country's top-selling manufacturer.

LG's mission is to make customers happy worldwide by creating products to change their lives, no matter where they live. In India, LG rolled out refrigerators with larger vegetable- and water-storage compartments, surge-resistant power supplies, and brightly colored finishes that reflect local preferences (red in the south, green in Kashmir). Some of LG's Indian microwaves have dark-colored interiors to hide masala stains. In Iran, LG offers a microwave oven with a preset button for reheating shish kebabs—a favorite dish. In the Middle East, the company unveiled a gold-plated 71-inch flat-screen television that sells for $80,000—a tribute to the region's famous affinity for gilded opulence. And in Russia, where many people entertain at home during the country's long winters, LG developed a karaoke phone that can be programmed with the top 100 Russian songs, whose lyrics scroll across the screen when they're played. The phone sold more than 220,000 handsets in the first year.

Thus, understanding cultural traditions, preferences, and behaviors can help companies not only to avoid embarrassing mistakes but also to take advantage of cross-cultural opportunities.

The Impact of Marketing Strategy on Cultures

Whereas marketers worry about the impact of culture on their global marketing strategies, others may worry about the impact of marketing strategies on global cultures. For example, social critics contend that large American multinationals such as McDonald's, Coca-Cola, Starbucks, Nike, Microsoft, Disney, and MTV aren't just "globalizing" their brands, they are "Americanizing" the world's cultures.

> Down in the mall, between the fast-food joint and the bagel shop, a group of young people huddle in a flurry of baggy combat pants, skateboards, and slang. They size up a woman teetering past wearing DKNY, carrying *Time* magazine in one hand and a latte in the other. She brushes past a guy in a Yankees baseball cap who is talking on his Motorola cell phone about the Martin Scorsese film he saw last night.

> It's a standard American scene—only this isn't America, it's Britain. U.S. culture is so pervasive, the scene could be played out in any one of dozens of cities. Budapest or Berlin, if not Bogota or Bordeaux. Even Manila or Moscow. As the unrivaled global superpower, America exports its culture on an unprecedented scale. . . . Sometimes, U.S. ideals get transmitted—such as individual rights, freedom of speech, and respect for women—and local cultures are enriched. At other times, materialism or worse becomes the message and local traditions get crushed.[23]

"Today, globalization often wears Mickey Mouse ears, eats Big Macs, drinks Coke or Pepsi, and does its computing [with Microsoft] Windows [software]," says Thomas Friedman, in his book *The Lexus and the Olive Tree.*[24] Critics worry that, under such "McDomination," countries around the globe are losing their individual cultural identities. Teens in India watch MTV and ask their parents for more westernized clothes and other symbols of American pop culture and values. Grandmothers in small European villas no longer spend each morning visiting local meat, bread, and produce markets to gather the ingredients for dinner. Instead, they now shop at Wal-Mart Supercenters. Women in Saudi Arabia see American films and question their societal roles. In China, most people never drank coffee before Starbucks entered the market. Now Chinese consumers rush to Starbucks stores "because it's a symbol of a new kind of lifestyle." Similarly, in China, where McDonald's operates 80 restaurants in Beijing alone, nearly half of all children identify the chain as a domestic brand.

Such concerns have sometimes led to a backlash against American globalization. Well-known U.S. brands have become the targets of boycotts and protests in some international markets. As symbols of American capitalism, companies such as Coca-Cola, McDonald's, Nike, and KFC have been singled out by antiglobalization protestors in hot spots all around the world, especially when anti-American sentiment peaks.

Despite such problems, defenders of globalization argue that concerns of "Americanization" and the potential damage to American brands are overblown. U.S. brands are doing very well internationally. In the most recent Millward Brown Optimor survey of global consumer brands, 11 of the top 15 brands were American-owned.[25] And based on a recent study of 3,300 consumers in 41 countries, researchers concluded that consumers did not appear to translate anti-American sentiment into antibrand sentiment. ▲Many iconic American brands are prospering globally, even in some of the most unlikely places:[26]

> It's lunchtime in Tehran's tony northern suburbs, and around the crowded tables at Nayeb restaurant, elegant Iranian women in Jackie O sunglasses and designer jeans let their table chatter glide effortlessly between French, English, and their native Farsi. The only visual clues that these lunching ladies aren't dining at some smart New York City eatery but in the heart of Washington's Axis of Evil are the expensive Hermès scarves covering their blonde-tipped hair in deference to the mullahs. And

▲ Many iconic American brands are prospering globally, even in some of the most unlikely places. At this Tehran restaurant, American colas are the drink of choice. Coke and Pepsi have grabbed about half the national soft drink sales in Iran.

the drink of choice? This being revolutionary Iran, where alcohol is banned, the women are making do with Coca-Cola. Yes, Coca-Cola. It's a hard fact for some of Iran's theocrats to swallow. They want Iranians to shun "Great Satan" brands like Coke and Pepsi. Yet, the two American brands have grabbed about half the national soft drink sales in Iran, one of the Middle East's biggest drink markets. "I joke with customers not to buy this stuff because it's American," says a Tehran storekeeper, "but they don't care. That only makes them want to buy it more."

More fundamentally, most studies reveal that the cultural exchange goes both ways—America gets as well as gives cultural influence:[27]

Hollywood dominates the global movie market—capturing 90 percent of audiences in some European markets. However, British TV is giving as much as it gets in serving up competition to U.S. shows, spawning such hits as *The Office, American Idol*, and *Dancing with the Stars*. And although West Indian sports fans are now watching more basketball than cricket, and some Chinese young people are daubing the names of NBA superstars on their jerseys, the increasing popularity of American soccer has deep international roots. Even American childhood has increasingly been influenced by Asian and European cultural imports. Most kids know all about the Power Rangers, Tamagotchi and Pokémon, Sega and Nintendo. And J. K. Rowling's so-very-British Harry Potter books are shaping the thinking of a generation of American youngsters, not to mention the millions of American oldsters who've fallen under their spell as well. For the moment, English remains cyberspace's dominant language, and having Web access often means that third-world youth have greater exposure to American popular culture. Yet these same technologies enable Balkan students studying in the United States to hear Webcast news and music from Serbia or Bosnia.

American companies have also learned that to succeed abroad they must adapt to local cultural values and traditions rather than trying to force their own. Disneyland Paris flopped at first because it failed to take local cultural values and behaviors into account. According to a Euro Disney executive, "When we first launched, there was the belief that it was enough to be Disney. Now we realize that our guests need to be welcomed on the basis of their own culture and travel habits."[28] That realization has made Disneyland Paris the number-one tourist attraction in Europe—with twice as many visitors each year as the Eiffel Tower. The movie-themed Walt Disney Studios Park now blends Disney entertainment and attractions with the history and culture of European film. A show celebrating the history of animation features Disney characters speaking six different languages. Rides are narrated by foreign-born stars speaking in their native tongues.

Thus, globalization is a two-way street. If globalization has Mickey Mouse ears, it is also wearing a French beret, talking on a Nokia cell phone, buying furniture at IKEA, driving a Toyota Camry, and watching a Sony big-screen plasma TV.

Deciding Whether to Go Global (pp 563–564)

Not all companies need to venture into international markets to survive. For example, most local businesses need to market well only in the local marketplace. Operating domestically is easier and safer. Managers don't need to learn another country's language and laws.

They don't have to deal with unstable currencies, face political and legal uncertainties, or redesign their products to suit different customer expectations. However, companies that operate in global industries, where their strategic positions in specific markets are affected strongly by their overall global positions, must compete on a regional or worldwide basis to succeed.

Any of several factors might draw a company into the international arena. Global competitors might attack the company's home market by offering better products or lower prices. The company might want to counterattack these competitors in their home markets to tie up their resources. The company's customers might be expanding abroad and require international servicing. Or the company's home market might be stagnant or shrinking, and foreign markets may present additional sales and profit opportunities. For example, to offset declines in the U.S. soda market, Coca-Cola and Pepsi are rapidly expanding their presence in emerging markets such as Russia and China. And whereas Whirlpool's North American sales slipped by 1 percent last year, its European sales jumped 12 percent.[29]

Before going abroad, the company must weigh several risks and answer many questions about its ability to operate globally. Can the company learn to understand the preferences and buyer behavior of consumers in other countries? Can it offer competitively attractive products? Will it be able to adapt to other countries' business cultures and deal effectively with foreign nationals? Do the company's managers have the necessary international experience? Has management considered the impact of regulations and the political environments of other countries?

Because of the difficulties of entering international markets, most companies do not act until some situation or event thrusts them into the global arena. Someone—a domestic exporter, a foreign importer, a foreign government—may ask the company to sell abroad. Or the company may be saddled with overcapacity and need to find additional markets for its goods.

Deciding Which Markets to Enter (pp 564-565)

Before going abroad, the company should try to define its international *marketing objectives and policies*. It should decide what *volume* of foreign sales it wants. Most companies start small when they go abroad. Some plan to stay small, seeing international sales as a small part of their business. Other companies have bigger plans, seeing international business as equal to or even more important than their domestic business.

The company also needs to choose in *how many* countries it wants to market. Companies must be careful not to spread themselves too thin or to expand beyond their capabilities by operating in too many countries too soon. Next, the company needs to decide on the *types* of countries to enter. A country's attractiveness depends on the product, geographical factors, income and population, political climate, and other factors. The seller may prefer certain country groups or parts of the world. In recent years, many major new markets have emerged, offering both substantial opportunities and daunting challenges.

After listing possible international markets, the company must carefully evaluate each one. It must consider many factors. ▲For example, P&G's decision to enter the Chinese toothpaste market with its Crest is a no-brainer: China's huge population makes it the world's largest toothpaste market. And given that only 20 percent of China's rural dwellers now brush daily, this already huge market can grow even larger. Yet P&G must still question whether market size *alone* is reason enough for investing heavily in China.

P&G should ask some important questions: Can Crest compete effectively with dozens of local competitors, Colgate, and a state-owned brand managed by Unilever? Will the Chinese government remain stable and supportive? Does China provide for the

▲ P&G's decision to enter the Chinese toothpaste market with Crest is a no-brainer: China is the world's largest toothpaste market. But P&G must still question whether market size alone is reason enough for investing heavily in China.

needed production and distribution technologies? Can the company master China's vastly different cultural and buying differences? Crest's current success in China suggests that it could answer yes to all of these questions.[30]

"Just 10 years ago, Procter & Gamble's Crest brand was unknown to China's population, most of whom seldom—if ever—brushed their teeth," says one analyst. "Now P&G . . . sells more tubes of toothpaste there than it does in America, where Crest has been on store shelves for 52 years." P&G achieved this by sending researchers to get a feel for what urban and rural Chinese were willing to spend and what flavors they preferred. It discovered that urban Chinese are happy to pay more than $1 for tubes of Crest with exotic flavors such as Icy Mountain Spring and Morning Lotus Fragrance. But Chinese living in the countryside prefer the 50-cent Crest Salt White, since many rural Chinese believe that salt whitens the teeth. Armed with such insights, Crest now leads all competitors in China with a 25 percent market share.

Possible global markets should be ranked on several factors, including market size, market growth, cost of doing business, competitive advantage, and risk level. The goal is to determine the potential of each market, using indicators such as those shown in ● **Table 19.1**. Then the marketer must decide which markets offer the greatest long-run return on investment.

● TABLE | 19.1   Indicators of Market Potential

Demographic characteristics	Sociocultural factors
Education	Consumer lifestyles, beliefs, and values
Population size and growth	Business norms and approaches
Population age composition	Cultural and social norms
	Languages

Geographic characteristics	Political and legal factors
Climate	National priorities
Country size	Political stability
Population density—urban, rural	Government attitudes toward global trade
Transportation structure and market accessibility	Government bureaucracy
	Monetary and trade regulations

Economic factors

GDP size and growth

Income distribution

Industrial infrastructure

Natural resources

Financial and human resources

Author Comment | A company has many options for entering an international market, from simply exporting its products to working jointly with foreign companies to holding its own foreign-based operations.

Deciding How to Enter the Market (pp 566–568)

Once a company has decided to sell in a foreign country, it must determine the best mode of entry. Its choices are *exporting*, *joint venturing*, and *direct investment*. ⬤ **Figure 19.2** shows three market entry strategies, along with the options each one offers. As the figure shows, each succeeding strategy involves more commitment and risk, but also more control and potential profits.

Exporting

Exporting
Entering a foreign market by selling goods produced in the company's home country, often with little modification.

The simplest way to enter a foreign market is through **exporting**. The company may passively export its surpluses from time to time, or it may make an active commitment to expand exports to a particular market. In either case, the company produces all its goods in its home country. It may or may not modify them for the export market. Exporting involves the least change in the company's product lines, organization, investments, or mission.

Companies typically start with *indirect exporting*, working through independent international marketing intermediaries. Indirect exporting involves less investment because the firm does not require an overseas marketing organization or network. It also involves less risk. International marketing intermediaries bring know-how and services to the relationship, so the seller normally makes fewer mistakes.

Sellers may eventually move into *direct exporting*, whereby they handle their own exports. The investment and risk are somewhat greater in this strategy, but so is the potential return. A company can conduct direct exporting in several ways: It can set up a domestic export department that carries out export activities. It can set up an overseas sales branch that handles sales, distribution, and perhaps promotion. The sales branch gives the seller more presence and program control in the foreign market and often serves as a display center and customer-service center. The company can also send home-based salespeople abroad at certain times in order to find business. Finally, the company can do its exporting either through foreign-based distributors who buy and own the goods or through foreign-based agents who sell the goods on behalf of the company.

Joint Venturing

Joint venturing
Entering foreign markets by joining with foreign companies to produce or market a product or service.

A second method of entering a foreign market is **joint venturing**—joining with foreign companies to produce or market products or services. Joint venturing differs from exporting in that the company joins with a host country partner to sell or market abroad. It differs from direct investment in that an association is formed with someone in the foreign country. There are four types of joint ventures: licensing, contract manufacturing, management contracting, and joint ownership.

Licensing

Licensing
A method of entering a foreign market in which the company enters into an agreement with a licensee in the foreign market.

Licensing is a simple way for a manufacturer to enter international marketing. The company enters into an agreement with a licensee in the foreign market. For a fee or royalty, the licensee buys the right

Direct investment—owning your own foreign-based operation—affords greater control and profit potential, but it's often riskier.

⬤**FIGURE | 19.2**
Market Entry Strategies

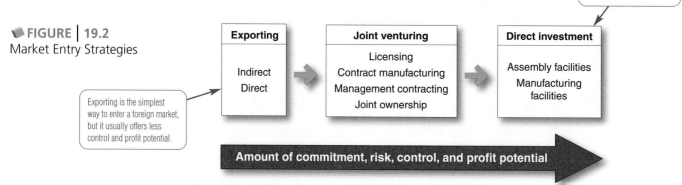

Exporting is the simplest way to enter a foreign market, but it usually offers less control and profit potential.

Exporting	Joint venturing	Direct investment
Indirect Direct	Licensing Contract manufacturing Management contracting Joint ownership	Assembly facilities Manufacturing facilities

Amount of commitment, risk, control, and profit potential

▲ Licensing: Tokyo Disneyland Resort is owned and operated by the Oriental Land Company (a Japanese development company), under license from The Walt Disney Company.

Contract manufacturing
A joint venture in which a company contracts with manufacturers in a foreign market to produce the product or provide its service.

Management contracting
A joint venture in which the domestic firm supplies the management know-how to a foreign company that supplies the capital; the domestic firm exports management services rather than products.

Joint ownership
A joint venture in which a company joins investors in a foreign market to create a local business in which the company shares joint ownership and control.

to use the company's manufacturing process, trademark, patent, trade secret, or other item of value. The company thus gains entry into the market at little risk; the licensee gains production expertise or a well-known product or name without having to start from scratch.

Coca-Cola markets internationally by licensing bottlers around the world and supplying them with the syrup needed to produce the product. In Japan, Budweiser beer flows from Kirin breweries and Marlboro cigarettes roll off production lines at Japan Tobacco, Inc. ▲ Tokyo Disneyland Resort is owned and operated by Oriental Land Company under license from The Walt Disney Company.

Licensing has potential disadvantages, however. The firm has less control over the licensee than it would over its own operations. Furthermore, if the licensee is very successful, the firm has given up these profits, and if and when the contract ends, it may find it has created a competitor.

Contract Manufacturing

Another option is **contract manufacturing**—the company contracts with manufacturers in the foreign market to produce its product or provide its service. Sears used this method in opening up department stores in Mexico and Spain, where it found qualified local manufacturers to produce many of the products it sells. The drawbacks of contract manufacturing are decreased control over the manufacturing process and loss of potential profits on manufacturing. The benefits are the chance to start faster, with less risk, and the later opportunity either to form a partnership with or to buy out the local manufacturer.

Management Contracting

Under **management contracting**, the domestic firm supplies management know-how to a foreign company that supplies the capital. The domestic firm exports management services rather than products. Hilton uses this arrangement in managing hotels around the world.

Management contracting is a low-risk method of getting into a foreign market, and it yields income from the beginning. The arrangement is even more attractive if the contracting firm has an option to buy some share in the managed company later on. The arrangement is not sensible, however, if the company can put its scarce management talent to better uses or if it can make greater profits by undertaking the whole venture. Management contracting also prevents the company from setting up its own operations for a period of time.

Joint Ownership

Joint ownership ventures consist of one company joining forces with foreign investors to create a local business in which they share joint ownership and control. A company may buy an interest in a local firm, or the two parties may form a new business venture. Joint ownership may be needed for economic or political reasons. The firm may lack the financial, physical, or managerial resources to undertake the venture alone. Or a foreign government may require joint ownership as a condition for entry.

Hershey recently formed a joint venture with Indian-based Godrej Beverages and Foods to make and distribute its chocolates in that country. ▲ When it comes to selling chocolate in India, Hershey will need all the help it can get from its new local partner.[31]

"Humans may have first cultivated a taste for chocolate 3,000 years ago," comments one observer, "but India [has] just gotten around to it. Compared to the sweet-toothed Swiss and Cadbury-crunching Brits, both of whom devour about 24 pounds of chocolate per capita annually, Indians consume a paltry 5.8 ounces." Indian consumers currently favor a traditional candy known as mithai, and it will take a significant and culturally savvy marketing effort to persuade them to transfer their

▲ Hershey recently formed a joint venture with Indian-based Godrej Beverages and Foods to make and distribute its chocolates in that country.

allegiance to chocolate. To make things even tougher, two global giants—Nestlé and Cadbury—already hold a 90 percent share of Indian chocolate between them. Still, given the sheer size of the Indian population, if consumers can be persuaded to acquire a taste for chocolate, the rewards for Hershey and Godrej could be substantial. Either company could have decided to go it alone, but both will likely benefit greatly from the joint venture. Godrej gains a highly respected global brand; Hershey reaps the benefits of a local partner that understands the intricacies of the Indian market.

Joint ownership has certain drawbacks. The partners may disagree over investment, marketing, or other policies. Whereas many U.S. firms like to reinvest earnings for growth, local firms often prefer to take out these earnings; and whereas U.S. firms emphasize the role of marketing, local investors may rely on selling.

Direct Investment

Direct investment
Entering a foreign market by developing foreign-based assembly or manufacturing facilities.

The biggest involvement in a foreign market comes through **direct investment**—the development of foreign-based assembly or manufacturing facilities. For example, HP has made direct investments in a number of major markets abroad, including India. It recently opened a second factory near Delhi to make PCs for the local market. Thanks to such commitments, HP has overtaken the favorite local brand, HCL, and now controls more than 21 percent of the market in India.[32]

If a company has gained experience in exporting and if the foreign market is large enough, foreign production facilities offer many advantages. The firm may have lower costs in the form of cheaper labor or raw materials, foreign government investment incentives, and freight savings. The firm may improve its image in the host country because it creates jobs. Generally, a firm develops a deeper relationship with government, customers, local suppliers, and distributors, allowing it to adapt its products to the local market better. Finally, the firm keeps full control over the investment and therefore can develop manufacturing and marketing policies that serve its long-term international objectives.

The main disadvantage of direct investment is that the firm faces many risks, such as restricted or devalued currencies, falling markets, or government changes. In some cases, a firm has no choice but to accept these risks if it wants to operate in the host country.

Author Comment | The major global marketing decision usually boils down to this: How much, if at all, should we adapt our marketing strategy and programs to local markets? How would the answer differ for Boeing versus Hershey?

Deciding on the Global Marketing Program (pp 568–575)

Companies that operate in one or more foreign markets must decide how much, if at all, to adapt their marketing strategies and programs to local conditions. At one extreme are global companies that use **standardized global marketing**, using largely the same marketing strategy approaches and marketing mix worldwide. At the other extreme is an **adapted global marketing**. In this case, the producer adjusts the marketing strategy and mix elements to each target market, bearing more costs but hoping for a larger market share and return.

Standardized global marketing
An international marketing strategy for using basically the same marketing strategy and mix in all the company's international markets.

The question of whether to adapt or standardize the marketing strategy and program has been much debated in recent years. On the one hand, some global marketers believe that technology is making the world a smaller place and that consumer needs around the world are becoming more similar. This paves the way for "global brands" and standardized global marketing. Global branding and standardization, in turn, result in greater brand power and reduced costs from economies of scale.

Adapted global marketing
An international marketing strategy for adjusting the marketing strategy and mix elements to each international target market, bearing more costs but hoping for a larger market share and return.

On the other hand, the marketing concept holds that marketing programs will be more effective if tailored to the unique needs of each targeted customer group. If this concept applies within a country, it should apply even more across international markets. Despite global convergence, consumers in different countries still have widely varied cultural backgrounds. They still differ significantly in their needs and wants, spending power, product preferences, and shopping patterns. Because these differences are hard to change, most marketers adapt their products, prices, channels, and promotions to fit consumer desires in each country.

However, global standardization is not an all-or-nothing proposition. It's a matter of degree. Most international marketers suggest that companies should "think globally but act locally"—that they should seek a balance between standardization and adaptation. The corporate level gives global strategic direction; regional or local units focus on individual consumer differences across global markets. Simon Clift, head of marketing for global consumer-goods giant Unilever, puts it this way: "We're trying to strike a balance between being mindlessly global and hopelessly local."[33]

McDonald's operates this way. It uses the same basic fast-food look, layout, and operating model in its restaurants around the world but adapts its menu to local tastes. In Japan, it offers up Ebi Filet-O-Shrimp burgers and fancy Salad Macs salad plates. In Korea it sells the Bulgogi Burger, a grilled pork patty on a bun with a garlicky soy sauce. In India, where cows are considered sacred, McDonald's serves McChicken, Filet-O-Fish, McVeggie (a vegetable burger), Pizza McPuffs, McAloo Tikki (a spiced-potato burger), and the Maharaja Mac—two all-chicken patties, special sauce, lettuce, cheese, pickles, onions on a sesame-seed bun.

Similarly, to boost sales of Oreo cookies in China, Kraft Foods has tweaked its recipes and marketing programs to meet the tastes of Chinese consumers. It even developed a brand new Chinese version of the all-American classic (see **Real Marketing 19.1**).

Product

Five strategies allow for adapting product and marketing communication strategies to a global market (see **Figure 19.3**).[34] We first discuss the three product strategies and then turn to the two communication strategies.

Straight product extension
Marketing a product in a foreign market without any change.

Straight product extension means marketing a product in a foreign market without any change. Top management tells its marketing people, "Take the product as is and find customers for it." The first step, however, should be to find out whether foreign consumers use that product and what form they prefer.

Straight extension has been successful in some cases and disastrous in others. Kellogg cereals, Gillette razors, Heineken beer, and Black & Decker tools are all sold successfully in about the same form around the world. But General Foods introduced its standard powdered JELL-O in the British market only to find that British consumers prefer a solid wafer or cake form. Likewise, Philips began to make a profit in Japan only after it reduced the size of its coffeemakers to fit into smaller Japanese kitchens and its shavers to fit smaller Japanese hands. Straight extension is tempting because it involves no additional product development costs, manufacturing changes, or new promotion. But it can be costly in the long run if products fail to satisfy foreign consumers.

> The real question buried in this figure is this: How much should a company standardize or adapt its products and marketing across global markets?

FIGURE | 19.3
Five Global Product and Communications Strategies

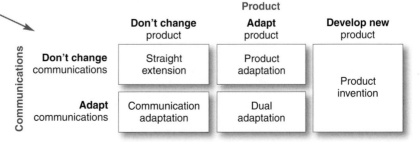

	Product		
Communications	**Don't change** product	**Adapt** product	**Develop new** product
Don't change communications	Straight extension	Product adaptation	Product invention
Adapt communications	Communication adaptation	Dual adaptation	

Real Marketing 19.1

Oreos and Milk, Chinese Style

Unlike its iconic American counterpart, the most popular Oreo in China is long, thin, four-layered, and coated in chocolate. Still, the two kinds of Oreos, sold half a world apart, have one important thing in common: Both are now best-sellers. But taking the dark chocolate American treasure to China has been no easy journey for Kraft Foods. Although the Oreo has long been the top-selling cookie in the United States, to make Oreos sell well in the world's most populous nation, Kraft has had to completely reinvent the popular cookie.

Oreos were first introduced in the United States in 1912, but it wasn't until 1996 that Kraft introduced Oreos to Chinese consumers. It began by selling the same Oreos in China that it markets in the United States—the ones that Americans love to twist apart to lick the creamy centers or dunk in milk until they're soggy. However, after nine years of trying mostly U.S. marketing themes and programs on Chinese consumers, Oreo sales remained flat. Albert Einstein's definition of insanity—doing the same thing repeatedly and expecting different results—"characterized what we

were doing," says Kraft Foods International's vice president of marketing. To make things happen, he concluded, it was time for a major Oreo makeover.

First up: Kraft changed the Oreo management team. Whereas previous decisions about Oreo marketing in China had been made at arm's length by people in Kraft's Northbrook, Illinois, headquarters, the company now handed the task of remaking the brand to an entrepreneurial team of local Chinese managers. The team began with in-depth research on Chinese consumers that yielded some interesting findings. First, the team learned, the Chinese weren't big cookie eaters. Despite China's immense population, the Chinese biscuit and cookie market was one-third the size of the U.S. market. Second, Chinese consumers weren't much enamored with the Oreos that Americans have come to crave. Traditional Oreos were too sweet for Chinese tastes. Also, standard packages of 14 Oreos, priced at 72 cents, were too expensive for most Chinese food budgets.

To make Oreo cookies sell well in China, Kraft completely reinvented the popular all-American classic. Kraft has now begun selling the popular Chinese wafers elsewhere in Asia, as well as in Australia and Canada.

So for starters, the company developed 20 prototypes of reduced-sugar Oreos and tested them with Chinese consumers before arriving at a formula that tasted right. Kraft

---

Product adaptation

Adapting a product to meet local conditions or wants in foreign markets.

Product adaptation involves changing the product to meet local conditions or wants. For example, Finnish cell phone maker Nokia customizes its cell phones for every major market. Developers build in rudimentary voice recognition for Asia where keyboards are a problem and raise the ring volume so phones can be heard on crowded Asian streets. Nokia is also making a major push to create full-featured but rugged and low-cost phones that meet the needs of less-affluent consumers in large developing countries such as India, China, and Kenya.[35]

Looking for ways to make cell phones practical for people living in developing countries, Nokia has trekked to far corners of the globe, from the narrow alleys of Mumbai to the vast slums of Nairobi. The result is a slew of new features especially designed for places with harsh weather and harsher living conditions. One example: The company created dustproof keypads—crucial in dry, hot countries with many unpaved roads, as Nokia executives learned from visits to customers' homes in India. Low price is also important. On a recent visit to slums outside Nairobi, members of the emerging markets team discovered that many people form buying clubs, pooling their money to buy handsets one at a time until every member has one. Now Nokia is looking for ways to encourage this form of self-financing. Communal finance is a far cry from manufacturing mobile phones, but Nokia knows it has to try all sorts of product and service ideas if it wants to capture its share of the industry's next 1 billion customers.

also introduced packages containing fewer Oreos for just 29 cents. However, some Chinese consumers still found even the reformulated Oreos too sweet. Said one 30-year-old consumer in the eastern part of Beijing, he liked the cookie but "many of my friends think I am a bit weird to stick to Oreo cookies—most think them too sweet to be accepted."

Kraft's research also revealed that Chinese consumers have a growing thirst for milk, which Kraft wasn't fully exploiting. So Kraft began a grassroots marketing campaign to educate Chinese consumers about the American tradition of pairing milk with cookies. The company created Oreo apprentice programs at 30 Chinese universities that drew 6,000 student applications. Three hundred of the applicants were trained to become Oreo brand ambassadors. Some of the students rode around Beijing on bicycles, outfitted with wheel covers resembling Oreos, and handed out cookies to more than 300,000 consumers.

Other ambassadors held Oreo-themed basketball games to reinforce the idea of dunking cookies in milk. Television commercials showed kids twisting apart Oreo cookies, licking the cream center, and dipping the chocolate cookie halves into glasses of milk. Kraft CEO Irene Rosenfeld calls the bicycle campaign "a stroke of genius that only could have come from local managers. [Letting] our local managers deal with local conditions will be a source of competitive advantage for us."

The product and marketing changes made a difference and Oreo sales in China improved. However, Kraft knew that if it was really serious about capturing a bigger share of the Chinese biscuit market, it needed to do more than just tweak its U.S. Oreo recipe and marketing. It needed to remake the Oreo itself.

So in 2006, Kraft introduced a second Oreo in China, one that looked almost nothing like the original. The new Chinese Oreo consisted of four layers of crispy wafer filled with vanilla and chocolate cream, coated in chocolate. The new Oreo was designed not only to satisfy the cravings of China's consumers, but also stand up to the challenges of selling and distributing across China's vast landscape. Kraft even developed a proprietary handling process to ensure that the chocolate product could withstand the cold climate in the north and the hot, humid weather in the south, yet still be ready to melt in the customer's mouth.

Kraft's efforts to reshape the Oreo brand and its marketing have paid off. Within a year of introduction, Oreo WaferSticks became the best-selling biscuit in China, outpacing HaoChiDian, a biscuit brand made by Chinese company Dali. The new Oreos are also outselling traditional round Oreos in China, and Kraft has begun selling the wafers elsewhere in Asia, as well as in Australia and Canada. Over the past two years, Kraft has doubled its Oreo revenues in China.

What's more, Kraft has learned, its "think globally, act locally" approach applies not just to Oreos and not just in China but to all of its products worldwide. For example, to take advantage of the European preference for dark chocolate, Kraft is introducing dark chocolate in Germany under its Milka brand. Research in Russia showed that consumers there like premium instant coffee, so Kraft is positioning its Carte Noire freeze-dried coffee as upscale by placing it at film festivals, fashion shows, and operas. And in the Philippines, where iced tea is popular, Kraft last year launched iced-tea-flavored Tang. As a result of such moves, international business now represents 40 percent of Kraft's total sales. Kraft's profit in the European Union last year rose 48 percent, and profits in developing countries rose 57 percent, far outpacing U.S. profit growth.

Source: Adapted from portions of Julie Jargon, "Kraft Reformulated Oreo, Scores in China," *Wall Street Journal*, May 1, 2008, p. B1. Also see www.kraft.com, accessed October 2008.

Product invention

Creating new products or services for foreign markets.

Product invention consists of creating something new for a specific country market. This strategy can take two forms. It might mean maintaining or reintroducing earlier product forms that happen to be well adapted to the needs of a given country. Or a company might create a new product to meet a need in a given country. For example, Sony added the "U" model to its VAIO personal computer line to meet the unique needs of Japanese consumers. It found that Japanese commuters had difficulty using standard laptops on crowded rush-hour trains—standing commuters have no laps. So it created the U as a "standing computer." The U is lightweight and small: only seven inches wide with a five-inch diagonal screen. And it includes a touch screen and small keyboard that can be used while standing or on the move.[36]

Promotion

Companies can either adopt the same communication strategy they use in the home market or change it for each local market. Consider advertising messages. Some global companies use a standardized advertising theme around the world. Of course, even in highly standardized communications campaigns, some adjustments might be required for language and cultural differences. For example, Guy Laroche uses virtually the same ads for its Drakkar Noir fragrances in Europe as in Arab countries. However, it subtly tones down the Arab versions to meet cultural differences in attitudes toward sensuality. And although McDonald's uses its standardized "I'm lovin' it" theme worldwide, it varies its interpretations of the theme in different countries. In China, for instance, it presents the Quarter Pounder as a lot more than just a big U.S.-style burger.[37]

> Many Chinese hold the traditional view that eating beef boosts energy and heightens sex appeal. The word "beef" in Chinese has connotations of manliness, strength, and skill. That's the message McDonald's is sending Chinese consumers as it tries to seduce them into eating more hamburgers. One racy Quarter Pounder poster hanging in restaurants features a close-up of a women's lips. "Flirt with your senses," the sign says. The burger chain's Quarter Pounder TV commercials are even steamier. In one, a man and a woman eat the burgers, and close-up shots of the woman's neck and mouth are interspersed with images of fireworks and spraying water. As the actors suck their fingers, the voice-over says: "You can feel it. Thicker. You can taste it. Juicier." A series of light-hearted print ads in trendy magazines lay out scenarios in which beef saves the day. In one, a young man frets that five women he has met online want to go out on dates with him the next day. The ad offers some solutions: Hire four friends. Split up the meetings. Or "have enough beef tonight" to "be able to handle five princesses tomorrow."

Colors also are changed sometimes to avoid taboos in other countries. Purple is associated with death in most of Latin America, white is a mourning color in Japan, and green is associated with jungle sickness in Malaysia. Even names must sometimes be adjusted. The global name for Microsoft's new operating system, Vista, turns out to be a disparaging term for a frumpy old woman in Latvia. And in the Americas, Mitsubishi changed the Japanese name of its Pajero SUV to Montero—it seems that *pajero* in Spanish is a slang term for sexual self-gratification. (See **Real Marketing 19.2** for more on language blunders in international marketing.)

Communication adaptation
A global communication strategy of fully adapting advertising messages to local markets.

Other companies follow a strategy of **communication adaptation**, fully adapting their advertising messages to local markets. Kellogg ads in the United States promote the taste and nutrition of Kellogg's cereals versus competitors' brands. In France, where consumers drink little milk and eat little for breakfast, Kellogg's ads must convince consumers that cereals are a tasty and healthful breakfast. In India, where many consumers eat heavy, fried breakfasts, Kellogg's advertising convinces buyers to switch to a lighter, more nutritious breakfast diet.

Similarly, Coca-Cola sells its low-calorie beverage as Diet Coke in North America, the United Kingdom, and the Middle and Far East but as Coke Light elsewhere. According to Diet Coke's global brand manager, in Spanish-speaking countries Coke Light ads "position the soft drink as an object of desire, rather than as a way to feel good about yourself, as Diet Coke is positioned in the United States." This "desire positioning" plays off research showing that "Coca-Cola Light is seen in other parts of the world as a vibrant brand that exudes a sexy confidence."[38]

Media also need to be adapted internationally because media availability and regulations vary from country to country. TV advertising time is very limited in Europe, for instance, ranging from four hours a day in France to none in Scandinavian countries. Advertisers must buy time months in advance, and they have little control over airtimes. However, cell phone ads are much more widely accepted in Europe and Asia than in the United States. Magazines also vary in effectiveness. For example, magazines are a major medium in Italy but a minor one in Austria. Newspapers are national in the United Kingdom but are only local in Spain.[39]

Price

Companies also face many considerations in setting their international prices. For example, how might Black & Decker price its power tools globally? It could set a uniform price all around the world, but this amount would be too high a price in poor countries and not high enough in rich ones. It could charge what consumers in each country would bear, but this strategy ignores differences in the actual costs from country to country. Finally, the company could use a standard markup of its costs everywhere, but this approach might price Black & Decker out of the market in some countries where costs are high.

Real Marketing 19.2

Watch Your Language!

Many global companies have had difficulty crossing the language barrier, with results ranging from mild embarrassment to outright failure. Seemingly innocuous brand names and advertising phrases can take on unintended or hidden meanings when translated into other languages. Careless translations can make a marketer look downright foolish to foreign consumers.

The classic language blunders involve standardized brand names that do not translate well. When Coca-Cola first marketed Coke in China in the 1920s, it developed a group of Chinese characters that, when pronounced, sounded like the product name. Unfortunately, the characters actually translated as "bite the wax tadpole." Now, the characters on Chinese Coke bottles translate as "happiness in the mouth."

Several modern-day marketers have had similar problems when their brand names crashed into the language barrier. Chevy's Nova translated into Spanish as *no va*—"it doesn't go." GM changed the name to Caribe (Spanish for Caribbean) and sales increased. Microsoft's new operating system, Vista, turns out to be a disparaging term for a frumpy old woman in Latvia. Rolls-Royce avoided the name Silver Mist in German markets, where *mist* means "manure." Sunbeam, however, entered the German market with its Mist Stick hair-curling iron. As should have been expected, the Germans had little use for a "manure wand." IKEA marketed a children's workbench named FARTFULL (the word means "speedy" in Swedish)—it soon discontinued the product.

Interbrand of London, the firm that created household names such as Prozac and Acura, recently developed a brand-name "hall of shame" list, which contained these and other foreign brand names you're never likely to see inside the local Safeway: Krapp toilet paper (Denmark), Crapsy Fruit cereal (France), Poo curry powder (Argentina), and Pschitt lemonade (France).

Global language barriers: Some standardized brand names do not translate well globally.

Travelers often encounter well-intentioned advice from service firms that takes on meanings very different from those intended. The menu in one Swiss restaurant proudly stated, "Our wines leave you nothing to hope for." Signs in a Japanese hotel pronounced, "You are invited to take advantage of the chambermaid." At a laundry in Rome, it was, "Ladies, leave your clothes here and spend the afternoon having a good time."

Advertising themes often lose—or gain—something in the translation. The Coors beer slogan "get loose with Coors" in Spanish came out as "get the runs with Coors." Coca-Cola's "Coke adds life" theme in Japanese translated into "Coke brings your ancestors back from the dead." The milk industry learned too late that its American advertising question "Got Milk?" translated in Mexico as a more provocative "Are you lactating?" In Chinese, the KFC slogan "finger-lickin' good" came out as "eat your fingers off." And Motorola's Hellomoto ring tone sounds like "Hello, Fatty" in India. Even when the language is the same, word usage may differ from country to country. Thus, the

British ad line for Electrolux vacuum cleaners— "Nothing sucks like an Electrolux"—would capture few customers in the United States.

So, crossing the language barrier involves much more than simply translating names and slogans into other languages. You can't uproot a concept and just translate it and put it into another market," says one translation consultant. "It's not really about translating word for word, but actually adapting a certain meaning." Beyond just word meanings and nuances, international marketers must also consider things like phonetic appeal and even associations with historical figures, legends, and other factors. The consultant points to the Chinese adaptation of the name for eBay's online free classified ads service—Kijiji (which means "village" in Swahili)—as a localization success story. "In Chinese, the three characters used to phonetically represent the Kijiji name map almost exactly to the English pronunciation," she says. "Plus, they have the meaning of people pulling together to share things, which is totally descriptive of the business and brand."

Sources: Quotes from Randall Frost, "Lost in Translation," *Brandchannel.com*, November 13, 2006. For the above and other examples, see David A. Ricks, "Perspectives: Translation Blunders in International Business," *Journal of Language for International Business,* 7:2, 1996, pp. 50–55; Martin Croft, "Mind Your Language," *Marketing,* June 19, 2003, pp. 35–39; Mark Lasswell, "Lost in Translation," *Business 2.0,* August 2004, pp. 68–70; "Lost in Translation," *Hispanic,* May 2005, p. 12; Ross Thomson, "Lost in Translation," *Medical Marketing and Media,* March 2005, p. 82; and Eric Pfanner, "Marketers Take a Fresh Look at the Language Barrier," *International Herald Tribune,* July 22, 2007.

Regardless of how companies go about pricing their products, their foreign prices probably will be higher than their domestic prices for comparable products. A Gucci handbag may sell for $60 in Italy and $240 in the United States. Why? Gucci faces a *price escalation* problem. It must add the cost of transportation, tariffs, importer margin, wholesaler margin, and retailer margin to its factory price. Depending on these added costs, the product may have to sell for two to five times as much in another country to make the same profit.

▲ The Internet is making global price difference more obvious, forcing companies toward more standardized international pricing.

To overcome this problem when selling to less-affluent consumers in developing countries, many companies make simpler or smaller versions of their products that can be sold at lower prices. For example, in China and other emerging markets, Dell sells its simplified Dell EC280 model for $340 dollars, and P&G sells everything from shampoo to toothpaste in less costly formulations and smaller packages at more affordable prices.

Another problem involves setting a price for goods that a company ships to its foreign subsidiaries. If the company charges a foreign subsidiary too much, it may end up paying higher tariff duties even while paying lower income taxes in that country. If the company charges its subsidiary too little, it can be charged with *dumping*. Dumping occurs when a company either charges less than its costs or less than it charges in its home market. For example, U.S. nail makers recently accused foreign nail makers—especially those in China and the United Arab Emirates—of dumping excess supplies of nails in the United States, hurting the domestic steel nail market. In over the past three years, imports of nails from the two countries have grown 70 percent, forcing U.S. manufacturers to close facilities and lay off workers. The U.S. International Trade Commission agreed, and the U.S. Commerce Department is imposing duties as high as 118 percent on steel nail imports from the offending countries.[40] Various governments are always watching for dumping abuses, and they often force companies to set the price charged by other competitors for the same or similar products.

Recent economic and technological forces have had an impact on global pricing. ▲For example, the Internet is making global price differences more obvious. When firms sell their wares over the Internet, customers can see how much products sell for in different countries. They can even order a given product directly from the company location or dealer offering the lowest price. This is forcing companies toward more standardized international pricing.

Distribution Channels

Whole-channel view

Designing international channels that take into account the entire global supply chain and marketing channel, forging an effective global value delivery network.

The international company must take a **whole-channel view** of the problem of distributing products to final consumers. ◆**Figure 19.4** shows the two major links between the seller and the final buyer. The first link, *channels between nations*, moves company products from points of production to the borders of countries within which they are sold. The second link, *channels within nations*, moves the products from their market entry points to the final consumers. The whole-channel view takes into account the entire global supply chain and marketing channel. It recognizes that to compete well internationally, the company must effectively design and manage an entire *global value delivery network*.

Channels of distribution within countries vary greatly from nation to nation. There are large differences in the numbers and types of intermediaries serving each country

◆**FIGURE | 19.4**
Whole-Channel Concept for International Marketing

Distribution channels between and within nations can vary dramatically around the world. For example, in the United States, Nokia distributes phones through a network of sophisticated retailers. In rural India, it maintains a fleet of Nokia-branded vans that prowl the rutted country roads.

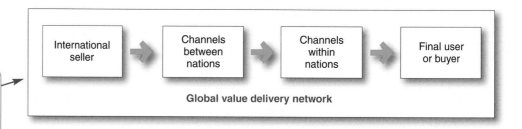

| International seller | → | Channels between nations | → | Channels within nations | → | Final user or buyer |

Global value delivery network

▲ Distribution channels vary greatly from nation to nation. In its efforts to sell rugged, affordable phones to Indian consumers, Nokia forged its own distribution structure, including a fleet of distinctive blue Nokia-branded vans that prowl rutted country roads to visit remote villages.

market, and in the transportation infrastructure serving these intermediaries. For example, whereas large-scale retail chains dominate the U.S. scene, much retailing in other countries is done by many small, independent retailers. In India, millions of retailers operate tiny shops or sell in open markets. ▲ Thus, in its efforts to sell rugged, affordable phones to Indian consumers, Nokia has had to forge its own distribution structure.[41]

In India, Nokia estimates there are 90,000 points-of-sale for its phones, ranging from modern stores to makeshift kiosks. That makes it difficult to control how products are displayed and pitched to consumers. "You have to understand where people live, what the shopping patterns are," says a Nokia executive. "You have to work with local means to reach people—even bicycles or rickshaws." To reach rural India, Nokia has outfitted its own fleet of distinctive blue Nokia-branded vans that prowl the rutted country roads. Staffers park these advertisements-on-wheels in villages, often on market or festival days. There, with crowds clustering around, Nokia reps explain the basics of how the phones work and how to buy them. Nokia has extended the concept to minivans, which can reach even more remote places.

Similarly, Coca-Cola adapts its distribution methods to meet local challenges in global markets. For example, in rural China, an army of more than 10,000 Coca-Cola sales reps make regular visits to small retailers, often on foot or bicycle. To reach the most isolated spots, the company even relies on teams of delivery donkeys. In Montevideo, Uruguay, where larger vehicles are challenged by traffic, parking, and pollution difficulties, Coca-Cola recently purchased 30 small, efficient three-wheeled ZAP alternative transportation trucks. The little trucks average about one-fifth the fuel consumption and scooted around congested city streets with greater ease. If the model works well in Montevideo, Coca-Cola may adopt it in other congested urban areas that pose similar challenges.[42]

Author Comment | Many large companies, regardless of their "home country," now think of themselves as truly *global* organizations. They view the entire world as a single borderless market. For example, although headquartered in Chicago, Boeing is as comfortable selling planes to Lufthansa or Air China as to American Airlines.

Deciding on the Global Marketing Organization (pp 575–576)

Companies manage their international marketing activities in at least three different ways: Most companies first organize an export department, then create an international division, and finally become a global organization.

A firm normally gets into international marketing by simply shipping out its goods. If its international sales expand, the company organizes an *export department* with a sales manager and a few assistants. As sales increase, the export department can expand to include various marketing services so that it can actively go after business. If the firm moves into joint ventures or direct investment, the export department will no longer be adequate.

Many companies get involved in several international markets and ventures. A company may export to one country, license to another, have a joint ownership venture in a third, and own a subsidiary in a fourth. Sooner or later it will create *international divisions* or subsidiaries to handle all its international activity.

▲ Many large companies view the entire world as a single borderless market. Boeing is headquartered in Chicago, but is as comfortable selling planes to Lufthansa and Air China as to American Airlines.

International divisions are organized in a variety of ways. An international division's corporate staff consists of marketing, manufacturing, research, finance, planning, and personnel specialists. It plans for and provides services to various operating units, which can be organized in one of three ways. They can be *geographical organizations*, with country managers who are responsible for salespeople, sales branches, distributors, and licensees in their respective countries. Or the operating units can be *world product groups*, each responsible for worldwide sales of different product groups. Finally, operating units can be *international subsidiaries*, each responsible for its own sales and profits. Many firms have passed beyond the international division stage and become truly *global organizations*. ▲For example, well over half of Boeing's airplane sales are made outside the United States. Although headquartered in Chicago, the company employs more than 159,300 people in 70 countries. Boeing is as comfortable selling planes to Lufthansa or Air China as to American Airlines.

Global organizations stop thinking of themselves as national marketers who sell abroad and start thinking of themselves as global marketers. The top corporate management and staff plan worldwide manufacturing facilities, marketing policies, financial flows, and logistical systems. The global operating units report directly to the chief executive or executive committee of the organization, not to the head of an international division. Executives are trained in worldwide operations, not just domestic *or* international operations. The company recruits management from many countries, buys components and supplies where they cost the least, and invests where the expected returns are greatest.

Today, major companies must become more global if they hope to compete. As foreign companies successfully invade their domestic markets, companies must move more aggressively into foreign markets. They will have to change from companies that treat their international operations as secondary to companies that view the entire world as a single borderless market.

REVIEWING Objectives AND KEY Terms

Companies today can no longer afford to pay attention only to their domestic market, regardless of its size. Many industries are global industries, and firms that operate globally achieve lower costs and higher brand awareness. At the same time, global marketing is risky because of variable exchange rates, unstable governments, protectionist tariffs and trade barriers, and several other factors. Given the potential gains and risks of international marketing, companies need a systematic way to make their global marketing decisions.

market's *economic*, *political-legal*, and *cultural characteristics*. The company must then decide whether it wants to go abroad and consider the potential risks and benefits. It must decide on the volume of international sales it wants, how many countries it wants to market in, and which specific markets it wants to enter. This decision calls for weighing the probable rate of return on investment against the level of risk.

OBJECTIVE 1 **Discuss how the international trade system and the economic, political-legal, and cultural environments affect a company's international marketing decisions. (pp 554–565)**

A company must understand the *global marketing environment*, especially the international trade system. It must assess each foreign

OBJECTIVE 2 **Describe three key approaches to entering international markets. (pp 566–568)**

The company must decide how to enter each chosen market—whether through *exporting*, *joint venturing*, or *direct investment*. Many companies start as exporters, move to joint ventures, and finally make a direct investment in foreign markets. In *exporting*, the company enters a foreign market by sending and selling products through international marketing intermediaries (indirect exporting) or the company's own department, branch, or sales representative or agents (direct exporting). When establishing a *joint venture,* a company enters foreign markets by joining with foreign companies to produce or market a product or service. In *licensing,* the company enters a foreign market by contracting with a licensee in the foreign market, offering the right to use a manufacturing process, trademark, patent, trade secret, or other item of value for a fee or royalty.

OBJECTIVE 3   **Explain how companies adapt their marketing mixes for international markets.** (pp 568–575)

Companies must also decide how much their products, promotion, price, and channels should be adapted for each foreign market. At one extreme, global companies use *standardized global marketing* worldwide. Others use an *adapted global*

marketing, in which they adjust the marketing strategy and mix to each target market, bearing more costs but hoping for a larger market share and return. However, global standardization is not an all-or-nothing proposition. It's a matter of degree. Most international marketers suggest that companies should "think globally but act locally"—that they should seek a balance between standardization and adaptation.

OBJECTIVE 4   **Identify the three major forms of international marketing organization.** (pp 575–576)

The company must develop an effective organization for international marketing. Most firms start with an *export department* and graduate to an *international division.* A few become *global organizations,* with worldwide marketing planned and managed by the top officers of the company. Global organizations view the entire world as a single, borderless market.

KEY Terms

OBJECTIVE 1

Global firm (p 555)
Economic community (p 557)
Countertrade (p 560)

OBJECTIVE 2

Exporting (p 566)
Joint venturing (p 566)

Licensing (p 566)
Contract manufacturing (p 567)
Management contracting (p 567)
Joint ownership (p 567)
Direct investment (p 568)

OBJECTIVE 3

Standardized global marketing (p 568)

Adapted global marketing (p 568)
Straight product extension (p 569)
Product adaptation (p 570)
Product invention (p 571)
Communication adaptation (p 572)
Whole-channel view (p 574)

DISCUSSING & APPLYING THE Concepts

Discussing the Concepts

1. Explain what is meant by the term *global firm* and list the six major decisions involved in international marketing. (AASCB: Communication)

2. Identify examples of economic communities and discuss their roles in international trade. (AACSB: Communication)

3. Name and define the four types of country industrial structures. (AACSB: Communication)

4. Discuss different forms of countertrade and explain why it is a growing practice. (AACSB: Communication)

5. Discuss the three ways to enter foreign markets. Which is the best? (AACSB: Communication; Reflective Thinking)

6. Discuss the possible product strategies used for adapting to a global market. (AACSB: Communication)

Applying the Concepts

1. Visit the Web site of the Brazilian Embassy in Washington, D.C., at www.brasilemb.org. What do you learn about doing

business in Brazil? (AACSB: Communication; Use of IT; Reflective Thinking)

2. The United States restricts trade with Cuba. Visit the U.S. Department of the Treasury at www.ustreas.gov/offices/enforcement/ofac to learn more about economic and trade sanctions. Click on the "Cuba Sanctions" link to learn more about the trade restrictions on Cuba. Are these tariff, quota, or embargo restrictions? To what extent do these trade restrictions allow U.S. businesses to export their products to Cuba? (AACSB: Communication; Use of IT; Reflective Thinking)

3. Visit the Central Intelligence Agency's *World Factbook* at https://www.cia.gov/library/publications/the-world-factbook/. In a small group, select a country and describe the information provided about that country on this site. How is this information useful to marketers? (AACSB: Communication; Use of IT; Reflective Thinking)

FOCUS ON Technology

Most small to midsize businesses have small or nonexistent information technology departments, but to remain competitive, all need cutting-edge computing capabilities. The global market for these IT needs is estimated at $500 billion, so IBM, a goliath company that does not yet serve this market, is developing a Global Applications Marketplace (also called Blue Business Platform) for small businesses. Through this platform, a small business can search and purchase software applications from independent software vendors around the world. However, local IBM partners will install and manage the applications for the business. When businesses enter information and receive recommendations through the Global Applications Marketplace, they receive product reviews along with access to an online IBM advisor. IBM is setting up hundreds of local vendor partners—called "innovation centers"—around the world, several of them in emerging markets. The Global Applications Marketplace is designed much like Apple's iTunes—customers will need an IBM server to use the system, just like consumers must have iPods to purchase music and movies from iTunes. While IBM is making the world available to small businesses, IBM's local channel partners bring it to their doorstep.

1. Read more about this initiative at www-03.ibm.com/press/us/en/pressrelease/24111.wss. Explain how IBM is delivering value for small to midsize businesses. How is it delivering value to independent software vendors? (AACSB: Communication; Use of IT; Reflective Thinking)

2. Who will be IBM's competitors in this market space? What advantage does IBM offer over these competitors? (AACSB: Communication; Reflective Thinking)

FOCUS ON Ethics

Advertising agency TBWA Worldwide came under fire in the months leading up to the 2008 Summer Olympics held in China for showing two sides of China in unrelated advertisements. On one side, ads developed for Adidas by TBWA's Beijing office showed athletes being lifted up by thousands of fans to depict Chinese pride. On the other side, ads developed by the agency's Paris office for Amnesty International depicted China's dark human rights side by showing Chinese athletes being tortured by authorities with the copy, "After the Olympic Games, the fight for human rights must go on." This second side is the one that Chinese authorities do not want the world to see, and it's the one that marketers supporting the games are tip-toeing around. Protests arose in cities around the world where the Olympic torch traveled—the route was even secretly altered in San Francisco amid fears of violent protests. China's Lenovo, the world's fourth largest PC firm, spent more than $100 million on Olympics sponsorship and related marketing activities in hopes of boosting sales in major markets like the United States. Other companies, such as Coca-Cola, McDonald's, and Samsung, were major sponsors of the Olympics, but fear of worldwide backlash for supporting China remains.

1. Was it right for businesses to sponsor the Olympic Games held in a country known for human rights violations? (AACSB: Communication; Ethical Reasoning)

2. Did sponsorship of the China Olympic Games help or harm businesses supporting them? (AACSB: Communication; Reflective Thinking)

MARKETING BY THE Numbers

Apple agreed to allow Hutchinson Telecommunications International (also known as Hong Kong 3) to sell its iPhone in Hong Kong beginning in 2008. Consumers there can purchase an 8 GB iPhone for HK$2,938 (that is, 2,938 Hong Kong dollars) with a 24-month service contract of HK$188 per month or receive a free iPhone with a 24-month service contract of HK$498 per month. The first plan offers 5,000 MB of voice and data, and the second provides 2,200 minutes of airtime and unlimited data. For more discussion of the financial and quantitative implications of marketing decisions, see Appendix 2, Marketing by the Numbers.

1. Determine the total revenue generated by a customer over the life of each 24-month contract option. Which one generates more revenue for Hong Kong 3? (AACSB: Communication; Analytical Reasoning)

2. Using a currency conversion Web site such as www.xe.com/ucc, convert the revenue generated by both plans to U.S. dollars. Compare this with iPhone plans available in the United States. Do U.S. consumers pay more or less? (AACSB: Communication; Use of IT)

VIDEO Case

Nivea

In 1911, German company Nivea introduced the revolutionary Nivea Crème in a simple blue tin. Today, that Crème is the centerpiece of a wide range of personal care products. The product line includes everything from soap, shampoo, and shaving products to baby care products, deodorant, and sunscreen. From small beginnings, the company's products are sold today in more than 150 countries worldwide.

But despite this global presence, most Nivea consumers believe that the products they buy are produced and marketed locally. Why? Although Nivea looks for commonalities between consumers around the globe, the company's marketers also recognize the differences between consumers in different markets. So Nivea adapts its marketing mix to reach local consumers while keeping its message consistent everywhere products are sold. This

globally consistent, locally customized marketing strategy has sold more than 11 billion tins of the traditional Nivea Crème.

After viewing the video featuring Nivea, answer the following questions about the company and the global marketplace:

1. Which of the five strategies for adapting products and promotion for the global market does Nivea employ? How does it do so?

2. Visit Nivea's Web site, www.nivea.com, and tour the sites for several different countries. How does Nivea market its products differently in different countries? How does the company maintain the consistency of its brand?

3. How is Nivea's consistent brand message relevant to different target markets?

COMPANY Case

Nokia: Envisioning a Connected World

What brand of cell phone do you have? If you're living in the United States, chances are it isn't a Nokia. But if you're living anywhere else in the world, it probably is. While the Finnish electronics company grabs only a single-digit slice of the U.S. cell phone pie, it dominates the global cell phone market with close to a 40 percent share.

Few companies dominate their industries the way that Nokia does. Half of the world's population holds an active cell phone—one in three of those phones is a Nokia. In 2007 alone, Nokia sold 437 million phones. That's 26 percent more phones than it sold the year before and almost as many phones as were sold by its four closest rivals—Samsung, Motorola, Sony-Ericsson, and LG—combined!

You might think that Nokia has accomplished this feat by being the product leader, always introducing the latest cutting-edge gadget. But Nokia has actually been slow to take advantage of design trends such as clamshell phones, "candy-bar" phones that slide open and closed, and ultrathin, blingy, multifunction phones. Rather, Nokia has risen to global dominance based on a simple, age-old strategy: sell basic products at low prices. Although Nokia markets a huge variety of cell phone models, it is best known for its trademarked easy-to-use block handset. Nokia mass-produces this basic reliable hardware cheaply and ships it in huge volumes to all parts of the world.

FROM PAPER TO CELL PHONES

While Finland's largest company leads the world's most high-tech industry, it is not a new company. In fact, Nokia started humbly in 1865 as a wood-pulp mill. A few mergers and a hundred years or

so later, the Nokia Corporation was making not only paper products, but bicycle and car tires, footwear, computers, televisions, and communications cables and equipment. Starting in the 1960s, one Nokia division made commercial and military mobile radios, a business unit that ultimately morphed into the cell phone giant that Nokia is today.

In 1984, Nokia marketed one of the world's first transportable phones, the Talkman. It weighed 11 pounds. Within three years, Nokia had slimmed the phone down to only 28 ounces. But that smaller model, the Cityman, cost a whopping $5,000! Believe it or not, even at that price, Nokia could hardly keep up with demand.

But the 1990s brought on a mobile phone explosion that vastly exceeded even the most optimistic predictions. The growth was accompanied by many challenges. During that period, Nokia focused on logistics and scale, two competencies that now serve as Nokia's major competitive advantages.

GAINING STRENGTH AS THE VOLUME LEADER

Based in Finland, Nokia's single most profit- and revenue-generating region is Europe. But the company's global strategy has been likened to that of Honda decades ago. Honda started by focusing on developing markets with small motorbikes. As the economies of such countries emerged and people could afford cars, they were already loyal to Honda.

Nokia has followed that same model. It sells phones in more than 150 countries. In most of those countries, it is the market leader. Nokia has a real knack for forging regional strategies based on the overall needs of consumers. But Nokia has filled its coffers by understanding the growth dynamics of specific emerging markets. Soren Peterson, Nokia's senior vice president of mobile phones, understands that concept more than anyone. He spends a great deal of his time studying the needs of consumers in emerging markets. And for the most part, these consumers need cheap phones.

Recognizing the need to make less expensive cell phones, Petersen is on a crusade throughout his company. Although it has been a bit of a battle, Petersen has convinced others that Nokia can make as much profit as the competition without charging more than $72 retail per phone. As a result, Nokia has relentlessly pursued the goal of bringing down costs and making phones less expensive.

Petersen cites an example of one cost-cutting tactic that sparked a chain of events at Nokia. While on a visit to Kenya, he stopped by an "excessively rural storefront," where he noticed that all products were displayed in plastic bags. When he asked the merchant where the boxes and manuals had gone, the man replied, "Make good fire."

Petersen quickly realized that packaging for many areas of the world barely needed to "last the journey." Packaging changes resulted in a savings of $147 million a year. "These numbers alone lit up a whole new drive within the business for these kinds of things," Petersen reported. Illustrating the magnitude of the large-scale manufacturer, Petersen explained that one cent in cost represents a million dollars for Nokia.

Among other notable discoveries for emerging markets, Petersen recognized that although many such customers spend a significant portion of their salary on one device, many of them will never know how to read or write. This led to an icon-based address book rather than the usual text-based version. Now, millions of people around the world identify their contacts by simple pictures, such as a soccer ball or a flower. And once it realized that many people in less-developed countries share their phones with up to a half-dozen other people, Nokia also added multiple phone books to its devices.

Because cell phone demand is growing so rapidly in emerging nations, Nokia will do well if it just holds its current market share in such countries. In India, for example, millions of people each month are buying their first cell phone. But Nokia isn't just holding on in such countries. In China alone, Nokia sold more than 70 million phones in 2007, a 38 percent increase over the previous year and a 35 percent share of the Chinese market. China also represented one-sixth of Nokia's unit sales.

Nokia shipped 150 million phones to emerging markets in 2007. For every five phones Nokia sells, one of them is an entry-level device, up from one in ten only two years ago. Most of those entry-level phones end up in developing countries. So whereas Europe accounts for 39 percent of Nokia's net sales, Asia, Latin America, Africa, and the Middle East account for 56 percent. The United States, with its market structure driven by the network carriers, produces only 5 percent of Nokia sales. With cell phone volume growing faster in developing regions, the gap will likely widen even more in coming years.

CAPITALIZING ON MARKET LEADERSHIP

Just as Honda used strength gained from selling motorbikes in emerging countries to establish itself as a manufacturer of virtually every kind of passenger vehicle, Nokia aims to do the same in the mobile phone industry. Although Nokia remains committed to the entry-level market and to emerging nations, it has developed a comprehensive global strategy. According to the company's own vision statement, that strategy has three facets: growing the number of people using Nokia devices, transforming the devices people use, and building new businesses.

For the first part of this plan, Nokia projects that global cell phone usage will almost double by 2015 to 5 billion users. Even if Nokia simply holds its current share of the market, that means that approximately 1.7 billion people will be holding Nokia phones, 67 percent more than today.

As for transforming the devices that people use, Nokia is becoming more than just an entry-level phone provider. Of its 112,000 employees, 30,000 of them work in research and development. Nokia hopes that as its customers in developing nations gain the resources, they will trade up and stay with Nokia. It's also aware of the changing needs and trends in Europe, the United States, and the rest of the developed world.

To that end, Nokia may just become the first company to release a serious contender to Apple's iPhone. Internally code-named the "Tube," Nokia's new phone should hit the market in the second half of 2008. The company says only that its smart phone will feature many of the trademarks associated with its next-generation series of phones, including a global positioning system, Java application support, Web browsing, 3G data transmission speeds, and of course, a touch screen.

Whereas Apple's iPhone sales of more than 4 million units in less than a year have more than met expectations, one Nokia vice president was heard to say, "We've done that since we've had dinner last Friday." But whereas Apple's sales represent a very small share of the total market, Nokia's answer to this product indicates a recognition that this niche may grow into something much more substantial.

Nokia has also been experimenting with nanotechnology and flexible materials. At the Museum of Modern Art in New York, it recently unveiled a phone called the "Morph" as part of a "Design and the Elastic Mind" exhibit. The phone literally flexes and twists—you can wrap it around your wrist like a watch. Although this exact phone may never reach the market, it suggests that future Nokia phones might become far thinner, more stretchable, more durable, and more energy-efficient.

Nokia also recognizes that the biggest trends in mobile devices are music, navigation, and gaming. Focusing on these activities, it is collaborating with the best minds in the business to find ways to add value for the consumer. Nokia appears poised to take advantage of the convergence of the Internet, media, and the cell phone. In fact, at its 2008 stockholder meeting, Nokia announced a shift to the Internet business as a whole. It no longer wants to be seen as just a phone company. It wants to be a company that keeps people connected to everything important in their lives, whether that's other people, information, commerce, or entertainment.

This new emphasis creates a very logical transition to the third leg of Nokia's strategy, building new businesses. Last year, Nokia sold more than 200 million camera phones (far more than Canon's camera sales) and 146 million music phones (Apple sold only 52 million iPods). Thus, through its mobile handsets, Nokia can claim to sell more computers, portable music players, and cameras than any other company. However, it has yet to find a way to secure a steady income stream from its devices once they are in place.

Nokia is spending a lot of money and resources on an ambitious plan that it calls "Ovi." The goal is to accomplish something that has eluded many mobile network operators—building a profitable business in mobile services. Nokia has acquired software companies like digital map maker Navteq. It hopes that satellite location services will be big in the future, charting a new path to sales and profits. Nokia has also lured executives from Yahoo!, Microsoft, eBay, and IBM to help build this business venture.

In expanding beyond the borders of its more traditional business, Nokia has a lot going for it. Beyond selling lots of phones, it is also one of the most trusted brands in the world. With a brand value of more than $33 billion, Nokia is now the fifth most valuable brand in the world. "The trust is so high, it has less trouble than other brands getting a customer back who may have tried out a competing brand," says a branding expert. And Anssi Vanjoki, head of Nokia's multimedia business group, quickly points out that the company's push into new products and services is not a case of the brand stretching for acceptance in new segments, like Volkswagen trying to sell luxury cars. Rather, it is all simply a natural extension of the company's product line to better meet the needs of its customers. "[We're] delivering on what our customers expected from us all along—there's a big difference in terms of managing your brand."

Questions for Discussion

1. Does Nokia have a truly global strategy, rather than just a series of regional strategies? Explain.

2. Consider the different global marketing environments discussed in the text. How do these environments differ in developing versus developed countries?

3. Discuss Nokia's global strategy in terms of the five global product and communications strategies.

4. Can competitors easily replicate Nokia's global strategy? Why or why not?

5. Will Nokia's planned expansion into other products and services work? Explain.

Sources: Lionel Laurent, "Nokia Still Looks Strong," *Forbes*, April 17, 2008, accessed online at www.forbes.com; Matt Kapko, "Nokia World: Strategies for the U.S., Emerging Markets," *RCR Wireless News*, December 17, 2007, p. 16; James Ashton, "Emerging Markets Help Nokia to Win Race For Mobile Supremacy," *Sunday Times (London)*, January 27, 2008, p. 11; David Kiley, "Best Global Brands," *BusinessWeek*, August 6, 2007, p. 56; Lionel Laurent, "Nokia Intends to Take a Bite Out of Apple," *Forbes*, April 9, 2008, accessed online at www.forbes.com; and www.nokia.com, accessed September 2008.

Chapter 20

Part 1   Defining Marketing and the Marketing Process (Chapters 1, 2)
Part 2   Understanding the Marketplace and Consumers (Chapters 3, 4, 5, 6)
Part 3   Designing a Customer-Driven Strategy and Mix (Chapters 7, 8, 9, 10, 11, 12, 13, 14, 15, 16, 17)
Part 4   Extending Marketing (Chapters 18, 19, 20)

Sustainable Marketing

Social Responsibility and Ethics

Chapter PREVIEW

In this final chapter, we'll examine the concepts of sustainable marketing, meeting the needs of consumers, businesses, and society—now and in the future—through socially and environmentally responsible marketing actions. We'll start by defining sustainable marketing and then look at some common criticisms of marketing as it impacts individual consumers and other businesses. Next, we'll examine consumerism, environmentalism, and other citizen and public actions that promote sustainable marketing. Finally, we'll see how companies themselves can benefit from proactively pursuing sustainable marketing practices that bring value not just to individual customers but to society as a whole. You'll see that sustainable marketing actions are more than just the right thing to do; they're also good for business.

First, let's look at an example of sustainable marketing in action. When it comes to socially and environmentally responsible practices, few companies meet the standard set by outdoor gear and apparel maker Patagonia. Here's a story about this forward-looking company's latest eco-initiative, called the Footprint Chronicles.

It seems like a typical Southern California scene: On a sunny afternoon, a camera-toting woman has tracked her subjects to an obscure corner of South Los Angeles, and she's snapping photos like a paparazzo. But she's no celeb stalker—her subjects are towers of Turkish cotton and pallets of organic yarn. Jill Dumain, director of environmental analysis for apparel company Patagonia, is investigating one of the company's T-shirt suppliers, Nature USA. It's part of an initiative called the Footprint Chronicles, an effort to document and share with customers information about the environmental effects of every link in the company's supply chain.

Going green is an increasingly big part of business these days, but you wouldn't expect Patagonia to have to worry much. It's a longtime leader in sustainability, founded in 1973 by environmentalist Yvon Chouinard. From the start, Patagonia has pursued a passionately held social responsibility mission.

> For us at Patagonia, a love of wild and beautiful places demands participation in the fight to save them, and to help reverse the steep decline in the overall environmental health of our planet. Our reason for being is to make the best product and cause no unnecessary harm—to use business to inspire and implement solutions to the environmental crisis. Yet we're keenly aware that everything we do as a business—or have done in our name—leaves its mark on the environment. As yet, there is no such thing as a sustainable business but every day we take steps to lighten our footprint and do less harm.

As early as 1991, before it was fashionable, Patagonia began a comprehensive Environmental Review Process, in which it examined all of the methods and materials used in making the company's clothing. Each year since 1985, the company has given away 10 percent of its pretax profits to support environmental causes. Today, it donates its time, services, and at least 1 percent of sales or 10 percent pretax profits, whichever is greater, to hundreds of grassroots environmental groups all over the world who work to help reverse the environmental tide.

Yet in this new age of consumer awareness, as customers have become eco-savvier, Patagonia has gotten more and more questions about its products' origins that it can't answer. "The green marketplace has become crowded," says Dumain. "We've had to learn to communicate in circles that are very different than they were 10 to 15 years ago, which is good." Good in more ways than one: The footprint project, intended as a consumer-education experiment, has put the company's design and manufacturing process under the eco-microscope. Patagonia has been forced to examine how green it actually is—and where it can improve.

In May 2007, Chouinard challenged a group of 10 employees to

Green gumshoe Jill Dumain, Patagonia's director of environmental analysis, leads the company's eco-efforts.

track five products from the design studio to the raw-materials stage to Patagonia's Nevada distribution center. His gumshoes canvassed the globe, from observing yarn spinners in Thailand and visiting a 50,000-employee footwear factory in China to touring a fiber-manufacturing facility in North Carolina. In the fall of that year, Patagonia quietly went live with a microsite at patagonia.com that features detailed footprint information and videos (also available on YouTube). The paths of 10 more products, including the Nature USA organic-cotton T-shirt, went up in 2008.

Patagonia vowed to share whatever it found, good and bad. One positive surprise was the low energy expenditure of transporting the company's products, usually thought to be a dirty part of the process. Patagonia discovered that shipping by sea represented less than 1 percent of the total energy used in its supply chain. "If we had followed environmental chatter and spent all that time shortening our supply chains, it would have had a huge impact on our product quality," Dumain says. "To realize that our conservation efforts needed to be focused elsewhere was really freeing."

Patagonia's actual manufacturing, however, devoured more energy than expected and sometimes created eco-unfriendly by-products. For instance, as the team tracked the production of the Eco Rain Shell jacket, it focused on perfluorooctanoic acid (PFOA)—a chemical that accumulates in the bloodstream and may be toxic—which is found in water-repellent membranes and coatings used in Patagonia parkas. The company believed that using PFOA-free materials would sacrifice performance. But that was little comfort to consumers who learned about PFOA through the Patagonia's own Footprint Chronicles Web site. One customer wrote an e-mail demanding that "Eco" be dropped from the product's name.

The footprint-chronicling process highlights the complexity of modern technology. Patagonia is trying to remove PFOA from its lines—by fall, the PFOA-containing membranes will be replaced by polyester and polyurethane, with no performance lost, it says—but it has not found a viable alternative to the existing coatings. "We don't want to sacrifice quality for environmental reasons," Dumain says. "If a garment is thrown away sooner due to a lack of durability, we haven't solved any environmental problem."

> When it comes to sustainable marketing, few companies can meet the standard set by outdoor gear and apparel maker Patagonia. Its latest eco-initiative, The Footprint Chronicles, raises the sustainability bar even further.

Patagonia's footprint efforts reflect a newly refined understanding of corporate social responsibility. "You're now responsible for the impacts of your suppliers," says the executive editor of the blog Greenbiz.com, "and sometimes your suppliers' suppliers, your customers, and their customers."

> Patagonia's reason for being is to make the best product and cause no unnecessary harm—to use business to inspire and implement solutions to the environmental crisis.

Patagonia admits that its findings are limited; only primary materials are traced, and no packaging is evaluated. The company also allows that by making production information public, it gives its competitors access too. Dumain concludes that the benefits of openness outweigh the costs, because the company wants to spur others to action: "Our influence is larger than our impact. If we're willing to share that information, it [multiplies exponentially]."

Dumain notes that a group of firms with progressive sustainability agendas—Stonyfield Farm, Aveda, Ben & Jerry's, Seventh Generation—have long informally shared best practices. "These companies have been working together for years to raise the [environmental responsibility] bar," says the manager of natural-resources use at Ben & Jerry's. "That's where Patagonia is with these Footprint Chronicles—that's the new bar."[1]

Responsible marketers discover what consumers want and respond with market offerings that create value for buyers in order to capture value in return. The *marketing concept* is a philosophy of customer value and mutual gain. Its practice leads the economy by an invisible hand to satisfy the many and changing needs of millions of consumers.

Not all marketers follow the marketing concept, however. In fact, some companies use questionable marketing practices that serve their own rather than consumers' interests. Moreover, even well-intended marketing actions that meet the current needs of some consumers may cause immediate or future harm to other consumers or the larger society. Responsible marketers must consider whether their actions are *sustainable* in the longer run.

Objective Outline

Consider the sale of sport-utility vehicles (SUVs). These large vehicles meet the immediate needs of many drivers in terms of capacity, power, and utility. However, SUV sales involve larger questions of consumer safety and environmental responsibility. For example, in accidents, SUVs are more likely to kill both their occupants and the occupants of other vehicles. Research shows that SUV occupants are three times more likely to die from their vehicle rolling than are occupants of sedans.[2] Moreover, gas-guzzling SUVs use more than their fair share of the world's energy and other resources and contribute disproportionately to pollution and congestion problems, creating costs that must be borne by both current and future generations.[3]

This chapter examines *sustainable* marketing and the social and environmental effects of private marketing practices. First, we address the question: What is sustainable marketing and why is it important?

Sustainable Marketing (pp 584–585)

> **Author Comment** | Marketers must think beyond immediate customer satisfaction and business performance toward strategies that preserve the world for future generations.

Sustainable marketing calls for meeting the present needs of consumers and businesses while also preserving or enhancing the ability of future generations to meet their needs. **Figure 20.1** compares the sustainable marketing concept with other marketing concepts we studied in earlier chapters.[4]

The *marketing concept* recognizes that organizations thrive from day to day by determining the current needs and wants of target group customers and fulfilling those needs and wants more effectively and efficiently than the competition. It focuses on meeting the company's short-term sales, growth, and profit needs by giving customers what they want now. However, satisfying consumers' immediate needs and desires doesn't always serve the future best interests of either customers or the business.

For example, McDonald's early decisions to market tasty but fat- and salt-laden fast foods created immediate satisfaction for customers and sales and profits for the company. However, critics assert that McDonald's and other fast-food chains contributed to a longer-term national obesity epidemic, damaging consumer health and burdening the

Sustainable marketing
Marketing that meets the present needs of consumers and businesses while also preserving or enhancing the ability of future generations to meet their needs.

584

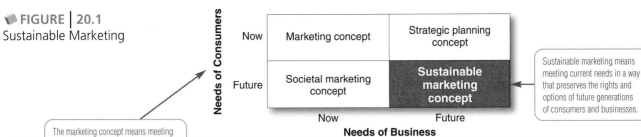

⬛ FIGURE | 20.1
Sustainable Marketing

The marketing concept means meeting the current needs of both customers and the company. But that can sometimes mean compromising the future of both.

Sustainable marketing means meeting current needs in a way that preserves the rights and options of future generations of consumers and businesses.

national health system. In turn, many consumers began looking for healthier eating options, causing a slump in the fast-food industry. Beyond issues of ethical behavior and social welfare, McDonald's was also criticized for the sizable environmental footprint of its vast global operations, everything from wasteful packaging and solid waste creation to inefficient energy use in its stores. Thus, McDonald's strategy was not sustainable in terms of either consumer or company benefit.

Whereas the *societal marketing concept* identified in Figure 20.1 considers the future welfare of consumers and the *strategic planning concept* considers future company needs, the *sustainable marketing concept* considers both. Sustainable marketing calls for socially and environmentally responsible actions that meet both the immediate and future needs of customers and the company.

For example, in recent years, ▲McDonald's has responded with a more sustainable "Plan to Win" strategy of diversifying into salads, fruits, grilled chicken, low-fat milk, and other healthy fare. Also, after a seven-year search for healthier cooking oil, McDonald's phased out traditional artery-clogging trans fats without compromising the taste of its french fries. And the company launched a major multifaceted education campaign—called "it's what i eat and what i do . . . I'm lovin' it"—to help consumers better understand the keys to living balanced, active lifestyles.

The "Plan to Win" strategy also addresses environmental issues. For example, it calls for food-supply sustainability, reduced and environmentally sustainable packaging, reuse and recycling, and more responsible store designs. McDonald's has even developed an environmental scorecard that rates its suppliers' performance in areas such as water use, energy use, and solid waste management.

McDonald's more sustainable strategy is benefiting the company as well as its customers. Since announcing its Plan to Win strategy, McDonald's sales have increased by 57 percent and profits have nearly tripled. And for the past three years, the company has been included in the Dow Jones Sustainability Index, recognizing its commitment to sustainable economic, environmental, and social performance. Thus, McDonald's is well-positioned for a sustainably profitable future.[5]

Truly sustainable marketing requires a smooth-functioning marketing system in which consumers, companies, public policy makers, and others work together to ensure socially responsible and ethical marketing actions. Unfortunately, however, the marketing system doesn't always work smoothly. The following sections examine several sustainability questions: What are the most frequent social criticisms of marketing? What steps have private citizens taken to curb marketing ills? What steps have legislators and government agencies taken to promote sustainable marketing? What steps have enlightened companies taken to carry out socially responsible and ethical marketing that creates sustainable value for both individual customers and society as a whole?

BE OPEN TO NEW POSSIBILITIES.

NEW ASIAN SALAD i'm lovin' it

▲ Sustainable marketing: McDonald's "Plan to Win" strategy has both created sustainable value for customers and positioned the company for a profitable future.

Author | In most ways, we all
Comment | benefit greatly from
marketing activities. However, like
most other human endeavors,
marketing has its flaws. Here, we
present both sides of some of the
most common criticisms of marketing.

Social Criticisms of Marketing (pp 586–594)

Marketing receives much criticism. Some of this criticism is justified; much is not. Social critics claim that certain marketing practices hurt individual consumers, society as a whole, and other business firms.

Marketing's Impact on Individual Consumers

Consumers have many concerns about how well the American marketing system serves their interests. Surveys usually show that consumers hold mixed or even slightly unfavorable attitudes toward marketing practices. Consumer advocates, government agencies, and other critics have accused marketing of harming consumers through high prices, deceptive practices, high-pressure selling, shoddy or unsafe products, planned obsolescence, and poor service to disadvantaged consumers. Such questionable marketing practices are not sustainable in terms of long-term consumer or business welfare.

High Prices

Many critics charge that the American marketing system causes prices to be higher than they would be under more "sensible" systems. They point to three factors—*high costs of distribution*, *high advertising and promotion costs*, and *excessive markups*.

High Costs of Distribution. A long-standing charge is that greedy channel intermediaries mark up prices beyond the value of their services. Critics charge that there are too many intermediaries, that intermediaries are inefficient, or that they provide unnecessary or duplicate services. As a result, distribution costs too much, and consumers pay for these excessive costs in the form of higher prices.

How do resellers answer these charges? They argue that intermediaries do work that would otherwise have to be done by manufacturers or consumers. Markups reflect services that consumers themselves want—more convenience, larger stores and assortments, more service, longer store hours, return privileges, and others. In fact, they argue, retail competition is so intense that margins are actually quite low. For example, after taxes, supermarket chains are typically left with barely 1 percent profit on their sales. If some resellers try to charge too much relative to the value they add, other resellers will step in with lower prices. Low-price stores such as Wal-Mart, Costco, and other discounters pressure their competitors to operate efficiently and keep their prices down.

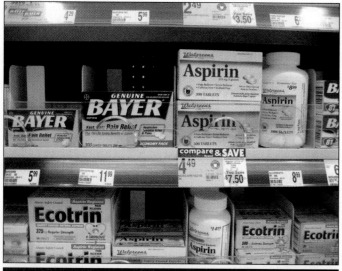

▲ A heavily promoted brand of aspirin sells for much more than a virtually identical nonbranded or store-branded product. Critics charge that promotion adds only psychological value to the product rather than functional value.

High Advertising and Promotion Costs. Modern marketing is also accused of pushing up prices to finance heavy advertising and sales promotion. ▲For example, a few dozen tablets of a heavily promoted brand of pain reliever sell for the same price as 100 tablets of less-promoted brands. Differentiated products—cosmetics, detergents, toiletries—include promotion and packaging costs that can amount to 40 percent or more of the manufacturer's price to the retailer. Critics charge that much of the packaging and promotion adds only psychological value to the product rather than functional value.

Marketers respond that advertising does add to product costs. But it also adds value by informing potential buyers of the availability and merits of a brand. Brand name products may cost more, but branding gives buyers assurances of consistent quality. Moreover, consumers can usually buy functional versions of products at lower prices. However, they *want* and are willing to pay more for products that also provide psychological benefits—that make them feel wealthy, attractive, or special. Also, heavy advertising and promotion may be necessary for a firm to match competitors' efforts—the business would lose "share of mind" if it did not match competitive spending. At the same time, companies are cost conscious about promotion and try to spend their money wisely.

Excessive Markups. Critics also charge that some companies mark up goods excessively. They point to the drug industry, where a pill costing five cents to make may cost the consumer $2 to buy. They point to the pricing tactics of funeral homes that prey on the confused emotions of bereaved relatives and to the high charges for auto repair and other services.

Marketers respond that most businesses try to deal fairly with consumers because they want to build customer relationships and repeat business. Most consumer abuses are unintentional. When shady marketers do take advantage of consumers, they should be reported to Better Business Bureaus and to state and federal agencies. Marketers also respond that consumers often don't understand the reasons for high markups. For example, pharmaceutical markups must cover the costs of purchasing, promoting, and distributing existing medicines plus the high research and development costs of formulating and testing new medicines. As pharmaceuticals company GlaxoSmithKline states in its ads, "Today's medicines finance tomorrow's miracles."

Deceptive Practices

Marketers are sometimes accused of deceptive practices that lead consumers to believe they will get more value than they actually do. Deceptive practices fall into three groups: pricing, promotion, and packaging. *Deceptive pricing* includes practices such as falsely advertising "factory" or "wholesale" prices or a large price reduction from a phony high retail list price. *Deceptive promotion* includes practices such as misrepresenting the product's features or performance or luring the customers to the store for a bargain that is out of stock. *Deceptive packaging* includes exaggerating package contents through subtle design, using misleading labeling, or describing size in misleading terms.

Deceptive practices have led to legislation and other consumer protection actions. For example, in 1938 Congress reacted to such blatant deceptions as Fleischmann's Yeast's claim to straighten crooked teeth by enacting the Wheeler-Lea Act giving the Federal Trade Commission (FTC) power to regulate "unfair or deceptive acts or practices." The FTC has published several guidelines listing deceptive practices. Despite new regulations, some critics argue that deceptive claims are still the norm. ▲Consider the glut of "environmental responsibility" claims marketers are now making:

Are you a victim of "greenwashing"? Biodegradable, eco-friendly, recycled, green, carbon neutral, carbon offsets, made from sustainable resources—such phrases are popping up more and more on products worldwide, leading many to question their validity. Last year, for example, the FTC has started reviewing its "Green Guides"—voluntary guidelines that it asks companies to adopt to help them avoid breaking laws against deceptive marketing. "We have seen a surge in environmental claims," says a lawyer at the FTC's Bureau of Consumer Protection. TerraChoice Environmental Marketing, which advises companies on green positioning, reviewed claims companies made about 1,018 widely sold goods. Using measures created by government agencies, TerraChoice concluded that all but one of the claims were false or could be misleading. "There is a lot going on there that just isn't right," says one environmental trend-watcher. "If truly green products have a hard time differentiating themselves from fake ones, then this whole notion of a green market will fall apart," says a Terra Choice executive.[6]

▲ Deceptive practices: Despite plenty of regulation, some critics argue that deceptive claims are still the norm. Consider all of those "green marketing" claims.

The toughest problem is defining what is "deceptive." For instance, an advertiser's claim that its powerful laundry detergent "makes your washing machine 10 feet tall," showing a surprised homemaker watching her appliance burst through her laundry room ceiling, isn't intended to be taken literally. Instead, the advertiser might claim, it is "puffery"—innocent exaggeration for effect. One noted marketing thinker, Theodore Levitt, once claimed that advertising puffery and alluring imagery are bound to occur— and that they may even be desirable: "There is hardly a company that would not go down in ruin if it refused to provide fluff, because nobody will buy pure functionality. . . . Worse, it denies . . . people's honest needs and values. Without distortion, embellishment, and elaboration, life would be drab, dull, anguished, and at its existential worst."[7]

However, others claim that puffery and alluring imagery can harm consumers in subtle ways. Think about the popular and long-running MasterCard Priceless commercials that paint pictures of consumers fulfilling their priceless dreams despite the costs. Similarly, Visa invites consumers to "Enjoy life's opportunities." Both suggest that your credit card can make it happen. But critics charge that such imagery by credit card companies encourages a spend-now-pay-later attitude that causes many consumers to *over*use their cards. The critics point to statistics showing that 60 percent of Americans are carrying a continuing balance on their credit cards and that 11.8 million bank credit card accounts are now delinquent. One in every seven Americans today is dealing with a debt collector because they can't make their payments.[8]

Marketers argue that most companies avoid deceptive practices. Because such practices harm their business in the long run, they simply aren't sustainable. Profitable customer relationships are built upon a foundation of value and trust. If consumers do not get what they expect, they will switch to more reliable products. In addition, consumers usually protect themselves from deception. Most consumers recognize a marketer's selling intent and are careful when they buy, sometimes to the point of not believing completely true product claims.

High-Pressure Selling

Salespeople are sometimes accused of high-pressure selling that persuades people to buy goods they had no thought of buying. It is often said that insurance, real estate, and used cars are *sold*, not *bought*. Salespeople are trained to deliver smooth, canned talks to entice purchase. They sell hard because sales contests promise big prizes to those who sell the most.

But in most cases, marketers have little to gain from high-pressure selling. Such tactics may work in one-time selling situations for short-term gain. However, most selling involves building long-term relationships with valued customers. High-pressure or deceptive selling can do serious damage to such relationships. For example, imagine a Procter & Gamble account manager trying to pressure a Wal-Mart buyer, or an IBM salesperson trying to browbeat a General Electric information technology manager. It simply wouldn't work.

Shoddy, Harmful, or Unsafe Products

Another criticism concerns poor product quality or function. One complaint is that, too often, products are not made well and services are not performed well. A second complaint is that many products deliver little benefit, or that they might even be harmful.

For example, think again about the fast-food industry. Many critics blame the plentiful supply of fat-laden, high calorie fast-food fare for the nation's rapidly growing obesity epidemic. Studies show that some 66 percent of American adults and 17 percent of children are overweight or obese. The number of people in the United States who are 100 pounds or more overweight quintupled between 2000 and 2005, from 1 adult in 200 to 1 in 40. This weight increase comes despite repeated medical studies showing that excess weight brings increased risks for heart disease, diabetes, and other maladies, even cancer.[9]

The critics are quick to fault what they see as greedy food marketers who are cashing in on vulnerable consumers, turning us into a nation of overeaters. Some food marketers

▲ Harmful products: Is Hardee's being socially irresponsible or simply practicing good marketing by giving customers a big juicy burger that clearly pings their taste buds? Judging by the nutrition calculator at its Web site, the company certainly isn't hiding the nutritional facts.

are looking pretty much guilty as charged. ▲Take Hardee's, for example:[10]

At a time when other fast-food chains such as McDonald's, Wendy's, and Subway were getting "leaner," Hardee's introduced the decadent Thickburger, featuring a third of a pound of Angus beef. It followed up with the *Monster* Thickburger: two-thirds of a pound of Angus beef, four strips of bacon, and three slices of American cheese, all nestled in a buttered sesame-seed bun slathered with mayonnaise! The Monster Thickburger weighs in at a whopping 1,410 calories and 107 grams of fat, far greater than the government's recommended fat intake for an entire day. Surely, you say, Hardee's made a colossal blunder here. Not so! Since introducing the Thickburger, Hardee's has experienced healthy sales increases and even fatter profits.

So, should Hardee's hang its head in shame? Is it being socially irresponsible by aggressively promoting overindulgence to ill-informed or unwary consumers? Or is it simply practicing good marketing, creating more value for its customers by offering a big juicy burger that clearly pings their taste buds and letting them make their own choices? Critics claim the former; industry defenders claim the latter. Hardee's diligently targets young men aged 18 to 34, consumers capable of making their own decisions about health and well-being. And Hardee's certainly isn't hiding the nutritional facts. Here's how it describes Thickburgers on its Web site:

There's only one thing that can slay the hunger of a young guy on the move: the Thickburger line at Hardee's. With nine cravable varieties, including the classic Original Thickburger and the monument to decadence, the Monster Thickburger, quick-service goes premium with 100% Angus beef and all the fixings. . . . If you want to indulge in a big, delicious, juicy burger, look no further than Hardee's.

Hardee's even offers a nutrition calculator on its Web site showing the calories, fat, and other content of all its menu items. In this case, as in many matters of social responsibility, what's right and wrong may be a matter of opinion.

A third complaint concerns product safety. Product safety has been a problem for several reasons, including company indifference, increased product complexity, and poor quality control. For years, Consumers Union—the nonprofit testing and information organization that publishes the *Consumer Reports* magazine and Web site—has reported various hazards in tested products: electrical dangers in appliances, carbon monoxide poisoning from room heaters, injury risks from lawn mowers, and faulty automobile design, among many others. The organization's testing and other activities have helped consumers make better buying decisions and encouraged businesses to eliminate product flaws.

However, most manufacturers *want* to produce quality goods. The way a company deals with product quality and safety problems can damage or help its reputation. Companies selling poor-quality or unsafe products risk damaging conflicts with consumer groups and regulators. Unsafe products can result in product liability suits and large awards for damages. More fundamentally, consumers who are unhappy with a firm's products may avoid future purchases and talk other consumers into doing the same. Thus, quality missteps can have severe consequences and are not consistent with sustainable marketing. Today's marketers know that good quality results in customer value and satisfaction, which in turn creates sustainable customer relationships.

Planned Obsolescence

▲Critics also have charged that some companies practice planned obsolescence, causing their products to become obsolete before they actually should need replacement. They accuse some producers of using materials and components that will break, wear, rust, or rot sooner than they should. One writer put it this way: "The marvels of modern technology include the development of a soda can which, when discarded, will last forever—and a . . . car, which, when properly cared for, will rust out in two or three years."[11]

Others are charged with continually changing consumer concepts of acceptable styles to encourage more and earlier buying. An obvious example is constantly changing clothing fashions. Still others are accused of introducing planned streams of new products that make older models obsolete. Critics claim that this occurs in the consumer electronics and computer industries. For example, consider this writer's tale about an aging cell phone:[12]

▲ Planned obsolescence: Almost everyone, it seems, has a drawer filled with the detritus of yesterday's hottest product, now reduced to the status of fossils.

Today, most people, myself included, are all agog at the wondrous outpouring of new technology, from cell phones to iPods, iPhones, laptops, BlackBerries, and on and on. ▲Even though I am techno-incompetent and like to think I shun these new devices, I actually have a drawer filled with the detritus of yesterday's hottest product, now reduced to the status of fossils. I have video cameras that use tapes no longer available, laptops with programs incompatible with anything on today's market, portable CD players I no longer use, and more. But what really upsets me is how quickly some still-useful gadgets become obsolete, at least in the eyes of their makers.

I recently embarked on an epic search for a cord to plug into my wife's cell phone to recharge it. We were traveling and the poor phone kept bleating that it was running low and the battery needed recharging. So, we began a search—from big-box technology superstores to smaller suppliers and the cell phone companies themselves—all to no avail. Finally, a salesperson told my wife, "That's an old model, so we don't stock the charger any longer." "But I only bought it last year," she sputtered. "Yeah, like I said, that's an old model," he replied without a hint of irony or sympathy. So, in the world of insanely rapid obsolescence, each successive model is incompatible with the previous one it replaces. The proliferation and sheer waste of this type of practice is mind-boggling.

Marketers respond that consumers *like* style changes; they get tired of the old goods and want a new look in fashion. Or they *want* the latest high-tech innovations, even if older models still work. No one has to buy the new product, and if too few people like it, it will simply fail. Finally, most companies do not design their products to break down earlier, because they do not want to lose customers to other brands. Instead, they seek constant improvement to ensure that products will consistently meet or exceed customer expectations. Much of the so-called planned obsolescence is the working of the competitive and technological forces in a free society—forces that lead to ever-improving goods and services.

Poor Service to Disadvantaged Consumers

Finally, the American marketing system has been accused of serving disadvantaged consumers poorly. For example, critics claim that the urban poor often have to shop in smaller stores that carry inferior goods and charge higher prices. The presence of large national chain stores in low-income neighborhoods would help to keep prices down. However, the critics accuse major chain retailers of "redlining," drawing a red line around disadvantaged neighborhoods and avoiding placing stores there.

Similar redlining charges have been leveled at the insurance, consumer lending, banking, and health care industries. Home and auto insurers have been accused of assigning higher premiums to people with poor credit ratings. The insurers claim that individuals with bad credit tend to make more insurance claims, and that this justifies charging them higher premiums. However, critics and consumer advocates have accused the insurers of a new form of redlining.

▲ Critics have accused mortgage lenders of "reverse redlining," targeting disadvantaged consumers with subprime mortgages that they couldn't afford.

Says one writer, "This is a new excuse for denying coverage to the poor, elderly, and minorities."[13]

More recently, consumer advocates have charged that mortgage companies have been taking advantage of the working poor, especially African Americans, by offering them subprime mortgages rather than fixed-rate mortgages to purchase homes. Subprime mortgages, also known as adjustable rate mortgages, have attractive low initial interest rates, but the rates fluctuate after a set time, usually upward. Recently, as the interest rates climbed and home values fell, many owners who could no longer afford their mortgage payments saw their homes go into foreclosure, creating a subprime mortgage crisis.

Many critics charge that such subprime loans should be treated as bias crimes. ▲They claim that mortgage lenders used "reverse redlining." Instead of staying away from people in poor urban areas, they targeted and exploited them, especially working-class black consumers, by steering them toward subprime loans even though many qualified for safer fixed-rate loans. A recent report issued by United for a Fair Economy claims that people of color are three times more likely than other groups to have subprime loans. It estimates that the subprime mortgage crisis will drain $213 billion in wealth from black Americans—the "greatest wealth loss in modern U.S. history." In response, the NAACP filed a racial discrimination suit against 18 mortgage providers, including WaMu, Citi, and GMAC.[14]

Clearly, better marketing systems must be built to service disadvantaged consumers. In fact, many marketers profitably target such consumers with legitimate goods and services that create real value. In cases in which marketers do not step in to fill the void, the government likely will. For example, the FTC has taken action against sellers who advertise false values, wrongfully deny services, or charge disadvantaged customers too much.

Marketing's Impact on Society as a Whole

The American marketing system has been accused of adding to several "evils" in American society at large. Advertising has been a special target—so much so that the American Association of Advertising Agencies once launched a campaign to defend advertising against what it felt to be common but untrue criticisms.

False Wants and Too Much Materialism

Critics have charged that the marketing system urges too much interest in material possessions, and that Americans' love affair with worldly possessions is not sustainable. People are judged by what they *own* rather than by who they *are*. This drive for wealth and possessions hit new highs in the 1980s and 1990s, when phrases such as "greed is good" and "shop till you drop" seemed to characterize the times.

In the current decade, many social scientists have noted a reaction against the opulence and waste of the previous decades and a return to more basic values and social commitment. However, our infatuation with material things continues.

> If you made a graph of American life since the end of World War II, every line concerning money and the things that money can buy would soar upward, a statistical monument to materialism. Inflation-adjusted income per American has almost tripled. The size of the typical new house has more than doubled. A two-car garage was once a goal; now we're nearly a three-car nation. Designer everything, personal electronics, and other items that didn't even exist a half-century ago are now affordable. Although our time spent shopping has dropped in recent years to just three hours a week, American households currently spend on average $1.22 for every $1 earned. Some consumers will let nothing stand between them and their acquisitions. Recently, in a Florida

Wal-Mart, post-Thanksgiving shoppers rushing to buy DVD players (on sale for $29) knocked down a woman, trampled her, and left her unconscious.[15]

The critics do not view this interest in material things as a natural state of mind but rather as a matter of false wants created by marketing. Businesses hire Madison Avenue to stimulate people's desires for goods, and Madison Avenue uses the mass media to create materialistic models of the good life. People work harder to earn the necessary money. Their purchases increase the output of American industry, and industry in turn uses Madison Avenue to stimulate more desire for the industrial output.

Thus, marketing is seen as creating false wants that benefit industry more than they benefit consumers. "In the world of consumerism, marketing is there to promote consumption," says one marketing critic. It is "inevitable that marketing will promote overconsumption, and from this, a psychologically, as well as ecologically, unsustainable world." ▲Some critics even take their concerns to the streets.[16]

▲ Materialism: With the zeal of a street-corner preacher and the schmaltz of a street-corner Santa, Reverend Billy—founder of the Church of Stop Shopping—will tell anyone who will listen that people are walking willingly into the hellfires of consumption.

For a decade Bill Talen, also known as Reverend Billy, has taken to the streets, exhorting people to resist temptation—the temptation to shop. With the zeal of a street-corner preacher and the schmaltz of a street-corner Santa, Reverend Billy will tell anyone willing to listen that people are walking willingly into the hellfires of consumption. Reverend Billy, leader of the Church of Stop Shopping believes that shoppers have almost no resistance to the media messages that encourage them, around the clock, to want things and buy them. He sees a population lost in consumption, the meaning of individual existence vanished in a fog of wanting, buying, and owning too many things, ultimately leading to a "Shopocalypse." Sporting a televangelist's pompadour, a priest's collar, and a white megaphone, Reverend Billy is often accompanied by his gospel choir when he strides into stores he considers objectionable or shows up at protests like the annual post-Thanksgiving Buy Nothing Parade in front of Macy's in Manhattan. When the choir, which is made up of volunteers, erupts in song, it is hard to ignore: "Stop shopping! Stop shopping! We will never shop again!"

Such criticisms overstate the power of business to create needs. People have strong defenses against advertising and other marketing tools. Marketers are most effective when they appeal to existing wants rather than when they attempt to create new ones. Furthermore, people seek information when making important purchases and often do not rely on single sources. Even minor purchases that may be affected by advertising messages lead to repeat purchases only if the product delivers the promised customer value. Finally, the high failure rate of new products shows that companies are not able to control demand.

On a deeper level, our wants and values are influenced not only by marketers but also by family, peer groups, religion, cultural background, and education. If Americans are highly materialistic, these values arose out of basic socialization processes that go much deeper than business and mass media could produce alone.

Too Few Social Goods

Business has been accused of overselling private goods at the expense of public goods. As private goods increase, they require more public services that are usually not forthcoming. For example, an increase in automobile ownership (private good) requires more highways, traffic control, parking spaces, and police services (public goods). The overselling of private goods results in "social costs." For cars, some of the social costs include traffic congestion, gasoline shortages, and air pollution. For example, Americans lose 3.7 billion hours a year in traffic jams. In the process, they waste 2.7 billion gallons of fuel and emit millions of tons of greenhouse gases.[17]

A way must be found to restore a balance between private and public goods. One option is to make producers bear the full social costs of their operations. The government could require automobile manufacturers to build cars with more efficient engines and better pollution-control systems. Automakers would then raise their prices to cover the extra costs. If buyers found the price of some cars too high, however, the producers of these cars would disappear. Demand would then move to those producers that could support the sum of the private and social costs.

A second option is to make consumers pay the social costs. ▲For example, many cities around the world are starting to charge "congestion tolls" in an effort to reduce traffic congestion. To unclog its streets, the city of London now levies a congestion charge of $16 per day per car to drive in an eight-square-mile area downtown. The charge has not only reduced traffic congestion within the zone by 21 percent and increased cycling by 43 percent; it also raises money to shore up London's public transportation system.[18]

Based on London's success, cities such as San Diego, Houston, Seattle, and Denver have turned some of their HOV (high-occupancy vehicle) lanes into HOT (high-occupancy

▲ Balancing private and public goods: In response to lane-clogging traffic congestion like that above, London now levies a congestion charge. The charge has reduced congestion by 30 percent and raised money to shore up the city's public transportation system.

toll) lanes for drivers carrying too few passengers. Regular drivers can use the HOT lanes, but they must pay tolls ranging from $.50 off-peak to $9 during rush hour. The U.S. government has recently proposed a bill that would create rush-hour fees in congested urban areas across the country. If the costs of driving rise high enough, the government hopes, consumers will travel at nonpeak times or find alternative transportation modes, ultimately helping to curb America's oil addiction.[19]

Cultural Pollution

Critics charge the marketing system with creating *cultural pollution*. Our senses are being constantly assaulted by marketing and advertising. Commercials interrupt serious programs; pages of ads obscure magazines; billboards mar beautiful scenery; spam fills our inboxes. These interruptions continually pollute people's minds with messages of materialism, sex, power, or status. A recent study found that 63 percent of Americans feel constantly bombarded with too many marketing messages, and some critics call for sweeping changes.[20]

Marketers answer the charges of "commercial noise" with these arguments: First, they hope that their ads reach primarily the target audience. But because of mass-communication channels, some ads are bound to reach people who have no interest in the product and are therefore bored or annoyed. People who buy magazines addressed to their interests—such as *Vogue* or *Fortune*—rarely complain about the ads because the magazines advertise products of interest.

Second, ads make much of television and radio free to users and keep down the costs of magazines and newspapers. Many people think commercials are a small price to pay for these benefits. Consumers find many television commercials entertaining and seek them out—for example, ad viewership during the Super Bowl usually equals game viewership. Finally, today's consumers have alternatives. For example, they can zip or zap TV commercials on recorded programs or avoid them altogether on many paid cable or satellite channels. Thus, to hold consumer attention, advertisers are making their ads more entertaining and informative.

Marketing's Impact on Other Businesses

Critics also charge that a company's marketing practices can harm other companies and reduce competition. Three problems are involved: acquisitions of competitors, marketing practices that create barriers to entry, and unfair competitive marketing practices.

Critics claim that firms are harmed and competition reduced when companies expand by acquiring competitors rather than by developing their own new products. The large number of acquisitions and the rapid pace of industry consolidation over the past several decades have caused concern that vigorous young competitors will be absorbed and that competition will be reduced. In virtually every major industry—retailing, entertainment, financial services, utilities, transportation, automobiles, telecommunications, health care— the number of major competitors is shrinking.

Acquisition is a complex subject. Acquisitions can sometimes be good for society. The acquiring company may gain economies of scale that lead to lower costs and lower prices. A well-managed company may take over a poorly managed company and improve its efficiency. An industry that was not very competitive might become more competitive after the acquisition. But acquisitions can also be harmful and, therefore, are closely regulated by the government.

Critics have also charged that marketing practices bar new companies from entering an industry. Large marketing companies can use patents and heavy promotion spending or tie up suppliers or dealers to keep out or drive out competitors. Those concerned with antitrust regulation recognize that some barriers are the natural result of the economic advantages of doing business on a large scale. Other barriers could be challenged by existing and new laws. For example, some critics have proposed a progressive tax on advertising spending to reduce the role of selling costs as a major barrier to entry.

Finally, some firms have in fact used unfair competitive marketing practices with the intention of hurting or destroying other firms. They may set their prices below costs, threaten to cut off business with suppliers, or discourage the buying of a competitor's products. Various laws work to prevent such predatory competition. It is difficult, however, to prove that the intent or action was really predatory.

In recent years, Wal-Mart has been accused of using predatory pricing in selected market areas to drive smaller, mom-and-pop retailers out of business. Wal-Mart has become a lightning rod for protests by citizens in dozens of towns who worry that the mega-retailer's unfair practices will choke out local businesses. However, whereas critics charge that Wal-Mart's actions are predatory, others assert that its actions are just the healthy competition of a more efficient company against less efficient ones.

For instance, when ▲Wal-Mart recently began a program to sell generic drugs at $4 a prescription, local pharmacists complained of predatory pricing. They charged that at those low prices, Wal-Mart must be selling under cost to drive them out of business. But Wal-Mart claimed that, given its substantial buying power and efficient operations, it could make a profit at those prices. The $4 pricing program was not aimed at putting competitors out of business. Rather, it was simply a good competitive move that served customers better and brought more of them in the door. Legislators in several states appear to agree. For example, Wisconsin lawmakers are proposing legislation that would do away with the state's minimum markup law on prescription drugs, allowing Wal-Mart to make its low generic drug prices available in that state.[21]

▲ Wal-Mart prescription pricing: Is it predatory pricing or is it just good business?

Author | Sustainable marketing
Comment | isn't the province of only businesses and governments. Through consumerism and environmentalism, consumers themselves can play an important role.

Consumer Actions to Promote Sustainable Marketing (pp 595–601)

Sustainable marketing calls for more responsible actions by both businesses and consumers. Because some people view business as the cause of many economic and social ills, grassroots movements have arisen from time to time to keep business in line. The two major movements have been *consumerism* and *environmentalism*.

Consumerism

American business firms have been the target of organized consumer movements on three occasions. The first consumer movement took place in the early 1900s. It was fueled by rising prices, Upton Sinclair's writings on conditions in the meat industry, and scandals in the drug industry. The second consumer movement, in the mid-1930s, was sparked by an upturn in consumer prices during the Great Depression and another drug scandal.

The third movement began in the 1960s. Consumers had become better educated, products had become more complex and potentially hazardous, and people were unhappy with American institutions. Ralph Nader appeared on the scene to force many issues, and other well-known writers accused big business of wasteful and unethical practices. President John F. Kennedy declared that consumers had the right to safety and to be informed, to choose, and to be heard. Congress investigated certain industries and proposed consumer-protection legislation. Since then, many consumer groups have been organized and several consumer laws have been passed. The consumer movement has spread internationally and has become very strong in Europe.

But what is the consumer movement? **Consumerism** is an organized movement of citizens and government agencies to improve the rights and power of buyers in relation to sellers. Traditional *sellers' rights* include:

Consumerism
An organized movement of citizens and government agencies to improve the rights and power of buyers in relation to sellers.

- The right to introduce any product in any size and style, provided it is not hazardous to personal health or safety; or, if it is, to include proper warnings and controls

- The right to charge any price for the product, provided no discrimination exists among similar kinds of buyers

- The right to spend any amount to promote the product, provided it is not defined as unfair competition

- The right to use any product message, provided it is not misleading or dishonest in content or execution

- The right to use any buying incentive programs, provided they are not unfair or misleading

Traditional *buyers' rights* include:

- The right not to buy a product that is offered for sale

- The right to expect the product to be safe

- The right to expect the product to perform as claimed

Comparing these rights, many believe that the balance of power lies on the seller's side. True, the buyer can refuse to buy. But critics feel that the buyer has too little information, education, and protection to make wise decisions when facing sophisticated sellers. Consumer advocates call for the following additional consumer rights:

- The right to be well informed about important aspects of the product

- The right to be protected against questionable products and marketing practices

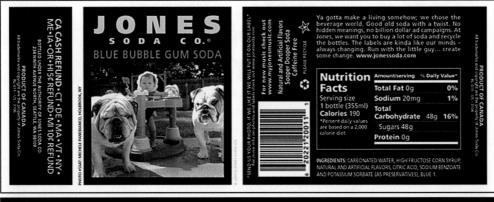

▲ Consumer desire for more information led to labels with useful facts, from ingredients and nutrition facts to recycling and country of origin information. Jones Soda even puts customer-submitted photos on its labels.

- The right to influence products and marketing practices in ways that will improve the "quality of life"

- The right to consume now in a way that will preserve the world for future generations of consumers

Each proposed right has led to more specific proposals by consumerists. ▲The right to be informed includes the right to know the true interest on a loan (truth in lending), the true cost per unit of a brand (unit pricing), the ingredients in a product (ingredient labeling), the nutritional value of foods (nutritional labeling), product freshness (open dating), and the true benefits of a product (truth in advertising). Proposals related to consumer protection include strengthening consumer rights in cases of business fraud, requiring greater product safety, ensuring information privacy, and giving more power to government agencies. Proposals relating to quality of life include controlling the ingredients that go into certain products and packaging and reducing the level of advertising "noise." Proposals for preserving the world for future consumption include promoting the use of sustainable ingredients, recycling and reducing solid wastes, and managing energy consumption.

Sustainable marketing is up to consumers as well as to businesses and governments. Consumers have not only the *right* but also the *responsibility* to protect themselves instead of leaving this function to someone else. Consumers who believe they got a bad deal have several remedies available, including contacting the company or the media; contacting federal, state, or local agencies; and going to small-claims courts. Consumers should also make good consumption choices, rewarding companies that act responsibly while punishing those that don't.

Environmentalism

Environmentalism

An organized movement of concerned citizens and government agencies to protect and improve people's current and future living environment.

Whereas consumerists consider whether the marketing system is efficiently serving consumer wants, environmentalists are concerned with marketing's effects on the environment and with the environmental costs of serving consumer needs and wants. **Environmentalism** is an organized movement of concerned citizens, businesses, and government agencies to protect and improve people's current and future living environment.

Environmentalists are not against marketing and consumption; they simply want people and organizations to operate with more care for the environment. The marketing system's goal, they assert, should not be to maximize consumption, consumer choice, or consumer satisfaction, but rather to maximize life quality. And "life quality" means not only the quantity and quality of consumer goods and services, but also the quality of the environment. Environmentalists want current and future environmental costs included in both producer and consumer decision making.

The first wave of modern environmentalism in the United States was driven by environmental groups and concerned consumers in the 1960s and 1970s. They were concerned with damage to the ecosystem caused by strip-mining, forest depletion, acid rain, global warming, toxic and solid wastes, and litter. They also were concerned with the loss of recreational areas and with the increase in health problems caused by bad air, polluted water, and chemically treated food.

The second environmentalism wave was driven by government, which passed laws and regulations during the 1970s and 1980s governing industrial practices impacting the environment. This wave hit some industries hard. Steel companies and utilities had to

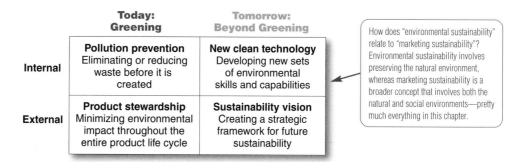

FIGURE | 20.2

The Environmental Sustainability Portfolio

Source: Stuart L. Hart, "Innovation, Creative Destruction, and Sustainability," *Research Technology Management*, September–October 2005, pp. 21–27.

	Today: Greening	**Tomorrow: Beyond Greening**
Internal	**Pollution prevention** Eliminating or reducing waste before it is created	**New clean technology** Developing new sets of environmental skills and capabilities
External	**Product stewardship** Minimizing environmental impact throughout the entire product life cycle	**Sustainability vision** Creating a strategic framework for future sustainability

How does "environmental sustainability" relate to "marketing sustainability"? Environmental sustainability involves preserving the natural environment, whereas marketing sustainability is a broader concept that involves both the natural and social environments—pretty much everything in this chapter.

Environmental sustainability
A management approach that involves developing strategies that both sustain the environment and produce profits for the company.

invest billions of dollars in pollution control equipment and costlier fuels. The auto industry had to introduce expensive emission controls in cars. The packaging industry had to find ways to improve recyclability and reduce solid wastes. These industries and others have often resented and resisted environmental regulations, especially when they have been imposed too rapidly to allow companies to make proper adjustments. Many of these companies claim they have had to absorb large costs that have made them less competitive.

The first two environmentalism waves have now merged into a third and stronger wave in which companies are accepting more responsibility for doing no harm to the environment. They are shifting from protest to prevention, and from regulation to responsibility. More and more companies are adopting policies of **environmental sustainability**. Simply put, environmental sustainability is about generating profits while helping to save the planet. Environmental sustainability is a crucial but difficult societal goal.

Some companies have responded to consumer environmental concerns by doing only what is required to avert new regulations or to keep environmentalists quiet. Enlightened companies, however, are taking action not because someone is forcing them to, or to reap short-run profits, but because it is the right thing to do—for both the company and for the planet's environmental future.

Figure 20.2 shows a grid that companies can use to gauge their progress toward environmental sustainability. In includes both internal and external "greening" activities that will pay off for the firm and environment in the short run and "beyond greening" activities that will pay off in the longer term. At the most basic level, a company can practice *pollution prevention*. This involves more than pollution control—cleaning up waste after it has been created. Pollution prevention means eliminating or minimizing waste before it is created. Companies emphasizing prevention have responded with internal "green marketing" programs—designing and developing ecologically safer products, recyclable and biodegradable packaging, better pollution controls, and more energy-efficient operations.

For example, Nike produces PVC-free shoes, recycles old sneakers, and educates young people about conservation, reuse, and recycling. General Mills shaved 20 percent off the paperboard packaging for Hamburger Helper, resulting in 500 fewer distribution trucks on the road each year. Sun Microsystems created its Open Work program that gives employees the option to work from home, preventing nearly 29,000 tons of CO_2 emissions, while at the same time saving $67.8 million in real-estate costs and increasing worker productivity by 34 percent. And UPS continues to develop a "green fleet" of alternative-fuel vehicles to replace its old fleet of diesel delivery trucks. In 2009 it will deploy 200 new next-generation hybrid electric delivery vehicles to join the roughly 2,000 low-carbon, hybrid and compressed natural gas vehicles already in use. The hybrid vehicles produce 45 percent better fuel economy and a dramatic decrease in vehicle emissions.[22]

At the next level, companies can practice *product stewardship*—minimizing not just pollution from production and product design but all environmental impacts throughout the

Pollution prevention: UPS is developing a "green fleet" of alternative-fuel vehicles that produce 45 percent better fuel economy and a dramatic decrease in vehicle emissions.

full product life cycle, and all the while reducing costs. Many companies are adopting *design for environment (DFE)* and *cradle-to-cradle* practices. This involves thinking ahead to design products that are easier to recover, reuse, recycle, or safely return to nature after usage, becoming part of the ecological cycle. DFE and cradle-to-cradle practices not only help to sustain the environment, they can also be highly profitable for the company.

An example is Xerox Corporation's Equipment Remanufacture and Parts Reuse Program, which converts end-of-life office equipment into new products and parts. Equipment returned to Xerox can be remanufactured reusing 70 to 90 percent by weight of old machine components, while still meeting performance standards for equipment made with all new parts. The program creates benefits for both the environment and for the company. So far, it has diverted nearly two billion pounds of waste from landfills. And it reduces the amount of raw material and energy needed to produce new parts. Energy savings from parts reuse total an estimated 320,000 megawatt hours annually—enough energy to light more than 250,000 U.S. homes for the year.[23]

Today's "greening" activities focus on improving what companies already do to protect the environment. The "beyond greening" activities identified in Figure 20.2 look to the future. First, internally, companies can plan for *new clean technology*. Many organizations that have made good sustainability headway are still limited by existing technologies. To create fully sustainable strategies, they will need to develop innovative new technologies. ▲For example, Coca-Cola is investing heavily in research addressing many sustainability issues:[24]

> From a sustainability viewpoint for Coca-Cola, an aluminum can is an ideal package. Aluminum can be recycled indefinitely. Put a Coke can in a recycling bin, and the aluminum finds its way back to a store shelf in about six weeks. The trouble is, people prefer clear plastic bottles with screw-on tops. Plastic bottles account for nearly 50 percent of Coke's global volume, three times more than aluminum cans. And they are not currently sustainable. They're made from oil, a finite resource. Most wind up in landfills or, worse, as roadside trash. They can't be recycled indefinitely because the plastic discolors. To attack this waste problem, Coca-Cola will invest about $44 million to build the world's largest state-of-the-art plastic-bottle-to-bottle recycling plant. As a more permanent solution, the company is researching new ideas like bottles made from corn or bioplastics.
>
> Coke is also investing in new clean technologies to solve other environmental issues. For example, about ten million or so vending machines and refrigerated coolers use potent greenhouse gases called HFCs to keep Cokes cold. To eliminate them, the company invested $40 million in research and formed a refrigeration alliance with McDonald's and even competitor PepsiCo. Coca-Cola has also promised to become "water neutral" by researching ways to help its bottlers waste less water and ways to protect or replenish watersheds around the world.

Finally, companies can develop a *sustainability vision*, which serves as a guide to the future. It shows how the company's products and services, processes, and policies must evolve and what new technologies must be developed to get there. This vision of sustainability provides a framework for pollution control, product stewardship, and new environmental technology for the company and others to follow.

Most companies today focus on the upper-left quadrant of the grid in Figure 20.2, investing most heavily in pollution prevention. Some forward-looking companies practice product stewardship and are developing new environmental technologies. Few companies have well-defined sustainability visions. However, emphasizing only one or a few quadrants in the environmental sustainability grid can be shortsighted. Investing only in the left half of the grid puts a company in a good position today but leaves it vulnerable in the future. In contrast, a heavy emphasis on the right half suggests

▲ New clean technologies: Coca-Cola is investing heavily to build a state-of-the-art plastic-bottle-to-bottle recycling plant. It's also researching new alternatives such as bottles made from corn or bioplastics.

that a company has good environmental vision but lacks the skills needed to implement it. Thus, companies should work at developing all four dimensions of environmental sustainability.

Wal-Mart, for example, is doing just that. Through its own environmental sustainability actions and its impact on the actions of suppliers, Wal-Mart has emerged in recent years as the world's super "eco-nanny" (see **Real Marketing 20.1**). Alcoa, the world's leading producer of aluminum, is also setting a high sustainability standard. For four years running it has been named one of the most sustainable corporations in the annual *Global 100 Most Sustainable Corporations in the World* ranking:

> Alcoa has distinguished itself as a leader through its sophisticated approach to identifying and managing the material sustainability risks that it faces as a company. From pollution prevention via greenhouse gas emissions reduction programs to engaging stakeholders over new environmental technology, such as controversial hydropower projects, Alcoa has the sustainability strategies in place needed to meld its profitability objectives with society's larger environmental protection goals. . . . Importantly, Alcoa's approach to sustainability is firmly rooted in the idea that sustainability programs can indeed add financial value. Perhaps the best evidence is the company's efforts to promote the use of aluminum in transportation, where aluminum—with its excellent strength-to-weight ratio—is making inroads as a material of choice that allows automakers to build low-weight, fuel-efficient vehicles that produce fewer tailpipe emissions. This kind of forward-thinking strategy of supplying the market with the products that will help solve pressing global environmental problems shows a company that sees the future, has plotted a course, and is aligning its business accordingly. Says CEO Alain Belda, "Our values require us to think and act not only on the present challenges, but also with the legacy in mind that we leave for those who will come after us . . . as well as the commitments made by those that came before us."[25]

Environmentalism creates some special challenges for global marketers. As international trade barriers come down and global markets expand, environmental issues are having an ever-greater impact on international trade. Countries in North America, western Europe, and other developed regions are generating strict environmental standards. In the United States, for example, more than two dozen major pieces of environmental legislation have been enacted since 1970, and recent events suggest that more regulation is on the way. A side accord to the North American Free Trade Agreement (NAFTA) set up the Commission for Environmental Cooperation for resolving environmental matters. The European Union has passed "end-of-life" regulations affecting automobiles and consumer electronics products. And the EU's Eco-Management and Audit Scheme (EMAS) provides guidelines for environmental self-regulation.[26]

However, environmental policies still vary widely from country to country. Countries such as Denmark, Germany, Japan, and the United States have fully developed environmental policies and high public expectations. But major countries such as China, India, Brazil, and Russia are in only the early stages of developing such policies. Moreover, environmental factors that motivate consumers in one country may have no impact on consumers in another. For example, PVC soft-drink bottles cannot be used in Switzerland or Germany. However, they are preferred in France, which has an extensive recycling process for them. Thus, international companies have found it difficult to develop standard environmental practices that work around the world. Instead, they are creating general policies and then translating these policies into tailored programs that meet local regulations and expectations.

Public Actions to Regulate Marketing

Citizen concerns about marketing practices will usually lead to public attention and legislative proposals. New bills will be debated—many will be defeated, others will be modified, and a few will become workable laws.

Real Marketing 20.1

Wal-Mart:
The World's Super Eco-Nanny

When you think of the corporate "good guys"—companies that are helping to save the world through sustainable actions—you probably think of names like Patagonia, Timberland, Ben & Jerry's, Honest Tea, Whole Foods Market, or Stonyfield Farm. But hold on to your seat. When it comes to sustainability, perhaps no company in the world is doing more good these days than Wal-Mart. That's right—big, bad, Wal-Mart.

Critics have long bashed Wal-Mart for a broad range of alleged social misdeeds, from unfair labor practices to destroying small communities. So many consumers are surprised to learn that the world's largest company is also the world's biggest crusader for the cause of saving the world for future generations. When it comes to sustainability, Wal-Mart is rapidly emerging as the world's super "eco-nanny." In the long run, Wal-Mart's stated environmental goals are to use 100 percent renewable energy, to create zero waste, and to sell only products that sustain the world's resources and environment. Toward that goal, not only is Wal-Mart greening up its own operations, it's also urging its vast network of suppliers to do the same.

Wal-Mart operates more than 7,350 stores around the world, and its huge stores are gluttons for energy and other resources. So even small steps toward making stores more efficient can add up to huge environmental savings. But Wal-Mart isn't settling for small steps—it's moving in large leaps to develop new eco-technologies. In 2005, the giant retailer opened two experimental superstores in McKinney, Texas, and Aurora, Colorado, designed to test dozens of environmentally friendly and energy-efficient technologies:

A 143-foot-tall wind turbine stands outside a Wal-Mart Supercenter in Aurora, Colorado. Incongruous as it might seem, it is clearly a sign that something about this particular store is different. On the outside, the store's facade features row upon row of windows to allow in as much natural light as possible. The landscaping uses native, drought-tolerant plants well adapted to the hot, dry Colorado summers, cutting down on watering, mowing,

and the amount of fertilizer and other chemicals needed. Inside the store, an efficient high-output linear fluorescent lighting system saves enough electricity annually from this store alone to supply the needs of 52 single-family homes. The store's heating system burns recovered cooking oil from the deli's fryers. The oil is collected, mixed with waste engine oil from the store's Tire and Lube Express, and burned in the waste-oil boiler. All organic waste, including produce, meats, and paper, is placed in an organic waste compactor, which is then hauled off to a company that turns it into mulch for the garden. These and dozens more technological touches make the supercenter a laboratory for efficient and Earth-friendly retail operations.

For Wal-Mart, sustainability is about more than just doing the right thing. Above all, it makes good business sense— "driving out hidden costs, conserving our natural resources for future generations, and providing sustainable and affordable products for our customers so they can save money and live better."

After evaluating these experimental stores, Wal-Mart is now rolling out new high-efficiency stores, each one saving more energy than the last. A newly opened Las Vegas store uses 45 percent less energy than a standard Wal-Mart. Moreover, Wal-Mart is eagerly spreading the word by encouraging visitors and sharing what it learns—even with competing companies. "We had Target in here not too long ago, and other retail chains and independents have also taken a tour of the store," notes the Aurora store manager. "This is not something we're keeping to ourselves. We want everyone to know about it."

At the same time that Wal-Mart presses forward with its own sustainability initiatives, it's laying down the law to suppliers. To demonstrate Wal-Mart's environmental leadership and determination, CEO Lee Scott recently called a meeting of 250 other CEOs. At the meeting, Scott outlined Wal-Mart's plans for holding its 61,000 suppliers accountable for reducing their "carbon footprints" and for eliminating excessive packaging. And in a show of force few governments could

pull off, the company also "urged" another 600 supplier executives to attend a Wal-Mart-sponsored seminar on sustainability. When imposing its environmental demands on suppliers, Wal-Mart "has morphed into . . . a sort of privatized Environmental Protection Agency, only with a lot more clout," says an industry observer. "The EPA can levy [only] a seven-figure fine; Wal-Mart can wipe out more than a quarter of a business in one fell swoop."

With its immense buying power, Wal-Mart can humble even the mightiest supplier. Take, for example, the super-concentrated liquid laundry detergent market. Procter & Gamble and other detergent makers have long had the capability to formulate concentrated detergents. But it wasn't until Wal-Mart declared that it would sell nothing but super-concentrated detergents that P&G decided to invest $100 million to make them, even in the face of uncertain financial returns. Wal-Mart's decision will result in smaller plastic detergent containers, conserving raw materials and

Continued on next page ▼

Real Marketing 20.1 Continued ▼

eliminating millions and millions of tons of solid waste each year.

Because of Wal-Mart's size, even small supplier product and packaging changes have a substantial environmental impact. For example, to meet Wal-Mart's requests, P&G developed a mega roll technology for its Charmin brand, which combines the sheets of four regular toilet paper rolls into one small roll. The seemingly minor change saves 89.5 million cardboard rolls and 360,000 pounds of plastic packaging wrap a year. It also allows Wal-Mart to ship 42 percent more units on its trucks, saving about 54,000 gallons of fuel a year. Wal-Mart also pressured General Mills to straighten the once curly noodles in boxes of Hamburger Helper. This small change eliminated thousands of pounds of packaging.

Wal-Mart is working with the Carbon Disclosure Project, an independent not-for-profit environmental organization, to measure the amount of energy consumed in creating products throughout its supply chain. About 3,400 suppliers of more than 13,000 products

are participating in the project. Accordingly, Wal-Mart has developed a packaging scorecard that rates the vendors and will soon be used to guide Wal-Mart purchasing decisions. Wal-Mart has also established more than a dozen "sustainable value networks." These networks connect Wal-Mart people with suppliers, advocacy groups, academics, and independent experts who work together on "hot-button" environmental issues in various product categories, such as greenhouse gases, logistics, packaging, and alternative fuels.

So there you have it—Wal-Mart the eco-nanny. Wal-Mart's sustainability efforts have earned praise from even its harshest critics. As one skeptic begrudgingly admits, "Wal-Mart

has more green clout than anyone." But for Wal-Mart, leading the eco-charge is about more than just doing the right thing. Above all, it also makes good business sense. More efficient operations and less wasteful products are not only good for the environment, they save Wal-Mart money. Lower costs, in turn, let Wal-Mart do more of what it has always done best—save customers money.

Says a Wal-Mart executive, "We've laid the foundation for a long-term effort that will transform our business by driving out hidden costs, conserving our natural resources for future generations, and providing sustainable and affordable products for our customers so they can save money and live better."

Sources: Quotes, adapted extract, and other information from Jack Neff, "Why Wal-Mart Has More Green Clout Than Anyone," *Advertising Age*, October 15, 2007, p.1; "Wal-Mart Says Latest High-Efficiency Store Cuts Energy Use 45%," *Environmental Leader*, March 18, 2008, accessed at www.environmentalleader.com; Danielle Sacks, "Working with the Enemy," *Fast Company*, September 2007, pp. 74–81; Joseph Tarnowski, "Green Monster," *Progressive Grocer*, April 1, 2006, pp. 20–26; Ylan Q. Mui, "Wal-Mart Green Chief to Shift Jobs," *Washington Post*," October 20, 2007, p. D2; YlanQ. Mui, "At Wal-Mart, 'Green' Has Various Shades," *Washington Post*, November 16, 2007, p. D1; and "Sustainable Value Networks," accessed at http://walmartstores.com/Sustainability/7672.aspx, November 2008.

Many of the laws that affect marketing are listed in Chapter 3. The task is to translate these laws into the language that marketing executives understand as they make decisions about competitive relations, products, price, promotion, and channels of distribution. 🔖**Figure 20.3** illustrates the major legal issues facing marketing management.

🔖**FIGURE | 20.3**
Major Marketing Decision Areas that May Be Called Into Question Under the Law

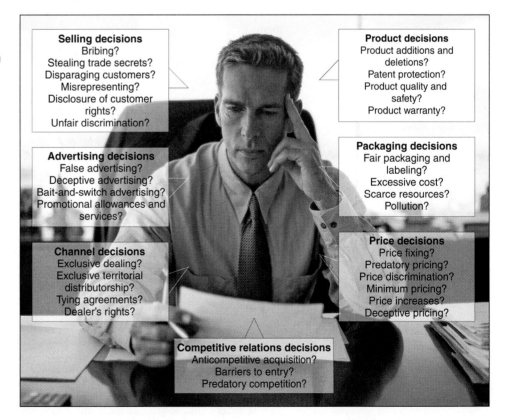

Selling decisions
Bribing?
Stealing trade secrets?
Disparaging customers?
Misrepresenting?
Disclosure of customer rights?
Unfair discrimination?

Product decisions
Product additions and deletions?
Patent protection?
Product quality and safety?
Product warranty?

Advertising decisions
False advertising?
Deceptive advertising?
Bait-and-switch advertising?
Promotional allowances and services?

Packaging decisions
Fair packaging and labeling?
Excessive cost?
Scarce resources?
Pollution?

Channel decisions
Exclusive dealing?
Exclusive territorial distributorship?
Tying agreements?
Dealer's rights?

Price decisions
Price fixing?
Predatory pricing?
Price discrimination?
Minimum pricing?
Price increases?
Deceptive pricing?

Competitive relations decisions
Anticompetitive acquisition?
Barriers to entry?
Predatory competition?

Author Comment | In the end, marketers themselves must take responsibility for sustainable marketing. That means operating in a responsible and ethical way to bring immediate and future value to customers.

Business Actions Toward Sustainable Marketing (pp 602–609)

At first, many companies opposed consumerism, environmentalism, and other elements of sustainable marketing. They thought the criticisms were either unfair or unimportant. But by now, most companies have grown to embrace the new consumer rights, at least in principle. They might oppose certain pieces of legislation as inappropriate ways to solve specific consumer problems, but they recognize the consumer's right to information and protection. Many of these companies have responded positively to sustainable marketing as a way to create greater immediate and future customer value and to strengthen customer relationships.

Sustainable Marketing Principles

Under the sustainable marketing concept, a company's marketing should support the best long-run performance of the marketing system. It should be guided by five sustainable marketing principles: *consumer-oriented marketing, customer-value marketing, innovative marketing, sense-of-mission marketing,* and *societal marketing.*

Consumer-Oriented Marketing

Consumer-oriented marketing
The philosophy of sustainable marketing that holds that the company should view and organize its marketing activities from the consumer's point of view.

Consumer-oriented marketing means that the company should view and organize its marketing activities from the consumer's point of view. It should work hard to sense, serve, and satisfy the needs of a defined group of customers, both now and in the future. All of the good marketing companies that we've discussed in this text have had this in common: an all-consuming passion for delivering superior value to carefully chosen customers. Only by seeing the world through its customers' eyes can the company build lasting and profitable customer relationships.

Customer-Value Marketing

Customer-value marketing
A principle of sustainable marketing that holds that a company should put most of its resources into customer-value-building marketing investments.

According to the principle of **customer-value marketing**, the company should put most of its resources into customer-value-building marketing investments. Many things marketers do—one-shot sales promotions, cosmetic packaging changes, direct-response advertising—may raise sales in the short run but add less *value* than would actual improvements in the product's quality, features, or convenience. Enlightened marketing calls for building long-run consumer loyalty and relationships by continually improving the value consumers receive from the firm's market offering. By creating value *for* consumers, the company can capture value *from* consumers in return.

Innovative Marketing

Innovative marketing
A principle of sustainable marketing that requires that a company seek real product and marketing improvements.

The principle of **innovative marketing** requires that the company continuously seek real product and marketing improvements. The company that overlooks new and better ways to do things will eventually lose customers to another company that has found a better way. ▲An excellent example of an innovative marketer is Nintendo:[27]

After Sony and Microsoft kicked the Mario out of Nintendo's GameCube in the Video Game War of 2001, the smallest of the three game platform makers needed a new plan. "Nintendo took a step back from the technology arms race and chose to focus on [customers and] the fun of playing, rather than cold tech specs," says the president of Nintendo of America. The resulting Wii system, with its intuitive motion-sensitive controller and interactive games, appealed not only to teen boys typically targeted by the game industry but also to their sisters, moms, dads, and even grandparents. The result: the perpetually sold-out Wii system quickly outsold both the PlayStation 3 and Xbox 360. But get this: Unlike its competitors—which lose money on each console and earn it back on software—Nintendo actually turns a profit on its consoles, makes more selling games, then takes in still more in licensing fees. "Not to sound too obvious," says the Nintendo executive, "but it makes good business sense to make a profit on the products you sell." Wall Street thinks so too. The company's stock has more than doubled over the past year.

Innovative marketing: Nintendo's customer-focused innovation not only attracted new gamers and bruised competitors Sony and Microsoft, "it has opened doors of creativity throughout the video-game business."

Sense-of-mission marketing

A principle of sustainable marketing that holds that a company should define its mission in broad social terms rather than narrow product terms.

Nintendo's upset is doing more than attracting new gamers and bruising Sony and Microsoft. Says the president of Sega of America, "It has opened doors of creativity throughout the video-game business."

Sense-of-Mission Marketing

Sense-of-mission marketing means that the company should define its mission in broad *social* terms rather than narrow *product* terms. When a company defines a social mission, employees feel better about their work and have a clearer sense of direction. Brands linked with broader missions can serve the best long-run interests of both the brand and consumers. For example, Dove wants to do more than just sell its beauty care products. It's on a mission to discover "real beauty" and to help women be happy just the way they are:[28]

It all started with a Unilever study that examined the impact on women of images seen in entertainment, in advertising, and on fashion runways. The startling result: Only 2 percent of 3,300 women and girls surveyed in 10 countries around the world considered themselves beautiful. Unilever's conclusion: It's time to redefine beauty. So in 2004, Unilever launched the global Dove Campaign for Real Beauty, with ads that featured candid and confident images of real women of all types (not actresses or models) and headlines that made consumers ponder their perceptions of beauty. Among others, it featured full-bodied women ("Oversized or Outstanding?"), older women ("Gray or Gorgeous?") and a heavily freckled woman ("Flawed or Flawless?"). The following year, as the campaign's popularity skyrocketed, Dove introduced six new "real beauties" of various proportions, in sizes ranging from 6 to 14. These women appeared in ads wearing nothing but their underwear and big smiles, with headlines proclaiming, "New Dove Firming: As Tested on Real Curves." "In Dove ads," says one advertising expert, "normal is the new beautiful."

The Dove Campaign for Real Beauty quickly went digital, with a campaignforrealbeauty.com Web site and award-winning viral videos with names such as "Evolution" and "Onslaught" that attacked damaging beauty stereotypes. As the campaign has taken off, so have sales of Dove products. But the people behind the Dove brand and the Campaign for Real Beauty have noble motives beyond sales and profits. According to a Unilever executive, Dove's bold and compelling mission to redefine beauty and reassure women ranks well above issues of dollars and cents. "You should see the faces of the people working on this brand now," he says. "There is a real love for the brand."

Some companies define their overall corporate missions in broad societal terms. For example, defined in narrow product terms, the mission of Unilever's Ben & Jerry's unit might be "to sell ice cream." However, Ben & Jerry's states its mission more broadly, as one of "linked prosperity," including product, economic, and social missions. From its beginnings, Ben & Jerry's championed a host of social and environmental causes, and it donated a whopping 7.5 percent of pretax profits to support worthy causes. By the mid-1990s, Ben & Jerry's had become the nation's number-two superpremium ice cream brand.

However, having a "double bottom line" of values and profits is no easy proposition. Throughout the 1990s, as competitors not shackled by "principles before profits" missions invaded its markets, Ben & Jerry's growth and profits flattened. In 2000, after several years of less-than-stellar financial returns, Ben & Jerry's was acquired by giant food producer Unilever. Looking back, the company appears to have focused too much on social issues at the expense of sound business management. Cohen once commented, "There came a time when I had to admit 'I'm a businessman.' And I had a hard time mouthing those words."[29]

FIGURE | 20.4
Societal Classification of Products

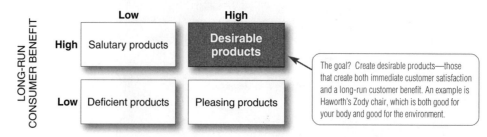

IMMEDIATE SATISFACTION

	Low	High
High	Salutary products	**Desirable products**
Low	Deficient products	Pleasing products

LONG-RUN CONSUMER BENEFIT

The goal? Create desirable products—those that create both immediate customer satisfaction and a long-run customer benefit. An example is Haworth's Zody chair, which is both good for your body and good for the environment.

Societal marketing
A principle of sustainable marketing that holds that a company should make marketing decisions by considering consumers' wants, the company's requirements, consumers' long-run interests, and society's long-run interests.

Deficient products
Products that have neither immediate appeal nor long-run benefits.

Pleasing products
Products that give high immediate satisfaction but may hurt consumers in the long run.

Salutary products
Products that have low appeal but may benefit consumers in the long run.

Desirable products
Products that give both high immediate satisfaction and high long-run benefits.

▲ Desirable products: Haworth's Zody office chair is not only attractive and functional but also environmentally responsible.

Such experiences taught the socially responsible business movement some hard lessons. The result is a new generation of activist entrepreneurs—not social activists with big hearts who hate capitalism, but well-trained business managers and company builders with a passion for a cause. Founded by businesspeople who are proud of it, the new mission-driven companies are just as dedicated to building a viable, profitable business as to shaping the mission. They know that to "do good," they must first "do well" in terms of successful business operations.

Societal Marketing

Following the principle of **societal marketing**, a company makes marketing decisions by considering consumers' wants and interests, the company's requirements, and society's long-run interests. The company is aware that neglecting consumer and societal long-run interests is a disservice to consumers and society. Alert companies view societal problems as opportunities.

Sustainable marketing calls for products that are not only pleasing but also beneficial. The difference is shown in **Figure 20.4**. Products can be classified according to their degree of immediate consumer satisfaction and long-run consumer benefit. **Deficient products**, such as bad-tasting and ineffective medicine, have neither immediate appeal nor long-run benefits. **Pleasing products** give high immediate satisfaction but may hurt consumers in the long run. Examples include cigarettes and junk food. **Salutary products** have low immediate appeal but may benefit consumers in the long run; for instance, bicycle helmets or some insurance products. **Desirable products** give both high immediate satisfaction and high long-run benefits, such as a tasty *and* nutritious breakfast food.

Examples of desirable products abound. GE's Energy Smart compact fluorescent lightbulb provides good lighting at the same time that it gives long life and energy savings. Toyota's hybrid Prius gives both a quiet ride and fuel efficiency. Maytag's front-loading Neptune washer provides superior cleaning along with water savings and energy efficiency. ▲ And Haworth's Zody office chair is not only attractive and functional but also environmentally responsible:

Let's talk about your butt—specifically, what it's sitting on. Chances are, your chair is an unholy medley of polyvinyl chloride and hazardous chemicals that drift into your lungs each time you shift your weight. It was likely produced in a fossil-fuel-swilling factory that in turn spews toxic pollution and effluents. And it's ultimately destined for a landfill or incinerator, where it will emit carcinogenic dioxins and endocrine-disrupting phthalates, the kind of hormone-mimicking nasties that give male fish female genitalia and small children cancer (or is it the other way around?). Now, envision what you might be sitting on in 2016. Actually, never mind: Office-furniture outfit Haworth already built it. It's called the Zody, and it's made without PVC, CFCs, chrome, or any other toxic fixin's. Ninety-eight percent of it can be recycled; some 50 percent of it already has been. The energy used in the manufacturing process is completely offset by wind-power credits, and when the chair is ready to retire, the company will take it off your hands and reuse its components. And the award-winning Zody's not just good for the environment, it's also good for your body. It was the first chair to be endorsed by the American Physical Therapy Association.[30]

Companies should try to turn all of their products into desirable products. The challenge posed by pleasing products is that they sell very well but may end up hurting the consumer. The product opportunity, therefore, is to add long-run benefits without reducing the product's pleasing qualities. The challenge posed by salutary products is to add some pleasing qualities so that they will become more desirable in consumers' minds.

Marketing Ethics

Good ethics is a cornerstone of sustainable marketing. In the long run, unethical marketing harms customers and society as a whole. Further, it eventually damages a company's reputation and effectiveness, jeopardizing the company's very survival. Thus, the sustainable marketing goals of long-term consumer and business welfare can be achieved only through ethical marketing conduct.

Conscientious marketers face many moral dilemmas. The best thing to do is often unclear. Because not all managers have fine moral sensitivity, companies need to develop *corporate marketing ethics policies*—broad guidelines that everyone in the organization must follow. These policies should cover distributor relations, advertising standards, customer service, pricing, product development, and general ethical standards.

The finest guidelines cannot resolve all the difficult ethical situations the marketer faces. ● **Table 20.1** lists some difficult ethical issues marketers could face during their careers. If marketers choose immediate sales-producing actions in all these cases, their marketing behavior might well be described as immoral or even amoral. If they refuse to go along with *any* of the actions, they might be ineffective as marketing managers and unhappy because of the constant moral tension. Managers need a set of principles that will help them figure out the moral importance of each situation and decide how far they can go in good conscience.

● TABLE | 20.1   Some Morally Difficult Situations in Marketing

1. You work for a cigarette company. Public policy debates over the past many years leave no doubt in your mind that cigarette smoking and cancer are closely linked. Although your company currently runs an "If you don't smoke, don't start" promotion campaign, you believe that other company promotions might encourage young (although legal age) nonsmokers to pick up the habit. What would you do?

2. Your R&D department has changed one of your products slightly. It is not really "new and improved," but you know that putting this statement on the package and in advertising will increase sales. What would you do?

3. You have been asked to add a stripped-down model to your line that could be advertised to pull customers into the store. The product won't be very good, but salespeople will be able to switch buyers up to higher-priced units. You are asked to give the green light for the stripped-down version. What would you do?

4. You are thinking of hiring a product manager who has just left a competitor's company. She would be more than happy to tell you all the competitor's plans for the coming year. What would you do?

5. One of your top dealers in an important territory recently has had family troubles, and his sales have slipped. It looks like it will take him a while to straighten out his family trouble. Meanwhile you are losing many sales. Legally, on performance grounds, you can terminate the dealer's franchise and replace him. What would you do?

6. You have a chance to win a big account that will mean a lot to you and your company. The purchasing agent hints that a "gift" would influence the decision. Your assistant recommends sending a big-screen HDTV television to the buyer's home. What would you do?

7. You have heard that a competitor has a new product feature that will make a big difference in sales. The competitor will demonstrate the feature in a private dealer meeting at the annual trade show. You can easily send a snooper to this meeting to learn about the new feature. What would you do?

8. You have to choose between three ad campaigns outlined by your agency. The first (a) is a soft-sell, honest, straight-information campaign. The second (b) uses sex-loaded emotional appeals and exaggerates the product's benefits. The third (c) involves a noisy, somewhat irritating commercial that is sure to gain audience attention. Pretests show that the campaigns are effective in the following order: c, b, and a. What would you do?

9. You are interviewing a capable female applicant for a job as salesperson. She is better qualified than the men just interviewed. Nevertheless, you know that in your industry some important customers prefer dealing with men, and you will lose some sales if you hire her. What would you do?

But *what* principle should guide companies and marketing managers on issues of ethics and social responsibility? One philosophy is that such issues are decided by the free market and legal system. Under this principle, companies and their managers are not responsible for making moral judgments. Companies can in good conscience do whatever the market and legal systems allow.

A second philosophy puts responsibility not on the system but in the hands of individual companies and managers. This more enlightened philosophy suggests that a company should have a "social conscience." Companies and managers should apply high standards of ethics and morality when making corporate decisions, regardless of "what the system allows." History provides an endless list of examples of company actions that were legal but highly irresponsible.

Each company and marketing manager must work out a philosophy of socially responsible and ethical behavior. Under the societal marketing concept, each manager must look beyond what is legal and allowed and develop standards based on personal integrity, corporate conscience, and long-run consumer welfare. A clear and responsible philosophy will help the company deal with knotty issues such as the one faced by 3M:

In late 1997, a powerful new research technique for scanning blood kept turning up the same odd result: Tiny amounts of a chemical 3M had made for nearly 40 years were showing up in blood drawn from people living all across the country. If the results held up, it meant that virtually all Americans may be carrying some minuscule amount of the chemical, called perfluorooctane sulfonate (PFOS), in their systems. Even though at the time they had yet to come up with a definitive answer as to what harm the chemical might cause, the company reached a drastic decision. In mid-2000, although under no mandate to act, 3M voluntarily phased out products containing PFOS and related chemicals, including its popular Scotchgard fabric protector. This was no easy decision. Since there was as yet no replacement chemical, it meant a potential loss of $500 million in annual sales. 3M's voluntary actions drew praise from regulators. "3M deserves great credit for identifying the problem and coming forward," says an Environmental Protection Agency administrator. "It took guts," comments another government scientist. "The fact is that most companies . . . go into anger, denial, and the rest of that stuff. [We're used to seeing] decades-long arguments about whether a chemical is really toxic." For 3M, however, it wasn't all that difficult a decision—it was simply the right thing to do. The company has since introduced reformulated Scotchgard products that it claims work even better than the original formula—and sell just as well.[31]

As with environmentalism, the issue of ethics presents special challenges for international marketers. Business standards and practices vary a great deal from one country to the next. For example, whereas bribes and kickbacks are illegal for U.S. firms, they are standard business practice in many South American countries. One recent study found that companies from some nations were much more likely to use bribes when seeking contracts in emerging-market nations. The most flagrant bribe-paying firms were from India, Russia, and China. Other countries where corruption is common include Iraq, Myanmar, and Haiti. The least corrupt were companies from Iceland, Finland, New Zealand, and Denmark.[32]

The question arises as to whether a company must lower its ethical standards to compete effectively in countries with lower standards. The answer: No. Companies should make a commitment to a common set of shared standards worldwide. For example, John Hancock Mutual Life Insurance Company operates successfully in Southeast Asia, an area that by Western standards has widespread questionable business and government practices. Despite warnings from locals that Hancock would have to bend its rules to succeed, the company set out strict guidelines. "We told our people that we had the same ethical standards, same procedures, and same policies in these countries that we have in the United States, and we do," says Hancock Chairman Stephen Brown. "We just felt that things like payoffs were wrong—and if we had to do business that way, we'd rather not do business." Hancock employees feel good about the consistent levels of ethics. "There may be countries where you have to do that kind of thing," says Brown. "We haven't found that country yet, and if we do, we won't do business there."[33]

Many industrial and professional associations have suggested codes of ethics, and many companies are now adopting their own codes. For example, the American Marketing Association, an international association of marketing managers and scholars, developed the code of ethics shown in ● **Table 20.2**. Companies are also developing programs to teach managers about important ethics issues and help them find the proper responses. They hold ethics workshops and seminars and set up ethics committees. Furthermore, most major U.S. companies have appointed high-level ethics officers to champion ethics issues and to help resolve ethics problems and concerns facing employees.

● TABLE | 20.2　American Marketing Association Code of Ethics

ETHICAL NORMS AND VALUES FOR MARKETERS PREAMBLE

The American Marketing Association commits itself to promoting the highest standard of professional ethical norms and values for its members. Norms are established standards of conduct that are expected and maintained by society and/or professional organizations. Values represent the collective conception of what people find desirable, important and morally proper. Values serve as the criteria for evaluating the actions of others. Marketing practitioners must recognize that they not only serve their enterprises but also act as stewards of society in creating, facilitating and executing the efficient and effective transactions that are part of the greater economy. In this role, marketers should embrace the highest ethical norms of practicing professionals and the ethical values implied by their responsibility toward stakeholders (e.g., customers, employees, investors, channel members, regulators and the host community).

GENERAL NORMS

1. Marketers must do no harm. This means doing work for which they are appropriately trained or experienced so that they can actively add value to their organizations and customers. It also means adhering to all applicable laws and regulations and embodying high ethical standards in the choices they make.

2. Marketers must foster trust in the marketing system. This means that products are appropriate for their intended and promoted uses. It requires that marketing communications about goods and services are not intentionally deceptive or misleading. It suggests building relationships that provide for the equitable adjustment and/or redress of customer grievances. It implies striving for good faith and fair dealing so as to contribute toward the efficacy of the exchange process.

3. Marketers must embrace, communicate and practice the fundamental ethical values that will improve consumer confidence in the integrity of the marketing exchange system. These basic values are intentionally aspirational and include honesty, responsibility, fairness, respect, openness and citizenship.

ETHICAL VALUES

Honesty—to be truthful and forthright in our dealings with customers and stakeholders.

• We will tell the truth in all situations and at all times.

• We will offer products of value that do what we claim in our communications.

• We will stand behind our products if they fail to deliver their claimed benefits.

• We will honor our explicit and implicit commitments and promises.

Responsibility—to accept the consequences of our marketing decisions and strategies.

• We will make strenuous efforts to serve the needs of our customers.

• We will avoid using coercion with all stakeholders.

• We will acknowledge the social obligations to stakeholders that come with increased marketing and economic power.

• We will recognize our special commitments to economically vulnerable segments of the market such as children, the elderly and others who may be substantially disadvantaged.

Fairness—to try to balance justly the needs of the buyer with the interests of the seller.

• We will represent our products in a clear way in selling, advertising and other forms of communication; this includes the avoidance of false, misleading and deceptive promotion.

• We will reject manipulations and sales tactics that harm customer trust.

• We will not engage in price fixing, predatory pricing, price gouging or "bait-and-switch" tactics.

• We will not knowingly participate in material conflicts of interest.

(continued)

● **TABLE** | **20.2**   American Marketing Association Code of Ethics—*continued*

Respect—to acknowledge the basic human dignity of all stakeholders.

• We will value individual differences even as we avoid stereotyping customers or depicting demographic groups (e.g., gender, race, sexual orientation) in a negative or dehumanizing way in our promotions.

• We will listen to the needs of our customers and make all reasonable efforts to monitor and improve their satisfaction on an ongoing basis.

• We will make a special effort to understand suppliers, intermediaries and distributors from other cultures.

• We will appropriately acknowledge the contributions of others, such as consultants, employees and coworkers, to our marketing endeavors.

Openness—to create transparency in our marketing operations.

• We will strive to communicate clearly with all our constituencies.

• We will accept constructive criticism from our customers and other stakeholders.

• We will explain significant product or service risks, component substitutions or other foreseeable eventualities that could affect customers or their perception of the purchase decision.

• We will fully disclose list prices and terms of financing as well as available price deals and adjustments.

Citizenship—to fulfill the economic, legal, philanthropic, and societal responsibilities that serve stakeholders in a strategic manner.

• We will strive to protect the natural environment in the execution of marketing campaigns.

• We will give back to the community through volunteerism and charitable donations.

• We will work to contribute to the overall betterment of marketing and its reputation.

• We will encourage supply chain members to ensure that trade is fair for all participants, including producers in developing countries.

IMPLEMENTATION

Finally, we recognize that every industry sector and marketing subdiscipline (e.g., marketing research, e-commerce, direct selling, direct marketing, advertising) has its own specific ethical issues that require policies and commentary. An array of such codes can be accessed through links on the AMA Web site. We encourage all such groups to develop and/or refine their industry and discipline-specific codes of ethics to supplement these general norms and values.

Source: Reprinted with permission of the American Marketing Association.

PricewaterhouseCoopers (PwC) is a good example. In 2002, PwC established a global ethics office and comprehensive ethics program, headed by a high-level global ethics officer. The ethics program begins with a code of conduct, called "The Way We Do Business." PwC employees learn about the code of conduct and about how to handle thorny ethics issues in comprehensive ethics training programs, which start when the employee joins the company and continue through the employee's career. The program also includes an ethics help line and regular communications at all levels. "It is obviously not enough to distribute a document," says PwC's CEO, Samuel DiPiazza. "Ethics is in everything we say and do."[34]

Still, written codes and ethics programs do not ensure ethical behavior. Ethics and social responsibility require a total corporate commitment. They must be a component of the overall corporate culture. According to PwC's DiPiazza, "I see ethics as a mission-critical issue . . . deeply imbedded in who we are and what we do. It's just as important as our product development cycle or our distribution system. . . . It's about creating a culture based on integrity and respect, not a culture based on dealing with the crisis of the day. . . . We ask ourselves every day, 'Are we doing the right things?'"[35]

The Sustainable Company

At the foundation of marketing is the belief that companies that fulfill the needs and wants of customers will thrive. Companies that fail to meet customer needs or that intentionally or unintentionally harm customers, others in society, or future generations will decline. Sustainable companies are those that create value for customers through socially, environmentally, and ethically responsible actions.

Sustainable marketing goes beyond caring for the needs and wants of today's customers. It means having concern for tomorrow's customers in assuring the survival and success of the business, shareholders, employees, and the broader world in which they all live. Sustainable marketing provides the context in which companies can build profitable customer relationships by creating value *for* customers in order to capture value *from* customers in return, now and in the future.

REVIEWING Objectives AND KEY Terms

Well—here you are at the end of your introductory marketing journey! In this chapter, we've closed with many important *sustainable marketing* concepts related to marketing's sweeping impact on individual consumers, other businesses, and society as a whole. You learned that sustainable marketing requires socially, environmentally, and ethically responsible actions that bring value not just to present-day consumers and businesses, but also to future generations and to society as a whole. Sustainable companies are those that act responsibly to create value for customers in order to capture value from customers in return, now and in the future.

OBJECTIVE 1 **Define *sustainable marketing* and discuss its importance.** (pp 584–585)

Sustainable marketing calls for meeting the present needs of consumers and businesses while still preserving or enhancing the ability of future generations to meet their needs. Whereas the marketing concept recognizes that companies thrive by fulfilling the day-to-day needs of customers, sustainable marketing calls for socially and environmentally responsible actions that meet both the immediate and future needs of customers and the company. Truly sustainable marketing requires a smooth-functioning marketing system in which consumers, companies, public policymakers, and others work together to ensure responsible marketing actions.

OBJECTIVE 2 **Identify the major social criticisms of marketing.** (pp 586–594)

Marketing's *impact on individual consumer welfare* has been criticized for its high prices, deceptive practices, high-pressure selling, shoddy or unsafe products, planned obsolescence, and poor service to disadvantaged consumers. Marketing's *impact on society* has been criticized for creating false wants and too much materialism, too few social goods, and cultural pollution. Critics have also criticized marketing's *impact on other businesses* for harming competitors and reducing competition through acquisitions, practices that create barriers to entry, and unfair competitive marketing practices. Some of these concerns are justified; some are not.

OBJECTIVE 3 **Define *consumerism* and *environmentalism* and explain how they affect marketing strategies.** (pp 595–601)

Concerns about the marketing system have led to *citizen action movements*. *Consumerism* is an organized social movement intended to strengthen the rights and power of consumers relative to

sellers. Alert marketers view it as an opportunity to serve consumers better by providing more consumer information, education, and protection. *Environmentalism* is an organized social movement seeking to minimize the harm done to the environment and quality of life by marketing practices. The first wave of modern environmentalism was driven by environmental groups and concerned consumers, whereas the second wave was driven by government, which passed laws and regulations governing industrial practices impacting the environment. The first two environmentalism waves are now merging into a third and stronger wave in which companies are accepting responsibility for doing no environmental harm. Companies now are adopting policies of *environmental sustainability*—developing strategies that both sustain the environment and produce profits for the company. Both consumerism and environmentalism are important components of sustainable marketing.

OBJECTIVE 4 **Describe the principles of sustainable marketing.** (pp 602–605)

Many companies originally opposed these social movements and laws, but most of them now recognize a need for positive consumer information, education, and protection. Under the sustainable marketing concept, a company's marketing should support the best long-run performance of the marketing system. It should be guided by five sustainable marketing principles: *consumer-oriented marketing*, *customer-value marketing*, *innovative marketing*, *sense-of-mission marketing*, and *societal marketing*.

OBJECTIVE 5 **Explain the role of ethics in marketing.** (pp 605–609)

Increasingly, companies are responding to the need to provide company policies and guidelines to help their managers deal with questions of *marketing ethics*. Of course even the best guidelines cannot resolve all the difficult ethical decisions that individuals and firms must make. But there are some principles that marketers can choose among. One principle states that such issues should be decided by the free market and legal system. A second, and more enlightened principle, puts responsibility not on the system but in the hands of individual companies and managers. Each firm and marketing manager must work out a philosophy of socially responsible and ethical behavior. Under the sustainable marketing concept, managers must look beyond what is legal and allowable and develop standards based on personal integrity, corporate conscience, and long-term consumer welfare.

KEY Terms

OBJECTIVE 1
Sustainable marketing (p 584)

OBJECTIVE 3
Consumerism (p 595)
Environmentalism (p 596)

Environmental sustainability (p 597)

OBJECTIVE 4
Consumer-oriented marketing (p 602)
Customer-value marketing (p 602)
Innovative marketing (p 602)

Sense-of-mission marketing (p 603)
Societal marketing (p 604)
Deficient products (p 604)
Pleasing products (p 604)
Salutary products (p 604)
Desirable products (p 604)

DISCUSSING & APPLYING THE Concepts

Discussing the Concepts

1. What is sustainable marketing? Explain how the sustainable marketing concept differs from the marketing concept and the societal marketing concept. (AASCB: Communication)

2. Marketing's impact on individual consumers has been criticized. Discuss the issues relevant to this impact. (AACSB: Communication)

3. Discuss the types of harmful impact that marketing practices can have on competition and the associated problems. (AACSB: Communication)

4. Can an organization focus on both consumerism and environmentalism at the same time? Explain. (AACSB: Communication)

5. Describe the five sustainable marketing principles and explain how companies benefit from adhering to them. (AACSB: Communication)

6. Good ethics is the cornerstone of sustainable marketing. Explain what this means and discuss how companies practice good ethics. (AACSB: Communication)

Applying the Concepts

1. The U.S. Consumer Product Safety Commission (CPSC) protects consumers from unsafe products. Visit www.cpsc.gov to learn about this agency. Discuss a recent product recall. (AACSB: Communication; Use of IT; Reflective Thinking)

2. In a small group, discuss each of the morally difficult situations in marketing presented in Table 20.1. Which philosophy is guiding your decision in each situation? (AACSB: Communication; Ethical Reasoning)

3. Recent public concerns over children and the Internet resulted in the Children's Online Privacy Protection Act (COPPA). Among other things, this act requires Web sites that are visited by children under the age of 13 to post a privacy policy detailing any personally identifiable information collected from those children. Learn more about this law and discuss the consumer need it meets. Survey three Web sites targeted to children and evaluate whether they meet the requirements of the law. (AACSB: Communication; Use of IT; Reflective Thinking)

FOCUS ON Technology

Do you share video files with others on the Internet? If you do, you're taking up a huge hunk of bandwidth, which can cause degraded service for other customers. As a result, Internet providers, such as Comcast, may be blocking or slowing down Internet traffic of some customers—a practice referred to as network management. However, if a recent Federal Communications Commission ruling stands, these practices will stop. In 2008, the FCC ruled that Comcast wrongly blocked video file sharing activities of customers, violating the agency's Net neutrality principle. This principle holds that consumers should have unfettered access to the Internet. But the reality is that some consumers use an

inordinate amount of bandwidth. Some cable and phone companies are experimenting with "Internet metering"—making customers pay for the amount of bandwidth used.

1. Learn more about the Federal Communications Commission's Net neutrality principle, passed in 2005, and write a brief report explaining it. (AACSB: Communication)

2. Discuss this issue from the point of view of the broadband network providers who commonly use network management practices. Suggest other solutions to this problem. (AACSB: Communication; Reflective Thinking)

FOCUS ON Ethics

R&B singer Chris Brown's "Forever" tune claimed the number-four spot on *Billboard* magazine's Hot 100 in July 2008. "Tonight is the night to join me in the middle of ecstasy. . . . Cause we only got one night. Double your pleasure. Double your fun." If that last part sounds familiar, it's because it comes from Wrigley's Doublemint gum's timeless jingle. "Forever" is an extended version of a new Doublemint jingle, but it was released months before the commercial without indication that it was also a commercial jingle. Actually, the song and the jingle not only share the "Double your pleasure/Double your fun" element, but the

melody is the same. Mr. Brown was paid by Wrigley to write and perform the song and jingle.

1. Was Wrigley's sponsorship of the song and later release of the jingle deceptive? (AACSB: Communication; Ethical Reasoning)

2. Discuss other examples of product placement—that is, brands appearing in songs, movies, television programs, or video games. Are these different than Mr. Brown's and Wrigley's "Forever"? (AACSB: Communication; Reflective Thinking)

MARKETING BY THE Numbers

"High-low" pricing is popular with retailers but considered deceptive by some. Using this practice, retailers set initial prices very high for a short period and then discount the merchandise for the majority of the selling season. Critics complain that the supposed discounted price is in reality the regular price. For example, in the 1990s, the North Carolina Attorney General's office charged JCPenney with inflating regular prices for jewelry and then dropping the prices—advertising discounts up to 60 percent off "regular" prices. In reality, JCPenney was selling the jewelry at a typical industry markup.

1. Refer to Appendix 2, Marketing by the Numbers, to answer the following questions. If JCPenney's cost for a piece of

jewelry is $50 and it was marked up five times the cost, what is the "high" retail price? What is the "low" sales price if the price is reduced 60 percent off the "regular" price? What is JCPenney's markup percentage on cost at this price? What is its markup percentage on the "low" selling price? (AACSB: Communication; Analytical Reasoning)

2. The judge in the JCPenney case ruled that the retailer did not violate any state laws and that one retailer cannot be singled out because most jewelry competitors promote sales prices in a similar way. Is it ethical for retailers to use this pricing tactic? (AACSB: Communication; Reflective Thinking)

VIDEO Case

Land Rover

The automotive industry has seen better days. Many auto companies are now facing declining revenues and negative profits. Additionally, because of its primary dependence on products that consume petroleum, the auto industry has a big environmental black eye, especially companies that primarily make gas-guzzling trucks and SUVs.

During the past few years, however, Land Rover has experienced tremendous growth in revenues and profits. It is currently selling more vehicles than ever worldwide. How is this possible for a company that only sells SUVs? One of the biggest reasons is Land Rover's strategic focus on social responsibility and environmentalism. Land Rover believes that it can meet consumer needs for luxury all-terrain vehicles while at the same time providing a vehicle that is kinder to the environment. As a corporation, it is also working feverishly to reduce its carbon emissions, reduce

waste, and reduce water consumption and pollution. With actions like this, Land Rover is successfully repositioning its brand away from the standard perceptions of SUVs as environmental enemies.

After viewing the video featuring Land Rover, answer the following questions about the company's efforts toward social responsibility:

1. Make a list of social criticisms of the automotive industry. Discuss all of the ways that Land Rover is combating those criticisms.

2. By the textbook's definition, does Land Rover practice "sustainable marketing"?

3. Do you believe that Land Rover is sincere in its efforts to be environmentally friendly? Is it even possible for a large SUV to be environmentally friendly? Present support for both sides of these arguments.

COMPANY Case

ExxonMobil: Social Responsibility in a Commodity Market

One fine spring day in 2008, Joe Tyler watched the numbers on the gas pump speedily climb higher and higher as he filled up his 2002 Toyota at the neighborhood Exxon station. When his tank was full, what he saw shocked him right down to the core of his wallet. It had just cost him $43.63 to fill up his economy car. How could this be? Sure, the tank was completely empty and took almost 11 gallons. And, yes, gas prices were on the rise. But at $4.04 per gallon, this was the first time that a fill-up had cost him more than $40.

In the past, Joe hadn't usually looked at his gas receipts. Even though gas prices had risen dramatically over the past few years, it had still been relatively cheap by world standards; still cheaper than bottled water. And his Toyota rolled along consistently at 32–34 miles per gallon. Until now, Joe didn't think that his gas expenses were affecting his budget all that much. But crossing the $40 line gave him a wake-up call. Although it was far less than the $100 fill-ups he'd heard about for SUV drivers in places like Los Angeles where gas prices were among the highest in the country, it didn't seem that long ago that he'd routinely filled his tank for not much more than $10. In fact, he remembered paying around $1.20 a gallon to fill this same car when it was new in early 2002. Now, he was starting to feel the frustration expressed by so many other gas buyers. What had happened?

Not long before Joe's epiphany about gas prices, a man named Lee Raymond was retiring after 13 years as the chairman and CEO of ExxonMobil. He probably wasn't too concerned about how much it cost him to fill up his own car—or his jet for that matter. Including all his pension payoffs and stock options, Raymond's retirement package was valued at a mind-boggling $400 million. And why not? While at the helm of the giant oil company, Raymond had kept ExxonMobil in one of the top three spots on *Fortune*'s 500 list year after year. By the end of 2007, ExxonMobil had been the most profitable company in America, setting a new record every year. While Joe and other consumers were going through pain at the pumps, Exxon had racked up $40 billion in profits on $372 billion in sales. ExxonMobil's fourth-quarter revenues alone exceeded the annual gross domestic product of some major oil producing nations, including the United Arab Emirates and Kuwait.

Was it just a coincidence that ExxonMobil and the other major oil companies were posting record numbers at a time when consumers were getting hit so hard? Most consumers didn't think so—and they cried "foul." In an effort to calm irate consumers, politicians and consumer advocates were calling for action. Maria Cantwell (D-WA) was one of four U.S. senators who backed legislation that would give the government more oversight of oil, gas, and electricity markets. "Right now excuses from oil companies on why gas prices are so high are like smoke and mirrors," Senator Cantwell said. "The days of Enron taught us the painful lesson that fierce market manipulation does happen and I don't want

American consumers to have to experience that again." In a House of Representatives hearing in 2008, Congresswoman Maxine Waters (D-CA) even threatened the CEOs of the largest oil companies with nationalizing their companies if things did not change.

Several state attorney generals also launched investigations. Even the Bush administration demanded a federal investigation into gasoline pricing. In a speech to the country, President Bush said, "Americans understand by and large that the price of crude oil is going up and that [gas] prices are going up, but what they don't want and will not accept is manipulation of the market, and neither will I." But no investigation into the pricing activities of U.S. oil companies had ever produced any evidence of substantial wrongdoing. The FTC had found isolated examples of price gouging, as in the wake of 2005 hurricanes Katrina and Rita. But most of those were explainable and the FTC had never found evidence of widespread market manipulation.

DEMAND AND SUPPLY: IS IT REALLY THAT SIMPLE?

Although the many parties disagree on where to place the blame for skyrocketing gas prices, there is a high level of consistency among economists and industry observers. They agree that crude oil and even gasoline are commodities. Like corn and pork bellies, there is little if any differentiation in the products producers are turning out. And even though ExxonMobil has tried hard to convince customers that its gasoline differs from other brands based on a proprietary cocktail of detergents and additives, consumers do not generally perceive a difference. Thus, the market treats all offerings as the same.

Walter Lukken, a member of the U.S. Commodity Futures Trading Commission, has stated publicly what many know to be true about the pricing of commodities. In testimony before Congress on the nature of gasoline prices, Mr. Lukken said, "The commission thinks the markets accurately reflect tight world energy supplies and a pickup in growth and demand this year." But is it really as simple as demand and supply?

Let's look at demand. In the early 2000s, when oil was cheap, global demand was around 70 million barrels a day (mbd). Eight years later, world consumption had risen to 87 mbd. Many environmentalists point the finger at the driving habits of North Americans and their gas-swilling SUVs—and with good reason. The United States continues to be one of the world's leading petroleum consumers, with an appetite that grows every year. And as much as U.S. consumers cry about high gas prices, they've done little to change how much gas they consume.

However, although the United States consumes more gas than any other country, this consumption has grown only moderately. Over the past decade, the rise in global demand for oil has been much more the result of the exploding needs of emerging economies. The biggest contributors are China and India, which together account for 37 percent of the world's population. Both countries have a growing appetite for oil that reflects their rapid economic growth. With manufacturing and production increasing and with more individuals trading in bicycles for cars, China and India have the fastest growing economies in the world, with annual growth rates of 10 percent and 8 percent, respectively.

Now, let's look at supply. Recent spikes in the global price of crude are occurring at a time when rising demand coincides with constrained supply. Supply constraints exist at various levels of production, including drilling, refining, and distributing. In past decades, oil companies have had little incentive to invest in exploration and to expand capacity. Oil has been cheap, and environmental regulations created more constraints. Oil producing countries claim that they are producing at or near capacity. Many analysts support this, noting that global consumption of oil is pressing up against the limits of what the world can produce.

Similar constraints place limits on other stages of the supply chain. For example, U.S. refineries no longer have the capacity to meet the country's demand for petroleum-based fuels. Not only has no new refinery been built in over 30 years, but the total number of refineries has actually shrunk. Many point to government regulation and public resistance as the reasons for this. And as regulations dictate more gasoline blends for different regions, refineries feel an even greater pinch, and distribution lines experience bottlenecks.

But as much as supply and demand account for fluctuations in gas prices, there is a third factor. At a time when supply is stretched so tightly across a growing level of demand, price volatility may result more from the global petroleum futures trading than from anything else. Modern futures markets function on speculation. When factors point to a rise in prices, traders buy futures contracts in hopes of profiting. When oil seems overvalued, they sell. The net effect of all the buying and selling is a constant tweaking of oil prices, which reflects both the fundamental supply-demand situation as well as the constantly changing risk of a major political crisis or natural disaster.

Some policymakers and consumer advocates have pointed to speculative futures trading as a cause of high gas prices. But according to Walter Lukken, "Blaming the futures markets for high commodity prices is like blaming a thermometer for it being hot outside." Although it is true that the oil futures trading can artificially inflate prices in the short term, economists have found that such activities have more of a stabilizing effect in the long run. Speculators absorb risk, often stepping in when nobody else wants to buy or sell. In fact, as with other commodities, the more traders in a given commodity market, the smaller the gap between the buying and selling price for petroleum. This reduces costs for companies at all stages of the value chain, which should ultimately lower prices for customers. Accordingly, if not for the global oil futures market, price spikes and crashes would probably be even bigger and occur more frequently.

THE ANATOMY OF THE PRICE OF A GALLON OF GAS

Consumers like Joe Tyler wonder not only what makes the price of gas go up, but just how much of the price of each gallon they buy goes into Big Oil's coffers. They might be surprised to learn the breakdown on the price of a gallon of gas. Roughly 58 percent of the retail price of gas covers the cost of crude. In 2004, the price of crude was only about $35 a barrel. That price nearly quadrupled by 2008. Thus, it should come as no surprise that gasoline prices have risen in tandem.

Of course, there are other costs that contribute to the price of a gallon of gas. Distribution and marketing swallow 10 percent. Refining costs are good for another 8.5 percent. And then there are taxes. In the United States, the excise tax on gasoline varies from state to state. But on average, state and federal sales taxes account for 15 percent of the retail price.

This leaves less for oil companies than most consumers might imagine. In 2007, the oil industry as a whole made a net profit of about 8.5 percent. Although this was higher than the average for all industries, it was less than half the profit margins for health care, financial services, and pharmaceuticals. Still, the absolute profits for big oil companies are among the highest of all industries. ExxonMobil representatives are quick to point out a simple reason: scale. ExxonMobil had the highest profits in 2007 because it had the highest revenues. And when a company like General Motors (number four on the *Fortune* 500) actually loses $38 billion, ExxonMobil's $40 billion net profit really stands out.

WHAT TO DO?

If gas prices are determined in the way that so many experts say, it seems odd that so many people point the finger of scandal. Yet, given the impact of gas prices on personal budgets and national economies, it is understandable that people want answers. But even if the investigations were to actually produce evidence of wrongdoing, many experts believe that this would only distract from examining the real factors that govern the price of oil.

Proposed solutions for gas price woes span a very broad spectrum. At one end, some call for extreme government intervention and regulation. On the other end are those who suggest that no action be taken. "I don't think the government should be involved, trying to change the supply-and-demand equation here," said Evan Smith, a fund manager with U.S. Global Investors in San Antonio. "I really don't think anything they might do will [make] much of a difference anyway." In a time of such turmoil, ExxonMobil must consider not only how it might help alleviate the problem, but also how actions by others might impact its operations.

Questions for Discussion

1. Consider and discuss the impact of the rising price of gasoline on as many other products and services as possible.

2. How does the information in this case relate to the common criticism that marketing causes prices to be higher than they normally would?

3. Is ExxonMobil acting responsibly with respect to pricing its product? Can it keep its prices stable (or even lower them) when the market price is increasing? Should it even try?

4. From the perspective of social responsibility, what role does the consumer play in the price of gas?

5. How would you "fix" the problem of rising gas prices? Consider solutions for different groups, including governments, corporations, nonprofit groups, and consumers. What are the advantages and disadvantages of your proposed solutions?

Sources: Peter Coy, "First Housing, Now Oil," *BusinessWeek*, June 9, 2008, accessed at www.businessweek.com; "A Primer on Gasoline Prices," brochure from the Energy Information Administration, May 2008, accessed at www.eia.doe.gov; Patricia Hill, "Market Fuel Prices Drop, Relief Ahead as Demand Slows and Supplies Rise," *Washington Times*, April 28, 2006, p. A01; Katherine Reynolds Lewis, "Oil Market Is Running on Fear," *New Orleans Times-Picayune*, May 6, 2006, p. M1; "High Gasoline Prices Not Due to Manipulation, Regulators Say," *Calgary Herald*, April 28, 2006, p. E5; and "High Oil Prices Drive Up Exxon Mobil's Profit," *Associated Press*, May 3, 2006, accessed at www.msnbc.com.

Marketing Plan

The Marketing Plan: An Introduction (pp A1–A2)

As a marketer, you'll need a good marketing plan to provide direction and focus for your brand, product, or company. With a detailed plan, any business will be better prepared to launch a new product or build sales for existing products. Nonprofit organizations also use marketing plans to guide their fund-raising and outreach efforts. Even government agencies put together marketing plans for initiatives such as building public awareness of proper nutrition and stimulating area tourism.

The Purpose and Content of a Marketing Plan

Unlike a business plan, which offers a broad overview of the entire organization's mission, objectives, strategy, and resource allocation, a marketing plan has a more limited scope. It serves to document how the organization's strategic objectives will be achieved through specific marketing strategies and tactics, with the customer as the starting point. It is also linked to the plans of other departments within the organization. Suppose that a marketing plan calls for selling 200,000 units annually. The production department must gear up to make that many units, the finance department must arrange funding to cover the expenses, the human resources department must be ready to hire and train staff, and so on. Without the appropriate level of organizational support and resources, no marketing plan can succeed.

Although the exact length and layout will vary from company to company, a marketing plan usually contains the sections described in Chapter 2. Smaller businesses may create shorter or less formal marketing plans, whereas corporations frequently require highly structured marketing plans. To guide implementation effectively, every part of the plan must be described in considerable detail. Sometimes a company will post its marketing plan on an internal Web site, which allows managers and employees in different locations to consult specific sections and collaborate on additions or changes.

The Role of Research

Marketing plans are not created in a vacuum. To develop successful strategies and action programs, marketers need up-to-date information about the environment, the competition, and the market segments to be served. Often, analysis of internal data is the starting point for assessing the current marketing situation, supplemented by marketing intelligence and research investigating the overall market, the competition, key issues, and threats and opportunities issues. As the plan is put into effect, marketers use a variety of research techniques to measure progress toward objectives and identify areas for improvement if results fall short of projections.

Finally, marketing research helps marketers learn more about their customers' requirements, expectations, perceptions, and satisfaction levels. This deeper understanding provides a foundation for building competitive advantage through well-informed segmentation, targeting, differentiation, and positioning decisions. Thus, the marketing plan should outline what marketing research will be conducted and how the findings will be applied.

The Role of Relationships

The marketing plan shows how the company will establish and maintain profitable customer relationships. In the process, however, it also shapes a number of internal and external relationships. First, it affects how marketing personnel work with each other and with other departments to deliver value and satisfy customers. Second, it affects how the company works with suppliers, distributors, and strategic alliance partners to achieve the objectives listed in the plan. Third, it influences the company's dealings with other stakeholders, including government regulators, the media, and the community at large. All of these relationships are important to the organization's success, so they should be considered when a marketing plan is being developed.

From Marketing Plan to Marketing Action

Companies generally create yearly marketing plans, although some plans cover a longer period. Marketers start planning well in advance of the implementation date to allow time for marketing research, thorough analysis, management review, and coordination between departments. Then, after each action program begins, marketers monitor ongoing results, compare them with projections, analyze any differences, and take corrective steps as needed. Some marketers also prepare contingency plans for implementation if certain conditions emerge. Because of inevitable and sometimes unpredictable environmental changes, marketers must be ready to update and adapt marketing plans at any time.

For effective implementation and control, the marketing plan should define how progress toward objectives will be measured. Managers typically use budgets, schedules, and performance standards for monitoring and evaluating results. With budgets, they can compare planned expenditures with actual expenditures for a given week, month, or other period. Schedules allow management to see when tasks were supposed to be completed—and when they were actually completed. Performance standards track the outcomes of marketing programs to see whether the company is moving toward its objectives. Some examples of performance standards are market share, sales volume, product profitability, and customer satisfaction.

Sample Marketing Plan for Sonic (pp A2–A10)

This section takes you inside the sample marketing plan for Sonic, a hypothetical start-up company. The company's first product is the Sonic 1000, a multimedia, cellular/Wi-Fi-enabled smartphone. Sonic will be competing with Apple, Nokia, Research in Motion, Motorola, and other well-established rivals in a crowded, fast-changing marketplace for smartphones that combine communication, entertainment, and storage functionality. The annotations explain more about what each section of the plan should contain and why.

Executive Summary

Executive summary
This section summarizes the main goals, recommendations, and points as an overview for senior managers who will read and approve the marketing plan. A table of contents usually follows this section, for management convenience.

Sonic is preparing to launch a new multimedia, dual-mode smartphone, the Sonic 1000, in a mature market. Our product offers a competitively unique combination of advanced features and functionality at a value-added price. We are targeting specific segments in the consumer and business markets, taking advantage of opportunities indicated by higher demand for easy-to-use smartphones with expanded communications, entertainment, and storage functionality.

The primary marketing objective is to achieve first-year U.S. sales of 500,000 units. The primary financial objectives are to achieve first-year sales revenues of $75 million, keep first-year losses to less than $8 million, and break even early in the second year.

Current Marketing Situation

Current marketing situation
In this section, marketing managers discuss the overall market, identify the market segments that they will target, and provide information about the company's current situation.

Sonic, founded 18 months ago by two entrepreneurs with experience in the PC market, is about to enter the maturing smartphone market. Multifunction cell phones, e-mail devices, and wireless communication devices have become commonplace for both personal and professional use. Research shows that the United States has 262 million wireless phone subscribers, and 85 percent of the population owns a cell phone.

Competition is therefore more intense even as demand flattens, industry consolidation continues, and pricing pressures squeeze profitability. Worldwide, Nokia is the smartphone leader, holding 45 percent of the global market. The runner-up is Research in Motion, maker of the BlackBerry, with 13 percent of the global market. In the U.S. market, BlackBerry is the market leader (with a 42 percent share) and Apple, maker of the iPhone, is the runner-up (with a 20 percent share). To gain market share in this dynamic environment, Sonic must carefully target specific segments with features that deliver benefits valued by each customer group.

Market description

Describing the targeted segments in detail provides context for the marketing strategies and detailed action programs discussed later in the plan.

Benefits and product features

Table A1.1 clarifies the benefits that product features will deliver to satisfy the needs of customers in each targeted segment.

Market Description

Sonic's market consists of consumers and business users who prefer to use a single device for communication, information storage and exchange, and entertainment on the go. Specific segments being targeted during the first year include professionals, corporations, students, entrepreneurs, and medical users. ● **Table A1.1** shows how the Sonic 1000 addresses the needs of targeted consumer and business segments.

Buyers can choose between models based on several different operating systems, including systems from Microsoft, Symbian, and BlackBerry, plus Linux variations. Sonic licenses a Linux-based system because it is somewhat less vulnerable to attack by hackers and viruses. Hard drives and removable memory cards are popular smartphone options. Sonic is equipping its first entry with an ultra-fast 20-gigabyte removable memory card for information and entertainment storage. This will also allow users to transfer photos and other data from the smartphone to a home or office computer. Technology costs are decreasing even as capabilities are increasing, which makes value-priced models more appealing to consumers and to business users with older devices who want to trade up to new, high-end multifunction units.

● **TABLE** | **A1.1**   Segment Needs and Corresponding Features/Benefits of Sonic

Targeted Segment	Customer Need	Corresponding Feature/Benefit
Professionals (consumer market)	• Stay in touch conveniently and securely while on the go • Perform many functions hands-free without carrying multiple gadgets	• Built-in cell phone and push-to-talk to communicate anywhere at any time; wireless e-mail/Web access from anywhere; Linux-based operating system less vulnerable to hackers • Voice-activated applications are convenient; GPS function, camera add value
Students (consumer market)	• Perform many functions hands-free without carrying multiple gadgets • Express style and individuality	• Compatible with numerous applications and peripherals for convenient, cost-effective communication and entertainment • Wardrobe of smartphone cases
Corporate users (business market)	• Security and adaptability for proprietary tasks • Obtain driving directions to business meetings	• Customizable to fit corporate tasks and networks; Linux-based operating system less vulnerable to hackers • Built-in GPS allows voice-activated access to directions and maps
Entrepreneurs (business market)	• Organize and access contacts, schedule details, business and financial files • Get in touch fast	• Hands-free, wireless access to calendar, address book, information files for checking appointments and data, connecting with contacts • Push-to-talk instant calling speeds up communications
Medical users (business market)	• Update, access, and exchange medical records • Photograph medical situations to maintain a visual record	• Removable memory card and hands-free, wireless information recording reduces paperwork and increases productivity • Built-in camera allows fast and easy photography, stores images for later retrieval

Product review
The product review summarizes the main features for all of the company's products, organized by product line, type of customer, market, or order of product introduction.

Product Review

Our first product, the Sonic 1000, offers the following standard features with a Linux OS:

- Built-in dual cell phone/Internet phone functionality and push-to-talk instant calling

- Digital music/video/television recording, wireless downloading, and playback

- Wireless Web and e-mail, text messaging, instant messaging

- Three-inch color screen for easy viewing

- Organizational functions, including calendar, address book, synchronization

- Global positioning system for directions and maps

- Integrated 4-megapixel digital camera

- Ultra-fast 20-gigabyte removable memory card with upgrade potential

- Interchangeable case wardrobe of different colors and patterns

- Voice recognition functionality for hands-free operation

First-year sales revenues are projected to be $75 million, based on sales of 500,000 Sonic 1000 units at a wholesale price of $150 each. During the second year, we plan to introduce the Sonic 2000, also with Linux OS, as a higher-end smartphone product offering the following standard features:

- Global phone and messaging compatibility

- Translation capabilities to send English text as Spanish text (other languages to be offered as add-on options)

- Integrated 8-megapixel camera with flash

Competitive review
The purpose of a competitive review is to identify key competitors, describe their market positions, and briefly discuss their strategies.

Competitive Review

The emergence of lower-priced smartphones, including the Apple iPhone, has increased competitive pressure. Competition from specialized devices for text and e-mail messaging, such as BlackBerry devices, is a major factor, as well. Key competitors include the following:

- *Nokia.* The market leader in smartphones, Nokia offers a wide range of products for consumers and professionals. It recently purchased the maker of the Symbian operating system and made it into a separate foundation dedicated to improving and promoting this mobile software platform. Many of Nokia's smartphones offer full keyboards, similar to Research in Motion models, but stripped-down models are available for users who do not require the full keyboard and full multimedia capabilities.

- *Apple.* The stylish, popular iPhone 3G has a 3.5-inch color screen and is well-equipped for music, video, and Web access, as well as having communication, calendar, contact management, and file management functions. Its global positioning system technology can pinpoint a user's location. Also, users can erase data with a remote command if the smartphone is lost or stolen. However, AT&T is the only U.S. network provider. The iPhone is priced at $199 and up, with a two-year service contract.

- *RIM.* Research in Motion makes the lightweight BlackBerry wireless multifunction products that are especially popular among corporate users. RIM's continuous innovation and solid customer service support clearly strengthen its competitive standing as it introduces smartphones with enhanced features and communication capabilities. RIM's newer smartphones come equipped with the BlackBerry OS.

- *Motorola.* Motorola, a global giant, has been losing U.S. market share to Apple and Research in Motion, in particular, because it has slowed the pace of new product introduction. One of its top smartphone models is the slender, lightweight quad-band Q, which incorporates e-mail and text message functions, photo caller identification, a full keyboard, camera with flash, removable memory, updated multimedia audio/video/image capabilities, dual stereo speakers, and more. After rebate, the Q is priced at $149.99 with a two-year AT&T Wireless contract, although the retail price without a contract is considerably higher.

- *Samsung.* Value, style, function: Samsung is a strong competitor, offering a variety of smartphones for consumer and business segments. Some of its smartphones are available for specific telecommunications carriers and some are "unlocked," ready for any compatible telecommunications network. Its Instinct is a smartphone with features similar to the iPhone. Like the iPhone, service agreements are only available through one provider—Sprint. After a mail-in rebate of $100, the Instinct's introductory price is $129.99 with a two-year contract.

Despite this strong competition, Sonic can carve out a definite image and gain recognition among the targeted segments. Our voice-recognition system for completely hands-off operation is a critical point of differentiation for competitive advantage. Also, offering GPS as a standard feature gives us a competitive edge compared with similarly priced smartphones. Moreover, our product is speedier than most and runs the Linux OS, which is an appealing alternative for customers concerned about security. ● **Table A1.2** shows a sample of competitive products and prices.

Channels and logistics review

In this section, marketers list the most important channels, provide an overview of each channel arrangement, and identify developing issues in channels and logistics.

Channels and Logistics Review

Sonic-branded products will be distributed through a network of retailers in the top 50 U.S. markets. Among the most important channel partners being contacted are

- *Office supply superstores.* Office Max and Staples will both carry Sonic products in stores, in catalogs, and online.

- *Computer stores.* Independent computer retailers in major cities will carry Sonic products.

- *Electronics specialty stores.* Circuit City and Best Buy will feature Sonic products.

- *Online retailers.* Amazon.com will carry Sonic products and, for a promotional fee, will give Sonic prominent placement on its home page during the introduction.

● TABLE | A1.2   Sample of Competitive Products and Pricing

Competitor	Model	Features	Price
Nokia	E61i	Quad-band for worldwide phone, e-mail, and Internet access, backlit keyboard, corporate and personal e-mail integration, 2.8-inch screen, 2-megapixel camera, memory card, Symbian OS.	$355 without phone contract
Apple	iPhone 3G	Sleek styling, big screen, fast Internet functions, one-touch calling, GPS navigation, integrated personal and corporate e-mail, open and edit Microsoft Office files, 2-megapixel camera, no keyboard, Apple Mac operating system.	$199 with phone contract
RIM	BlackBerry Curve	Phone, wireless e-mail and Internet access, 2-megapixel camera, built-in maps and GPS, audio and video recording, expandable memory, keyboard, case color options, BlackBerry OS.	$149.99 with rebate, phone contract
Motorola	Q	Extremely thin and light, with keyboard, quad-band functionality for worldwide use, integrated camera including flash, e-mail and texting functions, Bluetooth connections, multimedia capabilities, voice-activated dialing, Windows OS.	$449.99 without phone contract
Samsung	Instinct	Phone plus e-mail and speedy Internet access, voice-guided GPS, 3.1-inch touch-screen, expandable memory, 2-megapixel camera, live TV, video recording and transmission, FM radio, no keyboard, proprietary operating system.	$129.99 with rebate, phone contract

Initially, our channel strategy will focus on the United States; according to demand, we plan to expand into Canada and beyond, with appropriate logistical support.

Strengths, Weaknesses, Opportunities, and Threat Analysis

Sonic has several powerful strengths on which to build, but our major weakness is lack of brand awareness and image. The major opportunity is demand for multimedia smartphones that deliver a number of valued benefits, eliminating the need for customers to carry more than one device. We also face the threat of ever-higher competition from consumer electronics manufacturers, as well as downward pricing pressure. ● **Table A1.3** summarizes Sonic's main strengths, weaknesses, opportunities, and threats.

Strengths

Strengths are internal capabilities that can help the company reach its objectives.

Strengths

Sonic can build on three important strengths:

1. *Innovative product.* The Sonic 1000 offers a combination of features that would otherwise require customers to carry multiple devices: speedy, hands-free dual-mode cell/Wi-Fi telecommunications capabilities, GPS functions, and digital video/music/TV program storage/playback.

2. *Security.* Our smartphone uses a Linux-based operating system that is less vulnerable to hackers and other security threats that can result in stolen or corrupted data.

3. *Pricing.* Our product is priced lower than competing multifunction models—none of which offer the same bundle of features—which gives us an edge with price-conscious customers.

Weaknesses

Weaknesses are internal elements that may interfere with the company's ability to achieve its objectives.

Weaknesses

By waiting to enter the smartphone market until some consolidation of competitors has occurred, Sonic has learned from the successes and mistakes of others. Nonetheless, we have two main weaknesses:

1. *Lack of brand awareness.* Sonic has no established brand or image, whereas Apple and others have strong brand recognition. We will address this issue with aggressive promotion.

2. *Physical specifications.* The Sonic 1000 is slightly heavier and thicker than most competing models because it incorporates multiple features, offers sizable storage capacity, and is compatible with numerous peripheral devices. To counteract this weakness, we will emphasize our product's benefits and value-added pricing, two compelling competitive strengths.

● TABLE | A1.3   Sonic's Strengths, Weaknesses, Opportunities, and Threats

Strengths	Weaknesses
• Innovative combination of functions in one portable, voice-activated device • Security due to Linux-based operating system • Value pricing	• Lack of brand awareness and image • Heavier and thicker than most competing models
Opportunities	**Threats**
• Increased demand for multimedia, multifunction smartphones • Cost-efficient technology	• Intense competition • Downward pricing pressure • Compressed product life cycle

Opportunities

Sonic can take advantage of two major market opportunities:

1. *Increasing demand for multimedia smartphones with multiple functions.* The market for multimedia, multifunction devices is growing much faster than the market for single-use devices. Growth will accelerate as dual-mode capabilities become mainstream, giving customers the flexibility to make phone calls over cell or Internet connections. Smartphones are already commonplace in public, work, and educational settings, which is boosting primary demand. Also, customers who bought entry-level models are replacing older models with more advanced models.

2. *Cost-efficient technology.* Better technology is now available at a lower cost than ever before. Thus, Sonic can incorporate advanced features at a value-added price that allows for reasonable profits.

Threats

We face three main threats at the introduction of the Sonic 1000:

1. *Increased competition.* More companies are entering the U.S. market with smartphone models that offer some but not all of the features and benefits provided by Sonic's product. Therefore, Sonic's marketing communications must stress our clear differentiation and value-added pricing.

2. *Downward pressure on pricing.* Increased competition and market-share strategies are pushing smartphone prices down. Still, our objective of seeking a 10 percent profit on second-year sales of the original model is realistic, given the lower margins in this market.

3. *Compressed product life cycle.* Smartphones have reached the maturity stage of their life cycle more quickly than earlier technology products. We have contingency plans to keep sales growing by adding new features, targeting additional segments, and adjusting prices as needed.

Objectives and Issues

We have set aggressive but achievable objectives for the first and second years of market entry.

First-Year Objectives

During the Sonic 1000's initial year on the market, we are aiming for unit sales volume of 500,000.

Second-Year Objectives

Our second-year objectives are to sell a combined total of one million units of our two models and to achieve breakeven early in this period.

Issues

In relation to the product launch, our major issue is the ability to establish a well-regarded brand name linked to a meaningful positioning. We will have to invest heavily in marketing to create a memorable and distinctive brand image projecting innovation, quality, and value. We also must measure awareness and response so we can adjust our marketing efforts as necessary.

Marketing Strategy

Sonic's marketing strategy is based on a positioning of product differentiation. Our primary consumer target is middle- to upper-income professionals who need one portable device to coordinate their busy schedules, communicate with family and colleagues, get driving directions, and be entertained on the go. Our secondary consumer target is high school, college, and graduate students who want a multimedia, dual-mode device. This segment can be described demographically by age (16–30) and education status.

Our primary business target is mid- to large-sized corporations that want to help their managers and employees stay in touch and input or access critical data when out of the office. This segment consists of companies with more than $25 million in annual sales and more than 100 employees. We are also targeting entrepreneurs and small business owners as well as medical users who want to update or access patients' medical records while reducing paperwork.

Positioning

A positioning built on meaningful differentiation, supported by appropriate strategy and implementation, can help the company build competitive advantage.

Marketing tools

These sections summarize the broad logic that will guide decisions made about the marketing tools to be used during the period covered by the plan.

Positioning

Using product differentiation, we are positioning the Sonic as the most versatile, convenient, value-added smartphone for personal and professional use. Our marketing will focus on the hands-free operation of multiple communication, entertainment, and information capabilities differentiating the Sonic 1000.

Product Strategy

The Sonic 1000, including all the features described in the earlier Product Review section, will be sold with a one-year warranty. We will introduce a more compact, powerful high-end model (the Sonic 2000) during the following year. Building the Sonic brand is an integral part of our product strategy. The brand and logo (Sonic's distinctive yellow thunderbolt) will be displayed on the product and its packaging, and reinforced by its prominence in the introductory marketing campaign.

Pricing Strategy

The Sonic 1000 will be introduced at $150 wholesale/$199 estimated retail price per unit. We expect to lower the price of this first model when we expand the product line by launching the Sonic 2000, to be priced at $175 wholesale per unit. These prices reflect a strategy of (1) attracting desirable channel partners and (2) taking share from Nokia, Research in Motion, and other established competitors.

Distribution Strategy

Our channel strategy is to use selective distribution, marketing Sonic smartphones through well-known stores and online retailers. During the first year, we will add channel partners until we have coverage in all major U.S. markets and the product is included in the major electronics catalogs and Web sites. We will also investigate distribution through cell-phone outlets maintained by major carriers such as Verizon Wireless. In support of our channel partners, Sonic will provide demonstration products, detailed specification handouts, and full-color photos and displays featuring the product. Finally, we plan to arrange special payment terms for retailers that place volume orders.

Marketing Communications Strategy

By integrating all messages in all media, we will reinforce the brand name and the main points of product differentiation. Research about media consumption patterns will help our advertising agency choose appropriate media and timing to reach prospects before and during product introduction. Thereafter, advertising will appear on a pulsing basis to maintain brand awareness and communicate various differentiation messages. The agency will also coordinate public relations efforts to build the Sonic brand and support the differentiation message. To create buzz, we will host a user-generated video contest on our Web site. To attract, retain, and motivate channel partners for a push strategy, we will use trade sales promotions and personal selling. Until the Sonic brand has been established, our communications will encourage purchases through channel partners rather than from our Web site.

Marketing research

This section shows how marketing research will be used to support development, implementation, and evaluation of strategies and action programs.

Marketing Research

Using research, we are identifying the specific features and benefits that our target market segments value. Feedback from market tests, surveys, and focus groups will help us develop the Sonic 2000. We are also measuring and analyzing customers' attitudes toward competing brands and products. Brand awareness research will help us determine the effectiveness and efficiency of our messages and media. Finally, we will use customer satisfaction studies to gauge market reaction.

Marketing organization
The marketing department may be organized by function, as in this sample, by geography, by product, or by customer (or some combination).

Action programs
Action programs should be coordinated with the resources and activities of other departments, including production, finance, purchasing, and so on.

Marketing Organization

Sonic's chief marketing officer, Jane Melody, holds overall responsibility for all of the company's marketing activities. 🕮 **Figure A1.1** shows the structure of the eight-person marketing organization. Sonic has hired Worldwide Marketing to handle national sales campaigns, trade and consumer sales promotions, and public relations efforts.

Action Programs

The Sonic 1000 will be introduced in February. Following are summaries of the action programs we will use during the first six months of next year to achieve our stated objectives.

January We will launch a $200,000 trade sales promotion campaign and exhibit at the major industry trade shows to educate dealers and generate channel support for the product launch in February. Also, we will create buzz by providing samples to selected product reviewers, opinion leaders, influential bloggers, and celebrities. Our training staff will work with retail sales personnel at major chains to explain the Sonic 1000's features, benefits, and advantages.

February We will start an integrated print/radio/Internet campaign targeting professionals and consumers. The campaign will show how many functions the Sonic smartphone can perform and emphasize the convenience of a single, powerful handheld device. This multimedia campaign will be supported by point-of-sale signage as well as online-only ads and video tours.

March As the multimedia advertising campaign continues, we will add consumer sales promotions such as a contest in which consumers post videos to our Web site, showing how they use the Sonic in creative and unusual ways. We will also distribute new point-of-purchase displays to support our retailers.

April We will hold a trade sales contest offering prizes for the salesperson and retail organization that sells the most Sonic smartphones during the four-week period.

May We plan to roll out a new national advertising campaign this month. The radio ads will feature celebrity voices telling their Sonic smartphones to perform functions such as initiating a phone call, sending an e-mail, playing a song or video, and so on. The stylized print and online ads will feature avatars of these celebrities holding their Sonic smartphones.

🕮 **FIGURE | A1.1**
Sonic's Marketing Organization

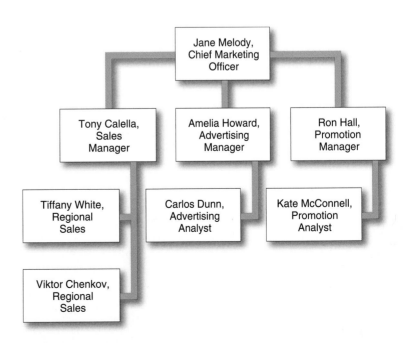

June Our radio campaign will add a new voice-over tag line promoting the Sonic 1000 as a graduation gift. We will also exhibit at the semiannual electronics trade show and provide channel partners with new competitive comparison handouts as a sales aid. In addition, we will tally and analyze the results of customer satisfaction surveys for use in future promotions and to provide feedback for product and marketing activities.

Budgets

Budgets

Managers use budgets to project profitability and plan for each marketing program's expenditures, scheduling, and operations.

Total first-year sales revenue for the Sonic 1000 is projected at $75 million, with an average wholesale price of $150 per unit and variable cost of $100 per unit for a unit sales volume of 500,000. We anticipate a first-year loss of up to $8 million on the Sonic 1000 model. Break-even calculations indicate that the Sonic 1000 will become profitable after the sales volume exceeds 650,000, early in the product's second year. Our break-even analysis of Sonic's first smartphone product assumes per-unit wholesale revenue of $150 per unit, variable cost of $100 per unit, and estimated first-year fixed costs of $32,500,000. Based on these assumptions, the break-even calculation is

$$\frac{32,500,000}{\$150 - \$100} = 650,000\,\text{units}$$

Controls

Controls

Controls help management assess results after the plan is implemented, identify any problems or performance variations, and initiate corrective action.

We are planning tight control measures to closely monitor quality and customer service satisfaction. This will enable us to react very quickly in correcting any problems that may occur. Other early warning signals that will be monitored for signs of deviation from the plan include monthly sales (by segment and channel) and monthly expenses. Given the market's volatility, we are developing contingency plans to address fast-moving environmental changes such as new technology and new competition.

Marketing Plan Tools

Pearson Prentice Hall offers two valuable resources to assist you in developing a marketing plan:

- *The Marketing Plan Handbook* by Marian Burk Wood explains the process of creating a marketing plan, complete with detailed checklists and dozens of real-world examples.

- *Marketing Plan Pro* is an award-winning software package that includes sample plans, step-by-step guides, an introductory video, help wizards, and customizable charts for documenting a marketing plan.

Sources: Background information and market data adapted from Laura M. Holson, "Phone Giants Fight to Keep Subscribers," *New York Times,* July 23, 2008, p. C1; Olga Kharif and Roger O. Crockett, "Motorola's Market Share Mess," *BusinessWeek,* July 10, 2008, www.businessweek.com; "Follow the Leader," *Economist,* June 14, 2008, pp. 78–80; Chris Nutall et al., "Apple Set to Slash iPhone Prices to Lift Sales," *Financial Times,* June 10, 2008, p. 20; Walter S. Mossberg, "Samsung Instinct Doesn't Ring True as an iPhone Clone," *Wall Street Journal,* June 12, 2008, p. D1; "Smartphones Get Smarter, Thanks in Part to the iPhone," *InformationWeek,* July 21, 2007; "Hospital Uses PDA App for Patient Transport," *Health Data Management,* June 2007, p. 14.

Marketing by the Numbers

Marketing managers are facing increased accountability for the financial implications of their actions. This appendix provides a basic introduction to measuring marketing financial performance. Such financial analysis guides marketers in making sound marketing decisions and in assessing the outcomes of those decisions.

The appendix is built around a hypothetical manufacturer of high-definition consumer electronics products—HDInhance. In the past, HDInhance has concentrated on making high-definition televisions for the consumer market. However, the company is now entering the accessories market. Specifically, HDInhance is introducing a new product—a Blu-ray high-definition optical disc player (DVD) that also plays videos streamed over the Internet. In this appendix, we will discuss and analyze the various decisions HDInhance's marketing managers must make before and after the new product launch.

The appendix is organized into *three sections*. The *first section* introduces pricing, break-even, and margin analysis assessments that will guide the introduction of HDInhance's new product. The *second section* discusses demand estimates, the marketing budget, and marketing performance measures. It begins with a discussion of estimating market potential and company sales. It then introduces the marketing budget, as illustrated through a *pro forma* profit-and-loss statement followed by the actual profit-and-loss statement. Next we discuss marketing performance measures with a focus on helping marketing managers to better defend their decisions from a financial perspective. In the *third section*, we analyze the financial implications of various marketing tactics, such as increasing advertising expenditures, adding sales representatives to increase distribution, lowering price, or extending the product line.

Each of the three sections ends with a set of quantitative exercises that provide you with an opportunity to apply the concepts you learned to situations beyond HDInhance.

Pricing, Break-Even, and Margin Analysis (pp A11–A16)

Pricing Considerations

Determining price is one of the most important marketing mix decisions, and marketers have considerable leeway when setting prices. The limiting factors are demand and costs. Demand factors, such as buyer-perceived value, set the price ceiling. The company's costs set the price floor. In between these two factors, marketers must consider competitors' prices and other factors such as reseller requirements, government regulations, and company objectives.

Current competing high-definition DVD/Internet streaming products in this relatively new product category were introduced in 2007 and sell at retail prices between $500 and $1,200. HDInhance plans to introduce its new product at a lower price in order to expand the market and to gain market share rapidly. We first consider HDInhance's pricing decision from a cost perspective. Then we consider consumer value, the competitive environment, and reseller requirements.

Fixed costs

Costs that do not vary with production or sales level.

Variable costs

Costs that vary directly with the level of production.

Total costs

The sum of the fixed and variable costs for any given level of production.

Cost-plus pricing (or markup pricing)

A standard markup to the cost of the product.

Relevant costs

Costs that will occur in the future and that will vary across the alternatives being considered.

Break-even price

The price at which total revenue equals total cost and profit is zero.

Return on investment (ROI) pricing (or target-return pricing)

A cost-based pricing method that determines price based on a specified rate of return on investment.

Determining Costs

Recall from Chapter 10 that there are different types of costs. **Fixed costs** do not vary with production or sales level and include costs such as rent, interest, depreciation, and clerical and management salaries. Regardless of the level of output, the company must pay these costs. Whereas total fixed costs remain constant as output increases, the fixed cost per unit (or average fixed cost) will decrease as output increases because the total fixed costs are spread across more units of output. **Variable costs** vary directly with the level of production and include costs related to the direct production of the product (such as costs of goods sold—COGS) and many of the marketing costs associated with selling it. Although these costs tend to be uniform for each unit produced, they are called variable because their total varies with the number of units produced. **Total costs** are the sum of the fixed and variable costs for any given level of production.

HDInhance has invested $10 million in refurbishing an existing facility to manufacture the new product. Once production begins, the company estimates that it will incur fixed costs of $20 million per year. The variable cost to produce each device is estimated to be $250 and is expected to remain at that level for the output capacity of the facility.

Setting Price Based on Costs

HDInhance starts with the cost-based approach to pricing discussed in Chapter 10. Recall that the simplest method, **cost-plus pricing** (or **markup pricing**), simply adds a standard markup to the cost of the product. To use this method, however, HDInhance must specify expected unit sales so that total unit costs can be determined. Unit variable costs will remain constant regardless of the output, but *average unit fixed costs* will decrease as output increases.

To illustrate this method, suppose HDInhance has fixed costs of $20 million, variable costs of $250 per unit, and expects unit sales of 1 million units. Thus, the cost per unit is given by the following:

$$\text{Unit cost} = \text{variable cost} + \frac{\text{fixed costs}}{\text{unit sales}} = \$250 + \frac{\$20,000,000}{1,000,000} = \$270$$

Note that we do *not* include the initial investment of $10 million in the total fixed cost figure. It is not considered a fixed cost because it is not a *relevant* cost. **Relevant costs** are those that will occur in the future and that will vary across the alternatives being considered. HDInhance's investment to refurbish the manufacturing facility was a one-time cost that will not reoccur in the future. Such past costs are *sunk costs* and should not be considered in future analyses.

Also notice that if HDInhance sells its product for $270, the price is equal to the total cost per unit. This is the **break-even price**—the price at which unit revenue (price) equals unit cost and profit is zero.

Suppose HDInhance does not want to merely break even, but rather wants to earn a 25% markup on sales. HDInhance's markup price is as follows:[1]

$$\text{Markup price} = \frac{\text{unit cost}}{(1 - \text{desired return on sales})} = \frac{\$270}{1 - .25} = \$360$$

This is the price that HDInhance would sell the product to resellers such as wholesalers or retailers to earn a 25% profit on sales.

Another approach HDInhance could use is called **return on investment (ROI) pricing** (or **target-return pricing**). In this case, the company *would* consider the initial $10 million investment, but only to determine the dollar profit goal. Suppose the company wants a 30% return on its investment. The price necessary to satisfy this requirement can be determined by the following:[2]

$$\text{ROI price} = \text{unit cost} + \frac{\text{ROI} \times \text{investment}}{\text{unit sales}} = \$270 + \frac{0.3 \times \$10,000,000}{1,000,000} = \$273$$

That is, if HDInhance sells its product for $273, it will realize a 30% return on its initial investment of $10 million.

In these pricing calculations, unit cost is a function of the expected sales, which were estimated to be 1 million units. But what if actual sales were lower? Then the unit cost would be higher because the fixed costs would be spread over fewer units, and the realized percentage markup on sales or ROI would be lower. Alternatively, if sales are higher than the estimated 1 million units, unit cost would be lower than $270, so a lower price would produce the desired markup on sales or ROI. It's important to note that these cost-based pricing methods are *internally* focused and do not consider demand, competitors' prices, or reseller requirements. Because HDInhance will be selling this product to consumers through wholesalers and retailers offering competing brands, the company must consider markup pricing from this perspective.

Setting Price Based on External Factors

Whereas costs determine the price floor, HDInhance also must consider external factors when setting price. HDInhance does not have the final say concerning the final price to consumers—retailers do. So it must start with its suggested retail price and work back. In doing so, HDInhance must consider the markups required by resellers that sell the product to consumers.

In general, a dollar **markup** is the difference between a company's selling price for a product and its cost to manufacture or purchase it. For a retailer, then, the markup is the difference between the price it charges consumers and the cost the retailer must pay for the product. Thus, for any level of reseller

$$\text{Dollar markup} = \text{selling price} - \text{cost}$$

Markups are usually expressed as a percentage, and there are two different ways to compute markups—on *cost* or on *selling price*:

$$\text{Markup percentage on cost} = \frac{\text{dollar markup}}{\text{cost}}$$

$$\text{Markup percentage on selling price} = \frac{\text{dollar markup}}{\text{selling price}}$$

To apply reseller margin analysis, HDInhance must first set the suggested retail price and then work back to the price at which it must sell the product to a wholesaler. Suppose retailers expect a 30% margin and wholesalers want a 20% margin based on their respective selling prices. And suppose that HDInhance sets a manufacturer's suggested retail price (MSRP) of $599.99 for its product.

Recall that HDInhance wants to expand the market by pricing low and generating market share quickly. HDInhance selected the $599.99 MSRP because it is lower than most competitors' prices, which can be as high as $1,200. And the company's research shows that it is below the threshold at which more consumers are willing to purchase the product. By using buyers' perceptions of value and not the seller's cost to determine the MSRP, HDInhance is using **value-based pricing**. For simplicity, we will use an MSRP of $600 in further analyses.

To determine the price HDInhance will charge wholesalers, we must first subtract the retailer's margin from the retail price to determine the retailer's cost ($600 − ($600 × 0.30) = $420). The retailer's cost is the wholesaler's price, so HDInhance next subtracts the wholesaler's margin ($420 − ($420 × 0.20) = $336). Thus, the **markup chain** representing the sequence of markups used by firms at each level in a channel for HDInhance's new product is as follows:

Suggested retail price:	$600
minus retail margin (30%):	−$180
Retailer's cost/wholesaler's price:	$420
minus wholesaler's margin (20%):	−$ 84
Wholesaler's cost/HDInhance's price:	$336

By deducting the markups for each level in the markup chain, HDInhance arrives at a price for the product to wholesalers of $336.

Markup

The difference between a company's selling price for a product and its cost to manufacture or purchase it.

Value-based pricing

Offering just the right combination of quality and good service at a fair price.

Markup chain

The sequence of markups used by firms at each level in a channel.

Break-Even and Margin Analysis

The previous analyses derived a value-based price of $336 for HDInhance's product. Although this price is higher than the break-even price of $270 and covers costs, that price assumed a demand of 1 million units. But how many units and what level of dollar sales must HDInhance achieve to break even at the $336 price? And what level of sales must be achieved to realize various profit goals? These questions can be answered through break-even and margin analysis.

Determining Break-Even Unit Volume and Dollar Sales

Break-even analysis

Analysis to determine the unit volume and dollar sales needed to be profitable given a particular price and cost structure.

Based on an understanding of costs, consumer value, the competitive environment, and reseller requirements, HDInhance has decided to set its price to wholesalers at $336. At that price, what sales level will be needed for HDInhance to break even or make a profit? **Break-even analysis** determines the unit volume and dollar sales needed to be profitable given a particular price and cost structure. At the break-even point, total revenue equals total costs and profit is zero. Above this point, the company will make a profit; below it, the company will lose money. HDInhance can calculate break-even volume using the following formula:[3]

$$\text{Break-even volume} = \frac{\text{fixed costs}}{\text{price} - \text{unit variable cost}}$$

Unit contribution

The amount that each unit contributes to covering fixed costs—the difference between price and variable costs.

The denominator (price – unit variable cost) is called **unit contribution** (sometimes called contribution margin). It represents the amount that each unit contributes to covering fixed costs. Break-even volume represents the level of output at which all (variable and fixed) costs are covered. In HDInhance's case, break-even unit volume is as follows:

$$\text{Break-even volume} = \frac{\text{fixed cost}}{\text{price} - \text{variable cost}} = \frac{\$20,000,000}{\$336 - \$250} = 232,558.1 \text{ units}$$

Thus, at the given cost and pricing structure, HDInhance will break even at 232,559 units.

To determine the break-even dollar sales, simply multiply unit break-even volume by the selling price:

$$\text{BE}_{\text{sales}} = \text{BE}_{\text{vol}} \times \text{price} = 232,559 \times \$336 = \$78,139,824$$

Contribution margin

The unit contribution divided by the selling price.

Another way to calculate dollar break-even sales is to use the percentage contribution margin (hereafter referred to as **contribution margin**), which is the unit contribution divided by the selling price:

$$\text{Contribution margin} = \frac{\text{price} - \text{variable cost}}{\text{price}} = \frac{\$336 - \$250}{\$336} = 0.256 \text{ or } 25.6\%$$

Then,

$$\text{Break-even sales} = \frac{\text{fixed costs}}{\text{contribution margin}} = \frac{\$20,000,000}{0.256} = \$78,125,000$$

Note that the difference between the two break-even sales calculations is due to rounding.

Such break-even analysis helps HDInhance by showing the unit volume needed to cover costs. If production capacity cannot attain this level of output, then the company should not launch this product. However, the unit break-even volume is well within HDInhance's capacity. Of course, the bigger question concerns whether HDInhance can sell this volume at the $336 price. We'll address that issue a little later.

Understanding contribution margin is useful in other types of analyses as well, particularly if unit prices and unit variable costs are unknown or if a company (say, a retailer) sells many products at different prices and knows the percentage of total sales variable costs represent. Whereas unit contribution is the difference between unit price and unit variable costs, total contribution is the difference between total sales and total variable costs. The overall contribution margin can be calculated by the following:

$$\text{Contribution margin} = \frac{\text{total sales} - \text{total variable costs}}{\text{total sales}}$$

Regardless of the actual level of sales, if the company knows what percentage of sales is represented by variable costs, it can calculate contribution margin. For example, HDInhance's unit variable cost is $250, or 74% of the selling price ($250 ÷ $336 = 0.74). That means for every $1 of sales revenue for HDInhance, $0.74 represents variable costs, and the difference ($0.26) represents contribution to fixed costs. But even if the company doesn't know its unit price and unit variable cost, it can calculate the contribution margin from total sales and total variable costs or from knowledge of the total cost structure. It can set total sales equal to 100% regardless of the actual absolute amount and determine the contribution margin:

$$\text{Contribution margin} = \frac{100\% - 74\%}{100\%} = \frac{1 - 0.74}{1} = 1 - 0.74 = 0.26 \text{ or } 26\%$$

Note that this matches the percentage calculated from the unit price and unit variable cost information. This alternative calculation will be very useful later when analyzing various marketing decisions.

Determining "Breakeven" for Profit Goals

Although it is useful to know the break-even point, most companies are more interested in making a profit. Assume HDInhance would like to realize a $5 million profit in the first year. How many units must it sell at the $336 price to cover fixed costs and produce this profit? To determine this, HDInhance can simply add the profit figure to fixed costs and again divide by the unit contribution to determine unit sales:[4]

$$\text{Unit volume} = \frac{\text{fixed cost} - \text{profit goal}}{\text{price} - \text{variable cost}} = \frac{\$20,000,000 + \$5,000,000}{\$336 - \$250} = 290,697.7 \text{ units}$$

Thus, to earn a $5 million profit, HDInhance must sell 290,698 units. Multiply by price to determine dollar sales needed to achieve a $5 million profit:

$$\text{Dollar sales} = 290,698 \text{ units} \times \$336 = \$97,674,528$$

Or use the contribution margin:

$$\text{Sales} = \frac{\text{fixed cost} + \text{profit goal}}{\text{contribution margin}} = \frac{\$20,000,000 + \$5,000,000}{0.256} = \$97,656,250$$

Again, note that the difference between the two break-even sales calculations is due to rounding.

As we saw previously, a profit goal can also be stated as a return on investment goal. For example, recall that HDInhance wants a 30% return on its $10 million investment. Thus, its absolute profit goal is $3 million ($10,000,000 × 0.30). This profit goal is treated the same way as in the previous example:[5]

$$\text{Unit volume} = \frac{\text{fixed cost} + \text{profit goal}}{\text{price} - \text{variable cost}} = \frac{\$20,000,000 + \$3,000,000}{\$336 - \$250} = 267,442 \text{ units}$$

$$\text{Dollar sales} = 267,442 \text{ units} \times \$336 = \$89,860,512$$

Or

$$\text{Dollar sales} = \frac{\text{fixed cost} + \text{profit goal}}{\text{contribution margin}} = \frac{\$20,000,000 + \$3,000,000}{0.256} = \$89,843,750$$

Finally, HDInhance can express its profit goal as a percentage of sales, which we also saw in previous pricing analyses. Assume HDInhance desires a 25% return on sales. To determine the unit and sales volume necessary to achieve this goal, the calculation is a little different from the previous two examples. In this case, we incorporate the profit goal into the unit contribution as an additional variable cost. Look at it this way: If 25% of each sale must go toward profits, that leaves only 75% of the selling price to cover fixed costs. Thus, the equation becomes:[6]

$$\text{Unit volume} = \frac{\text{fixed cost}}{\text{price} - \text{variable cost} - (0.25 \times \text{price})} \text{ or } \frac{\text{fixed cost}}{(0.75 \times \text{price}) - \text{variable cost}}$$

So,

$$\text{Unit volume} = \frac{\$20,000,000}{(0.75 \times \$336) - \$250} = 10,000,000 \text{ units}$$

$$\text{Dollar sales necessary} = 10,000,000 \text{ units} \times \$336 = \$3,360,000,000$$

Thus, HDInhance would need more than $3 billion in sales to realize a 25% return on sales given its current price and cost structure! Could it possibly achieve this level of sales? The major point is that although break-even analysis can be useful in determining the level of sales needed to cover costs or to achieve a stated profit goal, it does not tell the company whether it is *possible* to achieve that level of sales at the specified price. To address this issue, HDInhance needs to estimate demand for this product.

Before moving on, however, let's stop here and practice applying the concepts covered so far. Now that you have seen pricing and break-even concepts in action as they related to HDInhance's new product, here are several exercises for you to apply what you have learned in other contexts.

Marketing by the Numbers Exercise Set One

Now that you've studied pricing, break-even, and margin analysis as they relate to HDInhance's new-product launch, use the following exercises to apply these concepts in other contexts.

1.1 Sanborn, a manufacturer of electric roof vents, realizes a cost of $55 for every unit it produces. Its total fixed costs equal $2 million. If the company manufactures 500,000 units, compute the following:
a. Unit cost
b. Markup price if the company desires a 10% return on sales
c. ROI price if the company desires a 25% return on an investment of $1 million

1.2 An interior decorator purchases items to sell in her store. She purchases a lamp for $125 and sells it for $225. Determine the following:
a. Dollar markup
b. Markup percentage on cost
c. Markup percentage on selling price

1.3 A consumer purchases a toaster from a retailer for $60. The retailer's markup is 20%, and the wholesaler's markup is 15%, both based on selling price. For what price does the manufacturer sell the product to the wholesaler?

1.4 A vacuum manufacturer has a unit cost of $50 and wishes to achieve a margin of 30% based on selling price. If the manufacturer sells directly to a retailer who then adds a set margin of 40% based on selling price, determine the retail price charged to consumers.

1.5 Advanced Electronics manufactures DVDs and sells them directly to retailers who typically sell them for $20. Retailers take a 40% margin based on the retail selling price. Advanced's cost information is as follows:

DVD package and disc	$2.50/DVD
Royalties	$2.25/DVD
Advertising and promotion	$500,000
Overhead	$200,000

Calculate the following:
a. Contribution per unit and contribution margin
b. Break-even volume in DVD units and dollars
c. Volume in DVD units and dollar sales necessary if Advanced's profit goal is 20% profit on sales
d. Net profit if 5 million DVDs are sold

Demand Estimates, the Marketing Budget, and Marketing Performance Measures (pp A17–A18)
Market Potential and Sales Estimates

HDInhance has now calculated the sales needed to break even and to attain various profit goals on its new product. However, the company needs more information regarding demand in order to assess the feasibility of attaining the needed sales levels. This information is also needed for production and other decisions. For example, production schedules need to be developed and marketing tactics need to be planned.

The **total market demand** for a product or service is the total volume that would be bought by a defined consumer group, in a defined geographic area, in a defined time period, in a defined marketing environment, under a defined level and mix of industry marketing effort. Total market demand is not a fixed number but a function of the stated conditions. For example, next year's total market demand for high-definition DVD/Internet streaming devices will depend on how much Samsung, Sony, LG, and other producers spend on marketing their brands. It also depends on many environmental factors, such as government regulations, economic conditions, and the level of consumer confidence in a given market. The upper limit of market demand is called **market potential**.

One general but practical method that HDInhance might incorporate for estimating total market demand uses three variables: (1) the number of prospective buyers, (2) the quantity purchased by an average buyer per year, and (3) the price of an average unit. Using these numbers, HDInhance can estimate total market demand as follows:

$$Q = n \times q \times p$$

where

Q = total market demand
n = number of buyers in the market
q = quantity purchased by an average buyer per year
p = price of an average unit

A variation of this approach is the **chain ratio method**. This method involves multiplying a base number by a chain of adjusting percentages. For example, HDInhance's product is designed to play high-definition DVD movies on high-definition televisions as well as play videos streamed from the Internet. Thus, consumers who do not own a high-definition television will not likely purchase this player. Additionally, only households with broadband Internet access will be able to use the product. Finally, not all HDTV households will be willing and able to purchase the new product. HDInhance can estimate U.S. demand using a chain of calculations like the following:

Total number of U.S. households

× The percentage of U.S. households owning a high-definition television
× The percentage of U.S. households with broadband Internet access
× The percentage of these households willing and able to buy this device

ACNielsen, the television ratings company, estimates that there are almost 113 million TV households in the United States.[7] Experts estimate that 38% of TV households will own HDTVs by the end of 2008.[8] Research also indicates that 50% of U.S. households have broadband Internet access.[9] Finally, HDInhance's own research indicates that 87% of HDTV households possess the discretionary income needed and are willing to buy a device such as this. Then, the total number of households willing and able to purchase this product is

113 million households × 0.38 × 0.50 × 0.87 = 18.7 million households

Total market demand
The total volume that would be bought by a defined consumer group, in a defined geographic area, in a defined time period, in a defined marketing environment, under a defined level and mix of industry marketing effort.

Market potential
The upper limit of market demand.

Chain ratio method
Estimating market demand by multiplying a base number by a chain of adjusting percentages.

Because HDTVs are relatively new and expensive products, most households have only one of these televisions, and it's usually the household's primary television.[10] Thus, consumers who buy a high-definition DVD player/Internet streaming device will likely buy only one per household. Assuming the average retail price across all brands is $750 for this product, the estimate of total market demand is as follows:

$$18.7 \text{ million households} \times 1 \text{ device per household} \times \$750 = \$14 \text{ billion}$$

This simple chain of calculations gives HDInhance only a rough estimate of potential demand. However, more detailed chains involving additional segments and other qualifying factors would yield more accurate and refined estimates. Still, these are only *estimates* of market potential. They rely heavily on assumptions regarding adjusting percentages, average quantity, and average price. Thus, HDInhance must make certain that its assumptions are reasonable and defendable. As can be seen, the overall market potential in dollar sales can vary widely given the average price used. For this reason, HDInhance will use unit sales potential to determine its sales estimate for next year. Market potential in terms of units is 18.7 million (18.7 million households × 1 device per household).

Assuming that HDInhance wants to attain 2% market share (comparable to its share of the HDTV market) in the first year after launching this product, then it can forecast unit sales at 18.7 million units × 0.02 = 374,000 units. At a selling price of $336 per unit, this translates into sales of $125,664,000 (374,000 units × $336 per unit). For simplicity, further analyses will use forecasted sales of $125 million.

This unit volume estimate is well within HDInhance's production capacity and exceeds not only the break-even estimate (232,559 units) calculated earlier, but also the volume necessary to realize a $5 million profit (290,698 units) or a 30% return on investment (267,442 units). However, this forecast falls well short of the volume necessary to realize a 25% return on sales (10 million units!) and may require that HDInhance revise expectations.

To assess expected profits, we must now look at the budgeted expenses for launching this product. To do this, we will construct a pro forma profit-and-loss statement.

The Profit-and-Loss Statement and Marketing Budget (pp A18–A19)

All marketing managers must account for the profit impact of their marketing strategies. A major tool for projecting such profit impact is a **pro forma** (or projected) **profit-and-loss statement** (also called an **income statement** or **operating statement**). A pro forma statement shows projected revenues less budgeted expenses and estimates the projected net profit for an organization, product, or brand during a specific planning period, typically a year. It includes direct product production costs, marketing expenses budgeted to attain a given sales forecast, and overhead expenses assigned to the organization or product. A profit-and-loss statement typically consists of several major components (see ● **Table A2.1**):

Pro forma (or projected) profit-and-loss statement (or income statement or operating statement)
A statement that shows projected revenues less budgeted expenses and estimates the projected net profit for an organization, product, or brand during a specific planning period, typically a year.

- *Net sales*—gross sales revenue minus returns and allowances (for example, trade, cash, quantity, and promotion allowances). HDInhance's net sales for 2008 are estimated to be $125 million, as determined in the previous analysis.

- *Cost of goods sold* (sometimes called *cost of sales*)—the actual cost of the merchandise sold by a manufacturer or reseller. It includes the cost of inventory, purchases, and other costs associated with making the goods. HDInhance's cost of goods sold is estimated to be 50% of net sales, or $62.5 million.

- *Gross margin (or gross profit)*—the difference between net sales and cost of goods sold. HDInhance's gross margin is estimated to be $62.5 million.

● TABLE | A2.1   Pro Forma Profit-and-Loss Statement for the 12-Month Period Ended December 31, 2008

			% of Sales
Net Sales		$125,000,000	100%
Cost of Goods Sold		62,500,000	50%
Gross Margin		$ 62,500,000	50%
Marketing Expenses			
Sales expenses	$17,500,000		
Promotion expenses	15,000,000		
Freight	12,500,000	45,000,000	36%
General and Administrative Expenses			
Managerial salaries and expenses	$ 2,000,000		
Indirect overhead	3,000,000	5,000,000	4%
Net Profit Before Income Tax		$ 12,500,000	10%

- *Operating expenses*—the expenses incurred while doing business. These include all other expenses beyond the cost of goods sold that are necessary to conduct business. Operating expenses can be presented in total or broken down in detail. Here, HDInhance's estimated operating expenses include *marketing expenses* and *general and administrative expenses*.

Marketing expenses include sales expenses, promotion expenses, and distribution expenses. The new product will be sold though HDInhance's sales force, so the company budgets $5 million for sales salaries. However, because sales representatives earn a 10% commission on sales, HDInhance must also add a variable component to sales expenses of $12.5 million (10% of $125 million net sales), for a total budgeted sales expense of $17.5 million. HDInhance sets its advertising and promotion to launch this product at $10 million. However, the company also budgets 4% of sales, or $5 million, for cooperative advertising allowances to retailers who promote HDInhance's new product in their advertising. Thus, the total budgeted advertising and promotion expenses are $15 million ($10 million for advertising plus $5 million in co-op allowances). Finally, HDInhance budgets 10% of net sales, or $12.5 million, for freight and delivery charges. In all, total marketing expenses are estimated to be $17.5 million + $15 million + $12.5 million = $45 million.

General and administrative expenses are estimated at $5 million, broken down into $2 million for managerial salaries and expenses for the marketing function and $3 million of indirect overhead allocated to this product by the corporate accountants (such as depreciation, interest, maintenance, and insurance). Total expenses for the year, then, are estimated to be $50 million ($45 million marketing expenses + $5 million in general and administrative expenses).

- *Net profit before taxes*—profit earned after all costs are deducted. HDInhance's estimated net profit before taxes is $12.5 million.

In all, as Table A2.1 shows, HDInhance expects to earn a profit on its new product of $12.5 million in 2008. Also note that the percentage of sales that each component of the profit-and-loss statement represents is given in the right-hand column. These percentages are determined by dividing the cost figure by net sales (that is, marketing expenses represent 36% of net sales determined by $45 million ÷ $125 million). As can be seen, HDInhance projects a net profit return on sales of 10% in the first year after launching this product.

Marketing Performance Measures
(pp A20–A24)

Now let's fast-forward a year. HDInhance's product has been on the market for one year and management wants to assess its sales and profit performance. One way to assess this performance is to compute performance ratios derived from HDInhance's **profit-and-loss statement** (or **income statement** or **operating statement**).

Whereas the pro forma profit-and-loss statement shows *projected* financial performance, the statement given in ● **Table A2.2** shows HDInhance's *actual* financial performance based on actual sales, cost of goods sold, and expenses during the past year. By comparing the profit-and-loss statement from one period to the next, HDInhance can gauge performance against goals, spot favorable or unfavorable trends, and take appropriate corrective action.

The profit-and-loss statement shows that HDInhance lost $1 million rather than making the $12.5 million profit projected in the pro forma statement. Why? One obvious reason is that net sales fell $25 million short of estimated sales. Lower sales translated into lower variable costs associated with marketing the product. However, both fixed costs and the cost of goods sold as a percentage of sales exceeded expectations. Hence, the product's contribution margin was 21% rather than the estimated 26%. That is, variable costs represented 79% of sales (55% for cost of goods sold, 10% for sales commissions, 10% for freight, and 4% for co-op allowances). Recall that contribution margin can be calculated by subtracting that fraction from one $(1 - 0.79 = 0.21)$. Total fixed costs were $22 million, $2 million more than estimated. Thus, the sales that HDInhance needed to break even given this cost structure can be calculated as follows:

$$\text{Break-even sales} = \frac{\text{fixed costs}}{\text{contribution margin}} = \frac{\$22{,}000{,}000}{0.21} = \$104{,}761{,}905$$

If HDInhance had achieved another $5 million in sales, it would have earned a profit.

Although HDInhance's sales fell short of the forecasted sales, so did overall industry sales for this product. Overall industry sales were only $2.5 billion. That means that HDInhance's **market share** was 4% ($100 million ÷ $2.5 billion = 0.04 = 4%), which was higher than forecasted. Thus, HDInhance attained a higher-than-expected market share but the overall market sales were not as high as estimated.

Analytic Ratios

The profit-and-loss statement provides the figures needed to compute some crucial **operating ratios**—the ratios of selected operating statement items to net sales. These ratios let marketers compare the firm's performance in one year to that in previous years

Profit-and-loss statement (or income statement or operating statement)
A statement that shows actual revenues less expenses and net profit for an organization, product, or brand during a specific planning period, typically a year.

Market share
Company sales divided by market sales.

Operating ratios
The ratios of selected operating statement items to net sales.

● TABLE | A2.2   Profit-and-Loss Statement for the 12-Month Period Ended December 31, 2008

			% of Sales
Net Sales		$100,000,000	100%
Cost of Goods Sold		55,000,000	55%
Gross Margin		$ 45,000,000	45%
Marketing Expenses			
Sales expenses	$15,000,000		
Promotion expenses	14,000,000		
Freight	10,000,000	39,000,000	39%
General and Administrative Expenses			
Managerial salaries and expenses	$ 2,000,000		
Indirect overhead	5,000,000	7,000,000	7%
Net Profit Before Income Tax		($1,000,000)	(1%)

(or with industry standards and competitors' performance in that year). The most commonly used operating ratios are the *gross margin percentage,* the *net profit percentage,* and the *operating expense percentage.* The *inventory turnover rate* and *return on investment (ROI)* are often used to measure managerial effectiveness and efficiency.

Gross margin percentage
The percentage of net sales remaining after cost of goods sold—calculated by dividing gross margin by net sales.

The **gross margin percentage** indicates the percentage of net sales remaining after cost of goods sold that can contribute to operating expenses and net profit before taxes. The higher this ratio, the more a firm has left to cover expenses and generate profit. HDInhance's gross margin ratio was 45%:

$$\text{Gross margin percentage} = \frac{\text{gross margin}}{\text{net sales}} = \frac{\$45,000,000}{\$100,000,000} = 0.45 = 45\%$$

Note that this percentage is lower than estimated, and this ratio is seen easily in the percentage of sales column in Table A2.2. Stating items in the profit-and-loss statement as a percent of sales allows managers to quickly spot abnormal changes in costs over time. If there was previous history for this product and this ratio was declining, management should examine it more closely to determine why it has decreased (that is, because of a decrease in sales volume or price, an increase in costs, or a combination of these). In HDInhance's case, net sales were $25 million lower than estimated, and cost of goods sold was higher than estimated (55% rather than the estimated 50%).

Net profit percentage
The percentage of each sales dollar going to profit—calculated by dividing net profits by net sales.

The **net profit percentage** shows the percentage of each sales dollar going to profit. It is calculated by dividing net profits by net sales:

$$\text{Net profit percentage} = \frac{\text{net profit}}{\text{net sales}} = \frac{-\$1,000,000}{\$100,000,000} = -0.01 = -1.0\%$$

This ratio is easily seen in the percent of sales column. HDInhance's new product generated negative profits in the first year, not a good situation given that before the product launch, net profits before taxes were estimated at more than $12 million. Later in this appendix, we will discuss further analyses the marketing manager should conduct to defend the product.

Operating expense percentage
The portion of net sales going to operating expenses—calculated by dividing total expenses by net sales.

The **operating expense percentage** indicates the portion of net sales going to operating expenses. Operating expenses include marketing and other expenses not directly related to marketing the product, such as indirect overhead assigned to this product. It is calculated by

$$\text{Operating expense percentage} = \frac{\text{total expenses}}{\text{net sales}} = \frac{\$46,000,000}{\$100,000,000} = 0.46 = 46\%$$

This ratio can also be quickly determined from the percent of sales column in the profit-and-loss statement by adding the percentages for marketing expenses and general and administrative expenses (39% + 7%). Thus, 46 cents of every sales dollar went for operations. Although HDInhance wants this ratio to be as low as possible, and 46% is not an alarming amount, it is of concern if it is increasing over time or if a loss is realized.

Inventory turnover rate (or stockturn rate)
The number of times an inventory turns over or is sold during a specified time period (often one year)—calculated based on costs, selling price, or units.

Another useful ratio is the **inventory turnover rate** (also called **stockturn rate** for resellers). The inventory turnover rate is the number of times an inventory turns over or is sold during a specified time period (often one year). This rate tells how quickly a business is moving inventory through the organization. Higher rates indicate that lower investments in inventory are made, thus freeing up funds for other investments. It may be computed on a cost, selling price, or unit basis. The formula based on cost is as follows:

$$\text{Inventory turnover rate} = \frac{\text{cost of goods sold}}{\text{average inventory at cost}}$$

Assuming HDInhance's beginning and ending inventories were $30 million and $20 million, respectively, the inventory turnover rate is as follows:

$$\text{Inventory turnover rate} = \frac{\$55,000,000}{(\$30,000,000 + \$20,000,000)/2} = \frac{\$55,000,000}{\$25,000,000} = 2.2$$

That is, HDInhance's inventory turned over 2.2 times in 2008. Normally, the higher the turnover rate, the higher the management efficiency and company profitability. However, this rate should be compared to industry averages, competitors' rates, and past performance to determine if HDInhance is doing well. A competitor with similar sales but a higher inventory turnover rate will have fewer resources tied up in inventory, allowing it to invest in other areas of the business.

Return on investment (ROI)
A measure of managerial effectiveness and efficiency—net profit before taxes divided by total investment.

Companies frequently use **return on investment (ROI)** to measure managerial effectiveness and efficiency. For HDInhance, ROI is the ratio of net profits to total investment required to manufacture the new product. This investment includes capital investments in land, buildings, and equipment (here, the initial $10 million to refurbish the manufacturing facility) plus inventory costs (HDInhance's average inventory totaled $25 million), for a total of $35 million. Thus, HDInhance's ROI for this product is as follows:

$$\text{Return on investment} = \frac{\text{net profit before taxes}}{\text{investment}} = \frac{-\$1,000,000}{\$35,000,000} = -.0286 = -2.86\%$$

ROI is often used to compare alternatives, and a positive ROI is desired. The alternative with the highest ROI is preferred to other alternatives. HDInhance needs to be concerned with the ROI realized. One obvious way HDInhance can increase ROI is to increase net profit by reducing expenses. Another way is to reduce its investment, perhaps by investing less in inventory and turning it over more frequently.

Marketing Profitability Metrics

Given the above financial results, you may be thinking that HDInhance should drop this new product. But what arguments can marketers make for keeping or dropping this product? The obvious arguments for dropping the product are that first-year sales were well below expected levels and the product lost money, resulting in a negative return on investment.

So what would happen if HDInhance did drop this product? Surprisingly, if the company drops the product, the profits for the total organization will decrease by $4 million! How can that be? Marketing managers need to look closely at the numbers in the profit-and-loss statement to determine the *net marketing contribution* for this product. In HDInhance's case, the net marketing contribution for the product is $4 million, and if the company drops this product, that contribution will disappear as well. Let's look more closely at this concept to illustrate how marketing managers can better assess and defend their marketing strategies and programs.

Net Marketing Contribution

Net marketing contribution (NMC)
A measure of marketing profitability that includes only components of profitability controlled by marketing.

Net marketing contribution (NMC), along with other marketing metrics derived from it, measures *marketing* profitability. It includes only components of profitability that are controlled by marketing. Whereas the previous calculation of net profit before taxes from the profit-and-loss statement includes operating expenses not under marketing's control, NMC does not. Referring back to HDInhance's profit-and-loss statement given in Table A2.2, we can calculate net marketing contribution for the product as follows:

$$\text{NMC} = \text{net sales} - \text{cost of goods sold} - \text{marketing expenses}$$

$$= \$100 \text{ million} - \$55 \text{ million} - \$41 \text{ million} = \$4 \text{ million}$$

The marketing expenses include sales expenses ($15 million), promotion expenses ($14 million), freight expenses ($10 million), and the managerial salaries and expenses of the marketing function ($2 million), which total $41 million.

Thus, the product actually contributed $4 million to HDInhance's profits. It was the $5 million of indirect overhead allocated to this product that caused the negative profit. Further, the amount allocated was $2 million more than estimated in the pro forma profit-and-loss statement. Indeed, if only the estimated amount had been allocated, the product would have earned a *profit* of $1 million rather than losing $1 million. If HDInhance drops the product, the $5 million in fixed overhead expenses will not disappear—it will simply have to be allocated elsewhere. However, the $4 million in net marketing contribution *will* disappear.

Marketing Return on Sales and Investment

To get an even deeper understanding of the profit impact of marketing strategy, we'll now examine two measures of marketing efficiency—*marketing return on sales* (marketing ROS) and *marketing return on investment* (marketing ROI).[11]

Marketing return on sales (or **marketing ROS**) shows the percent of net sales attributable to the net marketing contribution. For our product, ROS is as follows:

$$\text{Marketing ROS} = \frac{\text{net marketing contribution}}{\text{net sales}} = \frac{\$4,000,000}{\$100,000,000} = 0.04 = 4\%$$

> **Marketing return on sales (or marketing ROS)**
> The percent of net sales attributable to the net marketing contribution—calculated by dividing net marketing contribution by net sales.

Thus, out of every $100 of sales, the product returns $4 to HDInhance's bottom line. A high marketing ROS is desirable. But to assess whether this is a good level of performance, HDInhance must compare this figure to previous marketing ROS levels for the product, the ROSs of other products in the company's portfolio, and the ROSs of competing products.

Marketing return on investment (or **marketing ROI**) measures the marketing productivity of a marketing investment. In HDInhance's case, the marketing investment is represented by $41 million of the total expenses. Thus, marketing ROI is as follows:

> **Marketing return on investment (or marketing ROI)**
> A measure of the marketing productivity of a marketing investment—calculated by dividing net marketing contribution by marketing expenses.

$$\text{Marketing ROI} = \frac{\text{net marketing contribution}}{\text{net marketing expenses}} = \frac{\$4,000,000}{\$41,000,000} = 0.0976 = 9.76\%$$

As with marketing ROS, a high value is desirable, but this figure should be compared with previous levels for the given product and with the marketing ROIs of competitors' products. Note from this equation that marketing ROI could be greater than 100%. This can be achieved by attaining a higher net marketing contribution and/or a lower total marketing expense.

In this section, we estimated market potential and sales, developed profit-and-loss statements, and examined financial measures of performance. In the next section, we discuss methods for analyzing the impact of various marketing tactics. However, before moving on to those analyses, here's another set of quantitative exercises to help you apply what you've learned to other situations.

Marketing by the Numbers Exercise Set Two

2.1 Determine the market potential for a product that has 50 million prospective buyers who purchase an average of 3 units per year and price averages $25. How many units must a company sell if it desires a 10% share of this market?

2.2 Develop a profit-and-loss statement for the Westgate division of North Industries. This division manufactures light fixtures sold to consumers through home improvement and hardware stores. Cost of goods sold represents 40% of net sales. Marketing expenses include selling expenses, promotion expenses, and freight. Selling expenses include sales salaries totaling $3 million per year and sales commissions (5% of sales). The company spent $3 million on advertising last year, and freight costs were 10% of sales. Other costs include $2 million for managerial salaries and expenses for the marketing function and another $3 million for indirect overhead allocated to the division.
  a. Develop the profit-and-loss statement if net sales were $20 million last year.
  b. Develop the profit-and-loss statement if net sales were $40 million last year.
  c. Calculate Westgate's break-even sales.

2.3 Using the profit-and-loss statement you developed in question 2.2b, and assuming that Westgate's beginning inventory was $11 million, ending inventory was $7 million, and total investment was $20 million (including inventory), determine the following:
  a. Gross margin percentage
  b. Net profit percentage
  c. Operating expense percentage
  d. Inventory turnover rate
  e. Return on investment (ROI)
  f. Net marketing contribution
  g. Marketing return on sales (marketing ROS)

　　h. Marketing return on investment (marketing ROI)
　　i. Is the Westgate division doing well? Explain your answer.

Financial Analysis of Marketing Tactics (pp A24–A28)

Although the first-year profit performance for HDInhance's new product was less than desired, management feels that this attractive market has excellent growth opportunities. Although the sales of HDInhance's product were lower than initially projected, they were not unreasonable given the size of the current market. Thus, HDInhance wants to explore new marketing tactics to help grow the market for this product and increase sales for the company.

　　For example, the company could increase advertising to promote more awareness of the new product and its category. It could add salespeople to secure greater product distribution. HDInhance could decrease prices so that more consumers could afford its product. Finally, to expand the market, HDInhance could introduce a lower-priced model in addition to the higher-priced original offering. Before pursuing any of these tactics, HDInhance must analyze the financial implications of each.

Increase Advertising Expenditures

Although most consumers understand DVD players, they may not be aware of high-definition DVD players that also stream video from the Internet. Thus, HDInhance is considering boosting its advertising to make more people aware of the benefits of this device in general and of its own brand in particular.

　　What if HDInhance's marketers recommend increasing national advertising by 50% to $15 million (assume no change in the variable cooperative component of promotional expenditures)? This represents an increase in fixed costs of $5 million. What increase in sales will be needed to break even on this $5 million increase in fixed costs?

　　A quick way to answer this question is to divide the increase in fixed cost by the contribution margin, which we found in a previous analysis to be 21%:

$$\text{Increase in sales} = \frac{\text{increase in fixed cost}}{\text{contribution margin}} = \frac{\$5,000,000}{0.21} = \$23,809,524$$

Thus, a 50% increase in advertising expenditures must produce a sales increase of almost $24 million to just break even. That $24 million sales increase translates into an almost 1 percentage point increase in market share (1% of the $2.5 billion overall market equals $25 million). That is, to break even on the increased advertising expenditure, HDInhance would have to increase its market share from 4% to 4.95% ($123,809,524 ÷ $2.5 billion = 0.0495 or 4.95% market share). All of this assumes that the total market will not grow, which might or might not be a reasonable assumption.

Increase Distribution Coverage

HDInhance also wants to consider hiring more salespeople in order to call on new retailer accounts and increase distribution through more outlets. Even though HDInhance sells directly to wholesalers, its sales representatives call on retail accounts to perform other functions in addition to selling, such as training retail salespeople. Currently, HDInhance employs 60 sales reps who earn an average of $50,000 in salary plus 10% commission on sales. The product is currently sold to consumers through 1,875 retail outlets. Suppose HDInhance wants to increase that number of outlets to 2,500, an increase of 625 retail outlets. How many additional salespeople will HDInhance need, and what sales will be necessary to break even on the increased cost?

Workload method
An approach to determining sales force size based on the workload required and the time available for selling.

One method for determining what size sales force HDInhance will need is the **workload method**. The workload method uses the following formula to determine the sales force size:

$$NS = \frac{NC \times FC \times LC}{TA}$$

where

NS = number of salespeople

NC = number of customers

FC = average frequency of customer calls per customer

LC = average length of customer call

TA = time an average salesperson has available for selling per year

HDInhance's sales reps typically call on accounts an average of 20 times per year for about 2 hours per call. Although each sales rep works 2,000 hours per year (50 weeks per year × 40 hours per week), they spent about 15 hours per week on nonselling activities such as administrative duties and travel. Thus, the average annual available selling time per sales rep per year is 1,250 hours (50 weeks × 25 hours per week). We can now calculate how many sales reps HDInhance will need to cover the anticipated 2,500 retail outlets:

$$NS = \frac{2,500 \times 20 \times 2}{1,250} = 80 \text{ salespeople}$$

Therefore, HDInhance will need to hire 20 more salespeople. The cost to hire these reps will be $1 million (20 salespeople × $50,000 salary per sales person).

What increase in sales will be required to break even on this increase in fixed costs? The 10% commission is already accounted for in the contribution margin, so the contribution margin remains unchanged at 21%. Thus, the increase in sales needed to cover this increase in fixed costs can be calculated by

$$\text{Increase in sales} = \frac{\text{increase in fixed cost}}{\text{contribution margin}} = \frac{\$1,000,000}{0.21} = \$4,761,905$$

That is, HDInhance's sales must increase almost $5 million to break even on this tactic. So, how many new retail outlets will the company need to secure to achieve this sales increase? The average revenue generated per current outlet is $53,333 ($100 million in sales divided by 1,875 outlets). To achieve the nearly $5 million sales increase needed to break even, HDInhance would need about 90 new outlets ($4,761,905 ÷ $53,333 = 89.3 outlets), or about 4.5 outlets per new rep. Given that current reps cover about 31 outlets apiece (1,875 outlets ÷ 60 reps), this seems very reasonable.

Decrease Price

HDInhance is also considering lowering its price to increase sales revenue through increased volume. The company's research has shown that demand for most types of consumer electronics products is elastic—that is, the percentage increase in the quantity demanded is greater than the percentage decrease in price. It has also been found that when the price of HDTVs goes down, the quantity of accessory products like DVD players demanded increases because they are complementary products.

What increase in sales would be necessary to break even on a 10% decrease in price? That is, what increase in sales will be needed to maintain the total contribution that HDInhance realized at the higher price? The current total contribution can be determined by multiplying the contribution margin by total sales:[12]

$$\text{Current total contribution} = \text{contribution margin} \times \text{sales} = .21 \times \$100 \text{ million} = \$21 \text{ million}$$

Price changes result in changes in unit contribution and contribution margin. Recall that the contribution margin of 21% was based on variable costs representing 79% of sales. Therefore, unit variable costs can be determined by multiplying the original price by this percentage: $336 × 0.79 = $265.44 per unit. If price is decreased by 10%, the new price is $302.40. However, variable costs do not change just because price decreased, so the contribution and contribution margin decrease as follows:

	Old	**New (reduced 10%)**
Price	$336	$302.40
− Unit variable cost	$265.44	$265.44
= Unit contribution	$ 70.56	$ 36.96
Contribution margin	$ 70.56/$336 = 0.21 or 21%	$ 36.96/$302.40 = 0.12 or 12%

So a 10% reduction in price results in a decrease in the contribution margin from 21% to 12%.[13] To determine the sales level needed to break even on this price reduction, we calculate the level of sales that must be attained at the new contribution margin to achieve the original total contribution of $21 million:

$$\text{New contribution margin} \times \text{new sales level} = \text{original total contribution}$$

So,

$$\text{New sales level} = \frac{\text{original contribution}}{\text{new contribution margin}} = \frac{\$21,000,000}{0.12} = \$175,000,000$$

Thus, sales must increase by $75 million ($175 million – $100 million) just to break even on a 10% price reduction. This means that HDInhance must increase market share to 7% ($175 million ÷ $2.5 billion) to achieve the current level of profits (assuming no increase in the total market sales). The marketing manager must assess whether or not this is a reasonable goal.

Extend the Product Line

As a final option, HDInhance is considering extending its product line by offering a lower-priced model. Of course, the new, lower-priced product would steal some sales from the higher-priced model. This is called **cannibalization**—the situation in which one product sold by a company takes a portion of its sales from other company products. If the new product has a lower contribution than the original product, the company's total contribution will decrease on the cannibalized sales. However, if the new product can generate enough new volume, it is worth considering.

To assess cannibalization, HDInhance must look at the incremental contribution gained by having both products available. Recall that in the previous analysis we determined that unit variable costs were $265.44 and unit contribution was just over $70. Assuming costs remain the same next year, HDInhance can expect to realize a contribution per unit of approximately $70 for every unit of the original product sold.

Assume that the first model offered by HDInhance is called HD1 and the new, lower-priced model is called HD2. HD2 will retail for $400, and resellers will take the same markup percentages on price as they do with the higher-priced model. Therefore, HD2's price to wholesalers will be $224 as follows:

Retail price:	$400
minus retail margin (30%):	− $120
Retailer's cost/wholesaler's price:	$280
minus wholesaler's margin (20%):	− $ 56
Wholesaler's cost/HDInhance's price	$224

Cannibalization
The situation in which one product sold by a company takes a portion of its sales from other company products.

If HD2's variable costs are estimated to be $174, then its contribution per unit will equal $50 ($224 − $174 = $50). That means for every unit that HD2 cannibalizes from HD1, HDInhance will *lose* $20 in contribution toward fixed costs and profit (that is, contribution$_{HD2}$ − contribution$_{HD1}$ = $50 − $70 = –$20). You might conclude that HDInhance should not pursue this tactic because it appears as though the company will be worse off if it introduces the lower-priced model. However, if HD2 captures enough *additional* sales, HDInhance will be better off even though some HD1 sales are cannibalized. The company must examine what will happen to *total* contribution, which requires estimates of unit volume for both products.

Originally, HDInhance estimated that next year's sales of HD1 would be 600,000 units. However, with the introduction of HD2, it now estimates that 200,000 of those sales will be cannibalized by the new model. If HDInhance sells only 200,000 units of the new HD2 model (all cannibalized from HD1), the company would lose $4 million in total contribution (200,000 units × –$20 per cannibalized unit = –$4 million)—not a good outcome. However, HDInhance estimates that HD2 will generate the 200,000 of cannibalized sales plus an *additional* 500,000 unit sales. Thus, the contribution on these additional HD2 units will be $25 million (i.e., 500,000 units × $50 per unit = $25 million). The net effect is that HDInhance will gain $21 million in total contribution by introducing HD2.

The following table compares HDInhance's total contribution with and without the introduction of HD2:

	HD1 only	HD1 and HD2
HD1 contribution	600,000 units × $70 = $42,000,000	400,000 units × $70 = $28,000,000
HD2 contribution	0	700,000 units × $50 = $35,000,000
Total contribution	$42,000,000	$63,000,000

The difference in the total contribution is a net gain of $21 million ($63 million − $42 million). Based on this analysis, HDInhance should introduce the HD2 model because it results in a positive incremental contribution. However, if fixed costs will increase by more than $21 million as a result of adding this model, then the net effect will be negative and HDInhance should not pursue this tactic.

Now that you have seen these marketing tactic analysis concepts in action as they related to HDInhance's new product, here are several exercises for you to apply what you have learned in this section in other contexts.

Marketing by the Numbers Exercise Set Three

3.1 Kingsford, Inc., sells small plumbing components to consumers through retail outlets. Total industry sales for Kingsford's relevant market last year were $80 million, with Kingsford's sales representing 10% of that total. Contribution margin is 25%. Kingsford's sales force calls on retail outlets and each sales rep earns $45,000 per year plus 1% commission on all sales. Retailers receive a 40% margin on selling price and generate average revenue of $10,000 per outlet for Kingsford.

a. The marketing manager has suggested increasing consumer advertising by $300,000. By how much would dollar sales need to increase to break even on this expenditure? What increase in overall market share does this represent?

b. Another suggestion is to hire three more sales representatives to gain new consumer retail accounts. How many new retail outlets would be necessary to break even on the increased cost of adding three sales reps?

c. A final suggestion is to make a 20% across-the-board price reduction. By how much would dollar sales need to increase to maintain Kingsford's current contribution? (See endnote 13 to calculate the new contribution margin.)

d. Which suggestion do you think Kingsford should implement? Explain your recommendation.

3.2 PepsiCo sells its soft drinks in approximately 400,000 retail establishments, such as supermarkets, discount stores, and convenience stores. Sales representatives call on each retail account weekly, which means each account is called on by a sales rep 52 times per year. The average length of a sales call is 75 minutes (or 1.25 hours). An average salesperson works 2,000 hours per year (50 weeks per year × 40 hours per week), but each spends 10 hours a week on nonselling activities, such as administrative tasks and travel. How many salespeople does PepsiCo need?

3.3 Hair Zone manufactures a brand of hair-styling gel. It is considering adding a modified version of the product—a foam that provides stronger hold. Hair Zone's variable costs and prices to wholesalers are as follows:

	Current Hair Gel	New Foam Product
Unit selling price	2.00	2.25
Unit variable costs	.85	1.25

Hair Zone expects to sell 1 million units of the new styling foam in the first year after introduction, but it expects that 60% of those sales will come from buyers who normally purchase Hair Zone's styling gel. Hair Zone estimates that it would sell 1.5 million units of the gel if it did not introduce the foam. If the fixed cost of launching the new foam will be $100,000 during the first year, should Hair Zone add the new product to its line? Why or why not?

Careers in Marketing

Now that you have completed this course in marketing, you have a good idea of what the field entails. You may have decided you want to pursue a marketing career because it offers constant challenge, stimulating problems, the opportunity to work with people, and excellent advancement opportunities. But you still may not know which part of marketing best suits you—marketing is a very broad field offering a wide variety of career options.

This appendix helps you discover what types of marketing jobs best match your special skills and interests, shows you how to conduct the kind of job search that will get you the position you want in the company of your choice, describes marketing career paths open to you, and suggests other information resources.

Marketing Careers Today (pp A29–A30)

The marketing field is booming with nearly a third of all Americans now employed in marketing-related positions. Marketing salaries may vary by company, position, and region, and salary figures change constantly. In general, entry-level marketing salaries usually are only slightly below those for engineering and chemistry but equal or exceed starting salaries in economics, finance, accounting, general business, and the liberal arts. Moreover, if you succeed in an entry-level marketing position, it's likely that you will be promoted quickly to higher levels of responsibility and salary. In addition, because of the consumer and product knowledge you will gain in these jobs, marketing positions provide excellent training for the highest levels in an organization.

Overall Marketing Facts and Trends

In conducting your job search, consider the following facts and trends that are changing the world of marketing.

Focus on customers: More and more, companies are realizing that they win in the marketplace only by creating superior value for customers. To capture value from customers, they must first find new and better ways to solve customer problems and improve customer brand experiences. This increasing focus on the customer puts marketers at the forefront in many of today's companies. As the primary customer-facing function, marketing's mission is to get all company departments to "think customer."

Technology: Technology is changing the way marketers work. For example, price coding allows instantaneous retail inventorying. Software for marketing training, forecasting, and other functions is changing the ways we market. And the Internet is creating new jobs and new recruiting rules. Consider the explosive growth in new media marketing. Whereas advertising firms have traditionally recruited "generalists" in account management, "generalist" has now taken on a whole new meaning—advertising account executives must now have both broad and specialized knowledge.

Diversity: The number of women and minorities in marketing continues to rise. They also are rising rapidly into marketing management. For example, women now outnumber men by nearly two to one as advertising account executives. As marketing becomes more global, the need for diversity in marketing positions will continue to increase, opening new opportunities.

Global: Companies such as Coca-Cola, McDonald's, IBM, Wal-Mart, and Procter & Gamble have become multinational, with manufacturing and marketing operations in hundreds of countries. Indeed, such companies often make more profit from sales outside the United States than from within. And it's not just the big companies that are involved in international marketing. Organizations of all sizes have moved into the global arena. Many new marketing opportunities and careers will be directly linked to the expanding global marketplace. The globalization of business also means that you will need more cultural, language, and people skills in the marketing world of the twenty-first century.

Not-for-profit organizations: Increasingly, colleges, arts organizations, libraries, hospitals, and other not-for-profit organizations are recognizing the need for effectively marketing their "products" and services to various publics. This awareness has led to new marketing positions—with these organizations hiring their own marketing directors and marketing vice presidents or using outside marketing specialists.

Looking for a Job in Today's Marketing World (pp A30–A36)

To choose and find the right job, you will need to apply the marketing skills you've learned in this course, especially marketing analysis and planning. Follow these eight steps for marketing yourself: (1) Conduct a self-assessment and seek career counseling, (2) examine job descriptions, (3) explore the job market and assess opportunities, (4) develop search strategies, (5) prepare a résumé, (6) write a cover letter and assemble supporting documents, (7) interview for jobs, and (8) follow-up.

Conduct a Self-Assessment and Seek Career Counseling

If you're having difficulty deciding what kind of marketing position is the best fit for you, start out by doing some self-testing or get some career counseling. Self-assessments require that you honestly and thoroughly evaluate your interests, strengths, and weaknesses. What do you do well (your best and favorite skills) and not so well? What are your favorite interests? What are your career goals? What makes you stand out from other job seekers?

The answers to such questions may suggest which marketing careers you should seek or avoid. For help in making an effective self-assessment, look for the following books in your local bookstore: Shoya Zichy, *Career Match: Connecting Who You Are with What You Love to Do* (AMACOM Books, 2007) and Richard Bolles, *What Color Is Your Parachute 2008?* (Ten Speed Press, 2007). Many Web sites also offer self-assessment tools, such as the Keirsey Temperament Theory and the Temperament Sorter, a free but broad assessment available at AdvisorTeam.com. For a more specific evaluation, CareerLeader.com offers a complete online business career self-assessment program designed by the Directors of MBA Career Development at Harvard Business School. You can use this for a fee.

For help in finding a career counselor to guide you in making a career assessment, Richard Bolles's *What Color Is Your Parachute 2008?* contains a useful state-by-state sampling. CareerLeader.com also offers personal career counseling. (Some counselors can help you in your actual job search, too.) You can also consult the career counseling, testing, and placement services at your college or university.

Examine Job Descriptions

After you have identified your skills, interests, and desires, you need to see which marketing positions are the best match for them. Two U.S. Labor Department publications (available in your local library or online)—the *Occupation Outlook Handbook* (www.bls.gov/oco) and the *Dictionary of Occupational Titles* (www.occupationalinfo.org)—describe the duties involved in various occupations, the specific training and education needed, the availability of jobs in each field, possibilities for advancement, and probable earnings.

Your initial career shopping list should be broad and flexible. Look for different ways to achieve your objectives. For example, if you want a career in marketing management, consider the public as well as the private sector, and local and regional as well as national and international firms. Be open initially to exploring many options, then focus on specific industries and jobs, listing your basic goals as a way to guide your choices. Your list might include "a job in a start-up company, near a big city on the West Coast, doing new-product planning with a computer software firm."

Explore the Job Market and Assess Opportunities

At this stage, you need to look at the market and see what positions are actually available. You do not have to do this alone. Any of the following may assist you.

Career Development Centers

Your college's career development center is an excellent place to start. In addition to checking with your career development center or specific job openings, check the current edition of the National Association of Colleges and Employers *Job Outlook* (www.jobweb.com). It contains a national forecast of hiring intentions of employers as they relate to new college graduates. More and more, college career development centers are also going online. For example, the Web site of the undergraduate career services of Indiana University's Kelley School of Business has a list of career links (http://ucso.indiana.edu/cgi-bin/students/careerResources) that can help to focus your job search.

In addition, find out everything you can about the companies that interest you by consulting business magazines, Web sites, annual reports, business reference books, faculty, career counselors, and others. Try to analyze the industry's and the company's future growth and profit potential, advancement opportunities, salary levels, entry positions, travel time, and other factors of significance to you.

Job Fairs

Career development centers often work with corporate recruiters to organize on-campus job fairs. You might also use the Internet to check on upcoming career fairs in your region. For example, visit Monster Career Fairs at www.nationalcareerfairs.com/monster. You may find other opportunities at online career fairs such as The Wall Street Journal Virtual Career Fair at www.wsj-classified.com/vcf.

Networking and the Yellow Pages

Networking—asking for job leads from friends, family, people in your community, and career centers—is one of the best ways to find a marketing job. Studies estimate that 60 to 90 percent of jobs are found through networking. The idea is to spread your net wide, contacting anybody and everybody.

The phone book's yellow pages are another effective way to job search. Check out employers in your field of interest in whatever region you want to work, then call and ask if they are hiring for the position of your choice.

Cooperative Education and Internships

According to a survey by CBcampus.com, CareerBuilder.com's college job search site, employers on average give full-time employment offers to about 61 percent of students who have had internships with their companies. Many company Internet sites have separate internship areas. For example, check out InternshipPrograms.com, MonsterTRAK.com, CampusCareerCenter.com (www.campuscareercenter.com/students/intern.asp), InternJobs.com, and InternAbroad.com. If you know of a company for which you wish to work, go to that company's corporate Web site, enter the human resources area, and check for internships. If none are listed, try e-mailing the human resources department, asking if internships are offered.

The Internet

A constantly increasing number of sites on the Internet deal with job hunting. You can also use the Internet to make contacts with people who can help you gain information on companies and research companies that interest you. The Riley Guide offers a great introduction to what jobs are available (www.rileyguide.com). CareerBuilder.com, Monster.com, and Yahoo! HotJobs (http://hotjobs.yahoo.com) are good general sites for seeking job listings. Other helpful sites are DisabilityInfo.gov and HireDiversity.com, which contain information on opportunities for African Americans, Hispanic Americans, Asian Americans, and Native Americans.

Most companies have their own Web sites on which they post job listings. This may be helpful if you have a specific and fairly limited number of companies that you are keeping your eye on for job opportunities. But if this is not the case, remember that to find out what interesting marketing jobs the companies themselves are posting, you may have to visit hundreds of corporate sites.

Professional Networking Sites

Many companies have now begun to take advantage of social networking sites to find talented applicants. From Facebook to LinkedIn, social networking has become professional networking. For example, Ernst & Young has a career page on Facebook (www.facebook.com/ernstandyoungcareers) to find potential candidates for entry-level positions. For job seekers, online professional networking offers more efficient job targeting and reduces costs associated compared with traditional interaction methods such as traveling to job fairs and interviews, printing résumé, and other expenses.

However, although the Internet offers a wealth of resources for searching for the perfect job, be aware that it constitutes a two-way street. Just as job seekers can search the Web to find job opportunities, employers can search for information on job candidates. A recent Execunet survey found that a growing number of job searches are being derailed by "digital dirt"—information mined from online social networking sites that reveals unintended or embarrassing anecdotes and photos. Web searches also can sometimes reveal inconsistencies and résumé inflation. According to the Execunet survey, 77 percent of recruiters interviewed use search engines to learn more about candidates. Some 35 percent said they've eliminated a candidate based on information that they uncovered.[1]

Develop Search Strategies

Once you've decided which companies you are interested in, you need to contact them. One of the best ways is through on-campus interviews. But not every company you are interested in will visit your school. In such instances, you can write, e-mail, or phone the company directly or ask marketing professors or school alumni for contacts.

Prepare Résumés

A résumé is a concise yet comprehensive written summary of your qualifications, including your academic, personal, and professional achievements, that showcases why you are the best candidate for the job. Since an employer will spend an average of 15 to 20 seconds reviewing your résumé, you want to be sure that you prepare a good one.

In preparing your résumé, remember that all information on it must be accurate and complete. Résumés typically begin with the applicant's full name, telephone and fax numbers, and mail and e-mail addresses. A simple and direct statement of career objectives generally appears next, followed by work history and academic data (including awards and internships), and then by personal activities and experiences applicable to the job sought.

The résumé sometimes ends with a list of references the employer may contact (at other times, references may be listed separately). If your work or internship experience is limited, nonexistent, or irrelevant, then it is a good idea to emphasize your academic and nonacademic achievements, showing skills related to those required for excellent job performance.

There are three types of résumés. Reverse *chronological* résumés, which emphasize career growth, are organized in reverse chronological order, starting with your most recent job. They focus on job titles within organizations, describing the responsibilities required for each job. *Functional* résumés focus less on job titles and work history and more on assets and achievements. This format works best if your job history is scanty or discontinuous. *Mixed,* or *combination,* résumés take from each of the other two formats. First, the skills used for a specific job are listed, then the job title is stated. This format works best for applicants whose past jobs are in other fields or seemingly unrelated to the position.

Your local bookstore or library has many books that can assist you in developing your résumé. Popular guides are Brenda Greene, *Get the Interview Every Time: Fortune 500 Hiring Professionals' Tips for Writing Winning Résumés and Cover Letters* (Dearborn Trade, 2004) and Susan Britton Whitcomb's *Résumé Magic: Trade Secrets of a Professional Résumé Writer* (JIST Works, 2006). Computer software programs, such as *RésuméMaker* (ResumeMaker.com), provide hundreds of sample résumés and ready-to-use phrases while guiding you through the résumé preparation process. America's Career InfoNet (www.acinet.org/acinet/resume/resume_intro.asp) offers a step-by-step résumé tutorial, and Monster (http://content.monster.com/resume/home.aspx) offers résumé advice and writing services. Finally, you can even create your own personalized online résumé at sites such as optimalresume.com.

Electronic Résumés

Use of the Internet as a tool in the job search process is increasing, so it's a good idea to have your résumé ready for the online environment. You can forward an electronic résumé to networking contacts or recruiting professionals through e-mail. You can also post it in online databases with the hope that employers and recruiters will find it.

Successful electronic résumés require a different strategy than paper résumés. For instance, when companies search résumé banks, they search key words and industry buzz words that describe a skill or core work required for each job, so nouns are much more important than verbs. Two good resources for preparing electronic résumés are Susan Ireland's Electronic Résumé Guide (http://susanireland.com/eresumeguide) and The Riley Guide (www.rileyguide.com/eresume.html).

After you have written your electronic résumé, you need to post it. The following sites may be good locations to start: Monster.com (www.monster.com) and Yahoo! HotJobs (http://hotjobs.yahoo.com). However, use caution when posting your résumé on various sites. In this era of identity theft, you need to select sites with care so as to protect your privacy. Limit access to your personal contact information and don't use sites that offer to "blast" your résumé into cyberspace.

Résumé Tips

- Communicate your worth to potential employers in a concrete manner, citing examples whenever possible.

- Be concise and direct.

- Use active verbs to show you are a doer.

- Do not skimp on quality or use gimmicks. Spare no expense in presenting a professional résumé.

- Have someone critique your work. A single typo can eliminate you from being considered.

- Customize your résumé for specific employers. Emphasize your strengths as they pertain to your targeted job.

- Keep your résumé compact, usually one page.

- Format the text to be attractive, professional, and readable. Times New Roman is often the font of choice. Avoid too much "design" or gimmicky flourishes.

Write Cover Letter, Follow Up, and Assemble Supporting Documents

Cover Letter

You should include a cover letter informing the employer that a résumé is enclosed. But a cover letter does more than this. It also serves to summarize in one or two paragraphs the contents of the résumé and explains why you think you are the right person for the position. The goal is to persuade the employer to look at the more detailed résumé. A typical cover letter is organized as follows: (1) the name and position of the person you are contacting; (2) a statement identifying the position you are applying for, how you heard of the vacancy, and the reasons for your interest; (3) a summary of your qualifications for the job; (4) a description of what follow-ups you intend to make, such as phoning in two weeks to see if the résumé has been received; (5) an expression of gratitude for the opportunity of being a candidate for the job. America's Career InfoNet (www.acinet.org/acinet/resume/resume_intro.asp) offers a step-by-step tutorial on how to create a cover letter, and Susan Ireland's Web site contains more than 50 cover letter samples (http://susanireland.com/coverletterindex.htm).

Follow-Up

Once you send your cover letter and résumé to perspective employers via the method they prefer—e-mail, their Web site, fax, or regular mail—it's often a good idea to follow up. In today's market, job seekers can't afford to wait for interviews to find them. A quality résumé and an attractive cover letter are crucial, but a proper follow-up may be the key to landing an interview. However, before you engage your potential employer, be sure to research the company. Knowing about the company and understanding its place in the industry will help you shine. When you place a call, send an e-mail, or mail a letter to a company contact, be sure to restate your interest in the position, check on the status of your résumé, and ask the employer about any questions they may have.

Letters of Recommendation

Letters of recommendation are written references by professors, former and current employers, and others that testify to your character, skills, and abilities. Some companies may request letters of recommendation, to be submitted either with the résumé or at the interview. Even if letters of recommendation aren't requested, it's a good idea to bring them with you to the interview. A good reference letter tells why you would be an excellent candidate for the position. In choosing someone to write a letter of recommendation, be confident that the person will give you a good reference. In addition, do not assume the person knows everything about you or the position you are seeking. Rather, provide the person with your résumé and other relevant data. As a courtesy, allow the reference writer at least a month to complete the letter and enclose a stamped, addressed envelope with your materials.

In the packet containing your résumé, cover letter, and letters of recommendation, you may also want to attach other relevant documents that support your candidacy, such as academic transcripts, graphics, portfolios, and samples of writing.

Interview for Jobs

As the old saying goes, "The résumé gets you the interview; the interview gets you the job." The job interview offers you an opportunity to gather more information about the organization, while at the same time allowing the organization to gather more information about you. You'll want to present your best self. The interview process consists of three parts: before the interview, the interview itself, and after the interview. If you pass through these stages successfully, you will be called back for the follow-up interview.

Before the Interview

In preparing for your interview, do the following:

1. Understand that interviewers have diverse styles, including the "chitchat," let's-get-to-know-each-other style; the interrogation style of question after question; and the tough-probing "why, why, why" style, among others. So be ready for anything.

2. With a friend, practice being interviewed and then ask for a critique. Or, videotape yourself in a practice interview so that you can critique your own performance. Your college placement service may also offer "mock" interviews to help you.

3. Prepare at least five good questions whose answers are not easily found in the company literature, such as "What is the future direction of the firm?" "How does the firm differentiate itself from competitors?" "Do you have a new-media division?"

4. Anticipate possible interview questions, such as "Why do you want to work for this company?" or "Why should we hire you?" Prepare solid answers before the interview. Have a clear idea of why you are interested in joining the company and the industry to which it belongs. (See Susan Ireland's site for additional interview questions: http://susanireland.com/interviewwork.html)

5. Avoid back-to-back interviews—they can be exhausting and it is unpredictable how long they will last.

6. Prepare relevant documents that support your candidacy, such as academic transcripts, letters of recommendation, graphics, portfolios, and samples of writing. Bring multiple copies to the interview.

7. Dress conservatively and professionally. Be neat and clean.

8. Arrive 10 minutes early to collect your thoughts and review the major points you intend to cover. Check your name on the interview schedule, noting the name of the interviewer and the room number. Be courteous and polite to office staff.

9. Approach the interview enthusiastically. Let your personality shine through.

During the Interview

During the interview, do the following:

1. Shake hands firmly in greeting the interviewer. Introduce yourself, using the same form of address that the interviewer uses. Focus on creating a good initial impression.

2. Keep your poise. Relax, smile when appropriate, and be upbeat throughout.

3. Maintain eye contact, good posture, and speak distinctly. Don't clasp your hands or fiddle with jewelry, hair, or clothing. Sit comfortably in your chair. Do not smoke, even if it's permitted.

4. Along with the copies of relevant documents that support your candidacy, carry extra copies of your résumé with you.

5. Have your story down pat. Present your selling points. Answer questions directly. Avoid either one-word or too-wordy answers.

6. Let the interviewer take the initiative but don't be passive. Find an opportunity to direct the conversation to things about yourself that you want the interviewer to hear.

7. To end on a high note, make your most important point or ask your most pertinent question during the last part of the interview.

8. Don't hesitate to "close." You might say, "I'm very interested in the position, and I have enjoyed this interview."

9. Obtain the interviewer's business card or address and phone number so that you can follow up later.

A tip for acing the interview: Before you open your mouth, find out *what it's like* to be a brand manager, sales representative, market researcher, advertising account executive, or other position for which you're interviewing. See if you can find a "mentor"—someone in a position similar to the one you're seeking, perhaps with another company. Talk with this mentor about the ins and outs of the job and industry.

After the Interview

After the interview, do the following:

1. After leaving the interview, record the key points that arose. Be sure to note who is to follow up and when a decision can be expected.

2. Analyze the interview objectively, including the questions asked, the answers to them, your overall interview presentation, and the interviewer's responses to specific points.

3. Immediately send a thank-you letter or e-mail, mentioning any additional items and your willingness to supply further information.

4. If you do not hear within the specified time, write, e-mail, or call the interviewer to determine your status.

Follow-Up Interview

If your first interview takes place off-site, such as at your college or at a job fair, and if you are successful with that initial interview, you will be invited to visit the organization. The in-company interview will probably run from several hours to an entire day. The organization will examine your interest, maturity, enthusiasm, assertiveness, logic, and company and functional knowledge. You should ask questions about issues of importance to you. Find out about the working environment, job role, responsibilities, opportunities for advancement, current industrial issues, and the company's personality. The company wants to discover if you are the right person for the job, whereas you want to find out if it is the right job for you. The key is to determine if the right *fit* exists between you and the company.

Marketing Jobs (pp A36–A40)

This section describes some of the key marketing positions.

Advertising

Advertising is one of today's hottest fields in marketing. In fact, *Money* magazine lists a position in advertising as among the 50 best jobs in America.

Job Descriptions

Key advertising positions include copywriter, art director, production manager, account executive, and media planner/buyer.

- *Copywriters* write advertising copy and help find the concepts behind the written words and visual images of advertisements.

- *Art directors,* the other part of the creative team, help translate the copywriters' ideas into dramatic visuals called "layouts." Agency artists develop print layouts, package designs, television layouts (called "storyboards"), corporate logotypes, trademarks, and symbols. *Production managers* are responsible for physically creating ads, in-house or by contracting through outside production houses.

- *Account development executives* research and understand clients' markets and customers and help develop marketing and advertising strategies to impact them.

- *Account executives* serve as liaisons between clients and agencies. They coordinate the planning, creation, production, and implementation of an advertising campaign for the account.

- *Account planners* serve as the voice of the consumer in the agency. They research consumers to understand their needs and motivations as a basis for developing effective ad campaigns.

- *Media planners (or buyers)* determine the best mix of television, radio, newspaper, magazine, digital, and other media for the advertising campaign.

Skills Needed, Career Paths, and Typical Salaries

Work in advertising requires strong people skills in order to interact closely with an often-difficult and demanding client base. In addition, advertising attracts people with strong skills in planning, problem solving, creativity, communication, initiative, leadership, and presentation. Advertising involves working under high levels of stress and pressure created by unrelenting deadlines. Advertisers frequently have to work long hours to meet deadlines for a presentation. But work achievements are very apparent, with the results of creative strategies observed by thousands or even millions of people.

Because they are so sought after, positions in advertising sometimes require an MBA. But there are many jobs open for business, graphics arts, and liberal arts undergraduates. Advertising positions often serve as gateways to higher-level management. Moreover, with large advertising agencies opening offices all over the world, there is the possibility of eventually working on global campaigns.

Starting advertising salaries are relatively low compared to some other marketing jobs because of strong competition for entry-level advertising jobs. You may even want to consider working for free to break in. Compensation will increase quickly as you move into account executive or other management positions. For more facts and figures, see the Web pages of *Advertising Age,* a key ad industry publication (www.adage.com, click on the Job Bank link), and the American Association of Advertising Agencies (www.aaaa.org).

Brand and Product Management

Brand and product managers plan, direct, and control business and marketing efforts for their products. They are involved with research and development, packaging, manufacturing, sales and distribution, advertising, promotion, market research, and business analysis and forecasting.

Job Descriptions

A company's brand management team consists of people in several positions.

- *Brand managers* guide the development of marketing strategies for a specific brand.

- *Assistant brand managers* are responsible for certain strategic components of the brand.

- *Product managers* oversee several brands within a product line or product group.

- *Product category managers* direct multiple product lines in the product category.

- *Market analysts* research the market and provide important strategic information to the project managers.

- *Project directors* are responsible for collecting market information on a marketing or product project.

- *Research directors* oversee the planning, gathering, and analyzing of all organizational research.

Skills Needed, Career Paths, and Typical Salaries

Brand and product management requires high problem-solving, analytical, presentation, communication, and leadership skills, as well as the ability to work well in a team. Product management requires long hours and involves the high pressure of running large projects. In consumer goods companies, the newcomer—who usually needs an MBA—joins a brand team as an assistant and learns the ropes by doing numerical analyses and watching senior brand people. This person eventually heads the team and later moves on to manage a larger brand, then several brands.

Many industrial goods companies also have product managers. Product management is one of the best training grounds for future corporate officers. Product management also offers good opportunities to move into international marketing. Product managers command relatively high salaries. Because this job category encourages or requires a master's degree, starting pay tends to be higher than in other marketing categories such as advertising or retailing.

Sales and Sales Management

Sales and sales management opportunities exist in a wide range of profit and not-for-profit organizations and in product and service organizations, including financial, insurance, consulting, and government organizations.

Job Descriptions

Key jobs include consumer sales, industrial sales, national account manager, service support, sales trainers, sales management, and telesellers.

- *Consumer* sales involves selling consumer products and services through retailers.

- *Industrial sales* involves selling products and services to other businesses.

- *National account managers (NAM)* oversee a few very large accounts.

- *Service support* personnel support salespeople during and after the sale of a product.

- *Sales trainers* train new hires and provide refresher training for all sales personnel.

- *Sales management* includes a sequence of positions ranging from district manager to vice president of sales.

- The *teleseller* (not to be confused with the home consumer telemarketer) offers service and support to field salespeople.

Salespeople enjoy active professional lives, working outside the office and interacting with others. They manage their own time and activities. And successful salespeople can be very well paid. Competition for top jobs can be intense. Every sales job is different, but some positions involve extensive travel, long workdays, and working under pressure. You can also expect to be transferred more than once between company headquarters and regional offices. However, most companies are now working to bring good work–life balance to their salespeople and sales managers.

Skills Needed, Career Paths, and Typical Salaries

Selling is a people profession in which you will work with people every day, all day long. In addition to people skills, sales professionals need sales and communication skills. Most sales positions also require strong problem-solving, analytical, presentation, and leadership abilities as well as creativity and initiative. Teamwork skills are increasingly important.

Career paths lead from salesperson to district, regional, and higher levels of sales management and, in many cases, to the top management of the firm. Today, most entry-level sales management positions require a college degree. Increasingly, people seeking selling jobs are acquiring sales experience in an internship capacity or from a part-time job before graduating. Sales positions are great springboards to leadership positions, with more CEOs starting in sales than in any other entry-level position. This possibly explains why competition for top sales jobs is intense.

Starting base salaries in sales may be moderate, but compensation is often supplemented by significant commission, bonus, or other incentive plans. In addition, many sales jobs include a company car or car allowance. Successful salespeople are among most companies' highest paid employees.

Other Marketing Jobs

Retailing

Retailing provides an early opportunity to assume marketing responsibilities. Key jobs include store manager, regional manager, buyer, department manager, and salesperson. *Store managers* direct the management and operation of an individual store. *Regional managers* manage groups of stores across several states and report performance to headquarters. *Buyers* select and buy the merchandise that the store carries. The *department manager* acts as store manager of a department, such as clothing, but on the department level. The *salesperson* sells merchandise to retail customers. Retailing can involve relocation, but generally there is little travel, unless you are a buyer. Retailing requires high people and sales skills because retailers are constantly in contact with customers. Enthusiasm, willingness, and communication skills are very helpful for retailers, too.

Retailers work long hours, but their daily activities are often more structured than some types of marketing positions. Starting salaries in retailing tend to be low, but pay increases as you move into management or some retailing specialty job.

Marketing Research

Marketing researchers interact with managers to define problems and identify the information needed to resolve them. They design research projects, prepare questionnaires and samples, analyze data, prepare reports, and present their findings and recommendations to management. They must understand statistics, consumer behavior, psychology, and sociology. A master's degree helps. Career opportunities exist with manufacturers, retailers, some wholesalers, trade and industry associations, marketing research firms, advertising agencies, and governmental and private nonprofit agencies.

New-Product Planning

People interested in new-product planning can find opportunities in many types of organizations. They usually need a good background in marketing, marketing research, and sales forecasting; they need organizational skills to motivate and coordinate others; and they may need a technical background. Usually, these people work first in other marketing positions before joining the new-product department.

Marketing Logistics (Physical Distribution)

Marketing logistics, or physical distribution, is a large and dynamic field, with many career opportunities. Major transportation carriers, manufacturers, wholesalers, and retailers all employ logistics specialists. Increasingly, marketing teams include logistics specialists, and marketing managers' career paths include marketing logistics assignments. Coursework in quantitative methods, finance, accounting, and marketing will provide you with the necessary skills for entering the field.

Public Relations

Most organizations have a public relations staff to anticipate problems with various publics, handle complaints, deal with media, and build the corporate image. People interested in public relations should be able to speak and write clearly and persuasively, and they should have a background in journalism, communications, or the liberal arts. The challenges in this job are highly varied and very people-oriented.

Not-for-Profit Services

The key jobs in not-for-profits include marketing director, director of development, event coordinator, publication specialist, and intern/volunteer. The *marketing director* is in charge of all marketing activities for the organization. The *director of development* organizes, manages, and directs the fund-raising campaigns that keep a not-for-profit in existence. An *event coordinator* directs all aspects of fund-raising events, from initial planning through implementation. The *publication specialist* oversees publications designed to promote awareness of the organization.

Although typically an unpaid position, the *intern/volunteer* performs various marketing functions, and this work can be an important step to gaining a full-time position. The not-for-profit sector is typically not for someone who is money-driven. Rather, most not-for-profits look for people with a strong sense of community spirit and the desire to help others. Therefore, starting pay is usually lower than in other marketing fields. However, the bigger the not-for-profit, the better your chance of rapidly increasing your income when moving into upper management.

Other Resources (p A40)

Professional marketing associations and organizations are another source of information about careers. Marketers belong to many such societies. You may want to contact some of the following in your job search:

Advertising Women of New York, 25 West 45th Street, New York, NY 10036. (212) 221-7969 (www.awny.org)

American Advertising Federation, 1101 Vermont Avenue, NW, Suite 500, Washington, DC 2005. (800) 999-2231 (www.aaf.org)

American Marketing Association, 311 South Wacker Drive, Suite 5800, Chicago, IL 60606. (800) AMA-1150 (www.marketingpower.com)

Market Research Association, 110 National Drive, 2nd Floor, Glastonbury, CT 06033. (860) 682-1000 (www.mra-net.org)

National Association of Sales Professionals, 37577 Newburgh Park Circle, Livonia, MI 48152. (877) 800-7192 (www.nasp.com)

National Management Association, 2210 Arbor Boulevard, Dayton, OH 45439. (937) 294-0421 (www.nma1.org)

National Retail Federation, 325 Seventh Street NW, Suite 1100, Washington, DC 20004 (800) 673-4692 (www.nrf.com)

Product Development and Management Association, 15000 Commerce Parkway, Suite C, Mount Laurel, NJ 08054. (800) 232-5241 (www.pdma.org)

Public Relations Society of America, 33 Maiden Lane, Eleventh Floor, New York, NY 10038. (212) 460-1400 (www.prsa.org)

Sales and Marketing Executives International, PO Box 1390, Sumas, WA 98295-1390. (312) 893-0751 (www.smei.org)

The Association of Women in Communications, 3337 Duke Street, Alexandria, VA 22314. (703) 370-7436 (www.womcom.org)

References

CHAPTER 1

1. Quotes and other information from Jonah Bloom, "Stengel Exhorts 4As: It's Not About Telling and Selling," *Advertising Age*, March 1, 2007, accessed at http://adage.com/4asmedia07/article?article_id=115259; Robert Berner, "Detergent Can Be So Much More," *BusinessWeek*, May 1, 2006, pp. 66–67; Jack Neff, "New Tide Campaign Goes Beyond Stains," *Advertising Age*, February 13, 2006, p. 16; "For P&G, Success Lies in More Than Merely a Dryer Diaper," *Advertising Age*, October 15, 2007, p. 30; "Case Study: Tide Knows Fabrics Best," accessed at www.thearf.org/awards/ogilvy-current-winners.html, April 2008; and "P&G: Our Purpose, Values, and Principles," accessed at www.pg.com/company/who_we_are/ppv.jhtml, November 2008.

2. Statement made in an address to the American Association of Advertising Agencies conference, accessed via Jonah Bloom, "Stengel Exhorts 4A's: It's Not About 'Telling and Selling'" *Advertising Age*, March 1, 2007, at http://adage.com/print?article_id=115259.

3. See "Markets: Since Launch of First Generation of iPod, Apple Inc. Has Sold More Than 88.7 Million Units Worldwide," *Associated Press Financial Wire*, March 14, 2007; Adam L. Penenberg, "All Eyes on Apple," *Fast Company*, December 2007–January 2008, pp. 83–91.

4. As quoted in Carolyn P. Neal, "From the Editor," *Marketing Management*, January–February 2006, p. 3.

5. The American Marketing Association offers the following definition: "Marketing is the activity, set of institutions, and processes for creating, communicating, delivering, and exchanging offerings that have value for customers, clients, partners, and society at large." Accessed at www.marketingpower.com/mg-dictionaryview1862.php?, November 2008. Also see, Lisa M. Keefe, "Marketing Defined," *Marketing News*, January 15, 2008, pp. 28–29.

6. Geoff Colvin, "Selling P&G," *Fortune*, September 17, 2007, pp. 163–169. For other examples, see Tim Laseter and Larry Laseter, "See for Yourself," *Strategy + Business*, Autumn 2007, pp. 20–24.

7. Information from Douglas Quentua, "Revising a Name, but Not a Familiar Slogan," *New York Times*, January 17, 2008; and www.adcouncil.org/default.aspx?id=224, November 2008.

8. See Theodore Levitt's classic article, "Marketing Myopia," *Harvard Business Review*, July–August 1960, pp. 45–56. For more recent discussions, see Yves Doz, Jose Santos, and Peter J. Williamson, "Marketing Myopia Re-Visited: Why Every Company Needs to Learn from the World," *Ivey Business Journal*, January–February 2004, p. 1; "What Business Are You In?" *Harvard Business Review*, October 2006, pp. 127–137; and John D. Nicholson and Philip J. Kitchen, "The Development of Regional Marketing—Have Marketers Been Myopic?" *International Journal of Business Studies*, June 2007, pp. 107–125.

9. Information from a recent "The Computer Is Personal Again" advertisement and www.hp.com/personal, August 2008.

10. See Ben Elgin, "How 'Green' Is That Water?" *BusinessWeek*, August 13, 2007, p. 68.

11. See Larry Edwards, et al., "75 Years of Ideas," *Advertising Age*, February 14, 2005, p. 14; "America's Most Admired Companies," *Fortune*, accessed at http://money.cnn.com/magazines/fortune/mostadmired/2007/index.html, August 2007; "The Top 10 PR Endeavors," *PR News*, October 30, 2006, p.1; and www.jnj.com/our_company/our_credo/index.htm, December 2008.

12. Quotes and information from Blanca Torres, "Jeans' Genes Part of Price Tag Formula," *Knight Ridder Tribune Business News*, November 8, 2006, p. 1; "Paige Denim Week," *Toronto Fashion Monitor*, October 30, 2006, accessed at http://toronoto.fashion-monitor.com/events.php/56; Megan Kaplan, "Haute Mama," *Knight Ridder Tribune Business News*, March 22, 2007, p. 1; and www.paigepremiumdenim.com, November 2008.

13. For more on how to measure customer satisfaction, see D. Randall Brandt, "For Good Measure," *Marketing Management*, January–February 2007, pp. 21–25.

14. Portions adapted from Julie Barker, "Power to the People," *Incentive*, February 2008, p. 34 and Carmine Gallo, "Employee Motivation the Ritz-Carlton Way," *BusinessWeek*, February 29, 2008, accessed at www.businessweek.com. Also see "The World's Best Hotels—Where Luxury Lives," *Institutional Investor*, November 2007, p. 1; and http://corporate.ritzcarlton.com/en/About/Awards.htm#Hotel, November 2008.

15. Information about the Harley Owners Group accessed at www.hog.com, September 2008. For more on loyalty programs, see Yuping Liu, "The Long-Term Impact of Loyalty Programs on Consumer Purchase Behavior and Loyalty," *Journal of Marketing*, October 2007, p. 19; and "Reward Programs Pay for Customer Loyalty, but Fail to Engage, According to Allegiance, Inc.," *Business Wire*, February 28, 2008.

16. Quotes and other information from "Gunning for the Best Buy," *Knight Ridder Tribune Business News*, May 28, 2006, p. 1; Gary McWilliams, "Analyzing Customers, Best Buy Decides Not All Are Welcome," *Wall Street Journal*, November 8, 2004, p. A1; Shirley A. Lazo, "Let's Go Shopping," *Barron's*, June 26, 2006, p. 28. Matthew Boyle, "Best Buy's Giant Gamble," *Fortune*, April 3, 2006, pp. 69–75; Marc Millstein, "Best Buy Quest to Master Customer Centricity," *Chain Store Age*, December 2007, pp. 2A+; "Best Buy Co., Inc.," *Hoover's Company Records*, March 1, 2008, p. 10209; and www.bestbuy.com, October 2008.

17. Andrew Walmsley, "The Year of Consumer Empowerment," *Marketing*, December 20, 2006, p. 9.

18. Walmsley, "The Year of Consumer Empowerment," p. 9; and "Who's in Control?" *Advertising Age*, January 28, 2008, p. C9.

19. Helen Coster, "Crowd Control," *Forbes*, November 26, 2007, pp. 38–39; and "Top 100 Global Marketers," *Advertising Age*, November 19, 2007, p. 4.

20. Adapted from information in Jonathan Birchall, "Just Do It, Marketers Say," *Los Angeles Times*, April 30, 2007, accessed at http://articles.latimes.com/2007/apr/30/business/ft-brands30. Other facts and information from Louise Story, "New Advertising Outlet: Your Life," *New York Times*, October 14, 2007; Nicholas Casey, "Nike, New Coach Chase Serious Runners," *Wall Street Journal*, December 6, 2007, p. B7; and "Consumer Experiences: Nike," *Fast Company*, March 8, 2008, pp. 94–95.

21. Matthew Creamer, "John Doe Edges Out Jeff Goodby," *Advertising Age*, January 8, 2007, pp. S4–S5. Also see Karen E. Klein, "Should Your Customers Make Your Ads?" *BusinessWeek*, January 2, 2008, www.businessweek.com.

22. Philip Kotler and Kevin Lane Keller, *Marketing Management*, 13th ed. (Upper Saddle River, NJ: Prentice Hall, 2009), p. 11.

23. For more on the relationship between customers satisfaction, loyalty, and company performance, see Fred Reichheld, *The Ultimate*

Question: Driving Good Profits and True Growth (Boston: Harvard Business School Press, 2006); Bruce Cooil, et al., "A Longitudinal Analysis of Customer Satisfaction and Share of Wallet: Investigating the Moderating Effects of Customer Characteristics," *Journal of Marketing*, January 2007, pp. 67–83; Murali Chandrahsekaran, Kristin Rotte, Stephen S. Tax, and Rajdeep Grewal, "Satisfaction, Strength, and Customer Loyalty," *Journal of Marketing Research*, February 2007, pp. 153–163; and Leonard L. Berry, Lewis P. Carbone, "Build Loyalty Through Experience Management," *Quality Progress*, September 2007, pp. 26+.

24. "Stew Leonard's," *Hoover's Company Records*, July 15, 2007, pp. 104–226; and www.stew-leonards.com/html/about.cfm, November 2007.

25. For interesting discussions on assessing and using customer lifetime value, see Rajkumar Venkatesan, V. Kumar, and Timothy Bohling, "Selecting Valuable Customers Using a Customer Lifetime Value Framework," Marketing Science Institute, Report No. 05–121, 2005; Sunil Gupta, et al., "Modeling Customer Lifetime Value," *Journal of Service Research*, November 2006, pp. 139–146; "Determining 'CLV' Can Lead to Making Magical Marketing Decisions," *BtoB*, May 7, 2007, p. 18; and Detlef Schoder, "The Flaw in Customer Lifetime Value," *Harvard Business Review*, December 2007, p. 26.

26. See www.brandkeys.com/awards/cli08.cfm, April 2008; www.llbean.com/customerService/aboutLLBean/guarantee.html, November 2008.

27. Erick Schonfeld, "Click Here for the Upsell," *Business 2.0*, July 11, 2007, accessed at http://cnnmoney.com; and "Getting Shoppers to Crave More," *Fortune Small Business*, August 24, 2007, p. 85.

28. Don Peppers and Martha Rogers, "Customers Don't Grow on Trees," *Fast Company*, July 2005, pp. 26.

29. See Roland T. Rust, Valerie A. Zeithaml, and Katherine A. Lemon, *Driving Customer Equity* (New York: Free Press 2000); Robert C. Blattberg, Gary Getz, and Jacquelyn S. Thomas, *Customer Equity* (Boston, MA: Harvard Business School Press, 2001); Rust, Lemon, and Zeithaml, "Return on Marketing: Using Customer Equity to Focus Marketing Strategy," *Journal of Marketing*, January 2004, pp. 109–127; Rust, Zeithaml, and Lemon, "Customer-Centered Brand Management," *Harvard Business Review*, September 2004, p. 110; Robert P. Leone, et al., "Linking Brand Equity to Customer Equity," *Journal of Service Marketing*, November 2006, pp. 125–138; Julian Villanueva and Dominique Hanssens, *Customer Equity: Measurement, Management and Research Opportunities* (Hanover, MA: Now Publishers Inc., 2007); and Roland T. Rust, "Seeking Higher ROI? Base Strategy on Customer Equity," *Advertising Age*, September 10, 2007, pp. 26–27.

30. This example is adapted from information in Rust, Lemon, and Zeithaml, "Where Should the Next Marketing Dollar Go?" *Marketing Management*, September–October 2001, pp. 24–28. Also see David Welch and David Kiley, "Can Caddy's Driver Make GM Cool?" *BusinessWeek*, September 20, 2004, pp. 105–106; and Jean Halliday, "Comeback Kid Cadillac Stalls after Shop Swap," *Advertising Age*, September 24, 2007, p. 1.

31. Werner Reinartz and V. Kumar, "The Mismanagement of Customer Loyalty," *Harvard Business Review*, July 2002, pp. 86–94. For more on customer equity management, see Michael D. Johnson and Fred Selnes, "Customer Portfolio Management: Toward a Dynamic Theory of Exchange Relationships," *Journal of Marketing*, April 2004, pp. 1–17; Sunil Gupta and Donald R. Lehman, *Managing Customers as Investments* (Philadelphia: Wharton School Publishing, 2005); Roland T. Rust, Katherine N. Lemon, and Das Narayandas, *Customer Equity Management* (Upper Saddle River, NJ: Prentice Hall, 2005); and Kathy Stevens, "Using Customer Equity Models to Improve Loyalty and Profits," *Journal of Consumer Marketing*, vol. 23, 2006, p. 379.

32. Brian Morrissey, "Is Social Media Killing the Campaign Micro-Site?" November 12, 2007, accessed at www.mediaweek.com.

33. Statistics from www.internetworldstats.com/stats.htm, accessed March 2008; "Internetic World in the Year 2015," February 7, 2007, accessed at www.weboma.com; and "Dawn of the Web Potato," *Fortune*, September 17, 2007, p. 52. The following extract from "The Way We Were in 2007," *The Week*, December 28, 2007–January 11, 2008, p. 26.

34. See Allison Enright, "Get Clued In: Mystery of Web 2.0 Resolved," *Marketing News*, January 15, 2007, pp. 20–22. Also see Jessica Tsai, "Power to the People," *Customer Relationship Management*, December 2007, pp. 28+.

35. "JupiterResearch Forecasts Online Retail Spending Will Reach $144 Billion in 2010, a CAGR of 12% from 2005," February 6, 2006, accessed at www.jupitermedia.com/corporate/releases/06.02.06-newjupresearch.html.

36. See Kerry Capell, "The Arab World Wants Its MTD," *BusinessWeek*, October 22, 2007, pp. 79–81; and Tom Lowry, "The Game's the Thing at MTV Networks," *BusinessWeek*, February 18, 2008, p. 51. Additional information from annual reports and other information found at www.mcdonalds.com, www.viacom.com, and www.nikebiz.com, October 2008.

37. Adapted from information in Don Frischmann, "Nothing Is Insignificant When It Comes to Brand Fulfillment," *Advertising Age*, January 21, 2008, p. 16.

38. Quotes and information found at www.patagonia.com/web/us/contribution/patagonia.go?assetid=2329, August 2008.

39. For examples, and for a good review of nonprofit marketing, see Philip Kotler and Alan R. Andreasen, *Strategic Marketing for Nonprofit Organizations*, 6th ed. (Upper Saddle River, NJ: Prentice Hall, 2003); Philip Kotler and Karen Fox, *Strategic Marketing for Educational Institutions* (Upper Saddle River, NJ: Prentice Hall, 1995); Philip Kotler, John Bowen, and James Makens, *Marketing for Hospitality and Tourism*, 3rd ed. (Upper Saddle River, NJ: Prentice Hall, 2003); and Philip Kotler and Nancy Lee, *Marketing in the Public Sector A Roadmap for Improved Performance* (Philadelphia: Wharton School Publishing, 2007).

40. See David Williams, "St. Jude Gets Record Donation from PGA," www.commercialappeal.com, November 16, 2007; and information from various pages at www.stjude.org, accessed April 2008.

41. "100 Leading National Advertisers," *Advertising Age*, June 25, 2007, p. S4. For more on social marketing, see Philip Kotler, Ned Roberto, and Nancy R. Lee, *Social Marketing: Improving the Quality of Life*, 2nd ed. (Thousand Oaks, CA: Sage Publications, 2002).

CHAPTER 2

1. Quotes and other information from Stuart Elliott, "Marketers Are Putting NASCAR on Different Kinds of Circuits," *New York Times*, February 15, 2008; Paul Farriss, "NASCAR Rides the Fast Track," *Marketing*, April 11, 2005, pp. 11–12; Mark Woods, "Readers Try to Explain Why Racin' Rocks," *Florida Times Union*, February 16, 2003, p. C1; Tony Kontzer, "Backseat Drivers—NASCAR Puts You in the Race," *InformationWeek*, March 25, 2002, p. 83; Jenny Kincaid, "NASCAR Beefs Up Its Brand Loyalty," *Knight Ridder Tribune Business News*, April 1, 2006, p. 1; Frank Litsky, "Bill France, Who Built NASCAR into Phenomenon, Dies," *International Herald Tribune*, June 6, 2007, p. 20; Barry Janoff, "NASCAR's 50th Daytona 500 Offers Golden Opportunities," *Brandweek*, February 4, 2008, p. 14; and www.NASCAR.com, September 2008.

2. For more on mission statements, see Joseph Peyrefitte and Forest R. David, "A Content Analysis of Mission Statements of United States Firms in Four Industries," *International Journal of Management*, June 2006, pp. 296–301; Jeffrey Abrahams, *101 Mission Statements from*

Top Companies (Berkeley, CA: Ten Speed Press, 2007); and Jack and Suzy Welch, "State Your Business," January 14, 2008, p. 80.

3. Mission statements are from, Cold Stone Creamery, www. coldstonecreamery.com/assets/pdf/secondary/Pyramid1. pdf; and eBay, http://pages.ebay.com/aboutebay/thecompany/ companyoverview.html, accessed September 2008.

4. Jack and Suzy Welch, "State Your Business; Too Many Mission Statements Are Loaded with Fatheaded Jargon. Play It Straight," *BusinessWeek*, January 14, 2008, p. 80.

5. See the BASF Innovations Web page, accessed at www.corporate. basf.com/en/innovationen/?id=Z_l-HA6M0bcp4PX, July 2008.

6. See "BASF Innovative Agricultural Products to Asian Growth Markets," February 28, 2007, accessed at www.corporate. basf.com/en/presse/mitteilungen/pm.htm?pmid=2586&id=Z_l-HA6M0bcp4PX; and "BASF in Greater China," accessed at www.greater-china.basf.com/apw/GChina/GChina/en_GB/portal, April 2008.

7. The following discussion is based in part on information found at www.bcg.com/publications/files/Experience_Curve_IV_ Growth_Share_Matrix_1973.pdf, December 2008.

8. For an interesting discussion on managing growth, see Matthew S. Olson, Derek van Bever, and Seth Verry, "When Growth Stalls," *Harvard Business Review*, March 2008, pp. 51–61.

9. H. Igor Ansoff, "Strategies for Diversification," *Harvard Business Review*, September–October 1957, pp. 113–124.

10. Information about Crocs in this discussion are from Kris Hudson, "Crocs on the Catwalk," *Wall Street Journal*, February 13, 2007, p. C1; Taesik Yoon, "Crocs Still Have Bite," *Forbes*, www.forbes.com, April 4, 2007; and www.crocs.com, accessed April 2008. Crocs and Croslite are trademarks of Crocs, Inc.

11. Michael E. Porter, *Competitive Advantage: Creating and Sustaining Superior Performance* (New York: Free Press, 1985); and Michel E. Porter, "What Is Strategy?" *Harvard Business Review*, November–December 1996, pp. 61–78; Also see "The Value Chain," accessed at www.quickmba.com/strategy/value-chain, July 2008; and Philip Kotler and Kevin Lane Keller, *Marketing Management* (Upper Saddle River, NJ: Prentice Hall, 2009) pp. 35–36 and pp. 252–253.

12. Kotler, *Kotler on Marketing* (New York: The Free Press, 1999), pp. 20–22; and Marianne Seiler, "Transformation Trek," *Marketing Management*, January–February 2006, pp. 32–39.

13. "McDonald's Fetes 50th Birthday, Opens Anniversary Restaurant," *Knight Ridder Tribune Business News*, April 15, 2005, p. 1; and information from www.mcdonalds.com/corp.html, September 2008.

14. Quotes and other information from Jeffery K. Liker and Thomas Y. Choi, "Building Deep Supplier Relationships," *Harvard Business Review*, 2004, pp. 104–113; Lindsay Chappell, "Toyota Aims to Satisfy Its Suppliers," *Automotive News*, February 21, 2005, p. 10; "Toyota Recognizes Top Suppliers for 2007," *PR Newswire*, March 4, 2008; and www.toyotasupplier.com, November 2008.

15. Jack Trout, "Branding Can't Exist Without Positioning," *Advertising Age*, March 14, 2005, p. 28.

16. "100 Leading National Advertisers," special issue of *Advertising Age*, June 23, 2008, p. 10.

17. The four Ps classification was first suggested by E. Jerome McCarthy, *Basic Marketing: A Managerial Approach* (Homewood, IL: Irwin, 1960). For the 4Cs, other proposed classifications, and more discussion, see Robert Lauterborn, "New Marketing Litany: 4P's Passé C-Words Take Over," *Advertising Age*, October 1, 1990, p. 26; Don E. Schultz, "New Definition of Marketing Reinforces Idea of Integration," *Marketing News*, January 15, 2005, p. 8; and Phillip Kotler, "Alphabet Soup," *Marketing Management*, March–April 2006, p. 51.

18. For more discussion of the CMO position, see Pravin Nath and Vijay Mahajan, "Chief Marketing Officers: A Study of Their Presence in Firms' Top Management Teams," *Journal of Marketing*, January 2008, pp. 65–81; and Philip Kotler and Kevin Lane Keller, *Marketing Management*, (Upper Saddle River: NJ: Prentice Hall, 2009), pp. 11–12.

19. For more on brand and product management, see Kevin Lane Keller, *Strategic Brand Management*, 3rd ed. (Upper Saddle River, NJ: Prentice Hall, 2008).

20. Adapted from Diane Brady, "Making Marketing Measure Up," *BusinessWeek*, December 13, 2004, pp. 112–113; with information from "Kotler Readies World for One-on-One," *Point*, June 2005, p. 3. Also see Darryl E. Owens, "Champion ROI to Prove Worth," *Marketing News*, March 1, 2007, pp. 13, 22.

21. Mark McMaster, "ROI: More Vital Than Ever," *Sales & Marketing Management*, January 2002, pp. 51–52. Also see Gordon A. Wyner, "Beyond ROI," *Marketing Management*, June 2006, pp. 8–9; James Lenskold, "Unlock Profit Potential," *Marketing Management*, May–June, 2007, pp. 26–31; Steven H. Seggie, Erin Cavusgil, and Steven Phelan, "Measurement of Return on Marketing Investment: A Conceptual Framework and the Future of Marketing Metrics," *Industrial Marketing Management*, August 2007, pp. 834–841.

22. See David Skinner and Doug Brooks, "Move from Metrics Overload to Actionable Insights," *Advertising Age*, May 28, 2007, pp. 14–15; and Gregor Harter, Edward Landry, and Andrew Tipping, "The New Complete Marketer," *Strategy + Business*, Autumn 2007, pp. 79–87.

23. For more discussion, see Bruce H. Clark, Andrew V. Abela, and Tim Ambler, "Behind the Wheel," *Marketing Management*, May–June 2006, pp. 19–23; Christopher Hosford, "Driving Business with Dashboards," *BtoB*, December 11, 2006, p. 18; and Allison Enwright, "Measure Up: Create a ROMI Dashboard That Shows Current and Future Value," *Marketing News*, August 15, 2007, pp. 12–13.

24. For a full discussion of this model and details on customer-centered measures of return on marketing investment, see Roland T. Rust, Katherine N. Lemon, and Valerie A. Zeithaml, "Return on Marketing: Using Customer Equity to Focus Marketing Strategy," *Journal of Marketing*, January 2004, pp. 109–127; Roland T. Rust, Katherine N. Lemon, and Das Narayandas, *Customer Equity Management* (Upper Saddle River, NJ: Prentice Hall, 2005); David Tiltman, "Everything You Know Is Wrong," *Marketing*, June 13, 2007, pp. 28–29; Roland T. Rust, "Seeking Higher ROI? Base Strategy on Customer Equity," *Advertising Age*, September 10, 2007, pp. 26–27; and Valerie P. Valente, "Redefining ROI," *Advertising Age*, January 28, 2008, p. C7.

25. Deborah L. Vence, "Return on Investment," *Marketing News*, October 15, 2005, pp. 13–14.

CHAPTER 3

1. Quotes and other information from or adapted from Claudia Deutsch, "A Big Red X No Longer Marks the Spot," *New York Times*, January 8, 2008, p. C11; Nanette Byrnes, "Xerox' New Design Team: Customers," *BusinessWeek*, May 7, 2007, p. 72; "Xerox Unveils Biggest Change to Its Brand in Company History," January 7, 2008, Xerox news release, accessed at www.Xerox.com; Paula Lehman, "The Issue: Putting the 'R' Back in R&D," *BusinessWeek*, March 18, 2008, accessed at www.businessweek. com/managing/content/mar2008/ca20080318_765446.htm; and "About Xerox," accessed at www.xerox.com, October 2008.

2. Robert J. Bowman, "Home Depot Turns Its Attention to Supplier Performance Management," SupplyChainBrain.com, June 2006; and https://suppliercenter.homedepot.com, accessed April 2008.

3. Information from Robert J. Benes, Abbie Jarman, and Ashley Williams, "2007 NRA Sets Records," accessed at www.chefmagazine.com/nra.htm; September 2007; and www.cokesolutions.com, accessed November 2008.

4. World POPClock, U.S. Census Bureau, accessed online at www.census.gov, September 2008. This Web site provides continuously updated projections of the U.S. and world populations.

5. See from Frederik Balfour, "Educating the 'Little Emperors': There's a Big Market for Products That Help China's Coddled Kids Get Ahead," *BusinessWeek*, November 10, 2003, p. 22; Clay Chandler, "Little Emperors," *Fortune*, October 4, 2004, pp. 138–150; and "Hothousing Little Tykes," *Beijing Review*, May 5, 2005, accessed at www.bjreview.cn/EN/En-2005/05-18-e/china-5.htm; and "China's 'Little Emperors,'" *Financial Times*, May 5, 2007, p. 1.

6. Adapted from information in Janet Adamy, "Different Brew: Eyeing a Billion Tea Drinkers, Starbucks Pours It On in China," *Wall Street Journal*, November 29, 2006, p. A1. Also see "Where the Money Is," *Financial Times*, May 12, 2007, p. 8; and Loretta Chao, "Politics and Economics: China to Retain Its One-Child Policy," *Wall Street Journal*, March 11, 2008, p. A7.

7. U.S. Census Bureau projections and POPClock Projection, U.S. Census Bureau, accessed at www.census.gov, September 2008.

8. Louise Lee, "Love Those Boomers," *BusinessWeek*, October 24, 2005, pp. 94–102; Tom Ramstack, "The New Gray: Boomers Spark Retirement Revolution," *Washington Times*, December 29, 2005, p. A1; Ken Wheaton, "Marketers Would Be Foolish to Ignore Boomer Audience," *Advertising Age*, June 4, 2007, p. 26; and Abbey Klaassen, "Media Players to Go After Free-Spending Boomers," *Advertising Age*, September 3, 2007, pp. 3+.

9. Adapted from information in Claudia H. Deutsch, "Not Getting Older, Just More Scrutinized," *New York Times*, October 11, 2006, accessed at www.nyt.com; and Madhusmita Bora, "Gadgety Grandparents," *McClatchy-Tribune Business News*, February 24, 2008.

10. Dee Depass, "Designed with a Wink, Nod at Boomers," *Minneapolis-St. Paul Star Tribune*, April 1, 2006, p. 1. Also see Victoria Knight, "Advisers Link Physical, Financial Health," *Wall Street Journal*, January 17, 2007, p. B3C.

11. Jack Neff, "Unilever Resuscitates the Demo Left for Dead," *Advertising Age*, May 28, 2007, pp. 1, 26; and Judann Pollack, "Boomers Don't Want Your Pity, but They Do Demand Your Respect," *Advertising Age*, October 8, 2007, p. 24.

12. Stuart Elliott, "Flower Power in Ad Land," *New York Times*, April 11, 2006. p. G2; and Jack Willoughby, "Good Morning, Ameriprise: A Financial-Services Giant Awakens," *Barron's*, August 21, 2006, pp. 15–16. Also see Laura Petrecca, "More Marketers Target Boomers' Eyes, Wallets," *USA Today*, February 26, 2007, p. 6B; and Karla Freeman, "How to Attract the Baby Boomer Market," *Accounting Technology* January 2008, p. 2.

13. Scott Schroder and Warren Zeller, "Get to Know Gen X and Its Segments," *Multichannel News*, March 21, 2005, p. 55; Jim Shelton, "When Children of Divorce Grow Up," *Knight Ridder Tribune Business News*, March 4, 2007, p. 1; and James H. Barnett III and Ana Veciana-Suarez, "The Leaders of Today Are Diverse Group," *McClatchy-Tribune Business News*, January 21, 2008.

14. Based on Jennifer Alsever, "For Gen X, It's Time to Grow Up and Get a Broker," www.msnbc.msn.com/id/21083120, November 9, 2007; and "Schwab's (Gen) X Files," *Brandweek*, December 17, 2007, p. 18; and information from Charles Schwab, June 2008.

15. Julie Liesse, "Getting to Know the Millennials," *Advertising Age*, July 9, 2007, pp. A1–A6; and "The Millennials," *Time*, Spring 2008, p. 55.

16. John Jullens, "Marketers: Meet the Millennial Generation," *Strategy + Business*, Spring 2007, pp. 16–18. Also see "Generation Y Research: What Makes 'y' Tick," *Brand Strategy*, February 5, 2007, p. 38.

17. Sharon Jayson, "Totally Wireless on Campus," *USA Today*, October 2, 2006, accessed at www.usatoday.com/tech/news/2006-10-02-gennext-tech_x.htm. Also see Barbara Rose, "Generation Y a Learning Experience for Firms," *Chicago Tribune*, March 4, 2007; and Carlos Grande, "Targeting the Millennial Mindset," *Financial Times*, February 19, 2008, p. 15.

18. Example adapted from Jack Neff, "Tide's 'Washday Miracle': Not Doing Laundry," *Advertising Age*, November 12, 2007, p. 12; with information from www.swashitout.com, accessed September 2008.

19. See "America's Families and Living Arrangements: 2006," U.S. Census Bureau, accessed at www.census.gov/population/www/socdemo/hh-fam.html, September 2007.

20. See Paul Nyhan, "Stay-Home Dads Connect with New Full-Time Job; Pay Stinks, but Benefits Are Great," *Seattle Post-Intelligencer*, April 25, 2006, p. A1; U.S. Census Bureau, "Single-Parent Households Showed Little Variation Since 1994, Census Bureau Reports," March 27, 2007, accessed at www.census.gov/Press-Release/www/releases/archives/families_households/009842.html; and U.S. Census Bureau, "Facts for Features," March 2008, accessed at www.census.gov/Press-Release/www/releases/archives/facts_for_features_special_editions/011179.html.

21. "Peapod Is in the 'Growth'ery Business: 10 Millionth Order Delivered, 10 Million Hours Saved," *PR Newswire*, February 7, 2007, p. 1; and information from www.peapod.com/corpinfo/GW_index.jhtml; September 2008.

22. U.S. Census Bureau, "Geographical Mobility/Migration," accessed at www.census.gov/population/www/socdemo/migrate.html, September 2008.

23. See U.S. Census Bureau, www.census.gov/population/www/estimates/aboutmetro.html, accessed June 2008; Gordon F. Mulligan and Alexander C. Vias, "Growth and Change in Micropolitan Areas," *The Annals of Regional Science*, June 2006, p. 203; and Madeline Johnson, "Devilish Definitions as Urban Masses Evolve, New Terms and Labels Are Emerging to Try to Describe and Distinguish Them," *Financial Times*, December 29, 2007.

24. Kate Lorenz, "What's the Advantage to Telecommuting," accessed at www.cnn.com, April 27, 2007. Also see "Number of Worldwide Mobile Workers Increasing," *Workspan*, March 2008, p. 19; Sue Shellenbarger, "Some Companies Rethink That Telecommuting Trend," *Wall Street Journal*, February 28, 2008, p. D1.

25. See Fahmida Y. Rashid and Mario Morejon, "Cisco WebEx MeetMeNow—Conferencing with Compatibility," *CRN*, November 19, 2007, p. 43; "WebEx Communications, Inc.," *Hoover's Company Records*, March 15, 2008, p. 99024; and "About WebEx," accessed at www.webex.com/companyinfo/company-overview.html, July 2008.

26. "Educational Attainment," U.S. Census Bureau, January 2008, accessed at www.census.gov/population/www/socdemo/educ-attn.html.

27. See U.S. Bureau of Labor Statistics, "Labor Force, Employment, and Earnings," p. 416, accessed at http://landview.census.gov/prod/2001pubs/statab/sec13.pdf, June 2004; and U.S. Department of Labor, *Occupational Outlook Handbook, 2008–09 Edition*, accessed at www.bls.gov/oco/home.htm.

28. See Mike Swift, "State's Diversity a Cue for U.S.," *McClatchy-Tribune Business News*, February 12, 2008.

29. See Laurel Wentz, "Energizer's Bunny Marches to New Beat," *Advertising Age*, November 5, 2007, p. S3; Leila Cobo, "Energizer Teams with Latin Acts for Staying Power," *Reuters*, January 4, 2008; and Laurel Wentz, "Pop Culture with a Twist," *Advertising Age*, January 21, 2008, p. S11.

30. For these and other statistics, see www.rivendellmedia.com/ngng/executive_summary/NGNG.PPT and www.gaymarket.com/ngng/ngng_reader.html, accessed April 2008; and www.planetoutinc.com/sales/market.html, accessed September 2008.

31. For these and other examples, see Edward Iwata, "More Marketing Aimed at Gay Consumers," *USA Today*, November 2, 2006, accessed at www.usatoday.com; Andrew Hampp, "An Ad in Which Boy Gets Girl . . . or Boy," *Advertising Age*, August 6, 2007, p. 4; and "Delta Airlines Sponsors City Navigaytour Gay and Lesbian Travel Guides," *Business Wire*, December 6, 2007.

32. Andrew Adam Newman, "Web Marketing to a Segment Too Big to Be a Niche," *New York Times*, October 30, 2007, p. 9.

33. Andrew Adam Newman, "Web Marketing to a Segment Too Big to Be a Niche," p. 9; "Disaboom.com Unveils Expanded Content Platform and Marketing Campaign," *PR Newswire*, January 24, 2008; and information from Ford, July 2008.

34. Gavin Rabinowitz, "Carmaker in India Unveils $2,500 Car," *USA Today*, January 10, 2008, accessed at www.usatoday.com; Gavin Rabinowitz, "India's Tata Motors Unveils $2,500 Car, Bringing Car Ownership Within Reach of Millions," *Associated Press*, January 10, 2008; and Mark Phelan, "Automaker Tata's Presence Already Felt in Detroit Area," *McClatchy-Tribune Business News*, March 17, 2008.

35. See Arik Hesseldahl, "What's Eating Apple?" *BusinessWeek*, February 25, 2008, p. 36; and "Not-So-Big Spenders," *Marketing Management*, January/February 2008, p. 5.

36. Mark Dolliver, "How the Rise of Inequality Fosters a New Culture of Antagonism," *Adweek*, December 17, 2007, pp. 30–31, 37.

37. Kelly Nolan, "Mass Movement of High Fashion," *Retailing Today*, January 8, 2007, pp. 4–6; Eric Wilson and Michael Barbaro, "Can You Be Too Fashionable?" *New York Times*, June 17, 2007, p. 1; Elizabeth Wellington, "Mirror, Mirror: Discounted to Distraction," *Philadelphia Inquirer*, November 4, 2007, p. M1; and Yelena Moroz, "Mass Fashion in Focus: Cheap Chic Fever Quickly Catching On," *Retailing Today*, February 11 2008, p. 1.

38. Andrew Zolli, "Business 3.0," *Fast Company*, March 2007, pp. 64–70.

39. Steve Bronstein, "50 Ways to Green Your Business (and Boost Your Bottom Line)," *Fast Company*, November 2007, pp. 90–99.

40. Adapted from Lorraine Woellert, "HP Wants Your Old PC Back," *BusinessWeek*, April 10, 2006, pp. 82–83; with information from "HP Recycles Nearly 250 Million Pounds of Products in 2007— 50 Percent Increase Over 2006," February 5, 2008, accessed at www.hp.com/hpinfo/newsroom/press/2008/080205a.html.

41. See "RFID Market Nears $7B," *Journal of Commerce Online Edition*, July 9, 2007; Scott Denne, "After Being Overhyped, RFID Starts to Deliver," *Wall Street Journal*, November 7, 2007, p. 5F; "Wal-Mart Expands RFID Requirements," *McClatchy-Tribune Business News*, January 30, 2008; "Sam's Club Gets Serious about RFID," *Modern Materials Handling*, March 2008, p. 18; and information accessed online at www.autoidlabs.org, September 2008.

42. See "Slowing Economy Dampens 2008 R&D Spending," *R&D Magazine*, February 2008, pp. F3–F15.

43. See Jack Neff, "Unilever, P&G War Over Which Is Most Ethical," *Advertising Age*, March 3, 2008, p. 1; "Hilary Swank Donates Her Hair to Pantene Beautiful Lengths," PR Newswire, November 2, 2007; and information from www.beautifullengths.com, accessed April 2008.

44. Wendy Meillo, "The Greed for Goodwill," *Adweek*, March 13, 2006, p. 14; and "The Growth of Cause Marketing," accessed at www.causemarketingforum.com/page.asp?ID=188, August 2008.

45. Adapted from descriptions found at www.yankelovich.com/products/lists.aspx, November 2006.

46. Ronald Grover, "Trading the Bleachers for the Couch," *BusinessWeek*, August 22, 2005, p. 32. Also see, "Examine the Impact Cocooning Is Having on Consumer Markets," *Business Wire*, February 22, 2007; and Paul Kagan, "Home Theatre 101," *Boxoffice*, January 2008, pp. 52–53.

47. "Decked Out," *Inside*, Spring 2006, pp. 76–77. See also "Meet Me at the Oasis; From Saunas to Spas, People Are Turning Their Homes into a Personal Paradise," *Ottawa Citizen*, April 18, 2007, p. E8.

48. Laura Feldmann, "After 9/11 Highs, America's Back to Good Ol' Patriotism," *Christian Science Monitor*, July 5, 2006, p. 1; and "Lifestyle Statistics: Very Proud of Their Nationality," accessed at www.nationmaster.com, April 2008.

49. L. A. Chung, "New Greetings of Hybrid Fans: Aloha, LOHAS," *Mercury News*, April 29, 2005, accessed at www.mercurynews.com/mld/mercurynews/news/columnists/la_chung/11520890.htm; with information from www.lohas.com, accessed April 2008.

50. See "Wal-Mart Launches Live Better Index with First Focus on the Environment," April 17, 2007, accessed at www.walmartfacts.com/articles/4960.aspx; "Updated Wal-Mart Live Better Index Reveals More Americans Embrace Earth Friendly Products," *PR Newswire*, October 22, 2007; and www.livebetterindex.com/sustainability.html, accessed April 2008.

51. "Earthbound Farm Facts," www.earthboundfarm.com, accessed September 2008.

52. See Joanne Friederick, "Evolution Leads to Niches," *Gourmet News*, September 2007, p. 22.

53. Quotes from Myra Stark, "Celestial Season," *Brandweek*, November 16, 1998, pp. 25–26; and Becky Ebankamp, "The Young and Righteous," *Brandweek*, April 5, 2004, p. 18. Also see "Where 'California' Bubbled Up; American Spirituality," *The Economist*, December 22, 2007, p. 75; and Suzanne Sataline, "The Changing Faiths of America; Study Shows Big Declines Among Major Denominations," *Wall Street Journal*, February 26, 2008, p. D1.

54. See Philip Kotler, *Kotler on Marketing* (New York: Free Press, 1999), p. 3; and Kotler, *Marketing Insights from A to Z* (Hoboken, NJ: John Wiley & Sons, 2003), pp. 23–24.

55. Based on information found at www.breakthechain.org/exclusives/oscarmayer.html and www.kraftfoods.com/oscarmayer/hoaxes_rumors, November 2008.

CHAPTER 4

1. Portions adapted from Bill Breen, "The Mind Reader," *Fast Company*, October 2006, pp. 70–74; with other information and quotes from Christina Williams, "The Leader by Design," *Oregon Business*, May 1, 2007, p. 36; Richard Read, "Introducing the No-Name Behind Your TV," *Knight Ridder Tribune Business News*, February 4, 2007, p. 1; and www.ziba.com and www.cleret.com, accessed September 2008.

2. Unless otherwise noted, quotes in this section are from the excellent discussion of customer insights found in Mohanbir Sawhney, "Insights into Customer Insights," accessed at www.redmond.nl/hro/upload/Insights_into_Customer_Insights.pdf, March 15, 2007. The Apple iPod example is also adapted from this article.

3. See Charles Babcock, "Data, Data, Everywhere," *InformationWeek*, January 9, 2006, pp. 49–53; Holly Wright, "Data Overload," *Marketing Direct*, June 2006, pp. 43–46; and Mary Hayes Weier, "HP Data Warehouse Lands in Wal-Mart's Shopping Cart," *InformationWeek*, August 6, 2007, pp. 31–32.

4. Michael Fassnacht, "Beyond Spreadsheets," *Advertising Age*, February 19, 2007, p. 15.

5. Quotes from Mohanbir Sawhney, "Insights into Customer Insights," p. 3; and Robert Schieffer and Eric Leininger, "Customers at the Core," *Marketing Management,* January/February 2008, pp. 31–37.

6. For more discussion, see Robert Schieffer and Eric Leininger, "Customers at the Core," *Marketing Management,* January/February 2008, pp. 31–37.

7. See Steve Wills and Sally Webb, "Measuring the Value of Insight—It Can and Must Be Done," *International Journal of Market Research,* vol. 49, no. 2, 2007, pp. 155–165.

8. See Samar Farah, "Loyalty Delivers," *Deliver,* September 1, 2006, www.delivermagazine.com/the-magazine/2006/09/01/loyalty-delivers; Jennifer Brown, "Pizza Hut Delivers Hot Results Using Data Warehousing," *Computing Canada,* October 17, 2003, p. 24; and www.yum.com/investors/fact.asp, accessed September 2008.

9. See Jean Halliday, "Car Talk: Ford Listens in on Consumers' Online Chatter," *Advertising Age,* February 5, 2007, pp. 3, 34. Also see Sean Hargrave, "Measuring Buzz: Ears to the Ground," *New Media Age,* January 17, 2008, p. 21.

10. See Richard L. Wilkins, "Competitive Intelligence: The New Supply Chain Edge," *Supply Chain Management Review,* January/February 2007, pp. 18–27.

11. Fred Vogelstein and Peter Lewis, "Search and Destroy," *Fortune,* May 2, 2005.

12. James Curtis, "Behind Enemy Lines," *Marketing,* May 21, 2001, pp. 28–29. Also see Brian Caufield, "Know Your Enemy," *Business 2.0,* June 2004, p. 89; Michael Fielding, "Damage Control: Firms Must Plan for Counterintelligence," *Marketing News,* September 15, 2004, pp. 19–20; and Bill DeGenaro, "A Case for Business Counterintelligence," *Competitive Intelligence Magazine,* September–October 2005, pp. 5+; and Jim Middlemiss, "Firms Look to Intelligence to Gain a Competitive Edge," *Law Times,* March 5, 2007, accessed at www.lawtimesnews.com.

13. See "What's Hot: Axe Extends its Aromatic Reach," *Drug Store News,* December 11, 2006, p. 67; David Colman, "Younger, and Faster to Pick Up the Scent," *New York Times,* July 26, 2007, p. 5; and information from www.unilever.com/ourbrands/personalcare/Axe.asp, July 2008.

14. For more on research firms that supply marketing information, see Jack Honomichl, "Honomichl Top 50," special section, *Marketing News,* June 15, 2008, pp. H1–H67. Other information from www.infores.com; www.smrb.com; www.acnielsen.com; and www.yankelovich.com/products/monitor.aspx, August 2008.

15. See http://us.infores.com/page/solutions/market_content/infoscan, accessed April 5, 2008.

16. Example adapted from an example in David Kiley, "Shoot the Focus Group," *BusinessWeek,* November 14, 2005, pp. 120–121. Also see Richard G. Starr and Karen V. Fernandez, "The Mindcam Methodology: Perceiving Through the Native's Eye," *Quantitative Market Research,* Spring 2007, pp. 168+.

17. Example adapted from information in Rhys Blakely, "You Know When It Feels Like Somebody's Watching You . . ." *Times,* May 14, 2007, p. 46; and Nandini Lakshman, "Nokia: It Takes a Village to Design a Phone for Emerging Markets," *BusinessWeek,* September 10, 2007, p. 12.

18. Spencer E. Ante, "The Science of Desire," *BusinessWeek,* June 5, 2006, p. 100; and Rhys Blakely, "You Know When It Feels Like Somebody's Watching You . . ." *Times,* May 14, 2007, p. 46.

19. David Kiley, "Shoot the Focus Group," *BusinessWeek,* p. 120. Also see Peter Noel Murray, "Focus Groups Are Valid When Done Right," *Marketing News,* September 1, 2006, pp. 21, 25.

20. Adapted from information in Kenneth Hein, "Hypnosis Brings Groups into Focus," *Brandweek,* May 23, 2008, p. 4.

21. Emily Spensieri, "A Slow, Soft Touch," *Marketing,* June 5, 2006, pp. 15–16.

22. Adam Woods, "Get to the Truth with Web 2.0," *Revolution,* December 2007, p. 39.

23. Gelb, "Online Options Change Biz a Little—and a Lot," *Marketing News,* November 1, 2006, p. 23.

24. Johnson, "Forget Phone and Mail: Online's the Best Place to Administer Surveys," p. 23. See also, "Get to the Truth with Web 2.0," *Revolution,* December 4, 2007, p. 40.

25. Based on information found in Jeremiah McWilliams, "A-B Sees Web As Fertile Ground for Advertising Efforts," *St. Louis Post-Dispatch,* December 19, 2007.

26. Based on information found www.channelm2.com/HowOnlineQualitativeResearch.html; accessed September 2008.

27. John B. Horrigan, and Aaron Smith, "Home Broadband Adoption 2007," Pew Internet & American Life Project, June 2007, www.pewinternet.org/pdfs/PIP_Broadband%202007.pdf.

28. For more on Internet privacy, see Jessica E. Vascellaro "They've Got Your Number (and a Lot More), *Wall Street Journal,* March 13, 2007, pp. D1–D2; "Comment: Do Consumers Really Want Their Privacy?" *New Media Age,* December 13, 2007, p. 12; and Jim Puzzanghera, "Internet; Tough Cookies for Web Surfers Seeking Privacy," *Los Angeles Times,* April 19, 2008, p. C1.

29. See "Creating Computers That Know How You Feel," www.almaden.ibm.com/cs/BlueEyes/index.html, accessed November 2008.

30. See Josh Goldstein, "Branding on the Brain," *News & Observer,* December 6, 2006, p. 9E; and Jack Neff, "This Is Your Brain on Super Bowl Spots," *Advertising Age,* February 11, 2008, pp. 1, 21.

31. This example is adapted from Rebecca Harris, "Brain Waves," *Marketing,* June 5, 2006, pp. 15–17. Also see Douglas L. Fugate, "Neuromarketing: A Layman's Look at Neuroscience and Its Potential Application to Marketing Practice," *Journal of Consumer Marketing,* 2007, p. 385–394.

32. For more on neuromarketing, see Tameka Kee, "NeuroFocus Unveils 'Best Practices,' for Getting into Consumers' Brains," *MediaPost Publications,* April 23, 2008, accessed at http://publications.mediapost.com; Steve McClellan, "Mind over Matter: New Tools Put Brands in Touch with Feelings," *Adweek,* February 18, 2008, accessed at www.adweek.com; and Stewart Elliott, "Is the Ad a Success? The Brain Waves Tell All," *New York Times,* March 31, 2008.

33. "Analysis: Customer Relationship Management Set to Grow," *Precision Marketing,* November 2, 2007, p. 12.

34. Mike Freeman, "Data Company Helps Wal-Mart, Casinos, Airlines Analyze Customers," *San Diego Union Tribune,* February 24, 2006.

35. Quotes and other information from Suzette Parmley, "Wooing with Loyalty," *Philadelphia Inquirer,* February 28, 2007; Sudhir H. Kale and Peter Klugsberger, "Reaping Rewards," *Marketing Management,* August 2007, pp. 14–17; and Harrah's annual reports and other information accessed at http://investor.harrahs.com/phoenix.zhtml?c=84772&p=irol-sec, August 2008.

36. Michael Krauss, "At Many Firms, Technology Obscures CRM," *Marketing News,* March 18, 2002, p. 5. Also see William Boulding et al., "A Customer Relationship Management Roadmap: What Is Known, Potential Pitfalls, and Where to Go," *Journal of Marketing,* October 2005, pp. 155–166; Deborah L. Vence, "CRM: You Know What It Stands for, but Do You Know What It Means?" *Marketing News,* September 15, 2007, p. 12; and "Study: Marketers Stink When It Comes to CRM," *Brandweek,* April 14, 2008, p. 7.

37. See "Value Added with mySAP CRM: Benchmarking Study," accessed at www.sap.com/solutions/business-suite/crm/pdf/Misc_CRM_Study.pdf, June 2008.

38. See Darell K. Rigby and Vijay Vishwanath, "Localization: The Revolution in Consumer Markets," *Harvard Business Review,* April 2006, pp. 82–92; and information found at www.partnersonline. com, September 2008.

39. Adapted from information in Ann Zimmerman, "Small Business; Do the Research," *Wall Street Journal,* May 9, 2005, p. R3; with information from www.bibbentuckers.com, accessed July 2008.

40. Zimmerman, "Small Business; Do the Research," *Wall Street Journal,* p. R3.

41. For some good advice on conducting market research in a small business, see "Marketing Research . . . Basics 101," accessed at www. sba.gov/starting_business/marketing/research.html, August 2008; and "Researching Your Market," U.S. Small Business Administration, accessed at www.sba.gov/idc/groups/public/documents/sba_ homepage/pub_mt8.pdf, November 2008.

42. See Jack Honomichl, "2006 Revenue Growth Remains Flat," *Marketing News,* August 15, 2007, p. H3.

43. See ACNielsen International Research Web site, accessed at www2.acnielsen.com/company/where.php, September 2008.

44. Phone, PC, and other country media stats are from http:// devdata.worldbank.org/query/default.htm and www.nationmaster. com; July 2008.

45. Subhash C. Jain, *International Marketing Management,* 3rd ed. (Boston: PWS-Kent, 1990), p. 338. For more discussion on international marketing research issues and solutions, Micheal Fielding, "Shift the Focus: Ethnography Proves Fruitful in Emerging Economies," *Marketing News,* September 1, 2006, pp. 18, 20; Robert B. Young and Rajshekhar G. Javalgi, "International Marketing Research: A Global Project Management Perspective," *Business Horizons,* March–April 2007, pp. 113–122; and Gordon A. Wyner, "The World Isn't Flat Yet," *Marketing Research,* Summer 2007, p. 6.

46. Portions of this example are adapted from "Listening to the Internet," *The Economist,* March 11, 2006, p. 8. Other information from Louise Story, "To Aim Ads, What Is Keeping Closer Eye on You," *New York Times,* March 10, 2008; and www.nielsenbuzzmetrics. com, accessed August 2008.

47. Abbey Klaassen and Ira Teinowitz, "An Ad App You'll Love (and Privacy Groups Will Hate)," *Advertising Age,* November 5, 2007, pp. 3–4; Thomas Claburn, "Call Off the Wolves," *InformationWeek,* November 12, 2007, pp. 69+; and Anick Jesdanun, "Study: Online Privacy Concerns Increase," *Associated Press,* January 16, 2008.

48. "ICC/ESOMAR International Code of Marketing and Social Research Practice," accessed at www.esomar.org/index.php/ codes-guidelines.html, July 2008. Also see "Respondent Bill of Rights," accessed at www.cmor.org/rc/tools.cfm?topic=4, July 2008.

49. Jaikumar Vijayan, "Disclosure Laws Driving Data Privacy Efforts, Says IBM Exec," *Computerworld,* May 8, 2006, p. 26. Also see Thornton A. May, "The What and Why of CPOs," *Computerworld,* November 27, 2006, p. 18.

50. Information accessed at www10.americanexpress.com/sif/cda/ page/0,1641,14271,00.asp, July 2008.

51. Cynthia Crossen, "Studies Galore Support Products and Positions, But Are They Reliable?" *Wall Street Journal,* November 14, 1991, pp. A1, A9. Also see Allan J. Kimmel, "Deception in Marketing Research and Practice: An Introduction," *Psychology and Marketing,* July 2001, pp. 657–661; Alvin C. Burns and Ronald F. Bush, *Marketing Research* (Upper Saddle River, NJ: Prentice Hall, 2005), pp. 63–75; and Jack Neff, "Who's No. 1? Depends on Who's Analyzing the Data," *Advertising Age,* June 12, 2006, p. 8.

52. Information accessed at www.casro.org/codeofstandards.cfm#intro, September 2008.

CHAPTER 5

1. Quotes and other information from Vito J. Racanelli, "Bound for Hog Heaven," *Barron's,* November 26, 2007, p. 20–22; Greg Schneider, "Rebels with Disposable Income; Aging Baby Boomers Line Up to Buy High-End Versions of Youthful Indulgences," *Washington Post,* April 27, 2003, p. F1; Ted Bolton, "Tattooed Call Letters: The Ultimate Test of Brand Loyalty," accessed online at www.boltonresearch.com, April 2003; "Harley Davidson Reports Fourth Quarter and Full Year Results for 2007, *PR Newswire,* January 25, 2008; and the Harley-Davidson Web site at www. Harley-Davidson.com, October 2008.

2. GDP figures from *The World Fact Book,* February 7, 2008, accessed at www.cia.gov/cia/publications/factbook/. Population figures from the World POPClock, U.S. Census Bureau, www.census.gov, September 2008. This Web site provides continuously updated projections of the U.S. and world populations.

3. Don E. Schultz, "Lines or Circles" *Marketing News,* November 5, 2007, p. 21.

4. Statistics from Mike Swift, "State's Diversity a Cue for U.S.," *McClatchy-Tribune Business News,* February 12, 2008; Deborah L. Vence, "Segmentation: Multicultural—Scratch the Surface," *Marketing News,* February 15, 2007, pp. 17–18; and Andrew V. Hernandez, "Growing Market: As the Hispanic Population and Buying Power Increases, Area Businesses Look to Tap into the Market," *McClatchy-Tribune Business News,* October 13, 2007.

5. See "Nielsen Reveals Hispanic Consumer Shopping Behavior Insights," *Business Wire,* September 24, 2007.

6. Adapted from information found in Della de Lafuente, "The New Weave," *Adweek,* March 3, 2008, pp. 26–28.

7. See Deborah L. Vence, "Scratch the Surface," *Marketing News,* February 2007, pp. 17–18; "Buying Power Among African Americans to Reach $1.1 Trillion by 2012," *PR Newswire,* February 6, 2008; and U.S. Census Bureau reports accessed online at www.census.gov, September 2007.

8. Quote from "Queen Latifah Turns CoverGirl," February 2, 2006, accessed at http://blogs.chron.com/shopgirl/archives/2006/02/ queen_latifah_t.html. Facts from Cliff Peale, "P&G Showed the Way: Company's Ads Targeted to Blacks Paid Off," *Cincinnati Enquirer,* February 25, 2007, accessed at http://news.enquirer.com; and www.covergirl.com/products/collections/queen, accessed November, 2008.

9. Cliff Peale, "Procter & Gamble Campaigns for Black Consumers Paying Off," *Cincinnati Inquirer,* March 6, 2007, accessed at www. clarionledger.com. Also see, Michael Bush, "P&G Unveils 'My Black Is Beautiful' Campaign," *PRWeek,* December 3, 2007, p. 5.

10. See David Dodson, "Minority Groups' Share of $10 Trillion U.S. Consumer Market Is Growing Steadily," Terry College of Business News & Announcements, July 31, 2007, www.terry.uga.edu/news/ releases/2007/minority_buying_power_report.html; and U.S. Census Bureau reports accessed at www.census.gov, October 2008.

11. "Annual Asian American Consumer Behavior Study Reveals Key Findings in Retail, Automobile, Insurance, and Telecom Industries," DiversityBusiness.com, May 7, 2007, www. diversitybusiness.com/news/supplierdiversity/45200672.asp. Example based on conversations with PNC Bank, May 2007.

12. Information accessed at www.census.gov, August 2008. Also see Sherry L. Jarrell, "Picture of Retiree Spending Is Changing," *Marketing News,* September 15, 2006, p. 40; and "Mature Market in the U.S.," *M2 Presswire,* March 2, 2007.

13. "Boom Time of America's New Retirees Feel Entitled to Relax— and Intend to Spend," *Financial Times,* December 6, 2007, p. 9.

14. For a discussion of influencers, see Clive Thompson, "Is the Tipping Point Toast?" *Fast Company,* February 2008, pp. 75–105; Edward Keller and Jonathan Berry, *The Influentials* (New York: The Free Press, 2003); and Daniel B. Honigman, "Who's on First?" *Marketing News* November 1, 2007, pp. 14–17. The study results and quotes are from Kenneth Hein, "Report Explores What Influences the Influencers," *Brandweek,* February 5, 2007, p. 13; Ryan Mcconnell, "Spread the News: Word-Of-Mouth Worth $1 Billion," *Advertising Age* November 15, 2007, p. 4; and Megan Mcilroy, "Family, Friends Most Influential on Shoppers," *Advertising Age,* April 9, 2008, accessed at www.adage.com.

15. Extract adapted from Robert Berner, "I Sold It Through the Grapevine," *BusinessWeek,* May 29, 2006, pp. 32–34; and Melanie Wells, "Kid Nabbing," *Forbes,* February 2, 2004, p. 84. Also see Jack Neff, "P&G, Unilever Are Ready to Clutter," *Advertising Age,* June 11, 2007, p. 4. Data on Vocalpoint from www.vocalpoint.com, July 2008.

16. Adapted from Anya Kamenetz, "The Network Unbound," *Fast Company,* June 2006, pp. 69–73. Also see Brad Stone, "Social Networking's Next Phase," *New York Times,* March 3, 2007, accessed at www.nytimes.com; and Chuck Brymer, "The Birds and the Bees," *Adweek,* January 7, 2008, p. 16.

17. See Alana Semuels, "Small Business; This Advertising Shop Knows Jack," *Los Angeles Times,* February 7, 2008, p. C1; Jen Haberkorn, "Facebook, MySpace See Ads Invasion," *Washington Times,* August 17, 2007, p. C9; Nicole Maestri, "Wal-Mart Using Facebook to Win Back-to-School Sales," August 8, 2007, accessed at www.reuters.com.

18. Allison Enright, "How the Second Half Lives," *Marketing News,* February 15, 2007, pp. 12–14; Mike Shields, "CNN to Launch Bureau in Second Life Virtual World," *Media Week.com,* October 29, 2007, accessed at www.mediaweek.com; and http://secondlife.com, July 2008.

19. Leslie Brooks Suzukamo, "Serious Joints Silly as Companies, Others See YouTube Marketing Promise," *McClatchy-Tribune Business News,* January 10, 2008; Stuart Elliott, "For Marketing, the MVP Might Be YouTube," *New York Times,* February 5, 2008, accessed at www.nytimes.com; Alana Semuels, "Small Business; This Advertising Shop Knows Jack," *Los Angeles Times,* February 7, 2008, p. C1; and Elizabeth A. Sullivan, "H.J. Heinz Company," *Marketing News,* February 1, 2008, p. 10.

20. Adapted from Kim Hart, "Online Networking Goes Small, and Sponsors Follow," *Washington Post,* December 29, 2007, p. D1.

21. Hart, "Online Networking Goes Small, and Sponsors Follow," p. D1.

22. See Yuval Rosenberg, "Building a New Nest," *Fast Company,* April 27, 2007, p. 48; and http://capessa.com/members/aboutus.aspx, October 2008.

23. Quote from Anya Kamenetz, "The Network Unbound," *Fast Company,* June 2006, p. 73. Also see Julie Bosman, "Chevy Tries a Write-Your-Own-Ad Approach," *New York Times,* April 4, 2006, p. C1.

24. See Scott Hidebrink, "Women and the Automotive Aftermarket," *Motor Age,* September 2007, pp. 60+; and "Finance and Economics: A Guide to Womenomics," *The Economist,* April 15, 2006, p. 80.

25. Jeff James, "Nickelodeon, Chrysler Announced a Deal to Promote '08 Minivans," June 27, 2007 accessed at www.about.com; and Anthony Crupi, "Nickelodeon, Chrysler Join Forces to Reach Families," *Brandweek,* June 26, 2007, accessed at www.brandweek.com.

26. Alice Dragoon, "How to Do Customer Segmentation Right," *CIO,* October 1, 2005, p. 1. For another example, see Teri Koenke, "Destroying Demographics: The New Art of Strategic Customer Communications." *U.S. Banker,* October 2006, pp. 22–23.

27. Information from www.spearshoes.com, December 2008.

28. Portions adapted from Linda Tischler, "How Pottery Barn Wins with Style," *Fast Company,* June 2003, pp. 106–113; and Carole Sloan, "Lifestyle Specialists Enjoy Strong Year," *Furniture Today,* August 28, 2006, p. 28; with information from www.potterybarn.com, www.potterybarnkids.com, and www.pbteen.com, October 2008.

29. Jennifer Aaker, "Dimensions of Measuring Brand Personality," *Journal of Marketing Research,* August 1997, pp. 347–356. Also see Aaker, "The Malleable Self: The Role of Self Expression in Persuasion," *Journal of Marketing Research,* May 1999, pp. 45–57; and Audrey Azoulay and Jean-Noel Kapferer, "Do Brand Personality Scales Really Measure Brand Personality?" *Journal of Brand Management,* November 2003, p. 143.

30. See "Apple Debuts New 'Get a Mac' Ads," *Apple Matters,* January 17, 2007; and "Apple 'Get a Mac' Ad Campaign Seen Taking Toll on Microsoft's Reputation," *MacDailyNews,* March 20, 2008, accessed at www.macdailynews.com.

31. See Mark Tadajewski, "Remembering Motivation Research: Toward an Alternative Genealogy of Interpretive Consumer Research," *Marketing Theory,* December 2006, pp. 429–466; and Leon G. Schiffman and Leslie L. Kanuk, *Consumer Behavior,* 9th ed. (Upper Saddle River, NJ: Prentice Hall, 2007), chapter 4.

32. See Abraham. H. Maslow, "A Theory of Human Motivation," *Psychological Review,* 50 (1943), pp. 370–396. Also see Maslow, *Motivation and Personality,* 3rd ed. (New York: HarperCollins Publishers, 1987); and Barbara Marx Hubbard, "Seeking Our Future Potentials," *Futurist,* May 1998, pp. 29–32.

33. Louise Story, "Anywhere the Eye Can See, It's Likely to See an Ad," *New York Times,* January 15, 2007, accessed at www.nytimes.com; and Matthew Creamer, "Caught in the Clutter Crossfire: Your Brand," *Advertising Age,* April 1, 2007, p. 35.

34. Bob Garfield, "'Subliminal' Seduction and Other Urban Myths," *Advertising Age,* September 18, 2000, pp. 4, 105; and Lewis Smith, "Subliminal Advertising May Work, but Only If You're Paying Attention," *Times,* March 9, 2007. For more on subliminal advertising, see Alastair Goode, "The Implicit and Explicit Role of Ad Memory in Ad Persuasion: Rethinking the Hidden Persuaders," *International Journal of Marketing Research,* vol. 49, no. 2, 2007, pp. 95–116; Don E. Shultz, "Subliminal Ad Notions Still Resonate Today," *Marketing News,* March 15, 2007, p. 5; Cynthia Crossen, "For a time in the 50s, a Huckster Fanned Fears of an Ad 'Hypnosis,'" *Wall Street Journal,* November 5, 2007, p. B1; and Beth Snyder Bulik, "This Brand Makes You More Creative," *Advertising Age,* March 24, 2008, p. 4.

35. Quotes and information from "Ogilvy Public Relations Worldwide and BzzAgent Forge Strategic Alliance to Offer Clients More Word-of-Mouth Communications Solutions," *PR Newswire,* January 10, 2008; Duglas Pruden and Terry G. Vavra, "Controlling the Grapevine," *Marketing Management,* July–August 2004, pp. 25–30; and Yubo Chen and Jinhong Xie, "Online Consumer Review: Word-of-Mouth as a New Element of Marketing Communication Mix," *Management Science,* March 2008, pp. 477–491.

36. See Leon Festinger, *A Theory of Cognitive Dissonance* (Stanford, CA: Stanford University Press, 1957); Schiffman and Kanuk, *Consumer Behavior,* pp. 219–220; "Cognitive Dissonance and the Stability of Service Quality Perceptions," *Journal of Services Marketing,* 2004, p. 433+; Cynthia Crossen, "'Cognitive Dissonance' Became a Milestone in the 1950s Psychology," *Wall Street Journal,* December 12, 2006, p. B1; and Mohammed N. Nadeem, "Post-Purchased Dissonance: the Wisdom of the Repeat Purchases" *Journal of Global Business Issues,* Summer 2007, pp. 183–194.

37. The following discussion draws from the work of Everett M. Rogers. See his *Diffusion of Innovations,* 5th ed. (New York: Free Press, 2003).

38. See Glen Dickson, "Nielsen Gives Fuzzy Picture of HDTV Penetration," *Broadcasting & Cable,* October 30, 2007, accessed at www.broadcastingandcable.com.

CHAPTER 6

1. Quotes and other information from "GE Transportation Endorses New Tier 3 and 4 Emission Regulations," *Business Wire,* March 14, 2008; "General Electric Signs Contract to Supply 310 Evolution Series Locomotives to Kazakhstan," *Business Wire,* September 28, 2006; Jim Martin, "GE to Seal $650 Million Deal," *Knight Ridder Tribune Business News,* September 28, 2006, p. 1; Rick Stouffer, "GE Locomotives: 100 Years and Still Chuggin'," *Knight Ridder Tribune Business News,* September 23, 2007; David Lustig, "GE Unveils Hybrid Loco," *Railway Gazette International,* July 2007, p. 1; "Collaborating with Partners," accessed at www.getransportation.com, May 2008; and various pages at www.ge.com, accessed October 2008.

2. See Kerry Capell, "How the Swedish Retailer Became a Global Cult Brand," *BusinessWeek,* November 14, 2005, p. 103; Greta Guest, "Inside IKEA's Formula for Global Success," *Detroit Free Press,* June 3, 2006; IKEA, *Hoover's Company Records,* April 1, 2008, p, 42925; "IKEA Group Stores," accessed www.ikea-group.ikea.com/?ID=11, April 2008; and "Our Vision: A Better Everyday Life," accessed at www.ikea.com, December 2008.

3. Patrick J. Robinson, Charles W. Faris, and Yoram Wind, *Industrial Buying Behavior and Creative Marketing* (Boston: Allyn & Bacon, 1967). Also see James C. Anderson and James A. Narus, *Business Market Management,* 2nd ed. (Upper Saddle River, NJ: Prentice Hall, 2004), chapter 3; and James C. Anderson, James A. Narus, and Wouter van Rossum, "Customer Value Propositions in Business Markets," *Harvard Business Review,* March 2006, pp. 91–99; and Philip Kotler and Kevin Lane Keller, *Marketing Management,* 13th ed. (Upper Saddle River, NJ: Prentice Hall, 2009), chapter 7.

4. Example adapted from information found in "Nikon Focuses on Supply Chain Innovation—and Makes New Product Distribution a Snap," UPS case study, accessed at www.ups-scs.com/solutions/case_studies/cs_nikon.pdf, July 2008. See also Roger Morton, "Keeping the Supply Chain in Focus," *Logistics Today,* July 2007, pp. 12+.

5. See Frederick E. Webster Jr. and Yoram Wind, *Organizational Buying Behavior* (Upper Saddle River, NJ: Prentice Hall, 1972), pp. 78–80. Also see James C. Anderson and James A. Narus, *Business Market Management: Understanding, Creating and Delivering Value* (Upper Saddle River NJ: Prentice Hall, 2004), chapter 3; Jorg Brinkman and Markus Voeth, "An Analysis of Buying Center Decisions Through the Sales Force," *Industrial Marketing Management,* October 2007, p. 998; and Philip Kotler and Kevin Lane Keller, *Marketing Management,* 13th ed. (Upper Saddle River, NJ: Prentice Hall, 2009), pp. 188–191.

6. Jennifer Lawinski, "Good Checkup—Avent's HealthPath University Puts VARs in Touch with How Things Work at a Hospital," *CRN,* August 20, 2007, p. 57.

7. See Frederick E. Webster, Jr., and Yoram Wind, *Organizational Buying Behavior,* pp. 33–37.

8. Robinson, Faris, and Wind, *Industrial Buying Behavior,* p. 14.

9. For this and other examples, see Kate Maddox, "10 Great Web Sites," *BtoB Online,* September 11, 2006; accessed at www.btobonline.com; and Karen J. Bannan, "10 Great Web Sites," September 10, 2007, accessed at www.btobonline.com. Other information from www.sun.com, September 2008.

10. Michael A. Verespej, "E-Procurement Explosion," *Industry Week,* March 2002, pp. 25–28. For more information on e-procurement, see Amit Gupta, "E-Procurement Trials and Triumphs," *Contract Management,* January 2008, pp. 28–35; and Christian Tanner, et al., "Current Trends and Challenges in Electronic Procurement: an Empirical Study," *Electronic Markets,* February 2008, pp. 6–18.

11. Information from www.shrinershq.org/Hospitals/Hospitals_for_Children/Facts; and www.tenethealth.com, October 2008.

12. Michael Myser, "The Hard Sell," *Business 2.0,* December 2006, pp. 62–65.

13. See "About Food Away from Home," accessed at www.fafh.com, April 2008.

14. "Federal IT Spending to Rebound in 2009," *Techweb,* March 29, 2007; Budget of the United States Government, FY 2007, Office of Management and Budget, Department of Homeland Security, www.whitehouse.gov/omb/budget/fy2007/dhs.html, accessed February 2008.

15. Ari Vidali, president of Envisage Technologies, personal communication, July 6, 2006.

16. See "GSA Organization Overview," accessed as www.gsa.gov, December 2008; and VA Office of Acquisition & Material Management, accessed at www1.va.gov/oamm, December 2008.

CHAPTER 7

1. Adapted from Ruple Parekh, "Febreze Sniffs Out New Target: Dorm Dwellers," *Advertising Age,* October 29, 2007, p. 12; with quotes and information from Leslie Benson, "Forget Laundry Day, Use Febreze," *GCI,* February 2008, p. 8; "Ten Years Marks Milestone for Procter & Gamble's Febreze Brand," *PR Newswire,* June 4, 2008; and www.whatstinks.com, accessed September 2008.

2. For these and other examples, see Jesse Harlin, "Speaking in Tongues—Localizing at Home and Abroad," *Game Developer,* November 2007, p. 40; and Philip Kotler and Kevin Lane Keller, *Marketing Management,* 13th ed. (Upper Saddle River, NJ: Prentice Hall, 2009), pp. 210–211.

3. Based on information from Patti Bond, "Home Depot to Test Superstores, Ministores," *Atlanta Journal-Constitution,* March 23, 2007.

4. See "Wal-Mart's Smaller Grocery Format on the Way," *ProgressiveGrocer.com,* January 15, 2008; and Jonathan Birchall, "Wal-Mart Unveils First New Format in a Decade with Small Store Brand," *Financial Times,* May 16, 2008, p. 1.

5. See Beth Snyder Bulik, "Forget the Parents: HP Plans to Target Teenagers Instead," *Advertising Age,* July 30, 2007, p. 8; and www.parentalmindcontrol.org, accessed June 2008.

6. Solvej Schou, "Sisters Doing It for Themselves," Associated Press, March 12, 2007; and www.daisyrock.com, accessed November 2008.

7. Adapted from information found in Laura Koss-Feder, "At Your Service," *Time,* June 11, 2007, p. 1.

8. Adapted from information found in Laura Koss-Feder, "At Your Service," *Time,* June 11, 2007, p. 1.

9. Information from www.smartertravel.com, www.rssc.com, and www.royalcaribbean.com, accessed June 2008.

10. See Louise Story, "Finding Love and the Right Linens," *New York Times,* December 13, 2006, accessed at www.nytimes.com; and www.williams-sonoma.com/cust/storeevents/index.cfm, accessed September 2008.

11. Kate MacArthur, "BK Rebels Fall in Love with King," *Advertising Age,* May 1, 2006, pp. 1, 86; Kenneth Hein, "BK 'Lifestyle' Goods Aim for Young Males," *Adweek,* June 12, 2006, p. 8; and Janet Adamy, "Man Behind the Burger King Turnaround: Chidsey Says Identifying His Restaurant's Superfan Helped Beef Up Its Offerings," *Wall Street Journal,* April 2, 2008, p. B1.

12. See Manish Bhatt and Raghu Bhat, "Building a Brand, Creating a Cult," *LiveMint.com*, February 12, 2008, accessed at www.livemint. com/2008/02/12231611/Building-a-brand-creating-a-c.html; Chris Maxcer, "A Menagerie of Mac Fanatic Must-Haves," *MacNewsWorld*, November 19, 2007, www.macnewsworld.com/ story/60367.html; and Asher Moses, "Doco Puts Macheads Under the Microscope," *Sydney Morning Herald*, February 19, 2008, accessed at www.smh.com.

13. See the "PRIZM NE Lifestyle Segmentation System" brochure and other cluster information, accessed at www.claritas.com/claritas/ Default.jsp?ci=3&si=4&pn=prizmne, July 2008.

14. Information from https://home.americanexpress.com/home/ open.shtml, August 2008.

15. See Thomas L. Powers and Jay U. Stirling, "Segmenting Business-to-Business Markets: A Micro-Macro Linking Methodology," *Journal of Business & Industrial Marketing*, April 15, 2008, pp. 170–177.

16. Raed Rafei, "Cola Makers Target Mideast," *Los Angeles Times*, February 4, 2008, accessed at www.latimes.com; "Uganda; Carol Mgasha Is MTV VJ," *Africa News*, September 17, 2007; "Music on the Coke Side of Life," September 18, 2007, accessed at www.cokemusic. com.mt/subsites/news.htm; and Charles R. Taylor, "Lifestyle Matters Everywhere," *Advertising Age*, May 19, 2008, p. 24.

17. See Michael Porter, *Competitive Advantage* (New York: Free Press, 1985), pp. 4–8, 234–236. For more recent discussions, see Stanley Slater and Eric Olson, "A Fresh Look at Industry and Market Analysis," *Business Horizons*, January–February 2002, p. 15–22; Kenneth Sawka and Bill Fiora, "The Four Analytical Techniques Every Analyst Must Know: 2. Porter's Five Forces Analysis," *Competitive Intelligence Magazine*, May–June 2003, p. 57; and Philip Kotler and Kevin Lane Keller, *Marketing Management*, 13th ed. (Upper Saddle River, NJ: Prentice Hall, 2009), pp. 342–343.

18. See Suzanne Kapner, "How Fashion's VF Supercharges Its Brands," *Fortune*, April 14, 2008, pp. 108–110; and www.vfc.com, accessed October 2008.

19. Store information found at www.walmartstores.com, www. wholefoodsmarket.com; and www.kroger.com, accessed June 2008.

20. See Gerry Khermouch, "Call It the Pepsi Blue Generation," *BusinessWeek*, February 3, 2003, p. 96; Phyllis Furman, "Mist-Takes Made Again: New Ads for Sierra Mist," *Knight Ridder Tribune Business News*, April 10, 2006, p. 1; and Duane D. Stanford, "Coke, Pepsi Cola Sales Down, Other Sodas Grow," *Cox News Service*, March 8, 2007.

21. Quotes and information from Sidra Durst, "Shoe In," *Business 2.0*, December 2006, p. 54; Kimberly Weisul, "A Shine on Their Shoes," *BusinessWeek*, December 12, 2006, p. 84; Connie Gentry, "Cultural Revolution," *Chain Store Age*, December 2007, pp. 32–33; Brian Morrissey, "Communal Branding," *Adweek*, May 12, 2008, pp. 8–9; and "About Zappos," accessed at www.zappos.com/about.zhtml, October 2008.

22. Examples from in Darell K. Rigby and Vijay Vishwanath, "Localization: The Revolution in Consumer Markets," *Harvard Business Review*, April 2006, pp. 82–92. Also see Jenny McTaggart, "Wal-Mart Unveils New Segmentation Scheme," *Progressive Grocer*, October 1, 2006, pp. 10–11.

23. See Arundhati Parmar, "On the Map," *Marketing News*, February 15, 2008, pp. 13–15; and information from http:// mysbuxinteractive.com, accessed July 2008.

24. For these and other examples see Lynnley Browning, "Do-It-Yourself Logo for Proud Scion Owners," *New York Times*, March 24, 2008, accessed at www.nytimes.com; and Mike Beirne, "Mars Gives M&M's a Face," *Brandweek*, May 22, 2008, accessed at www.brandweek.com.

25. See Gigi Stone, "Advertisers Try New Way to Get into Your Head," December 16, 2006, accessed at http://abcnews.go.com/ WNY/print?id=2731799; and Steve Miller, "Who Said That?" *Brandweek*, January 30, 2007, accessed at www.brandweek.com.

26. Adapted from portions of Fae Goodman, "Lingerie Is Luscious and Lovely—for Grown-Ups: But Is the Pink?" *Chicago Sun-Times*, February 19, 2006, p. B2; and Stacy Weiner, "Goodbye to Girlhood," *Washington Post*, February 20, 2007, p. HE01. Also, see Jayne O'Donnell, "As Kids Get Savvy, Marketers Move Down the Age Scale," *USA Today*, April 11, 2007, accessed at www.usatoday.com; and Maybeth Hicks, "No Secret: Victoria Pink Turns Mom's Cheeks Red," *Washington Times*, January 13, 2008, p. D1.

27. Andrew Adam Newman, "Youngsters Enjoy Beer Ads, Arousing Industry's Critics," *New York Times*, February 13, 2006, p. C15; Katy Bachman, "Study: Radio Alcohol Ads Reaching Young Ears," *Mediaweek*, September 18, 2007, accessed at www. mediaweek.com; and www.adbowl.com, accessed March 2008.

28. See "Reported Dollar Loss from Internet Crime Reaches All-Time High," April 3, 2008, accessed at www.ic3.gov/media/2008/ 080403.htm.

29. Jack Trout, "Branding Can't Exist Without Positioning," *Advertising Age*, March 14, 2005, p. 28.

30. Adapted from a positioning map prepared by students Brian May, Josh Payne, Meredith Schakel, and Bryana Sterns, University of North Carolina, April 2003. SUV sales data furnished by WardsAuto.com, June 2008. Price data from www.edmunds.com, June 2008.

31. Based on information found in Michael Myser, "Marketing Made Easy," *Business 2.0*, June 2006, pp. 43–44; Steve Smith, "Staples' Sales Rise While Office Depot's Drop," *Twice*, March 10, 2008, p. 62; and "Staples, Inc." *Hoover's Company Records*, June 1, 2008, p. 14790.

32. See Bobby J. Calder and Steven J. Reagan, "Brand Design," in Dawn Iacobucci, ed. *Kellogg on Marketing* (New York: John Wiley & Sons, 2001) p. 61. The Mountain Dew example is from Alice M. Tybout and Brian Sternthal, "Brand Positioning," in Iacobucci, ed., *Kellogg on Marketing*, p. 54. Also see Philip Kotler and Kevin Lane Keller, *Marketing Management*, 13th ed. (Upper Saddle River, NJ: Prentice Hall, 2009), pp. 315–316.

33. For a fuller discussion, see Philip Kotler and Kevin Lane Keller, *Marketing Management*, 13th ed. (Upper Saddle River, NJ: Prentice Hall, 2009), chapter 10.

CHAPTER 8

1. Quotes and other information from Damon Hodge, "Tourism Chief Aims to Continue Vegas' Hot Streak," *Travel Weekly*, February 12, 2007, p. 64; Parija Kavilanz "Hot In '07: Google, Vegas. Not: Paris, Britney," accessed at www.cnnmoney.com, January 12, 2007; Greg Lindsay, "Players Place Bets on Brands," *Advertising Age*, June 5, 2006; Bob Garfield, "This Time, Vegas Tourism Gets the Credit It Deserves," *Advertising Age*, August 21, 2006, p. 25; Theresa Howard, "Vegas Goes for Edgier Ads," *USA Today*, August 3, 2003, accessed at www.usatoday.com; and Kitty Bean Yancey, "$40B Thrown into Vegas Development Kitty," *USA Today*, January 18, 2008, p. 7D. The extract examples are adapted from Tamara Audi, "Vegas Plans a New Push to Attract More People," *Wall Street Journal*, January 7, 2008, p. B2.

2. Based on information from Philip Kotler and Kevin Lane Keller, *Marketing Management*, (Upper Saddle River, NJ; Prentice Hall, 2009), p. 272; and Lani Haywood, "A Model of Change," *Bank Systems & Technology*, March 2008, p. 24.

3. "Athletes Help Brands Win Big," *Marketing News*, March 15, 2008, p. 17.

4. See Diane Brady, "It's All Donald, All the Time," *BusinessWeek*, January 22, 2007, p. 51; and "Being Like a Celebrity Is Easier Than You Think," *PR Newswire*, June 3, 2008.

5. Based on information from Sonia Reyes, "Faster Than a Ray of Light," *Brandweek*, October 9, 2006, pp. M28–M31; Grant McCracken, "Rachael Ray: Branding Goddess?" *This Blog Sits at the Intersection of Anthropology and Economics*, October 17, 2006, accessed at www.cultureby.com/trilogy/2006/10/rachael_ray_bra.html; Alec Foege, "The Rachael Way," *Adweek*, March 5, 2007, pp. SR22–SR24; "Food Network Orders More Helpings of Rachael Ray," *McClatchy-Tribune Business News*, December 17, 2007; and Racheal Ray, "10 Questions," *Time*, April 28, 2008, p. 6.

6. Information from www.cnto.org/aboutchina.asp, April 2008. Also see www.TravelTex.com, and www.visitcalifornia.com, October 2008.

7. Accessed online at www.social-marketing.org/aboutus.html, August 2008.

8. See Rob Gould, and Karen Gutierrez, "Social Marketing Has a New Champion," *Marketing News*, February 7, 2000, p. 38. Also see Alan R. Andreasen, *Social Marketing in the 21st Century* (Thousand Oaks, CA: Sage Publications, 2006); Philip Kotler and Nancy Lee, *Social Marketing: Improving the Quality of Life*, 3rd ed. (Thousand Oaks, CA: Sage Publications, 2008); and www.social-marketing.org, November 2008.

9. Quotes and definitions from Philip Kotler, *Kotler on Marketing* (New York: Free Press, 1999), p. 17; and www.asq.org, July 2008.

10. Quotes and other information from Regina Schrambling, "Tool Department; The Sharpest Knives in the Drawer," *Los Angeles Times*, March 8, 2006, p. F1; Arricca Elin SanSone, "OXO: Universal Design Innovator," *Cooking Light*, April 2007, p. 118; and www.oxo.com/OA_HTML/oxo/about_what.htm, July 2008.

11. See "Supermarket facts," accessed at www.fmi.org/facts_figs/?fuseaction=superfact, April 2008; and "Wal-Mart Facts," accessed at www.walmartfacts.com/StateByState/?id=2, April 2008.

12. "The Oyster Awards," *Consumer Reports*, March 2007, p. 12. See also Michael Antonucci, "Ouch! Why Do They Package Stuff Like That?" *McClatchy-Tribune Business News*, January 18, 2008; and Elsa Wenzel, Killing the Oyster Pack," April 7, 2008, accessed at http://news.cnet.com/8301-11128_3-9912173-54.html.

13. Sonja Reyes, "Ad Blitz, Bottle Design Fuel Debate over Heinz's Sales," *Brandweek*, February 12, 2007, accessed at www.brandweek.com/bw/news/recent_display.jsp?vnu_content_id=1003544497.

14. Example adapted from "Pepsi's New Set of Cans," *Creativity*, March 2007, p. 76; with quote from Martinne Geller, "PepsiCo Invites Designers to New Pepsi Challenge," *San Diego Union-Tribute*, April 4, 2007, accessed at www.SignOnSanDiego.com. Also see www.pepsigallery.com and "Pepsi Launches Creative Challenge with MyClick Application," *Telecomworldwire*, April 14, 2008.

15. See Jena McGregor, "Customer Service Champs," *BusinessWeek*, March 5, 2007, pp. 52–64; and David Welch, "Looser Rules, Happier Clients," *BusinessWeek*, March 5, 2007, p. 62.

16. See the HP Total Care site at http://h71036.www7.hp.com/hho/cache/309717-0-0-225-121.html, accessed December 2008.

17. Information accessed online at www.marriott.com, August 2007.

18. See "McAtlas Shrugged," *Foreign Policy*, May–June 2001, pp. 26–37; and Philip Kotler and Kevin Lane Keller, *Marketing Management*, 13th ed. (Upper Saddle River, NJ: Prentice Hall, 2009), p. 254.

19. See Jack Trout, "'Branding' Simplified," *Forbes*, April 19, 2007, accessed at www.forbes.com.

20. For more on Y&R's Brand Asset Valuator, see "Brand Asset Valuator," Value Based Management.net, www.valuebasedmanagement.net/methods_brand_asset_valuator.html, accessed February 2008; W. Ronald Lane, Karen Whitehill King, and J. Thomas Russell, *Kleppner's Advertising Procedure*, 17th ed. (Upper Saddle River, NJ: Prentice Hall, 2008), p. 105; and Chelsea Greene, "Using Brands to Drive Business Results," Landor, accessed at www.wpp.com/WPP/Marketing/ReportsStudies/Usingbrandstodrivebusinessresults.htm, March 2008.

21. Al Ehrbar, "Breakaway Brands," *Fortune*, October 31, 2005, pp. 153–170. Also see "DeWalt Named Breakaway Brand," *Snips*, January 2006, p. 66.

22. See Millward Brown Optimor, "BrandZ Top 100 Most Powerful Brands 2008," accessed at www.brandz.com/output, July 2008.

23. See Scott Davis, *Brand Asset Management*, 2nd ed. (San Francisco: Jossey-Bass, 2002). For more on brand positioning, see Philip Kotler and Kevin Lane Keller, *Marketing Management*, 13th ed. (Upper Saddle River, NJ: Prentice Hall, 2009), chapter 10.

24. Adapted from information found in Geoff Colvin, "Selling P&G," *Fortune*, September 17, 2007, pp. 163–169; and "For P&G, Success Lies in More Than Merely a Dryer Diaper," *Advertising Age*, October 15, 2007, p. 20.

25. See Nirmalya Kumar and Jan-Benedict E. M. Steenkamp, *Private Label Strategy* (Boston, MA: Harvard Business School Press, 2007), pp. 1–12; Vanessa L. Facenda, "A Swift Kick to the Privates," *Brandweek*, September 3, 2007, pp. 24+; and Janet Groeber, "Emphasizing Quality, Price and Value, Supermarkets Say Goodbye to Generics and Hello to Proprietary Programs," *Stores*, February 2008, accessed at www.stores.org/Current_Issue/2008/02/Edit1.asp.

26. See Noreen O'Leary, "New and Improved Private Label Brands," *Adweek*, October 22, 2007, pp.16+; and Teresa F. Lindeman, "Store Brands Get a Boost," *McClatchy-Tribune Business News*, May 21, 2008.

27. Noreen O'Leary, "New and Improved Private Label Brands," *Adweek*, October 22, 2007, pp. 16+.

28. Nirmalya Kumar and Jan-Benedict E. M. Steenkamp, *Private Label Strategy* (Boston, MA: Harvard Business School Press, 2007), p. 5.

29. "Dora the Explorer Takes the Lead as Sales Growth Elevates Property to Megabrand Status as Number-One Toy License in 2006," *PR Newswire*, February 8, 2007; Clint Cantwell, "$187 Billion Global Licensing Industry Comes to Life at Licensing International Expo 2008," *Business Wire*, June 6, 2008; and "Nickelodeon Expands Product Offerings and Debuts New Properties for Kids and Teens at Licensing 2008 International Show," June 10, 2008, accessed at http://biz.yahoo.com/prnews/080610/nytu056.html?.v=101.

30. Quote from www.apple.com/ipod/nike, August 2008.

31. Quote from www.apple.com/ipod/nike, August 2008.

32. Gabrielle Solomon, "Cobranding Alliances: Arranged Marriages Made by Marketers," *Fortune*, October 12, 1998, p. 188; "Martha Stewart Upgrading from Kmart to Macys," *FinancialWire*, April 26, 2006, p. 1; and James Mammerella, "Martha Stewart Narrows Loss," *Home Textiles Today*, November 7, 2007, p. 28.

33. For more examples of good and bad brand extensions, see Kenneth Hein, "Line Extensions to Cross the Line and '07," *Brandweek*, December 10, 2007, p. 4. For more discussion on the use of line and brand extensions and consumer attitudes toward them, see Philip Kotler and Kevin Lane Keller, *Marketing Management* (Upper Saddle River, NJ: Prentice Hall, 2009), p. 262.

34. "100 Leading National Advertisers," *Advertising Age*, June 25, 2007, accessed at http://adage.com/article?article_id=118648.

35. Quotes from Stephen Cole, "Value of the Brand," *CA Magazine*, May 2005, pp. 39–40; and Lawrence A. Crosby and Sheree L. Johnson, "Experience Required," *Marketing Management*, July/August 2007, pp. 21–27.

36. See Kevin Lane Keller, *Strategic Brand Management* (Upper Saddle River, NJ: Prentice Hall, 2008), chapter 10.

37. See CIA, *The World Factbook*, accessed at https://www.cia.gov/cia/publications/factbook/index.html, August 2008; and information from the Bureau of Labor Statistics, www.bls.gov, accessed August 2008.

38. Adapted from information in Leonard Berry and Neeli Bendapudi, "Clueing in Customers," *Harvard Business Review*, February 2003, pp. 100–106; with information accessed www.mayoclinic.org, August 2008. See also Leonard L Berry and Kent D. Selman, "Building a Strong Services Brand: Lessons from Mayo Clinic," *Business Horizons*, May–June 2007, pp. 199–209.

39. See James L. Heskett, W. Earl Sasser Jr., and Leonard A. Schlesinger, *The Service Profit Chain: How Leading Companies Link Profit and Growth to Loyalty, Satisfaction, and Value* (New York: Free Press, 1997); Heskett, Sasser, and Schlesinger, *The Value Profit Chain: Treat Employees Like Customers and Customers Like Employees* (New York: Free Press, 2003); and John F. Milliman, Jeffrey M. Ferguson, and Andrew J. Czaplewski, "Breaking the Cycle," *Marketing Management*, March–April 2008, pp. 14–17.

40. William C. Johnson and Larry G. Chiagouris, "So Happy Together," *Marketing Management*, March–April 2006, pp. 47–50.

41. Adapted from information in Jeffrey M. O'Brien, "A Perfect Season," *Fortune*, pp. 62–66.

42. O'Brien, "A Perfect Season," p. 66.

43. See "Prescription Drug Trends," Kaiser Family Foundation, May 2007, accessed at www.kff.org/rxdrugs/3057.cfm; and "UPS Fact Sheet," accessed at http://pressroom.ups.com/mediakits/factsheet/0,2305,866,00.html, August 2008.

44. Based on information in Robert Rappa and Evan Hirsch, "The Luxury Touch," *Strategy+Business*, Spring 2007, pp. 32–37.

45. Brian Hindo, "Satisfacton Not Guaranteed," *BusinessWeek*, June 19, 2006, pp. 32–36. Also see Frances X. Frei, "Breaking the Trade-Off Between Efficiency and Service," *Harvard Business Review*, November 2006, pp. 93–99.

CHAPTER 9

1. Quotes and other information in this Apple story from Betsy Morris, "What Makes Apple Golden?" *Fortune*, March 17, 2008, pp. 68–74; Brent Schlender, "How Big Can Apple Get," *Fortune*, February 21, 2005, pp. 67–76; "Apple," *BusinessWeek*, March 26, 2007, p. 84; "The World's Most Innovative Companies," *BusinessWeek*, May 14, 2007, p. 55; Adam L. Penenberg, "All Eyes on Apple," *Fast Company*, December 2007/January 2008, pp. 83+; and financial reports and other information accessed at www.apple.com, April 2008.

2. Calvin Hodock, "Winning the New-Products Game," *Advertising Age*, November 12, 2007, p. 35.

3. Information and examples from Robert M. McMath and Thom Forbes, *What Were They Thinking? Money-Saving, Time-Saving, Face-Saving Marketing Lessons You Can Learn from Products That Flopped* (New York: Times Business, 1999), various pages; Beatriz Cholo, "Living with Your 'Ex': A Brand New World," *Brandweek*, December 5, 2005, p. 4; and www.arborstrategy.com/asg/newproductworks/about-newproductworks.html, October 2008.

4. "IBM Taps Into Its Workers' Bright Ideas," *Irish Times*, October 27, 2006, p. 12; and Luke Collins, "Embedding Innovation into the Firm," *Research Technology Management*, March–April, 2007, pp. 5–6.

5. John Peppers and Martha Rogers, "The Buzz on Customer-Driven Innovation," *Sales & Marketing Management*, June 2007, p. 13.

6. See Rik Kirkland, "Cisco's Display of Strength," *Fortune*, November 12, 2007, pp. 90–100; and "Cisco on Cisco: Web 2.0 in the Enterprise," accessed at www.cisco.com, September 2008.

7. Based on material from Anna Fifield, "Samsung Sows for the Future with Its Garden of Delights," *Financial Times*, January 4, 2008, p. 13; and Peter Lewis, "A Perpetual Crisis Machine," *Fortune*, September 19, 2005, pp. 58–67. Also see "Camp Samsung," *BusinessWeek Online*, July 3, 2006, accessed at www.businessweek.com.

8. Example from http://ideo.com-/portfolio/re.asp?x=19009472, accessed July 2008.

9. See Chris Reidy, "100,000 Heads Are Better Than One," *Boston Globe*, August 21, 2006, p. E1; and information from www.innocentive.com, accessed April 2008.

10. Cliff Saran, "Wake Up to the Dawn of Web 2.0," *Computer Weekly*, June 5, 2007.

11. Paul Gillin, "Get Customers Involved in Innovations," *BtoB*, March 12, 2007, p. 111. See also Patricia B. Seybold, *Outside Innovation: How Your Customers Will Co-Design Your Company's Future* (New York: Collins, 2006); and Patricia B Seybold's blog: http://outsideinnovation.blogs.com, accessed April 2007.

12. Based on quotes and information from Robert D. Hof, "The Power of Us," *BusinessWeek*, June 20, 2005, pp. 74–82. See also Robert Weisman, "Firms Turn R&D on Its Head, Looking Outside for Ideas," *Boston Globe*, May 14, 2006, p. E1.

13. "Bill Invites Customers to Share Ideas and Original Video via Dell IdeaStorm and StudioDell," February 16, 2007, accessed at www.dell.com. Also see www.ideastorm.com.

14. Information accessed online at www.avon.com, August 2008.

15. Quotes from Robert Gray, "Not Invented Here," *Marketing*, May 6, 2004, pp. 34–37; and Betsy Morris, "What Makes Apple Golden?" *Fortune*, March 17, 2008, pp. 68–74.

16. See George S. Day, "Is It Real? Can We Win? Is It Worth Doing?" *Harvard Business Review*, December 2007, pp. 110–120.

17. Information for this example obtained from www.teslamotors.com, April 2008; and Alan Pierce, "Seeing Beyond Gasoline Powered Vehicles," *Tech Directions*, April 2008, pp. 10–11.

18. Examples adapted from those found in Carol Matlack, "The Vuitton Machine," *BusinessWeek*, March 22, 2004, pp. 98–102; and Linda Grant, "Gillette Knows Shaving—and How to Turn Out Hot New Products," *Fortune*, October 14, 1996, pp. 207–210. See also Anna Van Pragh, "One of These Bags Cost £23,000 . . . the Other a Snip at £116. Can You Tell the Difference?" *Daily Mail (London)*, March 10, 2007.

19. "KFC Fires Up Grilled Chicken," March 23, 2008, accessed at www.money.cnn.com.

20. Jack Neff, "Is Testing the Answer?" *Advertising Age*, July 9, 2001, p. 13; and Dale Buss, "P&G's Rise," *Potentials*, January 2003, pp. 26–30. For more on test marketing, see Philip Kotler and Kevin Lane Keller, *Marketing Management*, 13th ed. (Upper Saddle River, NJ: Prentice Hall, 2008), pp. 587–590.

21. Information on BehaviorScan accessed at http://us.infores.com/page/manufacturers/market_performance/behaviorscan_testing, August 2008.

22. Example developed from information found in Allison Enright, "Best Practices: Frito-Lay Get Real Results from a Virtual World," *Marketing News*, December 15, 2006, p. 20; and "Decision Insight: Simushop," accessed at www.decisioninsight.com, September 2008.

23. See Steve McClellan, "Unilever's Sunsilk Launch Goes Far Beyond the Box," *Adweek*, August 21–28, 2006, p. 9.

24. Jeremy Mullman, "Copying Corona: Miller, Bud Want Their Fun in the Sun," *Advertising Age*, January 29, 2007, p. 1; David Kesmodel, "Miller Gives Lime-and-Salt Beer a Shot at Boosting Sales," *Wall Street Journal*, June 12, 2007, accessed at www.wsj.com; Mike Beirne, "A Distinct Chill Has Been Cast Over the Beer

Category," *Brandweek*, September 3, 2007, p. 11; Jeremy Mullman, "Miller Chill Featured on 'Live' Ad on 'Late Night,'" *Advertising Age*, October 1, 2007, p. 6; and David Kesmodel, "Miller to Bring 'Chill' to Australia," *Wall Street Journal*, November 12, 2007, p. B6.

25. See Beth Snyder Bulik, "$500 Million for Vista? Wow," *Advertising Age*, January 29, 2007, pp. 1, 30.

26. Robert G. Cooper, "Formula for Success," *Marketing Management*, March–April 2006, pp. 19–23; and Barry Jaruzelski and Kevin Dehoff, "The Global Innovation of 1000," *Strategy + Business*, Issue 49, fourth quarter, 2007, pp. 68–83.

27. Adapted from information in Barry Jaruzelski and Kevin Dehoff, "The Global Innovation of 1000," *Strategy + Business*, Issue 49, fourth quarter, 2007, pp. 68–83.

28. Lawrence A. Crosby and Sheree L. Johnson, "Customer-Centric Innovation," *Marketing Management*, March–April 2006, pp. 12–13.

29. Teressa Iezzi, "Innovate, But Do It for Customers," *Creativity*, September 2006, pp. 8–11.

30. Portions adapted from Chuck Salter, "Google: The Faces and Voices of the World's Most Innovative Company," *Fast Company*, March 2008, pp. 74–88.

31. This definition is based on one found in Bryan Lilly and Tammy R. Nelson, "Fads: Segmenting the Fad-Buyer Market," *Journal of Consumer Marketing*, vol. 20, no. 3, 2003, pp. 252–265.

32. See Katya Kazakina, Robert Johnson, "A Fad's Father Seeks a Sequel," *New York Times*, May 30, 2004, p. 3.2; Debbie Howell, "Retailers Piece Together New Crafting Opportunities," *DSN Retailing Today*, January 23, 2006, pp. 11–12; Tom McGhee, "Spotting Trends, Eschewing Fads," *Denver Post*, May 29, 2006; John Schwartz, "The Joy of Silly," *New York Times*, January 20, 2008, p. 5; and www.crazyfads.com, accessed September 2008.

33. Youngme Moon, "Break Free from the Product Life Cycle," *Harvard Business Review*, May 2005, pp. 87–94.

34. See Constantine von Hoffman, "Glad Gives Seal of Approval to Alternate Wrap Uses," *Brandweek*, November 27, 2006, p. 10; and www.1000uses.com, accessed September 2008.

35. For a more comprehensive discussion of marketing strategies over the course of the product life cycle, see Philip Kotler and Kevin Lane Keller, *Marketing Management*, 13th ed. (Upper Saddle River, NJ: Prentice Hall, 2008), pp. 278–290.

36. See "Verdict Warns Drug Makers Not to Suppress Known Risks," *Tampa Tribune*, August 23, 2005, p. 10; "Year-by-Year Analysis Reveals an Overall Compensatory Award of $1,500,000 for Products Liability Cases," *Personal Injury Verdict Reviews*, July 3, 2006; "Manufacturers Hit Hard by Litigation; Survey Reveals 91% Faced New Lawsuits Last Year," *Control Engineering*, December 2007, p. 28; and Heather Won Tesoriero, "Merck's Prospects Brighten for Vioxx Settlement," *Wall Street Journal*, January 19, 2008, p. A3.

37. Example based on information provided by Nestle Japan Ltd., May 2008; with additional information from http://en.wikipedia.org/wiki/Kit_Kat and the Japanese Wikipedia discussion of Kit Kat at http://ja.wikipedia.org, accessed November 2008.

38. Information accessed online at www.deutsche-bank.com, July 2008.

39. Information accessed online at www.interpublic.com and www.mccann.com, August 2008.

40. See "2007 Global Powers of Retailing," *Stores*, January 2007, accessed at www.stores.org; "Wal-Mart International Operations," accessed at www.walmartstores.com, April 2008; and information accessed at www.carrefour.com/english/groupecarrefour/profil.jsp, July 2008.

CHAPTER 10

1. Quotes and other information from Anna Sowa, "Trader Joe's: Why the Hype?" *McClatchy-Tribune Business News*, March 27, 2008; Deborah Orr, "The Cheap Gourmet," *Forbes*, April 10, 2006, pp. 76–77; Monica Chen, "'Crew' Readies Trader Joe's," *Durham Herald-Sun*, November 29, 2007, p. 1; "Trader Joe's Company," *Hoover's Company Records*, April 15, 2008, p. 47619; and information from www.traderjoes.com, November 2008.

2. George Mannes, "The Urge to Unbundle," *Fast Company*, February 27, 2005, pp. 23–24. Also see Stuart Elliott, "Creative Spots, Courtesy of a Stalled Economy," *New York Times*, April 11, 2008.

3. Linda Tischler, "The Price Is Right," *Fast Company*, November 2003, pp. 83–91. See also Elizabeth A. Sullivan, "Value Pricing: Smart Marketers Know Cost-Plus Can Be Costly," January 15, 2008, p. 8.

4. For more on the importance of sound pricing strategy, see Thomas T. Nagle and John Hogan, *The Strategy and Tactics of Pricing: A Guide to Growing More Profitably* (Upper Saddle River, NJ: Prentice Hall, 2007), chapter 1.

5. John Tayman, "The Six-Figure Steal," *Business 2.0*, June 2005, pp. 148–150; and www.automotive.com/2008/12/bentley/continental/pricing/index.html, April 2008.

6. These and other examples found at Stuart Elliott, "Creative Spots, Courtesy of a Stalled Economy," *New York Times*, April 11, 2008; and www.vw.com/rabbit/en/us/#, April 2008.

7. Example adapted from Anupam Mukerji, "Monsoon Marketing," *Fast Company*, April 2007, p. 22.

8. Elizabeth A. Sullivan, "Value Pricing: Smart Marketers Know Cost-Plus Can Be Costly," *Marketing News*, January 15, 2008, p. 8. Also see Venkatesh Bala and Jason Green, "Charge What Your Products Are Worth," *Harvard Business Review*, September 2007, p. 22.

9. Here accumulated production is drawn on a semilog scale so that equal distances represent the same percentage increase in output.

10. The arithmetic of markups and margins is discussed in Appendix 2, Marketing by the Numbers.

11. Joshua Rosenbaum, "Guitar Maker Looks for a New Key," *Wall Street Journal*, February 11, 1998, p. B1; and information accessed online at www.gibson.com, September 2008.

12. See Nagle and Hogan, *The Strategy and Tactics of Pricing*, chapter 7.

13. Comments from www.yelp.com/biz/annie-blooms-books-portland, accessed May, 2008.

14. See Robert J. Dolan, "Pricing: A Value-Based Approach," *Harvard Business School Publishing*, 9-500-071, November 3, 2003.

CHAPTER 11

1. Quotes and other information from: Beth Snyder Bulik, "Kodak Develops New Model: Inexpensive Printer, Cheap Ink," *Advertising Age*, March 12, 2007, p. 4; Clive Akass, "Kodak Inkjets Shake Industry," *Personal Computer World*, April 2007, accessed at www.pcw.co.uk/personal-computer-world/news/2174253/kodak-halves-cost-photo-prints; David Pogue, "Paying More for a Printer but Less for Ink," *New York Times*, May 17, 2007, p. C1; Stephen H. Wildstrom, "Kodak Moments for Less," *BusinessWeek*, May 14, 2007, p. 24; William M. Bulkeley, "Kodak's Strategy for First Printer—Cheaper Cartridges," *Wall Street Journal*, February 6, 2007, p. B1; Keith J. Winstein, "Kodak Forecasts Increase in Revenue, Pinning Optimism on Inkjet Printers," *Wall Street Journal*, February 8, 2008, p. B4; "Consumer Launch Campaign of the Year 2008," *PRweek*, March 10, 2008, p. S11; and www.kodak.com, accessed September 2008.

2. For comprehensive discussions of pricing strategies, see Thomas T. Nagle and John E. Hogan, *The Strategy and Tactics of Pricing*, 4th ed. (Upper Saddle River, NJ: Prentice Hall, 2007).

3. See Philip Kotler and Kevin Lane Keller, *Marketing Management*, 13th ed. (Upper Saddle River, NJ: Prentice Hall, 2008), pp. 383–384; and Chris Tribbey, "HDTV Prices Projected to Drop 15% in 2008," *Home Media Magazine*, January 20–January 26, 2008, p. 10.

4. Adapted from information found in Mei Fong, "IKEA Hits Home in China; The Swedish Design Giant, Unlike Other Retailers, Slashes Prices for the Chinese," *Wall Street Journal*, March 3, 2006, p. B1; and "IKEA to Open Three Stores in China in 2008," *Sinolcast China Business Daily News*, August 31, 2007, p. 1.

5. See Susan Berfield, "Sleek. Stylish. Samsonite?" *BusinessWeek*, February 26, 2007, p. 106.

6. Information from www.meadwestvaco.com, accessed September 2008.

7. See Nagle and Hogan, *The Strategy and Tactics of Pricing*, pp. 244–247; Bram Foubert and Els Gijsbrechts, "Shopper Response to Bundle Promotions for Packaged Goods," *Journal of Marketing Research*, November 2007, pp. 647–662; Roger M. Heeler, et al., "Bundles = Discount? Revisiting Complex Theories of Bundle Effects," *Journal of Product & Brand Management*, vol. 16, no. 7, 2007, pp. 492–500; and Timothy J. Gilbride, et al, "Framing Effects in Mixed Price Bundling," *Marketing Letters*, June 2008, pp. 125–140.

8. See data from "Continental Airlines Reports March 2008 Operational Performance," Continental Financial and Traffic Releases, accessed at www.continental.com/company/investor/news.asp. Also see Benjamin Marcus and Chris K. Anderson, "Revenue Management for Low-Cost Providers," *European Journal of Operational Research*, July 1, 2008, p. 258.

9. Based on information from Eric Anderson and Duncan Simester, "Mind Your Pricing Cues," *Harvard Business Review*, September 2003, pp. 96–103. Also see Heyong Min Kim and Luke Kachersky, "Dimensions of Price Salience: A Conceptual Framework for Perceptions of Multi-Dimensional Prices," *Journal of Product and Brand Management*," 2006, vol. 15, no. 2, pp. 139–147; and Monika Kukar-Kinney, et al, "Consumer Responses to Characteristics of Price-Matching Guarantees," *Journal of Retailing*, April 2007, p. 211.

10. For more discussion, see Manoj Thomas and Vicki Morvitz, "Penny Wise and Pound Foolish: The Double-Digit Effect in Price Cognition," *Journal of Consumer Research*, June 2005, pp. 54–64; Alex Mindlin, "For a Memorable Price, Trim Syllables," *New York Times*, August 14, 2006, accessed at www.nytimes.com; Christine Harris and Jeffery Bray, "Price Endings and Consumer Segmentation," *Journal of Product & Brand Management* vol. 16, no. 3, 2007, pp. 200–205; Wilson Rothman, "The Weird Science of Pricing" *Money*, April 2007, p. 127; and Keith S. Coulter and Robin A. Coulter, "Distortion of Price Discount Perceptions: The Right Digit of Fact," *Journal of Consumer Research*, August 2007, pp. 162–171.

11. Karyn McCormack, "Price War Leaves AMD Reeling," *BusinessWeek Online*, January 25, 2007, p. 4; and Chris Nuttall, "AMD Suffers Further Losses Amid Price War with Rival Intel," *Financial Times*, October 19, 2007, p. 18.

12. Example adapted from Louise Story, "Online Pitches Made Just for You," *New York Times*, March 6, 2008.

13. Based on information found in Bruce Einhorn, "Grudge Match in China," *BusinessWeek*, April 2, 2007, pp. 42–43; "Struggling Dell Enters Partnership," *ChinaDaily.com.cn*, September 25, 2007; and "Dell Continues to Expand Retail Presence in China," *Business Wire*, April 17, 2008.

14. Example adapted from information found in Ellen Byron, "Fashion Victim: To Refurbish Its Image, Tiffany Risks Profits," *Wall Street Journal*, January 10, 2007, p. A1; and Aliza Rosenbaum and John Christy, "Financial Insight: Tiffany's Boutique Risk; By Breaking Mall Fast, High-End Exclusivity May Gain Touch of Common," *Wall Street Journal*, October 20, 2007, p. B14.

15. Jack Neff, "Viva Viva! K-C Boosts Brand's marketing," *Advertising Age*, June 11, 2007, p. 4.

16. For discussions of these issues, see Dhruv Grewel and Larry D. Compeau, "Pricing and Public Policy: A Research Agenda and Overview of Special Issue," *Journal of Public Policy and Marketing*, Spring 1999, pp. 3–10; and Michael V. Marn, Eric V. Roegner, and Craig C. Zawada, *The Price Advantage* (Hoboken, NJ: John Wiley & Sons, 2004), Appendix 2.

17. Julie Jargon, "Retailers' Lawsuits Accuse Candy Makers of Fixing Prices," *Wall Street Journal*, April 1, 2008, p. B3; "Germany Raids Offices of Candy Makers," *Wall Street Journal*, February 12, 2008, p. A15; and Alia McMullen, "Chocolate Giants Sued for Collusion," *Financial Post*, February 19, 2008, p. FP1.

18. "Predatory-Pricing Law Passed by New York Governor," *National Petroleum News*, December 2003, p. 7; Brenden Timpe, "House Rejects Bill to Protect Gas Stations from Wal-Mart-Style Competition," *Knight Ridder Tribune Business News*, March 26, 2005, p. 1; Charles Ashby, "Senate OKs Bill to Allow Below-Cost Fuel," *Knight Ridder Tribune Business News*, March 14, 2007, p. 1; and Martin Sipkoff, "Wal-Mart, Other Discounters Facing Predatory-Pricing Concerns," *Drug Topics*, April 2, 2007, pp. 10–12.

19. "FTC Guides Against Deceptive Pricing," accessed at www.ftc.gov/bcp/guides/decptprc.htm, December 2008.

CHAPTER 12

1. The "e" logo, Enterprise, and "We'll Pick You Up" are registered trademarks of Enterprise Rent-A-Car Company. Quotations and other information from "Enter Enterprise," *Business Travel News*, April 23, 2007; Carol J. Loomis, "The Big Surprise Is Enterprise," *Fortune*, July 24, 2006, p. 140; Carol J. Loomis, "Enterprise Pulls Up at the Airport," *Fortune*, July 23, 2007, p. 50; Darren Everson, "Car-Rental Companies Learn to Share," *Wall Street Journal*, February 7, 2008, p. D1; and www.hertz.com and http://aboutus.enterprise.com/press_room/fact_sheets.html, October 2008.

2. See "No Time to Rest for Goodyear," *Tire Business*, February 13, 2006, p. 8; Kevin Kelleher, "Giving Dealers a Raw Deal," *Business 2.0*, December 2004, pp. 82–84; Jim MacKinnon, "Goodyear Tire & Rubber Company," *Knight Ridder Tribune Business News*, April 8, 2007, p. 1; and Jim MacKinnon, "Goodyear Boasts of Bright Future," *McClatchy-Tribune Business News*, April 9, 2008.

3. Information accessed at www.kroger.com, www.safeway.com, and www.luxottica.com/english/profilo_aziendale/index_keyfacts.html, October 2008.

4. Adapted from information found in Kerry Capell, "Fashion Conquistador," *BusinessWeek*, September 4, 2006, pp. 38–39; Miguel Helft, "Fashion Fast Forward," *Business 2.0*, May 2002, p. 60; Kasra Ferdows, Michael A. Lewis, and Jose A. D. Machuca, "Rapid-Fire Fulfillment," *Harvard Business Review*, November 2004, pp. 104–110; Cecilie Rohwedder and Keith Johnson, "Pace-Setting Zara Seeks More Speed to Fight Its Rising Cheap-Chic Rivals," *Wall Street Journal*, February 20, 2008, p. B1; and the Inditext Press Kit, accessed at www.inditex.com/en/press/information/press_kit, October 2008.

5. Franchising facts from www.franchise.org/content.asp?contentid=379 and www.azfranchises.com/franchisefacts.htm; July 2008.

6. See Melinda Liu, "Just Beware of the White Lightning; Car Culture Is Booming in China," *Newsweek*, November 19, 2007, p. E24; and http://english.sinopec.com/about_sinopec/our_business/refining_selling/, accessed July 2008.

7. Information accessed at www.mind-advertising.com/ch/nestea_ch.htm, September 2007.

8. See Paolo Del Nibletto, "Dell Stuck in the Middle," *Computer Dealer News*, March 21, 2008, p. 12.

9. Quotes and information from Normandy Madden, "Two Chinas," *Advertising Age*, August 16, 2004, pp. 1, 22; Russell Flannery, "China: The Slow Boat," *Forbes*, April 12, 2004, p. 76; Jeff Berman, "U.S. Providers Say Logistics in China on the Right Track," *Logistics Management*, March 2007, p. 22; and Jamie Bolton, "China: The Infrastructure Imperative," *Logistics Management*, July 2007, p. 63.

10. Nanette Byrnes, "Avon Calls. China Opens the Door," *BusinessWeek Online*, February 28, 2006, p. 19; Mei Fong, "Avon's Calling, but China Opens Door Only a Crack," *Wall Street Journal*, February 26, 2007, p. B1; "Direct-Selling Giants to Dig Chinese Market," *SinoCast China Business Daily News*, August 3, 2007, p. 1; and "Cosmetic Changes in China Market," www.Chinadaily.com.cn, October 11, 2007.

11. See Steven Burke, "Samsung Launches Revamped Partner Program." *CRN*, February 12, 2007, accessed at www.crn.com/it-channel/197005419; and "Program Details: Samsung Electronics America, IT Division," *VAR Business 2007 Partner Programs Guide*, accessed at www.crn.com/var/apps/2007/ppg/ppg_details.jhtml?c=54, July 2007.

12. For a full discussion of laws affecting marketing channels, see Anne Coughlin, Erin Anderson, Louis W. Stern, and Adel El-Ansary, *Marketing Channels*, 7th ed. (Upper Saddle River, NJ: Prentice Hall, 2006), chapter 10.

13. Ari Natter, "Freight Costs Rising," *Traffic World*, April 14, 2008; Neil Shister, "Redesigned Supply Chain Positions Ford for Global Competition," *World Trade*, May 2005, pp. 20–26; and supply chain facts from www.cscmp.org/Website/AboutCSCMP/Media/FastFacts.asp; July 2008.

14. Shlomo Maital, "The Last Frontier of Cost Reduction," *Across the Board*, February 1994, pp. 51–52; and information accessed online at www.walmartstores.com, October 2008.

15. William Hoffman, "Supplying Sustainability," *Traffic World*, April 7, 2008.

16. Gail Braccidiferro, "One Town's Rejection Is Another's 'Let's Do Business,'" *New York Times*, June 15, 2003, p. 2; Dan Scheraga, "Wal-Smart," *Chain Store Age*, January 2006 supplement, pp. 16A–21A; and facts from www.walmart.com, October 2008.

17. Example adapted from Evan West, "These Robots Play Fetch," *Fast Company*, July/August 2007, pp. 49–50.

18. See "A Worldwide Look at RFID," *Supply Chain Management Review*, April 2007, pp. 48–55; Owen Davis, "Time to Roll with RFID," *Supply & Demand Chain Executive*, February–March 2007, p. 56; and "Wal-Mart Says Use RFID Tags or Pay Up," *Logistics Today*, March 2008, p. 4.

19. Transportation percentages and other figures in this section are from Bureau of Transportation Statistics, "Freight in America," January 2006, accessed at www.bts.gov/publications; and Bureau of Transportation Statistics, "Pocket Guide to Transportation 2008," February 2008, accessed at www.bts.gov/publications/pocket_guide_to_transportation/2008.

20. See Laurie Sullivan, "Hey, Wal-Mart, A New Case of Pampers Is on the Way," *InformationWeek*, January 23, 2006, p. 28; Connie Robbins Gentry, "No More Holes at Krispy Kreme," *Chain Store Age*, July 2006, pp. 64–65; "Collaborative Supply Chain Practices and Evolving Technological Approaches," *Supply Chain Management*, May 2007, pp. 210–220; and Yuliang Yao and Martin Dresner, "The Inventory Value of Information Sharing, Continuous Replenishment, and Vendor-Managed Inventory," *Transportation Research*, May 2008, p. 361+.

21. See "The 2007 Supply & Demand Chain Executive 100," *Supply & Demand Chain Executive*, May 2007; accessed at www.sdcexec.com/print/Supply-and-Demand-Chain-Executive/2007-Supply-and-Demand-Chain-Executive-100/1$9672; and David Blanchard, "Sterling Commerce Shifts from EDI to the Supply Chain," *Supply Chain and Logistics*, December 2007, p. 50.

22. "Whirlpool: Outsourcing Its National Service Parts Operation Provides Immediate Benefits," accessed at www.ryder.com/pdf/MCC633_Whirlpool_single.pdf, October 2008.

23. John Paul Quinn, "3PLs Hit Their Stride," *Logistics Management/Supply Chain Management Review*, July 2006, pp. 3T–8T; and "U.S. and Global Third-Party Logistics (3PL) Market Analysis Is Released," *PR Newswire*, April 12, 2007.

CHAPTER 13

1. Quotes and other information from "Costco vs. Sam's Club," *Consumer Reports*, May 2007, pp. 16–19; Matthew Boyle, "Why Costco Is So Addictive," *Fortune*, October 25, 2006, pp. 126–132; Anthony Bianco, "Wal-Mart's Midlife Crisis," *BusinessWeek*, April 30, 2007, pp. 46–55; John Helyar, "The Only Company Wal-Mart Fears," *Fortune*, November 24, 2003, pp. 158–166; Reena Jana, "The Revenge of the Generic," *BusinessWeek*, December 27, 2006, accessed at www.businessweek.com/innovate/content/dec2006/id20061227_049239.htm; Pat Regnief, "Hunting Big Savings at Costco," *Money*, June 22, 2006; Andrew Bary, "Everybody's Store," *Barron's*, February 12, 2007, pp. 29–32; Merrill Markoe, "Life Lessons: Love for Sale?" *Real Simple*, January 2008, pp. 52–57; and www.costco.com, November 2008.

2. Quotes from "Ogilvy Gets Activated," *MediaPost Publications*, January 8, 2007, accessed at publications.mediapost.com/index.cfm?fuseaction=Articles.showArticle&art_aid=53477; and "OgilvyAction Takes Regional Marketers to the Last Mile," January 23, 2008, accessed at www.entrepreneur.com/tradejournals/article/173710015.html. Retail sales statistics from "Annual Revision of Monthly Retail and Food Services: Sales and Inventories—January 1992–2007," U.S. Census Bureau, March 2007, p. 3; and www.census.gov/mrts/www/mrts.html, accessed May 2008.

3. For more on shopper marketing, see Grocery Manufacturers Association and Deloitte Consulting, *Shopper Marketing: Capturing a Shopper's Mind, Heart, and Wallet*, 2007; Jack Neff, "What's in Store: The Rise of Shopper Marketing," *Advertising Age*, October 1, 2007, pp. 1, 42; and Bob Holston, "Avoid Shopper Marketing Pitfalls," *Advertising Age*, March 31, 2008, pp. 20–21.

4. Jo-Ann Heslin, "Supermarkets—Are They on the Endangered Species List?" *HealthNewsDigest.com*, March 30, 2008, www.healthnewsdigest.com/news/Food_and_Nutrition_690/Supermarkets_—_Are_They_On_The_Endangered_Species_List.shtml.

5. Blanca Torres, "4th Quarter Profit soars at Safeway," *Knight Ridder Tribune Business News*, February 23, 2007, p. 1; Justin Hibbard, "Put your Money Where Your Mouth Is," *BusinessWeek*, September 18, 2007, pp. 61–63; and "Safeway Feels Impact of Generics," *Drug Store News*, March 3, 2008, pp. 4+.

6. "Convenience Store Industry Sales Top $569 Billion, NACS Reports," April 11, 2007, accessed online at www.nacsonline.com.

7. See John Lofstock and Kate Quackenbush, "The Power 25," *Convenience Store Decisions*, October 2007, pp. 18+; "Sheetz Hits the Mark," *Retail Merchandiser*, September–October 2007, pp. 28–32; "Stan Sheetz Recognized Among Most Influential Retail Leaders in the World," *PR Newswire*, January 29, 2008; "Sheetz, Inc.," *Hoover's Company Records*, May 1, 2008, p. 43078; and www.sheetz.com/main/about/definition.cfm, accessed November 2008.

8. Statistics based on information from "SN Top 75 2007," http://supermarketnews.com/profiles/top75/; accessed June 2008; http://walmartstores.com/FactsNews/NewsRoom/6852.aspx, accessed June, 2008; and "Industry Overview: Grocery Stores and Supermarkets," *Hoover's Company Records*, accessed at www.hoovers.com/grocery-stores-and-supermarkets/—ID__84—/free-ind-fr-profile-basic.xhtml, June 2008.

9. Elizabeth Woyke, "Buffett, the Wal-Mart Shopper," *BusinessWeek*, May 14, 2007, pp. 66–67.

10. Company information from www.mcdonalds.com/corp.html and www.subway.com/subwayroot/AboutSubway/index.aspx, September 2008.

11. Quotes from "Sears Rethinks Amidst Revenue Decline," *Brandweek*, March 17, 2008, p. 12; and Natalie Zmuda, "Sears Wants to Dust off Brand," *Advertising Age*, April 7, 2008, p. 8.

12. The Whole Foods example is based on quotes and information from Diane Brady, "Eating Too Fast at Whole Foods," *BusinessWeek*, October 24, 2005, pp. 82–84; Kim Wright Wiley, "Think Organic," *Sales & Marketing Management*, January–February 2007, pp. 54–59; "Whole Food Market, Inc.," *Hoover's Company Records*, May 1, 2008, p. 10952, p.1; and www.wholefoods.com, September 2008.

13. JCPenney Annual Report 2007, accessed at www.jcpenney.net.

14. Adapted from information found in Katie Hafner, "Inside Apple Stores, a Certain Aura Enchants the Faithful," *New York Times*, December 27, 2007.

15. Jerry Useem, "Simply Irresistible," *Fortune*, March 19, 2007, p. 107.

16. Information from www.hollywood-rodeo-drive.com, accessed June 2008; and www.bijan.com, accessed November 2008.

17. For definitions of these and other types of shopping centers, see "Dictionary of Marketing Terms," American Marketing Association, accessed at www.marketingpower.com/mg-dictionary.php, September 2007.

18. Ryan Chittum, "Mall-Building Industry Takes Stock," *Wall Street Journal*, May 17, 2006, p. B7; Kelsey Volkmann, "Business Malls Evolving to Imitate Traditional Downtowns," *Associated Press*, January 31, 2007, p. 1; and the International Council of Shopping Centers, "U.S. Mall Report," April 2007, accessed at www.icsc.org; and "Birth, Death, and Shopping," *The Economist*, December 22, 2007.

19. Dean Starkman, "The Mall, Without the Haul—'Lifestyle Centers' Slip Quietly into Upscale Areas, Mixing Cachet and 'Curb Appeal,'" *Wall Street Journal*, July 25, 2001, p. B1; Paul Grimaldi, "Shopping for a New Look: Lifestyle Centers Are Replacing Enclosed Malls," *Providence Journal (Rhode Island)*, April 29, 2007, p. F10; and Laura Klepacki, "Open-Air Shopping with the Works," *Chain Store Age*, March 2008, pp. 136+.

20. See Amy Barrett, "A Retailing Pacesetter Pulls Up Lame," *BusinessWeek*, July 12, 1993, pp. 122–123; John Helyar, "The Only Company Wal-Mart Fears," *Fortune*, November 24, 2003, pp. 158–166; and Jessica Long, "San Diego's Wealthiest: Sol Price," *San Diego Business Journal*, December 10, 2007, p. 28.

21. Mylene Mangalindan, "Surge Seen in U.S. Online Sales," *Globe & Mail (Canada)*, April 8, 2008, p. B11.

22. Nanette Byrnes, "More Clicks at the Bricks," *BusinessWeek*, December 17, 2007, pp. 50–51.

23. "Facts About America's Top 500 E-Retailers," *Internet Retailer*, accessed online at www.internetretailer.com/top500/facts.asp, April 2008.

24. Adapted from portions of Don Davis, "M Is for Multi-channel," *Internet Retailer*, June 2007, www.internetretailer.com/internet/marketing-conference/30566-m-multi-channel.html; with information from www.macys.com, accessed June 2008.

25. See "The *Fortune* 500," *Fortune*, May 5, 2008, p. F1.

26. Examples adapted from information found in Nanette Byrnes, "More Clicks at the Bricks," *BusinessWeek*, December 17, 2007, pp. 50–51; and www.shopbloom.com, September 2008.

27. "Wal-Mart International Operations," March 28, 2008, accessed online at http://walmartstores.com/media/factsheets/fs_2203.pdf; and "The *Fortune* 500," *Fortune*, May 5, 2008, p. F1.

28. See "2008 Global Powers of Retailing," *Stores*, January 2008, accessed at www.nxtbook.com/nxtbooks/nrfe/stores-globalretail08.

29. "Top 250 Global Retailers," *Stores*, January 2008, accessed at www.nxtbook.com/nxtbooks/nrfe/stores-globalretail08; and information from www.walmartstores.com and www.carrefour.com, accessed April 2008.

30. Example adapted from information in Josh Bernoff, "Social Networking Needs CMO Lead," *Advertising Age*, April 28, 2008, p. 129.

31. Adapted from information in Josh Bernoff, "Social Networking Needs CMO Lead," *Advertising Age*, April 28, 2008, p. 129.

32. See the Grainger 2008 Fact Book and other information accessed at www.grainger.com, September 2008.

33. See Dale Buss, "The New Deal," *Sales & Marketing Management*, June 2002, pp. 25–30; Colleen Gourley, "Redefining Distribution," *Warehousing Management*, October 2000, pp. 28–30; Steve Konicki and Eileen Colkin, "Attitude Adjustment," *InformationWeek*, March 25, 2002, pp. 20–22; Stewart Scharf, "Grainger: Tooled Up for Growth," *BusinessWeek Online*, April 25, 2006, p. 8; and John Nank, "W. W. Grainger Inc.: Industrial Strength," *Smart Business Chicago*, September 2007, p. 14.

34. Information from "About Us" and "Supply Management Online," accessed online at www.mckesson.com, October 2008.

35. Facts accessed at www.supervalu.com, October 2008.

36. See www.mckesson.com/static_files/McKesson.com/CorpIR/PDF_Documents/2007%20Form%2010-K%20BM.pdf, p. 101, accessed October 2008.

CHAPTER 14

1. Portions adapted from Jack Neff, "Digital Marketer of the Year: Unilever," *Advertising Age*, March 17, 2008, p. 50. Also see Jack Neff, "K-C, Unilever Turn Down TV to Ramp Up ROI," *Advertising Age*, February 25, 2008, p. 1; and Stephanie Kang, "Media & Marketing: Hellmann's Spreads Message with Flay," *Wall Street Journal*, May 23, 2008, p. B9.

2. The first four of these definitions are adapted from Peter D. Bennett, *The AMA Dictionary of Marketing Terms*, 2nd ed. (New York: McGraw-Hill, 1995). Other definitions can be found at www.marketingpower.com/_layouts/Dictionary.aspx, accessed December 2008.

3. Bob Garfield, "The Chaos Scenario," *Advertising Age*, April 4, 2005, pp. 1, 57+; and Garfield, "The Chaos Scenario 2.0: The Post-Advertising Age," *Advertising Age*, March 26, 2007, pp. 1, 12–13.

4. Chase Squires and Dave Gussow, "The Ways in Which We Watch TV Are Changing Right Before Our Eyes," *St. Petersburg Times*, April 27, 2006; and Geoff Colvin, "TV Is Dying? Long Live TV!" *Fortune*, February 5, 2007, p. 43.

5. Bob Garfield, "The Chaos Scenario 2.0: The Post-Advertising Age," *Advertising Age*, March 26, 2007, pp. 1, 12–13.

6. Brian Steinberg and Suzanne Vranica, "As 30-Second Spot Fades, What Will Advertisers Do Next?" *Wall Street Journal*, January 3, 2006, p. A15; Warren Berger, "A Hard Sell," *Business 2.0*, May 2007, pp. 91–96; and Megan Mcilroy, "Serving Other Media with TV Ups Appetite for Products," *Advertising Age*, June 2, 2008, accessed at http://adage.com/print?article_id127454.

7. TV advertising stats from "Lisa Snedeker, "Ad Spending Goes Limp as 2007 Ends," *Media Life*, March 28, 2008, www.medialifemagazine.com/artman2/publish/Media_economy_57/Ad_spending_goes_limp_as_2007_ends.asp. Quotes from Mike Shaw, "Direct Your Advertising Dollars Away from TV at Your Own Risk," *Advertising Age*, February 27, 2006, p. 29; and Bob Liodice, "TV Make Strides While Marketers Experiment Widely," *Advertising Age*, March 24, 2008, pp. 16–17.

8. Adam Armbruster, "TV Central in Mixology of Multimedia," *TelevisionWeek*, March 3–March 10, 2008, p. 30; and Bob Liodice, "TV Make Strides While Marketers Experiment Widely," *Advertising Age*, March 24, 2008, pp. 16–17.

9. Bob Garfield, "Lee Chow on What's Changed Since '1984,'" *Advertising Age*, June 11, 2007, p. 3.

10. Dan Hill, "CMOs, Win Big by Letting Emotions Drive Advertising," *Advertising Age*, August 27, 2007, p. 12.

11. "Brand Design: Cracking the Colour Code," *Marketing Week*, October 11, 2007, p. 28.

12. Jonah Bloom, "The Truth Is: Consumers Trust Fellow Buyers Before Marketers," *Advertising Age*, February 13, 2006, p. 25.

13. Linda Tischler, "What's the Buzz?" *Fast Company*, May 2004, p. 76; Matthew Creamer, "BzzAgent Seeks to Turn Word of Mouth into a Saleable Medium," *Advertising Age*, February 2006, p. 12; Lisa van der Pool, "Word of Moth Marketing Takes Off," *Boston Business Journal*, November 24, 2007; "BzzAgent Reaches 34M Consumers," *Boston Business Journal*, December 17, 2007; and www.bzzagent.com, accessed October 2008.

14. See Kate Fitzgerald, "Women's Golf Extends Its Footprint," *Advertising Age*, January 29, 2007, p. S4; Tim Arango, "Lebron, Inc.," *Fortune*, December 10, 2007, pp. 100–108; and "Athletes Help Brands Win Big," *Marketing News*, March 15, 2008, p. 17.

15. Eugenia Levenson, "When Celebrity Endorsements Attack," *Fortune*, October 17, 2005, p. 42; Charlie Gillis, "Thee Shill of Victory," *Maclean's*, February 27, 2006, p. 40; and Cathy Yingling, "Beware the Lure of Celebrity Endorsers," *Advertising Age*, September 24, 2008, p. 19.

16. For more on advertising spending by company and industry, see http://adage.com/datacenter/datapopup.php?article_id=119881, accessed September 2008.

17. For more on setting promotion budgets, see W. Ronald Lane, Karen Whitehill King, and J. Thomas Russell, *Kleppner's Advertising Procedure*, 17th ed. (Upper Saddle River, NJ: Prentice Hall, 2008), chapter 6.

18. See Brian Steinberg, "Super Bowl Busts Ratings Record on 'The Greatest Day Ever' for Fox," *Advertising Age*, February 11, 2008, p. 21; Sergio Ibarra, "Weekly Prime-Time Ratings—Week of Feb. 18–Feb. 24," *Television Week*, March 3, 2008, p. 34; and Lisa de Moraes, "'Idol' Takes a Ratings Dip—Albeit a Slight One—in Season Opener," *Washington Post*, January, 17, 2008, p. C7.

19. Roy Chitwood, "Making the Most out of Each Outside Sales Call," February 4, 2005, accessed at http://seattle.bizjournals.com/seattle/stories/2005/02/07/smallb3.html; and "The Cost of the Average Sales Call Today Is More Than $400," *Business Wire*, February 28, 2006.

20. Based on Matthew P. Gonring, "Putting Integrated Marketing Communications to Work Today," *Public Relations Quarterly*, Fall 1994, pp. 45–48. Also see Philip Kotler and Kevin Lane Keller, *Marketing Management*, 13th ed. (Upper Saddle River, NJ: Prentice Hall, 2009), pp. 491–493.

21. For more on the legal aspects of promotion, see Lane, King, and Russell, *Kleppner's Advertising Procedure*, chapter 25; and William L. Cron and Thomas E. DeCarlo, *Dalrymple's Sales Management*, 9th ed. (New York: Wiley, 2006), chapter 10.

CHAPTER 15

1. Quotes and other information from Linda Tischler, "Clan of the Caveman," *Fast Company*, June 2007, pp. 105–108; Jim Lovel, "Loving the Lizard," *Adweek*, October 24, 2005, pp. 32–33; Suzanne Vranica, "How a Gecko Shook Up Insurance Ads," *Wall Street Journal*, January 2, 2007, p. B1; Mya Frazier, "GEICO's $500M Outlay Pays Off," *Advertising Age*, July 9, 2007, p. 8; "GEICO," *Advertising Age*, October 15, 2007, p. 50; "GEICO Earns Top Spot Again for Customer Loyalty on Brand Keys Index," *BusinessWire*, March 27, 2008; Lisa Gschwandtner, "Hard Sell, Soft Landing," *Selling Power*, April 2008, pp. 58–63; and information provided by GEICO, October 2008.

2. Data on U.S. and global advertising spending obtained at http://adage.com/datacenter/#top_marketers;_adspend_stats, accessed September 2008.

3. For these and other examples, see Kate MacArthur, "Why Big Brands Are Getting Bigger," *Advertising Age*, May 2007, p. 6.

4. For more on advertising budgets, see Ronald Lane, Karen King, and Thomas Russell, *Kleppner's Advertising Procedure*, 17th ed. (Upper Saddle River, NJ: Prentice Hall, 2008), chapter 6.

5. For more discussion, see John Consoli, "Heavy Lifting," *MediaWeek*, March 3, 2008.

6. "Commercial Conundrum," *Marketing Management*, April 2006, p. 6; and "Number of Magazines by Category," accessed at www.magazine.org/editorial/editorial_trends_and_magazine_handbook/1145.cfm, April 2008.

7. Louise Story, "Anywhere the Eye Can See, It's Likely to See an Ad," *New York Times*, January 15, 2007, accessed at www.nytimes.com; and Matthew Creamer, "Caught in the Clutter Crossfire: Your Brand," *Advertising Age*, April 1, 2007, pp. 1, 35.

8. See http://adage.com/images/random/0907/2007_Ad_Age_TV_Price_Survey.pdf, accessed June 2008; Meg James and Maria Elena Fernandez, "Ad Buyers Hooked on 'Idol' Too," *Los Angeles Times*, January 13, 2008, p. 1; and Steve McClellan, "Super Bowl Spots Hit 3 Mil," *Adweek*, June 5, 2008, accessed at www.adweek.com.

9. Ken Krimstein, "Tips for the Ad World," *Forbes*, October 16, 2006, p. 34; and Bob Garfield, "The Chaos Scenario 2.0: The Post-Advertising Age," *Advertising Age*, March 26, 2007, pp. 1, 12–13.

10. John Consoli, "Broadcast, Cable Ad Clutter Continues to Rise," *MediaWeek*, May 4, 2006, accessed at www.mediaweek.com.

11. Ronald Grover, "The Sound of Many Hands Zapping," *BusinessWeek*, May 22, 2006, p. 38; Daisy Whitney, "DVR, Broadband Users Take Control," *Television Week*, October 29, 2007, p. 10; "Attack of the Pod People," *Adweek.com*, March 24, 2008; Jack Neff, "Study Finds Mixed DVR Effects," *Advertising Age*, March 24, 2008, p. 8; and Brian Morrissey, "Can Online Video Queue or DVR Cure DVR Commercial Skipping?" *Adweek*, May 8, 2008, accessed at www.adweek.com.

12. See Steve McKee, Advertising: Less Is Much More," *BusinessWeek Online*, May 10, 2006, accessed at www.businessweek.com; and Stewart Elliott, "Now, the Clicking Is to Watch the Ads, Not Skip Them," *New York Times*, August 17, 2007, accessed at www.nytimes.com.

13. For this and other examples, see Wendy Tanaka, "D.I.Y Ads," *Red Herring*, January 29, 2007, accessed at www.redherring.com/Article.aspx?a=20955&hed=D.I.Y.+Ads; and Lee Gomes, "Tips from Web Greats on Becoming a Legend in Your Spare Time," *Wall Street Journal*, November 14, 2007, p. B1.

14. See Brian Steinberg, "Super Bowl Advertisers Hand Amateurs the Ball," *Wall Street Journal*, January 12, 2007, p. B1; "How All the Ads Ranked in *USA Today*'s Super Bowl Ad Meter," *USA Today*, February 5, 2007, accessed at www.usatoday.com; "Fans Full

22-Year-Old Singer/Songwriter Kina Grannis Winner in Doritos Crash the Super Bowl Challenge," PR Newswire, February 3, 2008, and http://216.178.38.116/doritoscrashthesuperbowl, accessed June 2008.

15. Louise Story, "Can a Sandwich Be Slandered?" *New York Times*, January 29, 2008, accessed at www.nytimes.com.

16. Tanaka, "D.I.Y Ads," p. 3; and Laura Petrecca, "Madison Avenue Wants You! (Or at Least Your Videos)," *USA Today*, June 21, 2007, p. 1B.

17. Allison Enright, "Let Them Decide," *Marketing News*, June 1, 2006, pp. 10–11.

18. Enright, "Let Them Decide," pp. 10–11; and "Who's in Control?" *Advertising Age*, January 28, 2008, p. C1.

19. Stuart Elliot, "New Rules of Engagement," *New York Times*, March 21, 2006, p. C7; Abbey Klaassen, "New Wins Early Battle in Viewer-Engagement War," *Advertising Age*, March 20, 2006, p. 1; Mike DiFranza, "Rules of Engagement," *MediaWeek*, January 15, 2007, p. 9; Andrew Hampp, "Water Cooler," *Advertising Age*, April 16, 2007, p. 32; Megan McIlroy, "So Much for Engagement; Buys Are Still Based on Eyes," *Advertising Age*, January 14, 2008, p. 1; and Betsy Cummings, "Marketers Size Up New Metric System," *Brandweek*, April 6, 2008, Accessed at www.brandweek.com.

20. For these and other examples and quotes, see Chris Walsh, "Ads on Board," *Rocky Mountain News*, February 27, 2007; David Kiley, "Rated M for Mad Ave," *BusinessWeek*, February 26, 2006, pp. 76–77; Cliff Peale, "Advertising Takes Many Forms," *Cincinnati Enquirer*, December 3, 2006, accessed at http://news.enquirer.com; Louise Story, "Anywhere the Eye Can See, It's Likely to See an Ad," *New York Times*, January 15, 2007, p. A12; and Adam Remson, "School Buses Latest Victim of Ad Creep," *Brandweek*, February 4, 2008, p. 4.

21. Adapted from information found in Claudia Wallis, "The Multitasking Generation," *Time*, March 27, 2006, accessed at www.time.com; Curtis L. Taylor, "Teens' Balancing Act: New Study Shows Young People Are Spending More Time Multitasking," *Knight Ridder Tribune Business News*, December 16, 2006, p. 1; John Harlow, "How We Squeeze 31 Hours into a Day," *Times* (London), April 13, 2008, p. 8; and Tanya Irwin, "Study: Kids Are Master Multitaskers on TV, Web, Mobile," *MediaPost Publications*, March 10, 2008, accessed at www.mediapostpublications.com.

22. *Newsweek* and *BusinessWeek* cost and circulation data accessed online at http://mediakit.businessweek.com and www.newsweekmediakit.com, September 2008.

23. See "Pounds 10M Domino Effect Cheers Up Guinness," *Daily Record*, February 15, 2008; and Frank Ahrens, "$2 Million Airtime, $13 Ad," *Washington Post*, January 31, 2007, p. D1.

24. See Stuart Elliot, "How Effective Is This Ad, in Real Numbers? Beats Me," *New York Times*, July 20, 2005, p. C8; Jack Neff, "Half Your Advertising Isn't Wasted,—Just 37.3 Percent," *Advertising Age*, August 7, 2006, pp. 1, 32; Ben Richards and Faris Yakob, "The New Quid pro Quo," *Adweek*, March 19, 2007, p. 17; and Kate Maddox, "ROI Takes Center Stage at CMO Summit," *BtoB*, February 11, 2008, p. 3.

25. David Tiltman, "Everything You Know Is Wrong," *Marketing*, June 13, 2008, pp. 28+.

26. Stuart Elliot, "How Effective Is This Ad, in Real Numbers? Beats Me," p. C8; and "Taking Measure of Which Metrics Matter," *BtoB*, May 5, 2008.

27. Information on advertising agency revenues from "Top 10 Worldwide Ad Agencies," *Advertising Age*, May 5, 2008, accessed at http://adage.com/datacenter/datapopup.php?article_id=126731; and "World's Top 50 Agency Companies," May 5, 2008, accessed at http://adage.com/datacenter/datapopup.php?article_id=126706.

28. Adapted from information in Geoffrey A. Fowler, Brian Steinberg, and Aaron O. Patrick, "Mac and PC's Overseas Adventures," *Wall Street Journal*, March 1, 2007, p. B1.

29. See Alexandra Jardine and Laurel Wentz, "It's a Fat World After All," *Advertising Age*, March 7, 2005, p. 3; George E. Belch and Michael A. Belch, *Advertising and Promotion*, (New York: McGraw-Hill/Irwin, 2004), pp. 666–668; Jonathan Cheng, "China Demands Concrete Proof of Ads," *Wall Street Journal*, July 8, 2005, p. B1; Cris Prystay, "India's Brewers Cleverly Dodge Alcohol-Ad Ban," *Wall Street Journal*, June 15, 2005, p. B1; Dean Visser, "China Puts New Restrictions on Cell Phone, E-Mail Advertising," *Marketing News*, March 15, 2006, p. 23; Steve Inskeep, "Ban Thwarts 'Year of the Pig' Ads in China," *National Public Radio*, February 6, 2007; Maxine Frith, "It Worked in Canada to Ban Junk Food Ads and Now the Call Is on TV in Australia," *Sun Herald (Sydney)*, March 16, 2008, p. 14.

30. Adapted from Scott Cutlip, Allen Center, and Glen Broom, *Effective Public Relations*, 9th ed. (Upper Saddle River, NJ: Prentice Hall, 2006), chapter 1.

31. See Jeff Manning and Kevin Lane Keller, "Got Advertising That Works?" *Marketing Management*, January–February 2004, pp. 16–20; Alice Z. Cuneo, "Now Even Cellphones Have Milk Mustaches," *Advertising Age*, February 26, 2007, p. 8; "Got Milk? Campaign Searches for America's First-Ever 'Chief Health Officer,'" *Business Wire*, May 6, 2008; and information from www.bodybymilk.com and www.whymilk.com, September 2008.

32. "Consumer Launch Campaign of the Year 2008," *PRWeek*, March 6, 2008, accessed at www.prweekus.com/Consumer-Launch-Campaign-of-the-Year-2008/article/100570.

33. Al Ries and Laura Ries, "First Do Some Publicity," *Advertising Age*, February 8, 1999, p. 42. Also see Al Ries and Laura Ries, *The Fall of Advertising and the Rise of PR* (New York: HarperBusiness, 2002). For points and counterpoints and discussions of the role of public relations, see O. Burtch Drake, "'Fall' of Advertising? I Differ," *Advertising Age*, January 13, 2003, p. 23; David Robinson. "Public Relations Comes of Age," *Business Horizons*, May–June 2006, pp. 247+; and Noelle Weaver, "Why Advertising and PR Can't Be Separated," *Advertising Age*, May 14, 2007, accessed at www.adage.com.

34. "Aveeno Case Study," accessed at www.ogilvypr.com/case-studies/aveeno.cfm, October 2008; And see www.youtube.com/watch?v=hfn8Dz_13Ms.

35. See "Butterball Turkey Talk-Line Fact Sheet," accessed at www.butterball.com, November 2008.

36. Paul Holmes, "Senior Marketers Are Sharply Divided about the Role of PR in the Overall Mix," *Advertising Age*, January 24, 2005, pp. C1–C2.

CHAPTER 16

1. Quotes and other information from "*Fortune* Ranks CDW First in Wholesalers: Electronics on America's Most Admired Company List," *Business Wire*, March 10, 2008; Jeff O'Heir, "Michael Krasny—IT Sales Innovator." *Computer Reseller News*, November 18, 2002; Ed Lawler, "Integrated Campaign Winner: CDW Computer Centers," *BtoB*, December 9, 2002, p. 20; Chuck Salter, "The Soft Sell," *Fast Company*, January 2005, pp. 72–73; Paolo Del Nibletto, "CDW Goes to Class," *Computer Dealer News*, May 25, 2007, p. 20; "CDW Corporation," *Hoover's Company Records*, May 1, 2008, p. 16199; and www.cdw.com, September 2008.

2. Based on information in Jennifer J. Salopek, "Bye, Bye, Used Car Guy," *T+D*, April 2007, pp. 22–25. Also see "Prepare to Win," *Selling Power*, April 2008, p. 27.

3. For more on "salesperson-owned loyalty," see Robert W. Palmatier, et al. "Customer Loyalty to Whom? Managing the

Benefits and Risks of Salesperson-Owned Loyalty," *Journal of Marketing Research*, May 2007, pp. 185–199.

4. This extract and strategies that follow are based on Philip Kotler, Neil Rackham, and Suj Krishnaswamy, "Ending the War Between Sales and Marketing," *Harvard Business Review*, July–August 2006, pp. 68–78. Also see Timothy Smith, Srinath Gopalakrishna, and Rabikar Chatterjee, "A Three-Stage Model of Integrated Marketing Communications at the Marketing-Sales Interface," *Journal of Marketing Research*, November 2006, pp. 564–579; and Christian Homburg, Ove Jensen, and Harley Krohmer, "Configurations of Marketing and Sales: a Taxonomy," *Journal of Marketing*, March 2008, pp. 133–154.

5. See "Lear Corp. Honored by GM as Supplier of the Year," *St. Charles County Business Record*, May 10, 2006, p. 1; Andy Cohen, "Top of the Charts: Lear Corporation," *Sales & Marketing Management*, July 1998, p. 40; "Lear Corporation," *Hoover's Company Records*, June 15, 2008, p. 17213; and www.lear.com, accessed June 2008.

6. "Selling Power 500," accessed at www.sellingpower.com/sp500/index.asp, October 2007.

7. For more on this and other methods for determining sales force size, see Mark W. Johnston and Greg W. Marshall, *Sales Force Management*, 9th ed. (Boston: McGraw-Hill Irwin, 2009), pp. 152–156.

8. Theodore Kinni, "The Team Solution," *Selling Power*, April 2007, pp. 27–29.

9. Roy Chitwood, "Making the Most out of Each Outside Sales Call," February 4, 2005, accessed at http://seattle.bizjournals.com/seattle/stories/2005/02/07/smallb3.html; and "The Cost of the Average Sales Call Today Is More Than $400," *Business Wire*, February 28, 2006.

10. Carol Krol, "Telemarketing Team Rings Up Sales for Avaya," *BtoB*, October 10, 2005, p. 34. For more on the Avaya's sales strategy, see Julia Chang, "On Top of the World," *Sales & Marketing Management*, January–February 2006, pp. 31–36.

11. See Martin Everett, "It's Jerry Hale on the Line," *Sales & Marketing Management*, December 1993, pp. 75–79. Also see Irene Cherkassky, "Target Marketing," *BtoB*, October 2006, pp. 22–24.

12. Adapted from Chuck Salter, "The Soft Sell," *Fast Company*, January 2005, pp. 72–73. See also "Minding Our Business," *Multichannel Merchant*, March 2006, p. 1.

13. Jennifer J. Salopek, "Bye, Bye, Used Car Guy," *T+D*, April 2007, pp. 22–25; and William F. Kendy, "No More Lone Rangers," *Selling Power*, April 2004, pp. 70–74. Also see Michelle Nichols, "Pull Together—Or Fall Apart," *BusinessWeek Online*, December 2, 2005, accessed at www.businessweek.com; and Theodore Kinni, "The Team Solution," *Selling Power*, April 2007, pp. 27–29.

14. "Customer Business Development," accessed at www.pg.com/jobs/jobs_us/work_we_offer/advisor_overview.jhtml?sl=jobs_advisor_business_development, November 2008.

15. For more information and discussion, see Benson Smith, *Discover Your Strengths: How the World's Greatest Salespeople Develop Winning Careers* (New York: Warner Business Books, 2003); Kevin McDonald, "Therapist, Social Worker or Consultant?" *CRN*, December 2005–January 2006, p. 24; Tom Reilly, "Planning for Success," *Industrial Distribution*, May 2007, p. 25; Dave Kahle, "The Four Characteristics of Successful Salespeople," *Industrial Distribution*, April 2008, p. 54; and www.gallup.com/consulting/1477/Sales-Force-Effectiveness.aspx, accessed October 2008.

16. Geoffrey James, "The Return of Sales Training," *Selling Power*, May 2004, pp. 86–91. See also Rebecca Aronauer, "Tracking Your Investment," *Sales & Marketing Management*, October 2006, p. 13; Geoffrey James, "Training: A Wise Choice," *Selling Power*, January–February 2007, pp. 88–90; and James, "Return on Your Sales Training Investment," *Selling Power*, October 2007, p. 102. Also see Ashraf M. Attia, et al., "Global Sales Training: in Search of Antecedent, Mediating, and Consequence Variables," *Industrial Marketing Management*, April 2008, pp. 181+.

17. David Chelan, "Revving Up E-Learning to Drive Sales," *EContent*, March 2006, pp. 28–32. Also see "E-Learning Evolves into Mature Training Tool," *T+D*, April 2006, p. 20; Rebecca Aronauer, "The Classroom vs. E-Learning," *Sales & Marketing Management*, October 2006, p. 21; and Harry Sheff, "Agent Training Beyond the Classroom," *Call Center Magazine*, April 2007, p. 18.

18. From David Chelan, "Revving Up E-Learning to Drive Sales," *EContent*, March 2006, pp. 28–32; and "International Rectifier Drives Sales with Global E-Leaning Initiative," GeoLearning case study, accessed at www.geolearning.com/main/customers/ir.cfm, October 2008.

19. Joseph Kornak, "'07 Compensation Survey: What's It All Worth?" *Sales & Marketing Management*, May 2007, pp. 28–39.

20. See Henry Canady, "How to Increase the Times Reps Spend Selling," *Selling Power*, March 2005, p. 112; George Reinfeld, "8 Tips to Help Control the Hand of Time," *Printing News*, January 9, 2006, p. 10; and David J. Cichelli, "Plugging Sales 'Time Leaks,'" *Sales & Marketing Management*, April 2006, p. 23; Rebecca Aronauer, "Time Well Spent," *Sales & Marketing Management*, January–February 2007, p. 7; and Dave Bradford, "Finding More Time for Selling," *Electrical Wholesaling*," April 2007, pp. 66–67.

21. See Gary H. Anthes, "Portal Powers GE Sales," *Computerworld*, June 2, 2003, pp. 31–32. Also see Betsy Cummings, "Increasing Face Time," *Sales & Marketing Management*, January 2004, p. 12; David J. Cichelli, "Plugging Sales 'Time Leaks,'" *Sales & Marketing Management*, April 2006, p. 23; and Henry Canaday, "How to Boost Sales Productivity and Save Valuable Time," *Agency Sales*, November 2007, p. 20.

22. For extensive discussions of sales force automation, see the May 2005 issue of *Industrial Marketing Management*, which is devoted to the subject; Gary K. Hunter and William D. Perreault, "Making Sales Technology Effective," *Journal of Marketing*, January 2007, pp. 16–34; and Mary M. Long, Thomas Tellefsen, and J. David Lichtenthal, "Internet Integration into the Industrial Selling Process: A Step-By-Step Approach," *Industrial Marketing Management*, July 2007, pp. 676–689; and Anupam Agarwal, "Bringing Science to Sales," *Customer Relationship Management*, March 2008, p. 16.

23. Based on information from Thomaselli, "Pharma Replacing Reps," *Advertising Age*, January 2005, p. 50; and Matthew Arnold, "Is There a Doctor on the Web?" *Medical Marketing and Media*, 2008, pp. 10–11. Also see Mary M. Long, Thomas Tellefsen, and J. David Lichtenthal, "Internet Integration into the Industrial Selling Process: A Step-By-Step Approach," *Industrial Marketing Management*, July 2007, pp. 676–689.

24. Quotes from Bob Donath, "Delivering Value Starts with Proper Prospecting," *Marketing News*, November 10, 1997, p. 5; and Bill Brooks, "Power-Packed Prospecting Pointers," *Agency Sales*, March 2004, p. 37. Also see Gerhard Gschwandtner, "The Basics of Successful Selling," *Selling Power*, 25th anniversary issue, 2007, pp. 22–26; and Maureen Hrehocik, "Why Prospecting Gets No Respect," *Sales & Marketing Management*, October 2007, p. 7.

25. Quotes in this paragraph from Lain Ehmann, "Prepare to Win," *Selling Power*, April 2008, pp. 27–29.

26. Adapted from Charlotte Huff, "EXTREME Makeover," *Workforce Management*, May 8, 2006, p. 1. Also see "iLevel Performance Home Educates Homebuyers on What to Look For in a Home's Structural Framing," *PR Newswire*, April 29, 2008; and www.ilevel.com, accessed November 2008.

27. Phil Sasso, "Listening in for More Sales," *Professional Distributor*, December 2007, pp. 18–19. Also see Gerhard Gschwandtner, "The Basics of Successful Selling," *Selling Power*, 25th anniversary issue, 2007, pp. 22–26; and Robert L. Bailey, "Story of Two Salespeople," *Rough Notes*, April 2008, p. 142.

28. Betsy Cummings, "Listening for Deals," *Sales & Marketing Management*, August 2005, p. 8. Also see Michele Marchetti, "Listen to Me!" *Sales and Marketing Management*, April 2007, p. 12.

29. Adapted from Izabella Iizuka, "Not Your Father's Presentation," *Sales & Marketing Management*, March/April 2008, pp. 33–35.

30. *Shopper-Centric Trade: The Future of Trade Promotion* (Wilton, CT: Cannondale Associates, October 2007), p. 15.

31. Based on information and quotes from Helen Leggatt, "PostPoints Rewards Readers for Reading," *Biz Report: Loyalty Marketing*, April 2, 2007, accessed at www.bizreport.com; and www.washingtonpost.com/postpoints, October 2008.

32. See "Savings for All Ages," September 6, 2007, accessed at www.pmalink.org/press_releases/default.asp?p=pr_09062007; and "CMS Reports Annual Coupon Distribution to 286 Billion," accessed at www.couponinfonow.com/Couponing/2007trendsoverview.cfm, May 2008.

33. Quotes and other information from Alan J. Liddle, "Hardee's Connects with Mobile Device Users, Offer Discounts," *Nation's Restaurant News*, May 14, 2007, p. 16; Alice Z. Cuneo, "Package-Goods Giants Roll Out Mobile Coupons," *Advertising Age*, March 10, 2008, p. 3; Alex Palmer, "Cellular Savings," *Incentive*, April 2008, p. 69; and www.cellfire.com, August 2008.

34. See "McDonald's Debuts *American Idol*-Inspired Toys in Happy Meals and Mighty Kid Meals," *PR Newswire*, April 18, 2007; and Ken Barnes, "Idol Links with McDonald's for Happy Meal Toys 2.0," April 11, 2008, accessed at http://blogs.usatoday.com/idolchatter/2008/04/idol-links-with.html.

35. See "2007 Promotion Products Fact Sheet," at Promotion Products Association International Web site, www.ppai.org, accessed May 2008.

36. Adapted from information found in Betsey Spethmann, "Doritos Experiments with Sampling and Sweeps," *Promo*, June 19, 2007, accessed at http://promomagazine.com/contests/news/doritos_experiments_sampling_sweeps_061907.

37. "Exclusive PQ Media Research: Branded Entertainment Defies Slowing Economy," February 12, 2008, accessed at www.pqmedia.com/about-press-20080212-bemf.html.

38. Martha T. Moore, "Charmin Rolls Out 20 Restrooms in Times Square," *USA Today*, November 11, 2006, accessed at www.usatoday.com/news/nation/2006-11-21-charmin_x.html; and Irene Chang, "Charmin Brings Back NYC Public Restrooms," *PRWeek*, December 10, 2007, p. 5.

39. *Shopper-Centric Trade: The Future of Trade Promotion* (Wilton, CT: Cannondale Associates, October 2007), p. 15.

40. See the Consumer Electronics Association Press Web site, www.cesweb.org/press/default_flash.asp, accessed May 2008; and the Bauma Web site, www.bauma.de, October 2008.

CHAPTER 17

1. Quotes and other information from Josh Quittner, "The Charmed Life of Amazon's Jeff Bezos," *CNNMoney.com*, April 15, 2008, accessed at www.cnnmoney.com; Joe Nocera, "Putting Buyers First? What a Concept," *New York Times*, January 5, 2008; Jena McGregor, "Bezos: How Frugality Drives Innovation," *BusinessWeek*, April 28, 2008, p.64; and annual reports and other information found at www.amazon.com, accessed October 2008.

2. For these and other direct marketing statistics in this section, see Direct Marketing Association, *The DMA Statistical Fact Book, 30th edition*, June 2007, pp. 223–224; Direct Marketing Association, *The Power of Direct Marketing: 2007–2008 Edition*, June 2008; and a wealth of other information accessed at www.the-dma.org, December 2008.

3. Roy Chitwood, "Making the Most out of Each Outside Sales Call," February 4, 2005, accessed at http://seattle.bizjournals.com/seattle/stories/2005/02/07/smallb3.html; and "The Cost of the Average Sales Call Today Is More Than $400," *Business Wire*, February 28, 2006.

4. Portions adapted from Mike Beirne, *Brandweek*, October 23, 2006, p. 22; and Jason Voight, "Southwest Keeps Fans from Straying," *Adweek*, August 20, 2007, access data adweek.com. Other information from "Southwest Airlines Celebrates Anniversary of DING!" *PR Newswire*, February 28, 2008; www.blogsouthwest.com and "What Is DING!?" accessed at www.southwest.com/ding, December 2008.

5. Daniel Lyons, "Too Much Information," *Forbes*, December 13, 2004, p. 110; Mike Freeman, "Data Company Helps Wal-Mart, Casinos, Airlines Analyze Data," *Knight Ridder Business Tribune News*, February 24, 2006, p. 1; and Mary Hayes Weier, "HP Data Warehouse Lands in Wal-Mart's Shopping Cart," *InformationWeek*, August 6, 2007, p. 31.

6. Quotes from Scott Horstein, "Use Care with the Database," *Sales & Marketing Management*, May 2006, p. 22; with information from Travis E. Poling, "*BusinessWeek* Says USAA Is Best in Nation When It Comes to Customer Service," *Knight Ridder Tribune Business News*, April 9, 2007, p. 1; Geoffrey Brewer, "The Customer Stops Here," *Sales & Marketing Management*, March 1998, pp. 31–36; *Hoover's Company Records*, June 15, 2008, p. 40508; "USAA Receives Highest Customer Advocacy Score," June 6, 2008, accessed at www.usaa.com/inet/ent_utils/McStaticPages?key=2008_06_forrester_awa; and www.usaa.com, October 2008.

7. Direct Marketing Association, *The Power of Direct Marketing: 2007–2008 Edition*, June 2008.

8. David Ranii, "Compact Discs, DVDs Get More Use as Promotional Tool," *Knight Ridder Tribune Business News*, May 5, 2004, p. 1; "DVD & CD Serious Cardz Increase Response Rate Over 1000% Over Traditional Direct Marketing," *Market Wire*, January 10, 2007, p.1; and Emily Maltby, "A Marketing Tool That Fits in Your Wallet," *FSB*, April 2007, p. 76.

9. Jack Neff, "P&G, Unilever Are Ready to Clutter," *Advertising Age*, June 11, 2007, p. 4.

10. Emily Bryson York, "This Isn't the Holiday Catalog You Remember," *Advertising Age*, October 29, 2007.

11. Ylan Q. Mui, "Paging Through the Holidays," *Washington Post*, December 1, 2007, p. D1.

12. See Karen E. Kleing, "Making It with Mail-Order," *BusinessWeek*, January 23, 2006, accessed at www.businessweek.com; and Direct Marketing Association, *The Power of Direct Marketing: 2007–2008 Edition*, June 2008.

13. See "About Lillian Vernon," accessed at www.lillianvernon.com, September 2008.

14. Direct Marketing Association, *The Power of Direct Marketing: 2007–2008 Edition*, June 2008.

15. "Off the Hook," *Marketing Management*, January–February 2008, p. 5; and www.donotcall.gov, accessed October 2008.

16. Ira Teinowitz, "'Do Not Call' Does Not Hurt Direct Marketing," *Advertising Age*, April 11, 2005, pp. 3, 95.

17. Teinowitz, "'Do Not Call' Does Not Hurt Direct Marketing," p. 3.

18. See Brian Steinberg, "Read This Now!; But Wait! There's More! The Infomercial King Explains," *Wall Street Journal*, March 9, 2005, p. 1; and Natasha Singer, "Why Kids Have All the Acne," *New York Times*, October 18, 2007, p. G1.

19. Jack Neff, "What Procter & Gamble Learned from Veg-O-Matic," *Advertising Age*, April 10, 2006, pp. 1, 65; and Jack Neff, "P&G Turns Lights Out on DRTV Players," *Advertising Age*, March 19, 2007, p. 3.

20. Steve McLellan, "For a Whole New DRTV Experience, Call Now," *Adweek*, September 5, 2005, p. 10; Jack Neff, "What Procter & Gamble Learned from Veg-O-Matic," p. 1; and "Analysis: Can DRTV Really Build Brands Better than Image Ads?" *Precision Marketing*, February 9, 2007, p. 11.

21. Adapted from portions of Elizabeth Esfahani, "A Sales Channel They Can't Resist," *Business 2.0*, September 2005, pp. 91–96; with information from Stacey Burling, "The Ultimate Sell Job," *Knight Ridder Tribune Business News*, February 18, 2007, p. 1; and Laura Petrecca, "QVC Shops for Ideas for Future Sales," *USA Today*, May 5, 2008, p. 1B.

22. Jenni Mintz, "DVD Rental Kiosks Gained Popularity in Stores," *McClatchy-Tribune Business News*, April 10, 2008.

23. "Interactive: Ad Age Names Finalists," *Advertising Age*, February 27, 1995, pp. 12–14.

24. Stephanie Kang, "Consumers Come Calling, Literally, for the Holidays," *Wall Street Journal*, November 16, 2007, p. B5; Daniel B. Honigman, "On the Verge: Mobile Marketing Will Make Strides," *Marketing News*, January 15, 2008, pp. 18–21; and "Nielsen Says Mobile Ads Growing, Consumers Respond," *Reuters*, March 5, 2008, accessed at www.reuters.com.

25. Alice Z. Cuneo, "Scramble for Content Drives Mobile," *Advertising Age*, October 24, 2005, p. S6; "Where Are Those Mobile Ads?" *International Herald Tribune*, May 4, 2008; and CTIA: The Wireless Association, June 2008, accessed at www.ctia.org.

26. Alice Z. Cuneo, "So Just What Is Mobile Marketing?" *Advertising Age*, March 17, 2008, p. 36. The following example is adapted from Paul Davidson, "Ad Campaigns for Your Tiny Cellphone Screen Get Bigger," *USA Today*, August 9, 2006, accessed at www.usatoday.com/tech/wireless/2006-08-08-mobile-ads_x.htm.

27. For this and other examples, see Alice Z. Cuneo, "Marketers Get Serious About the "Third Screen," *Advertising Age*, July 11, 2005, p. 6; Louise Story, "Madison Avenue Calling," *New York Times*, January 20, 2007, accessed at www.nytimes.com; and Stephanie Kang, "Retailers Come Calling, Literally, for the holidays," *Wall Street Journal*, November 30, 2007, p. B5.

28. See Davidson, "Ad Campaigns for Your Tiny Cellphone Screen Get Bigger," p. 2; Julie Schlosser, "Get Outta My Phone," *Fortune*, February 10, 2007, p. 20; Emily Burg, "Acceptance of Mobile Ads on the Rise," *MediaPost Publications*, March 16, 2007, accessed at http://publications.mediapost.com; Steve Miller and Mike Beirne, "The iPhone Effect," *Adweek.com*, April 28, 2008; and Spencer E. Ante, "The Call for a Wireless Bill of Rights," *BusinessWeek*, March 31, 2008, pp. 80–81.

29. Adapted from information found in Raymund Flandez, "Calling All Customers," *Wall Street Journal*, April 30, 2007, p. R7.

30. Evie Nagy, "Podding Along," *Billboard*, May 10, 2008, p. 14.

31. For these and other examples, see Karyn Strauss and Derek Gale, Hotels, March 2006, p. 22; Kate Calder, "Hot Topic Cranks Its Music Biz," *Kidscreen*, May 2007, p. 22; and "Official Disneyland Resort Podcasts," http://disneyland.disney.go.com/disneyland, accessed July 2008.

32. Shahnaz Mahmud, "Survey: Viewer Crave TV Ad Fusion," *Adweek.com*, January 25, 2008.

33. Adapted from Alice Z. Cuneo, "Nike Setting the Pace in Interactive-TV Race" *Advertising Age*, August 13, 2007, p. 3. For other information and examples, see Cliff Edwards, "I Want My iTV," *BusinessWeek*, November 19, 2007, pp. 54–63; and Suzanne Vranica, "Unilever Bets on Interactivity; Company Steps up iTV Ads in a Bid to Engage Viewers," *Wall Street Journal*, May 14, 2008, p. B13.

34. For these and other statistics on Internet usage, see "Nielsen Online Reports Topline U.S. Data for April 2008," Nielsen/NetRatings, May 15, 2008, accessed at www.nielsen-netratings.com; and "Global Index Chart," www.nielsen-netratings.com/press.jsp?section=pr_netv&nav=3, accessed May 30, 2008.

35. See Les Luchter, "Study: Internet 2nd Most Essential Medium, but #1 in Coolness," June 27, 2007, accessed at www.publications.mediapost.com; and Gail Schiller, "Ads More Wired, Survey Finds," *The Reporter*, December 28, 2007, accessed at http://hollywoodreporter.com.

36. See "America's Top Ten Retail Businesses," accessed at www.internetretailer.com/top500/list.asp, August 2008.

37. See Tom Sullivan, "A Lot More Than Paper Clips," *Barron's*, April 16, 2007, pp. 23–25; and information from www.officedepot.com, September 2008.

38. See Shop.org, Forrester Research Inc., *The State of Retailing Online 2007*, accessed at www.forrester.com/SORO; and Jen Haberkorn, "Web Sales May Hit $204 Billion," *Washington Times*, April 8, 2008, p. C8.

39. "JupiterResearch Forecasts Online Retail Spending Will Reach $144 Billion in 2010, a CAGR of 12% from 2005," February 6, 2006, accessed at www.jupitermedia.com/corporate/releases/06.02.06-newjupresearch.html; and "Online Sales to Climb Despite Struggling Economy," National Retail Federation, April 8, 2008, accessed at www.nrf.com/modules.php?name=News&op=viewlive&sp_id=499.

40. Information for this example accessed at http://quickenloans.quicken.com, September 2008.

41. Information for this example accessed at www.dell.com/html/us/segments/pub/premier/tutorial/users_guide.html, August 2008.

42. See "eBay Inc.," *Hoover's Company Records*, June 1, 2008, p. 56307; and facts from eBay annual reports and other information accessed at www.ebay.com, September 2008.

43. Beth Snyder Bulik, "Who Blogs?" *Advertising Age*, June 4, 2007, p. 20.

44. Adapted from "Max Colchester, "Nescafé Brews Buzz via Blogs," *Wall Street Journal*, November 23, 2007, p. B3.

45. See David Ward, "GM Blog Keeps Everyone Up to Speed," *PRWeek*, April 3, 2006, p. 7; "Welburn: Calm Down, Camaro Complainers," *Automotive News*, January 14, 2008, p. 42; and Michelle Martin, "GM Keeps Pace with Customers Through Blogs," *Crain's Detroit Business*, May 12, 2008, p. 35.

46. Pete Blackshaw, "Irrational Exuberance? I Hope We're Not Guilty," *Barcode Blog*, August 26, 2005, accessed at www.barcodefactory.com/wordpress/?p=72.

47. Laurie Peterson, "When It Comes to Blogs, It Pays to Listen," *MediaPost Publications*, September 29, 2006, accessed at www.publications.com; and Michael Bush, "Starbucks Gets Web 2.0 Religion, But Can It Convert Nonbelievers?" *Advertising Age*, March 24, 2008, p. 1.

48. Carolyn Kepcher, "Bad Service? Point, Click, Complain," *New York Daily News*, May 12, 2008; and Kermit Pattison, "Does a New Website Hold the Secret to Great Customer Service?" *Fast Company*, April 2008, www.fastcompany.com/articles/2008/04/interview-muller.html.

49. Adapted from Jack Neff, "Media Owners Take Heed: P&G's Staid Old Web Site Has you Licked," *Advertising Age*, December 4, 2007, pp. 1, 38.

50. Adapted from Jena McGregor, "High-Tech Achiever: MINI USA," *Fast Company*, October 2004, p. 86, with information from www.miniusa.com, September 2007.

51. Jeffrey F. Rayport and Bernard J. Jaworski, *e-Commerce* (New York: McGraw-Hill, 2001), p. 116. Also see Goutam Chakraborty, "What Do Customers Consider Important in B2B Websites?" *Journal of Advertising*, March 2003, p. 50; and "Looks Are Everything," *Marketing Management*, March/April 2006, p. 7.

52. Adapted from Brooks Barnes, "In Overhaul, Disney.com Seeks a Path to More Fun," *New York Times*, June 25, 2008.

53. Internet Advertising bureau, *IAB Internet Advertising Revenue Report*, May 2008, accessed at www.iab.net/insights_research/iab_news_article/299656.

54. Jonathan Lemonnier, "What Is Rich Media?" *Advertising Age*, March 17, 2008, p. 48.

55. Internet Advertising Bureau, *IAB Internet Advertising Revenue Report*, May 2008, accessed at www.iab.net/insights_research/iab_news_article/299656.

56. Abbey Klaassen and Megan McIlroy, "Search," *Advertising Age*, March 17, 2008, p. 43; and www.teapartay.com, accessed June 2008.

57. Danielle Sacks, "Down the Rabbit Hole," *Fast Company*, November 2006, pp. 86–93.

58. Adapted from information found in Jeff Gordon, "Good Cheer: OfficeMax's Viral Campaign Revels in Its Elfin Glory and Returns Happy Results," *Marketing News*, March 15, 2008, pp. 24–28.

59. Chaddus Bruce, "Big Biz Biddies Up to Gen Y," *Wired*, December 20, 2006, accessed at www.wired.com; "Masterclass: The Revolution Masterclass on Social Networking Sites," *Revolution*, January 25, 2007, accessed at www.brandrepublic.com.

60. See "U.S. E-Mail Marketing Spending and User Data," *Digital Marketing and Media Fact Pack*, supplement to *Advertising Age*, April 23, 2007, p. 44; Alex Moskalyuk, "E-mail Marketing Spending to Reach $2.1 Bln by 2012," *ZDNet.com*, January 7, 2008, http://blogs.zdnet.com/ITFacts/?p=13581.

61. Jon Swartz, "Despite Filters, Tidal Wave of Spam Bears Down on e-Mailers," *USA Today*, November 23, 2008, p. 6B; "Spam Turns 30 and Never Looked Healthier," *TechWeb*, May 2, 2008; and Symantec, *The State of Spam, A Monthly Report—May 2008*, accessed at www.symantec.com/business/theme.jsp?themeid=state_of_spam.

62. Adapted from Regina Brady, "Profitable E-Mail," *Target Marketing*, April 2007, pp. 21–22.

63. William Hupp, "E-Mail," *Advertising Age*, March 17, 2008, p. 48.

64. "Sweepstakes Groups Settles with States," *New York Times*, June 27, 2001, p. A14; "PCH Reaches $34 Million Sweepstakes Settlement with 26 States," *Direct Marketing*, September 2001, p. 6; and Steve Higgins, "Reader's Digest Will Pay Up in Connecticut Sweepstakes Settlement," *Knight Ridder Tribune Business News*, March 29, 2005, p. 1.

65. See Internet Crime Complaint Center, "Internet Crime Report 2007," accessed at www.ic3.gov/media/annualreport/2007_IC3Report.pdf.

66. "Jon Swartz, "Despite Filters, Tidal Wave of Spam Bears Down on e-Mailers," *USA Today*, November 23, 2008, p. 6B.

67. See "Consumer Security Fears Continue to Rise in Banking Industry," *Business Wire*, December 14, 2006; and Tom Wright, "Online Card Use Stirs Fears Despite Relatively Low Fraud," *Cards and Payments*, April 2007, p. 16.

68. "Net Threats," *Consumer Reports*, September 2007, p. 28. Excerpt adapted from Ben Elgin, "The Plot to Hijack Your Computer," *BusinessWeek*, July 17, 2006, p. 40. Also see Joseph Menn, "Online Tunes are More Risky than Web Porn," *Los Angeles Times*, June 4, 2007, p. C3.

69. "Net Threats," *Consumer Reports*, September 2007, p. 28.

70. See Damon Darlin, "Don't Call. Don't Write. Let Me Be," *New York Times*, January 20, 2007; Ira Tenowitz and Ken Wheaton, "Do Not Call," *Advertising Age*, March 12, 2007, pp. 1, 44; Louise Story, "FTC to Review Online Ads and Privacy," *New York Times*, November 1, 2007; and Saul Hansell, "Is Google Violating a California Privacy Law?" *New York Times*, May 30, 2008.

71. See Jennifer DiSabatino, "FTC OKs Self-Regulation to Protect Children's Privacy," *Computerworld*, February 12, 2001, p. 32; Ann Mack, "Marketers Challenged on Youth Safeguards," *Adweek*, June 14, 2004, p. 12; "Xanga.com to Pay $1 Million for Violating Children's Online Privacy Protection Act," *Computer and Internet Lawyer*, December 2006, pp. 38–39; and "COPPA Protects Children But Challenges Lie Ahead," *US Fed News*, February 27, 2007.

72. Information on TRUSTe accessed at www.truste.com, October 2008.

73. Information on the DMA Privacy Promise obtained at www.dmaconsumers.org/privacy.html, November 2008.

CHAPTER 18

1. Quotes and other information from Gene Marcial, "Nike: Set for Two Great Leaps," *BusinessWeek*, April 14, 2008, p. 78; Matt Woolsey, "Nike's Game Plan: Growth in China, India," *Forbes*, May 2, 2007, accessed at www.forbes.com; and annual reports and other sources at www.nikebiz.com, accessed October 2008.

2. Logitech annual report, accessed at http://ir.logitech.com/annuals.cfm, June 2008.

3. For more on Encyclopaedia Britannica competitive positioning, see Paula Berinstein, "Wikipedia and Britannica: The Kid's All Right (And So's the Old Man)," *Searcher*, March 2006, pp. 16–27; "Encyclopedia Britannica, Inc.," *Hoover's Company Records*, May 1, 2008, p. 40871; and http://corporate.britannica.com, accessed October 2008.

4. Adapted from Taylor Clark, "Who's Afraid of the Big Bad Starbucks?" *The Week*, January 18, 2008, p. 46.

5. See Michael Porter, *Competitive Advantage: Creating and Sustaining Superior Performance* (New York: Free Press, 1998), chapter 6.

6. Based on Devin Leonard, "The Player," *Fortune*, March 20, 2006, p. 54; "The Slow Death of Digital Rights," *The Economist*, October 13, 2007; and information from www.apple.com, accessed May 2008.

7. Adapted from information found in "Blue Ocean Strategy: Making the Competition Irrelevant," accessed at www.blueoceanstrategy.com/resources/press.php, June 2008; and W. Chan Kim and Renée Mauborgne, *Blue Ocean Strategy* (Boston: Harvard Business School Press, 2005).

8. The Stonyfield Story is adapted from Margaret Menge, "Guerilla Marketing Works for NH's Stonyfield Farms," *New Hampshire Union Leader*, November 7, 2005; with information from "From Seven Cows in a Leaky Barn to the World's Top Organic Yogurt Maker," *PR Newswire*, April 29, 2008; and www.stonyfield.com, September 2008.

9. Michael E. Porter, *Competitive Strategy: Techniques for Analyzing Industries and Competitors* (New York: Free Press, 1980), chapter 2; and Porter, "What Is Strategy?" *Harvard Business Review*, November–December 1996, pp. 61–78. Also see Richard Allen and others, "A Comparison of Competitive Strategies in Japan and the United States," *S.A.M. Advanced Management Journal*, Winter 2006,

pp. 24–36; and Stefan Stern, "May the Force Be with You and Your Plans for 2008," *Financial Times*, January 8, 2008, p. 14.

10. Philip Kotler and Kevin Lane Keller, *Marketing Management*, 12th ed. (Upper Saddle River, NJ: Prentice Hall, 2006), p. 243.

11. See Michael Treacy and Fred Wiersema, "Customer Intimacy and Other Value Disciplines," *Harvard Business Review*, January–February 1993, pp. 84–93; Michael Treacy and Mike Wiersema, *The Discipline of Market Leaders: Choose Your Customers, Narrow Your Focus, Dominate Your Market* (New York: Perseus Press, 1997); Fred Wiersema, *Customer Intimacy: Pick Your Partners, Shape Your Culture, Win Together* (Santa Monica, CA: Knowledge Exchange, 1998); Wiersema, *Double-Digit Growth: How Great Companies Achieve It—No Matter What* (New York: Portfolio, 2003); and Edward M. Hindin, "Learning from Leaders: Questions to Ask and Rules to Follow," *Health Care Strategic Management*, August 2006, pp. 11–13.

12. For more discussion, see Philip Kotler and Kevin Lane Keller, *Marketing Management*, 13th ed. (Upper Saddle River, NJ: Prentice Hall, 2009), chapter 11.

13. Based on information found in Andrew Adam Newman, "The Skinny on Males Dieting," *Adweek*, April 7–April 14, 2008, pp. 24–27; and www.nutrisystem.com, accessed September 2008.

14. Adapted from information found in Jack Neff, "Why Unilever Lost the Laundry War," *Advertising Age*, August 6, 2007, pp. 1, 25; and "Bidders Eye Unilever's US Detergent Arm," *Financial Times*, April 9, 2008, p. 24.

15. See "Consumers Can Get More Camera for Less Money," *USA Today*, January 30, 2008, p. 8B; and Betsy McKay, "Soft-Drink Sales Volume Slipped Faster Last Year," *Wall Street Journal*, March 13, 2008, p. B6.

16. "*Fortune* 500: Largest U.S. Corporations," *Fortune*, May 5, 2008, pp. F1–F2.

17. Adapted from David J. Bryce and Jeffrey H. Dyer, "Strategies to Crack Well-Guarded Markets," *Harvard Business Review*, May 2007, pp. 84–91.

18. Based on information from Janet Frankston Lorin, "Kosher Food Brand Is Branching Out," *Los Angeles Times*, December 11, 2006, p. C3; Stuart Elliott, "Manischewitz Wants to Move to a Mainstream Aisle," *New York Times*, July 7, 2006; "R.A.B. Food Group," *Hoover's Company Records*, May 15, 2008, p. 56,134; and www.rabfoodgroup.com, accessed September 2008.

19. "Alberto-Culver Company," *Hoover's Company Records*, May 15, 2008, p. 10048; Jim Kirk, "Company Finds Itself, Finds Success: Alberto-Culver Adopts Strategy of Knowing Its Strengths and Promoting Small Brands, Rather Than Tackling Giants," *Chicago Tribune*, January 22, 1998, p. B1; and www.alberto.com, accessed September 2008.

CHAPTER 19

1. Quotes and other information from: Janet Adamy, "Steady Diet: As Burgers Boom in Russia, McDonald's Touts Discipline," *Wall Street Journal*, October 16, 2007, p. A1; Fern Glazer, "NPD: QSR Chains Expanding Globally Must Also Act Locally," *Nation's Restaurant News*, October 22, 2007, p. 18; and information from www.mcdonalds.com/corp, accessed September 2008.

2. Data from Michael V. Copeland, "The Mighty Micro-Multinational," *Business 2.0*, July 28, 2006, accessed at http://cnnmoney.com; "Fortune 500," *Fortune*, May 5, 2008, pp. F1–F2; and "List of Countries by GDP," *Wikipedia*, accessed at http://en.wikipedia.org/wiki/List_of_countries_by_GDP_%28nominal%29, July 2008.

3. *Global Economic Prospects, 2007*, World Bank, June 3, 2005, accessed at www.worldbank.org; CIA, *The World Factbook*, accessed at https://www.cia.gov, June 2008; and Jonathan Lynn, "World Trade Growth to Slow Further This Year," www.reuters.com, April 17, 2008, www.reuters.com/article/topNews/idUSL1692469520080417.

4. Information from www.michelin.com/corporate, www.jnj.com, and www.caterpillar.com, October 2008.

5. Steve Hamm, "Borders Are So 20th Century," *BusinessWeek*, September 22, 2003, pp. 68–73; and "Otis Elevator Company," *Hoover's Company Records*, June 15, 2008, p. 56332.

6. Adapted from information in Brian Bremner and Dexter Robests, "How Beijing Is Keeping Banks at Bay," *BusinessWeek*, October 2, 2006, p. 42. Also see Ge Jianguo, WTO and Revision of China's Foreign Banking Regulations," *Banking Law Journal*, June 2007, p. 536.

7. "What Is the WTO?" accessed at www.wto.org/english/thewto_e/whatis_e/whatis_e.htm, September 2008.

8. See *WTO Annual Report 2005*, accessed at www.wto.org, September 2007; and World Trade Organization, "10 Benefits of the WTO Trading System," accessed at www.wto.org/english/thewto_e/whatis_e/whatis_e.htm, September 2008.

9. Peter Coy, "Why Free-Trade Talks Are in Free Fall," *BusinessWeek*, May 22, 2006, p. 44; and "EU Officials Still Hopes for Doha Meeting in May," *Journal of Commerce*, April 25, 2008.

10. "The EU at a Glance," accessed online at http://europa.eu/abc/index-en.htm, September 2008.

11. "Economic and Monetary Union (EMU)," accessed at http://europa.eu/abc/12lessons/lesson_7/index_en.htm, September 2008.

12. See David J. Bailey, "Misperceiving Matters: Elite Ideas and the Failure of the European Constitution," *Comparative European Politics*, April 2008, pp. 33+; and CIA, *The World Factbook*, accessed at https://www.cia.gov, June 2008.

13. Statistics and other information from CIA, *The World Factbook*, accessed at https://www.cia.gov, June 2008; and "NAFTA Analysis 2007" and "NAFTA—A Success for Trade," Office of the United States Trade Representative, October 2007, accessed at www.ustr.gov/Trade_Agreements/Regional/NAFTA/Section_Index.html.

14. See Angela Greiling Keane, "Counting on CAFTA," *Traffic World*, August 8, 2005, p. 1; "Integrating the Americas: FTAA and Beyond," *Journal of Common Market Studies*," June 2005, p. 430; Alan M. Field, "Spinning Its Wheels," *Journal of Commerce*, December 3, 2007; CIA, *The World Factbook*, accessed at https://www.cia.gov, June 2008; "Foreign Trade Statistics," accessed at www.census.gov, June 2008.

15. See "Former Ecuador President Borja Accepts S. America Union Presidency," *Xinhua General News Service*, May 9, 2007; and "Union of South American Nations," *Wikipedia*, accessed at http://en.wikipedia.org/wiki/South_American_Community_of_Nations, July 2008.

16. Adapted from information found in Clay Chandler, "China Deluxe," *Fortune*, July 26, 2004, pp. 148–156; "Brand Strategy in China: Luxury Looks East," *Brand Strategy*, June 12, 2007, p. 56; and "More Academic Focus on Luxury Product Craze," *Chinadaily.com.cn*, January 22, 2008.

17. See "Venezuelan Financial Analyst Says Inflation Could Spark Political Instability," *BBC Worldwide Monitoring*, January 24, 2008; and "Venezuela," www.buyusa.gov, accessed May 2008.

18. Ricky Griffin and Michael Pustay, *International Business*, 5th ed. (Upper Saddle River, NJ: Prentice Hall, 2008), pp. 522–523.

19. For other examples, see Emma Hall, "Do You Know Your Rites? BBDO Does," *Advertising Age*, May 21, 2007, p. 22.

20. Jamie Bryan, "The Mintz Dynasty," *Fast Company*, April 2006, pp. 56–61; and Viji Sundaram, "Offensive Durga Display Dropped," *India-West*, February 2006, p. A1.

21. For other examples and discussion, see www.executiveplanet.com, December 2008; *Dun & Bradstreet's Guide to Doing Business Around the World* (Upper Saddle River, NJ: Prentice Hall, 2000); Richard Pooley, "When Cultures Collide," *Management Services*, Spring 2005, pp. 28–31; Terri Morrison and Wayne A. Conaway, *Kiss, Bow, or Shake Hands* (Avon, MA: Adams Media, 2006); and Helen Deresky, *International Management*, 6th ed. (Upper Saddle River, NJ: Prentice Hall, 2008).

22. See Elizabeth Esfahani, "Thinking Locally, Succeeding Globally," *Business 2.0*, December 2005, pp. 96–98, Evan Ramstas, "LG Electronics' Net Surges 91 Percent as Cell Phone Margins Improve," *Wall Street Journal*, January 25, 2006, p. B2; and www.lge.com, October 2008.

23. Adapted from Mark Rice-Oxley, "In 2,000 Years, Will the World Remember Disney or Plato?" *Christian Science Monitor*, January 15, 2004, p. 16.

24. Thomas L. Friedman, *The Lexus and the Olive Tree: Understanding Globalization* (New York: Anchor Books, 2000).

25. "The 100 Most Powerful Brands 2008," www.millwardbrown.com/Sites/optimor/Content/KnowledgeCenter/BrandzRanking.aspx, accessed June 2008.

26. Eric Ellis, "Iran's Cola War," *Fortune*, March 5, 2007, pp. 35–38. Also see Robert Berner and David Kiley, "Global Brands," *BusinessWeek*, August 1, 2005, pp. 86–94.

27. Portions adapted from information found in Mark Rice-Oxley, "In 2,000 Years, Will the World Remember Disney or Plato?" *Christian Science Monitor*, January 15, 2004, p. 16. See also, Liz Robbins, "The NBA and China Hope They've Found the Next Yao," *New York Times*, June 25, 2007, accessed at www.nytimes.com; and Fara Warner, "Hidden Dragons," *Brandweek*, July 2, 2007, p. 18.

28. See Paulo Prada and Bruce Orwall, "A Certain 'Je Ne Sais Quoi' at Disney's New Park—Movie-Themed Site Near Paris Is Multilingual, Serves Wine—and Better Sausage Variety," *Wall Street Journal*, March 12, 2002, p. B1; and "Euro Disney S. C. A.," *Hoover's Company Records*, May 15, 2008, p. 42391. Hong Kong Disneyland faced similar problems. See Merissa Marr and Geoffrey A. Fowler, "Chinese Lessons for Disney," *Wall Street Journal*, June 12, 2006, p. B1; and Benjamin Scent, "Double-Digit Percentage Gain in Disneyland Attendance," *The Standard*, May 8, 2008.

29. Lisa LaMotta, "McDonald's Golden in International Markets," *Forbes*, February 8, 2008, accessed at www.*forbes*.com.

30. See Noreen O'Leary, "Bright Lights, Big Challenge," *Adweek*, January 15, 2007, pp. 22–28; and Dexter Roberts, "Scrambling to Bring Crest to the Masses," *BusinessWeek*, June 25, 2007, p. 72.

31. Adapted from information found in the Vicky McCrorie, "Hershey: Hoping to Taste Success in India," *Food Business Review*, April 2007, accessed at www.food-business-review.com; and Jennifer Fishbein, "Chocolatiers Look to Asia for Growth," *BusinessWeek*, January 18, 2008, accessed at www.businessweek.com.

32. Bruce Einhorn and Nandini Lakshman, "PC Makers Are Racing to India," *BusinessWeek*, October 1, 2007, p. 48.

33. Quotes from Pankaj Ghemawat, "Regional Strategies for Global Leadership," *Harvard Business Review*, December 2005, pp. 97–108; and Ben Laurance, "Unilever Learns to Join the Dots," *Sunday Times*, March 18, 2007, p. B1. Also see Ghemawat, "Managing Differences," *Harvard Business Review*, March 2007, pp. 59–68.

34. Warren J. Keegan, *Global Marketing Management*, 7th ed. (Upper Saddle River, NJ: Prentice Hall, 2002), pp. 346–351. Also see Phillip Kotler and Kevin Lane Keller, *Marketing Management*, 13th ed. (Upper Saddle River, NJ: 2009), pp. 596–615.

35. Adapted from Jack Ewing, "First Mover in Mobile: How It's Selling Cell Phones to the Developing World," *BusinessWeek*, May 14, 2007, p. 60.

36. See Douglas McGray, "Translating Sony into English," *Fast Company*, January 2003, p. 38; James Coates, "Chicago Tribune Binary Beat Column," *Chicago Tribune*, January 9, 2005, p. 1; and http://vaio-online.sony.com/prod_info/vgn-u8g/index.html, accessed June 2008.

37. Adapted from Gordon Fairclough and Janet Adamy, "Sex, Skin, Fireworks, Licked Fingers—It's a Quarter Pounder Ad in China," *Wall Street Journal*, September 21, 2006, p. B1.

38. Kate MacArthur, "Coca-Cola Light Employs Local Edge," *Advertising Age*, August 21, 2000, pp. 18–19; "Case Studies: Coke Light Hottest Guy," Advantage Marketing, msn India, accessed at http://.advantage.msn.co.in, March 15, 2004; and www.youtube.com/watch?v=Tu5dku6YkHA, accessed June 2008.

39. See Alicia Clegg, "One Ad One World?" *Marketing Week*, June 20, 2002, pp. 51–52; Ira Teinowitz, "International Advertising Code Revised," *Advertising Age*, January 23, 2006, p. 3; George E. Belch and Michael A. Belch, *Advertising and Promotion: An Integrated Marketing Communications Perspective*, 7th ed. (New York: McGraw Hill, 2007), chapter 20; and Shintero Okazaki and Charles R. Taylor, "What Is SMS Advertising and Why Do Multinationals Adopt it?" *Journal of Business Research*, January 2008, pp. 4–12.

40. Bill Addison, "Nail Dumping Tariffs Approved," *Home Channel News*, February 11, 2008, pp. 4–5.

41. Adapted from Jack Ewing, "First Mover in Mobile: How It's Selling Cell Phones to the Developing World," *BusinessWeek*, May 14, 2007, p. 60.

42. See Leslie Chang, Chad Terhune, and Betsy McKay, "A Global Journal Report; Rural Thing—Coke's Big Gamble in Asia," *Wall Street Journal*, August 11, 2004, p. A1; and "Coca-Cola Rolls Out New Distribution Model with ZAP," www.zapworld.com/zap-coca-cola-truck, January 23, 2008.

CHAPTER 20

1. Adapted from Alissa Walker, "Measuring Footprints," *Fast Company*, April 2008, pp. 59–60; with information from www.patagonia.com/web/us/patagonia.go?assetid=2047&ln=140 and www.patagonia.com/web/us/footprint/index.jsp, accessed November 2008.

2. For lots of information on SUV safety, see www.citizen.org/autosafety/suvsafety, accessed December 2008.

3. For lots of information on SUV safety and environmental performance, see www.citizen.org/autosafety/suvsafety, accessed July 2008.

4. The figure and the discussion in this section are adapted from Philip Kotler, Gary Armstrong, Veronica Wong, and John Saunders, *Principles of Marketing: European Edition*, 5th ed. (London: Pearson Publishing, 2009), chapter 2.

5. McDonald's financial information and other facts from www.mcdonalds.com/corp/invest.html and www.mcdonalds.com/corp/about/factsheets.html, accessed September 2008.

6. Heather Green, "How Green Is That Gizmo?" *BusinessWeek*, December 31, 2007, p. 36; and Tom Wright, "False 'Green' Ads Draw Global Scrutiny," *Wall Street Journal*, January 30, 2008, p. B4. See also Louise Story, "FTC Asks if Carbon-Offset Money Is Winding Up True Green," *New York Times*, January 9, 2008, sec. C, p. 1.

7. Theodore Levitt, "The Morality (?) of Advertising," *Harvard Business Review*, July–August 1970, pp. 84–92. For counterpoints, see Heckman, "Don't Shoot the Messenger," *Marketing News*, May 24, 1999, pp. 1, 9.

8. "Elizabeth Warren on the Credit Card Industry," NRP's *Fresh Air*, March 27, 2007, accessed at www.npr.org/templates/story/story.php?storyId=9156929; and Jennifer Levitz, "Hi, My Name Is Fred, And I'm Addicted to Credit Cards," *Wall Street Journal*, June 10, 2008, p. A1.

9. See Rand Health, "Obesity and Disability: The Shape of Things to Come," 2007, accessed at www.rand.org/pubs/research_briefs/2007/RAND_RB9043-1.pdf.

10. Based on information from www.hardees.com/menu, accessed September 2008.

11. Cliff Edwards, "Where Have All the Edsels Gone?" *Greensboro News Record*, May 24, 1999, p. B6. Tim Cooper, "Inadequate Life? Evidence of Consumer Attitudes to Product Obsolescence," *Journal of Consumer Policy*, December 2004, pp. 421–448; David Hunter, "Planned Obsolescence Well Entrenched in Society," *Knoxville News-Sentinel*, August 15, 2005, p. B5; Atsuo Utaka, "Planned Obsolescence and Social Welfare," *Journal of Business*, January 2006, pp. 137–147; and Jessiac Harbert and Caleb Pari Heeringga, "Camp Out for Days to Be First to Buy Apple iPhones," *Knight Ridder Tribune Business News*, June 30, 2007, p. 1.

12. Adapted from David Suzuki, "We All Pay for Technology," *Niagara Falls Review*, March 15, 2007, p. A4.

13. See Brian Grow and Pallavi Gogoi, "A New Way to Squeeze the Weak?" *BusinessWeek*, January 28, 2002, p. 92; Judith Burns, "Study Finds Links in Credit Scores, Insurance Claims," *Wall Street Journal*, February 28, 2005, p. D3; Erik Eckholm, "Black and Hispanic Home Buyers Pay Higher Interest on Mortgages, Study Finds," *New York Times*, June 1, 2006, p. A22; and Frank Phillips, "Battle Brewing on Auto Insurance," *Knight Ridder Tribune Business News*, July 1, 2007, p. 1.

14. Jeff Dickerson, "One Step Forward; Three Steps Back," *Atlanta Tribune: The Magazine*, May 2008, p. 68; Harry Alford, "Subprime Scandal—The Largest Hate Crime in History," *New York Beacon*, April 3–9, 2008, p. 12; Edward R. Culvert, "Sub-Prime Loans Should Be Treated as Bias Crimes," *Culvert Chronicles*, March 13–19, 2008, p. 1; NAACP Mortgage Class Action Fast Tracked," *PR Newswire*, March 10, 2008.

15. Information from "Shop 'til They Drop?" *Christian Science Monitor*, December 1, 2003, p. 8; Gregg Easterbrook, "The Real Truth About Money," *Time*, January 17, 2005, pp. 32–35; and "Bankers Encourage 'Consumer Generation' to Save," *Texas Banking*, March 2006, pp. 25–26. For more on materialism as it relates to quality of life, see James A. Roberts and Aimee Clement, "Materialism and Satisfaction with Over-All Quality of Life Domains," *Social Indicators Research*, May 2007, pp. 72–92; and William Kilbourne and Gregory Pickett, "How Materialism Affects Environmental Beliefs, Concern, and Environmentally Responsible Behavior," *Journal of Business Research*, September 2008, pp. 885–893.

16. The quote is from Oliver James, "It's More Than Enough to Make You Sick," *Marketing*, January 23, 2008, pp. 26–28. Portions Or Reverend Billy example adapted from Constance L. Hays, "Preaching to Save Shoppers from 'Evil' of Consumerism," *New York Times*, January 1, 2003, p. C1; and "A Preacher's Plea to Stop the 'Shopocalypse,'" *Knight Ridder Tribune Business News*, December 11, 2006. Also see Trevor Butterworth, "'Stop, Stop Shopping' The Reverend Billy Is No Ordinary Evangelical Preacher," *Financial Times*, December 1, 2007, p. 2.

17. See Michael Kanellos, "A Nationwide Map of Traffic Jams," *CNET News.com*, September 11, 2007, accessed at http://news.cnet.com/8301-10784_3-9776535-7.html.

18. See www.tfl.gov.uk/roadusers/congestioncharging/6710.aspx, accessed July 2008.

19. See John D. McKinnon, "Politics & Economics: Bush Plays Traffic Cop in Budget Request," *Wall Street Journal*, February 5, 2007, p. A6; "A Rush-Hour Tax on Urban Drivers," *Christian Science Monitor*, February 7, 2007; and Rich Saskal, "Washington: First HOT Lane Opens Up," *Bond Buyer*, May 9, 2008, p. 9.

20. See Allison Linn, "Ads Inundate Public Places," *MSNBC.com*, January 22, 2007; and Bob Garfield, "The Chaos Scenario 2.0: The Post-Advertising Age," *Advertising Age*, March 26, 2007, pp. 1, 12–13.

21. For more discussion, see Martin Sipkoff, "Wal-Mart, Other Discounters Facing Predatory-Pricing Concerns," *Drug Topics*, April 2007, pp. S10–S11; Guy Bolton, "Legislator Targets Drug Prices: Bill Would Eliminate Minimal Markup Law," *McClatchy-Tribune Business News*, December 31, 2007; and "Wal-Mart Expands $4 Prescription List in Colorado," *PR Newswire*, June 5, 2008.

22. For these and other examples, see Mark Borden et al., "50 Ways to Green Your Business," *Fast Company*, November 2007, pp. 90–99; and "UPS Places Largest Order Ever for Hybrid Electric Trucks," UPS press release, May 13, 2008, accessed at www.pressroom.ups.com.

23. Information from "Because We Can't Remanufacture the Earth . . .," March 2005, accessed at www.xerox.com/downloads/usa/en/e/ehs_remanufacture_2005.pdf; "Environmental Solutions That Work," April 2007, accessed at www.xerox.com/downloads/usa/en/e/Environmental_Overview.pdf; and "Nurturing a Greener World Through Sustainable Innovation and Development," *2007 Report on Global Citizenship*, accessed at www.xerox.com/Static_HTML/citizenshipreport/2007/nurturing-page9-2.html.

24. Based on information from Marc Gunther, "Coca-Cola's Green Crusader," *Fortune*, April 28, 2008, p. 150.

25. Adapted from "The Top 3 in 2005," *Global 100*, accessed at www.global100.org, July 2005. See also "Alcoa Again Named One of the World's Most Sustainable Companies at Davos," January 1, 2008, accessed at www.aloca.com; and information from www.global100.org, August 2008. For further information on Alcoa's sustainability program, see Alcoa's Sustainability Report, found at www.alcoa.com.

26. See "EMAS: What's New?" accessed at http://europa.eu.int/comm/environment/emas, August 2008; "Special Report: Free Trade on Trial—Ten Years of NAFTA," *The Economist*, January 3, 2004, p. 13; Daniel J. Tschopp, "Corporate Social Responsibility: A Comparison Between the United States and Europe," *Corporate Social-Responsibility and Environmental Management*, March 2005, pp. 55–59; "Three Countries Working Together to Protect our Shared Environment," Commission for Environmental Cooperation, accessed at www.cec.org/who_we_are/index.cfm?varlan=english, August 2007.

27. Chuck Salter, "Fast 50 the World's Most Innovative Companies," *Fast Company*, March 2008, pp. 73+.

28. See Laurel Wentz, "'Evolution' Win Marks Dawn of New Cannes Era," *Advertising Age*, June 25, 2007, p. 1; Theresa Howard, "Ad Campaign Tells Women to Celebrate How They Are," *USA Today*, August 7, 2005, accessed at www.usatoday.com; "Beyond Stereotypes: Rebuilding the Foundation of Beauty Beliefs," February 2006, accessed at www.campaignforrealbeauty.com; "Cause: Conscience Marketing. You Stand for Something. Shouldn't Your Brand?" *Strategy*, June 2007, p. 22; Maeve Hosea, "Case Study—Dove: Beneath the Skin," *Brand Strategy*, May 8, 2008, p. 20; and information found at www.campaignforrealbeauty.com, September 2008.

29. Information from Mike Hoffman, "Ben Cohen: Ben & Jerry's Homemade, Established in 1978," *Inc.*, April 30, 2001, p. 68; and the Ben & Jerry's Web site at www.benjerrys.com, September 2008.

30. Adapted from Chip Giller and David Roberts, "Resources: The Revolution Begins," *Fast Company*, March 2006, pp. 73–78. Also see Joseph Ogando, "Green Engineering," *Design News*, January 9, 2006, p. 65; and information accessed online at www.haworth.com, October 2008.

31. Joseph Webber, "3M's Big Cleanup," *BusinessWeek*, June 5, 2000, pp. 96–98. Also see "What You Should Know About 3M's "Next Generation" Scotchgard Protector Products," accessed at http://solutions.3m.com/wps/portal/3M/en_US/Scotchgard/Home/Resources/Environmental, August 2008.

32. See *Global Corruption Report 2008*, Transparency International, accessed at www.transparency.org/publications/gcr/download_gcr#download.

33. John F. McGee and P. Tanganath Nayak, "Leaders' Perspectives on Business Ethics," *Prizm*, first quarter, 1994, pp. 71–72. Also see Adrian Henriques, "Good Decision—Bad Business?" *International Journal of Management & Decision Making*, 2005, p. 273; and Marylyn Carrigan, Svetla Marinova, and Isabelle Szmigin, "Ethics and International Marketing: Research Background and Challenges," *International Marketing Review*, 2005, pp. 481–494.

34. See Samuel A. DiPiazza, "Ethics in Action," *Executive Excellence*, January 2002, pp. 15–16; Samuel A. DiPiazza, Jr., "It's All Down to Personal Values," accessed online at www.pwcglobal.com, August 2003; and "Code of Conduct: The Way We Do Business," accessed at www.pwc.com/ethics, December 2008. [PricewaterhouseCoopers (www.pwc.com) provides industry-focused assurance, tax, and advisory services to build public trust and enhance value for its clients and their stakeholders. More than 130,000 people in 148 countries across its network share their thinking, experience, and solutions to develop fresh perspectives and practical advice. "PricewaterhouseCoopers" refers to the network of member firms of PricewaterhouseCoopers International limited, each of which is a separate and independent legal entity.]

35. DiPiazza, "Ethics in Action," p. 15.

APPENDIX 2

1. This is derived by rearranging the following equation and solving for price: Percentage markup = (price − cost) ÷ price.

2. The equation is derived from the basic profit = total revenue − total cost equation. Profit is set to equal the return on investment times the investment (ROI × I), total revenue equals price times quantity (P × Q), and total costs equals quantity times unit cost (Q × UC): ROI × I = (P × Q) − (Q × UC). Solving for P gives P = ((ROI × I) ÷ Q) + UC.

3. The break-even volume equation can also be derived from the basic profit = total revenue − total cost equation. At the break-even point, profit is equal to zero, and it is best to separate fixed and variable costs: 0 = (P × Q) − TFC − (Q × UVC). Solving for Q gives Q = TFC ÷ (P − UVC).

4. As in the previous note, this equation is derived from the basic profit = total revenue − total cost equation. However, unlike the break-even calculation, in which profit was set to equal zero, we set the profit equal to the dollar profit goal: Dollar profit goal = (P × Q) − TFC − (Q × UVC). Solving for Q gives Q = (TFC + dollar profit goal) ÷ (P − UVC).

5. Again, using the basic profit equation, we set profit equal to ROI × I : ROI × I = (P × Q) − TFC − (Q × UVC). Solving for Q gives Q = (TFC + (ROI × I)) ÷ (P − UVC).

6. Again, using the basic profit equation, we set profit equal to 25% of sales, which is 0.25 × P × Q: 0.25 × P × Q = (P × Q) − TFC − (Q × UVC). Solving for Q gives Q = TFC ÷ (P − UVC − (0.25 × P)) or TFC ÷ ((0.75 × P) − UVC).

7. "US Television Households Increase 1.3% for 2007–2008," www.marketingcharts.com/television/us-television-households-increase-13-for-2007-2008-season-1385, accessed August 25, 2008.

8. "HDTV Penetration and Sales Figures," www.parksassociates.blogspot.com/2008/02/hdtv-penetration-and-sales-figures.html, accessed August 25, 2008.

9. "Broadband Internet to Reach 77 Percent of Households by 2012," www.tmcnet.com/voip/ip-communications/articles/35393-gartner-broadband-internet-reach-77-percent-households-2012.htm, accessed August 25, 2008.

10. Daisy Whitney, "'06 HDTV Sales to Outpace Analog," *Television Week*, October 31, 2005, pp. 19–24.

11. See Roger J. Best, *Market-Based Management*, 4th ed. (Upper Saddle River, NJ: Prentice Hall, 2005).

12. Total contribution can also be determined from the unit contribution and unit volume: Total contribution = unit contribution × unit sales. Total units sold were 297,619 units, which can be determined by dividing total sales by price per unit ($100 million ÷ $336). Total contribution = $70 contribution per unit × 297,619 units = $20,833,330 (difference due to rounding).

13. Recall that the contribution margin of 21% was based on variable costs representing 79% of sales. Therefore, if we do not know the price, we can set it equal to $1.00. If the price equals $1.00, 79 cents represents variable costs and 21 cents represents unit contribution. If the price is decreased by 10%, the new price is $0.90. However, variable costs do not change just because the price decreased, so the unit contribution and contribution margin decrease as follows:

	Old	New (reduced 10%)
Price	$1.00	$0.90
− Unit variable cost	$0.79	$0.79
= Unit contribution	$0.21	$0.11
Contribution margin	$0.21/$1.00 = 0.21 or 21%	$0.11/$0.90 = 0.12 or 12%

APPENDIX 3

1. See "Companies Give 'Web Search' a New Meaning," *CFO.com*, April 21, 2008, accessed at http://backwww.CFO.com.

Glossary

Action programs Action programs should be coordinated with the resources and activities of other departments, including production, finance, purchasing, and so on.

Adapted global marketing An international marketing strategy for adjusting the marketing strategy and mix elements to each international target market, bearing more costs but hoping for a larger market share and return.

Administered VMS A vertical marketing system that coordinates successive stages of production and distribution, not through common ownership or contractual ties, but through the size and power of one of the parties.

Adoption process The mental process through which an individual passes from first hearing about an innovation to final adoption.

Advertising Any paid form of nonpersonal presentation and promotion of ideas, goods, or services by an identified sponsor.

Advertising agency A marketing services firm that assists companies in planning, preparing, implementing, and evaluating all or portions of their advertising programs.

Advertising budget The dollars and other resources allocated to a product or company advertising program.

Advertising media The vehicles through which advertising messages are delivered to their intended audiences.

Advertising objective A specific communication *task* to be accomplished with a specific *target* audience during a specific period of *time*.

Advertising strategy The strategy by which the company accomplishes its advertising objectives. It consists of two major elements: creating advertising messages and selecting advertising media.

Affordable method Setting the promotion budget at the level management thinks the company can afford.

Age and life-cycle segmentation Dividing a market into different age and life-cycle groups.

Agent A wholesaler who represents buyers or sellers on a relatively permanent basis, performs only a few functions, and does not take title to goods.

Allowance Promotional money paid by manufacturers to retailers in return for an agreement to feature the manufacturer's products in some way.

Alternative evaluation The stage of the buyer decision process in which the consumer uses information to evaluate alternative brands in the choice set.

Approach The step in the selling process in which the salesperson meets the customer for the first time.

Attitude A person's consistently favorable or unfavorable evaluations, feelings, and tendencies toward an object or idea.

Baby boomers The 78 million people born during the baby boom following World War II and lasting until 1964.

Basing-point pricing A geographical pricing strategy in which the seller designates some city as a basing point and charges all customers the freight cost from that city to the customer.

Behavioral segmentation Dividing a market into groups based on consumer knowledge, attitudes, uses, or responses to a product.

Belief A descriptive thought that a person holds about something.

Benchmarking The process of comparing the company's products and processes to those of competitors or leading firms in other industries to identify "best practices" and find ways to improve quality and performance.

Benefit segmentation Dividing the market into groups according to the different benefits that consumers seek from the product.

Brand A name, term, sign, symbol, design, or a combination of these that identifies the products or services of one seller or group of sellers and differentiates them from those of competitors.

Brand equity The differential effect that knowing the brand name has on customer response to the product or its marketing.

Brand extension Extending an existing brand name to new product categories.

Brand personality The specific mix of human traits that may be attributed to a particular brand.

Break-even analysis Analysis to determine the unit volume and dollar sales needed to be profitable given a particular price and cost structure.

Break-even price The price at which total revenue equals total cost and profit is zero.

Break-even pricing (target profit pricing) Setting price to break even on the costs of making and marketing a product, or setting price to make a target profit.

Broker A wholesaler who does not take title to goods and whose function is to bring buyers and sellers together and assist in negotiation.

Budgets Managers use budgets to project profitability and plan for each marketing program's expenditures, scheduling, and operations.

Business analysis A review of the sales, costs, and profit projections for a new product to find out whether these factors satisfy the company's objectives.

Business buyer behavior The buying behavior of the organizations that buy goods and services for use in the production of other products and services or to resell or rent them to others at a profit.

Business buying process The decision process by which business buyers determine which products and services their organizations need to purchase, and then find, evaluate, and choose among alternative suppliers and brands.

Business portfolio The collection of businesses and products that make up the company.

Business promotions Sales promotion tools used to generate business leads, stimulate purchases, reward customers, and motivate salespeople.

Business-to-business (B2B) online marketing Businesses using B2B Web sites, e-mail, online catalogs, online trading networks, and other online resources to reach new business customers, serve current customers more effectively, and obtain buying efficiencies and better prices.

Business-to-consumer (B2C) online marketing Businesses selling goods and services online to final consumers.

Buyer-readiness stages The stages consumers normally pass through on their way to purchase, including awareness, knowledge, liking, preference, conviction, and purchase.

Buyers The people in the organization's buying center who make an actual purchase.

Buying center All the individuals and units that play a role in the purchase decision-making process.

Buzz marketing Cultivating opinion leaders and getting them to spread information about a product or service to others in their communities.

By-product pricing Setting a price for by-products in order to make the main product's price more competitive.

Cannibalization The situation in which one product sold by a company takes a portion of its sales from other company products.

Captive-product pricing Setting a price for products that must be used along with a main product, such as blades for a razor and film for a camera.

Catalog marketing Direct marketing through print, video, or digital catalogs that are mailed to a select customers, made available in stores, or presented online.

Category killer Giant specialty store that carries a very deep assortment of a particular line and is staffed by knowledgeable employees.

Causal research Marketing research to test hypotheses about cause-and-effect relationships.

Chain ratio method Estimating market demand by multiplying a base number by a chain of adjusting percentages.

Chain stores Two or more outlets that are commonly owned and controlled.

Channel conflict Disagreement among marketing channel members on goals and roles—who should do what and for what rewards.

Channel level A layer of intermediaries that performs some work in bringing the product and its ownership closer to the final buyer.

Channels and logistics review In this section, marketers list the most important channels, provide an overview of each channel arrangement, and identify developing issues in channels and logistics.

Click-and-mortar companies Traditional brick-and-mortar companies that have added online marketing to their operations.

Click-only companies The so-called dotcoms, which operate only online without any brick-and-mortar market presence.

Closing The step in the selling process in which the salesperson asks the customer for an order.

Co-branding The practice of using the established brand names of two different companies on the same product.

Cognitive dissonance Buyer discomfort caused by postpurchase conflict.

Commercial online databases Computerized collections of information available from online commercial sources or via the Internet.

Commercialization Introducing a new product into the market.

Communication adaptation A global communication strategy of fully adapting advertising messages to local markets.

Competitive advantage An advantage over competitors gained by offering greater

customer value, either through lower prices or by providing more benefits that justify higher prices.

Competitive marketing strategies Strategies that strongly position the company against competitors and that give the company the strongest possible strategic advantage.

Competitive review The purpose of a competitive review is to identify key competitors, describe their market positions, and briefly discuss their strategies.

Competitive-parity method Setting the promotion budget to match competitors' outlays.

Competitor analysis The process of identifying key competitors; assessing their objectives, strategies, strengths and weaknesses, and reaction patterns; and selecting which competitors to attack or avoid.

Competitor-centered company A company whose moves are mainly based on competitors' actions and reactions.

Complex buying behavior Consumer buying behavior in situations characterized by high consumer involvement in a purchase and significant perceived differences among brands.

Concentrated (niche) marketing A market-coverage strategy in which a firm goes after a large share of one or a few segments or niches.

Concept testing Testing new-product concepts with a group of target consumers to find out if the concepts have strong consumer appeal.

Consumer buyer behavior The buying behavior of final consumers—individuals and households that buy goods and services for personal consumption.

Consumer market All the individuals and households who buy or acquire goods and services for personal consumption.

Consumer product A product bought by final consumer for personal consumption.

Consumer promotions Sales promotion tools used to boost short-term customer buying and involvement or to enhance long-term customer relationships.

Consumer-generated marketing Marketing messages, ads, and other brand exchanges created by consumers themselves—both invited and uninvited.

Consumer-oriented marketing The philosophy of sustainable marketing that holds that the company should view and organize its marketing activities from the consumer's point of view.

Consumer-to-business (C2B) online marketing Online exchanges in which consumers search out sellers, learn about their offers, and initiate purchases, sometimes even driving transaction terms.

Consumer-to-consumer (C2C) online marketing Online exchanges of goods and information between final consumers.

Consumerism An organized movement of citizens and government agencies to improve the rights and power of buyers in relation to sellers.

Contract manufacturing A joint venture in which a company contracts with manufacturers in a foreign market to produce the product or provide its service.

Contractual VMS A vertical marketing system in which independent firms at different levels of production and distribution join together through contracts to obtain more economies or sales impact than they could achieve alone.

Contribution margin The unit contribution divided by the selling price.

Controls Controls help management assess results after the plan is implemented, identify any problems or performance variations, and initiate corrective action.

Convenience product A consumer product that customers usually buy frequently, immediately, and with a minimum of comparison and buying effort.

Convenience store A small store, located near a residential area, that is open long hours seven days a week and carries a limited line of high-turnover convenience goods.

Conventional distribution channel A channel consisting of one or more independent producers, wholesalers, and retailers, each a separate business seeking to maximize its own profits even at the expense of profits for the system as a whole.

Corporate VMS A vertical marketing system that combines successive stages of production and distribution under single ownership—channel leadership is established through common ownership.

Corporate (or brand) Web site. A Web site designed to build customer goodwill, collect customer feedback, and supplement other sales channels, rather than to sell the company's products directly.

Cost-based pricing Setting prices based on the costs for producing, distributing, and selling the product plus a fair rate of return for effort and risk.

Cost-plus pricing Adding a standard markup to the cost of the product.

Countertrade International trade involving the direct or indirect exchange of goods for other goods instead of cash.

Creative concept The compelling "big idea" that will bring the advertising message strategy to life in a distinctive and memorable way.

Cultural environment Institutions and other forces that affect society's basic values, perceptions, preferences, and behaviors.

Culture The set of basic values, perceptions, wants, and behaviors learned by a member of society from family and other important institutions.

Current marketing situation In this section, marketing managers discuss the overall market, identify the market segments that they will target, and provide information about the company's current situation.

Customer database An organized collection of comprehensive data about individual customers or prospects, including geographic, demographic, psychographic, and behavioral data.

Customer equity The total combined customer lifetime values of all of the company's customers.

Customer insights Fresh understandings of customers and the marketplace derived from marketing information that become the basis for creating customer value and relationships.

Customer lifetime value The value of the entire stream of purchases that the customer would make over a lifetime of patronage.

Customer relationship management The overall process of building and maintaining profitable customer relationships by delivering superior customer value and satisfaction.

Customer relationship management (CRM) Managing detailed information about individual customers and carefully managing customer "touch points" in order to maximize customer loyalty.

Customer sales force structure A sales force organization under which salespeople specialize in selling only to certain customers or industries.

Customer satisfaction The extent to which a product's perceived performance matches a buyer's expectations.

Customer value analysis Analysis conducted to determine what benefits target customers value and how they rate the relative value of various competitors' offers.

Customer-centered company A company that focuses on customer developments in designing its marketing strategies and on delivering superior value to its target customers.

Customer-centered new-product development New-product development that focuses on finding new ways to solve customer problems and create more customer-satisfying experiences.

Customer-perceived value The customer's evaluation of the difference between all the benefits and all the costs of a marketing offer relative to those of competing offers.

Customer-value marketing A principle of sustainable marketing that holds that a company should put most of its resources into customer value-building marketing investments.

Deciders People in the organization's buying center who have formal or informal power to select or approve the final suppliers.

Decline stage The product life-cycle stage in which a product's sales decline.

Deficient products Products that have neither immediate appeal nor long-run benefits.

Demand curve A curve that shows the number of units the market will buy in a given time period, at different prices that might be charged.

Demands Human wants that are backed by buying power.

Demographic segmentation Dividing the market into groups based on variables such as age, gender, family size, family life cycle, income, occupation, education, religion, race, generation, and nationality.

Demography The study of human populations in terms of size, density, location, age, gender, race, occupation, and other statistics.

Department store A retail organization that carries a wide variety of product lines—each line is operated as a separate department managed by specialist buyers or merchandisers.

Derived demand Business demand that ultimately comes from (derives from) the demand for consumer goods.

Descriptive research Marketing research to better describe marketing problems, situations, or markets, such as the market potential for a product or the demographics and attitudes of consumers.

Desirable products Products that give both high immediate satisfaction and high long-run benefits.

Differentiated (segmented) marketing A market-coverage strategy in which a firm decides to target several market segments and designs separate offers for each.

Differentiation Actually differentiating the market offering to create superior customer value.

Direct investment Entering a foreign market by developing foreign-based assembly or manufacturing facilities.

Direct marketing Direct connections with carefully targeted individual consumers to both obtain an immediate response and cultivate lasting customer relationships—the use of direct mail, the telephone, direct-response television, e-mail, the Internet, and other tools to communicate directly with specific consumers.

Direct marketing channel A marketing channel that has no intermediary levels.

Direct-mail marketing Direct marketing by sending an offer, announcement, reminder, or other item to a person at a particular physical or virtual address.

Direct-response television marketing Direct marketing via television, including *direct-response television advertising* (or *infomercials*) and *home shopping channels*.

Discount A straight reduction in price on purchases during a stated period of time.

Discount store A retail operation that sells standard merchandise at lower prices by accepting lower margins and selling at higher volume.

Disintermediation The cutting out of marketing channel intermediaries by product or service producers, or the displacement of traditional resellers by radical new types of intermediaries.

Dissonance-reducing buying behavior Consumer buying behavior in situations characterized by high involvement but few perceived differences among brands.

Distribution center A large, highly automated warehouse designed to receive goods from various plants and suppliers, take orders, fill them efficiently, and deliver goods to customers as quickly as possible.

Diversification A strategy for company growth through starting up or acquiring businesses outside the company's current products and markets.

Downsizing Reducing the business portfolio by eliminating products of business units that are not profitable or that no longer fit the company's overall strategy.

Dynamic pricing Adjusting prices continually to meet the characteristics and needs of individual customers and situations.

E-procurement Purchasing through electronic connections between buyers and sellers—usually online.

Economic community A group of nations organized to work toward common goals in the regulation of international trade.

Economic environment Factors that affect consumer buying power and spending patterns.

Engel's laws Differences noted over a century ago by Ernst Engel in how people shift their spending across food, housing, transportation, health care, and other goods and services categories as family income rises.

Environmental sustainability A management approach that involves developing strategies that both sustain the environment and produce profits for the company.

Environmentalism An organized movement of concerned citizens and government agencies to protect and improve people's current and future living environment.

Ethnographic research A form of observational research that involves sending trained observers to watch and interact with consumers in their "natural habitat."

Event marketing Creating a brand-marketing event or serving as a sole or participating sponsor of events created by others.

Exchange The act of obtaining a desired object from someone by offering something in return.

Exclusive distribution Giving a limited number of dealers the exclusive right to distribute the company's products in their territories.

Execution style The approach, style, tone, words, and format used for executing an advertising message.

Executive summary This section summarizes the main goals, recommendations, and points as an overview for senior managers who will read and approve the marketing plan. A table of contents usually follows this section, for management convenience.

Experience curve (learning curve) The drop in the average per-unit production cost that comes with accumulated production experience.

Experimental research Gathering primary data by selecting matched groups of subjects, giving them different treatments, controlling related factors, and checking for differences in group responses.

Exploratory research Marketing research to gather preliminary information that will help define problems and suggest hypotheses.

Exporting Entering a foreign market by selling goods produced in the company's home country, often with little modification.

Factory outlet An off-price retailing operation that is owned and operated by a manufacturer and that normally carries the manufacturer's surplus, discontinued, or irregular goods.

Fad A temporary period of unusually high sales driven by consumer enthusiasm and immediate product or brand popularity.

Fashion A currently accepted or popular style in a given field.

Fixed costs Costs that do not vary with production or sales level.

FOB-origin pricing A geographical pricing strategy in which goods are placed free on board a carrier; the customer pays the freight from the factory to the destination.

Focus group interviewing Personal interviewing that involves inviting six to ten people to gather for a few hours with a trained interviewer to talk about a product, service, or organization. The interviewer "focuses" the group discussion on important issues.

Follow-up The last step in the selling process in which the salesperson follows up after the sale to ensure customer satisfaction and repeat business.

Franchise A contractual association between a manufacturer, wholesaler, or service organization (a franchiser) and independent businesspeople (franchisees) who buy the right to own and operate one or more units in the franchise system.

Franchise organization A contractual vertical marketing system in which a channel member, called a franchiser, links several stages in the production-distribution process.

Freight-absorption pricing A geographical pricing strategy in which the seller absorbs all or part of the freight charges in order to get the desired business.

Gatekeepers People in the organization's buying center who control the flow of information to others.

Gender segmentation Dividing a market into different groups based on gender.

General need description The stage in the business buying process in which the company describes the general characteristics and quantity of a needed item.

Generation X The 45 million people born between 1965 and 1976 in the "birth dearth" following the baby boom.

Geographic segmentation Dividing a market into different geographical units such as nations, states, regions, counties, cities, or neighborhoods.

Geographical pricing Setting prices for customers located in different parts of the country or world.

Global firm A firm that, by operating in more than one country, gains R&D, production, marketing, and financial advantages in its costs and reputation that are not available to purely domestic competitors.

Good-value pricing Offering just the right combination of quality and good service at a fair price.

Government market Governmental units—federal, state, and local—that purchase or rent goods and services for carrying out the main functions of government.

Gross margin percentage The percentage of net sales remaining after cost of goods sold—calculated by dividing gross margin by net sales.

Group Two or more people who interact to accomplish individual or mutual goals.

Growth stage The product life-cycle stage in which a product's sales start climbing quickly.

Growth-share matrix A portfolio-planning method that evaluates a company's strategic business units in terms of its market growth rate and relative market share. SBUs are classified as stars, cash cows, question marks, or dogs.

Habitual buying behavior Consumer buying behavior in situations characterized by low-consumer involvement and few significantly perceived brand differences.

Handling objections The step in the selling process in which the salesperson seeks out, clarifies, and overcomes customer objections to buying.

Horizontal marketing system A channel arrangement in which two or more companies at one level join together to follow a new marketing opportunity.

Idea generation The systematic search for new-product ideas.

Idea screening Screening new-product ideas in order to spot good ideas and drop poor ones as soon as possible.

Income segmentation Dividing a market into different income groups.

Independent off-price retailer An off-price retailer that is either independently owned and run or is a division of a larger retail corporation.

Indirect marketing channel Channel containing one or more intermediary levels.

Individual marketing Tailoring products and marketing programs to the needs and preferences of individual customers—also labeled "one-to-one marketing," "customized marketing," and "markets-of-one marketing."

Industrial product A product bought by individuals and organizations for further processing or for use in conducting a business.

Influencers People in an organization's buying center who affect the buying decision; they often help define specifications and also provide information for evaluating alternatives.

Information search The stage of the buyer decision process in which the consumer is aroused to search for more information; the consumer may simply have heightened attention or may go into an active information search.

Innovative marketing A principle of sustainable marketing that requires that a company seek real product and marketing improvements.

Inside sales force Inside salespeople who conduct business from their offices via telephone, the Internet, or visits from prospective buyers.

Institutional market Schools, hospitals, nursing homes, prisons, and other institutions that provide goods and services to people in their care.

Integrated logistics management The logistics concept that emphasizes teamwork, both inside the company and among all the marketing channel organizations, to maximize the performance of the entire distribution system.

Integrated marketing communications (IMC) Carefully integrating and coordinating the company's many communications channels to deliver a clear, consistent, and compelling message about the organization and its products.

Intensive distribution Stocking the product in as many outlets as possible.

Interactive marketing Training service employees in the fine art of interacting with customers to satisfy their needs.

Intermarket segmentation Forming segments of consumers who have similar needs and buying behavior even though they are located in different countries.

Intermodal transportation Combining two or more modes of transportation.

Internal databases Electronic collections of consumer and market information obtained from data sources within the company network.

Internal marketing Orienting and motivating customer-contact employees and supporting service people to work as a team to provide customer satisfaction.

Internet A vast public web of computer networks that connects users of all types all around the world to each other and to an amazingly large "information repository."

Introduction stage The product life-cycle stage in which the new product is first distributed and made available for purchase.

Inventory turnover rate (or **stockturn rate**) The number of times an inventory turns over or is sold during a specified time period (often one year)—calculated based on costs, selling price, or units.

Joint ownership A joint venture in which a company joins investors in a foreign market to create a local business in which the company shares joint ownership and control.

Joint venturing Entering foreign markets by joining with foreign companies to produce or market a product or service.

Learning Changes in an individual's behavior arising from experience.

Licensing A method of entering a foreign market in which the company enters into an agreement with a licensee in the foreign market, offering the right to use a manufacturing process, trademark, patent,

trade secret, or other item of value for a fee or royalty.

Lifestyle A person's pattern of living as expressed in his or her activities, interests, and opinions.

Line extension Extending an existing brand name to new forms, colors, sizes, ingredients, or flavors of an existing product category.

Local marketing Tailoring brands and promotions to the needs and wants of local customer groups—cities, neighborhoods, and even specific stores.

Macroenvironment The larger societal forces that affect the microenvironment—demographic, economic, natural, technological, political, and cultural forces.

Madison & Vine A term that has come to represent the merging of advertising and entertainment in an effort to break through the clutter and create new avenues for reaching consumers with more engaging messages.

Management contracting A joint venture in which the domestic firm supplies the management knowhow to a foreign company that supplies the capital; the domestic firm exports management services rather than products.

Manufacturers' sales branches and offices Wholesaling by sellers or buyers themselves rather than through independent wholesalers.

Market The set of all actual and potential buyers of a product or service.

Market challenger A runner-up firm that is fighting hard to increase its market share in an industry.

Market description Describing the targeted segments in detail provides context for the marketing strategies and detailed action programs discussed later in the plan.

Market development A strategy for company growth by identifying and developing new market segments for current company products.

Market follower A runner-up firm that wants to hold its share in an industry without rocking the boat.

Market leader The firm in an industry with the largest market share.

Market nicher A firm that serves small segments that the other firms in an industry overlook or ignore.

Market offering Some combination of products, services, information, or experiences offered to a market to satisfy a need or want.

Market penetration A strategy for company growth by increasing sales of current products to current market segments without changing the product.

Market potential The upper limit of market demand.

Market segment A group of consumers who respond in a similar way to a given set of marketing efforts.

Market segmentation Dividing a market into distinct groups of buyers who have different needs, characteristics, or behaviors, and who might require separate products or marketing programs.

Market share Company sales divided by market sales.

Market targeting The process of evaluating each market segment's attractiveness and selecting one or more segments to enter.

Market-centered company (targeting) A company that pays balanced attention to both customers and competitors in designing its marketing strategies.

Market-penetration pricing Setting a low price for a new product in order to attract a large number of buyers and a large market share.

Market-skimming pricing Setting a high price for a new product to skim maximum revenues layer by layer from the segments willing to pay the high price; the company makes fewer but more profitable sales.

Marketing The process by which companies create value for customers and build strong customer relationships in order to capture value from customers in return.

Marketing channel A set of interdependent organizations that help make a product or service available for use or consumption by the consumer or business user.

Marketing channel design Designing effective marketing channels by analyzing consumer needs, setting channel objectives, identifying major channel alternatives, and evaluating them.

Marketing channel management Selecting, managing, and motivating individual channel members and evaluating their performance over time.

Marketing concept The marketing management philosophy that holds that achieving organizational goals depends on knowing the needs and wants of target markets and delivering the desired satisfactions better than competitors do.

Marketing control The process of measuring and evaluating the results of marketing strategies and plans and taking corrective action to ensure that objectives are achieved.

Marketing environment The actors and forces outside marketing that affect marketing management's ability to build and maintain successful relationships with target customers.

Marketing implementation The process that turns marketing strategies and plans into marketing actions in order to accomplish strategic marketing objectives.

Marketing information system (MIS) People and procedures for assessing information needs, developing the needed information, and helping decision makers to use the information to generate and validate actionable customer and market insights.

Marketing intelligence The systematic collection and analysis of publicly available information about consumers, competitors, and developments in the marketing environment.

Marketing intermediaries Firms that help the company to promote, sell, and distribute its goods to final buyers.

Marketing logistics (physical distribution) Planning, implementing, and controlling the physical flow of materials, final goods, and related information from points of origin to points of consumption to meet customer requirements at a profit.

Marketing management The art and science of choosing target markets and building profitable relationships with them.

Marketing mix The set of controllable tactical marketing tools—product, price, place, and promotion—that the firm blends to produce the response it wants in the target market.

Marketing myopia The mistake of paying more attention to the specific products a company offers than to the benefits and experiences produced by these products.

Marketing organization The marketing department may be organized by function, as in this sample, by geography, by product, or by customer (or some combination).

Marketing research The systematic design, collection, analysis, and reporting of data relevant to a specific marketing situation facing an organization.

Marketing return on investment (or *marketing ROI*) A measure of the marketing productivity of a marketing investment—calculated by dividing net marketing contribution by marketing expenses.

Marketing return on sales (or **marketing ROS**) The percent of net sales attributable to the net marketing contribution—calculated by dividing net marketing contribution by net sales.

Marketing strategy The marketing logic by which the business unit hopes to create customer value and achieve profitable customer relationships.

Marketing strategy development Designing an initial marketing strategy for a new product based on the product concept.

Marketing tools These sections summarize the broad logic that will guide decisions made about the marketing tools to be used during the period covered by the plan.

Marketing Web site A Web site that engages consumers in interactions that will move them closer to a direct purchase or other marketing outcome.

Markup The difference between a company's selling price for a product and its cost to manufacture or purchase it.

Markup chain The sequence of markups used by firms at each level in a channel.

Maturity stage The product life-cycle stage in which sales growth slows or levels off.

Merchant wholesaler An independently owned business that takes title to the merchandise it handles.

Microenvironment The actors close to the company that affect its ability to serve its customers—the company, suppliers, marketing intermediaries, customer markets, competitors, and publics.

Micromarketing The practice of tailoring products and marketing programs to the needs and wants of specific individuals and local customer groups—includes *local marketing and individual marketing.*

Millennials (or **Generation Y**) The 83 million children of the baby boomers, born between 1977 and 2000.

Mission statement A statement of the organization's purpose—what it wants to accomplish in the larger environment.

Modified rebuy A business buying situation in which the buyer wants to modify product specifications, prices, terms, or suppliers.

Motive (drive) A need that is sufficiently pressing to direct the person to seek satisfaction of the need.

Multichannel distribution system A distribution system in which a single firm sets up two or more marketing channels to reach one or more customer segments.

Natural environment Natural resources that are needed as inputs by marketers or that are affected by marketing activities.

Need recognition The first stage of the buyer decision process, in which the consumer recognizes a problem or need.

Needs States of felt deprivation.

Net marketing contribution (NMC) A measure of marketing profitability that includes only components of profitability controlled by marketing.

Net profit percentage The percentage of each sales dollar going to profit—calculated by dividing net profits by net sales.

New product A good, service, or idea that is perceived by some potential customers as new.

New task A business buying situation in which the buyer purchases a product or service for the first time.

New-product development The development of original products, product improvements, product modifications, and new brands through the firm's own product-development efforts.

Nonpersonal communication channels Media that carry messages without personal contact or feedback, including major media, atmospheres, and events.

Objective-and-task method Developing the promotion budget by (1) defining specific objectives; (2) determining the tasks that must be performed to achieve these objectives; and (3) estimating the costs of performing these tasks. The sum of these costs is the proposed promotion budget.

Objectives and issues The company's objectives should be defined in specific terms so management can measure progress and plan corrective action if needed to stay on track. This section describes any major issues that might affect the company's marketing strategy and implementation.

Observational research Gathering primary data by observing relevant people, actions, and situations.

Occasion segmentation Dividing the market into groups according to occasions when buyers get the idea to buy, actually make their purchase, or use the purchased item.

Off-price retailer A retailer that buys at less-than-regular wholesale prices and sells at less than retail. Examples are factory outlets, independents, and warehouse clubs.

Online advertising Advertising that appears while consumers are surfing the Web, including display ads, search-related ads, online classifieds, and other forms.

Online focus groups Gathering a small group of people online with a trained moderator to chat about a product, service, or organization and gain qualitative insights about consumer attitudes and behavior.

Online marketing Company efforts to market products and services and build customer relationships over the Internet.

Online marketing research Collecting primary data online through Internet surveys, online focus groups, Web-based experiments, or tracking consumers' online behavior.

Online social networks Online social communities—blogs, social networking Web sites, or even virtual worlds—where people socialize or exchange information and opinions.

Operating expense percentage The portion of net sales going to operating expenses—calculated by dividing total expenses by net sales.

Operating ratios The ratios of selected operating statement items to net sales.

Opinion leader Person within a reference group who, because of special skills, knowledge, personality, or other characteristics, exerts social influence on others.

Opportunities Opportunities are external elements that the company may be able to exploit to its advantage.

Optional-product pricing The pricing of optional or accessory products along with a main product.

Order-routine specification The stage of the business buying process in which the buyer writes the final order with the chosen supplier(s), listing the technical specifications, quantity needed, expected time of delivery, return policies, and warranties.

Outside sales force (or *field sales force*) Outside salespeople who travel to call on customers in the field.

Packaging The activities of designing and producing the container or wrapper for a product.

Partner relationship management Working closely with partners in other company departments and outside the company to jointly bring greater value to customers.

Percentage-of-sales method Setting the promotion budget at a certain percentage of current or forecasted sales or as a percentage of the unit sales price.

Perception The process by which people select, organize, and interpret information to form a meaningful picture of the world.

Performance review The stage of the business buying process in which the buyer assesses the performance of the supplier and decides to continue, modify, or drop the arrangement.

Personal communication channels Channels through which two or more people communicate directly with each other, including face to face, on the phone, through mail or e-mail, or even through an Internet "chat."

Personal selling Personal interactions between a customers and the firm's sales force for the purpose of making sales and building customer relationships.

Personality The unique psychological characteristics that lead to relatively consistent and lasting responses to one's own environment.

Pleasing products Products that give high immediate satisfaction but may hurt consumers in the long run.

Political environment Laws, government agencies, and pressure groups that influence and limit various organizations and individuals in a given society.

Portfolio analysis The process by which management evaluates the products and businesses that make up the company.

Positioning Arranging for a product to occupy a clear, distinctive, and desirable place relative to competing products in the minds of target consumers.

Positioning statement A statement that summarizes company or brand positioning—it takes this form: *To (target segment and need) our (brand) is (concept) that (point-of-difference).*

Postpurchase behavior The stage of the buyer decision process in which the consumers take further action after purchase, based on their satisfaction or dissatisfaction.

Preapproach The step in the selling process in which the salesperson learns as much as possible about a prospective customer before making a sales call.

Presentation The step in the selling process in which the salesperson tells the "value story" to the buyer, showing how the company's offer solves the customer's problems.

Price The amount of money charged for a product or service, or the sum of the values that customers exchange for the benefits of having or using the product or service.

Price elasticity A measure of the sensitivity of demand to changes in price.

Primary data Information collected for the specific purpose at hand.

Pro forma (or **projected**) **profit-and-loss statement** (or **income statement** or **operating statement**) A statement that shows projected revenues less budgeted expenses and estimates the projected net profit for an organization, product, or brand during a specific planning period, typically a year.

Problem recognition The first stage of the business buying process in which someone in the company recognizes a problem or need that can be met by acquiring a good or a service.

Product Anything that can be offered to a market for attention, acquisition, use, or consumption that might satisfy a want or need.

Product adaptation Adapting a product to meet local conditions or wants in foreign markets.

Product bundle pricing Combining several products and offering the bundle at a reduced price.

Product concept A detailed version of the new-product idea stated in meaningful consumer terms.

Product concept The idea that consumers will favor products that offer the most quality, performance, and features and that the organization should therefore devote its energy to making continuous product improvements.

Product development A strategy for company growth by offering modified or new products to current market segments.

Product development Developing the product concept into a physical product in order to ensure that the product idea can be turned into a workable market offering.

Product invention Creating new products or services for foreign markets.

Product life cycle The course of a product's sales and profits over its lifetime. It involves five distinct stages: product development, introduction, growth, maturity, and decline.

Product line A group of products that are closely related because they function in a similar manner, are sold to the same customer groups, are marketed through the same types of outlets, or fall within given price ranges.

Product line pricing Setting the price steps between various products in a product line based on cost differences between the products, customer evaluations of different features, and competitors' prices.

Product mix (or **product portfolio**) The set of all product lines and items that a particular seller offers for sale.

Product position The way the product is defined by consumers on important attributes—the place the product occupies in consumers' minds relative to competing products.

Product quality The characteristics of a product or service that bear on its ability to satisfy stated or implied customer needs.

Product review The product review summarizes the main features for all of the company's products, organized by product line, type of customer, market, or order of product introduction.

Product sales force structure A sales force organization under which salespeople specialize in selling only a portion of the company's products or lines.

Product specification The stage of the business buying process in which the buying organization decides on and specifies the best technical product characteristics for a needed item.

Product/market expansion grid A portfolio-planning tool for identifying company growth opportunities through market penetration, market development, product development, or diversification.

Production concept The idea that consumers will favor products that are available and highly affordable and that the organization should therefore focus on improving production and distribution efficiency.

Profit-and-loss statement (or income statement or operating statement) A statement that shows actual revenues less expenses and net profit for an organization, product, or brand during a specific planning period, typically a year.

Promotion mix (marketing communications mix) The specific blend of advertising, sales promotion, public relations, personal selling, and direct-marketing tools that the company uses to persuasively communicate customer value and build customer relationships.

Promotional pricing Temporarily pricing products below the list price, and sometimes even below cost, to increase short-run sales.

Proposal solicitation The stage of the business buying process in which the buyer invites qualified suppliers to submit proposals.

Prospecting The step in the selling process in which the salesperson or company identifies qualified potential customers.

Psychographic segmentation Dividing a market into different groups based on social class, lifestyle, or personality characteristics.

Psychological pricing A pricing approach that considers the psychology of prices and not simply the economics; the price is used to say something about the product.

Public Any group that has an actual or potential interest in or impact on an organization's ability to achieve its objectives.

Public relations Building good relations with the company's various publics by obtaining favorable publicity, building up a good corporate image, and handling or heading off unfavorable rumors, stories, and events.

Pull strategy A promotion strategy that calls for spending a lot on advertising and consumer promotion to induce final consumers to buy the product, creating a demand vacuum that "pulls" the product through the channel.

Purchase decision The buyer's decision about which brand to purchase.

Push strategy A promotion strategy that calls for using the sales force and trade promotion to push the product through channels. The producer promotes the product to channel members who in turn promote it to final consumers.

Reference prices Prices that buyers carry in their minds and refer to when they look at a given product.

Relevant costs Costs that will occur in the future and that will vary across the alternatives being considered.

Retailer A business whose sales come primarily from retailing.

Retailing All activities involved in selling goods or services directly to final consumers for their personal, non-business use.

Return on advertising investment The net return on advertising investment divided by the costs of the advertising investment.

Return on investment (ROI) A measure of managerial effectiveness and efficiency—net profit before taxes divided by total investment.

Return on investment (ROI) pricing (or target-return pricing) A cost-based pricing method that determines price based on a specified rate of return on investment.

Return on marketing investment (or marketing ROI) The net return from a marketing investment divided by the costs of the marketing investment.

Sales force management The analysis, planning, implementation, and control of sales force activities. It includes designing sales force strategy and structure and recruiting, selecting, training, supervising, compensating, and evaluating the firm's salespeople.

Sales promotion Short-term incentives to encourage the purchase or sale of a product or service.

Sales quota A standard that states the amount a salesperson should sell and how sales should be divided among the company's products.

Salesperson An individual representing a company to customers by performing one or more of the following activities: prospecting, communicating, selling, servicing, information gathering, and relationship building.

Salutary products Products that have low appeal but may benefit consumers in the long run.

Sample A segment of the population selected for marketing research to represent the population as a whole.

Secondary data Information that already exists somewhere, having been collected for another purpose.

Segmented pricing Selling a product or service at two or more prices, where the difference in prices is not based on differences in costs.

Selective distribution The use of more than one, but fewer than all, of the intermediaries who are willing to carry the company's products.

Selling concept The idea that that consumers will not buy enough of the firm's products unless it undertakes a large-scale selling and promotion effort.

Selling process The steps that the salesperson follows when selling, which include prospecting and qualifying, preapproach,

approach, presentation and demonstration, handling objections, closing, and follow-up.

Sense-of-mission marketing A principle of sustainable marketing that holds that a company should define its mission in broad social terms rather than narrow product terms.

Service Any activity or benefit that one party can offer to another that is essentially intangible and does not result in the ownership of anything.

Service inseparability A major characteristic of services—they are produced and consumed at the same time and cannot be separated from their providers.

Service intangibility A major characteristic of services—they cannot be seen, tasted, felt, heard, or smelled before they are bought.

Service perishability A major characteristic of services—they cannot be stored for later sale or use.

Service retailer A retailer whose product line is actually a service, including hotels, airlines, banks, colleges, and many others.

Service variability A major characteristic of services—their quality may vary greatly, depending on who provides them and when, where, and how.

Service-profit chain The chain that links service firm profits with employee and customer satisfaction.

Share of customer The portion of the customer's purchasing that a company gets in its product categories.

Shopping center A group of retail businesses planned, developed, owned, and managed as a unit.

Shopping product A consumer product that the customer, in the process of selection and purchase, usually compares on such bases as suitability, quality, price, and style.

Social class Relatively permanent and ordered divisions in a society whose members share similar values, interests, and behaviors.

Social marketing The use of commercial marketing concepts and tools in programs designed to influence individuals' behavior to improve their well-being and that of society.

Societal marketing A principle of sustainable marketing that holds that a company should make marketing decisions by considering consumers' wants, the company's requirements, consumers' long-run interests, and society's long-run interests.

Societal marketing concept The idea that a company's marketing decisions should consider consumers' wants, the company's requirements, consumers' long-run interests, and society's long-run interests.

Spam Unsolicited, unwanted commercial e-mail messages.

Specialty product A consumer product with unique characteristics or brand identification for which a significant group of buyers is willing to make a special purchase effort.

Specialty store A retail store that carries a narrow product line with a deep assortment within that line.

Standardized global marketing An international marketing strategy for using basically the same marketing strategy and mix in all the company's international markets.

Store brand (or **private brand**) A brand created and owned by a reseller of a product or service.

Straight product extension Marketing a product in a foreign market without any change.

Straight rebuy A business buying situation in which the buyer routinely reorders something without any modifications.

Strategic group A group of firms in an industry following the same or a similar strategy.

Strategic planning The process of developing and maintaining a strategic fit between the organization's goals and capabilities and its changing marketing opportunities.

Strengths Strengths are internal capabilities that can help the company reach its objectives.

Style A basic and distinctive mode of expression.

Subculture A group of people with shared value systems based on common life experiences and situations.

Supermarket A large, low-cost, low-margin, high-volume, self-service store that carries a wide variety of grocery and household products.

Superstore A store much larger than a regular supermarket that offer a large assortment of routinely purchased food products, nonfood items, and services.

Supplier development Systematic development of networks of supplier-partners to ensure an appropriate and dependable supply of products and materials for use in making products or reselling them to others.

Supplier search The stage of the business buying process in which the buyer tries to find the best vendors.

Supplier selection The stage of the business buying process in which the buyer reviews proposals and selects a supplier or suppliers.

Supply chain management Managing upstream and downstream value-added flows of materials, final goods, and related information among suppliers, the company, resellers, and final consumers.

Survey research Gathering primary data by asking people questions about their knowledge, attitudes, preferences, and buying behavior.

Sustainable marketing Marketing that meets the present needs of consumers and businesses while also preserving or enhancing the ability of future generations to meet their needs.

SWOT analysis An overall evaluation of the company's strengths (S), weaknesses (W), opportunities (O), and threats (T).

Systems selling (or **solutions selling**) Buying a packaged solution to a problem from a single seller, thus avoiding all the separate decisions involved in a complex buying situation.

Target costing Pricing that starts with an ideal selling price, then targets costs that will ensure that the price is met.

Target market A set of buyers sharing common needs or characteristics that the company decides to serve.

Team selling Using teams of people from sales, marketing, engineering, finance, technical support, and even upper management to service large, complex accounts.

Team-based new-product development An approach to developing new products in which various company departments work closely together, overlapping the steps in the product development process to save time and increase effectiveness.

Technological environment Forces that create new technologies, creating new product and market opportunities.

Telephone marketing Using the telephone to sell directly to customers.

Territorial sales force structure A sales force organization that assigns each salesperson to an exclusive geographic territory in which that salesperson sells the company's full line.

Test marketing The stage of new-product development in which the product and marketing program are tested in realistic market settings.

Third-party logistics (3PL) provider An independent logistics provider that performs any or all of the functions required to get its client's product to market.

Threats Threats are current or emerging external elements that could potentially challenge the company's performance.

Total costs The sum of the fixed and variable costs for any given level of production.

Total market demand The total volume that would be bought by a defined consumer group in a defined geographic area in a defined time period in a defined marketing

environment under a defined level and mix of industry marketing effort.

Trade promotions Sales promotion tools used to persuade resellers to carry a brand, give it shelf space, promote it in advertising, and push it to consumers.

Undifferentiated (mass) marketing A market-coverage strategy in which a firm decides to ignore market segment differences and go after the whole market with one offer.

Uniform-delivered pricing A geographical pricing strategy in which the company charges the same price plus freight to all customers, regardless of their location.

Unit contribution The amount that each unit contributes to covering fixed costs—the difference between price and variable costs.

Unsought product A consumer product that the consumer either does not know about or knows about but does not normally think of buying.

Users Members of the buying organization who will actually use the purchased product or service.

Value chain The series of departments that carry out value-creating activities to design, produce, market, deliver, and support a firm's products.

Value delivery network The network made up of the company, suppliers, distributors, and ultimately customers who "partner" with each other to improve the performance of the entire system in delivering customer value.

Value proposition The full positioning of a brand—the full mix of benefits upon which it is positioned.

Value-added pricing Attaching value-added features and services to differentiate a company's offers and charging higher prices.

Value-based pricing Setting price based on buyers' perceptions of value rather than on the seller's cost.

Variable costs Costs that vary directly with the level of production.

Variety-seeking buying behavior Consumer buying behavior in situations characterized by low consumer involvement but significant perceived brand differences.

Vertical marketing system (VMS) A distribution channel structure in which producers, wholesalers, and retailers act as a unified system. One channel member owns the others, has contracts with them, or has so much power that they all cooperate.

Viral marketing The Internet version of word-of-mouth marketing—Web sites, videos, e-mail messages, or other marketing events that are so infectious that customers will want to pass them along to friends.

Wants The form human needs take as shaped by culture and individual personality.

Warehouse club An off-price retailer that sells a limited selection of brand name grocery items, appliances, clothing, and a hodgepodge of other goods at deep discounts to members who pay annual membership fees.

Weaknesses Weaknesses are internal elements that may interfere with the company's ability to achieve its objectives.

Wheel-of-retailing concept A concept that states that new types of retailers usually begin as low-margin, low-price, low-status operations but later evolve into higher-priced, higher-service operations, eventually becoming like the conventional retailers they replaced.

Whole-channel view Designing international channels that take into account the entire global supply chain and marketing channel, forging and effective global value delivery network.

Wholesaler A firm engaged primarily in wholesaling activities.

Wholesaling All activities involved in selling goods and services to those buying for resale or business use.

Word-of-mouth influence Personal communication about a product between target buyers and neighbors, friends, family members, and associates.

Workload method An approach to determining sales force size based on the workload required and the time available for selling.

Zone pricing A geographical pricing strategy in which the company sets up two or more zones. All customers within a zone pay the same total price; the more distant the zone, the higher the price.

Credits

Index